ENCYCLOPEDIA OF ARABIC LITERATURE

ENCYCLOPEDIA OF ARABIC LITERATURE

Volume 2

Edited by

Julie Scott Meisami

and

Paul Starkey

London and New York

First published 1998
by Routledge
11 New Fetter Lane, London EC4P 4EE
29 West 35th Street, New York, NY 10001

Reprinted 1999

Routledge is an imprint of the Taylor & Francis Group

Typeset in Times and Helvetica by
Mathematical Composition Setters Ltd, Salisbury, UK

Printed and bound in Great Britain by
TJ International Ltd, Padstow, Cornwall

British Library Cataloguing in Publication Data
A catalogue record for this book is available from the British Library

Library of Congress Cataloging-in-Publication Data
A catalog record for this book is available on request

ISBN 0-415-18571-8 (vol. 1)
ISBN 0-415-18572-6 (vol. 2)

ISBN 0-415-06808-8 (set)

Contents

List of contributors
vi

Introduction
x

List of abbreviations
xiii

English transliteration system
xvii

Volume 1: entries A–J
1–420

Volume 2: entries K–Z
421–829

Glossary
830

Chronological tables
835

Index
842

Contributors

Kamal Abu-Deeb
School of Oriental and African Studies, London

Farida Abu-Haidar
London

Roger Allen
University of Pennsylvania

Lourdes Alvarez
Bard College, New York

Mona T. Amyuni
American University of Beirut

Ali Asani
Harvard University

Aziz al-Azmeh
Institute of Advanced Study, Berlin

Thomas Bauer
University of Erlangen, Germany

Constance E. Berkley
Vassar College, New York

Marcel Bois
Algeria

Marilyn Booth
University of Illinois

Gert Borg
University of Nijmegen, The Netherlands

C.E. Bosworth
University of Manchester

Issa J. Boullata
McGill University

William M. Brinner
University of California, Berkeley

Pierre Cachia
Columbia University

Giovanni Canova
University of Venice

M.G. Carter
University of Oslo

Peter Clark
British Council, London

Lawrence I. Conrad
Wellcome Institute, London

Miriam Cooke
Duke University, North Carolina

John Cooper
University of Cambridge

Michael Cooperson
University of California, Los Angeles

Francesca Maria Corrao
Oriental Institute, University of Naples

Jack A. Crabbs, Jr
California State University, Fullerton

Elton L. Daniel
University of Hawaii

Francois de Blois
Royal Asiatic Society, London

Ed C.M. de Moor
University of Nijmegen, The Netherlands

Jean Déjeux
*

Rina Drory
Tel Aviv University

Peter G. Emery
Sultan Qaboos University, Oman

Gerhard Endress
Ruhr University, Bochum, Germany

Jean Fontaine
Tunisia

Bassam K. Frangieh
Yale University

A. Giese
Arlington, Massachusetts

Lois A. Giffen
University of Utah

Michael Glünz
Switzerland

Walid Hamarneh
University of Texas at Austin

Parveen Hasanali
St Thomas University, Canada

Wolfhart P. Heinrichs
Harvard University

C. Hillenbrand
University of Edinburgh

R. Hillenbrand
University of Edinburgh

Hassan Hilmy
Hassan II University, Casablanca

John O. Hunwick
Northwestern University

R. Husni
University of Durham

Robert Irwin
School of Oriental and African Studies, London

Renate Jacobi
Freie Universität, Berlin

Philip F. Kennedy
New York University

Hilary Kilpatrick
Lausanne

R.A. Kimber
University of St Andrews

Alexander Knysh
University of Exeter

Hermann Landolt
McGill University

Oliver Leaman
Liverpool John Moores University

Stefan Leder
Martin Luther University, Halle-Wittenberg, Germany

James E. Lindsay
Colorado State University

Ulrich Marzolph
Enzyklopädie des Märchens, Göttingen

J.S. Meisami
University of Oxford

M. Mikhail
New York University

James E. Montgomery
University of Cambridge

Shmuel Moreh
Bar Ilan University, Ramat Gan

R.L. Nettler
Oxford Centre for Hebrew and Jewish Studies

Ian R. Netton
University of Leeds

C. Nijland
Netherlands Institute for the Near East

M.R. Nourallah
University of Westminster

Robin C. Ostle
University of Oxford

Nick Pelham
BBC World Service

Carl Petry
Northwestern University

D. Pinault
Santa Clara University, California

Wadād al-Qāḍī
University of Chicago

B. Radtke
Rijksuniversiteit of Utrecht

D.M. Reid
Georgia State University

D.S. Richards
University of Oxford

Lutz Richter-Bernburg
Leipzig University

A. Rippin
University of Calgary

Geoffrey Roper
Cambridge University Library

Everett K. Rowson
University of Pennsylvania, Philadelphia

J. Sadan
Tel Aviv University

Philip C. Sadgrove
University of Manchester

Raymond P. Scheindlin
Jewish Theological Seminary of America, New York

Gregor Schoeler
Orientalisches Seminar, University of Basel

Tilman Seidensticker
Friedrich Schiller University, Jena

David Semah
*

John L. Sharpe
William R. Perkins Library, Duke University, North Carolina

M. I. Shoush
University of Edmonton

P.J. Sluglett
University of Utah

Pieter Smoor
Institute for Modern Near Eastern Studies, University of Amsterdam

Reuven Snir
University of Haifa

F. Sobieroj
Friedrich-Schiller–Universität, Jena

Sasson Somekh
Tel Aviv University

Abdul-Nabi Staif
University of Damascus

Paul Starkey
University of Durham

Willem Stoetzer
University of Leiden

Yasir Suleiman
University of Edinburgh

Shawkat M. Toorawa
RRAALL, University of Mauritius

Ahmad Ubaydli
CMES, University of Cambridge

Geert Jan H. van Gelder
University of Groningen

Wiebke Walther
Eberhard Karls University, Tübingen

David J. Wasserstein
Tel Aviv University

Otfried Weintritt
Albert Ludwigs University, Freiburg im Breisgau

Bernard Weiss
University of Utah

Owen Wright
School of Oriental and African Studies, London

Michael J. L. Young
*

M. Zakeri
Johann Wolfgang Goethe University, Germany

K. Zebiri
School of Oriental and African Studies, London

* The contributor is now deceased

Introduction

The *Encyclopedia of Arabic Literature* has been a long time in the making. The first idea for a biographical dictionary in English of Arab personalities down the ages appears to have been put forward in the second half of the 1980s. In subsequent discussion this rather general idea was modified to a more specific proposal, centring on writers of literature in Arabic, and preliminary entry lists were drawn up on this basis in around 1987 by Philip Sadgrove with the involvement of Roger Allen – lists which proved valuable when the present editors assumed responsibility for the work in 1990. Taking as its model the series of literary *Companions* published by the Oxford University Press, the *Encyclopedia* was at this stage known as the *Companion to Arabic Literature*, and indeed it continues to be so known to many; the change in title was made at a somewhat later stage, as it became clear that the projected scope of the work brought it within the ambit of the series of *Encyclopedias* – both literary and other – already embarked on by Routledge.

Little needs to be said about the scope or rationale for a publication of this type. Although several reference sources of relevance to the field have existed for some time in European languages, there has been no work in English (or any other language, to our knowledge) which has covered in a single volume the most important authors, works, genres, key terms and issues in the Arabic literary tradition – classical, transitional and modern. At one end of the spectrum, the monumental English and French versions of the first and second editions of the *Encyclopaedia of Islam* have been an indispensable reference tool for scholars and others interested in the writers and literature of the classical (and, to a more limited extent, the transitional) periods of Arabic literature, but have made no attempt to cover more modern developments in any depth. At the other end of the spectrum, Volume III of Jaroslav Průšek's *Dictionary of Oriental Literatures*, published in 1974, covers the literatures of West Asia and North Africa including the modern period; but its greater linguistic and geographical range inevitably means that the literature of any individual language cannot be covered in any great detail. We therefore see the current publication as filling an important gap.

In compiling the *Encyclopedia*, our aim has been so far as possible to emphasize the state of the art of current scholarship on Arabic literature, relying on recent research and less on received traditional opinion. We have accordingly tried to provide an up-to-date assessment of the tradition by incorporating the latest views on the authors and subjects represented, which we hope will be less subject to rapid obsolescence than more traditionally oriented works. To what extent we have succeeded, must of course be for others to judge. In making our selection of entries, we have taken it as our assumption that the main users of the *Encyclopedia* will be students and academics working in Arabic language and literature and, more generally, in the fields of Middle Eastern culture, history and philosophy; to these may be added students and academics working in other Middle Eastern literatures, and students of comparative literature, non-Western literatures and world literature.

Inevitably, in a publication of this sort, there will be gaps, and specialists in particular fields will no doubt wish to draw attention to omissions which they regard as important. Some omissions have of course been inevitable: given the need to keep the volume to a manageable size, it has simply not been possible to include everything. In other cases, entries which appeared on the editors' original list have unfortunately had to be abandoned when we failed to find contributors able and willing to produce suitable entries; while in other cases (fortunately only a few), promised contributions simply did not materialize. On the other side of the coin, a few entries have been included which may strike most readers as rather unexpected; proffered by enthusiastic contributors, they on occasion simply seemed too interesting to turn down. Particular difficulties were experienced in the case of living authors whose literary reputations are not yet secure; in general, writers who have come to prominence later than 1980 have not been included, but it has not been possible to operate a rigid cut-off date on any sensible basis and the inclusion or omission of contemporary authors is inevitably slightly arbitrary. Equally arbitrary has been the inclusion of some North African writers writing mainly (or in a few cases, exclusively) in French, where the general cultural context has suggested an exception to the usual principle that 'Arabic literature' is 'literature written in Arabic'. For the medieval period, the scope of 'literature' has not been restricted to *belles-lettres* but has been extended to other types of writing – history, biography, geography, philosophy and so on – as medieval writers and readers did not make the same distinctions between various types of 'literature' as do modern ones.

The principles on which the volume has been organized are largely self-explanatory. Medieval and transitional period authors have been entered under their *shuhra* (the best known element of their name), with cross-references where necessary. Modern authors have been entered under the final, or family, element of their name, with cross-references in the few cases where readers might perhaps have expected to find the entry elsewhere. For the medieval and transitional periods, dates have been given according to both the Islamic (AH/*hijrī*) and Christian (AD/CE/*mīlādī*) calendars, but for the modern period *hijrī* dates have not been included. Cross-references (in bold) within entries, and 'See also' references at the end of some entries, indicate other, related entries. For transliteration from Arabic and Persian the *International Journal of Middle East Studies* system has been used, as set out in detail on page xvii. Further information on Arabic names and some other technical points may be found in the Glossary (pp. 830–4); for further information on chronology, readers should consult the dynastic tables on pp. 835–41.

For reasons of space, no attempt has been made to compile exhaustive bibliographies for individual entries. The primary object has been to list translations and to refer the reader, where possible, to other secondary sources for further information on the subject of the entry; entries for classical authors may list published editions of the writer's main works, but this has not been thought practicable in the case of modern writers. In deciding which secondary sources to list, the primary emphasis has been on accessibility; in the context of the present volume, this has inevitably led to a certain preference for English-language works, for which I hope that we may be forgiven. In general, unless they are of particular importance, references to standard works such as the *Encyclopaedia of Islam*, Brockelmann's *Geschichte der arabischen Literatur* (*GAS*), Sezgin's *Geschichte des arabischen Schrifttums*, etc., have not been included in the bibliographies.

It remains to thank all those who have contributed in whatever way to the volume. Our primary thanks go to the contributors themselves and to the two editorial advisers, Professor Roger Allen and Professor Renate Jacobi, who have provided much valuable advice at various stages of the operation, as well as contributing several entries on their own account. Among contributors, it would in general be invidious to single out particular individuals, but special thanks are due, for the modern period, to Dr Philip Sadgrove and Professor Shmuel Moreh, who have each taken responsibility for more entries than could reasonably have been demanded of them, and, for the medieval period, to Dr G.H.J, van Gelder and Dr Philip Kennedy, who similarly contributed more than could or should have been expected, and to Dr Thomas Bauer and Dr Gert Borg, who stepped in at the last minute to take on entries which had not materialized. Three contributors, Dr Jean Déjeux of Paris, Dr Michael Young of the University of Leeds and Dr David Semah of the University of Haifa, have sadly not lived to see their entries in print. Finally, thanks are due to Dr Cathy Hampton and Dr Alma Giese, who translated several entries from French and German respectively, and to the succession of staff at Routledge who have shepherded the volume through the various stages of production with a seemingly almost inexhaustible patience – especially to Mark Barragry, who was responsible for getting the project off the ground in its present form, and to Denise Rea, who finally persuaded us that the volume had to see the light of day. For whatever imperfections remain, we are of course responsible.

Julie Scott Meisami, University of Oxford
Paul Starkey, University of Durham

Abbreviations: books

ʿAbbās Festschrift
Studia Arabica et Islamica, Festschrift for Iḥsān ʿAbbās. Ed. W. al-Qāḍī. Beirut 1981.

Aghānī
Abū al-Faraj al-Iṣbahānī, *Kitāb al-Aghānī*. Editions: Bulaq 1285/1869; Cairo 1323/1905; Beirut 1960; Cairo 1345–94/1927–74.

Ahlwardt, *Divans*
W. Ahlwardt, *The Divans of the Six Ancient Arabian Poets*, London 1870.

Arabicus Felix
Arabicus Felix: Luminosus Britannicus: Essays in Honour of A.F.L. Beeston on his Eightieth Birthday. Ed. Alan Jones, Reading 1991.

Ayalon Festschrift
Studies in Islamic History and Civilization in Honour of Professor David Ayalon. Ed. M. Sharon. Jerusalem/Leiden 1986.

Baneth Festschrift
Studia Orientalia Memoriae D.H. Baneth dedicata. Jerusalem 1979.

Browne Festschrift
A Volume of Oriental Studies Presented to E.G. Browne on His 60th Birthday. Ed. T.W. Arnold and R.A. Nicholson. Cambridge, Eng. 1922.

CHALABL
The Cambridge History of Arabic Literature: ʿAbbāsid Belles-Lettres. Ed. Julia Ashtiany *et al.* Cambridge 1990.

CHALMAL
The Cambridge History of Arabic Literature: Modern Arabic Literature. Ed. M.M. Badawi, Cambridge 1992.

CHALRLS
The Cambridge History of Arabic Literature: Religion, Learning and Science in the ʿAbbāsid Period. Ed. M.J.L. Young *et al.* Cambridge 1991.

CHALUP
The Cambridge History of Arabic Literature: Arabic Literature to the End of the Umayyad Period. Ed. A.F.L. Beeston *et al.* Cambridge 1983.

Chauvin, *Bibliographie*
V. Chauvin, *Bibliographie des ouvrages arabes et relatifs aux Arabes publiées dans l'Europe chrétienne de 1810 à 1883*. 4 vols, Liege/Leipzig 1892–1909; rpt. Paris 1985.

CHIr
The Cambridge History of Iran.

Fihrist
Ibn al-Nadīm, *al-Fihrist*. Editions: ed. G. Flügel, 2 vols, Leipzig 1871–72, rpt. Cairo 1948; Cairo 1938; (Dodge) *The Fihrist of al-Nadīm*, ed. and trans. Bayard Dodge, 2 vols, New York 1970.

HIP
History of Islamic Philosophy. Ed. Oliver Leaman. Routledge 1997.

Nöldeke Festschrift
Orientalische Studien Theodor Nöldeke zum 70. Geburtstag gewidmet. Giessen 1906. 2 vols.

Sachau Festschrift
Festschrift Eduard Sachau zum siebzigsten Geburtstage gewidmet. Ed. G. Weil. Berlin 1915.

Spuler Festschrift
Studien zur Geschichte und Kultur des Vorderen Orients. Ed. H.R. Roemer and Albrecht Noth. Leiden 1981.

UEAI Proceedings
Proceedings of the Congresses of the Union Européenne des Arabisants et Islamisants.

Wagner Festschrift
Festschrift Ewald Wagner zum 65. Geburtstag, 2: Studien zur arabischen Dichtung. Ed. W. Heinrichs & G. Schoeler. Beirut 1994.

Abbreviations: journals and reference works

Abh. Akad. Wiss. und Lit. Mainz
Abhandlungen der Akademie der Wissenschafts und Literature, Mainz

Abh. G.W. Göttingen
Abhandlungen der Gesellschaft der Wissenschaften zu Göttingen

_AI_
Annales Islamologiques

AIEO
Annales de l'Institut d'Etudes Orientales (Algiers)

_AI[U]ON_
Annali del Istituto [Universitario] Orientale di Napoli

AKM
Abhandlung für die Kunde des Morgenlandes

_AO_
Acta Orientalia

ArO
Archiv Orientální

_AS_
Asiatische Studien

BEO
Bulletin d'Études Orientales

BGA
Bibliotheca Geographorum Arabicorum

BIFAO
Bulletin de l'Institut Français d'Archéologie Orientale du Caire

BJRL
Bulletin of the John Rylands Library

BSOAS
Bulletin of the School of Oriental and African Studies, University of London

CHM
Cahiers d'Histoire Mondiale

_EI^1_
Encyclopaedia of Islam (First edition; + *Supplement*)

_EI^2_
Encyclopaedia of Islam (Second edition; + *Supplements*)

EIr
Encyclopaedia Iranica

_EJ_
Encyclopaedia Judaica

_EM_
Enzyklopädie des Märchens

ERE
Encyclopaedia of Religion and Ethics

_FO_
Folia Orientalia

GAL
Carl Brockelmann, *Geschichte der arabischen Literatur* . . . 2 vols, Leiden 1943–49.

GAL(S)
Supplementbanden. 3 vols, Leiden 1937–42.

GAP
Grundriss der arabische Philologie. Vol. 1: *Sprachwissenschaft*, ed. W. Fischer; vol. 2, *Literaturwissenschaft*, ed. H. Gätje; vol. 3: *Supplement.* 3 vols, Wiesbaden 1982–91.

GAS
Fuat Sezgin, *Geschichte des arabischen Schrifttums.* Leiden 1967–

IBLA
Revue de l'Institut des Belles Lettres Arabes (Tunis)

IJMES
International Journal of Middle Eastern Studies

IC
Islamic Culture

IOS
Israel Oriental Studies

IQ
Islamic Quarterly

IS
Islamic Studies

JA
Journal Asiatique

JAL
Journal of Arabic Literature

JAOS
Journal of the American Oriental Society

JCOI
Journal of the Cama Oriental Institute

JCS
Journal of Cuneiform Studies

JE
Jewish Encyclopaedia

JIS
Journal of Islamic Studies

JNES
Journal of Near Eastern Studies

JPHS
Journal of the Pakistan Historical Society

JRAS
Journal of the Royal Asiatic Society

J[R]ASB
Journal and Proceedings of the [Royal] Asiatic Society of Bengal

JSAI
Jerusalem Studies in Arabic and Islam

JSS
Journal of Semitic Studies

MFOB
Mélanges de la Faculté Orientale de l'Université de St. Joseph (Beirut)

MMII
Majallat al-Majmaʿ al-ʿIlmī al-ʿIrāqī

MMMA
Majallat Maʿhad al-Makhṭūṭāt al-ʿArabiyya

MO
Le monde oriental

MSOS
Mitteilungen des Seminars für Orientalische Sprachen

MW
The Muslim World

OC
Oriens Christianus

OLZ
Orientalische Literaturzeitung

OM
Oriente Moderno

OP
Orientalia Pragensia

ParOr
Parole de l'Orient

PEPP
The New Princeton Encyclopedia of Poetry and Poetics. Ed. Alex Preminger and T.F. Brogan, Princeton 1993.

PO
Patrologia Orientalis

QSA
Quaderni di Studi Arabi

RAAD
Revue de l'Academie Arabe de Damas

REI
Revue des Études Islamiques

REJ
Revue des Études Juives

RH
Revue Historique

RHR
Revue de l'Histoire des Religions

RIMA
Revue de l'Institut des Manuscrits Arabes

RO
Revue Orientale

ROr
Rocznik Orientalistyczny

RSO
Rivista degli studi orientali

SA
Studia Arabica

SAV
Schweizerisches Archiv für Volkskunde

SBAW
Sitzungsberichte der Bayerischen Akademie der Wissenschaften

SI
Studia Islamica

TAPS
Transactions of the American Philological Society

WI
Die Welt des Islams

WO
Die Welt des Orients

WZH
Wissenschaftliche Zeitschrift der Universität Halle

WZKM
Wiener Zeitschrift für die Kunde des Morgenländes

ZDMG
Zeitschrift der Deutschen Morganländischen Gesellschaft

ZGAIW
Zeitschrift für Geschichte der Arabisch-Islamischen Wissenschaften

English transliteration system

Consonants†

	A	P		A	P		A	P
ء	ʾ	ʾ	ژ	—	zh	گ	—	g
ب	b	b	س	s	s	ل	l	l
پ	—	p	ش	sh	sh	م	m	m
ت	t	t	ص	ṣ	ṣ	ن	n	n
ث	th	s	ض	ḍ	ż	ه	h	h
ج	j	j	ط	ṭ	ṭ	و	w	v *or* u
چ	—	ch	ظ	ẓ	ẓ	ى	y	y
ح	ḥ	ḥ	ع	ʿ	ʿ	ة	-a[1]	
خ	kh	kh	غ	gh	gh			
د	d	d	ف	f	f			
ذ	dh	z	ق	q	q			
ر	r	r	ك	k	k *or* g			
ز	z	z						

[1] (-at in construct state)

†*Column Headings:* A = Arabic, P = Persian

Vowels

		Arabic and Persian
Long	ا or ى	ā
	و	ū
	ي	ī
Doubled	ـِيّ	iyy (final form ī), etc.
	ـُوّ	uww (final form ū), etc.
Diphthongs	ـَو	aw
	ـَى	ay
Short	ـَ	a
	ـُ	u
	ـِ	i

K

Ka'b al-Aḥbār (d. between 32–5/652–5)

Abū Ishāq ibn Māti' Ka'b al-Aḥbār was a Jew from **Yemen**. He accepted Islam in 17/638, and fanciful legends, both Christian and Muslim, about his conversion abound. Often confusing rabbis with monks, these legends were used to show deliberate tampering by Jews (or Christians) with the original Biblical texts supposedly predicting the coming of Muḥammad and Islam.

Little is known of Ka'b's life except for reports of his relations with the second and third caliphs, 'Umar and 'Uthmān. After coming to Medina, but before his conversion, he accompanied 'Umar to Jerusalem in 15/636, where he helped to identify the site of the ancient Jewish temple which the Christians were supposedly attempting to conceal. 'Umar, however, is said to have rebuked Ka'b for his veneration of that site. He later became a champion of 'Uthmān, leading to bitter conflicts with the latter's pietist opponents, especially Abū Dharr. After 'Uthmān's death Mu'āwiya tried to attract him to **Damascus**, but he seems to have withdrawn to Homs, where he died.

Considered the earliest authority on Jewish tradition in Islam, and often cited in ***ḥadīth*** on biblical lore and law, statements of the rabbis, and legendary tales of the *Haggadah*, Ka'b's reputation varies greatly, from the somewhat negative views of pietists as reported by early historians, to positive acceptance by collectors of the ***Legends of the Prophets***, for whom he was an essential first-hand authority. Even among their accounts, and among some present-day Muslim scholars, however, one finds condemnation of some of his transmitted lore as un-Islamic.

Further reading

Hirschberg, H.Z., 'Ka'b al-Aḥbār', *EJ*, vol. 10, 488.

Hirschfeld, H., 'Ka'b al-Aḥbār', *JE*, vol. 7, 400.

Ibn Ḥajar al-'Asqalānī, *Tahdhīb al-tahdhīb*, Hyderabad (1907), vol. 1, 438–40.

Perlmann, M., 'A legendary story of Ka'b al-Aḥbār's conversion to Islam', in *The Joshua Starr Memorial Volume*, New York (1953) 85–99.

Wolfensohn (Ben-Zeev), I., *Ka'ab al-Aḥbār: Jews and Judaism in the Islamic Tradition* (in Arabic), Jerusalem (1976).

W.M. BRINNER

See also: *Isrā'īliyyāt*

Ka'b ibn Zuhayr (first/seventh century)

Son of the poet **Zuhayr ibn Abī Sulmā** and himself a poet of repute in pre- and (mainly) early Islamic times. He owes his fame to a poem addressed to the Prophet **Muḥammad** in which he apologizes after having satirized Islam. Muḥammad accepted his excuse and allegedly rewarded him with a mantle (*burda*) which gave the poem its name. Ka'b's *Burda* (also called *Bānat Su'ād* after its opening words) is a carefully structured ***qaṣīda*** of fifty-eight lines. A *nasīb* describing a beloved's beauty and falseness is followed by a *raḥīl* (description of a desert journey) with the detailed portrait of a swift camel. The last part contains the poet's excuse and, connected through a lion episode, a very short eulogy of the Prophet and his tribe Quraysh. The *Burda* became one of the most famous Arabic poems and was the subject of numerous commentaries and imitations. Its attractiveness lies not only in its indisputable literary qualities, but also in the fact that it stands as a symbol for the reconciliation of Islam and pre-Islamic traditions. Ka'b's other poems, often melancholic in tone, display a lot of originality especially in their portrayal of desert journeys and animals, but are not devoid of some clumsy expressions.

Text editions

La Bânat So'âd, R. Basset (ed. and trans.), Algiers (1910).
Beiträge zur arabischen Poesie, Oskar Rescher (trans.), vol. 4, pt 1, Istanbul (1950), 32–41; vol. 4, pt 3, Istanbul (1959–60), 99–175.
Dīwān, Cairo (1950); Tadeusz Kowalski (ed.), Cracow (1950).

Further reading

Bauer, Thomas, *Altarabische Dichtkunst*, Wiesbaden (1992), vol. 1, 122–4; vol. 2, 127–70.
Sells, Michael J., '*Bānat Su'ād*: translation and introduction', *JAL* 21 (1990), 140–54.

T. BAUER

al-Kāfiyājī (d. 879/1474)

Muḥyī al-Dīn Muḥammad ibn Sulaymān al-Kāfiyājī was a scholar whose interests and writings covered a broad spectrum but whose importance lies chiefly in his works on grammar and logic. His mastery of logic is reflected in his treatises on various subjects, which attempt to arrange the subject matter on the basis of principles of formal logic. In some cases, as in his treatises on mysticism and historiography, his writings give the impression of a conscious attempt to found new disciplines.

Further reading

Rosenthal, Franz, *A History of Muslim Historiography*, 2nd edn, Leiden (1968), 245–62, 547–80.

B. WEISS

al-Kalābādhī, Abū Bakr Muḥammad ibn Isḥāq (d. *c.*385/995)

A prominent writer on early **Sufism** and a ***ḥadith*** specialist. Few details of his life are known; his *nisba* refers to the Kalābādh quarter of Bukhārā. Al-Kalābādhī's main work, *Kitāb al-Ta'arruf li-madhhab ahl al-taṣawwuf* (*The Doctrine of the Ṣūfīs*), was an early Ṣūfī manual of 'self-explanation'. The book explained the doctrine, origins, concepts and practices of Sufism, imparting information while conveying its message of Sufism's roots in Islam and its essential theological 'orthodoxy'. To this end, al-Kalābādhī employed a new Ṣūfī literary style of open and sober explication of esoteric ideas and practices. His discussion of Ṣūfī technical terms is a model of this genre. The *Ta'arruf* was influential in reducing the tension between Sufism and 'orthodoxy' after the **al-Ḥallāj** drama. Its place as a major source for the early history of Sufism is assured, as well as its standing as a great expositor of Sufism to non-Ṣūfī Islam.

Text editions

The Doctrine of the Sufis, A.J. Arberry (trans.), Cambridge (1932).
Kitāb al-Ta'arruf li-madhhab ahl al-taṣawwuf, 'Abd al-Ḥalīm Maḥmūd (ed.). Cairo (1960).

R.L. NETTLER

al-Kalā'ī (sixth/twelfth century)

Muḥammad ibn 'Abd al-Ghafūr al-Kalā'ī was a literary critic. Although he belonged to a well-known Arab family of statesmen and writers in Seville, and he himself became a vizier, almost nothing is known of him. He was a friend of **Ibn Bassām al-Shantarīnī**, who died 542/1147. He is the author of *Iḥkām ṣan'at al-kalām* (*The Perfection of the Art of Speech*), which deals with prose style (e.g. the various forms of rhymed prose or ***saj'*** and prose genres such as **artistic prose**, the sermon (***khuṭba***) and the ***maqāma***. He is concerned more with stylistic embellishment (for which he employs an original terminology) than with matters of content.

Text edition

Iḥkām ṣan'at al-kalām, Muḥammad Riḍwān al-Dāya (ed.), Beirut (1966).

Further reading

al-Dāya, Muḥammad Riḍwān, *Ta'rīkh al-naqd al-adabī fī al-Andalus*, Beirut (1968), 401–31.

G.J.H. VAN GELDER

Kalām

Kalām, which literally means 'speech', or 'talk', is the common designation among Muslims historically for theological discourse. Generally, the term is combined with *'ilm* to form the phase *'ilm al-kalām*, 'the science of theological discourse'. Arabic terms that more closely approximate 'theology' in their literal meaning, viz. *ilāhiyyāt* and *lāhūt* (often following *'ilm*), are put to other uses. *Ilāhiyyāt* commonly refers to metaphysics as developed by the Muslim Peripatetic philosophers, and *lāhūt* is commonly used among Christians. The only real alternative to *'ilm al-kalām* as a designation for theology among Muslims is *'ilm uṣūl al-dīn*, 'the science of the foundations of religion',

Although theological discussion in the first two centuries of Islam is marked by wide diversity and great fluidity, later theological thought crystallized into three major schools: **Mu'tazilī**, Ash'arī and Māturīdī. The Mu'tazilī was the earliest of the three to emerge, and though itself diverse in its earlier development it came to be associated with certain fundamental notions, the most prominent of which were the unity of God and justice. What was distinctive about the Mu'tazilī approach to these ideas was their particular brand of rationalism: the unity of God meant for them that the eternality of the **Koran** (an idea precious to many Muslims) had to be denied and that justice – right and wrong – had to be rooted in human rational intuition.

The Ash'arī school – named after the person claimed as its founder, Abū al-Ḥasan **al-Ash'arī** – embraced the cause of rationalist inquiry but with different results: it claimed to be able to demonstrate the eternality of the divine speech and other divine attributes and to demolish the idea of a rationalist ethics with the very tools of discursive argumentation that had been used by the Mu'tazilīs. The Māturīdī school, which arose soon after the Ash'arī, leaned toward Ash'arī positions on major issues but took a middle-of-the-road stance on subordinate issues not dealt with here.

A great many religious scholars in medieval Islam considered argumentation over certain issues debated by these schools, such as the status of the divine attributes, to be forbidden and actively opposed *kalām*. This anti-*kalām* movement, which waxed and waned during successive centuries, was in many ways a school of thought in its own right.

Further reading

Watt, W.M., *The Formative Period of Islamic Thought*, Edinburgh (1973), 180–250, 279–318.

Wolfson, H.A., *The Philosophy of the Kalam*, Cambridge, Mass. (1976).

B. WEISS

Kalb *see* tribes

Kalīla wa-Dimna

A famous collection of didactic fables, mostly of Indian origin. The book, which takes its name from those of the two jackals who figure in its first story (and which are corruptions of Sanskrit Karaṭaka and Damanaka respectively), was translated into Arabic by **Ibn al-Muqaffa'** around the middle of the second/eighth century from an original in Middle Persian ('Pahlawī') which in turn had been compiled by the physician Burzōy (Arabicized: Barzūya) during the reign of the Sasanian emperor Khusrōy (Arabic: Kisrā) I Anūshīrwān (531–79). The Sasanian original is lost, but we do have a Syriac translation made directly from the Middle Persian, most probably in the sixth century, and by confronting it with the Arabic version we can form a fairly precise picture of the contents of their common source. This, like the Syriac translation, evidently contained ten frame-stories (each with a number of inserted sub-stories, and sometimes even sub-sub-stories). The first five ('The lion and the ox', 'The ring-dove and her companions', 'The owls and the crows', 'The ape and the tortoise', 'The ascetic and the weasel') are a translation of the five chapters of the *Pañcatantra*, the most celebrated story-book in Sanskrit. The next three ('The mouse and the cat', 'The king and the bird', 'The lion and the jackal') are taken from the twelfth book of the *Mahābhārata*, the Indian national epic. One ('The king and his eight dreams') is derived from a lost Buddhist Sanskrit source (the story survives in Tibetan, Pali and Chinese Buddhist versions), while the last chapter ('The king of the mice and his ministers') was apparently written by Burzōy himself.

The Arabic version of Ibn al-Muqaffa' began (at least in its original form) with an introduction by the Arabic translator extolling the book of *Kalīla wa-Dimna* as an indispensable store-house of political wisdom. Like all the other chapters it is interspersed with sub-stories, evidently the work of the translator himself. This was followed by a brief account of how Burzōy journeyed to India in search of medicinal herbs, but brought back books instead (published and translated in de Blois, 81–7; the story of Burzōy's journey as found in the printed editions is spurious). The third chapter was Burzōy's own autobiographical introduction, doubtless translated from the Middle Persian original (though lost in the Syriac version); this contains a very remarkable passage rejecting all established religions and preaching asceticism. These three introductory sections are followed by the translation of the ten stories contained in the Sasanian original, but after 'The lion and the ox' someone (most probably Ibn al-Muqaffaʿ himself) inserted a sequel of his own composition describing the trial and punishment of the treacherous jackal, Dimna. At the end of the book there are four stories that were probably not part of Burzōy's compilation: two ('The traveller and the goldsmith' and 'The king's son and his companions') are of Indian origin, the other two ('The lioness and the horseman' and 'The ascetic and his guest') have not been traced to any earlier source.

Kalīla wa-Dimna has always enjoyed great popularity in the Near East and has frequently been copied; unfortunately it has in the process undergone radical reworking. The existing manuscripts, the oldest of which are from the seventh/thirteenth century (500 years after the time of translation), differ radically from one another in virtually every sentence. Moreover, some of the genuine chapters listed above are missing from most of the manuscripts, while certain spurious chapters have been inserted at the beginning and end of the existing copies. The process of textual degradation has been continued by modern editors, who, in the mistaken belief that they were dealing with a children's book, have felt it necessary to alter some of the more ribald stories.

The Arabic work, like its principal source, the Sanskrit *Pañcatantra*, presents itself as a handbook for kings, a textbook of political science (see further **Mirrors for Princes**). The stories are embedded in a dialogue between an Indian king and the 'philosopher' B.y.d.n.' (later corrupted to Bīdpāy, Pīlpāy, etc.); each chapter begins by relating how the king asks the 'philosopher' to tell a story to illustrate a particular political lesson and how the latter proceeds to do so. Most of the stories have animals as their actors, although some deal with humans, but even in the animal stories the characters talk and behave like humans and not (as in the Aesopic fables) as stylized animals. The stories themselves are interupted by a large number of wise maxims, corresponding, in the case of the stories taken ultimately from the *Pañcatantra*, mostly to the verses which are inserted at regular intervals into the Sanskrit prose text. The lesson conveyed at least by the ten 'original' stories is decidedly utilitarian and indeed Machiavellian – success in politics depends on being able to outwit one's enemies – but the amoral tenor of the book is mitigated to a considerable extent by Burzōy's autobiography, as well as by the five additional stories added (apparently) by Ibn al-Muqaffaʿ. But in the end it is unlikely that anyone ever learnt either politics or morals from this book; the supposed pedagogical content is little more than an ostensible justification for what to a Muslim reader would otherwise have seemed a trivial work of entertainment.

The maxims in *Kalīla wa-Dimna* were copiously anthologized in the classic Arabic ***adab*** collections and the whole book was several times recast in rhymed couplets. The earliest known versification was by **Abān ibn ʿAbd al-Ḥamīd al-Lāḥiqī** (d. *c.*200/815); some fragments of this version have been preserved by Abū Bakr **al-Ṣūlī**. The sixth/twelfth century versification by **Ibn al-Habbāriyya** (who also wrote a versified imitation of *Kalīla wa-Dimna* entitled *Kitāb al-ṣādigh wa-al-bāʿim*) was lithographed in Bombay in 1887 while some later reworkings remain unpublished. *Kalīla wa-Dimna* has often been imitated, giving rise to a whole genre of books about wise (and not so wise) animals; the most important of these is doubtless **Abū al-ʿAlāʾ al-Maʿarrī**'s *Risālat al-ṣāḥil wa-al-shāḥij*. In the Middle Ages the book was translated from Arabic into several other languages (Greek, a second time into Syriac, Old Spanish, twice into Hebrew and several times into Persian); the earliest of these translations are older than the oldest surviving Arabic manuscripts and are thus of great importance for textual criticism. The earlier of the Hebrew versions was translated into Latin in the seventh/thirteenth century and this Latin version was in turn rendered into most of the vernacular languages of Europe, where it exerted considerable influence.

Many of the Arabic (and Persian) manuscripts of *Kalīla wa-Dimna* are beautifully illustrated; the book has thus an important place also in the history of Islamic art.

Text edition

The only published Arabic text that is based on sound editorial principles is the edition by L. Cheikho, Beirut (1905) (not to be confused with the same editor's bowdlerized 'school edition'!), which reflects a fairly decent manuscript dated 749/1339. All the other editions have been tampered with or 'corrected' by the editors.

There is no adequate English translation, but a good French version by A. Miquel is available (Paris, 1957).

For full discussion and further literature see F. de Blois, *Burzōy's Voyage to India and the Origin of the Book of Kalīlah wa Dimnah*, London (1990).

F. DE BLOIS

See also: didactic literature; fables; translation, medieval

Kamāl al-Dīn ibn al-ʿAdīm *see* Ibn al-ʿAdīm, Kamāl al-Dīn

kāmil *see* prosody

Kāmil, ʿĀdil (1916–)

Egyptian novelist. Like Najīb **Maḥfūẓ**, a disciple of the Egyptian Fabian Salāma **Mūsā**, Kāmil began his career as a novelist by writing a historical work, *Malik al-shuʿāʿ* (1945), based on the life and beliefs of the Pharaoh Akhenaten. This book won a prize for historical fiction in 1942. The novel that he submitted for a prize in 1944, *Millīm al-akbar*, was entirely different, being a realistic work that explored the state of Egyptian society through the lives of two young Egyptians from different social backgrounds. This novel (which some critics believe to have inspired Maḥfūẓ to move in the same direction) was Kāmil's final contribution to Egyptian fiction, after which he resumed his legal career.

Further reading

Jād, ʿAli B., *Form and Technique in the Egyptian Novel, 1912–71*, London (1983), 153–7, 166–8.

Kilpatrick, Hilary, *The Modern Egyptian Novel*, London (1974), 60–5.

Sakkūt, Hamdi, *The Egyptian Novel and its Main Trends from 1913–1952*, Cairo (1971), 79–84, 108–11.

R. ALLEN

Kāmil, Muṣṭafā (1874–1908)

Egyptian historian, nationalist and founder of the Egyptian National Party (al-Ḥizb al-Waṭanī). A law-school graduate of the University of Toulouse, Kāmil began in the 1890s, with the khedive's secret encouragement, to agitate for the withdrawal of the British from Egypt. A strong believer in education, he originated the idea of establishing a Western-style university in Egypt. This became the Egyptian University (al-Jāmiʿa al-Miṣriyya), set up one year after Kāmil's death and now the University of Cairo.

Kāmil's works are too numerous to list, since he spent all his adult life writing and making speeches. (Most of these are contained in his party newspaper, *al-Liwāʾ*.) His most important historical work is the two-volume *al-Masʾala al-sharqiyya* (1898) – the first distinctly modern, interpretative and analytical historical study to emerge from Egypt.

Kāmil was also a trend-setter stylistically. He abandoned the ***sajʿ*** conventions of earlier times and pioneered, with Qāsim **Amīn**, the adoption of a new 'direct style'.

Further reading

Crabbs, J.A., *The Writing of History in Nineteenth-century Egypt*, Detroit (1984), 146–66.

J. CRABBS

kān wa-kān

A form of non-classical poetry which probably originated in **Baghdad** in the fifth/eleventh century and remained in vogue until the eighteenth century. Its name ('there was once', i.e. 'once upon a time') is explained as being a formula used in tales and fables, the alleged original subject of this kind of verse. Famous preachers such as **Ibn al-Jawzī** (511–97/1117–1201) and Shams al-Dīn al-Kūfī (623–75/1226–77) employed the *kān wa-kān* in their sermons. A ***qaṣīda*** in *kān wa-kān* consists of a number of stanzas (*bayt*) with four members (*ʿuḍw*) or hemistichs (*miṣrāʿ*) each, the last of which ends in a long vowel+consonant representing the rhyme (*bcda*, *efga*, etc.). Single stanzas occur and may indeed have been the original form, but *qaṣīda*s with up to forty stanzas are frequently found. Al-Shaybī's collection contains 173 pieces totalling 1,490 stanzas. According to **Ibn Saʿīd al-Maghribī** (d. 685/1286), its metrical pattern is a form of *mujtathth* (– – v – / v – –), but, on the basis of paradigms mentioned by al-Banawānī (d. *c*.860/1456) and further developed by Aḥmad al-Darwīsh (d. before 1801), al-Shaybī arguably concludes that the pattern is accentual.

Further reading

García Gómez, E., 'Un poema paremiológico (...) en kān wa-kān (...)', *al-Andalus* 36 (1971), 329–72.

Hoenerbach, W., *Die Vulgärarabische Poetik ... des Ṣafīyaddīn Ḥillī*, Wiesbaden (1956).
al-Qurayshī Riḍā Muḥsin, *al-Funūn al-shi'riyya ghayr al-mu'raba 3: al-kān wa-kan wa-al-qūmā*, Baghdad (1977).
al-Shaybī, Kāmil Muṣṭafā, *Dīwān al-kān wa-kān fī al-shi'r al-sha'bī al-'Arabī al-qadīm*, Baghdad (1987).

W. STOETZER

Kanafānī, Ghassān (1936–72)

Palestinian novelist, literary critic, political journalist and artist. The son of a lawyer in Acre, Kanafānī's early education was in French schools. In 1948 his family was uprooted and moved to Syria. Kanafānī trained as a teacher and studied Arabic literature at Damascus University. Having been expelled for political activity, he joined relatives in Kuwait, working as a journalist until invited to Beirut in 1960 by George Habash to contribute to Arab nationalist newspapers. In 1969 he became official spokesman of Habash's organization, the Popular Front for the Liberation of Palestine, and editor of its journal *al-Hadaf*. He was killed by a car bomb planted by Israeli agents.

Kanafānī left seven novels (three of them unfinished), five collections of short stories, some plays, and studies of Palestinian resistance literature and Zionist literature. He was the first of a new generation of Palestinian writers who, not content with depicting the tragedy of the refugees, sought to foster national consciousness and explore paths of liberation for their people. Uniquely at the time, he ignored taboos to write of the Palestinians in Israel and of Israeli Jewish culture. His portrayal of an elderly Israeli couple, refugees from European anti-semitism, in the novel *'Ā'id ilā Ḥayfā*, was a pioneering attempt to go beyond the stereotyped representation of 'the enemy' common in Palestinian fiction of that period.

Kanafānī's main contribution to Arabic literature is in his fiction. His earliest stories established exploration of the Palestinian predicament and commitment to the struggle for a more dignified life for the refugees as a major theme of his work. As his talent matured, he employed, to increasing effect, powerful images and symbols and bitter irony to convey his perception of the betrayal that the Palestinians had suffered, their own weakness and their unwillingness to revolt against injustice and take responsibility for their future. His two most successful novels, *Rijāl fī al-shams* (1963) and *Mā tabaqqā lakum* (1966) reveal a remarkable awareness of modern techniques of stream of consciousness, flashback and changes in narrative perspective. The later *'Ā'id ilā Ḥayfā* (1969) reflects Kanafānī's adoption of a Marxist ideology and, concomitantly, of socialist-realist techniques of writing. Even then, however, his capacity to convey the attitudes and behaviour of the Palestinian peasant turned refugee, represented by Umm Sa'd in the cycle of stories named after her (1969), springs from a mastery of dialogue and pace independent of any specific political commitment.

Both the Palestinian and the classical Arabic literary heritage influenced Kanafānī's writing. The latter inspired the setting and characters of the play *al-Bāb* (1964), while the importance that some of the novels and short stories accord the desert, even when reinterpreted in modern terms, recalls its place in pre- and early Islamic poetry. The unfinished *al-'Āshiq* bears traces of the 'magic realism' associated in Palestinian literature with Imīl **Ḥabībī**. By contrast, some themes recurrent in Kanafānī's fiction, such as the interplay of coincidence and human weakness and gullibility, reflect a sense of the absurd. Kanafānī's constant drive to innovate, the quality of his writing, and his ability to convey the universal dimension of his people's tragedy and struggle explain the continuing popularity of his work in the Arab world and abroad.

Text editions

All That's Left to You, Mayy Jayyusi and Jeremy Reed (trans), Austin, Texas (1990).
Men in the Sun, Hilary Kilpatrick (trans), Washington, DC (1985).
Palestine's Children, Barbara Harlow (trans), Washington, DC (1985).

Further reading

Fischer, Wolfdietrich (ed.), *Männer unter tödlicher Sonne. Ghassan Kanafanis Werk heute*, Würzburg (1995).
Raḍwān, 'Āshūr, *al-Ṭarīq ilā al-khayma al-ukhrā*, Beirut (1977).
Siddiq, Muhammad, *Man is a Cause: Political Consciousness and the Fiction of Ghassān Kanafānī*, Seattle and London (1984).
Wild, Stefan, *Ghassan Kanafani: Life of a Palestinian*, Wiesbaden (1975).

H. KILPATRICK

Karagöz *see* shadow play; theatre and drama

Karāma, Buṭrus (1774–1851)

Syrian Greek Catholic court poet and teacher. Born in Homs, he died in Istanbul. He was employed in the chancellery of ʿAlī Pasha al-Asʿad, governor of Acre, for five years, then went to Mount Lebanon, becoming in 1813 court poet and private secretary to Prince Bashīr al-Shihābī, and finally his deputy in charge of the Lebanon. He taught the prince's sons Turkish and Arabic. When the prince left for exile in Malta in 1840, he accompanied him, before going to Istanbul as court interpreter. His published works include a collection of Andalusian ***Muwashshaḥāt*** (1864) (including his own attempts at the genre), and his **dīwān**, *Sajʿ al-ḥamāma fī dīwān al-muʿallim Buṭrus Karāma* (1898). Although arguably the best poet of his age, he is criticized for his ornate phraseology and style.

Further reading

Ebied R.Y., and Young, M.J.L., 'Buṭrus Karāma', *EI*[2], Supp., fascs. 3–4, 162.

P.C. SADGROVE

al-Kāshānī, ʿAbd al-Raḥmān *see* ʿAbd al-Raḥmān al-Qāshānī

Kateb, Yacine (1929–89)

Algerian poet, novelist and playwright writing in French. Born in Constantine, Kateb studied first at **Koran** school, then at French school and at the grammar school in Sétif. On 8 May 1945 he took part in the nationalist demonstration that took place in that town. He was arrested several days later and put in prison, where he met many militant leaders of the national movement. This experience shocked him. He then went through a period of romantic agony over his cousin Nedjma, whom he loved but who was already married. Expelled from grammar school, he left for Bône, where he published *Soliloques* (1946) – poems on the revolution and on love. He became attached to the Algerian Communist Party, then left for France, where he held various jobs, and where he published *Nedjma* in 1956. He died in Grenoble.

In *Nedjma*, Kateb had wanted to write a novel showing the tough side of Algeria – quite the opposite of what the critics expected from him. Without any real idea of the technique that he ought to adopt, he was trying to blend prose, poetry and drama. He wrote an A–Z of ideas, went back over them and added to them, adopting a different point of view every time. Each time he moved house, he began the same stories again, in an almost circular fashion, scribbling some 400 pages, from which he extracted *Nedjma*, then published the rest in 1966 under the title *Le Polygone étoilé*. In a flourish of lyricism he plunged into the realm of myth, using fragments from ancient Algerian history and claiming that a large part of his work was 'subconscious'. His cousin Nedjma became, in a sense, the symbol of the homeland of Algeria taken over by others – a virgin suffering for centuries the violation of conquest. In the novel his cousin–sister is coveted by four cousins, all from the generation who sacrificed themselves on 8 May 1945, so that the work may be seen in a sense as an 'autobiography in the plural'.

The same sense of tragedy is expressed in the dramatic work *Le Cercle des représailles* (1959), which includes 'Le Cadavre encerclé', 'Les Ancêtres redoublent de férocité', and a farce, 'La Poudre d'intelligence'. *L'Oeuvre en fragments* (1986) is a collection of various, previously unpublished texts. From 1971, Kateb also put on unpublished plays in colloquial Algerian Arabic. He is widely regarded as one of the most important modern Maghribi writers, although he himself recognized that his reputation was built around one central work.

Text editions

Intelligence Powder, S.J. Vogel (trans.), New York (1985).
Nedjma, R. Howard (trans.), New York (1961).

Further reading

Abdoun, M.-I., *Kateb Yacine*, Paris and Algiers, (1983).
Arnaud, J., *Recherches sur la littérature maghrébine de langue française*, vol. 2, *Le cas de Kateb Yacine*, Paris (1986).
Bonn, C., *Kateb Yacine*, 'Nedjma', Paris (1990).

J. DÉJEUX

kātib *see* secretaries

Kātib, Yāsīn *see* Kateb, Yacine

Kātib Çelebi *see* Ḥājjī Khalīfa

al-Kātib al-Siqillī *see* at-Ballanūbī

al-Kattānī (1858–1927)

Muḥammad ibn Ja'far al-Kattānī was a Moroccan historian, biographer, Ṣūfī and jurist, who became known as an implacable critic of French colonialism and a spokesman for the pan-Islamic movement. Born in Fez into a celebrated family of scholars and notables of Sharifian background, al-Kattānī initially pursued a typical scholarly career. His early works deal with such traditional themes as his family's genealogy, ***fiqh*** and ***ḥadīth***. His voluminous biographical collection *Salwat al-anfās* was dedicated to the saints, notables, rulers and *'ulamā'* of his native city; it testifies to al-Kattānī's spectacular proficiency in Maghribī historiography and intimate knowledge of the local hagiographical tradition. In this work al-Kattānī took pains to provide a rationale for, and a guide to, the veneration of the saints' shrines. Based on a thorough study of earlier historical sources and meticulous 'field' observations, *Salwat al-anfās* is often regarded as a model work of its genre. It gave rise to a number of imitations devoted to the celebrities of other Maghribī cities.

A witness to the French occupation of Morocco, al-Kattānī was outraged by the compliance and docility of the Moroccan rulers, who did nothing to organize a resistance to it. He expressed his protest by emigrating to Medina (1328/1910). From his exile, he invited his compatriots to follow his example, claiming that a Muslim cannot stay in the land ruled by the 'infidels'. When he moved to **Damascus**, he became involved in the anti-French struggle waged by Syrian Muslims. Despite his unswerving loyalty to Ṣūfī piety, he concurred on many points with the pan-Islamic and nationalist programmes advanced by **Shakīb Arslān** and Rashīd **Riḍā**, both of whom were ardent opponents of mystical Islam. Like these leaders, in his later works, al-Kattānī advocated for the renewal and reform of Islam, which he viewed as the only force capable of stemming Christian encroachments on Muslim lands.

Text editions

'Ilān al-ḥujja, Damascus (1990).
Naṣīḥat ahl al-Islām, Rabat (1989).
al-Risāla al-mustaṭrifa, Cairo (n.d.).
Salwat al-anfās, 3 vols, Fez (1316 AH).

Further reading

Lévi-Provençal, E., *Les Historiens des chorfa*, Paris (1922), 377–86

A. KNYSH

al-Kayyālī, Sāmī (1898–1972)

Syrian literary scholar and historian, editor and translator. Al-Kayyālī was born and educated in Aleppo, where he held several administrative posts and edited his influentual journal *al-Ḥadīth* (1927-60). He had close links with writers and institutions in Egypt and travelled widely in the Arab world, Europe and the United States, producing several books based on his journeys. He was a prolific writer, with some twenty books and dozens of articles to his credit. In addition to several collections of essays on Arabic literature, culture and history, he published works on **al-Jāḥiẓ, Abū al-'Alā' al-Ma'arrī**, Ṭāhā **Ḥusayn** and others. His widely used biographical and bibliographical survey of contemporary Syrian literature was published in Cairo in 1959, and in a revised, expanded edition in 1968.

Further reading

Ṣalībā, Jamīl, *Ittijāhāt al-naqd al-ḥadīth fī Sūriyya*, Cairo (1969).
Sulaymān, Nabīl, *al-Naqd al-adabī fī Sūriyya*, Beirut (1980).

A.-N. STAIF

al-Khafājī, Aḥmad ibn Muḥammad (*c*.979–1069/*c*.1571–1695)

Shihāb al-Dīn Aḥmad ibn Muḥammad al-Khafājī was an Egyptian scholar who spent much of his career as a legal official in the Ottoman empire before settling down to a literary life in **Cairo**. His many works include a ***dīwān*** of poetry, a supercommentary on **al-Bayḍawī's Koran** commentary; two works of literary biography, which are useful in that they give specimens of contemporary Arabic poetry and provide autobiographical details on the author; and, perhaps most valuable and original, his *Shifā' al-ghalīl* on foreign words borrowed into the Arabic language, complementing the earlier *al-Mu'arrab* of **al-Jawālīqī** and also providing examples of common solecisms in Arabic speech.

Text editions

Shifā' al-ghalīl, Cairo (1371/1952).
Ṭirāz al-majālis, Cairo (1284//1868).

C.E. BOSWORTH

al-Khafājī, Ibn Sīnān *see* Ibn Sīnān al-Khafājī

Khafīf see prosody

Khaïr-Eddine, Mohammed (1941–)

Moroccan poet and novelist writing in French. Born in 1941 in Tafraout in the Anti-Atlas, Khaïr-Eddine's native language was Berber; he then learned Arabic and French, but chose to write in French. In 1964 he published his manifesto *Poésie toute*, then left for France where he spent ten years before returning to Morocco in 1979. He returned to France in 1990. He has witten six novels, including *Agadir* (1967), *Corps négatif* (1968), *Moi, l'aigre* (1970) and *Le Déterreur* (1973), in which literary genres are mixed and the rebel poet-novelist pours out his wrath on all those who have attacked his work. Among his collections of poetry is *Soleil arachnide* (1969).

J. DÉJEUX

al-Khāl, Yūsuf (1917–87)

Syrian, later Lebanese, poet, translator and literary critic. Born in 'Amar al-Ḥuṣn, al-Khāl moved with his family to Tripoli (Lebanon), where his father was in charge of the Evangelical churches. He was educated at the American School there, at the American College in Aleppo, and from 1940 at the American University of Beirut, where he studied philosophy and was influenced by the prominent Lebanese philosopher Charles Malik. He joined the Syrian National Socialist Party in his youth; the teachings of Anṭūn **Sa'āda** had a lasting effect on his poetry and writings, even after he ceased to be officially connected with the party.

Al-Khāl spent much of his life working in journalism and publishing, with short spells teaching in secondary schools and at the American University of Beirut. He worked in New York in the UN's information department from 1948 to 1952 and was editor of the New York-based *al-Hudā* from 1952 to 1955. After returning to Lebanon, he launched the periodical *Shi'r* in 1957, one of the most influential publications in modern Arab cultural history, and began to distinguish himself both as a poet and literary agitator and as a father figure for a new generation of writers. His influence on the modernist movement in Arabic poetry may be compared with that of Ezra Pound on the imagist movement; significantly, al-Khāl's first volume of mature poetry (*al-Bi'r al-mahjūra*, 1958) opens with a poem, 'Ezra Pound', in which al-Khāl announces to Pound that he 'would be resurrected *here*, having been crucified by the Jews *out there*'.

Before embarking on the *Shi'r* project, al-Khāl had published a volume of poetry and a verse play heavily imbued with semi-romantic and symbolist imagery and a sense of belonging to a civilization whose glory had waned but which was now seeking rebirth. At this point, the West does not appear in his poetry as a problematic, but as a light interacting with the civilization from which it had derived its greatness. Already, myth and ritual permeated his poetry. From the mid-1950s, however, his poetry became freer and less concerned with immediate political and social issues, while remaining involved in the 'struggle of the modern' to create a new world: a new poetic language and a new social order. He developed a metaphysical tone, a spirit of search and yearning, and a Christian vision of man and society which continued the spirit of Jubrān Khalīl **Jubrān** (whose work *The Prophet* he later retranslated into Arabic). A combination of biblical imagery, ancient Syrian myth, and a language rich in the vocabulary and atmosphere of prayer, gave his poetry its most intimate qualities and distinguished his work from the rest of the *Shi'r* group. Al-Khāl's contribution to the emergence of a mythical dimension in Arabic poetry was crucial, and the so-called 'Tammūzī' poets owe much to his pioneering spirit and to his translations from English and American poetry. His deep-rootedness in the Christian tradition expressed itself later when he undertook the translation of the Bible, of which the New Testament was published in

1979; he died before completing the project, which has since been assumed by his close friend, the poet Fu'ād Rifqa.

Al-Khāl's poetry is distinguished by its more contemplative tone and falling rhythms, in contrast with the ideologically motivated tones of the period. Some of his poems in *al-Bi'r al-mahjūra* (1958) and *Qaṣā'id fī al-arba'īn* (1960) remain without parallel in their metaphysical depth. His greatest influence, however, came through his work, in collaboration with **Adūnīs** and other younger poets, on *Shi'r*, which played a pivotal role in the development of modern Arabic writing. His prose produced during the last two decades of his life is among the finest of this period and his *Rasā'il ilā Don Kishūt* are imbued with a mystical tone which masks a passionate belief in the possibilities of rebirth at a time when civil war, loss of faith and even cynicism were the dominant impulses in life and writing. With the recent eclipse of the literature of ideologies, a reassessment of al-Khāl's work will almost certainly resituate him as one of the small number of truly major figures in modern Arabic literature.

Further reading

Khair Beik, Kamāl, *Ḥarakat al-ḥadātha fī al-shi'r al-'Arabī al-mu'āṣir*, Beirut (1982) (French original, Paris, 1978).

KAMAL ABU-DEEB

Khalaf al-Aḥmar (d. *c.*180/796)

Early 'Abbāsid poet and famous ***rāwī*** of early poetry. Abū Muḥriz Khalaf Ibn Ḥayyān was a *mawlā* of Farghānian descent, born in **Basra**. Among his teachers was **Abū 'Amr ibn al-'Alā'**. He is praised by the critics and anthologists for his poetry, particularly his ***rajaz*** verse on snakes. **Abū Nuwās** reputedly transmitted his poetry, but his ***dīwān*** is not preserved, although a number of poems are found in various anthologies. Lost, too, is his work *Jibāl al-'Arab* (*'The Mountains of the Arabs'*). He was particularly famous as a great specialist in and transmitter of pre-Islamic poetry. Together with his older colleague and teacher **Ḥammād al-Rāwiya** he forms an important link between the pre-scholarly stage of transmitting early poetry and the following generation of scholarly philologians. As in the case of Ḥammād, there are some early reports that Khalaf was suspected of, or even confessed to, having made poetry in the ancient style and attributing it to famous poets. The most famous example of this is the great elegiac *lāmiyya* by **Ta'abbaṭa Sharran**; sometimes he is also said to have authored the equally famous poem (the *Lāmiyyat al-'Arab*) by **al-Shanfarā**. Their authorship is still a matter of dispute, a majority of scholars now favouring the basic authenticity of the poems in question.

Text editions

Ahlwardt, W., *Chalef alahmar's Qasside*, Greifswaldi (1859).
See also studies on the authenticity of early Arabic verse, in particular the poems by Ta'abbaṭa Sharran and al-Shanfarā. A work on syntax attributed to Khalaf al-Aḥmar, *Muqaddima fī al-naḥw*, 'Izz al-Dīn al-Tanūkhī (ed.), Damascus (1961), is unlikely to be by him.

G.J.H. VAN GELDER

al-Khalī' *see* al-Ḥusayn ibn al-Ḍaḥḥāk

al-Khalī' al-Raqqī

Al-Khalī' al-Raqqī died, according to some, *c.*280/893 but said by others to have been still alive in the days of the **Ḥamdānid** Sayf al-Dawla (r. 333–56/945–67); a North Syrian poet stemming from **Ibn Qays al-Ruqayyāt** who can hardly be traced any more. His ***dīwān***, which was said to encompass 300 leaves at the end of the fourth/tenth century, is lost. Nothing more than half a dozen poems with a maximum length of four lines is transmitted in the sources.

T. SEIDENSTICKER

Khālid ibn Yazīd al-Kātib (d. 262/876 or 269/883)

Poet mainly of ***ghazal*** from **Baghdad**. His family was of Khurāsānī origin. He worked as a *kātib* connected with the army in Baghdad and in the frontier area with Byzantium. He was known as a composer of love poems already, apparently in the time of **Hārūn al-Rashīd**. Almost all his poems are very short; he greatly favoured a compass of four lines. In his poetry and in his life he is the typical love-stricken poet, pining for love first from youth, then from old age as well. He died at a very advanced age.

Further reading

Arazi, Albert, 'La poésie d'amour dans le Dīwān de Ḫālid b. Yazīd *al-kātib*', *RSO* 53 (1979), 235–68; 54 (1980), 29–49.
——, *Amour divin et amour profane dans l'Islam médiéval à travers le Dīwān de Khālid al-Kātib*, Paris (1990) (edition and study).
Bencheikh, Jamel E., 'Les secrétaires poètes et animateurs de cénacles aux IIe et IIIe siècles de l'Hégire', 263 (1975), 265–315, esp. 310–12.

G.J.H. VAN GELDER

al-Khālidī, Muḥammad ibn Hishām *see* al-Khālidiyyān

al-Khālidī, Rawḥī (1864–1913)

Literary critic. Born into a prominent Jerusalem family, al-Khālidī attended Jamāl al-Dīn **al-Afghānī's** circle in the Ottoman capital and later studied Arabic and European culture in Paris. He served as Ottoman consul in Bordeaux, and was elected for three consecutive terms as Jerusalem's Deputy in the Ottoman Parliament after the declaration of the Ottoman Constitution in 1908.

Al-Khālidī wrote several books and many articles on subjects as varied as chemistry, the history of Zionism, linguistics and literature. He is best known, however, for his book *Tārīkh 'ilm al-adab 'ind al-Ifranj wa-al-'Arab wa-Victor Hugo*. Considered by many as the first successful attempt in Arabic at applied comparative literature, it was first published in 1902–3 as a series of articles in ***al-Hilāl***, then as a book under a pseudonym for fear of Ottoman oppression, before a third edition appeared in 1912 under the author's real name.

Further reading

al-Khaṭīb, Ḥ., *Rawḥī al-Khālidī rā'id al-adab al-'Arabī al-muqāran*, Amman (1985).

A.-N. STAIF

al-Khālidī, Sa'īd ibn Hishām *see* al-Khālīdīyyān

al-Khālidiyyān

Abū Bakr Muḥammad (d. 380/990) and Abū 'Uthmān Sa'īd (or Sa'd, d. *c.*390/1000) ibnā Hāshim al-Khālidiyyān were two brothers, both poets and anthologists. Born near al-Mawṣil, they lived in **Basra** and in Aleppo, as librarians at the court of the **Ḥamdānid** ruler Sayf al-Dawla. Some of their poetry has been preserved in anthologies such as *Yatīmat al-dahr* by **al-Tha'ālibī**. Part of their verse was composed in collaboration, as were all of their prose works. They were accused (largely unjustly, it seems) of plagiary by their rival, the poet **al-Sarī al-Raffā'**. *Al-Ashbāh wa-al-naẓā'ir* (not identical, as is sometimes claimed, with their *Ḥamāsat shi'r al-muḥdathīn*) is a loosely structured critical anthology of poems and fragments with identical motifs by pre- and early Islamic poets, at times compared with the same motifs as they occur in the poetry of the ***muḥdathūn***; the general drift is to show the superiority of the older poets. They also compiled some monographs or anthologies devoted to 'modern' poets, such as **Bashshār ibn Burd**, **Muslim ibn al-Walīd**, **Abū Tammām**, **al-Buḥturī** and **Ibn al-Rūmī**.

Text editions

al-Ashbāh wa-al-naẓā'ir min ash'ār al-mutaqaddimīn wa-al-Jāhiliyya wa-al-mukhaḍramīn, al-Sayyid Muḥammad Yūsuf (ed.), 2 vols, Cairo (1958, 1965).
Dīwān, Sāmī al-Dahhān (ed.), Damascus (1969).
al-Mukhtār min shi'r Bashshār, selection by al-Khālidiyyān, commentary by Ismā'īl ibn Aḥmad al-Tujībī, Muḥammad Badr al-Dīn al-'Alawī (ed.), Aligarh (1934).
al-Tuḥaf wa-al-hadāyā, Sāmī al-Dahhān (ed.), Cairo (1952).

G.J.H. VAN GELDER

Khalīfa, Saḥar (1941–)

Palestinian novelist. Born in Nablus, Saḥar Khalīfa's novels are dominated by her feminism and by her experience of life under Israeli occupation in the West Bank. In her first novel, *Lam na'ud jawārī lakum* (1974), she highlights the reality of the Palestinian female in her attempts to challenge the norms of her male-dominated society. More successfully artistically is *al-Ṣabbār* (1976), where she shows the tension between, on the one hand, the older generation of West Bank Palestinians who acquiesce in Israeli occupation and, on the other, the defiant younger generation eager to break out of the stifling paternalism of traditional society. The two themes of nationalist and feminist liberation are more fully integrated in *'Abbād al-shams*

(1980), the protagonists of which are two women, Rafīf and Sa'diyya – a significant departure from *al-Ṣabbār*, whose main character is male. Her fourth novel, *Mudhakkirāt imra'a ghayr wāqi'iyya* (1986), returns to the theme of personal and social freedom for Palestinian women – suggesting, however, that women's liberation is a distant dream, mainly because of the unremitting indoctrination that women have passively endured.

In her 1990 novel, *Bāb al-sāḥa*, she deals with the position of Palestinian women in their own society. However, she significantly departs from previous practice by using colloquial Arabic in dialogue. Not unexpectedly this made her the object of strong criticism by the literary establishment.

Text edition

Wild Thorns, T. LeGassick and Elizabeth Fernea (trans), London (1985).

Y. SULEIMAN

al-Khalīl ibn Aḥmad (*c*.100-75/718–91)

Abū 'Abd al-Raḥmān al-Khalīl ibn Aḥmad al-Farāhīdī al-Azdī was a famous grammarian and lexicographer, the founder of Arabic phonetics and prosody; he grew up and died in **Basra**. Of the works attributed to him, the lexicon *Kitāb al-'ayn* has been preserved. His authorship of this work is not unchallenged in the Arabic tradition, but the plan of the dictionary is thought to be purely Khalilian. Words are placed under their roots, but the roots come in bundles in which all permutations are grouped together. These bundles themselves, as well as the roots within each bundle, are ordered according to the Khalilian row, a sequence of Arabic consonants devised by al-Khalīl according to their place of articulation, which runs as follows: *' ḥ h kh gh q k j sh ḍ ṣ s z ṭ d t ẓ dh th r l n f b m w alif y '*. This system provides for a network that comprises all existing (*musta'mal*) and theoretical (*muhmal*) root combinations. The arrangement implies that roots with the letter *'ayn* are all together in the first chapter.

Hierarchical and permutational organization is also characteristic of al-Khalīl's prosodical system (*'arūḍ*), where the circles are bundles of permutationally related metres (see **prosody**). As a grammarian al-Khalīl played a fundamental role through his pupil **Sībawayhi**.

Further reading

Wild, S. *Das Kitâb al-'Ain und die arabische Lexikographie*, Wiesbaden (1965).

W. STOETZER

See also: grammar and grammarians; lexicography, medieval

Khalīl ibn Aybak al-Ṣafadī *see* al-Ṣafadī, Khalīl ibn Aybak

Khallāṣ, Jīlālī (1952–)

Algerian novelist and short-story writer, bilingual in French and Arabic. Born in Aïn Defla, Khallāṣ spent five years as a teacher before beginning work in publishing and at the Ministry of Culture in 1976. He has published four collections of short stories and two novels, in addition to stories for children and essays; he has also translated into Arabic works by Tahar **Djaout** (*Les Chercheurs d'os*) and Rachid **Boujedra** (*Topographie idéale pour une agression caractérisée*). In 1990 he founded the literary review *al-Riwāya*. Khallāṣ's essays have paved the way for modern literary criticism in Algeria; he is passionately interested in the millenial history of Algeria, and has sought in his writings to create a futuristic vision which draws both on myths and on real events.

M. BOIS

al-Khamīsī, 'Abd al-Raḥmān (1920–)

Egyptian socialist poet and short-story writer. Born in Port Said, al-Khamīsī worked in professions as varied as grocer, bus conductor, song composer, actor, teacher, radio announcer, film producer and translator. He spent the years 1954–6 in prison.

Al-Khamīsī started his literary career as a romantic poet at an early age. In 1958 he published *Ashwāq insān*, a collection of romantic poetry composed between 1938 and 1958. He also published short stories in newspapers and translated European short stories into Arabic. Most of his own stories (which draw on his own experiences) deal with the misery of the poor urban classes, sex, brutality, madness and drugs. His style is simple, direct and journalistic, with colloquial dialogues. His collections include: *Alf layla al-jadīda* (2 vols, n.d.), *al-Aʿmāq* (1950), *Yawmiyyāt majnūn, al-Mukāfiḥūn, Ṣayḥāt al-shaʿb* (which contains stories about the national and popular struggle against the British in Egypt), and *Qumṣān al-dam* (1953). Some of his stories have been translated into Russian.

Further reading

ʿAwaḍ, L., *Dirāsāt fī adabinā al-ḥadīth*, Beirut (1961), 169–80.

Moreh, S., and Milson, M., *Modern Arabic Literature: A Research Bibliography 1800–1980*, Jerusalem (1993), 180.

Qabbish, A., *Tārīkh al-shiʿr al-ʿArabī al-ḥadīth*, n.p. (1971), 709.

S. MOREH

khamriyya

Wine poetry. Descriptions of wine and banquets are already found in pre-Islamic poetry. Characteristically, connections between the early *khamriyyāt* poets and the court and town of **Ḥīra** – an ancient centre for the wine trade – can often be established (**ʿAdī ibn Zayd, Ṭarafa ibn al-ʿAbd**, **al-Aʿshā**, al-Aswad ibn Yaʿfur). However, these wine descriptions can as yet scarcely be found in independent poems where this happens to be the case, as in several pieces composed by ʿAdī ibn Zayd from Ḥīra, it cannot be determined whether they were, indeed, originally independent poems or fragments of ***qaṣīda***s. In the ancient Arabic *qaṣīda*, banquet scenes are mainly to be found in two places: in the self-praise (***fakhr***) part in which poets (e.g, **ʿAlqama ibn ʿAbada**, al-Aʿshā) boast about having taken part in banquets (which clearly points to their being an aristocratic amusement); and in the description of the beloved, where the 'independent' comparison of her saliva with wine often results in a detailed wine scene description (e.g. ʿAdī ibn Zayd, al-Aswad ibn Yaʿfur). The choice of motifs in the ancient Arabic descriptions of banquets may be exemplified by an analysis of two detailed wine scenes by ʿAdī ibn Zayd (d. *c.*600) and al-Aʿshā (d. *c.*9/630).

(ʿAdī): *nasīb* with a description of the beloved's saliva – metaphorization of the saliva by wine – comparison of its colour (red) with blood – characterization of the wine's transparency – mention of the Jewish merchant who aged it and then sold it in the market – description of the buyer (a generous young man) – drinking scene (in the early morning) with mention of the female cup-bearer – comparison of the wine with a rooster's eye.

(Al-Aʿshā in the *fakhr* part of a *qaṣīda*): Boasting with frequent visits to the tavern – mention of the meat cook and the boon companions – mention of the drinkers lying propped up (on their sides) as well as the flowers that are being used as decoration for the banquet – description of the wine, its flavour, the intoxication of the drinkers, the banquet's musical framework and the songstress.

Most of these motifs can be found again in the fully developed wine poetry of the **ʿAbbāsid** period.

During the early Islamic period wine poetry at first receded somewhat, partly perhaps, because of the Islamic prohibition of wine, although the Prophet **Muḥammad**'s court poet **Ḥassān ibn Thābit** (d. *c.*50/670?) composed verses on wine even after his conversion. Meanwhile, one poet comes to our attention who described his banquets while being fully conscious of his sinfulness: **Abū Miḥjan al-Thaqafī** (d. *c.*16/637). The tension between sinful actions and repentance later became a constant part of the reservoir of motifs in wine poetry and is particularly to be found in **Abū Nuwās**.

After having been founded in the immediate vicinity of al-Ḥīra, the town of **Kufa** seems to have taken over the role of al-Ḥīra as centre of the wine trade. It is noticeable that most of the poets of the **Umayyad** period who composed verses on wine either came from Kufa or had connections with it. The Christian poet **al-Akhṭal** (d. *c.*92/710), one of the main representatives of Umayyad wine poetry, spent his youth in Kufa (probably having been born in Ḥīra). In his poetry wine descriptions are almost always found within the framework of *qaṣīda*s, as in the poetry of al-Aʿshā, to whom he is also closely connected in the choice of motifs for his banquet scenes. Independent wine poems on a larger scale can be found for the first time among a group of minor poets, almost all of whom are from Kufa (**Abū Jilda al-Yashkurī, al-ʿUqayshir al-Asadī**, Mālik ibn Asmāʾ ibn Khārija, ʿAmmār Dhū Kināz). Most of these poets also composed love poems and obscene poetry which often cannot be separated from the wine poetry. The Umayyad caliph **al-Walīd ibn Yazīd** (d. 126/744), who may have been the most prominent composer of independent wine poems before Abū Nuwās, is said to have had a high regard for 'Ammār Dhū Kināz, and it seems that he himself has his place in the Ḥīra–Kufa tradition. On the other hand, al-Walīd's *khamriyyāt* are already so similar to those of Abū Nuwās that one of his poems ended up in the latter's *dīwān*. In the poetry of al-Walīd, a large amount of motifs typical of the wine poetry of Abū Nuwās are found in exactly the same form. The call to enjoy life, the comparison of the wine with precious metals and fire, and especially blasphemous thoughts and the simultaneous hope for forgiveness.

Among the wine poets active in the Umayyad period as well as in early **'Abbāsid** times should be mentioned **Abū al-Hindī** (d. *c.*133/750) and **Muṭī' ibn Iyās** (d. 169/785), both from Kufa. Abū al-Hindī, who later moved to **Khurasan**, in one case prepared the way for a type of wine-poem in which a **dialogue** between the drinkers and the vintner is the main characteristic and which later plays an important role in Abū Nuwās. Muṭī' is the first wine poet of the ***muḥdath*** school. It seems that he and **Muslim ibn al-Walīd** (d. 208/823), (again originating from Kufa), imported the genre to Baghdad and propagated it there.

The most important Arabic wine-poet of all times is Abū Nuwās (d. *c.*200/815). His poetry is closely connected to that of his predecessors, especially al-Walīd ibn Yazīd and Abū al-Hindī; therefore, Abū Nuwās is not strictly speaking an innovator. However, his *khamriyyāt* exceed all their predecessors by far in terms of quantity, versatility and quality. There is a very free choice of motifs for wine poems, and even later no rigid pattern developed (as it did in the case of the hunting-poems). The introductory part of many *khamriyyāt* consists of a rebuke of the fault-finders or the call for submitting to the pleasures of the wine instead of weeping over deserted camps (as was done so often by the old tribal poets in the beginnings of their *qaṣīdas*). Many poems have as their main theme the description of the wine, its appearance (comparisons with light, precious stones), its scent, its age and its effect on the drinkers. Much space is also taken by the description of the male or female cup-bearer who serves the wine, of the male or female singer who entertains the drinker, of the flowers with which the inn is decorated or the garden in which the banquet takes place. The description that has acquired much fame is that of a golden drinking bowl of the Sassanian period that is decorated with figurative motifs. In some of his longer poems Abū Nuwās speaks in a quite realistic way about himself and his boon companions setting out in the dark night and rousing and persuading the (Christian, Zoroastrian or Jewish) vintner to sell wine to them. The dialogue with the vintner is then followed by a description of the wine and the nocturnal banquet which lasts until early morning. There are other poems that have a melancholic tone, because they contain the poet's memories of the pleasures of his youth long past. The religious dimension which appears time and again in the *khamriyyāt* (tension between being conscious of one's sins and hope for forgiveness) has already been mentioned. A large number of Abū Nuwās's poems end with a quotation from a song that usually is put into the mouth of a female singer. Once, a poem ends with a sentence in Persian. One may perhaps regard this convention as the model for the Andalusian ***muwashshaḥ*** poets who, as a rule, ended their poems with a quotation (*kharja*), often from a song, in the Andalusian dialect, or in Romance.

All of the later wine poets are dependent on Abū Nuwās without adding many innovations. One of his most important imitators is **Ibn al-Mu'tazz** (d. 296/908), whose ***dīwān*** contains a chapter on *khamriyyāt*. Ibn al-Mu'tazz's most famous wine-poem is his *muzdawija* (a poem consisting of rhymed couplets) *Fī dhamm al-ṣabūḥ* (*On Blaming the Early Morning Drink*). In the *dīwān*s of many other poets (**al-Buḥturī, Ibn al-Rūmī**), wine poems or verses about wine in poems of other genres can be found sporadically. The *dīwān* of **Ṣafī al-Dīn al-Ḥillī** (d. *c.*750/1350) still contains a special chapter on *khamriyyāt*.

Wine and carousals form the major theme in many Andalusian poems, particularly also in strophic poems (*muwashshaḥs*, **Ibn Quzmān**'s ***zajal***s). Here again Abū Nuwās's gamut of motifs is omnipresent.

The motifs of wine poetry (like those of love poetry) undergo a new interpretation in the poetry of the mystics. With them, wine becomes a symbol of divine love and drunkenness becomes mystical ecstasy. There are mystical *khamriyyāt*, the most famous example of which is the poem by **Ibn al-Fāriḍ** (d. 632/1235) which is known by the name *khamriyya*. (See further **Ṣūfī literature: poetry**.)

Further reading

Bencheikh, J.E., 'Khamriyya', *EI²*.
Hamori, Andras, *On the Art of Medieval Arabic Literature*, Princeton (1974), 37–77.
Harb, F., 'Wine Poetry (*Khamriyyāt*)', in *CHALABL*, 219–34.
Ḥāwī, Ī., *Fann al-shi'r al-khamrī*, Beirut (n.d.).
Schoeler, G., 'Bashshār ibn Burd, Abū 'l-'Atāhiya, Abū Nuwās', in *CHALABL*, 275–299.
Wagner, E., *Abū Nuwās: Eine Studie zur arabischen Literatur der frühen 'Abbāsidenzeit*, Wiesbaden (1964), 143–62, 189–308.
——, *Grundzüge der klassischen arabischen Dichtung*, Darmstadt (1987–8), vol. 2, 34–46.

G. SCHOELER; trans. A. GIESE

al-Khansā' (d. after 644)

The greatest early Arabic elegiac poet. Tumāḍir bint 'Amr, nicknamed al-Khansā' ('Snub-nose', epithet also of a gazelle), of the tribe Sulaym, was reportedly praised for her verse by her contemporary **al-Nābigha al-Dhubyānī**; later poets such as **Jarīr ibn 'Aṭiyya** and **Bashshār ibn Burd** also admired her. Her fame rests mainly on the extraordinary series of elegies made for her two brothers, Ṣakhr and Mu'āwiya, who died before the coming of Islam. The former died after a lingering illness due to a wound received in a tribal skirmish, the latter was killed in another raid. Lamenting the dead (*niyāḥā*) was traditionally a female speciality; al-Khansā' was instrumental in raising it to the level of high-status poetry (*qarīḍ*) by using its metres and rhyme form instead of ***saj'*** or forms of ***rajaz*** (see ***rithā'***). The poems, technically accomplished, are relatively accessible by their direct appeal to the emotions. Most poems include many themes, some relating to the poet herself (weeping, addressing the eyes), others to the lamented brother and his virtues, or to the tribe, who are urged to avenge the deceased.

Text editions

Dīwan, L. Cheikho (ed.), Beirut (1896); 'Abd al-Salām al-Ḥūfī (ed.), Beirut (1985); Ibrāhīm 'Iwaḍayn (ed.), Cairo (1986); Anwar Abū Suwaylim (ed.), Amman (1988).

Further reading

Bonebakker, S.A., 'Mubarrad's version of two poems by al-Khansā'', Wagner Festschrift, vol 2, 90–119.
Gabrieli, G., *I tempi, la vita e il canzoniere della poetessa araba al-Ḫansā'*, Rome (1944).
Jones, Alan, *Early Arabic Poetry. I:* Marāthī *and* Ṣu'lūk *poems*, Reading (1992), 89–101
Nöldeke, T., *Beiträge zur Kenntnis der Poesie der alten Araber*, Hannover (1864), 152–82.
Rhodokanakis, N., *Al-Ḫansā' und ihre Trauerlieder*, Wien (1904).

G.J.H. VAN GELDER

al-Khāqānī, 'Alī (1912–79)

Iraqi **Shī'ī** literary historian. Al-Khāqānī was born and educated in al-Najaf, where he edited the journal *al-Bayān* from 1946 to 1950. In 1959 he founded the al-Bayān Publishing House in **Baghdad**. Al-Khāqānī collected the poetry and biographies of poets (particularly Shī'īs) from a number of towns – among his publications being *Shu'arā' al-Ḥilla aw Bābiliyyāt* (5 vols, al-Najaf, 1951–2), *Shu'arā' al-Gharī aw al-Najafiyyāt* (12 vols, al-Najaf, 1954–6) and *Shu'arā' Baghdād min ta'sīsihā ḥattā al-yawm* (2 vols., Baghdad, 1962). He also edited the ***dīwāns*** of several Shī'ī poets, including those of Ḥaydar **al-Ḥillī** and Muḥammad Riḍā al-Naḥwī, and collected dialect poetry in his *Funūn al-adab al-sha'bī* (5 vols, Baghdad, 1962–3).

W. WALTHER

al-Kharā'iṭī, Muḥammad ibn Ja'far (d. 327/938)

Abū Bakr Muḥammad ibn Ja'far al-Kharā'iṭī was a traditionist and compiler of books which may be described as a kind of pious ***adab*** literature. He is said to have been 'of the people of Surra Man Ra'ā' (Samarra). He collected ***ḥadīth*** there and in **Baghdad** and was regarded by most experts as a reliable transmitter, especially valued for his longevity – linking him with the first half of the third century AH – as well as for his taste for subjects that attracted general interest. He died at Askelon, aged about 90. His compilation of *ḥadīth*, anecdotes and verses on love, *I'tilāl al-qulūb* (*The Malady of Hearts*), seems to have played a key part as a source and inspiration for later Ḥanbalī theory of love (see **love theory**).

Text editions

Hawātif al-jinnān wa-'ajīb mā yuḥkā 'an al-kuhhān, M.A. 'Abd al-'Azīz (ed.), Beirut (1989).
I'tilāl al-qulūb, The Malady of Hearts, Arabic edn. and English trans. with introduction and notes by L.A. Giffen (in process).

Kitāb Faḍīlat al-shukr lillāh 'alā ni'matih, M.M. Ḥāfiẓ (ed.), Damascus (1982).
Makārim al-akhlāq wa-ma'ālīhā, S.S.I Khānaqāwī *et al.* (eds), 2 vols, Cairo (1991).
al-Muntaqā min Makārim al-akhlāq, G. Budayr and M.M. Ḥāfiẓ (eds), Damascus (1986) (selections).

Further reading

Giffen, L.A., *Theory of Profane Love Among the Arabs*, New York (1971), 15–16, 74–8 and index.
Leder, S., *Ibn al-Jawzī und seine Kompilation wider die Leidenschaft*, Beirut (1984).
Vadet, J.-C., 'Littérature courtoise et transmission du ḥadīṯ, un exemple: Muḥammad b. Ǧa'far al-Ḫarā'iṭī', *Arabica* 7 (1960), 140–66 (but see additions and emendations to his description of the contents of *I'tilāl al-qulūb* in Giffen, *op. cit.* 75, n.14).

L.A. GIFFEN

Khārijīs, Khārijī literature

Khārijīs (ar. *al-khawārij*; sing. *al-khārijī*, 'dissenters', 'schismatics'), groups of Muslim warriors that seceded (*kharaja*) from the army of **'Alī ibn Abī Ṭālib** in 37–8/657–8, after he had agreed to compromise with Mu'āwiya, the Muslim ruler of **Syria** who contested 'Alī's claims to the caliphate. Defeated by 'Alī's troops at Nahrawān (Iraq) in 38/658, the Khārijīs, most of whom were Arabs of tribal background, became his implacable enemies. They declared war on 'Alī and his followers, and finally assassinated him in **Kufa** (60/661). From then on they fought against every Muslim government that appeared. Under Mu'āwiya's successors, the Khārijīs formed a piously-minded opposition to the increasingly secularized **Umayyad** state. They claimed that the caliphal incumbents had strayed from the right path, forfeited their allegiance to Islam and therefore must be treated as illegitimate usurpers of power. The Khārijīs sought to depose these unworthy and sinful rulers and replace them with the most pious and knowledgeable leader (Imām), regardless of his origin ('even if he were a black slave'). According to the Khārijīs, Muslims who co-operated with impious rulers had committed a grievous sin. The Khārijīs called upon Muslims to rally around a pious commander, who should be elected by a free vote, and to dissociate themselves from the deluded remainder of the Muslim community.

As time went on, leaders of the Khārijī groupings based in **Basra** and Kūfa adopted different interpretations of these basic principles. The extreme version of Khārijism was represented by the Azraqīs (*al-azāriqa*). They regarded each Muslim who had committed a grave sin as an apostate and polytheist. In keeping with this view, they classified all those refusing to join their rebellion as enemies of Islam, who should be put to death together with their families. This ferocious principle did not fail to estrange the Khārijī extremists from the main body of Muslims. Most of them perished in battles against caliphal troops.

A more tolerant stance towards the non-Khārijī Muslims was taken by the 'quietists' (*al-qa'ada*), who constituted two major groups, *al-ibāḍiyya* and *al-ṣufriyya*. Their leaders rejected the excesses of the Azraqīs, and held that under unfavourable circumstances the Khārijī should refrain from rebellion, waiting for a more propitious moment to proclaim the imamate. The moderate wing of the Khārijī movement proved more viable. The communities of *al-ibāḍiyya* and *al-ṣufriyya* managed to survive the tumult of the Umayyad era and founded several Khārijī states throughout the Muslim world. They continued to exist throughout the **'Abbāsid** era and some have survived until our day.

The Khārijīs left a considerable literary corpus, preserved by Arab historians and later Khārijī writers. The early history of the movement found a vivid reflection in the poetry and orations of the leaders of the movement as well as its rank-and-file members, including women. The ascendancy of poetic word among the Khārijīs is not surprising, for the movement started among the warriors of Arab extraction who were well versed in the tradition of pre-Islamic poetry. Yet the contents of Khārijī verses indicate a decisive rupture with the pre-Islamic age. They did not accentuate tribal allegiances and the **bedouin** code of honour, preaching instead the overriding loyalty to Islamic values. Their poetry and orations were Islam-oriented and free from the themes of the tribal past. In contrast to the elaborate verses of the conventional court poets of the age, Khārijī poetry was characterized by greater directness and simplicity. It sprang from immediate experience and genuine religious sentiment. Khārijī poets provided vivid descriptions of the exceptional courage and piety displayed by their departed comrades; they reproach themselves for not having followed their fallen heroes through death by martyrdom; they defy danger and exhibit intense loathing for earthly existence.

As other Arabic poetry of the time, that of the Khārijīs became conventionalized to a high degree and is, at times, repetitious. Yet some of its representatives stood out as real masters of the genre. Two of them, Abū Bilāl Mirdās (d. 61/680–1) and Qaṭarī ibn Fujā'a (d. 78–9/698–9), led the reckless uprisings against the Umayyads and fell in battle. Their verses 'breathe a stern religious enthusiasm' and 'a truly Arabian sentiment of valour' (R.A. Nicholson, *A Literary History of the Arabs*, Cambridge, 1956, 212–13). The feats and heroic death of Abū Bilāl and Qaṭarī were eulogized by perhaps the greatest Khārijī poet, 'Imrān ibn Ḥittān (d. 84/703), who clung to a less militant version of Khārijism. Despite his ascetic renunciation of the unjust world around him, 'Imrān was still attached to the delights and beauty of earthly existence. His verses oscillate finely between his conflicting commitments, revealing a deep, and contradictory, world outlook. Spirited praises of the Khārijīs and their ideals were composed by the professional poet **al-Ṭirimmāḥ** (d. early second/eighth century). His attachment to Khārijism was, however, rather lukewarm. Instead of renouncing this world in search of the bliss of the hereafter, al-Ṭirimmāḥ readily plunges into life's intrigues and succumbs to its allures. He was also fond of praising himself and his tribe.

As the civil war in the caliphate began to subside, the puritanical and revolutionary message carried by Khārijī poetry gradually lost its appeal. It was replaced by the poetic works that resonated better with the buoyant, worldly mentality prevalent in the 'Abbāsid period.

For centuries, men of letters in the small Khārijī states of South Arabia and North Africa wrote historical and biographical works glorifying the feats of the early Khārijīs and the exceptional merits of local community leaders. Generally, their literary output, including poetry, was confined to theology and jurisprudence (e.g. Ibn al-Naẓar, who lived in the sixth/twelfth century).

Text edition

Shi'r al-Khawārij, Iḥsān 'Abbās (ed.), 3rd edn, Beirut (1974).

Further reading

Bellamy, J., 'The impact of Islam on early Arabic poetry', in *Islam: Past Influence and Present Challenge*, A. Welch and P. Cachia (eds), Edinburgh (1979), 141–67.

Ḍayf, Shawqī, *Ta'rīkh al-adab al-'Arabī. Vol. 2. al-'Aṣr al-Islāmī*, 6th edn, Cairo (n.d.), 302–14.

Gabrieli, F., 'La poesia harigita nel secolo degli Omayyadi', *RSO* 20 (1943), 331–72.

Madelung, W., *Religious Trends in Early Islamic Iran*, New York (1988), 54–76.

Pellat, C., 'Djāḥiẓ et les Khāridjites', *FO* 12 (1970), 195–209.

A. KNYSH

kharja see muwashshaḥ

al-Kharrāṭ, Idwār (1926–)

Egyptian novelist, short-story writer and translator. Born in Alexandria into a Coptic Christian family, al-Kharrāṭ graduated in law from Alexandria University. Detained from 1948 to 1950 for political activities, he later worked for an insurance company. Although he apparently began writing in the 1940s, his first collection of short stories (*Ḥīṭān 'āliya*) was not published until 1958. He began to come to prominence in literary circles during the 1960s, and for a time edited the literary and cultural magazine *Gallirī 68*, which brought together a new generation of Egyptian writers united by a feeling of disillusion following the Arab defeat in the Six-Day War of 1967.

Al-Kharrāṭ's writing reflects his own experience as a Copt in a predominantly Muslim society, and many of his works contain autobiographical elements. His first novel, *Rāma wa-al-tinnīn* (1979), revolves around the relationship between the Copt Mīkhā'īl and the Muslim Rāma – a relationship that ranges between the overtly sexual and the mystical, and which constitutes a daring theme in view of the taboos on marriage between Muslim women and non-Muslim men. The theme is continued in *al-Zaman al-ākhar* (1985), in which Mīkhā'īl and Rāma resume their relationship after a chance meeting at a conference. More successful artistically is the semi-autobiographical *Turābuhā za'farān* (1985), which relives the memories of Mīkhā'īl as a boy in the Alexandria of the 1930s and 1940s – the city that also provides the setting for the slightly older Mīkhā'īl of *Yā banāt Iskandariyya* (1990).

Despite al-Kharrāṭ's associations with other members of the so-called Egyptian 'generation of the sixties', he remains a unique voice in modern Egyptian literature. His modernistic works make considerable demands on the reader, exploiting the lexical possibilities of the Arabic language to the full in a meandering style which often relies on image and memory rather than logical connection to advance the narrative. Although in works such as *Rāma wa-al-tinnīn* this characteristic at times threatens to make the work unreadable, at its best his language combines qualities of richness, subtlety and precision.

In addition to his novels and several volumes of short stories, al-Kharrāṭ is also a distinguished literary translator, who has translated several major works from English and French into Arabic.

Text editions

City of Saffron, Frances Liardet (trans.), London (1989).

Girls of Alexandria, Frances Liardet (trans.), London (1993).

Further reading

al-Nowaihi, M., 'Memory and imagination in Edwar al-Kharrat's *Turābuhā Za'farān*', *JAL* 24 (1994), 34–57.

P. STARKEY

al-Khāshīn, Fu'ād (1925–)

Lebanese Druze lyrical, romantic and erotic poet. Born in al-Shuwayfāt, al-Khāshīn graduated from the Lebanese Teachers' Seminary in 1946 and worked as a teacher from 1946 to 1952. He then emigrated to Venezuela (1953–60), where he joined the Lebanese literary society 'Usrat al-Jabal al-Mulham' ('The Group of the Inspired Mountain').

Al-Khāshīn's poetry tends to mystical love, using Druze religious symbols as well as Mediterranean mythology. He employs various strophic forms, with short metres and changing rhymes. Like Nizār **Qabbānī**, his poetry depicts the erotic whims of women. Khāshīn was among the pioneer poets who employed one metre in lines of irregular lengths and an irregular rhyme scheme, as in his poem *Anā lawlākī* (*al-Adīb*, October 1946, republished in his love anthology *Siwār al-yāsamīn*, Beirut, 1961). In other respects, however, his poetry of this period appears conventional. His other works include *Ghābat al-zaytūn* (Beirut, 1963), in which he sings to the olive tree in al-Shuwayfāt and to nature; *Ma'bad al-shawq* (Beirut, 1966); and *Ṣalwāt al-shaykh al-azraq* (Beirut, n.d.). The last-mentioned includes al-Khāshīn's epic on the Phoenician–Greek mythological love of *Adūnīs wa-'Ashtārūt* (Beirut, 1965), which was awarded a prize by the Lebanese Ministry of Education.

Further reading

al-Khāzin, W. and Ilyās, N., *Kutub wa-udabā'*, Beirut (1970).

Moreh, S., *Modern Arabic Poetry 1800–1970*. Leiden (1976), 206–7.

Qabbish, A., *Tārīkh al-shi'r al-'Arabī al-ḥadīth*, n.p. (1971), 727.

S. MOREH

al-Khashshāb, Ismā'īl (d. 1814)

Egyptian historian. A relatively insignificant historian of the early nineteenth century, al-Khashshāb was a close friend of **al-Jabartī** and a regular member of the governing councils (*dawāwīn*) set up by the French during the occupation of 1798–1801. He reputedly helped al-Jabartī obtain access to documents of the Superior Court (Dār al-Maḥkama al-Kabīra); and since it was his job to record the official minutes of council meetings, he must have had intimate knowledge of affairs of state. According to al-Jabartī, he tried on the basis of this knowledge to write a history of the French occupation. But if indeed he succeeded, the work has yet to be found.

Further reading

Crabbs, J.A., *The Writing of History in Nineteenth-century Egypt*, Detroit (1984), 45, 58.

J. CRABBS

Khaṭāba *see* oratory and sermons

Khaṭīb *see* oratory and sermons

al-Khaṭīb al-Baghdādī (392–463/1002–71)

Aḥmad ibn 'Alī ibn Thābit Abū Bakr al-Khaṭīb al-Baghdādī was a famous *ḥadīth* scholar and historian of **Baghdad**. Born the son of a preacher in a village near Baghdad, he began his studies of the **Koran** and ***ḥadīth*** very early in Baghdad, and later travelled extensively in search of *ḥadīth*. In Baghdad, he began a career of teaching and preaching which earned him great fame. His conversion from Ḥanbalism to Shāfi'ism and adherence to Ash'arism, however, earned him the hatred and opposition of the strong Ḥanbalīs in Baghdad. In 445/1053 he undertook a two-year journey to **Syria** and Mecca. Five years later, he fled to **Damascus**, where he spent eight years lecturing in its Umayyad Mosque and in other Syrian towns, particularly Tyre. A personal accident led to the rise of the Damascene Shī'īs against him, so he fled to Tyre, then returned to Baghdad, where he died.

Al-Khaṭīb wrote many influential books on *ḥadīth* scholarship which have survived, like *Taqyīd al-'ilm*, *al-Riḥla fī ṭalab al-ḥadīth* and *al-Kifāya fī ma'rifat uṣūl 'ilm al-riwāya*, and some literary works, such as his *al-Bukhalā'* (see Fedwa Malti-Douglas, *The Structures of Avarice*, Leiden, 1985). His reputation, however, rests largely on his monumental 14-volume biographical dictionary *Ta'rīkh Baghdād*, which contains almost 8,000 biographies of men and women, particularly *ḥadīth* scholars, who were associated with Baghdad in any way until his time.

Text editions

Ta'rīkh Baghdād (Cairo, 1931; offset edn, Beirut, 1968); there is a separate edition and French translation by G. Salomon of the introductory chapter on the topography of Baghdad (*L'Introduction topographique à l'histoire de Baghdad*, Paris, 1904).

Ta'rīkh madīnat Dimashq, 'Umar ibn Gharāma al-'Amrawī (ed.), Beirut: (1995), vol. 5, 31–41.

Further reading

Ibn Khallikān, *Wafayāt al-a'yān*, Iḥsān 'Abbās (ed.), Beirut (1968), vol. 1, 92.

al-'Ishsh, Yūsuf, *al-Khaṭīb al-Baghdādī mu'arrikh Baghdād wa-muḥaddithuhā*, Damascus (1945).

Rosenthal, F., *A History of Muslim Historiography*, Leiden (1952), *passim*.

Yāqūt, *Mu'jam al-udabā'*, D.S. Margoliouth (ed.), Cairo (1923–30), vol. 1, 246.

W. AL-QĀḌĪ

See also: biography, medieval

Khaṭīb Dimashq *see* al-Khaṭīb al-Qazwīnī

al Khaṭīb al-Iskāfī *see* al-Iskāfī

al-Khaṭīb al-Qazwīnī (666–739/1268–1338)

Abū 'Abd Allāh (and: Abū al-Ma'ālī) Muḥammad ibn 'Abd al-Raḥmān Jalāl al-Dīn al-Khaṭīb al-Qazwīnī, also known as Khaṭīb Dimashq (the Preacher of Damascus), was a legal scholar and rhetorician. In spite of his Persian place-of-origin name al-Qazwīnī, he was of pure Arab descent. He was trilingual in Arabic, Persian and Turkish, but wrote only in Arabic. In his legal and religious career he was rather successful; in 706/1307 he was made preacher and *imām* at the Umayyad Mosque in Damascus; in 724/1324 he attained a high judgeship in **Syria**; and three years later he was appointed Shāfi'ī chief judge in **Cairo** under the Mamlūk ruler al-Nāṣir ibn Qalāwūn. He became an influential figure at the latter's court, and he saw to it that the poor and destitute under his jurisdiction were generously supported by the proceeds from pious foundations. In trouble because of a profligate son of his, he was transferred back to **Damascus** where he died soon afterwards. In spite of his literary interests, not a single line of poetry is credited to him.

His fame rests on two works on rhetoric, *Talkhīṣ al-Miftāḥ* (*Summary of the 'Key'*) and *al-Īḍāḥ* (*The Clarification*). The first is an epitome of the *Miftāḥ al-'ulūm* (*Key of the Sciences*) by **al-Sakkākī** (d. 626/1229), although not of the entire book – which deals with all aspects of language: morphology, syntax, rhetoric, argumentation and prosody – but only the third part, rhetoric. The *Īḍāḥ* was written later as an expanded version of the *Talkhīṣ*. Al-Qazwīnī is not uncritical of al-Sakkākī; among the changes he introduces are the following: (a) the 'science of rhetorical figures' (*'ilm al-badī'*; see ***badī'***) is added on an equal footing to the 'science of [syntactic] meanings' (*'ilm al-ma'ānī*, approx. 'stylistics'; see also ***ma'nā***) and the 'science of illustration' (*'ilm al-bayān*, approx. 'theory of imagery') to constitute the 'science of eloquence' (*'ilm al-balāgha*); (b) a section on the taxonomy of plagiarism (see ***sariqa***) is added.

The *Talkhīṣ* became the basic textbook for rhetorical studies in the *madrasa*s of the later Middle Ages up to modern times. Its popularity is shown by the plethora of commentaries, supercommentaries, glosses and versifications devoted to it. The most famous commentaries are the *Concise* and the *Expanded Commentary* (*al-Sharḥ al-mukhtaṣar* and *al-Sharḥ* *al-muṭawwal*) by Sa'd al-Dīn **al-Taftāzānī** (d. 792/1390).

Text editions

al-Īḍāḥ, Muḥammad 'Abd al-Mun'im Khafājī (ed.), 3rd edn, Beirut (1391/1971).

Talkhīṣ al-Miftāḥ, 'Abd al-Raḥmān al-Barqūqī (ed.), Cairo (1904) (and numerous reprints).

Further reading

Maṭlūb, Aḥmad, *al-Qazwīnī wa-shurūḥ al-Talkhīṣ* (*Al-Qazwīnī and the Commentaries on the* Talkhīṣ), Baghdad (1387/1967).

von Mehren, A.F.M., *Die Rhetorik der Araber*, Vienna (1853), rpt Hildesheim and New York (1970), a well-known reference work mainly based on the *Talkhīṣ*.

W.P. HEINRICHS

See also: commentaries; rhetoric and poetics

al-Khaṭīb al-Tibrīzī (421–502/1030–1109)

Abū Zakariyyā' Yaḥyā ibn 'Alī al-Khaṭīb al-Tibrīzī was a philologist, a great authority on poetry; he was usually known as al-Khaṭīb al-Tibrīzī, although **Yāqūt** insists this ought to be Ibn al-Khaṭīb. He left his native Tabriz in order to study philology and ***ḥadīth***; **Abū al-'Alā' al-Ma'arrī** was among his teachers. For a time he was a teacher in **Egypt**, then he moved to **Baghdad** where he taught at the Niẓāmiyya Academy until his death. According to a report given by Yāqūt, he was addicted to wine and often drunk when teaching; apparently this did not impair his scholarly reputation. **Al-Jawālīqī** was his most famous pupil. He wrote several highly respected commentaries on ancient poetry, such as the ***Mu'allaqāt***, the ***Mufaḍḍaliyyāt***, the *Lāmiyya* attributed to **al-Shanfarā** and three commentaries differing in length on the *Ḥamāsa* by **Abū Tammām,** as well as commentaries on **'Abbāsid** poets, e.g. Abū Tammām's *Dīwān*, **Ibn Durayd**'s *Maqṣūra*, the *Dīwān* of **al-Mutanabbī** and *Saqṭ al-zand* by Abū al-'Alā' al-Ma'arrī. Judging by his commentaries, his main interests were grammar and lexicography. He made some poetry himself, with little success. His *al-Kāfī* is a compendium on **prosody** and ***badī'***. Other works, on grammar, lexicography and Koranic **exegesis**, are lost or preserved in manuscript.

Text editions

al-Kāfī fī al-'arūḍ wa-al-qawāfī, al-Ḥassānī Ḥasan 'Abd Allāh (ed.), *MMMA* 12 (1966), 1–250.

al-Wāfī, 'Umar Yaḥyā and Fakhr al-Dīn Qabāwa (eds), 3rd edn, Damascus (1979).

G.J.H. VAN GELDER

Khatibi, Abdelkebir (1938–)

Moroccan novelist, poet, essayist and playwright writing in French. Born in 1938 in El Jadida on the Atlantic coast, Khatibi pursued his studies to university level and was assigned to the Centre for Scientific Research in Rabat. In his work he seeks to promote an alternative approach to one of his favourite themes: that of identity and difference. *La Mémoire tatouée* (1971) is the 'autobiography of a decolonised man'; *Le Livre du sang* (1979) deals with pagan mysticism and eroticism; while *Amour bilingue* (1983) plays on the idea of the stranger, woman and language. *Maghreb pluriel* (1983), *La Blessure du nom propre* (1974) and *Penser Maghreb* (1993) are a series of brilliant essays, in which Khatibi shows a great openness to the wider world.

Text edition

Love in Two Languages, R. Howard (trans.), London (1990).

J. DÉJEUX

al-Khaṭṭābī, Ḥamd ibn Muḥammad (319–86 or 388/931–96 or 988)

Abū Sulaymān Ḥamd ibn Muḥammad al-Khaṭṭābī al-Bustī was the author of a treatise on ***i'jāz al-Qur'ān***. His *ism* is sometimes given as Aḥmad; as a result. Yāqūt devotes two different chapters to him. A religious scholar as well as a littérateur, he was known in his own days especially for his works on ***ḥadīth***, some of which are preserved in manuscript. His *Bayān i'jāz al-Qur'ān* is an important treatise on the inimitability of the **Koran**. He died in his birthplace, Bust.

Text editions

Bayān i'jāz al-Qur'ān, in *Thalāth rasā'il fī i'jāz al-Qur'ān*, Muḥammad Khalaf Allāh and Muḥammad Zaghlūl Sallām (eds.), 2nd edn, Cairo (1968), 19–72.

Al-Ḫaṭṭābī et l'inimitabilité du Coran: traduction et introduction au Bayān i''ǧāz al-Qur'ān, Claude-France Audebert (trans.), Damascus, (1982).

G.J.H. VAN GELDER

khayāl

In classical Arabic literature and lexicography, the word *khayāl* (or *khiyāl*) originally means 'figure, phantom (of the lover seen at night or in a dream), disembodied spirit, ghost, spectre; imagination; reflection, illusion, phantom, apparition, fantasy, vision; shadow, human shape, statue, scarecrow'. In *Lisān al-'Arab*, *khayāl* is defined as *al-shakhṣ wa-al-ṭayf* ('figure and phantom'); in the ***Naqā'iḍ***, the word is used once as 'scarecrow to frighten wolves away from the sheep', and once as a 'hobby-horse figure' (*kurraj*) (*The Naḳā'iḍ of Jarīr and al-Farazdaḳ*, A.A. Bevan (ed.), Leiden (1905–9), vol. 3, 362, 1, 246).

Sometimes *khayāl* is used as a synonym of *ḥikāya*, *tamthīl* and *la'ba*, revealing a meaning that passed unnoticed by many scholars of Arabic theatre, i.e. 'a live theatrical performance', 'acting' and 'miming', besides the usual meaning of 'figure of a hobby-horse', used to simulate duals and fights performed to the music of flute and tambourine. In this case *khayāl* is used with the verb *akhraja*, e.g. *akhraja fī al-khayāl* ('he performed a live play'). On one occasion, *khayāl* is used in the sense of 'exchanging sharp retorts'. When *khayāl* is used without the word *ẓill*, to denote a 'shadow play', some writers used to emphasize that they meant the latter sense so as not to confuse their readers.

During the third/ninth century *khayāl* was used as a synonym of *ḥikāya* (imitation, mime or live play) presented by the *ḥākiya* or *muḥākī* (mime artist, imitator, live actor) and of the **Umayyad** term *lā'ib* and *la''āb*. By the beginning of the fifth/eleventh century it had completely replaced the term *ḥikāya*. When, at the end of the tenth or the beginning of the eleventh century, the **shadow play** arrived from the Far East by way of Muslim merchants and travellers to the Muslim world, the Arabs added the word *al-ẓill* ('the shadow') to the well-established term *khayāl* ('live play'), and used the new term (*khayāl al-ẓill*) to describe the shadow play, in which the shadows of puppets or leather figures, manipulated by a shadow presenter, were cast on a curtain by the light of a lamp or candle.

For this reason, from the fifth/eleventh century onwards it was difficult to distinguish between the presenter of a shadow play and a live actor. Both were called *khayālī* or *mukhāyil*. According to Pedro de Alcala (*Vocaulista aravigo en lietra castellana*, Granada, 1505), in Muslim Spain the term for live actor (*la''āb*) was *representador de momos*, and the head of a troup of actors, the Eastern *rayyis al-muḥabbiẓīn* (maestro), was called *kabīr la''āb al-khiyāl*, and in Spanish *momo principal*.

According to our present knowledge, from the seventh/thirteenth century onwards the term *muḥabbiẓ* was used to denote a live actor, in order to distinguish him from the shadow-play presenter. In Egypt during the nineteenth century, a live actor was called Ibn Rābiya, and his troupe (probably his children) was called Awlād Rābiya. Later on, every live actor was called Ibn Rābiya and the troupe of actors was called Awlād Rābiya. The most famous actor of this type is Aḥmad al-Fār (see Landau, J.M., 'Popular Arabic Plays, 1909', *JAL* [1986] 120–5.) Not only did the term *muḥabbiẓ* distinguish between a live actor and a presenter of shadow plays, but also the verb *akhraja* and derivatives were used to denote a live play performance.

There are very few descriptions of *khayāl* plays. The earliest live plays are attributed to a Jewish actor near **Kufa**, named Baṭrūnī or Bustānī, during the second half of the second/seventh century, who might have been a continuator of the tradition of actors or mimes in Mesopotamia from the pre-Islamic period. Few names of *khayāl* plays are known in Arabic literature. The longest description of a play is from the time of al-Mahdī (775–85), on the *Trial of the Caliphs*; **Ibn Shuhayd** (d. 1034) mentions the *Play of the Jew*; **Ibn Quzmān** (d. 1160) the *Play of the Villager*; **Ibn Mawlāhum al-Khayālī** (thirteenth century) mentions the *Play of Umm Qāwishtī*; **Ibn al-Ḥājj** (d. 1336) the *Play of the Judge*. Some of these plays were recorded and given by the author to actors for performance, e.g. the *Ḥikāyat al-Khalanjī* by 'Alluwayh, the poet and singer. E.W. Lane gives a long description of a play about a Nāẓir (governor of a district) and the way in which the *fallāḥ*'s wife bribes officials in **Egypt**. The only full text of a play known to us is *Misṭara Khayāl, Munādamat Umm Mujbir*, composed by 'Abd al-Bāqī al-Isḥāqī (d. 1660), and al-Maqāma al-mukhtaṣara fī al-khamsīn mar'a, by Muḥammad ibn Mawlāhum al-Khayālī (ed. S. Moreh and J. Sadan) (in preparation).

Further reading

Moreh, S., 'Live theatre in medieval Islam', in Ayalon Festschrift, 565–611.

——, *Live Theatre and Dramatic Literature in the Medieval Arab world*, Edinburgh (1992).

Woidich, M. and Landau, J.M., *Arabisches Volkstheater in Kairo in Jahre 1909*, Beirut (1993).

S. MOREH

See also: acting and actors, medieval; theatre and drama, medieval

khayāl al-ẓill see shadow play

Khayr al-Dīn *see* al-Tūnisī, Khayr al-Dīn

al-Khayyāṭ, Abū al-Ḥasan ʿAlī ibn Muḥammad (fifth/eleventh century)

Abū al-Ḥasan ʿAlī ibn Muḥammad al-Rabaʿī al-Khayyāṭ was a famous panegyrist of the Kalbid court (947–1053); he was particularly known for his elegies to Yūsuf Thiqat al-Dawla (990–8) and his heir, the prince-poet Jaʿfar (998–1014/15) Al-Khayyāṭ was a 'modern' poet who preferred the description of reality to the imitation of classical models. He was a pupil of the famous Sicilian grammarian **al-Ballānūbī**, father of the homonymous poet. The lexicographer **Ibn al-Qaṭṭāʿ** compared his work to that of **Jarīr ibn ʿAṭiyya**, the famous poet of the **Umayyad** era. Iḥsān ʿAbbās has affirmed that the descriptive technique of al-Khayyāṭ is second only to that of **Ibn Ḥamdīs**.

Text editions

Di Matteo, I., 'Antologia di poeti arabi siciliani', in *Archivio Storico Siciliano* Palermo (1935), 1–28.

Rizzitano, U., 'Un compendio dell'antologia dei poeti arabo-siciliani'. *Accademia Nazionale dei Lincei, Memorie* 8 (1958), 334–78.

F.-M. CORRAO

al-Khayyāṭ, Yūsuf (?–1900)

Syrian actor, famous for his portrayal of female parts. In 1876 he took over the remnants of the troupe of Salīm **al-Naqqāsh** and Adīb **Isḥāq**, of which he had been a member, and performed for many seasons in Egypt in Alexandria and in **Cairo**. It is said that his first patron, Khedive Ismāʿīl, saw his performance of the play *al-Ẓalūm* in 1878 and, annoyed at its allusions to his oppressive rule, ordered his expulsion from Egypt. Al-Khayyāṭ was, however, soon performing again before the Khedive. In 1882 Sulaymān **al-Qardāḥī** took over the troupe; al-Khayyāṭ formed new troupes, joined by the famous actor and singer Salāma Ḥijāzī, but unable to sustain the rivalry of al-Qardāḥī and al-Qabbānī he stopped his theatrical activities and turned to commerce.

Further reading

Najm, Muḥammad Yūsuf, *al-Masraḥiyya fī al-adab al-ʿArabī al-ḥadīth, 1847–1914*, Beirut (1967), 103–6.

Sadgrove, P.C., *The Egyptian Theatre in the Nineteenth Century*, Reading (1996), 138–45, 150–2, 154–6.

P.C. SADGROVE

Khazraj *see* tribes

al-Khirnīq (d. perhaps *c.*600)

Early elegiac poet. Khirnīq (or al-Khirnīq) bint Badr ibn Hiffān (or Haffān) was a half-sister or an aunt of **Ṭarafa ibn al-ʿAbd**. A slim ***dīwān*** with a total of less than sixty lines is preserved in the redaction of **Abū ʿAmr ibn al-ʿAlāʾ**, with short poems or fragments of ***rithāʾ*** on her brother, her husband Bishr ibn ʿAmr and other relatives. To these can be added a small number of lines from other sources.

Text editions

Dīwān, Louis Cheikho (ed.), Beirut (1897); Ḥusayn Naṣṣār (ed.), Cairo (1969); Yusrī ʿAbd Allāh (ed.), Beirut (1990).

Further reading

Stetkevych, Suzanne P., *The Mute Immortals Speak*, Ithaca (1993), 168–76.

G.J.H. VAN GELDER

khiṭaṭ see historical literature

khiyāl *see* khayāl

Khoury, Elias *see* Khūrī, Ilyās

al-Khubzaruzzī (d. *c.*327/938)

Abū al-Qāsim Naṣr ibn Aḥmad al-Khubzaruzzī (Khubza'aruzzī, Khubzuruzzī, etc.), was an illiterate poet of Basra. He baked rice-bread (hence his name) in a shop in the Mirbad (camel market) of **Basra**, where **Ibn Lankak** and other élite poets of the city would visit him to hear his verse; for someone of such lowly social status to achieve such celebrity was clearly most unusual. He is said to have spent some time in **Baghdad**, and, according to a rather dubious rumour, was drowned by the military adventurer al-Barīdī after mocking him in a poem. He excelled primarily, however, in amorous verse (see ***ghazal***), which was directed exclusively to males; the young men of Basra are said to have competed for his poetic attentions. His style is described as simple and unsophisticated, but delicate and effective. His ***dīwān***, reportedly compiled by Ibn Lankak, survives in an unpublished Yemeni manuscript. His verses are also very widely quoted in later anthologies.

Further reading

Fullest accounts, with selections, in al-Tha'ālibī, *Yatīmat al-dahr*, Cairo (1956), vol. 2, 366–9, and al-Khaṭīb al-Baghdādī, *Ta'rīkh Baghdād*, Cairo (1931), vol. 13, 296–9.

E.K. ROWSON

Khuḍayyir, Muḥammad (1940–)

Iraqi prose writer. Born in **Basra**, he worked there as a teacher. In his short stories, which were collected in the anthologies *al-Mamlaka al-sawdā'* (Baghdad, 1972) and *Fī Darajat khamsa wa-arba'īn mi'awī* (Baghdad, 1978) he often mingles mythical or folk-tale motifs with realistic narrative to depict social reality in a symbolic way. His *Baṣriyyāt* (Nicosia, Damascus, 1996) consists of intellectual reflections and tales about Basra.

Text edition

'Ein Märchen am Ofen', in Walther, W. (ed.), *Erkundungen. 28 irakische Erzähler*, Berlin (1985), 76–87.

Further reading

al-Ṭālib, 'Umar Muḥammad, *al-Qiṣṣa al-qaṣīra al-ḥadītha fī al-'Irāq*, Mosul (1979), 480ff.

W. WALTHER

khulāṣa see abridgements

al-Khūlī, Amīn (1895–1966)

Egyptian writer. After studying religious law, al-Khūlī taught *balāgha* and *tafsīr* (see **exegesis**) at Cairo University. The author of books such as *Fann al-qawl* and *Mushkilāt ḥayātinā al-lughawiyya*, he is best known as an advocate of 'regionalism' (*al-naẓariyya al-iqlīmiyya*), as propounded in his *Fī al-adab al-Miṣrī* (1943). Laying emphasis on environment, he maintained that there is not one Arabic literature, but several regional literatures. This theory was rejected on ideological grounds by Sāṭi' **al-Ḥuṣrī**, the champion of Arab unity, and on literary grounds by al-Khūlī's student Shukrī Fayṣal in his MA thesis presented in 1948 under al-Khūlī's supervision.

Further reading

Fayṣal, S., *Manāhij al-dirāsa al-adabiyya*, Damascus (1965).
al-Ḥuṣrī, S., *Ārā' wa-aḥādīth fī al-lugha wa-al-adab*, Beirut (1958).

D. SEMAH

khurāfa (pl. *khurāfāt*)

In classical and medieval Arabic, a word designating stories and tales of a fantastic nature, often dealing with wonders and incredible events. In contrast to the canonized, official literature which claimed to be non-fictional, these stories were obviously regarded as overt fiction. All the same, they were tolerated by representatives of the official literary norms (who usually condemned fiction as a 'lie'), who considered *khurāfāt* to be entertainment consumed by women and youths, an audience of inferior social status.

In the **'Abbāsid** period, the *khurāfāt* were a recognized literary genre, based initially on translations from Persian (as also from Indian and Greek), and later on Arabic adaptations of Persian models, as well as original Arabic works. Collections of *khurāfāt* were popular in literary and royal circles, especially at the court of al-Muqtadir (908–32 AD). Contemporary sources mention the book *Hazār afsān (Thousand Fables*; in Arabic, *Alf khurāfa*) as a representative example of the genre; the work is apparently identified with the *Thousand and One Nights* (see ***Alf layla wa-layla***).

In *ḥadīth*, and especially in ***adab*** compilations, one can find a tradition called *ḥadīth khurāfa*, which explains, on the authority of the Prophet, the origin of the word *khurāfa* as the name of a person who was stolen by demons (*jinn*) in the *Jāhiliyya*, and when returned to the human world, told of his adventures. His stories, the Prophet emphasizes, were true. *Ḥadīth* techniques are employed here in an attempt to legitimize the type of fiction represented in the *khurāfāt* genre.

In modern Arabic, *khurāfāt* usually means 'nonsense, non-serious talk'.

Further reading

Abbot, N., 'A ninth-century fragment of the "Thousand Nights"', *JNES* 3 (1949), 149–64.

Drory, R., 'Three attempts to legitimize fiction in classical Arabic literature', *JSAI* 18 (1994) 146–64.

Fihrist (Dodge), vol. 2, 712–24.

Ghazi, M.F., 'La littérature d'imagination en arabe du IIe/VIIIe au Ve/XIe siècles', *Arabica* 4 (1957), 164–78.

Mez, A., *The Renaissance of Islam*, S.K. Bukhsh and D.S. Margoliouth (trans.), London (1937), 253–4.

R. DRORY

See also: fiction, medieval

Khurasan

The most important province of the eastern Islamic world, comprising eastern Iran, western Afghanistan and parts of Central Asia. In a broad sense, particularly in the early Islamic period, Khurasan often referred to all territories under Muslim rule east of the deserts of central Iran; more narrowly defined, it was bordered on the north by the Oxus River, on the south by the oasis of Sijistān (Sīstān) and its dependencies, and on the east by the Hindu Kush.

The Arab conquerors reached Marv, the Sasanian capital of the province, as early as 31/651, but full conquest and Islamicization proceeded only slowly. Very large numbers of Arab troops were transferred to Khurasan during the **Umayyad** period, and inter-tribal disputes, as well as conflicts between older and newer settlers, with increasing participation by local converts, dominate the local history and constitute the complex background for the emergence of the **'Abbāsid** revolution, won by Khurasanian troops who marched westward and toppled the Umayyads in 132/750. A number of prominent poets were associated with the tribes and their commanders in Umayyad Khurasan, and some important religious scholars settled particularly in Marv and Balkh, but one cannot yet speak of a true regional Arabic literature.

The prominence of Khurasan in the 'Abbāsid revolution was further enhanced when al-Ma'mūn, ruling the province from Marv, launched a successful rebellion against his brother, the caliph al-Amīn, in 198/813. Al-Ma'mūn subsequently appointed his general Ṭāhir ibn al-Ḥusayn governor of Khurasan, and the **Ṭāhirids** retained control of the province for most of the rest of the century, holding court first at Marv and then at Nishapur, and both patronizing and themselves contributing to the development of a local literary culture. After a rather disturbed period when Khurasan fell under the control of the **Ṣaffārids** of Sijistan, a truly indigenous Arabic tradition came to full flower under the **Sāmānids**, who ruled both Khurasan and Transoxania from their capital at Bukhara throughout the fourth/tenth century.

Although these regions remained overwhelmingly Persian-speaking, and both Ṣaffārids and Sāmānids to some extent encouraged the development of neo-Persian poetry and prose, Arabic remained the prestige language of poetry, literary and official prose, and scholarship. The Sāmānids amassed a major library at Bukhara, their viziers sponsored scholarship and patronized poets, and their chancery officials encouraged developments in artistic prose. Similar developments can be seen at such secondary centres as Balkh, Jurjan and, above all, Nishapur, which was by the end of the century the most important city in the East. In his *Yatīmat al-dahr* the Nishapuri **al-Tha'ālibī** offers us a panorama of Arabic poets and prose writers of this period in his native city and throughout Khurasan, including such luminaries as **Badī' al-Zamān al-Hamadhānī**, Abū Bakr **al-Khwārazmī**, **Abū al-Fatḥ al-Bustī**, and **al-'Utbī**, and makes it clear that, aside from court patronage, it was the urban élite, solidly **Sunnī** (Ḥanafī and Shāfi'ī) in religious orientation and trained in Arabic religious scholarship, that constituted the primary audience for, and supplied many important contributors to, Arabic letters. Both al-Tha'ālibī and his younger contemporary, the great scientist **al-Bīrūnī**, were aggressive partisans of Arabic against the growing rivalry of literary Persian; and while another giant of this extraordinary generation of Easterners, the philosopher **Ibn Sīnā**, did compose a few of his works in Persian, they are the exception to an enormous output in Arabic. Writers from further west remarked at this period on the purity of the Arabic of Khurasanis, which seems likely to be due at least in part to their isolation from any interference by a related vernacular; and surely the role played by a command of Arabic as a sharp demarcator of élite status contributed to the tenacity with which the urban notables pursued it.

At the imperial courts, however, Persian began to gain ground. When Sāmānid power disintegrated at the end of the fourth/tenth century, Khurasan fell to the Ghaznavid Maḥmūd (see **Ghaznavids**), and it was Maḥmūd's patronage of such Persian poets as Firdawsī, ʿUnṣurī and Farrukhī that marked the true beginning of the Persian renaissance. Arabic panegyrics of Maḥmūd are relatively rare, and although the sources speak of an attempt to switch the language of his chancery from Arabic to Persian as abortive, there must in fact have been there too a gradual increase in the importance of Persian at the expense of Arabic. After forty years of Ghaznavid rule, most of Khurasan fell to the invading **Saljūqs** in 431/1040, and with their further conquests in the west and establishment of capitals at **Rayy** and Isfahan the region reverted for a time to provincial status. The continuing importance of Arabic poetry and prose in Khurasan in this period is attested by **al-Bākharzī**, a protégé of the Saljūq viziers al-Kundurī and Niẓām al-Mulk, who compiled his *Dumyat al-qaṣr* as a sequel to al-Thaʿālibī's anthology. Al-Bākharzī gives selections from some sixty Khurasanian Arabic poets and prose writers; of these, however, very few achieved more than local fame, and, with the notable exception of the literary critic and theorist **ʿAbd al-Qāhir al-Jurjānī** from the neighbouring province of Jurjan, those who attained lasting renown owed it less to their literary talents than to their religious scholarship. In fact, it was the moderate Sufism and the Ashʿarī theology cultivated in Nishapur, represented by such writers as the mystic theoretician **al-Qushayrī** and the theologian al-Juwaynī, and culminating in the towering figure of **al-Ghazzālī**, that was the basis for Khurasan's chief contributions to Arabic letters in the later fifth/eleventh century.

In the first half of the sixth/twelfth century Khurasan was ruled directly by the Saljūq sultan Sanjar; as Saljūq power waned in the second half of the century, it was contested between the forces of the Ghūrids and the Khwārazmshāhs, the latter finally achieving full control for only a few years before the Mongol onslaught, beginning in 616/1219. During this period Arabic literature was completely overshadowed by Persian, especially in poetry, although Arabic poetry and fine prose continued to enjoy some patronage, and many writers were bilingual. Probably the most important writer of Arabic artistic prose in the East was Rashīd al-Dīn al-Waṭwāṭ at the court of the Khwārazmshāh (see **Khwārazm**). Scholarship in all fields continued to be cultivated in Arabic, although Persian made inroads here as well; aside from the purely religious disciplines of Prophetic tradition and Islamic law, representative scholars include the heresiographer **al-Shahrastānī** (d. 548/1153), the traditionist and historian **al-Samʿānī**, the bilingual philosopher, historian and littérateur ʿAlī ibn Zayd **al-Bayhaqī**, and the philologist and theologian **al-Zamakhsharī** and his followers in Khwārazm. Post-Mongol Arabic writing in the East was overwhelmingly religious in nature, although the study of **rhetoric and poetics** codified by the Khwārazmian **al-Sakkākī** was also continued by such figures as **al-Taftazānī** at the court of Tamerlane.

Further reading

Daniel, E., *The Political and Social History of Khurasan Under Abbasid Rule*, Minneapolis (1979).

Danner, V., 'Arabic literature in Iran', in *CHIr*, vol. 4, *From the Arab Invasion to the Saljuqs*, R.N. Frye (ed.), Cambridge (1975), 566–94.

EI², s.v.

Richter-Bernburg, L., 'Linguistic Shuʿūbīya and early neo-Persian prose', *JAOS* 94 (1974), 55–64.

al-Ṭāhir, ʿA.J., *al-Shiʿr al-ʿArabī fī al-ʿIrāq wa-bilād al-ʿAjam fī al-ʿaṣr al-Saljūqī*, 2 vols, Baghdad (1961).

al-Tūnjī, M., *Ḥawl al-adab fī al-ʿaṣr al-Saljūqī*, Benghazi (1974).

See also the selections in Thaʿālibī, *Yatīmat al-dahr*, Cairo (1956), vol. 4; idem, *Tatimmat al-yatīma*, A. Iqbāl (ed.), Tehran (1946); Bākharzī, *Dumyat al-qaṣr*, S.M. al-ʿĀnī (ed.), Baghdad (1971), vol. 2, 83–481; unfortunately, the Iranian section of the next in this series of anthologies, the *Kharīdat al-qaṣr* of ʿImād al-Dīn al-Iṣfahānī, covering the sixth/twelfth century, remains unpublished.

E.K. ROWSON

al-Khuraymī, Abū Ya'qūb *see* Abū Ya'qūb al-Khuraymī

Khurayyif, al-Bashīr (1917–83)

Contemporary Tunisian novelist and short-story writer, born in Nefta in southern Tunisia. Khurayyif studied at the Dār al-Jild school in Tunis and at the Khaldouniya, gaining a diploma in 1946. He then became a primary school teacher, teaching in Sened, Ariana, Aïn Draham and Tunis; he also worked as a shopkeeper in Souk al-Blat, and held various posts in the National Education Council, the Ministry of Cultural Affairs and in radio. Khurayyif is generally considered the foremost writer of the Tunisian realist tradition. He published his first story, 'Laylat al-Waṭya' in *al-Dustūr* in September 1937. In this story, a young girl finds herself in conflict with the forces of tradition; the author wrote the dialogue of this work in Tunisian dialect, leading to a stream of opposition from the critics and total silence on his part for several years. In 1958–9 the review *al-Fikr* published his first novel *Iflās aw ḥubbuk darbānī* in serial form. In this work the author portrays the sentimental and sexual education of a young man from the *petite bourgeoisie* living in a world evolving rapidly under the forces of modernity. The historical novel *Barq al-layl* (1961), named after a black slave who lived in the sixteenth century, is a hymn to the old town and a plea on behalf of the victims of racism. His masterpiece, however, is *al-Dijla fī 'arājīnihā* (1969), the events of which take place in the Nefta oasis between 1910 and 1930. The plot of the story revolves around the deaths of three people, all victims of an unscrupulous character's scheming and of the miserable conditions inherent in southern life. The woman in this story has the most attractive role, but the real hero is the palm tree.

Text edition

La Terre des passions brûlées, Hedi Djebnoun and Assia Djebar (trans), Paris (1986).

Further reading

Fontaine, J., *La Littérature tunisienne contemporaine*, Paris (1991).
Zmirli, F., *al-Kitāba al-qaṣaṣiyya 'inda al-Bashīr Khurayyif: al-ashkāl wa-al-dalālāt*, Tunis (1989).

J. FONTAINE

Khurayyif, Muḥyī al-Dīn (1932–)

Contemporary Tunisian poet, nephew of al-Bashīr. He was born in Nefta, an oasis in the south of the country. After teaching for a time he became responsible for folk literature at the Ministry of Cultural Affairs and while there, edited the work of poets making use of the oral tradition in the Tunisian Arabic dialect. In addition to numerous children's stories, he has published eight collections of poetry. His books mark successive stages in the development of his thought. In *Kalimāt lil-ghurabā'* (1970) he deals with the distressing plight of the destitute; he contemplates his own interior life in a quest for freedom in *Rubā'iyyāt* (1985); finds an area where love takes pride of place; and discovers, amidst the wind and rain, the essence of his past life (*al-Bidāyāt wa-al-nihāyāt*, 1987).

Further reading

al-Jābirī, M.S., *al-Shi'r al-Tūnusī al-mu'āṣir*, Tunis (1974).
——, *al-Shi'r al-Tūnusī al-ḥadīth*, Tunis (1976).

J. FONTAINE

al-Khūrī, Bishāra 'Abd Allāh *see* al-Akhṭal al-Ṣaghīr

Khūrī, Ḥunayn Ni'mat Allāh

Lebanese historian and member of the Syrian Learned Society (al-Jam'iyya al-'Ilmiyya al-Sūriyya) in Beirut in the 1870s. He translated from French Eugène Sue's novel *Le Morne au diable* (1874), and from an English version E.-P. Guizot's *Histoire de la civilisation en Europe* (1877), dedicating his translation to the Khedive Ismā'īl; he wrote an article on this subject for the society, as well as various articles on history for ***al-Muqtaṭaf*** magazine.

Further reading

Sarkīs, Yūsuf Ilyān, *Mu'jam al-maṭbū'āt al-'Arabiyya wa-al-mu'arraba*, Cairo (1928), vol. 1, 845.

P.C. SADGROVE

Khūrī, Ilyās [Elias Khoury] (1948–)

Lebanese novelist, essayist, literary critic and journalist. Born in Beirut into a Maronite family, Khūrī grew up in the Christian Ashrafieh area of Beirut, but quickly rebelled against his background. His militant engagement with the Left during the Lebanese Civil War of 1975–90 is reflected in his semi-autobiographical novel *al-Jabal al-ṣaghīr* (1977), as well as in his press editorials. *Zamān al-iḥtilāl* (1985) brings together a collection of vehement editorials which he wrote for the leftist Beiruti daily *al-Safīr* during the Israeli invasion of Lebanon in 1982. According to Khūrī, the writer is an integral part of his epoch; his freedom is not a personal matter, but is the liberty of the whole community.

The most interesting aspect of Khūrī's fiction is its perfect embodiment of war-torn Lebanon. Khūrī's fragmented, bleeding city is reflected in dismembered bodies, decimated houses and destroyed streets. The city is populated with shadows of people, whitewashed as in *al-Wujūh al-bayḍā'* (1981) or filled with the black boots of the enemy as in *Riḥlat Ghāndī al-ṣaghīr* (1989). His protagonist is often a stranger who has travelled a long time and has endlessly turned the gates of the city in an attempt to enter (*Abwāb al-madīna*, 1981). *Mamlakat al-ghurabā'* (1993) epitomizes alienation in the midst of an atavistic search for self and home.

Khūrī's writing is at the vanguard of the 'new novel' in Lebanon. His postmodernist style tears apart the normal conventions of prose, mixing anger and sarcasm with a desperate, lyrical nostalgia.

Text editions

Little Mountain, M. Tabet (trans.), Minneapolis (1989).

Gates of the City, P. Haidar (trans.), Minneapolis (1993).

M.T. AMYUNI

al-Khūrī, Iskandar al-Baytjālī (1890–1973)

Palestinian neo-classical poet, writer and jurist. Born into a Greek Orthodox family, al-Khūrī studied at the Russian boarding school in Nazareth and at the Roman Catholic Patriarchal College in Beirut. In 1908 with the declaration of the Ottoman constitution he joined the Greek Orthodox delegation to Constantinople demanding rights for the Arab Christian Orthodox communities. He subsequently taught Arabic and French in Jerusalem.

During the British Mandate al-Khūrī studied law and was later appointed as a justice of the peace. After 1948 he worked for the Red Cross in Bethlehem and Hebron, at the same time editing a column for *al-Difā'* and *al-Jihād* in Jerusalem (1949–67).

Al-Khūrī's collections of poetry include *al-Zafarāt* (1916); *Daqqāt qalb* (Jerusalem, 1923); *Mashāhid al-ḥayāh* (Jerusalem, 1927); *al-'Unqūd* (Jerusalem, 1946); *al-Ḥarb al-'ālamiyya al-thāniya* (Cairo, 1946); and *Alam wa-amal* (Jerusalem, 1961). In these, he expresses his Arab nationalist feelings, lamenting the Arab defeat of 1948. He also composed poetry for children, wrote a romantic novel on World War 1 in Palestine – *al-Ḥayāh ba'd al-mawt ... 1913–1918* (Jerusalem, 1920) – and translated novels from French and Russian.

After the Six-Day War of 1967, al-Khūrī published a collection of classical Arab anecdotes, *Adab wa-ṭarab* (Tel Aviv, 1972), and a volume of memoirs, *Dhikrayātī* (Jerusalem, 1972), whose publication he said was possible only because of the freedom of expression in Israel. Critical of Arab leadership, he asserted that the Arabs had exaggerated the horrors of the battle of Dīr Yāsīn (1948), and called for the Palestinian problem to be solved peacefully according to UN resolutions.

Further reading

Abū Ḥamad, *A'lām min arḍ al-salām*, Haifa (1979), no. 223.

al-Asad, Nāṣir al-Dīn, *al-Shi'r al-ḥadīth fī Filasṭīn wa-al-Urdunn*, Cairo (1961), 50–4.

Moreh, S. and Milson, M., *Modern Arabic Literature: A Research Bibliography 1800–1980*, Jerusalem (1993), 125.

Qabbish, A., *Tārīkh al-shi'r al-'Arabī al-ḥadīth*, n.p. (1971), 326–8.

al-Sawāfirī, K., *Al-Adab al-'Arabī al-mu'āṣir fī Filasṭīn*, Cairo (1979), 92–6.

al-'Ūdāt, *Min a'lām al-fikr wa-al-adab fī Filasṭīn*, 90–4.

S. MOREH

al-Khūrī, Khalīl (1836–1907)

Lebanese journalist, official and poet. Born in al-Shuwayfāt, he died in Beirut. He started

Arabic journalism in Syria in 1858 with the newspaper *Ḥadīqat al-akhbār*, and later ran the official paper *Sūriyya*. After the 1860 civil war he was a secretary to Fu'ād Pasha, the Ottoman Minister of Foreign Affairs sent to Syria to re-establish peace, and he subsequently held several other official positions. He wrote six *dīwāns*, a verse history of the Ottomans, and some historical works in prose. His occasional verses earned him the title of 'State Poet'. The first to attempt to free Syro-Lebanese poetry from the old outworn modes of expression, his influence on later writers seems none the less to have been small.

Further reading

Ayalon, A., *The Press in the Arab Middle East*, New York (1995), 23–4, 31–4.
Dāghir, Yūsuf As'ad, *Maṣādir al-dirāsāt al-adabiyya*, Beirut (1956), vol. 2, 344–7.

P.C. SADGROVE

Khūrī, Ra'īf (1912–68)

Lebanese literary critic and nationalist intellectual. After graduating from the American University of Beirut in 1932 Khūrī taught in Syria for two years then moved to Palestine where he participated in the popular uprising against the British and Zionists which preceded the so-called 'Big Strike'. He lost his job in Palestine as a result of his political activities and returned to Beirut where he joined the Ligue contre le Nazisme et le Fascisme headed by 'Umar **Fākhūrī**. In 1947 he visited the Soviet Union and wrote *al-Thawra al-Rūsiyya* (1984); but his relationship with the Soviet Union, and with Arab communists, was strained by their support for Palestinian partition, and his long-standing association with the leftist press, particularly *al-Ṭalī'a* and *al-Ṭarīq*, came to an end. The launching of *al-Ādāb* in 1953, however, provided Khūrī with an Arab nationalist alternative and he remained a regular contributor to it until his death.

Khūrī has some twenty books and dozens of articles to his credit. In addition to a poetic drama entitled *Thawrat Baydabā* (1936), and a number of short stories (some not collected), he produced several textbooks connected with Arabic literature, and a treatise on modern Arab thought (*al-Fikr al-'Arabī al-ḥadīth wa-athar al-thawra al-Faransiyya fī tawjīhih al-siyāsī wa-al-ijtimā'ī*) which stands as a classic of modern Arab intellectual history. He also wrote on Palestine, human rights and national consciousness. As a literary critic, he called for **commitment** to society rather than to a particular ideology, and for literature that functions as a critic of the establishment, particularly the state. Distinguished by his independent stands, he never hesitated to oppose leading figures such as Qusṭanṭīn **Zurayq** and Ṭāhā **Ḥusayn** (with whom he conducted a famous debate over the function of literature) for the sake of his beliefs.

Further reading

Idrīs, S., *Ra'īf Khūrī wa-turāth al-'Arab*, Beirut (1986).

A.-N. STAIF

al-Khūrī, Rashīd Salīm (al-Qarawī) (1887–1984)

Mahjar poet. Born in al-Barbāra (Lebanon), al-Khūrī received a good formal education, and taught in the American schools in Sidon and al-Mīna, and in al-Kulliyya al-Sharqiyya in Zahle. He emigrated to Brazil in 1913. In 1915 he was invited to São Paulo because the Arab community there was in need of a poet. He adopted the pen-name 'al-Shā'ir al-Qarawī' ('Qarawī' for short) after he had been disparagingly so named by a journalist.

Al-Khūrī's first volume of poetry, *al-Rashīdiyyāt*, was published in São Paulo in 1916. He became a member of al-'Uṣba al-andalusiyya and was its chairman from 1938 to 1942. His poetry is nationalistic, attacking the French mandate in Syria and Lebanon as well as Jewish colonization in Palestine. Al-Khūrī's ***dīwān*** was first published in São Paulo in 1952, and has been several times reprinted. He returned to Lebanon in 1958. Rashīd Salīm al-Khūrī's brother was the emigrant poet Qayṣar Salīm al-Khūrī, who took the pen-name 'al-Shā'ir al-Madanī' and whose *dīwān* was published in Damascus in 1966.

Text edition

Colo Materno, São Paulo (1980).

Further reading

al-Ḥāwī, Īliyā, *al-Shā'ir al-qarawī*, 4 vols, Beirut (1978).
Al-Thaqāfa: 'adad khāṣṣ 'an al-shā'ir al-Qarawī 1(6) (October 1958).

C. NIJLAND

khuṭba

Literally 'speech, oration', *khuṭba* was in Arab society and, earliest Islam a tribal political or sectarian rallying cry; the texts of some of these have come down to us and are prized as fine examples of oratory. (Many are to be found in **al-Jāḥiẓ**'s *al-Bayān wa-al-tabyīn.*) Subsequently, *khuṭba* came to designate the two sermons pronounced by the *khaṭīb* or preacher before the afternoon worship on Fridays and on certain other festivals in the religious calendar. Normally within the Islamic world, it should be pronounced in Arabic. In medieval Islamic times, collections of model sermons were composed for professional preachers, e.g, by **Ibn Nubāta al-Khaṭīb**. The term is sometimes used to mean 'exordium' (analogous to the *nasīb* of the ***qaṣīda***) and should, according to **ʿAbd al-Qāhir al-Jurjānī**, demonstrate the writer's eloquence and mastery of style (*Asrār al-balāgha*, Istanbul, 1954, 9–10).

Text edition

al-Jāḥiẓ, *al-Bayān wa-al-tabyīn*, 3rd edn, Cairo (1968), vol. 1.

Further reading

*EI*² art. s.v. (A.J. Wensinck).

C.E. BOSWORTH

See also: oratory and sermons

Khuzāʿa *see* tribes

Khwārazm

The region of the lower Oxus River and its delta, later known as the Khanate of Khiva and now a part of Uzbekistan. Surrounded by desert and steppe, Khwārazm preserved a distinctive identity and culture, and its own Iranian language, through the early Islamic centuries. Conquered by the Arabs in 93/712, it was only gradually Islamicized, and continued to be ruled by the Afrīghid dynasty of Khwārazmshāhs from their capital at Kāth through the fourth/tenth century, latterly under the nominal suzerainty of the **Sāmānids** of Bukhara. In 385/995 the Afrīghids were replaced by the Ma'mūnids of Gurganj (al-Jurjāniyya in Arabic), who ruled as Khwārazmshāhs until the region was conquered by Maḥmūd of Ghazna in 408/1017. Taken in turn by the Oghuz Turks and then the **Saljūqs**, Khwārazm was again ruled by a hereditary dynasty of Khwārazmshāhs beginning with the Saljūq governor Anūshtigin from about 470/1077. With the crumbling of Saljūq power, these Khwārazmshāhs built up an independent empire which by the early seventh/thirteenth century comprised most of Iran and Afghanistan as well as large parts of Central Asia. The Khwārazmian empire was the first Islamic state to endure the onslaught of the Mongols, who destroyed and devastated it in the years 617–28/1220–31.

In the early Islamic centuries a number of Khwārazmīs achieved fame outside their native land, notably the mathematician Muḥammad ibn Mūsā (*fl.* *c.*205/820), the Sāmānid official and author of the *Keys of the Sciences* Muḥammad ibn Aḥmad **al-Khwārazmī** (*fl*, *c.*370/980), and the poet and prose stylist Abū Bakr Muḥammad ibn al-ʿAbbās **al-Khwārazmī** (d. 383/993). Under the Ma'mūnids, the court at al-Jurjāniyya became an important centre of patronage, supporting a group of poets, prose writers and scholars, including **al-Thaʿālibī** and **Ibn Sīnā**, as well as **al-Bīrūnī**, whose history of his native land is unfortunately lost. Despite the increasing importance of Persian prose and, especially, poetry in the fifth/eleventh century, Arabic literature continued to thrive in Khwārazm, and produced a series of major writers and scholars under the Khwārazmshāhs of the sixth/twelfth century. The most important of these is unquestionably the **Muʿtazilī** theologian, philologist, and stylist **al-Zamakhsharī**, who, like al-Thaʿālibī and al-Bīrūnī a century earlier, aggressively vaunted the superiority of Arabic to Persian. Both his Muʿtazilism and his attachment to Arabic were equally promoted by his second-generation pupil **al-Muṭarrizī**, best known for his Arabic grammatical works and his commentary on the *Maqāmāt* of **al-Ḥarīrī**. Later representatives of Arabic philology include al-Muṭarrizī's pupil al-Qāsim ibn al-Ḥusayn, known as Ṣadr al-Afāḍil (d. 617/1220), who commented the *Maqāmāt*, the *Saqṭ al-zand* of **Abū al-ʿAlā' al-Maʿarrī**, and the *Kitāb al-Yamīnī* of **al-ʿUtbī**, and al-Qāsim's contemporary **al-Sakkākī**, author of the standard rhetorical handbook the *Key of the Sciences*.

Of more purely literary figures, the most significant is Rashīd al-Dīn al-Waṭwāṭ (Vaṭvāṭ) (d. 587/1191 at an advanced age), the court poet and secretary of the Khwārazmshāh Atsiz

(521–51/1127–56) and his two successors. Besides a large ***dīwān*** of Persian poetry and a theoretical work on poetics, also in Persian, al-Waṭwāṭ left an important collection of Arabic epistles, both diplomatic and personal, celebrated for their elaborate style. A final representative of the secretarial style of Arabic prose cultivated in Khwārazm is Shihāb al-Dīn al-Nasawī (d. 647/1249–50), secretary to the last Khwārazmshāh Jalāl al-Dīn, who composed a well-known biography of his master.

Text editions

Khwārazmian poets of the fourth/tenth and fifth/eleventh centuries are surveyed in al-Tha'ālibī, *Yatīmat al-dahr*, Cairo (1956), vol. 4, 194–255, and al-Bākharzī, *Dumyat al-qaṣr*, S.M. al-'Ānī (ed.), Baghdad (1971), vol. 2, 61–7.

EI^2, s.v.v. Khwārazm, Khwārazm-Shāhs.

al-Nasawī, *Sīrat al-sulṭān Jalāl al-Dīn*, Khwārazm, O. Houdas (ed.), Paris (1891) (trans. 1895).

Ṭāhā, H.H., *al-Adab al-'Arabi fi iqlīm Khwarazm*, Baghdad (1976).

al-Waṭwāṭ, *Majmū'at rasā'il Rashīd al-Dīn al-Waṭwāṭ*, Cairo (1315/1897–8).

E.K. ROWSON

al-Khwārazmī, Abū Bakr (323–83/934–93)

Abu Bakr Muḥammad ibn al-'Abbās al-Khwārazmī was a celebrated author of epistles in **artistic prose**, as well as of poetry. Born in **Khwārazm**, he travelled extensively, visiting many courts, including those of Sayf al-Dawla (see **Ḥamdānids**) in Aleppo and, in particular, the **Būyid** vizier **al-Ṣāḥib Ibn 'Abbād**, in Isfahan, **Rayy**, and Jurjan. In his later years he settled in Nishapur. He was a militant Imāmī **Shī'ī**, and in one of his most famous letters consoles the Shī'ī community in Nishapur on their persecution under the **Sunnī Sāmānids**. At the end of his life, he suffered a defeat in a literary contest with the upstart **Badī' al-Zamān al-Hamadhānī**, and died soon after. Reports that he was the nephew of the historian **al-Ṭabarī** are based on a misunderstanding.

Text editions

Ā'īnahwand, Ṣ., *Sharḥ risālat Abī Bakr al-Khwārazmī ilā jamā'at al-Shī'a bi-Naysābūr*, Beirut (1985).

Rasā'il Abī Bakr al-Khwārazmī, Beirut (1970).

(The poetic *Dīwān* remains unpublished).

Further reading

al-Dudd, S.I.M., *Abū Bakr al-Khwārazmī*, Cairo (1985).

Muṣṭafā, A.A., *Abū Bakr al-Khwārazmī*, Cairo (1985).

Rowson, E.K., 'Religion and politics in the career of Badī' al-Zamān al-Hamadhānī', *JAOS* 107 (1987), 658–70.

E.K. ROWSON

al-Khwārazmī, Abū Ja'far Muḥammad ibn Mūsā (early third/ninth century)

Abū Ja'far al-Khwārazmī was a scholar of the sciences. His name suggests that he came from the eastern province of **Khwārazm**, but apart from this all that is known of his life is that he enjoyed the patronage of the caliph al-Ma'mūn (r. 198–218/813–33) in **Baghdad**.

Al-Khwārazmī's work was important and innovative. He wrote the first Arabic treatise on arithmetic, in which he appears to have invented new terminology, and the first work on algebra and geometry, in which algebra was for the first time used to solve problems of geometry. He was also the author of the first Arabic books on the construction of sundials and the regulation of the time for prayers through mathematical tables; the *Zīj al-Sind-hind* (*Indian Astronomical Table*), which now survives only in Latin translation, is the earliest work of Arabic astronomy to survive complete to modern times. He also wrote a geography that comprises a revision of Ptolemy.

His scholarship in the exact sciences illustrates the character of the translation movement associated with the name of al-Ma'mūn, which involved not only translation of ancient texts into Arabic, but also pursuit of the work of the ancients in new directions (see further **translation, medieval**). Of particular interest is the way in which he made use of Indian scholarship, translated from Sanskrit, and sought to harmonize it with the heritage of the Greeks; this suggests that while Greek works were always favoured for translation, in al-Khwārazmī's day they were not yet as overwhelmingly authoritative as they were to become later on.

Further reading

King, David A., 'Al-Khwārizmī and new trends in mathematical astronomy in the ninth century', *Occasional Papers on the Near East, New York University, Kevorkian Center for Near Eastern Studies*, 2.

Rashed, Roshdi, 'Algebra', in *Encyclopedia of the*

History of Arabic Science, Roshdi Rashed (ed.), London (1996), vol. 2, 349–55.
Rosenfeld, B.A., *Muhammad ibn Musa al-Khorezmi*, Moscow (1983).

L.I. CONRAD

al-Khwārazmī, Muḥammad ibn Aḥmad ibn Yūsuf (d. 387/997)

Muḥammad ibn Aḥmad ibn Yūsuf al-Kātib al-Khwārazmī was an author at the **Sāmānid** court in Bukhara. He is well-known for his *Mafātiḥ al-'ulūm* (*Keys to the Sciences*), which takes a fairly traditional form in its encyclopaedic structure. It comprises Islamic law, theology, grammar, theory of writing, *ḥadīth*, and the secular sciences like logic, philosophy, medicine, astronomy, geometry, arithmetic, music and chemistry. The work, dedicated to the Sāmānid vizier Abū al-Ḥasan al-'Utbī and addressed to members of the secretarial class, provides interesting accounts of administrative procedure which may well furnish an accurate guide to the forms of organization that then prevailed in Persia. The importance of the book is that it shows what science was thought to comprise and gives an interesting picture of the richness of contemporary scientific thought, not only in its theoretical depth but also in its practical application.

Text editions

Liber mafâtîh al-'olûm, G. van Vloten (ed.), Leiden (1895), rpt (1968).
Mafātīḥ al-'ulūm, I. al-Ibyārī (ed.), Beirut (1984).

Further reading

Bosworth, C.E., 'A pioneer Arabic encyclopaedia of the sciences: al-Khwārizmi's *Keys of the Sciences*', *Isis* 54 (1963), 97–111.

O. LEAMAN

See also: encyclopaedias, medieval

kināya see rhetorical figures

Kinda *see* tribes

al-Kindī, Abū 'Umar (283–350/897–961)

Abū 'Umar Muḥammad ibn Yūsuf al-Kindī was a historian of Egypt, who spent his whole life there and devoted his literary efforts to the Islamic history of that country. He was born towards the end of the Ṭūlūnid period and died, a few years before the **Fāṭimid** conquest. Much of his output has been lost and is known only by quotation or title. Later writers, especially the compilers of the **Mamlūk** period, made frequent use of these works. They include one on the notable Egyptian ***mawālī*** or converted non-Arabs, an influential topographical work (*Khiṭaṭ Miṣr*), and monographs dealing with particular individuals or subjects of the early history of Islamic Egypt.

His extant work, in fact two separate works, is known as *The Governors and Judges of Egypt* (*Wulāt Miṣr wa-quḍātuhā*). This deals, individual by individual, with the representatives of the central caliphates and then the effectively independent dynasties, in the case of the 'governors' down to 334/946 and for the 'judges' down to 246/861. Leaving aside its historical and legal merit, the material, which is presented with full *isnād*s as in ***ḥadith*** scholarship, produces a jejune and repetitive literary effect.

Text edition

The Governors and Judges of Egypt, Rhuvon Guest (ed.), Leiden (1912).

D.S. RICHARDS

al-Kindī, Abū Yūsuf (d. after 252/865)

Abū Yūsuf Ya'qūb ibn Isḥāq al-Kindī was a scientist and philosopher. Coming from a distinguished family of the Kinda Arabs, he was connected with the caliphal court of **Baghdad** until the political changes of the mid-century; he was tutor of the **'Abbāsid** prince Aḥmad ibn al-Mu'taṣim, and both as a scientist and as a literary figure reflected the practical and intellectual interests of the autocratic aristocracy and its administrative élite. His enormous *oeuvre* encompasses the whole range of the Hellenistic sciences, made accessible during his lifetime through translations from Greek and Syriac, where al-Kindī appears to have been directing his own circle of translators. His activity marks the taking over, after the predominantly Iranian bias of the early 'Abbāsid administration, of Hellenism – allied with Arabism in ***adab*** – in the formative period of classical Islamic culture, and earned him the *laqab* of *faylasūf al-'Arab*, the 'Philosopher of the Arabs'.

In astronomy, his writings attended the final success of Ptolemy's *Almagest*, e.g. in his *Kitāb*

Fī al-ṣināʿa al-ʿuẓmā, and his descriptions of observational instruments. In astrology, while applying the Iranian 'world year' model, he used it for predicting the continuance of the Arab caliphate (*Risāla fī mulk al-ʿArab wa-kammiyyatih*). In optics, he contributed to the Euclidian geometry of vision and perspective in his *Iṣlāḥ al-manāẓir*. In musical theory, he presented the Greek doctrine of harmonic proportions (e.g., in his *Risāla fī khubr taʾlīf al-alḥān*). In pharmacology, he applied **Galen**'s doctrine of the 'forces' of the *simplicia* to develop a theory of the action of composite drugs and wrote various works on pharmacy, and on perfumes. In philosophy, he legitimized the rational sciences by demonstrating their consistency with the doctrine of God's unicity (*tawḥīd Allāh*) and, employing the creationist Neoplatonism of his sources, he built a philosophical ideology in harmony with Islam. His works on magic and the occult (e.g. *De radiis*, extant in a Latin version), as also his doctrine of the immortal soul and its return to the 'world of the intellect', are based on a system of cosmic sympathy in which the gnostic and hermetic tendencies of late Neoplatonism survive in a religion for intellectuals.

Text editions

For a complete listing of works by and about al-Kindī see N. Rescher, *Al-Kindī: An Annotated Bibliography*, Pittsburgh (1964), to which may be added the following:

L'Intellect selon Kindī, J. Jolivet, Leiden (1971).

'al-Kindī: *De radiis*', M.-T. d'Alverny and F. Hudry, *Archives d' histoire doctrinale et littéraire du Moyen Âge*, ann. 49: 1974, t. 41 (1975), 139–267.

Al-Kindī's Metaphysics, A.L. Ivry (ed.), Albany (1974).

Further reading

Endress, G. 'Al-Kindī über die Wiedererinnerung der Seele', *Oriens* 34 (1994), 174–221.

——, 'Die wissenschaftliche Literatur', *GAP*, vol. 3, 3–152.

Lindberg, D.C., 'Alkindi's critique of Euclid's theory of vision', *Isis* 62 (1971), 469–89.

Ullmann, M., *Die Medizin im Islam*, Leiden (1970), 123, 301f., 314.

——, *Die Natur- und Geheimwissenschaften in Islam*, Leiden (1972), 313f.

G. ENDRESS

al-Kirmānī, Ḥamīd al-Dīn Aḥmad ibn ʿAbd Allāh (d. *c*.411–12/1021)

Ismāʿīlī **Fāṭimid** *dāʿī* whose principal missionary activity was undertaken in Iran and Iraq. Because of this he gained the honorific title *Ḥujjat al-ʿIrāqayn*. Al-Kirmānī has been much esteemed for his scholarship. His *magnum opus* was his *Rāḥat al-ʿaql*. As a true Neoplatonist (see **Neoplatonism**) he followed in the footsteps of Iamblichus before him, and made Ismāʿīlī Arabic literature more complex by his multiplication of hypostases. Like **al-Fārābī** he held to an emanationist hierarchy of ten Intellects, and God is frequently characterized in a Neoplatonically negative way. From a literary and theological point of view, al-Kirmānī represents an Ismāʿīlī trend away from simplicity of doctrine and expression.

Text edition

Rāḥat al-ʿaql, Muṣṭafā Ghālib (ed.) Beirut (1967).

Further reading

De Smet, D., *La Quiétude de l'intellect. Néoplatonism et gnose ismaëlienne dans l'œuvre de Hamid al-Din al-Kirmani*, Leuven (1995).

Ivanow, W., *Ismaili Literature*, 2nd edn, Tehran (1963) 40–5.

Poonawala, I.K., *Biobibliography of Ismaʿili Literature*, California (1977), 94–102.

I.R. NETTON

See also: Ismāʿīlīs

al-Kisāʾī, Aḥmad ibn Sulaymān (seventh/thirteenth century)

Aḥmad ibn Sulaymān ibn Ḥumayd al-Kisāʾī al-Shāfiʿī is known as the author of a work on **love theory** (unedited) dedicated to the **Ayyūbid** ruler al-Malik al-Ashraf Abū al-Muẓaffar Mūsā ibn Sayf al-Dīn Abū Bakr (d. 634 or 5/1237). Since this ruler controlled the territory around Baʿalbak and **Damascus** beginning *c*.626 AH, al-Kisāʾī may have been a Damascene. Especially interesting is his forthright assertion that books on love should show a balance between attention devoted to love – the essence and meaning of love and its types and degrees – and accounts of the experiences of lovers.

Further reading

Giffen, L.A., *Theory of Profane Love among the Arabs*, New York (1971), 30–1, 67–9, Table 1, and index.

L.A. GIFFEN

al-Kisā'ī, Muḥammad ibn 'Abd Allāh (fifth/twelfth century?)

No definite identification of this author of a classical collection of the ***Legends of the Prophets*** genre is as yet possible. The above personal name is the one usually found in the various manuscript versions of the work, but he is not mentioned in any medieval Muslim biographical works. The seventeenth-century Ottoman bibliographer, **Ḥājjī Khalīfa**, is the only Muslim author to identify him explicitly as the grammarian and **Koran** scholar of the second/eighth century, 'Alī ibn Ḥamza al-Kisā'ī (*GAL* vol. 1, 115). In the latter's bibliography, however, one finds no mention of such a work.

In comparing al-Kisā'ī's *Kitāb bad' (khalq) al-dunyā wa-qiṣaṣ al-anbiyā'* with the other great work by **al-Tha'labī** one finds such great differences of sources, treatment and language that modern scholars have concluded that al-Kisā'ī's text is a reflection of a folk-like, perhaps oral tradition of tales transmitted by the *quṣṣāṣ*, or popular preachers, who were opposed and condemned by the *'ulamā'*. A recent doctoral dissertation (in Hebrew) by A. Schussman finds interesting parallels to an eighth-century Jewish midrashic work and concludes that authorship by the aforementioned grammarian, 'Alī ibn Ḥamza, should not be ruled out. The identification of the author is, thus, still obscure and even controversial, but the work is valuable and interesting for the view it offers of popular Islam.

Text editions

Die Prophetenlegenden des Muḥammed ben Abdallāh al-Kisāi, I. Eisenberg (trans), Bern (1898/1902).

The Tales of the Prophets of al-Kisa'i, W. Thackston (trans), Boston (1978).

Vita Prophetarum, I. Eisenberg (ed.), Leiden (1923).

Further reading

Nagel, T., "Al-Kisā'ī, ṣāḥib Ḳiṣaṣ al-Anbiyā'", *EI*², vol. 5, 176.

Schussman, A., *Stories of the Prophets in Muslim Tradition*, PhD dissertation (in Hebrew with English summary), Jerusalem (1981).

W.M. BRINNER

kitāb see books and book-making

kitāba see artistic prose; secretaries

Koran

The Arabic word *qur'ān*, applied to the Muslim scripture, is variously interpreted as (a scriptural) 'reading' or 'lesson', or as a verbal noun derived from *qara'a* 'he read', 'he recited'. A variety of other terms are used to refer to the Koran, e.g. *furqān*, from *faraqa* 'he divided', 'he distinguished (between)' (see further *EI*² arts. 'Ḳur'ān', 'Furḳān').

The Koran is believed by Muslims to be the revealed word of God in Arabic, dictated in segments by the angel Gabriel to the Prophet **Muḥammad** between the years 610 and 632. The revelations were memorized and recorded word for word and are today found in the text of the Koran in precisely the manner that God intended.

Consisting of 114 chapters, called *sūra*s, the Koran is arranged approximately in order of length from the longest chapter (some twenty-two pages of Arabic text for *Sūra* 2) through the shortest (only a single line for *Sūra* 108). Acting as an introduction to the text is the first chapter, called 'The Opening', *al-Fātiḥa*, which is a short segment used within the Muslim prayer ritual. Each chapter is divided into verses, *āyāt* (sg. *āya*), the total number being reckoned somewhere between 6,204 and 6,236, differing according to various schemes of counting. These verse divisions do not always correspond to the sense of the text but are generally related to the rhyme structure of the individual *sūra*s. The rhyme is constructed by a vowel plus the following final consonant at the end of each verse, although few chapters have a consistent rhyme scheme throughout and, in the longer narrative chapters, the rhyme is created by the use of stock phrases such as 'God is all-knowing, all wise'.

Twenty-nine chapters are preceded by disconnected letters of the Arabic alphabet, some single letters (Q = *qāf*, *Sūra* 50; N = *nūn*, *Sūra* 68) or up to five letters together (in *Sūra* 42). The significance of these letters has eluded traditional Muslim and modern scholarship alike. Also prefacing each chapter, with the exception of *Sūra* 9, is the *basmala*, 'In the name of God, the Merciful, the Compassionate'. This phrase acts as an opening to all Muslim religious statements and is found within the Koran itself as the opening phrase of the letter written by Solomon to the Queen of Sheba (*Sūra* 27: 30).

The text as it is generally found today indicates both the Arabic consonants and the vowels according to a standard system of notation, along with a variety of other marks connected to recitation practices and verse divisions. Early manuscripts of the Koran dating from the eighth and ninth centuries provide only the consonantal form of the Arabic, however.

Apart from the mechanical arrangement of the Koran by length of chapter, the organisational principle behind the text is unclear. Despite the best efforts of many people from both within and outside the faith perspective, the sense of an apparent random character and seemingly arbitrary sense of organisation is hard to overcome. There seem to be no historical, biographical, thematic, aesthetic or poetic criteria by which one can understand the overall structure of the work. To the source critic, the work displays all the tendencies of rushed editing with only the most superficial concern for the content, the editors/compilers apparently engaged only in establishing a fixed text of scripture.

The Muslim tradition has provided an explanation for why the Koran looks the way it does, although the contradictions created by the multiplicity of versions of the story have raised grave doubts on the part of many scholars as to their plausibility and motivation. Generally, Muḥammad himself is excluded from any role in the collection of the text. Zayd ibn Thābit, a companion of Muḥammad, is generally credited with an early collection of the scripture. Later, under the instructions of ʿUthmān, the third caliph after the death of Muḥammad (see **Orthodox caliphate**), the major collection of the text took place. Gathering together the text as it was written 'on palm leaves or flat stones or in the hearts of men', the complete text (deemed to have survived in full) was compiled, copied and distributed to the major centres of the early empire. Thus, within thirty years of the death of Muḥammad in 632, it is understood that the Koran existed in its fixed form. For Muslims, the emergence of the written text is moot; it is held that an oral tradition preserved the full text from the time of its revelation, the written form serving only as a mnemonic device supporting the memorization of the text.

The difficulties in understanding the text are by no means confined to matters related to its organization. Another issue that confronts most readers is the idea of the 'speaker' of the Koran. Muslim theology understands that God speaks throughout the Koran. Yet He refers to Himself in both the singular and plural first-person forms, as well as through a third-person omniscient narrator. Furthermore, statements that might be conceived to be those of Muḥammad are frequently preceded by the word 'Say', a stylistic device understood to be God giving the authorization for Muḥammad to speak through his own person while reciting the 'dictated words'. On occasion, the reader encounters passages where the voice of the text clearly cannot be God's, but the Muslim interpretative tradition has always been able to provide a corrective understanding to maintain a consistent presence of the divine voice throughout the text, even in a case such as *Sūra* 1.

A reading of the Koran shows that it has a thematic preoccupation with three major topics: law, the previous prophets and the final judgement. The three topics appear to presuppose on the part of their readers some Biblical knowledge along with a reference point within a native Arabian tradition.

Ruling over all of the Koran, and the reference point for all the developments of its major themes, is the figure of God, Allāh in Arabic. The all-mighty, all-powerful and all-merciful God created the world for the benefit of His creatures, has sent messages to them in the past to guide them in the way of living most befitting to them and to Him, has given them the law by which they should live and which has reached its perfection and completion in Islam, and will bring about the end of the world at a time known only to Him when all shall be judged strictly according to their deeds. The basic message is a familiar one from within the Judaeo-Christian tradition. This emphasis on the uniqueness of God, that He is the only god who exists, is presented both in opposition to the Jewish–Christian tradition and in opposition to the polytheist idolaters who worshipped spirits (*jinn*, 'genies'), offspring of God and various idols.

The God of the Koran is the God Who communicated to the prophets of the past. Most of the stories of the past prophets as recounted in the Koran are familiar from the Hebrew Bible and the New Testament but are presented shorn of the extensive narrative element. The Koran tends to present summaries of the stories in order to get directly to the religio-moral points lying behind them. A number of prophets are named in the Koran as having been commissioned or selected by God to spread the message of the true way of obedience to Him. A limited number of these people were given scriptures to share with their communities: Abraham, Moses, David and Jesus are clearly cited in this regard. Not all of the named prophets are familiar from the Biblical tradition (or at least their identification with personages of the past is less than clear); for example, Hūd, Ṣāliḥ, Shu'ayb and Luqmān are generally treated as prophets of the specifically Arabian context prior to Muḥammad.

The stories of these prophets are frequently recounted through a formulaic structure. The prophet is commissioned by God, and then confronts his people, only to be rejected by them. As a result, the people are destroyed and the prophet and any persons faithful to his message are saved by the mercy of God, The story of some of the prophets is told in more expansive form, for example in the case of Joseph which is recounted in *Sūra* 12 and is one of the most cohesive narratives found in the Koran. Elaborations within the story indicate that the Koran is not simply retelling biblical stories but is reflecting their popular form in the Near Eastern milieu of the seventh century. (See further ***Legends of the Prophets***.)

All of the prophets brought the same message of the coming judgement for those who do not repent and follow the law of God. The message is a simple and familiar one. All people shall die at their appointed time and then, at a point known only to God, the resurrection shall take place at which each person shall be judged according to the deeds that they have performed on earth. The scene of the judgement day and the hereafter is painted in graphic style within the Koran (see, for example, *Sūra* 56).

To be granted eternal existence in heaven, one must believe in the truth and the contents of the scripture and put those contents into action in day-to-day life. It is on the basis of one's intentional adherence to the will of God as expressed through legal requirements detailed in the Koran that one's fate in the hereafter will be determined. The Koranic law contains elements familiar from Jewish law such as the prohibition of pork and the institution of ritual slaughter, some purity regulations (especially as regards women) and the emphasis on the regulation of marriage, divorce and inheritance. As well, various emblems of Islam are mentioned in the Koran, but often only in an unelaborated form. The pilgrimage, the month of fasting, the institution of prayer and the idea of charity are all dealt with to varying degrees. Overall, the law is conceived as a gift given by God to humanity to provide guidance in living the proper, fully human life.

Conveying these Koranic themes are vast complexes of symbolic language, the ranges of which have not been catalogued through any contemporary literary perspective. The mix of Biblical and Arabian motifs render the task a difficult one. Some scholars have tended to interpret the text as reflecting the contemporary situation of Muḥammad, and thus pictured the symbolism in materialist terms; others have emphasized the Biblical (or general ancient Near Eastern) context and seen the language as reflecting the nature of monotheistic idiom in that milieu.

The Koran is, and has been from the beginning of the emergence of the religion, the primary source and reference point for Islam. Indeed, the Koran in its function as a source of authority is the defining element of Islamic identity. The emergence of the Muslim community is intimately connected with the emergence of the Koran as an authoritative text in making decisions on matters of law and theology.

Allusions and direct quotations to the Koran are pervasive in Muslim literature. While imitation of the Koran is considered both impossible and sinful (because it is God's word), the contents of the Koran and its particular form of classical Arabic create the substrata of literary production. The widespread knowledge of the Koran, traditionally instilled in most Muslim children through memorization, means that reverberations of the text are guaranteed to be felt by many readers. Direct quotations of the Koran and the use of some of the text's striking metaphors abound in literature from all ages.

Text edition

The Koran Interpreted, Arthur A. Arberry (trans.), London (1955), rpt Oxford (1964) (a scholarly translation, with the advantage of an excellent concordance, tied to the Arabic text: *A Concordance of the Qur'ān*, Hanna Kassis, Berkeley, 1983).

Further reading

Al-Azmeh, Aziz, 'Rhetoric for the senses: a consideration of Muslim paradise narratives', *JAL* 26

(1995), 215–31 (Koranic motif and its influence on Muslim literature broadly conceived).
Analyse conceptuelle du Coran sur cartes perforées, Allard, Michel, Paris (1963) (while primitive by today's standards of computer technology, this is still valuable for its conceptual analyses).
Rippin, A., 'The commerce of eschatology' in *The Qur'ān as Text*, S. Wild (ed.), Leiden (1996), 125–35 (on the symbolism of the Koran).
Le métaphor dans le Coran, Sabbagh, I., Paris (1943) (catalogues the literary figures of the text, although the framework within which this is done is rather limited).
The Teaching of the Qur'ān, Stanton, H.U.W., London (1919) (a useful summary with an account of its growth and a topical index).
Stewart, D.J., 'Saj' in the Qur'an', *JAL* 21 (1990), 102–39 (on the rhyme of the Koran).
Watt, W.M., *Bell's Introduction to the Qur'ān*, Edinburgh (1977) (provides a scholarly overview to the subject).

A. RIPPIN

See also: exegesis, Koranic; *i'jāz al-Qur'ān*

Kufa

After the conquest of Iraq, Kufa was founded in 17/638 as a permanent military establishment of the Arabs in Mesopotamia. Being, alongside **Basra**, one of the two early Arab city-encampments in Iraq, Kufa was a centre of conquering Islam. During the second half of the second/eighth century, it lost much of its importance, politically and culturally, to the new capital **Baghdad**. The settlement of Arab tribes in Kufa was of great multiplicity, and was further fractionated by the conflict between conquerors and newcomers. The presence, during four years, of the fourth caliph **'Alī ibn Abī Ṭālib** gave Kufa a lasting **Shī'ī** imprint. In consequence, the main political divisions of that time, i.e. the first/seventh century, concentrated here and found, as happened with specific local issues as well, eager and militant partisans. Kufa therefore won fame for being a hotbed of political unrest. The life and verses of Kufan poets, such as **A'shā Hamdān** (d. 83/702), **al-Kumayt ibn Zayd al-Asadī** (d. 126 or 127174), and, 'Kufan' to a lesser degree, **al-Ṭirimmāḥ** bear witness to these circumstances.

The immediate neighbourhood to the city of **Ḥīra**, which had attracted Arab poets from the Peninsula in pre-Islamic time and continued to be frequented for the sake of its taverns, may have furthered the development of a Kufan poetry in the early Islamic period that was urban, light-hearted, even frivolous in character. **Al-Uqayshir al-Asadī** (d. after 80/699), known for wine poetry as well as for his licentious love poetry (***mujūn***), as well as 'Ammār Dhū Kināz, represent a libertine element in Kufan society. Love and wine poetry also flourished with Ayman ibn Khuraym (d. 86/705), and **Muṭī' ibn Iyās** (d. 169/785) conveyed this tradition to **Baghdad**.

Most important for Arabic literature was Kufa's function as a magnificent platform for the exchange and formation of Arab traditions on the pre-Islamic past and tribal genealogy, on the heroic period of the conquest and the dramatic events of the 'Alid schism. Private circles and, to a degree which is hard to ascertain, the *kunāsa*, the vast market place for arriving caravans, served the reception and transmission of these traditions. Thousands of accounts of this kind, as well as anecdotal narrations about men of fame, have found their way into our sources through Kufan collectors of *akhbār*, for example, by 'Awāna ibn al-Ḥakam (d. 147/764), Abū Mikhnaf (d, 157/774), Abū al-Jarrā ibn 'Ayyāsh (d. 158/775), Sayf ibn 'Umar (d. 180/796), the Ibn al-Kalbīs, father Hishām (d. 146/763) and his son Muḥammad (d. 204/819; see **Ibn al-Kalbī**), and al-Haytham ibn 'Adī (d. 207/821), the latter spending most of his life in Baghdad. Notwithstanding the Shī'ī bias and the impact of tribal pride on some of these accounts, they represent, in general, a large variety of aspects. The materials handed down to us by these and other experts were, often in a very anecdotal manner, also concerned with poets and their poetry, a field in which **Ḥammād al-Rāwiya** (d. 155/772) won fame; philologically more solid were al-Sharqī al-Quṭāmī (d. *c.*150/767) and **al-Mufaḍḍal al-Ḍabbī**. Apart from this, an old popular form of edifying story-telling is preserved by Naṣr ibn Muzāḥim (d. 221/827). Among the prominent authorities of the first/eighth-century figures the *qāḍī* al-Sha'bī (d. 103/721). He is also an exponent of the juridical tradition in Kufa, which bore, as did its reformer **Abū Ḥanīfa** (d. 150/767), the eponym of the Ḥanafī law school, and his pupil Abū Yūsuf (d. 182/798).

The 'School of Kufa' in Arabic **grammar**, characterized by its anomalistic orientation towards the reality of spoken language, and thus supposedly of a typically Kufan inspiration, is however a fact of literary history. Its main advocates, **al-Farrā'** (d. 207/822), and, later, **Ibn al-ʿArābī** and **Thaʿlab**, did not live in Kufa.

Further reading

Athamina, Khalil, 'Aʿrāb and Muhājirūn in the environment of Amṣār', *SI* (1987), vol, 66, 5–25.

Blachère, Régis, *Histoire de la littérature arabe des origines à la fin du XVe siécle de J.C.*, 3 vols, Paris (1952–66), 514–36.

Djaït, Hichem, *al-Kufa, Naissance de la ville islamique*, Paris (1986).

Duri, A.A., *The Rise of Historical Writing Among the Arabs,* Lawrence I. Conrad (ed. and trans.), Princeton (1983), 41–9 and *passim.*

Leder, Stefan, *Das Korpus al-Haiṯam ibn ʿAdī*, Frankfurt (1991), 48–51, 292–5.

Meisami, J.S., 'Arabic *Mujūn* poetry: the literary dimension', in *Verse and the Fair Sex*, F. de Jong (ed.), Utrecht (1993), 8–30.

Nallino, C.-A., *La Littérature Arabe des origines à l'époque de la dynastie umayyade*, Ch. Pellat (trans.), Paris (1950), 221–32.

Schoeler, Gregor, 'Bashshār b. Burd, Abū 'l-ʿAtāhiyah and Abū Nuwās', in *CHALABL*, 275–99.

Wagner, Ewald, *Grundzüge der klassischen arabischen Dichtung*, 2 vols, Darmstadt (1987–8), vol. 2, 84.

S. LEDER

Kulthūm ibn ʿAmr al-ʿAttābī *see* al-ʿAttābī, Kulthūm ibn ʿAmr

al-Kumayt ibn Zayd al-Asadī (*c.*59–128/*c.*679–744)

The poet Abū al-Mustahill al Kumayt ibn Zayd al-Asadī was born in **Kufa**, and died there from a lethal injury. After being trained he became a teacher at the local mosque. Inspired by his acquaintance with poets like **al-Farazdaq**, **Ru'ba ibn al-ʿAjjāj** and **al-Ṭirimmāḥ**, and allegedly under pressure from his family, he started a career as a poet. After he joined the local **Zaydī** movement, a moderate branch of Shīʿism, he became an eloquent spokesman for this group. His poetry shows a strong tendency to be ideological and political, although it is very **bedouin**-like in diction and imagery, and is based on a thorough knowledge of ancient Arabic poetry.

Much of al-Kumayt's work aroused the anger of the politicians of his time, and consequently he came into conflict witb a local governor and with the **Umayyad** caliph Hishām ibn ʿAbd al-Malik, who sentenced him to death, but the sentence was never carried out. One of his famous works is a cycle of poems called the *Hāshimiyyāt*, a set of eleven panegyrics of various length on the Prophet, **ʿAlī, ibn Abī Ṭālib**, al-Ḥusayn, and Zayd ibn ʿAlī, in which he often quotes from *Jāhilī* poetry and from the **Koran**, which caused some later critics to accuse him of plagiarism. Another work, which ultimately caused his death, was the *Mudhahhaba*, a satire on the Southern Arab **tribes** from **Yemen**, who opposed the Northern Arab tribe of Muḍar, one of the conflicts that ultimately led to the downfall of the Umayyad dynasty. A final work from the apparently extensive but largely lost ***dīwān*** of this poet is the *Malḥama* in which he praises the tribe of Quraysh.

If his contradictory loyalties to the **Sunnī** Umayyads and the opposing Shīʿīs do not represent different stages in the development of his political ideas, al-Kumayt must be considered a hypocritical or at least enigmatic personality. His works, however, are greatly esteemed in Shīʿī circles, whose ideas they eloquently represent. He died from an injury inflicted by insurgent soldiers of Yemeni origin.

Text editions

Die Hašimijjāt, J. Horovitz (ed.), Leiden (1904).

al-Qaysī, Aḥmad ibn Ibrāhīm, *Sharḥ Hāshimiyyāt al-Kumayt*, Dā'ūd Sallūm and Nūrī Ḥammūdī al-Qaysī (eds), Beirut (1984).

Further reading

Madelung, W., 'The *Hāshimiyyāt* of al-Kumayt and Hāshimī Shīʿism', *SI* 70 (1989), 5–26.

Müller, Kathrin, *Kritische Untersuchungen zum Diwan des Kumait b. Zaid*, Freiburg im Breisgau (1979).

Najā, A.S., *al-Kumayt ibn Zayd al-Asadī, shāʿir al-Shīʿa al-siyāsī fī al-ʿaṣr al-Umawī*, Beirut (1957).

G. BORG

Kurd ʿAlī, Muḥammad Farīd (1876–1953)

Syrian intellectual and journalist. Born in **Damascus** the son of a Kurdish father and a Circassian mother, Muḥammad Kurd ʿAlī found work as a young man on the staff of the first Arabic newspaper in Damascus, *al-Shām*. He also contributed to the Cairo journal ***al-Muqtaṭaf***. In 1901 he moved to **Cairo**, and attended the lectures of Muḥammad **'Abduh** at **al-Azhar**. He went back to Damascus, but soon returned to Cairo, where he collaborated in editing the journals *al-Ẓāhir*, *al-Musāmarāt* and *al-Mu'ayyad*, and in 1905 founded the review *al-Muqtabas*. In 1908 he transferred it to Damascus, but in 1914 it was closed down by the Ottoman authorities. He visited Europe in 1908, 1913 and 1921–2. During his stay in Italy in 1913 he collected much of the material for his principal work, *Khiṭaṭ al-Shām* (Damascus, 1925). He was largely responsible for the founding of the Arab Language Academy of Damascus in 1919, having been inspired by the example of the Académie Française.

Further reading

GAL(S), vol. 3, 430–4.

Pellat, Ch., *EI*[2], s.v. Kurd 'Alī, and bibliography there cited.

M.J.L. YOUNG

Kushājim (d. *c.*360/970–1)

Abū al-Fatḥ Maḥmūd ibn al-Ḥusayn ibn Shāhak, known as Kushājim, was a poet, polymath and collator of literature. He was born in Ramla and lived in Mosul at the court of Abū al-Hayjā' 'Abd Allāh ibn Ḥamdān, then in Aleppo at the court of Sayf al-Dawla (see **Ḥamdānids**). As a panegyricist he was generously rewarded at the Ḥamdānid court for a poem on Ja'far ibn 'Alī ibn Ḥamdān. His verse is described by Blachère (in *Histoire de la littérature arabe*) as 'excessivley florid and enjoying a contemporary vogue'; he was closely associated with his son-in-law **al-Ṣanawbarī** and is one of the creators of nature poetry in Arabic, in which he evokes visual pleasure by his descriptions of gardens, flowers and trees. He also composed a number of prose works, including one on the etiquette of the ***nadīm***.

Text editions

Dīwān, Khayriyya Muḥammad Maḥmūd (ed.), Baghdad (1970).

Kitāb adab al-nadīm, Cairo (1920).

al-Maṣāyid wa-al-maṭārid, Muḥammad As'ad Ṭalas (ed.), Baghdad (1954).

Further reading

Giese, Alma, *Waṣf bei Kushājim*, Berlin (1981) (see also the bibliography therein).

P.F. KENNEDY

See also: nature, in classical poetry; *waṣf*

Kuthayyir (*c.*40–105/660–723)

Kuthayyir ibn 'Abd al-Raḥmān al-Mulaḥī was an ***'Udhrī*** poet of the middle **Umayyad** period, who resided mainly in the **Hijaz**. A malformed half-orphan, in his poems he was occupied with his unfulfilled love to a married woman named 'Azza whose name was in later times attached to his in the genitive case: 'Kuthayyir possessed by 'Azza'. During a sojourn in **Egypt** (to where 'Azza had moved with her husband) he made the acquaintance of the governor 'Abd al-'Azīz ibn Marwān, and this was the starting point of his relationships with the caliphs 'Abd al-Malik (d. 86/705), 'Umar II (d. 101/720) and Yazīd II (d. 105/724) attested by panegyrics. His allegedly ultra-**Shī'ī** ('Kaysānī') inclinations seem to be a later re-interpretation of a more personal affection for Muḥammad ibn al-Ḥanafiyya. A ***dīwān*** has not been preserved; the collection of fragments by 'Abbās contains 172 poems with about 2,000 verses. Favourite topics in his poetry are love and panegyrics. Infatuated by the unattainable 'Azza, he carries on the tradition of the *'Udhrī* poets to whom he is also linked as *rāwī* (transmitter) of **Jamīl** Buthayna. Unlike them, his attitude to the female sex is less adoring than defiant and demanding, and moreover he was not specialized in love poetry. In his panegyrics, the addressees are treated as friends equal in rank, not as patrons. His poetical diction has in modern times been called unaffected and easily understandable.

Text edition

Collections of fragments: *Sharḥ Dīwān Kuthayyir*, H. Pérès (ed.), 2 vols, Algiers and Paris (1928–30); *Dīwān*, I. 'Abbās (ed.), Beirut (1971).

Further reading

Blachère, R., *Histoire de la littérature arabe*, 3 vols, Paris (1952–66), 609–16.

al-Rabī'ī, A., *Kuthayyir 'Azza, ḥayātuhū wa-shi'ruh*, Cairo (1967).

Rubinacci, R. 'I versi politico-religiosi di Kuṯayyir

ʿAzza', in *Studi in onore di Francesco Gabrieli*, Rome (1984), 661–5.

T. SEIDENSTICKER

kuttāb *see* secretaries

al-Kutubī, Abū ʿAbd Allāh Muḥammad Ibn Shākir (686?–764/1287?–1363)

Syrian historian who was born in the village of Darayyā near **Damascus** and lived most of his life in that city. He held no official office, religious or civil, but earned his living from selling books; hence his soubriquet al-Kutubī, the 'book-man'. He is known for two works. 'Known' is perhaps not the word, because his large history, the *ʿUyūn al-tawārīkh (The Historical Springs)*, has been little studied and is still in various scattered manuscripts. The section that covers events that he himself lived through reaches the year 760/1359. His other work, which has been edited many times, is an alphabetically organized biographical dictionary. The author's expressed intention was to supplement the similar compilation of **Ibn Khallikān** – hence the title, *Fawāt al-Wafayāt*. It contains 600 notices, for many of which al-Kutubī relied heavily on earlier compilations.

Text edition

Fawāt al-Wafayāt, Iḥsān ʿAbbās (ed.), 4 vols, Beirut, (1973–4).

Further reading

Ashtor, E. 'Étude sur quelques chroniques mamloukes', *IOS* 1 (1971), 272–97 (see especially 277–84).

D.S RICHARDS

L

Laâbi, Abdellatif (1942–)

Moroccan novelist and dramatist writing in French. Born in Fez, Laâbi founded the review *Souffles* in 1966, which introduced new, experimental methods of writing into Morocco. Arrested in 1972, he was not freed until July 1980. He has lived in France since 1985. His first collections of poetry were *Race* (1967) and *L'Arbre de fer fleurit* (1974), the former characterized by a very abrupt style. Since then, his poetry has evolved into a more profound means of expression, as seen in the recent collections *Le Soleil se meurt* (1992) and *L'Etreinte du monde* (1993). His novel *Les Rides du lion* (1989) is a work of lucid self-criticism, representing a return to the expression of common human experience. *La Baptême chacaliste* (1987) and *Exercises de tolérance* (1993) represent a step into the world of militant theatre, in which the author speaks out against oppression. Laâbi's work is characterized by sincerity and an unusual awareness, which transcends chauvinistic and nationalistic issues.

J. DÉJEUX

Labakī, Ṣalāḥ (1916–55)

Lebanese poet, lawyer, journalist and politician. Born in Brazil, Labakī was brought up in B'abdāt (Mount Lebanon). He served as president of the Ahl al-Qalam literary society, and was convener of the first pan-Arab conference of writers at Beyt Meri (1954). He published a number of ***dīwān*s**, including *Urjūḥat al-qamar* (1938), *Mawā'īd* (1944), *Sa'm* (1949) and, posthumously, *Ghurabā'* (1956) and *Ḥanīn* (1961).

Labakī's poetry reflects romantic and symbolist influences current among his generation. It treats themes such as love, nature and death in a predictably Romantic fashion, while showing concern for *le mot juste*, organic unity and technique, and employing some novel images and unusual syntheses. Although he uses classical and neo-classical metres, Labakī nevertheless experiments with the ***muwashshaḥ***, sonnet and other stanzaic forms. The result is a distinct lyrical voice which, though overshadowed by a sense of futility and impending doom (partly influenced by Adīb **Maẓhar**), often registers an insistence on hope and renewal. Portraits of women are 'ethereal' in the Romantic vein, but at times Promethean and iconoclastic. Labakī's *Lubnān al-shā'ir* (1954) remains a perceptive account of modern literary trends in Lebanon and the **Mahjar**.

Further reading

Mūsā, Munīf, *al-Shi'r al-'Arabī al-ḥadīth fī Lubnān*, Beirut (1980).

M.R. NOURALLAH

Labīd ibn Rabī'a al-'Āmirī (d. *c.*41/661)

One of the most important poets from the time of the Prophet. Born in pre-Islamic times as a member of one of the leading clans of the tribe 'Āmir ibn Ṣa'ṣa'a, he was repeatedly engaged in diplomatic and political affairs. As his poetry displays a deep religious sensitivity, there is no reason to doubt reports according to which he became a pious Muslim. There are even some lines in praise of **Muḥammad** attributed to him. Less credible is the assertion that he stopped composing poetry after having embraced Islam, saying that the **Koran** would render poetry dispensable. He died in old age, a motive often treated in his poetry.

Labīd's fame rests on some of his ***qaṣīda*s**, the most famous being his *Mu'allaqa*, and on his laments on his brother Arbad. In his *qaṣīda*s, Labīd pays more attention to the unity of the poem than most of his contemporaries. His poems often display a reflective mood and show his susceptibility to the tensions and changes of his time. In some of his poems, one finds ideas close to Koranic concepts, such as the praise of God and submission to God's will. Also worth mentioning are his descriptions of thunderstorms and his beautiful and comparatively numerous animal episodes, which inspired **al-Shammākh** and **Dhū al-Rumma**. Among his laments on his brother Arbad, who had been struck by lightning, is a poem of twenty lines (no. 24), in which the traditional praise of the deceased gives way to a more general expression of grief and reflection on the destiny of man. This lament for the transitoriness of man, the futility of human enterprise and the hardships of old age became one of the most famous elegies of pre- and early Islamic poetry.

Text editions

Arberry, A.J., *The Seven Odes*, London (1957), 19–48.
Dīwān, Beirut (1966); Ḥ.N. al-Ḥittī (ed.) Beirut (1993).
Sharḥ Dīwān Labīd, Iḥsān ʿAbbās (ed.), Kuwait (1962).

Further reading

Bauer, Thomas, *Altarabische Dichtkunst*, Wiesbaden (1992), vol. 1, 217–20; vol. 2, 86–127.
Jones, Alan, *Early Arabic Poetry*, vol. 1, Oxford (1992), 80–8.
Müller, Gottfried, *Ich bin Labīd und das ist mein Ziel*, Wiesbaden (1981).
Sells, M., *Desert Tracings*, Middletown (1989), 32–44.

T. BAUER

See also: *Muʿallaqāt*

Lacheraf, Mostefa (1917–)

Algerian poet, essayist, novelist and political figure, writing in French. Born in Sidi Aïssa in Central Algeria, Lacheraf was brought up in a bicultural environment. He taught at the grammar school in Mostaganem, then at Louis le Grand in Paris while involving himself in the struggles of the nationalist movement. A political figure, he was appointed ambassador to Argentina in 1962, and subsequently ambassador to Mexico. In 1977 he became Minister of Education in Algeria, resuming the role of ambassador to Mexico in 1979. He was Algerian delegate to UNESCO in 1982. He is now retired and living in Algeria. Although Lacheraf has written poetry for reviews, his main literary output consists of critical essays, including *L'Algérie, nation et société* (1965) and *La Culture algérienne contemporaine* (1986). A number of his works were brought together in the collection *Ecrits didactiques* (1988). Lacheraf's ideas are always precise and coherent, and he expresses himself with clarity and frankness on the major issues of the day.

J. DÉJEUX

lafẓ and *maʿnā*

'Words' and 'meaning.' This is a basic dichotomy that is assumed by all disciplines dealing with language. In the controversy between (Aristotelian) logic and grammar which raged in the fourth/tenth century, the logicians claimed that they were dealing with the meanings common to all languages, while the grammarians dealt with the words of specific languages. This did not go down well with the grammarians, who rightly insisted that they were dealing with semantics as well, and who denied to logic all universality, claiming that it was nothing but Greek grammar. (See further **grammar and grammarians**.)

In literary criticism the meaning of *maʿnā* is usually narrowed down to 'poetic idea,' or 'motif,' in which case *lafẓ* is best rendered 'wording.' Since the number of motifs tended to be limited by convention, especially in the important 'ritual' genres such as praise, the idea soon arose that the 'same' idea could be expressed by various ways of wording it. This in turn led to the question: which was poetically more important, the meaning or the wording? The dominant opinion was that the wording should be given precedence, since this was the 'form' that the poet gave to his 'material', the motifs. Analogies from other crafts are commonly adduced here (e.g. goldsmith/poet fashions ring/wording from gold/meaning). (See further ***ṣināʿa***.) This basic assumption also underlies enterprises like catalogues of motifs with their various treatments (**Ibn Qutayba** [d. 276/889], **Abū Hilāl al-ʿAskarī** [d. 395/1005]) and the attitude toward plagiarism (see ***sariqa***), where the typology to a large extent reflects the various changes in the wording; if the changes improve the rendition of the motif, the plagiarism is approved.

The poetic ideas were, of course, not unimportant, and early criticism takes both, *lafẓ* and *ma'nā*, into account. Ibn Qutayba establishes four categories of quality: (1) both are good, (2) both are bad, (3) one is good and the other bad or (4) vice versa. Similarly, though richer in variants and less systematic, in **Ibn Ṭabāṭabā** (d. 322/934). **Qudāma ibn Ja'far** (d. 337/948), in accordance with the logical layout of his *Assaying of Poetry*, treats the virtues and defects of (a) the words, (b) the meaning, and (c) the combination of the two. The availability of this last category allows him to address, under the first rubric, the qualities of single words (phonetic smoothness, archaicness, and others) rather than the wording of the meaning of a whole verse. It seems that later authors were less circumspect; for we see **'Abd al-Qāhir al-Jurjānī** (d. 471/1078 or later) waging war against those who thought that *lafẓ* referred to the dimension of sound only, and proposing instead a *lafẓ–ma'nā* dichotomy within a larger dichotomy of 'sounds' (*ajrās al-ḥurūf*) and 'intention' (*gharaḍ*). Here *lafẓ* and *ma'nā* are completely congruent due to a 'form' (*ṣūra*) that shapes the semantic relations on the *ma'nā* side and the syntactic ones on the *lafẓ* side (slightly simplified). For him this is just an explication of the critical thought of the ancient authorities; *lafẓ* still takes precedence with him in the evaluation of poetry.

Ibn Rashīq al-Qayrawānī (d. 456/1063 or later) asserts that there were partisans of *ma'nā* as there were partisans of *lafẓ*. Ibn Rashīq explains, however, that the *ma'nā* in this context is not simply the meaning and the content of the line, but rather the *ma'nā al-ṣan'a*, 'the specific meaning of a line achieved by the application of a figure of speech', thus – with a grain of salt – a 'conceit.' In the mask of *ma'nā*, the *lafẓ* is still triumphant.

Further reading

Abu Deeb, Kamal, *Al-Jurjānī's Theory of Poetic Imagery*, Warminster (1979), index, s.vv. *lafẓ* and *ma'nā*.

Athamina, K., '*Lafẓ* in classical poetry', in *Studies in Medieval Arabic and Hebrew Poetics*, S. Somekh (ed.), Leiden (1991), 47–55.

Cantarino, V. *Arabic Poetics in the Golden Age*, Leiden (1975), 46–51.

Heinrichs, Wolfhart, *Arabische Dichtung und griechische Poetik*, Beirut and Wiesbaden (1969), 69–82.

W.P. HEINRICHS

See also: literary criticism, medieval; rhetoric and poetics

al-Lāḥiqī, Abān *see* Abān ibn 'Abd al-Ḥamīd al Lāḥiqī

al-Lāḥiqī, Ḥamdān ibn Abān *see* Ḥamdān ibn Abān al-Lāḥiqī

Lakhmids

An Arab tribal dynasty allied with the Sasanians and based at the Iraqi town of **Ḥīra** from the fourth to sixth centuries. Under their rule the town became not only the main base for military activity in defence of the Iraqi desert frontier, but also a lively cultural centre.

The Lakhmids were a major stimulus to Arabic poetry, and indeed, one unparalleled anywhere else in Arabia. From throughout Arabia, such eminent poets as **Imru' al-Qays**, **Zuhayr ibn Abī Sulmā**, **Ṭarafa ibn al-'Abd**, **Ḥātim al-Ṭā'ī**, **al-Nābigha al-Dhubyānī**, **al-Ḥārith ibn Ḥilliza** and **Labīd ibn Rabī'a** came to recite verse in praise of Lakhmid princes or to lament their deaths, and on occasion would mock them in poems. No clash with their enemies was too minor for commemoration in verse, and the amenities of their base at Ḥīra were likewise celebrated. Some of this poetry may have been retrojected from Islamic times, but much of it is so detailed, or devoted to such minor events, that later forgery seems unlikely or pointless.

The Lakhmids were also the object of a number of proverbs, and they may have been responsible for some degree of historical consciousness. The churches and monasteries of Ḥīra are said to have possessed books recording genealogical and chronological information on the Lakhmids. These books must have been Nestorian works written in Syriac, but Ḥīra was a major centre for Arabic culture as well and translations could easily have been made later. The influence of such works is perhaps to be seen in the detailed knowledge of the Lakhmids that one finds in such authors as **Ḥamza al-Iṣfahānī** (wrote 350/961).

The Lakhmids were buffeted by several serious incursions by the **Ghassānids** in the sixth century, and in 602 their rule was brought to an end when their last and most renowned ruler, al-Nu'mān ibn al-Mundhir, was killed by the Sasanians. Ḥīra, on the other hand, retained at least some of its cultural significance for another three centuries after its fall in the Arab conquest of Iraq in the 630s.

Further reading

ʿAbd al-Ghanī, ʿĀrif, *Ta'rīkh al-Ḥīra fī al-Jāhiliyya wa-al-Islām*, Damascus (1993).
Rothstein, Gustav, *Die Dynastie der Laḫmiden in al-Ḥīra*, Berlin (1899).
Shahid, Irfan, *Byzantium and the Arabs in the Sixth Century*, Washington, DC (1995) (see index).

L.I. CONRAD

lampoon *see* ***hijā'***

Laroui, Abdallah *see* al-ʿArawī, ʿAbd Allāh

Lāshīn, Maḥmūd Ṭāhir (1894–1954)

Egyptian prose writer. Born in **Cairo** into a Turko-Circassian family long settled in **Egypt**, Lāshīn was the brother of the dramatist Maḥmūd ʿAbd al-Raḥīm. He studied engineering at the Muhandiskhāna in Cairo, and from 1918 to 1953 was an employee in the Department of Public Works. Inspired by French and Russian realistic literature and by the Egyptian national movement of 1919, Lāshīn shared the views of other writers of the 'Modern School' (al-Madrasa al-Ḥadītha), and together with Ḥusayn **Fawzī** and Aḥmad Khayrī Saʿīd founded the literary review ***al-Fajr***, which appeared from 1925 to 1927. Together with Yaḥyā **Ḥaqqī** and Maḥmūd **Taymūr**, he is one of the most important representatives of the Modern School. Lāshīn published in *al-Fajr* a series of short stories marked by realism, modernism and local colour; these stories, together with some others, were republished in the collections *Sukhriyyat al-nāy* (1927) and *Yuḥkā ʿannā* (1930). His only novel, *Ḥawwā bilā Ādam*, appeared in 1934, and a final collection of short stories entitled *al-Niqāb al-ṭā'ir* in 1940. *Ḥawwā bilā Ādam* has been discussed by Kilpatrick as a fine psychological novel demonstrating the incompatibility of the traditional culture with the ideas of the ***nahḍa*** espoused by the writers of the Modern School. The main character, the well-educated middle-class Ḥawwā, falls in love with a younger man of an aristocratic family, then kills herself when she realizes that he will never be hers.

Further reading

Brugman, J., *An Introduction to the History of Modern Arabic Literature in Egypt*, Leiden (1984), 252–4.
Hafez, S., *The Genesis of Arabic Narrative Discourse*, London (1993), 215–68.
——, 'The maturation of a new literary genre', *IJMES* (1984), 367–89.
Ḥaqqī, Y., *Fajr al-qiṣṣa al-Miṣriyya*, Cairo (1975), 73–100, 207–69.
Kilpatrick, H., '*Ḥawwā bilā Ādam:* an Egyptian novel of the 1930s', *JAL* 4 (1973), 48–56.

E.C.M. DE MOOR

Laylā al-Akhyaliyya (d. *c.*85/704)

Poetess of the early **Umayyad** period, famous mainly for her elegies. Laylā's poetical life was dominated by the fact that her family refused to accept the brigand-poet Tawba ibn al-Ḥumayyir as her husband and married her to another man. Ancient ***dīwān***s are lost; the collection of fragments by al-ʿAṭiyya contains 47 pieces with 300 verses. A quarter of these poems are elegies on Tawba; one poem laments the death of the caliph ʿUthmān (d. 35/656). She also quarrelled with the poet **al-Nābigha al-Jaʿdī** in a series of poems, and composed panegyrics on the caliph Marwān I (d. 65/685) and the governor **al-Ḥajjāj ibn Yūsuf** (d. 95/714), with both of whom she had personal contact. She composed two small poems in the ***rajaz*** metre containing satire and praise of her tribe.

Text edition

Dīwān Laylā al-Akhyaliyya, K. I. al-ʿAṭiyya and J. al-ʿAṭiyya (eds), Baghdad (1967) (collection of fragments).

T. SEIDENSTICKER

al-Laythī, ʿAlī (*c.*1820–96)

Egyptian court poet. Born in Būlāq, he died in **Cairo**; his name was taken from that of al-Imām al-Layth, near whose tomb the family lived. After studying at **al-Azhar**, he went to Libya, where he became a Ṣūfī and disciple of Muḥammad ibn ʿAlī al-Sanūsī. Under Khedive Saʿīd, he was exiled to Aswan for teaching astrology and divination, but he later became a court poet and companion to the Khedives Ismāʿīl and Tawfīq. He was exiled to his estate for supporting the army in the ʿUrābī revolt, and although he later returned to the court, he did not regain his former popularity there. A leading poet of the old style, al-Laythī placed a curse on anyone publishing his ***dīwān***, thereby revealing his own reservations about his poetry.

Further reading

Brugman, J., *An Introduction to the History of Modern Arabic Literature in Egypt*, Leiden (1984), 7–8.
Dāghir, Yūsuf As'ad, *Maṣādir al-dirāsāt al-adabiyya*, Beirut (1956), iii/2, 1120–1.

P.C. SADGROVE

Lebanon, modern

Despite the pivotal position of Lebanon in the nineteenth-century Arabic ***nahḍa***, the country's present literary pre-eminence derives largely from the period following World War 2, when **Beirut** became the cultural and intellectual capital of the Middle East, attracting creative artists from all over the world. Numerous publishing houses and journals emerged during this period, including Suhayl **Idrīs**'s *al-Ādāb*, a magazine that called for **commitment** in artistic endeavour and which has been considered key in the subsequent development of Arabic literature.

Arabic and French have been equally important in the development of an authentic Lebanese literature during this period. Francophone writers include poets like Etel Adnan, Marouane Hoss, Claude Khal and Nadia Tueni, as well as novelists such as Andrée Chedid, André Bercoff and Evelyne Accad. Writers in Arabic include poets such as Yūsuf **al-Khāl**, Khalīl **Hāwī**, May Rīhānī and Henri Zghayb, as well as novelists such as Tawfīq **'Awwād**, Laylā Ba'labakkī, Ḥalīm **Barakāt**, Imilī **Naṣr Allāh**, Ilyās **Khūrī** and Ḥanān **al-Shaykh**.

Whereas men's writings of the 1950s and 1960s tend to revolve round political events connected with the Arab world, particularly Palestine, women's writings are more self-reflexive and concerned with the roles and status of women in modern society. The two best-known novels of this period are Ḥalīm Barakāt's *'Awdat al-ṭā'ir ilā al-baḥr* (1969) and Laylā Ba'labakkī's *Anā aḥyā* (1958).

The writings of the 1970s and 1980s have been dominated by the Lebanese Civil War which broke out in 1975. 'Awwād's *Ṭawāḥīn Bayrūt* (1975) was a prognostication of the devastation to come. The war spawned enormous literary activity, especially on the part of women. New writers were published and established writers found new ways to express their anger and grief. Among the novels that have attracted critical attention are Ilyās Khūrī's *al-Jabal al-ṣaghīr* (1978), Ḥanān al-Shaykh's *Ḥikāyat Zahra* (1980) and Etel Adnan's *Sitt Marie Rose* (1978). Novelists like Imilī Naṣr Allāh found that they could express themselves more effectively through the short story, as in *'al-Mar'a fī 17 qiṣṣa'* (1983), while others turned to poetry as a medium that allowed them to express otherwise forbidden emotions and political positions.

Further reading

Accad, Evelyne, *Sexuality and War. Literary Masks of the Middle East*, New York (1990).
Cooke, M,, *War's Other Voices: Women Writers on the Lebanese Civil War*, Cambridge (1988).

M. COOKE

legends

Legends as narratives about persons regarded as saints, or who were at least venerated because of their socio-religious reputation, are found already in the **Koran**, e.g. in legends about the Koranic prophets from Ādam to Yūsuf (Joseph) and Zakariyā', developed later into the *Qiṣaṣ al-anbiyā'* (***Legends of the Prophets***). There are other legendary motifs in the Koran concerning **Muḥammad**, although he is said to have said about himself 'I am only a human being like you'; but a non-Muslim will regard the ***Mi'rāj***, the Prophet's midnight journey from Mecca to Jerusalem or to the seven heavens on a beast named al-Burāq (see *Sūra*s 17:1; in the early **ḥadīth**) – which inspired Persian literature more than Arabic and became the topic of masterpieces of Islamic miniature painting – as a legend. Other legends widespread throughout the Near East in the time of Muḥammad, such as that of Solomon and the Queen of Sheba (Bilqīs), found their way into the Koran and were reworked many times in the mouths of street storytellers (*quṣṣāṣ*) in **Umayyad** and early **'Abbāsid** times and were reshaped again when written down.

One of the most famous Near Eastern legends, that of **Alexander the Great**, preserved in the *Pseudo-Kallisthenes*, inspired the legend of al-Khiḍr (al-Khaḍir) found in the Koran (18: 60ff., without being named) and later in **Ṣūfī literature**. Islamic eschatologia as found in the Koran and/or ***ḥadīth*** include peoples like Gog and Magog (Yā'jūj and Mā'jūj), figures like al-Dajjāl 'the deceiver' (the Antichrist), who will come at the End of Days for forty days (or years) to spread tyranny and injustice, followed by a general conversion to Islam. Then the Mahdī ('the rightly guided' and guiding) will come to restore religion, peace and justice. These ideas have especially inspired Ṣūfī and **Shī'ī literature**.

There are legendary places mentioned in the Koran like Iram Dhāt al-'Imād, 'Iram the many-columned' (89: 7), connected with the tribe of 'Ād, already mentioned in old Arabic poetry and later found in **folklore** and ***adab*** literature. Several stories in the ***sīra*** about the Prophet and members of his family, especially **'Alī ibn Abī Ṭālib** and his descendants, and about the Khulafā' al-Rāshidūn, the first four 'Rightly Guided Caliphs', can also be regarded as legends or at least as edifying religio-political stories.

Further reading

Norris, H.T., 'Fables and legends', in *CHALABL*, 136–45.

——, 'Fables and legends in pre- Islamic and early Islamic times', in *CHALUP*, 374–86.

Thackston, W.M., Jv., 'Islamische Mythologie, Schöpfungslegenden, Prophetengeschichte, Eschatologie', in *Orientalisches Mittelalter*, W. Heinrichs (ed.), Wiesbaden (1990), 186–201.

W. WALTHER

See also: Legends of the Elders; popular literature

Legends of the Elders

The Arabic *asāṭīr al-awwalīn* occurs in the **Koran** in the pejorative meaning 'untrue stories of the men of old', as a term with which the opponents of **Muḥammad** signified his words as lies (e.g. *Sūra*s 6: 25; 8: 31; 16: 24; 23: 83; 25: 5; 27: 68; 46: 17; 83: 13). *Asāṭīr* probably derives from Latin *historia* or Greek ἱστορία. Arab philologists defined the singular form as *usṭūra*. *Usṭūra* means today 'myth, legend' without pejorative connotation, at least concerning literature, after the revaluation of national traditions, including pre-Islamic ones, that has occurred since the confrontation with European cultural ideas and ideals. *Asāṭīr*/myths are analysed and explained under the influence of Freud, Lévy-Strauss, C.G. Jung and others. Myths and legends of different origin, including ancient Near Eastern, Jewish and Christian ones, are widely used as allusions and allegories in modern Arabic poetry, prose and drama.

Further reading

Ibn Dhurayl, 'Adnān, *al-Tafsīr al-jadalī lil-usṭūra*, Damascus (1973).

Khalīl, Khalīl Aḥmad, *Maḍmūn al-usṭūra fī al-fikr al-'Arabī*, Beirut (1973).

W. WALTHER

See also: legends

Legends of the Prophets (*Qiṣaṣ al-anbiyā'*)

Tales about Biblical, early Arabian, or general Near Eastern figures, most of whom are mentioned in the **Koran**, which became the basis for a Muslim literary genre. These legends can be found in four main sources: the ***ḥadīth***, or collection of the reports about the words and deeds of the Prophet **Muḥammad**; *tafsīr*, or Koran commentary; *ta'rīkh*, works of history, especially the universal histories of writers such as **al-Ṭabarī**; and particularly in the two main collections of such material, the *Qiṣaṣ al-anbiyā'* proper, by **al-Kisā'ī** and **al-Tha'labī**. Most nineteenth- and early twentieth-century Western scholars saw these legends as simple borrowings of Jewish or Christian tales reworked into an Islamic setting. More recently, however, using newer literary theoretical approaches, scholars see the evolution of these tales as reflections of much more complex phenomena and cultural interrelationships.

Islamic doctrine posits a belief in prophets (sg. *nabī*, pl. *nabiyyūn*, *anbiyā'*), each sent by God with a divine message to a people, especially *ahl al-kitāb*, 'people of the book'. The numbers of prophets sent vary greatly, but around eighteen are mentioned in various *sūra*s of the Koran, most of whom reflect Biblical figures not necessarily known as prophets in either Judaism or Christianity. Among these are: Noah, Idris (Enoch), Abraham, Lot, Isaac, Ishmael, Jacob, Joseph, Moses, Aaron, Shu'ayb (Jethro), David, Solomon, Job, Jonah, Zachariah, John (the Baptist) and Jesus. In addition there are ancient Arabian figures such as Hūd, Ṣāliḥ and Dhū al-Kifl.

Many of these Koranic references are very

brief and elliptic, seemingly relying on previous knowledge by the hearer of the whole story to which brief reference is made. This probably indicates, incidentally, a widespread acquaintance in pre-Islamic **Arabia** with a large number of stories found in the Hebrew Bible, the New Testament, and the cultural world of the ancient Near East in general. Hence the scholarly effort to trace the 'sources' of the tales. The Muslim collectors of the stories often state the line of transmission of a given tale or version as going back to early Jewish converts to Islam. This gave rise to a labelling of such tales as ***Isrā'īliyyāt***, a term that took on a rather negative aspect with the flourishing of a brilliant Islamic civilization connected with the vast, wealthy and powerful early **ʿAbbāsid** caliphate. Becoming culturally self-assured and independent, the *'ulamā'* tended to discourage and even forbid recourse to non-Muslim sources. These legends became more and more an inspiration for poetry, especially of the **Ṣūfīs**, the realm of popular religion, and of the visual arts.

The Legends served several purposes: for Muḥammad and his early followers they foreshadowed or reflected the actual experiences of the Prophet and his community, with **Sunnīs** and **Shīʿīs** making different use of the same tales. To the universal historians, when combined with pre-Islamic Iranian tradition and what was known of the Graeco-Roman world, they provided the historical background for the coming of Islam and its eventual victory. For the Koran commentators they supplied the necessary material to expand and interpret the brief, often enigmatic references in Koran and *ḥadīth.* It is in the work of the two collectors of these legends, al-Thaʿlabī and the still unidentified al-Kisā'ī, that we find the greatest disparity of approach: al-Thaʿlabī seeks to give as full and traditional an account as possible, enriched by reference to the material still available from the prevailing cultures of pre-Islamic Arabia and its Jewish and Christian inhabitants, primarily for religious edification; while al-Kisā'ī's accounts reflect a more imaginative, popular retelling of the tales aimed at attracting the attention of the listeners with the ultimate aim of instilling enthusiasm for Islam, its practices and its values. But even in al-Thaʿlabī we find large segments of the widespread legends of **Alexander the Great** and the tale of Buluqiyyā, both of which were more in the nature of popular entertainment than of religious preaching. The legends can be found in translations and adaptations to most of the 'Islamic languages': Persian, Urdu, Turkic languages, Swahili, Malay, etc., and contemporary versions in Arabic are widely popular today.

Further reading

Duri, A.A., *The Rise of Historical Writing Among the Arabs*, Princeton (1983), 122–35 and *passim.*

Firestone, R., *Journeys in Holy Lands*, Albany (1990), 13–21.

Khoury, R.G., *Les Légendes prophétiques dans l'Islam depuis le Ie jusqu'au IIIe siėle de l'Hégire* (edition and study of Abū Rifāʿa ʿUmāra al-Fārisī's *K. Bad' al-khalq wa-qiṣaṣ al-anbiyā'*), Wiesbaden (1978).

Nagel, T., *Die Qiṣaṣ al-anbiyā': Ein Beitrag zur arabischen Literaturwissenschaft*, Bonn (1967).

al-Najjār, M.W., *Qiṣaṣ al-anbiyā'*, Beirut (n.d.).

Pauliny, J., 'Einige Bemerkungen zu den Werken "Qiṣaṣ al-anbiyā" in der arabischen Literatur', in *Graecolatina et Orientalia*, Bratislava (1969), 11–22.

——, 'Zur Rolle der Quṣṣāṣ bei der Entstehung und Überlieferung der popularen Prophetenlegenden', *Asian and African Studies* (Bratislava), 10 (1974), 125–41.

Rosenthal, F., *A History of Muslim Historiography*, Leiden (1968), 335, 403–4.

——, 'The influence of the biblical tradition on Muslim historiography', in *Historians of the Middle East*, P.M. Holt and B. Lewis (eds), London (1962), 35–45.

Sidersky, D., *Les Origines des légendes musulmanes dans le Qoran et dans les vies des prophètes*, Paris (1929).

W.M. BRINNER

See also: popular literature

Leo Africanus (b. between 894 and 901/1489 and 1495)

Leo Africanus, or Giovanni Leone, formerly al-Ḥasan ibn Muḥammad al-Wazzānī, was born in Granada, but his family subsequently moved to Fez. As a young man he worked in a mental hospital in Fez and travelled extensively throughout North Africa. In 1518 he was captured by Sicilian corsairs and taken to Rome, where under the patronage of Leo X he converted to Christianity and learnt Latin. In 1526 he completed *The History and Description of Africa and the Notable Thinqs Therein Contained*, which he wrote in (poor) Italian on the basis of Arabic notes. It is an exceptionally lively and vivid survey, especially for Morocco. He also wrote a biographical dictionary, *Libellus de viris quibusdam illustribus apud Arabes* (1527). At the end of his life he returned to Tunis and probably died there. His life and travels form the basis of Amin Maalouf's novel *Léon l'Africain* (*Leo the African*, P. Sluglett (trans.), London, 1988).

Text edition

Description de l'Afrique, A. Épaulard (trans.), Paris (1956).

Further reading

Bovill, E.W., *The Golden Trade of the Moors*, 2nd edn, Oxford (1968).
Mauny, R., 'Note sur *Les grands voyages* de Leon l'Africain,' *Hespéris*, 41 (1954), 379–94.

R. IRWIN

Leone, Giovanni *see* Leo Africanus

letter-writing *see* artistic prose; secretaries

lexicography, medieval

Origins

Lexicography is a by-product of the realization that the intuitive knowledge of the meaning of words among the Arabs in the Prophet's lifetime was lost to the heterogeneous urban communities who formed the majority of the Islamic population, Pioneers such as **Abū ʿAmr ibn al-ʿAlāʾ** (d. 144–7/771–4) began soliciting information from the **bedouin** on the assumption that they preserved the authentic Koranic and pre-Koranic usage. The results, however, forerunners of the great dictionaries, were entirely secular word-lists, names of animals, meteorological features, near-homonyms, difficult genders and morphologies, etc., more useful to the collector of poetry than the religious scholar, for which reason some philologists shunned the subject.

Vocabularies and other more elaborate lists continued to be produced well into the fourth/tenth century, but already in the late second/eighth century a full-scale dictionary is ascribed to **al-Khalīl ibn Aḥmad** (d. 175/791). Some medieval lexicographers evidently regard al-Khalīl's friend al-Layth ibn al-Muẓaffar (d. 190/805) as the author, but in any case the *Kitāb al-ʿAyn*, named after the first letter in its alphabetical arrangement (see below), is the earliest dictionary.

Arrangement of dictionaries

All medieval Arabic dictionaries (though not Persian, Turkish, etc.) etymologize words into their constituent radicals, hence *aftaḥu* 'I open', *miftāḥ* 'key', *iftataḥa* 'was opened', for example, are all located under the root *f-t-ḥ*, more precisely its citation form, the simple perfect verb *fataḥa* 'he opened'. Moreover four alphabetical systems exist, viz:

1. *Permutative/phonological*: The alphabetical order is that of al-Khalīl's *Kitāb al-ʿAyn*, i.e. in ascending order of points of articulation (the conjectural Indian origins of this alphabet remain unproven), namely

   ʿ,ḥ,h,kh,gh,q,k,j,sh,ḍ,ṣ,s,z,ṭ,d,t,ẓ,dh,th,r, l,n,f,b,m,w,ā,y,ʾ,

   and each entry comprises all the permutations, both used (*mustaʿmal*) and unused (*muhmal*), of the given radicals. *F-t-ḥ* is thus found under *ḥ* in the group *ḥ-t-f* and its permutations (of which *f-ḥ-t* does not occur). This arrangement is followed in the *Muḥīṭ* of **al-Ṣāhib Ibn ʿAbbād** (d. 385/995), the *Bāriʿ* of **al-Qālī** (d. 356/965), the *Tahdhīb* of al-Azharī (d. 370/980) and the *Muḥkam* of Ibn Sīda (d. 458/1066).
2. *Permutative/alphabetical*: The order is that of the standard Arabic alphabet, viz.

   ʾ,b,t,th,j,ḥ,kh,d,dh,r,z,s,sh,ṣ,ḍ,ṭ,ẓ,ʿ,gh,f, q,k,l,m,n,h,w,y,

   and the roots are grouped into permutations as before, so that *f-t-ḥ* is now found under *t-ḥ-f* and its combinations. Only one dictionary uses this arrangement, the *Jamhara* of **Ibn Durayd** (d. 321/933), an expansion of the *Kitāb al-ʿAyn* supplemented by short monographs on such topics as foreign words, the theory of permutations (inspired directly by al-Khalīl's metrical circles; see **prosody**) and the relative frequency of the Arabic consonants.
3. *Alphabetical by first radical*: Each root is listed by its first radical in the standard alphabetical order, the internal sequence

being determined by the second and third radicals. Hence *f-t-ḥ* occurs between *f-t-j* and *f-t-kh*. An early but enigmatic example is the *Kitāb al-Jīm* of al-Shaybānī (d. 213/828), named after the letter *j* for still unknown reasons. Many specialized dictionaries, particularly collections of technical terms, favour this order, among them **al-Zamakhsharī**'s (d. 538/1144) *Asās al-balāgha*, noteworthy for its attention to metaphorical meanings.

Arabic dictionaries on the Western model from the nineteenth century onwards invariably follow this order, but two important medieval examples are the *Muʿjam maqāyīs al-lugha* and its abridgement *al-Mujmal*, both by **Ibn Fāris** (d. 395/1005). These are further complicated by being arranged cyclically, so that the first entry under *f* is *f-q-m* (the root whose second and third consonants occur *after f*), continuing until *f-y-n*, when the alphabet restarts and so eventually passes through *f-t-ḥ*. The arrangement is undoubtedly original but was never imitated. Ibn Fāris also provides a general root meaning for each set of radicals, an extremely interesting semantic experiment which has been adopted by the dictionary of the Arab Academy in Cairo.

4. *Alphabetical by last radical*: Each root is listed by its *last* radical in the standard alphabetical order, hence *f-t-ḥ* is found under *ḥ*, the internal sequence being determined by the first and second radicals. The innovation is often attributed to **al-Jawharī** (d. 393/1003) and his dictionary *al-Ṣiḥāḥ*, but earlier rhyming lists are known, e.g. by al-Bandanījī (d. 284/897). It is this arrangement which was followed by all succeeding major works. That these are also rhyming dictionaries is probably a coincidence: poets do not seem to have used them as such. Perhaps the ordering reflects the greater semantic weight of final radicals, which can serve to differentiate near-synonymous roots, e.g. *n-b-ṭ*, *n-b-ʿ*, *n-b-gh*; *q-ṭ-ʿ*, *q-ṭ-f*, *q-ṭ-m*, etc.

The classic dictionaries

The *Ṣiḥāḥ* of al-Jawharī may be regarded as the ancestor of the classic dictionaries both in its arrangement and scope and its importance for subsequent lexicography in East and West. The most notable productions after al-Jawharī are the *Lisān al-ʿArab* of **Ibn Manẓūr** (d. 711/1311), the *Qāmūs al-muḥīṭ* of **al-Fīrūzābādī** (d. 817/1415) and the massive *Tāj al-ʿarūs* of al-Murtaḍā **al-Zabīdī** (d. 1205/1791), the last subsuming the contents of virtually every previous work. The *Qāmūs* in particular has become the most widely used of all the dictionaries and has exercised considerable influence in the West (see **lexicography, modern**).

General characterization of Arabic lexicography

Modern scholarship has tended to be rather dismissive of Arabic lexicography, forgetting perhaps that European lexicography was just beginning when the *Tāj al-ʿarūs* had crowned a thousand-year tradition. Lexicography was a genuine science to the Arabs – *ʿilm al-lugha*, 'science of vocabulary' might be an acceptable translation – but its goals were akin to those of ***ḥadīth*** scholarship, to *preserve* meanings rather than analyse them, even of words that may never have existed (although their authenticity did not always go unchallenged). It is true that Arabic lexicography does not pursue the history or origin of words in the Western manner, still less their changes in form or meaning. Etymological science (*ʿilm al-ishtiqāq*) certainly exists, but it denotes the re-attachment of a word to its radicals: the root, formally speaking, is already known and all that is required is to account for this particular instance of it, sometimes involving rather tortuous reasoning reminiscent of medieval European etymologies. A science of semantics, *ʿilm al-waḍʿ*, emerged in the later Middle Ages, and it is probably time for a re-examination of the language sciences in the light of recent progress in Western linguistics.

Further reading

Carter, M.G., 'Lexicography', in *CHALRLS*, 107–117 (Bibliography 531).

Gätje, H., 'Arabische Lexikographie: ein Überblick', *Historiographia Linguistica* 12 (1985), 105–47.

Ghālī, W.R. and Naṣṣār, Ḥ., *al-Muʿjamāt al-ʿArabiyya*, Cairo (1971).

Haywood, J.A., *Arabic Lexicography, its History, and its Place in the General History of Lexicography*, 2nd edn, Leiden (1965).

Kraemer, J., 'Studien zur altarabischen Lexikographie', *Oriens* 6 (1953), 201–38.

Krenkow, F., 'The beginnings of Arabic lexicogra-

phy till the time of al-Jauhari, with special reference to the work of Ibn Duraid', *JRAS Centenary supplement* (1924), 255–70.
Marçais, W., 'La lexicographie arabe', *Notes et conférences*, Paris (1961).
Rundgren, F., 'La lexicographie arabe', in *Studies in Semitic Lexicography*, P. Fronzaroli (ed.), Florence (1973), 145–59.
Spitaler, A., review of J.A. Haywood, *Arabic Lexicography*, in *OLZ* 63 (1968), coll. 50–8.
Weiss, B., ''Ilm al-waḍ': an introductory account of a later Muslim philological science', *Arabica* 34 (1987), 339–56.
Wild, S., 'Die arabische Lexikographie', in *GAP*, vol. 2, 136–47 and see vol. 3, *Supplement*, W. Fischer (ed.), Wiesbaden (1992), 264–9.
——, *Das Kitāb al-'Ain und die arabische Lexikographie*, Wiesbaden (1965).

M.G. CARTER

lexicography, modern

Modern Arabic lexicography and the European tradition are so closely intertwined that they are best treated together. Although the two earliest Western examples, the *Vocabolista arauigo en letra castellana* of Pedro de Alcalá (1505) and the *Lexicon Arabicum* of Raphelengius (1613, posthumously), owe nothing to the Arabic lexica, every succeeding dictionary until Dozy's *Supplément* of 1881 is substantially dependent on Arabic models: Giggeius' *Thesaurus linguae arabicae* relies on **al-Fīrūzābādī**'s *Qāmūs*, the *Lexicon Arabico-Latinum* of Golius and Freytag's *Lexicon Arabico-Latinum* are both based on **al-Jawharī**'s *Ṣiḥāḥ*, while the greatest individual accomplishment in Western lexicography, Lane's *Madd al-Qāmūs, an Arabic English Lexicon*, is essentially a consolidation of all the medieval Arabic dictionaries.

Ironically, it was probably Lane's work that stimulated not only the appearance of several European dictionaries (notably Biberstein-Kazimirski and the worthy Belot – the latter virtually a translation of the *Qāmūs*, soon rendered into English as the familiar and still indispensable Hava) but also the first dictionaries by modern Arab lexicographers, e.g, the *Muḥīṭ al-muḥīṭ* of Buṭrus **al-Bustānī**, the *Bustān* of 'Abd Allāh **al-Bustānī** and the *Mu'jam matn al-lugha* of Aḥmad Riḍā (1872–1953). All these Arab works follow Western methods and principles of arrangement. The *Mu'jam al-kabīr* of the Arab Academy in Cairo is the most ambitious lexicographical undertaking of this kind so far, and is remarkable for citing **Ibn Fāris**'s general summaries of root meanings wherever possible. However, publication is proceeding rather slowly: only the third letter of the alphabet has been reached to date.

The *Wörterbuch der klassischen arabischen Sprache* is the first comprehensive dictionary to draw upon actual literary examples, but begins only where Lane left off (he died on the letter *qāf*). In this it differs from Blachère, Chouémi and Denizeau, *Dictionnaire arabe–français– anglais*, which ambitiously aims to cover both classical and modern Arabic. The greatest practical contribution to contemporary lexicography is Wehr's *Arabisches Wörterbuch für die Schriftsprache der Gegenwart*, also compiled from original data rather than earlier dictionaries: the English translation, *Dictionary of Modern Written Arabic*, has become the standard. There is no space here to discuss the many English–Arabic or colloquial dictionaries but mention must be made of Badawi/Hinds, *Dictionary of Colloquial Egyptian* for its brilliant presentation of the full range of Egyptian speech.

Further reading

Badawi, El-Said and Hinds, Martin, *Dictionary of Colloquial Egyptian*, Cairo (1981).
Belot, J.-P., *Al-Farā'id al-durriyya*, Beirut (1883), trans. J.D. Hava, Beirut (1899), many rpts.
Biberstein-Kazimirski, A. de, *Dictionnaire arabe–français*, Paris (1860), Cairo (1875), rpt (1960).
Blachère, R., Chouémi, M. and Denizeau, C., *Dictionnaire arabe–français–anglais (langue classique et moderne)*, Paris (1967–).
al-Bustānī, 'A., *Al-Bustān*, Beirut (1927).
al-Bustānī, B., *Muḥīṭ al-Muḥīṭ*, Beirut (1867–9).
Dozy, R., *Supplément aux dictionnaires arabes*, Leiden and Paris (1881), 2nd edn (1927), rpt (1967).
Freytag, G.W., *Lexicon Arabico-Latinum*, Halle (1830-7).
Fück, J., *Die arabischen Studien in Europa bis in den Anfang des 20. Jahrhunderts*, Leipzig (1955).
——, 'Zur arabischen Wörterbuchfrage', *ZDMG* 107 (1957), 340–7.
Gätje, H., 'Arabische Lexikographie: ein Überblick', *Historiographia Linguistica* 12 (1985), 104–47.
Ghālī, W.R. and Naṣṣār, Ḥ., *Al-Mu'jamāt al-'arabiyya*, Cairo (1971).
Giggeius, Antonius, *Thesaurus linguae arabicae*, Milan (1632).
Golius, Jacobus, *Lexicon Arabico-Latinum*, Leiden (1653).

Haywood, J.A., *Arabic Lexicography, its History. and its Place in the General History of Lexicography*, 2nd edn, Leiden (1965), 122–32, 137–8.
Lane, E.W., *Madd al-Qāmūs, Arabic–English Lexicon*, London (1863–93), rpt several times.
Al-Mu'jam al-kabīr, Cairo (1956–).
Raphelengius, Franciscus, *Lexicon Arabicum*, Leiden (1613).
Riḍā, Shaykh Aḥmad, *Mu'jam matn al-lugha*, Beirut (1958–61).
Sezgin, F., *GAS*, vol. 8 (1981), 1–6.
Vix, A., 'Survey of useful Arabic reference materials', *Al-'Arabiyya* (Journal of the American Association of Teachers of Arabic) 12 (1979), 44–57.
Wehr, H., *Arabisches Wörterbuch für die Schriftsprache der Gegenwart*, Wiesbaden (1952, 1958–9, 1985).
——, *Dictionary of Modern Written Arabic*, J.M. Cowan (ed.), Wiesbaden (1961, 1966, 1971 [1976 paper], 1979).
Wörterbuch der klassischen arabischen Sprache, Jörg Kraemer, Helmut Gätje, Anton Spitaler, Manfred Ullman, Wiesbaden (1970–).

M.G. CARTER

libraries, medieval

The transition from orality to scripturalness in Arabic letters, or, differently put, the rapid emergence of a written tradition in all fields since the middle of the second/eighth century, before long resulted in the establishment of libraries properly speaking as well. Remarkably enough, though, pre-modern Arabic does not have a specific single term for 'library' (cf. the modern *maktaba*), but uses the more generic *khizāna* ('storehouse'), either by itself or in compounds like *khizānat al-ḥikma* ('storehouse of wisdom'; see below) or, less emphatically, *khizānat al-kutub* ('storehouse of books').

The earliest reports about notable collections of books refer to the period of roughly the turn of the third/ninth century; this was a time of heady intellectual activity and experimentation, not the least aspect of which was the appropriation of 'foreign', i.e. Greek and, less massively, Hindu and Persian learning under the patronage of the **'Abbāsid** caliphs **Hārūn al-Rashīd** (170–95/786–809) and his son al-Ma'mūn (198–209/813–33). (See further **translation, medieval**.) Nor should a technological–material impulse for the dissemination of knowledge at about the same time go unmentioned; after the battle on the Ṭalās in 133/751, Chinese prisoners of war were instrumental in introducing the craft of paper-making into the caliphate – Samarkand became the eponymous manufacturing centre – and reputedly within a scant fifty years, the **Barmakid** Ja'far ibn Yaḥyā established the first paper-mill in **Baghdad**. In time, paper, very much cheaper than papyrus – not to mention vellum – made books significantly more affordable to wide strata of society.

The rate and scope of the translation activity that al-Rashīd and al-Ma'mūn, their successors, and other high-placed and wealthy patrons supported could not have been sustained without ready access to a collection of sources. Thus, their library (*khizānat*, 'storehouse', or **Bayt al-Ḥikma**, 'house of wisdom') grew into a research centre for the translator–scholars in the fields concerned. However, it was not a 'public' library, neither by ownership nor by accessibility: the former was private, and the latter was restricted to a privileged group of scholars. Private ownership and restricted access were typical of Islamic libraries even after the turn of the fifth/eleventh century, when the institution of mortmain (*waqf*) brought about a proliferation of libraries and generally opened their resources up to a wider public; yet it was the donor's (*wāqif*) prerogative to stipulate limitations to access. Furthermore, such trust libraries were not set up as institutions of learning in their own right; they were adjuncts to institutions either wholly or partially devoted to instruction, such as mosques, 'colleges' (*madrasas*) and hospitals. Their holdings, however, were not necessarily limited to the fields of specific concern to them, such as religious disciplines, jurisprudence (***fiqh***) or medicine.

From the time of Hārūn al-Rashīd and al-Ma'mūn onwards, biographers and chroniclers time and again mention extraordinarily large private holdings of books; the numbers are usually to be taken as symbolic (multiples of 'forty' or other traditional 'large figures') and in general the anecdotal nature of such reports hardly permits of an extraction of factual kernels from them. However, it is clear that literacy and, as a result, bibliophily, touched ever wider segments of the population. It was the needs of scholars and littérateurs rather than the pastime of rich dilettanti that supported the flourishing book trade of Baghdad and other centres of intellectual life; less wealthy scholars frequently earned, or supplemented, their livelihood as copiers and book dealers. Conversely, numerous book dealers qualified as scholars themselves. Perhaps their most brilliant representative was Muḥammad **Ibn al-Nadīm**, the author of the biobibliographical 'catalogue' – actually an encycopaedic conspectus of the arts and sciences of the period – *al-Fihrist*. Just as Ibn al-Nadīm offers a glimpse into the intellectual life of Būyid Baghdad, the extant description of the library of the Imāmī-Shīʿī scholar Raḍī al-Dīn ʿAlī ibn Mūsā ibn Ṭāwūs (589–664/1193–1266) highlights the range of interests of an admittedly wealthy but by no means outstandingly brilliant scholar of the waning ʿAbbāsid period. Precisely for its individual, private profile the richness of his holdings – comprising more than 1,500 titles – lends credence to the numerous adulatory reports about scholars' libraries in the biobibliographical sources.

As is to be expected, the most famous libraries of medieval Islam were princely collections; no survey can ignore them although, sadly, they have all vanished without a trace. Al-Ma'mūn's and his successors' libraries fell victim to the dynasty's decline under the **Būyids**, but the pattern repeated itself with the Būyid ʿAḍud al-Dawla's (r. 339–72/950–83) library in Shiraz as well as, for example, with the **Sāmānids**' in Bukhara, the Spanish **Umayyad** al-Ḥakam II's (r. 351–66/962–77) in Córdoba, and, best documented, with the **Fāṭimid** palace library in **Cairo** after their fall at the hands of Saladin in 567/1171 (Saladin, no uncultured boor himself, obviously could not be bothered with his 'heretic' **Ismāʿīlī** adversaries' estate). What holds true for the property of *amīr*s also goes for that of viziers: **Ibn al-ʿAmīd** and **al-Ṣāḥib Ibn ʿAbbād** were famed bibliophiles and employed highly qualified librarians (**Miskawayh** and Abū Ḥayyān **al-Tawḥīdī**), but their libraries survived as little as did that of Saladin's quasi-vizier **al-Qāḍī al-Fāḍil**, who bequeathed his sumptuous library to the *madrasa* he founded; *waqf* law, while stipulating the perpetuity of the foundation, did not assure its proper maintenance. Libraries, especially but not exclusively those owned by prominent and, for one reason or another, hated individuals, fell victim to sheer vandalism, but also to vengefulness and religious bigotry; they were thrown into the fire or soaked in water in order to 'cleanse' them of reprehensible contents. Mosques and *madrasa*s, on the other hand, did make for safer keeping of books than did private property, and all in all, an astounding number of medieval manuscripts has been preserved, especially from the post-Mongol period. Although no pre-Ottoman, pre-Ṣafavid or pre-Mughal princely library has survived, manuscripts owing their existence to courtly patronage have; a pre-900/1500 history of the Islamic book on the basis of the provenance of extant manuscripts – yet to be written – would yield a mine of information on the libraries of that period as well.

Princely and other generously appointed libraries boasted a specialized staff including librarians, craftsmen charged with the maintenance and production of books, and administrators; funds were allocated for acquisitions. Books were shelved in cabinets, and catalogued by subject; they were stacked lying sideways and for easy identification carried an abridged title on the cut edge. Miniatures such as those illustrating **al-Ḥarīrī**'s *Maqāmāt* give an idea of the physical appearance of library rooms. Architecturally, however, it was the interior appointments that turned unspecific structures into libraries; not until the Ottoman period were buildings purposely raised as libraries.

Further reading

Eche, Youssef, *Les Bibliothèques arabes publiques et semi-publiques en Mésopotamie, en Syrie et en Égypte au Moyen Age*, Damascus (1967)

Endress, Gerhard, 'Handschriftenkunde', in *GAP*, vol. 1, esp. 271–6, 306–10 (refs)

——, 'Die wissenschaftliche Literatur', in *GAP*, vol. 2, esp. 448–60.

Grabar, Oleg, *The Illustrations of the Maqamat*, Chicago (1984) (re MS Paris, Bibl. nat., Arabe 5847, fol. 5a).

Haarmann, Ulrich, 'The library of a fourteenth-century Jerusalem scholar', *Der Islam* 61 (1984), 327–33.

Kohlberg, Etan, *A Medieval Muslim Scholar at Work: Ibn Ṭāwūs and His Library*, Leiden (1992).

Lyons, Malcolm C. and Jackson, David E.P., *Saladin: The Politics of the Holy War*, Cambridge (1982), esp. 118 (re the Fāṭimid library).

Makki Sibai, Mohamed, *Mosque Libraries: an Historical Study*, London (1987).

Wasserstein, David J., 'The library of al-Ḥakam II al-Mustanṣir and the culture of Islamic Spain', *Manuscripts of the Middle East* 5/1990–1 (1993), 99–105.

L. RICHTER-BERNBURG

Libya *see* Maghrib

literary criticism, medieval

While the term *al-naqd al-adabī* is used by modern scholars to designate 'literary criticism', there is no single corresponding medieval Arabic term, just as there is no specific, overall term for 'literature'. *Naqd* (from *naqada*, 'to weigh', 'to assay', e.g. coinage), used by some medieval critics, signifies a process of evaluation, of determining the soundness of a piece of writing in accordance with a certain standard or criterion (*miʿyār*, a term also applied to coinage); writers concerned with evaluating literary style are often termed *nuqqād*. *Naqd*, however, denotes less a specific discipline than an approach: the distinguishing of good poetry or prose from bad, often combining both descriptive and prescriptive methods. As most medieval critics were associated with formalized 'sciences' such as philology, grammar, exegesis or logic, each of which had, by the fourth/tenth century, established both its own set of 'questions' (*masā'il*) for examination and its own methodology, the critics' treatment of matters bearing on aesthetics and stylistics varies with respect to the disciplinary contexts in which they occur.

From the earliest times the Arabs had a consuming interest in poetry, and many accounts of spontaneous evaluations of poetry and poets have been preserved. The old practice of ranking poets in classes according to their eloquence (often based on fragmentary citations: who, for example, composed the best verse describing a horse?) found an extension in early critical works generated by the movement to compile and record the ancient pre-Islamic and early Islamic poetry (chiefly from oral sources) in the third/ninth century, seen, for example, in **Ibn Sallām al-Jumaḥī**'s (d. *c.*232/847) *Ṭabaqāt fuḥūl al-shuʿarā'*, with its somewhat idiosyncratic ranking of poets in groups. Such works, along with anthologies like the ***Mufaḍḍaliyyāt***, contributed to the formation of a canon of poetic excellence based on the ancient poetry.

That poetry also provided a corpus drawn on by such disciplines as grammar, lexicography and exegesis for *shawāhid* (evidentiary examples) used to clarify problems of language; in these contexts it formed a standard for correct usage, and much subsequent criticism relied heavily on the criteria established by the philologists. (See further the entries on **exegesis**, **grammar and grammarians**, **lexicography**). Indeed, a primary focus of Arabic criticism was language, defined as a 'way' (*naḥw*) of behaviour and characterized by such 'speech acts' as statement, question, command and prohibition, semantic categories applied by **Thaʿlab** (d. 291/904) in his fourfold classification of poetry in the *Qawāʿid al-shiʿr*.

Although some philologists showed a preference for the Ancients, other writers extended the poetic canon to include the 'modern' poets (***muḥdathūn***), whose stylistic innovations became a subject of debate in the third/ninth and fourth/tenth centuries (see further **ancients and moderns**). **Ibn Qutayba** (d. 276/889) in his *Kitāb al-Shiʿr wa-al-shuʿarā'* urged that poetry be judged on its own merits, not by whether it was ancient or modern, and noted that what is now 'ancient' was once itself contemporary; his well-known description of the ***qaṣīda***, though often viewed as conservative, is, as scholars have pointed out, based on its **ʿAbbāsid** rather than its pre-Islamic form, and demonstrates an awareness that the function of its constituent parts is best realized by observing certain tried and tested conventions. **Ibn al-Muʿtazz** (d. 296/908) devoted his *Ṭabaqāt al-shuʿarā'* [*al-muḥdathīn*] to the moderns, and in his *Kitāb al-Badīʿ* set himself to analyse the chief features of their 'new style' (see further ***badīʿ***). **Ibn Ṭabāṭabā** (d. 322/934), treating the 'craft' (***ṣināʿa***) of poetry in his *ʿIyār al-shiʿr*, related the conventions of ancient poetry to the circumstances of its production, and contrasted the innovations of the moderns with the traditionalism of the ancients; while Abū Bakr **al-Ṣūlī** (d. *c.*335/946) in his *Akhbār Abī Tammām* stressed the continuity of Arabic poetry from pre-Islamic to modern times. The final stage of canon formation was perhaps **al-Marzūqī**'s (d. 421/1030) introduction to his commentary on **Abū Tammām**'s *Ḥamāsa*, in which, developing the ideas of earlier critics, he enunciated his formulation of the ***ʿamūd al-shiʿr***, the constituents of sound poetry. Abū Tammām, and later **al-Mutanabbī**, became the focus of critical discussions that centred around the 'excessive' use of figures of *badīʿ* and the comparative merits of the ancients and moderns, among them **al-Āmidī**'s (d. 370/980) *al-Wasāṭa bayna Abī Tammām wa-al-Buḥturī*, in which the two poets are held up as representatives of the 'artificial' and 'natural' styles respectively, and al-Qāḍī **al-Jurjānī**'s (d. 392/1002) *al-Muwāzana bayna al-*

Mutanabbī wa-khuṣūmih, which amounts to a detailed defence of that poet against criticisms on a variety of grounds.

Exegesis, which first addressed itself to the explication of difficulties encountered in the **Koran**, also evinced a concern for the nature of eloquence (*balāgha*) itself; and discussions of the ***iʿjāz al-Qur'ān***, the inimitability of Koranic language, produced a spate of works aimed at demonstrating this inimitability by comparing the style of the Koran to that of poetry – usually to demonstrate the inferiority of the latter, as in **al-Bāqillānī**'s (d. 403/1013) *Iʿjaz al-Qur'ān*. From exegesis also stemmed the distinction between the figurative and literal uses of language, which was widely discussed by such writers as **Abū ʿUbayda**, Ibn Qutayba and **al-Khaṭṭābi** (d. 386 or 8/996 or 8). (See further ***majāz***.) Exegesis produced much important theorizing, especially on the questions of imagery and metaphor, as seen especially in the works of **ʿAbd al-Qāhir al-Jurjānī** (d. 471/1078). (See further **metaphor**.)

The Arabic translations and discussions of **Aristotle** affected criticism in various ways. **Qudāma ibn Jaʿfar**'s (d. 337/948) *Naqd al-shiʿr*, which discusses the good and bad qualities of poetry according to a fourfold classification reminiscent of **Aristotle**, adapts Aristotelian moral categories as the proper topics for ***madīḥ*** (panegyric) and ***hijā'*** (invective); while **Isḥāq ibn Ibrāhīm ibn Wahb**'s (tenth century) *Kitāb al-Burhān* (long wrongly attributed to Qudāma) discusses poetry and prose from the standpoint of logic. The philosophers, heirs to the Aristotelian Organon in which poetry (like rhetoric) was classed as a branch of logic, concerned themselves with such matters as the truth of poetic statements (see **truth and poetry**), the use of poetic syllogisms and enthymemes, and the psychological and moral effects of poetry, the latter in the context of the role of **imagination** (*takhyīl*) in a system of psychology derived from Aristotle but considerably expanded by **Ibn Sīnā** (d. 428/1037). Al-Fārābī (d. 339/950) in his *Qawānīn al-shiʿr* defined poetic statements as neither true nor false, and introduced the concept of the poetic syllogism later to be expanded by Ibn Sīnā, who dealt with both poetry and rhetoric in his monumental *Kitāb al-shifā'*, a translation-cum-commentary of the Organon, as well as in other works on logic. The Andalusian **Ibn Rushd**, in his important 'Middle Commentary' on the Poetics (*Talkhīṣ Fann al-shiʿr*), defined poetic statements as imaginative (*aqāwīl mutakhayyila*), treated comparison as the chief means of conveying poetic meanings, and addressed himself to the moral effects of poetry. Although he had little influence on later Arab critics, Ibn Rushd's Aristotle was the basis for the Latin translation of the Poetics by Hermann Alemanus in 1256; his views thus passed to the medieval European Aristotelians (see J.B. Allen, 'Hermann the German's Averroistic Aristotle and medieval poetic theory', *Mosaic* 9(3) (1976), 67–81; O.B. Hardison Jr, 'The place of Averroes' commentary on the Poetics in the history of medieval criticism', in John L. Lievsay (ed)., *Medieval and Renaissance Studies*, Durham (1970), 57–81).

Many critics made claims to a specialized knowledge of poetry or, more broadly, stylistics, among them **Abū Hilāl al-ʿAskarī** (d. 395/1004), who in his *Kitāb al-Ṣināʿatayn* attempted to establish criteria for excellence in poetry and prose, and **Ibn Rashīq al-Qayrawānī** (d. 456 or 63/1063 or 71), who presented a wide variety of opinions on poetry, mediated by his own. Such writers brought criticism close to the status of a formalized discipline (*ʿilm*) based on acquired knowledge, recognized principles (*uṣūl*) and a specific methodology. Later criticism became increasingly prescriptive and normative, often concentrating on grammar (as in **al-Sakkākī**'s (d. 626/1229) *Miftāḥ al-ʿulūm*, which became the basis for many later abridgements and commentaries) and on ornament (*badīʿ*), producing compendia of ever growing lists of figures. An exception is the Maghribi **Ḥāzim al-Qarṭājannī** (d. 684/1285), whose *Minhāj al-bulaghā'* applies both a philosophical and a formal approach to the analysis of poetry.

Further reading

'Abbās, Iḥsān, *Ta'rīkh al-naqd al-adabī ʿinda al-ʿArab*, Beirut (1978).

Abu Deeb, Kamal, 'Literary criticism', in *CHALABL*, 339–87.

Black, Deborah L., *Logic and Aristotle's Rhetoric and Poetics in Medieval Arabic Philosophy*, Leiden (1990).

Bonebakker, S.A., 'Aspects of the history of literary rhetoric and poetics in Arabic literature', *Viator* 1 (1970), 75–95.

——, 'Poets and critics in the third century A. H.', in *Logic in Classical Islamic Culture*, G.E. von Grunebaum (ed.), Wiesbaden (1970), 85–111.

Cantarino, Vicente, *Arabic Poetics in the Golden Age*, Leiden (1975).

Heinrichs, Wolfhart, 'Literary theory: the problem of its efficiency', in *Arabic Poetics: Theory and Development*, G.E. van Grunebaum (ed.), Wiesbaden (1973), 19–69.
Kemal, Salim, 'Philosophy and theory in Arabic poetics', *JAL* 20 (1989), 128–47.
Kilito, Abd El-Fattah, 'Sur le métalangage métaphorique des poéticiens arabes', *Poétique* 38 (1979), 162–74.
Meisami, J.S., 'Arabic poetics revisited', *JAOS* 112 (1992), 254–68.
Stetkevych, S.P., *Abū Tammām and the Poetics of the 'Abbāsid Age*, Leiden (1991).
Trabulsi, Amjad, *La Critique poétique des Arabes*, Damascus (1955).
van Gelder, G.J.H., *Beyond the Line: Classical Arabic Literary Critics on the Coherence and Unity of the Poem*, Leiden (1982).
von Grunebaum, G.E., 'The aesthetic foundation of Arabic literature', *Comparative Literature* 4 (1952), 348–40.
——, 'Arabic literary criticism in the tenth century A.D.', *JAOS* 61 (1941), 51–7.

J.S. MEISAMI

See also: rhetoric and poetics

literary criticism, modern

Through most of the nineteenth century, even while creative prose writers were paving the way towards a functional, informative style, critics continued to champion the standards inherited from their immediate predecessors. These tolerated nothing less than the strictest fidelity to the classical language, favoured themes long held in honour by convention, and found their greatest delight in the expert handling of rhetorical 'schemes' developed by the masters of ***badīʿ***.

A change of direction was adumbrated by a protégé of the religious reformer Muḥammad **ʿAbduh**, Ḥusayn al-Marṣafī. The bulk of his *al-Wasīla al-adabiyya* (2 vols, 1872, 1875) was still concerned with grammar and rhetoric, but he also displayed a taste for poets of the more vigorous and less word-bound periods of the past, and he recognized the talent of a contemporary, Maḥmūd Sāmī **al-Bārūdī**, whose literary formation owed little to the scholastic tradition.

Substantive formulations of a new aesthetic were slow to come. Mostly, these took the form of free translations of contemporary European works, in which the theoretical elements were more or less faithfully transposed, but the illustrations were drawn from Arabic sources. Texts such as Herbert Spencer's *Philosophy of Style*, Winchester's *Principles of Literary Criticism*, Abercrombie's work of the same title, and René Wellek's *Concepts of Criticism* were dealt with in this manner by Jabr Ḍūmiṭ in 1898, by Aḥmad al-Shāyib in 1940, by Muḥammad 'Awaḍ Muḥammad in 1942 and by Muḥammad 'Aṣfūr in 1987 respectively. The later Arab critics such as Luwīs **ʿAwaḍ** or Kamāl Abū Dīb (b. 1942) have not been so dependent on single models, but have formed and expounded their own syntheses. All have remained convinced of the relevance of Western perceptions, however, so that all the 'isms' familiar to Western readers, including the language-based theories of mainly French origin, have their echoes in the Arab world. Out of the same impulse have grown some magisterial surveys (implying radical re-evaluation) of classical Arabic criticism, such as Muḥammad **Mandūr**'s *al-Naqd al-manhajī 'ind al-'Arab* (1948) and Iḥsān **ʿAbbās**'s *Tārīkh al-naqd al-adabī* (1971).

Even more influential than the theorists were those pioneering writers who shaped the taste of the reading public in a multitude of direct and indirect ways. The first half of the twentieth century in particular was dominated by a number of bold, energetic, self-assertive and prolific men of letters, such as Ṭāhā **Ḥusayn** and 'Abbās Maḥmūd **al-ʿAqqād**. Although these writers did not confine themselves to any one genre and never produced a fully worked-out exposition of their literary creeds, they were won over to Western culture – especially in its French, and to a lesser extent its British, manifestations – and gave free rein in their own output to the perceptions they thus acquired.

These writers were far from turning their back on their Arab heritage. Beginning with Jurjī **Zaydān**, they attempted vast histories and reappraisals of classical Arabic literature. Their generation did sterling service in editing ancient texts, the selection of which was no less significant than their content. In countless individual critiques, they judged the works of their forefathers and of their contemporaries alike by newly acquired criteria. No less formative were their own creations. There were differences between individuals and between rival schools, but because the sources from which they drank were comparatively limited, there was considerable cohesion in their approach: they were mostly Romantics.

Intellectuals of the next generation have

had the benefit not only of earlier pioneering work, but also of a wider choice of models and of greater maturity. Although their circumstances still do not favour narrow specialization, they do not scatter their energies on so wide a field. Creative writers like the poet **Adūnīs** are explicit in expounding their understanding of literature, but among those noted mainly for the solidity of their criticism are men such as Ghālī Shukrī, Ḥusayn **Muruwwa** and Luwīs ʿAwaḍ. They try to relate their concepts more intimately to the realities of their environment – the keywords being **commitment**, and a realism tinged in varying degrees with Marxism. The dominant sense is not one of regional distinctiveness, but of participation in a universal movement of ideas.

Further reading

Alif 2 (Spring 1982) (number devoted to 'Criticism and the avant-garde').

ʿAwaḍ, L., *al-Ishtirākiyya wa-al-adab*, Cairo (1968).

Cachia, P., *An Overview of Modern Arabic Literature*, Edinburgh (1991), 76–103.

Najm, M.Y., *Naẓariyyat al-naqd wa-al-funūn wa-al-madhāhib al-adabiyya fī al-adab al-ʿArabī al-ḥadīth*, Beirut (1961, 1985).

Yāghī, H., *al-Naqd al-adabī al-ḥadīth fī Lubnān*, Cairo (1968).

P. CACHIA

literature and the visual arts

Arabic secular literature plays only a minor role in Islamic art, although of course Koranic inscriptions in their thousands permeate all media – architecture, glassware, metalwork, ceramics and so on – and sanctify even the most mundane object. With the exception of book painting, which saw the principal expression of Arabic literature in visual terms because the pictures illustrate a specific text, the impact of Arabic literature on Islamic art was in general restricted to a few lines of poetry quoted on buildings, on metalware and on ivories, while **Mamlūk** textiles and **Sāmānid** ceramics also bear rhyming proverbs. Only rarely is this poetry of literary value, as in the case of the multiple quotations from the works of the Grenadine poet **Ibn Zamrak** (and possibly Ibn Jayyāb) at the Alhambra. In these inscriptions the building or the object often apostrophizes itself. A Córdoban ivory likens itself in *ramal* metre to a maiden's breast, while other Spanish ivories bear love-poems or vaunt their value as safe deposits. The Marinid *madrasa* of Sale in Morocco bears verses praising its door; the niche for a Nasrid vase compliments itself (presumably the vase is intended) on its beauty and splendour; the dome of the Hall of the Two Sisters in the Alhambra describes itself in terms of the Pleiades and the constellation of Gemini; a Mamlūk brass bowl states, 'My colour and workmanship are beautiful and flattering', and extols the excellence of its construction; while the fountain in the Court of the Lions in the Alhambra bears a long poem replete with references to royal victory and to Solomon. In other contexts the verses are of Shīʿī content or are benedictory, as in the case of a Mamlūk brass lunch box:

> On the owner be happiness and peace,
> And may his life last as long as the dove
> coos;
> May he receive of the outpouring of the
> spiritual world;
> The owner is Aḥmad ibn Muḥammad
> ibn Idrīs.

Several pieces of Mamlūk metalwork bear inscriptions with all or part of the following poetic text: 'You have reached the highest rank as regards greatness, and good fortune has associated with you on every side; may you not cease to be in demand and to stretch forth your right hand in the world by obtaining your wishes.' And a Zangid lid for a cylindrical box bears a corrupt text of two verses from the ***dīwān*** of the ***Jāhiliyya*** poet **al-Nābigha al-Dhubyānī**, written for the king of **Ḥira**, al-Nuʿmān ibn Mundhir:

> Don't you see that God has granted you
> a degree of power which makes all
> the kings (grovel at your feet)?
> For you are a sun; the kings, stars. When
> the sun rises no star will be seen.

Arabic poetry also became a favoured type of decoration in the private houses of the wealthy in the Levant during the eleventh/seventeenth and twelfth/eighteenth centuries, and is also found on later Islamic woodwork. Curiously enough, some of the most popular classics of medieval Arabic literature, such as the *Sīrat* ***ʿAntar*** and *The Thousand and One Nights* (***Alf layla wa-layla***), were never chosen by artists for book illustration, although some of the *Sīrat ʿAntar* images have found a ready market in modern folk art, for example in underglass paintings from **Tunisia**.

Arabic poetry, too, conspicuously unlike Persian poetry, did not develop a tradition of cycles of illustration. Nor, for that matter, did the vast majority of ***adab*** literature. One must conclude that there was no expectation on the part of writers of poetry or *belles-lettres* that their work would be illustrated. A rare exception is the *Jāmi' al-tawārīkh* of Rashīd al-Dīn, composed *c.*700/1300 and copied at the behest (and expense) of the author twice each year for transmission to the major cities of the Ilkhanid realm; contemporary fragments of this text survive in Edinburgh and London.

Texts of a scientific tenor, on the other hand, offered numerous popular subjects for painters of the seventh/thirteenth and eighth/fourteenth centuries, the period when most Arab book painting of quality was produced. Particularly favoured texts ranged over such topics as astronomy (al-Ṣūfī's *Kitāb ṣuwar al-kawākib al-thābita*), medicine and pharmacology (the Arabic translation of the *De Materia Medica* of Dioscorides), automata (works by al-Jazarī), bestiaries (by **al-Jāḥiẓ** and Ibn al-Durayhim), the cosmology of Zakariyyā' **al-Qazwīnī** (*Kitāb 'Ajā'ib al-makhlūqāt)*, handbooks of military exercises (al-Aqsarāyī's *Nihāyat al-su'l)* and farriery (Ibn Akhī Khuzām's *Kitāb al-Bayṭara* and a book of the same name by Aḥmad ibn al-Ḥusayn ibn al-Aḥnaf). Numerous other works known in only one or occasionally two illustrated copies fall into this same 'scientific' category – treatises on snakebite, medicine, calendrical systems, zoology and cosmology. In such texts, whether they were popular with painters or not, the illustrations had a specific purpose, namely to explain or amplify what the text said. They were not intended to serve as decoration. In this respect the painters of these manuscripts, some of whom may have been Christians, followed Byzantine precedent, in which the illustrations of secular manuscripts were subordinate to the text, and were indeed often reduced to scrawled explanatory diagrams.

Adab literature offered far fewer texts that were deemed suitable for illustration, and it remains puzzling why some *adab* texts were illustrated and others not. Here, too, several *unica* are known. One is the *Ḥadīth Bayāḍ wa-Riyāḍ*, a romance of courtly love originating in the Muslim West, whose paintings evoke the Andalusian cultural milieu most vividly (possibly Mālikī influence may explain why the tally of medieval illustrated manuscripts from the **Maghrib** and Muslim **Spain** is tiny in comparison with that from the central Islamic lands). Others are **al-Mubashshir ibn Fātik**'s *Mukhtār al-ḥikam*, an anthology of wisdom literature with appropriate images depicting the sages of times past, and **Ibn Ẓafar**'s *Ṣulwān al-mut'a*, a collection of animal fables.

But two texts in this category stand out for their popularity with illustrators, a factor that resulted in the evolution of sophisticated pictorial cycles. They are the animal fables known under the title ***Kalīla wa-Dimna***, and the Assemblies (itself a disputed translation) or *Maqāmāt* of **al-Ḥarīrī**. Over a score of illustrated manuscripts of these texts are known, and they take us to the heart of the painter's response to Arabic literature. That response, it has to be said, is not very profound; wherever possible, painters tend to seize on the obvious, and when the text is too complicated verbally they fix on peripheral details from it or draw directly on their own imaginations, sometimes to powerful effect. Thus the painting may be a commentary on the text rather than a direct illustration of it.

Kalīla wa-Dimna is in origin an Indian, not an Arabic, text whose great popularity ensured its translation into most of the major languages of the medieval world. The text is also noteworthy for its function as a **Mirror for Princes**, which gave it a political and moral function, despite its notional purpose of 'straight' entertainment. Nevertheless, the painters usually focused on animal rather than human subjects, even though the text offered ample scope for the latter. Presumably the lively, if not narrowly naturalistic, depiction of a wide variety of creatures constituted a major attraction of these manuscripts. Bold colours, lavish use of the silhouette mode and of the frontal plane only, and simplified conventional notations for landscape elements – all of them features that facilitated the legibility of the image – contribute to the ready appeal of these *Kalīla wa-Dimna* manuscripts, produced mostly in the seventh/thirteenth and eighth/fourteenth centuries in **Egypt**, **Syria** and Iraq. The simple narrative framework of the text, with its succession of brief independent tales, was ideally suited for illustration. The main protagonists are often identified by inscriptions, although it is not always clear whether these are contemporary. Once the iconography for a given scene had been established – a process that usually involved pruning the image of extraneous detail – it tended to become fixed and was copied with minimal alteration by subseqent painters. Thus it seems that generations of painters were not each challenged afresh by the text to produce their own personal interpretation of a scene, and this strong undertow of conservatism also explains why the same scenes were copied from one century to the next, even though the text offered hundreds of opportunities for new images.

Happily, the most popular book for illustration in all of Arabic literature was itself quintessentially Arab. This was the *Maqāmāt* of al-Ḥarīrī, which within a century of the author's death in 516/1122 was being transcribed in multiple illustrated copies, first in Syria and Iraq and then in Egypt. The plethora of illustrated versions should not, however, be attributed to the abilities of the painters, but to the runaway popularity of the text itself, a fashion that began in the lifetime of the author and lasted for centuries. Nevertheless, there is a major paradox here. The attraction of the text centred on its form rather than on its content, and specifically on its verbal pyrotechnics, for each tale or 'assembly' is the merest peg on which to hang grammatical disquisitions of stultifying length and complexity, puns, outlandish vocabulary and other features of narrowly linguistic and not generally literary interest. By and large, these are beyond the powers of the painters to illustrate. Accordingly, artists approached the text from another angle, and used its minimal references to a geographical location or a social milieu as a foundation for the close (and frequently satirical) observation of contemporary society. The fact that the *Maqāmāt* stories revolve around a confidence trickster, Abū Zayd, provides the necessary justification for this approach. As a result, the best of the illustrated *Maqāmāt* manuscripts, like those of Paris and St Petersburg, hold up a mirror to high and low life alike, to the world of the palace and the caravansarai, the judge's court and the tavern. These manuscripts are thus an unrivalled source for the minutiae of daily life in the seventh/thirteenth and eighth/fourteenth centuries, from the daily grind of village life to the great public processions and parades, with the fabled Eastern Isles adding a touch of exotic fantasy. Despite the survival of a dozen medieval illustrated versions, no standard iconography was ever evolved for this text, unlike the case of *Kalīla wa-Dimna*; the reasons for this remain obscure, but these internal differences point to the existence of numerous independent ateliers probably working for the market rather than for specific patrons. Possession of a copy of the *Maqāmāt* may well have been desirable as an indication of the owner's high level of education and culture – a matter of snob appeal – but in the case of illustrated copies one may further suggest that their main attraction was visual rather than intellectual. Their patrons may have been incapable of appreciating the finer points of the text; but when it came to pictures, they knew what they liked.

Further reading

Allan, J.W., 'Later Mamluk metalwork, II. A series of lunch-boxes', *Oriental Art* 17(2) (1971), 1–9.
Atil, E., *Renaissance of Islam: Art of the Mamluks*, Washington DC (1981).
Ettinghausen, R., *Arab Painting*, Geneva (1962).
Ferrandis, J., *Marfiles Arabes de Occidente*, Madrid (1935–40).
Ghouchani, A., *Inscriptions on Nishabur Pottery*, Tehran (1986).
Grabar, O., *The Alhambra*, London (1978).
——, *The Illustrations of the Maqamat*, Chicago and London (1984).
Grube, E.J. (ed.), *A Mirror for Princes from India: Illustrated Versions of the Kalilah wa Dimnah, Anvar-i Suhayli, Iyar-i Danish, and Humayun Nameh*, Bombay (1991).
Haldane, D., *Mamluk Painting*, Warminster (1978).
Rice, D.S., 'The brasses of Badr al-Dīn Lu'lu'', *BSOAS* 13(3) (1950), 627–34.
——, 'Two unusual Mamlūk metal works', *BSOAS* 20 (1957), 487–500.

R. HILLENBRAND

love poetry *see ghazal*

love theory

Love theory or 'theory of love' (Arabic: *naẓariyyat al-ḥubb*) is a modern term characterizing the content of a genre of Arabic essays and books devoted to profane (i.e. earthly) love and lovers written between the third/ninth and eleventh/seventeenth centuries. More than twenty works on love theory appeared, about one per generation, their authors emerging from both the Islamic East and the Islamic West. The most comprehensive deal with the nature of love, Arabic terms for love, its causes, its varieties, and the experiences that accompany it. Some significant contributors, however, focused on a particular kind of love or phenomenon (e.g. **al-Jāḥiẓ, al-Sarrāj, Mughulṭā'ī**. Most were not specialists in literature, but had been trained in Arabic letters as the foundation of a good education, as essential to a career in the bureaucracy as to one in the religious sciences. After the maturing of the genre, and with trends that developed over much of the learned culture, writing on love and lovers from about the eighth/fourteenth century took the form of lengthy anthologies whose authors strove to outdo their predecessors in taste and completeness. This kind of literature, centred upon the emotional, spiritual, ethical, social, and psychological aspects of 'being in love', is not to be confused with manuals of advice on the conduct of sexual relations (*bāh, nikāḥ*), often written by physicians, and sometimes bearing titles referring to 'the beloved'.

As the genre evolved, there was a tendency toward greater comprehensiveness and a typical organization. Discussion and opinion on the nature and phenomena of love was amplified with quotes from Arab poets who had expressed eloquently a certain idea; then the author would move on to anecdotes and stories about lovers, 'case studies' as it were, drawn from the written and oral fund of such narratives in circulation and serving to illustrate the many vicissitudes (*aḥwāl,* circumstances) experienced by those in love. The *Ṭawq al-ḥamāma* of **Ibn Ḥazm** of Córdoba (d. 456/1064) is unique in the history of love theory for its departures from the usual: the poetry he used to illustrate or reinforce his points was his own, and instead of the lore about famous lovers of the past he related anecdotes about love and lovers drawn largely from his own life and times or heard from acquaintances. These, together with a fresh personal style, symmetry of organization, a balance between the delightful and the earnestly moral, and the vivid glimpses offered into Andalusian society have made it a classic of world literature.

Lest anyone think love a subject too light and pleasurable for a serious scholar, one might make reference, as did Ibn Ḥazm, to the ***ḥadīth*** recommending a little recreation to prevent 'rusting' of the soul. Adding weight to the enterprise, authors related stories of love among revered members of the early Muslim community or other great figures of history, the theories of noted philosophers and physicians, and information from respected lexicographers, philologists, collectors of ***ḥadīth*** and *akhbār*, theologians and jurisprudents. As ***adab*** literature it must educate and edify as well as give enjoyment.

The approach of most writers in this field was literary and humanistic, in the spirit of the cherished Arab poetic tradition on love and the legendary loves of poets famed for their enduring and pure (*'udhrī*) love of a woman with whom their name was forever linked. (See further ***'Udhrī* poetry**.) In this context, *hawā* or *'ishq* meant the passionate obsession with thoughts of the beloved, love-sickness, or a kind of madness that might end in death. A love-smitten poet might speak in playful hyperbole of 'worshipping' the beloved and of turning in the direction of the beloved for prayer instead of the Ka'ba.

At least four authors did not share this literary concept of love which accepted erotic passion as a thing of potential beauty and heroism and the inspiration of poets and storytellers. These authors composed books forming a subtype on love theory, known now as 'Ḥanbalī theory of love', since their thought was shaped by their adherence to the tenets of that school of Islamic law and its doctrines in moral theology. Ḥanbalī theory of love was most fully developed in the *Dhamm al-hawā* of **Ibn al-Jawzī** (d. 597/1200) and the *Rawḍat al-muḥibbīn* of **Ibn Qayyim al-Jawziyya** (d. 751/1350), although the two differ in the details of their theory of love. While attracting readers with lore on love drawn from those popular sources and learned disciplines used by other writers, they emphasized the negative possibilities inherent in passion. One ought to avoid the snare of 'falling in love' by averting the eyes from 'strange' women and youths, citing sayings of the Prophet and Companions that enjoined this and similar precautions. They also saw worshipful adoration of one's beloved as too real in spiritual terms, depriving God of his rightful place. They found *'ishq*, or *hawā*, to present danger to both the body and soul, citing cases of lovers for whom tragic or unrequited love had been fatal or who been driven to commit fornication, adultery, apostasy, murder or suicide.

While in the literary and humanistic context *'ishq* and *hawā* both connoted the intense yearning of the lover for the beloved, each word carried negative associations in the moral theology of the Ḥanbalīs. **Mu'tazilīs** and mystics had used *'ishq* to describe the passionate yearning of the believer for God, and God's corresponding love for his creatures, a teaching abhorrent to Ibn al-Jawzī, who taught that love for God must be expressed by obedience to His law. As for God's 'love' or 'yearning' for his creatures, he asserted rather that God wills the good of the believers. Their low opinion of *hawā* was due to the word's being used in the **Koran** and *ḥadīth* to mean 'lust' (for women, possessions, power or any earthly thing) or 'craving'. Thus Ibn al-Jawzī took this term from the vocabulary of the preacher, a profession in which he had earned wide fame, and applied it unhesitatingly to condemn even the chaste, unconsummated passion celebrated in poetic and narrative art and in a long tradition of discourse and debate.

Further reading

Bell, J.N., *Love Theory in Later Ḥanbalite Islam*, Albany (1979).
Giffen, L.A., *Theory of Profane Love among the Arabs*, New York (1971).
——, 'Love poetry and love theory in medieval Arabic literature', in *Arabic Poetry: Theory and Development*, G.E. von Grunebaum (ed.), Wiesbaden (1973), 107–24.
Vadet, J.-C., *L'Esprit courtois en Orient dans les cinqs premiers siècles de l'Hégire*, Paris (1968), espec. Pt. 2.

L.A. GIFFEN

See also: courtly love

lughz

'Riddle'. An ancient genre, taking many forms both in prose and in verse. Instead of *lughz* (pl. *alghāz*) one also finds *uḥjiyya* (pl. *aḥājī*), *ta'miya* and ***mu'ammā***, terms that are not rarely used indiscriminately. The riddle may take the form of a question; in poetry, however, it often employs the old '*wāw rubba* formula' (the particle *wa-* followed by a genitive) which in ordinary poetry is used to introduce a description. It may be noted that much traditional descriptive poetry resembles riddles in its employ of paraphrastic 'kennings' rather than straightforward naming. Many an 'ekphrastic epigram' in the style of **al-Ma'mūnī** may be read as a riddle (see further **epigram**). Riddles may be found scattered in old stories attributed to the pre-Islamic **bedouins**, in the ***ḥadīth*** and elsewhere; and collected in chapters such as in *al-Zahra* (ch. 89) by **Ibn Dā'ūd al-Iṣbahānī**, *al-'Iqd al-farīd* by **Ibn 'Abd Rabbih**, or *Ḥilyat al-muḥāḍara* by **al-Ḥātimī**. The works of **Abū al-'Alā' al-Ma'arrī** are riddled with riddles. **Al-Ḥarīrī** built several of his *Maqāmat* on series of riddles; among his imitators in this respect was Nāṣīf **al-Yāzijī** in his *Majma' al-baḥrayn* (see further ***maqāma***). The various forms and terms are discussed by scholars of stylistics and ***badī'***, among them **Ibn Rashīq**, Ḍiyā' al-Dīn **Ibn al-Athīr** and **Ibn Ḥijja al-Ḥamawī**. Folk riddles in dialect are found in every Arab country (see **folklore**).

Further reading

Chyet, Michael L., '"A thing the size of your palm": a preliminary study of Arabic riddle structure', *Arabica* 35 (1988), 267–92.
Scott, Charles T., *Persian and Arabic Riddles: A Language-centered Approach to Genre-definition*, Bloomington and The Hague (1965).
Smoor, Pieter, 'Enigmatic allusion and double meaning in Ma'arrī's newly discovered *Letter of a Horse and a Mule*', *JAL* 12 (1981), 49–73, and 13 (1982), 23–52.
——, 'The weeping wax candle and Ma'arrī's wisdom-tooth: night thoughts and riddles from the *Gāmi' al-awzān*', *ZDMG* 138 (1988), 283–312.
Weil, Jürgen W., *Mädchennamen – verrätselt. Hundert Rätsel-Epigramme aus dem adab-Werk Alf ğāriya wa-ğāriya (7./13. Jh.)*, Berlin (1984).

G.J.H. VAN GELDER

See also: *mu'ammā*

Luqmān

Legendary pre-Islamic sage, incorporating various traits in later tradition. Known in the ***Jāhiliyya*** as one of the 'long-lived' (*al-mu'ammarūn*), the **Koran** (*Sūra* 31: 12: 'Indeed, We gave Luqmān [the book of] maxims') established Luqmān as the utterer of admonitions, proverbs and wise maxims, laying the foundation for his later interpretation as the '*ḥakīm* par excellence'. Bearing close resemblance to the wise Aḥiqar (Ḥaiqar), he is profusely attested in a wide range of works in the fields of wisdom literature and proverbs. Only with the age of translation (probably not before the seventh/thirteenth century) did Luqmān also come to be regarded as the author of **fables**, apparently identifying him with the Greek Aesop. This is, however, no indigenous Muslim Arabic tradition, since the Paris manuscript published by J. Derenbourg appears to be an adaptation of the Syriac version of Aesop originating in Christian circles in Mamlūk Syria.

Further reading

Chauvin, *Bibliographie* (Liege/Leipzig), vol 3, 1–38.
Cherbonneau, M., *Fables de Lokman*, Paris (1925).
Gutas, D. 'Classical Arabic wisdom literature: nature and scope', *JAOS* 101 (1981), 49–86.
——, 'Luqmān', in *EM*8 (1996), cols. 1288–91.
Heller, B. and Stillman, N.A., 'Luḳmān', *EI*[2] 5, 811–13.

U. MARZOLPH

See also: fables; proverbs

Luṭfī al-Sayyid, Aḥmad (1872–1963)

Egyptian intellectual, journalist, politician, editor and critic. Born in Daqhaliyya province, Luṭfī al-Sayyid studied at Law School, then worked as a civil servant where he made the acquaintance of the Khedive 'Abbās II. After resigning from the civil service in 1905, he helped to establish the Umma party and became editor of its newspaper *al-Jarīda* in 1907. He played a part in establishing the Egyptian University in 1925 and held important posts there, in **Dār al-Kutub** and in other ministerial positions. Though not a leading author himself, he played an important part in the development of Egyptian literature through his encouragement and influence on a younger generation of writers and through his work in education.

Further reading

Brugman, J. (1984), *An Introduction to the History of Modern Arabic Literature in Egypt*, Leiden (1984).
Hourani, A., *Arabic Thought in the Liberal Age, 1798–1939*, London (1962).

P. STARKEY

luzūm mā lā yalzam

Luzūm mā lā yalzam (synonyms: *i'nāt*, 'constraint' and *iltizām*, 'undertaking') arises when the poet follows non-obligatory (rhyme) precepts. Examples are found in the poetry of **Kuthayyir** (d. 105/723) and **Ibn al-Rūmī** (d. 283/896), but more particularly in the collection of philosophical poems *Luzūm mā lā yalzam* by **Abū al-'Alā' al-Ma'arrī** (363–449/973–1058), often referred to as the *Luzūmiyyāt*. In 113 sections (four for each rhyme consonant, plus the letter *alif*) all rhyme conditions are explored. Moreover, each poem has a non-obligatory rhyme feature, such as the rhyme consonant (*rawī*) being preceded by an identical consonant in all lines.

Further reading

Sperl, Stefan, *Mannerism in Arabic Poetry: A Structural Analysis of Selected Texts*, Cambridge (1989), 100–4.

W. STOETZER

See also: prosody

lyric poetry *see ghazal; qaṣīda*

M

maʿānī *see* *lafẓ* and *maʿnā*; *maʿnā*; rhetoric and poetics

al-Maʿarrī, Abū al-ʿAlāʾ *see* Abū al-ʿAlāʾ al-Maʿarrī

Maʿbad ibn Wahb *see* singers and musicians

macaronic verse *see* *mulammaʿa*

al-Madāʾinī (d. 228/842–3)

Abū al-Ḥasan ʿAlī ibn Muḥammad al-Madāʾinī was an important early historian. He was born and grew up in **Basra** at the beginning of the **ʿAbbāsid** period, lived for a time in al-Madāʾin (Ctesiphon), and settled finally in **Baghdad**. There he enjoyed the patronage of the famous musician Isḥāq ibn Ibrāhīm **al-Mawṣilī**, in whose house he died, aged over 90. He is said to have written more than 200 books on mainly historical topics, but hardly any have been preserved as separate works. He is, however, quoted extensively by later historians, above all by **al-Balādhurī** and **al-Ṭabarī**. He was well regarded as a reliable transmitter of ***ḥadīth***, and his work represents a significant advance in the systematic application of the methods and discipline of *ḥadīth* scholarship to the history of the period after the Prophet Muḥammad.

Text edition

Kitāb al-taʿāzī, B. el-Ouni (ed. and trans.), Göttingen (1984).

Further reading

Duri, A.A., *The Rise of Historical Writing among the Arabs*, L. Conrad (trans), Princeton (1983) (see index).

Rosenthal, F., *A History of Muslim Historiography*, Leiden (1952) (see index).

Yāqūt, *Muʿjam al-udabāʾ*, I. ʿAbbās (ed.), Beirut (1993), vol. 5, 309–18.

R.A. KIMBER

see also: historical literature

al-Madanī, ʿIzz al-Dīn (1938–)

Contemporary Tunisian playwright, novelist and short-story writer, born in Tunis. After completing his secondary education at the French grammar school in the capital and a year at university in Tunis, he went to Paris where he became a journalist. On his return to Tunis he held various posts: he has been in charge of the arts supplement of the newspaper *al-ʿAmal* and the periodical *al-Ḥayāh al-thaqāfiyya*; he has also run the Ibn Rashīq House of Culture, cultural programmes in the Tunis municipality, the Hammamet International Cultural Centre, the Carthage Festival, and served as Director of Theatre at the Ministry of Culture. In 1988 he won the Prix National for Arts. Al-Madanī's published literary output comprises a dozen volumes. He is generally considered to be the leading writer of Tunisian avant-garde literature in the 1960s, and is notorious for the few chapters of his unfinished novel *al-Insān al-ṣifr* (1968–71) which are characterized by an extreme iconoclasm. His most important work, however, is a tetralogy of plays (1970–7) in which he utilizes the Arab historical heritage to discuss themes of revolution and despotism.

Further reading

Fontaine, J., *La Littérature tunisienne contemporaine*, Paris (1991).

al-Midyūnī, M., *Masraḥ ʿIzz al-Dīn al-Madanī wa-al-Turāth*, Tunis (1984).

Starkey, P., 'Quest for freedom: the case of ʿIzz al-Dīn al-Madanī', *JAL* 26 (1995) 67–79.

Ṭarshūna, M., *Mabāḥith fī al-adab al-tūnusī al-muʿāṣir*, Tunis (1989).

J. FONTAINE

al-madhhab al-kalāmī

Lit. 'the theological approach', a term denoting a figure of speech which changes its meaning rather drastically during the history of rhetoric. It occurs first in **Ibn al-Muʿtazz** (d. 296/908) in his *Kitāb al-Badīʿ* (1935; see 53–7) who attributes the term to **al-Jāḥiẓ** (d. 255/868–9), in whose surviving works it has, however, not been found. The examples adduced by the author indicate that the term refers to the intricate argumentational style and jargon of the theologians as parodied in poetry. An example from his own poetry runs: 'I concealed [my] love for you to such an extent that I concealed my concealment; there was nothing I could do but mention it (i.e, my love) with my tongue.' The repetition and the slightly warped and surprising thinking are characteristic. It should be noted that the language of the theologians was one of the first technical jargons in Arabic, and was thus certain to attract the attention of language-conscious people. (See further ***kalām***.)

In the scholastic 'science of rhetorical figures' the term has acquired a different meaning, namely 'theological, i.e. dialectical, argumentation', as opposed to 'philosophical, i.e. apodictic, argumentation'. An example is **Koran** 21: 22: 'If there were in them (i.e. heaven and earth) gods rather than [one] God, the two of them would perish.' The reason for the change of meaning is vagueness of the original notion and subsequent semantic 'refill' of the term when logical ideas and parlance had made its way into rhetoric.

Al-madhhab al-kalāmī has also been interpreted as 'the conceptualizing mentality of the *mutakallimūn* and ... the true source of all that we would call *badīʿ*' (S.P. Stetkevych), but the textual basis for this would seem exiguous.

Further reading

Stetkevych, S.P., *Abū Tammām and the Poetics of the ʿAbbāsid Age*, Leiden (1991), 35–7.

von Mehren, A.F.M., *Die Rhetorik der Araber*, Copenhagen and Vienna (1853), rpt Hildesheim and New York (1970), 116–17.

Wansbrough, John, 'A note on Arabic rhetoric', in *Lebende Antike: Symposion für Rudolf Sühnel*, H. Meller and H.J. Zimmermann (eds), Berlin (1967), 55–63.

W.P. HEINRICHS

See also: *badīʿ*; rhetorical figures

madīd *see* prosody

madīḥ, madḥ

'Praise', 'eulogy': generic terms that refer to panegyric poetry and the panegyric section of the ***qaṣīda***. Panegyric is one of the oldest types of poetry: praise of gods, rulers, priests, chieftains, heroes, athletes and other figures is widespread throughout the world's literatures, and panegyric occupies a central place in Arabic poetry.

In the ***Jāhiliyya*** praise was dedicated to a tribal leader or other notable (among the *bedouin* poets), or to a ruler by poets who frequented the **Lakhmid** and **Ghassānid** courts or others further afield. Praise of tribal leaders focused on the virtues esteemed by tribal society: courage, noble lineage, liberality, hospitality, patience in adversity, forbearance towards enemies. Many of these qualities were transferred to Islamic panegyric; to them were added such specifically Islamic virtues as piety, right guidance, purity and support of the faith. Panegyric enjoyed a complementary relationship with other genres such as boasting (***fakhr***), invective (***hijāʾ***), and elegy (***rithāʾ***). The poet would boast of his own virtues and achievements in the same terms in which he praised others; he would satirize his opponents by stating that they possessed not those virtues but their opposite vices; and he would mourn a departed leader who exemplified those virtues.

Although the Prophet criticized false praise for deceiving people into thinking themselves better than they were, he encouraged panegyrists like **Ḥassān ibn Thābit**, who acted as propagandists in spreading the message of Islam, and rewarded the *Jāhilī* poet **Kaʿb ibn Zuhayr** with his own mantle for a *qaṣīda* in which that poet declared his new allegiance to Islam. The **Orthodox caliphs** are said to have disapproved of panegyric; but under the **Umayyads** panegyric regained its importance at the hands of poets like **Jarīr** and **al-Farazdaq**. From then on it became the most prestigious form of Arabic poetry and the standard of poetic excellence, and was the primary focus of the *qaṣīda*.

The formal and thematic divisions of the panegyric *qaṣīda* are considered to be *nasīb* (exordium), *raḥīl* (the desert journey to the patron; often omitted by later urban poets), and *madīḥ* (encomium, to which might be added a passage of boasting or of satire, or a petition); in royal panegyrics a *du'ā'* or prayer for the ruler's well-being might be added. The *qaṣīda*'s divisions were described by **Ibn Qutayba**; but while he maintained that this model was derived from the poetry of 'the Arabs', it in fact represents the **'Abbāsid** form of the *qaṣīda*. Moreover, although Ibn Qutayba cautioned poets against 'abandoning the ways of the Arabs' (e.g. by substituting, in the *raḥīl*, descriptions of gardens and urban landscapes for those of the desert) many poets did so; **Bashshār ibn Burd**, for example, described his journey by boat up the Tigris to the caliphal court.

The ***muḥdathūn*** ('moderns') introduced topics that reflected both the sophisticated urban, Islamic milieu of the court and traditions adopted from cultures (notably Persian) that had come under Islamic rule. The ruler is depicted less in tribal terms, as first among equals, than as absolute monarch, the deputy of God and leader of the Islamic community. He is the Imām who supports the faith both at home and abroad, exemplifying piety and combating the infidel in holy war. Not only his bounty but his very existence confers prosperity on his people. His campaigns and victories are celebrated, as are his peaceful achievements, for example his building of palaces and gardens, whose beauty and elegance mirror both the prosperity of the state he rules and the divine order of the cosmos.

Poets also praised other patrons: military commanders, religious leaders, judges, viziers, secretaries and so on. Praise played an important role in political and sectarian conflicts. Many poets devoted poems of praise to the Prophet and his family, a celebrated example being **al-Buṣīrī**'s *Qaṣīdat al-Burda*, modelled on Ka'b ibn Zuhayr's *qaṣīda* to the Prophet. Poets like **al-Ṣanawbarī** and the two **Sharīf**s, **al-Murtaḍā** and **al-Raḍī**, composed elegant poems in praise of **'Alī ibn Abī Ṭālib** and his descendants. Panegyrists of the **Fāṭimids** dwelt on their status as divinely inspired Imāms; those of the **Būyids** employed Persian terms such as *Shāhanshāh*, 'king of kings', to address their rulers. Nor were panegyrics always wholly serious: the Būyid poet **Ibn al-Ḥajjāj** composed light-hearted panegyrics in which the ruler is praised for his success with women and his qualities of bon-viveur. Other adaptations of panegyric took as their subjects cities or regions, or combined panegyric with ***waṣf*** to praise, for example, flowers. Humorous panegyrics (usually in the ***qiṭ'a*** form) might praise the poet's cat, or his robe, or a particularly succulent dish.

As the most prestigious poetic genre, *madīḥ* was the focus of the literary critics' attention when discussing the poetic art in general; they also treated its specific principles, topics and decorum. Not all agreed as to the proper qualities to be praised: **Qudāma ibn Ja'far**, for example, asserted that only the (Aristotelian) virtues merited praise, and that such topics as lineage or appearance, being accidental attributes, did not. His was, however, an idiosyncratic position. Poets were warned against beginning their *qaṣīda*s with lines that the addressee might find offensive or inauspicious. The critics generally agreed that hyperbole was appropriate in panegyric as long as it remained within the realm of possibility (thus, to say a person was unequalled in strength was acceptable; to say that he could move mountains was not). Persons should be praised for qualities appropriate to their office or position (a ruler for justice, a secretary for eloquence, a *qāḍī* for piety); improprieties or controversions of fact were to be avoided (one does not praise a judge for feasting and conviviality, or someone who has never seen a battle for bravery). The philosophers (e.g, **al-Fārābī**, **Ibn Sīnā**, **Ibn Rushd**) discussed praise in the context of the Aristotelian art of eulogy (i.e. tragedy, equated with *madīḥ*), and stressed its ethical function of inspiring the emulation of virtue and the performance of great deeds.

Western scholarship has often viewed panegyric as prince-pleasing flattery dedicated to unworthy patrons, composed in a bombastic style, and motivated by desire for personal gain. That there were poets whose motives were primarily material is undeniable (and was widely criticized). Yet taken as a whole, panegyric's reputation as the prestige genre of Arabic poetry is not undeserved. It presents less praise of an actual ruler than an ideal of kingship; moreover, because of its very conventionality, its potential for oblique criticism is unequalled, since the slightest departure from, or modification of, its conventions would be immediately perceived. Thus *madīḥ* should be recognized as a fascinating and highly flexible genre.

Further reading

Bencheikh, *Poétique arabe: essai sur les voies d'une création*, Paris (1965).

Sperl, Stefan, 'Islamic kingship and Arabic panegyric poetry in the early 9th century', *JAL* 8 (1979), 20–35.
——, *Mannerism in Arabic Poetry: A Structural Analysis of Selected Texts*, Cambridge (1989).
Stetkevych, S.P. *Abū Tammām and the Poetics of the 'Abbāsid Age*, Leiden (1991).
Trabulsi, Amjad, *La critique poétique des Arabes jusqu'au Ve siécle de l'hégire/XIe siècle de J.C.*, Damascus (1995), 220–8.
von Grunebaum, G.E., 'Aspects of Arabic urban literature mostly in the ninth and tenth centuries', *al-Andalus* 20 (1955), 259–81.

J.S. MEISAMI

al-Madīnī, Aḥmad (1948–)

Moroccan novelist, poet and short-story writer, writing in Arabic. Born in Casablanca, al-Madīnī graduated from the University of Fez. He worked for a time as a teacher in Casablanca before leaving for France, where he now lives. His first publication was a collection of short stories entitled *al-'Unf fī al-dimāgh* (1971). He has since produced several further collections of short stories, three novels (*Zaman bayn al wilāda wa-al-ḥulm*, 1976; *Warda lil-waqt al-Maghribī*, 1982; *al-Jināza*, 1987), and two volumes of poetry (*Bard al-masāfāt*, 1982; *Andalus al-raghba*, 1988).

H. HILMY

madrasa see education

Mafākhir al-Barbar

An anonymous work produced in the thirteenth century glorifying the Berbers of Morocco and al-Andalus. It survives in a unique manuscript in Rabat. It is based very largely on quotation from earlier authors, and includes long sections describing Berber activities and involvement in the politics of al-Andalus, both as soldiers in the service of, or in opposition to, Andalusi rulers, and as North African invaders of the peninsula (Almoravids or Almohads). The name of the author is not given in the text in the manuscript, but it is possible that the work is to be attributed to **Abū Ḥayyān** of Granada (654–745/1256–1344), the well-known traveller and writer on language, who was himself an arabized Berber. Other texts connected with him are associated with this manuscript. **Ibn 'Idhārī** has also been suggested as the author. The question remains open.

Text edition

Kitāb Mafākhir al-Barbar, E. Lévi-Provençal (ed.), Rabat (1934).

Further reading

Lévi-Provençal, E., 'Un nouveau récit de la conquête de l'Afrique par les arabes', *Arabica* 1 (1954), 17–43.
Shatzmiller, M., 'Une source méconnue de l'histoire des berbères: le *Kitāb al-Ansāb li-Abī Ḥayyān*', *Arabica* 30 (1983), 73–9.

D.J. WASSERSTEIN

Maghrib

'[The land of] the sunset', a term applied to the Western part of the Muslim world, primarily North Africa. From ancient times, the Maghrib was divided into several homogenous geographical and political entities: Tripolitania and Cyrenaica (Libya), East Maghrib (Ifrīqiya) and Far Maghrib (Morocco). Nowadays the Maghrib comprises four Arab countries: Libya, Tunisia, Algeria and Morocco, although Mauritania and Western Sahara are sometimes also included in this notion.

After the Arab conquest the Maghrib became part of the Western Islamic civilization that consisted of North Africa and al-Andalus (see **Spain**). Both geographical areas formed a cohesive cultural and economic whole that only ceased to exist with the Christian conquest of Granada in 899/1492. Muslim men of letters continually travelled across the Strait of Gibraltar to the extent that, for the medieval period, it is difficult to attribute them accurately to either al-Andalus or the Maghrib.

The rise of the lettered tradition in the Arabic language in the Maghrib was closely associated with the spread of religious learning. From the third/ninth century onwards most North African scholars adhered to the Sunnism of the Mālikī school of law. Other religious convictions, e.g. **Khārijism** and **Ismā'īlism**, proved ephemeral. The first Maghribī writers were mostly Mālikī jurists. Among them we find Darrās ibn Ismā'īl (d. 357/968) of Fez, who is credited with introducing into the Maghrib the *Mudawwana* by Saḥnūn (d. 240/854), the most widely read and commented textbook on Mālikī law. A rendition of this book by Ibn Abī Zayd al-

Qayrawānī of Ifrīqiya (d. 396/996) became a popular epitome of Mālikī ***fiqh*** studied throughout the Muslim West. Abū ʿImrān al-Fāsī (d. 430/1039), a scholar from Far Maghrib, supplemented the juridical theory of Mālikism with a full-fledged theology, based on the study of the **Koran** and traditions. He spent his last years at Qayrawān, the capital of the Zīrid rulers of Ifrīqiya which, together with Fez (and somewhat later also Marrakesh, Tlemcen and Bougie) were the chief centres of Islamic learning in the Maghrib. A Qayrawani scholar, Abū al-ʿArab Muḥammad (d. 334/945), was the author of a biographical collection of the *ʿulamā'* of east Maghrib, the first of its kind in Maghribī literature. In the later period Qayrawān produced many celebrated Mālikī theologians, e.g. Ibn ʿArafa (d. 803/1401), the author of a classical synopsis of the Mālikī canon.

Despite the predominance of Mālikism, the first great poet of the Muslim West, **Ibn Hānī' al-Andalusī** (d. 362/973), was an adherent of Ismāʿīlī teaching. He immortalized his name by the eloquent panegyrics to the glory of the **Fāṭimid** caliph al-Muʿizz, the conqueror of Ifrīqiya. Ibn Hānī''s arcane imagery and symbolism, impenetrable to the outsider, were firmly grounded in Ismāʿīlī esotericism.

Qayrawān was also famous for its more secular-minded scholars, including the Arab physician and philosopher **Ibn al-Jazzār** (d. 395/1004), whose *Viaticum* (*Zād al-musāfir*) was translated into Greek, Latin and Hebrew. Equally prominent was **Ibn Abī al-Rijāl** (d. 454/1062), astrologer at the Zīrid court. His bulky astrological compendium, *al-Bārī*ʿ, was popular in medieval Europe.

Zīrid patronage of arts gave rise to a literary school represented by Ibrāhīm **al-Ḥuṣrī** (d. 413/1022), **Ibn al-Rashīq** (d. 456/1063 or 463/1070) and **Ibn Sharaf** (d. 460/1067). Apart from being elegant poets, these men contributed in significant ways to nascent literary criticism. Ibn al-Rashīq's essay on Arabic poetics called *al-ʿUmda fī ṣināʿat al-shiʿr* became a classic textbook still used by the students of Arabic poetry. Among other Maghribī poets who consciously used literary theory to improve their creative work, one may mention **Ibn Khamīs** (d. 708/1308), whose love for rare words earned him the reputation of one of the 'stallions' (*fuḥūl*) of Arabic poetry. As a rule, most of the Maghribī scholars mentioned in this article were also poets and wrote extensively on ***adab*** and philology.

The genre of historical writing was developed by an outstanding Qayrawānī doctor **Ibn Raqīq** (d. after 418/1027). His chronicle of the Maghrib (now lost) was used by later writers, namely **Ibn ʿIdhārī** (d. after 712/1312) and **Ibn Khaldūn**. Another Tunisian historian, Ibn al-Ṣaghīr (d. in the early third/tenth century), wrote a chronicle of the sectarian state of the Ibāḍīs (see **Khārijīs**) based in Tahert. From then on, histories of local dynasties and cities became a salient feature of Maghribī literary life. A typical example is the *Rawḍ al-qirṭās* by **Ibn Abī Zarʿ** (d. in the first quarter of the eighth/fourteenth century). It recounts the history of Fez in conjunction with political developments in the rest of the Maghrib. Annalistic history was often amalgamated with the biographical genre. A typical work of this kind was written by Yaḥyā **Ibn Khaldūn** (d. 780/1379), brother of the great Arab historian, who dedicated it to his native city of Tlemcen. Yaḥyā's history is more than a mere account of political events; it includes lengthy poetical fragments and passages in rhymed prose. **Al-Maqqarī** (d. 1041/1632), another native of Tlemcen, perpetuated this tendency. In his *Nafḥ al-ṭīb* he provided a detailed account of Andalusian literature intricately combining elements of history, biobibliography and poetic anthology. From Tlemcen came another outstanding Maghribī historian and littérateur, **Ibn Marzūq** (d. 781/1379), whose monograph treats the history of the ruling dynasty of his native city. Ibn Marzūq was a polymath typical of the Maghribī scholarly élite. He wrote with equal facility on history, apologetics, religious morals, and law. The same is true of many other Maghribī *ʿulamā'* who were men of variegated interests and encyclopaedic knowledge. To one of them, **Ibn al-Qāḍī** (d. 1025/1616), we owe a work that presents us with the first general picture of the literary movement in medieval Morocco. The tenacity of this biography-cum-history with literary bent is evidenced by **al-Kattānī**'s (d. 1355/1926) *Salwat al-anfās* – an excellent biographical dictionary of the celebrated authors of Fez.

By far the most impressive sample of the historical genre belongs to **Ibn Khaldūn**, whose *Prolegomena* presents us with a comprehensive picture of Maghribī history and culture.

Geographical literature found an ingenious

exponent in **al-Idrīsī** (d. 459/1066), who left a remarkable summary of the Arab geography, illustrated with maps and tables. The greatest Arab traveller, **Ibn Baṭṭūṭa** (d. 770/1368 or 779/1377), was also a native of the Maghrib. His itineraries give illuminating descriptions of remote lands such as China, the Golden Horde, Sumatra, Bengal, **Yemen** and Africa. With the other Maghribī travellers, e.g. Ibn Rushayd (d. 721/1321), al-ʿAbdarī (seventh/thirteenth–eighth/fourteenth century), al-ʿAyyāshī (d. 1090/1679), and Ibn Zākār (d. 1120/1708), the genre of travel books (*riḥla*) was largely divested of its original meaning, becoming rather the pretext for displaying the author's literary and religious erudition. Nevertheless, *riḥla*s give us an illuminating insight into intellectual life and literary tastes of the medieval Maghrib. (See further **geographical literature; travel literature**.)

In the Far Maghrib, throughout the medieval period religion was the main source of creative inspiration. It left a deep imprint on both poetry and prose. The body of purely lyrical poetry was insignificant compared to the bulk of didactic, mystical or panegyrical verses. A rare example of religio-political poetry is provided by Ibn al-Muraḥḥal (d. 699/1300), who exhorted his co-religionists to fight the Christian *Reconquista*. Religious prose, originally focused on jurisprudence, underwent some changes due to the new theological trends which came on the heels of the religious reform initiated by **Ibn Tūmart** (d. 524/1130), the founder of the Almohad movement. His epistles elucidating the new creed, however, failed to impress the majority of the Maghribī scholars, who remained faithful to the Mālikī tradition. Yet even these conservative scholars eventually accepted elements of speculative theology and Sufism, both of which were discouraged under the Almoravid rule. Qāḍī ʿIyāḍ (d. 544/1149) of Ceuta stands out as the principal exponent of this reformed Mālikism. His works found an eager audience far beyond the limits of the Maghrib and became standard textbooks in the field. Later on, al-Wansharīsī (d. 914/1508) composed a real *summa* of Maghribī juridical literature entitled *al-Miʿyār al-mughrib*.

Sufism was another hallmark of the Almohad epoch and later Maghribī history as a whole. Although the diffusion of the mystical outlook originally occurred through the works of an Eastern scholar, **al-Ghazzālī** (d. 505/1111), it soon found many enthusiastic proponents among local scholars. Since most of the early Ṣūfī masters of the Maghrib were illiterate, their followers took pains to record their oral teachings.

From the late seventh/thirteenth century such followers began to compose voluminous hagiographies in which they described the exceptional piety, glorious deeds and miracles of the charismatic Ṣūfī leaders of the past. Most Ṣūfī writers adhered to the geographical principle: their books dealt with the Ṣūfī saints living in a particular region or city. Others gave biographical information on the holy families of noble descent (*shurfā*) or the followers of an eminent Ṣūfī teacher. The earliest works of this kind were *al-Tashawwuf ilā rijāl al-taṣawwuf* by Ibn al-Zayyāt (d. 628/1230 or 629/1231), dedicated to the saints of Marrakesh; *al-Maqṣad al-sharīf* by al-Bādisī (still living in 722/1322), a collection of the lives of the saints of Rīf; and *Uns al-faqīr* by **Ibn Qunfudh** (d. 809/1406 or 810/1407), which is devoted to the great mystic **Abū Madyan** and his numerous Maghribī followers. The hagiographical genre flourished, achieving maturity in the work of **Ibn Maryam** (d. 1014/1605) called *al-Bustān*, a sympathetic description of the deeds of the Ṣūfī saints of Tlemcen, both 'missionaries and visionaries, passing effortlessly from daily tasks to the most exalted piety'.

Ṣūfī philosophy, however, got only a lukewarm reception among Maghribī scholars. Although such giants of mystical thought as the Andalusians **Ibn al-ʿArabī** (d. 638/1240) and Ibn Sabʿīn (d. 668/1269 or 669/1271) temporarily stayed in the Maghrib, they finally preferred to leave for the East, which was far more tolerant of high theosophical speculation. Yet the more conventional Ṣūfīs of the Maghrib such as **Ibn ʿAbbād** (d. 792/1390) and Aḥmad Zarrūq (d. 879/1493) were prolific writers, whose works circulated widely among Ṣūfīs and scholars alike. The enormous Ṣūfī corpus produced in the Maghrib needs further study.

In the twelfth/eighteenth–thirteenth/nineteenth centuries the intense political contacts that developed between the Maghrib and Europe led to the re-emergence of *riḥla* literature. Travelogues, composed by many Maghribī diplomats, presented descriptions (sometimes fulsomely florid) of their missions to Europe and other Muslim countries (e.g. Ibn ʿUthmān al-Miknāsī, d. 1214/1799, and Abū al-ʿAlāʾ ibn Idrīs, d. 1296/1879).

The genre of political prose was introduced

by the progressive Tunisian statesman Khayr al-Dīn **al-Tūnisī** (d. 1307/1889), whose *Aqwam al-masālik* presents a synthesis of Ibn Khaldūn's sociology and the legacy of the French Enlightenment.

Nationalist ideology led to an intensive study and propagation of the Maghribī cultural heritage. It was advanced by a group of talented educators and reformers of Algerian extraction such as Mohammed Ben Cheneb (d. 1347/1929) and Ibn Bādīs (d. 1359/1940).

The French rule over the Maghrib (with the exception of Libya) that lasted more than a century had a strong impact on its cultural and intellectual life. Modern literary genres in **Tunisia**, **Algeria**, and **Morocco** took shape under the commanding influence of French culture, a phenomenon that became known as 'acculturation'. In some cases it was limited to the appropriation by Arab authors of the general trends peculiar to the European literary tradition, e.g. romanticism, symbolism and, later on, existentialism and surrealism. Anxious to preserve their cultural identity such authors continued to write in Arabic, availing themselves of the traditional genres and forms (e.g, the poets Abū al-Qāsim **al-Shābbī** of Tunisia and Muḥammad al-'Īd of Algeria).

On the other hand, already in the first decades of this century many Maghribī littérateurs wrote in French. For some of them this was a matter of principle, as they considered Arabic an obsolete language of theology *par excellence*, incompatible with the realities of the twentieth century. This tendency (which varied from country to country, being at its strongest in Algeria) gained momentum in the 1950–60s. During this period the Maghrib experienced the emergence of a copious Francophone literature, represented by a pleiad of talented prose writers: Mohammed **Dib**, Yacine **Kateb**, Mouloud **Mammeri**, Mouloud **Feraoun** in Algeria; Ahmed **Sefrioui** and Driss **Chraïbi** in Morocco; Albert Memmi in Tunisia. The same period produced a cohort of Francophone poets, including the Algerians Mourad Bourbounr, Rachid **Boujedra**, Nabile **Farès** and the bilingual poet Yousef Sebti; and the Moroccans Mohammed Khair-Eddine and Abdellatif **Laâbi**. Conversely, the development of modern Arabic poetry and prose was retarded by the lack of audience, for many educated Maghribīs did not know literary Arabic.

In Algeria the first real novels in Arabic appeared only in the late 1960s to early 1970s (e.g. 'Abd al-Ḥāmid **Benhedouga**'s *Rīḥ al-janūb*, published in 1971). Although in Morocco and Tunis the Arabic novel had emerged earlier, it still counts only three or four decades. Furthermore, for obvious reasons, its quality has generally been inferior to that of its more sophisticated Francophone counterpart.

The struggle for independence and the subsequent controversy over the orientations to be taken by the new sovereign states resulted in tensions between Francophone and Arabophone intellectuals. Their heated debates reflected broader issues than simply personal predilection for a language of artistic expression. The choice between Arabic and French was tantamount to the adoption of a specific cultural perspective and a corresponding model for future development. In Algeria, whose Arabic-speaking intelligentsia was decimated by the long war for national liberation and whose educated class was mostly Francophone, the authorities endeavoured to promote the revival of Arabic culture through forceful Arabization. This policy yielded controversial results, but on the whole achieved its aims. In Tunisia and Morocco Arabization was carried out on a modest scale, since both countries were not as thoroughly Gallicized as Algeria and had managed to sustain a greater cultural independence from the metropolis. The revival of Arabic education resulted in a considerable body of Arabophone literature, especially in Morocco and Tunisia. Naturally enough, Arabophone writers resorted to borrowing from, and imitation of, the more developed literary traditions of the Arab East, especially that of **Egypt**. This primarily applies to Libya, which was not subject to European acculturation and retained closer ties with the Arab world. At the same time, owing to their command of French, the writers of Tunisia, Algeria and Morocco are often better versed in the latest European literary fashions and intellectual fads than the Arab writers of the East. This accounts for intense experimentations with established literary forms and genres and the emergence in the Maghrib of a strong and influential literary avant-garde in both Arabic and French. Whereas in the previous decades Maghribī men of letters were largely preoccupied with realistic portrayal of the anti-colonial struggle and inculcating nationalist outlook, the more recent samples of Maghribī literature display the acute interest of the writers in the medieval

Islamic heritage and an attempt to put it to artistic use. This is especially true of the traditional Ṣūfī themes which readily yield themselves to a wide variety of creative interpretations in poetry and prose.

Further reading

Benjemaa, B., 'Bibliographie du roman maghrébin d'expression Arabe', *IBLA* 51 (1988), 283–91; 52 (1989), 95–104, 289–301.
Gannoun, A., *al-Nubūgh al-Maghribī*, 2 vols, Beirut (1960).
Guernier, E. (ed.), *Maroc*, Paris (1948), 524–42.
Hajji, M., *L'Activité intellectuelle au Maroc à l'époch saʿdide*, Rabat (1976–7).
Idris, H.R., *La Berbérie oriental sous les Zirides*, 2 vols, Paris (1962).
Khatibi, A., *Le Roman maghrébin*, Paris (1968).
Lakhdar, M., *La Vie littéraire au Maroc sous la dynastie ʿalawide*, Rabat (1971).
Lévi-Provençal, E., *Les Historiens des Chorfa, essai sur la littérature historique et bibliographique au Maroc du XVI*[ème] *au XX*[ème] *siècle*, Paris (1922).
Nwyia, P., *Ibn ʿAbbād de Ronda*, Beirut (1961).
Pantuček, S., *Tuniesische Literaturgeschichte*, Wiesbaden (1974).
Pérès, H., *La Littérature arabe et l'Islam par les textes, XIX*[e] *et XX*[e] *siècles*, Algiers (1938).
al-Rāʿī, ʿAlī, *al-Riwāya fī al-waṭan al-ʿArabī*, Cairo (1991).
(For more information on the medieval Maghribī writers mentioned in this article see *EI*[2] and the entries for individual authors. Also consult the following periodicals: *Journal of Maghrebi Studies* and *Research in African Literatures*.)

A. KNYSH

al-Maghribī, al-Ḥusayn ibn ʿAlī (370–418/981–1027)

Abū al-Qāsim al-Ḥusayn ibn ʿAlī al-Maghribī, usually known as al-Wazīr al-Maghribī, was a statesman, political intriguer and littérateur, the last member of a distinguished family of officials and secretaries in the service of the **ʿAbbāsids**, **Ḥamdānids** and **Fāṭimids**. His stormy career in politics brought him successively to several of the Arab and Kurdish courts of the Near East, but he found time to compose a ***dīwān*** of poetry and various prose works, including a short **Mirror for Princes** or treatise on statecraft, the *Kitāb al-siyāsa*, probably intended for the Kurdish Marwānid local ruler of Diyārbakr, whose text has survived. He was also in contact with the famous blind Syrian poet **Abū al-ʿAlāʾ al-Maʿarrī**, who refers to al-Maghribī in his works and who composed an elegy on his death; and his precious library survived for at least two centuries at Mayyāfāriqīn in Diyārbakr.

Further reading

EI [2] art. 'al-Maghribī, Banu' (P. Smoor).
Ibn Khallikān's Biographical Dictionary, M.G. de Slane (trans.), Paris (1842–71), vol. 1, 450–6.
Smoor, Pieter, *Kings and Bedouins in the Palace of Aleppo as Reflected in Maʿarrī's Works*, Manchester (1985), 17, 46.

C.E. BOSWORTH

al-Māghūṭ, Muḥammad (1934–)

Syrian poet. Born in Salamiyya, al-Māghūṭ received his primary and secondary education (in agriculture) locally before moving to **Damascus**. Early in his life he became involved with the Syrian National Socialist Party and was imprisoned for his political activities. In 1956 he fled to **Lebanon**, where he began to blossom as a poet and was again imprisoned; he returned to **Syria** in 1961, since when he has lived and written freely in Damascus.

With little formal education or knowledge of foreign languages, al-Māghūṭ invented his own poetic language, making the **prose poem** the hallmark of his art. The encouragement he received from the *Shiʿr* group – especially from **Adūnīs** – had a major impact on his career as a poet: his work is characterized by a wild imagination, coupled with an unusual degree of directness of emotion and expression and an overwhelming passion for life. His poetry (which includes three major collections: *Ḥuzn fī Ḍaw' al-Qamar*, 1959; *Ghurfa bi-Malāyīn al-Judrān*, 1964; *al-Faraḥ Laysa Mihnatī*, 1970) is the poetry of the deprived who refuse to be crushed – the poetry of the personal and the intimate in their most direct and piercing manifestations. For this reason, although he was at the heart of the *ḥadātha* movement, al-Māghūṭ remained for a long time a lone voice with few apparent disciples; his influence only began to make itself felt when the 'ideological' phase of modern Arabic poetry had exhausted its energy.

In addition to his poetry, al-Māghūṭ has also published fiction, drama and essays, all possessed by the same spirit: a tireless search for freedom, a cutting wit, a sharp eye for detail and a dark – at times surrealist – yet humorous vision of reality. From the early

1970s he devoted much of his energy to writing TV and film scripts of political and social satire, achieving an unrivalled position as a social satirist and enhancing his reputation as one of the most original writers of his generation.

Text edition

The Hunchbacked Sparrow, Leiden (1976).

Further reading

al-Daqqāq, U., *Funūn al-Adab al-Mu'āṣir fī Sūriyyā 1870–1970*, Damascus? (1971), 442-5.
Sa'īd, K., *al-Baḥth 'an al-Judhūr*, Beirut (1960), 71–80.
Maḥfūẓ, I., *Daftar al-Thaqāfa al-'Arabiyya al-Ḥadītha*, Beirut (1973).
Qabbish, A., *Tārīkh al-Shi'r al-'Arabī al-Ḥadīth*, n.p. (1971), 728.

KAMAL ABU-DEEB

maḥāsin wa-masāwi'

'Merits and faults', the name of a literary genre. From the very beginning of Arab culture there has been a fascination with linguistic antitheses, debates and poetical controversies (*mu'āraḍāt*). This inclination, reinforced by the art (inherited most probably from the Greeks) of manifesting contradictory sides of the same phenomenon, encouraged **al-Jāḥiẓ** in the third/ninth century to record oral debates in which, for instance, one person praises dogs and blames roosters, while his interlocutor praises the roosters and blames the dogs (similar antithetical topics used: goats/sheep, young men/maidens, belly/back). In the same period, the work *al-Maḥāsin wa-al-aḍdād*, belonging to this theme and ascribed to al-Jāḥiẓ, is not really his. In the fourth/tenth century, Ibrāhīm ibn Muḥammad **al-Bayhaqī** composed *al-Maḥāsin wa-al-masāwi'*, in which he elaborates and amplifies this genre (merits and faults of almost every conceivable matter, except for purely religious and moral subjects, where the strategy does not consist of displaying merits and faults of the same trait, but of praising beliefs and morals, while blaming unbelief and immorality). Geries (1977) has successfully described the growth at this stage of sporadic attempts and the formation of a genuine literary genre. **Al-Tha'ālibī** (d. 429/1038), in a series of works consecrated to this topic (the most elaborated of which is *al-Taḥsīn wa-al-taqbīḥ*), pretends to having established this literary branch, but when one examines his *al-Ẓarā'if* (MS Cairo, Dār al-Kutub: Adab Sh.-64), one may readily conclude that this author has independently arrived at formulating his works belonging to this genre through collecting tropes and ornate sayings for his anthologies intended to embellish the epistolary style of contemporary *kuttāb* (**secretaries**). Building upon a few chapters employing 'merits and faults' as one of many other other elements, he then began to devote entire compositions to this theme. In literary anthologies, the division of 'for' and 'against' (advantage and disadvantage) is sometimes used as a structural scheme which helps the compiler to render the text in a more attractive manner.

Further reading

Berque, J. and Charnay, J.-P., *L'Ambivalence dans la culture arabe*, Paris (1967).
Geries, I., *Un Genre littéraire arabe: al-maḥāsin wa-al-masāwi'*, Paris (1977).
Nawfal, M.M.Q., *Ta'rīkh al-mu'āraḍāt fī al-shi'r al-'Arabī*, Beirut (1983).

J. SADAN

Maḥbūb ibn Qusṭanṭīn *see* Agapius

al-Mahdī *see* 'Abbāsids

Maḥfūẓ, 'Iṣām (1930–)

Lebanese avant-garde, postmodern poet, playwright and critic. Like **Adūnīs**, Maḥfūẓ was involved in attempting to establish a new poetic theory for the *Shi'r* magazine group in its efforts to liberate Arabic poetry from the shackles of classical Arabic poetic conventions. He defended the use of colloquial Arabic in poetry and drama to enable the creative writer to express himself spontaneously, subconsciously creating his own irrational images and visions which reveal the chaos of his inner universe and fantasies. His collections of **free-verse** poems include *Ashyā' Mayyita* (1959), *A'shāb al-Ṣayf* (1961), *al-Ṣayf wa-Burj al-'Adhrā'* (1963) and *al-Mawt al-Awwal* (1973).

'Iṣām is also a talented playwright who has published several dramas on political problems in the Arab world, among them *al-Qatl* (1969), *Carte Blanche* (1971) and a play in colloquial Lebanese dialect *al-Zanzalakht*

(1969). *Al-Diktātūr* (1972) is a long dialogue between two characters denouncing military revolutions in the Arab world; while *Limādhā Rafaḍa Sarḥān Sarḥān mā Qālahu al-Zaʿīm ʿan Faraj Allāh al-Ḥulū fī Studio 71* (1972) deals with political assassination in the Arab world. He collected his critical articles in *Daftar al-Thaqāfa al-ʿArabiyya al-Ḥadītha* (1973).

Further reading

Ballas, S., *La Littérature arabe et le Conflit au Proche-Orient 1943–73*, Paris (1980), 255–7.

Moreh, S., *Modern Arabic Poetry 1800–1970*, Leiden (1976), 219, 221, 226, 287.

S. MOREH

Maḥfūẓ, Najīb (1911–)

The most illustrious writer of fiction in the Arab world today, Maḥfūẓ was selected in 1988 to receive the world's most public literary accolade, the Nobel Prize for literature. This award provided the capstone for a writing career that has spanned over five decades, during which he has produced some thirty-five novels and fourteen collections of short stories. Born in one of the old quarters of **Cairo**, Maḥfūẓ attended Cairo University and was embarking on a graduate programme in philosophy when, under the inspiration of writers including the prominent socialist Salāma **Mūsā**, he began to write short stories. Until his retirement in the early 1970s, Maḥfūẓ's life was thereafter divided between, on the one hand, the routines of a civil servant working in the cultural sector (including the cinema) – a career that lends authenticity to his frequent excursions into this setting in his fictions – and, on the other, the process of writing that bears the hallmarks of a keen follower of worldwide intellectual and literary trends and of a thoroughly methodical planner.

It is possible to identify several turning points in Maḥfūẓ's career. The first came in the early 1940s with his decision to abandon a planned project to write a number of historical novels set in Egypt (he had already written three) and instead to focus his attention on the conditions of his fellow Egyptians in the twentieth century. In their attention to authenticity of setting and character depiction, and in the way that they address the social and political issues confronting Egypt at the time, novels such as *al-Qāhira al-jadīda* (1946?) and *Zuqāq al-Midaqq* (1947) established a new yardstick for social-realist fiction in Arabic. The crowning point of this series is the justly famous *Trilogy* (1956–7), a work finished immediately before the Egyptian Revolution of 1952. Here forty years of Egyptian social and political upheaval are reflected in a lovingly detailed portrait of three generations of a single Egyptian family, their loves and hatreds, their professions, their religious crises and their involvement in a variety of political movements. This monumental work, for which Maḥfūẓ won the Egyptian State Prize in 1957, was published in a period that witnessed the Suez Crisis of 1956 and the increasing political prominence of Nasser and Egypt in the Arab world and beyond. It demonstrated in masterful fictional form the struggles that had led up to the Revolution; as such, literary work and period could not have been better matched, and this and other works by Maḥfūẓ were the subject of critical acclaim throughout the Arab world.

1959 may be seen as another pivotal year in Maḥfūẓ's career, in that it saw the publication, in the newspaper ***al-Ahrām***, of Maḥfūẓ's most controversial work, *Awlād Ḥāratinā*. To those readers who were anticipating a continuation of the tradition established by the *Trilogy* and its predecessors, this work clearly signalled a change in direction, although several critics have noted that its theme – the role of religion in a world dominated by science – and certain aspects of technique were already evident in earlier works. The furore aroused by this work was sufficient to have it banned in Egypt, although it was published in Lebanon in 1967; its status was also much discussed during the Nobel year of 1988 when Maḥfūẓ's support of Salman Rushdie in the wake of the publication of *The Satanic Verses* caused popular Islamic preachers in Egypt to re-examine *Awlād Ḥāratinā*.

Awlād Ḥāratinā serves as a bridge to a new phase in Maḥfūẓ's writing career, one marked by a greater concentration on the psychological make-up of the alienated individual within the newly emerging post-revolutionary society and a more terse and symbolic representation of the external realities within which such characters functioned. Beginning with *al-Liṣṣ wa-al-Kilāb* (1961) and culminating in *Mīrāmār* (1967), these novels can be seen as a crescendo of criticism of the course that the revolution took in this troubled decade. That course was brought to a grinding halt in the June War of 1967.

Maḥfūẓ's response to that devastating event was a series of highly cryptic and symbolic stories, many of them long, multi-sectioned and cyclical in structure. They portrayed a world full of self-doubt and recrimination, and, as often with Maḥfūẓ's works, superbly captured the mood of the moment.

With the advent to power of Sadat in 1970, retrospection became a preoccupation for many intellectuals; Maḥfūẓ's contribution in fictional form was *al-Marāyā* (1972), a montage of vignettes about a series of Egyptian 'characters' arranged in alphabetical order.

Following his retirement from the civil service, Maḥfūẓ accepted the invitation of *al-Ahrām* to write a weekly column, and this provided him with a forum for his ideas on both international and local issues. As Sadat's social and political agenda began to take Egypt in new directions, Maḥfūẓ made use of his works of fiction to address problems that were of somewhat local and ephemeral interest: the shortage of housing; the pervasiveness of opportunism among the newly emerging entrepreneurial class; the role of popular religion in contemporary Egyptian society, and the unhealthy cynicism of many intellectuals. While there are a few pieces from his output since the early 1970s that have attracted broad critical attention, including *Malḥamat al-Ḥarāfīsh* (1976) and *Riḥlat Ibn Faṭūma* (1982), Maḥfūẓ's work has been characterized by a tendency to repeat previous experiments rather than to branch out in new directions, and his pioneer status has been inherited by a younger generation of novelists.

From the outset Maḥfūẓ has insisted on using the standard literary language in his fictional works, rejecting resort to the colloquial language as a means of expressing dialogue. This has not prevented him from developing a pliable language of dialogue that replicates many of the structures of colloquial Arabic and indeed occasionally includes a colloquial word. It is in the process of adapting style to narrative purpose that Maḥfūẓ's craftsmanship as a writer may be most prominently seen.

With Maḥfūẓ, the Arabic novel has achieved a genuine maturity. His contributions to the genre in the 1940s and early 1950s laid the groundwork, and since that time both he and a younger generation of writers throughout the Arab world have been able to utilize it to comment on the many social and political developments in the region. Maḥfūẓ's status as a pioneer in this field is assured.

Text editions

Adrift on the Nile, Frances Liardet (trans.), London (1993).

Arabian Nights and Days, Denys Johnson-Davies (trans.), London (1995).

Autumn Quail, R. Allen (trans.), Cairo (1985).

The Beggar, K.W. Henry and N.K.N. al-Warraki (trans.), Cairo (1986).

The Beginning and the End, R. Awad (trans), Cairo (1985).

Children of the Alley, Peter Theroux (trans.), London (1996).

Children of Gebelawi, P. Stewart (trans.), London (1981).

The Day the Leader was Killed, M. Hashem (trans), Cairo (1989).

Echoes of an Autobiography, Denys Johnson-Davies (trans.), London (1997).

Fountain and Tomb, S. Sobhi, E. Fattouh and J. Kenneson (trans.), Washington (1988).

God's World, A. Abadir and R. Allen (trans.), Minneapolis (1973).

The Journey of Ibn Fattouma, D. Johnson-Davies (trans.), London (1992).

'*Al-Karnak*', in *Three Contemporary Egyptian Novels*, S. El-Gabalawy (trans.), Fredericton (1979).

Midaq Alley, T. Le Gassick (trans), Beirut (1966).

Miramar, F. Moussa-Mahmoud (trans.), London and Cairo (1978).

Mirrors, R. Allen (trans.), Minneapolis (1977).

One-Act Plays 1, N. Selaiha (trans.), Cairo (1989).

Palace of Desire, W.M. Hutchins, L.M. Kenny and O.E. Kenny (trans.), London (1991).

Palace Walk, W.M. Hutchins and O.E. Kenny (trans.), London (1990).

Respected Sir, R. El-Enany (trans.), London (1986).

The Search, M. Islam (trans.), Cairo (1987).

Sugar Street, W.M. Hutchins and A.B. Samaan (trans.), London (1992).

The Thief and the Dogs, T. Le Gassick and M.M. Badawi (trans.), Cairo (1984).

The Time and the Place and Other Stories, D. Johnson-Davies (trans.), New York (1991).

Wedding Song, O.E. Kenny (trans.), Cairo (1984).

Further reading

Abu-Haydar, J., '*Awlād Hāratinā* by Najib Mahfuz: an event in the Arab world', *JAL* 16 (1985), 119–31.

Allen, R., 'Some recent works of Najib Mahfuz: a critical analysis', *Journal of the American Research Center in Egypt* XIV (1977), 101–11.

El-Enany, R., *The Pursuit of Meaning*, London (1993).

Le Gassick, T., 'An analysis of *al-Hubb Taht al-Matar* (Love in the Rain), a novel by Najib Mahfuz', in R.C. Ostle (ed.), *Studies in Modern Arabic Literature*, Warminster (1973), 140–51.

Milson, M., 'Nagib Mahfuz and the quest for meaning', *Arabica* 17 (1970), 178–86.

——, 'Reality, allegory and myth in the work of Najib Mahfuz', *Asian and African Studies* 11(2) (Autumn 1976), 157–79.
——, 'Najib Mahfuz and Jamal 'Abd al-Nasir: the writer as political critic', *Asian and African Studies* 23(1) (March 1989), 1–22.
Naguib Mahfouz. From Regional Fame to Global Recognition, Michael Beard and Adnan Haydar (eds.), Syracuse (1993).
Peled, M., *Religion my own: the literary works of Najib Mahfuz*, New Brunswick and London (1984).
Somekh, S., *The Changing Rhythm*, Leiden (1973).

R. ALLEN

Mahjar literature

By 'Mahjar literature' is usually meant all writing in Arabic (with the exception of scientific writing) produced by Arab immigrants in North and South America, regardless of whether it is published in America itself or in the Arab East.

North America

The first Arab immigrants to North America in recent history arrived about 1850. From an early stage, journalism played an important part in reinforcing the identity of the Arab communities. In his article 'Bāqāt min al-maṭbū'āt al-'arabiyya al-ṣādira fī al-Amrīkatayn' (1981) Fawzī 'Abd al-Razzāq lists some 135 newspapers and magazines published in Arabic in the United States and Canada before 1980. The first Arabic newspaper, *Kawkab Amīrkā*, was founded in 1892 in New York and continued until 1908; the newspaper *al-Hudā*, established by Na'ūm Mukarzil in New York, was published from 1902 to 1976, and *al-Sā'iḥ*, established by 'Abd al-Masīḥ **Ḥaddād**, from 1912 to 1957. Other notable newspapers include *al-Bayān* (1910–60), which incorporated *al-Sā'iḥ* in 1957, and *Mir'āt al-gharb* (1899), which also later merged with *al-Bayān*.

The first literary magazine was Nasīb **'Arīḍa's** *al-Funūn*, which was published in New York from 1913 to 1918, with some interruptions. *Al-Funūn* served as a mouthpiece for young Arab authors such as Amīn **al-Rīḥānī**, Khalīl **Jubrān**, Mīkhā'īl **Nu'ayma**, Īlīyā **Abū Māḍī** and others, who later formed **al-Rābiṭa al-qalamiyya** in 1920. More successful was *al-Samīr*, published by Abū Māḍī from 1929 to 1936 as a fortnightly and then as a daily until 1957.

Arabic book production in North America was centred in New York. It began with the volume of poetry *al-Gharīb fī al-gharb*, by Mīkhā'īl Rustum (New York, 1895). This was followed by Yūsuf Nu'mān al-Ma'lūf's *Khazā'in al-Ayyām* (1899), by his *Asrār Yildiz* (1900), and by the stories of Salīm Sarkīs (1901, 1904). Amīn al-Rīḥānī and Khalīl Jubrān published their first works from 1902 onwards and 'Afīfa Karam's *Badī'a wa-Fu'ād* appeared in 1906. Other notable works to be published in the Mahjar were the ***dīwāns*** of Asad Rustum (1905, 1919); Īlīyā Ābū Māḍī (1919, 1925, 1940); Rashīd Ayyūb (1916, 1928, 1940); Ni'mat al-Ḥājj (1921); Mas'ūd Samāḥa (1938); Nadra Ḥaddād (1941); and Nasīb 'Arīḍa (1946).

From 1910 onwards – beginning with the works of al-Rīḥāni – North American Mahjar literature was also published in the Arab East. Although the most important periods of literary activity were before World War 1 and during the inter-war years, mention must also be made of Aḥmad Zakī **Abū Shādī**, who came to New York in 1946, where he established the Rābiṭat Minerva.

Latin America

Arab immigrants have also settled in Latin America, from Mexico to Argentina. The main centres of their literary activity have been São Paulo and Rio de Janeiro in Brazil, and Buenos Aires, Tucumán and Córdoba in Argentina. Fawzī 'Abd al-Razzāq (1984) lists 49 Arabic newspapers and 22 periodicals published at various times in São Paulo, and 35 newspapers and 21 periodicals in Buenos Aires; he also lists more than 200 book titles produced in São Paulo, some 70 titles in Buenos Aires and about 30 in Rio Janeiro.

The first Arabic newspaper to be published in Latin America was *al-Fayḥā* (São Paulo, 1895–); other important literary newspapers and periodicals include Shukrī al-Khūrī's *Abū al-Hawl* (1906–41), Mūsā Kurayyim's *al-Sharq* (1927–74) and Shukr Allāh **al-Jurr**'s *al-Andalus al-jadīda* (Rio de Janeiro, 1931–). In Buenos Aires Khalīl Sa'āda, father of the Syrian politician Anṭūn **Sa'āda**, published his *Jarīdat al-Rābiṭa al-Waṭaniyya al-Sūriyya* (1929–34). Among the first Arabic books published in Latin America were Jamīl Ṣafadī's *Majmū'at Barāzīl* (São Paulo, 1900), Shukrī al-Khūrī's *Finyānūs* (São Paulo, 1902) and the *dīwān* of Qayṣar Ibrāhīm al-Ma'lūf, *Tadhkār al-Mahājir* (São Paulo, 1905).

The first literary circle in Latin America was the Riwāq al-Ma'arrī, founded in 1900 by

Na'ūm Labakī, which attracted many itinerant merchants and which concentrated on reading and discussing works by contemporary Arab poets. It is not known exactly why or when this circle came to an end. In 1922 alumni of the American University of Beirut formed a circle to educate Arab immigrants and to make Arabic literature known through translation; this circle also organized an annual poetry festival. In 1933 al-'Uṣba al-andalusiyya was founded, bringing together poets such as Shafīq **al-Ma'lūf**, al-Shā'ir al-Qarawī (see Rashīd Salīm **al-Khūrī**) and Ilyās **Farḥāt** (the last of whom later withdrew from it); the circle, which lasted until 1953, published a prestigious literary journal *al-'Uṣba*, edited by Ḥabīb Mas'ūd. The gap left by the demise of *al-'Uṣba* was filled by *al-Marāḥil* (1955), founded by Maryānā Di'bil Fākhūrī, who also established Jāmi'at al-qalam, with its club, the Nādī al-udabā', in 1964. The Ḥoms Club, founded in São Paulo in 1920, has an important library of Mahjar literature and the Syrian Cultural Centre in São Paulo also houses a library.

In Argentina the first meeting of al-Rābiṭa al-adabiyya, convened by Jūrj **Ṣaydaḥ**, took place on 25 July 1949. An important factor in the formation of this circle – which also included Ilyās **Qunṣul**, Zakī **Qunṣul** and Jūrj Ṣawāyā – was the need to organize receptions for Arab delegations visiting Buenos Aires. This circle was succeeded by the Nadwat al-adab al-'Arabī, among whose founders was Yūsuf al-'Īd.

Further reading

'Abd al-Razzāq, Fawzī, 'Adab al-Mahjar: Bibliyūghrāfiyā lil-dirāsāt al-naqdiyya wa-al-maqālāt', *Mundus Arabicus (al-'Ālam al-'Arabī)* 1 (1981), 89–230.

——, 'Bāqāt min al-maṭbū'āt al-'Arabiyya al-ṣādira fī al-Amrīkatayn', *'Ālam al-kutub* 4(4) (1984), 603–46.

——, 'Kashshāf al-qism al-'Arabī min majallat *al-Marāḥil* al-Barāziliyya 1955–1980', *'Ālam al-kutub* 12(4) (1991), 546–76.

al-Badawī al-Mulaththam, *al-Nāṭiqūn bi-al-Ḍād fī Amīrkā*, Jerusalem (1946).

——, *al-Nāṭiqūn bi-al-Ḍād fī Amīrka al-janūbiyya*, 2 vols, Beirut (1956).

Farsūnī, Fu'ād, 'Ḥawl al-ḍabṭ al-bibliyūghrāfī li-adab al-mahjar wa-maṣādirihi', *'Ālam al-kutub* 4(4) (1984), 514–35.

McNulty, Francine N., 'Mahjar literature: an annotated bibliography of literary criticism and biography in Western languages', *Mundus Arabicus* 1 (1981), 65–88.

al-Nā'ūrī, 'Īsā, *Adab al-Mahjar*, 3rd edn, Cairo (1977).

Ṣaydaḥ, Jūrj, *Adabunā wa-udabā'una fī al-mahājir al-amīrkiyya*, 3rd edn, Beirut (1964).

C.NIJLAND

Maḥjūb, [Muḥammad] Aḥmad (1910–76)

Sudanese poet. Born in Omdurman, Maḥjūb graduated from Gordon Memorial College as an engineer. He later studied law and worked as an engineer, judge and lawyer. He held several ministerial posts and became prime minister after Sudanese independence in 1956.

Maḥjūb, who published several books of poetry and prose, was on the editorial board of *al-Fajr* for over ten years. His signed articles expressed his and the 'Fajr' group's conception of their hybrid cultural identity and its relationship to Sudanese literature and politics. He believed that cultural ideas could be utilized as the means of achieving ideal human relationships.

Text edition

Ahmed, O.H. and Berkley, C.E. (eds), *Anthology of Sudanese Poetry*, Washington, DC (1982).

Further reading

'Abd al-Hayy, M., *Conflict and Identity: The Cultural Poetics of Contemporary Sudanese Poetry*, Khartoum (1976).

Shoush, M.I., 'Some background notes on modern Sudanese poetry', *Sudan Notes and Records* 44 (1963), 21–42.

C. BERKLEY

Maḥmūd, Zakī Najīb (1905–93)

Egyptian literary critic, translator and essayist. Born in Mīt al-Khūlī, a village in Lower **Egypt**, he studied at the Teacher Training College in **Cairo**, then at the University of London, where he received his PhD in philosophy in 1947. For most of the rest of his life he taught at the University of Cairo, receiving several honours and prizes for his contributions to literature, culture and philosophy. Maḥmūd published forty-six books in Arabic, two books in English and over a thousand articles on Islamic and Western philosophy, literary criticism, arts and culture; in addition, he translated ten books from English, and published a two-volume autobiography, *Qiṣṣat Nafs* (1965) and *Qiṣṣat 'Aql* (1982). He founded and edited *al-Fikr al-Mu'āṣir* and from 1973 wrote weekly for ***al-Ahrām***. Throughout his life he called for rationalism and scientific thinking. In 1956 he married the well-known psychologist Munīra Ḥilmī.

Further reading

Ibdāʿ (Cairo) 11(10) (October 1993), 7–72.
Islām, ʿAẓmī, *et al., al-Duktūr Zakī Najīb Maḥmūd ... Kitāb Tadhkārī*, Kuwait (1987).
al-Jadīd fī ʿĀlam al-Kutub wa-al-Maktabāt (Amman) 3 (summer 1994), 8-30.

A.-N. STAIF

Maḥmūd ibn al-Ḥasan al-Warrāq *see* al-Warrāq, Maḥmūd ibn al-Ḥasan

Maimonides (Moses ben Maimon/Mūsā ibn Maymūn (529 or 32–601/1135 or 8–1204)

Rabbi, philosopher, and physician in **Cairo**. Maimonides was the son of a rabbinic judge in Córdoba. When Judaism was outlawed by the Almohads, the family fled, eventually reaching Fez, where they may have converted ostensibly to Islam. About 560/1165 they fled again to Palestine, where the father died; in the same year, the family arrived in Alexandria; two years later they settled in Fusṭāṭ. Until 1169, when his brother, who handled the family's business affairs, was drowned, Maimonides devoted himself to rabbinic and scientific studies and to community affairs; thereafter he acted as a physician (he treated the poet **Ibn Sanā' al-Mulk**) and teacher of medicine, both to Jews and Muslims. In 1185 he entered the **Ayyūbid** court as physician to **al-Qāḍī al-Fāḍil**, Saladin's chief minister; later he served as a physician to al-Malik al-Afḍal and other high officials.

With the establishment of the Ayyūbid dynasty in 1171 Maimonides became the official head of the Jewish community (*ra'īs al-Yahūd*). After an interruption of eighteen years (1177–95) he regained the position, in which he was succeeded by his descendants until 1381. As head of the Jewish community he brought about the domination of the Rabbanites over the Karaites and introduced various changes in liturgical practices (some of them, apparently, under the influence of Islamic practices). He also responded to inquiries on Jewish law and philosophy directed to him from all parts of the Islamic world, as well as from Provence.

Maimonides' *magnum opus* is his code of Jewish law, entitled *Mishne torah (The Repetition of the Law)*. This work, in Hebrew, is the first comprehensive Jewish code organized by strict thematic criteria and incorporating the principles of theology as a full part of the legal system. It aroused severe criticism, partly because it does not cite authorities for its rulings. Yet thanks to its masterful and comprehensive approach it became – and remains – one of the most widely studied books of rabbinic scholarship. As a preamble Maimonides wrote the *Sefer hamiṣvot* (*Book of Commandments*; in Arabic, despite the Hebrew title), a carefully reasoned compilation of the 613 fundamental commandments traditionally believed to be contained in the Pentateuch.

His other major works are in Arabic. The most influential was the *Dalālat al-ḥā'irīn* (*Guide of the Perplexed*), ostensibly a study of the figurative language in scripture but actually a complex exploration of the relationship between Jewish tradition and Aristotelian philosophy. Translated into Hebrew in his lifetime for the use of Jews outside the Arabic-speaking world, this work was influential in disseminating knowledge of Greek and Islamic philosophy among those communities, and it established Aristotelianism as the basis of medieval Jewish philosophy. Maimonides' synthesis of Greek and Jewish thought as expressed in the *Guide* and other works was the cause of bitter controversies within the Jewish communities. Later it was translated into Latin, thereby becoming accessible to the scholastics of the Church.

Earlier in his career Maimonides wrote an extensive commentary in Arabic on the Mishna with important excurses on the principles of Jewish law, eschatology and ethics. This work includes his creed, consisting of thirteen articles, which rapidly came to be authoritative throughout the Jewish world and was eventually incorporated into some versions of the liturgy in Hebrew translation, sometimes in verse. As the chief rabbinic authority of Fāṭimid Egypt, Maimonides wrote many responsa on rabbinic law (464 are extant; they are in both Hebrew and Arabic) and a number of pastoral letters including the *Risāla Yamaniyya* (*Epistle to Yemen*), dealing with the religious implications of the Jews' status as a subject people, messianism and false messiahs; and the *Maqāla fī tᵉḥiyat hametim* (*Epistle on Resurrection*), defending his opinions on eschatology, particularly the doctrine of resurrection, as expounded in his *Mishne torah*. In Hebrew he wrote the treatise *Igeret hash^{e}mad* (*Epistle on Apostasy*) in defence of the Jews in the Almohad realms who had feigned conversion to Islam and who wished to return to Judaism.

Maimonides also wrote on topics not of specifically Jewish interest. His first book was an Arabic treatise on logic. Later he composed numerous works on medical topics, of which the most famous are *Fuṣūl Mūsā*, a collection of medical aphorisms; *Sharḥ asmā' al-'uqqār*, containing the description of about 350 drugs with their names in many languages; *Fī tadbīr al-ṣiḥḥa*, on hygiene; treatises on haemorrhoids, sexual intercourse, asthma and depression, most of them written for his patients among the members of the royal family.

Text edition

The Guide of the Perplexed, S. Pines (trans.), L. Strauss (intro.), Chicago (1963).

Further reading

Goitein, S.D., 'The life of Maimonides in the light of the new discoveries' (in Hebrew), *P^{e}raqim* 4 (1966), 29ff.

Twersky, Isadore, *Introduction to the Code of Maimonides*, New Haven (1980).

Yellin, David and Abrahams, Israel, *Maimonides*, 2nd edn, New York (1972).

R.P. SCHEINDLIN

majāz

Lit. 'transit', a technical term pertaining to the interpretation of texts, with two different meanings:

1. In the early linguistic (as opposed to traditionist) exegesis of the **Koran**, the term means 'explanatory re-writing' in 'natural' language, of idiomatic passages in the Scripture. The implicit justification of this approach to the Holy Book may be formulated thus: (a) the Koran was sent down in 'clear Arabic speech' (26: 195); (b) the language of the ancient Arabs was full of idioms; (c) it follows that the Koran is also full of the same idioms. The first major undertaking in this direction is the *Majāz al-Qur'ān*, (*Explanatory Re-Writing in the Koran*) of the Basran philologist **Abū 'Ubayda** (d. 210/825). The author does not define *majāz*, but at the beginning of his work he does give a list of thirty-nine cases of deviation from the 'natural' language that can be found in the Koran. For each case he combines an abstract description with a Koranic example. In the main text he mostly uses the formula '[Koranic idiom] – its *majāz* is ["natural" equivalent]'. This use of the term *majāz* lingers on for a while and overlaps in time with the second meaning, before falling into desuetude. (See further **exegesis, Koranic**.)
2. The other meaning of *majāz* originated in the theological discussions of the **Mu'tazilī** movement and was used to eliminate the apparent anthropomorphisms contained in the Koran. It denoted something 'not truly real' (ontologically) or 'figurative' (semantically), and was soon coupled with *ḥaqīqa* as its counterpart meaning 'truly real' or 'proper', respectively. Thus, some said that attributes such as 'speech,' when applied to God, were *ḥaqīqa*, but *majāz* when applied to humans. Others maintained, on the contrary, that God's speech was not really speech as we know it and, therefore, was *majāz*, while only human speech was *ḥaqīqa*. Both approaches did the trick of separating the Divine from the human sphere. It is not, however, clear in the debates of the theologians whether this was considered to be happening on the level of being or that of language. Since for the later legal and literary theorists the *ḥaqīqa–majāz* dichotomy was the linguistic phenomenon of 'proper' vs. 'figurative' meaning, this may also be true of the theological discussions. On the other hand, the mystics considered *ḥaqīqa–majāz* to be ontological categories: to God belongs 'true reality' (*ḥaqīqa*) and to the world 'derivative reality' (*majāz*).

Ibn Qutayba (d. 276/889), philologist and anti-Mu'tazilī theologian, amalgamates the theological approach with that of Abū 'Ubayda: *majāz* is a linguistic phenomenon, its centre is the figurative use of language, but many other idiomatic uses treated by Abū 'Ubayda are also included. The legal theorists build on this in their hermeneutics: although *majāz* is first and foremost figurative speech, other phenomena like ellipsis and pleonasm are still part and parcel of *majāz*. The first preserved full-fledged treatment of *ḥaqīqa–majāz* is by the Ḥanafī jurist al-Jaṣṣāṣ (d. 370/981), and it remains an integral part of all later comprehensive treatments of legal methodology.

The literary scholars were slow to take up what the legal scholars had developed, although it afforded them an opportunity for a systematic presentation of figurative speech and imagery. After some inconsequential beginnings, it was **ʿAbd al-Qāhir al-Jurjānī** (d. 471/1078 or 474/1081) who offered several tightly reasoned statements on *majāz*, in his two major works. He rids the concept of its non-figurative components, ellipsis and pleonasm, and distinguishes two types of *majāz* (now: 'trope'), one based on similarity, i.e. the metaphor, the other on contiguity, i.e. the metonymy. In addition to these 'lexical tropes' (*majāz lughawī*) he recognizes for the first time a predication-based 'mental trope' (*majāz ʿaqlī*), in which all words are literal and only the predication is tropical (e.g. 'The days of separation have made my hair white', where the days are not the real agent). One major difference between the legal and the literary approach to *majāz* is that for the legal scholars, intent on interpreting the Koran, *majāz* is an integral part of the Arabic language and not open to analogy, while for a scholar like al-Jurjānī *majāz* is governed by 'rational laws', which are applicable in all languages. This difference mirrors the Koranic–interpretive vs. the poetic–creative approach to the problem.

Further reading

Almagor, Ella, 'The early meaning of *majāz* and the nature of Abū 'Ubayda's exegesis', in Baneth Festschrift, 307–26.
Heinrichs, Wolfhart, 'On the genesis of the *ḥaqīqa–majāz* dichotomy', *SI* 59 (1984), 111–40.
——, 'Contacts between scriptural hermeneutics and literary theory in Islam: the case of *majāz*', *ZGAIW* 7 (1991/92), 253–84.
Modarressi, H., 'Some recent analyses of the concept of *majāz* in Islamic jurisprudence', *JAOS* 106 (1986), 787–91.
Wansbrough, John, '*Majāz al-Qur'ân*: periphrastic exegesis', *BSOAS* 33 (1970), 247–66.

W.P. HEINRICHS

See also: literary criticism, medieval; metaphor

al-Majdhūb, [Muḥammad] al-Mahdī (1919–82)

Sudanese poet. Born in al-Damer into a family famous for the teaching and spreading of Islam, al-Majdhūb studied at Gordon Memorial College and worked as an accountant. The Sudanese 'Fajr' group's rediscovery of its communally rooted identity found its first real expression in his work. Uninfluenced by outside literary forces, he was the first Sudanese poet to express the cultural consciousness of belonging to both the 'Negro' and the Arab tradition. His long poem 'al-Sayra', published in *al-Sharāfa wa-al-hijra* (1973), treats the fusion of pagan and Islamic elements as though a cultural wedding were taking place.

Text edition

Ahmed, O.H. and Berkley, C.E. (eds), *Anthology of Sudanese Poetry*, Washington, DC (1982).

Further reading

ʿAbd al-Hayy, M., *Conflict and Identity: The Cultural Poetics of Contemporary Sudanese Poetry*, Khartoum (1976).
Shoush, M.I., 'Some background notes on modern Sudanese poetry', *Sudan Notes and Records* 44 (1963), 21–42.

C. BERKLEY

al-Majlisī, Muḥammad Bāqir (1037–1110/1627–99), known as ʿAllāma Majlisī

An outstanding scholar and collector of ***ḥadīth*** of the late Ṣafavid period, intimately involved in politics, al-Majlisī was the defining figure in the **Shiʿism** of his time. He was born into a family of scholars in Isfahan, where he lived and died, and where his father, Muḥammad Taqī (1003–70/1594–1659, 'Majlisī the First', as opposed to 'Majlisī the Second', Muḥammad Bāqir) had been a prominent religious leader before him. Staunchly anti-Sunnī and anti-Ṣūfī, Muḥammad Bāqir wrote several works in Persian on legal subjects as well as popular theology, but his enduring scholarly output was in Arabic. His *magnum opus*, the *Biḥār al-anwār*, completed only four years before his death, is an encyclopaedic collection of Shīʿī *ḥadīth* material, unrivalled in its extent. He also wrote a much-used commentary on al-Kulaynī's *al-Kāfī*, the *Mir'āt al-ʿuqūl*. Like his father, he was on good terms with the Ṣafavid monarchy, and was made *shaykh al-Islām* in 1098/1686 by Shāh Sulaymān (d. 1106/1694) and later *Mullābāshī* under his successor Sulṭān Ḥusayn (d. 1125/1713), from which positions he was able to wield unprecedented power over religious affairs. His opinion that Shīʿī *ʿulamāʾ* should always respect the ruler, even the tyrannical ruler, was influential up to the present century, when clerical involvement in opposition movements, culminating in the 1978–9 Islamic Revolution, made such views unpopular.

Text editions

Biḥār al-anwār, 25 vols (litho.), Tehran (1887–97); 110 vols, Tehran (1957–72) (vol. 105 contains a major traditional study of al-Majlisī by Ḥusayn ibn Muḥammad Taqī al-Nūrī al-Ṭabarsī).
Mirʾāt al-ʿuqūl, 26 vols, Sayyid Hāshim al-Basūlī and Sayyid Jaʿfar al-Ḥusaynī (eds), Tehran (1984–91).

Further reading

Pampus, Karl-Heinz, *Die Theologische Enzyklopädie Biḥār al-Anwār des Muḥammad Bāqir al-Mağlisī (1037–1110 AH/1627–1699 AD)*, Bonn (1979).

J. COOPER

Majnūn and Layla *see* Qays ibn al-Mulawwaḥ, al-Majnūn; *see also* *ʿUdhrī* poetry

al-Majrīṭī, Maslama ibn Aḥmad (d. *c.*398/1008)

Spanish philosopher, mathematician and astronomer who is of considerable interest in Arabic literature for the history of the *Rasāʾil* of the **Ikhwān al-Ṣafāʾ** (which, in one source, he claims to have authored himself!). However, he is generally considered to have been instrumental in introducing these epistles into Spain. It has also been claimed that he authored the summary of the *Rasāʾil*, known as the ***Risālat al-jāmiʿa***, but this seems unlikely. A lengthy epistle dealing with magic, astrology and related matters, the *Ghāyat al-ḥakīm* (translated into Latin under the title *Picatrix*) has also been attributed to him but, again, scholars now believe that this ascription is improbable. Whatever his mathematical and astronomical talents (he adapted the astronomical tables of **al-Khwārazmī** to the Córdoban meridian, and may have served as court astrologer to the caliph ʿAbd al-Raḥmān III al-Nāṣir), from the perspective of mainstream Arabic philosophical and theological literature al-Majrīṭī seems to be a source to whom much has been ascribed but whose actual authorship cannot be definitively proven. Be that as it may, he had a considerable impact in Muslim **Spain** by virtue of those who followed in his footsteps (he was the teacher of Ḥamīd al-Dīn **al-Kirmānī**, among others).

Text editions

Picatrix, The Latin Version of the Ghāyat al-Ḥakīm, David Pingree (ed.), London (1986).
ʻPicatrix,ʼ Das Ziel des Weisen von pseudo-Mağrīṭī, Hellmut Ritter and Martin Plessner (trans. into German from the Arabic), London (1962).

Further reading

Fakhry, Majid, *A History of Islamic Philosophy*, 2nd edn, London and New York (1983) (see index).
Ullmann, Manfred, *Die Natur- und Geheimwissenschaft in Islam*, Leiden (1972) (see index under ʻal-Mağrīṭīʼ and ʻPs. Mağrīṭīʼ).

I.R. NETTON/J.S. MEISAMI

al-Majūsī (d. late fourth/tenth century)

ʿAlī ibn al-ʿAbbās al-Majūsī was a medical writer on whom few personal details are available. He lived most of his life in southern Persia, studied medicine at Shīrāz, and dedicated his *magnum opus*, the *Kāmil al-ṣināʿa al-ṭibbiyya* (*The Complete Medical Art*) to the **Būyid** ruler ʿAḍud al-Dawla (r. 338–72/949–83). The *Kāmil* is a large medical compendium designed to provide an authoritative synthesis of the medical knowledge of the author's day. Beginning with a valuable introduction surveying past medical history, it divides medicine into theoretical and practical aspects, each covered by ten chapters on specialized topics. The book was specifically intended to supersede the works of **al-Rāzī**, and in this it was largely successful. Indeed, its organization and thoroughness were such that it immediately secured al-Majūsī's reputation; in the longer term, it ranked second only to the great *Qānūn* of **Ibn Sīnā**. It was translated into Latin by Constantine the African (d. before 1098) as *Liber pantegni*, and then again by Stephen of Antioch as *Liber regius* in 1127, and thus became very influential in Europe as well.

Text edition

Kāmil al-ṣināʿa al-ṭibbiyya, Cairo (1294/1877); repr. Frankfurt (1996).

Further reading

Burnett, Charles and Jacquart, Danielle (eds), *Constantine the African and 'Alī ibn al-'Abbās al-Mağūsī: The Pantegni and Related Texts*, Leiden (1994) (with further bibliography).
Sezgin, Fuat (ed.), *'Alī ibn al-'Abbās al-Majūsī (4th/10th cent.): Texts and Studies*, Frankfurt am Main (1996).
Ullmann, Manfred, *Die Medizin in Islam*, Leiden (1970), 140–6 (with further bibliography; Ullmann offers a translation of the Introduction and a summary table of contents).

L.I. CONRAD

al-Mak, 'Alī (1937–1992)

Sudanese short-story writer, poet and translator. Born in Omdurman, al-Mak graduated with honours in Arabic language and literature from Khartoum University. At his death he was director of the Arabic Language Translation Unit. His work reflects a social-realist view. Al-Mak's first short story appeared in the Khartoum bi-weekly *al-Ṣarāḥa* when he was only 16. His major poetic work, *Madīna min Turāb* (Khartoum, 1974), is a long prose poem which structurally resembles the classical ***qaṣīda***; the poem opens with the poet's description of the entryway to his 'beloved', the decaying Omdurman *sūq*.

Text edition

A City of Dust, al-Fatih Mahjub (trans.), C.E. Berkley (ed. and intro.), Washington DC (1982)

C. BERKLEY

al-Makkī, Abū Ṭālib (d. 386/996)

Abū Ṭālib Muḥammad ibn 'Alī al-Makkī was a Ṣūfī writer. Of Iranian origin, he grew up in Mecca, then lived in **Basra** and later in **Baghdad**, where he died. In Basra he attached himself to the Sālimiyya, the mystic theological school of Aḥmad ibn Sālim. Al-Makkī is the author of the *Qūt al-qulūb*, the most comprehensive handbook on classical Sufism. This work especially presents the traditions of Basran Sufism, i.e. those of the school of **Sahl al-Tustarī**, which were transmitted within the Sālimiyya. The book is also of particular importance because it served as the model for **al-Ghazzālī**'s *Iḥyā' 'ulūm al-dīn*. Indeed, one may go so far as to say that the *Iḥyā'* is in fact nothing more than a reworking of the *Qūt al-qulūb*.

Text editions

Die Nahrung der Herzen. Abū Ṭālib al-Makkīs Qūt al-qulūb, Richard Gramlich (trans.) 4 vols, Stuttgart (1992–5).
Qūt al-qulūb, Cairo: 1351/1932; 1381/1961.
(There are no critical editions of al-Makkī's work.)

B. RADTKE

maktab *see* education

maktaba *see* libraries

malāḥim

The ancient meaning of *malḥama*, pl. *malāḥim*, was 'bloody fight', 'battlefield'. **Muḥammad** himself was called *nabī al-malḥama*, an expression understood as meaning 'prophet of contention' (but also of reconciliation). The term acquired the further sense of prediction, eschatological prophecy, e.g. the *malḥamat Dāniyāl*. **Al-Jāḥiẓ** states that the first author of a *qaṣīdat al-malāḥim* was Ibn 'Aqb al-Laythī. **Ibn Khaldūn** notes that by *malāḥim* the **Maghrib** peoples meant prophecies concerning future wars and the duration of dynasties. Reverting to this concept, Sulaymān **al-Bustānī** has proposed the use of *malḥama* to signify *shi'r qaṣaṣī*, **epic poetry**, a term accepted among men of letters. The name *sīra sha'biyya* (see ***sīra* literature**) is, however, preferred for popular Arab epic cycles.

Further reading

Amīn, Muḥammad Shawqī, 'al-Malāḥim bayna al-lugha wa-al-adab', *'Ālam al-fikr* 16 (April–June 1985), 227–30.
de Sacy, S., *Chrestomathie arabe*, Paris (1826), 2: 298–302.
Fahd, T., *La Divination arabe*, Paris (1987).
Fodor, A., 'Malḥamat Dāniyāl', in *The Muslim East: Studies in Honour of J. Germanus*, Budapest (1974), 85–133.
Iliyādhat Hūmīrūs, Sulaymān al-Bustānī (trans.), Cairo (1904), 162–75.
al-Jizāwī, Sa'd al-Dīn, *al-Malḥama fī al-shi'r al-'Arabī*, Cairo (1967).

G. CANOVA

al-Malā'ika, Nāzik Ṣādiq (1923–)

Iraqi poet and critic. Born into a wealthy literary family in Baghdad, al-Malā'ika obtained a BA in Arabic language and literature from the Teachers' Training College there in 1944. In 1950 she received a year's scholarship to study literary criticism at the University of Princeton and in 1956 gained an MA in comparative literature from the University of Wisconsin. On her return to Baghdad she worked as a lecturer at the Teachers' Training College. In 1964 she moved with her husband 'Abd al-Hādī Maḥbūba to **Basra**, where they were instrumental in establishing the University of Basra. At the end of 1968 she returned to Baghdad. In 1970 she left Iraq and lectured at the University of Kuwait until her retirement in 1982. She is currently living in Iraq.

Like much of her early work, the poems in al-Malāi'ka's first collection, *'Āshiqat al-Layl* (1947), are characterized by their sensitivity, idealism and glorification of emotion, and the attendant dangers of disillusion and disappointment to which her emotions often led her. Alienated from society and with an intense yearning for a non-existent utopia, al-Malā'ika developed a pessimistic outlook towards life and death. Nature and, in particular, 'night' occupy a prominent position in her poetry; she refers to the latter as a friend who has the power to ease her pain and sadness. Al-Malā'ika's pessimism at this stage sprang from personal tragedy, coupled with her concern about world events, the destructiveness of war and the position of women in Arab society; as a result of these images and others, she is usually categorized as a 'Romantic' poet in her early work.

Al-Malā'ika was greatly influenced by Western literature and thought, especially the English Romantic poets. Her poem 'Ilā al-Shā'ir Keats' vividly demonstrates her love of, and fascination with, Keats' sonnets, in particular 'Ode to a nightingale'. It was mainly due to the influence of English poetry that she wrote her revolutionary introduction to her second collection, *Shaẓāyā wa-Ramād* (1949), in which she expressed the view that rhyme is an obstacle blocking the flow of poetic expression and argued that the traditional monorhyme of Arabic poetry prevented it from reaching the poetic heights of other world literatures. The collection contains nine poems written in **free verse**, the remainder following the traditional form of verses in two hemistichs. In addition to romanticism, the collection also shows the influence of literary movements such as realism and symbolism. Al-Malā'ika's third collection, *Qarārat al-Mawja* (1957), containing poems written between 1937 and 1953 in both free and traditional verse, heralds a shift from her intense romanticism. Her deep pessimism is here replaced by a more philosophical acceptance of the many sad aspects of life. The introduction contains a dialogue between the two opposing inner personalities of the old al-Malā'ika and the new.

In 1970 al-Malā'ika published for the first time her long poem *Ma'sāt al-Ḥayāh*, originally written in 1945 in 1,200 lines in rhyming couplets. It was accompanied by two revised editions of the poem written between 1950 and 1965 and entitled respectively *Ughniya lil-Insān 1* and *Ughniya lil-Insān 2*. The theme of the poem is the poet's search for happiness – in the palaces of the rich, in monasteries, among the country shepherds, among lovers and with criminals – followed by the realization that there is no happiness on earth. The first version vividly illustrates al-Malā'ika's early Romantic tendency and fear of death, and the three versions together chronicle the poet's personal and artistic development over some twenty years.

Al-Malā'ika's last two collections, *Yughayyiru Alwānahu al-Baḥr* (1977) and *Lil-Ṣalāh wa-al-Thawra* (1978), are – except for one poem – written entirely in free verse. In the final collection, she has freed herself from her Romanticism and has turned to religion and nationalism, which she sees as closely linked.

In addition to her collections of poetry, al-Malā'ika has published three books of criticism. The first, *Qaḍāyā al-Shi'r al-Mu'āṣir* (1962), deals with questions related to free verse. The second, *Muḥāḍarāt fī Shi'r 'Alī Maḥmūd* ***Ṭāhā*** (1965), subsequently re-titled *al-Ṣawma'a wa-al-Shurfa al-Ḥamrā'*, illustrates her critical methodology which fuses a strong theoretical foundation with a holistic evaluation of the entire collection. The third, *al-Tajzi'iyya fī al-Mujtama' al-'Arabī* (1974), includes a discussion of issues related to nationalism and society, including authenticity, modernism and romanticism.

Further reading

Badawi, M.M., 'Convention and revolt in modern Arabic poetry', in G.E. von Grunebaum (ed.), *Arabic Poetry: Theory and Development*, Wiesbaden (1973), 181–208.

——, *A Critical Introduction to Modern Arabic Poetry*, Cambridge (1975), 228–30.
Jayyusi, S.K., *Trends and Movements in Modern Arabic Poetry*, 2 vols, Leiden (1977), 551ff., etc.
Moreh, S., 'Technique and form in modern Arabic poetry up to World War II', in M. Rosen-Ayalon (ed.), *Studies in Memory of Gaston Wiet*, Jerusalem (1977), 415–34.

R. HUSNI

malḥama *see* epic poetry; *malāḥim*

Malḥas, Thurayyā (1925–)

Lebanese poetess, literary critic and university professor. Born in Amman to a Palestinian father and Caucasian mother, Malḥas studied Arabic and western literature and taught Arabic literature in Kulliyyat Bayrūt lil-Banāt, where she was nominated in 1965 to be head of the Arabic section. She has published poetry, prose and various literary and cultural studies on modern and classical subjects. Best known for her two symbolic and surrealist mystical anthologies of *shi'r manthūr* (see **prose poem**), *al-Nashīd al-Tā'ih* (Beirut, 1949) and *Qurbān* (Beirut, 1952), she has also published a poetry collection in English entitled *Prisoners of Time* (Beirut, 1952) as well as a collection of short stories (Beirut, 1962). Her most prominent critical study is *Mīkhā'īl Nu'ayma al-Adīb al-Ṣūfī* (Beirut, 1964) in which she analyses the mystic elements in **Nu'ayma**'s life and work. Her tendency to mysticism is also apparent in her book *al-Qiyam al-Rūḥiyya fī al-Islām* (Beirut, 1964).

Further reading

al-Khāzin, Wilyam and al-Yān, Nabīh, *Kutub wa-Udabā'*, Beirut (1970), 387–99.
Moreh, S., *Modern Arabic Poetry 1800–1970*, Leiden (1976), 302–3.

R. SNIR

Mālik ibn Anas (d. 179/796)

Famous early jurist from whom one of the four major **Sunnī** schools of law, the Mālikī, derives its name. Mālik lived and taught throughout his entire life in Medina, and the legal doctrine that he propounded represented to a large extent the consensus of legists of that city. His major contribution to the literature of Islamic jurisprudence was the *Muwaṭṭa'*, which exists in numerous recensions. This work records the commonly held doctrine of Medina, frequently supporting it with sayings of the Prophet **Muḥammad** or his Companions. It represents an important stage in the systemization of Islamic law.

Text edition

al-Muwaṭṭa', Cairo (1962).

Further reading

Dutton, Y., *Mālik's Use of the Qur'ān in the Muwaṭṭa'*, D Phil thesis, Oxford (1992).
Schacht, J, *Introduction to Islamic Law*, Oxford (1964), 43–4.

B. WEISS

See also: *fiqh*

Mālik ibn Nuwayra (d. 11/632)

Leading figure of the tribe Yarbū' (Tamīm). He was killed during the secession of **bedouin** tribes after the Prophet's death, apparently by order of the general Khālid ibn al-Walīd. Since Mālik professed himself a Muslim before his execution, Khālid's order gave rise to a political scandal. The few poems attributed to Mālik are of minor literary importance. Instead, he owes his fame to the elegies that his brother **Mutammim** composed upon his death.

For bibliography see **Mutammim ibn Nuwayra**.

T. BAUER

Malikshāh *see* Saljūqs

al-Ma'lūf, Fawzī (1899–1930)

Mahjar poet and dramatist, brother of Shafīq **al-Ma'lūf**. After attending the Kulliyya al-Sharqiyya in Zahle (his birthplace), and the École des Frères in Beirut, he went to São Paulo, Brazil, where he worked in industry and trade. In 1922 he founded the al-Muntadā al-Zaḥlī (Zahle Club) as a meeting place for the members of the Syrian and Lebanese colonies and had his plays performed in this club. His first play, *Ibn Ḥamīd aw suqūṭ Ghurnāṭa*, was written in 1926 and published in 1952 by al-ʿUṣba al-Andalusiyya in São Paulo. Fawzī al-Maʿlūf earned his fame with his long poem *Shāʿir fī ṭayyāra*, originally published in the São Paulo magazine *al-Jāliya*, and republished in book form in 1929 with the title *ʿAlā bisāṭ al-rīḥ*, with colour plates by the Russian painter A. Ignatovitch. His four collections of poetry – *Min qalb al-samāʾ*, *Taʾawwuhāt al-rūḥ*, *Aghānī al-andalus* and *Shuʿlat al-ʿadhāb* – were posthumously published as *Dīwān Fawzī al-Maʿlūf* in Beirut in 1957. A 500-page memorial volume, *Dhikrā Fawzī al-Maʿlūf*, was published in Zahle in 1931; he was further honoured with a bronze statue erected in Zahle in 1937, and by a rose planted for him in the Garden of the Poets in Alhambra, Granada.

Further reading

ʿAbd al-Shahīd, Ṣamūʾīl, *Fawzī al-Maʿlūf*, Beirut (1971).
al-Badawī al-Mulaththam, *Fawzī al-Maʿlūf*, Cairo (1953).
al-Ḥāwī, Īliyā, *Fawzī al-Maʿlūf*, Beirut (1973).

C. NIJLAND

al-Maʿlūf, ʿĪsā Iskandar (1869–1956)

Lebanese encyclopaedist, writer, poet, historian and journalist. Born in Kafr ʿUqāb, he was the father of the **Mahjar** poets Fawzī and Shafīq **al-Maʿluf**.

After a year of studying in al-Shuwayr English Secondary School, al-Maʿlūf taught at the Jesuit School and elsewhere in Lebanon, and in **Damascus**. He helped to edit the newspaper *Lubnān* and in 1911 established *al-Athar* magazine. As well as articles in various Egyptian, Lebanese and Syrian magazines, he published about ninety books, most printed in Lebanon or Syria. He also composed four plays, three of which were performed in 1893. He was a member of the Arabic Academy in Damascus (1919), and in 1928 was among the founders of the Lebanese Academy.

ʿĪsā published books on subjects as varied as the history of medicine among the Arabs (1921); the history of cities such as Zahle (1911) and Damascus (1924); the biographies of rulers such as al-Amīr Fakhr al-Dīn II (1927) and al-Amīr Bashīr (1914); and accounts of families such as the Maʿlūf family (1908), and the **Yāzijī** family (1944, 2 vols). After the death of his son Fawzī he collected his obituaries and elegies in *Dhikrā Fawzī al-Maʿlūf* (Zahle, 1931). He died in Zahle.

Further reading

al-Badawī al-Mulaththam, *ʿĪsā Iskandar al-Maʿlūf*, Cairo (1969).
Dāghir, Yūsuf Asʿad, *Maṣādir al-Dirāsāt al-Adabiyya*, Beirut (1956), III/2, 1246–55.
Ṣaydaḥ, George, *Adabunā wa-ʾUdabāʾunā fī al-Mahājir al-Amīrkiyya*, 2nd edn, Beirut (1957).

S. MOREH

al-Maʿlūf, Shafīq (1905–76)

Mahjar poet and journalist, brother of Fawzī **al-Maʿlūf**. Born in Zahle, he worked for a time as a journalist in **Damascus**. His first volume of poetry, *al-Aḥlām*, appeared in Beirut in 1926. In the same year he left for São Paulo, where he worked in the textile factory of his brothers Fawzī **al-Maʿlūf** and Iskandar. He took an active part in the foundation of the literary circle al-ʿUṣba al-Andalusiyya in 1933 and its monthly *al-ʿUṣba* in 1935, and was its chairman from 1942 to 1953.

In 1936 he published *ʿAbqar*, a long narrative poem in six cantos based on Arabian folklore. It describes the poet's visit to ʿAbqar, the home of the *jinn*, which is neither on earth nor in heaven or hell. A second edition, with six new cantos, appeared in 1949. The poem has been translated into both Spanish and Portuguese. Five new ***dīwāns*** appeared from 1951 onwards, and he also published volumes of short stories and essays.

Further reading

Nijland, C., 'A "new Andalusian" poem', *JAL* 18 (1987), 102–20.

C. NIJLAND

Maʿmar ibn al-Muthannā, Abū ʿUbayda *see* Abū ʿUbāyda Maʿmar ibn al-Muthannā

Mamlūks

A *mamlūk* is a military slave or freedman. Mamlūk sultans and *amīr*s, mostly of Kipchak Turkish and Circassian origin, governed **Egypt** and **Syria** from 648/1250 until 923/1517. Their military and servile background notwithstanding, some of the sultans and many of the *amīrs* were writers. Young *mamlūks* in the Citadel were instructed not only in the arts of war, but also in Arabic and Turkish, and some made copies of books in the royal library. Thus the Mamlūk system produced an unusually literate ruling élite. Quite a few *mamlūks* were qualified to issue *fatwās* and transmit *ḥadīths*. Among the *amīrs*, Sanjar al-Dawādārī (d. 699/1299–1300) wrote poetry, **Baybars al-Manṣūrī** wrote history, Ṭaybughā al-Ashrafī wrote a treatise on archery. The powerful *amīr* Yashbak ibn Mahdī wrote religious poetry in Arabic and so did his sultan, al-Ashraf Qaytbāy. The Sultan Qānsūḥ al-Ghawrī also wrote poetry in Arabic and Turkish and presided over regular literary soirées.

In the late seventh/thirteenth century the amīr Jamāl al-Dīn Mūsā ibn Yaghmūr presided over a salon of poets, and Baysarī al-Shamsī built up a great library of Arabic books. In the ninth/fifteenth century the sultans al-Mu'ayyad Shaykh and al-Ẓāhir Jaqmaq were noted book collectors, and Jaqmaq's son Prince Muḥammad was an expert on Arabic and Turkish poetry who turned the Cairo Citadel into a literary salon for a while. More generally, the sons of *mamlūks* (the *awlād al-nās*) served as cultural intermediaries between the ruling Turko-Circassian élite and the Arab civilians, and many of the former became writers, among them the historians Ibn al-Dawādārī and **Ibn Taghrībirdī** and the biographer Ibn Aybak **al-Ṣafadī**. Ibn Manglī (*fl.* 770s/1370s) wrote on occultism, politics, warfare and hunting, and Khalīl al-Ẓāhirī (d. 872/1468) wrote on court ceremonies and on dream interpretation.

The Mamlūk chancery gave employment to many Arab writers, among them the historians **Ibn ʿAbd al-Ẓāhir** and ʿIzz al-Dīn **Ibn Shaddād**, and the encyclopaedists **al-Nuwayrī**, **Ibn Faḍl Allāh al-ʿUmari** and **al-Qalqashandi**, as well as the poet **Ibn Ḥijja al-Ḥamawī**. The chancery style developed by the **Ayyūbid** administrator **al-Qāḍī al-Fāḍil** had a posthumous influence on writers which extended beyond the chancery. The biographer Ibn Ṣuqāʿī worked for the Mamlūk administration in Syria, as did Ibn Durrayhim (712–62/1312–66), who wrote on animals and on cryptography. Today the authors of the Mamlūk age are chiefly famous for their compilations of unoriginal and bulky histories, topographies and biographical dictionaries. Certainly it was an age of compendia, produced by such polygraphic compilators as **al-Maqrīzī** and Jalāl al-Dīn **al-Suyūṭī**. However, the view of authors of the period as merely industrious epigones is based on a very slight acquaintance with what was actually produced. The literature of entertainment, in particular, deserves more attention than it has hitherto received.

Typical of the period are such agreeable works of *belles-lettres* such as the *Maṭāliʿ al-budūr* by **al-Ghuzūlī** (d. 812/1415), an anthology of verse and prose, celebrating the joys of life (among them parties, gardens, chess, baths, songs and story-telling). The less reputable poet Taqī al-Dīn Abu Bakr al-Badrī (d. 1443) wrote books about beautiful boys, hashish and the beauty of eyes. The historians **Ibn ʿArabshāh** and Badr al-Dīn **al-ʿAynī** both produced anthologies of entertaining tales. Muḥammad al-Bilbaysī's eighth/fourteenth-century *al-Mulaḥ wa-al-ṭuraf* is a light-hearted kind of symposium in which members of various crafts sit around a table exchanging jokes. Prose erotica, making extensive use of ***adab*** materials, was produced by **al-Tīfāshī** (d. 1253), ʿAlī al-Baghdādī (early eighth/fourteenth century), and others. Muḥammad **al-Nawājī** (early ninth/fifteenth century) produced a collection of poetry devoted to beautiful boys.

Much of the poetry produced in this period had either a eulogistic or an instructional purpose. Thus **Ibn Nubāta al-Miṣrī** specialized in panegyrics to secular rulers, while **al-Būṣīrī**, **Ibn Abī Ḥajala** and Ibn Ḥijja produced poems in praise of the Prophet. Numerous authors turned treatises on law, medicine, chess, etc., into verse for (presumably) mnemonic purposes. The moralizing *Lāmiyya* and the verse treatises on grammar, law and dream interpretation by **Ibn al-Wardī** are entirely typical of the period. Love and love sickness attracted the attention of many writers, among them Ibn Abī Ḥajala, **Ibn Qayyim al-Jawziyya**, al-Ṣafadī and **Mughulṭa'i**.

Popular themes infiltrated 'mainstream' literature and even quite drab annals such as those of Mufaḍḍal ibn Abī Faḍā'il and **Ibn Iyās** are peppered with *mirabilia*, folkloric elements and post-classical colloquialisms. This was a golden age for popular literature. **Ibn Dāniyāl**, although he was a sophisticated member of the élite, drew on popular material and forms of expression for the scripts of his **shadow plays**. Although a version of ***Alf layla wa-layla*** was circulating in **'Abbāsid** times, the oldest manuscript of this story collection comes from the Mamlūk period and the bulk of the stories that swell out modern editions of this work seem to have been added in the same period. Similarly, although versions of such popular romances as those of **Sayf ibn Dhī Yazan**, **'Antar** and **Dhāt al-Himma** were circulating earlier, they were expanded and reworked in the Mamlūk period (see further **popular literature**; ***sīra* literature**). Street-corner actors performed bawdy farces which mocked the manners of the ruling élite. In the anonymous story, *The Battle of King Mutton and King Honey*, the foodstuffs of the poor fight with those of the élite. The buffoon poet 'Ali **Ibn Sūdūn** al-Bashbughawī (d. 868/1464) used to give public performances of his satirical verses and his *al-Maqāmāt al-habbaliyya* (*Foolish Assemblies*) in the streets of **Damascus**. (See further **acting and actors, medieval**.)

According to Tāj al-Dīn **al-Subkī**'s pietistic guide to everyday living, the *Kitāb mu'īd al-ni'am* (*c.*760/1360), scribes should refrain from copying works like the *Sīra* of 'Antar or works by licentious authors (*ahl al-mujūn*; see ***mujūn***). Curiously, the Mamlūk age is as notable for its puritan literature as it is for its pornography. Ḥanbalī polemicists such as **Ibn Taymiyya** and Ibn Qayyim al-Jawziyya attracted much popular support, and their writings have had an enormous influence on later fundamentalist movements. The Mālikī **Ibn al-Ḥajj** al-'Abdarī's *Madkhal*, a treatise on *bida'* (heretical innovations), is a rich source on the sorts of things that pious Cairenes were not supposed to do, but which the less pious often got up to. Throughout the period fundamentalists clashed repeatedly with **Ṣūfīs** over the merits or otherwise of the works of **Ibn al-'Arabī** and **Ibn al-Fāriḍ**. Al-Yāfi'ī (d. 768/1367) collected tales of Ṣūfī piety and miracles, but in general this was not a great age for Ṣūfī literature. Sufism and occultism overlapped in such works as revisions of al-Bunī's magical treatise the *Shams al-ma'ārif* and later pseudepigrapha attributed to him or to Ibn al-'Arabī. The age is notable for its occultist authors, among them the sorcerer Abū al-Qāsim' al-'Irāqī (*fl.* 660s/1260s) and the alchemists al-Jildakī (*fl.* 760s/1360s) and al-Ghamrī (d. 808/1405).

Further reading

Chamberlain, M., *Knowledge and Social Practice in Medieval Damascus, 1190–1350*, Cambridge (1995).
Haarmann, U., *Quellenstudien zur fruhen Mamlukenzeit*, Freiburg im Breisgau (1970).
——, 'Arabic in speech, Turkish in lineage: Mamluks and their sons in the intellectual life of fourteenth-century Egypt and Syria', *JSS* 33 (1988), 81–114.
Irwin, R., *The Middle East in the Middle Ages: The Early Mamluk Sultanate 1250–1382*, London (1986).
——, *The Arabian Nights Companion*, London (1994).
al-Jammāl, A.S., *al-Adab al-'āmmī fī Miṣr fī al-'asr al-Mamlūkī*, Cairo (1966).
Little, D.P., *History and Historiography of the Mamluks*, London (1986).
Lyons, M.C., *The Arabian Epic*, 3 vols, Cambridge (1995).
Qalqīlā, 'A.'A., *al-Naqd al-adabī fī al-'aṣr al-Mamlūkī*, Cairo (1972).
Sallam, M.Z., *al-Adab fī al-'aṣr al-mamlūkī*, 2 vols, Cairo (1971).
Shoshan, Boaz, 'High culture and popular culture in medieval Islam', *SI* 73 (1991), 67–107.
——, *Popular Culture in Medieval Cairo*, Cambridge (1993).
Thorau, P.T., *The Lion of Egypt: Sultan Baybars I and the Near East in the Thirteenth Century*, P.M. Holt (trans.), London (1922).

R. IRWIN

Mammeri, Mouloud (1917–89)

Algerian novelist, playwright, anthropologist and linguist writing in French. Born in Taourirt-Mimoun (Greater Kabylia), Mammeri studied at the Gouraud grammar school in Rabat, then at the Eugend school in Algiers. After World War II he taught literature in Algeria, first at school level, then at the University of Algiers. Until 1980 he was also the director of the Centre de Recherches Anthropologiques. He wrote four novels: *La Colline oubliée* (1952); *Le Sommeil du juste* (1955); *L'Opium et la bâton* (1965), on the subject of war; and *La Traversée* (1982), on the theme of disenchantment. His plays are entitled *Le Banquet* (1973) and *Le Foehn* (1982). Mammeri also played a very active role in the revival of Berber culture, translating ancient Kabyle poetry and publishing a Berber grammar (1986). He died in an accident in Ain Debla.

Further reading

Awal, 1990, nos 6–7, special issue: *Hommage à Mouloud Mammeri*, Paris.

El Hassar-Zeghari, L. and Louanchi, D., *Mouloud Mammeri*, Algiers (1982).

J. DÉJEUX

al-Ma'mūn *see* 'Abbāsids

al-Ma'mūnī, Abū Ṭālib (fourth/tenth century)

Abū Ṭālib 'Abd al-Salām ibn al-Ḥasan al-Ma'mūnī was an Arabic poet. Born in **Baghdad** after 343/953, he moved to **Rayy** in his youth, where he attended the court of the **Ṣāḥib Ibn 'Abbād**. He left due to intrigue and ended up, via Nishapur, at the **Sāmānid** court in Bukhara. **Al-Tha'ālibī** suggests that he had political ambitions, viz. to usurp the **'Abbāsid** caliphate; however, his poetry, which shows him to have been a pleasure-seeking man, does not chime with this. His poems constitute short specimens of ***waṣf***, and 'form an interesting document for the development of the sophisticated Persian style, showing it at an early stage and in Arabic guise' (Bürgel).

Further reading

Bürgel, J.C., *Die ekphrastischen Epigramme des Abū Ṭālib al-Ma'mūnī*, Göttingen (1965).

P.F. KENNEDY

Ma'n ibn Aws (d. *c.*73/692)

A ***mukhaḍram*** poet of the Banū Muzayna. He spent his life near Medina but travelled to **Basra** where he met **al-Farazdaq**. His eulogies on a number of early luminaries (including 'Āṣim ibn 'Umar ibn al-Khaṭṭāb and Sa'īd ibn al-'Āṣ) are noted for their **bedouin** style. Though ignored by early critics, his verse was considered by Mu'āwiya to be on a par with that of his elder fellow tribesman, **Zuhayr ibn Abī Sulmā**. This may be due to the inclusion in his poetry of passages of a moralistic nature.

Text editions

Gedichte des Ma'n b. Aus, P. Schwartz (ed.), Leipzig (1903); R. Geyer (ed.), *WKZM* 17 (1903), 246–70, 18 (1904), 27–29.

Rescher, O., *Beiträge zur arabische Poesie*, Istanbul (1956–8) 6, 2, 1–28.

Further reading

Kamāl, M., *Ma'n ibn Aws, ḥayātuhu, shi'ruhu, akhbāruh*, Cairo (1927).

P.F. KENNEDY

ma'nā

Throughout the literature of the Muslim religious sciences and the auxiliary linguistic sciences the term *ma'nā* refers to the meaning of a vocable (*lafẓ*). A vocable may consist of a word or component of a word (its form or radicals) or a formal structure such as a construct phrase, combination of word and definite article, or entire sentence (to name only a few examples). Language, in these sciences, is thus broken down into fundamental meaning-laden units. The relationship between ***lafẓ* and *ma'nā*** is considered to be fixed by convention or divine fiat, not by nature. Since some vocables have more than one meaning, communication through language occasions ambiguity, which must be resolved through contextual clues (*qarā'in*) so that a speaker's *intended* meaning (*murād*) may be grasped. Resolution of ambiguity is a chief concern of Muslim hermeneutics.

In rhetoric and literary criticism *ma'nā* refers variously to: the meaning of a word or statement in a specific verse, or of a trope; the particular form of a statement (i.e. a topos, as in collections of poetic *ma'ānī* such as those of **Abū Hilāl al-'Askarī** or **al-Sarī al-Raffā'**); the syntactic forms of statements (as in the 'science of *ma'ānī*' developed by **al-Sakkākī** and his followers); types of figurative expression, as in the theory of **'Abd al-Qāhir al-Jurjānī**. In philosophy it means a concept or idea (often in the Platonic sense), the 'essence' of a thing.

Further reading

Ait El Ferrane, M., *Die Ma'nā-Theorie bei 'Abdalqāhir al-Ǧurǧānī*, Frankfurt am Main (1990).

*EI*², art. 'Ma'nā'

Heinrichs, Wolfhart, *Arabische Dichtung und griechische Poetik*, Beirut and Weisbaden (1969), 62–82.

Mahdi, M., 'Language and logic in classical Islam', in *Logic in Classical Islam*, G.E. von Grunebaum (ed.), Wiesbaden (1970), 51–83.

Weiss, B.G., ''Ilm al-Waḍ': an introductory account of a later Muslim philological science', *Arabica* 34 (1987), 340–4.

B. WEISS

manāqib literature

A genre of biographical–hagiographical literature devoted to recounting and recording the *manāqib*, 'qualities and characteristics', *faḍā'il*, 'virtues', or *mafākhir*, *ma'āthir*, 'sources of pride' of notable individuals. The term *manāqib* could originally be employed in quite a neutral way, or even used to detail a person's bad characteristics, but very soon came to denote *par excellence* a laudatory biography, especially of a religious figure, detailing his charismatic attributes and, often, his miraculous powers of healing, etc. It thus comes to mean, in effect, 'hagiography'.

The biographies of the Prophet have some connection with the genre, and this term alternates with *manāqib/faḍā'il* for works on other outstanding personages of early Islam, such as those on the early caliphs and on ʿUmar ibn ʿAbd al-ʿAzīz by such authors as **Ibn ʿAbd al-Ḥakam** and **Ibn al-Jawzī**. The founders of the great law schools in Islam soon became the subjects of *manāqib* treatises, especially **Abū Ḥanīfa** and **al-Shāfiʿī**, while biographical dictionaries were composed of their disciples, often arranged in generations (*ṭabaqāt*), such as those of the Shāfiʿīs by **al-Subkī** and those of the Ḥanbalīs by Abū Yaʿlā al-Farrā' (451–526/1059–1133).

Hagiolatry of individual holy men and mystics and, from the sixth/twelfth century onwards, the institutionalization of the **Ṣūfī** orders or *ṭuruq*, both provided powerful stimuli for the development of *manāqib* literature, so that almost every ascetic or Ṣūfī *shaykh* of any note became the subject of either a special work or at least of a section within a wider book. Many such works are listed by the bibliographer **Ḥājjī Khalīfa**, and the genre continued almost up to the fourteenth/twentieth century, especially in regions where traditionalist Islam and the veneration of local saints were particularly strong, such as **Morocco** and other lands of the **Maghrib**.

Further reading

EI[2] art. 'Manāḳib' (C. Pellat).

C.E. BOSWORTH

See also: biography, medieval

Mandūr, Muḥammad (1907–65)

Egyptian literary critic, translator, lawyer and politician. Born in Kafr Mandūr (Lower Egypt), Mandūr studied law and literature at the Egyptian University, graduating with two Licences in 1929 and 1930. He then studied for nine years in France, where he received several graduate diplomas and a Licence in French and African literatures. He returned to Egypt in 1939 and taught at the University of Cairo before moving in 1942 to Alexandria, where he completed his doctorate (later published as *al-Naqd al-minhajī ʿind al-ʿArab*) under the supervision of Aḥmad **Amīn** in 1943. In 1944 Mandūr resigned his post and worked as an editor on various newspapers. He became a member of the Egyptian Parliament and from 1949 taught at the Institute of Dramatic Arts. He visited Romania and the USSR in 1956 and was greatly impressed by the socialist experience of both. He was awarded the State Prize for Literature in 1962.

Mandūr produced more than twenty books and many articles. In addition to his translation of Flaubert's *Madame Bovary* and other works, he is best known for his call for *al-adab al-mahmūs* ('whispered literature'), which he defended in his first major book *Fī al-mīzān al-jadīd* (1944), considered by many as a landmark in modern Arabic literary criticism. He is also noted for his textual analysis of modern Arabic literature, informed by the French critical tradition of *l'explication de textes*; for his later call – inspired by his visit to eastern Europe – for ideological criticism; for his influential work on classical Arabic literary theory, and for his widely read books on modern Arabic literature and criticism (especially Egyptian poetry and drama), including *Muḥāḍarāt ʿan Khalīl Muṭrān* (1954), *Muḥāḍarāt fī al-shiʿr al-Miṣrī baʿd Shawqī* (3 vols, 1955–8), *Masraḥiyyāt Shawqī* (1956), *Masraḥiyyāt ʿAzīz Abāẓa* (1958), *al-Masraḥ al-nathrī* (1959), *Masraḥ Tawfīq al-Hakīm* (1971) and *Fī al-masraḥ al-Miṣrī al-muʿāṣir* (1971). His books have for many years provided the most accessible résumés on Western literary genres and schools for Arab readers.

Throughout his career, Mandūr was motivated by a strong commitment to change in Arab society, strengthened by his political engagement before the 1952 revolution, and later by his visit to eastern Europe. He drew on a profound knowledge of Arabic culture and first-hand experience of its European counterpart, influencing several generations of Arab writers and critics, as well as students of Arabic literature (particularly drama) throughout the Arab world.

Further reading

Barrāda, Muḥammad, *Muḥammad Mandūr wa-tanẓīr al-naqd al-ʿArabī*, Beirut (1979).

Riyāḍ, Hinrī, *Muḥammad Mandūr rā'id al-adab al-ishtirākī*, Beirut (1983).
Semah, D., *Four Egyptian Literary Critics*, Leiden (1974).
Shukrī, Ghālī, *Muḥammad Mandūr: al-nāqid wa-al-manhaj*, Beirut (1981).

A.-N. STAIF

al-Manfalūṭī *see* Abū al-Nasr al-Manfalūṭī

al-Manfalūṭī, Muṣṭafā Luṭfī (1876–1924)

Egyptian writer and poet. Born in Manfalūṭ (southern Egypt), the son of an Islamic court judge, Manfalūṭī was sent at the age of 12 to **al-Azhar**, where he spent ten years. Like many Arab authors he started his career by writing poetry. In 1897 he was imprisoned for publishing a poem considered insulting to the Khedive ʿAbbās II. Manfalūṭī admired the reformist ideas of Muḥammad **ʿAbduh** and took his side in his dispute with the Egyptian government. In 1907 he started publishing a series of articles in the newspaper *al-Mu'ayyad* which were collected first under the title *al-Usbūʿiyyāt*, and later as *al-Naẓarāt*. These articles were published in three parts in 1910, 1912 and 1920. In 1915 followed a collection of short stories, *al-ʿAbarāt*, in which he tried to adapt four French and even one American story for the Egyptian reading public. In addition to these collections (many times reprinted), Manfalūṭī also wrote three original stories called *al-Yatīm*, *al-Ḥijāb* and *al-Hāwiya*.

In 1909 Manfalūṭī became Arabic editor at the Ministry of Education. From then on, his career was spent in government service, at the Department of Justice and at the Royal Court.

Manfalūṭī is widely recognized as having modernized Arabic prose writing, while retaining contacts with traditional style and ideas. He did not know French or English well, but was fascinated by Western literature, despite knowing it only through translations and adaptations. Curiously, he was able to publish Arabic versions of at least four long French works: *Cyrano de Bergerac* by Edmond Rostand (1921); *Pour la Couronne* by François Coppée (1920); *Paul et Virginie* by Bernadin de Saint-Pierre (1923); and *Sous les Tilleuls* by Alphonse Karr (1917?).

The most striking feature both of Manfalūṭī's original works and of his translations is their Romantic vein, which is dominated by melancholy and a mood of bewilderment, not to say sentimental pessimism. In this respect, as Jayyusi notes, he paved the way for the Romantic poetry of the 1920s and 1930s. His poems were published in 1912 as *Mukhtārāt al-Manfalūṭī*, and he also made contributions in the field of poetic and literary criticism.

Further reading

Brockelmann, *GAL(S)*, vol. 3, 195–202.
Brugman, J., *An Introduction to the History of Modern Arabic Literature in Egypt*, Leiden (1984), 83–8.
Gibb, H., *Studies on the Civilization of Islam*, London (1962).
Jayyusi, S.K., *Trends and Movements in Modern Arabic Poetry*, 2 vols, Leiden (1977), 140–4.
Vial, C., *EI*², s.v. 'Manfalūṭī'.
Ziriklī, K., *al-Aʿlām*, 3rd edn, Beirut (*c.*1970), vol. 7, 239–40.

E.C.M. de MOOR

Manṣūr, Anīs (1926?–)

Egyptian writer and journalist. Manṣūr graduated in 1947 from the philosophy department of Cairo University. His works include essays, short stories, travel literature, plays and translations, many of which have appeared in numerous editions. In 1963 he received the State Prize for his work *Ḥawla al-ālam fī mi'atay yawm*, which – according to UNESCO statistics – is one of the most widely read books in Arabic. Among his studies are *Waḥdī maʿa al-ākharīn*. Manṣūr's travel writings include *Aṭyab taḥiyyātī min Muskū*, *Laʿnat al-Farāʿina* and *Aʿjab al-riḥlāt fī al-tārīkh*; among his plays are *al-Aḥyā' al-mujāwira* and *Ḥilmak yā Shaykh Aʿlam*. Manṣūr, who has his own editorial column in ***al-Ahrām***, is also the translator of Arthur Miller's *After the Fall*, four plays by Dürrenmatt and a play by Jean Giraudoux.

Further reading

Shalabī, M., *Maʿa ruwwād al-fikr wa-al-fann*, Cairo (1982).

M. MIKHAIL

Manṣūr al-Namarī (d. 190/805)

Abū al-Faḍl (or Abū al-Qāsim) ibn Salam ibn al-Zibriqān al-Namarī, from the Banū Rabīʿa ibn Nizār, was a court poet of **Hārūn al-Rashīd**. He was attached also to both al-Faḍl ibn Yaḥyā al-Barmakī and Ja'far al-Barmakī (see **Barmakids**), as well as their nemesis al-Faḍl ibn Rabī'. Although **Ibn al-Nadīm** mentions a 100-leaf ***dīwān*** in the *Fihrist*, only 57 fragments (386 verses) survive in various sources. He composed, among other genres, a substantial amount of ***ghazal***, which is hard to distinguish from the manner of the *nasīb*, but mostly ***madīḥ***, for which he reworked the classical ***qaṣīda*** model. Though an **'Abbāsid** panegyricist, he was pro-'Alid – Shī'ī sources quote anti-'Abbāsid material. He represents well the era in which he lived, although one must search for signs of dissimulation in his official eulogies.

Text edition

Shi'r Manṣūr al-Namarī, T. al-'Ashshāsh (ed.), Damascus (1981).

P.F. KENNEDY

maqāma (pl. *maqāmāt*)

Classical Arabic literary genre, developed in the fourth/tenth century out of a cluster of ***adab*** prose genres which basically comprised all of the education and learning of court circles. The *maqāmāt* were usually composed in collections of short independent narrations written in ornamental rhymed prose (***saj'***) with verse insertions, which shared a common plot-scheme and two constant protagonists: the narrator and the hero. In each narration (*maqāma*) one familiar *adab* topos is usually chosen to be elaborated. The narration tells of an episode in which the hero, a vagrant and mendicant but also a man of letters and eloquence, appears in a certain public place (a market, a mosque, a cemetery, a public bath, a traveling caravan, etc.) in different guises, and tricks people into donating him money by manipulating their feelings and beliefs. As Beeston has put it:

> Despite his gifts of wit and eloquence, he is a hypocritical rascal – albeit a rather engaging one – and an unrestrained drunkard who, after a serious and moving religious homily, for example, which gains him alms from his auditory, dissipates the cash in low society at a tavern drinking wine; he himself is elderly, but occasionally has with him a youthful accomplice, whom he uses in playing crafty tricks for extracting money (Beeston, 1990, 133).

Usually the narrator witnesses the hero's adventures; and each episode ends with the narrator exposing the hero's identity, the hero justifying his behaviour, and their friendly departure. This is the basic scheme of a typical *maqāma*; naturally there are many variations to this scheme, depending on author and period.

The fact that the *maqāma* genre emerged in the wake of a literary institution that was highly established at the time – that of *adab* – bears significant implications for the nature and structure of the *maqāmāt*. The immense body of *adab* literature served as a literary reservoir from which the *maqāma* drew practically everything, from entire literary models to particular themes, motifs, situations, verses of poetry, figures of speech, clichés, ready rhymed-prose collocations and so on. Allusions to specific, often well-known texts from ***ḥadīth***, *adab* and poetry can also be found in the *maqāma*, sometimes functioning as a founding principle upon which an entire *maqāma* is structured (e.g. the *Maqāma of the Lion* by al-Hamadhānī). All these are processed in the *maqāma* and moulded into a new literary model, which is, however, essentially distinct from other traditional *adab* models in that it overtly proclaims itself to be fictional.

Fiction is on the whole rejected in official classical Arabic literature, which, governed by powerful religious–poetic norms, consistently claims the historicity of its texts (see **fiction, medieval**). When discussed, fiction would usually be condemned as a 'lie' that should not be accepted. Introducing, through the *maqāma*, a literary model that purports to be fictional was therefore quite an innovative act, albeit one announced in a highly cautious fashion – a fashion that tended towards obscuring the innovation rather than declaring it loudly. In the introductions to their works, authors of *maqāmāt* would often state that 'they themselves gave the names to the hero and the narrator, who otherwise never existed', meaning, in other words, that they employed invented, fictional rather than historical characters. But at the same time, they would be very careful to relate their works to well-accepted literary traditions like those of the fables of ***Kalīla wa-Dimna*** or of love poetry, in order to prove the legitimacy of their writings.

What, then, were the circumstances that turned such an unfavourable poetic idea of unabashed fiction into a possible literary option? The answer seems to lie, again, in the relation of the *maqāma* to its parent genre, *adab*. The first pieces of what were later to be recognized as '*maqāma* texts' were created with an obvious humorist intent. These were composed by **Badīʿ al-Zamān al-Hamadhānī** (d. 398/1008) as a sort of 'comic relief' at learned *adab* sessions in which serious *adab* materials were circulated and discussed. A tradition cited by al-Sharīshī, a famous comentator of **al-Ḥarīrī**'s *Maqāmāt*, states that at the end of such sessions al-Hamadhānī used to challenge his fellow companions by requesting them to suggest a theme or topos, on which he would improvise 'a *maqāma*'. His texts were thus created as parodic variations on familiar, often well-chewed pieces of *adab* knowledge. In order to mark the improvisations as merely 'fun' and distinguish them from the 'genuine' educational texts related by and about real historical figures, fictitious characters had to be introduced, and their fictionality be (to a certain degree) openly admitted.

The genre of *maqāmāt* emerged in **Khurasan**, where al-Hamadhānī first composed his *maqāmāt* in 387/997, in Nishapur. It hovered on the periphery of the canonized literature for about a hundred years, until the *maqāmāt* of al-Ḥarīrī (d. 516/1122) appeared on the scene and captured the literary taste of the period within a short time. The explicit praise of literary critics, the many commentaries written on his *maqāmāt* almost from the time that they were first published in **Baghdad**, and the testimonies of learned men who came from distant places, including **Spain**, to hear the authorized version of al-Ḥarīrī's *Maqāmāt* from his own mouth, all provide ample evidence of an almost immediate prestige and popularity. Al-Ḥarīrī's *Maqāmāt* became a symbol of Arabic eloquence and stylistic dexterity, and preserved their prominent status up until modern times.

The success of al-Ḥarīrī's *Maqāmāt* marked a change in the status of the *maqāma* and its establishment as a canonical literary genre. Al-Ḥarīrī's model overshadowed all previous models and was followed by later writers, who focused on language, style and edifying subject matter rather than on fiction, parody or satire. The successful acceptance of the *maqāma* into Arabic literature was thus accompanied by a process of extensive blurring of the genre's self-proclaimed fictionality. Its fictional world was gradually reduced to a mere skeleton, with its plot serving to connect now larger and more important presentations of information on a wide range of subjects. Adjusting itself to the normative classical poetics, the *maqāma* seemed to have lost its potential ability to significantly impact the established literature with the introduction of fiction. Despite the considerable prestige that the *maqāma* had won for itself, its literary model ultimately failed to fulfil a creative role in the dynamics of Arabic literature.

The prestigious status enjoyed by the *maqāma* in Arabic culture brought other, non-Arabic, communities within that culture to produce *maqāmāt* in their own languages. The twelfth and thirteenth centuries witnessed the appearance of *maqāmāt* in Persian, Hebrew (both in Spain and in the East) and Syriac. Although no evidence of *maqāmāt* translation into European languages such as Latin or Romance is extant, literary contacts between the *maqāma* and the adjacent Spanish picaresque literature have been conclusively established by modern research.

Further reading

Beaumont, Daniel, 'The Trickster and Rhetoric in the *Maqāmāt*,' *Edebiyât*, n.s., 5 (1994), 1–14.

Beeston, A.F.L., 'Al-Hamadhānī, al-Ḥarīrī and the *maqāmāt* genre', in *CHALABL*, 1990, 125–35.

Bosworth, C.E., *The Medieval Islamic Underworld*, Leiden (1976), vol. 1, 96–103.

Drory, R., 'Introducing fictionality into classical Arabic literature: the *maqāma*', in *Studies in Arabic and Comparative Poetics*, Wiesbaden (forthcoming).

Kilito, A., *Les Séances*, Paris (1983).

Malti-Douglas, F., '*Maqāmāt* and *adab*: "*Al-Maqāma al-Maḍīriyya*" of al-Hamadhānī', *JAOS* 105 (1985), 247–58.

Mattock, J., 'The early history of the *maqāma*', *JAL* 15 (1984), 1–17.

Nemah, H., 'Andalusian *maqāmāt*', *JAL* 5 (1974), 83–92.

Richards, D.S., 'The *maqāmāt* of al-Hamadhānī: general remarks and a consideration of the manuscript', *JAL* 12 (1991), 89–99.

Tarchouna, M., *Les Margitans dans les récits picaresques arabes et espagnols*, Tunis (1982).

Zakharia, K., 'Norme et fiction dans la genèse des Maqāmāt d'al-Ḥarīrī', *BEO* 46 (1994), 217–31.

R. DRORY

al-Maqdisī *see* al-Muqaddasī

Ma'qil ibn Dhirār, al-Shammākh *see* al-Shammākh

al-Maqqarī, Shihāb al-Dīn (*c.*986–1041/*c.*1577–1632)

Shihāb al-Dīn Aḥmad ibn Muḥammad al-Maqqarī was born into a scholarly family in Algeria; he lived in Morocco and died in **Egypt**. Of his numerous works (for lists see *GAL* and *EI*), three are particularly important: (a) *Rawḍat al-ās al-'atirat al-anfās fī dhikr man laqītuhu min a'lām al-ḥaḍratayn Marrākush wa-Fās*, containing biographies of many Moroccan scholars, and much on the education and life of the author; (b) *Azhār al-riyāḍ*, a biography of the *qāḍī* Iyāḍ (476–544/1083–1149); and (c) *Nafḥ al-ṭīb min ghuṣn al-Andalus al-raṭīb* (a partial translation was made by P. de Gayangos in the nineteenth century). This last is his most important work. It is in two parts: the first is a history of al-Andalus, valuable for its descriptions of the country and its scholars. The second is a biography of Lisān al-Dīn **Ibn al-Khaṭīb** (713–76/1313–75), the famous vizier of Nasrid Granada. Both the *Nafḥ* and the *Azhār* include many quotations from literary and historical works which are otherwise lost.

Text editions

Azhār al-riyāḍ, Cairo (1359–61/1939–42); Muḥammadiyya (1978–80).

de Gayangos, P., *The History of the Mohammedan Dynasties in Spain*, 2 vols., London (1840–3; includes partial translation of the *Nafḥ al-ṭīb*).

Nafḥ al-ṭīb min ghuṣn al-Andalus al-raṭīb, I. 'Abbas (ed.), 8 vols., Beirut (1968).

Rawdat al-ās al-'atirat al-anfās fī dhikr man laqītuhu min a'lām al-ḥaḍratayn Marrākush wa-Fās, Rabat (1383/1964).

D.J. WASSERSTEIN

al-Maqrīzī (766–845/1364–1441)

Taqī al-Dīn Aḥmad ibn 'Alī al-Maqrīzī was one of the great polymaths of the **Mamlūk** period. In addition to his official career, mainly as *muḥtasib* (market inspector) in **Cairo**, he devoted his life to recording the history and topography of **Egypt** in a series of large-scale works and smaller monographs. Although he was no great stylist, his writings are always interesting because of his eye for arresting details and the odd touch of melodrama in his historical writing, and because of his relatively greater attention to the economic and social background. His many works include: a history of the **Fāṭimids** (*Itti'āẓ al-ḥunafā'*); a chronicle of the **Ayyūbids** and the Mamlūks down to the end of his life (*Kitāb al-sulūk*); a large biographical dictionary, largely unpublished (*al-Muqaffā*), a monograph on the economy, finances and periodic famines of Egypt; and the indispensable topographical work generally known as *al-Khiṭaṭ*.

Text editions

Description ... de l'Égypte, U. Bouriant (trans.), Paris (1895–1900) (incomplete).

Histoire des Sultans Mamelouks de l'Égypte, E. Quatremère (trans.), Paris (1837–45).

Ighāthat al-umma bi-kashf al-ghumma, Cairo (1940).

Itti'āẓ al-ḥunafā-', Jamāl al-Dīn al-Shayyāl (ed.), Cairo (1967–73).

Kitāb al-Mawā'iẓ wa-al-i'tibār fi dhikr al-khiṭaṭ wa-al-āthār, Bulaq (1854), rpt Baghdad (n.d.).

Kitāb al-sulūk, M. Ziyāda *et al.* (eds), Cairo (1956–73)

D.S. RICHARDS

maqṣūra (*qaṣīda*) *see qaṣīda*

Mardam Bek, Khalīl (1895–1959)

Syrian poet, journalist, prose writer and editor of classical Arabic texts. Among other official positions, he was president of al-Rābita al-Adabiyya (1921) and of al-Majma' al-'Ilmī al-'Arabī (1953), and was minister of education in 1942, 1949 and 1952. In his life and writings, Mardam Bek reflects the advantages of the affluent class to which he belonged, as well as the influence of the **Kurd 'Alī** school with its scholarly and linguistic emphases. However, his involvement in the nationalist struggle against the French mandate and concern for pan-Arab unity, as well as his own restless personality and exposure to progressive Arab ideas and European literature, mark his otherwise traditional verse with a readiness to discuss contemporary issues. His better poems have, besides their neo-classical features, qualities of sensuousness and irony, and his influence extended even to poets as different in outlook as Nizār al-**Qabbānī**.

Mardam Bek's *Dīwān* was published posthumously in 1960. His son 'Adnān (1917–88) was a notable verse dramatist.

Further reading

Wizārat al-Thaqāfa wa-al-Irshād al-Qawmī, *al-'Urūba tukarrim dhikrā al-'Allāma Khalīl Mardam Bek*, Damascus (1960).

R. NOURALLAH

Mardān, Ḥusayn (1927–72)

Iraqi journalist and erotic poet. Born in Ba'qūba, he worked in journalism after graduating from secondary school, and was tried and imprisoned for publishing poems that the government censor considered as pornographic.

Mardān's poetry is lyrical, simple and fluent, depending on sensual feeling and emotional tension. Sex and prostitutes form its main themes. His *Qaṣā'id 'āriya* (Baghdad, 1949) and *al-Laḥn al-aswad* (1950) (2nd edn of both anthologies, 1955) aroused the criticism and anger of conservative circles in Iraq. Other collections of his poetry include *Rajul al-ḍabāb* (1951), *Ṭirāz khāṣṣ* and *Halāhil naḥwa al-shams* (1955), in which he dealt with political themes. He also published collections of short stories, including *Ṣuwar mur'iba* (1951), *'Azīzatī Fulāna* (1952) and *Ḥulm 'an al-ḥarb al-thālitha, 'Ishrūn qasīdat nathr* (1993), as well as literary criticism such as *Maqālāt fī al-naqd al-adabī* (1955).

Further reading

'Awwād, K., *Mu'jam al-mu'allifīn al-'Irāqiyyīn fī al-qarnayn al-tāsi' 'ashar wa-al-'ishrīn*, Baghdad (1969), vol. 1, 357.

Jayyusi, S.K., *Trends and Movements in Modern Arabic Poetry*, 2 vols, Leiden (1977), 473–4.

Sallūm, D., *Taṭawwur al-fikra wa-al-uslūb fī al-adab al-'Irāqī*, Baghdad (1955), 120–1, 192.

S. MOREH

al-Marghīnānī (fifth/eleventh century)

Abū al-Ḥasan Naṣr ibn al-Ḥasan al-Marghīnānī was a poet and critic. Very little is known of his life. He was born in Marghīnān in Transoxania and settled in Zawzan. **Al-Bākharzī** quotes some of his prose and poetry in his *Dumyat al-qaṣr*. He wrote a short treatise called *al-Maḥāsin fī al-naẓm wa-al-nathr* (*Beauties in Poetry and Prose*) which deals with tropes and figures of speech, and was used by Rādūyānī in his *Tarjumān al-balāgha*, the first work on the subject in Persian. Another work on stylistics, in the only surviving manuscript entitled *al-Badī'* and ascribed to al-Marghīnānī, is in fact by the sixth/twelfth century poet 'Alī ibn Aflaḥ.

Text edition

Two Arabic Treatises on Stylistics: al-Marghīnānī's al-Maḥāsin fī 'l-naẓm wa-'l-nathr, *and Ibn Aflaḥ's* Muqaddima, *formerly ascribed to al-Marghīnānī*, G.J. van Gelder (ed.), Istanbul (1987).

G.J.H. VAN GELDER

Mar'ī ibn Yūsuf (d. 1033/1624)

Mar'ī ibn Yūsuf ibn Abī Bakr ibn Aḥmad al-Karmī was a *muftī*, teacher, and author of works on Islamic law, biography, writing style, Koran commentary and theory of love (see **love theory**). Mar'ī was born in Tur Karm, now Tulkarm, near Nablus, and was educated in Jerusalem and **Cairo**. On love theory, his *Munyat al-muḥibbīn wa-bughyat al-'āshiqīn* sums up with a light touch some major issues that had emerged on this subject since the third/ninth centuries. Works of his on **Ibn Taymiyya** and on law have become classics.

Text editions

Badī' al-inshā'āt wa-al-ṣifāt fī al-mukātabāt wa-al-murāsalāt, Istanbul (1299/1882); Cairo (1319/1901) (many earlier editions); abridged version, Mosul (1866).

Dalīl al-ṭālib li-nayl al-maṭālib (a textbook on *fiqh*), in *Nayl al-ma'ārib fī Dalīl al-ṭālib* (a commentary on it by 'Abd al-Qādir 'Uthmān ibn 'Umar al-Dimashqī al-Shaybānī al-Taghlibī), Cairo (1324/1907); also in *Manār al-sabīl fī sharḥ al-Dalīl* (a commentary on it by Ibrāhīm ibn Muḥammad ibn Dūyān [1858/9–1934/5]), 'Iṣām Qala'jī (ed.), 2 vols, Riyadh (1985).

al-Kawākib al-durriyya fī manāqib al-mujtahid Ibn Taymiyya, in al-*Majmū' al-mushtamil 'alā al-durar al-ātiya*, M.S. 'Abd Allāh Ashqar (ed.), 2 vols, Kuwait (1985).

Further reading

Bell, J.N., *Love Theory in Later Ḥanbalite Islam*, Albany (1979), 182–99.

Giffen, L.A., *Theory of Profane Love among the Arabs*, New York (1971). 46–8, Table 1, and index.

L.A. GIFFEN

Marrāsh, Frānsīs (1836–73)

Melchite writer and poet, born and died in Aleppo. He studied medicine under an English physician, and furthered his studies in Paris (writing an account of his journey there); illness plagued him, however, and he returned home totally blind. His first published ***dīwān***, *Mir'āt al-ḥasnā'*, tried to introduce new themes into modern Arabic literature by describing modern mechanical innovations; *Mashhad al-aḥwāl* (1851) follows a philosophical path, dealing with the universe, nature and humankind. *Ghābat al-ḥaqq* (*The Forest of Truth*) (1865) is a vision of a dream world, describing an ideal state of spiritual freedom in constant war with a kingdom of bondage; the work is a fantastic blend of European ideas (the advantages of peace, the importance of liberty and equality) and a personal Christian belief in universal love. It was followed by the moralistic social romance *Durr al-ṣadaf fī gharā'ib al-ṣudaf* (1872). Marrāsh also wrote a treatise on medicine (1861), *Nature's Proof of the Existence of God and the Divine Law* (1892) and a history of extinct nations (1864). His original style is the first example of poetic prose in modern Arabic, and was later to influence **Jubrān**. Marrāsh has some claim to be regarded as the first truly universal Arab intellectual of modern times.

Further reading

Moosa, M., *The Origins of Modern Arabic Fiction*, Washington, DC (1983), 147–53.

Tomiche, N., 'Marrāsh, Fransīs...', *EI*[2] vol. 6, 598–9.

Wielandt, Rotraud, 'Fransīs Fatḥallāh Marrāshs Zugang zum Gedankengut der Aufklärung und der französischen Revolution' in *The Middle East and Europe: Encounters and Exchanges*, Amsterdam (1992), 116–46.

P.C. SADGROVE

marthiya see rithā'

Marwān ibn Abī Ḥafṣa (105–*c*.182/723–*c*.798)

Abū al-Simṭ Marwān ibn Sulaymān ibn Yaḥyā ibn Abī Ḥafṣa, of a non-Arab family with a certain tradition in poetry, was born in Yamama. His first established patron was Ma'n ibn Zā'ida, the governor of **Yemen**. The elegy Marwān composed when Ma'n died expressed his grief so effectively that he had some difficulty in finding a new patron, but eventually he gained the favour of the caliphs al-Mahdī and **Hārūn al-Rashīd**. He supported the **'Abbāsids'** political claims unequivocally, and they rewarded him accordingly. An unattractive personality (his meanness was pathological), he was a master of the classical style associated with the great **Umayyad** panegyricists. His language avoids obscurity and his syntax is economical; he aims at striking formulae and well-turned phrases to convey his political message. His poems have the rhythm of oratorical periods, and he is known to have spent much care on their composition, consulting philologists about the correctness of his diction. Most of his poetry is panegyric or elegiac, but a few occasional pieces on private affairs have also been preserved. Even if it is apocryphal that he was killed by a supporter of the 'Alids in revenge for one line of his debunking their claims to the caliphate, the story suggests the impact that his poetry had.

Text editions

Shi'r Marwān ibn Abī Ḥafṣa, Qaḥṭān Rashīd al-Tamīmī (ed.), Baghdad (1386/1966); Husayn 'Aṭwān (ed.), Cairo (1973).

Further reading

EI[2], art. 'Marwān' (J.-E. Bencheikh) gives both information and bibliography on Marwān and the family from which he came.

H. KILPATRICK

Marwān ibn Abī al-Janūb (d. after 247/861)

Poet from **Baghdad** (also known as Marwān al-Aṣghar). He was born into a family of poets, the most famous one being his grandfather, **Marwān ibn Abī Ḥafṣa**. He specialized in panegyric poetry, which he made for the caliphs al-Ma'mūn, al-Mu'taṣim, al-Wāthiq and al-Mutawakkil, currying the favour of the last-mentioned with his anti-**Shī'ī** poems. Al-Mutawakkil made him governor of al-Baḥrayn and al-Yamāma, but on the accession of al-Muntaṣir he fell from grace. With several poets, including **'Alī ibn al-Jahm**, he exchanged invective poems (***hijā'***). Most critics agree that his poetry was mediocre; little of it has been preserved.

Further reading

Bencheikh, J.E., 'Le cénacle poétique du calife al-Mutawakkil (m. 247): contribution à l'analyse

des instances de légitimation socio-littéraires', *BEO* 29 (1977), 33–52, esp. 39–41.
*EI*², art. 'Marwān'.

G.J.H. VAN GELDER

Marwānids *see* Umayyads

al-Marzubānī, Muḥammad ibn 'Imrān (*c.*297–384/910–94)

Abū 'Ubayd Allāh Muḥammad ibn 'Imrān al-Marzubānī was a literary scholar from **Baghdad**. He studied under famous philologians such as **Ibn Durayd** and Abū Bakr **al-Anbārī**. His literary gatherings were famous also as social events. His reputation as a scholar suffered somewhat from his predilection for wine. Only a small part of his vast biographical work on philologians, *al-Muqtabas*, has survived. Incompletely preserved also are his encyclopaedia of poets, *Mu'jam al-shu'arā'*, and his work on women poets, *Ash'ār al-nisā'*. Interesting is *al-Muwashshaḥ*, a collection and discussion of numerous points on which poets had been criticized. Of the many other works by him we only know the title and the size – often considerable – as given in **Ibn al-Nadīm**'s *Fihrist* or **Yāqūt**'s *Mu'jam al-udabā'*, such as *Ash'ār al-jinn* (*Poems of the Jinn*), *al-Riyāḍ* (*The Gardens*, on those madly in love), *al-Mustaṭraf* (*The Peculiar*, anecdotes on stupid people), *al-Shi'r* (on poetics), *al-Mufaṣṣal* (on eloquence) and *al-Marāthī* (*Elegies*).

Text editions

Ash'ār al-nisā', Sāmī Makkī al-'Ānī (ed.), Baghdad (1976).
Mu'jam al-shu'arā', 'Abd al-Sattār Aḥmad Farrāj (ed.), Cairo (1960).
al-Mukhtār min kitāb al-Muqtabas li-'Alī ibn Ḥasan ibn Mu'āwiya, facs. edn, Frankfurt am Main (1990).
Nūr al-qabas al-mukhtaṣar min al-Muqtabas/Die Gelehrtenbiographien des Abū 'Ubaidallah al-Marzubānī in der Rezension des Ḥāfiẓ al-Yaġmūrī, Rudolf Sellheim (ed.), Wiesbaden (1964).

G.J.H. VAN GELDER

al-Marzūqī (d. 421/1030)

Abū 'Alī Aḥmad ibn Muḥammad al-Marzuqī was a grammarian and literary scholar. Born in Isfahan, he is said to have earned his living as a weaver, before his study of grammar and poetry turned him into a respected scholar who was employed by some of the **Būyid** princes as a tutor for their children. His most famous work is an extensive commentary on the *Ḥamāsa* of **Abū Tammām** (*Sharḥ Dīwān al-Ḥamāsa, Commentary on the 'Bravery' Collection*). In the introduction he deals with a number of important issues in literary criticism, such as canons of choice for **anthologies**; the notion of ***'amūd al-shi'r***; the question of truth, falsehood and the golden mean in poetry; and the 'natural–artificial' dichotomy. His interest in the poetry of Abū Tammām is clear from a commentary on the difficult verses in the latter's ***dīwān***, *Sharḥ mushkil abyāt Abī Tammām al-mufrada* (*Commentary on the Difficult in Single Verses by Abū Tammām*), as well as a defence of the poet against his detractors, preserved only in fragments in later literature (*Kitāb al-Intiṣār min ẓalamat Abī Tammām, Getting Even with Those Who have Wronged Abū Tammām*). His extensive work on ancient Arab star lore, weather lore and time notions, *Kitāb al-Azmina wa-al-amkina* (*Times and Places*) deserves mention as well, since all these topics are intimately connected with the ancient literature.

Text editions

Kitāb al-Azmina wa-al-amkina, 2 vols, Hyderabad, Deccan (1332/1914) (a list of contents in *GAS*, vol. 7, 361–3).
Sharḥ dīwān al-Ḥamāsa, Aḥmad Amīn and 'Abd al-Sallām Hārūn (eds), 4 vols, 2nd edn, Cairo (1387/8–1967/8).
Sharḥ mushkil abyāt Abī Tammām al-mufrada aw Tafsīr ma'ānī abyāt shi'r Abī Tammām, Khalaf Rashīd Nu'mān (ed.), Beirut (1407/1987).

Further reading

Ajami, M., *The Alchemy of Glory*, Washington, DC (1988), 9–12.
Stetkevych, S.P., *Abū Tammām and the Poetics of the 'Abbāsid Age*, Leiden (1991), 257ff.

W.P. HEINRICHS

See also: literary criticism, medieval; *maṭbū'* and *maṣnū'*; truth and poetry.

al-Mas'adī, Maḥmūd (1911–)

Tunisian writer. Al-Mas'adī's creative writings date from the 1930s and 1940s but did not find their way into print until the appearance of *al-Sudd* in 1955. *Al-Sudd*, his best-known work, is usually thought of as a play which revolves around the two main characters, Ghaylān and Maymūna. In fact, it does not correspond to any established literary form: within the outer framework of the drama it alternates between lengthy narrative passages and blank verse. The whole work is a subtle satire on the conflicts that exist between traditional Muslim societies and social reformers and modernizers, whose fits of enthusiasm are often idealistic and unrealistic at one and the same time. The author achieves much of his satire through linguistic parodies of different elements of the Arab–Islamic tradition and this is undoubtedly one of the most original features of his work.

Al-Masʿadī was ahead of his time in that he wrote during a period when much of Arabic literature was obsessed with issues of political **commitment**, and the themes and styles of Arabic literature were adapted accordingly. He is no less concerned by such matters, but he chooses to approach them by remoulding timeless motifs and styles of Arabic literature around the dilemmas of a twentieth-century mentality. His works such as *Sindbād wa-al-ṭahāra*, *al-Musāfir* and *Ḥaddatha Abū Hurayra Qāl* (1973) represent some of the earliest exercises in reworking the classical heritage for modern literary purposes.

Together with Abū al-Qāsim **al-Shābbī**, al-Masʿadī is one of the two modern Tunisian writers with a widespread reputation in the Arab world. For many years before his retirement, he was minister of culture in Bourguiba's government.

Further reading

Ghāzī, Férid, *Le Roman et la nouvelle en Tunisie*, Tunis (1970).
Ostle, R.C., 'Maḥmūd al-Masʿadī and Tunisia's "lost generation"', *JAL* 8 (1977), 153–66.

R.C. OSTLE

al-Mashriq (1898–)

Oriental, historical, literary and scientific review, published by the Catholic Université Saint-Joseph in Beirut to support the Christian religion, promote oriental disciplines and help the diffusion of sciences. Its early directors were Father Luwīs **Shaykhū** (Cheikho), Father Henri Lammens and Father Aghnātyūs Khalīfa. It ceased publication briefly in World War 1 and in 1970 for a twenty-year period. Until his death, the major contributor was Shaykhū himself, who wrote more than 7,000 pages for the review; many of his major works first appeared there.

Further reading

Fihris al-Mashriq, 1898–1950; 1951–70.
Hechaïmé, Camille, *Bibliographie analytique du Père Louis Cheikho*, Beirut (1986).

P.C. SADGROVE

Maskīn al-Dārimī *see* Miskīn al-Dārimī

masks and masquerades

Smearing the face with soot or ashes, or whitening it with lime or flour, or wearing masks of animals or demonic features, was an integral part of dramatic rituals among many nations, including the Arabs. The use of masks in theatrical performances in Islam seems to be of both Byzantine and Persian origins and might be the origin of live theatre in Islam. In Arabic lexicography mask is called *samāja*, *wajh* and *qinaʿ*. *Samāja* is defined as 'foul, unseemly, or ugly', but in literary and historical works it has the meaning of 'mask and/or a man in masquerade'.

In the ***naqā'iḍ*** there is one of the earliest indications that actors with hobby-horses wore masks. In poem no. 42, verse 9, **Jarīr** (d. 114/733) mocks **al-Farazdaq** with his silk garment and bracelet, riding on his mule, indicating that he looks like a masquerading player or actor disguised with a mask of a monkey with moustaches, and imitating riding a horse with his hobby-horse. Such figures of actors disguised as monkeys and bears are preserved in a painting in the **Umayyad** palace of Quṣayr ʿAmra (see Ettinghausen, 1965).

The use of the term *samāja* in the sense of comic masks and/or masked actors is attested in Iraq and **Egypt** from the third/ninth to the fifth/eleventh centuries in the context of ***Nayrūz*** celebrations by Muslims and Copts from the time of the **ʿAbbāsid** caliph al-Muʿtaṣim (218–28/833–42) to the **Fāṭimid** caliph al-Ẓāhir (411–27/1020–35). However, during the ʿAbbāsid period in **Baghdad**, masked actors are mentioned as performing dances (*raqṣ* also means playing and acting) in the caliphs' palaces together with unmasked actors called *ṣafā'ina* (slapstick actors). During al-Mutawakkil's reign (233–48/847–62), a gallery was built to separate him from the masked actors, for reasons of security. During the Fāṭimid period the *samāja* performed in market places.

From the second half of the eleventh century the term *samāja*, for no obvious reason, was no longer mentioned in Arabic historiography, but rather the term *muharrij* (pl. *muharrijūn*), was used. Both terms, *samāja* and *muharrij*, were used in Spain and later in Europe as *mascara* and *moharrache* in the sense of buffoon and masquerade (see R. Dozy and W.H. Engelmann, *Glossaire des mots espagnols et portugais derivés de l'arabe*, 2nd edn, Amsterdam [1915] 509).

The *samāja* are said not only to perform dances but to imitate the behaviour of prostitutes. Actors with goats' masks performed *Kôsa nishin* (the ride of the thin-bearded man), a festival borrowed from Persia performing symbolic folk plays of 'temporary king' or 'false *amīr*', which illustrates the expulsion of winter or the driving out of the old year. Alternatively, the *muharrijūn* performed a *faṣl* (play) wearing animal masks or bearskins in cafés, market squares and palaces during celebrations of festivals and *mawlid*s (the Prophet's or a Muslim saint's birthday) to the end of the nineteenth century.

Further reading

And, Metin, *Culture. Performance and Communication in Turkey*, Tokyo (1987).

——, *Drama at the Crossroads: Turkish Performing Arts Link Past and Present, East and West*, Istanbul (1991).

Ettinghausen, R., 'The dance with zoomorphic masks', in *Arabic Studies in Honor of Hamilton A.R. Gibb*, G. Makdisi (ed.), Leiden (1965), 211–24.

Moreh, S., *Live Theatre and Dramatic Literature in the Medieval Islamic World*, Edinburgh (1992), 44–63.

——, 'Masks in medieval Arabic theatre', *Assaph C* 9 (1993), 89–94.

S. MOREH

See also: actors and acting, medieval; theatre and drama, medieval

maṣnū' (style, in poetry) *see* *maṭbū'* and *maṣnū'*

masraḥ, masraḥiyya *see* theatre and drama

al-Mas'ūdī (*c.*283–345/*c.*896–956)

Abū al-Ḥasan 'Alī ibn al-Ḥusayn al-Mas'ūdī was born **Baghdad** and died in **Cairo**. Erudite polymath and *adīb*, he travelled extensively in **India** (and possibly beyond India to the East), **Persia**, Armenia, **Arabia**, **Syria** and East Africa, and sailed the Indian Ocean, the Red Sea, the Mediterranean and the Caspian. Apart from this information, gleaned from his own works, little is known of his life or of the sources of his livelihood, except for statements by various writers on his 'Alid sympathies.

Many works have been attributed to al-Mas'ūdī, and he speaks of a number of works he wrote which he expanded, epitomized and reworked at various times and in many versions. What is certain is that he was the author of *Murūj al-dhahab* and of *Akhbār al-zamān*. All these works contain various components of exotic knowledge which formed the more cultivated fringes of ***adab***, courtly urbane secular culture: ethnography, ethnology, geography, natural science, antiquarianism, doxography, *mirabilia* and history proper. Overall, this material is classified in a very general way under headings that would today be called geographical and historical. The geographical material is divided according to the quaternary division of zones, of Persian provenance, which had little incidence in Arabic writing in which the Ptolemaic septenary division of *klimata* (*aqālīm*) was standard. In each quarter, climatic and ecological conditions, as well as astrological influences, produce people of particular temperaments and predispositions. Thus the geographical discussion is the occasion for ethnographical description and ethnological stereotyping, and for the description of various exotic aspects of nature and narratives of *mirabilia* (see ***'ajā'ib* literature**).

The historical narratives, also full of various digressions, take up the history of seven great nations – the Chaldeans, Indians, Chinese, Greeks, Persians and Egyptians, in addition to Arabian antiquities and the histories of lesser peoples narrated on the margins of these major histories. In all, the organization is regnal; with Islamic history, the organization is annalistic.

Both the geographical and historical sections betoken an extraordinary curiosity and massive erudition, sharpened and consolidated by acute personal witness. Al-Masʿūdī's knowledge of western Europe and of Frankish history was extraordinary. In all, an elevated spirit of humanism pervades his works, which mark a high point of the *adab* spirit of urbanity and culture. Cognizant of the relativity of cultures, alive to mutability and diversity, al-Masʿūdī's works provide a glimpse of the extraordinary breadth, diversity and catholicity of *dār al-Islam* in a manner that other works stunt.

Text editions

Kitāb al-tanbīh wa-al-ishrāf, M. de Goeje (ed.), Leiden (1893).

Le livre de l'avertissement et de la révision, Carra de Vaux (trans.), Paris (1897).

Meadows of Gold: The Abbasids, E.P. Lunde and C. Stone (trans.), London (1989).

Les prairies d'or (*Murūj al-dhahab wa-maʿādin al-jawhar*), C. Barbier de Meynard and Pavet de Courteille (eds and trans.), Paris (1861–77); edition revised and corrected by Ch. Pellat, (1966–79); translation revised by Ch. Pellat (1962–89); M.M. ʿAbd al-Ḥamīd, (ed.), Cairo (1948), rpt Sidon (1987).

Further reading

Khalidi, T., 'Masʿūdī's lost works: a reconstruction of their content', *JAOS* 94 (1974), 35–41.

——, *Islamic Historiography: The Histories of Al-Masʿudi*, Albany (1975).

Meisami, J.S., 'Masʿūdī and the fall of the Barmakids', *JRAS* (1989), 252–77.

Shboul, A., *Al-Masʿudi and his World: A Muslim Humanist and his Interest in Non-Muslims*, London (1979).

A. AL-AZMEH

See also: historical literature

Maṭar, Muḥammad ʿAfīfī (1935–)

Egyptian poet. Born in Ramlat al-Anjab in the province of Manūfiyya, Maṭar studied philosophy at Ain Shams University and worked as a teacher as well as in literary journalism. In his early career he faced the hostility of the Egyptian literary establishment (the General Egyptian Book Organization refusing to publish his poetry collection in 1963, for example) and spent about ten years working as an editor for the literary review ***al-Aqlām*** in Baghdad. Only recently, following recognition of his talent by the major Arab critics, has he also gained the recognition of the literary establishment in **Egypt**, where he received the State Prize for Literature in 1989. In 1991 he was arrested by the Egyptian authorities following his condemnation of the American intervention in Iraq, but was released after a protest by Arab intellectuals and writers. Maṭar published his first successful poems in the 1960s in Lebanese literary magazines, particularly *Shiʿr*. At first extensively influenced by **Adūnīs's** poetic vision, his subsequent poetic development has been independent and original. His poetry is complex and hermetic, with many obscure allusions and images from the Arab and Egyptian heritage. Many realistic village anecdotes from his childhood are employed in his poems, as is evident in his collection *Wa-al-nahr Yalbasu al-aqniʿa* (Baghdad, 1976). Among his other poetry collections are *Min daftar al-ṣamt* (Damascus, 1968), *Malāmiḥ min al-wajh al-Anbadūqilīsī* (Beirut, 1969) and *Kitāb al-arḍ wa-al-dam* (Baghdad, 1972). Until the early 1990s only one collection of his poetry (*Yataḥaddathu al-ṭamyu*, Cairo, 1977) had been published in Egypt itself – the subtitle, *Qaṣāʾid min al-khurāfa al-shaʿbiyya* (*Poems from Popular Folklore*), showing the interests of the poet in the late 1970s and early 1980s – but more recently, Egyptian publishing houses have expressed readiness to publish his work. In one of his last collections, *Rubāʿiyyat al-faraḥ* (London, 1990), his earlier poetic interests are interwoven with a heavy mystical tendency reminiscent of Adūnīs in his later poetic development. The same poetic vision is also expressed in his last collection *Fāṣilat īqāʿāt al-naml* (Cairo, 1993). Maṭar, who is regarded as one of the outstanding innovative poets of contemporary Egypt, has recently also been involved in a project aimed at introducing modern Arabic poetry to Arab youth; the first book published in the project concentrated on Maḥmūd Sāmī **al-Bārūdī**, with an introduction by Maṭar (1993).

Text edition

Modern Arabic Poetry: An Anthology, S.K., Jayyusi (ed.), New York (1987), 349–52.

Further reading

ʿAbd al-Ḥamīd, Shākir, 'al-Ḥulm wa-al Kīmyāʾ wa-al-kitāba: qirāʾa fī dīwān *Anta wāḥiduhā wa-hiya aʿḍāʾuk ntatharat* lil-shāʿir Muḥammad ʿAfīfī Maṭar' *Fuṣūl* 7 (October 1986–March 1987), 160–90.

Badawi, M.M., *Modern Arabic Literature and the West*, London (1985), 37.

Ghazūl, Firyāl, 'Fayḍ al-dalāla wa-ghumūḍ al-maʿnā', *Fuṣūl* 4(3) (April–June 1984), 175–89.

R. SNIR

maṭbūʿ and *maṣnūʿ*

'Natural' and 'artificial/artful', an opposition used for a typology of poets and poetry at the time of the 'moderns' of the **ʿAbbāsid** era. The term *maṭbūʿ* first applied to the poets and described them as 'naturally talented for poetry' (*maṭbūʿ ʿalā al-shiʿr*); by extension it was used also to characterize the poetry. Originally (e.g. in **Ibn Qutayba**), the opposite of this term was *mutakallif*, 'proceeding with difficulty (in composing poetry)'. This referred to a poet who laboriously constructed his lines and smoothed out their rough edges over a long period of time; the result was not necessarily bad, but was thought to betray its slow genesis (among the ancient poets **Zuhayr** and **al-Ḥuṭayʾa** are considered to be such slow workers, for which reason they were called 'the slaves of poetry' by the philologist **al-Aṣmaʿī** [d. 213/828].

With the rising tide of *badīʿ*, i.e. the application of rhetorical figures, in 'modern' poetry, a new aspect entered the debate: *ṣanʿa* (see ***ṣināʿa***). This term refers to the rhetorical or even concettistic 'crafting' of lines. The resulting line was called *maṣnūʿ*, rhetorically 'crafted', 'artful', or, for those who abhorred this development, 'artificial'. By extension the word was also applied to a poet who produced such lines, although in some early texts one also finds *ṣāḥib ṣanʿa*, 'a man of "crafting"'. The older term *mutakallif* came to be equated with the new term, especially by those who frowned on the new style.

Maṣnūʿ is the marked term of the opposition. This means that both types of poets are talented by nature; only the 'artful' poet is not content with the lines that come to his mind, but superimposes upon them one or the other rhetorical figure to make the content strange and novel. The *maṭbūʿ–maṣnūʿ* opposition became personified by **Abū Tammām** as the *maṣnūʿ* and his disciple **al-Buḥturī** as the *maṭbūʿ*. It should be noted, however, that there are no schools with these labels. The same poet may write verses in both categories, even within the same poem. The most that can be said is that a given poet has a tendency one way or the other.

Text editions

al-Āmidī, *al-Muwāzana*, al-Sayyid Aḥmad Ṣaqr (ed.), Cairo (1961–5), vol. 1, 6.

Ibn Qutayba, *Introduction au Livre de la poésie et des poètes*, M. Gaudefroy-Demombynes (ed. and trans.), Paris (1947), 15.

al-Marzūqī, *Sharḥ Dīwān al-Ḥamāsa*, Aḥmad Amīn and ʿAbd al-Salām Hārūn (eds), 2nd edn, Cairo (1968–72), vol. 1, 12.

Further reading

Ajami, Mansur, *The Neckveins of Winter: The Controversy over Natural and Artificial Poetry in Medieval Arabic Literary Criticism*, Leiden (1984).

Cantarino, Vicente, *Arabic Poetics in the Golden Age*, Leiden (1975), 59–61.

Heinrichs, Wolfhart, *Arabische Dichtung und griechische Poetik*, Beirut and Wiesbaden (1969), 52–5.

Schoeler, Gregor, *Einige Grundprobleme der autochthonen und der aristotelischen arabischen Literaturtheorie*, Wiesbaden (1975), 33–7.

Sperl, Stefan, *Mannerism in Arabic Poetry: A Structural Analysis of Selected Texts*, Cambridge (1989), 155–80.

W.P. HEINRICHS

See also: ancients and moderns; *badīʿ*; literary criticism, medieval; rhetoric and poetics

mathal *see* metaphor; proverbs

mathālib

Plural of *mathlaba*, meaning 'vices, shortcomings, defects, faults, shameful actions, unpraiseworthy traits'; hence the opposite of ***manāqib***, *maʾāthir*, *mafākhir*, *faḍāʾil*, *maḥāsin*. In classical Arabic literature, a satirical poem (***hijāʾ***) may be said to 'mention' the *mathālib* of someone. Technically, however, the *mathālib* genre is restricted to prose compilations, whose aim is to slander a group or an individual through describing their vices, and whose titles normally feature the term *mathālib* (rarely *akhlāq*/*akhbār*). The sources mention several such titles in the first four Hijrī centuries, all but one of which have not survived. These indicate that the genre addressed at the beginning mainly the vices of tribal Arab groups (e.g. **Ibn al-Kalbī**'s *Mathālib al-ʿArab* and al-Haytham ibn ʿAdī's *Mathālib Rabīʿa*), and hence its connection with the ***Shuʿūbiyya*** movement (see **Ibn al-Nadīm**'s description of ʿAllān al-Shuʿūbī's *al-Maydān fī al-mathālib*). Later, it addressed the vices of individuals, as in *Kitāb mathālib Abī Nuwās* by Aḥmad ibn ʿUbayd Allāh al-Thaqafī, and Abū Ḥayyān **al-Tawḥīdī**'s preserved *Mathālib/Akhlāq al-wazīrayn*, which represents the culmination of the genre.

Further reading

For titles by various authors, see *Fihrist* (ed. Flügel), 54, 96, 99, 105–6, 137, 148; Yāqūt, *Muʿjam al-udabāʾ*, D.S. Margoliouth (ed.), Cairo (1923–30) vol. 1, 227, vol. 2, 30, vol. 3, 93, vol. 7, 169, 219, 251, 265; Ibn Khallikān, *Wafāyat al-aʿyān*, I. ʿAbbās (ed.), Beirut (1968–72), vol. 5, 113, 239, vol. 6, 83, 106.

Pellat, Ch., 'Mathālib', *EI*[2], vol. 6, 828–9; and cf. idem, 'Hidjā'', *EI*[2], vol. 3, 352–5, and 'Manāqib', vol. 6, 349–57.

W. AL-QĀḌĪ

See also: biography, medieval; *manāqib* literature

Mattā ibn Yūnus (d. 328/940)

Abū Bishr Mattā ibn Yūnus was a translator and commentator of the works of **Aristotle**. A Nestorian Christian who studied and taught in Dayr Qunnā, he settled in **Baghdad** during the caliphate of al-Rāḍī (after 322/934), and through his Christian and Muslim disciples (**Yaḥyā ibn ʿAdī, al-Fārābī**) became one of the principle initiatators of the reception of Peripatetic philosophy through Arabic translations from Syriac.

His translations of Aristotle represent a revival of Aristotelian studies, and recovered an Aristotle more complete and – as against the early predominance of pseudepigraphic Neoplatonica – more authentic than had been known heretofore to Arabic readers, comprising all of the *Organon* of logic and the essential works of natural philosophy and metaphysics, and accompanied by the commentaries of Alexander of Aphrodisias, Themistius and Olympiodorus. The only surviving texts of Aristotle in his translation are: the *Posterior Analytics*, recognized as the high point and crown of logic; the *Metaphysics*, book xii, 1–7, containing the central chapters of Aristotle's theology; and the *Ars Poetica* – notorious for Mattā's ignorance of the Greek literary tradition, but transmitted and read as part of the logic. The commentaries of Mattā were in the form of more or less extensive notes (*taʿālīq*, i.e. *hypomnēmata*), still extant in school notes on the *Organon* and comments on Aristotle's *Physics*.

While Mattā was recognized as the scholarch of logic in his time, he had to confront a rising polemic against the claims of Greek logic and philosophy to universal truth, aggravated by the intrusion of 'logical' paradigms into the *uṣūl al-naḥw* of contemporary grammarians, and suffered defeat against the attack of the grammarian Abū Saʿīd **al-Sīrāfī** in a famous debate in the year 326/937–8, reported by Abū Ḥayyān **al-Tawḥīdī**.

Text editions

Manṭiq Arisṭū, ʿAbd al-Raḥmān Badawī (ed.), 2nd edn, Beirut and Kuwait (1980).

Tkatsch, J., *Die arabische Übersetzung der Poetik des Aristoteles*, Vienna and Leipzig (1928–32).

Further reading

Endress, G., 'Grammatik und Logik', *Sprachphilosophie in Antike und Mittelalter*, B. Mojsisch (ed.), Amsterdam (1986), 163–299.

Kühn, W., 'Die Rehabilitierung der Sprache durch den arabischen Philologen as-Sirafī', in *Sprachphilosophie in Antike und Mittelalter*, B. Mojsisch (ed.), Amsterdam (1986), 301–402.

Mahdi, M., 'Language and logic in classical Islam', in *Logic in Classical Islamic Culture*, G.E. von Grunebaum (ed.), Wiesbaden (1979), 51–83.

al-Tawḥīdī, Abū Ḥayyān, *Kitāb al-Imtāʿ wa-al-muʾānasa*, A. Amīn and A. al-Zayn (eds), Cairo (1939–44), vol. 1, 107–29 (contains the debate between Mattā and al-Sīrāfī).

Walzer, R., *Greek into Arabic*, Oxford (1962), 66, 77f., 99f, 102.

Zimmermann, F.W., (ed.), *Al-Farabi's Commentary and Short Treatise on Aristotle's De Interpretatione*, London (1978), ciii–cviii, cxxii–xccix.

G. ENDRESS

al-Maṭwī, Muḥammad al-ʿArūsī (1920–)

Contemporary Tunisian novelist and short-story writer, born in Métouia in southern Tunisia. He has worked as a teacher in the Zitouna University, as a cultural adviser in Cairo, as chargé d'affaires in Baghdad and ambassador in Saudi Arabia; he has also been general secretary of the Faculty of Theology and a Member of Parliament. Al-Maṭwī established the Nādī al-Qiṣṣa (Short Story Club) in 1964, founded his own review *Qiṣaṣ*, and acted as president of the Union des Ecrivains Tunisiens from 1981 to 1991. He has edited a number of classical texts and written children's stories, a play and two collections of poetry. While his short stories exhibit many different styles, his three novels – *Wa-min al-ḍaḥāyā* (1956), *Ḥalīma* (1956) and *al-Tūt al-murr* (1967) – are the leading examples of Tunisian realism.

Further reading

al-Kīlānī, M., *Ishkāliyyat al-riwāya*, Carthage (1990).
Lunt, L.G., 'Love and politics in the Tunisian novel', unpublished PhD thesis, Indiana University (1977).

J. FONTAINE

mawālī (sing. mawlā)

An Arabic word of many significations, some of a technical legal nature, but used in Arabic literary history to designate, in the early centuries of Islam, the non-Arabs – Persians, Aramaeans, Berbers, etc. – who converted to the new faith. They were assigned an inferior place in the political and social hierarchy of Islam as clients (*mawālī*) of the Arab tribesmen; but, in compensation, many of these *mawālī* exerted themselves to great effect in the fields of Arabic literary composition and scholarship, often acquiring a profound knowledge of Arabic and composing numerous works in such rarefied fields as Arabic grammar and lexicography, in addition to the more general aspects of ***adab***. The process began early, as may be seen in the works of the Persian *mawlā* of the second/eighth century **Ibn al-Muqaffaʿ**, and from then onwards, the works of genuine Arabs and non-Arabs are in most respects indistinguishable. Certain attitudes of the *mawālī* did, however, provoke a reaction from the Arabs and the defenders of the special role of the Arabs within Islam; for this, see ***Shuʿūbiyya***.

Further reading

*EI*² art. 'Mawlā' (P. Crone).
Goldziher, I., "Arab and 'Ajam', in *Muslim Studies*, C.R. Barber and M. Stern (trans.), London (1967), vol. 1, 98–136.

C.E. BOSWORTH

mawāliyā (also vocalized mawāliyyā and muwālayā)

One of the 'Seven Arts' (*al-funūn al-sabʿa*), i.e. forms of verse composition which include the classical ode (***qaṣīda***) but also the later multi-rhyme inventions, consistently made to add up to seven in the different treatises, although the components are not always the same. In the written sources, the *mawāliyā* is always ranked high on the ground that it lends itself to either the classical or the colloquial forms of the language although it is the uninflected compositions that are preferred.

The names of most of the non-classical 'arts' are of unknown origin, and are difficult to connect with Arabic roots. Probably for no other reason than a phonetic similarity with ***mawālī***, the non-Arab Muslims whose status was a thorny question in late **Umayyad** and early **ʿAbbāsid** times, late sources recount pretty anecdotes ascribing the invention of the *mawāliyā* to Wasitis or Baghdadis of the second/eighth century. The first reliable examples, however, belong to the seventh/thirteenth century.

All the early instances on record consist of four lines in the *basīṭ* metre with a single rhyme, the line here being the equivalent of a hemistich in classical prosody. This form is now known as the *rubāʿī* or *murabbaʿ* 'quatrain'. Later developments are the result of additions between the third and last lines, producing fixed form poems rhyming *aaaxa* – the *aʿraj*, 'lame' – or *aaabbba* – the *Baghdādī*, *Nuʿmānī*, *sabʿānī* or *musabbaʿ*, 'sevener'. Yet, another elaboration apparently peculiar to **Egypt** and occurring not earlier than the nineteenth century was the insertion of a sestet of alternating rhymes, called *ridfa*, 'riding pillion', after the first three lines, the resulting pattern being *aaabcbcbcddda*, often with an internal 'd' rhyme in the last line. This variety is called Ṣaʿīdī (Upper Egyptian) or *mardūf*.

In modern times, the *mawāliyā* has passed almost exclusively to the hands of folk artists, and is more commonly called *mawwāl*, the term previously applied to the composer of *mawāliyā*s. Furthermore, a *mawwāl* that boasts mere rhymes is termed *abyaḍ*, 'white' or 'blank'. More highly esteemed is the inflation of every rhyme into an elaborate paronomasia, called *zahr*, 'flower', achieved by deliberate distortion of the normal pronunciation; the *mawwāl* is then called 'red' or 'green', the distinction often – but not consistently – made being that the red has a sad theme and the green a joyful on one. On the other hand, the metre is often very cavalierly treated, although when regular it is always recognizably *basīṭ*.

In Egypt at least, the folk artists can, by multiplying the sestets of the *mardūf* or by using any variety of the *mawwāl* as a stanza, extend the length of a composition indefinitely. This is particularly convenient for the composition of narrative ballads, which usually run to hundreds of lines. Folk terminology, however, is extremely loose, and the word *mawwāl* is sometimes, by extension, applied to any narrative song, or to interpretative freesongs, with no set tune and no regular metre or rhyme scheme.

Text edition

al-Ḥillī, Ṣafī al-Dīn, *Die Vulgärarabische Poetik – al-Kitāb al-ʻĀṭil al-Ḥālī wal-Muraḫḫaṣ al-Ġālī*, W. Hoenerbach (ed.), Wiesbaden (1956).

Further reading

Cachia, P., *Popular Narrative Ballads of Modern Egypt*, Oxford (1989).

P. CACHIA

See also: popular literature; prosody

al-Māwardī, ʻAlī ibn Muḥammad (364–450/974–1058)

A jurist of the Shāfiʻī school, best known for his treatise on government entitled *Kitāb al-aḥkām al-sulṭāniyya.* This work provides, among other things, a theory of the caliphate which deals with the basis of caliphal authority, the procedures whereby a caliph is appointed to office and the qualifications and duties of a caliph. Al-Māwardī's methods of argument stand firmly within the tradition of Islamic jurisprudence, in contrast to the political writings of Muslim philosophers such as **al-Fārābī**.

Text editions

Le droit du califat, Comte L. Ostrorog (trans.), Beirut (1982).
Das kitab 'adab ed-dunjâ wa'ddîn', O. Rescher (trans.), 3 vols, Stuttgart (1932–3).
Kitāb al-aḥkām al-sulṭāniyya, Kuwait (1989).
al-Māwardī's Theory of the State, Q. Khan (trans.), Lahore (1983).
Les statuts gouvernementaux ou règles de droit public et administratif, E. Fagnan (trans.), Algiers (1983).

Further reading

Gibb, H.A.R., 'al-Māwardī's Theory of the Caliphate', *IC* 11 (1937), 291–302, rpt in *Studies in the Civilization of Islam*, Boston (1962), 151–65.
Laoust, H., 'La pensée et l'action politique d'al-Mawardi', *REI* 36 (1963), 11–92.
Rosenthal, E.I.J., *Political Thought in Medieval Islam*, Cambridge (1958), 27–37.

B. WEISS

mawʻiẓa see oratory and sermons

al-Mawṣilī, Ibrāhīm (125–88/742–804)

Abū Isḥāq Ibrāhīm ibn Maymūn (Māhān) al-Mawṣilī was a musician, composer and courtier. Of noble Persian descent, Ibrāhīm was born in ***Kufa***. He spent a turbulent youth, but early in life he developed an interest in singing. He visited Mosul (hence his *nisba* al-Mawṣilī) and **Rayy** in search of musical education, before going to **Basra**, where he attracted the notice of members of the **ʻAbbāsid** family. So outstanding a musician was bound to pursue his career at court. Ibrāhīm not only established himself as one of the best singers in **Baghdad**, he also took care to fill in the lacunas in his education so as to be a worthy companion of royalty. Despite al-Mahdī's determined opposition, he established a lasting friendship with the princes (later caliphs) al-Hādī and **Hārūn al-Rashīd**.

Ibrāhīm's lavish life-style was financed by a monthly salary, rewards from admirers, fees from teaching and the income from selling the slave-girls he trained. He and two other musicians are said to have drawn up the list of songs on which **Abū al-Faraj al Iṣbahānī**'s *Kitāb al-Aghānī* is based, although there is little to confirm this. Ibrāhīm was certainly one of the greatest musicians of the age, a performer and composer of genius with 900 songs to his credit, and an adherent of the 'classical' Hijazi school of singing. He seems always to have remained something of a non-conformist.

Further reading

Aghānī (Beirut), vol. 5, 154–258.
Neubauer, E., *Musiker am Hofe der Frühen Abbasiden*, Frankfurt am Main (1965), 47–9, 112–21, 182–3.
Sawa, G.D., *Music Performance Practice in the Early ʻAbbāsid Era*, Toronto (1989) (see index).

H. KILPATRICK

See also: singers and musicians

al-Mawṣilī, Isḥāq ibn Ibrāhīm Abū Muḥammad (150/767–235/850)

Musician, composer, musicologist, poet and courtier. The son of Ibrāhīm **al-Mawṣilī**, Isḥāq received an excellent education both in music and in the usual disciplines of Koran, ***ḥadīth***, philology, poetry and history. He sang before the caliphs from **Hārūn al-Rashīd** to al-Mutawakkil, and after his father's death was the acknowledged leader among singers at court. He compensated for his comparatively poor voice by thorough musical knowledge and gracefulness; he was also a brilliant lutenist.

Isḥāq followed his father in adhering to the Hijazi style of performance, and he systematized the Hijazi musical modes. He clashed with **Ibrāhīm ibn al-Mahdī**, who advocated an independent approach to the interpretation of the established repertoire and made much use of ornaments. Isḥāq was the author of books on many earlier singers as well as on an authoritative system of musical theory; he also compiled a famous list of songs for al-Wāthiq. In poetry he preferred the more old-fashioned Umayyads, to whom he devoted several works; he himself was quite a talented poet. A complicated character, he chafed at the label 'singer', yet it is as a singer that he is remembered, even in the *Arabian Nights*.

Text editions

Dīwān, M.A. al-'Izzī (ed.), Baghdad (1970).

Neubauer, Eckhard, *Musiker am Hof der frühen 'Abbāsiden*, Frankfurt am Main (1965), 64–7 (translation of part of Isḥāq's correspondence with Ibrāhīm ibn al-Mahdī).

Further reading

Bencheikh, J.E., 'Les musiciens et la poésie. Les écoles d'Isḥāq al-Mawṣilī (m. 225 H.) et d'Ibrāhīm Ibn al-Mahdī (m. 224 H.)', *Arabica* 22 (1975), 114–52.

H. KILPATRICK

mawsū'a *see* encyclopedias

mawwāl see mawāliya

al-Maydānī, Aḥmad ibn Muḥammad (d. 518/1124)

Abū al-Faḍl Aḥmad ibn Muḥammad al-Naysabūrī al-Maydānī was an Arab philologist, who was born, lived and studied in Nishapur, i.e. in a Persian-speaking environment. His teachers were philologists and specialists in the **Koran**, who had gained their knowledge during their travels. al-Maydānī has become famous through his *Majma' al-amthāl*, the most voluminous and popular collection of Arabic **proverbs**, based on fifty former collections, as he writes in his introduction. The proverbs are arranged alphabetically without strict consistency. Obsolete vocabulary is explained; the origin and the general meaning of the proverbs is frequently commented on by anecdotes. Thus the collection is also a socio-cultural source. Among his other works are the *Sharḥ* ***al-Mufaḍḍaliyyāt***, a commentary on that famous collection of poetry, and *al-Sāmi fī al-asāmī*, an Arabic–Persian dictionary, for which he himself wrote a commentary. The words are arranged in the categories *shar'iyyāt* (legal terms), *ḥayawānāt* (animate), *'ulwiyyāt* (heavenly) and *sufliyyāt* (earthly things). *Qayd al-awābid min al-fawā'id* is a critique of **al-Jawharī**'s dictionary *al-Ṣiḥāḥ*; *al-Hādī lil-shādī* is a syntax with Persian notes, divided into the parts nouns, verbs, particles. Al-Maydānī was a typical scholar of his time, compiling, arranging and commentating knowledge more than creating it.

Text edition

Arabum proverbia, G.W. Freytag (ed. and trans.), Bonn (1838–43) (includes text and translation).

Majma' al-amthāl, 4 vols, 2nd edn, Beirut (1987).

W. WALTHER

See also: proverbs

Maymūn ibn Qays *see* al-A'shā

Maẓhar, Adīb (1898–1928)

Lebanese poet, born into the al-Ma'lūf family. His early poems were traditional, but after he had discovered the French symbolist poets, especially Baudelaire, he began composing symbolist poems previously unknown in Arabic literature in the 1920s. His poem *Nashīd al-sukūn*, written under the influence of Baudelaire's *Correspondance*, is considered to be the first Arabic symbolist poem, employing various typically symbolist elements, particularly synaesthesia (i.e. the description of the perception of one sense modality in terms of another) and oxymoron. One of the central topics in his poetry is death, which he treated as a fascinating experience where the poet reveals a deep mystic desire for the 'soft, black claw of death'. Unlike other Arab symbolist poets, who concentrated on the element of music embodied in the single word, he was concerned less with polish and the choice of words than with conveying obliquely and symbolically a highly complex meaning, without losing the spontaneous nature of the experience and its relation to the depth of human anguish. Critics have argued that Maẓhar's contribution to the development of modern Arabic poetry has been overlooked. His small output and his early death (as well as the rise of other major Lebanese poets in the 1930s immediately after his death) have contributed to this neglect, and his experiments are still little known even in literary circles in the Arab world, compared to those of Saʿīd **ʿAql**.

Further reading

Aḥmad, Muḥammad Fattūḥ, *al-Ramz wa-al-ramziyya fī al-shiʿr al-muʿāṣir*, Cairo (1978), 192–6.

Jayyusi, S.K., *Trends and Movements in Modern Arabic Poetry*, Leiden (1977), 486–8.

R. SNIR

al-Māzinī *see* grammar and grammarians

al-Māzinī, Ibrāhīm ʿAbd al-Qādir (1890–1949)

Egyptian novelist, short-story writer, poet and critic. A significant figure in the development of modern Egyptian fiction, al-Māzinī was also, at different stages of his life, a teacher, journalist and translator.

Born into a relatively poor family, al-Māzinī attended teachers' college, where he met ʿAbd al-Raḥmān **Shukrī** who introduced him to a wide variety of Arabic and European literature. Al-Māzinī was much influenced, as was Shukrī, by the British Romantic poets and began to write and translate poems that reflected these readings. Throughout his career al-Māzinī was an inveterate borrower, both from his own works and those of others, and this led to charges of plagiarism.

During his early career as a teacher al-Māzinī and Shukrī joined ʿAbbās Maḥmūd **al-ʿAqqād** to share their interest in poetry and its criticism. Although the contacts between the poets were fruitful at first, Shukrī caused a split in the group by pointing out in print the nature of al-Māzinī's 'borrowings' in his poetry. In 1921 al-ʿAqqād and al-Māzinī published an important and iconoclastic work of criticism in two parts called *al-Dīwān*. The naming of the three poets as the '**Dīwān Group**' is the result of this publication, but, since al-Māzinī's savage attack on Shukrī in this publication led to the disintegration of the group, the label seems hardly appropriate.

By this time al-Māzinī had abandoned a teaching career in favour of journalism and translation. He began also to write short articles, vignettes and stories, in which his genius for character depiction and humour were given free rein. These works were gathered into several collections, of which the most famous are *Ṣundūq al-dunyā* (1929) and *Khuyūṭ al-ʿankabūt* (1935). Many of these tales show al-Māzinī's delight in absurd and farcical situations. In 'Ḥallāq al-qarya' a city-dweller holidaying in the countryside decides that he needs a shave; when the 'barber' arrives, it emerges that he is the local sheep-shearer. In 'al-Lugha al-ʿArabiyya bi-lā muʿallim' the narrator, astonished by the claims of a language-teaching manual he has bought for fun, decides to pose as a Maltese visitor and to tour Cairo using only the resources of the book. In 'Kayf aṣbaḥtu ʿifrītan min al-jinn', al-Māzinī exploits the fact that his own home was close to a graveyard to recount a tale of scaring a tomb-visitor out of his wits.

This talent for creating scenarios and filling them with a mischievous humour is also a distinctive feature of al-Māzinī's longer works of fiction. Most famous among them is *Ibrāhīm al-kātib* (1931), a novel that al-Māzinī began to serialize in 1925, then lost in part and reconstructed. This work, which won a prize for novel writing, was rightly regarded as a further major step in the development of the Arabic novel in Egypt after **Haykal**'s *Zaynab* (1913). While it shares with the earlier work a strong element of the autobiographical – reflected, in spite of the author's protests to the contrary, in the title – it differs from it in many other ways. The Egyptian countryside is no longer a stimulus for romantic reveries but now serves as the location for a rather supercilious picture of rustic values, where al-Māzinī's gift for characterization and vignette is much in evidence. The story tells the course of the narrator's love affairs, with three women: Marie, who nurses him through an illness, Shūshū, his cousin; and Laylā, who, though carrying his child, refuses to marry him once she learns of his affection for Shūshū. The novel concentrates more on individual scenes and character situations than on the development of a continuing dramatic plot, but, by providing a less idealized picture of Egyptian life and customs within a portrait of the life and loves of an Egyptian narrator, al-Māzinī clearly advanced the technique of the novel genre and set an example that was emulated by several other Egyptian writers during the 1930s.

Another novel, *Ibrāhīm al-thānī* (1943), returns to the same character, but this story of a married man and his infidelities lacks the interest and humour of the earlier work. More significant as contributions to the development of fictional genres are shorter works which show al-Māzinī's humorous talents to the full: *Thalāthat rijāl wa-mra'a* (1943), *Mīdū wa-shurakā'uhu* (1943) and *'Awd 'alā bad'* (1943). The first is concerned with attempts to woo Maḥāsin, the beautiful daughter of a tyrannical Circassian father. The second is a typically Māzinīan family farce, in which the author experiments to interesting effect with irony and the role of an interfering narrator. In the third work the narrator finds himself in a dream placed into a childhood role while still preserving the mentality of an adult; the resulting disjunctures allow al-Māzinī to use his penchant for humour to the fullest and to produce one of his most accomplished works of fiction.

Al-Māzinī's fiction is notable for the clear and uncluttered prose style in which it is couched. In the debate over the use of colloquial Arabic in dialogue, he chose not to follow the lead of Haykal who, in the limited amount of dialogue in *Zaynab*, had used colloquial Arabic. Al-Māzinī decided instead to adopt a form of the written language that managed to convey the spontaneity of speech while preserving the qualities of the written language. In this he was followed by one of his most noted admirers, Najīb **Maḥfūẓ**.

In the context of the development of Arabic fiction in Egypt, al-Māzinī's name is one that has receded into the background. At a crucial stage in that process, however, he made a major contribution to several aspects of fictional technique that provided a basis on which the next generation could build.

Text editions

Ibrahim the Writer, Magdi Wahba (trans.), Cairo (1976).

Al-Mazini's Egypt, William M. Hutchins (trans.), Washington (1983).

Further reading

Allen, Roger, *Modern Arabic Literature*, New York (1987), 214–19.

Badawi, M.M., 'Al-Māzinī the Novelist', *JAL* 4 (1973), 112–45.

——, *Critical Perspectives on Modern Arabic Poetry*, Cambridge (1975), 84–92, 105–9.

Brugman, J., *An Introduction to the History of Modern Arabic Literature in Egypt*, Leiden (1984), 138–47.

Jad, Ali B., *Form and Technique in the Egyptian Novel, 1912–71*, London (1983), 45–50, 88–9, 115–27.

Jayyusi, S.K., *Trends and Movements in Modern Arabic Poetry*, Leiden (1977), 152–63.

Kilpatrick, H., *The Modern Egyptian Novel: A Study in Social Criticism*, London (1974), 26–30.

Sakkut, H., *The Egyptian Novel and its Main Trends 1913–1952*, Cairo (1971), 22–7.

R. ALLEN

Mecca *see* Arabia; Hijaz

Medina *see* Arabia; Hijaz

metaphor

In poetry

A history of metaphor and its function in Arabic poetry (or literature in general) has not yet been written, and studies of metaphor in circumscribed corpora of texts, such as the *œuvre* of a particular poet, are few and far between. They are complemented by medieval theoretical and critical statements on *isti'āra* (see below).

In the imagery of pre-Islamic poetry (see ***Jāhiliyya***) there is a marked preponderance of similes, but metaphors do play an important role. Simple nominal substitution metaphors ('lion' for 'hero') are relatively rare, because ambiguity might arise; those that do exist are mostly commonplace and form a kind of poetic jargon. They are either based on worn-out similes like 'gazelle' for 'beautiful woman' or they are remnants of a former genitive metaphor like 'rope' for 'bond (of love)' from an original construct like 'rope of love'. Among the many other syntactic types of metaphors that exist in ancient poetry the most original and effective is the genitive metaphor, whether it be identifying ('the abyss of death') or attributive ('the claws of death'). This latter type in particular, where the metaphorical word often has no real equivalent (there is no part of death which could be compared with claws), attracted the attention of poetry experts rather early, and it was this type for which the later Arabic term for 'metaphor', *isti'āra* (lit. 'borrowing'), was originally coined. The vast majority of these 'borrowings' combine a concrete 'borrowed thing' ('claws') with an abstract new 'owner' ('death'). Death and fate are often and almost routinely personified in this way; the small poetic subgenre 'reviling fate' (*shatm al-dahr*) is rich in metaphors of this kind.

Jumping ahead to the 'modern' poetry of **'Abbāsid** times (see **ancients and moderns**), we find a considerable increase in the metaphorical 'jargon' especially in love poetry (see ***ghazal***) ('rose' for 'cheek', 'moringa branch' for '(upper) body', 'sand dunes' for 'buttocks'); however, contextual elements usually ensure correct understanding. More importantly, the 'loan' metaphor is still central to the poets' imagery and some recherché varieties develop, causing a major literary debate. These new and daring types were brought about by a different generating approach: while the ancient 'loan' metaphors were the result of an abbreviated analogy ('death takes hold of man' = 'predator sinks claws into victim' > 'death sinks claws in' and syntactic variations like 'claws of death'), the 'modern' poet often constructs such a metaphor by taking an existing figurative expression and moving, on the level of the analogue, to an adjacent element to incorporate it into his image ('his beauties lead the pupils towards him'; 'lead' being a weak metaphor from the realm of equitation, the poet moves to the adjacent element 'reins', which results in 'his beauties lead the reins of the pupils towards him' [Abū Nuwās]). The earliest interpretable occurrences of the term ***badī'*** (the 'novelty' of the 'modern' poets) refer to metaphors of this type; they may thus be considered central to the literary debate surrounding *badī'*. Apart from this type which, because of the intrusiveness of the new element, met some resistance in critical circles (see below), the poets also developed a type in which the new element was connected to the topic by way of simile, such as: 'the hills look at you with the eyes of the flowers' (where 'eyes' = 'flowers').

In theory

In early commentaries of ancient poetry, which normally deal with grammatical and lexical problems, one sometimes finds that non-literal usages such as metaphors are pointed out and labelled *mathal*, lit. 'likeness'. This very vague term (it also means, *inter alia*, 'proverb' and 'analogy') is soon replaced by several more precise terms. The one that comes closest to our notion of 'metaphor' is *isti'āra*, lit. 'borrowing'. It is, however, a specific type to which this name applies (see above). The poet **Labīd** wrote a famous line in which he said that the 'reins of the morning' were in the 'hand of the northwind' to indicate that the morning was cool and completely under the influence of the north wind. The early poetry experts considered that the poet had taken the 'hand' from a 'rider' and given it 'on loan' to the north wind (and similarly with the 'reins'). The borrowed element often has no equivalent in the topic (the 'hand' cannot really be compared to any part of the north wind) – the *isti'āra* is thus an imaginary ascription – but in other cases the borrowed element is metaphorically equated with an element of the topic. The transfer of the element into a new context is made possible by an underlying analogy between the old and the new context, but the early theorists show awareness of this fact only rarely.

Confronted with certain bolder varieties of 'loan' metaphors in 'Abbāsid 'modern' poetry, some critics became uneasy with the fact that the borrowed element was left dangling in the air, as it were, and they set up the requirement that it should be tied to the topic by an additional metaphorical equation based on a simile. Thus in the case of the 'eyes of the flowers with which the hills are looking' (see above) the 'eyes' are equated with the 'flowers' – an identifying genitive metaphor – while in the following, more dynamic example, 'the evening wind undoes the necklaces of the rainclouds', the 'necklaces' become metaphorically existent only when they become 'undone': the raindrops are being compared with pearls sliding from the string. This type in which the deep structure is a combination of an analogy (*tamthīl*) and a simile (*tashbīh*) is attested in a few examples already in ancient poetry, but becomes popular only in ʿAbbāsid times.

Metaphors that are derived from well-known simple similes (of the 'narcissus'-for-'eye' type) were for a long time not considered *istiʿāra*, but *tashbīh*, 'simile', even though the subject of comparison was not mentioned; the historical memory was sufficient to keep them in that category. Their recognition as *istiʿāra*, or the semantic extension of *istiʿāra* to cover such cases, was brought about (a) by the *tashbīh–tamthīl* combination metaphors just discussed and (b) the fact that, in Koranic studies, the term *istiʿāra* had a much wider field of application, namely any type of figurative usage (see **exegesis, Koranic**). Not surprisingly, **ʿAbd al-Qāhir al-Jurjānī** was instrumental in bringing about this change. He clearly distinguishes between metaphors based on simile and others based on analogy, but calls both of them *istiʿāra*. (In the case of a full-fledged sentence metaphor he also uses the term for analogy, *tamthīl*, which thus becomes ambiguous; to remove the ambiguity he sometimes calls it 'analogy in the way of metaphor', *al-tamthīl ʿalā ḥadd al-istiʿāra*.) Authors for whom the *istiʿāra* is first and foremost a one-word affair, mostly based on a simple simile (usually authors with a background of Koranic studies), tended to characterize the mechanism of the metaphor as 'the transference of a name/noun' (the name/noun 'lion' is transferred to a 'brave man'); others, more circumspect, considered that the entity to be transferred was the 'thing named' or the 'notion'. Al-Jurjānī after some wavering completely rejects the idea of 'transference' (*naql*) and replaces it by the notion that the metaphor is really a 'claim' (*daʿwā*) that the 'brave man' is a 'lion'.

Al-Sakkākī quotes an anonymous earlier authority as saying that metaphor is 'either making s.th. become s.th. else or making a thing belong to s.th. else'; this clearly refers to the simile metaphor and the 'loan' metaphor, respectively. But it is patently not one, but two definitions for two different entities. He himself prefers a unifying definition and for this purpose he uses the one-word simile-based metaphor as his unit of analysis. Thus the case of 'death sinking its claws in' consists of (a) a 'make-believe metaphor' (*istiʿāra takhyīliyya*), namely 'claws', so called because it makes one believe that there is a part of death that could be likened to the 'claws'; (b) a 'metaphor by allusion' (*istiʿāra bil-kināya*), i.e., 'death' which is actually no metaphor but alludes to the underlying 'predator' who is providing the 'claws'; and (c) a verb metaphor ('to sink in'). The unity of the image, which is safeguarded by the old idea of the 'loan' and likewise by the Jurjānian idea of the analogy-based metaphor, is now lost, but the analysis carries the day until modern times.

Further reading

Abu Deeb, Kamal, *Al-Jurjānī's Theory of Poetic Imagery*, Warminster (1979) (in particular 178–229).

Bonebakker, Seeger A., art. 'Istiʿāra', *EI*².

Heinrichs, Wolfhart, *The Hand of the Northwind: Opinions on Metaphor and the Early Meaning of Istiʿāra in Arabic Poetics*, Wiesbaden (1977).

——, '*Istiʿārah* and *badīʿ* and their terminological relationship in early Arabic literary criticism', *ZGAIW* (1984), 180–211.

——, 'Muslim b. al-Walīd und *badīʿ*', *Wagner Festschrift*, vol. 2, 211–45.

——, 'Paired metaphors in *muḥdath* poetry', in *Occasional Papers of the School of Abbasid Studies* 1 (1986), 1–22.

Jacobi, Renate, *Studien zur Poetik der altarabischen Qaṣide*, Wiesbaden (1971), 129–57.

Reinert, Benedikt, 'Probleme der vormongolischen arabisch-persischen Poesiegemeinschaft und ihr Reflex in der Poetik', in *Arabic Poetry, Theory and Development*, G.E. von Grunebaum (ed.), Wiesbaden (1973), 71–105.

Stetkevych, Suzanne P. *Abū Tammām and the Poetics of the ʿAbbāsid Age*, Leiden (1991) (see index under 'metaphor' and '*istiʿāra*').

W.P. HEINRICHS

See also: *badīʿ*; *majāz*

metonymy *see majāz*

metres, poetic *see* prosody

Miflāḥ, Muḥammad (1953–)

Algerian novelist and short-story writer, writing in Arabic. Miflāḥ studied law at the University of Oran and started publishing in national newspapers in 1973. To date, he has published two collections of short stories (*al-Sā'iq*, 1983, and *Asrār al-Madīna*, 1983) and some eight novels, including the prize-winning *al-Infijār* (1984) and *Humūm al-zaman al-fallāqī* (1986).

H. HILMY

Mihrajān

Mihrajān was the name of a festival celebrated among the pre-Islamic Zoroastrians of Persia, dedicated to the god Mir/Mithra and celebrated at the autumn equinox. In early Islam, and especially under the orientally influenced **'Abbāsid** caliphs, Mihrajān, like the New Year festival Nawrūz (see ***Nayrūz***), continued among the Muslims also as a festival, but shorn of its religious implications, substantially up to the Mongol invasions of the seventh/thirteenth century. Since its celebration was marked by present-giving, music and poetic declamation, there evolved a minor genre of poetry, the *Mihrajāniyyāt*, poems composed for and recited on these occasions; this was especially cultivated in Persian literature, but a number of examples in Arabic have also survived, including some attributed to the caliphs al-Ma'mūn and al-Mutawakkil.

Further reading

*EI*², art. 'Mihragān' (J. Calmard).

C.E. BOSWORTH

Mihyār al-Daylamī (d. 428/1036–7)

Mihyār ibn Marzuwayh (Marzūya) Abū al-Ḥusayn (or Ḥasan) al-Daylamī was a secretary and poet of the **Būyid** period. A Zoroastrian, in 394/1004 Mihyār was converted to Islam by **al-Sharīf al-Raḍī**, who educated him in both **Shī'ism** and in secretarial and poetic skills. Except for the little that can be gleaned from his ***dīwān***, information concerning his life and career is scant.

Mihyār wrote in all genres, including ***ghazal***, verse epistles to friends (*ikhwāniyyāt*) and ***rithā'***; his elegies on **'Alī ibn Abī Ṭālib** and al-Ḥusayn express his Shī'ī sentiments, while that on al-Sharīf al-Raḍī is considered his masterpiece. The bulk of his poems are panegyrics, often of extreme length; he also composed many brief **epigrams** and riddle-poems (see ***lughz***). Mihyār's style has been criticized as being artificial and derivative, and as marking the decline of Arabic poetry into imitative decadence. S. Sperl considers his poetry as representative of the 'mannerist' style; the length of his poems is attributed to his 'comprehensive style' which seeks 'to integrate all traditional topoi of court poetry into one poem' (1989, 48), his poems are doninated by metaphor, and he shows a predilection for the desert motifs of ancient poetry, reworked and defamiliarized in his own.

Text edition

Dīwān, Aḥmad Nasīm (ed.), 4 vols, Cairo (1925–31).

Further reading

Margoliouth, D.S., 'The poems of Mihyār the Dailemite', in *Oriental Studies in Honour of Cursetji Erachji Pavry*, London (1933), 286–92.

Mūsā, Muḥammad 'Alī, *Mihyār al-Daylamī*, Beirut (1961).

Sperl, Stefan, *Mannerism in Arabic Poetry: A Structural Analysis of Selected Texts*, Cambridge (1989), 1–6, 48–70 and *passim*.

J.S. MEISAMI

al-Mīkālī, Abū al-Faḍl *see* Abū al-Faḍl al-Mīkālī

Mimouni, Rachid (1945–95)

Algerian novelist and short–story writer, writing in French. Born in Boudouaou, Mimouni is one of the most widely read writers in the **Maghrib** today. His early novels published in Algeria, *Le Printemps n'en sera que plus beau* (1978), describing events during the war of independence, and *Une Paix à vivre* (1983), depicting life in Algeria after independence, have been overshadowed by his later masterpieces. In *Le Fleuve détourné* (1982), his first novel to be published in France, Mimouni's disenchantment with social and political conditions in Algeria can be detected, a disenchantment which becomes more intense in his next novel, *Tombéza* (1984). In *Une Peine à vivre* (1992), he probes into the mind of a despot, trying to understand the motivating force behind his ruthless actions. Mimouni frequently resorts to fables and legends in order to shed light on life in Algeria, as in his novel *L'Honneur de la tribu* (1989) and his collection of short stories

La Ceinture de l'Ogresse (1990), both translated into English.

Text editions

The Honour of the Tribe, London (1992).
The Ogre's Embrace, London (1993).

Further reading

Achour, C., *Anthologie de la littérature algérienne de langue française*, Paris (1990).
——, *Dictionnaire des oeuvres algériennes en langue française*, Paris (1991).
Bonn, C., *Anthologie de la littérature algérienne*, Paris (1990).

F. ABU-HAIDAR

Mīna, Ḥannā (1924–)

Syria's most prominent novelist, Mīna grew up in poor surroundings in the port city of Lattakia. He has worked in a variety of occupations, as stevedore, barber and journalist; he has been imprisoned for his political activities, and has spent time in exile. His earlier novels are works of social realism: *Al-Maṣābīḥ al-zurq* (1954), for example, traces the struggle against French colonial rule during World War 2, while in *Al-Shirā' wa-al-'āṣifa* (1966) the struggle is the same, but the backdrop is that of class conflict. In later works Mīna turns to a more symbolic analysis of class differences, as in *Al-Shams fī yawm ghā'im* (1973), and later to the autobiographical novel, as in *Baqāyā ṣuwar* (1974). The change from an over-obvious realism to a more subtle and refined vision is also reflected in Mīna's language; in his later works the use of style and symbol reveals the mastery of a writer who has now found a fruitful union between theme and medium.

Text editions

Fragments of Memory, L. Kenny and O. Kenny (trans), Austin (1993).
Sun on Cloudy Day, Bassam Frangieh and Clementina Brown (trans.), Colorado (1997).

Further reading

Allen, Roger, *The Arabic Novel*, 2nd edn, New York (1994).
'Hanna Minah' in *Encyclopedia of World Literature in the 20th Century*, vol. 5, New York (1993), 424–45.

R. ALLEN

mirabilia see *'aja'ib* literature

mi'rāj literature

The literature concerning the story of **Muḥammad's** ascension to heaven. Connected with Koranic allusions to the Prophet's *isrā'*, night journey, from 'the sacred place of worship to the farthest place' (Koran 17: 1), the story of the *mi'rāj* in various rescensions is elaborated in ***ḥadīth***, exegesis and other traditional literature. A common version tells that on the 27th of Rajab, in the tenth year of his prophecy, Muḥammad, sleeping in the mosque in Mecca, was suddenly taken by Gabriel to the farthest place of worship in Jerusalem. There Muḥammad conducted prayer in the presence of previous prophets. From the sacred rock in that mosque the ascent to heaven and closeness to God occurred on the prophet's noble steed, Burāq. Though popular in many circles and places, the *mi'rāj* story found particular favour with, and was most commented on by, the Ṣūfīs. For them, the framework story of *mi'rāj* signified the freeing of Muḥammad's soul from the dross of phenomenal existence and his attainment of closeness to God (*qurb*). Abū Yazīd al-Bisṭāmī (d. 234/848) introduced this conception of *mi'rāj* into Sufism, explicating *tawḥīd* through *mi'rāj*. Abū Yazīd's *mi'rāj* story appeared in several versions. Common to all of them was a stage-by-stage description of the *mi'rāj* as an expression of the stages of mystical experience. Because of his pivotal position in the history of Sufism, Abū Yazīd's mystical interpretation of the prophet's ascension was extremely influential on later Ṣūfī thought and literature. **Al-Ḥallāj**, **al-Junayd**, 'Aṭṭār, Shabistarī, **Najm al-Dīn Kubrā**, and Rūmī were but a few among the many who took up Abū Yazīd's teachings on *mi'rāj*.

Text editions

Ibn Ḥajar al-'Asqalānī, *The Isrā' and Mi'rāj: The Prophet's Night-Journey and Ascent to Heaven*, 'Abd Allāh Ḥajjāj (trans), London (1989) (compiled from *al-Fatḥ al-bārī*).
al-Qushayrī, *Kitāb al-Mi'rāj*, 'A.Ḥ. 'Abd al-Qādir (ed.), Cairo (1964).

Further reading

Abu Rabb, M., *The Life, Thought and Historical Importance of Abū Yazīd al-Bisṭāmī*, Dacca (1971).
Affifi, A.A., 'The story of the Prophet's ascent in Sufi thought and literature', *IC* 2 (1955).
Archer, J.C., *Mystical Elements in Muhammad*, New Haven (1924).

Bencheikh, J., *Le voyage nocturne de Mahomet*, Paris (1988).
*EI*², arts 'al-Isrā'', 'Mi'radj'.
Nicholson, R.A. 'An early Arabic version of the Mi'ráj of Abú Yazíd al-Bistámí', *Islamica* (1926), 402–15.
Schimmel, A., *And Muhammad is his Messenger*, Chapel Hill (1985), 158-75.
Widengren, Geo, *Muḥammad, the Apostle of God, and His Ascension*, Uppsala (1955).

R.L. NETTLER

Mirbad

Al-Mirbad is the name of a famous site outside **Basra**, originally a camel market (the word *mirbad* has been explained as 'enclosure for camels'), which served as a meeting-place for poets and orators, both **bedouin** and urban, declaiming their poems and speeches; a favourite haunt of philologists and grammarians studying Arabic from the horse's (or camel's) mouth. When people (including philologists and scholars of ***ḥadīth***) began to live at Mirbad itself, it developed into a suburb of Basra.

Further reading

Pellat, Charles, *Le Milieu baṣrien et la formation de Ǧâḥiẓ*, Paris (1953).
Scemama, O., 'Le rôle du Mirbad de Bassora dans le conservatisme poétique jusqu'au début du IIIe siècle', *IBLA* 20 (1957), 369–79.

G.J.H. VAN GELDER

Mirrors for Princes

A genre of Arabic prose writing (equally represented in many other Islamic literatures deriving from the Arabic) which purports to give advice (Ar. *naṣīḥa*, Pers. *andarz*, *pand*) to rulers, statesmen, governors and other officials on how they should comport themselves, i.e, what religious and ethical qualities should underpin their conduct, and on how best they can achieve their political or military or administrative aims; it thus corresponds to the similar genre of medieval European literature often referred to by its German name, *Fürstenspiegel*. Such works thus have a twofold intention: a practical one, the exercise of *Realpolitik* in public life, the approach in Renaissance Italian times of Machiavelli in his famous treatise *The Prince*, what in Arabic was called *siyāsa* or *tadbīr al-mulk*; and an ethical one, the making of this practice as far as possible conformable to the justice and righteousness that God requires of those of His creatures who happen to be entrusted with power over others. These two aspects appear in varying proportions in the Mirrors for Princes, while certain treatises are additionally of an Islamic homiletic nature, composed of popular religious tales (see ***Legends of the Prophets***), hagiography, proverbial sayings and aphorisms (*ḥikam*). A very wide conspectus of Islamic culture and thought is thus displayed in the Mirrors, so that they are revelatory of both ideal and practice in much of medieval Islamic life. A certain amount of information can be gleaned from them about Islamic administration, while those Mirrors that illustrate their narrative by a sprinkling of historical anecdotes, such as the relevant sections in **Ibn Qutayba's** Arabic *'Uyūn al-akhbār* and **Ibn 'Abd Rabbih**'s *al-'Iqd al-farīd*, and the **Saljūq** vizier Niẓām al-Mulk's Persian *Siyāsatnāma*, often supply direct historical information. Sometimes a counsel that seems theoretical or imprecise can be correlated with actual history; thus when the governor of **Khurasan** Ṭāhir Dhū al-Yamīnayn, in his letter of advice to his son (see below), warns him against letting a backlog of unfinished administrative chores pile up, we are reminded of a passage in **al-Ṭabarī**'s *History* in which the **'Abbāsid** caliph al-Hādī (169–70/785–6) is criticized by his minister for not receiving petitions or hearing complaints of his subjects for three whole days.

The genre is also important in that it constitutes a meeting-place for several contributing streams in Islamic ethics and ideas of statecraft, some of these streams being non-Islamic; it has, indeed, been said that the Mirrors reflect the convergence of Persian and Arabic heritages and traditions. The purely Arab–Islamic concept of power was that the caliph-Imām's authority derived from a sacred charge and was only legitimate when exercised in full conformity with the Islamic religious law or *sharī'a*, whose custodians were the *'ulamā'* or religious scholars. In later **Umayyad** and early 'Abbāsid times, however, Persian traditions of government, which hearkened back to the Sasanian emperors and beyond, were being incorporated into the purely Arabic fabric of the caliphate, the intermediaries here being largely the influential secretarial class [see **secretaries**]. These secretaries included many persons of Persian stock or cultural background whose educations had been moulded in the Persian imperial tradition of government, in which the emperor had a God-given power, manifested in the 'divine effulgence' (*farr*) around him, whose power over his subjects was unfettered by any earthly constraints and whose practical policies tended to give a significant role to opportunism and expediency. In this process of knowledge of the ancient Persian emperors and their attitudes to power coming into the Arab world, a key figure was the Persian secretary of the caliphs **Ibn al-Muqaffaʿ** and his translations from Middle Persian or Pahlavi into Arabic. As a result of his work and of other strands of information, the subsequent Mirrors for Princes are replete with anecdotes on the justice and firm government of rulers like Bahrām Chūbīn, Khusraw Anūshirvān and Khusraw Aparvīz (Parvīz) and of the wise minister Buzurjmihr, now held up as the ideal for Islamic viziers. Other influences on the Mirrors came from the Indian world in the shape of animal fables, those of Bidpay, appearing in Arabic as ***Kalīla wa-Dimna***, and from the ancient Greek and Hellenistic world, seen in the role ascribed to **Alexander the Great** as the exemplar, guided by his tutor **Aristotle**, of the wise ruler, and in the recommendation by Ṭāhir Dhū al-Yamīnayn, in his epistle to his son (see below), to practise the virtues of moderation and circumspection, the Aristotelian golden mean.

The earliest materials in Arabic classifiable as Mirrors are brief epistles (*rasā'il*), which feel their way towards the full development of the genre in complete treatises, or else they are component sections of larger ***adab*** collections. Ibn al-Muqaffaʿ's *Risāla fī al-ṣaḥāba* (*Epistle Concerning Courtiers*), from the earliest years of ʿAbbāsid rule, is more a topical political tract, drawing the ruler's attention to measures necessary to assure the stability of the régime, but his *al-Adab al-kabīr* is certainly a proto-Mirror, offering strictly practical advice, in the Persian *andarz* tradition and with no obvious Islamic religious component, to the ruler and his courtiers. The genre proper is undoubtedly reached in Ṭāhir's epistle addressed in 206/821 to his son ʿAbd Allāh when the latter was about to take up a provincial governorship. It is a sophisticated, theoretical exposition of the ethos of rulership and the qualities of the perfect ruler, tightly constructed and unadorned by historical examples or anecdotes, and emphasizes the ruler's dependence on God and on Islamic religion as the mainspring of all his doings. Preserved in a *History of Baghdad* by **Ibn Abī Ṭāhir Ṭayfūr**, its concision and terse style secured for it a contemporary fame, which lasted long enough for **Ibn Khaldūn** to include its text in his *Muqaddima* (*Prolegomena*) of five centuries later.

The *Kitāb al-tāj* (*Book of the Crown*), dedicated to a minister of the caliph al-Mutawakkil in the middle years of the third/ninth century and containing ethical and political counsels, is almost certainly wrongly attributed to **al-Jāḥiẓ**, but is nevertheless a rich source of information on the etiquette and court procedures of the Sasanian emperors; its very title is reminiscent of one of the Pahlavi works translated into Arabic by Ibn al-Muqaffaʿ (see above). Shortly after this, *Fürstenspiegel* material was incorporated in the lengthy *adab* works of Ibn Qutayba and Ibn ʿAbd Rabbih (see above), both of whom place an extended section on the *sulṭān* (meaning either the abstract idea of the goverment power or the person holding this) at the beginning of their books, dealing with the qualities and conduct of the ruler and how he should choose his courtiers and officials.

The genre was by now firmly established in Arabic literature and was treated by some of the major literary figures of the fifth/eleventh century (this century being also the one in which the two supreme Persian examples of the genre, Kay Kāvūs ibn Iskandar's *Qābūsnāma* and Niẓām al-Mulk's *Siyāsatnāma*, were written). The Shāfiʿī jurist from Iraq ʿAlī **al-Māwardī** wrote, as supplements to his classic work on public law the *Aḥkām al-sulṭāniyya*, two treatises on the duties of the vizier and on government, plus a Mirror with the specific title of *Naṣīḥat al-mulūk*, extant but so far unpublished. The philologist and littérateur of Nishapur ʿAbd al-Malik **al-Thaʿālibī** wrote a *Kitāb ādab al-mulūk al-Khwārazmshāhī* for a petty prince of Central Asia. The Mirror from this period that is best known, however, because of the attention paid to it by Western scholars, is that of the great theologian Abū Ḥāmid **al-Ghazzālī** (450–505/1058-1111), originally composed in Persian and given the general title of *Naṣīḥat al-mulūk*. It is divided into two parts. The first is strongly theologically oriented, giving an exposition of the Muslim creed and stressing the necessity of the ruler addressed (probably a Saljūq prince) being totally imbued with this faith; rulership is bestowed by God with no basis in human approbation, and the ruler will be fully accountable for his charge at the Last Judgement. All the illustrative examples here are from the history of the Prophet's career or early Islam. The second part is very different, in that it deals with the qualities of character, above all a sense of justice, required by monarchs, and is very much within the Persian ethical and political mould; the supporting anecdotes and sayings are drawn equally from Islamic history and from the Persian national tradition. It has, in fact, been surmised that this second part is by some unknown Persian author rather than by al-Ghazzālī. The whole work merits consideration here in that it was translated, apparently in the seventh/thirteenth century, into Arabic as *al-Tibr al-masbūk*, and this circulated widely, almost driving the Persian original out of circulation and forming the basis for subsequent Ottoman Turkish translations.

Various other Arabic Mirrors are known from times after this, some from the Muslim West like the *Sirāj al-mulūk* of Ibn Abī Randaqa **al-Ṭurṭushī** (d. 520/1126) or from the central Islamic lands like those of the **Ayyūbid** authors **Ibn Ẓafar** (d. 565/1169 or 568/1172–3) and **Sibṭ Ibn al-Jawzī** (d. 654/1257), all of a predominantly literary cast and well away from the Persian tradition.

Text editions

Bosworth, C.E., 'An early Arabic Mirror for Princes: Ṭāhir Dhū l-Yamīnain's epistle to his son 'Abdallāh (206/821)', *JNES* 29 (1970), 25–41.
pseudo-al-Jāhiẓ, *Le Livre de la couronne*, Ch. Pellat (trans.), Paris (1954).

Further reading

Bosworth, C.E., 'Administrative literature', in *CHALRLS*, 165–7.
Dawood, A.H., 'A comparative study of Arabic and Persian Mirrors from the second to the sixth century A.H.', unpublished PhD thesis, London (1965).
Lambton, A.K.S., 'Islamic Mirrors for Princes', *Quaderno dell'Accademia Nazionale dei Lincei* 160 (1971), 419–42.
Richter, G., *Studien zur Geschichte der älteren arabischen Fürstenspiegel*, Leipzig (1932).
Rosenthal, E.I.J., *Political Thought in Medieval Islam*, revised edn, Cambridge (1968), 67–83.

(C.E. BOSWORTH)

See also: Persia, culture and literature

al-Misaddī, 'Abd al-Salām (19??–)

Tunisian linguist and critic. Born in Sfax, al-Misaddī was educated at al-Zaytūna School, and graduated in language and literature from the Higher College of Education in Tunis. He taught in state schools before moving to teach at the Tunisian University, where he was the first holder of a state doctorate in Arabic language and literature. Combining a deep knowledge of the Arabic linguistic tradition with that of modern Western linguistics, he helped to generate an interest in linguistics and its application in the humanities (particularly literary criticism) not only in Tunisia but also in other parts of North Africa and the Arab world. Among his main works on linguistics and linguistic criticism are *al-Uslūbiyya wa-al-uslūb* (1977), *al-Tafkīr al-lisāni fī al-ḥaḍāra al-'Arabiyya* (1981), *Qirā'āt ma' al-Shābbī wa-al-Mutanabbī wa-al-Jāḥiz* (1984) and *al-Naqd wa-al-ḥadātha* (1983). His Arabic–French/French–Arabic dictionary, with its valuable introduction on terminology, was published in 1981.

Further reading

al-Zaydī, T., *Athar al-lisāniyyāt fī al-naqd al-'Arabī al-ḥadīth min khilāl ba'ḍ namādhijihi*, Tunis (1984).

A.-N. STAIF

Mis'ar ibn Muhalhil *see* Abū Dulaf Mis'ar ibn Muhalhil

Miskawayh (*c.*320–421/932–1030)

Abū 'Alī Aḥmad ibn Muḥammad Miskawayh was a philosopher and historian. A native of Iran, Miskawayh spent his early and middle age at the courts of the **Būyid** rulers of Iran and Iraq, and in the circles of their viziers: with **al-Muhallabī** (d. 352/963) at **Baghdad**, at **Rayy** as secretary and librarian of Abū al-Faḍl **Ibn al-'Amīd** (d. 360/970) and tutor of his son Abū al-Fatḥ (d. 366/976–7) whom he served, in turn, after his succession to office until his inglorious end. Entering the attendance of the *amīr* and king 'Aḍud al-Dawla, he accompanied him to Baghdad, but after his death in 372/983, and a period of changing fortunes, he returned to his native Iran (after 375/986). His position brought him into contact with many of the leading scholars and littérateurs of his time; his relationship with the *faylasūf al-udabā'*, Abū Ḥayyān

al-Tawḥīdī, whom he met in the *majlis* of the vizier Ibn Sa'dān (373–5/983–5), led to a remarkable exchange.

His literary activities as a critical historian and as a moral philosopher are closely connected. The very title of his historical work, the *Tajārib al-umam*, reflects a new paradigm: a lesson (*'ibra*) to be learnt from the 'Experiences of the Peoples'. While following the traditional chronicle of **al-Ṭabarī** in scope (starting with pre-Islamic Iran) and annalistic form, and drawing heavily on his predecessor's work for the earlier periods of Islam, he discarded the traditionist style, and for his own time recorded dynastic and local events as an acute observer and critic.

In his *œuvre* of philosophical ethics and of gnomical wisdom (***ḥikma***), Miskawayh sought to integrate the intellectual traditions united in classical Islamic civilization: Arabic 'logocentrism', Iranian wisdom and Greek rationalism. This integration is shown to be personified ideally in the universal learning of the vizier Ibn al-'Amīd (*Tajārib* ii.275–83) and the just rule of 'Aḍud al-Dawla, both of whom had made the fusion of Islamic and Iranian traditions their political programme, and it is further exemplified by Miskawayh in a gnomology of Arabic, Persian and Greek sayings and spiritual testaments under the Persian title *Jāwīdān khiradh* (*Perennial Wisdom*).

Against the practical wisdom of the gnomologia, the *Kitāb Tahdhīb al-akhlāq* (*The Refinement of Character*) is a systematic treatment of philosophic ethics: the autonomous ethics of the Platonic philosopher who finds in the encyclopaedia of the rational sciences the instruction for educating the parts of his soul toward purity and ultimate bliss, leading the sensual passions toward temperance, the emotions toward courage, and the faculty of reason toward wisdom. Though Aristotelian in many details of the moral categories (especially in the fourth part on *'adl*, 'justice', being the governing principle of the just mean), this philosophy is based on the Platonic view of the soul and its *a priori* knowledge. The immortality of the rational soul, along with the topics of divinity and prophecy, is also treated in a small monograph *al-Fawz al-aṣghar* (dedicated to 'Aḍud al-Dawla), using the traditional arguments of the Platonic and Neoplatonic tradition; the encyclopaedia of the sciences had been presented in an earlier piece going back to Alexandrian Aristotelianism, the *Tartīb al-sa'ādāt wa-manāzil al-'ulūm*, being the ideal curriculum for the 'Grades of Happiness'. The *Kitāb al-hawāmil wa-al-shawāmil*, giving Miskawayh's replies to questions submitted by Abū Ḥayyān al-Tawḥīdī (as also the *Maqāla fī māhiyyat al-'adl, On the Nature of Justice*), is an impressive example of the fertility of philosophic discourse in a time of change.

Text editions

The Eclipse of the 'Abbasid Caliphate (the latter part of the *Tajārib al-umam*), H.F. Amedroz and D.S. Margoliouth (eds and trans), Oxford (1920–21).

al-Fawz al-aṣghar, Cairo (1319/1901).

al-Ḥikma al-khālida, jāwīdān khirad, 'Abd al-Raḥmān Badawī (ed.), Cairo (1952).

Maqāla fī māhiyyat al-'adl, M.S. Khan (ed.), Leiden (1964).

The Refinement of Character, C.K. Zurayk (trans.), Beirut (1968).

Tahdhīb al-akhlāq, Q. Zurayq (ed.), Beirut (1966).

Tajārib al-umam (partial ed.), L. Caetani (ed.), Leiden (1907–17).

Tartīb al-sa'ādāt wa-manāzil al-'ulūm, 'Alī al-Ṭūbjī (ed.), Cairo (1917).

al-Tawḥīdī, Abū Ḥayyān, *Kitāb al-hawāmil wa-al-shawāmil*, A. Amīn and A. Ṣaqr (eds), Cairo (1951).

'Textes inédits de Miskawayh, édités et présentés', M. Arkoun (ed.), *AI* 5 (1963), 181–205.

Traité d'Éthique, M. Arkoun (trans), Damascus (1969).

Further reading

Arkoun, M., *Contribution à l'étude de l'humanisme arabe au IVe/Xe siècle: Miskawayh, philosophe et historien*, Paris (1970), 2nd edn. (1982).

——, 'Éthique et histoire d'après les *Tajārib al-umam*', in *Essais sur la pensée islamique*, 2nd edn, Paris (1984), 51–86.

Fakhry, M., *Ethical Theories in Islam*, Leiden (1991).

Khan, M.S., *Studies in Miskawayh's Contemporary History*, Chicago (1980) (pub. by University Microfilms International).

Kraemer, Joel, *Humanism in the Renaissance of Islam: The Cultural Revival during the Būyid Age*, Leiden (1986) (see index).

Walzer, R. 'Some aspects of Miskawaih's Tahdhīb al-akhlāq', *Greek into Arabic: Essays in Islamic Philosophy*, Oxford (1962), 220–35.

G. ENDRESS

Miskīn al-Dārimī (14–89/635–708)

Poet of the early **Umayyad** period who resided mainly in Iraq. Rabī'a ibn 'Āmir Miskīn ('the Poor'), a distinguished member of the Banū

Dārim, fought against the **Khārijīs** at Nahrawān in 43/663 and against the rebel al-Mukhtār in 66/685. He had personal relations with the caliph Muʿāwiya (41–60/661–80) whom he assisted by a poem in installing his son Yazīd as his successor (no. 17 edn Baghdad, 1970), and with Muʿāwiya's governor Ziyād ibn Abīhi. An ancient ***dīwān*** never seems to have existed; the collection of fragments edited in Baghdad in 1970 contains 55 pieces with 292 verses. The two satires included here are directed against ʿAbd al-Raḥmān, son of **Ḥassān ibn Thābit**, and as famous an adversary as the poet **al-Farazdaq**. In his poetry, Miskīn is notoriously inclined to coin maxims.

Text edition

Dīwān, K.I. al-ʿAṭiyya and ʿA. al-Jubūrī (eds), Baghdad (1970).

Further reading

al-Tilbānī, al-Sayyid ʿA., 'Il poeta omayyade Miskīn al-Dārimī', *AION* n.s. 29 (1979), 179–89.

T. SEIDENSTICKER

miṣrāʿ see prosody

al-Miṣrī, Ibrāhīm (1900–79)

Egyptian journalist, dramatist and prose writer. Al-Miṣrī's name is linked with the group of young Cairo writers and artists who in 1918 founded the 'New School of Arts and Literature' (*Madrasat al-funūn wa-al-ādāb al-jadīda*), the forerunner of the 'Modern School' (*al-Madrasa al-ḥadītha*). He published his first stories and articles in the reformist magazine ***al-Sufūr*** and the Modern School review ***al-Fajr***. In the 1930s he wrote essays on contemporary subjects, and in the 1940s and 1950s published many short stories in magazines and weeklies. He also wrote two plays for the theatre. His narrative work is marked by a social-realist, psychological and humorous approach, with a particular interest in women's questions.

Further reading

Brugman, J., *An Introduction to the History of Modern Arabic Literature in Egypt*, Leiden (1984), 248.
GAL(S), vol. 3, 279.
Khidr, A., *al-Qiṣṣa al-qaṣīra fī Miṣr*, Cairo (1966), 256–7.

E.C.M. DE MOOR

Morocco, modern

Modern Moroccan literature is characterized by its variety and linguistic diversity. Written in Arabic and French, it has also come to include published collections of Berber oral verse and narratives. As a French protectorate (1912–56), Morocco continued to produce literature in Arabic. The first works of fiction appeared in the 1920s. It was in the 1940s, however, that the Arabic novel and short story developed, reaching peaks of excellence in the 1960s and 1970s in the works of ʿAbd al-Karīm Ghallāb, Mubārak Rabīʿ and ʿAbd Allāh al-ʿIrwī. There were few Francophone works before 1949, when Ahmed **Sefrioui**'s collection of short stories, *Le Chapelet d'ambre*, appeared. Francophone novels, though fewer in number than their Arabic counterparts, have reached a wider audience, winning international acclaim for the writers Driss **Chraïbi** and Tahar **Ben Jelloun**. Poetry in Arabic has passed through several phases of development, and has come to include the prose poem and the revived Andalusian ***muwashshaḥ*** in its repertoire. The **free verse** movement, initiated in the late 1940s in the Arab East, was somewhat delayed in its appearance in Morocco by the *salafiyya* or traditionalist movement, one of whose champions was the political and literary figure ʿAllāl al-Fāsī. In 1952 Mohammed-Aziz Lahbabi, a bilingual writer, published his first collection of Francophone poetry, *Chants d'espérance*. This paved the way for a galaxy of Moroccan Francophone poets, such as Abdellatif **Laâbi**, founder of the periodical *Souffles* and its Arabic counterpart *Anfās* which, together with other literary periodicals, have given modern Moroccan literature an added impetus. Drama has been a popular art form in Morocco since the 1920s when the first theatre companies were formed. But it is thanks to the playwright al-Ṭayyib al-Ṣaddīqī, whose name has been synonymous with Moroccan theatre, that a theatrical tradition has been established. Al-Ṣaddīqī and Nabile Lahlou, some of whose plays have been written in French, have given Moroccan theatre both status and verve.

Text edition

Kaye, J., *Maghreb: New Writing from North Africa*, New York (1992).

Further reading

Farhat, A., *Aṣwāt thaqāfiyya min al-Maghrib al-ʿArabī*, Beirut (1984).

Gontard, M., *Violence du texte*, Paris (1981).
——, *Le Moi étrange: Littérature marocaine de langue française*, Paris (1993).
Mouzouni, L., *Le roman marocain de langue française*, Paris (1987).

F. ABU-HAIDAR

Moses ben Maimon *see* Maimonides

Moses ibn Ezra (*c.*1055–*c.*1135 CE)

Poet and critic in Granada and elsewhere. Born to a family of distinguished Jewish scholars and office-holders, Ibn Ezra studied Jewish religious law in Lucena; in Granada, he became the centre of a circle of Jewish intellectuals and poets and held public office with the title *ṣāḥib al-shurṭa* until the fall of al-Andalus to the Almoravids in 1090. When his brothers fled to Christian territory, he was left destitute in Granada. Eventually, he found his way to the Christian north, where he wrote ***qaṣīda***s to friends in al-Andalus complaining bitterly about his exile.

Ibn Ezra wrote several books in Arabic, two of which have been preserved: *Kitāb al-muḥāḍara wa-al-mudhākara*, on the history and practice of the Hebrew poetry of al-Andalus; and *Maqālat al-ḥadīqa fī maʿnā al-majāz wa-al-ḥaqīqa*, on the nature of figurative language and its use in the Bible. Both works reflect extensive knowledge of Arabic poetry and literary theory.

Ibn Ezra's secular Hebrew poetry, like that of his Andalusian Jewish contemporaries, derives its general principles and specific themes, images and techniques from Arabic. Ibn Ezra is the only one of the great Hebrew poets of al-Andalus to use the desert-camp motif in his *nasīb*s. His ***dīwān*** also contains a group of ***muwashshaḥāt*** with *kharja*s in both Arabic and Romance; in several cases, the Arabic *muwashshaḥāt* that served as his models have been identified. He displayed his mastery of the ***badīʿ*** style in his *Sefer haʿanaq*, a collection of short poems with *tajnīs* rhymes in ten chapters, covering ten common themes of Arabic poetry, such as love, wine-drinking, friendship and *zuhd*.

Text editions

Dīwān, vols 1–2, Ḥ. Brody (ed.), Berlin and Jerusalem (1939–41); vol. 3, Dan Pagis (ed.), Jerusalem (1977).
Selected Poems of Moses Ibn Ezra, Ḥ. Brody (ed.), S. Solis-Cohen (trans.), Philadelphia (1934).
Kitāb al-muḥāḍara wa-al-mudhākara, A.S. Halkin (ed. and trans.), Jerusalem (1975); Montserrat Abumalhan Mas (trans.), 2 vols, Madrid (1985–6).

Further reading

Fenton, Paul B., *Philosophie et exégèse dans le jardin de la métaphore de Moïse ibn ʿEzra*, Leiden (1997).
Pagis, Dan, *Shirat haḥol vetorat hashir lemoshe ibn ezra uvene doro*, Jerusalem (1970).

R.P. SCHEINDLIN

See also: Hebrew literature, relations with Arabic

al-Muʿallaqāt

Title of the most famous and celebrated anthology of pre-Islamic poetry. Among philologists, it was commonly known as 'the Seven Long Odes' (*al-Qaṣāʾid al-sabʿ al-ṭiwāl*). The name *Muʿallaqāt*, only one of several ornamental names applied to this collection (others being *al-Sumūṭ*, 'the strings of a necklace', or *al-Mudhahhabāt* 'the gilded ones'), is first attested in the *Jamhara* of **Abū Zayd al-Qurashī** (probably fourth/tenth century). Its meaning is doubtful (perhaps 'esteemed precious'). The often-told story according to which the poems were 'suspended' (*muʿallaqa*) in the Kaʿba in Mecca in pre-Islamic times is most certainly a later invention.

Efforts to assemble a canon of what could be considered the best pre-Islamic poems go back to **Umayyad** times. **Ḥammād al-Rāwiya** (d. *c.*155/772), who is generally considered to be the compiler of the 'Seven Odes', already seems to have drawn upon older collections. The poems selected for the *Muʿallaqāt* show a remarkable variety in style, content and structure, and in their poet's character and background, a fact that certainly contributed to the lasting fame of this anthology. There are, however, different traditions about which poems belong to the *Muʿallaqāt*. The most widespread tradition is represented by **Ibn al-Anbārī**'s (d. 328/940) commentary and contains the following poems:

1. **Imru' al-Qays** (metre: *ṭawīl*; rhyme: *-lī*; 82 lines), the most famous Arabic poem. Its structure does not fit conventional

categories; it starts with a *nasīb* (see ***qaṣīda***) which develops into a vivid portrayal of a series of erotic adventures in ***fakhr*** rather than in *nasīb* style. The second half of the poem is made up of the description of a horse in a hunting episode, and a concluding storm scene.

2. **Ṭarafa** (*ṭawīl*; *-lī*; 103 lines), the longest poem in the collection, a tripartite *qaṣīda*. Its *nasīb* is followed by a camel section consisting of the most famous and most detailed camel description in Arabic poetry. The poem ends with a *fakhr* in which the poet expresses his hedonistic *Weltanschauung*, saying that one has to grasp life's pleasures, such as wine and women, before death puts an end to it.
3. **Zuhayr** (*ṭawīl*; *-mī*; 59 lines), the shortest poem of the Seven, in principle a bipartite *qaṣīda* (*naṣīb* and *madīḥ*), but expanded by an epilogue of gnomical verses. Its central section is a panegyric on two men who had ended the War of Dāḥis (end of the sixth century) by making peace between the tribes 'Abs and Dhubyān. The poem's eirenic tone is in remarkable contrast to the prevailing martial character of ancient Arabic poetry.
4. **'Antara** (*kāmil*; *-mī*; 79 lines), a tripartite *qaṣīda* composed during the War of Dāḥis. It opens with a *nasīb* encompassing a variety of topics arranged in associative order. A camel description with a short ostrich episode links up to a *fakhr* in which 'Antara depicts himself in different combat scenes and treats several aspects of the ongoing war.
5. **'Amr ibn Kulthūm** (*kāmil*; *-īnā*; 94 lines), a bipartite *qaṣīda* which is probably the most magnificent example of tribal *fakhr* in Arabic literature. Its *nasīb* proper is preceded by a short wine scene and immediately linked to the poem's main theme, the glorification of the tribe Taghlib. 'Amr boasts about his tribe's prowess, boldness and ruthlessness in battle, its noble ancestors and its never-ending glory, and threatens the hostile tribe Bakr and the **Lakhmid** king 'Amr ibn Hind (554–70), swearing never to subject to him.
6. **al-Ḥārith ibn Ḥilliza** (*khafīf*; *-ā'ū*; 84 lines), a tripartite *qaṣīda* with only a short *nasīb* and an even shorter camel section. Its main part contains a refutation of accusations brought by the Taghlib against Bakr and praise of the latter tribe, recalling its glorious deeds of the past. The poem may owe its inclusion among the Seven Odes to the fact that the compiler felt the need for a counterbalance to the glorification of Taghlib in 'Amr's poem.
7. **Labīd** (*kāmil*; *-āmuhā*; 88 lines), a *qaṣīda* of an extraordinarily balanced structure. Its three main sections, all linked by transitional lines, are: a *nasīb*; a camel section consisting of both an onager and an oryx episode; and a mainly peaceful *fakhr* in which the poet emphasizes his own value to society on the one hand and the reliability of his tribe on the other. The poem's main theme, the struggle to overcome the pessimism caused by the transience of the world through reassurance of one's individual and social value, is perceptible in all its different parts.

A second tradition, which is represented in one of the two versions of the *Jamhara* of al-Qurashī, omits poems no. 5 and 6, and includes instead a poem by **al-A'shā** Maymūn (*basīṭ*; -lū; 64 lines), a *qaṣīda* consisting of a long and often quoted *nasīb* and a personal and tribal *fakhr*; and a poem by **al-Nābigha al-Dhubyānī** (*basīṭ*; *-dī*, *c.*50 lines), a tripartite laudatory *qaṣīda* with a long oryx episode in its camel section and a praise of the Lakhmid king al-Nu'mān ibn al-Mundhir (580–602). The grammarian al-Naḥḥās (d. 338/950) integrated both traditions and commented on all nine poems. Finally, **al-Khaṭīb al-Tibrīzī** (d. 502/1109) added the most famous poem by **'Abīd ibn al-Abraṣ** (irregular form of *basīṭ*; *-ūlū*; 48 lines) in order to yield a collection of ten poems.

Text editions

Abū Zayd al-Qurashī, *Jamharat ash'ār al-'Arab*, Muḥammad 'Alī al-Hāshimī (ed.), 2 vols, Damascus, 2nd edn (1986).

Fünf Mo'allaqāt, Th. Nöldeke (trans.), 3 vols, Vienna (1899–1901).

Ibn al-Anbārī, Abū Bakr Muḥammad, *Sharḥ al-qaṣā'id al-sab' al-ṭiwāl al-Jāhiliyyāt*, 'Abd al-Salām Muḥammad Hārūn, Cairo (1963).

al-Khaṭib al-Tibrīzī, *Sharḥ al-qaṣā'id al-'ashr*, Charles Lyall (ed.), Calcutta (1894).

al-Naḥḥās, Aḥmad ibn Muḥammad, *Sharḥ al-qaṣā'id al-tis' al-mashhūrāt*, Aḥmad al-Khaṭṭāb (ed.), 2 vols, Baghdad (1973).

The Seven Odes, Arberry, A.J. (trans.), London (1957).

(See also the entries for the individual poets mentioned.)

Further reading

Beeston, A.F.L., 'The Mu'allaqāt problem', in *CHALUP*, 111–13.
Kister, M.J., '*The Seven Odes*', *RSO* 44 (1970), 27–36.

T. BAUER

mu'ammā

(Lit. 'blinded, obscured'.) A form of riddle or puzzle. The term is often used indiscriminately as a synonym of ***lughz***. When a distinction is made, it is that in the latter the riddle is solved by correctly combining concepts and in the *mu'ammā* by combining the constituent letters of the word or name to be found. **Abū Nuwās** seems to have been the first to practise this form of riddle in his poetry, either as independent riddle poems or incorporated in other genres. Many examples from later periods may be found, although Ṭāshkubrīzāda remarks in his *Miftāḥ al-sa'āda* that this form of riddle is far more popular and more developed among the Persians. The term *mu'ammā* (or the verbal noun *ta'miya*) is also used for cryptography, secret writing or codes, on which the encyclopaedia by **al-Qalqashandī** has a chapter.

Further reading

Bosworth, C.E., 'The section on codes and their decipherment in Qalqashandī's *Ṣubḥ al-a'shā*', *JSS* 8 (1963), 17–33, rpt in his *Medieval Arabic Culture and Administration*, London (1982).
Wagner, Ewald, *Abū Nuwās, Eine Studie zur arabischen Literatur der frühen 'Abbāsidenzeit*, Wiesbaden (1965), 379–83.

G.J.H. VAN GELDER

See also: *lughz*

mu'āraḍa

(Lit. 'opposition, confrontation'.) In literature, the technical term for the imitation or emulation of a literary text, often with the dual purpose of honouring the model and trying to surpass it. In the case of poetry, metre and rhyme of the model – usually a well-known and admired poem – were adopted, as well as the subject matter. Unlike the ***naqā'iḍ***, such poems were not intended, or not primarily, as an attack on the poet of the model, although an agonistic element is rarely absent (cf. **poetic contests**). Sometimes the term *mu'āraḍa* is employed in the sense of *naqīḍa* and vice versa; the same technique and term may be found in the case of parodies of famous poems.

Occasionally found in pre- or early Islamic times, *mu'āraḍa* became increasingly common in **'Abbāsid** and later periods. An elaborate complex of *mu'āraḍa* poems is formed by the genre of ***badī'iyyāt***, lengthy poems in *basīṭ* metre, rhyming in *-mī*; the model, by **Ṣafī al-Dīn al-Ḥillī**, deriving its metre, rhyme, many rhyme-words and subject (praise of the Prophet **Muḥammad**) from the famous poem called *al-Burda* by **al-Būṣīrī**, which in turn shows the influence of a short poem by **Ibn al-Fāriḍ** and may perhaps be traced further back. In the early twentieth century, among neo-classical poets, it is still common; some fifty poems by Aḥmad **Shawqī** are modelled on poems from 'Abbāsid times.

Several people have been accused of attempting a *mu'āraḍa* of the **Koran**, which, the Koran being inimitable and unsurpassable, was deemed both impossible and blasphemous. Among the accused are **Ibn al-Muqaffa'**; **al-Mutanabbī**, who is said to have acquired his nickname, 'the would-be Prophet', from an episode in his younger years; and **Abū al-'Alā' al-Ma'arrī**, whose *al-Fuṣūl wa-al-ghāyāt* has been taken to be an emulation of the Koran.

Further reading

Peled, Mattitiahu, 'On the concept of literary influence in classical Arab criticism', *IOS* 11 (1991), 37–46 (esp. 43–6).
van Ess, J., 'Some fragments of the *mu'āraḍat al-Qur'ān* attributed to Ibn al-Muqaffa'', in 'Abbās Festschrift, 151–63.
——, *Theologie und Gesellschaft im 2, und 3, Jahrhundert Hidschra*, Berlin (1992), vol 2, 35–6 ('Die Parodie des Korans').
Wagner, Ewald, *Grundzüge der klassischen arabischen Dichtung*, Darmstadt (1987–8), vol. 1, 26, vol. 2, 34, 147–8.

G.J.H. VAN GELDER

al-Mu'ayyad fī al-Dīn al-Shīrāzī (*c.*390–470/*c.*1000–78)

Hibat Allāh ibn Mūsā al-Mu'ayyad fī al-Dīn al-Shīrāzī was an important **Ismā'īlī** missionary, author, poet and politician. A native of Shiraz, he was born into a Daylami Ismā'īlī family (his father was himself a *dā'ī*), and around 429/1037–8 entered the service of the **Būyid** prince Abū Kālījār al-Marzubān (r. 415–40/1024–48), whom he converted to

Fāṭimid Ismāʿīlism. His activities and influence made him unpopular in **Sunnī** quarters, as well as with the **ʿAbbāsids**; obliged to leave Persia in 438/1046, he made his way by a circuitous route to Fāṭimid **Cairo** where he arrived in 439/1047. It was not long before he secured the favour of the Fāṭimid caliph al-Mustanṣir (r. 427–87/1036–94), for whom he served as intermediary between the Fāṭimids and the Turkish general al-Basāsīrī in Iraq, who briefly occupied **Baghdad** in 450/1058 in the name of the Fāṭimids; his dealings with al-Basāsīrī are recounted in his autobiography (*Sīrat al-Mu'ayyad fī al-Dīn*). In that same year al-Mu'ayyad became chief missionary (*dāʿī al-duʿāt*), a post that he held, except for a brief intermission, almost up to the time of his death. In 454/1062 he was also appointed to head the Fāṭimid Dār al-ʿIlm, where he lectured to would-be missionaries. His thought and teachings are contained in his *Majālis*, each of whose eight volumes (still not fully published) contains one hundred lectures. Daftary describes these as 'the high watermark of Fāṭimid Ismāʿīlī thought' (1990, 214). They include al-Mu'ayyad's correspondence with the poet **Abū al-ʿAlā' al-Maʿarrī** on the subject of vegetarianism. R.A. Nicholson, who observed, 'Margoliouth [who published this correspondence] thinks that Maʿarrī cuts a poor figure in this correspondence. No doubt [al-Mu'ayyad] found his letters unsatisfying' (1969, 136), believed that al-Mu'ayyad sought a theological exegesis of al-Maʿarrī's vegetarianism. Al-Mu'ayyad also authored a number of treatises and a large poetic ***dīwān*** which still awaits critical study. On his death, al-Mu'ayyad was buried in the Dār al-ʿIlm, where he had taught for so many years; his funeral ceremonies were led by the caliph al-Mustanṣir himself.

Text editions

Dīwān, M.K. Ḥusayn (ed.), Cairo (1949).

Kraus, P., 'Beiträge zur islamischen Ketzergeschichte: Das Kitāb az-Zumurrud des Ibn ar-Rāwandī', *RSO* 14 (1933–4), 96–109 (inc. *majālis* 517–22, in refutation of Ibn al-Rāwandī).

al-Majālis al-Mu'ayyadiyya, Muṣṭafā Ghālib (ed.) (vols. 1 and 3), Beirut (1974–84); Ḥātim ibn Ibrāhīm al-Ḥamīdī (comp.), M. ʿAbd al-Qādir (ed.), Cairo (1975).

Margoliouth, D.S., 'Abū'l-ʿAlā' al-Maʿarrī's correspondence on vegetarianism', *JRAS* (1902), 289–332.

Mudhakkirāt, ʿĀrif Tāmir (ed.), Beirut (1983).

Sīrat al-Mu'ayyad fī al-Dīn Dāʿī al-Duʿāt, M. Kāmil Ḥusayn (ed.), Cairo (1949).

Further reading

Daftary, F., *The Ismāʿīlīs: Their History and Doctrines*, Cambridge (1990), esp. 213–15.

Nicholson, R.A., *Studies in Islamic Poetry*, rpt Cambridge (1969), esp. 134–6.

Poonawala, I.K., *Biobibliography of Ismāʿīlī Literature*, Malibu, CA (1977), 103–9.

I.R. NETTON/J.S. MEISAMI

mubālagha see rhetorical figures

Mubārak, ʿAlī (1823–93)

Egyptian historian, prose writer, educator and official. Born into an obscure family in the Delta, ʿAlī Mubārak rose to become Egypt's first native Minister of Education under ʿAbbās I, reaching the peak of his influence during the reign of Ismāʿīl, when he simultaneously headed the Ministries of Public Works, Education and Awqāf (Charitable Foundations). He founded both the Egyptian National Library (**Dār al-Kutub**) and the Egyptian Teachers' College (**Dār al-ʿUlūm**), now a branch of the University of Cairo.

Mubārak's most important literary effort was the encyclopaedic *al-Khiṭaṭ al-Tawfīqiyya* – a painstakingly catalogued description of all of Egypt's major cities, palaces, monuments, streets, mosques, canals, etc., that runs to twenty thick volumes. Although poorly organized, it is a factual goldmine for historians of nineteenth-century Egypt because of its comprehensiveness.

Mubārak also wrote a fascinating four-volume 'novel', *ʿAlam al-Dīn*, in which he traced the adventures of an Azhari *shaykh* (**al-Ṭahṭāwī?**), who goes abroad to learn of Europe's ways in the company of an English orientalist (Edward Lane?). *ʿAlam al-Dīn* may be considered the first modern Egyptian example of the *Erziehungsroman*; it is also the first modern Arabic literary work in which the action is advanced largely through dialogue – a distinction often mistakenly attributed to **al-Muwayliḥī**'s superior literary creation, *Ḥadīth ʿĪsā ibn Hishām*.

Further reading

Crabbs, J.A., *The Writing of History in Nineteenth-century Egypt*, Detroit (1984), 109–19.

Fliedner, S., *'Alī Mubārak und seine Ḫiṭaṭ* (Islamkundliche Untersuchungen, 140), Berlin (1990).

J. CRABBS

al-Mubarrad (*c.*210–85 or 286/*c.*815–98 or 899)

Abū al-'Abbās Muḥammad ibn Yazīd al-Mubarrad was a grammarian and philologist, and a leading authority of the 'school of **Basra**' in his time. Of Arab descent, he was born in Basra, where he was taught by al-Jarmī, al-Māzinī and Abū Ḥātim **al-Sijistānī**. According to **Yāqūt**, his nickname ought to be al-Mubarrid, but he is commonly known as al-Mubarrad. He moved to **Baghdad**, where he was involved in many disputes. The numerous anecdotes (not all of them of dealing with matters of grammar and philology) in which he plays a part are witness to his reputation. His great rival **Tha'lab**, representative of the 'school of **Kufa**', is said to have feared discussions with him. Some fifty titles are ascribed to him by the biographers. His main work on grammar is *al-Muqtaḍab*. More influential was *al-Kāmil*, which consists of a rather unordered collection of studies on grammar, lexicography, poetry (mainly by pre- or early Islamic poets, but also by the ***muḥdathūn***) and history; **Ibn Khaldūn** calls it one of the four classic works of ***adab***.

Text editions

al-Balāgha, Ramaḍān 'Abd al-Tawwāb (ed.), 2nd edn, Cairo (1985) (also ed. by Gustave von Grunebaum, as 'Al-Mubarrad's epistle on poetry and prose', *Orientalia* 10 (1941), 372–82).

al-Fāḍil, 'Abd al-'Azīz al-Maymanī (ed.), Cairo (1956).

al-Kāmil, William Wright (ed.), 2 vols, Leipzig (1874, 1892): al-Sayyid Shaḥāta and Muḥammad Abū al-Faḍl Ibrāhīm (eds.), 4 vols, Cairo (n.d.).

al-Muqtaḍab, Muḥammad 'Abd al-Khāliq 'Uḍayma (ed.), 4 vols, Cairo (1965–8).

al-Ta'āzī wa-al-marāthī, Muḥammad al-Dībājī (ed.), Damascus (1976).

Further reading

Bernards, M., *Changing Traditions: Al-Mubarrad's Refutation of Sībawayh and the Subsequent Reception of the* Kitāb, Leiden (1997).

Danecki, Janusz, 'Social functions of adab literature: the example of al-Mubarrad's al-Kāmil fī l-adab', in *Arabische Sprache und Literature im Wandel*, M. Fleischhammer (ed.), Halle (1979), 84–91.

G.J.H. VAN GELDER

al-Mubashshir ibn Fātik (fifth/eleventh century)

Abū al-Wafā' Mubashshir ibn Fātik, originally from **Damascus**, moved to **Egypt**, where in 440/1048 or 9 he composed his *Mukhtār al-ḥikam*, an anthology of sayings of the sages of antiquity which came to be highly influential as a source of both information and style. The biographies that accompany the sayings are almost entirely inaccurate, and the sayings themselves highly dubious, but the work represents an important aspect of Arabic literature, the recounting of 'words of wisdom'. It was frequently translated into European languages, and served as a source for Arabic writers ranging from **al-Shahrastānī** (d. 458/1153) right up to the circle of Mīr Dāmād.

Text editions

Bocados de Oro (medieval Spanish trans.), in *Mittelheilungen aus dem Escurial*, H. Knust (ed.), Tübingen (1879), 66–394.

Mukhtār al-ḥikam wa-maḥāsin al-kalim, 'Abd al-Raḥmān Badawī (ed.), (1958).

Further reading

Rosenthal, F., 'Al-Mubashshir ibn Fātik: prolegomena to an abortive edition', *Oriens* 13–14 (1960–1), 132–58.

O. LEAMAN

Muḍār see tribes

muḍāri' see prosody

al-Mufaḍḍal ibn Muḥammad al-Ḍabbī (d. after 163/780)

Philologist and anthologist. His exact date of birth (probably in the beginning of the second/eighth century in **Khurasan**) is unknown. He was an outstanding Arabic philologist who had a remarkable knowledge of ancient Arabic literature, so much so that he bore the honorary title of *rāwiya*. He was of Arab origin; his father was an authority on the events of the wars in Khurasan.

For most of his life al-Mufaḍḍal worked as a scholar, but around the year 145/762 he took part in a **Zaydī** uprising, led by Ibrāhīm ibn 'Abd Allāh, against the **'Abbāsid** caliph al-Manṣūr, during which he was captured by the caliph, pardoned through the intercession of his fellow tribesman Musayyab ibn Zuhayr, and finally released to become a teacher of the caliph-to-be, al-Mahdī. Later he settled in **Kufa** and worked as a philologist and teacher.

Al-Mufaḍḍal's main fields of specialization were *gharīb* (rare words and expressions in Arabic), grammar, genealogy and pre-Islamic Arab history. He set down his profound knowledge in a number of books on subjects such as Arabic proverbs, Arabic metres, the meaning of poetry, and a dictionary. His most important book, however, is the *Mufaḍḍaliyyāt*, one of the most significant collections of ancient Arabic poetry. His meticulous and precise method of transmitting Arabic poetry is illustrated in **Abū al-Faraj al-Iṣbahānī**'s *Kitāb al-Aghānī* through stories in which al-Mufaḍḍal criticizes his colleague, the famous collector of ancient Arabic poetry **Ḥammād al-Rāwiya**, whom he accuses of faulty transmissions and even of forgery.

Some of his outstanding pupils were his stepson, the famous philologist Muḥammad ibn Ziyād **(Ibn) al-Aʿrābī** (d. 230/845) and **Khalaf al-Aḥmar** (d. 180/796). It is not clear when al-Mufaḍḍal himself died, but all information indicates a date some years after 163/780.

Further reading

*EI*², s.v., for an extensive discussion with bibliography (I. Lichtenstädter).

Yāqūt, *Muʿjam al-udabāʾ*, Cairo (1980), vol. 19, 164–7.

G. BORG

See also: *al-Mufaḍḍalīyyāt*

al-Mufaḍḍalīyāt

The title of an anthology of ancient Arabic poetry attributed to the philologist **al-Mufaḍḍal al-Ḍabbī** (d. *c.*163/780 or a few years later). The original title of the work was *Kitāb al-Ikhtiyārāt* or *Kitāb al-Mukhtārāt* ('anthology' or 'choice collection'), but at an early date it was already named after its (main) compiler.

Regarding al-Mufaḍḍal's motive for compiling this collection, two different stories circulate. The first has it that Ibrāhīm ibn ʿAbd Allāh, a Shīʿī revolutionary and a poet, selected some 70 poems from a number of books in al-Mufaḍḍal's possession while he was in hiding with the latter from the caliph. Al-Mufaḍḍal states that after Ibrāhīm was eventually captured and killed, he himself added some poems of his own choice, until they numbered 128 in total, and edited them under his own name. In another story the **ʿAbbāsid** caliph al-Manṣūr heard his son al-Mahdī reciting a poem by the pre-Islamic poet al-Musayyab ibn ʿAlas while he was being tutored by al-Mufaḍḍal. This aroused the caliph's enthusiasm, and he asked al-Mufaḍḍal to compile an anthology of *muqillūn* (poets who composed only a small number of poems). This holds true for this work, because it only includes such poets. The reason for this choice may have been that the *muqillūn* were felt to be underrepresented in the major collections of poetry of that time.

Which one of these stories is true is subject to discussion, but the possibility cannot be ruled out that one event superseded the other, in that al-Mufaḍḍal used the selection made by Ibrāhīm but completed and edited it in definitive form at the caliph's wish. On the other hand, the second story is only too welcome as it disconnects the compilation of this important anthology from the **Zaydī** milieu. Also open to debate is the question of who added the poems to the original 70, al-Mufaḍḍal himself or his famous colleague and connoisseur of ancient Arabic poetry **al-Aṣmaʿī**, the compiler of a similar – and probably related – anthology, the *Aṣmaʿiyyāt*.

Five recensions of the *Mufaḍḍalīyāt* seem to have circulated, of which three have survived. The most reliable of these recensions – that of **al-Anbārī** on the authority of Abū ʿIkrima and **Ibn al-Aʿrābī**, who probably knew it directly from al-Mufaḍḍal – has been edited, and contains a total of 126 poems, to which another four have been added from other available manuscripts.

Within its limiting scope of *muqillūn* poets, the anthology offers a fairly representative image of the first two centuries of Arabic poetry as we know it now, although pre-Islamic poetry is a bit over-represented: 48 poets as against 20 who witnessed early Islam (i.e. 94 poems as against 32). It contains 61 polythematic odes (*qaṣāʾid*; see ***qaṣīda***) seven elegies (*marāthī*; see ***rithāʾ***) and 58 monothematic poems (*qiṭaʿ*; see ***qiṭʿa***). As to the order of the poems, no specific criterion seems to have been used, but as a whole the anthology reflects the spirit of pre-Islamic and early Islamic times: poets who conceive of themselves as heroes and as being led by the concept of virtuous manhood (*muruwwa*), although the change in society that Islam brought about is already echoed in verses expressing the acceptance of fate without submitting to it as the morale of pre-Islamic times would require.

Text editions

The Mufaḍḍaliyât, C.J. Lyall (ed.), Oxford (1918).
al-Mufaḍḍaliyyāt, A.A. Shākir and M.'A. Hārūn (eds), Cairo (1942), 3rd edn (1964).
Sharḥ al-Mufaḍḍaliyāt (with commentary of al-Tibrīzī). A.M. al-Bijāwī (ed.), Cairo (1977).

Further reading

al-Asad, Nāṣir al-Dīn, *Maṣādir al-shi'r al-Jāhilī*, 7th edn, Cairo (1988), 573–7.
*EI*², s.v., for an extensive discussion (R. Jacobi).

G. BORG

mufākhara see debate literature; poetic contests

Mughulṭā'ī (*c.*690–762/1291–1361)

'Alā' al-Dīn Abū 'Abd Allāh ibn Qilīj al-Bakjarī Mughulṭa'ī taught and wrote about ***ḥadīth*** and Ḥanafī law; although he was probably of Turkish descent, he wrote in Arabic. *Al-Zahr al-bāsim fī sīrat Abī al-Qāsim* is a biography of the Prophet drafted in response to al-Suhaylī's *Rawḍ al-unuf* (a commentary on **Ibn Hishām**'s life of the Prophet). Mughulṭā'ī is best known for his specialized biographical dictionary *al-Wāḍiḥ al-mubīn fī man ustushhida min al-muḥibbīn* (*The Clear and Eloquent in Speaking of Those Lovers Who Became Martyrs*), in which he argued for the soundness of certain *ḥadīth*s which asserted that those who died of a chaste love died as martyrs. However, manuscripts of this work were withdrawn from market because of an allegedly unflattering anecdote about 'Ā'isha.

Text editions

Spies, O., 'Al-Mughulta'i's Spezialwerk uber "Martyrer der Lieve"', in *Studien zur Geschichte und Kultur des nähen and fernen Ostens*, W. Heffening and W. Kirfel (eds), Leiden (1935), 145–55.
al-Wāḍiḥ al-mubīn fī man ustushhidā min al-muḥibbīn, O. Spies (ed.), vol. 1, (all published), Stuttgart (1936).

Further reading

Giffen, L.A., *Theory of Profane Love among the Arabs: The Development of the Genre*, New York (1971), 33–4, 80 and see index, s.v.

R. IRWIN

muhājāt see hijā'

al-Muhalhil ibn Rabī'a (fifth century)

'Adī ibn Rabī'a, called al-Muhalhil, 'he who weaves finely (poetry)', is one of the oldest known Arab poets. He must have lived at the end of the fifth century, and is credited with many poetic innovations. So it is reported that he was the first to compose a ***qaṣīda*** and to have told 'lies' in his poetry. He figures prominently in the saga about the war between the two sister-tribes Bakr and Taghlib, called the 'War of Basūs'. Kulayb, the tyrannic leader of the Taghlib, whose murder led to the war's outbreak, is said to have been al-Muhalhil's brother. After Kulayb was killed, al-Muhalhil composed elegies mourning his death and inciting his people to take revenge. These elegies constitute the main part of his remaining poems. Although the authenticity of many poems ascribed to him is more than doubtful, one can find some good examples of ancient Arabic heroic and elegiac style among them.

Further reading

Cheikho, L., *Kitāb shu'arā' al-Naṣrāniyya*, Beirut (1890), vol. 1, 151–81 (biography and poetic fragments).
Ḥusayn, Ṭāhā, *Fī al-adab al-Jāhilī*, Cairo (1927), 266–75.
Stetkevych, S.P., 'Ritual and sacrificial elements in the poetry of blood-vengeance: two poems by Durayd ibn al-Ṣimmah and al-Muhalhil ibn Rabī'a', *JNES* 45 (1986), 31–43.

T. BAUER

al-Muhallabī, al-Ḥasan ibn Muḥammad (291–352/903–63)

Abū Muḥammad al-Ḥasan ibn Muḥammad al-Muhallabī a former vizier of the **Būyids** of Iraq, was a descendant of the aristocratic Arab Muhallabid family of **Basra** and a leading literary figure of his age. He comanded armies and directed the *amīr* Mu'izz al-Dawla's ***dīwān*** in **Baghdad,** but also gathered round himself a brilliant literary circle which was frequented by such luminaries as the *qāḍī* Abū al-Qāsim al-Tanūkhī, father of the author al-Muḥassin **al-Tanūkhī**, the poet **Ibn al-Ḥajjāj**, the anthologist **Abū al-Faraj al-Iṣbahānī** and the stylist and historian Abū Isḥāq Ibrāhīm ibn

Hilāl **al-Ṣābi'** and by the later members of the poetic family of the Banū al-**Munajjim**. He himself was a fine literary stylist, as seen in his epistles and official decrees, and a poet, to whom a literary biographer like **al-Tha'ālibī** devoted a special section in his *Yatīmat al-dahr*.

Further reading

*EI*², s.v. (K.V. Zetterstéen–C.E. Bosworth).
Kraemer, Joel L, *Humanism in the Renaissance of Islam: The Cultural Revival During the Buyid Age*, Leiden (1986), 16, 54–5.

C.E. BOSWORTH

Muḥammad, the Prophet (d. 11/632)

As the Prophet of Islam, Muḥammad was a subject of intense interest in Arabic literature from early Islamic times, and is no less so today. The story of his life provided the background and context for much of what was said in the **Koran**, and described the triumph of the faith in its Arabian homeland. Records of his sayings, deeds, and reactions to various situations came to provide normative models for personal conduct, authoritative precedents in matters of law, and illustrative materials for interpretation of scripture.

Clearly, then, the literature that arose around the persona of Muḥammad was, from the beginning, inspired by the fervour and vitality of a world faith and culture in the making. Materials about the Prophet were subject to numerous and conflicting social, political, and religious influences, and the record produced by this dynamic must be seen not so much as documenting the history of Muḥammad's life as recording Islamic society's continuing effort to interpret his example in response to new developments and challenges. The literature on the Prophet thus represents an invaluable corpus attesting to Muslims' changing perceptions of the founder of their faith, as well as to the evolution of the literary and dialectical tools through which these views found expression.

Arabic literature is thoroughly permeated by the subject of Muḥammad, and it is only in the technical and scientific literature that he appears but rarely or not at all. Here only the specific topic of the development of his biography can be considered, but the materials and processes involved were also crucial to the ways in which he was perceived in other genres.

Any but the most extreme critique of the sources will allow for the conclusion that the impact of Muḥammad's prophetic career was already considerable in his own lifetime. It is not clear that his followers focused their immediate attention on him personally, as opposed to his teachings, but certainly it was in Medina, the base for his religious and political success in the wake of the Hijra (his move from Mecca), that systematic interest was first and most vigorously expressed in early **Umayyad** times. While some modern scholarship sees the earliest materials as largely factual, only reshaped later as an idealized image of Muḥammad emerged, it is now becoming clear that right from the beginning there was considerable variety in the information becoming available. On the one hand, there was a certain degree of written documentation in circulation, most particularly the so-called 'Constitution of Medina' and numerous letters of the Prophet, for some of which convincing cases for authenticity have recently been advanced. Individuals and tribes who had participated in important events were anxious to preserve the memory of their roles, and one frequently encounters reports that relate perfectly mundane and inconsequential matters or portray Muḥammad and others as acting precisely as one, on the basis of other evidence, would expect to find in traditional tribal **Arabia**. On the other hand, however, events revolving around the Prophet also attracted the attention of fanciful storytellers (*quṣṣāṣ*), poets interested in dramatic or didactic details, and propagandists seeking to defend him from critics or promote his religious credentials.

Accounts relating his life and teachings quickly became the venue for further tendentious arguments at a secondary level. Individuals and families vied to include the names of their ancestors in important events, as this would increase their own status as their descendants. Tribes were sensitive over their record of acceptance or hostility to Islam, and the descendants of the Muhājirūn and Anṣār used accounts to dispute the relative importance of themselves, Mecca, and Medina. Quite fantastic elements also came into circulation, such as miracle stories (some based on New Testament models) and poems attributed to unseen apparitions, to demons, or to Satan.

The impact of reshaping and invention was especially important in four areas. One was the reverberation of later political tensions in the materials on Muḥammad, in the form of accounts altered or invented to argue positions for or against Abū Bakr, ʿUmar, ʿUthmān (see **Orthodox Caliphs**), **ʿAlī ibn Abī Ṭālib** and his family, the **Umayyads**, and the **ʿAbbāsids**. A pro-ʿAlid tradition on the battle of Uḥud, for example, lists Abū Bakr, ʿUmar, and ʿUthmān among those who deserted at a decisive moment, but insists that ʿAlī stood firm at the Prophet's side. In extreme cases not just details, but even an entire event, could be introduced: the tradition for the expedition to Turaba, for example, appears to be a complete fiction created in order to provide the caliph ʿUmar ibn al-Khaṭṭāb with the honour of having led at least one expedition on the Prophet's behalf, since several had been led by ʿAlī. Another problematic area was that of arguments over matters of religious doctrine and practice. As new issues and problems arose in later times that could never have been of much concern to the early Muslim community in Medina, proponents of the various positions on such matters promoted their views by recasting or inventing accounts to show that Muḥammad had also held their particular interpretation. As a result, one routinely finds contradictory accounts in which Muḥammad upholds diametrically opposed positions on one and the same question or addresses different stages of a debate that in reality must have taken a very long time to develop.

Third, there was the problem of the relation of the *sīra* (biography of the Prophet) to the Koran. While it has traditionally been thought that much of the *sīra* represents efforts to provide *asbāb al-nuzūl* ('occasions of revelation') and other exegesis for obscure Koranic passages, recent research shows that in fact the *asbāb al-nuzūl* traditions only became such at a secondary stage, and that earlier they had no connection with the Koranic verses to which they were eventually linked. Efforts to bring *sīra* and Koran together in some systematic way thus involved the reshaping of much material in the former. Finally, there was the area of 'clarification of ambiguity' (*taʿyīn al-mubham*). With the increasing sophistication of Islamic society, audiences demanded ever clearer and more articulate responses to the questions they put to the literary tradition on the Prophet. Reports that provided such details thus appeared to be more informative than, and superior to, others; the result was the arbitrary accretion of much new detail into the tradition, even on completely trivial matters such as the colour of an animal or the name of a weapon.

These trends were paralleled by, and closely related to, two other developments: the transmission and differentiation of materials into specific genres and the rise of tools for the critical assessment of accounts. There has been much discussion in modern scholarship about the terminology applied to differing kinds of material concerning the Prophet, based on the assumed centrality of such terminological considerations to assessment of the origins and development of the materials themselves. While this assumption is not entirely unfounded, it must be borne in mind that specialized terminology usually emerges in a situation in which previously undifferentiated materials are being regarded and used in new and more sophisticated ways and therefore need to be referred to more precisely. One finds this paradigm in every branch of medieval Islamic scholarship: it is therefore difficult to credit the notion that from the very beginning there were already meaningful categories (much less genres) of *sīra*, ***ḥadīth***, and so forth.

The generality of materials on the Prophet seem at first to have been called *sīra*, in the sense of 'way of life'. This consisted of short narratives called *akhbār* ('items of information') or *ḥadīth* ('discussion') that dealt with specific topics, which were usually transmitted orally through family connections or from teacher to student. Reports on the same or on related subjects gradually came to be transmitted together; lists were compiled (e.g. of participants, casualties, or prisoners in various battles, expeditions, and other events); and by the late 1st/7th century a framework for the biography of the Prophet had been established. Though this may not have been the case from the beginning, the main benchmark was identified as the Hijra, and as in the study of the revelation of the Koran, which in many cases was being investigated by the same scholars, the Prophet's career was divided (perhaps arbitrarily) into Meccan and Medinan periods of identical or similar lengths. Events before and after the Hijra were then arranged according to a relative chronology, though demands for greater precision quickly resulted in exact dating, often to the day.

Materials organized within this framework were often profoundly kerygmatic; efforts were made, for example, to show that Muḥammad's mission had been predicted in the Bible and by various Arabian figures, and to demonstrate that God had specifically prepared him for prophethood and vouchsafed his mission from error. With the forthcoming conquests in mind, Arabia was presented retrospectively as a barren land from which the Arabs would be delivered as reward for their faith (see ***futūḥ***). Accounts of the Prophet's campaigns stressed the element of divine guidance and support, e.g. by deploying the Old Testament motif of the few defeating a mighty host by the will and command of God.

The prominence of these and similar issues, as well as the other tendentious trends discussed above and the general proliferation of new material, made it important to know where reports came from and on what authority; hence the stress on oral transmission. But from early on there was also an element of written tradition, and this gradually assumed greater importance. Teachers and collectors often kept written records of their materials, and students likewise took notes, often in detail. But though references in the sources speak frequently of a 'sheet' (*ṣaḥīfa*) or 'book' (*kitāb*), it is difficult to determine exactly what is intended unless the work in question has survived; a *ṣaḥīfa* can amount to hundreds of pages in a modern printed edition, while a *kitāb* can prove to be a set of notes without a coherent beginning or end and clearly never intended for general circulation.

That critical considerations were not lost sight of in this process can be seen in the fact that the discrete reports from which such collections were constructed nevertheless retained their individual identity. In particular, this identity was specifically asserted by attaching to a report the *isnād*, or chain of authorities, through whom it had been transmitted. Much controversy surrounds the use of the *isnād*, which could of course be falsified or altered as easily as the subject matter of a report. It has long been argued that 'weak' *isnād*s (e.g. stopping short of the time of the Prophet, or betraying gaps or anomalies of various kinds) are in fact the earlier ones, and that these were perfected and extended back to the Prophet later; recent research has called this theory into question, however, and Jewish models for citation of authorities would in any case have suggested a rigorous *isnād* form fairly early on.

The second/eighth century witnessed two developments that were decisive for the study of the life of Muḥammad. First, this study gradually divided into two perspectives that assumed specific identities as separate genres: *sīra* and *ḥadīth*. The reasons for this division appear to have been based on criticial methods and subject interests. Some compilers and collectors sought to assemble materials revolving around the persona of the Prophet himself; these collections came to be known as *sīra*, sharpening the old general sense of the word into the specific meaning of the 'life of the Prophet'. In such compilations the various reports were arranged according to the pre-Islamic, Meccan, and Medinan periods of Muḥammad's life, or, where this was not feasible, into topical categories (e.g. his merits, wives, letters, delegations received, etc.). As attention focused more sharply on content and on the conclusions that might be reached by comparing one report with another, there emerged a trend towards the combination of reports into larger more comprehensive ones; their contents were thereby amalgamated and synthesized and their authorities were listed together in a collective *isnād*.

While this was clearly an important step toward continuous historical narrative, it was opposed by other scholars on critical grounds. These authorities attached greater importance to the specific contents of individual accounts, studied them for their relevance to matters of doctrine and religious law, and compiled them into collections that came to be known as *ḥadīth*. In these compilations, traditions were listed separately in chapters devoted to such topics as ritual purity, marriage, divorce, *jihād*, fasting, and prayer; these were often exactly the same rubrics used in compilations of law, and illustrate the close relation between the two fields. Other collections emerging at the same time or slightly later adopted an arrangement according to the name of the earliest transmitter. As this shows, *ḥadīth* placed greater stress on criticism of *isnād*s than *sīra* did; use of the collective *isnād* was especially deplored, as it obscured the attested transmission of the original accounts from which the collective report had been compiled. It must not be thought, however, that *sīra* and *ḥadīth* collections were essentially different in the materials they contained: the same reports often appeared in both genres, and the scholars named as transmitters in them were largely identical. To the extent that their contents did differ, this was because savants of *ḥadīth* insisted on a more rigorous method of selection based on *isnād* criticism; weakly attested traditions that didactic considerations might allow into a *sīra* work would not appear in a *ḥadīth* collection, and such material as poetry and the fanciful lore of the storyteller, which often appeared in *sīra*, was almost completely expunged from *ḥadīth*. Miracle stories too were severely proscribed; though collected in abundance in various *sīra* works, they are rare in *ḥadīth*.

The second decisive trend, already implicit in the first, was the emergence in the second/eighth century of written compilations specifically intended for general circulation as the work of a specific collector or compiler. The first of these may have been the *sīra*, also known as *Mashāhid al-nabī* ('Events Witnessed by the Prophet'), by the famous Medinan scholar **al-Zuhrī** (d. 124/742). To a large extent, these works consisted of detailed sets of teachers' or students' notes, revised and edited by the student. A good illustration of how this process worked is available in the example of **Ibn Isḥāq** (d. 150/767). Of the many written versions of his materials transmitted by his students, one recension, that of the Kufan scholar al-Bakkā'ī (d. 183/799), was quoted by numerous later scholars; once it had been further edited by **Ibn Hishām** (d. 218/833), it became an authoritative interpretation of Muḥammad's life.

Several aspects of this mode of publication and circulation bear special emphasis. First, it created a certain degree of ambiguity and confusion as to who did or did not write certain books on a given subject; it is both asserted and denied, for example, that 'Urwa ibn al-Zubayr (d. 94/712) wrote a *Sīra* or *Maghāzī* book. This scholar is almost certainly too early to have done so; but it is perfectly feasible that lecture notes of his were handed down and edited in some form later on. Second, with this means of transmission it is difficult to identify an 'original' form of a book, since over a long career a teacher may have changed or augmented his materials significantly, leaving numerous students handing down different versions or parts of his work reflecting their own interests. One such version (as in the case of Ibn Hishām's recension of Ibn Isḥāq) could gain authoritative status in later times; but one cannot conclude from this that the text underlying it was what the original compiler wished to be regarded as his authoritative word on the subject. Third, for some early compilations it is possible that the stage of lecture notes passed directly to that of incorporation into another authority's book, i.e. without achievement of independent status in the interim. Certainly a student's redaction often served to deny the teacher's work any further independent identity. The *Kitāb al-Ṭabaqāt* by **al-Wāqidī** (d. 207/823), for example, began with an ambitious collection of traditions on the Prophet, but the whole work was quickly superseded by the redaction of his student and secretary **Ibn Sa'd** (d. 230/854). Finally, early *sīra* collections could also surface in the domain of *ḥadīth*. The materials of al-Zuhrī, for example, were selectively collected and redacted by his student Ma'mar ibn Rāshid (d. 154/770), whose compilation was in turn incorporated into a *ḥadīth* compendium, the *Muṣannaf* of al-San'ānī (d. 211/827), in a chapter on the Prophet's military campaigns.

The third/ninth century marked the definitive emergence of the classical interpretations of the life of Muḥammad and the appearance of definite sub-genres, which arose from the earlier trend for students to collect only those parts of a master's teaching that interested them. The range of special topics studied was very broad, and included such subjects as the Prophet's birth, maternal genealogy, call to be a prophet (*mab'ath*), wives, children, names, appearance, habits, the night journey (*isrā'*) and ascent to heaven (***mī'rāj***), and the events following his death.

Several of these sub-genres were particularly important. One was *maghāzī* ('military expeditions'), a term which had earlier been commonly used *pars pro toto* for several *sīra* collections but which eventually developed an identity of its own. The most important such collection was al-Wāqidī's *Kitāb al-Maghāzī* ('Book of Military Expeditions'); frequently pursued by others who followed him, the topic comprised a link to the study of the Arab conquests after Muḥammad's death. Other important sub-genres were those of *shamā'il* ('merits'), *khaṣā'is* ('special characteristics'), and *dalā'il al-nubuwwa* ('proofs of prophecy'). Though traditions along these lines were in circulation in the Umayyad period, and at that time comprised part of the salvation history with which the biography of Muḥammad was so intensely concerned, by the 'Abbāsid period this material had developed into specific sub-genres, to a large extent aimed at addressing criticisms of Muḥammad and Islam by non-Muslims, especially Christians. A work entitled *A'lām al-nubuwwa* (*Signs of Prophecy*) is attributed to the caliph al-Ma'mūn (r. 198–218/814–33); the first extant work, **al-Jāḥiẓ**'s (d. 255/868) *Ḥujaj al-nubuwwa* (*Proofs of Prophecy*), is an explicit response to Christian criticisms.

Many of these works, particularly those produced in later medieval times, were devotional texts for general use rather than works of formal scholarship. It was a matter of pious merit, for example, to be able to recite from memory a long poem on the names of those who fought at Badr. But the importance of the later *sīra* tradition, generally underappreciated in modern scholarship, bears special emphasis. *sīra* commentaries, though overall comprising a tradition far more limited than what one finds in law, Koranic exegesis, or *ḥadīth*, were individually often of astonishing magnitude and erudition. The commentary by al-Suhaylī (d. 581/1185) on Ibn Hishām inspired two supercommentaries of particular importance. That of **Mughulṭā'ī** (d. 762/1361) was a polemic against al-Suhaylī, but assembled a vast range of material, some very early, over which the author displays considerable talents as a textual and historical critic. The supercommentary of al-Bilbaysī (d. 937/1531) was more generous in outlook, but was even more ambitious than that of Mughulṭā'ī. Again, a vast range of materials is adduced and critiqued, and to judge from the extant first volume the complete work (assuming it was finished) must have consumed nearly 2,000 folios. Much the same applies to some of the very specialized *sīra* works of later medieval Islam. The work of Ibn Nāṣir al-Dīn (d. 742/1341) on the Prophet's birth and birthday festival (*mawlid*), for example, runs to hundreds of folios and again preserves a wealth of early material on a broad range of subjects.

Sīra scholarship manifested itself in many other fields. Comprehensive histories usually dealt with the subject in detail, and compendia in law, Koranic exegesis, and *ḥadīth*, as well as the later commentaries on them, collected large numbers of traditions. In inspiration and structure they basically adhered to forms that has already been established earlier, but as with the later works within the *sīra* tradition, they attest to the ongoing vitality of the field and the enduring interest of the educated public in whatever could be known about the founder of Islam.

As will be evident from the above, the study of the Prophet's life is a complex undertaking fraught with difficulties of various kinds. But it is no less clear that much work remains to be done; new methodologies and an expanding corpus of source material and modern research ensure that much of value and significance will yet emerge in this, one of the most important fields of medieval Arabic literature.

Further reading

The literature on Muḥammad is vast. Excellent starting points are:

Peters, Frank E., 'The quest of the historical Muḥammad', *IJMES* 23 (1991), 291–315.

Rubin, U., (ed.), *The Biography of Muḥammad*, in *The Formation of the Classical Islamic World*, Lawrence I. Conrad (ed.), vol. 4, London (1998) (with a valuable introduction and bibliography).

Conrad, Lawrence I., (ed.), *History and Historiography in Early Islamic Times: Studies and Perspectives*, Princeton (1997).

Several important collections of articles are:

Fahd, Toufic, (ed.), *La vie du prophète Mahomet*, Paris (1983).

Kister, M.J., *Studies in Jāhiliyya and Early Islam*, London (1980).

——, *Society and Religion from Jāhiliyya to Islam*, Aldershot (1990).

Sezgin, *GAS*, I. (The standard guide to sources).

The following works are valuable for their methodological discussions and appreciations of the material as literature:

al-Dūrī, 'Abd al-'Azīz, *Dirāsa fī Sīrat al-nabī*, Baghdad (1965).

——, *The Rise of Historical Writing among the Arabs*, Lawrence I. Conrad, (ed. and trans.), Princeton (1983), 22–41, 76–135.

Jarrar, Maher, *Die Prophetenbiographie im islamischen Spanien: Ein Beitrag zur Überlieferungs- und Redaktionsgeschichte*, Frankfurt am Main (1989).

Khalidi, Tarif, *Arabic Historical Thought in the Classical Period*, Cambridge (1994), 17–48.

Lecker, Michael, *Muslims, Jews and Pagans: Studies in Early Islamic Medina*, Leiden (1995).

Rubin, Uri, *The Eye of the Beholder: The Life of Muḥammad as Viewed by the Early Muslims (a Textual Analysis)*, Princeton (1995).

Schoeler, Gregor, *Charakter und Authentie der muslimischen Überlieferung über das Leben Mohammeds*, Berlin (1996).

Sellheim, Rudolf, 'Prophet, Calif und Geschichte: Die Muhammad-Biographie des Ibn Isḥāq', *Oriens* 18–19 (1967), 33–91.

Wansbrough, John, *The Sectarian Milieu*, London (1978).

Useful bibliographies are:

Anees, Munawwar Ahmad and Athar, Alia N. *Guide to Sira and Hadith Literature in Western Languages*, London (1986).

Geddes, C.L., *An Analytical Guide to the Biblio-*

graphies on Islam, Muḥammad, and the Koran*, Denver (1973).
(See also the individual entries on the authors discussed above.)

L.I. CONRAD

Muḥammad, Nadīm (1910–94)

Syrian poet. Born in ʿAyn Shqaq, he studied in Beirut and Montpellier, and briefly served as director of cultural centres in Hiffah and Lattakia. He published a number of *Dīwāns*, including *Ālām* (Part I: 1953, Parts II and III: 1985), *Farāshāt wa-ʿanākib* (1955), *Āfāq* (1958), *Firʿawn* (1963), *Alwān* (1965), *Rifāq yamḍūn* (1978), *Ṣurākh al-tha'r* (1979), *Furūʿ min uṣūl* (1993). Besides its obvious Romantic features, his verse reflects socialist and existentialist influences. Though written largely in two-hemistich lines it departs from neo-classical diction and imagery, demonstrating the author's interest in organic unity and varied rhymes. The expression of love occupies much of Nadīm Muḥammad's writing. Other favourite themes include the torments and joys of the poet's inner world; the suffering of the Syrian peasant under feudalism; the celebration of the pan-Arab struggle for independence and unity; and the quest for human dignity in a harsh world.

M.R. NOURALLAH

Muḥammad Bāqir al-Majlisī *see* al-Majlisī, Muḥammad Bāqir

Muḥammad ibn ʿAbd Allāh al-Kisā'ī *see* al-Kisā'ī, Muḥammad ibn ʿAbd Allāh

Muḥammad ibn ʿAbd al-Karīm al-Shahrastānī *see* al-Shahrastānī

Muḥammad ibn ʿAbd al-Malik, known as Ibn al-Zayyāt (173–233/789–848)

ʿAbbāsid vizier and man of letters. As vizier to the caliphs al-Muʿtaṣim and al-Wāthiq, he was notorious for his severity, and invented a torture device for extracting confessions, to which he himself fell fatally victim soon after the accession of the caliph al-Mutawakkil. He was considered the best of the 'secretarial' poets of his generation, and his ***dīwān*** survives in an anonymous recension; a collection of his letters is lost. He was also an important patron, the subject of panegyrics by **Abū Tammām** (on whose death he wrote an elegy) and **al-Buḥturī**, and the dedicatee of several works by **al-Jāḥiẓ**, including his *Animals* and *Jest and Earnest*.

Text edition

Aghānī, (Cairo) vol. 20, 46–56.
Dīwān, J. Saʿīd (ed.), Cairo (1949).
Ibn Khallikān, *Wafayāt al-aʿyān*, I. ʿAbbas (ed.), Beirut (1968–72) vol. 5: 94–103.

E.K. ROWSON

Muḥammad ibn ʿA'isha *see* Ibn ʿA'isha, Muḥammad

Muḥammad ibn Bashīr al-Riyāshī *see* al-Riyāshī

Muḥammad ibn al-Ḥasan al-Ḥātimī *see* al-Ḥātimī, Muḥammad ibn al-Ḥasan

Muḥammad ibn al-Ḥasan ibn al-Kattanī *see* Ibn al-Kattanī

Muḥammad ibn Idrīs al-Shāfīʿī *see* al-Shāfīʿī

Muḥammad ibn Kunāsa *see* Ibn Kunāsa

Muḥammad ibn Muḥriz al-Wahrānī *see* al-Wahrānī, Muḥammad ibn Muḥriz

Muḥammad ibn Munādhir *see* Ibn Munādhir

Muḥammad ibn Zakariyyā' al-Rāzī *see* al-Rāzī, Muḥammad ibn Zakariyyā'

Muḥammad al-Salāmī (336–93/948–1003)

Abū al-Ḥasan Muḥammad ibn ʿUbayd Allāh (or ʿAbd Allāh) al-Salāmī was a poet from **Baghdad**. His genealogy goes back to Makhzūm (Quraysh); his name al-Salāmī refers to his birthplace (Madīnat al-Salām, i.e. Baghdad). As a child he moved to Mosul, where he met other poets such as Abū ʿUthmān al-Khālidī (see **al-Khālidiyyān**) and **al-Babbaghā'**. Later he associated with, and was honoured by, **al-Ṣāḥib Ibn ʿAbbād** in Isfahan and ʿAḍud al-Dawla in Shiraz. **Al-Thaʿālibī** quotes extensively from his poetry in *Yatīmat al-dahr*.

Text edition

Shiʿr, Ṣabīḥ Radīf (ed.), Baghdad (1971).

G.J.H. VAN GELDER

al-Muḥāsibī (*c.*165–243/*c.*781–857)

Abū ʿAbd Allāh al-Ḥārith ibn Asad al-ʿAnazī al-Muḥāsibī was born in **Basra** and died in **Baghdad**. An influential **Ṣūfī** writer, al-Muḥāsibī was learned in the religious sciences, particularly in **Muʿtazilī** theology, He sought, however, to transcend rationalized religion in an ascetic and moral quest for enlightenment. Through rigorous spiritual scrutiny of the self (*muḥāsaba*), this quest characterized al-Muḥāsibī's Ṣūfī methodology and informed his literary style. His spiritual psychology of the religious emotions remained his hallmark. This may be seen, for example, in his *Treatise on the Beginning of One Who Returns in Repentance to God, Most High.* Here al-Muḥāsibī describes the external and internal acts of the repenter in worshipful communion with God. The structure of the *ṣalāt* (prayer) is clearly the formal model, while the emotional description is al-Muḥāsibī's internal Ṣūfī topos of the *ṣalāt*. A few lines in translation will illustrate the style and mood: 'When he [the penitent] had been standing long before his Lord and yearning to humble himself by throwing dust on his face in obeisance to Him, you should have seen him dropping down from his upright position with burning heart, throbbing breast and bated breath. Then he fell in prostration on his face, thinking of his Lord looking at him, tears streaming down his cheeks and pooling on his face, contrite and imploring his Lord, shouting, crying, moaning...' (*Kitāb Bad' man anāba ilā Allāh Taʿālā*, 15–16).

Text editions

Kitāb Bad' man anāba ilā Allāh Taʿālā, H. Ritter (ed.), Glückstadt (1935).

Kitāb al-Riʿāya li-ḥuqūq Allāh, Margaret Smith (ed.), London (1941).

Further reading

Maḥmūd, ʿAbd al-Ḥalīm, *al-Mohasibi*, Paris (1940).

Roman, A., *Une vision humaine des fins dernières: le Kitab al-Tawahhhum d'al-Muhasibi*, Paris (1978).

Smith, Margaret, *An Early Mystic of Baghdad: A Study of the Life and Teaching of Harith b. Asad al-Muhasibi*, London (1935).

van Ess, J., *Die Gedankenweit des Hariṯ al-Muḥāsibī*, Bonn (1961).

R.L. NETTLER

muḥdathūn, 'the moderns'

Name for the poets of the **ʿAbbāsid** period, in opposition to the ancient Arabic poets, i.e. poets of the ***Jāhiliyya***, ***mukhaḍramūn*** and **Umayyad** poets. **Bashshār ibn Burd** (d.167/783) is called 'father' of the moderns (Ibn Rashīq, *al-ʿUmda* I, 131). He was, however, already prominent during the late Umayyad period (*mukhaḍram al-dawlatayn*). Other prominent early *muḥdathūn* are **Muṭīʿ ibn Iyās** (d. 169/785), **Muslim ibn al-Walīd** (d. 208/823) and, above all, **Abū Nuwās** (d. *c.* 200/815). As the most remarkable characteristic of *muḥdathūn* poetry, the indigenous critics mention the frequent and conscious application of ***badīʿ***. Originally, this term was understood to be a certain kind of metaphor (example: 'hand of the Northwind'); later it came to mean a certain group of figures of speech (among others, paronomasia and antithesis) and finally the figures of speech in general.

The poetry of the *muḥdathūn* excels in a way of rhetoricizing that did not exist before. Remarkable is the often complicated technique of imagery (Abū Nuwās on the blossoms of the narcissus: 'as if, they were eyes, but different [from the human eye] in their colour; yellow instead of the black [of the pupil], and the lids are the white'). The image becomes more important than the object that it is meant to elucidate (Abū Nuwās: 'she wept by pouring pearls [tears] from narcissi [eyes]'). Frequently, similes and metaphors are further developed into 'phantastic interpretations' (*takhyīl*) (Abū Nuwās: 'The roses saw him picking roses, and so they imitated his blush', based on the comparison of cheeks with roses). Topoi of the ancient Arabs are still employed, but handled very consciously or transformed, and also often parodied (e.g. the weeping over the traces of the encampment in the *nasīb* at the beginning of the ***qaṣīda*** by Abū Nuwās). (See further **satire**.) **Abū Tammām** (d. 231/845) made excessive use of rhetorization and thereby evoked a discussion among the indigenous critics about his poetry.

Other innovations that have at times been attributed to the *muḥdathūn* and that were conditioned by societal changes (court and city instead of desert) had in fact often set in earlier, but were taken up, developed and cultivated by the *muḥdathūn* ('court *qaṣīda*' or 'secondary *qaṣīda*', instead of 'tribal *qaṣīda*', or 'primary, *qaṣīda*'; replacement of the *nasīb* of the *qaṣīda* by another topic, particularly a description of wine or spring; further development of the ***ʿUdhrī*** love poetry into **'courtly' love** poetry by Bashshār ibn Burd and **al-ʿAbbās ibn al-Aḥnaf**). (See further ***qaṣīda***.) The expansion of the system of genres (love, wine, ascetic, and hunting poetry as independent forms) had also already taken place during the Umayyad period (or even earlier). New creations of the (later) *muḥdathūn* are, essentially, only the independent descriptive poem (***waṣf***) and the nature poem (*rawḍiyya*, etc.). (See **nature, in classical poetry**.)

Further reading

Badawi, M.M., ''Abbasid poetry and its antecedents', in *CHALABL*, 146–66.

Bonebakker, S.A., 'Ibn al-Muʿtazz and *Kitāb al-Badīʿ*', in *CHALABL*, 388–411.

Heinrichs, W., 'Istiʿārah and badīʿ', *ZGAIW* 1 (1984), 180–211.

Jacobi, R., 'Die arabische Qaṣīde', *Neues Handbuch der Literaturwissenschaft. Orientalisches Mittelalter*, W. Heinrichs (ed.), Wiesbaden (1990), 226–30.

Wagner, E., *Grundzüge der klassich–arabischen Dichtung*, Darmstadt (1987–8), vol. 2, 89–130.

G. SCHOELER, trans. A. GIESE

See also: ancients and moderns; literary criticism, medieval; *maṭbūʿ* and *maṣnūʿ*; rhetoric and poetics

al-Muḥibbī (1061–1111/1651–99)

Muḥibb al-Dīn Muḥammad ibn al-Amīn al-Muḥibbī was a member of a family of scholars and jurists in **Damascus**, who flourished in the tenth-eleventh/sixteenth-seventeenth centuries. He spent his career in Ottoman Anatolia and in his native Damascus, but was also the author of a (so far unpublished) ***dīwān*** of poetry and, above all, of biographical works: a dictionary of the literary men and scholars of his age, the *Khulāṣat al-athar*, which contains nearly 1,300 entries and is a precious source on the literary life of a period which has not so far been thoroughly explored; *al-Iʿlām*, on notable figures from all ages, only partially extant; and a continuation of **al-Khafājī**'s own literary–biographical dictionary.

Further reading

Wüstenfeld, F., *Die Gelehrten-Familie Muḥibbi in Damaskus*, in *Abh. G.W. Göttingen*, phil.-hist. Cl. 30:3 (1884), 1–28.

C.E. BOSWORTH

Muḥyī al-Dīn ibn al-ʿArabī *see* Ibn al-ʿArabī

mujtathth see prosody

mujūn

'Libertinage, licentiousness'; a term used to describe both a mode of behaviour and a genre of medieval Arabic poetry and prose. Closely related to *khalāʿa*, the throwing off of societal restraints, *mujūn* refers behaviourally to open and unabashed indulgence in prohibited pleasures, particularly the drinking of wine and, above all, sexual profligacy. *Mujūn* literature describes and celebrates this hedonistic way of life, frequently employing explicit sexual vocabulary, and almost invariably with primarily humorous intent.

Despite certain antecedents, *mujūn* literature is essentially a product of the early **ʿAbbāsid** period. Pre-Islamic poetry sometimes describes sexual adventures (most notably in the *Muʿallaqa* of **Imruʾ al-Qays**), but without the graphic and waggish qualities of true *mujūn*; and while pre-Islamic and **Umayyad** abuse poetry (***hijāʾ***) is often extremely coarse, and can also provoke laughter, its defamatory intent sets it off clearly from *mujūn*'s essential lightheartedness. The rise in Umayyad **Arabia** of the ***ʿUdhrī*** school of love poetry, chaste and emotionally overwrought, provided a perhaps essential foil for *mujūn*'s anti-romantic and sometimes cynical stance, while the growing practice of *tashbīb*, embarrassing respectable ladies by composing love lyrics about them, prefigures *mujūn*'s delight in breaching the barriers of what can be said in polite company.

But it was in the very different social climate of early ʿAbbāsid **Basra** and **Baghdad** that true *mujūn* first flourished, and above all in the person of **Abū Nuwās**. Unabashedly defying both **bedouin** poetic conventions and Islamic prohibitions, this poet celebrated in exquisite verses the joys of the tavern and of seducing boys (and occasionally girls), often in the most vivid terms, and, along with other poets of his time, definitively established this new genre. Its status as such is quite clear from the two extant recensions of Abū Nuwās's ***dīwān***, both of which are organized by genre and accord a separate section to his *mujūniyyāt*, distinguished not only from panegyric and the like, but also from wine poems (***khamriyyāt***), love poetry about women (*mu'annathāt*), and love poetry about boys (*mudhakkarāt*). While the latter might seem by definition to be *mujūn*, it is less the illicitness of the subject than the presence of explicit vocabulary and graphic description that sets off the latter, regardless of the sex of the beloved.

Abū Nuwās and other *mujūn* poets such as **al-Ḥusayn ibn al-Ḍaḥḥāk** received considerable encouragement at the court of the dissolute caliph al-Amīn (193–8/809–13), and the trend was equally popular in the following generation under al-Mutawakkil (232–47/847–61). The cultivation of *mujūn* was closely associated with the world of entertainers and musicians, and particularly the cultivated singing slave girls (*qiyān*) traded among the aristocracy (see **singers and musicians**); but its wider appeal as literature, despite opposition in certain quarters, is clear from a well-known passage in **al-Jāḥiẓ**'s *Boasting-Match between Girls and Boys* in which he castigates prudes for their aversion to sexually explicit humour by documenting its appreciation among the pious ancestors.

The relationship between licentious behaviour and licentious literature was always an ambiguous one. **Ibn al-Muʿtazz** and others pointed out that many *mujūn* poets led lives quite different from those they depicted in their verses; on the other hand, **al-Thaʿālibī** described the wild weekly drinking parties at which the Baghdad judge **al-Tanūkhī** and his grey-bearded colleagues would cast off their otherwise carefully maintained dignity. In the late fourth/tenth century aristocratic society seems to have undergone a wave of *nostalgie de la boue*, illustrated by the scabrous tastes of the **Būyid** vizier **al-Ṣāḥib Ibn ʿAbbād** and above all by the extraordinary popularity of the Baghdad poet **Ibn al-Ḥajjāj**, whose poetry added to graphic sexual description a new element of scatalogical humour (see ***sukhf***). The culmination of this trend was the *Tale of Abū al-Qāsim al-Baghdādī* by the otherwise unknown **Abū al-Muṭahhar al-Azdī**, which manages to touch on every conceivable aspect of *mujūn* in its depiction of a rogue's disruption of a drinking party.

While such excesses became less common in later periods, that *mujūn* had by the fifth/eleventh century acquired a respectable niche in both poetry and prose literature is clear from its inclusion in literary encyclopaedias by such authors as **al-Tawḥīdī**, **al-Ābī** and **al-Rāghib al-Iṣfahānī**. Later writers noted for their cultivation of *mujūn* include the poet **Ibn al-Habbāriyya** in the **Saljūq** East and the prose humorist **al-Wahrānī** in **Ayyūbid Egypt** and **Syria**, both of whom exploited in particular the genre's potential for satire. The proportion of *mujūn* in the picaresque ***Maqāmāt*** of **Badīʿ al-Zamān al-Hamadhānī** and **al-Ḥarīrī** is surprisingly low; but it did become a favoured theme of the colloquial, stanzaic ***zajal*** verse form developed in Andalusia, notably by **Ibn Quzmān**, and later popularized in the East as well by such poets as **Ṣafī al-Dīn al-Ḥillī**. Ibn al-Ḥajjāj found a worthy successor in **Ibn Dāniyāl**, whose **shadow plays** mark a new surge in popularity for both *mujūn* and *sukhf*. That *mujūn* literature continued to be both appreciated and composed by respectable scholars and religious figures is clear from the existence of several works in the genre from the pen of the ninth/fifteenth-century polymath **al-Suyūṭī**. Also to be noted as overlapping with *mujūn* literature, but remaining generically distinct, are works of erotica, of which the best known are those by **al-Tīfāshī** and **al-Nafzāwī**.

Further reading

Bosworth, C.E., *The Medieval Islamic Underworld:*

The Banū Sāsān in Arabic Society and Literature, Leiden (1976), vol. 1, 63–79.
Ibn al-Muʿtazz, *Ṭabaqāt al-shuʿarāʾ*, ʿA.A. Farrāj (ed.), Cairo (1981), 306–9.
Meisami, J.S., 'Arabic *mujūn* poetry: the literary dimension', in *Verse and the Fair Sex: Studies in Arabic Poetry and in the Representation of Women in Arabic Literature*, F. De Jong (ed.), Utrecht (1993), 8–30.
Schoeler, G., 'Die Einteilung der Dichtung bei den Arabern', *ZDMG* 123 (1973), 9–55.
al-Thaʿālibī, *Yatīmat al-dahr*, Cairo (1956), vol. 2, 336f.

E.K. ROWSON

mukhaḍram

A term applied to persons living in the ***Jāhiliyya*** and in the time of Islam. It is derived from *khaḍrama*, 'to cut the ear of one's camel', and signifies, according to some lexicographers, 'cut off from disbelief'. In literary classification, *al-mukhaḍramūn* constitute the generation of poets between 'the pagans' (*al-Jāhiliyyūn*) and the 'Islamic poets' (*al-Islāmiyyūn*). In their verses the development of Umayyad poetry is anticipated in many respects (see also **Orthodox caliphate**). The designation was later extended to poets of the second/eighth century, *mukhaḍramūn al-dawlatayn*, 'poets of the two dynasties', i.e. the **Umayyads** and the **ʿAbbāsids**.

R. JACOBI

mukhammas see **strophic poetry**

mukhannathūn

A term given to all kinds of entertainers from the rise of Islam to the late medieval Arab world. Arabic lexicography defines the word *mukhannath* as 'effeminate person; homosexual; bisexual; male prostitute; powerless, impotent, weak [person]'. In literary works the term denotes persons often engaged in the entertainment professions, e.g. musicians (flautists, drummers, lutists, cymbal and tambourine players), dancers, hobby-horse players, etc.

In the time of **Muḥammad** there were four *mukhannathūn*. They did not practise homosexuality, but they spoke in a soft voice, dyed their hands and feet, and toyed or danced like women. Al-Fākihī says that the *mukhannathūn* were active in Mecca from the pre-Islamic period up to 252/866; they played with hobby-horses (*kurraj*) at feasts in various quarters (*Akhbār Makka*, Leipzig, 1858–61, vol. 2, 9–10). The association between *kurraj* and *mukhannathūn* was so strong that during later periods effeminate men came to be known as *kurrajīs*.

Later the term was also given to actors of live theatre. Some musicians, e.g. flautists, were called *Mukhannath*, such as al-Mukhannath al-Baghdādī al-Dallāl. From the third/ninth century onward actors were given the title of *Mukhannath*. The most important among them is ʿAbbāda al-Mukhannath, the favourite actor of al-Mutawakkil (d. 247/861). ʿAbbāda's pantomimic play, imitating **ʿAlī ibn Abī Ṭālib**, was a favourite, frequently acted, accompanied by musicians and singers, for the delight of the caliph:

> ʿAbbāda al-Mukhannath used to tie a pillow onto his stomach under his clothes, take off his headgear although he was bald, and dance before al-Mutawakkil while the singers would sing, 'The bald one with the paunch is coming, the caliph of the Muslims!' He would impersonate (*yaḥkī*) ʿAlī, upon him be peace, to the roaring [laughter] of al-Mutawakkil while the latter was drinking [wine]. (Ibn al-Athīr, *al-Kāmil fī al-taʾrīkh*, Beirut, 1965, vol. 7, 55).

Other plays by *mukhannathūn* involved not only dancing with props, but also dialogue and acting.

In *Thesaurus Syriacus* the Greek term *mimos* is given in Syriac according to Ibn Bahlūl (*c*.963 CE) as *mīmas* and *mīmsā* with their Arabic meaning as *al-mukhannath al-muḥākī al-maskharī* (the imitating comedian mimic), as well as *mukhannath, muḥākī, al-muḍḥik* (mime, imitator, comedian), a clear indication that the term *mukhannath* also became an established term for comic actors.

Further reading

Moreh, S., 'Live theatre in medieval Islam', in Ayalon Festschrift, 565–611.
——, *Live Theatre and Dramatic Literature in the Medieval Arab World*, Edinburgh and New York (1992), 25–7 and *passim*.
Rowson, E.K., 'The effeminates of early Medina', *JAOS* 111 (4) (1991), 671–93.
Shiloah, A., *Music in the World of Islam*, Hants (1995), 13.

S. MOREH

See also: actors and acting, medieval

Mukhāriq ibn Shihāb *see* singers and musicians

*mulamma*ʿ*a*

(Lit. 'brightly variegated, piebald'). A *mulammaʿa* is a poem in which more than one language is used: 'macaronic' verse, be it that the comical or burlesque aspect implied by this term is not always present. Early examples mixing Arabic and Persian are by **Abū Nuwās**, **Ibn Mufarrigh** and Ibn Abī Karīma (the last two quoted by **al-Jāḥiẓ**); **Ibn Dā'ūd al-Iṣbahānī** gives some more examples (Arabic with Persian, with – allegedly – a negro language and with Greek) in his *Zahra*. Ḍiyā' al-Dīn **Ibn al-Athīr** mentions a poem mixing Arabic, Persian, Turkish Greek and Armenian, twenty lines in each language. Arabic works of ***badī*ʿ** ignore it, but it is incorporated by the less monoglot Persians from Rādūyānī (fifth/eleventh century) onward. Al-Ḥarīzī, the Hebrew emulator of **al-Ḥarīrī**, included in his *Taḥkemoni* a poem in Hebrew, Aramaic and Arabic. Classical and colloquial Arabic are sometimes mixed with burlesque results, as in the poems by the modern Egyptian poet Ḥusayn Ṭantāwī which he calls *shiʿr ḥalamantīshī* (etymology unknown).

G.J.H. VAN GELDER

Mullā Ṣadrā (979 or 980–1050/ 1571 or 1572–1640)

Ṣadr al-Dīn Muḥammad ibn Ibrāhīm al-Shīrāzī (Mullā Ṣadra), called Ṣadr al-Muta'allihīn, or simply Ākhund, has been perhaps the single most important and influential philosopher in the Muslim world in the last four hundred years, although philosophical activity has been more or less restricted during this period to Iran and the Indian subcontinent. Born in Shiraz, he studied in Isfahan with the leading scholars of his time before retiring for a number of years' spiritual solitude and discipline to the village of Kahak near Qum, where he completed the first part of his major work, the *Asfār*. He was invited by the governor of Fars to return to Shiraz, where he taught for the remainder of his life. He died in **Basra** while on his seventh *ḥajj* on foot to Mecca. The author of over forty works, he was the culminating figure of the major revival of philosophy in Ṣafavid Iran. Devoting himself almost exclusively to metaphysics, he constructed a critical philosophy which brought together Peripatetic, Illuminationist and gnostic philosophy with **Shīʿī** theology within the compass of what he termed a 'metaphilosophy', whose source lay in the Islamic revelation and the mystical experience of reality as existence.

Mullā Ṣadrā's metaphilosophy was based on existence as the sole constituent of reality, and rejected any role for quiddities or essences in the external world. Existence was for him at once a single unity and an internally articulated dynamic process, the unique source of both unity and diversity. Proceeding from this single fundamental starting point, he was able to analyse, and to find original solutions to, many of the logical, metaphysical and theological difficulties which he had inherited from his predecessors. His major philosophical work is the *Asfār*, a complete presentation of his philosophical ideas which he began in Kahak and finished in Shiraz. In other areas of his scholarship mention should be made of a commentary on the *Uṣūl* of *al-Kāfī*, one of the most important collections of Shīʿī ***ḥadīth***, and commentaries on various sections of the **Koran**.

Text editions

al-Ḥikma al-ʿarshiyya, Ghulām Riḍā Āhanī (ed. with Persian paraphrase), Isfahan (1341/1962).
al-Ḥikma al-mutaʿāliya fī al-asfār al-ʿaqliyya al-arbaʿa, Riḍā Luṭfī, Ibrāḥīm al-Amīnī, Fatḥ Allāh al-Umīd *et al.* (eds), 9 vols, Tehran and Qum (1378–89?)/1958–69?), with various partial glosses; vol. 1, 2nd printing, Qum (1387/ 1967), with intro. by Muḥammad Riḍā al-Muẓaffar; Ḥasan Ḥasanzāda al-Āmutī (ed. and comm.), Tehran (1914–/1995–).
Kitāb al-mashāʿir (Le Livre des pénétrations métaphysiques), Henry Corbin (intro., ed. and trans.), Paris and Tehran (1964).
The Wisdom of the Throne: An Introduction to the Philosophy of Mulla Sadra, James Winston Morris (trans. with intro.), Princeton (1981).

Further reading

Nasr, Seyyed Hossein, *Sadr al-Din Shirazi and His Transcendent Theosophy: Background, Life and Works*, Tehran (1978).
Rahman, Fazlur, *The Philosophy of Mullā Ṣadrā*, Albany (1975).

J. COOPER

Munajjim family

A family of scholars and courtiers prominent in the flourishing literary and scientific life of the **ʿAbbāsid** court in the third/ninth century. The family was of Persian and Zoroastrian origin and is said to have had connections with the Sasanian court. Its first known member in Islamic times served the caliph al-Manṣūr as his *munajjim* (astronomer/astrologer), and the astronomical qualifications of his son Yaḥyā brought him a prominent position at the court of al-Ma'mūn, under whose auspices he converted to Islam. After Yaḥyā his sons and grandsons were commonly known as Ibn al-Munajjim. Of these the most prominent was his son ʿAlī ibn Yaḥyā **Ibn al-Munajjim**, whose success at court and accumulation of wealth and property provided the family with a secure material foundation for its intellectual pursuits. These tended away from astronomy towards poetry, music, literary history and theology. All of these were among the interests of ʿAlī's son Yaḥyā ibn ʿAlī ibn Yaḥyā, who lived from 241/855–6 to 300/912 and, like his father, was a regular companion of the ʿAbbāsid caliphs. He and his brother Hārūn compiled respectively a history and anthology of Arabic poetry, both of which were used by **Abū al-Faraj al-Iṣbahānī** in his *Kitāb al-Aghānī*. Members of two more generations of the family are known to have frequented the declining ʿAbbāsid court or that of the **Būyids**, and to have continued the family's literary and scientific interests.

Further reading

Fihrist (Dodge), vol. 1, 312–16.

Fleischhammer, M., 'Die Banū l-Munağğim, eine Bagdader Gelehrtenfamilie aus dem 2.-4. Jahrhundert d.H..', *WZH, Ges.-u. Sprachw. Reihe* 12 (1963), 215–20.

Stern, S.M., 'Abū ʿĪsā Ibn al-Munajjim's Chronology', in *Islamic Philosophy and the Classical Tradition*, S.M. Stern *et al.*, (eds), Columbia, SC (1972), 437–56.

R.A. KIMBER

al-Munakhkhal al-Yashkurī (sixth century)

A semi-legendary figure from pre-Islamic times. Several anthologies contain a poem that belongs to the ***fakhr*** genre (self-glorification) and in which the poet dedicates some lines to a vivid portrayal of his seduction of a beautiful girl. Its author's name is given as al-Munakhkhal from the tribe Yashkur, and a story is told according to which he was tortured to death on orders from the **Lakhmid** king al-Nuʿmān ibn al-Mundhir (580–602) on the suspicion of having had an affair with his wife. Both the story, and the poem related to it, exist in a variety of different versions. The poem was set to music by Ibrāhīm **al-Mawṣilī** and others.

Text editions

Aghānī (Beirut), vol. 9, 13–14, vol. 21, 3–11.

al-Aṣmaʿī, *Elaçmaʿijjāt*, W. Ahlwardt (ed.), Berlin (1902), 30–2.

Cheikho, L., *Kitāb shuʿarā' al-Naṣrāniyya, The Christian Poets*, Beirut (1990), vol. 1, 421–4.

T. BAUER

munāẓara *see* debate literature

Munīf, ʿAbd al-Raḥmān (1933–)

Saudi novelist, economist and intellectual. Born in Jordan, Munīf studied law in **Damascus** and **Cairo**, then gained a PhD in oil economics from Yugoslavia. He held Saudi citizenship until stripped of it for his political opposition to the Saudi regime. Munīf worked in the Syrian and Iraqi oil industries and became editor of the Iraqi monthly *al-Nifṭ wa-al-tanmiya*. While working in Syria, he published his first novel, *al-Ashjār wa-ightiyāl Marzūq*; this was followed by *Qiṣṣat ḥubb majūsiyya* and *Ḥīna taraknā al-jisr*. These three early novels, though giving evidence of talent, may be regarded as novels of apprenticeship.

It was with works such as *Sharq al-Mutawassiṭ* (1977), *al-Nihāyāt* (1978) and *Sibāq al-masāfāt al-ṭawīla: Riḥla ilā al-sharq* (1979) that Munīf started to acquire his own independent and original voice. *Sharq al-Mutawassiṭ* is a prison novel in which stream-of-consciousness technique is used to show the physical and psychological horrors resulting from torture of political prisoners; *al-Nihāyāt* is structured in an analogous manner to the desert; *Sibāq* – set in Iran during the Moṣaddeq period – is narrated by a British agent who witnesses the decline of British and the rise of American imperialism. In 1982 he published *ʿĀlam bi-lā kharā'iṭ*, which he co-authored with Jabrā Ibrāhīm **Jabrā**.

In 1984 Munīf published the first volume of a planned trilogy (which later became a quintet), *Mudun al-milḥ*. This huge novel of more than 2,500 pages – the story of a desert community changed by the discovery of oil – takes as its theme the destruction of traditional bonds and social life through enforced 'modernization' and, as such, is arguably one of the most important recent novels in Arabic. His interest in history is also clear in works such as *Sīrat madīna: 'Ammān fī al-arba'īnāt* (1994).

Text editions

Cities of Salt, Peter Theroux (trans.), New York (1989).
Endings, Roger Allen (trans.), London (1988).
The Trench, Peter Theroux (trans.), New York (1993).
Variations on Night and Day, Peter Theroux (trans.), New York (1993).

W. HAMARNEH

munsariḥ see prosody

al-Muqaddasī (fourth/tenth century)

Shams al-Dīn (?) Muḥammad ibn Aḥmad ibn Abī Bakr al-Bannā' al-Shāmī al-Muqaddasī, also known as al-Bashshārī, was born in Jerusalem in the decade of 330/941, and died no earlier than 381/991. On both paternal and maternal sides he was descended from families of master builders. He was a travelling merchant, and possibly an **Ismā'īlī** missionary; he is renowned as a geographical author. Except for his own work, *Aḥsan al-taqāsīm fī ma'rifat al-aqālīm* (*The Best Disposal, on Knowledge of the Provinces*, completed around 380/990), no biographical source for him is extant.

Al-Muqaddasī's *Disposal* accomplishes and at the same time transcends the Balkhī tradition of geography in the fourth/tenth century. The text has become emancipated from the accompanying maps, and while al-Muqaddasī naturally peruses his predecessors when and wherever possible, he is far more assured than even **Ibn Ḥawqal** in giving precedence to autopsy as a means of acquiring geographical knowledge. He defines geography as a noble discipline, worthy of a cultivated style, and indispensable to princes and their ministers as well as to merchants and, generally, to the complete gentleman. His interest is not limited to physical features and economic conditions of a given region but includes the social and denominational make-up of its inhabitants, which he observes with insight; his family background also gives him an open eye for the aesthetic qualities of architecture.

Text editions

Aḥsan al-taqāsīm, M.J. de Goeje (ed.), Leiden (1906) (= *BGA* 3); rpt Beirut (n.d.).
The Best Divisions for Knowledge of the Regions, B.A. Collins (trans.), Reading (1994).
La meilleure répartition pour la connaissance des provinces, (partial) A. Miquel (trans.), Damascus 1963.

L. RICHTER-BERNBURG

See also: geographical literature

muqaddima

A term generally meaning 'premise' in medieval Arabic. It was used most particularly in logic in a technical sense, but also in dialectical theology, and from the end of the sixth/eleventh century in legal theory (*uṣūl al-fiqh*; see ***fiqh***) to indicate the logical or quasi-logical character of legal deductions (*qiyās*) based on the 'roots' of jurisprudence (the **Koran**, ***ḥadīth*** and consensus). In modern Arabic, the term still preserves its technical sense, but is generally used in a wide literary sense to denote the 'preface' or 'introduction' to a book or other form of discourse. This genre-specific use of the term was rarely used for prefatory discourses that almost invariably preceded medieval Arabic texts on all subjects. In most cases, these prefatory discourses indicated the purpose – pious, controversial or otherwise – of composing the work, and an outline of its textual genealogy. Rare were the texts like the prefatory statement by **Miskawayh** to his *Tajārib al-umam*, where he discourses on the very nature of his subject, in this case, history.

Ibn Khaldūn's *Muqaddima* joined together these two senses of the word. It was composed as a separate literary component of a work on universal history, to which it constituted at once a prefatory discourse and a logical propdeutic. The *Muqaddima* purported to set out the methodological rules which would allow the historian to ply his craft properly. Such rules were meant to allow the historian to arrive at a conclusion as to the plausibility or implausibility of received narratives, and such conclusions are dependent on knowledge of the nature of the state, of its emergence and of its decline, as well as a consequential awareness of mutability and of the reality of change. The rules constitute the premises from which deductions of plausibility are derived.

Ibn Khaldūn's *Muqaddima* itself is tightly structured along quasi-logical lines, and its text flows as would a deductive process from the basic to the derivative. This is a multi-layered process of considerable complexity and rigour, deploying metaphysical categories, and the metaphysical restatement of certain legal categories, for the study of material derived from the historical experience of the Arabs, the Berbers and other peoples, as well as observations on Ibn Khaldūn's own time. The *Muqaddima* contains a virtual register of the knowledge available to Ibn Khaldūn from his personal political experience and the books he read on history, politics, *fiqh*, eschatology, philosophy and the natural sciences, and offers extraordinary direct glimpses of his time. The result is a very richly textured work which has been read in different senses by different people, most of whom have tended to ignore its primary feature – complexity – for the sake of rather simplistic univocal interpretations.

Further reading

al-Tahānawī, *Kashshāf iṣṭilāḥāt al-funūn*, M. Wajīh, A. Sprenger and W. Nassau Lees (eds), Calcutta (1854 ff; rpt Beirut, 1966, in 4 vols), AH 1215–18 (on the technical sense of the term).

Quatremère, Etienne, *Les Prolégomènes d'Ebn Khaledoun*, Paris (1858–68) (edition of Ibn Khaldūn's *Muqaddina*) and the 1900 vocalized Beirut edition *Muqaddimat al-ʿallāma Ibn Khaldūn*, based on that of N. Hūrīnī (vol. 1 of *Kitāb al-ʿIbar*, Būlāq, AH 1284), were consolidated together by A. Wāfī and published as *Muqaddimat Ibn Khaldūn* (4 vols, Cairo, 1957 ff.) The best translation of the *Muqaddima* is still that of W. McGuckin de Slane, *Les Prolégomènes d'Ibn Khaldoun* (3 vols, Paris, 1863 ff.). The English translation of F. Rosenthal, *Ibn Khaldūn: The Muqaddimah. An Introduction to History* (3 vols, Princeton, 1958; rpt. 1967) is serviceable but often unreliable. On this was based the abridgement of N.J. Dawood, *Ibn Khaldūn: The Muqaddimah* (London, 1967, pbk 1978).

(For the linguistic aspects of the term, the standard Arabic dictionaries may be consulted.)

A. AL-AZMEH

See also: historical literature

muqaṭṭaʿa see qiṭʿa

muqtaḍab see prosody

al-Muqtaṭaf (1876–1952)

One of the most distinguished monthly reviews; founded in **Beirut**, it moved to **Cairo** in 1885. Its first editors were Yaʿqūb **Ṣarrūf** and Fāris Nimr. *Al-Muqtaṭaf* was an encyclopaedic popularizing magazine largely filled with information on Western civilization taken from foreign newspapers and magazines and covering, *inter alia*, history, commerce, art, archaeology, science and biography. It also published novels and short stories, initially mainly translations, including Disraeli's *Tancred*, Scott's *Ivanhoe* and Ṣarrūf's own first novel, *A Girl in Egypt*. Many leading Egyptian and other writers were among its contributors.

Further reading

Farag, Nadia, 'The Lewis affair and the fortunes of *al-Muqtataf*', *MES* 8 (1972), 73–83.

Fihris al-Muqtaṭaf, Beirut (1967).

Kenny, L.M., 'East versus West in *al-Muqtataf*, 1875–1900', in Donald P. Little (ed.), *Essays on Islamic Civilization Presented to Niyazi Berkes*, Leiden (1976), 140–54.

P.C. SADGROVE

al-Muraqqish al-Akbar (sixth century CE)

Al-Muraqqish ('the embellisher') the Elder was the sobriquet of a poet from the Qays ibn Thaʿlaba clan (cf. **al-Aʿshā Maymūn**) who lived in the first half of the sixth century. His real name is not known for certain. He is more famous as hero of a love romance, according to which he died of unrequited love for his cousin Asmā', than for his poetry. However, since he is one of the oldest Arab poets known to us, his importance to literary history can hardly be overestimated. His poetry, which was collected by **al-Mufaḍḍal al-Ḍabbī**, shows the rather advanced stage that Arabic poetry had already reached in the beginning of the sixth century, but still is not devoid of archaic traits (e.g. metrical irregularities). The tripartite form of the ***qaṣīda*** was not yet known at his time, but he often uses the form of a *qaṣīda* in two sections, namely a *nasīb* followed by a message, mostly ***fakhr*** (self-glorification).

Text edition

Lyall, C.J. (ed.), *The Mufaḍḍalīyāt*, Oxford (1918–21), poems nos 45–54 and appendix.

Further reading

Blachère, Régis, 'Remarques sur deux élégiaques arabes du VIe siècle', *Arabica* 7 (1960), 30–40.

T. BAUER

al-Muraqqish al-Aṣghar (sixth century CE)

Muraqqish the Younger, nephew of **al-Muraqqish al-Akbar** and uncle of **Ṭarafa**, lived around the middle of the sixth century in the region of **Ḥīra**. Like his uncle, he is the hero of a love romance, his beloved being the princess Fāṭima, daughter of the **Lakhmid** king al-Mundhir. The few remnants of his poetry are preserved in the *Mufaḍḍaliyāt* (nos 55–9) and in other anthologies.

For bibliography see **al-Muraqqish al-Akbar**.

T. BAUER

al-Murr, Muḥammad Aḥmad (1955–)

Dubai-born short-story writer, whose family is connected by marriage to the Maktūms, the ruling family of Dubai. He was educated in Dubai and at Syracuse University, New York State, where he studied political science. He has read voraciously the literature of the world in English, but is also familiar with classical Arabic literature.

After returning to Dubai al-Murr worked in journalism. He has been editor of the English-medium daily newspaper, *Khaleej Times*, and is a regular writer for *al-Bayān*. A collection of broadcast talks on the Arabic of the Gulf was published in 1991.

During the 1980s Muḥammad al-Murr was a prolific writer of short stories. His first collection, *Ḥubb min naw' ākhar*, was published in Beirut in 1982. Ten other collections followed. His stories vividly portray the lives and values of the people of contemporary Dubai, their expectations and their adjustment to oil wealth. They are written with economy, occasionally nostalgic, sometimes funny, but are always perceptive and humane.

Text editions

Dubai Tales, Peter Clark (trans.), London and Boston (1991).
The Wink of the Mona Lisa, Jack Briggs (trans.), Dubai and London (1995).

P. CLARK

al-Murtaḍā al-Zabīdī *see* al-Zabīdī, al-Murtaḍā

Muruwwa, Ḥusayn (1909–87)

Lebanese literary critic, political activist and writer on Arab–Islamic philosophy. Born in a small village in south Lebanon, Muruwwa studied Islamic law, theology and Arabic literature for ten years at the religious university of al-Najaf (Iraq). He worked in Iraq for almost ten more years as a teacher of Arabic, while writing for the political and literary press in Iraq, **Syria**, **Lebanon** and **Egypt**. He was deported in 1949 by Nurī al-Sa'īd's government for having taken part in the popular uprising against the 1948 Portsmouth Agreement with Britain, and from then lived in Lebanon until his assassination by a rival militia group in Beirut.

Muruwwa was closely associated with the leftist press, particularly *al-Ṭarīq* and *al-Thaqāfa al-waṭaniyya* (both published in Beirut), and served as editor and later managing editor of *al-Ṭarīq*. He earned a doctorate from the University of Moscow for his thesis *al-Naz'āt al-māddiyya fī al-falsafa al-'Arabiyya al-Islāmiyya*, which was published in two massive volumes in 1978 and 1979. He joined the Lebanese Communist Party in the 1940s and was a member of its central committee when he died; he was also a founder member of the Arab Writers' Association established in **Damascus** in September 1954.

Most of Muruwwa's books are collections of essays and articles originally published over more than half a century. They include *Ma'a al-qāfila* (1953), *Qaḍāyā adabiyya* (1956), *Thawrat al-'Irāq* (1958) and *Turāthunā kayfa naqra'uh* (1985). These remain the most comprehensive reading of Arabic literature and culture from a Marxist perspective. Although Muruwwa's work underwent various changes of emphasis during the course of his career, his basic premises remained those of an orthodox Marxist, who viewed both his cultural heritage and contemporary literature from the perspective of historical materialism.

Further reading

al-'Ālim, Maḥmūd *et al.*, *Ḥusayn Muruwwa: shahādāt fī fikrih wa-niḍālih*, Beirut (1981).
Al-Ṭarīq (Beirut), 47 (2–3) (June 1980), special issue on Muruwwa.

A.-N. STAIF

Mūsā, Nabawiyya (1886–1951)

Egyptian educator, writer and feminist. Born into a family of modest means, Mūsā exemplified the new visibility of middle-class Egyptian females in the educational system in the first half of the twentieth century. After completing her teacher training, she fought to be allowed to sit for the state baccalaureate examination in 1907, the first Egyptian female to do so. A teacher and then headmistress in state schools, she was appointed as the Ministry of Education's chief inspector of girls' education in 1924. Dismissed two years later for criticizing the government curriculum for girls, she ran two private schools that she had founded. An early member of the Egyptian Feminist Union, she wrote on women's rights to education and work, in her *al-Mar'a wa-al-'amal* (1920) and *al-Āyāt al-bayyināt fi tarbiyat al-banāt* (n.d.), and later in the magazine she founded, *al-Fatāt* (1937–43). In that forum she published *Dhikrayātī*, a bold essay into autobiographical writing. Her poetry was published as *Dīwān al-fatāt* (1938) and she published one novel (*Riwāyat Nabhūtūb*). Imprisoned for her criticism of the Egyptian government in the political crisis of 1942, she retired thereafter from public life.

Further reading

Badran, Margot, 'Expressing feminism and nationalism in autobiography: the memoirs of an Egyptian educator', in Sidonie Smith and Julia Watson (eds), *De/Colonizing the Subject: The Politics of Gender in Women's Autobiography*, Minneapolis (1992), 270–93.

——, *Feminists, Islam and Nation: Gender and the Making of Modern Egypt*, Princeton (1994).

Kaḥḥāla, 'Umar Riḍā, *A'lām al-nisā' fī 'ālamay al-'Arab wa-al-Islām*, Cairo (1984), vol. 5, 163.

M. BOOTH

Mūsā, Ṣabrī (1932–)

Egyptian novelist, journalist and short-story writer. Ṣabrī Mūsā's first collection of short stories, *al-Qamīṣ*, was published in 1958. It was followed by *Lā aḥad ya'lam* (1962), *Ḥikāyāt Ṣabrī Mūsā* (1963) and *Wajhan li-ẓahr* (1966). In these short stories Mūsā developed a style that was seemingly straightforward but at the same time cunning and inimitable; there is a clear influence from journalese and Egyptian colloquial, functionalized to achieve an ironic stance and a paradoxical ending that challenges the expectations of the reader. Mūsā has also written three novels which break new ground in the Arabic tradition. *Ḥādith al-niṣf mitr* (1972) uses similar structural strategies as his short stories, but with a more meticulous structuring of novelistic time and the foregrounding of mimetic dialogue. *Fasād al-amkina* (1973) is an investigation of the relationship between man and place – an infatuation also seen in his travel books to parts of Egypt and to Paris and Greece. *Sayyid min ḥaql al-sabānikh* (1987) represents one of the few science fiction novels in Arabic. Mūsā also wrote the script for the film *al-Būstagī*, an important contribution to the development of the Egyptian cinema.

Text editions

The Incident, Hoda Ayyad (trans.), Cairo (1987).

Seeds of Corruption, Mona Mikhail (trans.), Boston (1980).

W. HAMARNEH

Mūsā, Salāma (1887–1958)

Egyptian Coptic prose writer and intellectual. Known primarily for his early studies on socialism and Fabianism, Salāma Mūsā supported the liberal movement in Arabic literature. After studying in England, he published a concise study of socialism (1912), in which he reflected on his experiences with the Fabian Society, whose philosophy he had adopted. In 1920, with Ḥusnī al-'Arabī and others, he founded the first socialist party in the Arab world, but joined the Wafd party after Sa'd Zaghlūl became leader, believing 'al-Wafdiyya', as he termed it, to be essentially a call to independence. His intellectual development during this period was recorded in his autobiographical work *Tarbiyat Salāma Mūsā* (1947). From 1930 he published the weekly magazine *Majallat al-Miṣrī*, and from 1934 to 1942 edited the monthly *al-Majalla al-Jadīda*.

Salāma Mūsā was a staunch modernizer and a popularizer of Western culture and science among the Arabs, expressing his views in numerous articles and books. Outspoken in his political stances, he believed that literature should create an environment in which freedom could grow, prosper and prevail; he characterized past writing in Arabic as 'regal'. His outspokenness on women's issues was shown in many of his works, including *al-Mar'a laysat lu'bat al-rajul* (1955). His continuing influence and ability to provoke controversy among Arab readers are evidenced by the many reprints of his books throughout the Arab world after his death.

Text edition

The Education of Salāmah Mūsā, L.O. Schuman (trans.), Leiden (1961).

Further reading

'Awad, L., *The Literature of Ideas in Egypt*, Part 1 (*Arabic Writing Today*, vol. 3), Atlanta (1986).

M. MIKHAIL

Mūsā ibn Maymūn *see* Maimonides

musammaṭ see strophic poetry

music and poetry, medieval

Despite the gradual emergence of important instrumental forms, music in the Islamic world has been (and still is) predominantly vocal, and vocal compositions have usually included, or consisted entirely of, settings of verse. The question thus arises of the nature of the relationship between the two with respect on the one hand to the social function of song and the possible interaction between singer and poet and, on the other, to the more technical issue of styles of text setting and aesthetics.

On occasion poet and composer/singer are one and the same: although Isḥāq **al-Mawṣilī** (235/850) is best known as the foremost **'Abbāsid** court musician of his age, he was also a more than competent poet. But his songs served to disseminate the works of many others too, and certain poets are known to have associated with famous singers who might help their verse gain popularity. It has, in consequence, been suggested that singers' practices and preferences may have encouraged some of the changes in theme, diction and technique that radically affected the development of poetry during the preceding **Umayyad** period and, in particular, may have contributed to the development and popularization of some of the shorter metres that were then coming to the fore. Given that singing a line normally takes longer that reciting it, the metrical hypothesis is initially attractive. But singers remained equally content to set verse in the longer metres, and there is insufficient evidence to substantiate the claim that musical rhythms could have had a significant impact on metrical developments. Despite the intriguing presence of a degree of terminological overlap there are functional differences between the two systems: certainly settings of poems in metre *x* are not restricted to or predominantly in cycle *y*, and while it would be possible to map metrical feet onto rhythmic cycles, for one musical authority at least this was a recipe for poor quality best avoided in practice.

Similarly, it is difficult to demonstrate any decisive influence on theme and diction. The most that can be said is that a poet composing verse to be sung would naturally concentrate on those themes most appropriate to the context of performance: the amatory, bacchic and panegyric thus take precedence over the martial, descriptive and satiric. Changes in diction may be seen partly as a function of such thematic specialization, partly as a reflection of wider social (and aesthetic) transformations to which musicians both contributed and reacted, but which they can hardly have instigated.

Given the nature of the historical record, our knowledge of how words were set to music is scanty. The earliest example of a notated song dates from the seventh/thirteenth century; there are too few later ones to trace subsequent developments with any confidence; and antecedent stages can only be guessed at on the basis of secondary sources, whether literary or theoretical. If text setting may be variously placed on a continuum running from subservience (the melody is conceived of as a means to enhance the meaning and emotional impact of the verse) to independence (the melody is an autonomous art form using the words as incidental phonetic material), what information we have points, not surprisingly, to an intermediate position, but with at the same time the suggestion of a tendency, during periods of increasing musical sophistication, to approach the latter extreme.

Of the styles of performing Arabic poetry before the second/eighth century we know very little. Even the distinction between such basic terms as *inshād*, 'recitation' and *tarannum*, 'cantillation' cannot be drawn with any precision. The existence of professional (if slave) singers, together with the gradual development of a complex indigenous terminology independent of that adopted from Greek theory, certainly points to song (*ghināʾ*) having its own formal determinants and aesthetic criteria, yet the definition of the expert musician offered by the Umayyad singer Ibn Surayj gives prominence to fidelity to the structure (and hence, we may assume, respect for the sense) of the verse. One could well imagine a subtle theoretical literature emerging out of the concerns expressed through his pithy formulations, but in the event mathematics and cosmology were to predominate, and styles of verse setting are only fitfully illustrated. There are persistent references to a 'heavy' and melodically florid and difficult style associated with the Arab tradition (which contrasts with a 'light' and simple Persian one), and by the seventh/thirteenth century we even have a reference to a singer who is claimed to have spent some two hours over a single line of verse.

The development of a markedly melismatic style, together with the attention to the minutiae of vocal timbre and technique revealed by the vocabulary paraded in specialist works, clearly points to the composer/performer becoming increasingly independent. Indeed, beginning in the ninth/fifteenth century and increasingly in the tenth/sixteenth, the Middle Eastern court repertoire as preserved in contemporary song-text collections (in which Arabic yields pride of place to Persian) is predominantly made up of pieces in which much of the composition consists of formulaic expressions extraneous to the verse and long strings of nonsense syllables in which the semantic content is zero and the artistic content, consequently, wholly musical. Moreover, the distribution of material demonstrates that, for the composer, the verse is subordinate to purely musical structural concerns. The setting may still respect, if not prosodic units, then at least the fundamental distinction between long and short syllables, and the words still need to be articulated with sufficient clarity to ensure comprehension, but they are increasingly pegs on which purely musical effects can be hung. Indeed, it appears that the dominant aesthetic preferred semantically important words to be left unadorned, while the more melismatic passages were associated with emotionally neutral grammatical elements. The eleventh/seventeenth-century Ottoman tradition shows, however, a reaction, moving to simpler syllabic settings, and it is possible that there may have been, through time, a number of stylistic swings back and forth between the two poles.

Further reading

Bencheikh, J.-E., 'Les musiciens et la poésie: les écoles d'Isḥāq al-Mawṣili ... et d'Ibrāhīm ibn al-Mahdī ... ', *Arabica* 22 (1975), 114–52.

Farmer, H.G., *A History of Arabian Music* (to the thirteenth century), London (1929), rpt (1967).

Neubauer, E., 'Tarannum und terennüm in Poesie und Musik', *Mélanges de l'Université Saint-Joseph* 48 (1973–4), 139–53.

Sawa, G.D., *Music Performance Practice in the Early ʿAbbāsid Era*, Toronto (1989).

Wright, O., 'Music in Muslim Spain', in *The Legacy of Muslim Spain*, S.K. Jayyusi (ed.), Leiden (1992), 555–79.

O. WRIGHT

See also: Abū al-Faraj al-Iṣbahānī; singers and musicians

Muslim ibn al-Ḥajjāj (202 [or 206?]–261/817 [or 821?]–875)

Collector of ***ḥadīth***. Born in Nishapur, Muslim travelled widely throughout the Islamic world in search of traditions related from **Muḥammad**. It is said that he heard a total of 300,000 of these, of which he selected some 3,000 and compiled them into a book known as *al-Jāmiʿ al-ṣaḥīḥ* (*The Reliable Collection* [of *ḥadīth*]) or simply *al-Ṣaḥīḥ* (*The Reliable* [*ḥadīth*]). This work, along with that of **al-Bukhārī** by the same name, became accepted by the **Sunnī** community as the most authentic collection of prophetic traditions, second only in authority to the **Koran**. Organized by legal topic, Muslim's work contains 52 'books' covering all the major aspects of Islamic law, the life of Muḥammad, theology, eschatology and **exegesis**. Numerous commentaries on the work exist. Muslim is also credited with a number of other works, none of which achieved any substantial significance.

Text editions

al-Jāmiʿ al-ṣaḥīḥ, M.F. ʿAbd al-Bāqī (ed.), 5 vols, Cairo (1955–6) (other editions exist; this is certainly the best one).

Juynboll, G.H.A., 'Muslim's introduction to his *Ṣaḥīḥ*, translated and annotated with an excursus on the chronology of the *fitna* and *bidʿa*,' *JSAI* 5 (1984), 263–302.

Ṣaḥīḥ Muslim, being Traditions of the Sayings and Doings of the Prophet Muḥammad, A.H. Siddiqui (trans.), 4 vols, Lahore, (1976).

Further reading

Burton, John, *An Introduction to the Ḥadīth*, Edinburgh (1994), 123–7.

A. RIPPIN

See also: *ḥadīth*

Muslim ibn al-Walīd (*c.*130–207/*c.*748–823)

Abū al-Walīd Muslim ibn al-Walīd al-Anṣārī was a poet and *mawlā* of the Anṣār; he was born and brought up in **Kufa**. He moved to **Baghdad** in the reign of **Hārūn al-Rashīd** before the **Barmakid** débâcle of 187/794. It was al-Faḍl ibn Yaḥyā al-Barmakī who introduced the poet to al-Rashīd. He subsequently became close to Yazīd ibn Mazyad al-Shaybānī during Hārūn's reign and later to al-Faḍl ibn Sahl who appointed him, during the reign of al-Ma'mūn, to be postmaster in Jurjān.

Muslim was among the finest poets of the early **ʿAbbāsid** period and, as one of the first masters of ***badīʿ***, he is held to have had a profound influence on **Abū Tammām**. Although his reputation is built on the use of *badīʿ* it was also the source of some criticism, i.e. where *jinās* (paronomasia) is overworked such as to produce six words from the same root in one verse. He composed in most of the major genres and his poetry is an admixture of **bedouin**/conservative and urban styles; he used the traditional progression of themes in ***madīḥ*** with some striking innovation, i.e. a boat trip on the Tigris replaces a *raḥīl* on camel-back. He disliked ***hijā'*** though he had some poetic adversaries, including **al-ʿAbbās ibn al-Aḥnaf** and al-Ḥakam ibn Qanbar; he composed elegies on Yazīd ibn Mazyad, his wife and Ḥammād ibn Sayyār (a line of which echoes the style of **al-Khansā'**). But the best of his descriptive talent probably lies in depictions of wine drinking and debauchery. Here one must be careful to draw a distinction between him and **Abū Nuwās**, to whom he has been likened; unlike the latter, Muslim was inclined to treat wine within the framework of poetry offered by other dominant themes, i.e. *madīḥ* or ***ghazal***. A comparison between poem 3 of his ***dīwān*** and any composite seduction ***khamriyya*** of Abū Nuwās illustrates the essential difference between the two poets. Muslim's poem of 35 lines is replete with metaphors that suggest the link between the bacchic and erotic registers of this kind of poetry; but the absence of a specific role for wine in a seduction narrative, so common a trait in Abū Nuwās, holds the two styles of bacchism apart.

His *ghazal* is strikingly similar in places to **ʿUmar ibn Abī Rabīʿa**, although he did not nurture the seeds of debauchery to be found in ʿUmar in the same way as Abū Nuwās and others of his contemporaries.

Text editions

Beiträge zur arabische Poesie, O. Rescher (trans.), Istanbul (1961), 2.

Dīwān, Sāmī al-Dahhān (ed.), Cairo (1957).

Further reading

Barbier de Meynard, M., 'Un poète arabe du IIème siècle de l'hégire', in *Actes du XIème Congrès International des Orientalistes*, Paris (1892), 1–21.

Heinrichs, W., 'Muslim ibn al-Walīd and *Badīʿ*', in *Wagner Festschrift*, vol. 2, 211–45.

Ibn ʿAlwān, Ḥasan, *Ṣarī al-Ghawānī*, Cairo (1949).

Sulṭān, Jamīl, *Muslim ibn al-Walīd, Ṣarīʿ al-Ghawānī*, Damascus (1932); 2nd edn, Beirut (1967).

Tarzī, Fu'ād, *Muslim ibn al-Walīd Ṣarīʿ al-Ghawānī*, Beirut (1961).

P.F. KENNEDY

See also: *khamriyya*

muṭābaqa *see* rhetorical figures

mutadārik *see* prosody

al-Mutalammis (sixth century CE)

Pre-Islamic poet and protagonist of an ancient Arab saga according to which he and his nephew **Ṭarafa** were attending the court of the **Lakhmid** king of **Ḥīra**, ʿAmr ibn Hind (554–69 AD). At the end of their stay, the king gives each of them a letter which they should hand over to the king's governor in Western **Arabia**. On the way, al-Mutalammis is seized by suspicions, opens his letter and finds out that it contains his own death-warrant. Thereupon he throws it away and flees. Ṭarafa, however, who delivers his letter faithfully to the governor, does not escape execution. Nearly all of the poetry ascribed to al-Mutalammis is related to episodes from his legendary life, so that it seems rather to be the illustration of a saga than the work of a single historical figure.

Text editions

Dīwān, Ḥasan Kāmil al-Ṣayrafī (ed.) in *RIMA* 14 (1968), 1–559.

Die Gedichte des Mutalammis, K. Vollers (ed. and trans.), Leipzig (1903).

T. BAUER

al-Mu'tamid ibn 'Abbād (431–88/1039–95)

Abū al-Qāsim Muḥammad al-Mu'tamid ('alā Allāh) ibn 'Abbād was the ruler of Seville, and a poet. Al-Mu'tamid succeeded his father as king of the *ṭā'ifa* kingdom of Seville in 461/1069, but paid tribute to García of Galicia and later to Alfonso VI of Castile. In 1086 he invited the Almoravid leader Yūsuf ibn Tashufīn to help defend the *ṭā'ifa* kingdoms against Alfonso, resulting in the Muslim victory in the battle of Zallaqa. The second invitation to the Almoravids in 1090 led to their occupation of al-Andalus and the end of the *ṭā'ifa* kingdoms. Al-Mu'tamid was exiled to Aghmāt, where he died in prison.

Devotee of poetry and patron of distinguished poets like **Ibn 'Ammār**, **Ibn al-Labbāna**, **Ibn Wahbūn**, **Ibn Ḥamdīs**, and Ibn Sirāj, al-Mu'tamid was himself the author of at least 188 monorhymed poems and one ***muwashshaḥ***. His extant poems, though mostly short, were highly regarded. His early verse is mostly on love and wine, but he has an important *rā'iyya* apologizing to his father for the loss of Malaga, and another addressed to Ibn al-'Ammār, recalling their friendship in Silves. His best verse was written in exile about his imprisonment and humiliation; it reflects the stages by which he grappled emotionally with imprisonment.

Text editions

Dīwān, Aḥmad Aḥmad Badawī and Ḥāmid 'Abd al-Majīd (eds), Cairo (1951); R. Souissi (ed.), Tunis (1975).

Monroe, J.T., *Hispano-Arabic Poetry: A Student Anthology*, Berkeley (1974), 194–201.

Poesias: Antología bilingüe, M.J. Rubiera Mata (trans.), Madrid (1982).

Further reading

Meisami, J.S., 'Unsquaring the circle: rereading a poem by al-Mu'tamid ibn 'Abbād', *Arabica* 35 (1988), 293–310.

Nykl, A.R., *Hispano-Arabic Poetry and its Relations with the Old Provençal Troubadours*, Baltimore (1946), 134–54, 181.

Pérès, Henri, *La Poésie andalouse en arabe classique au xie siècle*, 2nd edn, Paris (1953); index s.v. al-Mu'tamid, prince de Seville.

Scheindlin, R., *Form and Structure in the Poetry of al-Mu'tamid ibn 'Abbād*, Leiden (1974).

Souissi, R., *Al-Mu'tamid et son oeuvre poètique*, Tunis (1977).

R.P. SCHEINDLIN

See also: Spain

Mutammim ibn Nuwayra (first/seventh century)

Poet of early Islamic times who owes his fame to the elegies (***rithā'***) in which he lamented the death of his brother **Mālik ibn Nuwayra** and which rendered him a model of brotherly affection. Among his laments is one of the most celebrated elegies of ancient Arabic literature (cf. *Mufaḍḍaliyyāt*, no. 67), in which he deals, in a balanced manner, both with the loss that Mālik's death means for society, as well as with the expression of his own personal feelings. It consists of six sections: praise for the virtues of the deceased (generosity, restraint, bravery); a call to weep for Mālik in remembrance of his deeds; an expression of the poet's own grief; a benediction over the deceased's grave; the poet's justification of his grief; and an attack on a person who had abandoned Mālik's corpse.

Text editions

Collection of fragments in:

Jones, Alan, *Early Arabic Poetry*, Oxford (1992), vol. 1, 102–25.

Nöldeke, Theodor, *Beiträge zur Kenntnis der Poesie der alten Araber*, Hannover (1864) 87–151.

al-Ṣaffār, Ibtisām Marhūn, *Mālik wa-Mutammim ibnā Nuwayra al-Yarbū'ī*, Baghdad (1968).

T. BAUER

al-Mutanabbī (*c.*303–54/*c.*915–65)

Abū al-Ṭayyib Aḥmad ibn al-Ḥusayn al-Mutanabbī was a renowned panegyrist, associated chiefly with the **Ḥamdānid** ruler Sayf al-Dawla (r. 336–56/947–67). Al-Mutanabbī, whose father claimed south Yemenite origins, was born in **Kufa**; his family may have had **Shī'ī** (perhaps **Zaydī**) leanings. Brought up by his maternal grandmother, the poet was educated at a school with Shī'ī tendencies, and showed his poetic abilities at an early age. In 312/924 his family left Kufa, which had been sacked by the **Carmathians**, for an extended sojurn among the Banū Kalb in the oasis of Samawa. Returning in 315/927, al-Mutanabbī came under the protection of a Kufan notable, one Abū al-Faḍl al-Kūfī (described by Blachère as a 'hellenised bourgeois'; 1935, 30), who exerted considerable influence over the young poet.

In the same year the Carmathians again seized Kufa; and in 316/928 al-Mutanabbī and his family migrated to **Baghdad**, where he continued his activities as a would-be panegyrist. Around 318/950 he left Baghdad for **Syria,** where he spent the next three years as an itinerant panegyrist; he seems also to have preached some sort of revolutionary propaganda, and became involved with the **bedouin** clan of the Banū 'Adī, engaging in acts of brigandage which led to his arrest and imprisonment in Homs (Syria) in 322/933. He was, apparently, credited with claiming miracles, which earned him his sobriquet (al-Mutanabbī – 'one who claims to be a prophet').

Around 325/937 al-Mutanabbī was released from prison through the auspices of the Ikhshīdid governor Isḥāq ibn Kayghalagh, and resumed his wanderings in search of patronage. (Syria was then under the rather precarious control of the Ikhshīds, rivals to the Ḥamdānids.) He spent some time at the court of Badr ibn 'Ammār al-Kharshanī, the governor of Tiberias, before being forced by his rivals to flee to the Syrian desert. Around 330/941 he attached himself to the Ikhshīdid general al-Musāwir, praising him and other Ikhshīdid notables. When the Ḥamdānid Sayf al-Dawla entered Aleppo in 333/944 al-Mutanabī, after a brief stay in Tripoli, fled to **Damascus**.

When Sayf al-Dawla took Antioch in 337/948 al-Mutanabbī composed a panegyric celebrating his entry. He soon became established at Sayf al-Dawla's court, which under that ruler's patronage had become a flourishing cultural and literary centre, and remained there some nine years as his panegyrist. The ***qaṣīda*s** addressed to that ruler, known as the *Sayfiyyāt*, are remarkable for many innovative features commented on by anthologists and critics, among them his addressing his prince as one would a beloved, and his vivid narratives of battle. The poet acquired a circle of ardent admirers (including the young **Ibn Jinnī**, who was to rejoin him later in Baghdad), as well as many rivals and detractors, headed by Sayf al-Dawla's cousin **Abū Firās al-Ḥamdānī**, who spared no effort to defame and discredit the poet, and who combed his poems for evidence of plagiary, linguistic error and heretical beliefs.

Al-Mutanabbī's stay at Sayf al-Dawla's court – during which he (like other poets) often accompanied the ruler on his campaigns, described in detail in his *qaṣīda*s – marked the high point of his career; but it was not without its negative aspects. Sayf al-Dawla expected a constant stream of production from his poets, which must have exacerbated the increasing friction between poet and patron which was fuelled by the poet's detractors After several reconciliations, early in 346/957 there was a total rupture. Al-Mutanabbī, realizing that he could no longer rely on Sayf al-Dawla's support, determined to flee to **Egypt**, ruled by the Ikhshīdid regent Kāfūr, and in the summer of that year arrived in the Egyptian capital of Fusṭāṭ.

Fusṭāṭ too boasted its intellectual circles, which al-Mutanabbī seems to have had difficulty in penetrating. Many critics make much of his supposed repugnance for Kāfūr – a former black slave – but this may represent pro-Arab propaganda. Whatever the case, the poet composed a number of panegyrics to Kāfūr, who had apparently promised him a governorship in Syria, but who kept him dangling. Tensions between the two increased; a possible alternative presented itself in the general Abū Shujā' Fātik, whose untimely death in late 350/961 dashed the poet's hopes. (He later composed a lengthy and bitter elegy in which he lauded Fātik and lampooned Kāfūr.) In 350/early 962, al-Mutanabbī fled once more, this time from Fusṭāṭ to Iraq.

After spending a year in his native Kufa the poet set out for Baghdad, perhaps intending to proceed to Syria in the hope of reconciliation with Sayf al-Dawla. Baghdad, at that time ruled by Sayf al-Dawla's enemy the **Būyid** Mu'izz al-Dawla (d. 356/967), was the home of many brilliant intellectual circles, among them that of the vizier **al-Muhallabī**, to which al-Mutanabbī failed to gain entry due both to his refusal to compose the obligatory panegyric for the vizier and to the enmity of some of its members, including the poets **Ibn**

al-Ḥajjāj and **Ibn Lankak** and the philologist-critic **al-Ḥātimī**. The latter, in an attempt to demonstrate the poet's plagiarisms and heretical beliefs, engaged al-Mutanabbī in a poetic debate in which he seems to have come off decidedly second best.

On the move again, al-Mutanabbī returned briefly to Kufa, where he assisted in repelling another Carmathian attack (in 353/954) and composed some satirical verses against the Carmathian leader Ḍabba. Then, on the invitation of **Ibn al-ʿAmīd** (vizier of **al-Ṣāḥib Ibn ʿAbbād**), in 354/965 he went to that notable's court in Arrajan, where he composed several panegyrics for the vizier, and thence to the ccurt of ʿAḍud al-Dawla in Shiraz, addressing a number of poems to him as well. Then, longing to return to Iraq (and perhaps from there to Syria), he set out on his final journey, in the course of which he was set upon by bedouin brigands led by the uncle of Ḍabba the Carmathian, whom he had satirized in Kufa. The poet, his son and his travelling companions were killed, the caravan sacked, and the autograph manuscript of his poems, which he carried with him, dispersed by the desert winds.

Al-Mutanabbī's poetry inspired many commentaries and works of criticism. Many writers took it upon themselves to point out his plagiarisms and his heretical beliefs, among them al-Ṣāḥib Ibn ʿAbbād, whose *Kashf ʿan masāwī shiʿr al-Mutanabbī* (*c*.364/974) was perhaps motivated by the poet's refusal to come to his court at **Rayy**; as **al-Thaʿālibī** notes in his *Yatīmat al-dahr*, the Ṣāḥib himself plagiarized al-Mutanabbī by 'prosifying' the poet's verses in his own epistles. Al-Qāḍī **al-Jurjānī**'s *al-Wasāṭa*, composed in response to such criticisms, stressed the difference between commonplaces and plagiarisms and pointed out that even the Ancients 'borrowed' from one another. Al-Mutanabbī was often compared (usually to his detriment) to **Abū Tammām** and **al-Buḥturī**; **al-Sharīf al-Raḍī** in his commentary on the *Dīwān* maintained his superiority and praised the heroic quality of his poetry. Other major commentaries include those of his pupil and admirer Ibn Jinnī, **Abū al-ʿAlāʾ al-Maʿarrī**, al-ʿUkbarī and al-Wāḥidī (462/1060), the basis for published editions of the *Dīwān*. (For a complete list of works on al-Mutanabbī's 'plagiary' and of commentaries on the *Dīwān* see *GAS*, vol. 2, 487–96).

Al-Mutanabbī's fame rapidly spread to other parts of the Islamic world, in particular al-Andalus (see **Spain**) and Iran, where he was an important influence on the development of New Persian poetry. His supposed 'pro-Arab' bias has made him a favourite with modern critics of a nationalist or pan-Arab bent.

Text editions

Beiträge zur arabischen Poesie, O. Rescher (ed.), Istanbul (1961), vol. 3, part 1.

Dīwān, ʿA. ʿAzzām (ed.), Cairo (1363/1944); Buṭrus al-Bustānī (ed.), Beirut (1860) (many reprints).

Mutanabbi carmina cum commentario Wahidii, F. Dieterici (ed.), Berlin (1861).

Poems of al-Mutanabbī, A.J. Arberry (ed. and trans.), Cambridge (1967).

Further reading

al-Āmidī, *al-Ibāna ʿan sariqāt al-Mutanabbī...*, ʿUmar al-Dasūqī (ed.), Cairo (1961) (includes al-Ṣāḥib Ibn ʿAbbād's *al-Kashf ʿan masāwī shiʿr al-Mutanabbī*).

Blachère, R., *Un Poète arabe du IVᵉ siècle de l'Hégire..., Abou t-Tayyib al-Motanabbi*, Paris (1935).

Hamori, A., *The Composition of Mutanabbī's Panegyrics to Sayf al-Dawla*, Leiden (1992).

Heinrichs, W.P., 'The meaning of Mutanabbī', in *Poetry and Prophecy*, James L. Kugel (ed.), Ithaca (1990), 120–39, 231–9.

Latham, J.D., 'The elegy on the death of Abū Shujāʿ Fātik by al-Mutanabbī', in *Arabicus Felix*, 90–107.

al-Mutannabbī, recueil publié à l'occasion de son millénaire, Beirut (1936).

Shākir, Maḥmūd, *al-Mutanabbī*, 2nd edn, Cairo (1977).

al-Thaʿālibī, *Yatīmat al-dahr*, Cairo (1934), vol. 1, 126–240.

J.S. MEISAMI

mutaqārib see prosody

al-Muṭarrizī (538–610/1144–1213)

Abū al-Fatḥ Nāṣir ibn ʿAbd al-Sayyid al-Muṭarrizī was a grammarian, jurist and man of letters from **Khwārazm**. He wrote a few works on **grammar**, the most popular one being *al-Miṣbāḥ*, and a lexicon of technical terms used in ***ḥadīth*** and ***fiqh*** (called *al-Mughrib fī tartīb al-muʿrib*. His most famous work is his commentary entitled *al-Īḍāḥ* on the *Maqāmāt* of **al-Ḥarīrī**; it was extensively used by De Sacy in his edition of al-Ḥarīrī. The commentary has a preface dealing with *balāgha* (see **rhetoric and poetics**). Al-Muṭarrizī was called '*khalīfat* (the successor of) **al-Zamakhsharī**', because he covered a similar range of interests and was born, moreover, on the day that al-Zamakhsharī died.

Text edition

al-Īḍāḥ, Tabriz (1872).

Further reading

Reinaud, J. and Derenbourg, J., 'Introduction' to A.I. Sylvestre de Sacy, *Les Séances de Hariri publ. en arabe avec un commentaire choisi*, 2nd edn, Paris (1847–53), vol. 2, 57–60.

G.J.H. VAN GELDER

al-Mutawakkil al-Laythī (d. after 72/691)

Poet from the **Umayyad** period. He lived in **Kufa**, a member of the tribe Layth ibn Bakr (a subdivision of Kināna). He made panegyric poems for Mu'āwiya and his son Yazīd, as well as love poetry on his ex-wife Ruhayma, divorced at her request because of an illness, but cured afterwards. Some poems of **hijā'** and **fakhr** are also preserved. **Al-Akhṭal** met him when he visited Kufa and was impressed by his poetry.

Text edition

Shi'r al-Mutawakkil al-Laythī, Yaḥyā al-Jubūrī (ed.), Baghdad (1971).

G.J.H. VAN GELDER

Mu'tazilīs

The Mu'tazilīs were a theological school that flourished in the second/eighth and third/ninth centuries and lingered within certain circles for at least two hundred years thereafter. Some ideas espoused by the Mu'tazilīs may be found among the **Shī'īs**. The heyday of the school occurred under the sponsorship of the **'Abbāsid** state, which was initiated by the caliph al-Ma'mūn (r. 813–33) and maintained until the reactionary measures of the caliph al-Mutawakkil (r. 847–61) brought it to an end. Thereafter, as Islamic orthodoxy came to be more fully defined and institutionalized, the Mu'tazilī school was relegated to the periphery of Islamic religious thought and accorded the status of a heterodox movement.

Members of the Mu'tazilī school preferred to be known as the 'Champions of Monotheism and Justice' (*ahl al-tawḥīd wa-al-'adl*). They were advocates of a rationalist approach to theological discourse that saw these two concepts as poorly served by what they perceived to be the obscurantism of most of their fellow Muslims. Anxious to make Islam rationally defensible against the intellectual challenges of Christianity, crypto-Manichaeanism and other religious traditions, the Mu'tazilīs insisted upon placing the tools of discursive reasoning as known from Greek and Hellenistic sources in the service of Islam.

Their insistence that the **Koran** not be accorded the status of an eternal, uncreated Word of God is the most well-known aspect of their rationalist monotheism. It was tied to a more general conviction that the attributes of God (of which the Word or Speech of God was one) should not be regarded as realities in their own right to be predicated of the Godhead, since such predication is contrary to the perfect, simple unity of God. As for the Mu'tazilī rationalist ethics (subsumed under the heading of justice), this entailed the conviction that good and evil are known by the intellect apart from divine revelation and that the human conception of justice belongs within the realm of the good thus known such that God's acts will necessarily conform to it.

Although an orthodox theology formulated principally by the Ash'arī school would challenge these Mu'tazilī positions on equally rationalist grounds, the Mu'tazilī school proved to be a major stimulus to theological thought and continues to represent a heritage valued and to some extent utilized by Muslim thinkers.

Further reading

Nader, Albert N., *Le Système philosophique des Mu'tazila*, Beirut (1956).
van Ess, J., 'Mu'tazilah', in *Encyclopaedia of Religion*, Mircea Eliade (ed.), New York (1987), vol. 10, 220–9.
Watt, W.M., *The Formative Period of Islamic Thought*, Edinburgh (1973), 209–50, 297–302.

B. WEISS

See also: *kalām*

Muṭī' ibn Iyās (d. 169/785)

Abū Salmā Muṭī' ibn Iyās al-Kinānī of the Banū Du'il of Kināna was one of the libertines of **Kufa** known to the **Umayyad** caliph **al-Walīd ibn Yazīd**; he was the latter's ***nadīm*** and was probably influenced by his wine poetry. He subsequently had relations with the **'Abbāsid** princes until his death. He was accused of *zandaqa*, along with other Kufan poets, but, except for possible Shī'ī leanings, no theological opinions can be safely ascribed to him. In his poetry he could show a delicate sensitivity but also extreme vulgarity. His most famous poem, alluded to by **Abū Nuwās**, is an apostrophe on 'The Two Palms of Ḥulwān'. Other surviving poems (including a panegyric on Ghamr ibn Yazīd and an elegy on youth) are also echoed in Abū Nuwās and suggest his role in influencing the development of the ***khamriyya***.

Text editions

von Grunebaum, G.E., 'Three Arabic poets of the early Abbasid age (the collected fragments of Muṭī' ibn Iyās, Salm al-Khāsir and Abū 'š-Šamaqmaq)', *Orientalia*, 17 (1948), 160–204.

Further reading

Ḥāwī, I., *Fann al-shi'r al-khamrī*, Beirut (1981).

P.F. KENNEDY

Muṭrān, Khalīl (1872–1949)

Lebanese poet and journalist. Born in Ba'albek, Muṭrān was a typical member of the Syro-Lebanese intelligentsia of the nineteenth century, deeply involved in literature, politics, business affairs and the polymathic journalism which was a feature of the age. Pressure from the Ottoman authorities forced him to leave Beirut in 1890 and he then spent two years in Paris, the cultural capital of Europe at the time and a hotbed of political activity among its immigrant communities. Following one of the common migration paths from Greater **Syria**, he arrived in Alexandria in 1892 and spent the remainder of his life in **Egypt**. In common with other prominent fellow immigrants, he became well known as a journalist and worked for ***al-Ahrām*** before starting his own twice-monthly periodical *al-Majalla al-Miṣriyya* in 1900 and a daily paper *al-Jawā'ib al-Miṣriyya* in 1902.

Muṭrān's outstanding achievements lay in poetry, where his work was seminal for the development of the genre until the 1940s. His first volume of verse appeared in 1908. In the preface, Muṭrān reveals his commitment to innovative ideas such as the structural unity of the poem, the necessity of not allowing the old rules of rhyme and metre to dominate the poet's emotions, and the primacy of the creative imagination. In many ways Muṭrān never surpassed the achievements of his first ***dīwān*** in his subsequent writing. Although most of his work appears at first glance to be in the neo-classical mode, careful analysis reveals that a number of these pieces contain passages of profound personal introspection and empathic identification with natural surroundings in a manner typical of the European Romantics. Poems from the first *dīwān* such as 'Death of Two Loved Ones, 'Evening', 'The Weeping Lion' and 'Solitude in the Desert' are clear illustrations of this important development.

One of the most striking signs of Muṭrān's taste for innovation was his use of dramatic narrative verse in a way that was quite new in Arabic poetry. His poem about the two Napoleons, '1806–1870', was written when he was only 16 years old. Most of his compositions of this type demonstrate his passionate dislike of political despotism and his consciousness of social injustice in whatever form. 'Nero', 'The Great Wall of China' and 'The Death of Buzurjumuhr' are all allegorical protests against political tyranny, while 'The Martyred Child' is a description of the degradation to which urban corruption reduces a simple country girl. In addition to his own original compositions Muṭrān was a gifted translator, rendering into Arabic *The Merchant of Venice*, *Othello*, *Macbeth*, *Hamlet* and *Le Cid*.

The great enigma of Muṭrān's career is that he did not build on the achievements of his first *dīwān*, for much of his subsequent poetry reverted to competent but genteel neo-classicism. It is possible that the business misfortunes that almost ruined him in 1912 led him to devote most of his energies to non-literary matters: he became secretary to the Khedivial Agricultural Society, was involved with the planning of the Miṣr Bank, and was also an effective director of the National Theatre Company. As well as the official recognition that he received for his poetry – earning him the title of *shā'ir al-quṭrayn* ('Poet of Two Countries', i.e. Lebanon and Egypt) – he was also much revered by later poets such as **Abū Shādī** and the **Apollo Group** who developed to the full the Romantic tendencies that he had begun to introduce. His complete *dīwān* was published in Cairo in 1948–9.

Further reading

Badawi, M.M., *A Critical Introduction to Modern Arabic Poetry*, Cambridge (1975), 68–84.

CHALMAL, 84–8.

Jayyusi, S.K., *Trends and Movements in Modern Arabic Poetry*, Leiden (1977), 54–64.

Mandūr, M., *Muḥāḍarāt 'an Khalīl Muṭrān*, Cairo (1954).

Moreh, S., *Modern Arabic Poetry 1800–1970*, Leiden (1976), 59–65.

al-Ramādī, Jamāl al-Dīn, *Khalīl Muṭrān: shā'ir al-aqṭār al-'Arabiyya*, Cairo (n.d).

R.C. OSTLE

muwalladūn

The term *muwallad* (pl. *muwalladūn*) is originally taken from the language of husbandry, where it means 'crossbreed', 'bastard'. Applied to human beings, it referred to persons of mixed, Arab and non-Arab, blood. Since the important poets of early **'Abbāsid** times were mainly of mixed origin, Iranian and Greek ancestry being not uncommon, they were called *muwalladūn*; by semantic extension, the term *muwallad* is also applied to their poetry. Outside poetry, with the direction of semantic development unclear, the term is used to denote as 'post-classical' certain linguistic items, such as words, derivations and even proverbs. 'Post-classical' means: not belonging to the classical language of pre- and early Islamic texts.

The *muwalladūn* poets are also called ***muḥdathūn***, this from the point of view of being the 'Moderns' *vis-à-vis* the 'Ancients'. There is, however, a tendency somewhat later to use *muḥdathūn* for the early 'Abbāsid poets, while *muwalladūn* is applied to the later poets, the sequence of eras in indigenous Arabic literary history thus being: *Jāhiliyyūn* 'pre-Islamic'; *mukhaḍramūn*, 'straddling'; *Islāmiyyūn*, '[early] Islamic'; *muḥdathūn*, '[early] Moderns'; and *muwalladūn* '[later] Moderns'.

W.P. HEINRICHS

muwashshaḥ (pl. muwashshaḥāt)

A strophic poetic form, usually performed with musical accompaniment, which originated in Islamic **Spain** in the third/late ninth century. The *muwashshaḥ* became popular throughout the Islamic world and was adopted by poets in other languages, notably Hebrew. The question of the Andalusian *muwashshaḥ*'s relation to European poetry, in particular the Provençal troubadour lyric, has fuelled several centuries of animated debate. In the latter half of this century, the discovery of a corpus of bilingual poems (mainly Arabic–Romance, Hebrew–Arabic and Hebrew–Romance) has excited scholars in a wide range of fields, and spawned a new generation of controversies.

Tradition has it that this verse form was invented by Muqaddam ibn Mu'afa al-Qabrī late in the third/ninth century, but none of his works are extant. Although 'Ubāda **Ibn Mā' al-Samā'** (d. 419/1028 or 421/1030) was long held to be the author of the oldest attributable *muwashashaḥ*, we now have a poem by Abū al-Qāsim ibn al-'Aṭṭār (d. 387/997) which is likely earlier. However, our knowledge of the early period of *muwashshaḥ* composition is limited, and many questions remain unanswered or the object of intense speculation. To what degree was the metre of the poems determined by pre-existing Romance verse? Can their appearance be explained as an outgrowth of earlier, purely Arabic forms such as the *musammaṭ*? In the context of a polyglot, multicultural al-Andalus, to which many people now look as a kind of mirror of our own times, the questions of the metre of the *muwashshaḥ*, of defining the role and even the language of the *kharjas*, go far beyond the realm of literary–critical esoterica. The interpretation of the poems, and uncertainties about their origins, have been burdened by the weight of their symbolism as a point of contact between European and Arabic culture and sensibility, as a place to explore notions of cultural influence and borrowing, hybridity, tradition and innovation.

Although we know that many celebrated Andalusian poets composed *muwashshaḥāt*, these are generally not included in their ***dīwān***s. It seems clear that as a non-classical form, these compositions – songs, we must not forget – were deemed unworthy of inclusion in tomes of lofty verse. Instead, the vast majority of these poems that have come down to us were collected in books solely devoted to *muwashshaḥāt*. The two most important known sources of Andalusian Arabic *muwashshaḥāt*, the *'Uddat al-jalīs* of Ibn Bishrī and the *Jaysh al-tawshīḥ* of **Ibn al-Khaṭīb**, date to the eighth/fourteenth century, four centuries after these poems presumably were first composed. Ibn al-Khaṭīb, exiled in North Africa after falling out of favour at the court of Muḥammad V of Granada, includes in his anthology a lament for al-Andalus, *Jādaka al-ghaythu*, and the very project of collecting these songs, many of which are anonymous, seems to be motivated by the nostalgia of exile and a desire to preserve the popular culture of Islamic Spain, endangered by the growing power of the Christian '*reconquista*'.

Our most substantive sources on the origin and development of the *muwashshaḥ* are **Ibn Bassām**'s (d. 542/1147) *Dhakhīra*, **Ibn Sanā' al-Mulk**'s (d. 608/1211) *Dār al-ṭirāz* and **Ibn Khaldūn**'s (d. 808/1406) *Muqaddima*. Yet these accounts are several centuries removed from the beginnings of the form, which had already undergone substantial elaboration and refinement. Of these explanations, that of Ibn Sanā' al-Mulk, an Egyptian poet and anthologist, is most cited and could rightly be called a poetics of the genre. Yet Ibn Sanā' al-Mulk's authority is also often questioned by the same scholars who quote him, not only because of his lateness but because he never travelled to al-Andalus and did not know the colloquials spoken there (whether Andalusian Arabic or Romance).

By convention the *muwashshaḥ* usually consisted of five stanzas, with a complex rhyme scheme. Each stanza was divided into two parts: the *ghuṣn*, whose rhyme was distinctive to that strophe; and the *simṭ* or *qufl* – the terminology for the parts of the poem varies – which repeated a rhyme common to the whole poem. The poems often opened with a segment called the *maṭla'*, a kind of prelude which anticipated the rhyme of the *simṭ*. Those poems with this introductory *maṭla'* are *ṭamm* ('complete') and those without are called *aqra'* (lit. 'bald'). As time went on, the poems were further complicated by the addition of internal rhyme. Typically, the initial part (*ghuṣn*) of the last stanza introduced some form of poetic quotation in the last *simṭ*, which often took the form of an interjection by another character in the poem ('then she sang: ...', or 'my heart cried out like the girl who sang: ...'). This parting segment, called the *kharja* (pl. *kharajāt*, 'exit') or *markaz*, uses a popular vernacular, usually either colloquial Arabic or Romance or some mixture of these, rather than the classical Arabic (or Hebrew) of the rest of the poem. Thus a sample rhyme scheme:

muwashshaḥ tamm (with *maṭla'*)

.........a ....b]*maṭla'*
.........c]*ghuṣn*
.........c]*ghuṣn*
.........c]*ghuṣn*
.........a ....b]*simṭ*/*qufl*
.........d
.........d
.........d
.........a ....b
pattern repeats ...
.........g
.........g
.........g
.........a ....b]*kharja* (typically in colloquial Arabic or Romance)

The *maṭla'*/*simṭ*/*kharja* lines were often divided into two, three or four internally rhyming segments, not necessarily of the same length; the *ghuṣn* was also sometimes divided into two segments.

The typical subject matter of the *muwashshaḥāt* is not new to Arabic poetry: hopeless love, separation, love lost, the cruelty of the beloved. Panegyric poems and poems celebrating wine drinking are also common. Ṣūfī poets such as **Ibn al-'Arabī** and **al-Shushtarī** composed *muwashshaḥāt* with mystical themes. Ibn Sanā' al-Mulk stressed the importance of the *kharja* to the success of the composition as a whole: 'the *kharja* is the seasoning of the *muwashshaḥ*, its salt and its sugar', and it plays a variety of rhetorical functions in these poems. At times the beloved expresses in the *kharja* his or her own feelings of longing, resulting in a kind of duet of separation. Or the *kharja* functions as a sort of refrain that catches the spirit of the poem as a whole. In other cases it introduces an interruption by the coquettish or mocking voice of the beloved, which shatters the image of the idealized creature projected in the rest of the poem. The effect is intensified by the linguistic contrast between the 'high' Arabic of the poet and the 'low' or vulgar colloquial, which also serves to thematize differences of power and social class.

The *kharja* has been the nucleus of critical debate and interest in the *muwashshaḥ* in our era. These poems had figured in debates, dating back to the eighteenth century, about the part that Arabic poetry may have played in the development of the vernacular lyric in

Europe and the rise of **courtly love**. But it was not until 1948 that the poems became the object of intense critical scrutiny both in Europe and the Americas, as well as in the Arab world. In a seminal article, 'Les vers finaux en espagnol dans les muwaššaḥs hispano-hébraïques' (*Al-Andalus* 13 [1948], 299–349), Samuel Stern suggested Romance readings of previously undeciphered *kharajāt* in several Hebrew *muwashshaḥāt*.

Stern quickly followed his initial article with the announcement that he had found the first Arabic *muwasshaḥ* with a Romance *kharja* (*Al-Andalus* 14 [1949], 214–18). In 1952 García Gómez published an article on twenty-four Romance *kharja*s in Arabic *muwashshaḥāt*. The reading of the Arabic transliteration of Romance words and phrases – largely unvowelled, and in some cases written in a very poor hand – has proven a seductively difficult paleographical puzzle. Although the vast majority of extant *muwashshaḥāt* have colloquial Arabic *kharja*s, the poems with partial or wholly Romance *kharja*s have been the focus of intense speculation. Jones (1988), which serves to temper some of the exaggerated claims made for the Romance *kharja*s, is a meticulous paleographical examination of each of them, reviewing previous readings and suggesting new ones.

The metre of the poems, which does not conform to the standard Khalīlian system (see **prosody**) has been the subject of great debate. Some critics, notably García Gómez and Armistead, have argued that the poems actually conform to a syllabic-stress system – that is, the Romance metrical system – rather than the quantitative classical Arabic scansion. The Romance elements in the *kharja* and thematic parallels with some early Galician verses have led to the idea that the *kharja*s are taken from pre-existing, independent poems in Romance. Thus, embedded in the *muwashshaḥāt*, those couplets would then become the oldest recorded 'European' lyric (supplanting the Provençal lyric which had previously held that honour). Given that both Ibn Bassām and Ibn Sanā' al-Mulk assert that the *kharja* formed the base around which the rest of the *muwashshaḥ* was composed, their conclusion is that the *washshāḥ*s simply adopted the metre of the pre-existing Romance poem. Other scholars (Jones, S. Ghāzī, *et al.*), pointing to uncertainties in the vocalization of the texts, have argued that an extended Khalīlian system can account for the scansion with few difficulties. Corriente has tried to bridge the distance between these two theories, positing a kind of hybridized Andalusī scansion in which the long quantity in the Arabic metrical system is replaced with stress.

The dissemination of the *muwashshaḥ* is widely attested: aside from being adopted by Hebrew poets in al-Andalus, it also spread to North Africa and to the Eastern capitals of Islamic culture. The parallels in structure and rhyme scheme between the *muwashshaḥ* and the early poems of the first Provençal troubadour, Guilhelm IX of Acquitaine (d. 1127), as well as thematic coincidences between Arabic love poetry and the traditions of courtly love as practised by the troubadours, have been taken as evidence of the 'Arabic theory', the idea that Arabic poetry played an important role in the development of vernacular poetry in Europe. Many traditional *muwashshaḥāt* survived in the repertoire of North African singers to this century, and the conservative performance tradition may provide some clues about the past. A number of factors have led to a resurgence of interest in the *muwashshaḥ*, both popular and scholarly, in the Arab world. Whereas previously there was a significant bias towards studying only 'high' culture, in recent decades especially the academic study of oral tradition and all forms of popular expression has gained legitimacy. Recordings of traditional *muwashshaḥāt* by well-known singers have increased public awareness of the form far beyond North Africa. The scholarly debates about the origins and metrics of the *muwashshaḥ* have coincided with and participated in a larger polemic about the nature of the coexistence of the diverse ethnic and religious groups in Islamic Spain and relations between Europe and medieval Islamic civilization. The loss of al-Andalus – which has always played a large role in the Arab imagination, as an oasis of harmony and splendour, as symbol of a time when Europe looked to Islamic civilization for technology, philosophy and culture – seemed to resonate with the loss of Palestine. Ibn al-Khaṭīb's *Jādaka al-ghaythu*, playing on radios from Morocco to Saudi Arabia, was as much a modern-day lament as it was for the al-Andalus of long ago.

Text editions

Ibn Bishrī, *'Uddat al-jalīs*, A. Jones (ed.), Cambridge (1992).

Ibn al-Khaṭīb, *Jaysh al-tawshīḥ*, H. Nājī (ed.), Tunis (1967).

Ibn Sanā' al-Mulk, *Dār al-ṭirāz*, J. Rikābī (ed.), 2nd edn, Damascus (1977).
Modern anthologies:
Ghāzī, S. (ed.), *Dīwān al-muwashshaḥāt al-Andalusiyya*, Alexandria (1979).
Ḥilū, S. (ed.), *al-Muwashshaḥāt al-Andalusiyya*, Beirut (1965) (includes modern musical arrangements).
Inani, M.Z. (ed.), *Dīwān al-muwashshaḥāt al-Andalusiyya*, Alexandria (1982).

Further reading

Compton, L.F., *Andalusian Lyrical Poetry and Old Spanish Love Songs*, New York (1976) (contains a translation of Ibn Sanā' al-Mulk's *muwashshaḥ* anthology).
Corriente, F. and Sáenz-Badillos, A. (eds), *Poesia estrófica*, Madrid (1991) (contains an article detailing Corriente's theory of modified *'arūḍ*).
García Gómez, E., *Las jarchas romances de la serie arabe en su marco*, 3rd edn, Madrid (1990).
Hitchcock, R., *The Kharjas: A Critical Bibliography*, London (1977).
Jones, A., *Romance Kharjas in Andalusian Arabic Muwaššaḥ Poetry*, London (1988).
Monroe, J.T., *Hispano-Arabic Poetry: A Student Anthology*, Berkeley (1974) (contains English translations of several *muwashshaḥāt*).
Solà-Solé, J., *Corpus de poesía mozárabe*, Barcelona (1973).
Stern, S., *Hispano-Arabic Strophic Poetry*, Oxford (1974) (contains several of his articles and his dissertation).

L. ALVAREZ

See also: Hebrew literature, relations with Arabic; Spain; strophic poetry

al-Muwayliḥī, Ibrāhīm (1844–1906)

Egyptian political journalist. Closely associated with the Egyptian Khedive Ismā'īl, Ibrāhīm al-Muwayliḥī, like his more famous son Muḥammad **al-Muwayliḥī**, followed the Egyptian ruler into exile. After a period spent at the court of the Ottoman Sultan Abdülhamid in Istanbul (1885–95), Ibrāhīm returned to **Cairo** where he published his most famous work, *Mā hunālik*, first in the newspaper *al-Muqaṭṭam*, then as a book (1896). A tissue of fact, rumour and innuendo, the work is a savage indictment of Abdülhamid and the entire Ottoman court; it was immediately banned on orders from Istanbul. In 1898, he founded his own newspaper, *Miṣbāḥ al-Sharq*, which soon established a high reputation for itself, but it closed in 1903. Regarded by many as an inveterate political schemer, al-Muwayliḥī was also praised for the brilliance of his style.

Further reading

Hamza, 'Abd al-Laṭīf, *Adab al-maqāla al-ṣaḥafiyya fī Miṣr*, Cairo (1959), vol. 3.
Ramitch, Yūsuf, *Usrat al-muwayliḥī wa-atharuhā fī al-adab al-'Arabī al-ḥadīth*, Cairo (1980).
Widmer, Gottfried, 'Der Spiegel der Welt', *Die Welt des Islams* N.S. 3 (1954), 57ff.

R. ALLEN

al-Muwayliḥī, Muḥammad (1858?–1930)

Egyptian journalist and prose fiction writer. Son of Ibrāhīm **al-Muwayliḥī**, Muḥammad is remembered as the author of one of the pioneering works in the development of a fictional tradition in modern Arabic, *Ḥadīth 'Īsā ibn Hishām*, originally published in article form under the title 'Fatra min al-Zaman' between 1898 and 1902 and in book form in 1907. Privately educated in **Cairo**, Muḥammad was banished from **Egypt** for distributing political pamphlets in 1882 and joined his father in Italy, later travelling with him to France and England. After spending several years in Istanbul, Muḥammad returned to Cairo in 1887 and continued his career as a journalist. When the episodes of 'Fatra min al-zaman' began to appear on the front page of the al-Muwayliḥī family newspaper, *Miṣbāḥ al-Sharq*, they were an immediate success. This may be attributed both to their astute criticism of the absurdities of daily life in Egyptian society under British occupation and to their evocation of one of the most famous works of classical prose literature, the *maqāmāt* of **Badī' al-Zamān al-Hamadhānī**, through the name of the narrator, 'Īsā ibn Hishām, and the use of a highly ornate prose style. The initial set of episodes was published over a two-year period and was followed by a further set describing Paris. Since its initial publication in book form, *Ḥadīth 'Īsā ibn Hishām* has appeared in at least nine editions – the Paris episodes being added as 'al-Riḥla al-thāniya' to the 1927 edition. While neo-classical in form and style, the pungent criticism of society to be found in al-Muwayliḥī's work makes it an obvious bridge between the narrative genres of the classical period and the emergence of a fictional tradition in modern Arabic literature.

Further reading

Allen, Roger, *A Period of Time*, Exeter (1992).
Hawārī, Aḥmad Ibrāhīm, *Naqd al-mujtama' fī Ḥadīth 'Īsā ibn Hishām lil-Muwayliḥī*, Cairo (1981).
Ramitch, Yūsuf, *Usrat al-Muwayliḥī wa-atharuhā fī al-adab al-'Arabī al-ḥadīth*, Cairo (1980).

R. ALLEN

Muzāḥim ibn 'Amr al-'Uqaylī (second/eighth century)

Bedouin poet of the later **Umayyad** period. Muzāḥim can be dated only approximately as being a younger contemporary of **Jarīr**, **al-Farazdaq** and **Dhū al-Rumma**, all said to have called him a 'gifted boy'. Only a small fragment of an ancient ***dīwān*** is preserved; the collection of fragments by al-Qaysī and al-Ḍāmin contains 43 pieces with 480 verses. An affinity with **'Udhrī** poetry is established by the fact that in several poems Muzāḥim describes his unfulfilled love to a married woman. Remarkable are some descriptions of the sand grouse (*qaṭā*) of unusual length (in one case more than 35 lines).

Text editions

The Poetical Remains of Muzāḥim al-'Uqailī, F. Krenkow (ed. and trans.), Leiden (1920).
'Shi'r Muzāḥim al-'Uqaylī', N.Ḥ. al-Qaysī and Ḥ.S. al-Ḍāmin (eds), *RIMA* 22 (1976), 85–146.

T. SEIDENSTICKER

Muzarrid ibn Ḍirār al-Dhubyānī (first/seventh century)

Yazīd ibn Ḍirār of the Dhubyān, a member of the Ghaṭafān confederacy, was styled Muzarrid for his alleged use of the verb *zarrada*, 'to look sternly upon'. He had two younger brothers who were also ***mukhaḍram*** poets; **al-Shammākh**, the most famous of the three, and Juz' ibn Ḍirār, who composed a threnody for the caliph 'Umar and who is included in the **Ḥamāsa** of **Abū Tammām**. Muzarrid's ***dīwān***, which exists in a singleton manuscript, is fragmentary and his fame rests on his reputed prowess as a lampoonist who vituperated both his own people and his guests (cf. nos 3, 4 and 5). Two poems were featured in the ***Mufaḍḍaliyyāt*** as nos 15 and 17; the former is ***hijā'*** of the Banū Thawb and is connected in the sources with the caliph 'Uthmān; the latter, more generally attributed to Juz' ibn Ḍirār, is a *tour de force* in the pre-Islamic manner, in which the resplendent knight, Muzarrid, is contrasted with a wretchedly indigent hunter.

Text editions

Dīwān al-Muzarrid al-Ghaṭafānī, K.I. 'Atiyya (ed.), Baghdad (1962).
The Mufaḍḍaliyyāt, C.J. Lyall, (ed.), Oxford (1918).

Further reading

Bauer, T., 'Muzarrid's Qaṣide vom reichen Ritter und dem armen Jäger', in *Wagner Festschrift*, vol. 2, 42–71.

J.E. MONTGOMERY

muzdawija

A poem written in rhyming couplets with different rhymes in each couplet (*aa bb cc* ...), chiefly in the ***rajaz*** metre, although other metres (e.g. *ramal*) sometimes occur. It contrasts with the majority of Arabic verse which has a single rhyme throughout. In the *rajaz* type of *muzdawij* both twelve-syllable lines and lines with eleven syllables occur.

The *muzdawija* was practised from early **'Abbāsid** times and, on account of its easy rhyming scheme, it proved particularly suitable for long narrative and didactic poems. Important for the development of the genre was the versification of the fables of ***Kalīla wa-Dimna*** by **Abān al-Lāḥiqī** (d. *c*.200/815). **Abū al-'Atāhiya** (d. 211 or 13/826 or 8) is reported to have written a *muzdawija* called *Dhāt al-amthāl* containing 4,000 proverbs and sayings. Historical subjects are found in *muzdawija*s by **'Alī ibn al-Jahm** (d. 249/863) (world history in 660 lines), **Ibn al-Mu'tazz** (d. 296/908) (biography of the caliph al-Mu'taḍid in 838 lines) and by **Ibn 'Abd Rabbih** (d. 328/940) on the exploits of the caliph 'Abd al-Raḥmān III. This last *muzdawija* is found in the author's *al-'Iqd al-farīd*, which also contains a long treatise on metre and rhyme in *muzdawij* form. **Abū Firās al-Ḥamdānī** (d. 357/968) wrote a *muzdawija* on the pleasures of hunting. Famous works on **grammar** that use this form are *Mulḥat al-i'rāb* by **al-Ḥarīrī** (446–516/1054–1122) and **Ibn Mālik**'s (d. 672/1274) versified grammar *al-Alfiyya*. In all other branches of learning as well, *muzdawija*s are used as teaching texts. Several authors have made versifications of the biography of the Prophet **Muḥammad**.

In modern times *muzdawij* poems are

found in translations, such as a version of La Fontaine's *Fables* by Muḥammad ʿUthmān **Jalāl** (1829–98), and in original works by **Shawqī** (1868-1932) (e.g. his *Duwal al-ʿArab wa-ʿuẓamāʾ al-Islām* of more than 100 pages long) and **al-ʿAqqād** (1889–1964). The relationship of this form with the Persian *mathnawī* and its origin are discussed by von Grunebaum (1944, 22–14), Manfred Ullmann (1966, 46 ff.) and J.T.P. de Bruijn (*EI*², art. 'Mathnawī').

Further reading

Ullmann, M., *Untersuchungen zur Rağazpoesie*, Wiesbaden (1966).

von Grunebaum, G.E., 'On the origin and early development of Arabic *muzdawij* poetry', *JNES* 3 (1944), 9–13.

W. STOETZER

mystical literature *see* Ṣūfī literature

N

Nabarāwī, Sayzā (1897–1985)

Egyptian feminist and journalist. An activist associated with the Egyptian Feminist Union (EFU) founded in 1923, Sayzā Nabarāwī was first editor-in-chief of its French-language organ, *L'Egyptienne* (founded 1925). Born Zaynab Murād, she was taken to Paris as a child by a relative. Sayzā moved back to **Egypt** after this adoptive mother's suicide, continued her French-language education, and became a protegée of the EFU's founder, Hudā **Sha'rāwī**. Returning to **Cairo** from the 1923 International Women Suffrage Alliance conference in Rome, she followed fellow delegate Sha'rāwī's lead in publicly removing her face-veil, often considered a landmark symbolic act in Egyptian feminism. She edited and wrote for *L'Egyptienne* from 1925 until 1940, and also published in the EFU's Arabic-language organ, *al-Miṣriyya* (founded 1937). After Sha'rāwī's death (1947), Nabarāwī served as EFU president, but as the Free Officers' regime clamped down on independent political expression – including feminist activism – in the late 1950s, she was purged as an alleged communist. A decade later, she was active in the progressive international Democratic Federation of Women. She remained a feminist spokesperson into the 1980s.

Text edition

Nabarawi, Saiza, 'Double standard' (editorial in *l'Egyptienne*, April 1925), C. Petrey (trans.), in *Opening the Gates: A Century of Arab Feminist Writing*, Margot Badran and Miriam Cooke (eds), Bloomington and Indianapolis (1990).

Further reading

Badran, Margot, 'Competing agenda: feminists, Islam and the state in 19th and 20th century Egypt', in Deniz Kandiyoti (ed.), *Women, Islam and the State*, Philadelphia (1991).

——, *Feminists, Islam and Nation: Gender and the Making of Modern Egypt*, Princeton (1994).

M. BOOTH

nabaṭi poetry

Nabaṭī is the term applied to the vernacular (basically oral) poetry of the **bedouin** in different parts of the Arab world. As the name implies, this variety differs from *fuṣḥā* ('literary') Arabic in terms of linguistic structure, although in function and thematic development it represents a continuation of the 'heroic' age of classical poetry in **Arabia**. For Sowayan (1985) Najd is the homeland of *Nabaṭī* poetry and its preservation of many of the features of ***Jāhiliyya*** literature was largely due to the unchanged socioeconomic conditions of tribal life which persisted in central Arabia until the early years of the twentieth century (see **tribes**).

Sa'īd (1981) bases his claim that the *Nabaṭī* poetic tradition was spread through the Arab world by the migrations of the Banū Hilāl (in the fifth/eleventh century) on the linguistic, lexical and thematic uniformity of the poetry as well as the fact that the principal mode of recitation, from which the others derive, is termed *hilālī*. With the decline of the traditional bedouin way of life in Arabia and the consequent weakening of much-prized values such as valour in battle and tribal honour, *Nabaṭī* poetry and its exponents (the *gaṣṣāds*) were becoming increasingly neglected until they began to feature on radio and TV programmes in Arab Gulf states in the 1950s and 1960s. Today, the genre is well supported and patronized (notably by ruling families in the Arabian Gulf states) but it has yet to become an approved subject for academic research.

In spite of its apparently self-contained nature, *Nabaṭī* poetry has always intersected with the settled world, reflecting the symbiotic relationship between 'the desert and the town'. In the summer months when tribes were camped near wells, bedouin and townspeople frequently came together for poetic recitals. Famous *Nabaṭī* poets such as Muḥammad ibn Liʿbūn (d. 1247/1831) and Muḥammad al-ʿAwnī (d. 1342/1923) were essentially townspeople imbued with the spirit of the desert. Neither were *Nabaṭī* poets necessarily illiterate; many were well-versed in classical Arabic literature and employed literary devices such as *jinās* and *ṭibāq* in their compositions. The functions of *Nabaṭī* poetry parallel those of its classical precursor, the most popular being ***ghazal*** and *ḥamāsa*. The *gisīda* (***qaṣīda***), of variable length, is typically arranged in the form of two metrically identical hemistiches, each with a different rhyming letter. Metres, which regularly correspond to particular modes of recitation (e.g. *Hilālī* has *ṭawīl* metre), are generally classical ones adapted to the prosody of vernacular speech. The most popular metre is *al-masḥūb*, perhaps so termed because it is slow and long-drawn out (see further **prosody**). Performance may be individual (accompanied or not by the *rabāb*), communal (e.g. *sāmrī*) or mixed (e.g. *arḍah*, war dance, and *mrādd*, poetic duelling).

Two aspects that merit further research concern (a) mode of composition and (b) lexis. Saʿīd (1981) describes *Nabaṭī* poetry as spontaneous and free from artifice while Sowayan stresses the degree to which poems are polished (*mḥakkak*). Saʿīd also asserts that the vocabulary of *Nabaṭī* poetry is the everyday language of the bedouin; but there is evidence that poets deliberately reject everyday words in their compositions. If Sowayan is correct, classical (i.e. pre-Islamic) and *Nabaṭī* poetry are located at opposite ends of a continuum of elevated poetic diction, understood by all but perceived as distinct from day-to-day speech.

Further reading

Ḍayf, S., *Ta'rīkh al-adab al-ʿArabī*, vol. 5, Cairo (1983).

al-Ḥāmid, A.A., *Fī al-shiʿr al-muʿāṣir fī al-Mamlaka al-ʿArabiyya al-Saʿūdiyya*, Riyadh (1986).

al-Saʿīd,T., *al-Shiʿr al-Nabaṭī*, Kuwait (1981).

Sowayan, S.A., *Nabaṭī Poetry: The Oral Poetry of Arabia*, Berkeley (1985).

P.G. EMERY

See also: Arabia; bedouin

al-Nābigha al-Dhubyānī (sixth century)

Ziyād ibn Muʿāwiya al-Nābigha al-Dhubyānī was a pre-Islamic poet, famous for his panegyrics upon **Lakhmid** and **Ghassānid** kings. He must have been adult at the time of the battle of Ḥalīma (554), where he intervened on behalf of the prisoners from his tribe. He was associated with several Lakhmids, especially with al-Nuʿmān III Abū Qābūs (580–602), the last king of **Ḥīra**. After losing al-Nuʿmān's favour, allegedly on account of a poem in praise of the queen, he fled to the Ghassānid court. From there he sent poetic apologies to Ḥīra and eventually became reconciled to al-Nuʿmān, whose illness is alluded to in a short poem (Ahlwardt No. 28). The date of al-Nābigha's death is unknown.

Al-Nābigha's ***dīwān*** is preserved in several recensions and appears authentic on the whole. It consists of twenty monothematic poems (see ***qiṭʿa***) and eleven panegyric odes (see ***qaṣīda***), and contains references to Christian rites and two fables, which suggests the influence of Ḥīra. His panegyrics are composed in a highly developed style and reveal a fine sense of climax, e.g. his famous comparison of Nuʿmān with the Euphrates (Ahlwardt No. 5, 44–7). The ode is included in some recensions of the ***Muʿallaqāt***. Although al-Nābigha never lost interest in affairs of his tribe, as evidenced by several poems offering political advice, he can hardly be called a **bedouin** poet in the true sense, but should be regarded as the first great court poet in Arabic literature.

Text editions

Dīwān, in *The Diwans of the Six Ancient Arabic Poets*, W. Ahlwardt (ed.), London (1970 [1878]); H. Derenbourg (ed. and trans.) Paris (1868); K. al-Bustānī (ed.), Beirut (1963); Shukrī Fayṣal (ed.), Beirut (1968); ʿAbbās ʿAbd al-Sātir (ed.), Beirut (1964); Lyall, C., *Translations of Ancient Arabic Poetry*, London (1885), 95–102.

Further reading

Ḥusayn, Ṭāhā, *Fī al-adab al-Jāhilī*, Cairo (1927), rpt (1952), 376–87.

Jacobi, Renate, *Studien zur Poetik der altarabischen Qaṣide*, Wiesbaden (1971), 95–9, 179–82, 196–203.

Montgomery, James, 'Arkhilokhos, al-Nābigha al-Dhubyānī and a Complaint Against Blacksmiths; or, a funny thing happened to me ...,' *Edebiyât*, n.s. 5 (1994), 15–49.

R. JACOBI

al-Nābigha al-Ja'dī (d. *c.*63/683)

Ḥibbān ibn Qays ibn 'Abd Allāh, known as al-Nābigha ('the Copious Genius') of the tribe of Ja'da (of the 'Āmir ibn Ṣa'ṣa'a), was a ***mukhaḍram*** poet actively involved in the political and military incidents of the **Orthodox caliphate** and possibly of the early **Umayyad** period. He is reckoned a 'Methuselah': his fragments display a fondness for the topic of senescent infirmity together with sporadic reference to his old age. He participated in his tribe's delegation to the Prophet in 9/630, whereupon he recited poem 3, of which three versions survive, the longest numbering 120 verses. Nos 2, 5, 6, 11 and 12 are examples of politically motivated tribal ***fakhr***. His pro-'Alid sympathies led to his presence at the battle of Ṣiffīn, the confiscation of his property and seizure of his family by Mu'āwiya, to whom he addressed an aggressive *i'tidhār* (apology; poem 1), and his subsequent exile to Isfahan where he died. He was renowned for his horse descriptions, of which poem 2, 11–33, is a fine example, and for his tendency to be bested in flytings (***naqā'iḍ***): nos 7a and 7b are lampoons composed on such occasions. Poem 8 is a hymn to Allāh, the authorship of which is disputed. A complete manuscript of his ***dīwān*** has not yet surfaced.

Further reading

Nallino, M., 'An-Nābiġa al-Ǧa'dī et le sue poesie, I: Notizie biografiche', *RSO* 14 (1934), 135–90, 384–432.

——, *Le Poesie di an-Nābiġa al-Ǧa'dī*, Rome (1953).

J.E. MONTGOMERY

al-Nābigha al-Shaybānī (d. *c.*126/744)

'Abd Allāh ibn al-Mukhāriq al-Nābigha al-Shaybānī was a poet of the middle and late **Umayyad** period who resided mainly in Iraq. Surnamed 'the Nābigha (genius) of the Banū Shaybān', he had a Christian mother and is himself said to have been a Christian by an ancient Arabic scholar while modern research tends to consider him a Muslim. He had relations with several Umayyad caliphs from 'Abd al-Malik (65–86/685–715) to al-Walīd II (125–6/743–4), as his poems show. In anthologies and biographical works he is rarely quoted or mentioned. The edition of Ya'qūb, based on an ancient ***dīwān***, contains twenty poems with 1,164 lines; four of these poems are longer than eighty lines.

Text edition

Dīwān, A. Nasīm (ed.), Cairo (1932) (unsatisfactory); 'A.I. Ya'qūb (ed.), Damascus (1987); for a further edition see R. Weiper, *ZGAIW* 2 (1985), 260.

Further reading

Blachère, Régis, *Histoire de la littérature arabe*, Paris (1952–66), vol. 3, 505–6.

T. SEIDENSTICKER

al-Nābulusī, 'Abd al-Ghanī *see* 'Abd al-Ghanī ibn Ismā'īl al-Nābulusī

nadīm

An Arabic term meaning 'boon companion'. The office of *nadīm* (whose origins can be traced back to Sasanian Iran) was an important one in medieval Arab court society, and became institutionalized under the **'Abbāsids**, especially under the caliphs al-Hādī and **Hārūn al-Rashīd**. The *nadīm*s constituted a special class; familiars of the ruler who accompanied and entertained him in his solitary moments, at his private literary and musical gatherings and drinking parties, in gaming (principally chess), hunting, on his travels and so on, they enjoyed great prestige and influence at court, The office was not restricted to the nobility, but open to anyone of talent, and was often held by poets (e.g. **al-'Abbās ibn al-Aḥnaf**, **Abū Nuwās**), littérateurs (Abū Bakr **al-Ṣūlī**), singers (Ibrāhīm **al-Mawṣilī**), as well as princes (**Ibrāhīm ibn al-Mahdī**); it sometimes became hereditary, as in the cases of the Banū **Munajjim** and the Banū Ḥamdūn.

The *nadīm* was expected to have many and varied talents, and a large literature grew up expounding the *adab al-nadīm* (see ***adab***), the requirements and etiquette of the *nadīm* (for a partial listing see Chejne, 1965, 328–9). He must be physically fit, of good appearance, and well dressed; well acquainted with the **Koran**, ***ḥadīth***, **grammar**, poetry, music and history, as well as the military arts, cookery and horse breeding, and games such as backgammon and chess. He must be able to entertain the ruler in whatever way the moment calls for, be a good talker and storyteller, able to improvise poetry and perhaps to play a musical instrument; above all, he must be worthy of trust, and be relied upon not to reveal his ruler's secrets, and must be sufficiently manly and skilled at arms to be able to defend him.

Among the authors who wrote on the subject were the singer Isḥāq **al-Mawṣilī** (credited with three works) and his son Ḥammād; **Ibn Kurradādhbih**, the geographer and author on music; **Jaḥẓa**, who served as *nadīm* (and something of a court jester) to the caliph al-Mu'tamid; and the poet **Kushājim**, who was also secretary, astrologer and master chef to the **Ḥamdānid** ruler Sayf al-Dawla. Except for two works by Kushājim, and Ibn Bābā al-Qāshī's (d, after 500/1106–7) *Kitāb ra's māl al-nadīm*, which exists in manuscript, few works on the subject have survived.

Text edition

pseudo-al-Jāḥiẓ, *Le Livre de la couronne*, C. Pellat (trans.), Paris (1954), 99–178 (contains a lengthy chapter on the *nadīm*).

Kushājim, *Adab al-nadīm*, Bulaq (1298/1881); published as *Adab al-nudamā' wa-laṭā'if al-ẓurafā'*, Alexandria (1329/1911).

Further reading

Chejne, A.J., 'The boon companion in early 'Abbāsid times', *JAOS* 85 (1965), 327–35.

J.S. MEISAMI

al-Nadīm *see* ibn al-Nadīm

al-Nadīm, 'Abd Allāh (1843/4–96)

Radical Egyptian poet, *zajjāl* and propagandist. Born in Alexandria, he died in Istanbul. He worked as a telegraph officer and spent some years in the Delta as an itinerant versifier (*udabātī*), earning the epithet of *nadīm* (boon companion). He later participated in the secret Union de la Jeunesse Egyptienne, challenging Riyāḍ Pasha's authoritarian government. Al-Nadīm was headmaster of the school of an Islamic charitable society that he founded in 1879, for which he wrote two plays in colloquial: *al-'Arab*, and *al-Waṭan wa-ṭāli' al-tawfīq*. He contributed to several newspapers, founding his own satirical ***al-Tankīt wa-al-Tabkīt*** (June–October 1881) and *al-Ṭā'if*, organ of the 'Urābists (November 1881–September 1882). Accused of participating in the 'Urābī rebellion, he spent nine years in hiding. In 1891 he was arrested and exiled but was pardoned by the new Khedive, and returned to Cairo and founded the satirical magazine *al-Ustādh* (1892–3), opposed to the British occupation. These activities led to a second period of exile, during which Sultan 'Abd al-Ḥamīd thought to silence him, appointing him to the Education Ministry, then Inspector of Publications; he ended his life in Istanbul. Al-Nadīm is an important figure, not only in the history of Egyptian nationalism, but also in the development of modern Arabic prose, for he pioneered the use of a less ornamental, more direct prose style, venturing so far as to write entire articles in the colloquial. Selections from his works have been published.

Further reading

Hafez, S., *The Genesis of Arabic Narrative Discourse*, London (1993), 1, 13–33.

Sadgrove, P.C., 'al-Nadīm, al-Sayyid 'Abd Allāh', EI^2, vol. 7, 852.

——, *The Egyptian Theatre in the Nineteenth Century*, Reading (1996), 145–9, 152–5, 161, 163.

P.C. SADGROVE

al-Nafzāwī (*fl.* ninth/fifteenth century)

Abū 'Abd Allāh Muḥammad ibn 'Umar al-Nafzāwī was the author of *The Perfumed Garden*, the best-known work of Arabic erotica in the West. Of his life virtually nothing is known. His book, an expansion of an earlier, briefer work that he had composed on the same subject, was commissioned by the Ḥafṣid vizier in Tunis, Muḥammad ibn 'Awāna al-Zawāwī, some time after 813/1410. It is a fairly typical representative of Arabic sex manuals, treating such topics as desirable and undesirable qualities in men and women, Arabic sexual vocabulary, positions of sexual intercourse, ways to enhance sexual pleasure, and medical questions regarding impotence, pregnancy and abortion, all these points being illustrated by traditional anecdotes, some quite salacious, drawn from a large variety of earlier sources. Its particular fame in the West is largely a matter of chance. A French translation appeared in Algiers in 1876, and was in turn translated into English by Sir Richard Burton in 1886.

Text editions

The Glory of the Perfumed Garden (London, 1975), (purporting to be a translation of the 'missing' final sections of the text; this remains to be clarified).

The Perfumed Garden, Sir Richard Burton (trans.), London (1886) and frequently reprinted (notably, London, 1963, with introduction by A.H. Walton).

al-Rawḍ al-ʿāṭir fī nuzhat al-khāṭir, J. Jumʿa (ed.), London (1990) (first critical edition of the text).

Further reading

Brunschvig, R., *La Berbérie orientale sous les Hafsides*, Paris, (1947), vol. 2, 172f.

al-Khayr, H., *Shahādāt wa-mukhtārāt min al-Rawḍ al-ʿāṭir fī nuzhat al-khāṭir, al-shaykh Muḥammad ibn Muḥammad al-Nafzāwī*, Damascus (1983).

E.K. ROWSON

Nāgī, Ibrāhīm *see* Nājī, Ibrāhīm

al-nahḍa

Nahḍa, usually translated in English as 'renaissance' or 'revival', is a term first used by Jurjī **Zaydān** and others to describe the process of Arabic literary and cultural renewal which occurred during the second half of the nineteenth, and early years of the twentieth, centuries. The 'revival' was associated with a number of interrelated factors, both political and intellectual: on a political level, they included the progressive enfeeblement of the Ottoman Empire and the growth of European influence in the Middle East, and, on an intellectual level, the consequent attempts by Muslim and other Arab intellectuals to reassess the relationship between Europe and the Arab Muslim world and to redefine the place of Islam within a modern society. In political terms, these various currents had an important outcome in the growth of Arab nationalism in its various forms; in literary terms, their main outcome was the substitution of Western *genres* – novel, short story, drama etc. – for traditional Arab forms as the main (though not the sole) vehicles for literary expression in prose, with a corresponding shift away from traditional themes and formal conventions in poetry.

Geographically, the countries mainly associated with the *nahḍa*, at least in its early phases, are **Egypt** and Greater **Syria** (including **Lebanon**). The cultural background and consequent contribution of these two areas to the movement differed considerably, however. For Egypt, Napoleon's invasion of 1798 has traditionally been held to mark the beginning of modern cultural development, and although the significance of this date for the socio-economic development of the country has become the focal point for some of the liveliest debates in Middle Eastern history, its status as a cultural turning-point remains difficult to ignore. From then until the British occupation beginning in 1881–2, Egypt was effectively an autonomous country, and the reigns of Muḥammad ʿAlī (1805–48) and Ismāʿīl (1863–79) in particular saw important developments which, while often not involving cultural objectives as such, had important cultural and literary side-effects: these included the dispatch of Egyptians to the West to study, a more widespread European presence in Egypt itself, the spread of Western-style education, the growth in the number of translations and adaptations from Western languages, and the progressive substitution of Arabic for Turkish as the language of administration. In Syria and Lebanon, the presence of indigenous Christian communities with long-standing links to the West implied a different starting-point, and their relationship with the Ottoman Empire remained a more complex one for most of the nineteenth century. Paradoxically, the civil disturbances arising from the periodic inter-communal strife in Lebanon themselves made a positive contribution to the movement, as émigrés sought sanctuary not only in the **Mahjar** but also in Egypt, where they helped to stimulate the search for new forms of literary expression; their contribution was particularly important in the fields of the **theatre** and the **press**.

The development of new literary forms and sensibilities implied by the *nahḍa* in the second half of the nineteenth century coincided with the growth of a wider reading public, itself the product of changes in educational patterns. In this context, the Arabic press was playing an increasingly important role, both politically and culturally, not only helping to forge a new sense of national consciousness, but also providing a training ground for young writers – a role it has continued to play to the present day. Associated with these developments were changes in the Arabic language itself, involving the evolution of a modern, less involved, prose style and a vocabulary capable of dealing with modern concepts in a manner accessible to a wide reading public.

Largely for economic reasons, the essay and article remained the dominant prose form of this period; but for longer narrative, Jurjī Zaydān and other writers were increasingly beginning to turn to Western forms. In this respect, Muḥammad **al-Muwayliḥī**'s *Ḥadīth 'Īsā ibn Hishām* (serialized between 1898 and 1902) occupies a pivotal position, as perhaps the last great Arabic masterpiece in ***maqāma*** form. A decade or so later, Muḥammad Ḥusayn **Haykal**'s *Zaynab* (1913) holds the distinction of being the first Western-style Egyptian novel with a contemporary Egyptian setting; by the time of **Tawfīq al-Ḥakīm**'s *'Awdat al-rūḥ* (1933) the adaptation of Western fictional techniques to an Arab environment was effectively complete. A similar timescale holds roughly good for the theatre, where the early efforts of Mārūn **al-Naqqāsh** and others in Syria and Lebanon, and of Ya'qūb **Ṣanū'** in Egypt in the 1870s, failed to bear fruit in the establishment of an Arabic dramatic tradition of literary value; most troupes continued to rely heavily on musical and melodramatic productions, and on adaptations of Western plays in which faithfulness to the original counted for little, if anything. Only with the plays of Ibrāhīm **Ramzī**, Anṭūn **Yazbak** and Muḥammad **Taymūr** around the time of World War 1 do we see significant steps being taken to create a genuinely Arab, or Egyptian, theatre. In poetry, traditionally regarded by the Arabs as the most highly-prized literary form, the same factors led initially not to any radical change in poetic structure but rather to a more gradual development in sensibility, accompanied by a conscious attempt to revitalize contemporary poetry by reaching back to the great models of the classical Arabic heritage. The resulting neo-classical movement found its first great poetic exponent in Maḥmūd Sāmī **al-Bārūdī** and was subsequently developed most notably in Egypt and Iraq. It was not until the rise of the Romantic movement, however, foreshadowed in the work of the Syro-Egyptian Khalīl **Muṭrān**, that Arabic poetry began in earnest to free itself from its traditionally rigid metrical and rhyme structure.

Although no rigid 'end-date' can be given for the *nahḍa*, by the 1920s at latest most of the initial problems involved in adapting Western literary forms for use in an Arab context had been tackled, and the groundwork laid for the future development of modern Arabic literature in the remainder of the twentieth century. At the same time, on the political level, many Arab countries found themselves under Western occupation, with their hopes of liberty dashed. The subsequent development of Arabic literature has continued to witness a close relationship between political and intellectual currents, but in a different overall context.

Further reading

Cachia, P., *An Overview of Modern Arabic Literature*, Edinburgh (1990).

CHALMAL, especially chapter 1.

Gibb, H.A.R. 'Studies in Contemporary Arabic Literature I: The Nineteenth Century', *Bulletin of the School of Oriental Studies*, (1928), 4, 745–60.

Hourani, A., *Arabic Thought in the Liberal Age, 1798–1939*, London (1962).

Stetkevych, J., *Modern Arabic Literary Language: Lexical and Stylistic Development*, Chicago (1970).

P. STARKEY

Nahj al-Balāgha (*The Way of Eloquence*)

An anthology of orations, sermons, epistles, apothegms, maxims, etc., traditionally attributed to the fourth Rightly-Guided caliph **'Alī ibn Abī Ṭālib** (r. 35–40/656–61). The work is written in an eloquent and polished style, and has been regarded by Muslims as one of the outstanding works of Arabic prose literature. There have, however, been lively controversies from medieval Islamic times onwards regarding its authorship, given that the style of much of the *Nahj* shows a maturity of expression and a confidence in the handling of words truly remarkable for its allegedly early date, virtually contemporary with or stemming from not much after the definitive compilation of the **Koran** itself.

For the **Shī'īs**, partisans of the claims of 'Alī and his house to the caliphate and imamate, the authenticity of the *Nahj* is an article of faith; but a **Sunnī** writer like **Ibn Abī al-Ḥadīd** (see below) was equally convinced of its essential genuineness as being written by 'Alī and compiled from his writings over three centuries later by **al-Sharīf al-Raḍī**. Other medieval scholars, such as **Ibn Khallikān**, thought that it had been compiled in **Baghdad** by one of the two brothers, al-Sharīf al-Raḍī or **al-Sharīf al-Murtaḍā**, and then possibly attributed to 'Alī. All this leaves unresolved the question of how much, if any, of the *Nahj* was genuinely written by 'Alī. Undoubtedly, considerable parts of it, and especially the historical sections and the orations and sermons, could have been written by the caliph himself, and there are passages whose supporting *isnād*s or chains of guarantors are complete and go back to 'Alī's time. A judicious view would be that the *Nahj* might well contain material traceable back to 'Alī, but that it was put together in its present form at the beginning of the fifth/eleventh century, most likely by al-Sharīf al-Raḍī.

The *Nahj* early attracted a host of commentaries, abridgements and selections, the outstanding commentary being the monumental *Sharḥ Nahj al-balāgha* of the Iraqi author Ibn Abī al-Ḥadīd which he wrote 644–9/1246–51; this author seems to have been basically a Sunnī but with **Mu'tazilī** sympathies which might have inclined him to look favourably on the Shī'īs. There have also been numerous translations, especially into Persian.

Text edition

Nahj al-balāgha (many printings, commentaries, translations, etc.).

Further reading

*EI*² art. 'Nahdj al-balāgha' (M. Djebli).
Veccia Vaglieri, L., 'Sul "Nahǧ al-balāġah" e sul suo compilatore aš-Šarīf ar-Rāḍī', *AIUON*, n.s. 8 (1958), 1–46.

C.E. BOSWORTH

See also: Shī'ī literature

naḥw see grammar and grammarians

Naimy, Mikhail *see* Nu'ayma, Mīkhā'īl

al-Najafī, Aḥmad al-Ṣāfī (1897–1977)

Iraqi poet. Born in al-Najaf to an Iraqi father and a Lebanese mother, al-Najafī left for Tehran in 1920 because of the British occupation of Iraq and remained there until 1927 working as a journalist, teacher and translator of 'Umar Khayyām's *Rubā'iyyāt*. After three years in Baghdad he went to **Lebanon** for health reasons and was briefly imprisoned in 1941 in Beirut by the allies for his poetic support for Rashīd al-Kīlānī. Only in 1976 did he return to Baghdad, having been wounded in the Lebanese Civil War. Al-Najafī published twenty collections of poetry during his lifetime, a more complete ***dīwān*** being published in Baghdad after his death. His neo-classical poems comprise praises of the beauty of towns and landscapes in **Syria** and Lebanon; ironical, humorous or critical descriptions, e.g. of the refreshing effects of tea, or the tortures caused by a mosquito at night; satires against those who mocked his ascetic and chaotic lifestyle; and praises of his poetical skill in the face of the literary critics.

Further reading

Barhūmī, Khalīl, *Aḥmad al-Ṣāfī al-Najafī: shā'ir al-ghurba wa-al-alam*, Beirut (1993).
Sharāra, 'Abd al-Laṭīf, *al-Ṣāfī: dirāsa taḥlīliyya*, Beirut (1981).

W. WALTHER

al-Najāshī (d. shortly after 49/669)

Mukhaḍram poet. Qays (or Sim'ān) ibn 'Amr, of the Bal-Ḥārith, called 'the Negus' on account of his dark appearance or his Ethiopian mother, was known especially for his invective verse, directed against clans or tribes (Banū 'Ajlān, Quraysh) and individuals (**Ibn Muqbil**, Mu'āwiya ibn Abī Sufyān). The ***naqā'iḍ*** exchanged between him and 'Abd al-Raḥmān, the son of **Ḥassān ibn Thābit**, were collected by **al-Madā'inī**.

Text edition

Shi'r, S. al-Na'īmī (ed.), *MMII* 13 (1966), 95–127.

Further reading

'Askar, Quṣayy al-Shaykh, *al-Najāshī, shā'ir Ṣiffīn*, Beirut (1988).
al-Bakkār, Ṣāliḥ and al-Ghurāb, Sa'd, 'Al-Najāshī al-Ḥārithī: akhbāruhu wa-ash'āruh', *Ḥawliyyāt al-Jāmi'a al-Tūnisiyya* 21 (1982), 105–201.
Schulthess, F., 'Über den Dichter al-Naǧāšī und einige Zeitgenossen', *ZDMG* 54 (1900), 421–74.

G.J.H. VAN GELDER

Nājī, Hilāl (1929–)

Iraqi poet, critic, editor and scholar. Born in al-Qarna, Nājī studied at the faculty of law, graduating in 1951. He left Iraq in 1959 after being accused of involvement in a plot to assassinate ʿAbd al-Karīm Qāsim. After the coup of 1963 he returned to Iraq where he joined the diplomatic service and was nominated for the Iraqi embassies in Spain and later in Iran and Tunis. Nājī ended his career at the Foreign Ministry in Baghdad as the head of the section responsible for Arab countries and the Gulf. He was recently elected as the President of the Iraqi Association of Writers. His poetry, written both in conventional form and in *shiʿr ḥurr* (**free verse**), deals with universal humanistic topics as well as national themes. Among his poetry collections is *al-Fajr ātin yā ʿIrāq* (1962). As a scholar Nājī rescued from oblivion **al-Zahāwī**'s *al-Nazaghāt aw al-shakk wa-al-yaqīn*, publishing it in his book *al-Zahāwī wa-dīwānuhu al-mafqūd* (Cairo, 1963). He has also produced a book on contemporary Yemeni poets (1966) and edited several texts from the classical Arabic and Islamic heritage.

Further reading

ʿIzz al-Dīn, Yūsuf, *Shuʿarāʾ al-ʿIrāq fī al-Qarn al-ʿIshrīn*, Baghdad (1969), 359–76.

R. SNIR

Nājī, Ibrāhīm (1898–1953)

Egyptian Romantic poet. Born in **Cairo** in relatively comfortable circumstances, Nājī graduated in 1923 from the School of Medicine. He worked as a doctor until his death, but at the same time managed to sustain his consuming interest in literature. To this extent his career bears similarities to that of his contemporary and mentor **Abū Shādī**.

Nājī gained recognition for his poetry through the **Apollo Group** of which he became vice-president, and through the pages of *Apollo* itself. Although acquainted with English, French and German literature, the major foreign influence on his work was that of nineteenth-century French Romantic poetry. He produced three collections of verse: *Warāʾ al-ghamām* (1934), *Layālī al-Qāhira* (1944) and a posthumous volume, *al-Ṭāʾir al-jarīḥ*, which appeared in 1957. The second of these, *Layālī al-Qāhira*, shows clear signs of being derived from *Les Nuits* by Alfred de Musset. His complete *Dīwān* was published in Cairo in 1961.

The particular contribution for which Nājī is remembered is his amatory poetry, which had not been a particularly successful part of the work of either **Muṭrān** or the ***Dīwān Group*** poets. He created an intriguing and successful fusion between the age-old tradition of highly sensual Arabic love poetry, and something that is closer to the spiritual, more ethereal love poetry of the European Romantic style. His work alternates between short love lyrics not unlike the classical ***qiṭʿa***, which usually reproduce a specific moment or experience of amorous pleasure, and longer, more complex poems of pessimistic endurance in an overall context of previous loves or unrequited passion. One of the most attractive features of Nājī's work is the extent to which he adapts old motifs to contemporary situations. His best-known poems, such as 'al-ʿAwda', 'al-Firāq', 'Waqfa ʿalā dār' and 'al-Aṭlāl', are nothing less than the infusing of classical themes with the spirit of Western Romanticism, usually with a fine sense of creative irony and self-deprecating humour. This ability to play creatively with the tradition was enjoyed by very few Arab poets between the neo-classical period and the 'new poetry' of the 1950s.

Further reading

Badawi, M.M., *A Critical Introduction to Modern Arabic Poetry*, Cambridge (1975), 129–37.
CHALMAL, 115–18.

R.C. OSTLE

Najm, Aḥmad Fuʾād *see* Nigm, Aḥmad Fuʾād

Najm al-Dīn al-Kubrā (540–618/1145 or 6–1220 or 1)

Najm al-dīn al-Kubrā Aḥmad ibn ʿUmar al-Khīwaqī al-Khwārazmī, Ṣūfī writer who was born in Khiva and died there during the Mongol invasion. Originally a scholar of ***ḥadīth***, he travelled in the western Islamic lands and underwent a conversion to Sufism. His most important teacher was ʿAmmār al-Bidlīsī. After returning to his homeland, he pursued a very active teaching career as a Ṣūfī *shaykh*. He is taken to be the founder of the Kubrawiyya Ṣūfī order. Kubrā (the title reflects his argumentative skill) has left us works on Sufism in both Arabic and Persian. His most important works in Arabic are: his Koranic commentary, the *ʿAyn al-ḥayāt*, which he never completed; *al-Uṣūl al-ʿashara*, which deals with the mystic path; *Fawā'iḥ al-jamāl wa-fawātiḥ al-jalāl*, which chiefly discusses visions.

Kubrā belongs to the post-classical phase of Sufism. He drew on the whole of earlier Ṣūfī tradition and combined it with Neoplatonic, Gnostic and Hermetic elements. The most distinctive features of his teachings, however, was his preoccupation with visions, which also remained characteristic of the school he left behind.

Text edition

'Traités mineures', M. Molé (ed.), *AI* 4 (1963), 1–78.

Further reading

Meier, Fritz, *Die Fawā'iḥ al-ǧamāl wa-fawātiḥ al-ǧalal des Naǧm ad-dīn al-Kubrā*, Wiesbaden (1957) (a fundamental exhaustive treatment of the subject).

B. RADTKE

Nakhla, Rashīd (1873–1939)

Lebanese poet, writer and journalist. Nakhla, who held several administrative posts in Jīzīn and the province of Ṣūr, wrote both literary and folk poetry. In 1933 he was elected the 'prince of ***zajal*** poetry' in Lebanon. His popular songs in colloquial Lebanese influenced the lyrical Romantic and symbolist poets in Lebanon. Nakhla founded *al-Shaʿb* newspaper in 1912, edited *al-Arza* newspaper and helped to edit *Jarīdat Lubnān*. Among his works are his long story *Muḥsin al-Hazzān* (Beirut, 1936) and his popular poetry collected by his son Amīn Nakhla as *Muʿannā Rashīd Nakhla* (Beirut, 1947).

Further reading

Dāghir, Yūsuf Asʿad, *Maṣādir al-dirāsāt al-adabiyya*, Beirut (1956), II/1, 742–3.
al-Kayyālī, Sāmī, *al-Rāḥilūn*, Cairo (1937?), 147–52.

S. MOREH

Nakhla, Rufā'īl (18??–19??)

Lebanese Jesuit theologian, philologist, scientist, historian and poet. Nakhla was the director of *Risālat Qalb Yasūʿ*, in which he published several articles on prose, poetry, theology, history and society. He also published scientific articles in *al-Mashriq*. Nakhla started publishing poetry in 1904. His anthology, *Aghānī al-manfā* (2nd edn, Beirut, 1965) contains many strophic Catholic hymns in Arabic; to this anthology he added articles in praise of his poetic talents by Khalīl **Muṭrān**, Mīkhā'īl **Nuʿayma** and others. He also published a dictionary of Arabic synonyms entitled *Qāmūs al-mutarādifāt wa-al-mutajānisāt* (Beirut, 1957).

Further reading

Moreh, S., *Modern Arabic Poetry 1800–1970*, Leiden (1976), 23.
Shaykhū, L., *Tārīkh al-ādāb al-ʿArabiyya fī al-rubʿ al-awwal min al-qarn al-ʿishrīn*, Beirut (1926), 159.

S. MOREH

al-Nāmī, Abū al-ʿAbbās (*c.*309–99/*c.*921–1008)

Abū al-ʿAbbās Aḥmad ibn Muḥammad al-Nāmī was a poet from al-Maṣṣīṣa (Cilicia). He became a famous poet in Aleppo in the time of Sayf al-Dawla, especially after the departure of **al-Mutanabbī**, with whom he had some altercations. Although **al-Thaʿālibī** counts him among the 'master poets' (*fuḥūla*) of his time, poetry came to him with difficulty and very slowly; some amusing anecdotes are given in *al-Wāfī* by **al-Ṣafadī**. Little of his poetry has survived. He also produced *Amālī* on philological subjects.

Text edition

Shiʿr, Ṣabīḥ Radīf (ed.), Baghdad (1970).

G.J.H. VAN GELDER

al-Namir ibn Tawlab (d. before 23/644)

A ***mukhaḍram*** poet and a distinguished aristocrat of the tribe of ʿUkl, a member of the Ribāb alliance (Tamīm); he was a 'Methuselah' who grew senile in his dotage. He is famed for his visit to the Prophet Muḥammad, and subsequent receipt of a letter from him. His poetry is the epitome of *Jāhilī* aristocratic verse (see ***jāhiliyya***), eschewing ***madīḥ*** and shunning ***hijā'***, eloquent of diction, audacious of thematic development, aphoristic in its acceptance of the inevitable, didactic in its presentation of al-Namir's code of conduct. Indeed, it is often compared with the poetry of **Ḥātim al-Ṭā'ī**, the pre-Islamic paradigm of altruism and munificence. As such, it proved to be popular with the philologists and anthologists. Especially interesting are nos 19, 25, 31, 42 and 44, reflections on personal worth and mortality, and no. 38, an incomplete threnody in the style of the poets of **Hudhayl**, in which the death of the ibex symbolizes the inevitability of fate. The dedicatee may be identical with that of no. 8, viz. the poet's brother al-Ḥārith ibn Tawlab.

Text editions

Krenkow, F., 'Three poems by an-Namir b. Taulab al-'Uklī', *RO* 17 (1951–2), 122–37.

Shi'r al-Namir ibn Tawlab, N.H. al Qaysī (ed.), Baghdad (1969).

J.E. MONTGOMERY

naqā'iḍ

'Contradicting poems, flytings' (sing. *naqīḍa*), poems in which tribal or personal insults are exchanged. This form of poetic duelling is therefore part of ***hijā'*** (see also ***mathālib***). The poems usually come in pairs, employing the same metre and rhyme. The genre has its origin in pre-Islamic times, in the slanging matches between members of opposing clans or tribes. It culminated in the **Umayyad** period, when **al-Akhṭal**, **al-Farazdaq** and **Jarīr** exchanged their famous series of *naqā'iḍ* in the course of several decades. The poems may be short and monothematic; but many are relatively long and in ***qaṣīda*** form, with a remarkable combination of themes: amatory, vaunting and invective verse. The 'rebutting' or 'undoing' (which may have been the original meaning of the verb *naqaḍa*) does not imply a point-by-point refutation of the poem of one's opponent. Instead of defending himself against abuse and slander the poet usually prefers a counter-attack. Rich in historical and political allusions, their political significance is second to their function as entertainment, which is provided by means of humorous descriptions, grotesque exaggerations and gross obscenities. They were often recited to great effect, either publicly, for instance at the **Mirbad** of **Basra**, or smaller gatherings, as at the Umayyad court. Their style and diction may range from the lofty to the near-colloquial. They were admired by philologians, critics and the general public alike. Several collections of *naqā'iḍ* (also called *munāqaḍāt*) were made from the eighth century onwards, some of them with philological commentaries; the most important one being the commentary by **al-Sukkarī** of *Naqā'iḍ Jarīr wa-al-Farazdaq* in the recension of **Abū 'Ubayda**.

In later times the *naqā'iḍ* are personal or sectarian rather than tribal. On the whole poets preferred, in their invective exchanges, independent **epigrams** that do not answer to the formal strictures (identical rhyme and metre) of the true *naqā'iḍ*. Sometimes the term *naqīḍa* is employed for what is more properly called a ***mu'āraḍa*** or emulation; see, for example, the first volume of the *Dīwān* of **Abū Nuwās** (ed. Wagner, 24–105) where the invective element is often absent. The old tribal form of poetic duelling survived, with little change, into modern times; witness the Arabian *riddiyyih* described by Sowayan – two poets alternately improvising a few lines with the same metre and rhyme.

Further reading

Abbott, Nabia, *Studies in Arabic Literary Papyri, vol. 3, Language and Literature*, Chicago (1972) (see index s.v. '*Naqā'iḍ*' and 'Satire').

al-Shāyib, Aḥmad, *Ta'rīkh al-naqā'iḍ fī al-shi'r al-'Arabī*, Cairo (1946).

Sowayan, Saad Abdullah, *Nabaṭi Poetry: The Oral Poetry of Arabia*, Berkeley (1985), 142–4.

(For a list of ancient compilations and commentaries of *naqā'iḍ*, see *GAS*, vol. 2, 62–3; for editions see under the individual poets.)

G.J.H. VAN GELDER

al-naqd al-adabī see literary criticism

naqīḍa see *naqā'iḍ*

al-Naqqāsh, Mārūn (1817–55)

Maronite dramatist, usually considered the first modern Arab playwright. Born in Sidon, he died in Tarsus. He was chief clerk in the Customs in Beirut. He went on business in 1846 to **Egypt**, and then Italy, where he discovered the world of theatre and opera, and wrote three high-quality plays, mainly in literary Arabic. The first Arabic play in the Levant was his *al-Bakhīl*, set in Beirut but inspired by Molière's *L'Avare*. It was performed at the end of 1847 on a stage in his home. Men and boys played the female parts. His second play *Abū al-Ḥasan al-Mughaffal*, from the ***Alf layla wa-layla*** story of a caliph 'for-a-day', was performed in 1850 before the Ottoman Governor, and is generally considered the first original play in Arabic. He performed his last play *al-Ḥasūd al-salīṭ* in 1853 in his own theatre beside his house. With a Syrian setting, this too was inspired by Molière, describing the actions of a jealous suitor, whose beloved is promised to another by her father. His plays were published in a posthumous collection, *Arzat Lubnān* (1869), by his brother Niqūlā **al-Naqqāsh**. Mārūn al-Naqqāsh inclined to musical theatre, as this was more appreciated by his fellow citizens and established a framework for the Arab theatre, coining the stage terminology that was to remain in vogue throughout most of the nineteenth century.

Further reading

Badawi, M.M., *Early Arabic Drama*, Cambridge (1988), 43–54.
al-Khozai, M.A., *The Development of Early Arabic Drama 1847–1900*, London (1984), 31–78.
Landau, J.M., *Studies in the Arab Theater and Cinema*, Philadelphia (1958), 57–61.
——, 'al-Naḳḳās͟h, Mārūn...', EI^2, vol. 7, 930.

P.C. SADGROVE

al-Naqqāsh, Niqūlā (1825–94)

Maronite lawyer, translator, teacher, dramatist, poet and journalist, born and died in Beirut. He worked in the Customs; was involved in banking and commerce, and was appointed secretary to the Governor of Beirut; he was also a member of the Beirut Commercial Court. In 1877 he was elected a member of the Ottoman Parliament. He was editor of *al-Najāḥ* magazine (1872), and founded *al-Miṣbāḥ* (1880), mouthpiece of the Maronite Bishop Yūsuf al-Dibs. He also translated many Ottoman legal works. The only person to follow in the footsteps of his brother Mārūn **al-Naqqāsh**, he presented his plays after his death, publishing them in *Arzat Lubnān* with a study on the theatre. His own plays include *al-Shaykh al-jāhil*, a play on the pre-Islamic knight Rabī'a ibn Zayd al-Muqaddam, *al-Muwaṣṣī*, and *al-Majnūn bi al-ghaṣb*.

Further reading

Dāghir, Yūsuf As'ad, *Maṣādir al-dirāsāt al-adabiyya*, Beirut (1956), iii/2, 1346–8.
Khouéiri, J., *Théâtre arabe: Liban, 1847–1860*, Louvain (1984), 82–4.

P.C. SADGROVE

al-Naqqāsh, Salīm Khalīl (1850–84)

Maronite writer, dramatist and journalist. Born in Beirut, he died in Alexandria. He was director of the Customs in Beirut (1876). Khedive Ismā'īl invited him to form a troupe to perform plays in Egypt, the first Lebanese troupe to go there. In Beirut he put actresses on the stage for the first time, despite strong criticism. He performed the plays of his uncle Mārūn **al-Naqqāsh**; his own adaptation of plays by Corneille and Racine; Verdi's *Aïda* (to which he added popular Arab airs); *al-Ẓalūm*, an intrigue set in an oriental court; Adīb **Isḥāq**'s *Gharā'ib al-ittifāq* (set in India) and his *Charlemagne*; and *Zénobie* by l'abbé d'Aubignac. When the troupe failed, **al-Afghānī** persuaded him to become a journalist. Salīm helped to edit the weekly *Miṣr* founded by Isḥāq, and founded the daily *al-Tijāra* (1878) with him. Both papers were strongly nationalist, and were suspended for their criticism of the government and of foreign interference. Salīm secured concessions for the daily *al-Maḥrūsa* and the weekly *al-'Aṣr al-jadīd* (1880). For opposing 'Urābī, *al-Maḥrūsa* was suspended in June 1882 and Salīm forced to flee. He returned to Egypt in 1884 and *al-Maḥrūsa* reappeared. His history of these troubled times, *Miṣr lil-Miṣriyyīn* was published after his death.

Further reading

Badawi, M.M., *Early Arabic Drama*, Cambridge (1988), 53–6.
Landau, J.M., *Studies in the Arab Theater and Cinema*, Philadelphia (1958), 63–5.
Khouéiri, J., *Théâtre arabe: Liban, 1847–1960*, Louvain (1984), 85–94.
Sadgrove, P.C., 'Salīm b. K͟halīl al-Naḳḳas͟h', EI^2, vol. 8, 992–3.
——, *The Egyptian Theatre in the Nineteenth Century*, Reading (1996), 126–33, 142–3, 145.

P.C. SADGROVE

al-Nāshi' al-Akbar (d. 293/893)

Abū al-'Abbās 'Abd Allāh ibn Muḥammad ibn Shirshīr al-Nāshi' al-Akbar was a **Mu'tazilī** theologian, grammarian, poet and critic. He was born in al-Anbār and was active in **Baghdad** and **Egypt**, where he died. A versatile scholar and poet, he was at home in both the 'Arabic' and the 'non-Arabic' sciences. He wrote works of a theological nature and on **grammar**. He was famous for hunting poetry (see *ṭardiyya*). A didactic poem on various subjects is said to have consisted of 4,000 lines in monorhyme. A book on poetry (*Naqd al-shi'r*) is known only from quotations. Also lost is his *Debate between Gold and Glass*.

Text editions

Dīwān, Hilāl Nājī (ed.), *al-Mawrid* 11(1) (1982), 89–104, 11(2) (1982), 61–78, 11(3) (1982) 43–74, 11(4) (1982) 27–54, 12(1) (1983) 57–78.

van Ess, Josef, *Frühe mu'tazilitische Häresiographie: Zwei Werke des Nāšī' al-akbar*, Beirut and Wiesbaden (1971).

G.J.H. VAN GELDER

al-Nāshi' al-Aṣghar (271–365 or 366/884–976)

'Alī ibn 'Abd Allāh ibn Waṣīf al-Nāshi' al-Aṣghar was a poet from **Baghdad**. The son of a perfume seller, he worked as a maker of copper ornaments, and became a **Shī'ī** theologian, although he was noted for his ***mujūn***. Most of his poetry ('innumerable poems', it is said) was devoted to the Shī'ī genre of panegyrics on the 'Alids; other poems were made for contemporary rulers, among them the caliph al-Rāḍī, Sayf al-Dawla, Kāfūr al-Ikhshīdī, **Ibn al-'Amīd** and 'Aḍud al-Dawla. Tall, robust, loud-voiced and fond of argumentation and jesting, he is reported to have lived into his nineties while still in possession of a strong set of teeth. Of his poetry only fragments survive.

G.J.H. VAN GELDER

Nashwān ibn Sa'īd al-Ḥimyarī (d. 573/1178)

Abū Sa'īd Nashwān ibn Sa'īd ibn Nashwān al-Ḥimyarī was a theologian, philologist, poet and historian. A member of a nobel Yemeni family from Ḥawt near Sanaa, Nashwān was for years a *qāḍī* before engaging in an attempt to establish himself as ruler of an area between Sanaa and Saada. He adhered to **Zaydī** and **Mu'tazilī** views. He wrote a **Koran** commentary and compiled several works on theological, historical, philological and other topics.

Best known are his 'Himyarite Poem' (*al-Qaṣīda al-Ḥimyariyya*) and his dictionary *Shams al-'ulūm wa-dawā' kalām al-'Arab min al-kulūm* (*The sun of Wisdom and Remedy for the Arabic Language's Lesions*). The former, an *ubi sunt* poem, enumerates historical and mythical Yemeni rulers in a series of episodes; it totals 135 lines. Nashwān, or perhaps his son, compiled a commentary on it. The *Shams al-'ulūm* goes far beyond a usual dictionary in the amount of explanatory information that it includes about individual words; much of this has a marked Yemeni bias.

Nashwān is interesting both as a promoter of a specifically Yemeni cultural consciousness and as a writer who made an unexpected use of existing literary forms to convey a very wide range of information.

Text editions

al-Qaṣīda al-Ḥimyariyya, A. von Kremer (ed. and trans.), Leipzig (1865); R. Basset (ed.), Algiers (1914).

Shams al-'ulūm (letters *alif* to *shīn*), 'A.A. al-Jarāfī (ed.), Beirut (1982).

H. KILPATRICK

nasīb see *qaṣīda*

Nāṣif, (Muḥammad) Ḥifnī (1855–1919)

Writer, poet and judge. Born in the outskirts of **Cairo**, he died in that city. He studied at **al-Azhar** and the École Khédiviale de Droit, where he later taught. He was imprisoned for his speeches during the 'Urābī revolt. Nāṣif played a part in the foundation of the Egyptian University (1908) and the Arab Academy in **Damascus** (1919), his lectures at the University on the history of the Arabic script being subsequently published. He lectured on the dialects of Egyptian tribes to the Orientalists Congress in Vienna (1886), and from *c*.1909–1912 was Inspector General of Arabic teaching at the Ministry of Education. His published works include his ***dīwān*** (1937); prose writings (1960); a work on women's emancipation in Islam (1924); and a commentary on **al-Suyūṭī**'s *al-Fatḥ al-qarīb*, on the *shawāhid* of **Ibn Hishām**'s great treatise on syntax (1902). He also edited the *dīwān* of the Egyptian poetess 'Ā'isha **al-Taymūriyya** (1840–1902). His daughter was the poet Malak Ḥifnī Nāṣif (*Bāḥithat al-Bādiya*).

Further reading

Ghunaym, Maḥmūd, *Ḥifnī Nāṣif: buṭūlatuh fī mukhtalif al-mayādīn*, Cairo (1965).

P.C. SADGROVE

Nasīm, Aḥmad (1878–1938)

Egyptian poet. Educated in a Turkish primary school and Egyptian Arabic secondary school, Nasīm studied at **al-Azhar** and subsequently worked in **Dār al-Kutub** where he was involved in the publication of classical poetry collections. Although his poetry belongs to the neo-classical trend, some of his poems reveal a Romantic influence (especially those poems published in 1933 in the magazine *Apollo*). Nasīm was intensely involved in political life, writing national and patriotic poems as a contribution to the struggle for independence. His ***dīwān*** was published in two parts: the first (1908) consists of poetry of occasions, and the second (1910) of nationalist poems previously published in the National Party's newspaper *al-Liwā'*. In the dedication of the second part he styles himself *shā'ir al-Ḥizb al-Waṭanī* (the poet of the National Party). He is also known as *shā'ir al-waṭaniyyāt* (the poet of nationalism).

Further reading

Brugman, J., *An Introduction to the History of Modern Arabic Literature in Egypt*, Leiden (1984), 53–4.

R. SNIR

Nāṣir, Kamāl (1925–73)

Palestinian poet, journalist, playwright and political activist. Born in Bir Zeit into a devout but artistically inclined Christian family, he studied at the American University of Beirut and joined the Ba'th Party, becoming briefly a member of the Jordanian Parliament. Forced to flee Jordan in 1957, he lived in various Arab countries until he joined the PLO's Executive Committee in 1969. He was assassinated by Israeli agents. Nāṣir's poetry has not achieved the popularity of some other Palestinian 'resistance poets'. His sonorous and patriotic verse, which blends neo-classical, Romantic and socialist influences, often reflects some impatience with technique coupled with a temperamental preference for action. The use of symbol, fashionable among his contemporaries, is only sketchy in his verse. In some of his more subdued, 'confessional' poems, however, alienation and defiance, despair and hope, battle for mastery of the poet's psyche. Intimations of further poetic maturity in his later poems remained unfulfilled owing to his untimely death.

M.R. NOURALLAH

Naṣīr al-Dīn al-Ṭūsī (597–672/1201–74)

Muḥammad ibn Muḥammad Naṣīr al-Dīn al-Ṭūsī was a Shī'ī scholar and political dabbler. Born into a Twelver Shī'ī family in Ṭūs (in **Khurasan**), al-Ṭūsī rose to prominence in the service of the **Ismā'īlī** governor of Quhistan, Muḥtasham Nāṣir al-Dīn 'Abd al-Raḥīm ibn Abī Manṣūr, whose court astrologer he was, and for whom he wrote a number of works (most of them in Persian), including one of the major works of Islamic ethical writing, the *Akhlāq-i Nāṣirī* (*Nasirean Ethics*), which has been described as 'the best known ethical digest to be composed in mediaeval Persia, if not in all mediaeval Islam' (Wickens, 1964, 10), and which, while heavily indebted to the *Tahdhīb al-akhlāq* of **Miskawayh** (d. 421/1029), greatly expands and deepens the scope of that work. He continued in Ismā'īlī employment in Quhistan and at their headquarters at Alamut until the second wave of Mongol incursions under Hūlāgū (Hülegü), when he defected to the Mongol leader (and was instrumental in his destruction of Alamut), whom he accompanied in the capacity of adviser to the conquest of **Baghdad**. He served as vizier and supervisor of *waqf*s under Hūlāgū and his successor Abāqā until his death, and founded the important observatory at Maragha (in Azarbaijan). His writings include works on astronomy, ethics and philosophy, including a commentary on *al-Ishārāt wa-al-tanbīhāt* of **Ibn Sīnā** (d. 428/1037), whom he defended against the criticisms of **Fakhr al-Dīn al-Rāzī** (d. 606/1209). The precise nature of al-Ṭūsī's beliefs has been a matter of dispute; his autobiography (in Persian) suggests that at one period in his life he embraced Ismā'īlī beliefs, but may later have reverted to Twelver **Shī'ism**.

Text editions

Ibn Sīnā, *al-Ishārāt wa-al-tanbīhāt*, Tehran (1983) (includes al-Ṭūsī's commentary).
Naṣīr al-Dīn Ṭūsī's Memoir on Astronomy (al-Tadhkira fī 'Ilm al-Hay'a), F.J. Ragib (ed. and trans.), New York (1993).
The Nasirean Ethics, G.M. Wickens (trans.), London (1964).
Tajrīd al-manṭiq, Beirut (1988).

Further reading

Fakhry, Majid, *Ethical Theories in Islam*, Leiden (1991).

Horton, M., *Die philosophischen Ansichten von Rázi und Túsi*, Bonn (1910).
——, *Die spekulative und positive Theologie des Islam nach Rázi und ihre Kritik durch Túsi*, Leipzig (1912).
Poonawala, I.K., *Biobibliography of Ismāʿīlī Literature*, Malibu, CA (1977), 260–3.
Ullmann, M., *Die Natur- und Geheimwissenschaft in Islam*, Leiden (1972), 127, 341f.

I.R. NETTON/J.S. MEISAMI

Naṣr Allāh, Imilī (Emily) (1938–)

Lebanese novelist and short-story writer. Born in Kfeir in South Lebanon, Naṣr Allāh's overriding concern is the question of emigration. She was among the first of her generation of women to leave the village for her education. In the 1950s, she worked her way through the American University of Beirut by publishing newspaper articles. In 1962, she published her first novel, *Ṭuyūr aylūl*, a fictionalized autobiography laced with legends. The novel explores the fate of women who defy convention by leaving home to gain education and a career. It quickly became popular and part of the Lebanese secondary school curriculum. Now in its ninth printing, it has been translated into German. Her next writings were implicitly and explicitly directed at children to whom she felt a strong sense of responsibility. Soon after the outbreak of the Lebanese Civil War, she wrote *Tilka al-dhikrayāt* (1980). This novel marks a change in Naṣr Allāh's thinking: emigration when its destination is outside Lebanon is to be proscribed. *Al-Iqlāʿ ʿaks al-zaman* (1981), a novel she claimed to have been writing for almost twenty years as a sequel to *Ṭuyūr aylūl*, is even more unequivocal: the Lebanese must earn the right to retain their citizenship by staying on the war-torn land. Between 1982 and 1990, her entire literary output was in the form of short stories, all of which use the Lebanese Civil War as pretext or context. All focus on the impact of the war on the lives of women.

Text editions

Flight Against Time, Issa J. Boullata (trans.), Charlottetown (1987).
A House not her Own, T. Khalil-Khouri (trans.), Charlottetown (1992).

Further reading

Cooke, M., *War's Other Voices: Women Writers and the Lebanese Civil War*, Cambridge (1988).

M. COOKE

nathr *see* prose

al-nathr al-fannī *see* artistic prose

nature, in classical poetry

Descriptions of nature (in the wider sense) can already be found in the oldest Arabic poetry. Among other things, the poets describe the desert, at first mostly within ***fakhr*** (self-praise), later on in the *raḥīl* part of the ***qaṣīda*** ('How many a desert in which the mirage is glittering'; **ʿAmr ibn Qamīʾa**), the long night, the early morning, a thunderstorm (**Imruʾ al-Qays** in the *Muʿallaqa*), hunting animals and hunting scenes, and particularly, of course, the camel (the most famous description being in **Ṭarafa**'s *Muʿallaqa*). Most of these topics are also treated in the later Arabic poetry; in addition, there are descriptions of atmospheric phenomena (clouds, snow), mountains, trees, fruit, etc. In **al-Mutanabbī**'s (d. 354/965) *Dīwān* there are to be found two unusual nature descriptions: a description of the valley of Bawwān through which the poet rode on his way to the **Būyid** ʿAḍud al-Dawla in Shiraz, and a description of Lake Tiberias.

However, the description of flowers, gardens and spring was to become Arabic nature poetry *par excellence*. The topic devlops into its own genre in the **ʿAbbāsid** period (*zahriyyāt* or *nawriyyāt*, *rawḍiyyāt*, and *rabīʿiyyāt*). Descriptions of flowers and meadows are already sporadically found in *Jāhilī* poetry. Thus, it was possible for the comparison of the beloved's scent with a flowering meadow in the *nasīb* of the *qaṣīda* to be developed into a detailed description of the meadow itself and its flowers (e.g. in **ʿAntara**'s *Muʿallaqa*). Furthermore, in the description of the deserted campsites (*aṭlāl*), one might describe the vegetation sprouting after the rain (e.g. in **Labīd**'s *Muʿallaqa*). Those poets, finally, who were connected with the court of **Ḥīra** (particularly **al-Aʿshā**) describe, in the wine scenes of their *qaṣīdas*, the flowers that were used as decoration for the inn (roses, narcissi). It is mainly here that one has to look for the origins of the later *zahriyyāt*. Hereafter, the development of the flower and garden description takes place, above all, within the framework of wine poetry (see ***khamriyya***). **Abū Nuwās** (d. *c*.200/815) inserted a frequently quoted description of narcissi into a wine poem ('[a wine] next to freshly picked narcissi, as if they were eyes, when we turn our eyes to them ...'). Some of Abū Nuwās's wine poems already contain more verses with a description of flowers than of wine.

Abū Tammām (d. 231/845) takes up the tradition of nature description in the prologue of the *qaṣīda* and leads it to its first climax. In a famous poem of praise, a *rā'iyya*, he completely replaces the *nasīb* with a long and rich description of spring. This method of Abū Tammām's formed a precedent in a unique way; he was followed in this by later Arabic poets (**Ibn al-Rūmī**, **al-Buḥturī**, **al-Ṣanawbarī**), as well as by Hebrew, Persian and Ottoman poets. In the Persian *qaṣīda*, a description of spring is the most frequently used topic for the prologue.

Al-Buḥturī (d. 284/897) repeatedly describes within the framework of the ***madīḥ*** part of his *qaṣīda*s the garden (and the palace) of the one praised. In a famous *qaṣīda* he develops out of the praise one of the most beautiful descriptions of spring in Arabic poetry (connecting thought: 'Unto you came the merry spring').

Al-Buḥturī's contemporary Ibn al-Rūmī (d. *c*.283/896) is even more famous as a nature poet. He was the first to compose (in addition to *qaṣīda* prologues containing descriptions of flowers and spring) longer independent poems on flowers. A dispute (*munāẓara*) between rose and narcissus in which the narcissus is granted superiority deserves special attention (see **debate literature**). Ibn al-Rūmī's *munāẓara* was often imitated or 'refuted' respectively. There are, however, a number of garden poems by Ibn al-Rūmī that are as remarkable as this flower poem and that, due to the feeling of nature displayed in them, go completely beyond the usual scope (see below).

Ibn al-Muʿtazz (d. 296/908) draws, above all, 'epigrammatic sketches' and 'poetic snapshots' (von Grunebaum) of flowers (the poems are to be found in the chapter *awṣāf*, 'descriptions', of his *dīwān*), but also takes up the tradition of garden descriptions within wine poetry (compare his well-known *muzdawija fī dhamm al-ṣabūh*, which begins with a long description of flowers and a garden which later forms the background for the banquet).

In the poetry of al-Ṣanawbarī (d. 334/945–6) the poems on nature form a genre of their own. In addition to short nature poems like Ibn al-Muʿtazz's, he also composed numerous long *qaṣīda*s with spring, a garden, a landscape, a dispute or a war among flowers being the main, if not the only topic. Furthermore, the description of nature is integrated into almost all the other genres used by him.

The description of nature is one of the preferred topics of the Andalusian Arabs. One of the oldest Spanish–Arabic anthologies (by **Abū al-Walīd al-Ḥimyarī**; d. *c*.440/1048) is named *al-Badīʿ fī waṣf al-rabīʿ*. It contains exclusively poems on flowers, gardens and spring. The most important nature poet is **Ibn Khafāja** (see below) who therefore was given the epithet 'Ṣanawbarī of the West'.

The feeling for nature in later Arabic poetry is for the most part purely optic, directed toward the decorative. Acoustic perceptions and those pertaining to the sense of smell are found much more seldom than visual perceptions. The most important devices for description are simile and metaphor, through which chiefly the colour or the form of the flower are illustrated. Donors of the image are most often precious stones and metals ('roses like rubies'), but also parts of the human body ('roses like cheeks'). Occasionally, the objects of nature are personified (Ibn al-Rūmī: 'The rose blushed out of shame ...'). Completely outside the usual scope are some of Ibn al-Rūmī's garden poems in which the poet describes nature living its own life; moving man by its splendour and forcing him to praise God; reviving man by the fragrance of its flowers and diverting him by the singing of its birds; averting sorrow from the sorrowful by a cool breeze, etc.

Arabic nature poetry reaches another climax with the Andalusians **Ibn Zaydūn** (d. 463/1071) and Ibn Khafāja (d. 533/1138). In one of Ibn Zaydūn's poems on his beloved **Wallāda**, nature participates in the poet's longing ('as if it [the breeze] was moved by compassion for me, and therefore became gentle out of pity'). The poetry of Ibn Khafāja, in which the description of nature makes up a large, if not the largest part, has in addition to the usual topics (flowers, gardens), more frequently than in the poetry of earlier poets, other objects of nature (i.e. trees, rivers, clouds, hills, fire). His nature scenes, which are frequently connected with love scenes, are often richly developed (in one case: description of the night and the early morning, of the flowers on a hill and at a watercourse; all of this within the frame of a love scene). Ibn Khafāja's feeling for nature is characterized by nature's almost always being personified and/ or brought into rapport with human beings ('[A cloud], that minted white dirhams of flowers which the fingertips of the twigs have handed to *you*'). Frequently, he projects human feelings and acts onto a natural object. His most famous poem is devoted to a mountain which he lets recite a moving monologue about transitoriness. Another of Ibn Khafāja's artistic devices is the projection of macrocosmic phenomena into the garden context ('An *arāk* tree that has pitched over us a dewy sky, while the celestial bodies of the goblets have been brought into circulation'). Next to the epics of the Persian poet Niẓāmī (d. 605/ 1209), Ibn Khafāja's nature poems belong to those poetical works within Islamic literature that have a special appeal to European taste.

Further reading

Bürgel, J.-C., 'Man, nature and cosmos as intertwining elements in the poetry of Ibn Khafāja', *JAL* 14 (1983), 31–45.

al-Nowaihi, Magda M., *The Poetry of Ibn Khafājah: A Literary Analysis*, Leiden (1993).

Schoeler, G., *Arabische Naturdichtung*, Beirut (1972).

——, 'Ibn al-Kattānī's *Kitāb at-Tašbīhāt* und das Problem des 'Hispanismus' der andalusisch–arabischen Dichtung', *ZDMG* 129 (1979), 43–97.

von Grunebaum, G.E., 'The response to nature in Arabic poetry', *JNES* 4 (1945), 137–51.

G. SCHOELER; trans. A. GIESE

See also: *waṣf*

al-Nawājī (788–859/1386–1455)

Egyptian poet and man of letters. Muḥammad Ibn Ḥasan ibn 'Alī ibn 'Uthmān al-Nawājī, who taught ***ḥadīth*** at two *madrasas* in **Cairo**, was a respected poet in his day. Besides poetry he wrote several anthologies, chiefly about poetry and stylistics. His most famous work, *Ḥalbat al-kumayt*, a literary celebration of wine and connected themes, remained popular in spite of pious attacks.

Text editions

Ḥalbat al-kumayt, Būlāq (1276/1859); Cairo (1299/1881, 1357/1939).

Muqaddima fī ṣinā'at al-naẓm wa-al-nathr, Beirut (1972).

Further reading

Semah, David, 'al-Muwashshaḥāt fī *'Uqūd al-la'āl* lil-Nawājī', *al-Karmil* 4 (1983), 69–92.

van Gelder, Geert Jan, 'A Muslim encomium on wine: *The Racecourse of the Bay (Ḥalbat al-kumayt)* by al-Nawāğī (d. 859/1455) as a post-classical Arabic work', *Arabica* 42 (1995), 222–34.

G.J.H. VAN GELDER

al-Nawawī (631–76/1233–77)

Muḥyī al-Dīn Yaḥyā ibn Sharaf al-Nawawī was a renowned ***ḥadīth*** scholar and jurist of the Shāfi'ī school. He spent his entire life in or near **Damascus**, and is noted for having stood up against the sultan Baybars by refusing to issue a legal opinion (*fatwā*) supporting certain of his acts. His pious and ascetic lifestyle become proverbial. In *ḥadīth* studies he is famed for his commentaries on the collections of **al-Bukhārī** and **Muslim** and for popular selection of *ḥadīth*s entitled *Kitāb al-arba'īn*. His commentary on Muslim's collection contains as an introduction a useful overview of *ḥadīth* studies as cultivated down to his time. His reputation in jurisprudence is based largely on his compendium of law entitled *Minhāj al-ṭālibīn* which, together with commentaries written later upon it, have become pre-eminent among the law books of the Shāfi'ī school.

Text editions

The Biographical Dictionary of Illustrious Men ..., F. Wüstenfeld (ed.), Göttingen (1842–7).

Gardens of the Righteous, M.Z. Khan (ed. and trans.), London (1975).

Une Herméneutique de la tradition islamique: le commentaire des Arba'ūn an Nawawīya, L. Pouzet (ed. and trans.), Beirut (1982).

Kitāb al-arba'īn wa-sharḥuh, al-Maḥalla al-Kubrā (1987).

Minhaj et talibin, E.G. Howard (trans.) (1914), rpt Lahore (1977).

al-Nawawī's Forty Hadith, E. Ibrahim and D. Johnson-Davies (trans), Damascus (1976).

al-Taqrīb fī fann al-ḥadīth, Cairo (1968).

Further reading

Wüstenfeld, F., *Über das Leben und die Schriften des Scheich Abū Zakarijā Jahjā al-Nawawī*, Göttingen (1949).

B. WEISS

al-Nawbakhtī

Nisba of a family of scientists and **Shī'ī** religious scholars of Iranian origin (second–fourth/eighth–tenth centuries). Nawbakht al-Fārisī (d. *c.*160/777) was one of the Persian astrologers appointed by the caliph al-Manṣūr to determine the auspices for the foundation of the **'Abbāsid** capital, **Baghdad**, in 145/762. His son Abū Sahl al-Faḍl (d. 170/786?) was astrologer to the caliphs al-Manṣūr and al-Rashīd and wrote several treatise on the art.

From the time of the lesser *Ghayba* (occultation) of the Shī'ī Imām members of the Nawbakhtī family played an important role as intellectual and political leaders of the Imāmiyya at Baghdad during the caliphate of al-Muqtadir (295–320/908–32): Ibn Rūḥ (d. 326/938), a Nawbakhtī on his mother's side, was the third *wakīl* of the Hidden Imām; Abū Sahl Ismā'īl ibn 'Alī (d. 311/924) and his nephew, Abū Muḥammad al-Ḥasan ibn Mūsā (d. between 300 and 310/912 and 923), were the founders of Imāmī *kalām*. The latter is best known for his book on the Shī'ī sects, *Firaq al-Shī'a*, and a general heresiography of Islam (known from citations only), *Kitāb al-Ārā' wa-al-diyānāt*, but he was also a student of Hellenistic philosophy and sciences, and a defender of astrology; his son, Abū al-Ḥasan Mūsā ibn al-Ḥasan ibn Kibriyā', wrote two astrological monographs (324–5/936–7).

Text editions

Kitāb al-Kāmil (fī asrār al-nujūm): horóscopos históricos, A. Labarta (ed. and trans.), Madrid (1982).

Die Sekten der Schia (Firaq al-Shī'a), H. Ritter (ed.), Leipzig and Istanbul (1931).

Further reading

Iqbāl, 'Abbās, *Khāndān-i Nawbakhtī*, Tehran (1311/1933), 3rd edn (1978).

Ullmann, M., *Die Natur- und Geheimwissenschaften im Islam*, Leiden (1972), 303.

G. ENDRESS

Nawrūz see Nayrūz

Nayrūz

The Arabized form of Persian *Nawrūz*, 'New Year', originally a festival of the Zoroastrians of Persia, traditionally celebrated at the spring equinox. The popular celebrations, marked by the exchange of presents, sprinkling of water, the wearing of new clothes and something like a saturnalia or carnival in the streets, continued in Islamic Persia but also in such Arab lands as Iraq, **Syria** and **Egypt** until late medieval times. They included the declaiming and singing of poetry, hence there exists in both Perisan and Arabic poetry a class of verse, *nayrūziyyāt*, composed on the occasion of these festivities, often specifically at the courts of the rulers. Also, the grammarian **Ibn Fāris** wrote a treatise, the *Kitāb al-Nayrūz*, so far unpublished.

Further reading

von Grunebaum, G.E., *Muhammadan Festivals*, New York (1951), rpt (1976), 53–6.

C.E. BOSWORTH

naẓm

(Lit. 'the ordering of pearls on a string to form a necklace'.) Used metaphorically to describe textual ordering of two different kinds. The first is 'ordering of words-*cum*-meanings' or, more freely, 'style'. In this sense it seems to have grown out of the discussions of the dogma of ***i'jāz al-Qur'ān***. **Al-Khaṭṭābī** (d. 388/998), in his treatise *Explanation of the Inimitability of the Koran*, postulates a triad of elements that make up 'speech' (*kalām*), namely 'words (*lafẓ*) as carriers, meaning (*ma'nā*) subsisting in them, and a connection (*ribāṭ*) that orders (*nāẓim*) both of them'. The third element is usually called *naẓm*. In all three elements the **Koran** is the superior text. The relationship between the three is metaphorically described (the various 'types of ordering' are a 'bridle on the words and a rein on the meanings'), but there is little explicit discussion of the workings of *naẓm*.

Al-Bāqillānī (d. 403/1013), in his *Inimitability of the Koran*, enumerates ten aspects of its *naẓm*, but these are very general considerations (such as 'the Koran is *sui generis* as a literary genre', 'the Arabs had not produced any eloquent text of such enormous length', 'the Koran is homogeneously eloquent', and 'the transition from one topic to the next in the Koran is unrivalled'), and the strict correlation between *naẓm* and the two other elements of speech, 'words' and 'meaning', is absent. **'Abd al-Qāhir al-Jurjānī** (d. 471/1078 or 474/1081), in his *Proofs for the Inimitability*, is closer to al-Khaṭṭābī, but goes beyond him by filling the notion of *naẓm* with real content. He defines it as 'minding the meanings of syntactic relations', and in several tightly reasoned chapters he exemplifies its workings by drawing attention to the role of word order or the functional meaning of certain particles. The 'ordering' creates a shape/form (*ṣūra*) in the mind and, parallel to it, in the language; through it the semantic (*maʿnā*) and the syntactic–stylistic (*lafẓ*) side of a proposition (*kalām*) become mirror images. The old and, according to al-Jurjānī, misunderstood dichotomy of **lafẓ and maʿnā** is thus reinterpreted: *lafẓ* is split up into the 'word and sound material', on the one hand, and the syntactically formed 'wording', on the other; likewise, *maʿnā* is divided into a vague 'intention' and a strictly formed 'meaning', mirrored by the 'wording'.

The other meaning of *naẓm* is 'metrical speech' or, as a process, 'versification'. If used as the opposite of *nathr*, 'prose' (lit. 'scattering of pearls'), it refers to any metrical text, whether real poetry or didactic versification. But not seldom it forms an opposition with *shiʿr*, 'poetry', thus referring specifically to didactic versification. As such, it can also be used as an adverse criticism of what claims to be poetry. With the ascendancy of **strophic poetry** in the fourth/tenth century and after, the term *shiʿr* is sometimes restricted to monorhyme poetry, the most traditional and most prestigious kind, with the result that *naẓm* is applied to strophic poetry. The various meanings can be seen in the following diagram:

naẓm = metrical speech

shiʿr = true poetry *naẓm* = didactic versification

shiʿr = monorhyme poetry *naẓm* = strophic poetry

The line between poetry and didactic versification is sometimes not easy to draw. Mystical poetry may belong on both sides. Even highly educated authors tend to blur the distinction: **al-Ṣafadī** (d. 764/1363), wanting to refute the idea that there are, in Arabic literature, no really long poems like the *Shāhnāma* of the Persians, points among other things to the *Shāṭibiyya*, a long didactic poem on the Seven Readings of the Koran; and **Ṣafī al-Dīn al-Ḥillī** (d. probably 749/1348) includes a selection of mnemonic verse in his *dīwān*.

Text editions

ʿAbd al-Qāhir al-Jurjānī, *Dalāʾil al-iʿjāz*, Maḥmūd Muḥammad Shākir (ed.), Cairo (1404/1984).

al-Bāqillānī, *Kitāb Iʿjāz al-Qurʾān*, al-Sayyid Aḥmad Ṣaqr (ed.), Cairo (1963), 35–48.

al-Khaṭṭābī, *Bayān iʿjāz al-Qurʾān*, in *Thalāth rasāʾil fī iʿjāz al-Qurʾān*, Muḥammad Khalaf Allāh and Muḥammad Zaghlūl Salām, (eds) Cairo (n.d), 19–65, here 24, 33.

al-Khaṭṭābī et l'inimitabilité du Coran, C.F. Audebert (trans.), Damascus (1982).

Futher reading

Abu Deeb, Kamal, *Al-Jurjānī's Theory of Poetic Imagery*, Warminster (1979), 24–64.

von Grunebaum, G.E., *Kritik und Dichtkunst*, Wiesbaden (1955), see index s.v.

W.P. HEINRICHS

See also: poetry, classical

al-Naẓẓām, Ibrāhīm ibn Sayyār (d. 836 or 845)

Abū Isḥaq Ibrāhīm ibn Sayyār al-Nazzam was a theologian of the **Muʿtazilī** school with strong leanings toward the natural sciences inherited from the Greeks. He was vigorously opposed by many of his fellow Muʿtazilīs for holding the view that God initially created the world with hidden potentialities that would subsequently become manifest. This way of thinking was in conflict with the predominant tendency among Muʿtazilīs and Muslim theologians in general to view God's creation as continuous, and it soon acquired the character of a heresy.

Text edition

Das Kitâb an-Nakṯ des Naẓẓâm und seine Rezeption im Kitâb al-Futyâ des Ǧâḥiẓ, J. van Ess (ed. and trans.), Göttingen (1972).

Further reading

Eberhardt, D., *Der sensualistische Ansatz und das Problem der Veränderung in der Philosophie Muʿammars und an-Nazzams*, Tübingen (1979).

van Ess, J., *Theology and Science: The Case of Abū Isḥāq an-Naẓẓām*, Ann Arbor (1979).

——, *Theologie und Gesellschaft im 2. und 3. Jh. Hidschra*, Berlin and York (1991–2), vol. 3, 296–419.

B. WEISS

neo-Platonism *see* Platonism

neo-classicism

A school of poetry which emerged in the second half of the nineteenth century, and which sought to revive the style and spirit of classical Arabic poetry. Closely connected with the ideals of the ***nahḍa***, the new poetry served to emphasize national and Islamic ideals by recalling the glories of the classical Arabic literary heritage; as such, it represented an act of literary self-assertion in the face of the Western influences which had begun to encroach on the Middle East since the beginning of the nineteenth century.

On a literary level, the neo-classical trend marked a reaction against the diction, style and poetic forms which had prevailed during the so-called 'transitional period' from the destruction of Baghdad in 1258 to the French occupation of Egypt in 1798, when word-play had been considered by many poets the best way to display their skill and talent. Believing that the classical poets had exhausted every possible theme and idea, they transformed poetry into an intellectual game – an intelligent, but essentially frivolous, form of entertainment. In contrast, the new poetics aimed to emulate the conventions and basic canons of classical Arabic poetry, including the use of ***muʿāraḍa*** (the imitation of a classical poem using the same metre, rhyme and theme with the intention of surpassing it).

The credit for initiating the new movement is usually accorded to Maḥmūd Sāmī **al-Bārūdī**, who, in his best poems, succeeds in articulating an individual experience within the constraints of traditional Arabic poetic forms. Al-Bārūdī's lead was followed in Egypt by Ismāʿīl **Ṣabrī**, Aḥmad **Shawqī**, Muḥammad Ḥāfiẓ **Ibrāhīm** and Walī al-Dīn **Yakan** and in Iraq by Jamāl Ṣidqī **al-Zahāwī**, Maʿrūf **al-Ruṣāfī**, Aḥmad al-Ṣāfī **al-Najafī** and Muḥammad Mahdī **al-Jawāhirī**.

Much of the output of the neo-classicists was 'public' poetry of one sort or another, written for particular social or political occasions and often composed to emphasize national ideals; at its most effective, this style of poetry attained a power and forcefulness uniquely suited to the purpose of the composition. At the other end of the spectrum, attempts by some neo-classicists to use the specific themes and imagery of the pre-Islamic ***qaṣīda*** in a contemporary context (e.g. by weeping over the deserted encampment of the poet's beloved) occasionally produce a ludicrous effect. Although individual poets continued to write in the neo-classical style for some time, by the 1930s the influence of modernist critics and poets seeking to combine conventional Arabic poetics with modern European theories had begun to gain ground, and neo-classicism yielded to **romanticism** as the dominant trend in Arabic poetry.

Further reading

Badawi, M.M., *A Critical Introduction to Modern Arabic Poetry*, Cambridge (1975).

Brugman, J., *An Introduction to the History of Arabic Literature in Egypt*, Leiden (1984).

Gibb, H.A.R., *Studies on the Civilization of Islam*, London (1962).

Jayyusi, S.K., *Trends and Movements in Modern Arabic Poetry*, 2 vols, Leiden (1977).

Moreh, S., *Modern Arabic Poetry 1800–1970*, Leiden (1976).

——, *Studies in Modern Arabic Prose and Poetry*, Leiden (1988).

Somekh, S., 'The Neo-classical Arabic Poets', in *CHALMAL*, 36–81.

S. MOREH/P. STARKEY

See also: poetry, modern

al-Niffarī (fourth/tenth century)

Muḥammad ibn ʿAbd al-Jabbār al-Niffarī was a Ṣūfī author, not usually mentioned in the Ṣūfī biographical dictionaries. His *nisba* indicates that his family origin was in Mesopotamia. He has left to posterity two larger works which were only put together in their final form after his death: the *Kitāb al-mawāqif* and the *Kitāb al-mukhāṭabāt*. In addition, some fragments of his other writings survive. **Ibn al-ʿArabī** refers to him by varying names, and ʿAfīf al-Dīn al-Tilimsānī (d. 690/1291) has written a commentary on him. Al-Niffarī's style is obscure and difficult, reminding one of **al-Ḥallāj**.

Text editions

The Mawáqif and Mukháṭabát of Muḥammad Ibn ʿAbdi 'l-Jabbár al-Niffarí with other fragments, Arthur J. Arberry (ed. and trans.), London (1935).

Nwyia, Paul (ed.), *Trois œuvres inédites de mystiques musulmans*, Beirut (1972), 183–324.

Further reading

Nwyia, Paul, *Exégèse coranique et langage mystique*, Beirut (1971), 348–407.

B. RADTKE

Nigm [Najm], Aḥmad Fu'ād (1929–)

Egyptian colloquial poet. Because of his uncompromising advocacy of the rights of the poor and underprivileged in his country, Nigm has often found himself at odds with the governmental apparatus, to the extent of being arrested and imprisoned on several occasions. Following the 1967 June War, Nigm (along with his companion, the famous blind singer, Shaykh Imām) abandoned his more covert modes of distributing his resistance poetry (such as by cassette or publication outside Egypt) and took his message directly to the public. Since that time he has spent further intervals in prison and others in hiding, but his poems continue to capture in memorable verse the political pulse of the Egyptian people. Among his more famous collections are: *Baladī wa-ḥabībatī* (1973), *Ughniyat al-ḥubb wa-al-ḥayāh* (1978), *Anā fayn* (1979), *'Īshī yā Maṣr* (1979), *al-'Anbara* (1982) and *Ṣundūq al-dunyā* (1985).

Further reading

Abdel-Malek, Kamal, *A Study of the Vernacular Poetry of Ahmad Fu'ad Nigm*, Leiden (1990).

R. ALLEN

al-Nīsābūrī, al-Ḥasan ibn Muḥammad (d. 406/1015)

Scholar and compiler of a famous work on 'wise fools' of the later Sāmānid period, who lived in **Khurasan**. Besides a book on Koranic philology, only al-Nīsābūrī's well-known *Kitāb 'Uqalā' al-majānīn* has been preserved. Within the branch of monographs on certain types of human characters, he was not the first to compile such a work, but the books of his forerunners and followers seem to be lost. In numerous anecdotes, the 'wise fools' appear primarily as ascetic or witty; excused by their 'madness', they can utter things that normal people would not dare to say.

Text editions

'Uqalā' al-majānīn, Muḥammad Baḥr al-'Ulūm (ed.), Najaf (1968).

Loosen, Paul, *Die Weisen Narren des Naisābūrī*, Strassburg (1912) (printed also in *Zeitschrift für Assyriologie und verwandte Gebiete* 27 (1912), 184–229) (partial translation).

Further reading

Dols, M.W., *Majnūn: The Madmen in Medieval Islamic Society*, Oxford (1992), 349–65.

Kindlers Neues Literatur Lexikon, Walter Jens (ed.), Munich (1991), vol. 12, 473–4 (S. Grotzfeld).

T. SEIDENSTICKER

North Africa *see* Maghrib

Nu'ayma, Mīkhā'īl (1889–1989)

Mahjar poet, prose writer, essayist and literary critic. Born in Biskinta (Lebanon), Nu'ayma attended the Russian school there, continuing his studies at the Russian training college in Nazareth, where he became a schoolmate of Nasīb **'Arīḍa**. In 1906 he was elected to attend the Diocesan Seminary in Poltava, Ukraine, where his involvement in a students' strike was punished by his removal from the Seminary and the postponement of his final examination for a year until 1911. In Poltava he studied the great works of modern Russian literature, became an admirer of the social ideas of Tolstoy and began to write poetry in Russian.

In autumn 1911 Nu'ayma joined his elder brothers living in the United States. He enrolled as a student of law and English literature in the University of Washington, Seattle, taking two bachelor's degrees in 1916. During this period he became acquainted with theosophy, which left a deep imprint on him and his work. He also contributed his first critical essays to 'Arīḍa's *al-Funūn* in New York, explaining what he considered the hallmarks of good poetry. 'Arīḍa invited him to come to New York to edit the journal with him. However, the financial basis of this enterprise was fragile, and Nu'ayma was forced to find employment with the Russian mission purchasing arms at the Bethlehem steel factory, until the Russian revolution intervened. He was then drafted into the US Army and sent to France, reaching the front line a few days before the Armistice of 11 November 1918. On returning to the United States, Nu'ayma wrote the charter for **al-Rābiṭa al-qalamiyya**, founded on 28 April 1920 with Nu'ayma as its secretary. He worked as a travelling salesman until 1932, when he returned to Lebanon and devoted himself to writing.

Nu'ayma produced more than thirty

volumes of poetry, narrative prose, drama, biography, autobiography, literary criticism and essays. His first book, *al-Ābā' wa-al-banūn*, was published in New York in 1917; it was followed by a volume of literary criticism, *al-Ghirbāl* (Cairo, 1923), in which he attacked Khalilian prosody as creating insurmountable obstacles for the free expression of emotion. For his biography of **Jubrān** (Arabic version, Beirut, 1934; English version, New York, 1950) he followed the style of the *biographie romancée* developed by Maurois, Strachey and others; the book, which spoke freely about Jubrān's weaknesses, was interpreted by some as an attack on him.

Among Nu'ayma's narrative works *The Book of Mirdad* (English version, Beirut, 1948; Arabic, *Kitāb Mirdād*, Beirut, 1952) deserves special mention. Nu'ayma considered this book the summit of his thought, explaining the human path to eternity. Impressive is his three-volume autobiography *Sab'ūn* (Beirut, 1959–60), the first volume of which is devoted to his years in Biskinta, Nazareth and Poltava, the second to his stay in the United States and the third to his years in Lebanon. Nu'ayma's collected works were published in eight volumes (Beirut, 1970–4).

Text editions

The Memories of a Vagrant Soul, New York (1952).
A New Year, J.T. Perry (trans.), Leiden (1974).
Till We Meet ..., Bangalore (1957).

Further reading

Naimy, N., *Mikhail Naimy*, Beirut (1967).
Nijland, C., *Mīkhā'īl Nu'aymah: Promoter of the Arabic Literary Revival*, Istanbul (1975).

C. NIJLAND

Nūr, Mu'āwiya Muḥammad (1909–41)

Sudanese essayist, short-story writer and literary critic. Born into a well-known family, Nūr was educated in Khartoum, **Cairo** and **Beirut**, then worked as a journalist in Cairo, where he rose to be literary editor of *Miṣr* newspaper and formed important contacts, particularly with 'Abbās Maḥmūd **al-'Aqqād**. In his criticism, he applied Western standards to Arabic literature and called for Arabic literature to explore new fields such as comedy and literary correspondence. Nūr maintained throughout his life a great interest in other cultural pursuits, including music, painting and Islamic and Western philosophy. His short stories belong to the school of social realism; he was one of the first Sudanese authors to use the technique of psychological analysis in his works of fiction.

In 1935, as a result of depression and overwork, Nūr fell victim to mental illness from which he continued to suffer until his death. His collected works were published in Khartoum in 1970.

M.I. SHOUSH

Nūrī, 'Abd al-Malik (1921–)

Iraqi short-story writer. After studying at the American University of Beirut, he graduated in the Faculty of Law of Baghdad University and became a journalist on the progressive newspaper *al-Ahālī*. He later served as an official in the Ministry of Justice and in the Iraqi diplomatic service in Japan, Indonesia and Czechoslovakia. His collections of short stories *Rusul al-insāniyya* (1946) and *Nashīd al-arḍ* (1954) are characterized by a profound psychological insight. They employ a poetical, sometimes ironical, language to cast light on problems of Arab/Iraqi society such as the role of women as victims of patriarchal repression (as in *Faṭṭūma*) or the tragic consequences of superstition and the veneration of saints (as in *Rīḥ al-janūb*), or corruption in the bourgeois classes.

Text edtion

'Südwind', in W. Walther (ed.), *Erkundungen. 28 irakische Erzähler*, Berlin (1985), 5–15.

Further reading

al-Ṭālib, 'Umar Muḥammad, *al-Qiṣṣa al-qaṣīra al-ḥadītha fī al-'Irāq*, Mosul (1979), 269ff.

W. WALTHER

al-Nūrī, Abū al-Haṣan (or Abū al-Ḥusayn) (d. 295/907–8)

A well-known member of the **Baghdad** school of Sufism and a friend of **al-Ḥallāj** and **al-Junayd**. In the dictionaries and handbooks on Sufism he is frequently mentioned in anecdotes and numerous dicta are attributed to him. His commentary on the **Koran** was incorporated into **al-Sulamī**'s *Ḥaqā'iq al-tafsīr*. Also preserved is his small treatise *Risālat maqāmāt al-qulūb*.

Text edition

Nwyia, Paul, 'Textes mystiques inédits d'Abū-l-Ḥasan al-Nūrī (m. 295/907)', *Mélanges de l'Université Saint-Joseph* 44 (1968), 115–54.

Further reading

Nwyia, Paul, *Exégèse coranique* et langage mystique, Beirut (1970) 316–48.

B. RADTKE

Nuṣayb ibn Rabāḥ (d. *c.*108/726)

Abū al-Hajnā' (or Abū Miḥjan) Nuṣayb ibn Rabāḥ was an **Umayyad** poet. He praised a number of Umayyad caliphs and officials (including 'Umar ibn 'Abd al-'Azīz) in relatively short and direct poems which reduce the role of the *nasīb* to a minimum. His imagery, however, is complex and given to expanded conceits. In love poetry he is the first to treat the grieving dove motif. The nature of this love poetry is that of *nasīb* disengaged from the ***qaṣīda***; it is ***'Udhrī*** in tone but given to descriptions that echo the manner of descriptive interludes in pre-Islamic poetry.

Text editions

Rizzitano, U., 'La poesia di Abū Miḥğan Nuṣayb ibn Rabāḥ e necessità di uno studio più completo sui poeti minori del secolo Umayyade', *Actes du XXème Congrès Internationale des Orientalistes*, (1938), 316–18.
Shi'r Nuṣayḅ, D. Sallūm (ed.), Baghdad (1957).
Verses collected and published by U. Rizzitano, *RSO* 20 (1943), 421–72; 22 (1945) 23–35.

P.F. KENNEDY

al-Nuwayhī, Muḥammad (1917–80)

Egyptian literary critic and university professor. Born in Mīt Hibaysh, a village near Tanta, al-Nuwayhī spent four years in the Department of Arabic Literature at the Egyptian University, attaching himself to Ṭāhā **Ḥusayn** who became his mentor. He earned his doctorate in 1942 from the University of London, securing a temporary senior lectureship there in 1943, and in 1947 moved to the Sudan. where the Gordon Memorial College was being transformed into the University of Khartoum. Al-Nuwayhī was associated with this university until 1956, publishing three books during that period including *Thaqāfat al-nāqid al-adabī* (1949), in which he argued that the successful critic of modern Arabic literature must be well grounded in all the modern sciences, including psychology. He subsequently studied the connection between psychology and literature in *Nafsiyyat Abī Nuwās* (1953), in which he employed psychoanalysis to clarify **Abū Nuwās'** personality. Al-Nuwayhī soon became an influential literary critic whose ideas and methods were pioneering, though not always warmly received. One of his critics was his mentor Ṭāhā Ḥusayn, who argued that it was absurd to apply psychoanalysis to the study of ancient poets of whom we have little evidence. In 1956 al-Nuwayhī returned to **Egypt**, where he was given an appointment at the American University in Cairo. He was one of the most important defenders of *shi'r ḥurr (***free verse**), arguing that the new form was the only way to revive Arabic poetry. In his book *Qaḍiyyat al-shi'r al-jadīd* (Cairo, 1964) he advocated a type of poetry that reflected daily life and speech; he considered that the new poetic form would prepare the way for a new type of rhythm and metre based on stress, arguing that the use of the new **prosody** – which he termed *al-niẓām al-nabrī* – would inject new blood into the Arabic language and preserve it from domination by the colloquial.

Further reading

Green, A.H., *In Quest of an Islamic Humanism: Arabic and Islamic Studies in Memory of Mohamed al-Nowaihi*, Cairo (1984), ix–xxiv.
Jayyusi, S.K., *Trends and Movements in Modern Arabic Poetry*, Leiden (1977), 638–9.
Moreh, S., *Modern Arabic Poetry 1800–1970*, Leiden (1976), 263–6.
Semah, D., *Four Egyptian Literary Critics*, Leiden (1974), 148, 195–201.

R. SNIR

al-Nuwayrī, (667–732/1279–1332)

Shihāb al-Dīn Aḥmad ibn 'Abd al-Wahhāb al-Nuwayrī was an encyclopaedist. The son of a civil servant, al-Nuwayrī was born in Upper **Egypt** but studied in **Cairo**, where he distinguished himself in jurisprudence and calligraphy. He followed in his father's footsteps, serving as a financial administrator in **Syria** and Egypt, where he ended by having responsibility for two provinces. A change of heart led him to abandon the secretary's profession for study of the humanities, which he had earlier scorned, and he composed his great encyclopaedia, the *Nihāyat al-arab fī funūn al-adab* (*The Heart's Desire in the Arts of Culture*), partly for his own use as an *aide-mémoire* of what he had read.

The *Nihāyat al-arab* consists of five Books, each one of which is divided into five sections which themselves contain several subsections: (1) the Heavens and the Earth, including a description of the world; (2) Man, his nature and especially his self-expression through poetry, and his institutions of government; (3) the Animal World; (4) the Vegetable World; (5) History. This last Book is by far the longest, occupying twenty-one of the work's thirty-one volumes. The whole reflects a carefully thought-out view of man and his place in the world and history. Unlike his sources, which include the major works of Arabic literature then extant, al-Nuwayrī avoids digressions, abbreviating his material where necessary and never losing sight of the plan of his book. Rather than writing to conserve the memory of a threatened civilization, he was probably trying to encourage the formation of a class of humanist secretaries at the height of **Mamlūk** power.

Text edition

Nihāyat al-arab fī funūn al-adab, vols 1–27, Cairo (1923–85).

Further reading

Chapoutot-Remadi, Mounira, 'An-Nuwayrī, encyclopédiste et chroniqueur de l'époque mamlûke', in *Les Africains*, C.-A. Julien *et al.* (eds), Paris (1978), vol. 10, 315–39.

H. KILPATRICK

See also: encyclopedias, medieval

Nuzhat al-udabā' (*Entertainment of the Educated*)

Collection of anecdotes, probably compiled by one Muḥammad ibn Aḥmad Iyās al-Ḥanafī in the middle of the eleventh/seventeenth century. The work is divided into 28 chapters containing about 540 anecdotes. They treat subjects such as teachers, grammarians, alleged prophets, **bedouins**, stingy persons, homosexuals and prostitutes as well as the most famed popular heroes of Arabic jokelore, **Juḥā**, **Abū al-ʿAynā'**, Muzabbid and **Ashʿab** (and notably **al-Jāḥiẓ**); the book ends with chapters on fables and popular sayings. In arrangement and content, the book shows a close similarity to **al-Ābī**'s *Nathr al-durr*. Contrary to G. Flügel's' verdict (*ZDMG* 14 [1860], 534–8), who regarded *Nuzhat al-udabā'* as a revolting accumulation of obscenities, the book does deserve attention as an exemplary compilation of the Ottoman period. It was extensively used for European translations of jocular prose by J. von Hammer-Purgstall and R. Basset, thus decisively contributing to the European conception of Arabic humour in the nineteenth and twentieth centuries.

Further reading

Flügel, G., 'Einige bisher wenig oder gar nicht bekannte arabische und türkische Handschriften', *ZDMG* 14 (1860), 527–46.
Marzolph, U., *Arabia ridens*, Frankfurt am Main (1992), vol.1, 67–71.

U. MARZOLPH

O

ode *see* *qaṣīda*

oral composition

Originally, Arabic poetry was oral poetry, meaning that it was composed by the tribe's poet without the help of writing. In the same manner, it was recited and passed on by the poet himself or his ***rāwī*** (transmitter). The fact that poets made use of writing utensils while composing a poem has been securely attested for the first time in the case of the **Umayyad** poets **Jarīr** and **al-Farazdaq**, or rather their *rāwī*s, but even earlier transmitters and poets may occasionally have made notes to assist their memory. On the other hand, until the early **ʿAbbāsid** period and even thereafter one has still to reckon with the fact that poets often composed their poetry without the help of writing. This is especially true for impromptu poetry (*badīhan, irtijālan*). (See **improvisation in poetry**.) Throughout the Middle Ages the recitation of poetry was done from memory, as is sometimes still done today.

The early ʿAbbāsid poet **Abū Nuwās** (d. *c*.200/815) seems to have written down at least part of his poems in an unsystematic way. It is said that in his estate there were copy-books and papers which had among them copies of some of his poems. However, none of the early ʿAbbasid poets yet prepared an edition of their ***dīwān***s. It was not until the fifth/eleventh century that the poets got into the habit of composing their works for future publication as a book.

The older ancient Arabic poetry shares many characteristics with the oral poetry of other peoples, such as infrequent enjambement, stereotyped topics and motifs (typical scenes from **bedouin** life, recurrence of animal descriptions, etc.), and formulaic phrases, mainly at the beginning of a ***qaṣīda*** and in the transition from one topic to another. The (real or apparent) similarity of these characteristics with those of the improvised epic poetry of illiterate folk-singers among the southern Slavs and of the Homeric poems, which have been investigated by M. Parry and A. Lord, has among American Arabists (J.T Monroe, M. Zwettler) resulted in the attempt to understand ancient Arabic poetry in the light of the so-called oral poetry theory of Parry and Lord. This theory states that in the presence of the above-mentioned characteristics – especially strong formulaicness – one may conclude that the poetry in question has been produced by oral improvisation because the impromptu poet, who is pressed for time while composing his poem, has to refer to prefabricated formulas, stereotyped topics, etc. This means that in this form of poetry composition and recitation are one and the same.

If the oral poetry theory were applicable to ancient Arabic poetry, then even the most complicated polythematic *qaṣīda*s would be improvised poems, presented in a different version with every recitation. However, some proponents of this theory concede that a *qaṣīda* consisted of a more or less solid core memorized by the poet or the transmitter and on which he is said to have improvised at each recitation.

At first glance the applicability of the oral poetry theory to ancient Arabic poetry seems to be confirmed by the fact that many *qaṣīda*s exist in different versions (recensions) with numerous variants. However, serious doubts have been raised against it. These are directed against the premature and grossly overstated identification of the anonymous, disinterested, popular epic poetry with the *qaṣīda* poetry which is always tied to the name of an author, usually has a specific goal and often shows individual styles. (See further ***qaṣīda***.) Above all, however, the *qaṣīda* cannot in general be considered improvised poetry because of inherent characteristics such as complicated metres that are subject to strict rules, the same rhyme throughout the entire poem, and conscious application of figures of speech in prominent places. Moreover, reports have come down to us that speak against it, according to which the poets would work on a *qaṣīda* for a long period of time, in individual cases up to a year. The poems that are improvised are in most cases not *qaṣīda*s, but short pieces (***qiṭʿa***s), and they are often composed in ***rajaz***, the most simple metre. Besides, the frequency of formulas is not nearly as extensive as has been claimed. What has been identified as a formula very often turns out to be a conscious resumption, a quotation, a recurring stereotypical phraseology, etc., and often occurs in different metres; it therefore cannot have been employed by the poet as a stopgap under the pressure of time.

In the case of the ancient Arabic *qaṣīda* we are dealing thus with a special kind of oral poetry for which a carefully planning poet is characteristic, and if one looks for a comparison this poetry could most easily be put on the same level with the old Icelandic poetry of the scalds or the lyrics of the troubadours. The different versions of specific poems and the richness in variants can be partly explained by the long oral, or at any rate philologically uncontrolled, transmission. Additionally, the poets may occasionally have revised their *qaṣīda*s and successively 'published' different versions of them. Finally, it is known that some *rāwī*s thought it to be their right to treat the transmitted poetry rather liberally. Sometimes they were even invited by their masters to improve the poems in certain places. However, the various versions of a *qaṣīda* arising from revision and correction by poets and *rāwī*s cannot at all be compared with the improvisations of the singers of the tales that are newly created in each new performance.

Further reading

Bauer, T., *Altarabische Dichtkunst*, parts 1–2, Wiesbaden (1992).

Bloch, A., 'Formeln' in der altarabischen Dichtung', *AS* 43 (1989), 95–119.

Monroe, J.T., 'Oral composition in pre-Islamic poetry', *JAL* 3 (1972), 1–53.

Schoeler, G., 'Die Anwendung der oral poetry-Theorie auf die arabische Literatur', *Der Islam* 58 (1981), 205–36.

Wagner, E., *Grundzüge der klassischen arabischen Dichtung*, Darmstadt (1987–8), vol. 1, 21–5.

Zwettler, M., *The Oral Tradition of Classical Arabic Poetry*, Columbus (1978).

G. SCHOELER; trans. A. GIESE

oratory and sermons

Oratory (*khaṭāba*) was an important feature of tribal life in early Arabia, where eloquence was highly valued. The tribal spokesman (*khaṭīb*) would rally the tribe to battle, revile its opponents, recall ancestral feats and virtues, and (like the tribal poet) often served as messenger between parties. Samples of such early orations, which often contained moralizing passages, exhortations to valour, and the like, and were prized as models of eloquence, are preserved, for example, in the *Kitāb al-bayān wa-al-tabyīn* of **al-Jāḥiẓ**. In Islamic times, oratory continued to play an important role in political and sectarian conflicts; the **Khārijīs**, for example, produced a number of impressive orators (as they did poets), and the **Umayyad** governor and general **al-Ḥajjāj ibn Yūsuf** was famed for his eloquence.

Oratory and the preaching of sermons (*waʿẓ*) became closely allied in the Islamic period. The term *khaṭīb* came to designate an Islamic preacher, specifically one charged with delivering the Friday sermon (*khuṭba*). The Prophet in his lifetime had delivered this sermon, and the question of his succession revolved in part around who was best qualified to take over this function. The official *khaṭīb* directed himself to the congregation, as the spokesman for the ruler, whose name was pronounced in the Friday *khuṭba* in confirmation of his rule (the **ʿAbbāsid** revolution was openly proclaimed when Abū Muslim preached the *khuṭba* in their name in **Khurasan**); it was also customary for the ruling caliph to deliver the *khuṭba* and lead the public prayer which followed. With the growth of urban centres the *khaṭīb* often became the chief spokesman for his town.

Another type of preacher might also address the congregation: the *wāʿiẓ*, whose task it was to instil pious teachings, to exhort and admonish, in his sermon (*waʿẓ*, *mawʿiẓa*; the two terms are attested in the **Koran**, which itself is referred to as *waʿẓ* or *mawʿiẓa*, and in pre-Islamic poetry). As in earlier times (for example, in the case of the Ḥīran poet **ʿAdī ibn Zayd**), another function of the *wāʿiẓ* was to address himself to sovereigns, reminding them of the transience of this world and the necessity for piety and just rule. Other terms designating preachers were *qāṣṣ* (pl. *quṣṣāṣ*; literally, 'story-teller'), whose preaching was based on Koranic stories and ***Legends of the Prophets***) and *mudhakkir* ('one who calls to recollection', i.e. admonishes) (for a discussion of terminology see Pedersen, 1948). Such preachers might accompany warriors into the field to rouse them to battle, and they played an important role in sectarian disputes. Or they might be attached to the mosque, where they would hold regular sessions on certain days. Their preaching did not, however, constitute part of the Friday sermon. There were also popular, itinerant preachers who addressed public gatherings in the streets, and who often came in for criticism for their ignorance and charlatanry from more respectable preachers such as the famous Ḥanbalī **Ibn al-Jawzī**, who left a valuable work on the subject (perhaps intended as a work of instruction; cf. 1971, 68).

Many preachers were major religious scholars, and some held official positions such as that of *qāḍī*. Popular preachers were often associated with pietistic, ascetic and, later, mystical tendencies. The style of sermons gradually developed from the simple and direct admonitions of, for example, the ascetic **al-Ḥasan al-Baṣrī**, who addressed his sermons to kings and commoners alike (and from whose style the poetry of **Abū al-ʿAtāhiya** takes much of its inspiration) to the more rhetorical and ornamental style characteristic of **Ibn Nubāta al-Khaṭīb** or Ibn al-Jawzī, in which rhymed prose (***sajʿ***) became an increasingly important element. Sermons of all sorts were collected and anthologized as models of style; they were often heavily ornamented with quotations from Koran and ***ḥadīth***, proverbs and poetry, the latter drawn from a wide variety of sources: the Ḥanbalī Ibn al-Jawzī, for example, often quotes the Shīʿī poet **Mihyār al-Daylamī**, while Ṣūfī preachers might use verses by such 'libertines' as **Abū Nuwās** to convey topics related to, for example, the intoxication of mystical love. Many writers also composed works on the principles of preaching and the qualities, both professional and moral, required of preachers.

Text editions

Ibn al-Jawzī, *Kitāb al-Quṣṣāṣ wa'l-Mudhakkirīn*, Merlin L. Swartz (ed. and trans.), Beirut (1971).

Ibn al-Ukhuwwa, *The Maʿālim al-Qurba fī Aḥkām al-Ḥisba*, R. Levy (ed.), London (1938), 65–7 (on rules concerning preachers).

Further reading

EI[2], arts 'Khaṭīb', 'Qāṣṣ'.

Pedersen, J., 'The Islamic preacher: *wāʿiẓ, mudhakkir, qāṣṣ*', in *Ignace Goldziher Memorial Volume*, S. Löwinger and J. Somogyi (eds), Budapest (1948), vol. 1, 226–51.

J.S. MEISAMI

See also: *khuṭba*; story-telling

Orthodox caliphate

The period of the first four caliphs, *al-Rāshidūn*, 'those who walk in the right way': Abū Bakr al-Ṣiddīq (reigned 11–13/632–4), ʿUmar ibn al-Khaṭṭāb (reigned 13–23/634–44), ʿUthmān ibn ʿAffān (reigned 23–35/644–56), **ʿAlī ibn Abī Ṭālib** (reigned 35–40/656–60). All of them were companions of the Prophet and related to him by marriage. It was a time of internal strife and civil war, resulting in the first schisms of Islam, and also of great military expansion, i.e. the foundation of an Islamic empire extending over Sasanian Iran, **Syria**, Palestine and **Egypt**. Islamic tradition regards the Orthodox caliphate as the golden age of Islam, when the *sunna* (see **Sunnīs**) of the Prophet was fully observed.

Abū Bakr, during his short caliphate, was mainly engaged in suppressing the 'apostasy' (*ridda*) of Arab tribes whose allegiance to Islam had ended with Muḥammad's death. His successor ʿUmar, one of the most gifted administrators in early Islam, laid the basis of the fiscal system and instituted the ***dīwān***, a register listing members of Arab tribes who were entitled to endowments. The financial organization of Medina was later introduced in all principle cities of the Muslim empire. ʿUmar also directed the conquests of Iran and the Byzantine territories of the Fertile Crescent and Egypt, which were completed under ʿUthmān. He was assassinated in 34/644 out of private revenge. The caliphate of ʿUthmān was a matter of dispute from the beginning, since a strong 'party' (*shīʿa*, see **Shīʿīs**) had supported ʿAlī, Muḥammad's cousin and son-in-law, father of his only male descendents, Ḥasan and Ḥusayn, by his daughter Fāṭima. ʿUthmān sought to strengthen his position by favouring members of his clan, the Banū Umayya (see **Umayyads**), thereby paving the way for their rise to power. His nepotism resulted in growing discontent, in an alliance of conflicting forces against him, and eventually in ʿUthmān's murder while he was praying in his house. His lasting achievement is the final redaction of the **Koran**.

The events leading to ʿUthmān's death mark the beginning of civil war, the first 'trial' (*fitna*) of the Islamic community. ʿAlī was proclaimed caliph, but was soon opposed by his former allies, among them ʿĀ'isha, daughter of Abū Bakr, Muḥammad's young and active widow. The opponents were defeated in the 'Battle of the Camel' (36/656), named after the camel on which ʿĀ'isha was riding, when she incited her party during the fight. A more serious opponent proved to be Muʿāwiya, governor of Syria and spokesman of the Umayyad clan, who demanded revenge for ʿUthmān's murder. He refused to pay homage to ʿAlī, who was not involved in the murder himself, but protected the culprits. Their armies met at Ṣiffīn (37/657), a battle famous in history, because the Syrians, when luck turned against them, hoisted copies of the Koran on their lances, thereby inviting the combatants to resolve the conflict by arbitration. When ʿAlī agreed to this, a considerable part of his adherents 'dissented' (*kharaja*, see **Khārijīs**), thus weakening his forces. They were defeated by him at Nahrawān (38/658), but remained an important political faction, especially in the Umayyad period. The arbitration took place at ʿAdhruḥ (38/659), the legal point being the justification of ʿUthmān's murder, which implied the legitimacy of ʿAlī's caliphate. Before any further military encounters, ʿAlī was murdered (40/660) by a Khārijī taking revenge for Nahrawān, and Muʿāwiya was proclaimed caliph without serious opposition, choosing **Damascus** as his residence. Thus with the end of the Orthodox caliphate the Hijaz ceased to be the political centre of Islam. (See further **Hijaz**.)

Poetic traditions of the ***jāhiliyya*** continued during the time of the Prophet and the Orthodox caliphs on the whole, the influence of Islam being limited to occasional allusions and the introduction of Koranic formulas (cf. Farrukh, 1937). But there are also significant changes on the formal and on the conceptual level. Poets of the period, the ***mukhaḍramūn***, were apt to introduce their individual experience and to transform conventional genres accordingly. (See further **genres.**) The ***qaṣīda*** in praise of **Muḥammad** and his successors is still **bedouin** in character, excepting some religious eulogies. There is an important structural change, however, motivated by its panegyrical function (see ***madīḥ***), the gradual development of the *raḥīl*, the poet's 'desert journey' to his patron, alongside the former description of his camel (cf. Jacobi, 1982). Political events are predominantly reflected in the ***qiṭʿa***. Invectives against Muḥammad are answered by poets in his employment, e.g. **Ḥassān ibn Thābit**, and during the *ridda* and the first civil war, tribal ***hijā'*** is used by the opponents in its traditional function. The Arab conquests, on the other hand, gave rise to a new development of ***fakhr***, i.e. Muslim warriors describe their hardships and celebrate their victories (cf. Nallino, 1950, 811–82). At the same time, poets deplore the 'emigration' of their tribesmen from the Arabian Peninsula (see **Hudhayl**). In addition to *fakhr* and *hijā'*, new monothematic genres emerged, e.g. the wine poem (see ***khamriyya***), if the verses of **Abū Miḥjan** are authentic, and the love poem (see ***ghazal***). It first appears in the *dīwān* of Abū Dhū'ayb (see Hudhayl), one of the most innovative poets of the time. As evidenced in his verses, the pre-Islamic concept of love, mainly a retrospect of former pleasures and a love affair in the past, is now sometimes replaced by a more emotional attitude, implying perseverance in love and faithfulness after separation. Viewed in its entirety, the poetry of the *mukhaḍramūn* constitutes the first stage of a process involving the gradual dissolution of the pre-Islamic oral tradition (see **oral composition**).

Further reading

Blachère, Régis, *Histoire de la littérature arabe*, Paris (1952–66), vol. 2.
Farrukh, O., *Das Bild des Frühislam in der arabischen Dichtung von der Higra bis zum Tode ʿUmars*, Erlangen (1937).
Jacobi, R., 'The camel-section of the panegyrical ode', *JAL* 13 (1982), 1–22.
Nallino, A., *La Littérature arabe*, Paris (1950).
al-Qāḍī, N.ʿA., *Shiʿr al-futūḥ al-Islāmiyya fī ṣadr al-Islām*, Cairo (1965).
Serjeant, R.B., 'Early Arabic prose', in *CHALUP*, 114–53.

R. JACOBI

Ouettar, Tahar *see* Waṭṭār, al-Ṭahir

P

pageantry

The custom of celebrating festive occasions by wearing decorated clothes was practised in the pre-Islamic period in Mecca. **Ibn Hishām** and **al-Wāqidī** say that the people of Mecca used to borrow their jewellery from the Jewish family of merchants al-Ḥuqayq in order to decorate themselves at weddings and other festive occasions.

With the rise of 'realism' in **ʿAbbāsid** art and literature, authors and artists showed interest in daily life, peculiar persons, stock types, professionals, officials and artisans, rather than in pre-Islamic heroes and subjects. This interest began with **al-Jāḥiẓ** and reached its peak around the end of the fourth/tenth century and later, especially during ʿAbbāsid and **Būyid** rule in **Baghdad** and the **Fāṭimid** and **Mamlūk** periods in **Cairo** and **Damascus**.

The practice of representing everyday life in a quasi-theatrical form was also reflected in pageantry. Pageants took place on occasions such as feasts, *mawlid*s, the sending of the *maḥmal* to Mecca, the accession of a new ruler, and weddings and circumcisions of sons of caliphs, sultans and other grandees. The city was decorated with silk and colourful fabrics, flags and lamps. Salvos of firearms (*shunnuk*) were fired and fireworks (*ḥarrāqāt*) were displayed.

These pageants were composed of diverse presentations by artisans and trade guilds, demonstrating their trades on coaches driven by men and animals. Scenes depicting daily life were displayed, such as sailors with a ship on wheels, millers working with stone hand-mills, weavers with looms, blacksmiths, sweet-makers, bakers, etc., with fortress-shaped constructions. The pageants were accompanied by processions of fully armed men, magnificently attired, with harnessed horses, and musicians (including flautists and drummers), singers, dancers (***mukhannathūn***) and itinerant actors (*mukhāyila* or *mukhāyilūn*; see ***khayāl***), acrobats, clowns, hobby-horse (*kurraj*) actors (whose plays were termed *khayāl* or *ḥikāya*), monkey-keepers, animal trainers, magicians, jugglers, and dolls and figures made of wood, clay and camphor.

During the Ottoman period, some sultans ordered albums of miniature paintings of pageantry, such as *The Album of Ahmed I* (1603–17), representing such pageants, marching in the streets of Istanbul.

Further reading

And, Metin, *A History of Theatre and Popular Entertainment in Turkey*, Ankara (1963–4), 17–22.

Moreh, S., *Live Theatre and Dramatic Literature in the Medieval Arab World*, Edinburgh and New York (1992).

Shoshan, B., *Popular Culture in Medieval Cairo*, Cambridge (1993) 67–78.

S. MOREH

Pahlavī *see* Persia

Palestinian poetry

Like its counterparts elsewhere in the Arab world, modern Palestinian poetry has its roots in the nineteenth-century ***nahḍa***. During the nineteenth century and for the first half of the twentieth century, the traditional forms and themes of the classical Arabic ***qaṣīda*** continued to characterize most Palestinian poetry – albeit at an ever-decreasing rate – and with a few exceptions such as Ibrāhīm **Ṭūqān**, most poetry of this period is derivative in tone, sentiment and imagery.

The nationalist identity of Palestinian poetry began to develop at the beginning of the twentieth century, as an expression of the aspirations of the Palestinians for freedom and the realization that their country was targeted for the establishment of the Jewish 'national home'. Palestinian poetry sought to articulate the fears of the Palestinians in the face of this onslaught as well as their diminishing hopes for national salvation within an independent Palestine. Palestinian poets provided perceptive analyses of their society and the dangers it faced, whether externally induced by the colonial powers or internally generated by forces of decay and corruption, and the lack of commitment of the traditional Palestinian leadership. Counterbalancing this overwhelming sense of frustration are numerous calls to thwart the enemy's attempts to establish the Jewish 'national home' in Palestine. In this poetry – most effectively, in that of Ibrāhīm Ṭūqān and 'Abd al-Raḥīm 'Umar – love of the homeland (*waṭan*) and the duty to fight for national freedom find their ultimate expression in the character of the martyr (*shahīd*) who sacrifices himself for his own country. Also prominent is the vigorous expression, in the face of 'divide-and-rule' attempts by the enemy, of the indissoluble unity of all Palestinians regardless of their religious affiliations. Thus Wadī' al-Bustānī, while proudly proclaiming his adherence to Christianity, expresses his true love for the Prophet **Muḥammad** as a fellow Arab.

The traumatic events that led to the fragmentation of Palestine and Palestinian society and the establishment of Israel in 1948 did not initially lead to any radical change in the character of Palestinian poetry. The older generation of poets – among them Muḥammad al-'Adnānī and Burhān al-Dīn **al-'Abbūshī** – continued to dominate the scene. However, the reality of the Palestinians as refugees (*lāji'ūn*) in neighbouring countries provided an expanded thematic horizon in which the Palestinian as a hapless but defiant character occupies the scene. Cast in the form of the traditional Arabic poem, this poetry was mostly couched in old and tired imagery; at times, it reads like a 'party political broadcast' whose twin themes are inevitably the need to pursue the objectives of liberation (*taḥrīr*) and return (*'awda*).

All this changed at the hands of a group of young Palestinian poets who came to prominence first within Israel, where they used to live, and later in the Arab world at large in the aftermath of the 1967 defeat. The leading poets in this group – Maḥmūd **Darwīsh**, Samīḥ **al-Qāsim** and Ḥannā Abū Ḥannā (b. 1928) – came to be known as the 'resistance poets' and their poetry as 'resistance poetry' (*shi'r al-muqāwama*). Military rule, confiscation of land, arrest, imprisonment and other harsh measures made up the lives of these poets and fellow Palestinians who continued to live in that part of Palestine on which Israel was established. Initially, these poets expressed themselves through the traditional Arabic ***qaṣīda***, but, unlike Palestinian poets outside Palestine, they did so through a new mode of poetic delivery in which concern for 'man's inhumanity to man' is articulated through the use of fresh imagery, lyricism and an endearing sense of dignity and self-confidence. At this stage, Palestinian poetry in Israel was characterized by immediacy and thematic accessibility which may be seen as a natural outcome of the poet's image of himself as an integral part of a beleaguered community.

A major change in Palestinian poetry within Israel came about as a result of the switch from the traditional *qaṣīda* to **free verse** at the end of the 1950s. This new-found freedom was, both symbolically and materially, an important factor in the development of a new direction in Palestinian poetry, characterized by the use of a powerful symbolism whose motifs are drawn from sources including local folklore, Arab history and literature, Greek, Babylonian and ancient Egyptian mythologies, the **Koran** and the Bible. By drawing on all these sources for symbolic enrichment, Palestinian poets seemed to wish to proclaim the intertwined localism and universalism of their poetry in an effort to galvanize the widest possible support for their cause. To enhance its immediate appeal, the 'resistance poets' have also employed everyday speech and experimented with the idea of incorporating prose in poetry, but never at the expense of causing the fine line between poetry and prose to be blurred.

Text editions

Elmessiri, A.M. (ed.), *The Palestinian Wedding: A Bilingual Anthology of Contemporary Palestinian Poetry*, Washington (1982).

Jayyusi, S.K. (ed.), *Anthology of Modern Palestinian Literature*, New York (1992).

Y. SULEIMAN

panegyric *see* ***madīḥ***

parody *see* satire

paronomasia *see* rhetorical figures: *tajnīs*

patronage

Taken broadly to mean support, encouragement and championship, patronage of the poets of pre-Islamic and early Islamic **Arabia** was mainly provided by the tribe. Prestige and renown were conferred upon the poet in exchange for praise of the tribe's accomplishments and scathing satires of its enemies (See further ***jāhiliyya***). It was, however, the few who composed under different circumstances – the unaffiliated wandering *ṣuʿlūk* (see ***ṣaʿālīk***) poets, and those littérateurs attached to royal courts, al-Nuʿmān III's (d. 20/602), for instance (see **Lakhmids**) – that presaged the system that would supplant the tribal one. In an empire that consisted of an increasing number of centres of cultural patronage, because of the fragmentation of the caliphal state into successor and vassal courts, the littérateurs were transformed into itinerants who composed for the highest bidders, often in response to and conformity with the egotist and conservative needs of these patrons.

In the courts and homes of these patrons men of letters gathered. For the latter, support meant livelihood and sometimes fortune. The poet **al-Buḥturī** (d. 284/897), for instance, amassed great wealth and much property. (On the other hand, Ṭāhir ibn Muḥammad al-Hāshimī of Aleppo was so generous in his patronage that he one day found himself penniless.) For the patron, largesse was a way of conferring prestige on oneself, of demonstrating one's discernment and of appearing devoted to Arabic literature and Islamic culture. For those who were unlearned, such as the Turkish prince Bajkam (d. 329/941), patronage was a way of offsetting that deficiency. It was to his court that the literary biographer Abū Bakr **al-Ṣūlī** (d. *c.*335/945) turned after the **ʿAbbāsid** caliph al-Muttaqī (d. 333/944) abruptly declared that for companionship he needed only the **Koran**.

The courts of al-Nuʿmān and of even the most generous **Umayyads** were eclipsed by that of **Hārūn al-Rashīd** (d. 193/809), the ʿAbbāsid caliph who for centuries was to epitomize the noble patron. His court boasted not only poets, such as **Abū Nuwās** (d. 199/814) and **Muslim ibn al-Walīd** (d. 208/823), but also the musicians Ibrāhīm (d. 188/804) and Isḥāq (d. 235/850) **al-Mawṣilī**, the philologists **al-Aṣmaʿī** (d. 213/828) and **al-Kisā'ī** (d. 189/805), and the historian **al-Wāqidī** (d. 207/823).

Another legendary patron is Sayf al-Dawla (d. 356/967), the **Ḥamdānid** prince of Aleppo. His entourage included the philosopher **al-Fārābī** (d. 339/950), the great literary biographer and anthologist **Abū al-Faraj al-Iṣbahānī** (d. 356/967), the orator **Ibn Nubāta** (d. 374/984–5) and the distinguished panegyrist **al-Mutanabbī** (d. 354/965). So integral to the composition of the poet was the consideration of Sayf al-Dawla that one of al-Mutanabbī's lines consists entirely of a crescendo of imperatives culminating in the near-command 'Give!'

Among other patrons may be mentioned **al-Ṣāḥib Ibn ʿAbbād** (d. 385/995), chief minister to the Būyid Mu'ayyid al-Dawla and an outstanding bellettrist in his own right. His liberality and accomplishments were so significant that the literary historian **al-Thaʿālibī** (d. 429/1038) devotes an entire chapter of the *Yatīmat al-dahr* to recording praises of him. Although the **Saljūq** sultan Malik Shāh's (d. 485/1092) patronage was wide-ranging – he supported astronomers and observatories, mystics and *ribāṭ*s, jurisconsults and *madrasa*s – it is his minister, Niẓām al-Mulk (d. 485/1092), who is better remembered as a lavish patron. Ministers, secretaries, governors and military leaders were, in fact, well placed politically and financially to rival caliphs and princes in their patronage.

Occasionally patronage came from other quarters. The bon vivants ʿAbd Allāh ibn Jaʿfar and Ibn Abī ʿAtīq, for example, are cited as a source of support for musicians in second/eighth-century Medina (E. Rowson 'Effeminates of early Medina', *JAOS* 111 (1991), 679). Nor was patronage confined to individuals. The vizier Ibn Hubayra (d. after 560/1165) showed support for the entire Ḥanbalī guild of law. Al-Ma'mūn (d. 218/833) and his immediate successors actively prosecuted the **Muʿtazilī** cause and patronized prominent Muʿtazilīs. Several generations of **Munajjim**s served consecutive ʿAbbāsid caliphs as companions, tutors and poets. This practice of retaining members of a particular family was duplicated by Khedive Ismāʿīl when he went into exile in 1879 and had Ismāʿīl al-Muwayliḥī join him as tutor to his sons (R. Allen, 'Muwayliḥī', *EI*², vol. 7, 814).

In the case of religious scholars (*'ulamā'*), jurists (*fuqahā'*), mystics (Ṣūfīs), heretics and others, influence derived from the personal ties cultivated by these individuals, or by the institutions to which they were affiliated, with ordinary people. As this kind of patronage often depended on means, it might involve merchants, landowners and other wealthy patrons. In the realm of 'religious' patronage, however, patronage included the small gifts and stipends offered by the lay person to the prayer leader, or the charitable donation by a number of such persons to a charismatic or popular preacher. Needless to say, with time, patronage of almost every group or personage perceived as exercising authority fell under the control of the state, as with the benevolent patronage of Muslim legal scholarship and Ṣūfī orders by the Saljūqs and Zangids (notably Nūr al-Dīn, d. 570/1174), for instance.

On occasion, patron and patronized were divided ideologically. **'Umāra al-Yamanī** (d. 569/1174), who was befriended and supported by the **Fāṭimids** in spite of his **Sunnī** proclivities, composed a poem for Saladin describing his reversal of fortune after the fall from power of his deposed patrons. The celebrated ode apparently never reached Saladin: perhaps it would have saved the historian from crucifixion by his unrealized patron for allegedly plotting his overthrow (*Ibn Khallikān*'s *Biographical Dictionary*, M. de Slane [trans.], Paris [1842–71], vol. 2, 367–72).

Further reading

Aghānī, passim.

Bencheikh, J., 'Les secrétaires, poètes et animateurs de cénacles aux IIe et IIIe siècles de l'Hégire', *JA* 262 (1975), 265–315.

——, 'Le cénacle poétique du calife al-Mutawakkil (m. 247): Contribution à l'analyse des instances de légitimation socio-littéraires', *BEO* 29 (1977), 33–52.

CHALABL, 7–8, 21–2, 154–6, 276–7, 454–9.

Lapidus, I., *A History of Islamic Societies*, Cambridge (1988), 159–60, 176–7, 353.

Makdisi, G., *The Rise of Humanism in Classical Islam and the Christian West*, Edinburgh (1990), 232–47.

Nicholson, R.A., *A Literary History of the Arabs*, London (1921), 261–315.

Yāqūt, *Mu'jam al-udabā'*, I. 'Abbās (ed.), Beirut (1993), *passim.*

S.M. TOORAWA

Persia, culture and literature

The momentum of conquest after the Prophet's death in 10/632 carried the Arabs within a generation into the former Sasanian lands of Iraq and Persia and within a century into the lands of 'l'Iran extérieure', Transoxania and **Khwarazm**. Hence in Iraq and Persia, the Arabs became immediately the heirs of the Sasanians, at first in a military and political sense but later as cultural heirs also. The process of acculturation was easier here than in the lands conquered from the Byzantines, in the eastern Mediterranean region or from the Visigoths in **Spain**, since the former state church of Zoroastrianism was toppled and the overwhelming majority of Persians freely adopted the new faith of Islam. Arabs and Persians thus became co-religionists, and this facilitated for the Arabs acceptance of much of the older Persian secular culture. It was, of course, precisely in such fields as artistic expression and material culture (food habits, clothing, housing) that the Persians were patently superior to the Arabs, with their desert or small-town backgrounds.

As a countering force, however, there was a suspicion of things Persian among the ranks of the rigorist and pietistic Arab religious institution, the traditionists and *fuqahā'*, who held that everything necessary for salvation had come out of Arabia and was enshrined in the **Koran** and in the *sunna* of the Prophet and the early Muslims. Apart from the religious argument, literary expression was the only aspect of culture in which the Arabs could claim equality with, if not superiority over, the Persians: in the miracle of the Koran, naturally, but also in the glories of pre-Islamic and early Islamic poetry. Hence religious disapproval was reinforced by a vaunting of the Arab literary heritage when there arose in the third/ninth century a struggle over acceptance of the ancient Persian heritage within an Islam hitherto largely dominated by Arab ways of life and thought; this was the ***Shu'ūbiyya*** controversy, essentially a battle of books which ended in the tacit acceptance of the Persian strand within the fabric of Islamic civilization.

Yet despite what purist Arab scholars liked to think, Islam had never been a totally Arab creation; even the Koran contained several words of Persian origin, attesting a cultural symbiosis in pre-Islamic times in such regions as Iraq and eastern **Arabia**. The attractiveness to the Islamic state of the more advanced Persian governmental and administrative techniques was already visible in the last years of the **Umayyad** caliphate in **Damascus**. Once the **'Abbāsids** were installed in **Baghdad**, the acceptance of Persian practices and traditions proceeded apace under the leadership of the secretarial profession, which was dominated by non-Arab clients or ***mawālī*** (see **secretaries**). **Ibn al-Muqaffa'** was a key figure here, with his translations from Middle Persian or Pahlavi (known rather from later citations than as surviving independent works): of the collection of animal fables ***Kalīla wa-Dimna***, ultimately of Indian origin but mediated through late Sasanian Persia; of the *Khudāynāmak* (*Book of Kings*), the national history of Persia from legendary times to the virtual end of the Sasanian empire; of the *Book of the Crown*, mainly on the life of the great sixth-century CE emperor Khusraw Anūshirvān; and of the *Āyīnnāmak* (*Book of Customs and Usages*), on the etiquette (*āyīn*, here equivalent to the Arabic term ***adab***) of life at the royal court, with the monarch and his boon companions (see ***nadīm***). Other figures were also engaged in interpreting Persian literature and culture to an Arab–Islamic audience; the fourth/tenth century book list, the *Fihrist* of **Ibn al-Nadīm** mentions the names of many other translators, and we know that the Persian client **Abān al-Lāḥiqī** (d. 200/815–16), a protégé of the **Barmakids**, produced, among other things, a versified *Kalīla wa-Dimna* and an Arabic translation of the romance of ***Bilawhar wa-Yūdāsaf***, ultimately of Buddhist origin. Although the greater part of the classical Greek scientific and medical heritage came into Arabic through Christian and Sabian translators of Syria and Mesopotamia, a role played here by certain Persians, such as 'Umar ibn Farrukhān al-Ṭabarī (d. 199/815) and his son Abū Bakr Muḥammad, is recorded in the *Fihrist*. (See further **translation, medieval**.)

It is possible to discern from the works of **al-Jāḥiẓ** and **Ibn Qutayba**, both ardent defenders of of the Arab cause in the ***Shu'ūbiyya*** debates, how Persian ways and objects of material culture (the latter often denoted by the actual Persian names) were becoming familiar in third/ninth-century Iraq, the heartland of the caliphate. In his *Kitāb al-bukhalā'* (*Book of Misers*), al-Jāḥiẓ often mentions Persian foodstuffs and dishes, and one of the tales within the book, that of a certain al-Ḥārithī, deals with the etiquette of meals, in which the *dihqāns*, the class of Persian landowners, are praised for their delicate table manners; and Ibn Qutayba thought it necessary to include in his *Adab al-kātib* a chapter on 'foreign words (*a'jamī*, i.e. Persian; see ***'ajam***) used by the common people'.

By the fourth/tenth century, the assimilation of Persian culture into the mainstream of Islamic life was largely complete. What now emerged was a composite society in which the original Arab–Islamic component continued to be dominant in the religious and legal spheres, but in which Persian models had permeated much of the material culture of Muslims in the central and eastern Islamic lands, just as Greek ideas had been brought into the scientific and philosophical domains. In the political field, Persian concepts of kingship and statecraft, with a particular emphasis on *Realpolitik* as the moving spirit in the practical businesses of ruling, warfare and diplomacy, were adopted into the purely Islamic religious tradition of rulership being only legitimate when it was exercised in complete conformity with the religious law or *sharī'a* for the literary expositions of such ideas, see **Mirrors for Princes**.

Further reading

Bosworth, C.E., 'Iran and the Arabs before Islam', in *CHIr*, vol. 3, 609–12.
Browne, E.G., *Literary History of Persia*, Cambridge (1928), vol. 1, 251ff.
Frye, R.N., *The Golden Age of Persia: The Arabs in the East*, London (1975), 150–74.
Rypka, J., *et al.*, *History of Iranian Literature*, Dordrecht (1968), 126ff.

C.E. BOSWORTH

See also: Persian literature, relations with Arabic.

Persian literature, relations with Arabic

New Persian literature as we know it emerges tentatively in the third/ninth century and is clearly flourishing by the next; hence from this time onwards, it was at least theoretically possible for the two literatures, Arabic and New Persian, to interact. New Persian speech had, of course, never disappeared from Persia in the period after the Arab conquest and remained fairly current in Iraq after that province had been taken over from the Sasanians. **Umayyad** and early **'Abbāsid** authors used a certain number of Persian words in their compositions, while **Abū Nuwās** wrote several *Fārisiyyāt*, poems basically in Arabic but with an admixture of unassimilated Persian words. By the fourth/tenth century, as such literary anthologies as those of **al-Tha'ālibī** and **al-Bākharzī** show, there were a considerable number of of poets and writers in the Persian lands and in Transoxania who wrote equally fluently in both Arabic and Persian, i.e. they were, in the expression of the time, *dhawū al-lisānayn*, 'possessors of the two languages'. Notable figures here were the secretary **Abū al-Fatḥ al-Bustī**, and the Ziyārid prince Shams al-Ma'ālī Qābūs ibn Vushmgīr (d. 403/1012–13). Characteristic of the mingling of the two languages and cultures at this time are macaronic verses called ***mulamma'āt***, 'patchwork poems', either Arabic poetry with Persian words copiously inserted into it or with alternate verses in the two languages. We often find in the Arabic literature of 'Abbāsid times amusing word-plays between the two languages, especially where an Arabic and a Persian word were homologous in Arabic script, e.g. *mard* (Pers. 'man') and *murd* (Ar. 'downy-cheeked [pl.]'), i.e. of youths.

Arabic long retained its primacy in the Persian lands as the language *par excellence* for scholarship, in particular, for theology, law and philosophy, and was still used for these types of writing up to Ṣafavid times (tenth-eleventh/sixteenth-seventeenth centuries). Gradually, a technical vocabulary for scholarship developed also in Persian, but the needs of a wider, non-Arabophone readership early led to translations from such landmarks as **al-Ṭabarī**'s *History* and his Koran commentary (both abridged and/or adapted in the **Sāmānid** period). Certain works seem to have been produced in more or less simultaneous Arabic and Persian versions, such as **al-Bīrūnī**'s *Kitāb al-Tafhīm*, a treatise on astrology; which came first is uncertain. These were all made within the Persian-speaking lands themselves; but from **Saljūq** times onwards, Persian literature acquired a wider cultural prestige so that we find the Persian national epic, Firdawsī's poem the *Shāhnāma*, in 620–1/1223–4 translated into Arabic prose for an **Ayyūbid** ruler of **Damascus** (see **al-Bundārī**). Finally, one should note that Arabic literary expression almost certainly had an effect on New Persian literary form and content. The question of the origins of New Persian prosody is a vexed one, but it seems that New Persian poetry evolved from a Middle Persian metrical system that was basically syllabic and accentual, whereas by the third/ninth century New Persian poetry had fully developed quantitative metres and an end-rhymed verse scheme. This replacement of the old minstrel-type poetry by one with a more structured metrical framework must have developed under the influence of Arabic **prosody**, even though the Persians, in order to express the particular genius of their language, developed metres different from the Arabic ones and original verse forms like the rhymed couplet or *mathnawī* (cf. ***muzdawija***). Also, the style and content of the New Persian lyric and romantic poetry clearly depend on the 'new wave' in Arabic poetry of the early 'Abbāsid period, that of the ***muḥdathūn*** poets, so that the early **Ghaznavid** poets follow Arabic models in poetic structure and use the stylistic devices of Arabic rhetoric or ***badī'***.

Further reading

Bosworth, C.E., 'The Persian impact on Arabic literature', in *CHALUP*, 483–96.

Danner, V., 'Arabic literature in Iran', in *CHIr*, vol. 4, 566–94.

Inostrancev, K., *Iranian Influence on Moslem Literature*, Part I, G.K. Nariman (trans.), Bombay (1918).

C.E. BOSWORTH

See also: Persia, culture and literature

philology *see* grammar and grammarians

philosophical literature

There are many kinds of literature in Arabic which may be called philosophical. Some are obviously so and deal openly with either philosophers or philosophical topics. Others are so in the more subtle sense that they embody philosophical principles and arguments while not explicitly discussing philosophy. Once Greek texts came to be translated into Arabic (see **Greek literature**; **translation**), there arose the need to understand those texts and also to reconcile them with Islam, since, they had been written in a very different cultural environment from that of the Arabic-speaking world and required explication and religious justification, Many **commentaries** were written on the leading works of Greek philosophy, some very detailed and long, others brief and freer in scope.

As well as this sort of derivative exercise, it was also felt to be necessary to show how worthwhile the study of philosophy could be. Many works also came to be written defending philosophy from the charge of *kufr* or *bid'a* (unbelief or innovation), a charge made explicitly by **al-Ghazzālī** in his *Tahāfut al-falāsifa* (*Refutation of the Philosophers*). Since Greek philosophy seemed to be based upon principles which were thoroughly un-Islamic, it was not easy to show how philosophy and religion could be reconciled, and a good deal of effort went into this project.

Of great importance here was the way in which the different forms of reasoning were explicated. The sort of reasoning involved in philosophy was taken to be demonstrative, working from certain premisses via valid decision procedures to establish certain conclusions, and contrasting with the dialectical, rhetorical, poetical and other lesser forms of reasoning present in legal, theological, political and imaginative literature. A hierarchy of different forms of reasoning was established, with philosophy at the summit and the rest somewhere lower down, but in such a way that this did not imply that there was anything wrong with the lower forms. These simply represent to the widest possible audience where the truth lies, so that ordinary people (i.e. non-philosophers) are able to appreciate the truth because they can represent it to themselves in language that makes sense to them. The philosophers also seek the truth, but in more perfect and perspicuous ways than can the other segments of Islamic society.

Alongside these major theoretical works there were also many intellectually slighter but none the less important texts which discussed the lives of the philosophers or produced aphorisms and advice based loosely on philosophical argument (see ***ḥikma***). The purpose of these texts was to give advice on practical action and to relate that advice to earlier traditions and to the lives of great men of antiquity. These works are highly eclectic, and use Indian, Persian, Stoic, Cynic, Neoplatonic and other source material. One assumes that these were relatively popular texts, since to understand them one did not require any great philosophical ability, merely the capacity to relate the pithy comments of the past to one's own life and community. The accounts of the lives of the philosophers are similarly non-exacting, and the reader can readily link such descriptions to contemporary ethical and political problems concerning how one ought to live and how one should relate to one's community.

A crucial distinction between two types of Arabic philosophical literature should be made between *falsafa* and *ḥikma*. The former is the Arabic equivalent of the Greek *philosophia*, and represents the Peripatetic tradition in Islamic philosophy. The *falāsifa* were those who followed the methods of Plato, **Aristotle** and their followers in seeking to analyse theoretical problems. *Ḥikma*, 'wisdom', can also be translated as 'philosophy', and often was, yet there is a broader notion of philosophy being used here. *Ḥikma* can include the tradition of Arabic thought that is concerned with mystical thought and its various intellectual explanations. Although it is popularly argued that philosophical literature in the Islamic world came to an end with **Ibn Rushd** in 595/1198, this is only true of a particular kind of *falsafa*, since there was no cessation of the efforts of those thinkers interested in exploring religious, mystical and subjective concepts from a philosophical perspective. Although much of this work was carried out in Iran, it was often in Arabic and was part of a long and distinguished tradition of philosophical writings which exists to this day.

It would be a mistake to restrict philosophical literature in Arabic to only those works that are entirely philosophical. Philosophy became an important part of how a whole variety of the Islamic sciences were pursued, especially jurisprudence (***fiqh***) and theology (***kalām***). These disciplines are based upon argument, upon the drawing of conclusions from premisses, and it is clear that the participants in the major legal and theological controversies of the time employed, albeit often tacitly, a good deal of philosophical methodology. Even thinkers like **Ibn Taymiyya** and al-Ghazzālī who set out to challenge philosophy did so from a philosophical perspective. One might wonder why it was necessary to use philosophy in trying to establish positions in the Islamic sciences, especially when the thinkers were so concerned to argue from as strict an Islamic position as possible.

The answer surely is that the information that one gets by looking at religious sources and texts is in itself insufficient to solve a whole range of problems of interpretation which inevitably arise whenever one has to reconcile a text with the changing and indeterminate features of the world, and some decision procedure has to be established to carry this out. Clearly this involves philosophy, and in the early centuries of Islam philosophical method was employed very much with the view of successfully persuading other communities of the validity of Islam and the disadvantages of their own faiths. Here was a universal method of argument capable of discerning the true from the false, the valid from the invalid and so also able to persuade those with a very different view from one's own. Not only was philosophy used in arguments with those from other religions, but also across the Sunnī–Shī'ī divide, between different types of **Sunnīs** and **Shī'īs**, between the **Mu'tazilīs** and the Ash'arīs, and within theological and legal schools themselves.

In Western interpretations of philosophical literature a particular agenda has tended to be set that suggests that the conflict between faith and reason is a predominant concern of such literature. Even where it is not obvious that the text is about such a conflict, it can be perceived to exist under the surface of the text, and unravelling it is vital to understanding the text. It is certainly true that that conflict is often important, but it is mistaken to think of it as dominating the nature of philosophical literature in Arabic. Like philosophers in general, the Islamic philosophers were interested in exploring in their works a whole range of issues, some of which have little or no bearing on religion at all. Theological and legal questions are often imported to help initiate a range of questions which are not themselves primarily theological or legal, but which raise issues capable of analysis and clarification. It is tempting to try to bring philosophical literature in Arabic under some very general rubric such as that of the philosophy vs. religion debate, but the very variety of the topics considered makes this vacuous. The impact of this form of writing on the development of philosophy and science in the Christian and Jewish communities was significant, and much of the basis of the Renaissance may be traced to it. What characterizes philosophical literature in Arabic is a passionate concern for argument, and the belief that it is through argument that one will approach more closely to the truth.

Further reading

Badawi, 'A., *Histoire de la philosophie en Islam*, Paris (1972).
Butterworth, C. and Kessel, B.A. (eds), *The Introduction of Arabic Philosophy into Europe*, Leiden (1994).
Corbin, H., *History of Islamic Philosophy*, L. and P. Sherrard (trans), London (1993).
de Menasce, J., *Arabische Philosophie*, Berne (1948).
Fakhry, Majid, *A History of Islamic Philosophy*, 2nd edn, London and New York (1983).
Leaman, O., *An Introduction to Medieval Islamic Philosophy*, Cambridge (1985).
Martínez Lorca, A. (ed.), *Ensayos sobre la filosofīa en el-Andalūs*, Barcelona (1990).
Nasr, S., and Leaman, O. (eds) *HIP*, *passim*
Walzer, R., *Greek into Arabic*, Oxford (1962).
Watt, W.M., *Islamic Philosophy and Theology*, London (1962).

O. LEAMAN

plagiarism *see sariqa*

Plato *see* Platonism

Platonism

Platonism in a very broad sense has had a major influence upon much Arabic literature, but it is important to note that this tradition has often had little to do with Plato himself. Plato (Aflāṭūn) is often confused with **Galen** (Jālīnūs) and seen through the eyes of Plotinus, Proclus and Porphyry. Some philosophers, such as Shihāb al-Dīn **al-Suhrawardī**, (d. 587/1191), regarded him as a mystic, while Muḥammad ibn Zakarīyyā' **al-Rāzī** and **Miskawayh** saw him as an expert on magic, alchemy and astrology. The best-known Platonic texts were the *Republic*, *Laws*, *Phaedo*, *Crito* and *Timaeus*. The *Republic* was often used instead of the unavailable *Politics* of **Aristotle**. There were also available in Arabic a very extensive list of **commentaries** by a whole mixture of Neoplatonists. Plato and Aristotle were often taken to have presented the same sorts of doctrines, in the sense that it is possible, some argued, to detect basic common strands in their thought. Many Islamic philosophers did appreciate the differences in their views, however, and came to see that they represented very different philosophical perspectives.

Both **al-Fārābī** and **Ibn Rushd** use Plato's *Republic* to argue for the necessity of the ruler, the caliph, being a philosopher-king. They also seem to have no difficulty with the idea that the perfect state is in principle attainable, provided that the appropriate conditions are met by the ruler. He must be divinely inspired and a philosopher, but also an excellent politician, and able to address the community in language which it will understand. Thus he could move people to act in ways that he wishes, and since he is a perfect ruler he would know how people ought to act. It seems clear that **Muḥammad** is the paradigm of the perfect ruler, with the *sharīʿa* (Islamic law) playing the part of Plato's *Laws* and establishing the best possible organization of life in the state. Since the Prophet is no longer available, the next best alternative is a ruler who is inspired by him, capable of understanding how the state should be run and with the requisite physical and intellectual virtues.

The fact that it is so easy to combine Plato with a religious tradition such as Islam reveals something very important about Plato's thought: that it is predominantly religious. The confusion of Plato with Socrates (Sūqrāṭ) in Arabic literature emphasizes the religious side of the philosopher. Socrates is represented as an ascetic with a rather contemptuous attitude to this world (clearly modelled on Diogenes the Cynic). If one is unmoved at the prospect of one's own death then one can have an appropriately calm attitude to the death of the body, confident that one's real life in the intelligible world is unaffected.

The writer who comes closest to being an orthodox Platonist is undoubtedly al-Rāzī (d. 313 or 20/925 or 32), whose *al-Ṭibb al-ruḥānī* (*Spiritual Regimen*) presents a view of our relationship with the passions which Plato would more or less recognize as his own. Al-Rāzī presents a strong attack on hedonism and argues that over-stimulation of the physical senses can diminish spiritual capacities, in particular our capacity to relate to whom we really are, the intellectual part of us. Too powerful an attachment to this world damages our chances to improve and develop our immortal side, the only really important part of the human self. Al-Rāzī suggests that we think clearly about the causes of our passions, for then we shall be in a position to control them, which will in turn enable us to concentrate upon those aspects of our lives which are worth thinking about, and which certainly do not include anything to do with the world of generation and corruption. Most other writers on Plato tend to water down this position by the addition of Aristotelian qualifications with respect to the divide between the theoretical and the practical. Thus thinkers such as Ibn Rushd are prepared to use Plato, especially his *Republic*, but with caution because of the other-worldly nature of Plato's views. Even the fourth/tenth-century thinker Miskawayh, who uses so much Platonic language in his ethics, is obliged to combine it with Aristotelian overtones, so that the spiritual harmony that arises in the state of justice is not an entirely internal process but necessitates, as with Aristotle, a form of relationship with others. Although Plato is accorded great respect in Islamic philosophy, he is rarely allowed to stand by himself. In general he is supplemented with Aristotle, or with some individual or school of Neoplatonists.

Platonism contributed to two important trends in Islamic philosophy. The first is to the development of Neoplatonism. It is actually highly inaccurate to refer to Neoplatonism as just one school of philosophy; rather, it is a combination of a whole range of philosophical positions, but inevitably has a Platonic aspect to it. There will exist some theory of emanation according to which there is a hierarchy of reality, with some scope for ascending and descending. Although Neoplatonism does create some problems for the sort of account of creation that one finds in the **Koran**, these are not irresoluble and the model itself can easily be co-opted for religious purposes. The notion of a scale of being, of a link between the different ranks of being and of communication along the hierarchy fits nicely within an Islamic framework. The details of such a model were not established by Plato, but rather by Plotinus and his followers, and yet it is not called Neoplatonic for no reason. The idea of different levels of reality is recognizable in Plato, and the Neoplatonists might be seen to be filling in the details.

As for Peripatetic philosophy in the Islamic world, it is very difficult to distinguish between that philosophy and Neoplatonism. Even though many philosophers (like Ibn Rushd) suspected that they were not dealing with purely Platonic or Aristotelian views, they found it difficult to abandon Neoplatonism. It very much set the philosophical curriculum of the Arabic world and even counter-arguments had to be presented in terms acceptable by the theory itself. The Islamic philosophers were highly creative in their use of the Neoplatonic methodology and a dazzling variety of different systems and models was produced.

The other significant school of philosophy in Islam is the Ishrāqī or Illuminationist school. This is heavily dependent upon the emphasis that Plato lays on knowledge by acquaintance. To know something it is necessary to come into contact with its paradigm, a perfect example of it, which involves sharing in the characteristics of the known object. These characteristics consist of perfection and invariability, and the knowing subject cannot really remain a distinct thing apart from the known object. Such separation interferes with the possibility of knowledge, since to know the object the knower has to become like the object, or come into contact with the object. There is an important group of thinkers like **Ibn al-ʿArabī, al-Suhrawardī, Mullā Ṣadrā** and many **Ṣūfī** writers whose approach to the relationship between the knower and the known adopts the sort of Platonic form that we have observed here. The language of mysticism is largely based upon Platonic language, and this has also been a major trend in Islamic philosophy. The idea that to know something is possible only if one can actually be acquainted with the object of knowledge, and that that object of knowledge must be an eternally existing object or idea, makes possible the development of a variety of theories describing the possibility of such knowledge and the paths to it. One is reminded yet again of the religious nature of Plato's thought, and the ease with which it can be employed by a particular religious tradition to make sense of the route to knowledge of reality and its associated metaphysics.

Much Arabic philosophical literature is affected by Platonism, either directly through the influence of Plato himself or indirectly through what was thought to be his thought, and the creative development of his premisses and principles. This influence can be seen to be powerful in a wide range of different types of literature, not all philosophical, and its assessment is crucial for any understanding of that literature.

Text editions

Badawi, ʿA. (ed.), *Neoplatonici apud Arabes*, Cairo (1955).
——, (ed.), *Aflāṭūn fi al-Islām*, Tehran (1974).
Plato Arabus, R. Walzer (ed.), 3 vols, London (1952).

Further reading

Morewedge, P. (ed.), *Neoplatonism and Islamic Thought*, Albany (1992).

O. LEAMAN

poetic contests

Poetic contests were held in **bedouin** tribal society as well as urban literary circles, in order to settle disputes over precedence: either to determine who is the better poet, or, as often among tribal groups, which one is morally and physically superior; a poet may act as a spokesman of his tribe or clan. Among the commonly used terms are *mufākhara* (cf. ***fakhr***), *musājala* and *munāfara* (see also **debate literature**). In pre-Islamic times such contests took place publicly, at fairs such as that of **ʿUkāẓ**, before a judge. Prose might also serve as a medium, as in the famous contest between **ʿĀmir ibn al-Ṭufayl** – himself a poet – and his cousin ʿAlqama ibn ʿUlātha, but there, too, poetry and poets played important roles during the contest and its aftermath. A poetic contest was often fought by means of ***naqāʾiḍ***; or it might take the form of poets alternately improvising verses or hemistichs on a given subject (the terms used include *ijāza* and *tamlīṭ*); some examples, of dubious authenticity, are ascribed to early poets like **Imruʾ al-Qays**. The same poet is also said to have fought a contest with **ʿAlqama ibn ʿAbada** as to which was the better poet; the former's wife, serving as a referee, preferred ʿAlqama on the basis of his horse description (and was subsequently divorced by her husband). Many early philologists, among them **Abū ʿUbayda, al-Madāʾinī** and Hishām al-Kalbī, collected the *mufākharāt* and *munāfarāt* of the early Arabs. Bedouin poetic duels are still to be found in the twentieth century.

Public poetic contests in urban society might take place in the presence of caliphs or kings; often they are a purely literary affair. Famous is the lengthy literary contest, in poetry and prose, in 383/993–4 between **Badīʿ al-Zamān al-Hamadhānī** and Abū Bakr **al-Khwārazmī**, won (and recorded) by the former. Ideological and political issues were at stake in contests on, for instance, the superiority of Arabs or Persians (see ***Shuʿūbiyya***), but although poets might play a part, one cannot properly speak of a poetic contest in such cases.

Further reading

Relevant titles may be found in the bibliographies to the entries **debate literature**, ***fakhr*** and ***naqā'iḍ***.

G.J.H. VAN GELDER

poetics *see* rhetoric and poetics

poetry, medieval

Poetry (*shi'r*; see also ***naẓm***, 'verse') occupies a central place in Arabic literature. In the minimalist definition of Arabic literary criticism, poetry is 'rhymed, metrical speech indicating a meaning'; other definitions, however, testify to a broader conception of poetry.

Poetry is called the '***dīwān*** [register] of the Arabs', the record of their genealogies, battles, and great deeds, the repository of their values and of their traditional wisdom. **Abū Ḥātim al-Rāzī** (d. 322/934) combines this conception of poetry with formal criteria when he states in his *Kitāb al-zīna* that the Persians, like other non-Arab peoples, have no poetry: their 'songs' are neither 'metrical and regular', nor do they contain 'panegyric, satire or boasting; they do not describe wars and battles, do not fix genealogies, are not concerned with glorifying noble deeds and memorable actions, enumerating titles for glory or shame, describing horses, camels, wild animals, deserts, wind, rain, wanderings to find pasture', and other subjects too numerous to mention.

For the critics poetry is a branch of *balāgha*, eloquence, the divine gift to humankind and especially to the Arabs, the highest example of which is the **Koran**; for this reason the study of poetry figures importantly in studies of Koranic style (see ***i'jāz al-Qur'ān***). Poetry is perfect speech, the most eloquent and effective form of communication; it is both the register and the standard for correct usage. Poetry is a craft (***ṣinā'a***), an art whose rules, principles and conventions must be learned and mastered, and a profession practised by those who have acquired such skills – a craft (*ṣan'a*), states **'Abd al-Qāhir al-Jurjānī**, 'in which one makes use of thought'. Poetry is a form of knowledge: **Ibn Rashīq** states that the poet (*shā'ir*) is so called because he 'perceives [*yash'uru*] what others do not'.

For the philosophers, poetry, defined as 'imaginative statements' (*aqāwīl mukhayyila* or *takhyīliyya*; see **imagination**), differs from other types of statements (e.g. demonstrative, *burhāniyya*; sophistic, *safsaṭiyya*) in that it operates affectively, working on the imagination, to produce 'poetic assent' (*taṣdīq shi'rī*, in **Ibn Sīnā**'s term), and thus to motivate the performance of good actions and avoidance of bad. It thus occupies a neutral ground between truth and falsehood (see **truth in poetry**), being neither; although **al-Fārābī** defined poetic statements as being categorically false, this position was not maintained. Poetry's affective function is enhanced by its ability to create a sense of wonder in the hearer (see ***ta'jīb***), which strengthens its effect on the imagination.

Although some conservatives expressed disapprobation of poetry, it never lost its prestigious status. The celebrated Koranic condemnation of poets (26:224–7) was specifically directed at those pagan poets who opposed Muḥammad's mission and satirized him. Throughout the centuries poetry – courtly and non-courtly, secular and religious, ritualistic and occasional – remained the dominant form of Arabic literary expression, its status declining only in modern times with the appearance of new prose genres.

Further reading

Bencheikh, J.-E., *Poétique arabe: essai sur les voies d'une création*, Paris (1975).

Bonebakker, S.A., 'Religious prejudice against poetry in early Islam', *Medievalia et Humanistica*, n.s. 7 (1976), 77–99.

Cantarino, Vicente, *Arabic Poetics in the Golden Age*, Leiden (1975).

Kanazi, G., *Studies in the Kitāb aṣ-ṣinā'atayn of Abū Hilāl al-'Askarī*, Leiden (1989).

Kemal, Salim, 'Philosophy and theory in Arabic poetics', *JAL* 20 (1989), 128–47.

J.S. MEISAMI

See also: literary criticism, medieval; rhetoric and poetics

poetry, modern

It is convenient to think of the history of modern Arabic poetry as consisting of three principal divisions: neo-classical poetry, which enjoyed its heyday from 1870 until 1930 (see **neo-classicism**); Romantic poetry, which flourished between 1910 and 1950 (see **romanticism**); and the different types of modernist poetry that have been written since 1950. These dates should, however, be considered as general chronological indicators rather than precise points of change, as these various models of modern Arabic poetry have overlapped and co-existed.

Neo-classical poetry is so-called because it represents to a considerable extent the rediscovery of the classical heritage of Arabic poetry, in particular that of the high **ʿAbbāsid** period, through the work of such poets as **al-Mutanabbī**, **al-Buḥturī**, **Abū Tammām**, **Abū al-ʿAlāʾ al-Maʿarrī** and **al-Sharīf al-Raḍī**. Throughout the **Mamlūk** and Ottoman periods in the Arab world, traditional Arabic poetry had never ceased to be written in and around the urban centres where local rulers held court and where sources of patronage existed: thus it was that the court of the *amīr* Bashīr al-Shihābī at Bayt al-Dīn in the Lebanon employed poets such as Niqūlā **al-Turk** (1763–1828) and Buṭrus **Karāma** (1774–1851) who produced eulogies for the *amīr* and wrote verse about the significant events of their age. Nāṣīf **al-Yāzijī** (1800–77) was also employed there and was one of the first whose work suggested that the Arabic poetry of the late nineteenth century might be able to rediscover the power and vitality that it had exhibited in ʿAbbāsid times. Similar figures existed in **Damascus** and Aleppo in **Syria**, and in Baghdad, Mosul and Najaf in Iraq, but in the nineteenth century none was able to stake a claim to any special pre-eminence.

Egypt became the centre of neo-classical poetry largely because of the work of Maḥmūd Sāmī **al-Bārūdī** (1839–1904), Aḥmad **Shawqī** (1868–1932) and Ḥāfiẓ **Ibrāhīm** (1872–1932). Al-Bārūdī was an extraordinary example of a figure of political eminence as well as literary talent; Shawqī can justly be described as the last great court poet in the history of Arabic literature; while Ḥāfiẓ Ibrāhīm richly deserved the title of 'the people's poet' for the manner in which he used his art against some of the worst atrocities of the British in Egypt. The influential scholar and critic Shaykh Ḥusayn al-Marṣafī did much to make the reputation of al-Bārūdī through the praise that he lavished on his work and the comparisons that he made between al-Bārūdī's poetry and some of the best authors of the ʿAbbāsid period. Al-Bārūdī compiled a huge anthology of ʿAbbāsid poetry which was published posthumously in 1909, a valuable service at a time when printed editions of the ***dīwān***s of the major classical poets were not yet widely available.

Neo-classical poetry was at the height of its creativity at a time when Arabic prose was beginning to develop the new genres of the novel, the short story and the drama. Yet such was the power of the classical tradition that formal transformation was to come to poetry at a much later stage. In terms of the politics of culture, poetry was also an area in which it was easy for Arabs to feel pride in their past achievements, especially at a time when the West seemed so dominant in virtually every other sphere. Thus it is that neo-classical poetry is composed in the traditional metres of classical Arabic poetry and uses monorhyme, while its language and themes (*aghrāḍ*) are recognizably derived from ʿAbbāsid models. A high degree of intertextuality often exists between neo-classical poems and their ʿAbbāsid sources of inspiration. This style remained particularly successful in Iraq during the inter-war period at the hands of Maʿrūf **al-Ruṣāfī** (1875–1945), Jamīl Ṣidqī **al-Zahāwī** (1863–1936), and Muḥammad Mahdī **al-Jawāhirī** (1903–97). At its most successful, this verse adapts the old themes to telling effect, particularly in satire (***hijāʾ***) on social and political issues. At its worst, it is an anachronistic style which struggles, often in vain, to maintain a respectable position in rapidly changing social and political circumstances.

The Romantic poetry that dominated the Arab world during the period between the two world wars emerged somewhat undramatically from the neo-classical poetry which both preceded and co-existed with it. Indeed, in formal terms there is often little to distinguish between the two styles, for most romantic poetry continued to use regular schemes of traditional metre and rhyme. In spite of the fact that poets such as ʿAbd al-Raḥmān **Shukrī** (1886–1958) and Aḥmad Zakī **Abū Shādī** (1892–1955) introduced experiments to try to modify the traditional rules of **prosody**, these did not generally have any great impact on the form within which poets continued to write. The real distinction between the two styles lies much more in the realms of the themes and the language of poetry: while the neo-classical poets wrote within the recognizable tradition of classical Arabic poetry, their successors are much closer to the Romantic poetry of England and France in the eighteenth and nineteenth centuries.

A vital contribution to the development of Romantic poetry in the Arab world was made by the **Mahjar** group of Syro-Lebanese writers who had emigrated to North and South

America in the early years of the twentieth century and who developed a flourishing school of literature in Arabic, particularly in New York. The 'Pen Association' (**al-Rābiṭa al-qalamiyya**) was founded in 1920, bringing together a number of the poets and writers who had been writing in the Arabic journals and newspapers published in New York: the first president was Jubrān Khalīl **Jubrān** (1883–1931) and the secretary was Mikhā'īl **Nu'ayma** (1889–1988). A number of themes developed initially in the Mahjar were to become features of Arab Romantic poetry generally: (a) the desire not to conform to traditional social norms and institutions; (b) the celebration of scenes of natural beauty and intense emotional identification with such scenes, along with a tendency to regard towns and cities as centres of evil and corruption; (c) deep emotional introspection and a tendency to glory in the isolated state of the poet who, like the prophet without honour, is shunned by his contemporaries; (d) a strong sense of the neo-platonic duality of body and soul; (e) a tendency to write amatory poetry which is ethereal and spiritual rather than strongly physical. The Mahjar poets, being far removed from the traditional centres of scholasticism in the Arab world, wrote verse in language that was simple and readily accessible to the reader, and radically different from the lexicon of neo-classical poetry. In their hands, strophic forms became much more frequent, and simple rather than compound metres were usually preferred. Through the works of critics such as the Egyptian, Muḥammad **Mandūr**, Mahjar poetry became much admired in the Arab world and Nu'ayma's poem *Akhī*, written in 1917, was hailed as an example of what could be achieved with the new, less loudly rhetorical style of Arabic poetry.

A further dramatic break with the neo-classical tradition was effected in Egypt by the vitriolic attack unleashed on Aḥmad Shawqī by 'Abbās Maḥmūd **al-'Aqqād** (1889–1964) and Ibrāhīm 'Abd al-Qādir **al-Māzinī** (1890–1949) in *al-Diwān: Kitāb fī al-naqd wa-al-adab* (1921), but the high point for Romantic poetry came with the foundation of the **Apollo Group** in 1932 under the leadership of Aḥmad Zakī Abū Shādī. Around the periodical *Apollo* which was published and edited by Abū Shādi from 1932 to 1934, there grouped the poets who formed the core of the romantic movement: 'Alī Maḥmūd **Ṭāhā** (1902–49) much of whose enchanting verse was set to music and gained enormous popularity in the 1930s and 1940s; Ibrāhīm **Nājī** (1898–1953) who produced intriguing fusions of the classical and Romantic traditions in his love poetry; the Tunisian Abū al-Qāsim **al-Shābbī** (1909–34), who was a corresponding member of Apollo and whose brief and tragic creative life has Keatsian qualities.

Although Egypt was very much the centre of the Romantic movement, the style was widespread elsewhere also. In Syria and Lebanon, 'Umar **Abū Rīsha** (b. 1910) and Bishāra al-Khūrī (1884–1968) both enjoyed high reputations, while Ilyās **Abū Shabaka** (1903–47) goes well beyond the normal range of the Romantic experience in his tortured obsessions with sin and physical lust. The Sudanese **al-Tījānī Yūsuf Bashīr** (1910–37) and the Egyptian Muḥammad 'Abd al-Mu'ṭi al-Hamsharī (1908–38) also had careers which, although brief, demonstrated remarkable creative talents.

If the transition from the neo-classical to the Romantic mode was relatively undramatic, the same cannot be said of the rise of the new poetry which became widespread in the Arab world throughout the 1950s. It is as though the dramas that changed the political map of the Arab world had an organic relationship with the revolutions that changed the form and diction of modern Arabic poetry: the loss of Palestine in 1948, the Free Officers' Revolution in 1952 and the eventual disappearance of the colonial systems across North Africa are accompanied by the destruction of the prosodic system which had controlled Arabic poetry since pre-Islamic times. At the hands of the Iraqi poets Nāzik **al-Malā'ika** (b. 1923) and Badr Shākir **al-Sayyāb** (1926–64), the whole edifice of the regular monorhymed hemistich was deconstructed and replaced by a system of free repetition of a single foot in lines of irregular length, with or without rhyme. In the cases of less than gifted poets, this new freedom could and did lead to undisciplined vapid compositions where vogue was more important than talent and inspiration, but with al-Sayyāb and 'Abd al-Wahhāb **al-Bayātī** (b. 1926) in Iraq, **Adūnīs** (b. 1930) of **Syria**, Yūsuf **al-Khāl** (1917–87) and Khalīl **Ḥāwī** (1922–82) of Lebanon, and Ṣalāḥ **'Abd al-Ṣabūr** (1931–81) of Egypt, this freedom made possible new worlds of language, imagery and theme. Just as *Apollo* had been a rallying point for the romantic poets in the 1930s, so the *Shi'r* review founded in Beirut in

1957 by Yūsuf al-Khāl became the outlet in which most of the new poets published their work and developed their theories in the crucial years from 1957 to 1964. Although *al-Ādāb*, the review founded in 1953 by the Lebanese Suhayl **Idrīs**, well deserves its honourable place in the continuing quest for modernity and change in literature, unlike *Shi'r* it was not devoted exclusively to poetry, nor was it so single-mindedly avant-garde in all that it promoted.

The major formal division in the Arabic poetry produced since 1950 is that between **free verse** which still relies on a basic poetic foot, and **prose poems** in which there is no discernible metrical scheme. Both Amīn al-**Rīḥānī** (1876–1940) and Khalīl **Jubrān** (1883–1931) had experimented with prose poetry early in the twentieth century, but until the 1950s their experiments had not led to any significant further developments. Then the Palestinian Tawfīq **Ṣāyigh** (1924–71) and the Lebanese Unsī **al-Ḥājj** began to explore the possibilities of the even greater freedoms provided by the prose poem, and this interest spread to other major poets: Adūnīs in particular took to this form with enthusiasm, and by the end of the 1950s prose poetry was accepted as a legitimate form of poetic expression, although it has yet to displace the dominant presence of the single metrical foot.

These formal transformations of poetry were accompanied by greatly extended thematic ranges: old Semitic fertility myths were mingled with the crucifixion symbol, while the dichotomy of city and country was explored with new depth and insight. These poems also introduced historical characters who were in fact symbolic archetypes taken from a range of religions and civilizations. However, after the catastrophic military defeat of 1967, much of the excitement that had characterized the daring avant-garde endeavours since 1950 was replaced by crises of doubt and questionings about the nature of modernity (*ḥadātha*). **Ḥāwī**, **al-Sayyāb**, **al-Bayātī** and **Adūnīs** had provided visionary concepts of a world that might be saved by transcendental agents, or the people, or the visions of the poets themselves, or by a combination of all three; by the 1980s, poets could no longer allow themselves such visionary optimism. This realization has at least freed them from direct political preoccupations in their work. This is a liberation that may be just as significant for the future of modern Arabic poetry as were the formal prosodic liberations of the 1950s.

Further reading

Badawi, M.M., *A Critical Introduction to Modern Arabic Poetry*, Cambridge (1975).
CHALMAL, Chapters 2–4.
Jayyusi, S.K., *Trends and Movements in Modern Arabic Poetry*, 2 vols, Leiden (1977).
Khouri, M.A., *Poetry and the Making of Modern Egypt*, Leiden (1971).
Moreh, S., *Modern Arabic Poetry 1800–1970*, Leiden (1976).

R.C. OSTLE

poetry vs. prose

Traditionally, there is a rigid distinction between Arabic prose (*nathr*) and poetry (*shi'r*, or, with a true antonym, ***naẓm***). The two differ in form (poetry being metrical) and subject matter (poetry being the medium *par excellence* e.g. for praise, self-praise, blame, and amorous declarations). The language, too, differs, as in the treatment of pausal forms, diptotes or word order. Texts that, by modern standards, are clearly 'poetic', such as the rhymed and rhythmical (but unmetrical) utterances of the soothsayers (see ***saj'***), or parts of the **Koran**, were not considered as poetry. Poetry and prose often went together in various genres, such as the **Battle Days** of the Arabs, the ***sīra***, anthologies of ***adab***, the ***maqāmāt***, and ***Alf layla wa-layla***; in all these, poetry is used in a prose context, to point a moral or adorn a tale. With the development of literary prose, especially among the chancery officials (see **secretaries**), prose took on some of the characteristics of poetry, stylistically and even in subject matter. The science of stylistics (see **rhetoric and poetics**) usually deals with poetry and prose alike. The versification of prose (*'aqd*) and the reverse (*ḥall*) became art forms in themselves.

Although many poets were able prosaists and vice versa, the comparison between poetry and prose was eagerly taken up in the form of debates and essays, each having its advocates. Superiority might be pronounced on the basis of inherent characteristics or external qualities. Thus poetry might be preferred because of its metre and rhyme, or because it is a repository of wisdom, history and eloquence; or it might be deemed inferior because prose gives more freedom, because the Koran employs prose and Muḥammad was no poet, or because there are fewer good prose writers than poets, or because the poet, from **'Abbāsid** times onward, was said to be a kind of beggar with a lower status than the civil servant, writer of epistles.

In modern times, under Western influence, the boundaries between poetry and prose have changed, for instance with the rise of 'prose poetry', and the different status of fictional prose.

Text editions

Arazi, Albert, 'Une épître d'Ibrāhīm b. Hilāl al-Ṣābī sur les genres littéraires', in Ayalon Festschrift, 473–505.

al-Zu'bi, Ziyād al-Ramadan (ed.), *Abhāth al-Yarmūk* 11:1 (1993), 129–65.

Further reading

Moreh, S., *Modern Arabic Poetry 1800–1970*, Leiden (1976), 289–311 ('Prose as a medium of a new concept of poetry').

az-Zu'bī, Z.R., *Das Verhältnis von Poesie und Prosa in der arabischen Literaturtheorie des Mittelabbers*, Berlin (1987).

G.J.H. VAN GELDER

See also: poetry, medieval

popular literature (*al-adab al-sha'bī*)

From the point of view of comparative folk narrative research, popular literature in the narrow sense denotes the literary part of 'folklore', a term which – although its creator W.J. Thoms (1846) introduced it into scientific discussion to abolish such antiquated and complicated terms as 'popular literature' – has gained too broad a meaning to be used as synonymous. Popular literature in its traditional understanding designates a relatively fixed canon of literary products, such as **fables**, historical, demonological and religious legends, romantic and heroic epics, fairy tales, jokes and anecdotes as well as popular sayings and idioms, folk songs and ballads, children's rhymes and riddles. Contemporary research regards this restriction to specific genres as reducing the creative as well as the receptive factors of popular imagination beyond permissible borders. Towards the end of the twentieth century, popular literature might tentatively be conceived as the sum of *all* creative verbal activities, whether oral ('verbal art') or written, which are passed on by ways of unofficial channels and are initiated or appreciated by any considerable amount of people. The term 'popular literature' now encompasses not only the traditional stock of narrative and non-narrative genres, but also the huge bulk of literary production aimed at popular reception, such as devotional and trivial literature, chapbooks and penny-magazines, tracts on the interpretation of dreams or leaflets containing preprinted charms, as well as more recently widespread urban legends or even the so-called office-lore (xerox-lore). This way of apprehending popular literature is not so much linked to any literary genres, but is rather defined by the means of production and distribution on the one side, and by the sociological and psychological implications of the recipients on the other side.

As for Arabic literature, K. Petráček (1987) in a recent detailed sketch of popular literature distinguishes between the three literary levels of (1) classical literature (written in classical Arabic, aiming at the educated), (2) popular literature (originally oral, fixed in classical and middle Arabic, aiming primarily at uneducated members of the urban and rural middle classes), and (3) folklore (oral literature in the dialect, mainly aiming at uneducated rural and nomad population). Popular literature in this sense means a transitory state being defined among others by social condition (middle classes of urban and rural population), relation between producer and consumer (not identical: partly educated, sometimes collective producer), language (mixture of written and oral standards), and literary fixing (different stages of fixing, redactional changes in tradition).

As for the form of literary expression, popular literature might be formulated in prose (*nathr*), poetry (*shi'r*) or ***saj'*** (rhymed prose); its genres might be classified as epic, lyric or dramatic. Petráček goes on to list the combinations in which different forms of content (history, religion, heroic tales, erotica, etc.) and function (informative, propagandistic, devotional, entertaining, etc.) would have shaped specific concretized forms of popular literature: religious content together with heroic function would form *maghāzī* and ***futūḥ*** literature; heroic content together with social and political propaganda would result in ***sīra* literature** of the type of **Dhāt al-Himma**; geographical content together with informative and entertaining function would produce

***'ajā'ib* literature** or such collections as the voyages of **Sindbād**. This attempt at categorizing Arabic popular literature is valuable in its sociological and functional approach. On the other hand, it does have a number of drawbacks: no clear lines of distinction can be drawn between either contents or functions, and also smaller, but nevertheless important, categories of prose literature (fables, sayings, anecdotes, etc.) as well as forms of popular literature exclusively developed in the oral (modern prose) are admittedly left aside, let alone the more recent categories of popular literature listed in the general definition above.

Any future definition of popular literature in the Arabic world would first have to provide clear definitions of the compound's two constituents, namely 'popular' and 'literature'. 'Literature' clearly cannot simply be translated by '***adab***', which in Arabic culture, contrary to Western European notions, means a whole set of behavioural standards, but might rather be understood in a very broad sense as any form of standardized or standardizable verbal expression, preferably – but not necessarily – fixed in any of a number of 'literary' categories, often in writing. 'Popular', on the other hand, is obviously connected with some conception of 'people', who might be termed as any significant number of population, whether educated or not (but preferably not) in a classical sense. While it is dangerous to restrict the former term to any previously perceived set of literary genres, for the latter it must be kept in mind that 'popular' can potentially refer to producers as well as to recipients, while on the other hand either one might belong to a societal élite group likely to be excluded from the term 'people' by definition. Most important is the realization of the fact that collective production of popular literature, as viewed by Romantic interpretation in the nineteenth century, exists only in a very limited sense: every piece of popular literature is in the first place brought forth by an individual author, and only in the process of reception and tradition incorporates elements produced by or adapted to collective consciousness. These elements originate from a specific historical, social or educational background and are subject to various influences from different cultures or levels of society. Even though they can only be grasped by minute scrutiny of a number of different aspects, they constitute the decisive criteria for distinguishing 'popular' from any other kind of literature.

Most previous research in any field of Arabic popular literature, whether classical, transitional or modern, has so far concentrated on a comparatively small number of monumental products, the most prominent of them treated here in separate articles: the *Arabian Nights* (***Alf layla wa-layla***), epic and romantic *sīra* literature (**'Alī al-Zībaq**, **'Antara ibn Shaddād**, **Bahrām**, **Banū Hilāl**, Dhāt al-Himma, **Ḥamza al-bahlawān**, al-Malik al-Ẓāhir **Baybars**, **Sayf ibn Dhī Yazan**, **Zīr Sālim**), epic poetry, historical (*ayyām al-'arab*; [see **Battle Days**]) ***mathālib***, religious (*maghāzī*, ***futūḥ***, *mawālīd*, *qiṣaṣ al-anbiyā'* [see ***Legends of the Prophets***]) and humorous literature (***hazl***, **humour**; **Buhlūl**, **Juḥā**), fables (***Kalīla wa-Dimna***, **Luqmān**) and the like.

Further reading

Bausinger, H., *Formen der 'Volkspoesie'*, Berlin (1968), rpt (1980).

Budayr, H., *Athar al-adab al-sha'bī fī al-adab al-ḥadīth*, Cairo (1986).

El-Shamy, H.M., *Folk Traditions of the Arab World: A Guide to Motif Classification*, Bloomington and Indianapolis (1995), 2 vols.

Fanjul, S., *Literatura popular arabe*, Madrid (1977).

Heath, P., 'Arabische Volksliteratur im Mittelalter', in *Neues Handbuch der Literaturwissenschaft, vol. 5, Orientalisches Mittelalter*, W. Heinrichs (ed.), Wiesbaden (1990), 423–39.

al-Jawharī, M., *Dirāsāt al-fūlklūr al-'Arabī*, Cairo (1978).

Petráček, K., 'Volkstümliche Literatur', in *GAP*, vol. 2, 228–41.

Spies, O., 'Arabisch-islamische Erzählstaffe', in *EM*, cols 685–718.

U. MARZOLPH

See also: folklore; proverbs; *sīra* literature

preaching, preachers *see* oratory and sermons

the press

The first Arabic newspaper seems to have appeared in Muḥammad 'Alī's **Egypt**, an ephemeral weekly in Arabic and Italian published *c.*1822 at the École Polytechnique in Būlāq; it was followed by the still extant official gazette of the Egyptian government, *Vaḳā'i'-i Miṣrīye* (***al-Waqā'i' al-Miṣriyya***), published in Turkish and Arabic in **Cairo** in

1828. In Egypt, **Syria**, **Morocco** and **Algeria** the earliest journals had primarily served the foreign communities. The French expeditionary force had published in Cairo in 1798 the ***Courier de l'Égypte*** and ***La Décade égyptienne***, journal of the Institut d'Égypte. In 1832 the French occupation forces published in Algiers an official journal in Arabic and French, the *Moniteur algérien*. In the Lebanon the first Arabic journal was an annual review, *Majmūʿ fawāʾid li-nukhbat afāḍil* (1851), published by the American Protestant missionaries in Beirut, covering *inter alia* religious, scientific, historical and geographical subjects.

The late 1850s and early 1860s saw a sudden spate of non-governmental newspapers, beginning with *Mirʾāt al-aḥwāl* (*c.*1854), *al-Salṭāna* (1857) and the Lebanese Aḥmad Fāris **al-Shidyāq**'s highly successful ***al-Jawāʾib*** (1860) all in Istanbul, *Ḥadīqat al-akhbār* (1858) in Beirut, *Birjīs Bārīs* (*c.*1858) in Paris, and *ʿUṭārid* (1858) in Marseilles. Independent journalism flourished in Egypt from the reign of Khedive Ismāʿīl; the first such paper was the ***Wādī al-Nīl*** (1867) in Cairo. From then on newspapers and periodicals began to appear at an accelerating rate in Beirut, Cairo and Alexandria, the main centres of journalistic activity. A stream of Syro-Lebanese writers moved to Egypt; the famous ***al-Ahrām*** (1876) was founded by the Lebanese Taqlā brothers in Alexandria. However, the first newspapers in most Arab countries were the official gazettes: in Tunis *al-Rāʾid al-Tūnisī* (1860), in Damascus *Sūriyya* (1865), in Aleppo *Ghadīr al-Furāt* (1867), in western Tripoli *Ṭarābulus al-Gharb* (1866), in Iraq *al-Zawrāʾ* (1869), and in the peninsula *Yaman* (*c.*1872). Newspapers by the 1870s and 1880s were carrying polemical writing by political activists, religious and social reformers, written in less affected, functional prose style. Many of these writers, such as Adīb **Isḥāq**, Salīm **al-Naqqāsh**, ʿAbd Allāh **Nadīm** and Muḥammad **ʿAbduh**, had been followers of Jamāl al-Dīn **al-Afghānī**. Language experiments went as far as using the vernacular, as in Yaqʿūb **Ṣanūaʿ**'s satirical paper, *Abū Naẓẓāra Zarqāʾ* (1878), published in Cairo.

The first important commercial presses were founded in the 1860s and 1870s in Lebanon and Egypt, allowing these countries to attain the pre-eminence that they still enjoy as publishing centres. These presses made available editions of Arab classics, popular folk tales and a few contemporary ***dīwān***s to an increasingly receptive audience. At the same time, the press was encouraging a move away from traditional styles, both by publishing the first experiments in new genres (short story, novel and drama) and by publishing translations and imitations of French romances, thrillers, spy and, later, detective stories. This process gathered momentum, so that some two decades later there were about fifteen periodicals in Egypt and Lebanon specializing in publishing translations and original works of fiction.

The first of the great reviews, ***al-Muqtaṭaf*** (1876–1952), was founded in Beirut. It was followed by many others of note, including Jurjī **Zaydān**'s ***al-Hilāl*** (1892) and Ibrāhīm **al-Yāzijī**'s *al-Ḍiyāʾ* (1898), both in Cairo, the Jesuit *al-Mashriq* (1898) in Beirut, Muḥammad **Kurd ʿAlī**'s *al-Muqtabas* (1908) in Damascus, and Anastase Marie al-Karmilī's *Lughat al-ʿArab* (1911) in Baghdad. These reviews spread much sought-after knowledge on the whole range of human endeavour. With the new century there was soon a plethora of literary journals, both in the Middle East itself and in the **Mahjar**. In New York *al-Sāʾiḥ* (1912), later organ of the important literary society **al-Rābiṭa al-qalamiyya**, included works by avant-garde poets such as Jubrān Khalīl **Jubrān**, Mīkhāʾīl **Nuʿayma** and Īlyā **Abū Māḍī**; it was followed by ***al-Funūn*** magazine in 1913 and Abū Māḍī's *al-Samīr* (1929–56). In São Paulo *al-ʿUṣba al-Andalusiyya* (1928) magazine was the organ of another literary circle. In Egypt the ideas of the ***Dīwān* Group**, voicing radical views on modern poetic theory, appeared in Aḥmad **Luṭfī al-Sayyid**'s newspaper *al-Jarīda* (1907) and in the magazine *al-Bayān* (1911). *Al-Sufūr* (1915), published by a group of young authors including Muḥammad Ḥusayn **Haykal**, Ṭāhā **Ḥusayn**, Aḥmad **Amīn**, Muṣṭafa **ʿAbd al-Rāziq**, ʿĪsā **ʿUbayd** and Muḥammad **Taymūr**, was a precursor of the 'new school' (*al-madrasa al-ḥadītha*) of 'national literature' (*adab qawmī*).

Egyptian periodicals, such as Muḥammad Ḥusayn Haykal's weekly *al-Siyāsa al-usbūʿiyya* (1926), played an important part in the literary life of the 1920s and early 1930s. Salāma **Mūsā**'s *al-Majalla al-jadīda* (1929–42) led the call for literature to address the problems of the masses. Ṭāhā Ḥusayn helped to establish the prestigious literary review *al-Risāla* (1933), at the centre of the Egyptian and Arab literary movements in the 1930s and 1940s. *Apollo/ Abūllū* (1932–34), established by Aḥmad Zakī **Abū Shādī**, was the first periodical devoted entirely to poetry, poetic theory and poetry criticism; the **Apollo Group** embraced most of the younger generation of poets and critics in Egypt. With the help of the periodical press, the Egyptian novel slowly came of age. Novels were and are still being published through serialization; in 1959, one of Najīb **Maḥfūẓ**'s major works, *Awlād Ḥāratinā*, was first published on the pages of *al-Ahrām*.

The golden age of the Lebanese press in a climate of unparalleled freedom was the 1950s and 1960s. The monthly *al-Ādāb* (1953), edited by Suhayl **Idrīs**, was in the vanguard of those championing the cause of committed literature. The centre for poetic activity had also moved to the Lebanon, where the poet Yūsuf **al-Khāl** founded *Shi'r* (1957–69), and *Mawāqif* (1968), founded by the Syrian poet **Adūnīs**, tested the suitability of French innovations to Arabic literary production. Egypt was by no means eclipsed; there the poet Ṣalāḥ **'Abd al-Ṣabūr** edited the influential monthly *al-Kātib* (1961), and the monthly *al-Masraḥ* (1964) led serious debates on the theatre. These publications were paralleled elsewhere, in the Tunisian *al-Ḥayāh al-thaqāfiyya* (1975); in the quarterly *al-Aqlām* (1964) and the monthly *Āfāq 'Arabiyya* (1975), both in Baghdad; in the review of the Palestinian Union of Writers, *al-Karmil* (1978), and in the Moroccan avant-garde magazine *al-Thaqāfa al-jadīda* (1974), among others.

The movement of sections of the Arab media to London, Paris and Cyprus in the 1970s and 1980s has opened a vibrant new chapter, leading to the emergence of some of the most successful pan-Arab newspapers and magazines. Arab newspapers and reviews at home and abroad continue to provide a powerful medium for the development of modern Arab thought, and to act as a platform for the best talents in modern Arabic literature.

Further reading

Ayalon, Ami, *The Press in the Arab Middle East: A History*, New York (1995).

Canal, Albert, *La Littérature et la presse tunisienne de l'occupaiton à 1900*, Paris (1924).

*EI*², 'Djarīda', vol. 2, 464–72.

Fayyāḍ, Maḥmūd, *al-Ṣiḥāfa al-adabiyya bi-Miṣr wa-al-ittijāhāt al-qawmiyya, 1914–1940*, Cairo (1976).

Ḥamza, 'Abd al-Laṭīf, *al-Ṣiḥāfa wa-al-adab fī Miṣr*, Cairo (1955).

Ḥamza, Ṣalāḥ al-Dīn, *Majallat al-Risāla wa-dawruhā fī al-nahḍa al-adabiyya al-ḥadītha*, Cairo (1982).

Ḥasan, Muḥammad 'Abd al-Ghanī and al-Dasūqī, 'Abd al-'Azīz, *Rawḍat al-Madāris*, Cairo (1975).

Majed, Jaafar, *La Presse littéraire en Tunisie de 1904 à 1955*, Tunis (1979).

al-Mughāzī, Aḥmad, *al-Tadhawwuq al-fannī wa-al-fann al-ṣuḥufī al-ḥadīth, 1924–1952*, Cairo (1984).

Shalash, 'Alī, *Dalīl al-majallāt al-adabiyya fī Miṣr, 1939–1952*, Cairo (1985).

Shukrī, Fayṣal, *al-Ṣiḥāfa al-adabiyya wijha jadīda fī dirāsāt al-adab al-mu'āṣir wa-ta'rīkhih*, Cairo (1960).

P.C. SADGROVE

printing and publishing

Printing was practised in the Arab world probably as early as the fourth/tenth century. Block-prints on paper, papyrus and parchment, found in **Egypt**, survive in several collections, and further pieces have emerged from excavations. However, no literary or historical testimony to the craft seems to exist, except for two obscure references in Arabic poems of the fourth/tenth and eighth/fourteenth centuries to the use of *ṭarsh* to produce copies of amulets. According to Bulliet (1987), this non-classical Arabic term may have signified tin plates with engraved or repoussé lettering, used to produce multiple copies of Koranic and incantatory texts for sale to the illiterate poor. Their crude style, and errors in the Koranic texts, indicate that they were not produced by writers or scholars, and there is no evidence that the technique was ever used to produce Arabic books or substantial literary texts in any form. These remained the monopoly of scribes in the Arab world until the eighteenth century, and the origins of Arabic typography and printed book production are to be found not there but in Europe.

The first Arabic printed book, a Melkite prayer-book, was printed at Fano in Italy in 1514. European Arabic printing over the next three or more centuries was developed partly to serve the needs of Orientalists but also to produce books for export to the Arab and Muslim world. The **Koran** was printed at Venice in the 1530s (see Nuovo, 1990), probably as a commercial export venture, but there is no evidence that the edition ever achieved any circulation, and later 'secular' printed Arabic texts also met with resistance or indifference. Only among Christian communities did European Arabic editions, mostly of biblical or liturgical texts, gain some acceptance.

It was among these communities, too, that Arabic typography was eventually introduced into the Arab world – the first Arabic book printed there was a Melkite Psalter at Aleppo in 1706 – and it remained in Christian hands for over 100 years. Although Muslim Turkish book printing had started in Istanbul in 1728, the first Muslim Arab press was the Egyptian state press of Muḥammad ʿAlī at Būlāq, which did not start publishing until 1822. The reasons for this lateness must be sought both in the nature of Islamic societies and in the supreme religious and aesthetic role accorded to the written word within them. The segmentation and mechanization of the Arabic script by typesetting seemed tantamount to sacrilege; at the same time mass production of books challenged the entrenched monopolies of intellectual authority enjoyed by the learned class (ʻ*ulamā*ʼ), and threatened to upset the balance between that authority and the power of the state. This was one important reason that printing was eventually sponsored by modernizing rulers in the nineteenth century.

Much of the early output of the Būlāq Press in Arabic (see Riḍwān, 1953, 446–79) consisted of military and technical books, official decrees, grammars, manuals of epistolography and translations of European works. But in 1836 editions of ***Alf layla wa-layla*** and ***Kalīla wa-Dimna*** were published, and these were followed by a series of classical texts which served to revive interest in the Arabic literary heritage. Rifāʿa Rāfiʿ **al-Ṭahṭāwī** was active in promoting the use of the press for this purpose, as well as himself translating and writing new works for publication.

Meanwhile, many Christian missionary publications in Arabic, including secular didactic works, were imported into the Arab world in the second quarter of the nineteenth century, mostly from the British-run press in Malta (1825–42). These went mainly, but not exclusively, to the Christian communities, and helped to create a new readership for literary texts. One of the editors, translators and type-designers in Malta was the Lebanese writer Fāris **al-Shidyāq** who became an enthusiastic protagonist of the print revolution and later founded the Jawāʼib Press in Istanbul (1870–84). This specialized in well-produced editions of the Arabic classics, as well as publishing new works by himself and others. The missionary contribution was continued by the American and Jesuit presses in Beirut (started in 1836 and 1848 respectively), which also published new and old literature as well as religious and didactic works.

Printing and publishing burgeoned in the Arab world from the mid-nineteenth century onwards, with Arabic presses starting in Jerusalem (1847), Damascus (1855), Mosul (1856), Tunis (1860), Baghdad (1863), Sana'a (1877), Khartoum (1881), Mecca (1883) and Medina (1885), among others. Many of these presses, like that of ***al-Jawāʼib*** already mentioned, produced newspapers as well as books.

Since the late 1820s, some books had been printed not from type but by lithography. This was favoured especially in Morocco and among smaller private publishers in Egypt. Its perceived advantages were that scribal calligraphy could be directly reproduced, and that it enabled many small publishers to avoid expensive investments in type-founts.

The rapid transition in the nineteenth century from manuscripts to printed books and periodicals as the normal means of transmitting Arabic texts had profound effects on the development of Arab literary culture. Insufficient research has been done to enable us either to measure or to trace accurately these effects; but it seems likely that the much greater dissemination of texts, both new and old, together with the standardization and systematization of their presentation, and their permanent preservation, played a major role in promoting that cultural and national self-awareness that led to the ***nahḍa*** of the late nineteenth and early twentieth century.

The subsequent development of Arabic printing and publishing has been less significant than its beginnings. The early twentieth century saw a revival in Arabic typography, which was subsequently reinforced by the adoption by the major presses of 'linotype' methods, as well as by the greater mechanization of the presses themselves. These developments permitted considerable increases in output of books, magazines and newspapers. **Cairo** and **Beirut** remained the principal publishing centres throughout the transition from Ottoman and European rule to full independence and beyond. Both lost ground, however, in the 1970s and 1980s, because of declining quality, lack of investment and rising prices in Egypt (see Rizk and Rodenbeck, 1985, 102–8), and the ruinous strife in Lebanon. Other Arab countries have therefore become relatively more important, notably those of the **Maghrib** (with an important output in French as well as Arabic), Iraq until 1991 and most recently Saudi Arabia. The lack of a well-developed book trade in these countries has, however, hampered development, as have political and religious **censorship** and restrictions in some cases. As elsewhere, the spread of broadcast and electronic media, especially television and video, has had some adverse impact on the market for printed literature, but this has been largely offset by the rise in rates of literacy.

Further reading

Albin, M.W., 'Early Arabic printing: a catalogue of attitudes', *Manuscripts of the Middle East* 5 (1990–1), 114–22.

Balagna, J., *L'Imprimerie arabe en occident (XVIe, XVIIe et XVIIIe siècles)*, Paris (1984).

Bulliet, R.W., 'Medieval Arabic *ṭarsh*: a forgotten chapter in the history of printing', *JAOS*, 107 (1987), 427–38.

Demeerseman, A., *L'Imprimerie en Orient et au Maghreb: une étape décisive de la culture et de la psychologie islamiques*, Tunis (1954); also in *IBLA* 17 (1954), 1–48.

——, *La Lithographie arabe et tunisienne*, Tunis (1954); also in *IBLA* 16 (1953), 347–89.

Gdoura, W., *Le Début de l'imprimerie arabe à Istanbul et en Syrie: évolution de l'environnement culturel (1706–1787)*, Tunis (1985).

Heyworth-Dunne, J., 'Printing and translations under Muḥammad 'Alī of Egypt: the foundation of modern Arabic', *JRAS* (1940), 325–49.

Krek, M., *A Gazetteer of Arabic Printing*, Weston (USA), (1977).

Nuovo, A., 'A lost Arabic Koran rediscovered', *The Library*, Sixth Series, 12 (1990), 273–292; translation of 'Il Corano arabo ritrovato', *La Bibliofilia* 89 (1987), 237–71.

Riḍwān, Abū al-Futūḥ, *Tārīkh Maṭba'at Būlāq*, Cairo (1953).

Rizk, N.A. and Rodenbeck, J., 'The book publishing industry in Egypt', in P.G. Altbach *et al.* (eds), *Publishing in the Third World*, Portsmouth (USA) and London (1985), 96–110.

Roper, G., 'Arabic printing: its history and significance', *Ur* (1) (=1982), 23–30.

Ṣābāt, Khalīl, *Tārīkh al-ṭibā'a fī al-Sharq al-'Arabī*, 2nd edn, Cairo (1966).

Details of other sources can be found in two bibliographies: M. Krek, *A Bibliography of Arabic Typography*, Weston (USA) (1976); and Y. Safadi, 'Arabic printing and book production', *Arab Islamic Bibliography: The Middle East Library Committee Guide*, Hassocks (1977), 221–34.

G. ROPER

prose, non-fiction, medieval

The heyday of pre-modern, 'classical' Arabic prose was from the third/ninth to fifth/eleventh centuries. The emergence of major works as well as the elaboration of a highly sophisticated prose style, in which acoustic elements came to play an increasing part, fall in this period. It is a characteristic feature of prose literature that it consists to a large extent of collections, which contain speeches, utterances of widely varying kinds, narratives about people and events, and sometimes letters. Many of the texts are quoted from narrators or orators of the second/eighth century and earlier. From a historian's point of view, however, one has to be aware that they have undergone a process of transmission which may have affected their wording and composition. In any case, as examples of good style these texts represent a literary tradition that is shown to go back to early Islamic and pre-Islamic times.

Prose literature cannot be separated from the literary concept of ***adab***, since many of its works are permeated by the didactic intention of guidance to learning and refinement. The works of, for example, **Ibn 'Abd Rabbih** (d. 328/940), **Ibn Ḥamdūn** (d. 562/1167) or **Ibn Abī al-Ḥadīd** (d. 655/1257) are important compilations of prose texts (as well as poetry) mainly from the classical period. A more philological outlook prevailed in works such as *al-Kāmil* of **al-Mubarrad** (d. 285/898) or the *Amālī* of Abū 'Alī **al-Qālī** (d. 356/967), whose intention was the collection and explanation of rare expressions (*nawādir*). Numerous prose texts of exemplary character are also inserted into historiographical works such as the chronicle of **al-Ṭabarī** (d. 310/923), and in collections of anecdotal material, among which the *Kitab al-Aghānī* of **Abū al-Faraj al-Iṣbahānī** is of primary importance.

In order to facilitate orientation, two main lines of prose style may be distinguished: the short and concise style characterized by omissions and extremely brief allusions, and the ornate prose which indulges in stylistic devices. Whereas both types of style cannot be separated in terms of literary genres, and even have some traits in common, their chronological development suggests a line of demarcation. From the fourth/tenth century onwards, ornate prose increasingly dominated all types of literary expression except those confined to simple prose for daily or purely scientific use.

Speeches (***khuṭba***) figure in many sources as specimens of refined prose. In his *al-Bayān wa-al-tabyīn* **al-Jāḥiẓ** (d. 255/869) has collected much information on the significance and the art of orators of earlier times. Many of the leaders of Arab tribal society figure in the collections of *adab* literature as masters of rhetorical expression. In the light both of al-Jāḥiẓ's evaluation of oratory, and of later collections, this art was not confined to the speech or official address, but was also observed in short sayings. Particular themes related to special occasions, such as condolence (*ta'ziya*), exhortation (*waṣiyya*) or admonition (*maw'iẓa*), were treated with great care by orators and by the authors of *adab* collections as well. Brief and exceptional descriptions, such as those collected by **al-Washshā'** (d. 325/936) in his *al-Fāḍil*, were also constituent parts of eloquence. Moreover, witty sayings or more solemn aphorisms, sometimes juxtaposed with sayings of the Prophet (***ḥadīth***), are omnipresent in *adab* literature (e.g. in **al-Zamakhsharī**'s *Rabī' al-abrār*), and were were held in high esteem. Aphorisms are often presented as having been generated from controversy, and found expression in collections of 'dumbfounding retorts' (*al-ajwiba al-muskita*) like those of **Ibn Abī 'Awn** (d. 322/934) and **al-Ābī** (d. 421/1030). Sententious formulations of general meaning represent an authentic tradition of Arabic oratory, and were often intended to become proverbial sayings. **Proverbs** (*mathal*) themselves form a very well-documented branch of Arabic prose literature. Here, as in fictional anecdotes, the migration of motifs from different cultural backgrounds is evident. In contrast to this, gnomological literature (*ḥikam*; see ***ḥikma***) does more to reveal its origin by the quotation of the philosophers of antiquity.

Monorhyme at the end of short clauses (***saj'***) is a striking characteristic of brief forms of old Arabic tradition, such as priestly verdicts and arbiters' decisions. Probably they reflect the practice of the pre-Islamic soothsayer (*kāhin*). Rhyme is also used as a means of emphasis in speeches, but here the achievement of rhythm through the division of the text into short phrases and the use of all kinds of parallelism is more important. Like speeches, letters (*rasā'il*) of the pre-**'Abbāsid** period, preserved in *adab* collections in considerable quantity, show a predilection for brevity (***ījāz***) and frequent use of allusion and imagery. In general, the elevated style (*jazāla*), based on the application of clear, dignified and pithy expression, was held to be a distinction that any manifestation of literary pretensions ought to have. The preference for the extremely concise formulation, which may sometimes appear to come close to abbreviation – and was in fact carried to extremes in the short form of the answer (*tawqī'*) to supplications, questions, etc. – is a characteristic feature of early Arabic prose. It was gradually superseded by new elements of ornate prose style. Furthered by the institution of the state secretary (*kātib*; see **secretaries**), which demanded mastery of style as part of craftsmanship, style began to be perceived in terms of literary embellishment which was pursued through the expansion of parallelism into long phrases and the use of synonyms and assonances. This implied, in contrast to the brevity of the earlier prose style, the repetion of the same ideas in different forms.

'Abd al-Ḥamīd ibn Yaḥyā (d. 132/750) and **Ibn al-Muqaffa'** (d. *c.*139/757) generally represent the beginning of this development. They were also authors of memoranda in the form of epistles (*rasā'il*), which mark the foundation of a distinct branch of prose literature. Epistles that were dedicated to a (possibly fictitious) addressee became the medium of argument and presupposed or prepared discussion. This feature was developed, mainly by **al-Jāḥiẓ**, into essays on various topics of social and cultural life, and also shaped the form of philosophical and scientific treatises. These writings reflected the development of dialectics, which occurred particularly in connection with theological issues and was generally applied as a technique of discussion through the reversal of terms and concepts (see ***kalām***). The style of the *risāla* was later applied to an expanded form of the essay as it was mastered by the philosophical writer Abū Ḥayyān **al-Tawḥīdī** (d. 414/1023). Similar to the discursive style of the epistle is the collection of *quaestiones* (*masā'il*) which appeared in the field of science and philosophy, as well as in Islamic ***fiqh***. Both of these genres seem united in the correspondence between al-Tawḥīdī and **Miskawayh** (*al-Hawāmil wa-al-shawāmil*).

The **translation** of works of the Greek, and also of the Persian, heritage, and the exploration into the fields of medicine, exact sciences and philosophy, achieved great intensity and variety in the third/ninth century, when these activities enjoyed the patronage of

ʿAbbāsid caliphs and private sponsors. The work of such translators and authors as Isḥāq ibn Ḥunayn (d. 298/910) or the members of the **Bukhtīshūʿ family** contributed to the development of appropriate terminology and to the formation of highly differentiated techniques of expression. It is this linguistic faculty of Arabic that stands at the basis of its triumph and which made the Arabization of the Hellenistic and Sasanian cultures possible. Arabic thus became the natural medium of expression even for such authors as the philosopher and Christian theologian **Yaḥyā ibn ʿAdī** (d. 363/967), who also disposed of other languages.

Arabic literature is, in the light of this development, defined in terms of language, not as 'literature of the Arabs'. Its success was, of course, also due to the genuine inspiration offered by the linguistic treasure-house of old Arabic poetry. As well as the persuasive force of Islam itself, it was strengthened by the Koran as an example, even the ultimate example, of rhetorical perfection. For grammar and for the art of **rhetoric** (*balāgha*), the text of revelation served as orientation, and both disciplines developed in interaction with linguistical explications of the holy text. (See **grammar and grammarians:** ***iʿjāz al-Qur'ān***.)

As literature expanded into all branches of human knowledge, the concern with the communication of information was combined, for some of its domains, with the endeavour for artistic expression. The conscious exploration of the formal resources of language which characterizes ***badīʿ*** poetry also took place in various types of correspondence. Their authors, being secretaries who often mastered poetry as well, increasingly employed, in addition to different forms of parallelism, the art of subtle and complex metaphorical expression (*istiʿāra*; see **metaphor**). Extended similes became a common feature of prose. These elements, the effect of assonance, and the use of rhyme (*sajʿ*) were the main constituents of the ornate prose style (*inshā'*), as it was elaborated in the fourth/tenth century by the political and cultural élite, ministers and men of letters, such as Abū Isḥāq **al-Ṣābi'** (d. 384/984), **Ibn al-ʿAmīd** (d. 360/970) and **al-Ṣāḥib Ibn ʿAbbād** (d. 385/995). Official as well as informal correspondence was composed according to these standards, showing an admirable sense of rhythm and rhetorical intensity. Letters of famous authors as well as short passages (*fuṣūl*) of refined composition on various subjects (e.g. *Ghurar al-balāgha* by al-Ṣābi') were collected and became firmly established as models of prose literature. Besides the correspondence of the literati (see, for example, **Abū al-ʿAlā' al-Maʿarrī**, d. 449/1058), the literary production of the chancery is to be considered as an important part of literature and did not cease to preoccupy men of letters in both practice and theory, as Ḍiyā' al-Dīn **Ibn al-Athīr** (d. 637/1239) demonstrated with his *al-Mathal al-sā'ir*. After the fourth/eleventh century, treatises on all kinds of topics were adorned with rhetorical embellishment, and the excessive use of *inshā'* style apparently became conventional in prefaces (*muqaddimāt*) even of works of otherwise quite sober character. More or less moderate forms of *inshā'* are to be observed in many works in the field of humanities, i.e. geography, history and *adab*, including ethical writings and **Mirrors for Princes** (*naṣīḥat al-mulūk*). It comes as no surprise that works of courtly character, such as **ʿImād al-Dīn al-Kātib**'s (d. 597/1201) biography of Saladin, indulged in stylistic refinement, whereas authors of religious writings modelled their prose after the tradition of ***ḥadīth*** which adhered, apart from the particularities of vocabularity, to a much plainer style.

A rather plain prose style is also predominant in the countless short narrative texts found in compilations of the most varying nature. As a rule, the narrations that are commonly referred to as *khabar*, or *qiṣṣa*, are usually concise, straightforwardly constructed and realistic. Since their focus is quite narrow, they do not relate more than one or two events at the same time. In contrast to tales that contain legendary and fabulous elements, they appear to reproduce the words and deeds of actual people. The distinctive neutral mode of narration, which allots much space to the characters' direct speech, gives the impression of factuality and mimetic or 'dramatic' representation. This aspect is strengthened by the fact that the narratives are normally ascribed to eye-witnesses or reporters close to the events in question. Apart from the simple report of events, the commonest type of *khabar* narration is the anecdote that illustrates the traits and abilities of individuals. Such narrations are sometimes collected in works concerned with certain types of characters and their doings, such as stories about poets (*akhbār al-shuʿarā'*) or lovers, and are omnipresent in general collections of *adab* literature. However, anecdotes that cannot but be fictitious share the same narrative traits with seemingly reliable and realistic narratives. The distinction of 'real' from 'invented' is, therefore, not always clear. It has to be sorted out carefully even in historiographical collections, such as the works of **al-Balādhurī** and **al-Mas'ūdī**. Short humoristic tales (*nukta*), which are widespread, adhere to the same narrative form, with the exception that the characters are often anonymous. Stylistically different from this type of narration is the larger form of narratives of epic character. They may portray the deeds of a central character in successive episodes and may even contain several plots. Lengthy and hyperbolic descriptions, and the appearence of folkloric motifs, as they are employed here, are characteristic of a popular style of narrating. A precurser of narrative literature is the sermon and edifying tale of the preacher (*qāṣṣ*) of the early Islamic period. His stories contributed to the development of narrative material and reappear under different forms in Arabic literature. (See **oratory and sermons**; **story-telling**)

Further reading

For surveys on the history of classical Arabic literature, see:

Nallino, C.-A., *La Littérature arabe des origines a l'époque de la dynastie umayyade*, Charles Pellat (trans.), Paris (1950).

Blachère, R., *Histoire de la littérature arabe des origines à la fin du XVe siécle de J.C.*, 3 vols, Paris (1952–66).

Modern surveys and bibliographic references are given by the volumes of *CHAL* in *CHALUP*, *CHALABL*, etc., in *GAP*, vols 2 and 3.

See also:

Leder, Stefan, and Kilpatrick, Hilary, 'Classical Arabic prose literature: a researchers' sketch map', JAL 23 (1992), 2–26 (with a bibiliography of studies in Arabic).

S. LEDER

See also: artistic prose

prose poem (*qaṣīdat al-nathr*)

Out of respect for the distinction between Koranic verses (*āyāt mufaṣṣalāt*) and poetry (*shi'r*), Muslim scholars have traditionally drawn a sharp distinction between prose and poetry, even though writers of artistic prose (***adab***, *nathr fannī*) have frequently used rhyme (***saj'***), rhythm and other poetic techniques.

The main protagonists of modern efforts to bridge the gap between prose and poetry were Arab Christians, inspired by Arabic translations of the Bible, Christian liturgical literature and Romantic European poetry. In 1903, both **Jubrān**, who was influenced by the Christian Maronite style and French Romantic poetry, and Amīn **al-Rīḥānī**, who had read Walt Whitman, began to use prose as a medium for poetry. They argued that by discarding metre and rhyme, and by stressing emotional tension and the spontaneous expression of the poetic experience, writers could achieve a new medium to express their ideas. In place of rhythm and rhyme, such writers used a rhythm of thought, employing various types of parallelism and reiteration of words and ideas. The success of this technique (termed *shi'r manthūr*) led to its rapid spread: other terms used were *shi'r ḥurr*, *muṭlaq*, *ṭalq* and *ṭalīq*.

Writers of *shi'r manthūr* before *c.*1950 stressed imagination, sentiment and escape to nature. The new generation of poets known as the *Shi'r* group, led by Yūsuf **al-Khāl** and **Adūnīs**, rejected their idealistic, humanistic vision of the world in favour of a revolutionary poetry, in which the irrational and subconscious played a leading part. This new concept of poetry demanded new techniques. According to Adūnīs, the first advocate of *qaṣīdat al-nathr* (*poème en prose*), he discovered the prose poem in 1958 when translating a poem by Saint-John Perse. The new genre exposed a creative poetic experience with a universal vision, roving over the past and its buried civilizations: its images and vocabulary were precise and simple, though at the same time sometimes exotic, personal, irrational and obscure. Other members of the group such as Unsī **al-Ḥājj** – influenced by Suzanne Bernard's *La Poème en prose* (Paris, 1959) – argued that the prose poem was the best medium to express rejection (*rafḍ*), i.e. to revolt against the cultural heritage of the Arabic language and to challenge the stagnation in contemporary Arab life. Their efforts met with a mixed response, being received with enthusiasm by many modern poets but attacked by conservative critics on the grounds (*inter alia*) that they corrupted the Arabic language.

Further reading

Moreh, S., *Modern Arabic Poetry 1839–1970*, Leiden (1976), 289–311.

——, *Studies in Modern Arabic Prose and Poetry*, Leiden (1988), 1–31.

S. MOREH

prose, rhymed *see* ***saj'***

prosody (*'arūḍ*)

Classical Arabic verse, and most modern verse, is quantitative, i.e. based on the distinction between short syllables (consonant + short vowel) and long syllables (consonant + long vowel, or: consonant + short vowel + consonant). Over-long syllables occur in certain types of verse at the end of the line. Vowels at the end of the line are always scanned long irrespective of their quantity in prose. The third person singular pronoun *-hū*/ *-hī* can be either long or short, the first person singular pronoun *anā* can be scanned short + long or double short.

Metre

Compositions are normally in one metre, but metrical variation is produced by the presence of several variable positions within each metre. These are of two kinds: double short syllables in one line alternating with one long syllable in another line (typical of *wāfir*, *kāmil* and *mutadārik*), and a long syllable in one line alternating with a short syllable in another (typical of the other metres). The usual metre names are those given in the metrical theory of **al-Khalīl ibn Aḥmad**, who distinguished fifteen metres. (A sixteenth, *al-mutadārik*, was added by his successor al-Akhfash.) Most of the fifteen metre names represent two or more distinct types that cannot be used together in one poem and therefore count as separate metres. Al-Khalīl distinguished sixty-three such types. Those in common use are shown, with their current variations, in the table.

Form

Most compositions of classical poetry (*shi'r* or *qarīḍ*) are ***qaṣīda***s with a variable number of lines (rarely over a hundred) or ***qiṭ'a***s (smaller pieces up to about ten lines). Lines (*bayt*, pl. *abyāt*) can have up to thirty syllables divided over two more or less symmetrical hemistichs (*miṣrā'* or *shaṭr*) separated by a caesura. A foot is called *juz'* (pl. *ajzā'*). The last foot of the first hemistich is called *'arūḍ*, the last foot of the second hemistich is called *ḍarb*. The number of syllables per line is variable in *wāfir*, *kāmil* and *mutadārik* metre types but fixed in the other metres. A single rhyme occurs at the end of every line. First lines (*maṭla'*, pl. *maṭāli'*) often have rhyming hemistichs (*aa*, *ba*, *ca* ...), particularly in the *qaṣīda*; this is termed *taṣrī'*, and may occasionally be repeated elsewhere in the poem.

Another type of composition, called ***rajaz***, has no caesura and a maximum of twelve syllables to the line. It can have three short syllables in succession (*shi'r* admits of only two). It uses the *rajaz*-4 or *sarī'*-7 metre (twelve or eleven syllables) and is then called *mashṭūr* (reduced by a *shaṭr* 'hemistich') or the *rajaz*-5, *munsariḥ*-3 or *munsariḥ*-4 metre (eight or seven syllables), and is then called *manhūk*, 'emaciated'.

Rajaz also occurs as ***muzdawija*** with a rhyming pattern *aa bb cc* etc., in which *rajaz*-4 and *sarī'*-7 metres can be mixed together. Strophic forms, which arrived comparatively late in Arabic versification, include ***muwashshaḥ*** and ***zajal*** (see **strophic poetry**).

After 1948 the free verse movement in modern Arabic poetry tried to liberate itself from the fixed patterns of the single rhyme and the symmetry of classical poetry. The basic unit of verse is now the single foot (*taf'īla*). Basically, the feet employed by the modern poets are either those used in older poetry or close derivatives. (See **free verse**.)

Rhyme

Arab theorists distinguish five types of rhyme on a metrical basis. The rhyme is called *mutarādif* if the verse ends in an overlong syllable (as happens in the *ramal*-2, *sarī'*-1 and *mutaqārib*-2 metres). It is called *mutawātir* if the verse ends in two long syllables (in *ṭawīl*-1, *ṭawīl*-3, *madīd*-1, *madīd*-6, *basīṭ*-2, *basīṭ*-6, *wāfir*-1, *wāfir*-3, *kāmil*-2, *kāmil*-3, *kāmil*-5, *kāmil*-6, *hazaj*-1, *rajaz*-2, *ramal*-1, *ramal*-5, *sarī'*-3, *sarī'*-7, *khafīf*-1, *mujtathth*, *mutaqārib*-1 and one type of the *mutadārik* metre). It is called *mutadārik* if the verse ends in the sequence long–short–long (in *ṭawīl*-2, *madīd*-3, *kāmil*-1, *kāmil*-8, *sarī'*-2; *khafīf*-4 and *mutaqārib*-3). It is called *mutarākib* if the verse ends in the sequence long–short– short–long (in *madīd*-5, *basīṭ*-1, *wāfir*-2, *kāmil*-4, *munsariḥ*-1, *muqtaḍab* and one *mutadārik* type). Finally, the rhyme is called *mutakāwis* if the verse ends in the sequence long–short–short–short–long, which happens only occasionally in *rajaz* verse. A combination of *mutarākib* and *mutadārik* rhymes can occur in *rajaz* and *ramal*-3.

Most other rhyme concepts revolve around the *rawī*, the rhyming consonant, which represents the common element of any *qaṣīda*, after which it is called *kāfiyya* (if the *rawī* is a *kāf*), *bā'iyya* (if the *rawī* is a *bā'*) etc. (The *alif* can also act as *rawī*; in that case the poem is called a *maqṣūra*.) When the rhyme ends with the *rawī* (without any vowel following) the rhyme is called *muqayyada* ('fettered'). When the *rawī* is followed by other elements it is called *muṭlaqa* ('loose'). These elements may be: a long vowel; a short vowel + the letter *hā'*; or a short vowel + the letter *hā'* + a long vowel. The long vowel and the letter *hā'* after the *rawī* are called *waṣl* or *ṣila*; the long vowel after the the *hā' al-waṣl* is called *khurūj*. Under certain conditions also *tā'* and *kāf* can be used as *waṣl*.

With respect to elements preceding the *rawī*, the rhyme may be *murdafa* (the *rawī* is preceded by *alif*, *wāw* or *yā'*, called *ridf*), *mu'assasa* (the *rawī* is preceded by the *ta'sīs*, i.e. an *alif* separated from the *rawī* by another consonant, called *dakhīl*, and its vowel) or *mujarrada* (when there is neither *ridf* nor *ta'sīs*).

The rhyming consonant, like any other rhyme element of the poem (*waṣl*, *khurūj*, *ridf* and *ta'sīs*), is identical in all lines. However, both *wāw* and *yā'* may be used indiscriminately as *ridf* in one and the same poem (e.g. both *-ūbū* and *-ībū* may occur in one poem).

In philological commentaries the rhyme is often described by a combination of several of the above-mentioned technical terms, e.g. the rhyme of a line ending in *khuṭūb* is called *mutarādif muqayyad murdaf* (because it ends in an over-long syllable, a consonant and has a long vowel before the *rawī*); that of a line ending in *'alā ḥazanī* is called *mutarākib muṭlaq bi-waṣl mujarrad* (sequence long–short–short–long; ending in a long vowel; no *ridf* nor *ta'sīs*).

Violations of rhyming rules mentioned in Arabic works on rhyme include *sinād* (irregular vowel preceding the *rawī*), *iqwā'* (irregular vowel following the *rawī*), *ikfā'* (irregular *rawī*), *īṭā'* (repetition of the same rhyming word in the course of the *qaṣīda*) and *taḍmīn* (running on of a syntactical construction beyond one line into the next).

Licences

The language of poetry is characterized by the use of forms and syntactic structures that do not normally occur in prose. They are dealt with in the works on *ḍarūra* (pl. *ḍarā'ir* or *ḍarūrāt*), 'poetic licence', such as *Ḍarūrat al-shi'r* by Abū Sa'īd **al-Sīrāfī** (d. 368/979), *Mā yajūzu lil-shā'ir isti'māluhū fī ḍarūrat al-shi'r* by Muḥammad al-Qazzāz (d. 412/1021), *Ḍarā'ir al-shi'r* by Ibn 'Uṣfūr al-Ishbīlī (d. 663/1263) and *al-Ḍarā'ir wa-mā yaṣūghu lil-shā'ir dūna al-nāthir* by Maḥmūd Shukrī **al-Ālūsī** (1857–1923). Examples of frequently occurring poetic licences are the use of a long *-ū* after the pronouns *-hum*, *-him*, *kum*, *-tum*, *antum*; the shortening of the ending *-ī* of the first person singular (*yā 'ayni*, *yā rabbi*); the use of *hamzat al-waṣl* instead of *hamzat al-qaṭ'* (*law abṣarta* instead of *law 'abṣarta*); the use of *hamzat al-qaṭ'* instead of *hamzat al-waṣl* (*qultu 'idhhab*); diptotes receiving triptote declension (*maḥāsinan*); shortening of interrogative *-ma* after a preposition (*lim*, 'why?'); *-uwa* (in the subjunctive mood and the pronoun *huwa*) is often read as *-ū*; *-iya* (in the subjunctive mood) is often read as *-ī*; *-ī* (pronoun ending of the first person singular) is often read as *-iya*; words ending in *-ā'* are often read with *-ā* (*bahā* instead of *bahā'*).

Special conditions obtain in rhyme. In the *qāfiya muṭlaqa* any short vowel is lengthened and the endings *-in*, *-un* and *-an* are read as *-ī*, *-ū* and *-ā* respectively. In this case long *-ā* is written with *alif* or undotted *yā'*, but long *-ī* and long *-ū* are only written with *yā'* and *wāw* if these letters belong to the prose form of the word. Words ending in a consonant sometimes are pronounced with a long *-ī* (*zallat-ī*, 'she slipped'; *lam 'anam-ī*, 'I did not sleep').

Indigenous theory

The development of the Arabic science of versification (*'arūḍ*) and rhyme (*qāfiya*) can be traced back to al-Khalīl ibn Aḥmad. The plethora of Arabic metrical data has been elegantly reduced in al-Khalīl's theory to just five metrical circles. Each circle has inscribed on its circumference a leading metre in an ideal form (*baḥr*) divided up into relevant elements of scanning (e.g. *watid majmū'* [∪ —] and *sabab khafīf* [—]). Starting at a particular point of the circle either the leading metre or one of its permutations will emerge. Some of these permutations are posited as the ideal form of actual metres, others are considered *muhmal* (not in use). The first circle has

Current classical Arabic metres and their most common variations

ṭawīl-1:	u — u̲ / u — — — / u — u̲ / u — u — / / u — u / u — — — / u — u̲ / u — — —
ṭawīl-2:	u — u̲ / u — — — / u — u̲ / u — u — / / u — u̲ / u — — — / u — u̲ / u — u —
ṭawīl-3:	u — u̲ / u — — — / u — u̲ / u — u — / / u — u̲ / u — — — / u — u / u — —
madīd-1:	u̲ u — / — u̲ u — / u̲ u — — / / u̲ u — / — u̲ u — / — u — —
madīd-3:	u̲ u — / — u̲ u — / u u — / / u̲ u — / — — u — / — u —
madīd-5:	u̲ u — / u̲ — u — / u u — / / u̲ u — / u̲ — u — / u u —
madīd-6:	u̲ u — / u̲ — u — / u u — / / u̲ u — / u̲ — u — / — —
basīṭ-1:	u̲ — u — / u̲ u — / — — u — / u u — / / u̲ — u — / u̲ u — / — — u — / u u —
basīṭ-2:	u̲ — u — / u̲ u — / — — u — / u u — / / u̲ — u — / u̲ u — / — — u — / — —
basīṭ-6:	u̲ — u — / u̲ u — / u — — / / u̲ — u — / u̲ u — / u — —
wāfir-1:	u — u̲u̲ — / u — u̲u̲ — / u — — / / u — u̲u̲ — / u — u̲u̲ — / u — —
wāfir-2:	u — u̲u̲ — / u — u̲u̲ — / / u — u̲u̲ — / u — u u —
wāfir-3:	u — u̲u̲ — / u — u̲u̲ — / / u — u̲u̲ — / u — — —
kāmil-1:	u̲u̲ — u — / u̲u̲ — u — / u̲u̲ — u — / / u̲u̲ — u — / u̲u̲ — u — / u̲u̲ — u —
kāmil-2:	u̲u̲ — u — / u̲u̲ — u — / u̲u̲ — u — / / u̲u̲ — u — / u̲u̲ — u — / u̲u̲ — —
kāmil-3:	u̲u̲ — u — / u̲u̲ — u — / u̲u̲ — u — / / u̲u̲ — u — / u̲u̲ — u — / — —
kāmil-4:	u̲u̲ — u — / u̲u̲ — u — / u̲u̲ — / / u̲u̲ — u — / u̲u̲ — u — / u u —
kāmil-5:	u̲u̲ — u — / u̲u̲ — u — / u u — / / u̲u̲ — u — / u̲u̲ — u — / — —
kāmil-6:	u̲u̲ — u — / u̲u̲ — u — / / u̲u̲ — u — / u̲u̲ — u — / —
kāmil-8:	u̲u̲ — u — / u̲u̲ — u — / / u̲u̲ — u — / u̲u̲ — u —
hazaj-1:	u — — u̲ / u — — u̲ / / u — — u̲ / u — — —
rajaz-1:	u̲ u̲ u — / u̲ u̲ u — / u̲ u̲ u — / / u̲ u̲ u — / u̲ u̲ u — / u̲ u̲ u —
rajaz-2:	u̲ u̲ u — / u̲ u̲ u — / u̲ u̲ u — / / u̲ u̲ u — / u̲ u̲ u — / — — —
rajaz-3:	u̲ u̲ u — / u̲ u̲ u — / / u̲ u̲ u — / u̲ u̲ u —
rajaz-4:	u̲ u̲ u — / u̲ u̲ u — / u̲ u̲ u —
rajaz-5:	u̲ u̲ u — / u̲ u̲ u —
ramal-2:	u̲ u — — / u̲ u — — / u̲ u — / / u̲ u — — / u̲ u — — / u̲ u =
ramal-3:	u̲ u — — / u̲ u — — / u̲ u — / / u̲ u — — / u̲ u — — / u̲ u —
ramal-5:	u̲ u — — / u̲ u — — / / u̲ u — — / u̲ u — —
sarī'-1:	u̲ u̲ u — / — u̲ u — / — u — / / u̲ u̲ u — / — u̲ u — / — u =
sarī'-2:	u̲ u̲ u — / —̬ u̲ u — / — u — / / u̲ u̲ u — / — u̲ u — / — u —
sarī'-3:	u̲ u̲ u — / — u̲ u — / — u — / / u̲ u̲ u — / — u̲ u — / — —
sarī'-7:	u̲ u̲ u — / u̲ u̲ u — / u̲ — —
munsariḥ:	u̲ u̲ u — / — u̲ — / u — u u — / / u̲ u̲ u — / — u̲ — / u — u u —
khafīf-1:	u̲ u — — / u̲ — u — / u̲ u — — / / u̲ u — — / u̲ — u — / u̲ u — —
	[sometimes in either or in both hemistichs: u̲ u — — / u̲ — u — / — — —]
khafīf-4:	u̲ u — — / u̲ — u — / / u̲ u — — / u̲ — u —
muqtaḍab:	— u — / u — u u — / / — u — / u — u u —
mujtathth:	u̲ — u — / u̲ u — — / / u̲ — u — / u̲ u — —
	[sometimes in either or in both hemistichs: u̲ — u — / — — —]
mutaqārib-1:	u — u̲ / u — u̲ / u — — / u — (u̲) / / u — u̲ / u — u̲ / u — — / u — —
mutaqārib-2:	u — u̲ / u — u̲ / u — — / u — (u̲) / / u — u̲ / u — u̲ / u — — / u =
mutaqārib-3:	u — u̲ / u — u̲ / u — — / u — (u̲) / / u — u̲ / u — u̲ / u — — / u —
mutadārik:	u̲u̲ — / u̲u̲ — / u̲u̲ — / u̲u̲ — / / u̲u̲ — / u̲u̲ — / u̲u̲ — / u̲u̲ —

Key:

u short syllable	u̲u̲ either one long or two short syllables
— long syllable	(u̲) either one syllable or no syllable at all
u̲ either long or short syllable	/ foot division
= overlong syllable	/ / hemistich division.

Notes:

1. Traditionally the division between the first and second feet in *madīd* comes after the fourth syllable instead of after the third syllable as given above; in *munsariḥ* and *muqtaḍab* all feet have four syllables in traditional scansion.
2. Sequences of three short syllables do not normally occur in *shi'r*, but may occur in *rajaz* (*rajaz*-4, *rajaz*-5 and *sarī'*-7 metres). The short syllables of the variations of a foot such as u̲ u̲ u — in other metre types than these (e.g. *munsariḥ*, *sarī'*-2, *sarī'*-3) do therefore normally not apply simultaneously.
3. Both *rajaz*-4 and *sarī'*-7 are sometimes referred to as *manhūk al-rajaz*.
4. *Rajaz*-5 is sometimes referred to as *manhūk al-rajaz*.
5. *Basīṭ*-6 is also called *al-mukhalla'* or *-mukhalla' al-basīṭ*.
6. *Mutadārik* (also called *mutadārak*) has several other names. The variant given above is especially known as *khabab*.

the ideal form of the *ṭawīl*-metre:

[∪ —] — / [∪ —] — — / [∪ —] — / [∪ —] — —
1 2 3 4 5 6 7 8 9 10

The permutation that emerges as one starts from element no. 4 is the theoretical formula of the *basīṭ* metre:

— — [∪ —] / — [∪ —] / — — [∪ —] / — [∪ —]
4 5 6 7 8 9 10 1 2 3

It is theoretical because the end of the first hemistich (elements 2 and 3) is always ∪ ∪ — in practice, never — ∪ —. Arabic theory copes with this by introducing the concepts of *ziḥāf* and *ʿilla*, which, like transformational rules in generative grammar, recast the ideal metre into all practical surface structure variants. *ʿIlla* ('illness') is introduced for dealing with the shorter metre types (e.g. those of sixteen syllables per line) considered as pruned forms of the 'healthy' ideal metre. *Ziḥāf* ('dragging gait?') is used for explaining variation within any one of the sixty-three types.

Departures from the strict Khalīlian system are found in *ʿArūḍ al-waraqa* by **al-Jawharī** (d. *c*.393/1003) and in *Minhāj al-bulaghā'* by **Ḥāzim al-Qarṭājannī** (d. 684/1285).

Role of stress

Paradoxically, within what appears to be a quantitative system, the total quantity per line in most metres is not constant. A solution for this paradox has been advanced by Gotthold Weil. He postulated that metrical stress (ictus) neutralizes any quantitative variation wherever it occurs. In his theory the line is divided up into quantity-sensitive elements marked by stress contrasting with unstressed elements where quantity does not matter.

By contrast, W. Stoetzer has argued that a purely quantitative analysis without Weil's stress postulate is possible on the basis of the quantitative equivalence of *sabab* (one long syllable) and *watid* (short + long syllable). Such a way of calculating (in which the single short syllable has zero quantity) is in line with al-Khalīl's premises in which the independent short syllable is no scansion element. The role of stress in Andalusian *muwashshaḥ*s and *zajal*s is in debate. Authors such as **Ibn Bassām** (d. 543/1147) and **Ibn Sanā' al-Mulk** (d. 608/1211) explicitly tell us that the Andalusians used two different systems in their strophic poetry, one the traditional prosody, the other one a system outside this tradition, not made for ordinary recitation but for singing. This second system could well be stress-based.

Further reading

Bencheikh, J.-E., *Poétique arabe*, Paris (1975), rpt (1989).

Heinrichs, W., 'Poetik, Rhetorik, Literaturkritik, Metrik und Reimlehre', in *GAP*, vol. 2, 177–207.

Stoetzer, W., *Theory and Practice in Arabic Metrics*, Leiden (1989).

Weil, G., *EI*², art. ''Arūḍ'.

Wright, W., *A Grammar of the Arabic Language*, 3rd edn, Cambridge (1896–98, and reprints), vol. 2, 350–90.

Ya'qūb, Amīl Badī', *al-Muʿjam al-mufaṣṣal fī ʿilm al-ʿaruḍ wa-al-qāfiya wa-funūn al-shiʿr*, Beirut (1991).

W. STOETZER

proverbs

The meaning of the Arabic *mathal* (pl. *amthāl*), usually translated 'proverb', includes much more than the English term. Derived from a common Semitic root implying 'to compare, resemble, represent', it signifies, besides proverbs, similes, metaphors and parables. Collections of *mathal*s, beginning with the *Kitāb al-Amthāl* of Abū ʿUbayd (d. 224/838), contain all these genres. Many *mathal*s are commented by etiologic anecdotes; obsolete words and the general meaning are explicated when the editor considers it necessary.

As in ancient Near Eastern literatures and the Torah, *mathal*s were widely used in ancient and classical Arabic poetry and in ***adab*** works, beginning with those of **al-Jāḥiẓ** (d. 255/868–9), and folk literature (see **folklore**) throughout the centuries, as in everyday life until today. The *Maqāmāt* of **al-Ḥarīrī** (d. 516/1122) abound with proverbs, used here in word-, rhyme- and meaning-plays. *Adab* encyclopedias like the *ab ʿIqd al-farīd* of **Ibn ʿAbd Rabbih** (d. 328/940) contain a proverb chapter, because to know and use a certain amount of proverbs was part of the ideal of the civilized and educated ***adīb***. That short *mathal*s were applied as inscriptions on the signet-rings widespread in court circles in **Baghdad** in the third/ninth century, and understood probably either apotropaically or as maxims by those who wore them or received them as a gift, is testified to in the *Kitāb al-Muwashshā* of **al-Washshā'**.

The popularity of *mathal*s is explained by **al-Maydānī** (d. 518/1124), the collector of the most voluminous compilation of *mathal*s, by their concise formulation, their apt expression, their beautiful comparisons and their excellent allusions. He characterizes them as the summit of rhetoric; their meaning is regarded as common sense/wisdom (***ḥikma***). Generally they provide an indirect way of communication by allusion to historically or socio-culturally well-known facts or persons, to social experiences and moral or cultural standards. They do this sometimes in a humorous way, e.g. *al-dīk al-faṣīḥ min al-bayḍa yaṣīḥ*, 'The eloquent cock yells through the egg-shell'. The widespread use of *mathal*s was and is a kind of inner cultural agreement revealing socio-religious, anthropological and cultural conceptions, some conditioned by special social and historical circumstances, which – like the application of the proverb – had to be explained later, sometimes differently by different compilators. Others are of a more general human validity.

There are different social and historical layers of Arabic proverbs. The oldest, are of **bedouin** origin, revealing tribal ethics preserved in the early and even later patriarchic court or urban society, e.g. *Man ashbaha abāhu fa-mā ẓalama*, 'Who resembles his father cannot do wrong', or *unṣur akhāka ẓāliman aw maẓlūman*, 'Help your brother, whether he is right or wrong'. The *Ayyām al-'Arab* (**Battle Days**), the **Koran** and ***ḥadīth*** are also sources of proverbs inspired by ancient bedouin or Arab wisdom and adapted to new social circumstances. So the tribal 'brother' becomes the brother in belief: *al-Muslim mir'ātu akhīhi*, 'The Muslim is the mirror of his brother', i.e. must be sincere and frank towards his fellow in belief. A proverb like *man ṣaddaqa 'llāha najā*, 'Who believes in God, will be saved', attributed to **Muḥammad** as transmitted by Abū Hurayra, gives expression of the new faith.

There are *amthāl*, probably deriving from different socio-cultural layers, that contradict each other, thus revealing mental ambivalences, for example the Koranic *ṣabrun jamīlun*, 'Comely patience/forbearance (is my way)', or *al-ṣabru miftāḥ al-faraj*, 'Patience is the key to joy', and *idhā kunta sindānan fa-'ṣbir wa-idhā kunta miṭraqatan fa-awji'*, 'If you are an anvil, wait; if you are a hammer, hurt!' Well-known oriental wisdom, also found in the Old Testament, is ascribed to famous Muslim personalities: *man ḥaffara maghawwātan waqa'a fīhā*, 'Hoist with one's own petard' (literally, 'he who digs a pit will fall into it') is ascribed to the caliph 'Umar with an etiologic anecdote. Many *amthāl* are attributed to **'Alī ibn Abī Ṭālib**, the cousin and son-in-law of Muḥammad and 'father' of the **Shī'īs**. There are *amthāl* defining historical or intercultural topics connected with certain historical or legendary personalities, e.g. *ṣaḥīfat al-Mutalammis*. 'Letter of Uriah', or *mawā'īdu 'Urqūbin*, 'Empty promises' (a certain 'Urqūb in the ***jāhiliyya*** is known as charlatan), or *jazā' Sinimmār*, 'bad reward for a good act' (a Byzantine architect named Sinimmār is said to have built the castle of al-Khawarnaq near **Kufa** for a **Lakhmid** king, who killed him afterwards to prevent him from building a similar castle for another person). A large number of *amthāl* are comparisons built with an elative such as *arwā min ḍabbin/ḥayyatin*, 'thirstier than the lizard/serpent' (which in fact are seldom thirsty), *a'dal min al-mīzān*, 'More just than the scale'.

Already Abū 'Ubayd gives as the source of many *mathal*s *al-'āmma* or *al-nās*, 'the common people', i.e. he collected *amthāl* from people's conversation during his lifetime. While his collection contains about 1,200 *mathal*s arranged topically, al-Maydānī collected about 7,000, one-fifth of the kind *af'alu min*, elative comparisons, and about 1,500 characterized as *amthāl muwallada*, 'new/post-classical proverbs'. He arranged them alphabetically but without strict consistency, the *af'alu min* proverbs at the end of each chapter. Many proverbs are characterized by their terseness, e.g. *al-mar' bi-aṣgharayhi*, 'Man exists by his two smallest things' (i.e. his heart and his tongue), *al-ḥarbu may'amatun*, 'War makes widows', *ummu l-kādhibi bikrun*, 'The mother of the liar is a virgin' (when somebody utters something impossible). Word games with verbal and nominal sentences built on a certain number of syllables and characterized by a certain kind of stress and rhymed patterns are frequent, e.g. *man jāla nāla*, 'Who roams, achieves', *al-tajallud lā al-taballud*, 'Show patience, not stupidity'. So, if Arabic *mathal*s belong to the 'simple forms' (as, according to A. Jolles, proverbs do), most of them are at least highly refined and sophisticated in their combination of structure and meaning.

Since the seventh/thirteenth century we find *mathal* collections in Arabic dialects, e.g. the

Tunisian Abū Yaḥyā al-Zajjālī's (d. 694/1294) *Amthāl al-'awwām fī al-Andalus*. European interest in Arabic proverbs began in the tenth/sixteenth century. They are found in readers, grammars and exercise-books for European students of Arabic. The German Arabist G.W. Freytag edited the collection of al-Maydānī with a Latin translation between 1838 and 1843. Since the early nineteenth century travelling Arabists collected proverbs of different regions in different dialects and published them in the original and in translation. Arab intellectuals and researchers, although usually preferring the literary language, became interested in collecting, publishing and analysing dialect proverbs, perhaps because as gnomic/wisdom literature they are more respected as part of the authochthonous socio-cultural heritage than popular narratives intended for people's entertainment.

Further reading

Barakat, R.A., *A Contextual Study of Arabic Proverbs*, Helsinki (1980).

Kilānī, T. and 'Ashūr, N., *A Dictionary of Proverbs: English–Arabic*, Beirut (1991).

Littmann, E., *Morgenlandische Spruchweisheit*, Leipzig (1937).

Mahgoub, F.M., *A Linguistic Study of Cairene Proverbs*, The Hague (1968).

Sellheim, R., *Die klassischen arabischen Sprichwörtersammlungen insbesondere die des Abū 'Ubaid*, The Hague (1954).

——, *EI*², *'Mathal'*.

Sīnī, M.I., 'Abd al-'Azīz, N.M. and Sulaymān, M.A., *Mu'jam al-amthāl al-'Arabiyya*, Beirut (1992).

Westermarck, E., *Wit and Wisdom in Morocco*, London (1930).

Many collections and studies of proverbs of various regions have been published, especially in recent years; the following is only a sample.

Abdelkafi, M., *One Hundred Arabic Proverbs from Libya*, London (1968).

Attar, B., *Les Proverbes marocaines*, Casablanca (1992).

Ben Cheneb, M., *Proverbes populares du Maghreb*, new edition, A., Eddaikra, N. Nazih and A. Touderti (eds), Paris (1989–).

Burckhardt, J.L., *Arabic Proverbs, or, The Manners and Customs of the Modern Egyptians*, 3rd edn, London (1972).

Duvollet, R., *Proverbes et dictons arabes, Algérie, Tunisie, Maroc, Sahara*, Vesoul, France (1980).

Feghali, M.T., *Proverbes et dictons syro-libanais*, Paris (1938).

Furayha, Anis, *A Dictionary of Modern Lebanese Proverbs*, Beirut (1974).

Goitein, S.D., *Jemenica: Sprichworter und Redensarten aus Zentral-Jemen*, Leiden (1970).

Jayakar, A.S.G., *Omani Proverbs*, Cambridge (1987).

Kayyāl, Munīr, *Mu'jam durar al-kalām fī amthāl ahl al-Shām*, Beirut (1993).

Lunde, Paul, and Wintle, Justin, *A Dictionary of Arabic and Islamic Proverbs*, London (1984).

Shawwa, M.M., *Mawsū'at al-amthāl al-sha'biyya al-Filasṭīnīyya*, Cairo (1996–).

Sudays, Muḥammad ibn Sulaymān, *Mukhtārāt min al-amthāl al-Najdiyya al-ḥadītha*, Beirut (1993).

Taymūr, Aḥmad, *Egyptian Proverbs and Popular Sayings*, S. Elkhadem (trans.), Fredericton, N.B. (1987).

Yetiv, I., *1001 Proverbs from Tunisia*, Washington, DC. (1987).

W. WALTHER

puns *see* rhetorical figures: *tajnīs, tawriya*

puzzle *see* mu'ammā

Q

al-Qabbānī, Aḥmad Abū Khalīl (1841–1902)

Syrian playwright and actor. Born and died in **Damascus**. Either the Governor Ṣubḥī Pasha (1872–3) or Midḥat Pasha (1878–9), having seen one of his plays, is said to have encouraged him to perform in public; the latter asked Iskandar Faraḥ, a Customs clerk, to form a troupe with him. Religious *shaykhs* complained that his plays were heretical, prompting Sultan ʿAbd al-Ḥamīd to close his theatre in 1884. He went to **Egypt**, at the invitation of the Khedive and performed regularly in Alexandria and **Cairo**. He was the creator of Arab operetta and the father of melodrama. He wrote or adapted about a hundred pieces, including musicals, comedies and one-act farces. Many of the plays he performed were written by other Arab writers, or adapted from European classics, including works by Corneille, Racine, Voltaire and Victor Hugo. He helped to create the tradition of using the Arab folk and historical heritage as a source of dramatical inspiration, making use of the stories of **Hārūn al-Rashīd** in the ***Alf layla wa-layla*** and other such tales. He himself designed the costumes, sang, danced, and set the words of the plays to verse and music for his troupe. He returned with his troupe to Damascus, and also toured the Egyptian provinces; in 1892 they played at the Chicago Fair. It was rumoured that his rivals incited the mob to set fire to his new theatre in Cairo in 1900, and thus his troupe was forced to disperse.

Further reading

Badawi, M.M., *Early Arabic Drama*, Cambridge (1988), 56–64.

Karachouli, Regina, 'Abū Ḥalīl al-Qabbānī (1883–1902) – Damaszener Theatergründer und Prinzipal', *WI* 32 (1992), 83–98.

al-Khozai, M.A. *The Development of Early Arabic Drama 1847–1900*, London (1984), 80–121.

P.C. SADGROVE

Qabbānī, Nizār (1923–)

Syrian poet born in **Damascus** to a rich family, Nizār Qabbānī graduated from university with a law degree in 1945 and joined the Syrian foreign service as a diplomat, stationed first in **Egypt**, then successively in Turkey, the United Kingdom, Lebanon, **Spain** and China. In 1966 he resigned his post and took up residence in Beirut, where he was active in literary journalism and later established his own publishing house. The Lebanese civil war forced him to leave the country and live in Switzerland, but he continued to be active in Arab literary journalism and to publish his poetry.

Since his earliest poems, Qabbānī has written on love and women, and his powerfully imaginative language and elegant style established an early reputation in the 1940s and 1950s. His poems in *Qālat lī al-samrā'* (1944) and *Anti lī* (1950) are exquisite expressions of sensual desire, describing the beauty of the female with youthful vigour full of astonishing verbal imagery. His later poems, as in the collections *Qaṣā'id* (1956), *Ḥabībatī* (1961), *al-Rasm bi-l-kalimāt* (1966) and *Kitāb al-ḥubb* (1970), are more refined and more aware of the complex love relations between men and women, sometimes expressing in the woman's voice her revolt against man's insensitivity. The later love-poems of Qabbānī's mature years present love as an intimate relationship of equals, as in his *Ashʿār khārija ʿalā al-qānūn* (1972), *al-Ḥubb lā yufīq ʿalā al-ḍaw' al-aḥmar* (1983) and *Hākadhā aktub tārīkh al-nisā'* (1986) – these poems never losing their emotional intensity and fervour or their richly evocative images.

Some of Qabbānī's early poems dealt with social and political issues, but it was the 1967 Arab defeat by Israel that launched him on a series of poems in **free verse**, severely satirizing Arab regimes and their submissive peoples. The best-known of these poems is his 'Hawāmish 'alā daftar al-naksa'. The destruction and death occasioned by the Lebanese civil war brought further angry poems, as in his *Ilā Bayrūt al-unthā ma'a ḥubbī* (1976) and *Jumhūriyyat Junūnistān: Lubnān sābiqan* (1987). The *intifāḍa* (uprising) of the Palestinians against Israeli occupation inspired him to write several more political poems, including his *Thulāthiyyat aṭfāl al-ḥijāra* (1988). His latest poetry openly castigates the repression of Arab regimes and criticizes their breach of the human and civil rights of their people, as in his *Qaṣā'id maghḍūb 'alayhā* (1986) and *al-Sīra al-dhātiyya li-sayyāf 'Arabī* (1987). Qabbānī is arguably the most popular modern Arabic poet today.

Text editions

Asfour, J.M., *When the Words Burn: An Anthology of Modern Arabic Poetry 1945–1987*, Dunvegan, ON (1988), 93–103.
Boullata, I.J., *Modern Arab Poets 1950–1975*, Washington, DC (1976), 53–60.
Jayyusi, S.K., *Modern Arabic Poetry: An Anthology*, New York (1987), 368–79.
Khouri, M.A. and Algar, H., *An Anthology of Modern Arabic Poetry*, Berkeley (1974), 161–95.
al-Udhari, A., *Modern Poetry of the Arab World*, Harmondsworth (1986), 97–104.

Further reading

Badawi, M.M., *A Critical Introduction to Modern Arabic Poetry*, Cambridge (1975), 221–2.
Boullata, I.J., 'Qabbani, Nizar', in L.S. Klein (ed.), *Encyclopedia of World Literature in the 20th Century*, New York (1981–4), vol. 3, 613.

I.J. BOULLATA

al-Qāḍī 'Abd al-Jabbār (d. 415/1025)

al-Qāḍī 'Abd al-Jabbār ibn Aḥmad al-Asadābādī was a prominent later representative of the **Mu'tazilī** school of theological thought who served as judge (*qāḍī*) in **Rayy** during the period of **Būyid** rule. The discovery in **Yemen** and subsequent publication of his multi-volume theological work, *Kitāb al-mughnī*, has brought him into special prominence among scholars of recent decades, since so much has been gleaned from this work concerning the Mu'tazilī movement. Not extant is his major work on jurisprudence, *Kitāb al-'umad*, which was an important foundation for subsequent jurisprudential writing both among Mu'tazilīs and among orthodox Sunnis.

Text editions

al-Mughnī fī abwāb al-tawḥīd wa-al-'adl (various vols, various eds), Cairo (1960s+).
Penseurs musulmans et religions iraniennes: 'Abd al-Jabbār et ses devanciers (extracts from *al-Mughnī*), G. Monnet (trans.), Paris (1974).

Further reading

Bernand, M., *Le Problème de la connaissance d'après le mugnī du cadi 'Abd al-Ğabbar*, Algiers (1984).
Hourani, G., *Islamic Rationalism: The Ethics of 'Abd al-Jabbār*, Oxford (1971).
Peters, J.R., *God's Created Speech: A Study in the Speculative Theology of the Mu'tazili Qadî l-Qudât...*, Leiden (1976).

B. WEISS

See also: Mu'tazilīs

al-Qāḍī 'Alī ibn al-'Azīz al-Jurjānī *see* al-Jurjānī

al-Qāḍī al-Fāḍil (529–96/1135–1200)

'Abd al-Raḥīm ibn 'Alī al-Qāḍī al-Fāḍil was a celebrated statesman, epistolographer and poet. The son of a judge in Ascalon, he apprenticed in the chanceries of **Fāṭimid** Alexandria and **Cairo**, becoming head of chancery to Saladin in 566/1171. Although never officially named vizier, he remained Saladin's most important adviser for the rest of his career; after the latter's death in **Damascus**, he retired to Cairo, where he died. Although he wrote much poetry, and kept an official diary (preserved only in extracts), his literary fame rests on his vast correspondence, both official and private, which became the standard for stylistic elegance in prose for generations to come.

Text editions

Dīwān, A.A. Badawī and I. al-Ibyārī (eds), 2 vols, Cairo (1961).
Of numerous collections of his letters extant in manuscript, two have been published:
Rasā'il 'an al-ḥarb wa-al-salām, min tarassul al-Qāḍī al-Fāḍil, M. Naghash (ed.), 2nd edn, Cairo (1984).

Ibn ʿAbd al-Ẓāhir, *al-Durr al-naẓīm min tarassul ʿAbd al-Raḥīm*, A. Badawī (ed.), Cairo (1959).

Further reading

Helbig, A.H., *Al-Qāḍī al-Fāḍil, der Wezir Saladins*, Leipzig (1908).

E.K. ROWSON

al-Qāḍī al-Nuʿmān (d. 363/974)

Al-Qāḍī al-Nuʿmān ibn Muḥammad al-Maghribī was a famed **Ismāʿīlī** judge, theologian and apologist. His early life is largely unknown, but he was early an adherent of Shīʿism, entering the service of the **Fāṭimid** caliphs of North Africa and becoming the confidant and adviser of al-Manṣūr and al-Muʿizz at the new Fāṭimid capital in **Tunisia** of al-Manṣūriyya. His theologico-legal works, such as the *Daʿāʾm al-Islām*, are powerfully argued attempts to systematize Ismāʿīlī law, and to make this law and faith into an instrument of politics for the vigorous and expanding Fāṭimid state. He also engaged in public lecture sessions, *majālis*, and courses of instruction, *durūs*, endeavouring to make Ismāʿīlism and its institutions known to wider audiences in the **Maghrib**.

Text editions

Daʿāʾim al-Islām, Cairo (1951) (several rpts).
Kitāb Iftitāḥ al-daʿwā, Farhat Dachraoui (ed.), Tunis (1975) (rpt 1986); W. al-Qāḍī (ed.), Beirut (1975).
al-Majālis wa-al-musāyarāt, al-Ḥabīb al-Faqqī *et al.* (eds), Tunis (1978).

Further reading

Daftary, Farhad, *The Ismāʿīlīs: Their History and Doctrines*, Cambridge (1990), 249–53.
EI[2] art. 'al-Nuʿmān b. Abī ʿAbd Allāh Muḥammad' (F. Dachraoui).
Fyzee, A.A.A., 'Qadi al-Nuʿmān, the Fatimid jurist and author', *JRAS* (1934), 1–32.
Poonawala, Ismail K., 'Al-Qāḍī al Nuʿmān and Isma'ili Jurisprudence', in *Medieval Isma'ili History and Thought*, F. Daftary (ed.), Cambridge (1996), 117–43.

C.E. BOSWORTH

See also: Ismāʿīlīs

al-Qādirī, Muḥammad ibn al-Ṭayyib (1124–87/1712–73)

Noted Moroccan biographer and historian of the ʿAlawī dynasty. He was born into a noble family of Fez, claiming descent from the Prophet through the legendary Muslim saint **ʿAbd al-Qādir al-Jīlānī** (hence his *nisba*). The family had produced a number of historians, including al-Qādirī's grandfather ʿAbd al-Salām, the famous genealogist of the Sharifian families of Morocco. Not only did al-Qādirī inherit his grandfather's concern for the Maghribi Sharifian ancestry (he wrote a few works on this subject), he also completed a dictionary of the Moroccan celebrities of the eleventh/seventeenth century which was only contemplated by his grandfather. It is to this dictionary, *Nashr al-mathānī*, that al-Qādirī largely owes his fame.

The *Nashr*, and its earlier version entitled *Iltiqāṭ al-durar*, can be viewed as continuations of the earlier works of this kind, e.g. that of **Ibn al-Qāḍī**. Both *Nashr* and *Iltiqāṭ* are hybrids, consisting of biographical notices arranged by year of death and of the accounts of the most notable events of the same year. While the former part comprises biographies of the famous Moroccans of the eleventh/seventeenth and twelfth/eighteenth centuries, the chronicle portion combines dynastic and political history with the information on natural phenomena, epidemics and social life in ʿAlawī Morocco. Each part is equally valuable for the study of the first century of ʿAlawī rule in Morocco which, unlike subsequent centuries, produced only a handful of chroniclers. Both of al-Qādirī's works were extensively used by the Maghribi historians who lived in thirteenth / nineteenth–fourteenth / twentieth centuries, especially al-Zayyānī, al-Ḥawwāṭ, Akansūs, Aḥmad Ibn al-Ḥājj, al-Nāṣirī, Ibn Zaydān, and **al-Kattānī**.

Text editions

Iltiqāṭ al-durar, Hāshim al-ʿAlawī al-Fāsī (ed.), Beirut (1983).
Muḥammad al-Qādirī's Nashr al-mathānī: The Chronicles, N. Cigar (ed.), Oxford (1981).

Further reading

al-Kattānī, *Salwat al-anfās*, Fez (1316/1898), vol. 2, 351–2.
Lévi-Provençal, E., *Les Historiens des chorfa*, Paris (1922), 275–80, 319–26.

A. KNYSH

qāfiya see prosody

al-Qāhira see Cairo

Qaḥṭān see tribes

al-Qaʿīd, [Muḥammad] Yūsuf (1944–)

Contemporary Egyptian novelist and short-story writer. Born in the Delta region of a peasant background, al-Qaʿīd received his education entirely in **Egypt**, and worked as a teacher before moving into journalism; he also served in the Egyptian armed forces during the wars of 1967 and 1973.

His first novel, *al-Ḥidād* (1969), took as its main theme the conflict between the requirements of official justice and traditional patterns of family retribution. The novel was marked by a lively use of Egyptian colloquial, and by the author's technique of portraying events through the eyes of the participants themselves. The theme of family honour was continued in *Akhbār ʿizbat al-Manīsī* (1971), in which al-Qaʿīd also began to experiment more radically with the novelistic technique, employing 'flashback' techniques and using a 'supernarrator' to introduce and conclude the action – an experiment continued in *al-Bayāt al-shatawī* (1974), which tells of the events following the visit to an Egyptian village by a group of oil engineers.

Al-Qaʿīd's heightened social consciousness is still more evident in *Yaḥduth fī Miṣr al-āna* (1977), a novel set against the background of President Nixon's visit to Egypt in 1974, which was published at the author's own expense after being rejected by a number of Egyptian publishing houses. Similar difficulties attended the publication of *al-Ḥarb fī barr Miṣr*, written in 1975 but not published until 1978 in Beirut. The plot of this novel, which is set at the time of the 1973 War, revolves around an impersonation devised by a village headman to avoid his son's being drafted into the army; the young man is killed in action and the deception discovered, but the ensuing inquiry is stopped on orders from a Cairo official.

Al-Qaʿīd's most ambitious work is his trilogy *Shakāwā al-Miṣrī al-faṣīḥ* (1981–5), which revolves around a journey by an impoverished Cairene family from their home in the City of the Dead to the centre of **Cairo**, where they attempt to put themselves up for sale; there is a disturbance, arrests are made and an investigation follows; the novel describes the background to these events and their aftermath, ending with President Sadat's return to Egypt a year later from his visit to Jerusalem. These events provide a peg on which to hang a scathing critique of contemporary Egyptian society, and of Sadat's policies in both the domestic and the foreign spheres; while, on another level, the novel is an exploration of the creative process, which builds on al-Qaʿīd's earlier experiments with the novelistic technique. As such, it represents the culmination of a combination of social criticism and literary experimentation which al-Qaʿīd has made distinctively his own.

Text editions

News from the Meneisi Farm, M.-T.F. Abdel-Messih (trans.), Cairo (1987).

War in the Land of Egypt, L. Kenny, O. Kenny and C. Tingley (trans.), London (1986).

Further reading

Starkey, P.G., 'From the City of the Dead to Liberation Square', *JAL* 25 (1993), 62–74.

P. STARKEY

al-Qalamāwī, Suhayr (1911–)

Egyptian scholar, critic and short-story writer. Al-Qalamāwī was among the first female university graduates and Master's Degree holders in **Egypt**. She completed her studies in Arabic Literature at the Sorbonne. Joining the Department of Arabic in Cairo University's Faculty of Arts, she later served as its chairperson. In 1935, al-Qalamāwī had published the first volume of short stories by a woman to appear in Egypt, *Aḥādīth jaddatī*. It is structured as a series of conversations between the narrator and her grandmother, reminiscences of the past drawn forcefully into the present by the narrator's own concerns. Al-Qalamāwī went on to publish another collection, *al-Shayāṭīn talhū* (1964); more than eighty of her short stories have appeared in the periodical press, regularly in the journal *al-Hilāl* for a while. She has also published many studies on literary topics, including the landmark ***Alf layla wa-layla*** (1943). An early member of the Egyptian Feminist Union youth group al-Shaqīqāt, she later wrote on gender issues and was at one point president of the Pan-Arab Women's League. Active in support of literary endeavour in Egypt, she has served on high-level government committees on the arts and as director of the Egyptian General Organisation for Information, Publication, Distribution and

Printing. She is now Emeritus Professor of Arabic Literature at Cairo University.

Further reading

'Al-Ānisa Suhayr al-Qalamāwī tanālu darajat majīstīr fī al-Jāmi'a al-Miṣriyya', *al-Miṣriyya* 1(4) (April 1937).

'Introduction,' in Marilyn Booth (ed. and trans.), *My Grandmother's Cactus: Stories by Egyptian Women*, London (1991).

al-Shārūnī, Yūsuf (ed.), *al-Layla al-thāniya ba'da al-alf: Mukhtārāt min al-qiṣṣa al-nisā'iyya fī Miṣr*, Cairo (1975).

M. BOOTH

al-Qālī, Abū 'Alī Ismā'īl ibn al-Qāsim (288–356/901–67)

Philologist active in **Baghdad** and Córdoba. He was born in Malazgird (Manzikert). In the company of people from Erzurum/Qālīqalā (hence his name al-Qālī) he moved to Baghdad in 303/915–16, where he studied with **Ibn Durayd**, Abū Bakr **al-Anbārī** and others. In 328/939 he left for **Spain** on the invitation of the **Umayyad** prince (later caliph) al-Ḥakam, a great patron of the arts and scholarship. Al-Qālī was a key figure in the transmission of the eastern grammatical tradition to the west. He wrote several books on lexicography, **grammar** and poetry, most of which are lost. Only a small part is preserved of his large dictionary entitled *al-Bāri'*, which shows a strong influence of *al-'Ayn* by **al-Khalīl ibn Aḥmad**. Extremely popular were his *Dictations (al-Amālī)* which he wrote down in Córdoba; **Ibn Khaldūn** mentions this work as one of the four 'pillars' of the science of literature. It deals with numerous questions of lexicography, grammar and pre- and early Islamic poetry, for which it is an important source.

Text edition

al-Amālī, 4 vols, Cairo (1926) (vol. 3 contains *Dhayl al-Amālī wa-al-Nawādir* by al-Qālī; vol. 4 is *al-Tanbīh 'alā awhām Abī 'Alī fī Amālīh* by Abū 'Ubayd al-Bakrī). A commentary on *al-Amālī* by the same al-Bakrī is called *Simṭ al-la'ālī*, 4 vols, Cairo (1936).

G.J.H. VAN GELDER

al-Qalqashandī (756–821/1355–1418)

Shihāb al-Dīn Aḥmad ibn 'Alī al-Qalqashandī was an Egyptian scholar, jurist and chancery official in the **Mamlūk** administration in **Cairo**, serving under a chief secretary to the sultan from the famous Faḍl Allāh family (see **Ibn Faḍl Allāh al-'Umarī**), whom he praised in a ***maqāma*** on secretaryship. He wrote commentaries on Shāfi'ī law and ***adab*** works, but his greatest literary achievements were in the fields of the secretarial art (*kitāba*) and its ancillaries. His monumental (fourteen volumes in the printed edition) *Ṣubḥ al-a'shā* follows on from Ibn Faḍl Allāh's *Masālik al-abṣār* and is an encyclopaedic and exhaustive compendium of both the theoretical knowledge (history, geography, *adab*, **grammar**) vital for the compleat secretary and also the practical skills of calligraphy, preparation of official correspondence, etc.; not least of the book's values is al-Qalqashandī's inclusion of the texts of diplomatic documents, addressed to Muslim and non-Muslim potentates alike, which have been extensively utilized by modern historians. Two other works of his had a similar practical aim, one dealing with early Arab genealogy and history and another with the constitutional theory of the caliphate and its history.

Text editions

Die Geographie und Verwalten von Aegypten (part on Egypt), F. Wüstenfeld (trans.), Göttingen (1879).

Les Institutions des Fâtimides en Égypte (extracts), M. Canard (ed.), Algiers (1957),

Ma'āthir al-ināfa fī ma'ālim al-khilāfa, 'A.A. Farrāj (ed.), Kuwait (1964).

Nihāyat al-arab fi ma'rifat ansāb al-'Arab, I. al-Abyārī (ed.), 2nd edn, Cairo (1980).

Subh al-a'šā fī kitâbat al-inšâ (part on Spain), L. Seco de Lucena (trans.), Valencia (1975).

Ṣubḥ al-a'shā fī kitābat al-inshā', Cairo (1913–18).

Further reading

Björkman, W., *Beiträge zur Geschichte der Staatskanzlei im islamischen Ägypten*, Hamburg (1928).

Bosworth, C.E., 'A *maqāma* on secretaryship: al-Qalqashandī's *al-Kawākib al-durriyya fī'l-Manāqib al-Badriyya*', *BSOAS* 27 (1964), 291–8.

*EI*², art. 'al-Ḳalḳashandī' (C.E. Bosworth).

C.E. BOSWORTH

See also: encyclopedias, medieval; secretaries

al-Qalyūbī, Aḥmad ibn Aḥmad (d. 1069/1659)

A luminary of the scholarly world of his day on account of the wide breadth of his knowledge.

He well exemplifies a later Islamic type, the polyhistor conversant with diverse facets of the Islamic high cultural tradition in its most developed form, such as jurisprudence, *belles-lettres*, geography and medicine. Among his best-known works is an encyclopaedic collection of information about unusual events and phenomena commonly entitled *Nawādir al-Qalyūbī*.

Text editions

The Book of Anecdotes, Marvels, Pleasantries, Rarities, and Useful and Precious Extracts, W.N. Lees and Mawlawi Kabir al-Din (eds), Calcutta (1856).

Le Fantastique et le quotidien, R.R. Khawam (trans.), Paris (1981).

Nawādir al-Qalyūbī, Cairo (1923).

B. WEISS

Qarāmiṭa *see* Carmathians

al-Qarawī *see* al-Khūrī, Rashīd Salīm

al-Qardāḥī, Sulaymān (?–1909)

Maronite actor and producer. Early in 1882 his company, including the famous singers the Egyptian Salāma Ḥijāzī and the Syrian Murād Rūmānū, was founded in Alexandria from the remnants of the earlier troupes of Salīm **al-Naqqāsh** and Yūsuf **al-Khayyāṭ**, in which he had been an actor. During the ʿUrābī revolt he left **Egypt** and did not return until 1883, when his troupe began to perform regularly (in Alexandria, **Cairo** and the Egyptian provinces) the plays of Mārūn **al-Naqqāsh** and Salīm al-Naqqāsh, Adīb **Isḥāq**, Salīm **al-Bustānī** and other Arab playwrights, as well as adaptations from Western authors such as Shakespeare, Corneille and Molière. He also formed one of the first troupes to tour abroad, going to **Syria** and to the International Exhibition in Paris. His popularity declined with the increasing success of Iskandar Faraḥ's troupe, which had been joined by Ḥijāzī, but his performances were a great success in Tunis, where he arrived in 1908. Uncontestably the father of Arab theatre in **Tunisia**, after his death the members of his troupe stayed to form a new troupe, allowing Tunisians for the first time to appear on the stage.

Further reading

Ben Halima, Hamadi, *Un Demi-siècle de théâtre arabe en Tunisie (1907–1957)*, Tunis (1974), 38–45.

Landau, J.M., *Studies in the Arab Theater and Cinema*, Philadelphia (1958), 68–9.

Najm, M.Y., *al-Masraḥiyya fī al-adab al-ʿArabī al-ḥadīth*, Beirut (1956), 107–14.

Sadgrove, P.C., *The Egyptian Theatre in the Nineteenth Century*, Reading (1996), 143–5, 155–60.

P.C. SADGROVE

al-Qarṭājannī, Ḥāzim *see* Ḥāzim al Qarṭājannī

qaṣīda (pl. *qaṣāʾid*)

Generic term denoting a polythematic poem with identical metre and rhyme (see **prosody**), usually beginning with amatory verses, the *nasīb*, and ending with the poet's praise of himself or his tribe (see ***fakhr***), sometimes in combination with satire (see ***hijāʾ***), or with a panegyric (see ***madīḥ***). It was the principal genre of pre-Islamic bedouin poetry, the main expression of tribal norms and values. (See **bedouin**; ***jāhiliyya***).

The *qaṣīda* was cultivated by Islamic poets throughout the Middle Ages, although with major changes in structure and function, and has been assimilated by other Islamic literatures as well. The term is derived from *qaṣada*, 'to aim at, to intend', but the original meaning of the designation is unknown. A plausible explanation would be that *qaṣīda* denotes a poem composed in '*qaṣīd*', i.e. in one of the long metres with two complete hemistichs, the employment of which demanded professional skill, in contrast to mere improvisation. In medieval Arabic sources the term is applied to any poem of a certain length; according to **Ibn Rashīq** a *qaṣīda* must exceed seven (or ten) verses (*al-ʿUmda*, Cairo, 1963, vol. 1, 188). In the Western tradition, which will be followed here, the application of the term has been limited to the polythematic form, as opposed to the ***qiṭʿa***, the monothematic poem.

Pre-Islamic period

The earliest specimens of the genre probably date back to the end of the fifth century CE and give the impression of a well-established tradition. They were composed and transmitted orally and present several characteristics of oral poetry (see **oral composition**), e.g. a high percentage of formulaic expressions, semantic repetition, additive style and independence of detail, which means that each section of the ode retains a certain degree of autonomy (cf. Zwettler, 1978). A *qaṣīda* varies in length from about 30 to 100 verses. It consists of short narrative and descriptive units, sometimes introduced as comparisons, depicting typical situations of tribal life, the bedouin's most precious possessions, camel and horse, and the landscape and animal world of the desert. Although the poet always speaks in the first person, he does not refer to his individual experience, except in the concluding section, where he may treat issues of personal concern. In the preceding parts of the ode he recreates the collective experience of tribal society, thus offering a model for identification; he is the 'bedouin hero' who encounters problems and provides solutions in accordance with the accepted values of the tribe (cf. Hamori, 1974, 3–30).

The *nasīb*, the only kind of love poetry preserved from the ***jāhiliyya***, always refers to a relationship of the past. In spring, the season of abundant pasture, neighbouring tribes camp together and affairs are conducted between their members. This was evidently approved of by bedouin society, since poets boast of it in their self-praise. However, when the tribes separate lovers must part, for individual relations are subordinated to the interest of the group. The poet conforms to tribal demands, but his emotions are still involved. This is the situation treated in the *nasīb* by several conventional motifs. The most favourite motif is the poet's stopping at the 'traces' (*aṭlāl*) of a deserted campsite (*dār*, *manzil*), which he recognizes as the place where he once spent happy days with his beloved. He remembers her beauty, weeps and complains, but finally regains his equanimity and resolves to forget his futile sorrow. Other motifs fulfil the same function. The poet, while resting by night, is haunted by the 'vision' (*khayāl*, *ṭayf*) of his beloved, whom he knows to dwell in a distant place (cf. Jacobi, 1990). Or he observes the preparations of his beloved's tribe for departure, and watches her litter disappear in the distance (cf. Jacobi, 1971, 10–49).

After deciding to forget love and the beloved, the poet usually turns towards his camel for consolation. He elaborately describes its excellence and emphasizes its strength and endurance by comparing it to an animal of the desert, e.g. an antelope, a wild ass, an ostrich or, very rarely, an eagle. These comparisons often develop into lively narratives which represent the animals in their typical behaviour and surroundings. The sequence of *nasīb* and camel theme seems to have constituted an early convention in the history of the ode. The concluding sections reveal a higher degree of variation. The following patterns are most frequent: (a) the poet compensates the melancholy mood of the *nasīb*, enhanced by allusions to his old age and failing success with women, by memories of youthful pleasures and pursuits; (b) he treats a political issue of tribal life, often in connection with satirical verses and threats against his adversaries; (c) he ends with a panegyric upon a tribal chief or a **Lakhmid** or **Ghassānid** king. The last pattern is most important for the history of the *qaṣīda*, since it survives in Islamic court poetry (cf. Jacobi, 1971, 65–105).

The origin of the *qaṣīda* remains obscure, in spite of various theories attempting to explain its sequence of themes. At our present stage of knowledge it seems safe to assume that independent genres were first united by metre and rhyme. Subsequently the need was felt to motivate the transition from one theme to the other, until by degrees several patterns emerged, which were accepted and regarded as meaningful by poets of different tribes and thus formed a common tradition. A careful assessment of pre-Islamic texts further points to the fact that the combination of *nasīb* and camel theme existed as a convention before other sections were added to it, for the concluding passages of the ode seem to allow of greater variation than the first two sections. An exceptional case is the *qaṣīda* ending with a *madīḥ*. Some odes seem to be conceived as a narrative sequence from beginning to end. The poet, on his desert journey, stops at a deserted campsite. He indulges in memories and renews his sorrow, but then he continues his journey and finally reaches the *mamdūḥ*, the patron to whom he addresses his *madīḥ*. This pattern serves as a starting point for the later development of the ode.

Early Islamic period

In the first half of the first/seventh century, the time of the ***mukhaḍramūn***, the pre-Islamic oral tradition was still followed by professional poets, e.g. **Ḥassān ibn Thābit** and **Ka'b ibn**

Zuhayr, who composed panegyrics upon the Prophet in the bedouin manner. But there are also significant changes on the formal and conceptual level indicating that the system of tribal values was beginning to disappear. In the *nasīb* poets occasionally introduce individual elements and refer to a present love affair they want to continue after separation. The beloved is now sometimes represented as an individual person, who takes part in the relationship, instead of the stylized heroine of the *Jāhiliyya*. These changes are particularly apparent in the ***dīwān*** of Abū Dhu'ayb (see **Hudhayl**), one of the most innovative poets of the period. Another important change regards the structure of the ode. As evidenced in the poetry of **al-Aʿshā** and **al-Ḥuṭay'a**, the description of the poet's excellent camel begins to be replaced by his desert journey (*raḥīl*) to the *mamdūḥ*, whom he tries to impress by emphasizing the dangers of the ways and the hardship he undertook, in order to reach him. This development is continued and completed in the **Umayyad** *qaṣīda* (Jacobi, 1982, cf. 8–13).

Umayyad period

With the gradual dissolution of tribal society in the course of the first Islamic century, the *qaṣīda* lost its former significance as the expression of tribal ideals and values, but it remained the principal form cultivated by professional poets in the employment of the caliphs and their governors. The *nasīb* develops in contact with Umayyad ***ghazal*** poetry and presents a marked contrast to the pre-Islamic form. Poets continue to allude to conventional motifs, e.g. the 'deserted campsite' or the 'night vision', but the narrative structure of the *nasīb* is mostly dissolved, and the amatory theme, the poet's longing and sorrow, is more elaborately treated than before. The 'heroic' resolution to forget love and the beloved is abandoned. Lovers promise faithfulness after separation, and memories are evoked so as to motivate their present concern in the relationship. The *nasīb* is sometimes followed, without transition, by a satirical section, a new pattern which seems to have been appreciated by the Umayyad audience (cf. van Gelder, 1990).

As regards the structure of the ode, the most important development is the elaboration of the *raḥīl*. Umayyad poets, instead of describing their excellent camel, refer to a perilous desert journey and usually mention a group of travellers and their mounts, emphasizing the traces of hardship and weariness visible on men and animals. The destination, the patron, is always named, often repeatedly, so as to leave no doubt to whom the poet looks for an adequate reward. It seems further significant that elements of the *raḥīl* may he inserted into the *nasīb*. There are also panegyrical odes beginning with a *raḥīl*, which is sometimes ingeniously blended with the *madīḥ*. This is a favourite technique of **al-Farazdaq**, who composed half of his panegyrics without a *nasīb* (cf. Jacobi, 1982, 14–19). The Umayyad *madīḥ* is more elaborate, on the whole, than the pre-Islamic, and has been adapted to its new purpose, i.e. celebrating the religions and political significance of the caliphate. In contrast to the pre-Islamic *qaṣīda*, the Umayyad ode appears to be determined in all its sections by the panegyrical function, thus corresponding with remarkable precision to **Ibn Qutayba**'s famous description of the *qaṣīda* (*Kitab al-Shiʿr wa-l-shuʿarā'*, de Goeje, 1902, 14f.).

ʿAbbāsid period

The **ʿAbbāsid** *qaṣīda* constitutes a highlight in the history of the ode, for it reflects the rhetorical brilliance of the 'new style' (see ***badīʿ***), as well as the intellectual sophistication of the age. Court poets like **Abū Tammām** and **al-Buḥturī** composed their odes with great care and a view to the coherence of the entire text on different linguistic levels (cf. Stetkevych, 1991, 113–231; cf. also Sperl, 1989, 28–47). There is further a growing tendency towards a bipartite form consisting of *nasīb* and *madīḥ*, the *raḥīl* being omitted altogether or reduced to a mere introduction to the *madīḥ* (cf. Jacobi, 1982, 19–21). The *nasīb* assimilates elements from courtly *ghazal* poetry, but whereas the ʿAbbāsid *ghazal* is provided with an urban background, as a rule, love affairs in the *nasīb* are conducted in the romantic world of a bedouin environment, evoked by place names and allusions to the landscape of the **Hijaz**. Early ***muḥdathūn***, e.g. **Abū Nuwās** and **Muslim ibn al-Walīd**, sometimes introduce their odes with a bacchic scene or a description of flowers and gardens. There is also a short-lived fashion for an 'anti-*nasīb*', i.e. the ironical rejection of bedouin conventions and attitudes.

The *madīḥ*, especially if addressed to a caliph, is usually of considerable length and closely structured from beginning to end. According to Sperl's theory of the bipartite form (1989), *nasīb* and *madīḥ* constitute an antithesis (strophe and anti-strophe), whereby each element of the *nasīb* finds its opposition in the *madīḥ*. The poet's relation to his cruel capricious beloved is compensated by the caliph's grace and generosity, who turns his frustration and grief into happiness and bliss. But the analogy is not limited to the personal aspect. The transitoriness of human affairs, symbolized in the *nasīb* by the deserted 'traces' (*aṭlāl*), is counterbalanced by the cosmic power of the caliph to rejuvenate the earth. The technique of establishing an opposition or analogy between *nasīb* and *madīḥ* seems to be developed already by **Bashshār ibn Burd**, who uses it ingeniously for his own purpose (cf. Meisami, 1985). The same technique has been demonstrated for odes of the **Būyid** period (cf. Sperl, 1989, 48–70), but the later history of the *qaṣīda* remains to be investigated. The form has been used by poets up to the nineteenth century, and even after it has become obsolete, topoi from the *qaṣīda* are used by poets and understood by their readers until today.

Text editions

Ibn Qutayba, *Liber poësis et poëtarum*, M.J. de Goeje (ed.), Leiden (1902).
——, *Introduction au Livre de la poésie et des poètes*, Gaudefroy-Demombynes (ed. and trans.), Paris (1947).

Further reading

Badawi, M.M., 'From primary to secondary qaṣīdas: thoughts on the development of classical Arabic poetry', *JAL* 11 (1980), 1–31.
Bateson, M.C., *Structural Continuity in Poetry: A Linguistic Study of Five Pre-Islamic Odes*, Paris and The Hague (1970).
Bencheikh, Jamal-Eddine, *Poétique arabe: essais sur les voies d'une création*, Paris (1975).
Hamori, Andras, *On the Art of Medieval Arabic Literature*, Princeton (1974), 3–30.
——, *The Composition of Mutanabbī's Panegyrics to Sayf al-Dawla*, Leiden (1992).
Jacobi, R., *Studien zur Poetik der altarabischen Qaṣide*, Wiesbaden (1971).
——, 'The camel-section of the panegyrical ode', *JAL* 13 (1982), 1–22.
——, 'The khayāl motif in early Arabic poetry', *Oriens* 32 (1990), 50–64.
Meisami, J.S., 'The uses of the *qaṣīda*: thematic and structural patterns in a poem of Bashshār', *JAL* 16 (1985), 40–60.
Sperl, S.M., 'Islamic kingship and Arabic panegyric poetry in the early 9th century', *JAL* 8 (1979), 20–35.
——, *Mannerism in Arabic Poetry*, Cambridge (1989).
Sperl, S. and Shackle, C. (eds), *Qasida Poetry in Islamic Asia and Africa*, 2 vols, Leiden (1966).
Stetkevych, S.P., *Abū Tammām and the Poetics of the ʿAbbāsid Age*, Leiden (1991).
van Gelder, G.J.H., 'Genres in collision: *nasīb* and *hijā*', *JAL* 21 (1990), 14–25.
Zwettler, M., *The Oral Tradition of Classical Arabic Poetry*, Columbus (1978).

R. JACOBI

qaṣīdat al-nathr *see* prose poem

Qāsim, ʿAbd al-Ḥakīm (1935–90)

Egyptian novelist and short-story writer. Born into a peasant family in al-Bandara, Gharbiyya province, Qāsim attended a Coptic school for part of his education. He studied law at Alexandria University. Imprisoned as a communist by the Nasser regime, he was later employed in the civil service. In 1974 he was awarded a scholarship to study in West Berlin and spent several years there. After his return to **Egypt** in the early 1980s he worked as a journalist until his death from a stroke.

Qāsim was one of the experimentalists who started writing around 1960 and gained recognition after 1967, when defeat in the Six-Day War had shattered the prevailing political and cultural assumptions. He was not a prolific writer; he left three novels and four collections of novellas and short stories. Almost all his work is linked in some way to his personal experience as an intellectual of peasant origin struggling against the economic, cultural and emotional privations of life in the Egyptian city and village, and to his hatred of the misuse of power. He took themes and situations already treated in Egyptian literature and developed them by changing them significantly or applying new techniques to them. His style, with its considerable recourse to the colloquial, its poetic rhythms of repeated words and phrases, and its sparing use of connectives, is well suited to convey the emotional significance of the outside world to the main characters, a consistent concern of his.

His first novel to be published, *Ayyām al-insān al-sabʿa* (1969) traces a boy's progressive alienation from the traditional world of his family, steeped in religion and Islamic folklore; it is a remarkably profound treatment of a familiar theme. The earlier *Muḥāwala lil-khurūj* (1980) describes a love affair between an Egyptian and a European girl – the Cairo setting at the same time affording an opportunity for a critical examination of Egyptian society. A courageous attack on the forced conversion of Copts by Islamic fundamentalists is the subject of the novella *al-Mahdī* (1978). In *Qadar al-ghuraf al-muqbiḍa* (1982) the hero's itinerary from Egyptian village to German metropolis is established by means of minute descriptions of the rooms in which he lodges. Some of the later stories show a renewed interest in the possibilities of the classical Arabic literary heritage.

Text editions

Rites of Assent, Peter Theroux (trans.), Philadelphia (1995) (includes *al-Mahdī* etc.).

The Seven Days of Man, Joseph N. Bell (trans.), Cairo (1990).

Further reading

Kilpatrick, Hilary, 'Abd al-Ḥakîm Qâsim and the search for liberation', *JAL* 26 (1995), 50–66.

H. KILPATRICK

al-Qāsim, Samīḥ (1939–)

Palestinian poet and dramatist. Born into a Druze family in Zarqa (Jordan), al-Qāsim was educated in Rama and Nazareth. He worked for a time as a teacher in Israel and subsequently as a journalist in Haifa. One of the most prolific of the Palestinian 'resistance' poets, he has several times been imprisoned for his views. Like his lifelong friend Maḥmūd **Darwīsh**, his life and literary output are rooted in the events that led to the creation of Israel in 1948 and the fragmentation of Palestinian society.

A highly accomplished poet, al-Qāsim employed the traditional ***qaṣīda*** form in his early poetry of the late 1950s and early 1960s, but with a refreshingly new and crisp sense of purpose. This poetry is also characterized by an overwhelming desire to achieve thematic immediacy through, *inter alia*, the use of a defiant but well-measured lyricism. This lyricism is also present in his later poetry, for the most part composed in **free verse**.

Al-Qāsim regarded form and content as organically related elements in the poetic creation. His poetry is characterized by a rich array of symbolic motifs whose choice depends on a vision of the Palestinian situation in terms that, while firmly rooted in the local culture, expand to encompass other cultures in a universalizing mode of poetic expression. This explains his use of local and Greek mythologies, in addition to the **Koran** and the Bible, as sources from which to draw his motifs. In his use of the Koran, al-Qāsim often reinterprets traditional meanings, as for example with the characters of Iram and Ayyūb.

No less significant is al-Qāsim's creative use of ordinary language, including dialectal expressions, imitations of the language of the Koran and the Arabic version of the Bible, the insertion of expressions from other languages (mainly Hebrew), the use of dialogue, and the insertion of ordinary prose as a mode of expression for well-defined purposes. The cumulative effect is to promote immediacy in the appreciation of his poetry by its Palestinian audience and to enhance its wider appeal; in particular, the insertion of borrowed expressions represents an attempt to convey a sense in which Palestinian life has been punctured by an intruding reality. Another special feature of his poetry is the use of 'signature' poems – short and sometimes cryptic poems characterized by dense emotional content and allusive imagery.

Text editions

Jayyusi, Salma Khadra (ed.), *Anthology of Palestinian Literature*, New York (1992), 254–61.

Victims of a Map, Abdullah al-Udhari (trans.), London (1984), 50–85.

Y. SULEIMAN

al-Qāsim ibn ʿĪsā, Abū Dulaf al-ʿIjlī (d. *c.*227/842)

Arab general, poet and musician. Abū Dulaf came from a wealthy family of the Banū 'Ijl, settled near Hamadan. Of **Shīʿī** sympathies, he had an uneasy relationship with al-Ma'mūn but was a companion of al-Muʿtaṣim, who admired his singing. He led his own contingent in the war against Bābak and had a reputation for bravery that reached almost mythical dimensions. He was an extravagantly generous patron, and many poets and musicians made the journey to his town of Karaj; they were attracted not only by hope of gain but by the knowledgeable and sympathetic welcome that their work received. Abū Dulaf was the author of books on falconry, weapons, the policy of the ruler and other subjects connected with court life which have not survived. Fragments of his poetry have been preserved, simple but effective love lyrics and some *fakhr*, which strikes a heroic note. He may be considered as both a representative of **'Abbāsid** court culture and an embodiment of the old Arab virtues.

Further reading

Aghānī [3]8: 248–257.
*EI*², art. 'al-Ḳāsim b. 'Īsā' (J. Bencheikh).

H. KILPATRICK

qāṣṣ *see* oratory and sermons; story telling

Qaṭarī ibn al-Fujā'a *see* Khārijīs

qawādīsī or *qādūsī*

From Arabic *qādūs* (pl. *qawādīs*) 'water-wheel bucket', a verse form not mentioned by **al-Khalīl ibn Aḥmad**, with alternating ū- and ī-sounds after the rhyming consonant. In classical poetry such an alternation represents a case of *iqwā'*, one of the defects of rhyme. The etymology of the term is explained by comparing the movement of the water-wheel buckets which are constantly going up and down with the alternation of -ū and -ī (*raf'* meaning either raising or ū-sound and *khafḍ* either lowering or ī-sound). An example taken from a longer poem by Ṭalḥa ibn 'Ubayd Allāh al-'Awnī are the following verses:

> *kam li-dumā 'l-abkāri bi-'l-khabtayni min manāzili*
> *bi-muhjatī li-'l-wajdi min tadhkārihā manāzilu*
> *ma'āhidun ghayyarahā sawākibu 'l-hawāṭili*
> *lammā na'ā sākinuhā fa-'admu'ī hawāṭilu*

> (How many abodes there are of the beautiful virgins in Khabtayn / In my heart there are abodes of ardour when I remember them / Places transformed by pouring rain / Since their resident left my tears are heavy rain).

Against official theory the poet twice uses the same word twice (*manāzil*/*hawāṭil*), two cases of *īṭā'* (see **prosody**).

W. STOETZER

qayna, qiyān *see* singers and musicians

Qayrawan *see* Maghrib

Qays 'Aylān *see* tribes

Qays ibn 'Amr al-Najāshī *see* *al-Najāshī*

Qays ibn Dharīḥ (*c*.4–70/*c*.626–89)

Love poet of the *'Udhrī* type (see ***'Udhrī*** **poetry**), early Islamic and early **Umayyad** period. Qays, stemming from the Kināna tribe, resided mainly near Medina. He is said to have been a foster-brother of al-Ḥusayn ibn 'Alī (*c*.4–61/*c*.626–80), son of the fourth Orthodox caliph. According to the *akhbār*, his marriage with his much-beloved wife Lubnā remained childless. Qays was therefore pressed by his parents to divorce her and finally yielded to their demands. Although both he and Lubnā married again, Qays for the rest of his life remained faithful to his former love. Some traditions have Qays and Lubnā reunite while others pretend to know that they died separated from each other. As a proverbial mistress Lubnā is already mentioned in a verse of **al-'Abbās ibn al-Aḥnaf** (d. 188/803 or after 193/808; cf. Kračkovskij, 1955, 35). No copy of his ***dīwān*** has survived. The collection of fragments compiled by Naṣṣār contains 76 pieces with 449 verses. The fact that Qays ibn Dharīḥ carries the same name as **Qays ibn al-Mulawwaḥ** (al-Majnūn) al-'Āmirī seems to have caused confusion about authorship even beyond what is usual in the circle of *'Udhrī* poets.

Text edition

Naṣṣār, Ḥ., *Qays wa-Lubnā, shi'r wa-dirāsa*, Cairo (1960).

Further reading

Blachère, R., *Histoire de la littérature arabe*, Paris (1952–66), vol. 2, 649–50.

Kilpatrick, H., '*Ahbār manẓūma*: the romance of Qays and Lubnā in the *Aghānī*', in *Wagner Festschrift*, vol. 2, 350–61.
Kračkovskij, I.J., 'Die Frühgeschichte der Erzählung von Macnūn und Lailā in der arabischen Literatur', *Oriens* 8 (1955), 35, 45–6, 49.

T. SEIDENSTICKER

Qays ibn al-Khaṭīm (d. before 1/622)

Pre-Islamic poet from the clan Ẓafar of the tribe of Aws, which together with Jewish tribes and the Banū Khazraj inhabited the oasis Yathrib (later Medina). Qays was murdered by a Khazrajī shortly before the Hijra (622 AD). His *dīwān* (23 poems, together nearly 300 lines) contains occasional pieces and dipartite ***qaṣīda****s*. The latter comprise *nasīb* and a message in which the poet glorifies his prowess and that of his tribe and deals with the feuds in Yathrib, especially the *yawm Buʿāth*, a battle in which the hostilities between Aws and Khazraj culminated in about 617 CE. Qays also exchanged polemics with the Khazrajī poets **Ḥassān ibn Thābit** and **ʿAbd Allāh ibn Rawāḥa**. Although some of his *nasīb* lines were admired by later critics, his main importance lies less in his literary achievements than in his shedding light on the circumstances in Yathrib on the eve of Islam.

Text edition

Dīwān, Thaddäus Kowalski (ed. and trans.), Leipzig (1914); Nāṣir al-Din al-Asad (ed.), Cairo (1962).

T. BAUER

Qays ibn al-Mulawwaḥ, al-Majnūn (first/seventh century)

The poet Qays ibn al-Mulawwaḥ al-ʿAmirī, widely known under the epithet al-Majnūn or Majnūn Laylā, is said to have lived around the middle of the first/seventh century, and to have died, according to various statements, between 65/685 and 80/699. His love for Laylā is the main theme of his poetry, and is dealt with in numerous short narrations, which themselves contain and preserve a good part of the verses known to us. As the most common version of the story runs, Majnūn's love had developed since his childhood years, but Laylā's parents, resentful of his behaviour, married her elsewhere. This only intensified Majnūn's passion, which caused him to roam about in search of relief and led him into madness. Tolerating only wild beasts as company, he lived and died in the wilderness, far from human habitation. During his agony, poetic inspiration would never fail to meet him whenever he remembered Laylā.

Majnūn shares the general features of his unfortunate but faithful love with other poets of the *ʿUdhrī* ***ghazal*** (e.g. **Jamīl** Buthayna, **Qays ibn Dharīḥ**; see ***ʿUdhri*** **poetry**), but stands out from them through the exaltation of his attitude and through his madness, which may be seen as coming close to mystical experience. At the same time his mental affliction appears as a consequence of his rejection of social conventions. The story of Majnūn and Laylā therefore gained precedence over others of the same genre. It became most prominent in several oriental literatures and was depicted, quite independently from the Arabic poetry, by Persian romances in the most accomplished way. According to the rich poetic imagery already present in the classical Arabic model, the story of Majnūn and Laylā and of his poetry can be interpreted from various aspects and has thus inspired modern versions, e.g. by Aḥmad **Shawqī** and the *Riwāyat Majnūn Laylā* by M. Munjī Khayr Allāh.

The person of the poet and the origin of the stories about his love, and of his poetry, give rise to some questions. Doubts concerning the poet's name and even the existence of a historical Majnūn are recorded in the earliest sources for his poetry and life-story, **Ibn Qutayba**'s (d. 276/890) *al-Shiʿr wa-al-shuʿarā'*, and **Abū al-Faraj al-Iṣbahānī**'s (d. 356/967) *Kitāb al-Aghānī*. In consequence it seems to have become accepted among Orientalists that Majnūn is a legendary figure. As to its origin, our oldest extant source (Ibn Qutayba's *Shiʿr*) does not say much, but a kernel of the accounts given here may be traced back to the second half of the second/eighth century, when older popular stories were shaped into a literary version. Already at that stage, the essential characteristics of Majnūn are present, whereas the establishment of the historicity of the figure was avoided.

Apart from the sources mentioned, an important collection of accounts is reproduced by Jaʿfar ibn Aḥmad **al-Sarrāj** (d. 500/1106) in his *Maṣāriʿ al-ʿushshāq*. He persistently quotes Ibn al-Marzubān (d. 302/921) who is known as the author of *Akhbār al-Majnūn* (Yūsuf al-ʿUshsh, *al-Khaṭīb al-Baghdādī*, *mu'arrikh Baghdād wa-muḥaddithuh*, Damascus, 1364/1945, 106). A recension of his *dīwān*, which was spread throughout many manuscripts, is attributed to the fairly unknown Abū Bakr al-Wālibī. In fact, a person of this name belonging to the second half of the second/eighth century is occasionally mentioned (al-Qālī, *al-Amālī*, vol. 2, 126; *Maṣāri'*, vol. 2, 78). The collection of Majnūn's verses, however, many of which are also attributed to other poets, must have been put together later, as was suggested by Kratchkowsky, whose arguments have not been challenged. This does not exclude, contrary to this author's excessive scepticism, that some poetry of the first/seventh century has been preserved. In any case, a comprehensive critical evaluation of the material attributed to Majnūn has not yet been undertaken.

Many of the verses of Majnūn's ***dīwān*** are fine poetry and quite interesting. Due to Majnūn's particular intimacy with nature his verses contain descriptions of a **bedouin** environment. Moreover, his passion for Laylā often mingles with the longing for his homeland (*al-ḥanīn ilā al-awṭān*), since Najd shelters the souvenirs of his beloved. His verses witness, besides the effects of passion and the states of a love that cannot hope for earthly fulfilment, an absolute devotion to his experience which cannot be counterbalanced even by religion and which has become the characteristic of Majnūn Laylā.

Text edition

Dīwān, A.A. Farrāj (ed.), Cairo (n.d., *c.*1960).
Ḳays b. al-Mulavvaḥ (al-Macnūn) ve Dīvāni (the recension of al-Wālibī), Şevkiye İnalcik (ed.), Ankara (1967).
Majnûn: l'amour poème, choix de poèmes, André Miquel (trans.), Paris (1984).

Further reading

Aghānī (Cairo 1927–), vol. 2, 1–96.
Blachère, Régis, *Histoire de la littérature arabe*, 3 vols, Paris (1952–66), 657–60.
Dols, Michael W., *Majnūn: The Madman in Medieval Islamic Society*, D. Immisch (ed.), Oxford (1992).
*EI*², art. 'Madjnūn Laylā' (Ch. Pellat).
Ibn Qutayba, *al-Shi'r wa-al-shu'arā'*, Aḥmad M. Shākir (ed.), Cairo (1966), 563–73.
Khairallah, As'ad E., *Love, Madness and Poetry: An Interpretation of the Mağnūn Legend*, Wiesbaden (1980).
Kratchkowsky, I.J., 'Die Frühgeschichte der Erzälung von Macnūn und Lailā in der arabischen Literatur', H. Ritter (trans.), *Oriens* 8 (1955), 1–50.
Leder, Stefan, 'Frühe Erzählungen zu Mağnūn – Mağnūn als Figur ohne Lebensgeschichte', *Supplement der ZDMG zum XXIV. Deutschen Orientalistentag*, Wiesbaden (1990), 150–61.
——, 'Akhbār al-Majnūn al-qadīma-nash'atuhā wa-shakluhā al-qiṣaṣī', *Majallat Majma' al-lugha al-'Arabiyya bi-Dimashq* (1995), 17–34.
Miquel, André and Kemp, P., *Majnūn et Laylā, l'amour fou*, Paris (1984).
al-Sarrāj, *Maṣāri' al-'ushshāq*, Beirut (1378/1958), *passim*.

S. LEDER

al-Qazwīnī, Muḥammad ibn 'Abd al-Raḥmān *see* al-Khaṭīb al-Qazwīnī, Muḥammad

al-Qazwīnī, Zakariyyā' ibn Muḥammad (*c.*600–82/*c.*1203–83)

Born in Qazwīn, he served as judge (*qāḍī*) of Wāsiṭ and al-Ḥilla and is famous as an author on cosmography and geography. Al-Qazwīnī's career as official in the judiciary and his works attest to the careful, well-rounded education he enjoyed. His travels to Mesopotamia and **Syria** and through Iran may have been motivated by search of employment at least as much as of learning; in Iraq he did enter **'Abbāsid** service and subsequently gravitated into the orbit of the Ilkhanid governor of **Baghdad**, 'Aṭā-Malik Juvaynī (d. 682/1283), to whom he dedicated his cosmography.

Al-Qazwīnī's two works, the cosmography *'Ajā'ib al-makhlūqāt wa-gharā'ib al-mawjūdāt* (*Marvellous Things of Creation and Wondrous Things of Existence*) and the geographical dictionary *Āthār al-bilād wa-akhbār al-'ibād* (*Monuments of Places and History of God's Bondsmen*) are not so much the fruit of autopsy, but of extensive reading in the whole range of pertinent disciplines, such as (Aristotelian) physics, astronomy, mineralogy, botany, zoology, psychology, history, geography, etc. However, the impressive number of authors quoted in either book decreases dramatically once the author's primary proximate source – or sources – is identified; in the cosmography, provided no hitherto concealed text is yet to be uncovered, the most frequently quoted authors are **Abū Ḥāmid al-Gharnāṭī** and the anonymous author of the Persian *Tuḥfat al-gharāʾib* (*Gift of Wonders*); in the geography, the unacknowledged main authority is **Yāqūt**'s *Muʿjam al-buldān* (*Dictionary of Countries*). Obviously, neither al-Qazwīnī's sometimes cavalier handling of his sources nor his basically compilatory method – to the neglect of empirical investigation and learning – are unique to him; on the contrary, they represent the then current standard of scholarship. The tremendous popularity of his cosmography is documented by the rich manuscript tradition, including a fair number of lavishly illustrated copies, by repeated revisions and adaptations, and by translations into Persian and Turkish.

By naming 'mirabilia' in the very title, al-Qazwīnī may have uncannily captured the mood of his age; he justifies them in 'rational' terms as signs of God's creative power and of the cunning of the created being so that only the stupid would reject them. The inhabitants of the supralunar and the sublunar, terrestrial worlds include, other than the multifarious earthly life, angels and demons – *jinn*. Using the time-honoured device of analogical reasoning, al-Qazwīnī claims that everything in this world causes wonderment to the uninitiated, as it does to children, except that in growing up, man becomes familiar with most phenomena and their causes so that he no longer perceives them as wonders. He will equally learn to accept the as yet hidden causes of what appears inexplicable and miraculous to him. However, al-Qazwīnī declines responsibility in case a reader persists in his doubt: he cannot vouchsafe for the correctness of testimony that he himself did no more than transmit faithfully.

Al-Qazwīnī arranges his material alphabetically wherever possible; thus in the cosmography, mountains, rivers, minerals, gemstones and medicinal plants are listed in alphabetical order. In the geography, he follows the same pattern, except within the constraints of the seven latitudinal climes.

Text editions

ʿAjāʾib al-makhlūqāt, F. Wüstenfeld (ed.), Göttingen (1849); *Al-Qazwînî, Die Wunder des Himmels und der Erde* (partial), A. Giese (trans.), Stuttgart and Vienna (1986).

Āthār al-bilād, F. Wüstenfeld (ed.), Göttingen (1848).

Further reading

al-Ṣafadī, *al-Wāfī* (Leipzig, etc. 1931–), vol. 14, 206, no. 289.

L. RICHTER-BERNBURG

See also: *ʿajāʾib* literature; geographical literature

al-Qazzāz, Ibn ʿUbāda *see* Ibn ʿUbāda al-Qazzāz

al-Qifṭī *see* Ibn al-Qifṭī

Qiṣaṣ al-anbiyāʾ *see* *Legends of the Prophets*

Qiṣṣat al-amīr Ḥamza al-bahlawān *see* *Ḥamza al-bahlawān*

qiṭʿa

(Also *maqṭūʿa*, *muqaṭṭaʿa*). A term used to designate brief, usually monothematic poems, as opposed to the longer, often polythematic ***qaṣīda***. Generally translated as 'fragment' (the term is used in anthologies both for short poems and for excerpts from longer poems), this rendering is somewhat misleading, suggesting (as has often been proposed) that the *qiṭʿa* was derived by the 'splitting off' of one or another of the *qaṣīda*'s constituent elements (this was, perhaps, a fiction developed by the poets). It has also been suggested that the polythematic *qaṣīda* evolved from the accumulation of such 'fragments' into long poems. Neither theory provides a satisfactory explanation of the relationship between the two.

Pre-Islamic poets evidently composed both long and short poems; but it was in the early **ʿAbbāsid** period that the *qiṭʿa* underwent a conscious and deliberate development (see below), as *qiṭʿa*s were composed both by professional poets and by the cultured élite at large (in particular, court **secretaries**) for a wide variety of occasions and on a wide range of topics. As well as being employed for the 'major' genres of praise (***madīḥ***) and elegy (***rithāʾ***), the *qiṭʿa* became a popular vehicle for boasting (***fakhr***) and invective (***hijāʾ***), and was widely used for the newly developed wine poem (***khamriyya***), love poem (***ghazal***) and ascetic poem (*zuhdiyya*), as well as for erotic and obscene poetry (***mujūn***, ***sukhf***) and descriptive poetry (***waṣf***), often in the form of highly elaborate riddles (see ***lughz***). It was also used for brief **epigrammatic** poems, as well as for a variety of mundane purposes – invitations, thank-you notes, requests for gifts, apologies and so on. Mystical poets adapted the genres of the love and wine poems to express mystical themes.

The *qiṭ'a* is distinguished formally from the *qaṣīda* not only by its brevity but by the frequent absence of *taṣrī'* (introductory rhymed hemistich; see **prosody**) in its opening line. Although both *qiṭ'a* and *qaṣīda* treat common thematic topics, each exhibits distinct structural features which reflect different, and complementary, functions. The *qaṣīda* was composed for public recitation on formal, ceremonial occasions, the *qiṭ'a* for more informal gatherings (often to be sung), and was often improvised. **Ibn Rashīq** observed that the short poem is more appropriate for such occasions, as it 'rests easier on the ear', while the *qaṣīda* is better suited to more formal purposes (in particular, panegyric), and is moreover intended to be memorized. Thus while the *qaṣīda* features an elevated diction and a complexity of style often marked by the extensive use of rhetorical devices, the *qiṭ'a* tends towards simpler diction, less elaborate rhetoric, and greater lyricism.

Further reading

Badawi, M.M., 'From primary to secondary qaṣīdas: thoughts on the development of classical Arabic poetry', *JAL* 11 (1980), 1–31.
*EI*², art. 'Mukhtārāt' (A. Hamori).

J.S. MEISAMI

al-Qu'ayyid, [Muḥammad] Yūsuf *see* al-Qa'īd, [Muḥammad] Yūsuf

Qudāma ibn Ja'far (d. 337/948; other dates are also given)

Abū al-Faraj Qudāma ibn Ja'far al-Kātib al-Baghdādī was a scribe with philosophical interests, a philologist and a literary theorist. Originally a Christian, he became a Muslim under al-Muktafī, **'Abbāsid** caliph from 289/902 to 295/908. He held various medium-level administrative positions in the caliphal chanceries. In 320/932, he attended the famous debate, before the vizier **Ibn al-Furāt**, between the grammarian **al-Sīrāfi** and the logician **Mattā ibn Yūnus**; otherwise nothing much is known of his life.

Three of his fifteen works have survived. *Jawāhir al-alfāẓ* (*Word Jewels*), is a topically arranged dictionary of synonyms and near-synonyms to help the state scribe achieve *variatio* and choose the appropriate word. The introduction contains a list of fifteen figures of style with explanations and examples, said to be the 'best part of eloquence' for both poet and orator. Of *Kitāb al-Kharāj wa-ṣinā'at al-kitāba* (*The Book of Land Tax and the Scribe's Art*), only the last four parts have been preserved, dealing with administration, geography, taxation and government, the last part belonging partly to the **Mirrors for Princes** genre. The lost third part of the book dealt with *balāgha* 'eloquence'. In *Naqd al-shi'r*, (*The Assaying of Poetry*), the author sees himself as a pioneer, writing, as he does, the first book on the 'science of the good and the bad in poetry'. The structure of the book betrays his philosophical interests. He starts with a definition ('Poetry is metred and rhymed utterance pointing to a meaning'), which becomes standard in the later literature. This yields the four elements that make up poetry: metre, rhyme, wording and meaning. He then proceeds to describe the good qualities of these elements and of their various combinations, to be followed by a similar chapter dealing with the bad qualities. In his treatment of 'meaning' he restricts himself to the major 'aims', i.e. **genres**, of poetry (panegyric, invective, elegies, simile, description and love poetry). The 'modern' genres (such as bacchic poetry; see ***khamriyya***) are glaringly absent, which tallies well with the astonishing fact that the vast majority of his examples are taken from ancient poetry. Since he does not use the term ***badī'***, lit. 'something novel', to refer to some or all rhetorical figures, he may have wanted to stay clear of the controversy associated with this notion, although he is certainly not unaware of the differences between 'ancient' and 'modern' poetizing. One such issue is the debate about the licitness of hyperbole which, according to Qudāma, was raging at his time. Belonging to the larger genus of the 'poetic lie', hyperbole was rejected by some and enthusiastically defended by others, while Qudāma takes a moderate stand in favour of the hyperbole, provided that it survives the insertion of 'almost.' (See further **ancients and moderns**; **truth and poetry**.)

Qudāma is frequently quoted in the later literature on rhetorical figures, but his method of presentation is abandoned.

Text editions

Jawāhir al-alfāẓ, Muḥammad Muḥyī āl-Dīn 'Abd al-Ḥamīd (ed.), Cairo (1350/1932), rpt. Beirut (1399/1979).

Kitāb al-Kharāj wa-ṣinā'at al-kitāba, Muḥammad Ḥusayn al-Zubaydī (ed.), Baghdad (1981); facs. edn Fuat Sezgin, Frankfurt (1986).

Naqd al-shi'r, Seeger A. Bonebakker (ed.), Leiden (1956); partial trans. in Vicente Cantarino, *Arabic Poetics in the Golden Age*, Leiden (1975), 118–24.

Further reading

Abu Deeb, Kamal, 'Literary criticism', in *CHALABL*, 370–2.

Bonebakker, S.A., 'Introduction', *Naqd al-shi'r*, S.A. Bonebakker (ed.), Leiden (1956).

W.P. HEINRICHS

See also: literary criticism, medieval

qufl see muwashshaḥ

Qunṣul, Ilyās [Elias Konsol] (1914–81)

Mahjar poet and prose writer. Born in Yabrud (**Syria**), he went with his father to Brazil in 1924, and with his father and younger brother Zakī **Qunṣul** to Argentina in 1929. They began as peddlers, but Ilyās then found employment as editor-in-chief of *al-Jarīda al-Sūriyya al-Lubnāniyya* in Buenos Aires. His first volume of poetry, *al-Aslāk al-shā'ika*, was published in 1931 in Buenos Aires, followed by *al-'Abarāt al-multahiba* (Buenos Aires, 1931) and *'Alā madhbaḥ al-waṭaniyya* (Beirut, 1931). In 1937 he started the monthly *al-Manāhil*, which continued until 1940. He returned to Syria in 1954, publishing a number of prose works including *Dawlat al-majānīn* and *Ghālib Afandī* (both Damascus, 1955) and beginning a journal *al-Funūn* which folded in its first year. He returned to Argentina in 1957, where he engaged in trade and journalism.

Further reading

Juḥā, Farīd, *Ilyās Qunṣul ...*, Aleppo (1983).

C. NIJLAND

Qunṣul, Zakī [Zaki Konsol] (1916–1994)

Mahjar poet and journalist. Zakī Qunṣul attended school in Yabrud until 1925, when he left to help ease his family's financial difficulties. In 1929 he emigrated with his father to Brazil and from there to Argentina, where they became peddlers. In 1935 he was employed on *al-Jarīda al-Sūriyya al-Lubnāniyya*, where his brother Ilyas **Qunṣul** worked as editor-in-chief. He left the paper in 1939 after a dispute with the owner and again became a trader. His first volume of poetry, *Shaẓāyā*, was published in the same year. Zakī Qunṣul's second volume of poetry, *Su'ād*, was devoted to his first-born child, Su'ād, who died in 1952 at the age of eight months; in addition to several more volumes of poetry, he also wrote a play, *Taḥt samā' al-Andalus*.

Further reading

al-Yūnus, 'Abd al-Laṭīf, *Zakī Qunṣul, shā'ir al-ḥubb wa-al-ḥanīn*, Buenos Aires (1967).

C. NIJLAND

Qur'ān see Koran

Quraysh see tribes

al-Qurdāḥī, Sulaymān *see* al-Qardāḥī, Sulaymān

al-Qushayrī (376–465/986–1072)

Abū al-Qāsim 'Abd al-Karīm ibn Hawāzin al-Qushayrī was a well-known theologian and mystic. Born in Ustuwā in **Khurasan**, in Nishapur al-Qushayrī fell under the tutelage of the prominent Ṣūfī figure Abū 'Alī al-Daqqāq, from whom he received the bulk of his mystical learning (and whose daughter he married). He also studied ***kalām***, ***fiqh*** and *uṣūl al-fiqh* there. Al-Qushayrī was also involved in the political–theological disputes of his time, as in 446/1054 when he was imprisoned during the violent Ḥanafī-Shāfi'ī conflict. In 448/1058 he was summoned to **Baghdad** to teach ***ḥadīth*** in the palace of the caliph al-Qā'im. Returning to Khurasan, he settled in Ṭūs until the accession of the **Saljūq** sultan Alp Arslān in 455/1063, then returned to Nishapur where he died.

Of al-Qushayri's numerous works the two most important are his exegetical work the *Laṭā'if al-ishārāt*, and his general treatise on Sufism *al-Risāla al-Qushayriyya*. Al-Qushayrī's *tafsīr* was based on a method of revealing the esoteric side of Koranic words and expressions, seeing the exoteric linguistic forms as pointers towards their own hidden meanings; hence the *ishārāt* of the title. The *Risāla* was al-Qushayrī's most influential work and the one through which he gained his fame. Like other general Ṣūfī treatises, it gives much information about Sufism and its doctrine while portraying it as a true orthodox trend. Thus the main doctrinal lines in the *Risāla* are: presenting the Ṣūfī idea of *tawḥīd* (divine unity) as being consonant with the orthodox notion; relating esoteric knowledge to the *sharī'a*; denying there are any objectionable features in the basic Ṣūfī esoteric concepts and methods.

Text editions

Laṭā'if al-ishārāt, Cairo (1970).
'Qushayrī's *Tartīb al-Sulūk*', F. Meier (ed.), *Oriens* 16 (1963), 1–39.
al-Risāla al-Qushayriyya, with selections from Zakariyyā' al-Anṣārī's commentary *Iḥkām al-dalāla ...*, Cairo (1940); Pīr Muḥammad Ḥasan (ed.), Karachi (1964) (with several other treatises and Urdu translation).
Das Sendschreiben al-Qušayrī's über das Sufitum, R. Gramlich (trans.), Wiesbaden (1989).

R.L. NETTLER

See also: Ṣūfī literature: prose

quṣṣāṣ see oratory and sermons; story telling

Qusṭā ibn Lūqā al-Ba'albakī (d. *c.*300/912–13)

A prolific Syrian Christian translator and scholar of medicine and the exact sciences. His skills in these fields resulted in an invitation to **Baghdad**, where he served the caliph al-Musta'īn (r. 248–52/862–6) and joined the company of such colleagues as Abū Yūsuf **al-Kindī**, **Ḥunayn ibn Isḥāq** and **Thābit ibn Qurra**. Later he moved to Armenia at the behest of the prince Sanḥarīb (Sennacherib), and remained active there to the end of his life. Fluent in Arabic, Greek and Syriac, he produced numerous Arabic translations of Greek texts in various fields, and also wrote original works on topics in medicine, mathematics, philosophy, logic, music, astronomy, and weights and measures. These works, some of considerable importance, are for the most part short essays and make Qusṭā a typical figure of the more mature translation period, when translators were also writing brief works of their own on specific topics, more so than ambitious compendia and monographs.

Text editions

Qusṭā ibn Lūqā's Medical Regime for the Pilgrims to Mecca: The Risāla fī tadbīr safar al-ḥajj, Gerrit Bos (ed. and trans.), Leiden (1992) (with commentary and further bibliography).

Further reading

GAS, vol. 3, 270–4, vol. 5, 285–6 (both with lists of edited and manuscript works).
Samir, Khalil, *Une Correspondance islamo-chrétienne entre Ibn al-Munağğim, Ḥunayn ibn Isḥāq et Qusṭā ibn Lūqā*, Turnhout (1981).
Sezgin, Fuat (ed.), *Qusṭā ibn Lūqā (3rd/9th cent.): Texts and Studies*, Frankfurt am Main (1996).
Ullmann, Manfred, *Die Medizin in Islam*, Leiden (1970), 126–8.

L.I. CONRAD

See also: translation, medieval

al-Quṭāmī, (d. *c.*101/719)

Abū Sa'īd 'Umayr ibn Shiyaym (or Shuyaym) al-Taghlibī al-Quṭāmī was an **Umayyad** poet who, like **Muslim ibn al-Walīd**, was known as *Ṣarī' al-Ghawānī*. Little is known about his life. According to **'Abd al-Qāhir al-Jurjānī**, he was a Christian who converted to Islam, although Taghlib remained Christian until the **'Abbāsid** period. His poetry consists of ***waṣf***, ***madīḥ*** and ***ghazal***; **Ibn Sallām** placed him in the second *ṭabaqa* alongside poets such as **Dhū al-Rumma**, though he was in fact closer in inspiration to **Jarīr** and similar to **al-Akhṭal** in his *ghazal* and *nasīb*. He drew inspiration from the desert roots of Arab culture to the exclusion of its new urban context. Notably there are a number of aphorisms in his poetry.

Text edition

Dīwān des 'Umeir ibn Schujeim al-Quṭāmī, J. Barth (ed.), Leiden (1902); *Dīwān*, I. Sāmarrā'ī and A. Maṭlūb (eds), Beirut (1960).

Further reading

Ibn Sallām al-Jumaḥī, *Ṭabaqāt fuḥūl al-shu'arā'*, Cairo (1974), 452–7.

P.F. KENNEDY

Quṭb, Sayyid (1906–66)

Islamic writer and activist. After a traditional religious education, Quṭb studied literature at **Dār al-'Ulūm** in **Cairo** where he was exposed to the ideas of Egyptian liberal intellectuals and published several literary works which he later renounced. A scholarship trip to America (1949–50), where he apparently witnessed anti-Arab prejudice and signs of moral decay, left him disillusioned with Western civilization. Returning to **Egypt** he joined the Muslim Brotherhood and was rapidly promoted. Although imprisoned by Nasser's regime from 1954 to 1964, his Islamic writings were prolific (including a thirty-volume Koranic commentary), and he became the foremost Brotherhood thinker. With his growing disenchantment with the government, his later works became increasingly radical, dogmatic and exclusivist. His last work, *Ma'ālim fī al-ṭarīq*, asserts that the majority of Muslims are living in *jāhiliyya* (ignorance). Influenced by Mawdudi, he posited Islam as a comprehensive ideology and system, and his combination of rational dialectic and powerful rhetoric have ensured a continuing popularity for his works. After his execution in 1966, his thought inspired certain militant Islamic movements, including al-Takfīr wa-al-Hijra.

Text editions

In the Shade of the Qur'ān, Vol. 30, M. Salahi and A. Shamis (trans.), London (1979).
Milestones, Lahore (n.d.).
Social Justice in Islam, J.B. Hardie (trans.), New York (1970).

Further reading

Abu Rabi, I., 'Sayyid Qutb: from religious realism to radical social criticism', *IQ* (1984).
Choueiri, Y., *Islamic Fundamentalism*, London (1990), 93–160.
Haddad, Y., 'Sayyid Qutb: ideologue of Islamic revival', in J. Esposito (ed.), *Voices of a Resurgent Islam*, New York (1983).

K. ZEBIRI

Quwaydir, Shaykh Ḥasan ibn 'Alī (1789–1845/6)

Egyptian writer, poet, philologist and grammarian. Born in **Cairo**, he studied under Ḥasan **al-'Aṭṭār** and Shaykh Ibrāhīm al-Bājūrī at **al-Azhar**, writing a commentary on a metrical composition (*manẓūma*) on **grammar** by al-'Aṭṭār. Among his pupils was the poet Maḥmūd Ṣafwat **al-Sā'ātī**. He wrote treatises on plagiarism, and the art of letter writing. His ***muzdawija*** (strophic verse) on language was translated to Italian as *Dizionario dei triplici* (1899) by Errico Vitto, the Italian consul in Beirut.

Further reading

al-Sandūbī, Ḥasan, *A'yān al-bayān*, Cairo (1914), 17–26.5

P.C. SADGROVE

R

Rabīʻ, Mubārak (1935–)

Moroccan novelist and short-story writer, writing in Arabic. Born in Benmaʻashu, Rabīʻ currently teaches psychology at the University of Rabat. He first published in national newspapers in 1961. Since then, he has published several collections of short stories, including *Sīdnā Qder* (1969) and *Dam wa-dukhān* (1975), and a number of novels including *al-Ṭayyibūn* (1972), *Rifqat al-silāḥ wa-al-qamar* (1976), *al-Rīḥ al-shatawiyya* (1980) and *Badr zamānihi* (1983). *Rifqat al-silāḥ wa-al-qamar*, set on the Golan Heights during the 1973 Arab–Israeli war, won the Arab Language Academy's first prize in 1975.

H. HILMY

Rabīʻa see tribes

Rābiʻa al-ʻAdawiyya (d. 183/801)

A mystic from **Basra**. Her persona has been so transfigured by legendary and hagiographical elements that it is scarcely possible to recover any genuine historical information about her life. No prose works have been attributed to her, but some verses on worldly and divine love have come down to us under her name. These are considered to be the earliest of their kind to emerge in mystic circles. That they are actually of her authorship, however, remains highly improbable.

Further reading

Badawī, ʻAbd al-Raḥmān, *Shāhidat al-ʻishq al-ilāhī, Rābiʻa al-ʻAdawiyya*, Cairo (n.d.; 1952?).

Smith, Margaret, *Rābiʻa the Mystic and Her Fellow-Saints in Islam*, Cambridge (1928).

van Gelder, G.J., 'Rābiʻa's poem on the two kinds of love: a mystification?' in *Verse and the Fair Sex*, Fred de Jong (ed.), Utrecht (1993), 66–76 (with ample bibliography).

B. RADTKE

Rabīʻa ibn Maqrūm (d. shortly after 16/672 in advanced age)

One of the few major poets from the tribe Ḍabba in pre- and early Islamic times. Only few of his poems have been preserved (altogether about 200 lines), but these are of remarkable quality. The aged poet's melancholic reminiscences of the heroic deeds of his youth and two onager episodes which influenced later poets deserve special attention.

Text edition

The Mufaḍḍalīyāt, C.J. Lyall (ed.), Oxford (1918–21), poem nos 38, 39, 43, 113.

Shiʻr, Nūrī Ḥammūdī al-Qaysī (ed.) Baghdad (1968).

Further reading

Bauer, Thomas, *Altarabische Dichtkunst*, Wiesbaden (1992), vol. 1, 224f., vol. 2, 170–9.

T. BAUER

al-Rābiṭa al-qalamiyya [Arrabitah]

Mahjar literary circle founded in New York in 1920. Its name dates back to 11 May 1916, when the New York newspaper *al-Sā'iḥ* published a contribution by William Katsiflis with his name and the words 'member of al-Rabiṭa al-qalamiyya'. A contribution by Amīn **al-Rīḥānī** on 22 May was signed in the same way. Issues of Nasīb **ʻArīḍa**'s *al-Funūn* for July, August and September 1916 contained contributions by **Jubrān** and others using the same line, but 'al-Rābiṭa al-qalamiyya' was not referred to again until January 1919, when *al-Sā'iḥ* in its special issue for that year mentioned the existence of a group by that name.

The official founding session of the group took place on 28 April 1920. The members of the circle were divided into three categories:

1 Workers, that is the authors and poets. Their number was limited to twenty-four. They were required to have published

works of literary value, to be of irreproachable conduct, and to live in New York.
2 Sponsors, who supported the circle.
3 Correspondents, who were to possess the same qualities as the workers, but did not have to live in New York.

The motto of the circle was 'God has treasures beneath his throne, the keys to which are the tongues of the poets'.

The circle saw it as its task to publish literary works by the 'workers' and others, and to translate important literary works into Arabic. It decided to give prizes to encourage poets, authors and translators, and to publish an annual to which all the 'workers' would contribute. The first and only annual was published in 1921, but special issues of *al-Sā'iḥ* served as an effective replacement. The group ended after the death of **Jubrān** and the return to Lebanon of **Nu'ayma**.

C. NIJLAND

Raḍwān, Fatḥī (1911–)

Egyptian playwright, prose writer and politician. After attending the Faculty of Law at Cairo University, Fatḥī Raḍwān embarked on a political career as a member of Miṣr al-Fatāt, the nationalist group founded by Aḥmad Ḥusayn in 1933. In the early days of the 1952 revolution he was nominated minister of national guidance and in 1954 became minister of communications.

Raḍwān's output comprises more than forty volumes, including short stories, collections of essays, history, politics, and biographies of Mahatma Gandhi, Mussolini and Muṣṭafā Kāmil. His works, like the writings of Aḥmad Ḥusayn himself, were strongly influenced by national socialism. He began writing for the theatre in 1955. His plays deal with social, philosophical and political issues (somewhat in the manner of Tawfīq **al-Ḥakīm**), with some use of colloquial Arabic in the dialogue; among the most important are *Akhlāq lil-bay'* (1957), *Dumū' Iblīs* (1958) and *Shuqqa lil-ījār* (1959).

Text edition

'A god in spite of himself', P. Cachia (trans.), *JAL* 5 (1974), 108–26.

Further reading

Badawi, M.M., *Modern Arabic Drama in Egypt*, Cambridge (1987), 129–39.

Shalaby, M., *Ruwwād al-fikr wa-al-fann*, Cairo (1982).

M. MIKHAIL

al-Rāfi'ī, Muṣṭafā Ṣādiq (18??–1937)

Egyptian poet. Between 1902 and 1908 al-Rāfi'ī published several volumes of poetry in the classical tradition. In his prose writings he defended traditional Arabic philology and culture against the innovations of Ṭāhā **Ḥusayn**, **al-'Aqqād**, Salāma **Mūsā** and others, and argued for the revival of traditional Islamic values in the social and political domains. In his 'poetic prose' (which at times rises to the level of 'poetry in prose') he used the convention of putting into a chain all similes known to him to describe an object, juxtaposing personification and the description of nature to reflect his emotions and psychological moods. Among his works in this vein are *Ḥadīth al-qamar* (2nd edn, Cairo, 1922), *Rasā'il al-aḥzān* (Cairo, 1924) and *al-Saḥāb al-aḥmar* (Cairo, 1924). Al-Rāfi'ī was an opponent of *shi'r manthūr*, which he defined as being no more than *nathr fannī* ('artistic prose').

Further reading

Nawfal, Y., *Qirā'āt wa-muḥāwarāt*, Cairo (n.d.).

M. MIKHAIL

See also: prose poem

al-Rāghib al-Iṣfahānī (fifth/eleventh century)

Abū al-Qāsim al-Ḥusayn ibn Muḥammad al-Rāghib al-Iṣfahānī was a man of letters, theologian, philosopher and philologist. Exceptionally for a writer of considerable importance, al-Rāghib is ignored by biographical dictionaries. Internal evidence points to him having lived in Isfahan in the first half of the fifth/eleventh century. His works fall into four categories: theology and the study of sects; ethics and moral education; *tafsīr* (Koranic **exegesis**), with a linguistic orientation; philology and ***adab***. This last group contains the *Majma' al-balāgha*, (*Assembly of Eloquence*), akin to a handbook of synonyms with illustrative phrases, and especially the *Muḥāḍarāt al-udabā' wa-muḥāwarāt al-shu'arā' wa-al-bulaghā'* (*The Ready Replies of Cultured Men, and Poets' and Orators' Conversation*), a collection of sayings, anecdotes and poetry arranged according to subject and drawing widely on religious, philosophical and literary material. One of the main *adab* anthologies, it challenges the reader intellectually by its stress on antithesis, while avoiding the stylistic excesses of the then fashionable rhymed prose (***saj'***).

Text edition

Muḥāḍarāt al-udabā' wa-muḥāwarāt al-shu'arā' wa-al-bulaghā', 4 vols, Beirut (1961).

Further reading

Madelung, W., 'Ar-Rāġib al-Iṣfahānî und die Ethik al-Ġazālîs', in *Islamwissenschaftliche Abhandlungen Fritz Meier zum sechzigsten Geburtstag*, R. Gramlich (ed.), Wiesbaden (1974), 152–62.
Rowson, E., 'The categorization of gender and sexual irregularities in medieval Arabic vice lists', in *Bodyguards: The Cultural Politics of Gender Ambiguity*, J. Epstein and K. Straub (eds.), New York (1991), 50–79.
'Umar 'Abd al-Raḥmān al-Sarīsī, *Al-Rāghib al-Iṣfahānī wa-juhūduh fī al-lugha wa-al-adab*, Amman (1987).

H. KILPATRICK

See also: anthologies, medieval

al-Rāhib, Hānī (1939–)

Syrian novelist and short-story writer. Hānī al-Rāhib studied English literature in **Syria** and England, where he gained a PhD. He has taught at the universities of **Damascus**, Sana'a and Kuwait. His first two novels, *al-Mahzūmūn* (written while a student at the University of Damascus) and *Sharkh fī tārīkh ṭawīl* (1970), are marked by an obsession with the estrangement of the middle-class, educated individual, and by great sensitivity and care with regard to language. Later works such as *Alf layla wa-laylatān* (1977), *al-Wabā'* (1981), *al-Tilāl* (1988) and *Khaḍrā' ka-al-mustanqa'āt* (1992) treat similar issues with greater emphasis on social constraints and determinants, placing individuals and themes within their social and political contexts. The historical destinies of the *petite bourgeoisie* in Syria and its rise and fall politically and morally is the theme that permeates most of his work since the late 1970s. He has also written short stories and journalistic pieces and translated works from English into Arabic, including works by Arnold Kettle, African–American writers and the Israeli novelist Yael Dayan.

W. HAMARNEH

Rāhib, Rufā'īl Zakhūr *see* Zakhūr, Père Rufā'īl

raḥīl see qaṣīda

Rā'ī al-Ibl *see* al-Rā'ī al-Numayrī

al-Rā'ī al-Numayrī (d. *c.*96/714)

Abū Jandal 'Ubayd ibn Ḥusayn from the tribe Numayr, called al-Rā'ī or Rā'ī al-ibil 'the camel-herd', was a poet in the **Umayyad** period who composed poems in a traditional vein. He spent much effort on the description of camels and desert animals and even introduced new motives taken from a **bedouin** milieu such as the activities of a camel-herd, whence he got his nickname. This literary tendency culminated in the work of **Dhū al-Rumma**, al-Rā'ī's pupil and the transmitter of his poetry.

Text edition

Diwān, Reinhard Weipert (ed.), Beirut (1980).

Further reading

Weipert, R., *Studien zum Diwan des Rā'ī*, Freiburg (1977).

T. BAUER

rajaz

An Arabic metre based on the foot *mustaf'ilun* (⏑̲ ⏑̲ ⏑ —), or a poem employing this metre. It has been in use since the earliest times of Arabic literature and is thought to have its origin in ancient rhymed prose (***saj'***). Simple songs, such as those of the camel driver, the boatman, the weaver, the water-carrier and the housewife, are alleged to have often been in *rajaz*. Some scholars hold the view that *rajaz* is the metrical pattern out of which all other metres have evolved.

From a literary point of view, a distinction can be made between *rajaz* verse and *qarīḍ* poetry (in any of the other metres). The distinction is based on the fact that *rajaz* has (under normal circumstances) only one member without caesura, whereas the other metres have two, more or less symmetrical, hemistichs separated by a caesura. *Rajaz* lines are therefore generally only half the length of lines in other metres. (They are, however, frequently printed in pairs.) The recurring rhyme at the short interval of only three (sometimes only two) feet, as compared with six or eight feet in the other metres, imposes a severe strain on the *rajaz* poet, who will often be tempted to use unusual words and bizarre forms, which adds to giving *rajaz* poetry its own distinctive literary character. Thematically, *rajaz* verse was often considered to be inferior and therefore outside *qarīḍ*. From a metrical point of view, it shows a greater looseness: as against the prestigious classical metres, where metrical variation is restricted to a limited number of positions, a *rajaz* trimeter has as many as six syllables that can be either long or short.

The founder of Arabic metrical theory, **al-Khalīl ibn Aḥmad**, does not attribute any special status to *rajaz*. For him, the metre is regarded as belonging to *shi'r* as do all other metres, and a composition in this metre can be called a ***qaṣīda.*** This has led to a problem of nomenclature. The *rajaz* trimeter occurs in two forms with either twelve or eleven syllables. The dimeter occurs in a form of either eight or seven syllables. According to al-Khalīl, only the acatalectic (i.e. complete) forms are *rajaz*, whereas the catalectic or truncated forms belong to other metres: the eleven-syllable *rajaz* is called *sarī'* and the seven-syllable form *munsariḥ*. One therefore sometimes finds a line in the Khalilian *sarī'* metre introduced with the words: 'the *rajaz* poet says ... '. (See **prosody** for scansion data of Khalilian metre types.)

The *urjūza* or *rajaz* poem comes in two types: monorhyme (*a a a* ...) and rhyming couplets (*a a b b c c* ...). This last type is called ***muzdawij*** and an *urjūza* of this structure is a ***muzdawija***. For the versifier it has the advantage that the severe rhyme restrictions of the monorhyme *urjūza* do not apply.

As an easy metre of low prestige, considered good for improvisation in connection with everyday subjects, *rajaz* was looked down upon by professional pre-Islamic and early **Umayyad** poets. It gained in literary importance with the emergence of prestigious *rajaz* poets such as **al-'Ajjāj** (d. *c*.91/710), his son **Ru'ba** (d. 145/762) and **Abū al-Najm al-'Ijlī** (d. before 125/743), who composed long poems with traditional *qaṣīda* themes. (Al-'Ijlī wrote a famous *urjūza* with a description of a camel which came to be known as *umm al-rajaz*, 'the *rajaz* poem par excellence'.) Other Umayyad poets such as **Jarīr** (d. *c*.112/730) and **Dhū al-Rumma** (d. 117/735) composed *urjūza*s alongside their *qaṣīda*s.

Towards the end of the Umayyad period, the hunting scenes of the polythematic *qaṣīda* evolved into the well-defined genre of the ***ṭardiyyāt*** (hunting poems) with its fixed form, contents and lexicon and, almost exclusively, *rajaz* metre. Some thirty-eight hunting poems in *rajaz* (among them long pieces of over fifty lines) are in the ***dīwān*** of **Abū Nuwās** (d. 199 or 200/814 or 15), the most important representative of this genre. Other examples are **Ibn al-Mu'tazz** (d. 296/908), **Kushājim,** (d. 360/971?), and **Abū Firās al-Ḥamdānī** (d. 357/968).

Thereafter the importance of the monorhyme *rajaz* declined, but the *rajaz* metre was still extensively used in the *urjūza muzdawija* which had become a popular form with **Abān al-Lāḥiqī**'s versification of ***Kalīla wa-Dimna***.

Since the late 1950s the *rajaz* foot has been the basis of many modern poems in *shi'r ḥurr* (**free verse**) with lines of varying length and various endings.

Text editions

Materials for the Study of Rağaz Poetry, 2: Five Rağaz Collections (al-Aghlab al-'Iğlī, Bashīr, Ibn an-Nikth, Ğandal, Ibn al-Muthannā, Ḥumayd al-Arqaṭ, Ghaylān ibn Ḥurayth, J. Hameen Antilla (ed.), Helsinki (1995).

——, *3: Minor Rağaz Collections*, J. Hameen Antilla (ed.), Helsinki (1996).

Further reading

Ullmann, Manfred, *Untersuchungen zur Rağazpoesie*, Wiesbaden (1966).

W. STOETZER

See also: *muzdawija*; prosody

rajjāz al-'arab *see* **Abū al-Nājm al-'Ijli**

ramal *see* **prosody**

al-Rammāḥ ibn Abrad *see* ibn Mayyāda

Ramzī, Muḥammad Munīr (1925–45)

Egyptian poet. A graduate of English literature at Alexandria University, he died by committing suicide. As one of the contributors to *Apollo* (see **Apollo Group**), he was influenced by **Abū Shādī**'s poetic experiments and other members of the society as well as by English poetry. He composed poems combining different metres. In his poem *Naḥwa al-ghurūb* rhyme is absent and the different combinations of feet employed sometimes slip into conventional Arabic metres – a method which is very like that of English–American **free verse**. He also wrote poems of a Romantic nature without metre altogether.

Further reading

Badawi, M.M., *An Anthology of Modern Arabic Verse*, Beirut (1970), 230–6.
——, *A Critical Introduction to Modern Arabic Poetry*, Cambridge (1975), 227.
Moreh, S., *Modern Arabic Poetry 1800–1970*, Leiden (1976), 185–6.

R. SNIR

al-Raqāshī (d. *c.*200/815)

Abū al-ʿAbbās al-Faḍl ibn ʿAbd al-Ṣamad al-Raqāshī, a *mawlā* (see ***mawālī***) of the Banū Raqāsh of Bakr ibn Wāʾil, was born in **Basra** and moved to **Baghdad** where he had contact with **Hārūn al-Rashīd**; he devoted himself especially to the **Barmakids** and composed a moving elegy on al-Faḍl ibn Yaḥyā. Upon the death of Hārūn al-Rashīd he moved to **Khurasan**, attaching himself to Ṭāhir ibn al-Ḥusayn, (see **Ṭahirids**) and remained there until his own death. He was a 'natural' poet (*shāʿir maṭbūʿ*) of the quality of **Abū Nuwās**, with whom he exchanged ***naqāʾiḍ*** and like whom he was given to reprobate verse. His cynical temperament can be seen in a mock-heroic lampoon of **Abū Dulaf al-ʿIjlī** contained in **Ibn al-Muʿtazz**'s *Ṭabaqāt al-shuʿarāʾ*.

Text ediitons

Abū Nuwās, *Dīwān*, Ewald Wagner (ed.), Cairo etc. (1958–), vol. 1, 52–3, 57–62, 72.
Ibn al-Muʿtazz, *Ṭabaqāt al-Shuʿarāʾ*, ʿA.A. Farrāj (ed.), Cairo (1957), 226–7.

P.F. KENNEDY

al-Raqīq al-Nadīm (also known as Ibn al-Raqīq) (fifth/tenth century)

Abū Isḥāq Ibrāhīm ibn al-Qāsim al-Kātib al-Qayrawānī al-Raqīq al-Nadīm was a historian and philologist from Qayrawan; he was also a poet of some ability. His most notable work is *Quṭb al-surūr fī awṣāf al-khumūr*, an anthology of anecdotes and poetry about wine poets and their poetry, from the *Jāhiliyya* to the eleventh century. As a source it is the finest medieval work of its kind, although it lacks the literary sensitivity of **Ibn al-Muʿtazz**'s earlier and far shorter *Fuṣūl al-tabāshīr fī tamāthīl al-surūr*.

Text edition

Quṭb al-surūr fī awṣāf al-khumūr, Aḥmad al-Jundī (ed.), Damascus (1969).

P.F. KENNEDY

al-Raqīq al-Qayrawānī *see* Ibn al-Raqīq al-Qayrawānī

al-Rashīd *see* Hārūn al-Rashīd

rāwī (pl. *ruwāh*)

Reciter and transmitter of poetry. In the ***jāhiliyya*** famous poets usually had one or more *rāwī*s, who preserved and recited their verses. Since many *rāwī*s became well-known poets themselves, they presumably also served as an apprentice to their master. Lineages of poets and *rāwī*s, often in the same family, are known over several generations. In Islamic times oral transmission was gradually replaced by writing. There is evidence that **Umayyad** poets dictated to their *rāwī*s, who were also expected to touch up and correct their lines. A derivation of the term is *rāwiya*, 'grand transmitter', applied, as a rule, to collectors of early **bedouin** poetry in the second/eighth century e.g. **Ḥammād al-Rāwiya**.

Further reading

Zwettler, M., *The Oral Tradition of Classical Arabic Poetry*, Columbus (1978), (see index).

R. JACOBI

Rayy

Major city in northern Iran in the medieval period, near modern Tehran, capital of the province of al-Jibāl or al-Jabal. The home throughout its history of numerous important writers and thinkers, including the philosopher Abū Bakr **al-Rāzī** (d. 313/925) and the theologian **Fakhr al-Dīn al-Rāzī** (d. 606/

1209), Rayy was a particularly important centre for Arabic literature, rivalling **Baghdad**, in the late fourth/tenth century, when it became one of the three capitals of the **Būyids**. The viziers **Ibn al-ʿAmīd** and **al-Ṣāḥib Ibn ʿAbbād**, in addition to their own literary accomplishments, attracted an impressive group of poets and scholars to Rayy, and the Ṣāḥib's protégé **al-Ābī**, later himself vizier, composed an important anthology of Arabic prose, as well as a lost history of the city. Although the Būyid viziers' magnificent library was pillaged and partly destroyed when the **Ghaznavids** took the town in 420/1029, the tradition of Arabic *belles-lettres* was maintained by the secretarial class who served first the Ghaznavid governors and then the **Saljūq** sultans, after the city fell to Ṭughril Beg in 434/1042 and became temporarily his capital; a noteworthy example is Ibn Ḥassūl (d. 450/1058), who served as a **secretary** to all three dynasties, and composed his *Superiority of the Turks to Other Troops* for the Saljūqs as an attack on the Būyids. The city declined under the later Saljūqs, and Arabic literature was overshadowed, as throughout Iran, by Persian letters. Rayy barely survived the Mongol onslaught in 617/1220 and was abandoned soon thereafter.

Further reading

al-Bākharzī, *Dumyat al-qaṣr*, S.M. al-ʿĀnī (ed.), Baghdad and Najaf (1971), vol. 1, 367–74.

Ibn Ḥassūl, *Tafḍīl al-Atrāk ʿalā sā'ir al-ajnād*, ʿA. al-ʿAzzāwī (ed.), 'Ibni Hassulün Türkler hakkinda bir eseri', *Türk Tarih Kurumu Belleten* 4 (1940), 235–66 (Turkish), 1–51 (Arabic).

Kraemer, J., *Humanism in the Renaissance of Islam*, Leiden (1986), 241–72.

al-Thaʿālibi, *Yatīmat al-dahr*, Cairo (1956), vol. 3, 157–418.

——, *Tatimmat al-yatīma*, A. Eghbal (ed.), Tehran (1934), vol. 1, 92–144.

E.K. ROWSON

al-Rāzī, Abū Bakr Muḥammad ibn Zakariyyā (*c.*251–313/*c.*865–925)

Physician, alchemist and philosopher, known in the West as Rhazes. Born in **Rayy**, he taught and practised medicine at the hospitals of his native town and of **Baghdad**. In his medical work he was the first to undertake a complete stocktaking of the sources of Greek medicine transmitted in late Hellenism and translated into Arabic by the end of the third/ninth century. In handbooks on the lines of the *Corpus Galenicum*, he presented a systematic treatment of pathology and therapy enlarged by his own clinical records. Among his numerous manuals, introductory textbooks and small monographs, the following stand out. *Al-Ḥāwī fī al-ṭibb* (the *Liber Continens* of the Latin tradition) is a vast collection of excerpts from **Galen** and all the other medical authorities available to him, united in book form posthumously at the instance of the vizier **Ibn al-ʿAmīd** (d. 360/970). *Al-Ṭibb* (also *al-Kunnāsh*) *al-Manṣūrī* (dedicated to the **Sāmānid** al-Manṣūr ibn Isḥāq between 290/903 and 296/908) is a systematic treatment of medicine in ten books, and through the much-studied *Liber Nonus*, a pathology of the parts of the body *a capite ad calcem*, was most influential in early European medicine. *Al-Murshid*, one of his late works, is modelled on the Hippocratic *Aphorisms*, but is a much more clearly arranged introduction to the elements of the medical art.

His main works on alchemy, presented systematically and as a strictly rational science, are the *Kitāb al-Asrār* and the *Sirr al-asrār* (*Book of Secrets* and *Secret of Secrets*). As a philosopher, al-Rāzī defended the pursuit of wisdom through the rational sciences, being, as medicine is to the body, the 'Spiritual Physick' to the mind, in his *al-Ṭibb al-rūḥānī* (also written for al-Manṣūr); here, as in his treatise *al-Sīra al-falsafiyya*, he propagated the philosophers' way of life: relieved from sensual affections and seeking, through the quest of knowledge, the highest good attainable to humankind. The heritage of Platonism, pervading the philosophic tradition in the Arabic medical schools, produced a peculiar offshoot in his metaphysics, *al-ʿIlm al-ilāhī*: a unique system of hypostatized 'eternals', God, soul, matter – consisting of atoms – time and (void) space. His rejection of revealed religion precluded any further influence of his ideas in later Islamic thought.

Text editions

Abi Bakr ... Rhagensis (Razis) Opera Philosophica, P. Kraus (ed.), Cairo (1939) (all extant texts and fragments).

Guide du médecin nomade, El-Arbi Moubachir (trans.), Paris (1980).

al-Ḥāwī fī al-ṭibb, 23 vols, Hyderabad (1955–70).

al-Razi's Buch Geheimnis der Geheimnisse, J. Ruska (trans.), Berlin (1937); *Sirr al-asrār:*

neizvestnoe sočinenie ar-Rāzī 'Kniga tajny tajn', U.I. Karimov (ed. and trans.), Tashkent (1957).
The Spiritual Physick of Rhazes, A.J. Arberry (trans.), London (1950).

Further reading

al-Bīrūnī, 'Epître de Bērūnī contenant le répertoire des ouvrages de ar-Rāzī', (=*Risāla fī fihrist kutub Muḥammad ibn Zakariyyā' al-Rāzī*), P. Kraus (ed.), Paris (1936); M. Muḥaqqiq (ed. with Persian trans.), Tehran (1984–5).
M. Mayerhof, 'Thirty-three clinical observations by Rhazes', *Isis* 23 (1935), 321–72.
Muḥaqqiq, Mahdī, *Faylasūf-i Rayy*, 2nd edn, Tehran (1973) (biography, 1–49; works, 51–133).
Pines, S., *Beiträge zur islamischen Atomenlehre*, Grafenhainichen (1936).
Ullmann, M., *Die Medizin im Islam*, Leiden (1970), 128–38.
——, *Die Natur- und Geheimwissenschaften im Islam*, Leiden (1972), 210–13.

G. ENDRESS

al-Rāzī, Abū Ḥātim *see* Abū Ḥātim al-Rāzī

al-Rāzī, Fakhr al-Dīn *see* Fakhr al-Dīn al-Rāzī

religious poetry

Religious poetry does not constitute one of the major genres of classical Arabic poetry. Yet traces of religious expression exist in the earliest extant material; this crystallized eventually into the ***zuhdiyya*** (the ascetic poem) of the early **ʿAbbāsid** period. Mystical (or Ṣūfī) poetry, which had its roots in the **Umayyad** period, flourished later; it is in Sufism that an Islamic religious poetry acquired its most profound and sensitive voice.

Poetry was accorded small significance as a form of expression by the nascent Islamic community during the life-time of the Prophet **Muḥammad**, as Islam sought initially to disassociate the Koranic revelation from this medium. Since, however, *shiʿr* (specifically *qaṣīd*) remained unassailable as the register of a tribalism that was not dismantled by the new religion, Islam came slowly to impinge upon an otherwise essentially 'secular' domain.

Although religious poetry (notwithstanding the *zuhdiyya* of the early ʿAbbāsid period) was never acknowledged to constitute a major genre in later medieval works on poetics (these simply described the salient features of the earlier canon), religious elements did exist both in the ***qaṣīda*** and as an independent theme among certain poets, notably the Christian of **Ḥīra**, **ʿAdī ibn Zayd al-ʿIbādī** (d. *c.*600), and the Ḥanīf (monotheist) **Umayya ibn Abī al-Ṣalt** (d. 8/630). Both produced compositions of monotheistic sentiment and are precursors of the later *zuhdiyya*. On the whole, however, where *Jāhilī* poetry is contemplative, it gives voice to an anxiety about *al-dahr*/fate – the prime mover that commanded the mutability of life.

Collectively the early corpus provides a glimpse – not much more – of the composite system of belief (both pagan and monotheistic) among those who populated the Arabian peninsula in the sixth century. Pagan elements in poetry, i.e. celebration of the various idols of pre-Islamic **Arabia**, survive as scattered verses, a significant number of which are cited in **Ibn al-Kalbī**'s *Kitāb al-Aṣnām*. With those purely monotheistic sentiments that survive (especially in the case of Umayya ibn Abī al-Ṣalt) authenticity is an a issue, since a standard reflex among later Muslim and Orientalist commentators (both medieval and modern) has been to suggest that they are interpolations dating from a later period. The criteria for making such judgements in individual cases have not been properly established; a way forward is to look at religious elements in the context of other quasi-religious and more conspicuously *Jāhilī* sentiments, i.e. one must gauge to what extent religious elements that smack of Islamic belief were compatible with, and even suggested by, the panoply of ethics and virtues contained in *muruwwa*. This may, for example, help us to understand the eschatological references that have been received in the *Muʿallaqa* of **Zuhayr ibn Abī Sulmā**, a poem that constitutes a celebration of *muruwwa* in its broadest sense.

In the Islamic period what might be broadly termed a religious poetry must be divided into two categories: poetry that expressed a quasi-orthodox piety, on the one hand, and poetry that can be termed political insofar as it gave voice to the views of a heterodox minority, on the other.

A mainstream of religious poetry can be seen in ascetic poetry which preached a renunciation of worldly pleasures. The roots of asceticism, and thus the ascetic poem (*zuhdiyya*), are commonly discerned in **al-Ḥasan al-Baṣrī** (d.

110/728). From the same period al-Sābiq al-Barbarī has left to posterity a number of ascetic poems whose tenor is consonant with the attitudes of al-Ḥasan al-Baṣrī; the asceticism of these poems is supported, as in the case of **Ṣāliḥ ibn ʿAbd al-Quddūs** (d. 167/783–4) and **Abū al-ʿAtāhiya** (d. 211/826), by pious maxims and general wisdom, based on the mutability of life and, to this extent, akin to the contemplative maxims of pre-Islamic poetry.

Khārijī and **Shīʿī** poetry form a separate category of religious poetry in the early Islamic period. The ***dīwān*** of the Khārijīs is a poetry of propaganda which articulated the ideals of martyrdom; it borrowed in large measure the imagery of the ancient **bedouin** and heroic canon. As Gabrieli (1973) has observed: 'on the religious battlefield, poetry became the weapon of the opposition. Before ascetic and mystical poetry the Umayyad age knew religious poetry chiefly as the vehicle of dissidence, essentially of Kharijites and Shiʿites.' Khārijī poetry is coloured to a large extent by mourning over slain comrades and ***fakhr***; it is centred on the praise and the joyful contemplation of martyrdom, on cursing a wicked world, and on scorning death; it is seldom descriptive or given to narrative. This poetry is not arcane (in the manner of some Shīʿī poetry) but the clear expression of an ideology that rejects all artifice: 'Ṭirimmah is a good case in point: in the few verses of a Kharijite *Stimmung* he abandons all his *gharīb* and speaks out frankly and simply like his comrades in faith' (Gabrieli, 1973).

In the ʿAlid or Shīʿī milieu the *Hāshimiyyāt* of **al-Kumayt** must be mentioned. Religiosity here is of political import; his poems follow the *qaṣīda* framework but with short and conventional *nasīb*s and *raḥīl*s followed by lavish eulogies of the ʿAlids similar to those that were addressed to the bedouin Sayyids. Other significant Shīʿī poets are **Kuthayyir** (d. 105/723) and **al-Sayyid al-Ḥimyarī** (d. 173/789). Kuthayyir's poetry, mainly erotic, provides valuable early documentation of some Shīʿī *arcana*. Of al-Sayyid al-Ḥimyarī, Gabrieli (1973) writes: 'what we notice in most of his collection is the combination of archaic language and *tashayyuʿ*; the impact and the genuine character of socio-religious feeling are nullified by an artificial vocabulary bristling with *gharīb*, by the laborious imagery, and by the irritatingly involved style ... [This poetry] had an emasculated weakness when contrasted with the savage violence of the Kharijites.'

Above are traced briefly the lines of development of the most conspicuous categories of religious poetry in the early Islamic period. To some extent the above constitutes a standard view. However, a detailed survey of early Arabic poetry (pre-Islamic to ʿAbbāsid) offers a variety of religious material which, collectively, must needs have had an influence on the crystallization of a mainstream religious voice in poetry. Consideration must be given to: the religiosity of ***rithāʾ***, which borrowed the elegiac mode of pre-Islamic poetry (i.e. in the ***dīwān*** of **Labīd ibn Rabīʿa**); other Ḥanīf material; the poetry of some of the Companions (**Ḥassān ibn Thābit**, Kaʿb ibn Malik al-Anṣārī, **ʿAbd Allāh ibn Rawāḥa**); other sundry early Islamic material, ranging from the pronounced religiosity in the *nasīb*s of **al-Nābigha al-Jaʿdī** (d. *c.*63/683) to the expression of a social etiquette (influenced significantly by Islam) in such as the poetry of **Abū al-Aswad al-Duʾalī** (d. *c.*69/688). Some consideration as a separate category of religious poetry must also be given to the extended rhyming couplets of **Abān al-Lāḥiqī** (d. 187/803) and **ʿAlī ibn al-Jahm** (d. 249/863); this material sought principally to praise the ʿAbbāsids as the inheritors of the Biblical prophets of whom a schematic history is traced.

From the **Mamlūk** and early Ottoman periods attention must be drawn to a large body of religious poetry that revolved around the veneration and praise of the Prophet Muḥammad: *al-Madāʾiḥ al-nabawiyya*. Two poems, separated from each other by six centuries, are the finest and most celebrated examples of this tradition (which acquired a particularly strong vitality in Ṣūfī circles): the so-called 'Burda' of **Kaʿb ibn Zuhayr** (d. after 10/632) and the similarly labelled 'Burda' of Sharaf al-Dīn **al-Būṣīrī** (d. *c.*694/1294). The former poem, which was recited before the Prophet himself, is cast – as we would expect from its early date of composition – in the mould of the classical *qaṣīda*; it thus sowed the seeds for subsequent evocations of this archetypal model, and especially for the manipulation of the imagery of nostalgia (contained in the *nasīb*) to articulate the affective signature of this quasi-liturgical genre. To distinguish it briefly from the 'Burda' of Kaʿb we should note that al-Būṣīrī's poem was 'a true compendium of medieval prophetology' (Schimmel, 1985). Material extant in some of the larger Islamic manuscript collections reflects the importance of prophetic venerations right up to the modern period. Further, the relevant manuscript catalogues illustrate well the extent to which favourite poems (especially the 'Burda' of al-Būṣīrī) were themselves celebrated by means of pentastich amplifications (*takhāmīs*, sing. *takhmīs*) – and other such reworkings – which rarely departed from the sentiments of the original composition. The most notable examples of these stanzaic effusions date from the thirteenth to sixteenth centuries.

Further reading

'Abbās, I., *Shi'r al-Khawārij*, Beirut (n.d.).
Abdesselem, M., *Le Thème de la mort dans la poésie arabe des origines à la fin du III*ème*/IX*ème *siècle*, Tunis (1977).
'Awīs, Muḥammad, *al-Ḥikma fī al-shi'r al-'Arabī*, Asyut (1979) (see therein for sources, 327–30).
Bellamy, J.A., 'The impact of Islam on early Arabic poetry', in *Islam: Past Influence and Present Challenge*, Edinburgh (1979), 141–67.
Bravmann, M., *The Spirtual Background of Early Islam: Studies in Ancient Arabic Concepts*, Leiden (1972).
Farrukh, O., *Das Bilde des Frühislam in der arabischen Dichtung von der Hijra bis zum Tode des kalifen 'Umar*, Leipzig (1937).
Gabrieli, F., 'Religious poetry in early Islam', in *Arabic Poetry: Theory and Development*, G.E. von Grunebaum (ed.), Wiesbaden (1973), 5–17.
Hamori, Andras, 'Ascetic poetry (*zuhdiyyāt*)', in *CHALABL*, 265–74.
Hūfī, A.M., *al-Ḥayāt al-'Arabiyya fī al-shi'r al-Jāhilī*, Cairo (1949).
Izutsu, T., *God and Man in the Koran*, Tokyo (1964), Chapter 7, 'Jāhiliyya and Islam'.
Kannūn, A.A., *Sābiq al-Barbarī*, Damascus (1969).
Khan, Muhamad Rahatullah, *Vom Einfluß des Qu'āns auf die arabische Dichtung*, Leipzig (1983).
Kister, M.J., *Society and Religion from Jāhiliyya to Islam*, Aldershot (1990).
Mubārak, Zakī, *al-Madā'iḥ al-nabawiyya fī al-adab al-'Arabī*, Cairo (1943).
Ringgren, H., *Studies in Arabian Fatalism*, Uppsala (1955).
Rosenthal, Franz, *'Sweeter than Hope': Complaint and Hope in Medieval Islam*, Leiden (1983), 4–18.
Rubinacci, R., 'Political poetry', in *CHALABL*, 185–201.
Schimmel, Annemarie, *And Muhammad is His Messenger: The Veneration of the Prophet in Islamic Piety*, Chapel Hill and London (1985) (especially Chapter 10, 'Poetry in honor of the Prophet', 176–215).
Sperl, Stefan, *Mannerism in Arabic Poetry*, Cambridge (1989) (Chapters 2 and 4).
Vajda, G., 'Les zindîqs en pays d'Islam au début de la période abbaside', *RSO* 17 (1937), 173–224.
Wagner, Ewald, *Grundzüge, der klassischen arabischen Dichtung*, Band II, *Die arabische Dichtung in islamischer Zeit*, Darmstadt (1988), 120–30.

P.F. KENNEDY

See also: Ṣūfī literature: poetry

rhetoric and poetics

The terms 'rhetoric' and 'poetics' clearly refer to disciplines in the Classical and Western tradition; as such, they may be applied to the Arab situation only with a grain of salt. Closest to 'rhetoric' is the 'science of eloquence' (*'ilm al-balāgha*) which comprises the three fields of syntactical stylistics, theory of imagery and rhetorical figures. It achieved its definitive formulation in the later Middle Ages (seventh/thirteenth century and onwards). 'Poetics' would have its closest counterpart in the 'critique [lit. assaying] of poetry' (*naqd al-shi'r*); poetics is thus to be understood as a theory of criticism rather than a normative guideline as to how to compose good poetry. This branch of literature flourished in the fourth/tenth and fifth/eleventh centuries and was later, at least in part, absorbed into the 'science of eloquence'. In this sense, poetics and rhetoric form one large field of intellectual pursuit, as one meta-discourse dealing with literature. One might thus replace the two terms by speaking of 'literary theory'. It should be noted, however, that 'theory' here mostly means 'taxonomy', i.e. the enumeration, definition, exemplification and hierarchical classification of various cases.

The pre-systematic phase

Given the decidedly unprimitive character of the Arabic verbal arts before Islam, we can assume that a rather developed vocabulary to talk about these arts already existed early on. This would include terms denoting the 'professionals' of the various arts, such as the poet (*shā'ir*), the ***rajaz*** poet (*rājiz*), the declaimer of poetry (***rāwī***), the soothsayer (*kāhin*) who enunciates his trance sayings in rhymed prose (***saj'***), the composer of rhymed prose (*sāji'*) who is not a soothsayer, and the orator (*khaṭīb*). Another group of terms are the poetic **genres**: praise (***madīḥ***), self-praise (***fakhr***), invective (***hijā'***) and dirge (***rithā'***).

For the technical side of poetry it is safe to assume that some terms were general knowledge, such as 'line' (*bayt*, lit. 'tent') and 'hemistich' (*miṣrāʿ*, lit. 'tent-flap') and possibly *rawī* for the 'central rhyme consonant' (the case of *qāfiya* for 'rhyme' is unclear, because in the beginning the word seems to mean complete poems [cf. the English 'rhyme'] and still occasionally does so in later times). In addition, it is likely that the experts, i.e. the poets and the declaimers of poetry (the latter were often apprentices to the poets), had their own technical jargon. One set of terms that, in view of the strange vagueness of their definitions, seems to be rather archaic is the fivesome of 'rhyme mistakes', often simply called 'mistakes of poetry' (*ʿuyūb al-shiʿr*; the vagueness of this name is another sign for the antiquity of these terms). While most of the terms mentioned so far remain in use throughout the centuries, albeit with certain semantic developments, there is one set of terms, transmitted in early sources, that is explicitly attributed to the **bedouins** (*ʿarab*, not necessarily, but most likely pre-Islamic) and which is clearly already obsolescent at the time of the sources: this set defines four terms denoting certain categories of poetry (*qaṣīd*, *ramal*, *rajaz*, *khafīf*) by correlating them with (a) the length of the line and (b) real-life situations in which they are used. Since these correlations no longer exist in the later poetry, our view of pre-Islamic poetry may be somewhat distorted in this respect.

As far as literary criticism is concerned there is little hard evidence to go on. There are legendary reports and there is the poetry itself. The reports inform us about poetic contests that were regularly held at the annual market of **ʿUkāẓ** near Mecca with the famous poet **al-Nābigha al-Dhubyānī** as the umpire, and also about individual jousts, such as the one between the two very early poets **ʿAlqama** and **Imru' al-Qays**. We hear that the famous Seven Odes were written on cloth with golden ink and hung on the Kaʿba – this legend resulting from a misinterpretation of their name ***al-Muʿallaqāt*** as 'the suspended ones' rather than 'the ones considered precious'. In all of this, certain implicit criteria for the evaluation of the poetry must have been used. Similarly, the poetry itself shows (disregarding for a moment the problem of authenticity) that certain motifs, similes, descriptive techniques, etc., were used by one poet and then imitated by others, thus proving the success and popularity of the feature in question. Again, explicit criteria are not offered. The conscious artistry of the poets is especially obvious in the work of those whom the later philologist al-Aṣmaʿī called the 'slaves of poetry' and whose long poems are known as the 'one-year-olds' (*ḥawliyyāt*) and the 'scraped ones' (*muḥakkakāt*) because of the constant attention to their refinement over a long period of time.

The situation does not change much in early Islamic poetry. Two types of anecdotal evaluations of poetry are not uncommon. One is individual and consists of A asking B 'who is the best poet?' (or, more specifically, 'best panegyrist, satirist, etc.') and B answering 'so-and-so, where s/he says: [followed, usually, by one line of poetry]'. This one-line approach to aesthetic judgement remained popular for a long time. The other type is exemplified by generally valid propositions in which the production of poetry is correlated with certain states of mind. This 'psycho-literary' approach remains rudimentary. Finally, at this stage there are various attempts to define basic, but rather vague terms, such as *balāgha*, 'eloquence', *faṣāḥa*, 'purity of speech', and *bayān*, 'lucidity'; this is usually done in pithy sayings of a quasi-definitory character.

The beginnings of a technical literature

The first group of people to deal in a scholarly way with poetry and, to a lesser extent, also with other genres of literature was the philologists, especially in the two centres of language studies, **Basra** and **Kufa**. Their main objective was to safeguard the integrity of the corpus of ancient poetry by collecting the old poems and trying to eliminate spurious materials. This latter activity is called 'assaying' (*naqd*) – a term taken from the vocabulary of the money-changer and later used not only to distinguish the genuine from the spurious, but also the good from the bad, thus 'literary criticism'. The few reports we have about people performing this activity show it to be an intuitive knowledge, comparable to physiognomy (*firāsa*) and unteachable. Apart from creating vulgate editions (often a Kufan, a Basran, and – later – a mixed one) of tribal and individual ***dīwān***s, from producing commentaries explaining lexical and grammatical difficulties, and from compiling biographical notes on the poets, the philologists, from handling so many texts, gradually also assembled some critical and aesthetic notions and terms. After some beginnings in books on poets (**Ibn Sallām al-Jumaḥī** and **Ibn Qutayba**), they were presented in a short treatise by the Kufan grammarian **Tha'lab** (d. 291/904), called *Qawā'id al-shi'r* (*The Foundations of Poetry*). Although having the appearance of lecture notes with examples, the treatise is logically structured, leading from basic sentence types to content-defined genres, then on to certain rhetorical beauties of the line and finally to a typology of lines based on the interdependence, or lack of such, of the hemistichs. The most successful line is one in which the hemistichs can be understood completely independently of each other.

Historically much more important was another group of poetry experts, the 'modern' poets and literati of the **'Abbāsid** era (see ***muḥdathūn***). The rise of the new style in poetry which gradually developed into a typically mannerist type of poetic endeavour (poetic motifs engendering more sophisticated and complex motifs) was not greeted with equal enthusiasm in all quarters; conservatives spoke of the corruption of poetry and supporters felt impelled to write apologetic, or simply descriptive, accounts. In any case, the contrast between 'ancient' and 'modern' poetry was a strong stimulus to reflect on the essence of poetry in general and 'modern' poetics in particular. **Ibn al-Mu'tazz** (d. 296/908), himself one of the most important poets of the middle 'Abbāsid period, wrote his book about the 'new' (***badī'***) component(s) of 'modern' poetry for the express purpose of legitimizing them by proving that they were anything but new and thus protected by the model character of ancient poetry. In another work, an unpreserved but quoted book on plagiarisms (see ***sariqa***), he alleges that *one* specific misconstructed metaphor in a poem by the 'ancient' poet **Dhū al-Rumma** deceived the 'modern' poet **Abū Tammām**, who was at the centre of the 'new style' controversy, into adopting his particular way of writing poetry; in general terms, he falsely extended the model character of 'ancient' poetry to the few bad lines that occur in it. On a larger scale, the contrast between 'ancient' and 'modern' is seen by the poet **Ibn Ṭabāṭabā** (d. 322/934) in his *'Iyār al-shi'r* (*The Criterion of Poetry*) as one between truth and wit: the 'ancients' present the true nature of things, while the 'moderns' must offer subtlety, elegance and other such textual qualities without any regard for the realities – an altogether very apt, though exaggerated characterization of the literary mannerism that began to hold sway at his time. Similar ideas can be found in the introductory epistle that the littérateur and courtier Abū Bakr **al-Ṣūlī** (d. 335/946) prefixed to his biographical work on the *bête noire* Abū Tammām.

The influx of Greek science and philosophy in translation had an additional impact on nascent poetics, in two ways. One is the heightened insight into the desirability of a logical, systematic presentation of arguments, including certain methods to be used for the achievement of this goal (definition of terms, taxonomies on the basis of complete disjunctions, deductive and inductive reasoning). The prime example is the *Naqd al-shi'r* (*Assaying of Poetry*) by the logician and administrator **Qudāma ibn Ja'far** (d. 337/948; other dates are also given). He became proverbial for his knowledge of 'eloquence' (in **al-Ḥarīrī**'s *Maqāmāt*) and many of his terms and ideas were taken up again by later authors; but his systematic presentation of the 'good and bad in poetry' (definition of poetry that yields its four basic elements, description of the good qualities of these elements and their combinations, followed by the bad qualities) was hardly ever emulated. The same tendency of systematizing is noticeable on a larger scale in the 'divisions of the sciences' that began to proliferate in the fourth/tenth century, and in which literary theory is often briefly mentioned in one way or another. Although the model for the divisions of sciences was taken from philosophical literature, it was predominantly the state **secretaries** who produced them, as they were interested in philosophy as well as in questions of eloquence. In the same tradition we find the unique *The Demonstration Concerning the Various Levels of Unhiddenness* (*al-Burhān fī wujūh al-bayān*) by **Ibn Wahb**, an – otherwise unknown – member if the Banū Wahb family of scribes. Here various literary theoretical topics are embedded in a general theory of 'unhiddenness' on the four consecutive levels of being, thinking, speaking and writing.

The other influence of the Greek tradition did not make itself felt immediately: it is the translations of **Aristotle**'s *Rhetoric* and *Poetics* together with the discussions of their position within the Organon. Already the late Alexandrian Greek commentators of Aristotle's writings considered these two works to be in essence logical books and thus part of the

Organon. This tradition was continued by the philosophers writing in Arabic who, after some initial hesitation due to their having inherited conflicting justifications for the inclusion of rhetoric and poetics in the Organon, agreed on the notion that the purpose of rhetoric was persuasion (*iqnāʿ*) and that of poetry the evocation of mental images (*takhyīl*); furthermore, that it is persuasive and evocative propositions and syllogisms that characterize these two arts. However, both books remained in the domain of the philosophers for a long time, while the literary theorists did not pay any attention, except for Ḍiyāʾ al-Dīn **Ibn al-Athīr** (d. 638/1239) who criticizes **Ibn Sīnā** for the strange Grecoid theory he proposes with its uncalled-for logical tinge. It is only later and only in the Islamic West that the rhetorical and poetical writings of the philosophers are made use of for the formulation of literary theory, namely in the works of **Ḥāzim al-Qarṭājannī** (d. 684/1285), al-Sijilmāsī (wrote *c.*704/1304) and Ibn al-Bannāʾ (d. 721/1321). In spite of their shared sources, their several efforts differ greatly from each other.

Lastly, literary theory was influenced and partly shaped by the Koranic disciplines. Two issues were at the forefront here; the dogma of the inimitability of the **Koran** and the problem of correct interpretation of non-straightforward (i.e. figurative, elliptical, or any other obliquely referential) language in the scripture. The emphasis in the discussion of the inimitability lay on style (although this was not the only consideration): word order, word use, use of metaphors and figures of speech – all these were unsurpassed and unsurpassable in their degree of *balāgha*, 'eloquence'. Theologically, the unattainable degree of eloquence that the Koran was believed to embody constituted the miracle that proved the prophethood of Muḥammad. Every prophet is thought to be divinely authenticated by a miracle, but it is only in the case of Muḥammad that divine message and divine miracle are inextricably intertwined; the miracles of, say, Moses and Jesus were completely outside their message. Moreover, the miracle was considered to happen in that field in which the human mind had at that time reached its highest perfection: magic (*siḥr*) in the case of Moses, medicine (*ṭibb*) with Jesus, and eloquence (*balāgha*) in the Arabic ambience of the Prophet. The term for a prophetic miracle is *muʿjiza*, and from the same root derives the verbal noun ***iʿjāz*** used to denote the Koran's inimitability. The two terms mean 'incapacitator' and 'incapacitation', respectively. In the case of the Koran, this idea means that those who disbelieved in the mission of the Prophet were challenged to produce something like the Koran and, in spite of their great need to do so, were 'incapacitated', i.e. found incapable of imitating it.

It is not surprising that a literature developed somewhere between **grammar**, stylistics and the theory of figurative speech, which tried to prove this important dogma. The outstanding names to be mentioned here are **al-Rummānī** (d. 386/997), **al-Khaṭṭābī** (d. 388/998) and **ʿAbd al-Qāhir al-Jurjānī** (d. 471/1078 or 474/1081). The first in particular became very influential with his rather short treatise *al-Nukat fī iʿjāz al-Qurʾān* (*Subtle Points about the Inimitability of the Koran*). This was amply used by later literary theorists, sometimes without acknowledgement, and certainly at their own peril. This is where the second of the above-mentioned Koranic influences has to be considered. Koranic studies, within the framework of theological as well as legal thought, had developed a hermeneutics in order to deal with figurative and other non-direct utterances. The terminology used in this field partially overlapped with that in literary studies, but the meanings attached to a number of identical terms differed. Indiscriminate quoting, side by side, of these Koranic materials on the one hand and poetic materials on the other in comprehensive and compilatory works like those of **Abū Hilāl al-ʿAskarī** (d. after 395/1005) and **Ibn Rashīq** (d. 456/1063 or later) created contradictions and confusion. The cleaning up has to be credited to the efforts of ʿAbd al-Qāhir al-Jurjānī.

Poetry and prose

There are some indications that the state secretaries developed an independent terminology, different from that of the poetry experts, to deal with the technicalities of their ornate epistolography. In the *Mafātīḥ al-ʿulūm* (*Keys of the Sciences*), which is a topically arranged dictionary of technical terms, Muḥammad ibn Aḥmad **al-Khwārizmī** (wrote between 366/976 and 372/982) has a section on 'on the conventional terms of the epistolographers' and another on 'on the critique of poetry'. Both are lists of rhetorical figures; a few have the same name but denote slightly different phenomena, while in other cases there are different names for the same phenomenon. There are a few more lists dealing specifically with epistolography; however, they remain the exception in a discipline that increasingly considered the differences between poetry and prose just one of the presence or absence of metre and rhyme. Apart from this, both poetry and **artistic prose** partake in the same quality of *balāgha*, 'eloquence'. The poet and epistolographer **al-ʿAttābī** (d. *c*.208/823) coined a short formula expressing this view: *al-shiʿru rasāʾilu maʿqūdatun wa-al-rasāʾilu shiʿrun maḥlūl*, 'poetry is congealed epistles and epistles are dissolved poetry'. As a matter of fact, poets and secretaries often dealt with the same topics (such as praise, blame, elegy, congratulation); there was a fair amount of give and take, as far as motifs and conceits were concerned; and the transposition of poetic lines into prose and vice versa became a favourite exercise. While, as **al-Jāḥiẓ** had observed, in earlier times an eloquent person rarely had the gift for both poetry and ornate prose, the secretaries now tried their hands also at poetry, mostly in the less ritual genres, and it became ever more frequent that they left two ***dīwān***s, one of poems and one of epistles. The outcome of all this is that prose and poetry were mostly served by the same theory. The formal aspects of poetry, metre and rhyme, were treated in separate disciplines, prosody and rhyme theory, and were rarely dealt with in works of literary theory

There have, however, been some attempts to define poetic speech beyond the purely formal definition. These are based either on the way in which things are expressed (al-Zanjānī; Ḥāzim al-Qarṭājannī), or on the idea of poetic untruth (**Ibn Fāris**, **Ibn Ḥazm**), or, finally, on the idea of poetic obscurity (Ibrāhīm ibn Hilāl **al-Ṣābiʾ**). None of these attempts were historically successful.

Major themes in literary theory

These have already been treated in separate entries; see especially: **ancients and moderns**, ***badīʿ***, ***lafẓ* and *maʿnā***, ***maṭbūʿ* and *maṣnūʿ***, and ***sariqa***.

ʿAbd al-Qāhir al-Jurjānī and the formation of scholastic rhetoric (*ʿilm al-balāgha*)

Literary theory reached its pinnacle in the two works of al-Jurjānī, the *Mysteries of Eloquence* (*Asrār al-balāgha*) and the *Proofs for the [Koran's] Inimitability* (*Dalāʾil al-isāz*). The first is more poetically oriented and deals first and foremost with questions of imagery and tropes. Due to the confluence of poetic and Koranic notions of the properties of texts, the definition and terminology of even as central a term as metaphor had become rather confused and contradictory. Al-Jurjānī now clarifies the mutual relationships of the terms 'simile' (*tashbīh*, comparison of things), 'analogy' (*tamthīl*, comparison of facts), and simile-based as well as analogy-based 'metaphor' (*istiʿāra*). (For details see **metaphor**.) In addition, he refashions the term ***majāz*** in such a way that it no longer covers non-tropical idioms like ellipsis and pleonasm but is strictly applied to 'figurative usages'. As such it becomes the genus for both 'metaphor' as a trope based on a similarity and 'metonymy', (*majāz mursal*) as a trope based on contiguity. In fact, al-Jurjānī decries the use of the term *istiʿāra* to include 'metonymy', which was common in the Koranic disciplines. Finally, in the *Dalāʾil* he proposes the semantic distinction between 'meaning' (*maʿnā*) and 'meaning of the meaning' (*maʿnā al-maʿnā*); in the latter case the surface meaning is not intended, but points to another, intended, meaning. All figurative usages can be subsumed under this heading, but it also includes 'periphrasis' (*kināya*) which is non-figurative, despite the fact that the surface meaning is not intended ('rich in ashes of the cooking-pot' = 'hospitable'; the 'ashes' are real, but not the point of the phrase). The net result of all this is a neat semantic system of indirect expressions. It should be noted that the overall system is partly due to poetic interests and partly to concerns of Koranic interpretation. The lion's share of the *Dalāʾil* is, of course, devoted to the problem of the 'structuring' (***naẓm***) of the Koranic text, in which lies its inimitability. It thus deals with questions of word order, use of particles, and the like.

Al-Jurjānī's books were the result of sustained efforts of reflection and analysis; the author tackles many issues that had been clouded by popular misconceptions and misused terms. He often returned to the same topic and looked at it from another angle. As a result his books are rather unsystematically presented and not readily to be used as textbooks. This deficiency was removed first by the theologian **Fakhr al-Dīn al-Rāzī** and then by **al-Sakkākī**, both of whom brought some order and system to al-Jurjānī's luxuriant thinking. Historically more influential was al-Sakkākī. His *Key of the Sciences* (*Miftāḥ al-ʿulūm*) is a grandiose panorama of all the linguistic sciences, except lexicography. Its third chapter deals with 'stylistics' (*maʿānī*, lit. '[syntactic] meanings') and with 'imagery' (*bayān*, lit. 'clarity'), the two parts being based on al-Jurjānī's *Dalā'il al-iʿjāz* and *Asrār al-balāgha*, respectively. Most popular in the medieval instruction in this field became **al-Khaṭīb al-Qazwīnī**'s summary of this chapter in his *Epitome of the Key* (*Talkhīṣ al-Miftāḥ*). He added the 'rhetorical figures' (*badīʿ*) as a third discipline on an equal footing with *maʿānī* and *bayān* and called the overarching discipline 'the science of eloquence' (*ʿilm al-balāgha*). This 'science' is then studied and presented in a never-ending series of commentaries, super-commentaries, glosses, versifications, etc., up to modern times.

Further reading

Handbooks

de Tassy, Joseph Garcin, *Rhétorique et prosodie des langues de l'Orient musulman*, 2nd edn, Paris (1873), rpt Amsterdam (1970).

Rückert, Friedrich, *Grammatik, Poetik und Rhetorik der Perser*, W. Pertsch (ed.), Gotha (1874).

von Mehren, August Ferdinand Michael, *Die Rhetorik der Araber*, Copenhagen and Vienna (1853), rpt Hildesheim and New York (1970).

Overviews

Heinrichs, Wolfhart, 'Poetik, Rhetorik, Literaturkritik, Metrik und Reimlehre', *GAP*, vol. 2, 177–207.

——, 'Arabic poetics, classical', *The New Princeton Encyclopedia of Poetry and Poetics*, Alex Preminger and T.V.F. Brogan (eds), Princeton (1993), 82–4.

General studies

ʿAbbās, Iḥsān, *Ta'rīkh al-naqd al-adabī ʿind al-ʿArab*, 2nd edn, Beirut (1978).

Bencheikh, J.-E., *Poétique arabe, essai sur les voies d'une création*, Paris (1989) (a first-hand study of Arabic poetics, but using the medieval theorists as well).

Bonebakker, Seeger A., 'Aspects of the history of literary rhetoric and poetics in Arabic literature', *Viator* 1 (1970), 75–95.

Cantarino, Vicente, *Arabic Poetics in the Golden Age*, Leiden (1975).

Heinrichs, Wolfhart, 'Literary theory: the problem of its efficiency', in *Arabic Poetry: Theory and Development*, G.E. von Grunebaum (ed.), Wiesbaden (1973), 19–69.

Trabulsi, Amjad, *La Critique poétique des Arabes jusqu'au Ve siècle de l'Hégire (XIe siècle de J.C.)*, Damascus (1956).

Specific studies with general implications

Ajami, Mansour, *The Alchemy of Glory: The Dialectic of Truthfulness and Untruthfulness in Medieval Arabic Literary Criticism*, Washington, DC (1988).

Canard, Marius, 'Deux chapitres inédits de l'œuvre de Kratchkovsky sur Ibn al-Muʿtazz', *AIEO* 20 (1962), 21-111.

Heinrichs, Wolfhart, *Arabische Dichtung und griechische Poetik: Ḥāzim al-Qarṭāǧannīs Grundlegung der Poetik mit Hilfe aristotelischer Begriffe*, Beirut and Wiesbaden (1969).

Kanazi, George J., *Studies in the Kitāb aṣ-Ṣināʿatayn of Abū Hilāl al-ʿAskarī*, Leiden (1989).

van Gelder, G.H., *Beyond the Line: Classical Arabic Literary Critics on the Coherence and Unity of the Poem*, Leiden (1982).

Philosophical rhetoric and poetics

Black, Deborah L., *Logic and Aristotle's Rhetoric and Poetics in Medieval Arabic Philosophy*, Leiden (1990).

Dahiyat, Ismail M., *Avicenna's Commentary on the Poetics of Aristotle: A Critical Study with an Annotated Translation of the Text*, Leiden (1974).

Kemal, Salim, *The Poetics of Alfarabi and Avicenna*, Leiden (1991).

W.P. HEINRICHS

See also: literary criticism, medieval

rhetorical figures

The Arabic term for rhetorical figures is the collective noun *badīʿ*, and the discipline dealing with them is thus called *ʿilm al-badīʿ*. In **al-Khaṭīb al-Qazwīnī**'s (d. 739/1338) influential epitomes on rhetoric (*ʿilm al-balāgha*) it forms the third part of this 'science'. The following list of rhetorical figures is selected from al-Qazwīnī's larger work, *al-Īḍāḥ* (*The Clarification*). Some additional material is taken from other sources, mostly from the *Pillar* (*al-ʿUmda*) of **Ibn Rashīq** (d. 456/1063 or later). All examples in the list are poetic; al-Qazwīnī, of course, like most other rhetoricians, adduces numerous examples also from the **Koran** and ***ḥadīth***. The sigla A and M after the names of poets mean 'ancient' and 'modern' (i.e. **ʿAbbāsid**).

The rhetorical figures come from various backgrounds: the poets and critics had one set of terms, the scribes (epistolographers) another, and the Koranic scholars a third. The confluence of these traditions started with compilations like the *Kitāb al-ṣināʿatayn* (*Book of the Two Arts*) of **Abū Hilāl al-ʿAskarī** (d. after 395/1005). As a result many terms have two or more meanings, or the same rhetorical figure has two or more names. This has been pointed out below only in a few cases.

In the Qazwīnian tradition the figures are divided into two kinds, as they are anchored either in the meaning (*maʿnawī*) or in the wording (*lafẓī*).

Figures of the meaning

- *ʿaks*, 'reversing', also called *tabdīl*, 'exchanging', i.e. mentioning an idea involving two terms and then switching the two terms in a quasi-paradox. Examples: ʿAbd Allāh ibn al-Zabayr (A): 'And [fate] turned their [i.e. the women's] black hair white and their white faces black.' **Al-Mutanabbī** (M): 'There is no glory in this world for him whose wealth is little, and there is no wealth in this world for him whose glory is little.'
- Antithesis, see *muṭābaqa*.
- Apostrophe, see *iltifāt*.
- Correspondence, see *muqābala* under *muṭābaqa*.
- Digression, see *istiṭrād*.
- Double entendre, see *tawriya*.
- *Ghuluww*, see *mubālagha*.
- *Hazl yurād bihi jidd*, 'jest through which seriousness is intended'. **Abū Nuwās** (M): 'When a Tamīmī comes to you boasting, then say: Stop that! How is it with your lizard meals?' The Tamīm – and most other **bedouins** – were rumoured to be lizard eaters and were teased for it.
- *Ḥusn al-taʿlīl*, 'phantastic etiology', finding an interesting fictitious cause for a fact in reality. This is a popular device in 'modern' poetry, with a number of variants. A few examples: al-Mutanabbī (M): 'The clouds do not imitate his gift [i.e. by raining profusely]; rather they have been fever-struck by it [i.e. for having been shamed by his large gifts], and so their downpour is but fever-sweat.' Abū Ṭālib **al-Ma'mūnī** (M): 'He does not cherish a nap except out of hope that he might see the apparition of a nightly petitioner.' **Muslim ibn al-Walīd** (M): 'O you calumniator, whose evil deed has turned out well for us: fear of you has saved my eye's pupil from drowning [because he did not dare cry].'
- *Ighrāq*, see *mubālagha*.
- *Īhām*, see *tawriya*.
- *Īhām al-taḍādd*, see *muṭābaqa*.
- *Iltifāt*, 'turning aside', used in two meanings: (1) Abrupt change of grammatical person, especially from second to third and from third to second (the classical apostrophe). **Jarīr** (A): 'When were the tents at Dhū Ṭulūḥ? O tents, may you be watered by ample rain!' (2) An aside in the form of a parenthesis. **Kuthayyir** (A): 'If those who behave stingily – and you (fem.) are one of them! – could see you, they would learn from you how to procrastinate.'
- *Iqtibās*, lit. 'taking live embers (to start a new fire)', refers to a phrase borrowed from the Koran or *ḥadīth*. **Ibn al-Rūmī** (M): 'If I have erred in praising you as you have erred in denying me [my reward], then I have made my hopes dwell in a valley where is no sown land.' The last phrase is taken from *Sūra* 14:40: 'Our Lord [says Abraham], I have made some of my seed to dwell in a valley where is no sown land' (Arberry's translation).
- *Istikhdām*, 'employing (both meanings of a homonym)', either by using the word in one meaning and referring back to the other meaning with a pronoun, or by using the word with both meanings, so that for the purpose of translation it has to be repeated (this second sense is not in al-Qazwīnī). Example of the first kind: **al-Buḥturi** (M): 'May [the rain] drench the euphorbia grove and its inhabitants, even though they kindle it [i.e. the hot-burning fire of euphorbia wood] between my front and rear ribs.' The word *ghaḍā* means the euphorbia trees as well as the proverbially hot fire of euphorbia wood; in the present line the second meaning is, of course, used metaphorically for the pain of separation and yearning. Example of the second kind: **Abū Tammām** (M): 'When she walks, she leaves in your bosom twice the amount of *waswās* that is in her jewels.' With regard to the poet's bosom, *waswās* means 'temptation', whereas with regard to her jewels it is their 'jingling'.
- *Istitbāʿ*, lit. 'producing a consequence', i.e. one praise leads, or is made to lead, to another. Al-Mutanabbī (M): 'You have taken away so many lives that, were you to

combine them [in yourself], the world would be congratulated on your being eternal.'

- *Istithnā'*, see *ta'kīd al-madḥ*.
- *Istiṭrād*, 'digression', a brief aside often containing an ironic stab at someone. **Al-Samaw'al** (A): 'We are indeed a people who do not consider being killed a shame, when [the tribes of] 'Āmir and Salūl do consider it [thus].'
- *I'tilāf*, see *murā'āt al-naẓīr*.
- *Jam'*, 'combination' of several subjects for one predication. **Abū al-'Atāhiya** (M): 'Youth and leisure and wealth are a place of ruin for man, oh what ruin!'
- *Jam' ma'a tafrīq*, 'combination-cum-separation', subsumption of several subjects under one predicate with subsequent differentiation of an aspect. Rashīd al-Dīn al-Waṭwāṭ (M): 'Your face is like fire in its light and my heart is like fire in its heat.'
- *Jam' ma'a taqsīm*, 'combination-cum-division', a general statement about various cases followed by a detailing of these cases, or vice versa. Al-Mutanabbī (M): '[Sayf al-Dawla led the armies] until he had control of the suburbs of Kharshana, the Byzantines and [their] crosses and churches made utterly miserable through him: [destined] for captivity was what they had married, for massacring what they had given birth to, for plundering what they had gathered, for the fire what they had sown.'
- *Jam' ma'a taqsīm wa-tafrīq*, 'combination-cum-division plus separation'. **Ibn Sharaf al-Qayrawānī** (M): 'Of those who come for [their] needs there is a throng at his door [general statement about needy people]; this one has a situation and that one has another [separation, though vague]: for the obscure there will be a lofty position, for the destitute riches, for the guilty benevolence, and for the fearful a safe haven [division of needs and their fulfilment].'
- *Laff wa-nashr*, lit. 'rolling up and unrolling', an enumeration of terms followed by an enumeration of predicates or comments, the exact correlation between the two sets being left to the audience. The two sets are either parallel or chiastic. Example of parallelism: **Ibn Ḥayyūs** (M): 'The effect and the colour and the taste of the wine are in his eyes and his cheeks and his saliva'. Example of chiasm: Ibn Ḥayyūs (M): 'How can I retrieve my composure, since you are dune and branch and gazelle as to glance and body and buttocks.'
- ***al-Madhhab al-kalāmī***, 'dialectical argumentation'. See separate entry.
- *Mubālagha maqbūla*, 'acceptable hyperbole', with three sub-categories depending on whether the exaggerated fact is customarily possible (*tablīgh*), only hypothetically possible (*ighrāq*) or impossible (*ghuluww*). First case: al-Mutanabbī (M): 'I bring down any quarry that I chase with it [i.e. his horse], and I dismount from it, it being just like it is when I mount [i.e. no perspiration and exhaustion is discernible].' Second case: 'Amr ibn al-Ayham al-Taghlibī (A): 'We honour our guest, as long as he stays among us, and we let honour follow him, wherever he turns.' (The second behaviour is unusual and not required by the bedouin code of honour.) Third case: Abū Nuwās (M): 'You have frightened the infidels to such an extent that even [their] sperm drops that have not yet been created fear you.' This last sub-category is acceptable only under certain conditions: (1) If a word meaning 'almost' is added which brings it back into the realm of the possible: **Ibn Ḥamdīs** (M): 'For sheer speed it almost (*yakādu*) broke away from its shadow – if it had wished to leave a companion.' (2) If the line contains a beautiful phantastic reinterpretation of reality (*takhyīl*). Al-Arrajānī (M) on an endless night: 'It seems to me that the fiery stars have been nailed to the darkness and that my eyelids have been tied to them with my eyelashes.' (3) If the line is a joke. Anonymous (probably M): 'I become drunk yesterday when I decide to drink tomorrow! That is certainly strange!'

  Some older rhetoricians understand *mubālagha* more broadly as 'emphasis', of which 'hyperbole' would be one sub-category. One specific type of 'emphasis' is called *īghāl*, lit. 'penetrating deeply'; it consists in making the rhyme word give an additional push to the idea of the line. **Marwān ibn Abī Ḥafṣa** (M): 'They are the real people: when they speak, they hit the mark, when they are called for help, they answer, and when they give, they do it well and they do it copiously!'
- *Muqābala*, see *muṭābaqa*.
- *Murā'āt al-naẓīr*, lit. 'observance of the equivalent', i.e. harmonious choice of ideas or images, also called *tanāsub*, *i'tilāf* or *tawfīq*. Al-Buḥturī (M): '[emaciated camels] like curved bows, nay, like the

arrows, when whittled sharp, nay, like the bowstrings'. A series of similes with increasing hyperbole, all taken from the same semantic area, that of archery.

- *Muzāwaja*, 'pairing' of the contents of the protasis and apodosis of a conditional sentence by making two similar consequences dependent on them. Al-Buḥturī (M): 'When they fight each other at times and their blood flows abundantly, they remember they are relatives and their tears flow abundantly.'
- *Muṭābaqa*, antithesis, also called *ṭibāq* and *taḍādd*, inclusion of two contraries in one line or sentence. Examples: 'saved up' vs. 'spent' in **Ṭufayl ibn ʿAwf al-Ghanawī** (A): 'with [a horse] of a scowling face and uncut thigh veins [i.e. sound, not needing this treatment], which is being saved up to be spent for the day of battle'; and 'extinguished' vs. 'lit' in Ibn Rashīq (M): 'They extinguished the sun of the day, and they lit the stars of the tall lances in a sky of dust.' Note that in the second example the antithesis is part of a metaphorical structure which, however, is based on a real-world contrast of 'blotting out the sun' and 'making the lances flash'. If the antithesis is based entirely on metaphorical contrast, al-Qazwīnī classifies it as 'simulated antithesis' (*īhām al-taḍādd*), e.g. 'laughing' vs. 'weeping' in **Diʿbil** (M): 'Don't be surprised, O Salmā, at a man on whose head hoariness is laughing, but he is weeping.' If there is more than one term on each side of the antithesis, the resulting figure is called 'correspondence' or 'opposition' (*muqābala*), e.g. al-Mutanabbī (M): 'Generosity does not deplete wealth, when luck is approaching, nor does stinginess preserve wealth, when luck is receding.'
- Opposition, see *muqābala* under *muṭābaqa*.
- Phantastic etiology, see *ḥusn al-taʿlīl*.
- Pun, see *tawriya*.
- Retraction, see *rujūʿ*.
- *Rujūʿ*, lit. 'going back', retraction of what has been said. Yazīd **Ibn al-Ṭathriyya** (A): 'Isn't one glance paltry, when I cast it at you (fem.). Far from it! From you it is not a paltry thing.'
- *Tabdīl*, see *ʿaks*.
- *Tablīgh*, see *mubālagha*.
- *Taḍādd*, see *muṭābaqa*.
- *Taḍmīn*, 'incorporation' of an existing line of poetry, or part thereof, into one's own poetry. To avoid an accusation of plagiarism, it is often an outright quotation with citation of the original author; or else it is a famous line, in which case it is often used in such a way that its meaning is changed in the new context. The *taḍmīn* may also be put into the mouth of the songstress who is one of the personae of the wine poem; in this case the line is not used as a kind of prooftext, but is part of the description of the party.
- *Tafrīq*, 'separation', pointing out a distinction within the same activity when performed by different agents. Rashīd al-Dīn al-Waṭwāṭ (M): 'The gift of the clouds at some time in the rainy season is not like the gift of the prince on a day of generosity; for the gift of the prince is a camel-load of dinars and the gift of the clouds a drop of water.' The separation of the gifts, of course, presupposes the frequent comparison of the generous prince with the raincloud.
- *Tafwīf*, lit. 'application of stripes (cloth)', dividing a line into several related ideas expressed in phrases of more or less equal length. **Ibn Zaydūn** (M): 'Be arrogant and I will bear it, be arbitrary and I will endure it, lord it and I will be lowly, tease and I will submit, speak and I will listen, command and I will obey.'
- *Tajrīd*, 'abstracting a general attribute from an individual' according to the pattern of 'in him (individual) I have a true friend (general attribute)'. Qatāda ibn Maslama al-Ḥanafī (A): 'Should I stay alive, I will embark on a raid which will bring together much booty, unless [in me] a noble man should die.'
- *Tajāhul al-ʿārif*, 'feigned ignorance', also called *tashakkuk*, 'doubtfulness'. It is often based on metaphors taken literally. **Al-ʿArjī** (A): 'By God, O antelopes of the plain, tell me: is my Laylā one of you or is Laylā one of humankind?' This is based on the ubiquitous comparison of a beautiful woman with an antelope.
- *Ta'kīd al-madḥ bi-mā yushbih al-dhamm*, 'strengthening praise with what looks like blame', and vice versa. **Al-Nābigha al-Dhubyānī** (A): 'There is no fault in them, except that there are notches in their swords from fighting [enemy] squadrons.' Their swords being notched is, of course, no fault, because it proves their courage and fighting spirit. Since 'except that' is a typical phrase with this figure, it is also called *istithnā'*, 'exception.'

- *Tanāsub*, see *murā'āt al-naẓīr*.
- *Taqsīm*, 'division,' enumeration of cases followed by an explicit mutual characterization of each. Abū Tammām (M): 'It is either the Revelation [which restores order] or the edge of a thin sword, whose cutting edges sway the jugular veins [i.e. neck] of each swaying person. One [i.e. the Revelation] is the remedy of any illness on the part of reasonable people, and the other is the remedy of any illness on the part of ignorant persons.' As al-Qazwīnī remarks later on, *taqsīm* is used also in two other senses: (1) An enumeration of (often contrary) attributes together with the different situations to which they apply. Al-Mutanabbī (M): '[warriors] heavy, when they encounter [the enemy]; light, when they are called [for help]; [seemingly] numerous, when they attack; few, when they are counted'. (2) An enumeration of all possible cases, in logical terms a complete disjunction. **Zuhayr** (A): 'I know today's knowledge and yesterday's before it, but I am blind as to the knowledge of what will be tomorrow.'
- *Tardīd*, lit. 'letting ring' by repeating a word, but in a different context and creating a contrast. Not mentioned in al-Qazwīnī. Zuhayr (A): 'Whoever meets Harim – though he be impoverished – on any given day, he will meet magnanimity and generosity in him as [dominant] character traits.' **Al-Ḥusayn ibn al-Ḍaḥḥāk** (M): 'She has filled my eye with resplendent beauties, which have filled my heart with torment and sorrows.'
- *Tashakkuk*, see *tajāhul al-'ārif*.
- *Tawfīq*, see *murā'āt al-naẓīr*.
- *Tawriya*, lit. 'concealment', a *double entendre* or pun in which the obvious meaning of a homonym is not the intended one, also called *īhām*, 'delusion'. There are various sub-types depending on whether or not the line contains contextual elements pointing to the obvious, unintended meaning or to the less common, intended one. The most frequent type in poetry is the *tawriya* with contextual elements, which are often themselves *tawriyas*, referring to the obvious meaning. Al-Qāḍī 'Iyāḍ (M): '[It's a cool summer, as if] the gazelle/sun, because of its long duration, had become senile and thus could no longer distinguish between the kid/Capricorn and the lamb/Aries.' The obvious meaning of the word *ghazāla* is 'gazelle', whereas the intended meaning 'sun' is rare. The 'gazelle' lets the reader think that the words *jady* and *ḥamal* also have their animal meanings, and only after the context has forced him to understand *ghazāla* as 'sun' does he make an adjustment and recognize the astronomical meanings of the terms. With a series of *tawriyas* the poet can construct a second layer of meaning, which need not be as absurd as it is in the present case.
- *Ṭibāq*, see *muṭābaqa*.

Figures of the wording

- *Ishtiqāq*, see *jinās*.
- *Jinās*, also called *tajnīs*, 'paronomasia', with many sub-categories depending on the extent of the identity between the two terms that form the paronomasia. They may be two identical words with different meanings, one of which may be a combination of two words; they may be identical words in writing, but different in vocalization and diacritics; they may be only partially identical verging on alliteration; and the two words may be identical except for a reversed sequence of their letters. One special type is called *tajnīs ishtiqāq*, or simply *ishtiqāq*; here the two terms are two different derivatives of the same root (not necessarily linguistically correct), which makes the figure correspond to the classical *figura etymologica*. The paronomasia is possibly the most popular rhetorical figure. It is often used to extract 'meaning' from names by playing on their root.
- ***Luzūm mā lā yalzam***, see separate entry.
- *Mumāthala*, see *muwāzana*.
- *Muwāzana*, 'equilibrium', i.e. the words and phrases of the two hemistichs are of the same length and general syllabic structure, but do not rhyme. If, in addition, they are all of the same word form, the figure is called *mumāthala*, 'congruence.'
- Paronomasia, see *jinās*.
- *Qalb*, 'palindrome'.
- *Radd al-'ajuz 'alā al-ṣadr*, 'having the end echo the beginning', i.e. repeating the rhyme word in the first hemistich, often at the beginning of the line, or sometimes at the start of the second hemistich. It is also called *taṣdīr*. **Al-Uqayshir** (A): '[He is] coming quickly to his cousin to slap his face, but to one who applies to [his] gener-

osity not coming quickly.' This may be combined with paronomasia.

- ***Saj'***, normally 'rhymed prose', but it occurs also in poetry as internal rhyme in a line, otherwise called (but not by al-Qazwīnī) *tarṣī'*, lit. 'studding with jewels'. See separate entry.
- *Tajnīs*, see *jinās*.
- *Tarṣī'*, see *saj'*.
- *Taṣdīr*, see *radd al-'ajuz 'alā al-ṣadr*.
- *Taṣrī'*, 'giving the poem's rhyme also to the first hemistich of a line'. This is commonly done with the first line of the poem, but may recur at irregular intervals. The term is derived from *miṣrā'*, '(rhymed) hemistich'.

Figures in the theory of imagery

In al-Qazwīnī this is not part of *'ilm al-badī'* (see above), but forms the second part of rhetoric, called *'ilm al-bayān*, 'the science of clarity, or clarification'. The name has to do with the original function of similes and other figurative usages in the Koran. In the older works on poetics and rhetorical figures no similar distinction is made, and the various tropes and similes are included among the rhetorical figures.

- *Isti'āra*, see **metaphor** (separate entry).
- *Kināya*, 'periphrastic expression', an expression that is not figurative, but not intended on the surface level either, such as: 'he is rich in ashes of the cooking-pot' as a proposition about a hospitable man.
- ***Majāz***, 'figurative language', see separate entry.
- **Metaphor**, see separate entry.
- Metonymy, see *majāz mursal* under ***majāz*** (separate entry).
- Simile, see *tashbīh*.
- *Tamthīl*, 'analogy,' a comparison of two sets of terms, grammatically speaking two sentences, though mostly only implicitly. Al-Mutanabbī (M) addressing his prince: 'If you are above all men, though one of them – well, musk is part of the blood of the gazelle.' The relationship of the terms is as follows: You: men = musk: gazelle's blood, the rather complicated aspect of comparison being 'transformation of something common and copious into something valuable and unique so that the result is, and at the same time is not, of the same genus as the source material'. The analogue is often such that the resulting argument can only be called a mock analogy, because the insinuated aspect of comparison is not valid. Al-Buḥturī (M) taking up the topos of black and white hair: 'And the white colour of the falcon is of a more genuine beauty, if you consider it, than the raven's blackness.' Obviously, it is not just the whiteness of the hair that makes old age loathsome. Mock analogies belong to the category of *takhyīl*, 'phantastic reinterpretation of reality,' a phenomenon identified by **'Abd al-Qāhir al-Jurjānī**. If the subject of comparison in a *tamthīl* is suppressed, the result will be a sentence metaphor. This is likewise called *tamthīl*; the term is actually more often used in this sense than in the previous one. **Ibn Mayyāda** (A): 'Had you not placed me into your right hand? So do not place me after that into your left!'
- *Tashbīh*, 'simile', i.e. the comparison of two single terms, as opposed to *tamthīl*, 'analogy', the comparison of two sets of terms or, grammatically speaking, two sentences. A simile consists of four basic elements: the subject of comparison, its object, its particle and its aspect. Any one of these elements – except, of course, the object of comparison – can be suppressed. The aspect is mostly not mentioned, unless the poet wants to make some unusual point. Ibn al-Rūmī (M): 'O moonlike one in beauty [the usual] and in unattainability [unusual], be generous, for sometimes even a rock bursts forth with fresh water.' Suppression of the particle ('like', etc.) does not yield a metaphor, as it would in the Western tradition; the resulting equation (of the type 'Zayd is a lion') is still considered a simile, since both the subject and the object are mentioned. However, critics like 'Abd al-Qāhir al-Jurjānī were conscious of the fact that the alleged identity in cases like 'Zayd is a lion' was often used as a basis for elaborations in such a way that the particle of comparison could no longer be restored. Abū Ṭālib al-Ma'mūnī (M): 'I am a fire in the entrails of the night, [the night] is my smoke and the stars are sparks.' Even when the object of comparison was mentioned alone and thus became a metaphor, the historical consciousness of its being rooted in an original simile was such that it continued to be considered a simile for some time; correct comprehension was usually ensured by contextual elements, often additional similes

of the same type. Abū Nuwās (M): 'She is weeping, throwing pearls [tears] from narcissi [eyes] and beating roses [cheeks] with jujubes [henna-dyed fingertips].' The critics were also keen on discussing the ontological status of the object of comparison, whether it was perceived by the senses or by the mind or whether it was just a figment of the imagination. This last type was of some poetic importance, because it yielded fantastic images. **Al-Ṣanawbarī** (M): 'The red anemones, when they swayed downwards and righted themselves again, were like banners [made] of ruby unfurled on lances [made] of emerald.' There was, finally, a great interest in the cumulation of similes in one line. Here is one with four similes to the line: al-Mutanabbī (M): 'She appeared – a full moon; she swayed – a moringa branch; she exuded fragrance – ambergris; she gazed – a gazelle.'

Text editions

Ibn Rashīq, *al-'Umda fī maḥāsin al-shi'r wa-ādābih wa-naqdih*, Muḥammad Muḥyī al-Dīn 'Abd al-Ḥamīd (ed.), 2 vols, 3rd edn, Cairo (1383/1963).

al-Khaṭīb al-Qazwīnī, *al-Īḍāḥ*, Muḥammad 'Abd al-Mun'im Khafājī (ed.), 3rd edn, Beirut (1391/1971).

von Mehren, A.F.M., *Die Rhetorik der Araber*, Copenhagen and Vienna (1853), rpt Hildesheim and New York (1970).

Further reading

Bonebakker, Seeger, A., *Some Early Definitions of the Tawriya and Ṣafadī's* Faḍḍ al-Xitām 'an at-Tawriya wa-'l-Istixdām, The Hague and Paris (1966).

DeYoung, Terri, 'Language in looking-glass land: Samīḥ al-Qāsim and modernization of jinās', *JAOS* 112 (1992), 183–97.

Hamori, Andras, 'Notes on paronomasia in Abū Tammām's style', *JSS* 12 (1967), 89–90 (on *jinās*).

Jones, Alan, 'Final *taḍmīn* in the poems of Abū Nuwās', in *Arabicus Felix*, 61–73.

van Gelder, G.J.H., 'The abstracted self in Arabic poetry', *JAL* 14 (1983), 22–30 (on *iltifāt*).

Wansbrough, John, 'Arabic rhetoric and Qur'anic exegesis', *BSOAS* 31 (1968), 470–85 (on *laff wa-nashr*).

W.P. HEINRICHS

See also: *badī'*

rhyme *see* prosody

Riḍā, (Muḥammad) Rashīd (1865–1935)

Islamic modernist. Born in Qalamun (**Syria**), Riḍā went to **Cairo** to study with Muḥammad **'Abduh**, who greatly influenced him and whose biography he wrote in 1931. He was founder and editor of the journal *al-Manār*, published between 1898 and 1935, the main mouthpiece of the Islamic regeneration movement known as the Salafiyya, which held that the revival of Islam required recourse to the first or pious generation (*al-salaf al-ṣāliḥ*) of Islam, the period of the rightly guided caliphs. Riḍā was also president of the Syrian National Congress which proclaimed Fayṣal ibn Ḥusayn king of Syria in March 1920.

Riḍā was profoundly influenced by 'Abduh's notions of natural law, and in his earlier writings contended that there was no necessary contradiction between reason and revelation. In *al-Khilāfa aw al-Imāma al-'Uẓmā* (1923) he stressed the necessity for the continuity of the caliphate, both in order to uphold and enforce 'Islamic government' and to rejuvenate Islamic society. In later life he espoused a more dogmatic and less rational interpretation of Islam, becoming a strong supporter of the Wahhabi movement and of the Sa'udi monarchy.

Further reading

Hourani, A., *Arabic Thought in the Liberal Age 1798–1939*, London (1962).

Kerr, Malcolm, *Islamic Reform*, Berkeley (1966).

P. SLUGLETT

riddles *see mu'ammā*; *lughz*

Riḍwān, Faṭhī *see* Raḍwān, Fatḥī

al-Rīḥānī, Amīn (1876–1940)

Mahjar poet, prose writer and journalist. Born in Frayka (Lebanon), al-Rīḥānī accompanied his uncle to New York in 1888, his father and the rest of his family arriving in 1889. For reasons of health he returned to Lebanon in 1898, and was there from 1905 to 1910. After meeting **Jubrān** in Paris, he again returned to New York to work as a journalist, and in that capacity he crossed the Atlantic some twenty times to visit Europe and the Arab countries. He published some fifty works in Arabic and English.

Amīn al-Rīḥānī opened his literary career with a booklet entitled *al-Tasāhul al-dīnī* (Philadelphia, 1901), followed by *Nubdha fī al-thawra al-faransiyya* (New York, 1902) and *al-Muḥālafa al-thulāthiyya fī al-mamlaka al-ḥayawāniyya* (New York, 1902). The last of these – a fable based on the ideas of Darwin, Rousseau, Voltaire and the French Revolution – is an attack on the feudal system and on the clergy who supported it. *Al-Mukārī wa-al-kāhin* (New York, 1904) shows the donkeyman as the true believer, and the priest in need of contrition and conversion. His first book in English was a translation of selected quatrains of **Abū al-ʿAlāʾ al-Maʿarrī** (*The Quatrains of Abu 'l'Ala*, London, 1904).

Al-Rīḥānī collected his prose poems and shorter pieces in his *Rīḥāniyyāt* (4 vols, Beirut, 1910–23), subsequently re-edited and republished as the *Rīḥāniyyāt* (1956), *Qawmiyyāt* (1956), comprising the political pieces, and *Hutāf al-awdiya* (1955), in which most of his prose poems were brought together. In *Antum al-shuʿarāʾ* (Beirut, 1923) he censured the Arab poets for weeping too much instead of raising their voices against the French mandate. Al-Rīḥānī also differed with **Jubrān** and **Nuʿayma** on a number of important issues, including the belief in the spirituality of the East versus the materialism of the West.

From 1920 onward, al-Rīḥānī began to visit the Arab countries – these travels resulting in a number of books, including *Ta'rīkh Najd al-ḥadīth* (1928), *Mulūk al-ʿArab* (1929) and others. An English series also appeared from 1928 onwards, including *Ibn Saud of Arabia* (London, 1928), *Around the Coasts of Arabia* (London, 1930) and *Arabian Peak and Desert* (London, 1931).

Further reading

al-Ḥusayn, Muḥammad, *al-Muṭālaʿāt wa-al-murājaʿāt wa-al-nuqūd wa-al-rudūd*, 2 vols, Beirut (1913).
Rihani, Albert, *Where to Find Ameen Rihani: Bibliography*, Beirut (1979).

C. NIJLAND

riḥla see travel literature

risāla see artistic prose; prose, non-fiction, medieval

al-Risāla al-jāmiʿa

At the end of the collection of the *Rasā'il Ikhwān al-Ṣafā'* (*The Epistles of the Brethren of Purity*) there is a *risāla* which has the appearance of a conclusion or summary, and which is known as the *Risāla al-jāmiʿa*. Some have ascribed its authorship to Maslama ibn Aḥmad **al-Majrīṭī**, but there seems little doubt from its style that it is by the same author(s) as the rest of the *Rasā'il*. Its name appears in the list of contents, and one might think that it had the role of explaining the meaning of the *Rasā'il* as a whole, yet it certainly does not do this. When one considers the style of the *Rasā'il*, this is hardly surprising, given the anecdotal and very varied nature of that text. On the other hand, the *Risāla* does make an attempt at summing up the general message of the larger work in so far as this is possible, and like the larger work it hints at the necessity for the correct esoteric key to be applied before the genuine meaning can be extracted. There are some intriguing differences between the *Risāla* and the main text, and the precise nature of the relationship between them is still very much open to conjecture.

Text edition

al-Risāla al-jāmiʿa, J. Salībā (ed.), Damascus (1949).

Further reading

Nasr, S.H., *An Introduction to Islamic Cosmological Doctrines*, rev. edn, London (1978).
Netton, I., *Muslim Neoplatonists*, London (1982).
——, 'The Brethren of Purity' in *HIP*, S. Nasr and O. Leaman (eds.), London (1996), 247–51.

O. LEAMAN

See also: Ikhwān al-Ṣafā'

rithā'

The Arabic poetry of lamentation. In Arabic literary theory the term *rithā'* appeared relatively late (with **Ibn Rashīq**, d. between 456/1064 and 463/1070); the more common name was *marāthī* (sing. *marthiya*), dirge, lament, elegy.

The origin of this genre lay in pre-Islamic **Arabia**. As part of funerary rites women used to bewail their male next of kin in compositions in rhymed prose called *niyāḥas*, often in unison with other women of the tribe, but already among the oldest known pieces of

Arabic poetry we find examples of women using *qarīḍ* poetry (i.e. poetry in standard metres) for the same purpose (so: **al-Khirnīq**, d. *c.*600 CE). The reason for this shift in ambition, expressed in the choice of a high level means of communication, may have been that women wanted publicly and vehemently to urge their tribe to take blood revenge.

Although *marāthī* are not composed following the more or less strict set of themes and motives as in the case of the ***qaṣīda***, a kind of favourite structure can be observed: a poetess likes to begin her *marthiya* inducing her eyes to cry abundantly. This can be understood as a way of breaking the social constraint of *ṣabr* (equanimity). This opening theme is often followed by pieces of real or pseudo-dialogue leading to the main part: praise of the deceased and his personal and social virtues, thereby reiterating the desirable norms of behaviour. In the closing sections the poetess often makes general observations on fate, generalizing her deprivation as a possible destiny for others. Both praise and generalizing destiny can be understood as the poetess's legitimizing of her own sorrow and loss of self-control.

The most important poetess of this genre, **al-Khansāʾ** (d. *c.*665 CE), developed this genre from an expression, private in origin, to a panegyric of the pre-Islamic heroic type of man as an example for society in her laments on her two brothers, Ṣakhr and Muʿāwiya, which she recited for an audience at **ʿUkāẓ**.

Shortly after the beginning of Islam the tradition of women bewailing their next of kin in poetical works came to a halt, but professional male poets followed the trend set by al-Khansāʾ and began composing *marāthī* on heroes who were not necessarily next of kin, thus developing the genre to a prestigious work of art. From the **Umayyad** and ʿAbbāsid eras famous *marāthī* on distinguished public personalities have survived and the genre became very popular as a kind of poetical obituary. In this sense it even became a tool of political or religious rhetoric.

In later periods in both the east and in al-Andalus (see **Spain**), the genre developed into the lament as such, expressing sorrow over the destruction of cities or the loss of civilizations. Famous early examples include al-Khuraymī's lengthy lament over **Baghdad** following the civil war between al-Amīn and al-Maʾmūn (see **ʿAbbāsids**) and **Ibn al-Rūmī**'s poem on the sack of **Basra** by the Zanj. In **Shīʿī** tradition *marāthī* referring to the death of al-Ḥusayn became extremely popular.

Medieval Arab literary theorists have always closely associated the *marthiya* with the genre of ***madīḥ*** (panegyric), for which there are probably two reasons: they tended to overrate the panegyric element in the older *marthiya*, neglecting the original motives for this kind of poetry, and the genre itself developed in this direction in course of time.

Further reading

Borg, G. *Mit Poesie vertriebe ich den Kummer meines Herzens*, Nijmegen (1994).

Goldziher, I., 'Bemerkungen zur arabischen Trauerpoesie', *WZKM* 16 (1902), 307–39.

Jacobi, R., 'Bemerkungen zur frühislamischen Trauerpoesie', *WZKM* (1997) (forthcoming).

Jones, A., *Early Arabic Poetry*, vol. 1, *Marāthī and Ṣuʿlūk Poems*, Oxford (1992).

al-Shūrā, M.ʿA., *Shiʿr al-rithāʾ fī al-ʿaṣr al-Jāhilī*, Beirut (1983).

G. BORG

al-Riyāshī, Muḥammad ibn Bashīr (180–257/796–871)

Abū al-Faḍl al-ʿAbbās ibn al-Faraj Muḥammad ibn Bashīr al-Riyāshī was born in **Basra**; he studied under **al-Aṣmaʿī** and Abū Zayd al-Anṣārī, and read **Sībawayhi**'s *Kitāb* with al-Māzinī, who conceded al-Riyāshī's superiority in the lexical and literary aspects of this work. In 230/845 he moved to **Baghdad**, preferring to teach rather than accept a judgeship in Samarra from the caliph al-Mutawakkil. His pupils include **al-Mubarrad**, Ibn Durustawayhi, **Ibn Qutayba**, **Ibn Durayd**, **Ibn Abī al-Dunyā** and his own patron the vizier **al-Fatḥ ibn Khāqān**. He was killed by insurgents on his return to Basra. Although none of his works survive, he is praised by **al-Jāḥiẓ** as one of the three greatest Basran grammarians alive at the time.

Further reading

Ibn al-Qifṭī, *Inbāh al-ruwāh ʿalā anbāh al-nuḥāh*, M.A.F. Ibrāhīm (ed.), Cairo (1950–73), vol. 1, 248, vol. 2, 367–73.

al-Sīrāfī, *Akhbār al-naḥwiyyīn*, F. Krenkow (ed.), Paris (1936), 89–93.

M.G. CARTER

See also: grammar and grammarians

riwāya see *rāwī*; fiction

romances *see sīra* literature

romanticism

Romanticism in the context of Arabic literature is as elusive a term as it is in Western literatures. Arab literary critics and historians of Arabic literature have none the less employed the term, arabicized as *al-rūmanṭīqiyya* or *al-rūmansiyya*, and have used the concept very much as it has been used in Western literatures.

Some critics have argued that Romantic traits may be seen in the Arabic love poetry of the **Umayyad** period, where the poet pines chastely after an ever-inaccessible sweetheart, and in the urban poetry of the period with its nostalgic yearning for vanished desert life. It is not, however, until the twentieth century that we find a fully developed Romantic movement in Arabic literature, which reached its peak between the two world wars. Cultural influences from the West and indigenous socio-political conditions in the Arab world co-operated to create the atmosphere for the rise of Arabic Romantic poetry during this period.

In the first two decades of the twentieth century, pre-Romantic voices were heard in Egypt in some of the poems of Khalīl **Muṭrān**, ʿAbd al-Raḥmān **Shukrī**, ʿAbbās Maḥmūd **al-ʿAqqād** and Ibrāhīm ʿAbd al-Qādir **al-Māzinī**. Masters of the classical form, they rebelled against the constraints of its traditional thematic concerns and wanted their poetry to express their individual feelings. Thus, Muṭrān's poem 'al-Masā'' is not only a poem beautifully describing the sunset, but also a portrayal of his own despondent feelings at this moment of the day, painted in fresh colours and images on the changing canvas of nature which the poet perceives to be sad. To the individual vision of their poems, al-ʿAqqād and al-Māzinī added essays of literary criticism collected in their book *al-Dīwān* (1921), in which they castigated the traditional style and poetic values of established neo-classical poets such as Aḥmad **Shawqī**, and called for a break with hackneyed images and diction.

Meanwhile, Jubrān Khalīl **Jubrān** was leading a Romantic movement in the North American **Mahjar** that had deep effects on Arabic literature generally. He and other members of **al-Rābiṭa al-qalamiyya**, established in New York in 1920, were evolving a new style in which they experimented with rhyme, rhythm and language to express their own vision and individual feelings. This new movement influenced many in the Arab world, including the Syrian poet ʿUmar **Abū Rīsha** and the Tunisian Abū al-Qāsim **al-Shābbī**. Mīkhā'īl **Nuʿayma**'s *al-Ghirbāl* (1923) brings together his literary–critical essays denouncing traditional poetry and advocating the spirit of wonder, sincerity, adventure and innovation in poetic form and content which is typical of this group.

In Egypt, the **Apollo Group** established by Aḥmad Zakī **Abū Shādī** in 1932 attracted Egyptian Romantic poets such as ʿAlī Maḥmūd **Ṭāhā** and Ibrāhīm **Nājī** as well as poets from other parts of the Arab world. It popularized Romantic writing through its short-lived monthly, *Apollo*, influencing such poets as al-Shābbī, the Sudanese **al-Tijānī Yūsuf Bashīr** and others.

ʿAlī Maḥmūd Ṭāhā, the Lebanese Ilyās **Abū Shabaka** and a few others brought the Romantic movement to its highest expression beyond the end of World War 2, and streaks of it marked the early voices of younger poets like the Iraqis Badr Shākir **al-Sayyāb**, ʿAbd al-Wahhāb **al-Bayātī**, Nāzik **al-Malā'ika** and the Palestinian Fadwā **Ṭūqān**. But the Arab world was now ready for less ethereal sensibility and more earthy poetry; as the Middle East gradually achieved independence from colonial rule, romanticism gave way to poetry of social realism and to experimentation with **free verse** and prose poetry (see **prose poem**), expressing in a rebellious fashion the need for new structures in Arabic society and culture.

Text editions

Boullata, I.J., *Modern Arab Poets 1950–1975*, Washington, DC (1976).

Boullata, K., *Women in the Fertile Crescent: An Anthology of Modern Poetry by Arab Women*, Washington, DC (1978).

Jayyusi, S.K., *Modern Arabic Poetry: An Anthology*, New York (1987).

Khouri, M.A. and Algar, H., *An Anthology of Modern Arabic Poetry*, Berkeley (1974).

Orfalea, G. and Elmusa, S., *Grape Leaves: A Century of Arab American Poetry*, Salt Lake City (1988).

Further reading

Abdul-Hai, M., *Tradition and English and American Influence in Arabic Romantic Poetry*, London (1982).

Badawi, M.M., *A Critical Introduction to Modern Arabic Poetry*, Cambridge (1975), 68–203.

Bullāṭa, ʿĪsā Yūsuf, *al-Rūmanṭīqiyya wa-maʿālimuhā fī al-shiʿr al-ʿArabī al-ḥadīth*, Beirut (1960), Baghdad (1968).
Jayyusi, S.K., *Trends and Movements in Modern Arabic Poetry*, Leiden (1977), vol. 2, 361–474.

I.J. BOULLATA

Ru'ba ibn al-ʿAjjāj (d. 145/762)

One of the great poets of ***rajaz***. He specialized, like his equally famous father **al-ʿAjjāj**, in lengthy poems in *rajaz* metre. Coming from a **bedouin** background, he lived in various places and countries, settling in **Basra** towards the end of his life. He dedicated his odes to the **Umayyad** caliphs and other prominent people; a few poems were made for al-Saffāḥ and al-Manṣūr, the two first **ʿAbbāsid** caliphs. In other poems he celebrates his tribe or himself. His poetry was very popular with the philologians, both during his lifetime and afterwards, witness the many quotations in dictionaries and works on **grammar**. His poetry, however, is more than merely a treasure-trove for linguists. Stubbornly clinging to a metre generally despised as suitable only for second-rate poets, he describes his own art and himself with a mixture of humour and pride. His desert scenes are powerful in language and evocative in their imagery.

Text edition

Der Dīwān des Reǧezdichters Rūba ben El'aǧǧāǧ, W. Ahlwardt (ed.), Berlin (1903); *Dīwān des Reǧezdichters Rūba ben El'aǧǧāǧ*,W. Ahlwardt (trans.), Berlin (1904).

Further reading

Geyer, R., *Altarabische Diiamben*, Leipzig (1908).
——, 'Beiträge zum Dîwân des Ru'bah', *SBAW* (Vienna) 163 (1909), 1–79.
Ullmann, Manfred, *Untersuchungen zur Raǧazpoesie. Ein Beitrag zur arabischen Sprach- und Literaturwissenschaft*, Wiesbaden (1966), 29–37 and *passim*.

G.J.H. VAN GELDER

See also: *rajaz*

rubāʿiyya see dūbayt

Rūmān, Mīkhā'īl (1927–73)

Egyptian dramatist. Born in Upper Egypt, Rūmān studied science at the University of Cairo. Beginning in the early 1960s, he produced a series of radical plays on social and political themes, which depict the struggle of the individual against oppression, be it political, social or psychological. In all of these works the leading character is given the same name, Ḥamdī. The first of these plays, *al-Dukhān* (1962), presents him as a member of a lower middle-class family struggling to escape from drug addiction; in the one-act play *al-Wāfid* (1965), the author uses a hotel as a symbol of a totalitarian system, skilfully maintaining a Kafkaesque atmosphere until the hero's final desperate plea that he does not want to die. Controversial and hard-hitting, Rūmān's plays frequently encountered difficulties from the Egyptian censor.

Text edition

'The new arrival', in F. Abdel Wahab (ed.), *Modern Egyptian Drama*, Minneapolis (1976), 154–205.

Further reading

Badawi, M.M., *Modern Arabic Drama in Egypt*, Cambridge (1987).

P. STARKEY

al-Rummānī, ʿAlī ibn ʿĪsā (276–384/889–994)

Abū al-Ḥasan ʿAlī ibn ʿĪsā was a **Muʿtazilī** grammarian, rhetorician and theologian from **Baghdad**. (Ibn al-Nadīm's *Fihrist* gives 296/909 as his year of birth.) **Ibn Durayd** was among his teachers. According to some of his contemporaries, he incorporated too much logic in his grammatical speculations. Twenty-one titles are ascribed to him in **Yāqūt**'s *Muʿjam al-udabā'*, most of them dealing with **grammar**. Part of his commentary on **Sībawayh** has been edited. His commentary on the **Koran** is lost. The impact of his short but influential treatise on the inimitability of Koranic style (***iʿjāz al-Qur'ān***) is noticeable in the works of **al-Bāqillānī**, **Abū Hilāl al-ʿAskarī** and many others.

Text editions

al-Ḥudūd fī al-naḥw, in *Rasā'il fī al-naḥw wa-al-lugha*, Muḥammad Jawād and Y.Y. Maskūnī (eds), Baghdad (1969), 37–50.
al-Nukat fī iʿjāz al-Qur'ān, in *Thalāth rasā'il fi iʿjāz al-Qur'ān lil-Rummānī wa-al-Khaṭṭābī wa-ʿAbd al-Qāhir al-Jurjānī*, Muḥammad Khalaf Allāh and Muḥammad Zaghlūl Sallām (eds), 2nd edn, Cairo (1968), 73–113.

Sieben Kapitel des Šarḥ Kitāb Sībawaihi, E. Ambros (ed. and trans.), Vienna (1979).

Further reading

Foda, Hachem, 'La formule du sens. Essai sur *al-Nukat fī i'ǧāz al-Qur'ān* d'al-Rummānī', *Analyses-Théorie* 1 (1982), 43–78.
Tuske, L., 'Ar-Rummānī on eloquence (*balāġa*)' in *Proceedings 14th Congr. UEAI (Budapest, 1988)*, A. Fodor (ed.), Budapest (1995), II, 247–61.

G.J.H. VAN GELDER

See also: exegesis, Koranic; literary criticism, medieval

al-Ruṣāfī, Ma'rūf 'Abd al-Ghanī Maḥmūd (1875–1945)

Iraqi neo-classical poet. Born in the al-Ruṣāfa district of Baghdad, al-Ruṣāfī's early education was confined to the traditional *kuttāb* (Koranic school). He later joined al-Rushdiyya military school in Baghdad but left after three years, having failed the course. He then studied religion and linguistics under the scholar Shukrī al-Ālūsī for twelve years.

Al-Ruṣāfī began his career as a schoolteacher of Arabic. Following the declaration of the Ottoman Constitution of 1908 he went to Istanbul, where he lectured in Arabic and edited the newspaper *Sabīl al-Rashād*. In 1912 he represented the al-Muthanna district of Iraq in the Turkish Chamber of Deputies. He left Turkey for **Damascus** in 1919, but after a brief and unhappy period there went to Jerusalem, where he taught Arabic literature and enjoyed attention and respect. In 1921 he returned to Iraq, where he unwillingly accepted the post of vice-chairman of a committee on translation and arabization and edited the short-lived daily newspaper *al-Amal*.

Al-Ruṣāfī later held several posts as a teacher and inspector of Arabic. He became a member of Parliament in 1930. After 1937 he lived in self-imposed isolation, abandoning poetry, and was later forced to sell tobacco in a small shop in Baghdad. Although he died a poor man, his fame never diminished and he is now honoured by a bronze statue in al-Amīn Square in Baghdad.

Like **al-Zahāwī**, al-Ruṣāfī had no direct knowledge of European languages or literature, but his fluency in Turkish enabled him to read widely on Western literature and civilization. He began his literary career by publishing articles on social and political issues in Syrian and Egyptian journals such as ***al-Muqtaṭaf*** and *al-Mu'ayyad*. His first collection of poetry was published in 1910 and a second, larger collection in 1932; the best edition appeared in Cairo in 1958.

Al-Ruṣāfī's reputation in the Arab world is linked with the historical, political and social development of Iraq from the late nineteenth to the early decades of the twentieth century. His poetry aimed to educate, reform and awaken Iraq – and indeed, the whole Arab nation – by acting as its spokesman. At times he showed anger and frustration, as he reminded his people of their past glory, and he often clashed with the authorities, criticizing and rebuking them for their injustice and tyranny. At times, however, his poetry shows undercurrents of appeasement.

As a progressive poet, al-Ruṣāfī paved the way for the development of modern Iraqi poetry by introducing new values and ideas in his writing. He wrote much on Arabic prosody and criticized the chronological classification of poets, suggesting an alternative classification scheme based on innovation and excellence. The themes of his poetry cover a broad spectrum: political, philosophical and social issues, including the emancipation of women, and descriptions of various innovative ideas of the time. He showed a special interest in education, believing that a good poet should comprehend scientific thought and incorporate this in his poetry.

Although influenced by Turkish literature, al-Ruṣāfī generally adhered to the conventional forms of Arabic poetry, rejecting innovations such as blank verse. He tried to keep his poetry free from stylistic devices, attaching great importance to the unity of the poem. The nationalist sentiments of his poetry are couched in a language characterized by a simplicity that is readily comprehensible by the ordinary Iraqi.

Further reading

Badawi, M.M., *A Critical Introduction to Modern Arabic Poetry*, Cambridge (1975), 55–62.
Jayyusi, S.K., *Trends and Movements in Modern Arabic Poetry*, Leiden (1977), 181–8.

R. HUSNI

al-Ruṣāfī, Muḥammad ibn Ghālib, al-Raffā' (d. 572/1177)

Andalusi poet, from the neighbourhood of Valencia, active during the middle of the sixth/twelfth century; he died in Málaga. He worked in Granada and elsewhere, writing in praise of the first Almohad ruler, ʻAbd al-Mu'min, among others, but is said to have preferred to do without the support of patrons. His name al-Raffā' may indicate that he was a weaver, and he is said to have made a living from this, but it may be no more than a topos. He is said never to have married.

Text editions

Dīwān, I. ʻAbbās (ed), Beirut (1960).
Monroe, J.T., *Hispano-Arabic Poetry: A Student Anthology*, Berkeley (1974), 292–301.

Further reading

Ibn Saʻīd, *al-Mughrib fī ḥulā al-Maghrib*, S. Ḍayf (ed.), 2nd edn, Cairo, (n.d), vol. 2, 342–53 (with references to other biographical sources).
al-Dhahabī, *Siyar aʻlām al-nubalā'*, Beirut, 1981–8, vol. 21, 74 (where there are further references).

D.J. WASSERSTEIN

Rushdī, Rashād (1912–82)

Egyptian critic, college professor and dramatist. Rushdī obtained his doctorate in English literature from Leeds University in 1950 and chaired the Department of English Literature at Cairo University from 1952 to 1979. Among his publications is a critical work entitled *Readings and Studies in English Literature*. He wrote his first play, *al-Farāsha*, which was presented by al-Masraḥ al-Ḥurr, in 1959; this was followed by *Luʻbat al-ḥubb* (1961), *Riḥla khārij al-sūr* (1963) and *Khayāl al-ẓill* (1964). His later plays include *Itfarrag yā salām* (1965), *Ḥalāwit zamān* (1966), *Baladī yā baladī* (1968), *Nūr al-ẓalām* (1971), *Muḥākamat ʻAmm Aḥmad al-fallāḥ* (1974), *Shahrazād* (1975) and *ʻUyūn bahiyya* (1976). Rushdī, who headed the Masraḥ al-Ḥakīm from its inception in 1963, also served as editor-in-chief of *Majallat al-Masraḥ*, as well as of *Majallat al-Jadīd*. From 1969 to 1975 he presided over the Institute of Dramatic Arts and in 1981 became president of the Academy of Arts. Rushdī is credited with having introduced the New Criticism, as well as the study of T.S. Eliot and his pivotal influence on Arabic poetry, to the Arab reader and to the curriculum of the Cairo University English Department. A generation of writers, dramatists and literary critics graduated under his guidance.

Text edition

'A journey outside the wall', in F. Abdel Wahab (ed.), *Modern Egyptian Drama*, Minneapolis (1974).

Further reading

Badawi, M.M., *Modern Arabic Drama in Egypt*, Cambridge (1987), 182–8.

M. MIKHAIL

Rūz al-Yūsuf (1925–)

Egyptian illustrated literary weekly, named after its founder, the actress Fāṭima **al-Yūsuf**. Early issues contained news on the theatre and translations of short stories and poetry and included a section on women's affairs; it later also embraced the cinema, pictures, art books and fashion. Its contributors have included the writers Ibrāhīm ʻAbd al-Qādir **al-Māzinī**, Maḥmūd **Taymūr** and ʻAbbās **al-ʻAqqād**, as well as Fāṭima's son, Iḥsān **ʻAbd al-Quddūs**. Nationalized in 1960, *Rūz al-Yūsuf* has served as an outlet for the Egyptian government's anti-imperialist and other policies, and was popular with left-of-centre intellectuals during the Sadat period (1970–81).

Further reading

ʻAbduh, Ibrāhīm, *Rūz al-Yūsuf: Sīra wa-ṣaḥīfa*, Cairo (1961).

P.C. SADGROVE

S

Sa'āda, Anṭūn (1904–49)

Syrian nationalist writer. The leading advocate of the unity of geographical **Syria** and thus of Syrian as opposed to Arab nationalism, Sa'āda returned to the Middle East in 1929 from emigration in Brazil. He worked as a German teacher at the American University of Beirut, and in 1932 founded al-Ḥizb al-Sūrī al-Qawmī, the Syrian National Party. By 1935 the party had several thousand members in Syria and Lebanon.

In *Nushū' al-umam* (1938) Sa'āda expounded the view that the 'Syrians' constituted a distinct nation which included the population of the Fertile Crescent, together, in a subsequent formulation in 1947, with that of Iraq and Cyprus. Sa'āda was evidently influenced by some of the national and ethnic theories of Nazi Germany, but he explicitly rejected the notion that the Arabic language could serve as the basis for nationalism. His political activities and polemical writings resulted in his arrest and imprisonment for two years in 1936.

He left Lebanon in 1938, returning in 1947 to campaign once more for a unified Syrian nation. After a quixotic attempt to seize power in Lebanon from a base in Syria, he was tried and summarily executed by the Lebanese authorities in July 1949. His ideas and the movement that he founded remained influential at least until the 1960s, and still have currency in some quarters in Lebanon and Syria.

Further reading

Tibi, B., *Arab Nationalism*, London (1981).
Yamak, L.Z., *The Syrian Social National Party*, Cambridge, MA. (1966).

P.J. SLUGLETT

Sa'adiā Gaon (269–331/882–942)

Sa'adiā ben Yōsēf (Arabic: Sa'īd ibn Yūsuf) al-Fayyūmī was a Jewish scholar, thinker, writer and leader, who wrote both in Arabic and in Hebrew. Born in **Egypt**, he began his literary career there by composing a dictionary for Hebrew poetry (*Egrōn*). After a stay in Palestine, where he studied in Tiberias, he left for Mesopotamia, the Jewish political and intellectual centre of the time. Upon his own initiative he became involved in several theological and Halakhic controversies, thereby gaining political power which eventually led him to the position of head of the academy at Sūrā, which he held, with a six-year intermission, until his death.

In his own perception, Sa'adiā Gaon was the spiritual leader of the Jewish community in his generation. Displaying the acumen of a cultural planner and using political strategies, he managed to establish for himself a recognized cultural authority with which he was able to set up a new agenda for canonized Jewish literature (that is, its Rabbinic section), and restructure it in a way that was to change its face completely for generations to come. By introducing models of literary activity and writing that were innovative for Rabbinic culture but were staples of contemporary Arabic culture, and by acting to bring about their assimilation, his career radically altered the canonical Rabbinic literature.

Sa'adiā Gaon introduced a restructured Rabbinic literary system, in which the Bible (rather than the corpus of Oral Law) becomes both the focus of literary attention, with a new repertoire being created around it, and a literary and linguistic exemplar, whose status is inspired by the Arabic concept of *faṣāḥa*; a revitalized Hebrew liturgical poetry on which the status and functions of Arabic poetry have been imposed; a liturgical canon (*Siddūr*) based on norms appropriated from classicist Arabic literary criticism; a new, official, status for the written text, along with its basic writing models; and last, new Arabic (using Hebrew script) and Hebrew prose-writing models.

Sa'adiā Gaon's attempt to create a model for eloquent Hebrew prose based on the Bible is especially interesting, even though it was unsuccessful.

While the imprint of contemporary Arabic culture is discernible in all of them (either overtly or, in some cases, covertly), both the Hebrew and the Arabic models addressed Jewish problematics and were intended for the Jewish community. Being well versed in contemporary Arab learning, its contents and its modes of expression, Sa'adiā Gaon borrowed models of writing from the Arabic in order to express himself on Jewish matters, and insofar as he invoked aspects of Muslim learning, he did so by naturalizing them as part of the Jewish discourse.

Further reading

Drory, Rina, 'Bilingualism and cultural images: the Hebrew and the Arabic Introductions of Saadia Gaon's Sefer Ha-Egron', *IOS* 15 (1995), 11–23.

Malter, Henry, *Saadia Gaon: His Life and Works*, New York (1969), originally published (1926).

'Saadia Gaon', *EJ*, s.v., with further bibliography.

R. DRORY

ṣa'ālīk

Brigand poets in the pre-Islamic and early Islamic era. The word has often been translated as 'outlaws', but, strictly speaking, this is not correct because pre-Islamic **Arabia**, unlike medieval Europe, knew neither a written law nor a body to enforce it, a 'police force' that a *ṣu'lūk* could get into conflict with.

The *ṣa'ālīk* (or *luṣūṣ*, 'thieves') were outcasts in the sense that having been born into a tribe, they ceased to be tribe members, either by their own choice or by expulsion. So to understand the position of the *ṣa'ālīk*, one has to understand the status of a tribal member, the position that *ṣa'ālīk* gave up or were forced to give up.

A **bedouin** belonged to a family, but much more importantly to a tribe. The individual and the tribe were complementary entities in that the tribe demanded from the individual the best of his/her abilities but at the same time provided for all individual needs. The individual was also in a position to demand from the tribe the best it could offer, but he/she had a never-ending obligation to give away to the tribe all he/she could afford.

The morale *par excellence* of pre-Islamic Arabia was *muruwwa* (manliness), comparable to the Latin *virtus* and the Greek ἀνδρεία, a complex of vitues that reflected the close relationship between individual and tribal collective; some of these *muruwwa* virtues were tribe-oriented, such as *wafā'*, loyalty to the family and the tribe, and *karam*, extreme generosity, expecially towards the poor and needy – mostly orphans and widows – or even self-denial. The individual had to practise virtues like *ṣabr*, endurance in hardship and in battle; *ṣidq*, loyalty towards oneself or trustworthiness; *'irḍ*, honour or the enforcement of what was good (*ma'rūf*) and the struggle against or rejection of evil; and *ibā'*, rejection of all forms of dependence on authorities other than one's own tribe (see Müller, G., 1981, 82). These interdependent *muruwwa* virtues formed a closely knit structure, aimed at survival of the individual and of the tribe, a kind of social contract in which survival was understood as a mutual pact.

If, however, something between the individual and the tribal community went wrong, then the break-up would be just as complete and irreversible. This happened to a number of men: history has not always recorded on what grounds it happened, and the transmitted stories may be sketchy or even invented, but it seems that in most cases these men violated the strict code of behaviour that *muruwwa* involved, by, for instance, using forms of force or violence that exceeded the boundaries of *Jāhilī* values. When a man's fate was to become a *ṣu'lūk*, the only way he could provide for his living was theft, either from individuals, from tribes or caravans, or from someone else's crops in areas where agriculture was possible. The isolation of these *ṣa'ālīk*, who called themselves the wolves of the Arabs (*dhu'bān al-'Arab*), cannot have been complete, if only for the fact that the poetry they composed was recorded and subsequently transmitted, which could only have happened if they were in contact with other individuals.

There would be no reason to regard the poetry of the *ṣa'ālīk* as a special kind of poetry if it did not have common features as compared to the work of poets who stayed within their tribes. These typical features are both thematic and formal. A common formal feature is that practically none of the ***qaṣīda***s composed by *ṣa'ālīk* starts with the amatory introduction, the *nasīb*, the usual first part of a traditional *qaṣīda*. In the *qaṣīda* the first verse is usually a *maṭla'*, that is, a verse in which both hemistichs rhyme. As if to underline the absence of a *nasīb*, a *ṣu'lūk qaṣīda* never has a *maṭla'* verse. In other respects also the poetic forms of the *ṣa'ālīk qaṣīda*s tend to be less traditional.

More important are the thematic features that *ṣa'ālīk* poems have in common. Instead of boasting over the excellence of his tribe, the *ṣu'lūk* would obviously only express pride in himself, in his own endurance in poverty and hunger, his (self)-ordained independence and – remarkable enough in pre-Islamic poetry, because a pre-Islamic hero would never run away from danger – his swift foot when circumstances forced him to flee. Often the poet's loneliness is accentuated by creating fictitious dialogues with other animals of the desert, especially in the form of dialogues with a lone wolf (*dhi'b*) or with ghosts (*jinn*).

Most of the *ṣa'ālīk* lived in pre-Islamic Arabia, but this way of life is also attested in early Islam. Among the pre-Islamic *ṣa'ālīk* the poets **al-Shanfarā** (d. *c.*540 CE?), who composed one of the most renowned poems of Arabic literary history, the *Lāmiyyat al-'Arab*, and **Ta'abbaṭa Sharran** (d. *c.*550 CE?) are the most famous. They even seem to have been friends, because the latter composed a *marthiya* on al-Shanfarā. In the history of Arabic literature the *ṣu'lūk* **'Urwa ibn al-Ward** (d. *c.*615 CE) was portrayed as a Robin Hood *avant la lettre*, stealing from the rich in order to feed the poor.

With the rise of Islam the *ṣu'lūk* way of life came to an end, because – unlike in pre-Islamic times, when theft, especially between tribes, was more or less accepted – the new religion advocated law and order, imposing sanctions on stealing and robbery. Some of the last *ṣa'ālīk* poets were al-Qattāl al-Kilābī (d. shortly after 65/685) and Ṣakhr al-Ghayy (d. end of the first/seventh century).

The tradition of brigand poets reappears in the sect of the Assassins in seventh/twelfth and eighth/thirteenth century **Persia**, Iraq and **Syria**. Among these legendary thugs were some poets as well, although they were never called *ṣa'ālīk*. In a less violent form we can recognize the type of the sympathetic brigand poet in stories about thieves in the medieval cities of the Arab world, who were able to compose improvised poetry at the proper occasion.

Further reading

Jones, A., *Early Arabic Poetry*, vol. 1, *Marāthī and Ṣu'lūk Poems*, Oxford (1992), 27–8, 127–247.

Khulayyif, Y., *al-Shu'arā' al-ṣa'ālīk fī al-'aṣr al-Jāhilī*, Cairo (1959).

Müller, G., *Ich bin Labīd und das ist mein Zeil*, Wiesbaden, 1981.

Wagner, E., *Grundzüge der klassischen arabischen Dichtung*, vol. 1, Darmstadt (1988), 135–44.

G. BORG

See also: Arabia; bedouin; *jāhiliyya*; *qaṣīda*

al-Sā'ātī, Maḥmūd Ṣafwat (1825–81)

Egyptian court poet and judge, born in **Cairo**. He acquired his nickname from his skill at repairing watches. After going on the pilgrimage in 1845, he became a companion to the Sharif of Mecca, Prince Muḥammad ibn 'Awn, whom he accompanied to Cairo and Istanbul after his deposition in 1850. He subsequently held various government and court positions in Egypt. There are various editions of his ***dīwān*** (1859), in which he eulogized the Khedives Sa'īd, Ismā'īl and Tawfīq, and the family of 'Awn and the notables of Mecca. His poetry, modelled on classical poets, is far superior to that of his contemporaries and he is considered the leading Egyptian poet before **al-Bārūdī**.

Further reading

Brugman, J., *An Introduction to the History of Modern Arabic Literature in Egypt*, Leiden (1984), 8.

Dāghir, Yūsuf As'ad, *Maṣādir al-dirāsāt al-adabiyya*, Beirut (1956), iii/1, 524–5.

P.C. SADGROVE

al-Ṣābi', Abū Isḥāq Ibrāhīm ibn Hilāl (313–84/925–94)

Master stylist of epistolary prose. The scion of two notable families of physicians from the **Sabian** religious community of Ḥarrān (his maternal grandfather was **Thābit ibn Qurra**), throughout his life he resisted pressure from his patrons to convert to Islam. Initially employed by the **Būyid** vizier **al-Muhallabī** in **Baghdad**, he then served as head of chancery for the amīrs Mu'izz al-Dawla and 'Izz al-Dawla. In this position he incurred the wrath of the latter's cousin 'Aḍud al-Dawla, who imprisoned him for some years; it was at the latter's command that he composed his eulogistic history of the Būyid family, the

Kitāb al-Tājī, of which only a fragment has survived. His later years were apparently uneventful. His fame rests on his letters, both official and private, of which about one thousand are preserved in manuscript, although only a small number have been published. Composed in an elaborate rhymed prose (see ***saj'***), they served as a model for prose stylists of the next generation, who attempted to outdo them.

Text editions

Arazi, A., 'Une épître d'Ibrāhīm b. Hilāl al-Ṣābī sur les genres littéraires', Ayalon Festschrift, 473–505.

al-Mukhtār min Rasā'il Abī Isḥāq Ibrāhīm al-Ṣābī, S. Arslān (ed.), Ba'abdā (1898).

Rasā'il al-Ṣābī wa-al-Sharīf al-Raḍī, M.Y. Najm (ed.), Beirut (1961).

al-Tājī (extant fragment) in *Arabic Texts Concerning the History of the Zaydī Imāms of Ṭabaristān, Daylamān and Gīlān*, W. Madelung (ed.), Beirut (1987).

Further reading

Khan, M.S., 'A manuscript of an epitome of al-Ṣābī's *Kitāb al-Tāğī*', *Arabica* 12 (1965), 27–44.

Van Damme, M., 'Les sources écrites concernant l'oeuvre du secrétaire buyide Abū Isḥāq Aṣ-Ṣābī', *Actes du premier congrès d'étude des cultures mediterranéannes d'influence arabo-berbères*, Algiers (1974), 175–81.

E.K. ROWSON

al-Ṣābi', Hilāl ibn al-Muḥassin (359–448/969–1056)

Historian and **secretary**. In his writing he followed in the footsteps of his grandfather, the famous chancery official Abū Isḥāq Ibrāhīm ibn Hilāl **al-Ṣābi'**, under whom he apprenticed, and the latter's uncle, the historian Thābit ibn Sinān. Born and raised in **Baghdad**, he was the first of this famous **Sabian** family, originally from Ḥarrān, to convert to Islam, which he did in about 403/1013, while in the employ of the **Būyid** vizier Fakhr al-Mulk; when the latter fell from power, he settled on Hilāl a sum that allowed him to live in comfort for the rest of his life. Of Hilāl's *History*, which continued that of Thābit from 363/973 to 447/1055, only the section covering the years 389–93/999–1003 survives; of his book of *Wazirs*, we have only the section dealing with three of the viziers of al-Muqtadir (296–320/908–32). The most valuable of his extant works is an exposition on the protocol of the **'Abbāsid** court. His collection of model chancery letters has also been published; whether his own official correspondence survives in manuscript is as yet unclear. A number of other works are entirely lost.

Text editions

Ghurar al-balāgha, M. al-Dībājī (ed.), Casablanca (1980).

Rusūm dār al-khilāfa, M. 'Awwād (ed.), Baghdad (1964); E. Salem (English trans.), Beirut (1977).

Ta'rīkh (surviving fragment) in H.F. Amedroz and D.S. Margoliouth (eds and trans), *The Eclipse of the 'Abbāsid Caliphate*, Oxford (1920).

Tuḥfat al-umarā' fī ta'īrīkh al-wuzarā', 'A.A. Farrāj (ed.), Cairo (1958).

Further reading

Sourdel, D., 'L'originalité du *Kitāb al-Wuzarā'* de Hilāl al-Ṣābi'', *Arabica* 5 (1958), 272–92.

E.K. ROWSON

Sabians (Arabic *Ṣābi'ūn*)

A pagan sect, which flourished in Ḥarran in northern **Syria** from early times until approximately the mid-fifth/eleventh century. There were also Sabians in **Baghdad** and elsewhere. They espoused a Neoplatonic form of theology, and our Arabic sources tell us that some worshipped stars while others worshipped idols. Some scholars believe that they deliberately identified themselves with the *Ṣābi'ūn* mentioned in the **Koran** (see *Sūras* 2:62, 5:72, 22:17); in this way they are supposed to have escaped persecution and become eligible for treatment as *Ahl al-Kitāb*. Their primary interest for the development of Arabic literature lies in the renowned scholars with whom they filled the Islamic world. **Thābit ibn Qurra** (d. 288/901) was responsible for translating some of Archimedes' works into Arabic as well as the famous *Introduction to Arithmetic* by Nicomachus. His son, Sinān ibn Thābit (d. 331–32/943) flourished both as a doctor to the **'Abbāsid** court as well as a minor historian. Abū Isḥāq Ibrāhīm ibn Hilāl **al-Ṣābi'** and his grandson Hilāl ibn al-Muḥassin **al-Ṣābi'** were famous as court officials and historians. It is clear that the thought of the Sabians also had a considerable impact on some of the teachings of the **Ikhwān al-Ṣafā'**; and they are mentioned with interest by many notable Arab writers including **Ibn Ḥazm**, **al-Shahrastānī** and **al-Mas'ūdī**. From a literary point of view, the Sabians acted both as textual translators and as channels into the cultural milieu of Islam of a major alien culture and body of learning. It is for this reason, among others, that the heresiographers mention them with such interest; another must clearly be the appearance in the Koran of the word 'Sabians'.

Further reading

Corbin, H., 'Sabian temple and Ismailism', in *Temple and Contemplation*, P. Sherrard (trans.), London (1986), 132–82.

Dodge, Bayard, 'The Ṣābians of Ḥarrān', in *American University of Beirut Festival Book*, Fūad Sarrūf and Suha Tamim (eds), Beirut (1967), 59–85.

McAuliffe, J.D., 'Exegetical identification of the Ṣābi'ūn', *MW* 72 (1982), 95–106.

I.R. NETTON

Sa'd ibn Muḥammad al-Tamīmī *see* Hayṣa Bayṣa

Ṣabrī Pasha, Ismā'īl (1854–1923)

Egyptian neo-classical poet and official, born and died in **Cairo**. After obtaining a degree in law from Aix-en-Provence University, he pursued a career in the Egyptian courts; he was Governor of Alexandria (1896–9), and was then appointed under-secretary of state in the Ministry of Justice. The first modern poet to achieve a metaphysical quality, his remarkable personal poems represent the beginnings of modern lyricism. His most important poetry, *Dīwān Ismā'īl Ṣabrī Bāshā* (1938), was written in the twentieth century, but was eclipsed by the towering figure of **Shawqī**. Some of his short poems in colloquial have been set to music, and sung by 'Abduh al-Ḥamūlī. He also translated poems by Alfred de Musset, Lamartine and Verlaine.

Further reading

Brugman, J., *An Introduction to the History of Modern Arabic Literature in Egypt*, Leiden (1984), 33–5.

Jayyusi, S.K., *Trends and Movements in Modern Arabic Poetry*, Leiden (1977), 39–42.

Rizzitano, U., 'Ismā'īl Ṣabrī Pas̲h̲a', *EI*², vol. 4, 194–5.

P.C. SADGROVE

al-Sa'dāwī, Nawāl (1931–)

Egyptian psychiatrist, novelist and political activist. From a village in Lower **Egypt**, al-Sa'dāwī graduated from Cairo University Faculty of Medicine in 1955. She sparked controversy in 1972 with her study of sexual socialization and its effects on women, *al-Mar'a wa-al-jins*, and was dismissed from her senior Ministry of Health post. She had been publishing fiction since the late 1950s: by 1960, two short-story collections, *Ta'allamtu al-ḥubb* and *Laḥẓat ṣidq*, and her first novel, *Mudhakkirāt ṭabība*, had appeared. Since then, she has been a prolific novelist and short-story writer, exploring in realist and allegorical works of fiction the modes and effects of gender-based oppression in her society (e.g. in *Mawt al-rajul al-waḥīd 'alā al-arḍ*, 1976, trans. S. Hetata as *God Dies by the Nile*, 1985; and *Imra'a 'ind nuqṭat al-ṣifr*, 1975, trans. S. Hetata as *Woman at Point Zero*, 1983), and questioning Islamist programmes for women (*Suqūṭ al-Imām*, 1987, trans. S. Eber as *The Fall of the Imam*, 1988) and the social control that religious ideologies construct and perpetuate (*Jannāt wa-Iblīs*, 1992, translated as *The Innocence of the Devil*, 1994). More recently, *al-Ḥubb fī zaman al-nafṭ* (n.d.) probes the relationship between global economic imperatives and gender. She has published a volume of prison memoirs, *Mudhakkirātī fī sijn al-nisā'* (1983, trans. M. Booth as *Memoirs from the Women's Prison*, 1986), as well as two other memoirs, and her fiction manifests her interest in 'autobiographical' modes of writing. She has also published two plays. Al-Sa'dāwī's corpus has been widely translated and she has become a celebrated feminist spokesperson internationally. She has written several socio-medical studies in the vein of *al-Mar'a wa-al-jins*, informed by her medical practice as family doctor and psychiatrist, and other non-fiction works on aspects of gender in society (e.g. *'An al-mar'a*, 1988). In 1982 she founded the Arab Women Solidarity Association (AWSA), which has fought in court for the right to exist since it was ordered to be dissolved by a governmental administrative order in June 1991 (see her *Ma'raka jadīda fī qaḍiyyat al-mar'a*, 1992).

Further reading

Malti-Douglas, Fedwa, *Men, Women, and God(s): Nawāl El Saadāwī and Arab Feminist Poetics*, Berkeley (1995).

——, *Woman's Body, Woman's Word: Gender and Discourse in Arabo-Islamic Literature*, Princeton (1991).

Middle East Watch, 'Egyptian government moves to dissolve prominent Arab women's organization' (September 1991).

al-Saadawi, Nawāl, 'Reflections of a feminist,' in Margot Badran and Miriam Cooke (eds), *Opening the Gates: A Century of Arab Feminist Writing*, Bloomington and Indianapolis (1990).

M. BOOTH

al-Ṣafadī, Khalīl ibn Aybak (d. 764/1363)

The son of a Turkish *mamlūk*, born in Safad in the last decade of the thirteenth century. After a life as a government clerk in various Syrian towns and in **Cairo**, and as a prodigiously productive author, he died in **Damascus**. Apart from a vast amount of poetry, his many prose works are, in the typical fashion of the time, little more than enormously industrious compilations or more narrowly focused **anthologies**. Among his compositions one finds something in the nature of a huge commonplace book, which later authors quarried, works on lexicography and rhetorical devices, a ***maqāma*** on wine, a collection of literary epistles (including some of those received by him), and anthologies on erotic and pederastic themes.

The work for which he is most famous is entitled *al-Wāfī bil-Wafayāt*. This is a biographical dictionary of gigantic proportions, said to contain over 140,000 entries, which in principle are arranged alphabetically, except for the precedence given to the name Muḥammad. The modern edition of this, having reached many volumes, is still not completed. Two other smaller biographical works are excerpts from the main work. One, *A'yān al-'aṣr*, is devoted to contemporaries and the other, *Nakt al-himyān*, to noted blind persons. The work has an introduction, which discusses different dating systems, the conventions of personal naming, the general method followed by the author and an exhaustive list of his predecessors, historians and biographers.

Text editions

Das bibliographische Lexikon des Salaheddin Ḫalīl ibn Aibak as-Safadī, H. Ritter *et al.* (eds), vols 1–18 and 22, Wiesbaden (1932–88).

Nakt al-himyān fī nukat al-'umyān, Aḥmad Zakī (ed.), Cairo (1911), rpt (n.d.).

Further reading

Little, D.P., 'Al-Ṣafadī as biographer of his contemporaries', in *History and Historiography of the Mamlūks*, Variorum Reprints, London (1986), no. 1.

D.S. RICHARDS

Ṣaffārids

A Persian dynasty which reigned in Sijistān or Sistan (the region on the frontiers of modern Iran and southern Afghanistan) 253–393/862–1003. It was founded by Ya'qūb ibn al-Layth, a coppersmith (*ṣaffār*), who by his death in 265/879 had assembled a mighty empire in the eastern Islamic lands, from the frontiers of **India** to Khuzistan, challenging the **'Abbāsid** caliphs in Samarra for control of southwestern **Persia** and lower Iraq. His brother and successor 'Amr expanded these conquests into **Khurasan**, before meeting a decisive check in 282/900 from the **Sāmānids** of Transoxania, after which the succeeding Ṣaffārid amīrs were largely reduced to their native province of Sistan for the remainder of their existence.

The early Ṣaffārid amīrs were preoccupied with warfare, but the reigns of Ya'qūb and 'Amr are significant in that poetry in literary New Persian was cultivated at their court, and a few specimens survive of this; also, we know of at least one poet who praised them in Arabic and expressed in his verse their challenge to the 'Abbāsids as representatives of what might be called a 'proto-Iranian' nationalism. Moreover, the amīrs of the fourth/tenth century were enthusiastic patrons of Arabic learning; the philosopher **Abū Sulaymān al-Sijistānī** worked at their court; the globe-trotter **Abū Dulaf** apparently visited this last and wrote about it; they were praised by some of the leading writers of the age, such as **Badī' al-Zamān al-Hamadhānī**; and the last amīr, Khalaf ibn Aḥmad, achieved fame as patron of a hundred-volume **Koran** commentary which has not, however, survived.

Further reading

Bosworth, C.E., 'The Tahirids and Saffarids', in *CHIr*, vol. 4, 106–35.

——, *The History of the Saffarids of Sistan and the Maliks of Nimruz (247/861 to 949/1542–3)*, Costa Mesa, CA and New York (1994).

Noeldeke, T. 'Yakúb the coppersmith and his dynasty', in *Sketches from Eastern History*, London (1892).

Stern, S.M., 'Yaʿqūb the coppersmith and Persian national sentiment', in *Iran and Islam*, C.E. Bosworth (ed.), Edinburgh (1971), 535–55.

The Tārikh-e Sistān, Milton Gold (trans.), Rome (1976).

C.E. BOSWORTH

Ṣafī al-Dīn al-Ḥillī (667–*c.*750/1278–*c.*1349)

Abū al-Maḥāsin ʿAbd al-ʿAziz ibn Sarāyā Ṣafi al-Dīn al-Ḥillī was a poet and stylist from the ancient **Shīʿī** centre of Ḥilla in central Iraq. Though himself apparently a moderate Shīʿī, he was quite happy to spend the greater part of his career as eulogist at the courts of strongly **Sunnī** rulers like the Turkish Artuqids of Diyārbakr, the last **Ayyūbids** and the **Mamlūks** of **Egypt**. In the field of classical Arabic literature, he was famed as a writer of ***qaṣīda*s** and ***muwashshaḥ*s**, and these form the extensive poetic *dīwān* as we know it today. Among his poems there is a *Qaṣīda Sāsāniyya* on the devices of beggars, fraudulent Ṣūfīs and other tricksters, in which he employs a very recondite and difficult vocabulary in part deriving from various tongues of the Iraqi–Syrian–eastern Anatolian milieu where he worked (for another poem of this type, see **Abū Dulaf**). He further wrote a work in verse on rhetoric. Of particular interest as one of the few works of its type deemed worthy of a modern critical edition and of being made widely known is Ṣafī al-Dīn's treatise on the popular Arabic poetry of his time, illustrated with compositions of his own and of other writers in such genres as the ***zajal***, ***mawāliyā***, ***kān wa-kān*** and *qūmā*, the *Kitāb al-ʿĀṭil al-ḥālī*.

Further reading

Bosworth, C.E., *The Mediaeval Islamic Underworld: The Banū Sāsān in Arabic Society and Literature*, Leiden (1976), vol. 1, 132–49.

Hoenerbach, W., *Die vulgärarabische Poetik al-Kitāb al ʿĀṭil al Ḥālī wal Muraḫḫaṣ al Ġālī des Ṣafiyaddīn Ḥillī*, Wiesbaden (1956).

C.E. BOSWORTH

al-Ṣāḥib Ibn ʿAbbād (326–85/938–95)

Abū al-Qāsim Ismāʿīl ibn ʿAbbād al-Ṣāḥib was a **Būyid** vizier, prose stylist and poet, and the most important literary patron of his era. A protégé of Rukn al-Dawla's vizier **Ibn al-ʿAmīd**, he served as vizier to Rukn's son Mu'ayyid al-Dawla in Isfahan and **Rayy** and then to the latter's brother Fakhr al-Dawla in Jurjan and Rayy. A highly effective administrator, he also succeeded in attracting to his court a stunning array of poets, littérateurs and philologists, including **Abū al-Faraj al-Iṣbahānī**, Abū Bakr **al-Khwārazmī** and **Ibn Fāris**, although he failed to snare **al-Mutanabbī**. The library he assembled in Rayy was probably unequalled in its day, and he himself authored a large number of works, of which some fifteen survive and have been published. A staunch **Muʿtazilī** (he appointed **al-Qāḍī ʿAbd al-Jabbār**, the chief Muʿtazilī thinker of his day, chief judge in Rayy) and a **Zaydī Shīʿī**, he wrote several theological treatises; unlike his predecessor Ibn al-ʿAmīd, however, he was opposed to philosophy and the secular sciences. His philological writings include a dictionary (partially preserved) and a number of specialized monographs, including a detailed exposé of all the faults in al-Mutanabbī's verse. His own poetry, of which much survives, is generally unremarkable, and his real literary achievements were in prose. He was an influential proponent of the trend towards increasing elaborateness in **artistic prose**, and his own famed correspondence, both official and private, displays a persistent reliance on parallelism and rhyme (see ***sajʿ***), combined with complex word play, which contrasts with the more chaste style of his predecessor Ibn al-ʿAmīd and his contemporary the **Baghdad** secretary Ibrāhīm ibn Hilāl **al-Ṣābi'**, whom he saw as his chief rival. He is in fact held responsible for the corruption of Arabic prose by the more conservative **al-Tawḥīdī**, whose notorious *Faults of the Two Viziers* furthermore depicts him as vainglorious, hypocritical, lecherous and irredeemably corrupt. That he had a pronounced taste for low life and the prurient is clear from numerous anecdotes, as well as his patronage of such dubious figures as **Abū Dulaf**, who composed his poem on the beggars and tricksters and their argot at his request.

Text editions

Dīwān al-Ṣāḥib Ibn ʿAbbād, M.Ḥ. Āl Yāsīn (ed.), Beirut (1974).

al-Kashf ʿan masāwi' shiʿr al-Mutanabbī, M.Ḥ. Āl Yāsīn (ed.), Baghdad (1965).

al-Muḥīṭ bil-lugha, I (*ʿayn*), M.Ḥ. Āl Yāsīn (ed.), Baghdad (1965).

Rasā'il al-Ṣāḥib Ibn 'Abbād, 'A.W. 'Azzām and S. Ḍayf (eds), Cairo (1947).

Further reading

Āl Yāsīn, M.Ḥ., *al-Ṣāḥib Ibn 'Abbād*, Baghdad (1957).
*EI*², s.v. Ibn 'Abbād.
Kraemer, J., *Humanism in the Renaissance of Islam*, Leiden (1986), 259–72.
Pellat, Ch., 'Al-Ṣāḥib Ibn 'Abbād', in *CHALABL*, 96–111.
al-Tawḥīdī, *Akhlāq al-wazīrayn*, M. al-Ṭanjī (ed.), Damascus (1965), *passim*.
al-Tha'ālibī, *Yatīmat al-dahr*, Cairo (1956), vol. 3, 192–290.

E.K. ROWSON

Sahl al-Tustarī (203–83/818–96)

Sahl ibn 'Abd Allāh al-Tustarī, one of the greatest Ṣūfī masters of the third/ninth century, born in Tustar and died in **Basra**. **Al-Ḥallāj** was numbered among his students. His teachings were perpetuated especially in the school of the Sālimiyya which was founded by his student Muḥammad ibn Sālim and the latter's son Aḥmad. One of Aḥmad's students was Abū Ṭālib **al-Makkī** who composed the *Qūt al-qulūb*, the chief source for **al-Ghazzālī**'s *Iḥyā' 'ulūm al-dīn*. Sahl himself has left us no writings. His dicta were collected and published by his students. Most important is his **Koran** commentary which **al-Sulamī** incorporated into his own *Ḥaqā'iq al-tafsīr*. Besides what al-Sulamī preserved, a collection of dicta attributed to Sahl has come down to us which bears the title *Kalām Sahl*.

Further reading

Böwering, Gerhard, *The Mystical Vision of Existence in Classical Islam: The Qur'ānic Hermeneutics of the Sufi Sahl At-Tustarī*, Berlin (1980).

B. RADTKE

Sahl ibn Hārūn (d. 215/830)

Abū 'Amr Sahl ibn Hārūn was an author of Persian descent who stemmed from Dastmaysān in lower Iraq. He was a protégé of the **Barmakids** and served the caliphs **Hārūn al-Rashīd** and al-Ma'mūn, becoming director of the latter's **Bayt al-Ḥikma** or 'House of Wisdom' and receiving the sobriquet of 'the Buzurjmihr of Islam' for his wisdom and learning. He was a strong partisan of the ***Shu'ūbiyya***, and continued the tradition of **Ibn al-Muqaffa'** in bringing the Persian heritage into Arabic literature and culture. His ***adab*** compositions ranged from poetry and animal fables of the ***Kalīla wa-Dimna*** type to politics and statecraft, according to the titles of all these works preserved in later authors. **Al-Jāḥiẓ** admired him, and quotes from an epistle written by Sahl in praise of economy and circumspection in his own *Book of Misers*, such advocacy being regarded as a *Shu'ūbī* reply to the Arabs' famed virtues of liberality and hospitality.

Further reading

*EI*², s.v. (Mohsen Zakeri).
Goldziher, I., *Muslim Studies*, C.R. Barber and S.M. Stern (trans.), London (1967–71), vol. 1, 149.

C.E. BOSWORTH

Sa'īd, 'Alī Aḥmad *see* Adūnīs

al-Sa'īd, Amīna (1914–)

Egyptian journalist, short-story writer, feminist and translator. Born in Asyut, Amīna al-Sa'īd was among the first group of women to enter the English literature department of Cairo University. She started her press career in 1932 before graduating from college and in 1952 was chosen to be editor-in-chief of *Majallat Ḥawwā'* (the most widely distributed women's magazine in the Middle East), published by the al-Hilāl publishing house. In 1959 she became chairperson of the press syndicate board. She headed the executive board of ***al-Hilāl*** from 1975 to 1981, and since her retirement has served as consultant to the al-Hilāl publishing house. Amīna al-Sa'īd's writings are characterized by a direct and clear style which speaks to large audiences about the complex emotions and psychological make-up of women. Her works include *al-Jāmiḥa*, *Ākhir al-ṭarīq* (a collection of short stories) and *Wujūh fī al-ẓalām*, a collection of articles from *Ḥawwā'* dealing with the psychology and alienation of the Egyptian woman, particularly in the 1930s and 1940s. The main thrust of her writings addresses women's dilemmas within the struggle to change from a traditional to a more liberal role. From 1980 to 1986, as a member of the Consultative Assembly (Shūrā) she courageously demanded reforms to family law. Amīna al-Sa'īd has also written a book on Byron, and translated Rudyard Kipling's

Jungle Book and Louisa May Alcott's *Little Women.*

Further reading

Badran, Margot and Cooke, Miriam (eds), *Opening the Gates*, London (1990), 357–65.
Fawzī, M., *Adab al-aẓāfir al-ṭawīla*, Cairo (1987).

M. MIKHAIL

Sa'īd, Khālida (1932–)

Syrian literary critic. Born in Latakia, Sa'īd was educated in Banyas, **Damascus** and at the Lebanese University in Beirut, where she graduated in Arabic literature in 1965. In 1974 she gained a doctorate from the Sorbonne for a thesis on innovation in Arabic literature. An active member of the Syrian National Socialist Party, she was imprisoned in 1955 and 1956. In 1956 she moved to Lebanon with her husband **Adūnīs**, where she soon distinguished herself as one of the most perceptive critics within the *ḥadātha* movement which centred around the journal *Shi'r* founded in 1957 by Yūsuf **al-Khāl**. Sa'īd's *al-Baḥth 'an al-judhūr* (1960) was the first work of genuinely modernist criticism in the Arab world; few critics had a finer ability to discern the subtle patterns within a poetic text, or a sharper sense of contrast between new and conventional modes of expression. In the mid-1970s, with the emergence of a more sophisticated, anti-ideological criticism, Sa'īd was again a leading figure; her *Ḥarakiyyat al-ibdā'* (1979) helped to set the tone for a new critical movement in the Arab world.

A main concern in Sa'īd's work has been the need to transcend ideologically based criticism and to explore virgin territories of textual study, while participating in the radical search for modernity. She has also stood for a new role for women, rejecting the exclusivist categorization of their works as 'feminist'; at the same time, she has devoted much energy to women's issues, producing in 1991 a fine volume of studies entitled *al-Mar'a, al-Taḥarrur, al-Ibdā'*.

In addition to her writing, Sa'īd's career has been characterized by continuing political and social involvement. In 1959 she founded a centre for the abolition of illiteracy and she has worked as a teacher at levels from primary school to the academy. Since 1975 she has been professor of modern Arabic literature at the Lebanese University.

KAMAL ABU-DEEB

Saj'

'Rhymed prose', a term used generally to distinguish artistic prose, subject to certain constraints of rhythm and rhyme, from unadorned or 'free' (*mursal*) prose. Etymologically, the word referred to the cooing of pigeons, and was first applied linguistically to the oracular statements of pre-Islamic soothsayers (*kāhin*s), which consisted of series of short phrases exhibiting monorhyme but not regular metre. Whether the style of the **Koran**, whose periods are throughout characterized by similar stretches of monorhyme, could be labelled *saj'* was later controversial, but mainly for theological reasons involving the doctrine of its stylistic inimitability (see ***i'jāz al-Qur'ān***).

Although *saj'* in a narrow sense refers specifically to this phenomenon of recurrent rhyme, complications have arisen from its association with another form of prose organization, that of parallelism, whether semantic, syntactic, rhythmic (i.e. with parallel vowel sequences), or some combination of these. Such parallelism (usually termed *izdiwāj* when phrases are grouped in pairs, or *muwāzana* when rhythmically based) was characteristic of early Arabic **oratory** (*khuṭab*), which on occasion combined it with the rhyming phenomenon of *saj'*, as the *kāhin*s also sometimes used their *saj'* to mark parallel phrases.

In early artistic written prose, such as that of **al-Jāḥiẓ**, both phenomena play only a limited role, parallelism being exploited rather more than rhyme. The distinctive genre of **artistic prose** developed in the chanceries and generally held to have been initiated by the **Umayyad** secretary **'Abd al-Ḥamīd ibn Yaḥyā al-Kātib** displays a growing reliance on both through the third/ninth and early fourth/tenth centuries, together with an increasing use of rhetorical tropes borrowed from poetry. During the same period *saj'* appears more and more frequently in titles of belletristic works (becoming virtually *de rigueur* by the end of the fourth/tenth century) and in their introductory sections. A recognized turning point was reached about 350/960 with the celebrated epistles of the **Būyid** vizier **Ibn al-'Amīd**, encapsulated in the *saj'* formula that 'chancery prose [*kitāba*] began with 'Abd al-Ḥamīd and was sealed by Ibn al-'Amīd'. There followed a generation of virtuosi of prose stylistics, affected to a greater or lesser degree by the 'mania for *saj'*' with which the relatively conservative **al-Tawḥīdī** charged Ibn al-'Amīd's successor as vizier, **al-Ṣāḥib Ibn 'Abbād**. The consistent use of *saj'* and parallelism throughout a composition became characteristic not only of chancery prose, but also of private epistles and, not surprisingly, oratory, reaching its high point in the latter art in the sermons of **Ibn Nubāta al-Khaṭīb** (d. 374/984). Other authors found new venues for this sort of rhetorical prose, notably **al-'Utbī** in history and biography and, crucially, **Badī' al-Zamān al-Hamadhānī** (in the ***maqāma***), destined to become the premier showcase for *saj'* for centuries to come.

This rhetorical prose was now a serious rival to poetry, from which it had borrowed not only an entire panoply of rhetorical devices, but also to a large extent generic themes and occasions, military successes being celebrated with both odes and victory letters (*kutub futūḥ*), letters of condolence paralleling elegies, and the like. This convergence is marked by the popularity of debates over the relative merits of **prose** and poetry, the development of the genre of *nathr al-naẓm* in which existing verses were recast in elaborate prose (as well as the reverse), and the proliferation of handbooks cataloguing themes and phrases of potential use to the budding prose stylist as well as poet. Critical analysis of *saj'*, though never as highly developed as that of poetry, first appears in the introduction to one of these handbooks, **Qudāma ibn Ja'far**'s *Gems of Locution*, and was further refined in later centuries by such critics as **Abū Hilāl al-'Askarī**, Ḍiyā' al-Dīn **Ibn al-Athīr**, and **al-Qalqashandī**. A single example of the sort of complexity dealt with would be Qudāma's definition of *tarṣī'*, in which multiple *saj'* rhyme is combined with full morphological parallelism, as in the phrase *ḥattā 'āda ta'rīḍuka taṣrīḥā wa-ṣāra tamrīḍuka taṣḥīḥā* ('until your obscurity reverted to plain statement and your deficient rendering became sound').

By the beginning of the sixth/twelfth century, when **al-Ḥarīrī** composed his *Maqāmāt*, the most celebrated *saj'* work of all, the necessity of casting any prose with stylistic pretensions into *saj'* was thoroughly established for centuries to come. Later authors famed for their *saj'* style include **al-Qāḍī al-Fāḍil**, **'Imād al-Dīn al-Iṣfahānī**, and **Ibn 'Abd al-Ẓāhir**. The use of *saj'* also became common in popular prose literature such as ***Alf layla wa-layla***. The extent of its continuing grip on Arabic prose can be measured by its use in Muḥammad **al-Muwayliḥī**'s *Ḥadīth 'Īsā ibn Hishām* in the early twentieth century, by which time, however, the modern revolt which has now largely swept away this sort of artifice was already growing strong.

Text edition

Qudāma ibn Ja'far, *Jawāhir al-alfāẓ*, Beirut (1985), 2–10.

Further reading

Beeston, A.F.L., 'Parallelism in Arabic prose', *JAL* 5 (1974), 134–46.
——, 'The role of parallelism in Arabic prose', in *CHALUP*, 180–5.
Freimark, P., *Das Vorwort als literarische Form in der arabischen Literatur*, Diss. Münster (1967).
Horst, H., 'Besondere Formen der Kunstprosa', in *GAP*, vol. 2, 221–7.
Mubārak, Z., *La Prose arabe au IVᵉ siècle de l'Hégire (Xᵉ siècle)*, Paris (1931).
Stewart, D.J., *Saj'* in the Qur'ān: prosody and structure', *JAL* 21 (1990), 101–39.

E.K. ROWSON

See also: artistic prose; oratory and sermons

Sakākīnī, Widād (1913–86)

Short-story writer. Born in Sidon, **Lebanon**, Widād Sakākīnī lived most of her life in **Syria**. She came from an upper-class background, and by profession was a teacher.

She is best known for her short stories, but also published novels and literary criticism. Her collection of stories entitled *Marāyā al-nās* (Cairo, 1945) is reckoned as the earliest Syrian collection after Fu'ād **al-Shāyib**'s *Ta'rīkh jurḥ*. In it she deals with aspects of social life in Syria, and particularly in **Damascus**. Her work is of the realist school, and her literary method is much like that of 'Abd al-Salām **al-'Ujaylī**. Her later works include *al-Sitār al-marfū'* (Cairo, 1955) and *Aqwā min al-sinīn* (Damascus, 1978).

Further reading

al-Aṭrash, M.I., *Ittijāhāt al-qiṣṣa fī Sūriyya*, Damascus (1982).

M.J.L. YOUNG

al-Sakhāwī (830–902/1427–97)

Shams al-Dīn Muḥammad ibn 'Abd al-

Raḥmān al-Sakhāwī was an Egyptian Shāfi'ī author of the later **Mamlūk** period. He was the pupil of **Ibn Ḥajar al-'Asqalānī** and spent most of his career as a *mudarris* or professor at various of the **Cairo** colleges. He wrote some 200 works, a fair number of which are extant, in the fields of history, Koranic studies, tradition and ***adab***. Especially valuable for cultural history is his collection of biographies, essentially of scholars of his own century (namely the ninth/fifteenth), *al-Ḍaw' al-lāmi' fī a'yān al-qarn al-tāsi'*, despite attacks on it by his contemporaries and rivals for its uncritical, compilatory character – a characteristic, however, of the age. More incisive and original is his historiographical work, *al-I'lān bil-tawbīkh li-man dhamma ahl al-ta'rīkh*, in which he defends the study of history as a valuable ancillary to the religious sciences; its value for Mamlūk history is enhanced by his concentration on near-contemporary and contemporary authors for his examples.

Text editions

al-Ḍaw' al-lāmi' fī a'yān al-qarn al-tāsi', Ḥ. al-Qudsī (ed.), Cairo (1934–6).

al-I'lān bil-tawbīkh li-man dhamma ahl al-ta'rīkh, Damascus (1930–1).

Rosenthal, F. (trans.), 'The open denunciation of adverse criticisms on historians', in *A History of Muslim Historiography*, 2nd edn, Leiden (1968), 263–529.

Further reading

Lutfi, H., 'Al-Sakhāwī's Kitāb al-Nisā' as a source for the social and economic history of women in the fifteenth century', *MW* 71 (1981), 104–24.

C.E. BOSWORTH

al-Sakkākī (555–626/1160–1229)

Abū Ya'qūb Yūsuf ibn Abī Bakr al-Sakkākī was a grammarian and rhetorician from **Khwarazm**, and author of the influential compendium *Miftāḥ al-'ulūm*. Not much is known of his life, the last three years of which he is said to have spent in prison on the order of Jaghatay, son of Chinghiz Khan. His *Miftāḥ al-'ulūm* (*The Key to the Sciences*) is divided into three parts: morphology, syntax and rhetoric; with appendixes on argumentation (*istidlāl*) and **prosody**. The third part, on *ma'ānī* (see ***ma'nā***) and *bayān*, which summarizes and systematizes the insights of **'Abd al-Qāhir al-Jurjānī**, became extremely popular and many commentaries were made on it. Al-Sakkākī's presentation and many of his definitions and formulations became standard in the science of Arabic rhetoric, as it was studied especially in the eastern parts of the Arab world and among Persians and Turks. The popularity of the *Miftāḥ*, due to its systematic and scholastic character, was exceeded only by that of a much shorter and simpler compendium which was itself based on the third part of the *Miftāḥ*: *Talkhīṣ al-Miftāḥ* by Muḥammad ibn 'Abd al-Raḥmān **al-Khaṭīb al-Qazwīnī**.

Text edition

Miftāḥ al-'ulūm, Nu'aym Zarzūr (ed.), Beirut (1983).

Further reading

Maṭlūb, Aḥmad, *al-Balāgha 'ind al-Sakkākī*, Baghdad (1964).

Sellheim, R., *Arabische Handschriften: Materialien zur arabischen Literaturgeschichte*, Wiesbaden (1976), vol. 1, 299–324.

Simon, U.G., *Mittelalterliche arabische Sprachbetrachtung zwischen Grammatic und Rhetoric*: 'ilm al-ma'ānī bei as-Sakkākī, Heidelberg (1993).

Smyth, W., 'Controversy in a tradition of commentary: the academic legacy of al-Sakkākī's *Miftāḥ al-'ulūm*', *JAOS* 112 (1992), 589–97.

——, 'Some quick rules *ut pictura poesis:* the rules for simile in *Miftāḥ al-'ulūm*, Oriens 33 (1992), 215–19.

G.J.H. VAN GELDER

See also: commentaries; literary criticism, medieval; rhetoric and poetics

Salāḥ al-Dīn (Saladin) *see* Ayyūbids

Salāma ibn Jandal (seventh century CE)

A celebrated pre-Islamic warrior poet of the Sa'd ibn Zayd Manāt (Tamīm), famed for its poets, such as al-Mukhabbal and 'Abda ibn al-Ṭabīb. His brother Aḥmar was also a warrior poet. Salāma took part in his tribe's victory over Bakr in the battle of Jadūd but is not mentioned as having fought on the second day of Kulāb (*c*.612 CE). His *qaṣā'id* are largely chronicles of the *Ayyām* of his tribe (see **Battle Days**). They reveal a fondness for a binary structure, with a marked avoidance of *tashbīh* (simile), focusing instead on an aspect of the *nasīb*, such as senectitude (Qabāwa 1 = *Mufaḍḍaliyyāt* 22) – a structural technique later adopted by **ʿAbbāsid** poets – or departing howdahs (Qabāwa 4). In Qabāwa 2 the desert voyage is portrayed, explicitly, as a heroic journey, as much a feature of the pre-Islamic poet's noble character as addiction to *maysir*, largesse and martial prowess. He was noted for his horse descriptions: Qabāwa 1, 5–15, is a splendid and much admired example. The manuscript tradition of Salāma's ***dīwān*** is amply discussed by Qabāwa in his edition (p. 13–85).

Text editions

Dīwān, F. Qabāwa (ed.), Aleppo (1968).
The Mufaḍḍaliyyāt, C.J. Lyall (ed.), Oxford (1918).

J.E. MONTGOMERY

Ṣāliḥ, Ilyās (1836–86)

Syrian Melchite poet and historian, born and died in Latakia. He worked for a number of years as translator in the American consulate, was involved in business, and served as a judge in Latakia. He translated the Turkish imperial constitution and state laws into Arabic. His poetry, *Dīwān al-marḥūm Ilyās Ṣāliḥ al-Lādhiqī* (1910), consists mainly of conventional eulogy and elegy. He also published some translations of psalms used in Presbyterian churches (1875), and a *Khuṭba fī ḥaqīqat al-tadhhīb* (1886), and wrote a short manuscript on the history of Latakia. With Asʿad Dāghir he translated a historical novel by George Ebers, *Eine ägyptische Königstochter* (1899).

Further reading

Dāghir, Yūsuf Asʿad, *Maṣādir al-dirāsāt al-adabiyya*, Beirut (1956), iii/1, 675–6.

P.C. SADGROVE

Ṣāliḥ ibn ʿAbd al-Quddūs (d. *c.*167/783)

Preacher and poet of *zuhd* (see ***zuhdiyya***) from **Basra**. He was suspected of being a Manichaean heretic, *zindīq*, for which he was executed in **Baghdad** on the order – some say by the hands – of the caliph al-Mahdī, or **Hārūn al-Rashīd**, according to others. He is a key figure in the early development of ascetic and gnomic poetry. His preserved verse testifies to his piety rather than his heresy.

Text edition

al-Khaṭīb, ʿAbd Allāh, *Ṣāliḥ ibn ʿAbd al-Quddūs*, Baghdad (1967), 116–52.

Further reading

Goldziher, Ignaz, 'Ṣâliḥ b. ʿAbd-al-Ḳuddûs und das Zindîḳthum wahrend der Regierung des Chalifen al-Mahdî', in *Gesammelte Schriften*, Hildesheim (1967–73), vol. 3, 1–26 (first published 1892).
van Ess, Joseph, 'Die Hinrichtung des Ṣāliḥ b. ʿAbdalquddūs', in Spuler Festschrift, 53–66.
——, *Theologie und Gesellschaft im 2. und 3. Jahrhundert Hidschra*, Berlin (1992), vol. 2, 15–20.

G.J.H. VAN GELDER

Ṣāliḥ, al-Ṭayyib (1929–)

Sudanese novelist, short-story writer and essayist. Born in the Northern Sudan, Ṣāliḥ pursued his higher education in Khartoum and London, where he is still based. For many years he travelled widely as a UNESCO cultural delegate in the Arab world. He is not a prolific writer; his works, however, reflect a profound assimilation of Arab and Western cultures, and a technical mastery unique in contemporary Arabic literature. Ṣāliḥ started publishing short pieces as Sudan awoke to its independence in 1956. *Ḥafnat tamr* (1957) set his particular tone and created his central *persona*, who speaks intimately to the reader in the first person singular, recounting his story from childhood to old age throughout Ṣāliḥ's work. His departures to the North and returns to the South shape the pattern and rhythm of Ṣāliḥ's writings, and embody the Arab artist's contemporary predicament. In *Risāla ilā Aylīn* (1960) he wonders how his British wife could love a black Muslim Arab who bears in his heart the anxieties of a whole generation; and in *Dūmat Wad Ḥāmid* (1960) he creates the mythical village of Wad Ḥāmid which he carries in his imagination wherever he goes.

In 1966, Ṣāliḥ published *Mawsim al-hijra ilā al-shimāl*, a novel that made him famous overnight. This was followed shortly afterwards by *ʿUrs al-Zayn* (1967), a long short story which presents a microcosm of Sudanese life, where all contradictions are resolved through the creative spirituality of Zayn, the village buffoon. By contrast, Muṣṭafā Saʿīd, the colonizer's buffoon of *Mawsim* ..., sows seeds of destruction in both South and North. A novel of violent confrontation, *Mawsim* ... breaks away from the previous Romantic literature on the subject, redefining the South–North encounter as one of conflict and distortion. It thus stands both as a landmark in post-colonial literature, and as a turning point in the history of the Arabic novel. Dense and highly charged with violence, anger and passion, it is propelled forward by imagery, parallels, contrasts and syncopated rhythms, closer to a symphonic poem than to narrative prose.

Ṣāliḥ's last novel to date, *Bandarshāh* (2 vols, 1971), brings together the threads of his previous works. The narrator–artist is charged by his people to preserve their memory – a task that he performs with piety, compassion and nostalgia. The lively dialogue is rendered in colloquial Arabic, while a sensuous use of the literary language gives richness to the texture of the novel. At times Ṣāliḥ's prose reaches poetic heights, as migration becomes a metaphor for life itself, and human dramas are played out in an atmosphere of love, piety, simplicity and tolerance, in the rich **Ṣūfī** tradition of Sudan.

Text editions

Season of Migration to the North, D. Johnson-Davies (trans), London (1969).

The Wedding of Zein and Other Stories, T. Salih and D. Johnson-Davies (trans), London (1968).

Further reading

Amyuni, M.T. (ed.), *Tayeb Salih's Season of Migration to the North: A Casebook*, Beirut (1985).

M.T. AMYUNI

Sālim, 'Alī (1936–)

Egyptian dramatist. One of the most prominent satirists of his generation, 'Alī Sālim worked as an actor before turning to dramatic composition. Many of his plays take as their targets bureaucracy and corruption in contemporary Egypt, while at the same time depicting the plight of modern man. Among his best works are three one-act plays written between 1967 and 1968: *Bīr al-qamḥ*, *il-Bufayh*, and *Ughniya 'alā al-mamarr*. Of these, the Kafkaesque *il-Bufayh* shows a playwright pressurized by the authorities to change his work; while *Ughniya 'alā al-mamarr* revolves around the fate of five Egyptian soldiers facing death in Sinai after being cut off from their colleagues during the 1967 war. Among the most successful of his full-length plays is *Kūmidiyā Ūdīb* (1970), in which the author uses a loose version of the Oedipus story to launch a barbed attack on the tyranny of Nasser's regime.

Text editions

The Comedy of Oedipus, in S.K. Jayyusi and R. Allen (eds), *Modern Arabic Drama: An Anthology*, Bloomington (1995), 353–86.

Further reading

Badawi, M.M., *Modern Arabic Drama in Egypt*, Cambridge (1987), 197–205.

P. STARKEY

Sālim Abū al-'Ālā'

Sālim ibn 'Abd Allāh (or 'Abd Al-Raḥmān) Abū al-'Āla' was a well-known **secretary** in **Umayyad** times. A non-Arab client of one Umayyad or another, he began his training in the chancery in **Damascus** during the caliphate of 'Abd al-Malik ibn Marwān (65–85/684–704), where he became the mentor of **'Abd al-Ḥamīd ibn Yaḥyā al-Kātib**, to whom he gave his sister (or daughter) in marriage. By the time Hishām ibn 'Abd al-Malik became caliph in 105/723, he had become the head of the chancery. He was a confidant of Hishām and hence an influential figure during his reign. He witnessed the caliph's death in 125/742 and was the messenger who informed the then crown prince, **al-Walīd ibn Yazīd**, of his successorship to the caliphate. Al-Walīd retained him as his chief secretary, but that may not have lasted long, for his own son, 'Abd Allāh ibn Sālim, became a secretary to al-Walīd also during the latter's short reign. After that, nothing is known about him, nor do the sources mention the date of his death. Only few of his letters have survived, but he is credited, according to some sources, by having translated (or checked the translation of) the letters of **Aristotle** to **Alexander the Great** from the Greek (see ***Sirr al-asrār***).

Further reading

Biographies:

Fihrist (ed. Flügel), 117. Ibn 'Asākir, *Ta'rīkh madīnat Dimashq*, 'Umar ibn Gharāma al-'Amrawī (ed.), Beirut (1995), vol. 20, 79–81.

al-Jahshiyārī, *al-Wuzarā' wa-al-kuttāb*, Cairo (1938), 62–4, 68.
al-Ṣafadī, *al-Wāfī bil-wafayāt*, B. Radtke (ed.), Wiesbaden (1979), vol. 15, 86–7.
al-Ṭabarī, *Ta'rīkh al-rusul wa-al-muluk*, Leiden (1879–1901), ser. II, 838, 1649–52, 1750–51.
Studies:
'Abbās, Iḥsān, *'Abd al-Ḥamīd ibn Yaḥyā al-Katib wa-mā tabaqqā min rasā'ilih wa-rasā'il Sālim Abī al-'Alā'*, Amman (1988), 28–31, 303–19.
Grignaschi, M., 'Le roman épistolaire classique conservé dans la version arabe a de Sālim Abū-l-'Alā'', *Le Museon*, 80 (1967), 211–64.
——, 'Les "rasā'il arisṭāṭālīsa ilā-l-Iskandar" de Sālim Abū-l-'Alū' et l'activité culturelle à l'époque Omayyade', *BEO* 10 (1965–6), 7–83.

W. AL-QĀḌĪ

Saljūqs

A Turkic Muslim dynasty of nomadic origin who ruled a vast empire embracing lands already long Islamicized – parts of Central Asia, Iran and Iraq (1038–1194), **Syria** (1078–1117) – as well as new territory in Anatolia (1077–1307). Unity held until 511/1118; thereafter, centrifugal forces inherent in the Saljūqs' nomadic heritage fragmented the Great Saljuq empire.

The Saljūqs and their successor states, such as the Būrids of **Damascus** and the Zangids of Mosul, presented themselves as strict **Sunnī** rulers, governing on the Perso-Islamic model. The Saljūq sultans acquired the reputation of keen patrons of the arts. By the sixth/twelfth century the 'uncouth' image presented by the first sultan Ṭughril (d. 455/1063) had been superseded, for example, by that of the cultivated Maḥmūd (d. 525/1131), who was allegedly well versed in Arabic *belles-lettres*. The great vizier Niẓām al-Mulk, and other prominent Saljūq notables, extended the *madrasa* (educational) system. These institutions possessed fine libraries – the Arabic poet **al-Abīwardī** was librarian of the Niẓāmiyya in **Baghdad** – and provided an important forum for writers.

The Saljūq period witnessed significant and long-lasting developments in the sphere of Arabic *belles-lettres*. Political fragmentation after 511/1118 generated provincial courts, presided over by princes and amīrs, vying with each other in artistic patronage. But to a large extent New Persian became the preferred medium of expression for both poetry and prose in Saljūq territories. The impact of this trend on Arabic ***adab*** is still difficult to assess. The traditional view, propounded by the few who have ventured to look at Saljūq literature, holds that this diverting of the literary talents of ethnically Persian writers who had previously written with consummate skill in Arabic irrevocably damaged Arabic literature. This theory is, however, based on patchy survivals of both Arabic and Persian literary pieces, inadequate publication of those works that *are* extant, and the pro-Persian bias of scholars such as E.G. Browne. It may still prove to be well founded but much more research and proper evaluation of Saljūq literature are needed first. What is undoubtedly true is that Saljūq Iran saw the virtual demise of Arabic as the medium for *belles-lettres*, although Arabic remained supreme, even there, as the language of religion, natural science and philosophy. Arabic continued to be used for *belles-lettres* in Saljūq Arabophone areas, such as Iraq and Syria, but the rise of New Persian in the sphere of *adab* caused the formation of linguistic barriers between the world of Iran, northern **India** and Central Asia, and the territories further to the west where Arabic held sway; indeed, while writers who opted generally for Persian continued to show considerable proficiency in Arabic – Tirmidhī, Sanjar's court poet, knew Arabic extremely well – and would occasionally demonstrate these skills, Arabic-speaking areas were unable to keep abreast of developments in Persian poetry and prose and became cut off from that inspirational source.

The court poet was still a significant figure, although he was often obliged to travel widely in search of patronage and fame: this process is epitomized in the career of the Arabic poet al-Ghazzī, who worked in **Damascus**, Baghdad, **Khurasan** and Kirman and died in distant Central Asia. Arab littérateurs of the Saljūq period held important administrative posts and were subject to the vicissitudes of political fortune. Ṭughril's vizier, al-Kundurī, wrote Arabic poetry. The most famous work of the Arabic poet **al-Bākharzī** is a letter to al-Kundurī commiserating with him over his castration. The illustrious poet **al-Ṭughrā'ī** was vizier to the Saljūq prince Mas'ūd, but in spite of his advanced years was executed on charges trumped up by his enemies. Beneath its glittering virtuosity, his *Lāmiyyat al-'Arab* attacks the inferior breed of political figures who have superseded him in the corridors of power. Poets also monitored political events: landmarks in the Crusader/Muslim confrontation inspired emotionally charged verses by Syrian poets such as **Ibn al-Qaysarānī** and Ibn Munīr.

The Saljūq period produced many commentators, compilers, grammarians and philologists – **al-Zawzanī** and **al-Khaṭīb al-Tibrīzī** commented on classical Arabic poetry, **al-Maydānī** prepared his well-known collection of proverbs and **Ibn al-Anbārī** compiled well-respected philological and grammatical works. The *Kharīdat al-qaṣr* of **ʿImād al-Dīn al-Iṣfahānī** is an impressive anthology of sixth/twelfth-century Arab poets. **Al-Jawālīqī** wrote works aimed at the preservation of *fuṣḥā*; the high standards of grammatical and lexicographical knowledge required for impeccable Arabic poetry and prose, though still achievable at this time, became increasingly the preserve of a small scholarly élite.

Important Saljūq works of historiography and in the **Mirrors for Princes** genre were produced. These aimed at both entertainment and moral edification. The histories of ʿImād al-Dīn al-Iṣfahānī are especially noteworthy for their rhymed prose (***sajʿ***); his epitomizer, **al-Bundārī**, aiming at greater comprehensibility, nevertheless still produced a work in which style prevails over content. Other Saljūq historiographical works, which survive only in quotations in later authors, reveal a simpler narrative style. The Syrian *adīb* **ʿUsāma ibn Munqidh**, though skilled in high-flown literary Arabic, opted for a language closer to the Syrian colloquial in his famous memoirs.

The few existing Orientalist judgements on Saljūq Arabic literature have generally been negative: its poetry and rhymed prose are dismissed as pedantic, affected and lifeless. Yet scholarly work on Saljūq literature consists almost exclusively of biographical data on individual writers, the titles of their works and sweeping condemnatory comments. Saljūq literature still produced two works generally recognized as masterpieces of *belles-lettres* by subsequent generations of Arab audiences: the *Maqāmāt* of **al-Ḥarīrī** and the *Lāmiyyat al-ʿArab* of al-Ṭughrāʾī. The lasting popularity of the *Maqāmāt* is demonstrated by its being illustrated by Arab painters more often than any other work. The Saljūq period produced definitive works in the religious sciences, especially those of **al-Zamakhsharī** and **al-Ghazzālī**. Literary skills were not the exclusive preserve of *adab* writers. Indeed, the undoubted literary prowess of the *ʿulamāʾ* class, and notably al-Ghazzālī, enhanced the didactic aspects of their works.

Text editions

See the entries for the individual authors.

Further reading

Browne, E.G., *A Literary History of Persia*, Cambridge (1969), vol. 2, 165–364.

Cahen, C., 'The Historiography of the Seljuqid period', in *Historians of the Middle East*, B. Lewis and P.M. Holt (eds), London (1962), 59–79.

Gabrieli, F., *Arab Historians of the Crusades*, London (1978).

Gibb, H.A.R., *Arabic Literature*, Oxford (1974), 117–27.

Huart, C., *Arabic Literature*, London (1903), 63–200.

Nicholson, R.A., *A Literary History of the Arabs*, Cambridge (1969), 326, 329–36.

Sivan, E., *L'Islam et la Croisade*, Paris (1968).

al-Ṭāhir, ʿAlī Jawād, *al-Shiʿr al-ʿArabī fī al-ʿIrāq wa-balad al-ʿAjam fī al-ʿaṣr al-Saljūqī*, Baghdad (1958).

C. HILLENBRAND

Salm ibn ʿAmr al-Khāsir (d. 186/802)

Poet from **Basra**. He was a pupil and ***rāwī*** of **Bashshār**. He acquired his nickname ('the Loser'), it is said, when he sold a copy of the **Koran** in exchange for a book of verse; other explanations are also given. Accused of dissoluteness and even heresy, he was considered a poet with a natural talent (***maṭbūʿ***). He made panegyric poems, elegies and poems on his poverty (he left a fortune when he died).

Further reading

Najm, Yūsuf, (ed.), *Shuʿarāʾ ʿAbbāsiyyūn*, Beirut (1959), 91–120.

von Grunebaum, G.E., 'Three Arabic poets of the early Abbasid age: V. Salm al-Ḫâsir', *Orientalia* 19 (1950), 53–80; rpt in his *Themes in Medieval Arabic Literature*, London (1981).

G.J.H. VAN GELDER

samāʿ

Literally 'listening', *samāʿ* is used more specifically to denote listening to music, sometimes in general, sometimes with particular reference to the function of music in a Ṣūfī context. There is a considerable literature on the legal question of whether the production and consumption of (secular) music is permissible. Although music is nowhere mentioned in the **Koran**, there emerged, possibly from a complex of social reasons resulting in entertainment music being intimately associated with eroticism and wine-drinking, a hostile attitude on the part of a number of legists, apparent already in the earliest extant text on this topic, the *Dhamm al-malāhī* by **Ibn Abī al-Dunyā** (d. 281/894), in which music, branded as *ruqyat al-zinā*, 'fornication's charm', is lumped together with other reprehensible activities such as games of chance and sexual perversions. But the more negative authorities rarely proscribe music entirely: although entertainment music and its related instruments are to be shunned, the music and instruments used in life-cycle rituals and celebrations are normally deemed permissible. Works that marshal arguments for the defence draw essentially upon the same contradictory stock of ***ḥadīth*** material, offering different interpretations and sometimes concluding, rather more subtly, that music is itself neutral, approval or disapproval depending upon the ends to which it is put. For Ṣūfī authorities these can be positive: just as the imagery of love poetry is to be interpreted symbolically, so the music to which it is sung is to be considered a means towards achieving not physical ecstasy but heightened states of spiritual awareness.

Text editions

Macdonald, D.B., 'Emotional religion in Islam as affected by music and singing. Being a translation of a book of the *Iḥyā' 'ulūm al-dīn* of al-Ghazzālī, with analysis, annotation and appendices', *JRAS* (1901), 195–252 and 705–48; (1902), 1–28.

Robson, J., *Tracts on Listening to Music*, London (1938).

O. WRIGHT

See also: music and poetry; Ṣūfī literature, poetry

al-Sam'ānī (506–62/1113–66)

'Abd al-Karīm ibn Muḥammad al-Sam'ānī was a biographer of the later **'Abbāsid** period stemming from Marw in **Khurasan**. Al-Sam'ānī was instructed by his father and later by two uncles and supplemented his knowledge by extensive travel; he died in his home town. The most famous of his extant works is his monumental dictionary of the traditionists *al-Ansāb*, arranged alphabetically according to the *nisbas*. It gives ample information on pronunciation and derivation of names, biographical data and the names of teachers and pupils of the scholars discussed. Important for the history of medieval Islamic instruction is his *Adab al-imlā' wa-al-istimlā'*, a handbook on dictation as a means of transmission of knowledge.

Text editions

Adab al-imlā' wa-al-istimlā', in M. Weisweiler, *Die Methodik des Diktatkollegs*, Leiden (1952) (with German summary of contents).

al-Ansāb, facs. edn, D.S. Margoliouth (ed.), Leiden and London (1912); 'A. al-Mu'allimī *et al.* (eds), 13 vols, Hyderabad (1952–82); 'A.'U. al-Bārūdī (ed.), Beirut (1988).

T. SEIDENSTICKER

Sāmānids

An Iranian dynasty which ruled over the eastern provinces of the Islamic world throughout the fourth/tenth century. Descended from the early convert Sāmān, members of the family governed various cities in Transoxania under the third/ninth-century **'Abbāsid** caliphs, eventually adopting Bukhara as their capital. In 287/900 Ismā'īl ibn Aḥmad was appointed by the caliph governor of **Khurasan** as well as Transoxania, and he and his descendants ruled these lands until 389/999, when their northern provinces fell to the Qarakhānids and their southern ones to the **Ghaznavid** Maḥmūd.

Despite their effective independence, the Sāmānids always stressed their loyalty to the 'Abbāsid caliph in **Baghdad**, including his name on their coins and in the Friday sermons in their mosques. Correspondingly, they were emphatically **Sunnī** in their religious orientation, except for a brief period when Naṣr ibn Aḥmad (r. 301–31/914–43) favoured **Ismā'īlī** Shī'ism, a policy that led to his abdication. Politically, Sāmānid Sunnism stood in marked (and undoubtedly deliberate) contrast to the Shī'ism of their principal rivals, the **Būyid** rulers of western Iran and Iraq, who from 334/945 had the caliph in their tutelage, and with whom the Sāmānids were in more or less constant conflict.

Linguistically, the Sāmānids' realm was predominantly Persian speaking, and it was they who provided the initial encouragement for the Persian literary renaissance that was to come to full flower in the following century. Naṣr ibn Aḥmad patronized the first great Persian poet, Rūdakī, and his successors continued to support the development of Persian verse, not only in panegyric but in epic and other genres as well. They also promoted Persian prose, mainly in the form of translations from Arabic and largely for pious motives. These include **al-Ṭabarī**'s *History* and his magisterial work of Koranic **exegesis**, both translated at the behest of Manṣūr ibn Nūḥ (r. 350–66/961–76), the former by his vizier al-Bal'amī, and a Sunnī creed from the Ḥanafī school (predominant in Transoxania), composed in Arabic under Ismā'īl ibn Aḥmad (r. 279–95/892–907) and translated under Nūḥ ibn Manṣūr (r. 365–87/976–97).

But this activity in Persian does not represent a cultural offensive, like the ***Shu'ūbiyya*** movement further west, against the predominance of Arabic in literary culture. While Persian translations made important religious works more accessible to the masses, and Persian panegyrics may have spoken more directly to the rulers themselves, Arabic retained its religious cachet and its full prestige, even in secular writing. The court bureaucracy remained officially Arabic, and the chancery was an important locus for Arabic eloquence in both prose and poetry. Probably because of later Persianization, much of Sāmānid Arabic literature is lost to us, but we can gain some idea of its richness from **al-Tha'ālibī**'s anthology the *Yatīmat al-dahr*, which devotes three sections to the Sāmānid poets of Bukhara. There we learn that serious court patronage of Arabic poetry began under Naṣr ibn Aḥmad, and was at first heavily imitative of Iraqi styles. Several heads of the chancery were noted for both poetry and prose, including the father of the celebrated **Būyid** vizier **Ibn al-'Amīd** and his successor Abū al-Qāsim al-Iskāfī. Many court poets were supported by being given appointments in the intelligence service (*barīd*) in various provincial centres. A great many were drawn to Bukhara from other cities, including al-Mutayyam al-Ifrīqī from Tunis and Abū Ṭālib **al-Ma'mūnī** from Baghdad. Some poets composed verses in both Arabic and Persian; others translated Persian aphorisms into Arabic rhymed couplets (***muzdawija***). Particularly regrettable is the loss of the works of al-Sallāmī, which included a history of the governors of Khurasan as well as several literary anthologies.

Besides important prose works in the various religious genres, the Sāmānid court also encouraged scientific writing in Arabic. One of the several Sāmānid viziers of the Jayhānī family composed a geographical work much quoted by later authors (but unfortunately lost). Abū al-Ḥusayn al-'Utbī, vizier to Nūḥ ibn Manṣūr, was the dedicatee of Muḥummad ibn Aḥmad **al-Khwārazmī**'s *Keys of the Sciences*, a valuable glossary of technical terms, as well as of a work by the philosopher al-'Āmirī. The extraordinary richness of the Sāmānid library in Bukhara (later destroyed by fire) is described in a well-known passage from the autobiography of **Ibn Sīnā** (Avicenna), who was granted access to it after curing Nūḥ ibn Manṣūr of an illness.

Further reading

Frye, R. 'The Sāmānids', in *CHIr*, vol. 4, 136–61.

Richter-Bernburg, L., 'Linguistic Shu'ūbīya and early neo-Persian prose', *JAOS* 94 (1974), 55–64.

al-Tha'ālibī, *Yatīmat al-dahr*, Cairo (1956), vol. 4, 63–193; M.C. Barbier de Meynard (partial trans.), 'Tableau littéraire de Khorassan et de la Transoxiane au IVe siècle de l'hégire', *JA*, 5th series, vol. 1 (1853), 169–239, and vol. 3 (1854), 291–361.

Treadwell, W.L., *The Political History of the Samanid State*, D.Phil. thesis, Oxford (1991).

E.K. ROWSON

al-Samaw'al (sixth century CE)

Al-Samaw'al ('Samuel') ibn 'Ādiyā' was a pre-Islamic Jewish poet, proverbial for his loyalty. A story already known in pre-Islamic times (cf. poem no. 25 in the ***dīwān*** of **al-A'shā**) relates that al-Samaw'al refused to deliver weapons that had been entrusted to him by one of the enemies of the **Ghassānid** king even when the king threatened to kill al-Samaw'al's son. The author of the poems attributed to al-Samaw'al (nine poems, eighty-eight lines) is most certainly not identical with the proverbial figure. Some of the poems, esp. ode no. 23 of the *Aṣma'iyyāt* which refers to the Jewish religion, may nevertheless be of genuine Jewish pre- or early Islamic origin.

Text editions

Dīwān, Louis Cheikho (ed.), Beirut (1909); Muḥ. Ḥasan Āl Yāsīn (ed.), Baghdad (1955)

Der Dīwān des as-Samau'al ibn 'Ādiā', J.W. Hirschberg (trans.), Cracow (1931).

Further reading

Levi Della Vida, Giorgio, 'A proposito di as-Samaw'al', *RSO* 13 (1931), 53-72.

T. BAUER

Sāmī, Amīn (late nineteenth/early twentieth century)

Egyptian historian. Little is known of Sāmī's life apart from his public service. He was most active during the reigns of Tawfīq (1879–92) and ʿAbbās II (1892–1914), when he became director of both the khedival school at al-Nāṣiriyya and of **Dār al-ʿUlūm**. He was a member of the Egyptian senate until 1928.

Sāmī's most important literary effort was the *Nile Almanac* (*Taqwīm al-Nīl*), a hefty six-volume history of Egypt which appeared in instalments between 1919 and 1936. The most valuable sections of the *Taqwīm* are the final three volumes, which contain a wealth of detail on the history of Egypt from 1848 to 1879.

Further reading

Crabbs, J.A., *The Writing of History in Nineteenth-century Egypt*, Detroit (1984), 119–25.

J. CRABBS

al-Sammān, Ghāda (1942–)

Syrian novelist and short-story writer. Born in **Damascus**, Ghāda al-Sammān was raised after her mother's death by her father, Dr Aḥmad al-Sammān (d. 1966), professor and dean of the faculty of law at the University of Damascus, later rector of the university, then minister of education of Syria. After her secondary education, she obtained a BA in English literature at the University of Damascus and in 1964 moved to Beirut, where she completed her MA studies at the American University of Beirut. She carried out postgraduate research in London and toured several Western countries between 1967 and 1969. She then settled in Beirut, where she lectured before becoming a journalist. In 1977 she founded her own publishing house to publish and republish her works. The Lebanese civil war forced her to leave Lebanon in 1984 with her husband and son and to go to Paris, where she continues to write and run her busy Beirut publishing house.

Having been writing since 1961, she has produced some thirty books, most reprinted several times and some translated into European languages. Her six short-story collections include *ʿAynāk qadarī* (1962), *Lā baḥr fī Bayrūt* (1963), *Layl al-ghurabā'* (1966) and *Raḥīl al-marāfi' al-qadīma* (1973); a number of her short stories have appeared in an Italian collection (1992), and some have appeared in Spanish, Romanian, German, Persian, Russian and English translations. Her books of essays, culled from her prolific writings in periodicals, include *al-Sibāḥa fī Buḥayrat al-Shayṭān* (1979) and *ʿAyn ghayn tatafarras* (1980). She has also written **free-verse** poems, collected in *Iʿtiqāl laḥẓa hāriba* (1979) and others, and a number of these poems have appeared in Persian in an Iranian collection (1990). Her novels include *Bayrūt 75* (1975), *Kawābīs Bayrūt* (1976) and *Laylat al-milyār* (1986). Some of her insightful and often provocative interviews with the mass media have been published in her *al-Qabīla tastajwib al-qatīla* (1981).

Ghāda al-Sammān's writings express an unmitigated rebellion against all constraints of tradition. A strong feminist, she has emphasized the portrayal of the prevailing oppression of Arab women in her earlier fiction; her later works, however, show the problems of Arab women as part of the larger socio-political ills of Arab society, of which Arab men are also victims. Her great love for freedom, justice and human values has impelled her to support oppressed peoples, such as the Palestinians and others; to defend freedom of expression everywhere; and to declare her abhorrence of tyranny wherever it occurs – not least in the home and in government. Her command of the Arabic language makes her plea even more powerful. Ghāda al-Sammān is perhaps the most popular female Arab author today, and one of the few Arab novelists who (in works such as *Kawābīs Bayrūt*) have gone beyond the classical form of the novel. Her latest collection of short stories, *al-Qamar al-murabbaʿ* (1994), explores the fantastic in ten supernatural tales and her latest novel, *al-Riwāya al-mustaḥīla* (1997), chronicles Damascene life and society at mid-century as an indomitable girl becomes an ebullient teenager.

Text editions

Asfour, J.M., *When the Words Burn: An Anthology of Modern Arabic Poetry 1945–1987*, Dunvegan, ON (1988), 132–33.

Beirut '75, Nancy N. Roberts (trans), Fayetteville, AR (1995).

'Our constitution' in Margot Badran and Miriam Cooke (eds), *Opening the Gates: A Century of Arab Feminist Writing*, Bloomington and Indianapolis (1990), 137–43.
'The sexual revolution and the total revolution' in E.W. Fernea and B.Q. Bezirgan (eds), *Middle Eastern Women Speak*, Austin, TX (1978), 391–9.
'Street walker' in Manzalaoui, M., *Arabic Writing Today: The Short Story*, Cairo (1968), 317–27.
'Widow of the Wedding' in Kassem, C. and Hashem, M. (eds), *Flights of Fantasy*, Cairo (1985), 139–57.

Further reading

Accad, E., *Veil of Shame*, Sherbrooke (1978) 112–16.
Awwad, H., *Arab Causes in the Fiction of Ghadah al-Sammān (1961–1975)*, Sherbrooke (1983).
Boullata, I.J., *Trends and Issues in Contemporary Arab Thought*, Albany, NY (1990), 135–36.
Cooke, M., 'Beirut ... Theatre of the Absurd ...', *JAL* 13 (1982), 124–41.
——, *War's Other Voices*, Cambridge (1988), 43–50, 113–18, etc.
Zeidan, J.T., *Arab Women Novelists*, Albany, NY (1995), 191–205.

I.J. BOULLATA

ṣanʿa see ṣināʿa

al-Ṣanʿānī (d. 211/827)

Abū Bakr ʿAbd al-Razzāq ibn Hammām al-Ṣanʿānī was an early Yemeni scholar of ***ḥadīth*** and Koranic **exegesis**. Born in Sanaa, he travelled extensively and studied with some of the greatest authorities of his day. Later he had many students of his own; his traditions frequently appear in the great canonical collections of *ḥadīth*, and one commentator opined that only the Prophet himself was more popular as a teacher. It was often said that he harboured **Shīʿī** sympathies. His most important work was his *al-Muṣannaf*, a lengthy compendium of *ḥadīth* based mostly on books written by (or materials transmitted by) his three main teachers, with additions of his own from other sources. As each tradition is supported by an *isnād* (chain of transmitters), it is possible to distinguish and identify these sources thus to gain important insights into even earlier stages in the development of the materials he used. He also compiled a **Koran** commentary by making additions to a commentary by his teacher Maʿmar ibn Rāshid (d. 154/770) in Sanaa. Apart from an unpublished work on traditions transmitted by the Prophet's Companions, other works attributed to him probably refer to chapters of his *Muṣannaf* transmitted separately by his students. ʿAbd al-Razzāq's works are important not only for their early date and the old traditions that they contain, but also for the way in which they place their older strata within the grasp of modern research.

Text editions

al-Muṣannaf, Ḥabīb al-Raḥmān al-Aʿẓamī (ed.), Beirut (1390–1407/1970–87).
Tafsīr al-Qur'ān, Muṣṭafā Muslim Muḥammad (ed.), Riyadh (1410/1989).

Further reading

Motzki, Harald, *Die Anfänge der islamischen Jurisprudenz. Ihre Entwicklung in Mekka bis zur Mitte des 2./8. Jahrhunderts*, Stuttgart (1991), esp. 53–67; the results of Motzki's very important study are summarized in his 'The *Muṣannaf* of ʿAbd al-Razzāq al-Ṣanʿānī as a source of authentic *Aḥādīth* of the first century A.H.', *JNES* 50 (1991), 1–21; the full text of his study will shortly appear in English translation.

L.I. CONRAD

al-Ṣanawbarī (b. before 275/888, d. 334/945–6)

Abū Bakr Aḥmad ibn Muḥammad (less likely: Muḥammad ibn Aḥmad) al-Ḍabbī al-Anṭākī al-Ṣanawbarī was an **ʿAbbāsid** poet, probably born in Antioch and died in Aleppo; he belonged to the entourage of Sayf al-Dawla (d.356/967; see **Ḥamdānids**). He spent most of his life in Aleppo and its surroundings, but also visited **Damascus**.

Of his *dīwān*, which is said to have been compiled in alphabetical order by Abū Bakr **al-Ṣūlī** (d. 335/946), about a third has been preserved and published. It contains poems in all genres cultivated in the Arabic poetry of his time. His dirges on the Prophet's grandson al-Ḥusayn deserve special mention as they lead to the conclusion that al-Ṣanawbarī had **Shīʿī** tendencies. Above all, however, his poems on flowers, gardens and spring (*zahriyyāt, rawḍiyyāt, rabīʿiyyāt*) should be mentioned. Through these poems al-Ṣanawbarī's fame was established and his name was most closely connected with the concept of the *rawḍiyyāt*. Al-Ṣanawbarī describes single flowers (i.e. rose, narcissus, water lily, red anemone) as well as gardens with a variety of flowers, and spring with its scents and the singing of the birds, as well as complete landscapes. He also composed a dispute (*munāẓara*) between flowers and a poem describing a war among flowers. (See **debate literature**.) In addition, there are snow poems (*thaljiyyāt*) and poems containing descriptions of cities (Aleppo, Damascus). The descriptions of nature appear in independent forms, in short pieces ('epigrammatic sketches') as well as in long poems ('garden ***qaṣīda***s'). Often, however, they have been integrated into poems of other genres (e.g. they may form the prologue of panegyrics). Alongside the descriptive parts the longer poems sometimes also contain parts of a lyric–hymnic character in which the poet enthusiastically praises the beauty of the landscape that is being described. (See further **nature, in classical poetry**.)

Al-Ṣanawbarī's style is a model of late 'Abbāsid mannerism. His descriptions present an accumulation of contrived images and figures of speech. The most frequent objects of comparison for his similes and metaphors are precious stones and metals (see below), also parts of the human body ('roses are like cheeks, narcissi are like eyes'). For real characteristics the poet often invents phantastic etiologies (the stylistic device of *ḥusn al-ta'līl*) ('the rose was ashamed [therefore it is red]'), and in his objects of comparison he uses combinations of images that do not have an equivalent in reality (red anemones are like 'banners of ruby unfurled on lances of chrysolith'). In his art of poetic description dependent on **Ibn al-Rūmī** and **Ibn al-Mu'tazz**, al-Ṣanawbarī strongly influenced later Arabic nature poetry.

Text edition

Dīwān, I. 'Abbās (ed.), Beirut (1970).

Tatimmat Dīwān al-Ṣanawbarī, L. al-Ṣaqqāl and D. al-Khaṭīb (eds), Aleppo (1971).

Further reading

Badawi, M.M., 'Abbāsid poetry and its antecedents', in *CHALABL*, 164–6.

Hamori, A., *On the Art of Medieval Arabic Literature*, Princeton (1974), 78–98.

Schoeler, G., *Arabische Naturdichtung*, Beirut (1974), 273–341.

G. SCHOELER; trans. A. GIESE

Ṣanū', Ya'qūb (James Sanua) (1839–1912)

Egyptian Jewish journalist, dramatist and orator who wrote under the nom de plume Abū Naḍḍāra (The Man with Glasses). Born in **Cairo**, he died in Paris. After studying in Italy, Ṣanū' taught at the École des Arts et Métiers and at the École Polytechnique in Cairo. He successfully created a national theatre in **Egypt** in 1870, winning the sobriquet of 'le Molière Egyptien'. He is said to have written plays from farce to a tragedy in the vernacular, referring to the condition of the poor and attacking the government and the activities of the Khedive; his extant comedies, however, depict the middle and upper classes, dealing with the non-political subjects of love and marriage, quacks, the imitation of European customs, and the young defying their parents. His plays, which were written in colloquial Egyptian, were regarded as subversive and the authorities closed his theatre in 1872. Ṣanū' then decided to publish his own papers, starting with the humorous *La Moustique*, then *L'occhialino*, *Le Bavard égyptien*, and *Abū Naḍḍāra Zarqā'* (1877–78), a satirical paper in the vernacular, enlivened by cartoons, ridiculing the viceroy. Exiled to Paris, he continued publishing his paper in Arabic and French intermittently under various titles from 1878 to 1910. His paper, copies of which were smuggled into Egypt, attacked Khedive Ismā'īl for his corruption and ruthlessness, and his successor Tawfīq for his incompetence and greed. He consistently condemned the abuses of the British occupation, calling on France and Turkey to oust the British; Khedive 'Abbās II granted him an amnesty, but he refused to accept it until his whole country was freed. Ṣanū' is best remembered as the founder of politico-satirical theatre in Egypt; but he also published poetry, a few stories, pamphlets on his journeys, speeches, and poetry and prose extracts from his journals.

Further reading

Badawi, M.M., *Early Arabic Drama*, Cambridge (1988), 31–42.

Gendzier, Irene L., *The Practical Visions of Ya'qub Sanu'*, Cambridge, MA (1966).

al-Khozai, M.A., *The Development of Early Arabic Drama 1847–1900*, London 123–68.

Landau, J.M., 'Abū Naḍḍāra', *EI*², vol. 1, 141–2.

Sadgrove, P.C., *The Egyptian Theatre in the Nineteenth Century*, Reading (1996), 89–124.

P. SADGROVE

Sanua, James *see* Ṣanū', Ya'qūb

al-Saraqustī (d. 538/1143)

Abū al-Ṭāhir Muḥammad ibn Yūsuf al-Tamīmī al-Saraqustī, known as Ibn al-Ishtarkūnī, was an Arabic philologist, ***adab*** connoisseur, poet and writer. Born in Saragossa, he studied in Seville and in Córdoba, where he lived until his death. He wrote poetry, a dictionary arranged in a chain order (*al-Musalsal fī al-lugha*) and a collection of fifty ***maqāma***s (*al-Maqāmāt al-Luzūmiyya*, or *al-Saraqustiyya*), by which he is primarily known.

According to the short introduction to this collection, al-Saraqustī modelled his *Maqāmāt* on those of **al-Ḥarīrī** (d. 516/1122). Though composed in **Basra** not long before (*c*.495/1101), al-Ḥarīrī's *Maqāmāt* were introduced in **Spain** already in 502/1108 and rapidly gained a reputation there, to the extent that they became part of the contemporary Andalusian literary curriculum. In accordance with this model, the collection comprises fifty narrations (*maqāmāt*) in rhymed prose (***saj'***), sharing the same two protagonists: a narrator (al-Sā'ib ibn Tammām; occasionally the name of a second narrator, al-Mundhir ibn Ḥummām, is added to create the rhyme) and a hero, a witty but eloquent rogue (Abū Ḥabīb al-Sadūsī) who gains his alms by tricking his audience; both names obviously are modelled on those of al-Ḥarīrī's protagonists, al-Ḥārith ibn Hammām and Abū Zayd al-Sarūjī. Al-Saraqustī's intention to imitate, but at the same time to excel, al-Ḥarīrī is manifested in his choice of a particularly difficult pattern for his rhymed prose, which requires a two-consonant rhymeme where the norm is only one. Though a known rhyming ornament (***luzūm mā lā yalzam***, 'self-obligation where one is not obliged'), it is nevertheless rarely used because of the limitation imposed on the selection of rhyming words (but cf. the poems of **Abū al-'Alā' al-Ma'arrī**). The collection is called, after this pattern, *al-Maqāmāt al-Luzūmiyya*, but other complicated rhyming patterns are also to be found in it.

Despite their reputation as Andalusian, al-Saraqustī's *Maqāmāt* are actually very Eastern in nature, and rarely touch upon Andalusian subjects. They draw so heavily on the Eastern repertoire of literary themes to elaborate on fantastic themes of the *Arabian Nights* kind (*maqāma* no. 41), which are not to be found in al-Ḥarīrī's or other Eastern *Maqāmāt*. Thus in a *maqāma* on the merits of poets (no. 30) only Eastern poets are discussed, with no mention of local ones.

Text edition

al-Maqāmāt al-Luzūmiyya, Aḥmad Badr Ḍayf (ed.), Alexandria (1982)

Further reading

'Abbās, Ḥ., *Fann al-maqāma fī al-qarn al-sādis*, Cairo (1986), 99–108.

'Abbās, I., *Ta'rīkh al-adab al-Andalusī, 'aṣr al-ṭawā'if wa-al-Murābiṭīn*, Beirut (1974), 317–25.

'Awaḍ, Y.N., *Fann al-maqāmāt bayna al-mashriq wa-al-maghrib*, Beirut (1979), 288–93.

al-Dāyā, M.R., *Ta'rīkh al-naqd al-adabī fī al-Andalus*, Beirut (1968), 352–63.

Ferrando, I., 'La *Maqāma* de Tarifa de al-Saraquṣṭī', *Al-Qanṭara* 18 (1997), 137–51.

Nemah, H., 'Andalusian *Maqāmāt*', *JAL* 5 (1974), 88–92.

R. DRORY

Sarhank Pāshā, Ismā'īl (*c*.1854–1924)

Egyptian historian. Frequently overlooked but nevertheless important, Sarhank (like his father) pursued a career in the Egyptian navy, eventually reaching the rank of admiral. His three-volume *Ḥaqā'iq al-akhbār 'an duwal al-biḥār* appeared in 1895, 1898 and 1923. Volume 1 covered Arab (except for **Egypt**), Ottoman and European sea-power; volume 2 dealt with Egypt to the turn of the twentieth century; volume 3, improperly planned and executed, appeared in truncated form only one year before the author's own death. *Ḥaqā'iq al-akhbār* is nevertheless a highly useful and detailed work. It is also fascinating as a transitional piece – in form a 'medieval' chronicle, but with such a wealth of interpretative features as to make it seem 'modern'.

Further reading

Crabbs, J.A., *The Writing of History in Nineteenth-Century Egypt*, Detroit (1984), 136–43.

J. CRABBS

Sarī' *see* prosody

Ṣarī' al-Ghawānī *see* Muslim ibn al-Walīd

al-Sarī al-Raffā' (d. *c.*362/972)

Poet of the middle **'Abbāsid** period. Abū al-Ḥasan al-Sarī ibn Aḥmad earned a living in Mosul as a darner (*raffā'*), and later as a fisherman. His poetical gifts gave him access to the **Ḥamdānid** court in Mosul, then to Sayf al-Dawla's court in Aleppo and finally to some important personalities in **Baghdad**, such as the vizier **al-Muhallabī**, but somehow, all these relationships cooled sooner or later, perhaps in part due to his character, perhaps also to the influence of the **Khālidī** brothers. He died impoverished in Baghdad. His poetry, nearly a thousand lines, covers the usual range of genres; most important in number is laudatory poetry (***madīḥ***), satire (***hijā'***) and descriptive poetry (***waṣf***). In this latter genre, his contributions seem to be quite original. Important is a group of poems in which he describes fishermen and their nets; some of these pieces, as is the case with hunting poems (***ṭardiyyāt***), are composed in the ***rajaz*** metre and even show the typical introductory formulae known from *ṭardiyyāt*. Al-Sarī also compiled an anthology of poetry, the *Kitāb al-Muḥibb wa-al-maḥbūb wa-al-mashmūm wa-al-mashrūb*.

Text editions

Dīwān, Cairo (1936); Ḥ.Ḥ. al-Ḥasanī (ed.), Baghdad (1981).

Kitāb al-Muḥibb ..., M. Ghalāwunjī and M.Ḥ. al-Dhahabī (eds), 4 vols, Damascus (1986).

Further reading

Sadan, J., 'Maidens' hair and starry skies', in *Studies in Medieval Arabic and Hebrew Poetics* (*IOS* 11), S. Somekh (ed.), Leiden (1991), 57–88.

T. SEIDENSTICKER

sariqa (pl. *sariqāt*)

Lit. 'theft', in literary criticism 'plagiarism'. The term *sariqa* does cover 'plagiarism' in the strict sense of the word, but often goes far beyond this narrow application to indicate any kind of 'borrowing' and 'developing' of an existing motif. As such it should be seen in the larger context of intertextuality, alongside other phenomena such as quotation (*taḍmīn*) and allusion (*talmīḥ*). (See further **allusion and intertextuality**.) Due to the fact that the term came to cover both licit and illicit borrowings, the slightly paradoxical qualifications *sariqa ḥasana*, 'good theft', and *sariqa maḥmūda*, 'laudable theft', were introduced to mark cases considered successful by the critics. Or else they dispensed with the inappropriate term altogether and chose a neutral one, *akhdh*, 'taking'.

Plagiarism

Awareness of this phenomenon is attested early on. Since pre-Islamic poems are, as a rule, attributable to individual poets who take pride in their craft, literary theft is mentioned by them as something to which they do not have to resort. Alongside the general notion of 'theft', the term *intiḥāl*, 'ascribing (verses) to oneself', is specifically used here. Examples given in later handbooks show that this means claiming other poets' verses as one's own without further ado. A fair number of the cases adduced by the later critics look suspicious and need further study to ascertain whether (a) they may not constitute quotations, or whether (b) the victim of the plagiarism might not be an invention produced by intertribal hostilities. While the notions of 'theft' and 'appropriation' show that the idea of intellectual property was well developed, there is one strange phenomenon that, in a way, runs counter to this notion, and that is the behaviour of some famous poets called *ighāra*, lit. 'raiding'. This occurs only between contemporaries and entails that a minor poet (though possibly minor only in a certain genre) composes an outstanding line and is then forced by a major poet to relinquish it to him, on the pretext that he, the major poet, should have composed it. The victim, under threat of a stinging satire, would more often than not comply, although some are reported to have refused, with the end result that the line in question would be included in both ***dīwān***s. The most notorious poet in this respect was the Umayyad poet **al-Farazdaq**.

In the literate society of **'Abbāsid** times, outright plagiarism took the form of inserting extraneous material, often whole poems, into one's own *dīwān*. The term often used for this is *muṣālata*, a post-classical word possibly derived from *ṣilt*, a variant – by metathesis – of *liṣt*, 'robber'. Several poets were accused of this, but today it is very difficult to prove that theft took place and that it went from A to B, rather than from B to A. That a poem occurs in two or more different *dīwān*s can just as well be due to uncertain attribution on the part of the redactors.

It should be mentioned that, although the word *sariqa* is used for 'plagiarism', no *sariqa*, 'theft', in the legal sense of the word occurs, as the notion of intellectual ownership is unknown in Islamic law.

Borrowing

While outright plagiarism may have had some sensationalistic entertainment value for the literary critic and his public, it is only with the introduction of changes into the borrowed verse that discussions of truly literary interest arise. Two genres of critical literature were developed: one devoted to the classification and taxonomy of *sariqa*, the other concerned with the identification, collection, and – to a lesser extent – discussion of the *sariqāt* of individual poets.

The *sariqa* classifications form part of the books on poetics, although not all such books can boast of a relevant chapter. The classifications themselves are highly unhomogeneous in the early literature, before the classification becomes solidified in the scholastic 'science of eloquence' starting with **al-Khaṭīb al-Qazwīnī**, and many terms are used with diffuse meanings or – even more confusingly – with different meanings altogether. Some common notions, however, emerge. (a) The focus of the discussion is overwhelmingly the single line, which is, of course, the most common approach in literary criticism and theory. (b) There is discussion about what is plagiarizable and what is not. Universally known or well-worn motifs are in the public domain. The other extreme is individually attributable inventions of new motifs. These are rare and, as **Ḥāzim al-Qarṭājannī** says, 'infertile', because later poets would hardly dare to take them up again. Of greatest interest is the group of motifs between the two extremes, those that have been treated, developed and improved upon (or, possibly, ruined) by a series of poets. Here a charge of plagiarism can only be avoided if the later poet introduces changes that confer a certain novelty on the borrowed motif. This he could do by changing the context (different genre; combination of the borrowed motif with another) or by changing the wording. If, by doing the latter, he improves on the rendition of the motifs, he can lay greater claim to it than the original poet. According to Ḥāzim, these are four relationships between a poet and his motif: 'invention' (*ikhtirā'*), 'greater claim' (*istiḥqāq*), 'partnership' (*sharika*, which is either 'equal participation' [*ishtirāk*], when there is no quality difference between earlier and later poet, or 'falling short' [*inḥiṭāṭ*], if the later poet is not up to par), and finally 'plagiarism' (*sariqa*). (c) Part of the taxonomy of plagiarism is based on the ***lafẓ*** and ***ma'nā*** dichotomy: does the alleged plagiarizer take only the motif or also its wording? Taking both with only minimal changes of the wording is the worst kind of *sariqa*. (d) Plagiarism can only take place if the later poet consciously borrows from the earlier. Otherwise, identical or similar lines of poetry are due to a 'confluence of two minds' (*tawārud al-khāṭirayn*): two poets found the line independently of each other. In a poetic tradition that favours the mannerist treatment of a rather circumscribed number of motifs (especially in the prestigious official genres), this is not as far-fetched as it may sound. (e) An identical line could also be explained as a quotation (*taḍmīn*, lit. 'incorporation'). If it is not a very well-known line, the poet has to mark it as a quotation in order that it not be taken as a plagiarism.

The other branch of literature devoted to this topic is represented by the collection of plagiarisms of individual poets, either as separate books or as part of critical books dealing with one or more poets. Several controversial 'modern' poets have been made the target of such attacks: thus **Abū Nuwās**, **Abū Tammām** and especially **al-Mutanabbī** (at least six separate books have come down to us). The authors of these works are mostly rather reticent in naming and discussing their cases, confining themselves instead to adducing the original (mostly 'modern') and the plagiarism. However, they usually cast a very wide net including many 'laudable plagiarisms' and they often manage to find several 'originals', either because the 'plagiarizer' has effected a combination of two 'stolen' motifs or because they could not be sure of the correct pedigree. As a result, one is presented at times with veritable family trees of a motif. This, of course, makes these works rather valuable for historical and critical research into the development of certain motifs and, more importantly, into the general tendencies governing such development within a mannerist tradition of poetry.

From a literary–historical vantage point, one should perhaps distinguish three *sariqa* situations: (1) Plagiarizer and victim are 'ancient' poets. Here we have to reckon with a certain amount of false accusation, because the cases adduced are in reality quotations or formulae, or else the victim is the invention of a tribe that wants to diminish the stature of a famous poet from a hostile tribe. Some cases of 'raiding' (see above) may be historical. Other plagiarisms will probably not have survived the selection and transmission process. (2) The plagiarizer is 'modern', the victim 'ancient'. Due to the fact that 'ancient' poetry became a classical model and on the whole very well known to all poets and philologists, clear cases of theft should be exceedingly rare. (3) Both are 'modern' poets. Here *sariqa*, in the broadest sense of the term, became a way of life. In a mannerist tradition of poetry, it is precisely the conceit, based on the tradition of the motif, yet innovative, that has the poet walk a fine line between originality and plagiarism. **'Abd al-Qāhir al-Jurjānī** states that a plain rational motif (*ma'nā 'aqlī*) cannot be plagiarized, as it is everybody's property; only the irreal, imaginary, phantasmagorical motif (*ma'nā takhyīlī*), i.e. the conceit, can be.

Further reading

Bauer, Thomas, 'Formel und Zitat: Zwei Spielarten von Intertextualität in der altarabischen Dichtung', *JAL* 24 (1993), 117–38.

Bonebakker, Seeger A., 'Sariqa and formula: three chapters from Ḥātimī's *Ḥilyat al-Muḥāḍara*', *AI[U]ON* 46 (1986), 367–89.

——, 'Naḥala and Saraqa. A shift in meaning?', *Occasional Papers of the School of 'Abbāsid Studies* 5 (forthcoming).

Haddāra, Muḥammad Muṣṭafā, *Mushkilat al-sariqāt fī al-naqd al-'Arabī*, 2nd edn, Beirut (1975).

Henirichs, Wolfhart, *Arabische Dichtung und griechische Poetik*, Beirut and Wiesbaden (1969), 94–8 (on Ḥāzim al-Qarṭājannī).

——, 'An evaluation of *sariqa*', *QSA* 5–6 (1987–88), 357–68.

——, 'Literary theory: the problem of its efficiency'; in *Arabic Poetry: Theory and Development*, G.E. von Grunebaum (ed.), Wiesbaden (1973), 19–69 (the fourth part deals with 'plagiarism' cases from al-'Amīdī's *al-Ibāna 'an sariqāt al-Mutanabbī*, Ibrāhīm al-Dasūqī al-Bisāṭī [ed.], Cairo [1961]).

Peled, Mattitiahu, 'On the concept of literary influence in classical Arabic criticism', *IOS* 11 (1991), 37–46.

Ṭabāna, Badawī, *al-Sariqāt al-adabiyya, Dirāsa fī ibtikār al-a'māl al-adabiyya wa-taqlīdihā*, Cairo (n.d.).

von Grunebaum, Gustave E., 'Der Begriff des Plagiats in der arabischen Kritik', in *Kritik und Dichtkunst*, Wiesbaden (1955), 101–29 (revised version of 'The concept of plagiarism in Arabic theory', *JNES* 3 [1944], 234–53).

W.P. HEINRICHS

Sarkīs family

Maronite Lebanese family from 'Abayh. The following members are worthy of mention for their literary activities. **Ibrāhīm ibn Khaṭṭār** (1834–85), historian and poet. He compiled an anthology of poetry, a collection of proverbs, and composed more than seventy Protestant hymns. **Khalīl ibn Khaṭṭār** (1842–1915), journalist, poet and historian. He published in Beirut the *Lisān al-ḥāl* newspaper (1877), the monthly magazine *al-Mishkāh* (1878) and *al-Salwa* magazine (1914). He also wrote a description of a trip to America, Europe and Istanbul, and produced an anthology of poetry and a novel. **Salīm ibn Shāhīn** (1867–1926), nephew of Khalīl, journalist, novelist, poet and historian. Constrained by censorship, he accompanied Prince Amīn Arslān to Paris in 1892, helping to set up the Young Turk Society. He published various newspapers and magazines in Egypt and London, before fleeing to America, where he edited Arabic papers in Saint Lawrence, New York and Boston. After returning to Egypt he published his popular literary monthly *Majallat Sarkīs* (1905–24). He also wrote novels, and translated Mühlbeck's work on Marie-Antoinette from French.

Further reading

Dāghir, Yūsuf As'ad, *Maṣādir al-dirāsāt al-adabiyya*, Beirut (1956), ii, 454–7; iii/i, 532–4.

P.C. SADGROVE

al-Sarrāj, Abū Naṣr (d. 378/988)

Abū Naṣr 'Abd Allāh ibn 'Alī al-Sarrāj al-Ṭūsī was born and died in Ṭūs; very little else is known about his life. What is certain is that he travelled extensively. He is the author of the *Kitāb al-luma' fī al-taṣawwuf*, the best-known handbook on Sufism of the classical period. No other writings of his have survived or are known to have existed. The *Kitāb al-luma'* presents in sixteen books an image of Sufism that is orthodox and in line with the **Koran** and the *sunna*. In book 16, which concludes the work, extremist teachings and practices are singled out and eliminated from Sufism as al-Sarrāj wished to conceive of it.

Text editions

The Kitáb al-luma' fi 'l-taṣawwuf of Abú Naṣr 'Abdallah b. 'Alí al-Sarráj al-Ṭúsí, R.A. Nicholson (ed.), Leiden and London (1914).

Schlaglichter über das Sufitum. Abū Naṣr as-Sarrāǧs Kitāb al-luma' eingeleitet, R. Gramlich (ed. and trans.), Stuttgart (1990).

B. RADTKE

al-Sarrāj, Ja'far ibn Aḥmad (*c.*417–500/1026–1106)

Abū Muḥammad Ja'far ibn Aḥmad al-Sarrāj was a scholar from **Baghdad** in the later **'Abbāsid** period, famous for his anthology of poems and prose texts about love and lovers. In his *Maṣāri' al-'ushshāq* (*The Battlegrounds of the Lovers*), al-Sarrāj presents his material (each text preceeded by the chain of transmitters, *isnād*) without any recognizable organization. The book is important because of the ample use that later authors made of the material contained in it: **al-Biqā'ī** (ninth/fifteenth century) in his *Kitāb Aswāq al-ashwāq min Maṣāri' al-'ushshāq* expanded it, while his book was reworked and abridged in the carefully arranged *Tazyīn al-aswāq bi-tafṣīl tartīb Ashwāq al-'ushshāq* by Dā'ūd **al-Anṭākī** (tenth/sixteenth century). Many traditions were taken over by **Ibn al-Jawzī** in *Dhamm al-hawā* and from him by **Ibn Qayyim al-Jawziyya** in *Rawḍat al-muḥibbīn*. The fact that the material of the Ḥanbalī al-Sarrāj is quoted in these famous Ḥanbalī works on the moral aspects of love and on **love theory**, however, should not be over-estimated: 'The relatively small proportion of moralizing traditions suggests that al-Sarrāj's concerns were significantly different from those of his followers in the Ḥanbalite school' (Bell, 1979, 235).

Text editions

Maṣāri' al-'ushshāq, Istanbul (1302/1885); Cairo (1325/1907); Beirut (1958).

Further reading

Bell, J.N., 'al-Sarrāj's Maṣāri' al-'Ushshāq', *JAOS* 99 (1979), 235–48.

Giffen, L.A., *Theory of Profane Love Among the Arabs*, New York (1971), 25–7 and *passim*.

Leder, S., *Ibn al-Ǧauzī und seine Kompilation wider die Leidenschaft*, Beirut and Wiesbaden (1984), 98–101.

Vadet, J.C., *L'esprit courtois en Orient*, Paris (1968), 379–430, 477–86.

T. SEIDENSTICKER

See also: love theory

Sasanians *see* Persia

Ṣarrūf, Ya'qūb (1852–1927)

Lebanese journalist, novelist and translator. Born in al-Ḥadath, Ṣarrūf was educated at the Syrian Protestant College and taught in Lebanon before emigrating to Egypt in 1885. A Maronite who subsequently converted to Protestantism, he is best known as co-founder in 1876, with Fāris Nimr, of the journal *al-Muqtaṭaf*, which played an important part in disseminating scientific ideas in the Arab Middle East. In addition to numerous articles and translations, Ṣarrūf also published three novels, *Fatāt Miṣr*, *Fatāt al-Fayyūm* and *Amīr Lubnān* (1907); the last of these deals with the religious conflicts in Lebanon during the 1850s and 1860s.

Further reading

Fontaine, J., *EI*^{2}, s.v. Ṣarrūf, Ya'ḳūb.

P. STARKEY

satire, medieval

There is no exact equivalent in Arabic for 'satire'. To some extent, therefore, speaking of satire in Arabic literature is to impose a Western concept on a tradition that had its own system of modes and genres. ***Hijā'*** or *hajw* is often translated as 'satire', it is true. Although this is not rarely appropriate, *hijā'* is, strictly speaking, better rendered as 'invective'; moreover, it is normally restricted to poetry. Much invective poetry aims at ridicule, contempt and scorn, yet lacks a moral dimension which is the hallmark of true satire; conversely, there is a moralistic type of poetry that is called *hijā'* or *dhamm* ('blame') because it condemns or polemicizes, but which lacks the wit or sparkle usually associated with satire. However, even within the limits of the more restricted definition implied here, there is a considerable body of classical Arabic texts that may be called satirical. It is a mode that takes many forms, whether in poetry, prose, or mixed. As for poetry, see the entries on ***hijā'***, **epigram** and ***naqā'iḍ***. Here it may only be added that in

Arabic there is no tradition of formal satire in the style of Horace and Juvenal. As a general rule, the great poets of *hijā'* such as **Jarīr** and **Ibn al-Rūmī** are also among the major satirists.

The most characteristic form of Arabic verse satire is the short epigram. Similarly, the brief anecdote (*nādira*, pl. *nawādir*; other terms are also found) is perhaps the most typical form of satire in prose. Throughout the history of classical Arabic literature there is an abundance of *nawādir* that make fun of misers, spongers, schoolteachers, ***ḥadīth*** scholars, *qāḍīs*, physicians, **bedouins**, non-Arabs, poets, philologians, women, singing girls, simpletons, homosexuals, effeminate men and many other categories: anecdotes that pretend to be based on actual fact but are often obviously fictional and, like most jokes, anonymous. They are often collected in anthologies or monographs such as *al-Bukhalā'* (*The Misers*) by **al-Jāḥiẓ**, *al-Taṭfīl* (*Sponging*) by **al-Khaṭīb al-Baghdādī**, or *al-Ḥamqā wa-al-mughaffalīn* (*Fools and Simpletons*) by **Ibn al-Jawzī**. Several of al-Jāḥiẓ's works have satirical elements, and none more so than his unique *al-Tarbī' wa-al-tadwīr* (*Squaring and Circling*), on pseudo-science. As behoves a good satirist, he attacks not merely the addressee, but through him an attitude prevalent in his time. Other works by him satirize schoolteachers, snobs or civil servants. When he praises, his faint praise may be read, at least partly, as satire: see his *Manāqib al-Turk* (*The Good Qualities of the Turks*).

Among the more famous satirical monographs are Abū Ḥayyān **al-Tawḥīdī**'s *Mathālib al-wazīrayn* (*The Vices of the Two Viziers*), a medley of straightforward invective polemic and satirical sketches and anecdotes, and *al-Ghufrān* (*Forgiveness*) by **Abū al-'Alā' al-Ma'arrī**, a peculiar mixture of satire and philology. Among its merits is the fact that jest and earnest are not always easily distinguished, and that different categories of readers will discern different objects of the satire in it. The same applies to some of the ***maqāma***s of **Badī' al-Zamān al-Hamadhānī**, where parody and irony bring about a most attractive kind of satire. Since al-Hamadhānī's time the *maqāma* has often served as a vehicle of satire. Worthy of mention are those by **Ibn Nāqiyā** and **al-Wahrānī**. Longer than the normal *maqāma* are, for instance, *Ḥikāyat Abī al-Qāsim al-Baghdādī* by **Abū al-Muṭahhar al-Azdī**, which contains much satire, and **Ibn Buṭlān**'s *Da'wat al-aṭibbā'*, on quacks. The literary **debate**, which often employs the *maqāma* format, may serve as a vehicle for satire. A peculiar form, occasionally found, is the 'catalogue': a list of terms, often newly coined and provided with explanations, for particular foibles, such as the different kinds of bad table manners, or for the various categories of beggars and tricksters. Sub-literary satire could take the form of mime and **theatre**; interesting evidence has been collected by Shmuel Moreh (see also ***khayāl***). As for the **shadow play** or *khayāl al-ẓill*, we have some satirical texts by **Ibn Dāniyāl**. Many stories and sketches in *The Thousand and One Nights* (see ***Alf layla wa-layla***) satirize various types of people or circumstances.

Irony and parody are among the more common techniques employed in satire. Again, there are no exact equivalents in Arabic literary terminology. *Tahakkum* or *sukhriyya* ('mockery, derision') may be found as the nearest terms for 'irony'; in modern critical discourse the word *mufāraqa* is sometimes used. Arab literary critics and theorists discussed irony, parody and related concepts in various contexts; a key term in this respect is ***hazl***. Among the specialists in parody (in prose and poetry) is **Ibn Sūdūn**. It is in the nature of satire and irony that it may be missed or misunderstood and the object of a satirical work may be ambiguous. Thus *Hazz al-quḥūf* by **al-Shirbīnī** is, on the face of it, a satire on the peasants and peasant life in **Egypt**; but at the same time it seems to parody contemporary pedantic scholarship, and it has also been read as a satirical attack on contemporary social conditions in general. A much older example may perhaps be found in the preserved fragments attributed to the 'false prophet' Musaylima, contemporary with Muḥammad: they are usually quoted in order to ridicule Musaylima, but they could also be read as a parody of Koranic style.

Further reading

Bürgel, Johann Christoph, 'Von der kultur- und sozialgeschichtlichen Bedeutung der arabischen Satire', *Bustan* 11(2/3) (1970), 36–46.

Malti-Douglas, Fedwa, *Structures of Avarice: The* Bukhalā' *in Medieval Arabic Literature*, Leiden (1985).

Monroe, James T., *The Art of Badī' az-Zamān al-Hamadhānī as Picaresque Narrative*, Beirut (1983).

Sadan, Joseph, *al-Adab al-hāzil wa-nawādir al-thuqalā'*, Tel Aviv (1983).
——, 'An admirable and ridiculous hero: some notes on the bedouin in medieval Arabic belles lettres (...)', *Poetics Today* 10 (1989), 471–92.
van Gelder, Geert Jan, 'Arabic banqueters: literature, lexicography and reality', *Res Orientales* 4 (1992), 85–93.

G.J.H. VAN GELDER

Saudi Arabia *see* Arabia

Ṣaydaḥ, Jūrj (1893–1978)

Mahjar poet and literary critic. Born in **Damascus**, Ṣaydaḥ was educated at ʿAyn Ṭūra. He emigrated to **Egypt** in 1925, and from there moved to Venezuela in 1927. In 1948 he moved to Argentina, where he organized Arab literary life and founded the circle known as al-Rābiṭa al-adabiyya. He published his first volume of poetry, *Nawāfil*, in Buenos Aires in 1948. His most important contribution to Arabic literature is his *Adabunā wa-udabā'unā fī al-mahājir al-amīrkiyya* (Cairo, 1956; 3rd edn, Beirut, 1965), in which he presents a detailed survey of Mahjar literature. He returned to Lebanon in 1952, and in 1959 went to live in Paris, where he died.

C. NIJLAND

Sayf al-Dawla *see* Ḥamdānids

Sayf al-Dīn al-Āmidī *see* al Āmidī, Sayf al-Dīn

Sayf ibn Dhī Yazan, romance of

Sayf ibn Dhī Yazan is the Ḥimyarī noble who, in the sixth century CE, freed the **Yemen** from its Abyssinian invaders, with Persian help. The ancient core of the saga includes Arab and Iranian traditions. It acquires an Islamic coating with the inclusion of Sayf's prophecy about the imminent coming of the Arab Prophet, announced to the Meccan delegation led by ʿAbd al-Muṭṭalib. The folk romance of Sayf bears a very distant relationship to these events. Its composition is reckoned to date from the end of the sixth/fourteenth or fifteenth century; the ***rāwī*** gives his name as Abū al-Maʿālī. The setting described is Egyptian, with magic playing a predominant role. A powerful talisman, the 'Book of the Nile', had blocked the flow of the waters of the Nile. After the foundation of Yathrib, Sayf moves to Africa and completes a threefold mission: he gains possession of the talisman and deviates the course of the Nile from Abyssinia to **Egypt**; he subjugates the idolatrous sons of Ḥām; he procures the triumph of Abraham's monotheism.

Text editions

The Adventures of Sauf Ben Dhi Yazan. An Arab Folk Epic, L. Jayyusi (trans.), Bloomington/Indianapolis (1996).
Sīrat Sayf Ibn Dhī Yazan, Bulaq (1294/1877–8).

Further reading

Bey, Ali, *Sultan Saif-Zuliazan*, Constantinople (1847).
Browne, E.G., *A History of Persian Literature*, Cambridge (1928), vol. 1, 178–81.
Chelhod, J., "La geste du roi Sayf', *RHR* 171 (1967), 181–205.
Ibn Isḥāq, *The Life of Muhammad*, A. Guillaume (trans.), Lahore (1968), 30–3.
Khūrshīd, Fārūq, *Mughāmarāt Sayf Ibn Dhī Yazan*, 2 vols, Cairo (1964).
Lyons, M.C., *The Arabian Epic*, Cambridge (1995), 3: 586–641.
Manqūsh, Thurayyā, *Sayf Ibn Dhī Yazan bayna al-ḥaqīqa wa-al-usṭūra wa-al-amal*, Beirut (1978).
Norris, H.T., 'Sayf B. D̲ī Yazan and the Book of the history of the Nile', *QSA* 7 (1989), 125–51.
Paret, R. *Sīrat Saif Ibn Dhī Jazan*, Hannover (1924).
von Kremer, A. *Über die südarabische Sage*, Leipzig (1866), 92–4.
Wahb Ibn Munabbih, *Kitāb al-tījān fī mulūk Ḥimyar*, Sanaa, s. d., 317–21.

G. CANOVA

See also: *sīra* literature

Ṣāyigh, Tawfīq (1924–71)

Palestinian poet. Born in Khirba (southern Syria), Ṣāyigh was educated in Jerusalem and Beirut, and later studied English at Harvard University; he subsequently taught Arabic in London, Cambridge and California. Between 1962 and 1967, he edited the Beirut cultural review *al-Ḥiwār*. His own ouput, influenced by English and American rather than French poetry, is all in the form of prose poetry; it includes *Thalāthūn qaṣīda* (1954), *al-Qaṣīda K* (1960) and *Muʿallaqāt Tawfīq Ṣāyigh* (1963). In addition, Ṣāyigh published translations of American poetry, including a version of Eliot's *Four Quartets*.

Further reading

Jayyusi, S.K., *Trends and Movements in Modern Arabic Poetry*, Leiden (1977), 635–40.

P. STARKEY

al-Ṣayrafī, Ḥasan Kāmil (1908–84)

Egyptian poet. Born in Damietta, al-Ṣayrafī joined the Ministry of Agriculture, and worked as an editor of the Egyptian journal *al-Majalla*. A member of the committee of the **Apollo Group** and a prolific contributor to its journal, he was known for his melancholic poetry as well as his Romantic view of the role of the poet. Since his first collection *al-Alḥān al-ḍā'i'a* (Cairo, 1934), al-Ṣayrafī expressed in his poetry a gloomy tendency and feeling of frustration following the failure of love, mixed with symbolism. Egyptian critics even stated that his poetic vision considered tears as essential to the genuine poet. As a result of political and social developments in **Egypt** in the 1950s, however, his poetry became more down-to-earth and connected to reality. He also practised poetry in prose and was involved in the publication of classical poetry collections such as those of **al-Buḥturī** (1963) and **al-Mutallamis** (1970). In the early 1980s a new interest in the poetry of al-Ṣayrafī was aroused in Egyptian litereary circles, prompting studies of his poetry as well as publication of several of his collections by Dār al-Ma'ārif. Among these collections are *Zād al-musāfir* (1980), *Sharazād* (1980) and *'Awdat al-waḥy* (1980), in which the poems are written in the traditional ***qaṣīda*** form as well as astrophic forms.

Further reading

Fishwān, Muḥammad Sa'd, *Ḥasan Kāmil al-Ṣayrafī wa-tayyārāt al-tajdīd fī shi'rihi*, Cairo (1985).
Moreh, S., *Modern Arabic Poetry, 1800–1970*, Leiden (1976), 300–1.
al-Saḥartī, Muṣṭafā 'Abd al-Laṭīf, '*al-Alḥān al-Ḍā'i'a* lil-shā'ir Ḥasan Kāmil al-Ṣayrafī', *Apollo* (December 1934), 511–15.

R. SNIR

al-Sayyāb, Badr Shākir (1926–64)

Iraqi poet. One of the leaders of the **free verse** movement in the Arab world, al-Sayyāb left works of lasting importance despite his early death. Born in Jaykūr and educated in **Basra**, he graduated from the Higher Teachers' Training College in Baghdad in 1948. He became a teacher of English for a short period, then worked as a civil servant and a journalist. A communist until 1954 and later an Arab nationalist, he was arrested and dismissed from jobs several times during the monarchy and the republican regime in Iraq. In addition to political harassment and periods of self-exile in Iran and Kuwait, he suffered towards the end of his life from a degenerative disease of the nervous system, for which he received treatment in Baghdad, Beirut, London, Paris and Basra to no avail. He finally died in a Kuwait hospital and was buried in Zubayr (Iraq). In 1971 the Ba'thist government of Iraq erected a statue of him in Basra in his honour.

Al-Sayyāb was influenced early in his life by Baudelaire and the English Romantic poets – particularly Wordsworth, to whom he dedicated many of his first poems – as well as by the Arab Romantic poets of the 1940s, especially 'Alī Maḥmūd **Ṭāhā** and Ilyās **Abū Shabaka**. His early collections *Azhār dhābila* (1947) and *Asāṭīr* (1950) are full of love themes and sensuous poems on women and nature. His political poems of this early period were delivered orally at anti-government and anti-British rallies in Baghdad and sometimes published in local newspapers; they were collected posthumously in volumes such as *Qithārat al-rīḥ* (1971) and *A'āṣīr* (1972).

In one poem in *Azhār Dhābila* and several poems in *Asāṭīr* al-Sayyāb experimented with new rhythms based on the single foot (*taf'īla*) as the metrical unit, using as many feet per line as the thought required instead of the fixed six or eight feet per line of traditional verse. Rhyme in these poems was optional and often irregular. This poetic form, later called 'free verse' (*shi'r ḥurr*), was adopted by many young poets in Iraq and the rest of the Arab world. Al-Sayyāb himself wrote most of his later poetry in this form.

Al-Sayyāb's best poetry was produced in the 1950s and collected in his major opus, *Unshūdat al-maṭar* (1960). Still politically committed, he made more effective use of symbols and literary allusions, creating images of unusual beauty and power to express the Arab hope for a new life, free from exploitation and repression. He achieved his greatest success when, following T.S. Eliot and Edith Sitwell, he used myths of death and resurrection to embody his vision for the renewal of Arab society and culture, in poems that ingeniously fused personal and collective experiences.

Physically and psychologically crushed by disease in the 1960s, al-Sayyāb still wrote abundantly, but his poems now dwelt mostly on his personal predicament. Occasionally, however, they portrayed the human condition, existentially wavering between heroic hope in the face of death and resigned acceptance of destiny, and sometimes celebrated reminiscences of innocent childhood and past moments of love and happiness with rare insight, as in the collections *Manzil al-aqnān* (1963) and especially *Shanāshīl ibnat al-Jalabī* (1964). Al-Sayyāb's complete *Dīwān* was published in two volumes in Beirut, 1971–4.

Text editions

Asfour, J.M., *When the Words Burn: An Anthology of Modern Arabic Poetry 1947–1987*, Dunvegan, ON (1988), 138–45.
Boullata, I.J., *Modern Arab Poets 1950–1975*, Washington, DC (1976), 3–10.
Jayyusi, S.K., *Modern Arabic Poetry: An Anthology*, New York (1987), 427–42.
Khouri, M.A. and Algar, H., *An Anthology of Modern Arabic Poetry*, Berkeley (1974), 83–107.
Al-Udhari, A., *Modern Poetry of the Arab World*, Harmondsworth (1986), 29–34.

Further reading

'Abd al-Ḥalīm, M.A.S., 'Al-Sayyāb: a study of his poetry', in R.C. Ostle (ed.), *Studies in Modern Arabic Literature*, Warminster (1973), 69–85.
El-Azma, N., 'The Tammūzī movement and the influence of T.S. Eliot on Badr Shākir al-Sayyāb', *JAOS* 88 (1968), 671–8.
Badawi, M.M., *A Critical Introduction to Modern Arabic Poetry*, Cambridge (1975), 250–8.
Boullata, I.J. 'Badr Shakir al-Sayyab ...', *Middle East Forum* 46 (1970), 73–80.
——, 'Badr Shākir al-Sayyāb ...', *IJMES* 1 (1970), 248–58.
——, 'The poetic technique of Badr Shākir al-Sayyāb', *JAL* 2 (1971), 104–115.
——, *Badr Shākir al-Sayyāb: ḥayātuh wa-shi'ruh*, Beirut (1971).
Ḥāwī, I.S., *Badr Shākir al-Sayyāb: shā'ir al-anāshīd wa-al-marāthī*, 6 vols, Beirut (1973).
Tramontini, L., *Badr Šākir al-Sayyāb ...*, Wiesbaden (1991).

I.J. BOULLATA

al-Sayyid, Aḥmad Luṭfī *see* Luṭfī al-Sayyid, Aḥmad

al-Sayyid, Maḥmūd Aḥmad (1901–37)

Iraqi novelist and short-story writer. Son of a teacher in a Baghdad mosque, al-Sayyid translated literature from Turkish (and from Russian via Turkish), publishing his first, rather amateurish, longer story *Fī sabīl al-zawāj* in 1921. Like others of his earlier longer stories (e.g. *al-Sihām al-mutaqābila*, 1922), this mingles social criticism with declamations of socialist and even Marxian ideas, for example on the role of women in Arab or human society; the plots are full of action, but the characters lack development. *Jalāl Khālid* (1928) may be described as an *Entwicklungsroman* with autobiographical features. Several of his later stories such as *Ḥādithatān* or *Baddāī al-Fā'iz* from the collections *al-Ṭalā'i'* (1929) and *Fī sā'an min al-zamān* (1936) represent the first real masterpieces of the realistic Iraqi short story, depicting, for example, the social causes and consequences of blood revenge.

Text edition

'Zwei Ereignisse', in W. Walther (ed.), *Erkundungen. 28 irakische Erzähler*, Berlin (1985), 202–4.

Further reading

Aḥmad, 'Abd al-Ilāh, *Nash'at al-qiṣṣa wa-taṭawwuruhā fī al-'Irāq 1908–1939*, Baghdad (1986).
al-Ṭāhir, 'Alī Jawād, *Maḥmūd Aḥmad al-Sayyid, rā'id al-qiṣṣa al-ḥadītha fī al-'Irāq*, Beirut (1969).

W. WALTHER

al-Sayyid al-Ḥimyarī (105–73/723/89)

Abū Hāshim Ismā'īl ibn Muḥammad al-Sayyid al-Ḥimyarī **Shī'ī** poet, was born in **Basra** to Ibāḍī **Khārijī** parents. In his youth he became a Kaysānī (i.e. he believed in the return of Muḥammad ibn al-Ḥanafiyya) and attacked Murji'īs for suspending judgement in the case of **'Alī ibn Abī Ṭālib** – 'Imām of the true path' – and 'Uthmān. Some verses attributed to **Kuthayyir** (also a Kaysānī) about the hidden Imām (Muḥammad ibn al-Ḥanafiyya) are probably by him. After the **'Abbāsid** revolution he praised the new caliphs (al-Saffāḥ, al-Manṣūr and al-Mahdī). For forty years as a

Kaysānī he zealously celebrated the house of ʿAlī until, in 150/767–8, he recognized the fifth Imām (Jaʿfar al-Ṣādiq). As a *muḥdath* poet (see ***muḥdathūn***) he was considered to be on a par with **Bashshār ibn Burd** (and some say **Abū al-ʿAtāhiya**) in the simple elegance of his language. However, the political nature of his poetry (praise of Āl Hāshim, ʿAlī and al-Ḥusayn and occasional lampoons of some of the *Ṣaḥāba* and even ʿĀ'isha, the Prophet's wife) limited the circulation of his verse of which there is no extant ***dīwān***, although individual poems survive in various sources.

Text edition

Dīwān, S. Hādī Shukr (ed.), Beirut (1966).

Further reading

Barbier de Meynard, C., 'Le Seid Himyarite', *JA* 4 (1874), 159–258.
Gabrieli, F., 'Religious poetry in early Islam', in *Arabic Poetry: Theory and Development*, G.E. von Grunebaum (ed.), Wiesbaden (1973), 5–17.
al-Ḥakīm, Muḥammad Taqī, *Shāʿir al-ʿAqīda*, Baghdad (n.d.).
al-Marzubānī, Muḥammad ibn ʿImrān, *Akhbār al-Sayyid al-Himyarī*, M. Hādī al-Amīnī (ed.), Najaf (1965).

P.F. KENNEDY

Scheherazade *see Alf layla wa-layla*

Sebbar, Leila

Franco-Algerian writer, broadcaster and teacher living in France. Born in Aflou, Algeria, Sebbar wrote about the portrayal of 'the good African' (*le bon nègre*) in eighteenth-century French colonial literature before turning to fiction. This, together with the themes of exile, alienation and East–West relationships, characterizes her fictional output. She is the first novelist to draw attention to the lonely existence of first-generation Algerian immigrant women in France (*Fatima ou les Algériennes au square*, 1981), and the tormented world of their daughters (*Shérazade, 17 ans, brune, frisée, les yeux verts*, 1982). Her latest novel, *Le Silence des rives* (1993), is a further study of exile, as experienced by a man.

Text edition

Sherazade, Aged 17, Dark Curly Hair, Green Eyes, Missing, London (1991).

Further reading

Achour, C., *Anthologie de la littérature algérienne de langue française*, Paris (1990).
——, *Dictionnaire des oeuvres algériennes en langue française*, Paris (1991).
Bonn, C., *Anthologie de la littérature algérienne*, Paris (1990).

F. ABU-HAIDAR

secretaries

In the early Islamic centuries, the secretary (Ar. *kātib*, Pers. *dabīr*) was a vital figure in the administration of the caliphate and in those of its provincial successor states. The Prophet Muḥammad had used secretaries, including the future caliphs ʿAlī and Muʿāwiya, to write down the divine revelation, but after his death, the profession of secretary was intimately linked with the institution of the ***dīwān*** or register, thence government office or department, which required an expert staff to indite correspondence, prepare administrative instruments and to receive and record incoming taxation; there thus developed the specializations of chancery and treasury secretaries. The staffs of these *dīwāns*, taken over when the Arabs overran the former Byzantine and Persian lands, remained essentially non-Arab for one or two centuries, so that the ethos and culture of the secretarial class continued to be Greek or Coptic or Persian, even though many of these personnel became converts to Islam, as ***mawālī*** or clients.

Hence the ***adab***, the polite learning, of the secretaries became an amalgam of traditional Arab learning – the theological, legal and philological sciences – with that of the so-called ʿAjamī or non-Arab sciences (see ***ʿAjam***). Especially strong was the contribution of the Persians, whose governmental tradition went back far beyond that of the Arabs, backed by the **translation** activities of secretaries like **Ibn al-Muqaffaʿ**, who mediated Persian theories on statecraft and administrative procedures to the Arabs. Soon after the advent of the **ʿAbbāsids** in 132/750, the secretaries began to acquire an *esprit de corps* of their own, including even distinctive dress and hairstyle, and the Persian origin of so many of their ideas and practices at times made them an object of suspicion to the rigorist and pietistic class of Arab traditionists and religious lawyers; in one of his epistles, **al-Jāḥiẓ** denounces them for their arrogance, their reliance on Persian lore and precedent and their contempt for the

Koran. It was true that many of the secretaries, with their cosmopolitan background, tended to favour the ***Shuʿūbiyya*** movement, but the majority of them – outside the not inconsiderable minority of Christian and Jewish secretaries – remained faithful Muslims, loyal to the ideal of the Islamic caliphate.

Because the secretary had to have an encyclopaedic knowledge, both practical and theoretical, a rich literature of manuals and guides for them soon emerged. Already in the mid-second/eighth century the famous secretary of the last **Umayyads ʿAbd al-Ḥamīd al-Kātib** wrote an epistle addressed to secretaries. **Ibn Qutayba**'s *Adab al-kātib*, written in the mid-third/ninth century, was the first of several similar treatises on correct linguistic usage, whilst Abū Bakr **al-Ṣūlī** and Abū Ḥayyān **al-Tawḥīdī** composed works on penmanship and correct forms of address. Treatises on the *kharāj* or land tax, such as that of **Qudāma ibn Jaʿfar**, were primarily intended for financial secretaries. The genre eventually resulted in the vast **encyclopaedias** of secretarial practice compiled in the **Ayyūbid** and **Mamlūk** periods by authors like **al-Nuwayrī**, **Ibn Faḍl Allāh al-ʿUmarī** and **al-Qalqashandī**, which often provide the administrative and diplomatic historian of Islam with valuable material, since the chancery secretaries (*kuttāb al-inshāʾ*) were responsible for sending out documents from **Cairo** and **Damascus**, whose chanceries had, in Mamlūk times, international spheres of operation. Such works often include specimens of the letters and epistles of noted viziers and secretaries, and these had in many cases already been collected into special collections of correspondence (*munshaʾāt, mukātabāt*) for use as models by future generations.

There was a feeling in medieval Islam that skill in a profession was often transmitted hereditarily and that the relevant arcana could be handed down within families, whence arose several noted families of secretaries and viziers (since this last office was most often filled by those with secretarial training), like the **Barmakīds**, the Banū Wahb, the Banū Furāt, the **Nawbakhtīs** and the progeny of Niẓām al-Mulk. Such families might have special monographs devoted to them, as was the case with the Barmakīds, but more often they were included in that sub-genre of biographical writing that dealt with the 'classes' or generations of secretaries and officials, starting with the *Kitāb al-wuzarāʾ wa-al-kuttāb* (*Book of Viziers and Secretaries*) of the early fourth/tenth-century author **al-Jahshiyārī**; such works are valuable not only for information on administrative procedures but also for general cultural history.

Text edition

al-Jāḥiẓ, 'Une change contre les secrétaires d'état attribuée à Ǧāḥiẓ' (=*Risāla fī dhamm akhlāq al-kuttāb*), Ch. Pellat (trans.), *Hespéris* 43 (1956), 29–50.

Further reading

Björkman, W., *Beiträge zur Geschichte der Staatskanzlei im islamischen Ägypten*, Hamburg (1928).

Carter, M., 'The *Kātib* in fact and fiction', *Abr Nahrain* 11 (1971), 42–55.

EI^2, art. 'Kātib. i.' (R. Sellheim and D. Sourdel).

C.E. BOSWORTH

Sefrioui, Ahmed (1915–)

Moroccan novelist writing in French. Born in Fez to an arabicized family of Berber descent, Sefrioui held several important positions in the Moroccan historical monuments service. He began to publish in the 1940s. *Le Chapelet d'ambre* (1949), a collection of fairy tales, is full of mystical echoes, while the novel *La Boîte à merveilles* (1954) shows the inner aspects of social and family life based on strong Islamic values in Fez. *La Maison de servitude* (1973) describes a young man coming into conflict with modernity. Sefrioui's works tend to overlook issues of colonial politics, concentrating instead on the traditional Moroccan way of life in the 1950s. He sought to show the hidden 'wonders' that a foreigner would be unable to understand from the outside.

J. DÉJEUX

Serhane, Abdel (1950–)

Moroccan novelist and poet writing in French. Born in Azrou, Serhane first worked as a teacher in Kénitra before studying at the University of Rabat. From there he went to France, where he presented a doctoral thesis on the sexuality of Moroccan youth in traditional Moroccan culture. His three novels show an obsession with problems of sexuality and the complexes produced by them. *Messaouda* (1983) describes the havoc of a childhood dominated by an authoritarian father and the fear of incest. *Les Enfants des rues étroites* (1986) dwells on the downfall of adolescents at the hands of adults, while *Le Soleil des obscurs* (1992) marks a return to the theme of sexual deviance in his own country – the 'dehumanization of the masses led by the State', and 'hope turned into decay'. Serhane's outlook in his work is consistently bleak and his denunciations violent.

J. DÉJEUX

sermons *see* oratory and sermons

Seven Viziers see Sindbad, Book of

al-Shābbī, Abū al-Qāsim (1909–34)

Tunisian Romantic poet. Al-Shābbī received a traditional education in the Zaytouna Mosque in Tunis and, unusually among the Arab Romantics, knew no foreign language. He gleaned his knowledge of other literatures from translations and from reading articles and literary studies in Arabic. The *Apollo* review and its society (see **Apollo Group**) provided him with an important opening to the world beyond the borders of a **Tunisia** that was firmly controlled by the French Protectorate, and his work demonstrates that he was well acquainted with the latest developments in Egyptian literature and among the Syro-Lebanese writers of the **Mahjar**.

The fact that he received such a conservative cultural formation in the Zaytouna seems almost to have added to the strength of his reaction against it: in 1929 he delivered a lecture at the Khaldūniyya Institute in which he called into question the value of the whole literary heritage of classical Arabic. This was subsequently published as a pamphlet *al-Khayāl al-shiʿrī ʿinda al-ʿArab*, which was reviewed in the March 1933 issue of *Apollo*.

On one level, al-Shābbī's verse seems typical of the Romantic movement as a whole: it revolves around the agonies and ecstasies of existence and of love, and the painful mystery of death. Images of light and darkness connected with the dawn or the night reappear throughout his work, while his language has powerful, liturgical effects with repetitive patterns which reinforce the succession of these images. The themes of rebirth and redemption are often expressed through the symbol of the new dawn, and he became increasingly obsessed with his own mortality as he struggled against the heart disease which ended his life prematurely in 1934. What is special about his work is that he was able to transpose his own suffering on to a level that embraces the problems of his people and society as a whole. The most complete expression of this is his poem 'Irādat al-ḥayāh', which gained popularity in many countries of the Arab world. In 1934 he began to prepare for publication his only collection *Aghānī al-ḥayāh*, but death intervened and the book did not appear until 1955.

Further reading

Badawi, M.M., *A Critical Introduction to Modern Arabic Poetry*, Cambridge (1975), 157–68.
CHALMAL, 126–30.

R.C. OSTLE

al-Shābushtī (d. 399/1008 or somewhat earlier)

ʿAlī ibn Aḥmad (or Muḥammad ibn Isḥāq) al-Shābushtī was an Egyptian littérateur and poet. Virtually nothing is known of his life except that he served as librarian to the **Fāṭimid** caliph al-ʿAzīz. His poetic ***dīwān***, and all but one of his ***adab*** works, are lost, and his fame rests solely on his *Book of Monasteries*, itself incompletely preserved in a single manuscript. The surviving text of this work gives accounts of fifty-three monasteries, in Iraq, **Syria** and **Egypt**. The author includes basic geographical and historical information about each of these, but his primary interest is literary, and his regular procedure is to cite a poem describing each monastery and then add other verses by the same poet. Because Muslim poets were accustomed to visiting monasteries for pleasure outings, the cited verses are mostly in the genres of ***waṣf***, ***ghazal***, ***khamriyya*** and ***mujūn***. Presumably similar *Books of Monasteries* were also composed by **Abū al-Faraj al-Iṣbahānī**, **al-Khālidiyyān** and others, but they are all lost.

Text edition

Kitāb al-Diyārāt, G. ʿAwwād (ed.), 3rd edn, Beirut (1986); full references in the editor's introduction.

E.K. ROWSON

shadow-play

There are several terms in Arabic denoting shadow-play. The most frequently used is *khayāl al-ẓill*, while the terms *khayāl al-izār* and *khayāl al-sitāra* are less in use.

The earliest description of the shadow-play in the medieval Arab world is given by Ibn al-Haytham (d. 430/1039) in his book *Kitāb al-manāẓir*, but, without referring to its Arabic term *khayāl al-ẓill*: 'the sight perceives the [translucent] figures [of characters and animals] behind the screen, these figures being images which the presenter moves so that their shadows appear on the wall behind the screen and on the screen itself' (*Kitāb al-manāẓir*, Kuwait, 1983, 408). On the other hand, his Andalusian contemporary **Ibn Ḥazm** (d. 456/1064) described another type of shadow-play (*khayāl al-ẓill*) in which images are mounted on a rapidly revolving wooden wheel, so that one group of images (*tamāthīl*) disappears as another appears: 'thus, in this world too, one generation follows another' (*al-Akhlāq wa-al-siyar*, Beirut, 1961, 28). These two versions indicate that there were at least two types of shadow-plays: one in which the actor performs his plays with translucent figures behind the screen, with the light of lamps or candles behind them casting shadows on the white linen screen, the other (according to Ibn Ḥazm's description) a kind of a Chinese magic lantern, hence the term *ombres chinoises* or shadow-theatre. The third type is supplied by **al-Khafājī** in *Shifā' al-ghalīl* (Cairo, 1952, 73), who terms it *khayāl Ja'far al-Rāqiṣ*, 'the shadow-play of Ja'far the Dancer', who might be a live actor dancing or performing behind a screen with the light of a lamp casting the actors' shadows on the curtain.

The fact that the term ***khayāl*** was used as early as the end of the second/eighth century in the sense of 'play' or 'live performance', and was also given to the figure of a hobby-horse (*kurraj*; see **acting and actors, medieval**), while the shadow-play entered the Arab world some time in the late fourth/tenth century, using the term *khayāl al-ẓill*, proves that the latter arrived some time after the development of the profane live theatre (*khayāl*). Presumably when the shadow-play became established in the Arab world, the word *al-ẓill* (shadow) was added to *khayāl* (play, theatre) to describe the new art.

It seems that the shadow-play travelled from the Far East, mainly China and **India**, westward via Muslim merchants to the Muslim world, and spread to **Egypt** and Andalusia. According to **Ibn Iyās**, the shadow-play was well established in Egypt and from there was transported to Turkey. Ibn Iyās describes in his *Badā'i' al-zuhūr* (Wiesbaden, 1960–84, vol. 5, 192) a play performed in 1517 before the Ottoman Sultan Selim I by an Egyptian presenter of shadow-plays, depicting the hanging of the last **Mamlūk** sultan, Ṭūmān Bay. The sultan was so pleased with this shadow-play that he asked the player to accompany him to Istanbul to perform before his son. It is supposed that in this way the shadow-play was transplanted to Turkey. While in Egypt the shadow-play was prohibited several times by the Mamlūk sultans for reasons of piety, moral and political censorship, it flourished in Turkey and gained the popular name of *Karagöz*. From Turkey it spread once more to the Arab world, especially Syria, Egypt and North Africa, retaining the characters of the Turkish shadow-plays.

Modern scholars regarded the term *khayāl* as a shortened form of *khāyāl al-ẓill* (shadow-play). Failing to understand the difference between the two terms and their significance, they could find no evidence of live theatre in the medieval Arab world, and in consequence unconsciously ignored the fact that the Arabs had developed their own live theatre which was an oral art. This misunderstanding can be explained by the fact that Ṣūfī scholars and poets were able to see in the shadow-play a parable propounded by God, the *muḥarrik* (eternal [prime] mover) of his creatures: the *khayālī* or *mukhāyil* (the presenter) symbolizes God; the screen or curtain symbolizes the veil screening the hidden, pre-ordained future or the divine secret, the first character who summarizes the plot to the audience symbolizes Adam, the first human being; other characters symbolize the successive generations; while of the two boxes of the presenter, that on his right, from which he takes the figures to perform on the screen, symbolizes the womb, that on his left, in which he leaves his figures after their roles are ended, the tomb.

On the other hand, Muslim scholars did not see such a parable in live theatre. They considered the theatre as vulgar and the popular arts unworthy of scholarly attention, and denied it the status of literature. Medieval theatrical performances were mainly oral, given in colloquial or semi-colloquial Arabic and providing frivolous, impudent and debauched (*sukhf wa-mujūn*) entertainment. This is the main reason that Arab scholars excluded theatre (*khayāl*) from the realm of literature and ignored it in their discussions on religious problems. They discussed the importance of the shadow-play and only rarely mentioned live theatre, thus giving the impression that Arabs were not acquainted with it.

Further reading

And, Metin, *A History of Theatre and Popular Entertainment in Turkey*, Ankara (1963–4).
——, *Karagöz, théâtre d'ombres Turc*, Ankara (1977).
Ḥamāda, I., *Khayāl al-ẓill wa-tamthīliyyāt Ibn Dāniyāl*, Cairo (1963).
Jacob, G., *Geschichte des Schattentheaters im Morgen- und Albendland*, Osnabruck (1972).
Landau, J.M., *Studies in the Arab Theatre and Cinema*, Philadelphia (1958), 9–47.
——, *Shadow-plays in the Near East*, Jerusalem (1948).
Moreh, S., 'The shadow play (*Khayāl al-Ẓill*) in the light of Arabic literature', *JAL* 28 (1987), 46–61.
Reich, H., *Der Mimus, ein literar-entwickenlungs geschichtliicher Versuch*, Berlin (1903).
Sa'd, Fārūq, *Khayāl al-ẓill 'inda al-'Arabī*, Beirut (1993).

S. MOREH

See also: theatre and drama, medieval

al-Shāfi'ī (150–204/767–820)

Muḥammad ibn Idrīs al-Shāfi'ī was a major jurist of his time, out of whose circle of followers emerged the school of law that bears his name. He composed the first treatise on the principles of Muslim jurisprudence, entitled simply *al-Risāla*, and is often regarded as having laid the foundations of the classical theory of law and its sources (*uṣūl al-fiqh*). More specifically, he developed a system of jurisprudence that secured a prominent place for ***ḥadīth*** material as the second major source of law after the **Koran**. His larger work, *Kitāb al-Umm*, is a detailed record of the jurisprudential dialectic which took place in his time and has become an important source for the early history of Islamic jurisprudence. Al-Shāfi'ī also composed poetry, chiefly short poems (*muqaṭṭa'āt*; see ***qiṭ'a***) and **epigrams**, chiefly, but not exclusively, of a moralizing or homiletic nature; the collection edited by M.M. Bahjat includes a useful study of his style.

Text editions

Dīwān, ed. N. Zarzūr, Beirut (1984); ed. M.M. Khafājī, Cairo (n.d.).
al-Risāla, ed. M.M. Shākir, Cairo (1940).
Islamic Jurisprudence: Shāfi'ī's Risāla, Majid Khadduri (trans.), Baltimore (1961).
Shi'r al-Shāfi'ī, M.M. Bahjat (ed.), Baghdad (1986).
al-Umm, Cairo (1961).

Further reading

Schacht, J., *Introduction to Islamic Law*, Oxford (1964), 45–8.

B. WEISS

al-Shā'ir al-Qarawī *see* al-Khūrī, Rashīd Salīm

al-Shahrastānī, Muḥammad ibn 'Abd al-Karīm (479–548/1086–1153)

Ash'arī theologian and, with **Ibn Ḥazm**, one of Islam's most famous heresiographers. Little is known about his life but he was born in **Khurasan**, in a town called Shahrastān, where he lived, taught and wrote for most of his life, apart from periods of study in cities like Nishapur and **Baghdad**. The work for which he is best known is the famous *Kitāb al-Milal wa-al-niḥal*, which ranks in Arabic literature as a major medieval source book for the comparative study of religions. It attempts to treat as fairly as possible the various religions with which it deals. As Lawrence notes, 'what is singular about Shahrastānī is not his reportorial scope as an historian but his analytic skill as a theologian' (p. 7.).

Text editions

Kitāb muṣāra' at al-falāsifa, S.M. Mukhtār (ed.), Cairo (1976).
Madkhal ilā 'ilm al-fiqh, Beirut (1996).
al-Milal wa-al-niḥal, M.S. Kīlānī (ed.), Cairo (1977) (numerous other editions).
Book of Religious and Philosophical Sects, W. Cureton, (ed.), London (1846).
Kitāb al-Milal, Les dissidences de l'Islam, J.-C. Vadet (ed. and trans.), Paris (1984).
Livre des religions et des sectes, D. Gimaret and G. Monnot (trans.), 2 vols., Leuven (1986).
Muslim Sects and Divisions (The section on Muslim sects) in *Kitāb al-Milal wa l-Nihal*, A.K. Kazi and J.G. Flynn (trans.), London (1984).
Shahrastānī on the Indian Religions, Bruce B. Lawrence (trans.), The Hague (1976).

The Summa Philosophiae of al-Shahrastānī Kitāb Nihāyat al-iqdām fī ʿilm al-kalām, A. Guillaume (ed.), London (1934).

I.R. NETTON

Shā'ib, Fu'ād *see* al-Shāyib, Fu'ād

al-Shamʿa, Khaldūn (1941–)

Syrian short-story writer, translator and literary critic. Born in **Damascus**, he started his literary career as a short-story writer, translator and book reviewer before emerging as an avant-garde literary theorist in the early 1970s. Taking an active part in the affairs of the Arab Writers' Union, he wrote regularly for *al-Maʿrifa, al-Mawqif al-adabī* and other periodicals in **Syria** and the Arab world. His criticism, mostly inspired by the Anglo-American 'New Criticism', has been collected in three volumes: *al-Shams wa-al-ʿanqā'* (1974), *al-Naqd wa-al-ḥurriyya* (1977) and *al-Manhaj wa-al-muṣṭalaḥ* (1979). In the late 1970s he moved to London, where he worked as literary editor, and later editor-in-chief, of *al-Dustūr*; he is currently preparing a PhD thesis on **Adūnīs** at the University of London.

Further reading

Sulaymān, N., *al-Naqd al-adabī fī Sūriyya*, Part 1, Beirut (1980).
——, *Musāhama fī naqd al-naqd al-adabī*, Beirut (1983).

A.-N. STAIF

al-Shamardal (*fl.* *c.*101/720)

Al-Shamardal ibn Sharīk (or Shurayk) al-Yarbūʿī was a poet in the **Umayyad** age. His most frequently quoted poem is a lament upon his brother Wā'il (no. 12) who is portrayed as a **bedouin** hero very much in the pre-Islamic mould. Equally traditional in style are al-Shamardal's other elegies and ***qaṣīda***s; he played a more important role in the development of hunting poetry (***ṭardiyyāt***) in the ***rajaz*** metre. Among his poems is one of the earliest examples of a fully developed hunting *urjūza* (no. 20).

Text edition

Die Gedichte des Šamardal ibn Šarīk, T. Seidensticker (ed.), Wiesbaden (1983).

T. BAUER

al-Shammākh (first/seventh century)

Maʿqil ibn Ḍirār al-Shammākh was an innovative poet in early Islamic times. Remarkable is his skill in composing long poems using rare and difficult rhymes. His favourite subject was the onager episode, in which poets would describe a stallion onager chasing his mates to a drinking place where a hunter might be lurking. Al-Shammākh's episodes are among the most brillant and original examples of this genre. In his most famous poem (no. 8), he includes a description of manufacturing a bow in the hunting scene of an onager episode. In addition, he was one of the first poets who composed ***qaṣīda***s in the ***rajaz*** metre. He also influenced **Dhū al-Rumma**.

Text edition

Dīwān, Ṣalāḥ al-Dīn al-Hādī (ed.), Cairo (1968).

Further reading

Bauer, Thomas, *Altarabische Dichtkunst*, Wiesbaden (1992).

T. BAUER

Shams al-Dīn Muḥammad al-Dimashqī *see* al-Dimashqī, Shams al-Dīn

al-Shanfarā (d. *c.*550)

Pre-Islamic poet. His life, about which very little is known with certainty, was dominated, as the story goes, by his quest for revenge on the tribe of Salāmān. He is counted among the 'outlaws' (***ṣaʿālīk***), said to have been a friend of **Ta'abbaṭa Sharran**, and particularly famous for the great poem called *Lāmiyyat al-ʿArab*, which has been widely admired. Among the many commentaries on it are those by **Thaʿlab** and **al-Zamakhsharī**. According to **Ibn Durayd**, the poem is a pastiche made by **Khalaf al-Aḥmar**; the matter is still unresolved, most modern critics taking it to be a genuine **bedouin** product. It forcefully describes the poet as roaming alone and camel-less in the desert, his weapons his only friends, and feeling akin to the animals rather than his tribe. It celebrates many aspects of the bedouin ethos, even though its rejection of tribal values makes it not as representative of the 'Arabs' as its title suggests. Apart from some fragments, only one other poem by him is known (see ***al-Mufaḍḍaliyyāt***, no. 20).

Text editions

The *Lāmiyya* is included in many anthologies. Among other editions, see:

Bulūgh al-arab fī sharḥ Lāmiyyat al-ʿArab, Cairo (1989) (with commentaries by al-Zamakhsharī *et al.*)

Among the many translations (some of them in the titles below) see also:

Sells, Michael A., *Desert Tracings*, Middletown, Conn. (1989), 21–31.

Treadgold, Warren J., in *JAL* 6 (1975), 30–4.

Further reading

Gabrieli, Francesco, 'Sull'autenticità della Lāmiyyat-alʿArab', *RSO* 15 (1935), 358–61.

Jacob, Georg, *Schanfarà-Studien*, 2 vols., Munich (1914–15).

Jones, Alan, *Early Arabic Poetry*, vol. 1, 139–204, 260–8.

Nöldeke, Theodor, 'Zur Kritik und Erklärung der Qaṣîda Aśśanfarâ's (Lâmîyat al-ʿarab), *Beiträge zur Kenntnis der Poesie der alten Araber*, Hannover (1864), 200–22.

Stetkevych, Suzanne P., 'Archetype and attribution: al-Shanfarā and the *Lāmiyyat al-ʿArab,' The Mute Immortals Speak*, Ithaca (1993), 119–57; cf. also *IJMES* 18 (1986), 361–90.

G.J.H. VAN GELDER

al-Shantamarī (410–76/1019–83)

Yūsuf ibn Sulaymān al-Aʿlam al-Shantamarī, Andalusian philologist. He was born in Santa Maria de Algarve, lived in Córdoba from 433/1041, and died in Seville. He is often known as al-Aʿlam ('Harelip'). He is famous in particular for his commentaries – some of them published, others preserved in manuscript – on important collections of poetry, among them the ***dīwān***s of the 'six poets' (**al-Nābigha al-Dhubyānī**, **ʿAntara**, **Ṭarafa**, **Zuhayr**, **ʿAlqama** and **Imruʾ al-Qays**) and the *Ḥamāsa* by **Abū Tammām**. He also wrote commentaries on Abū Tammām's *dīwān*, on *al-Jumal* by **al-Zajjājī**, and on the lines of poetry in the *Kitāb* by **Sībawayh**; this work, written in 456/1064 and entitled *Taḥṣīl ʿayn al-dhahab*, was published in the Būlāq edition of *Kitāb Sībawayh*. He compiled his own *Ḥamāsa*, which is lost.

G.J.H. VAN GELDER

al-Shaʿrānī (d. 973/1565)

ʿAbd al-Wahhāb ibn Aḥmad al-Shaʿrānī was a leading Egyptian Ṣūfī writer, whose *Laṭāʾif al-minan* (*Subtleties of Blessings*) presents a powerful defence of Ṣūfī ideas. His version of Sufism is marked by a lack of sympathy with Shīʿism, and with a view of the *mahdī* as the son of Imām al-Ḥasan al-ʿAskarī (255/869) who is supposed to remain alive until he comes to meet Jesus in the future. Al-Shaʿrānī's thought is not, on the whole, very original, but he is an effective summarizer of other Ṣūfī positions, and his writings give a good idea of the sorts of debate that took place in his community in **Egypt** at that time.

Text editions

Asrār arkān al-Islām [etc.], ʿAbd al-Qādir Aḥmad ʿAṭā (ed.), Cairo (1980).

Laṭāʾif al-minan, Cairo (1321/1903).

Il libro dei doni, V. Vacca (trans.), Naples (1972).

al-Ṭabaqāt al-kubrā (*Lawāqiḥ al-anwār fī ṭabaqāt al-akhyār*), Cairo (1299/1881).

Further reading

Winter, Michael, *Society and Religion in Early Ottoman Egypt: Studies in the Writings of ʿAbd al-Wahhāb ibn Aḥmad al-Shaʿrānī*, New Brunswick, NJ (1982).

O. LEAMAN

Shaʿrāwī, Hudā (born Nūr al-Hudā Sulṭān) (1879–1947)

Egyptian feminist. The daughter of a wealthy landowner–politician and a Circassian woman, Shaʿrāwī grew up in the *ḥarīm* still typical of a rich nineteenth-century **Cairo** household, an experience she describes in *Mudhakkirāt rāʾidat al-marʾa al-ʿArabiyya al-ḥadītha* (ed. ʿAbd al-Ḥamīd Fahmī Mursī, Cairo, 1981). She was educated by tutors in Arabic, Persian, Turkish and French. At the age of 13 she was married to her much older cousin and guardian, ʿAlī Shaʿrāwī, but a year later instigated a separation. Gradually she became active in the cause of women through charity work, and she took the lead in founding the Intellectual Association of Egyptian Women (1914). As leader of the first nationalist demonstration by women in March 1919 and head of the Wafdist Women's Central Committee, she was at the centre of Egypt's political life. Sensing the need for a feminist organization, she founded the Egyptian Feminist Union in 1923, and was its president until her death. As part of her EFU mission, she founded two journals, *L'Egyptienne* (1925) and *al-Miṣriyya* (1937), in which she published essays and editorials. From Sha'rāwī's attendance at the 1923 International Women Suffrage Alliance conference in Rome (on returning from which she publicly removed her veil at Cairo railway station) to her becoming vice-president (1935) of the International Alliance of Women for Suffrage and Equal Citizenship, she sought international visibility for Egyptian feminists. Her memoirs, written in the 1940s but not published until long after her death, constitute an early example of Arab women's autobiographical writing.

Text edition

Harem Years: The Memoirs of an Egyptian Feminist, Margot Badran (ed. and trans.), London (1986) and New York (1987).

Further reading

Badran, Margot, *Feminists, Islam and Nation: Gender and the Making of Modern Egypt*, Princeton (1994).
al-Subkī, Āmāl Kāmil Bayyūmī, *al-Ḥaraka al-nisā'iyya fī Miṣr mā bayna al-thawratayni 1919 wa-1952*, Cairo (1986).

M. BOOTH

sharḥ, shurūḥ see commentaries

al-Sharīf al-'Aqīlī (*c.*350–450/960–1060)

Abū al-Ḥasan 'Alī ibn al-Ḥusayn Ḥaydara al-Sharīf al-'Aqīlī was an Egyptian poet of the **Fāṭimid** period. By birth of 'Alawī descent and of independent means, he was not obliged to compose poetry of praise for his living. Only once did he compose a panegyric, dedicated to a certain Abū al-Yumn 'Alī ibn Bashīr, a chancellor during the reign of the Fāṭimid Imām al-Ḥākim billāh. His wine poems describe aspects which accompany the drinking of good wine, such as inebriety and the expedition in search of a tavern or monastery where not only wine is offered, but also the enjoyment of women and young boys. In this genre the poet was influenced by **Abū Nuwās**. Other poems describe subjects like the Nile, a fresh garden (the genre of the *rawḍiyya*), a pond, and flowers which are compared to many-coloured jewels. His descriptions of drinking bouts gave offence to pious circles; and perhaps the poet himself was aware of this, as we find him expressing feelings of remorse in the brief ascetic poems used to close each section of an identical rhyme letter within his *dīwān*. Other poems, however, exhort to a mentality of *carpe diem*. His comparisons and metaphors were often construed around quotations from, and allusions to, well-known historical events, but they remain somewhat superficial.

Text edition

Dīwān, Zakī al-Maḥāsinī (ed.), Cairo, (n.d.; but not before 1953).

Further reading

Ibn Sa'īd, *al-Mughrib fī ḥulā al-Maghrib*, Zakī Muḥammad Ḥasan *et al.* (eds), Cairo (1953), 205–49.
Smoor, P., 'The poet's house: fiction and reality in the works of the "Fāṭimid" poets', *QSA* (Venice/Rome) 10 (1992), 45–62.

P. SMOOR

al-Sharīf al-Murtaḍā (355–436/967–1044)

'Alī ibn al-Ḥusayn ibn Mūsā, 'Alam al-Hudā, al-Sharīf al-Murtaḍā was born in **Baghdad** to a family descended on both sides from **Shī'ī** Imāms, in his father's case from the eighth Imām, Mūsā al-Kāẓim. He was the elder brother of the **Sharīf al-Raḍī**, from whom he took over the appointments of *naqīb* (syndic) of the Ṭālibids, head of the *maẓālim* courts, and leader of the *ḥajj* caravan. Al-Murtaḍā was one of the great scholars of his time, having among his teachers the Shaykh al-Mufīd (d. 413/1022) and among his students Abū Ja'far al-Ṭūsī (d. 460/1067). He is counted among the most important contributors to Imāmī ***kalām*** and *uṣūl al-fiqh*, as well as being a noted scholar in ***fiqh***. He was also a renowned ***adīb***, whose literary gatherings (*majālis*) were attended by the great literary figures of the day such as **Abū al-'Alā' al-Ma'arrī** and **Ibn Jinnī**. His *Ghurar al-fawā'id wa-durar al-qalā'id bil-muḥādarāt*, an ***adab*** work commonly known as *al-Amālī*, contains a literary and theological treatment of passages from the **Koran** and ***ḥadīth*** together with philological analyses and copious poetic illustration. He was an accomplished poet who left a ***dīwān***.

Text editions

Dīwān, Muṣṭafā Jawād and Rashīd al-Ṣaffār (eds), Cairo (1958).

Kitāb al-Amālī, Muḥammad Abū al-Faḍl Ibrāhīm (ed.), Cairo (1373/1954).

Sharḥ al-qaṣīda al-mudhahhaba fi madḥ Amīr al-Mu'minīn 'Alī ibn Abī Ṭālib lil-Sayyid al-Ḥimyarī, Muḥammad al-Khaṭīb (ed.), Beirut (1970).

Further reading

Muḥyi al-Dīn, 'Abd al-Razzāq, *Adab al-Murtaḍā min sīratihi wa-āthārih*, Baghdād (1957).

J. COOPER

al-Sharīf al-Raḍī (359–406/970–1015)

Abu al-Ḥasan Muḥammad ibn Abī Ṭāhir al-Ḥusayn ibn Mūsā, al-Sharīf al-Raḍī was born in **Baghdad** to a family descended on both sides from **Shī'ī** Imāms, in his father's case from the eighth Imām, Mūsā al-Kāẓim. He was the younger brother of the **Sharīf al-Murtaḍā**. His father held the offices of *naqīb* (syndic) of the Ṭālibids, head of the *maẓālim* courts, and leader of the *ḥajj* caravan. Al-Raḍī was appointed to all of these posts by the **Būyid** amīr Bahā' al-Dawla (r. 388–403/998–1012) when his father relinquished them, although the dates are disputed. Al-Raḍī was by all accounts a man of great moral probity and generosity, and more socially and politically committed than his brother, a fact that forced him to hand over his appointment as syndic to al-Murtaḍā in 394/1003–4 on account of the caliph's displeasure at his criticism of **'Abbāsid** rule in a poem. During the tenure by al-Raḍī and his brother, the post of syndic of the Ṭālibids was associated with considerable power and prestige. Unlike his brother, al-Raḍī became more renowned for his literary achievements than for his contributions to the Islamic sciences. Among his teachers in **grammar** and literature were Abū Sa'īd **al-Sīrāfī** (d. 368/979) and **Ibn Jinnī** (d. 392/1002). He is perhaps best known as the compiler of the celebrated ***Nahj al-balāgha***, a collection of sermons, epistles, exhortations and briefer utterances by **'Alī ibn Abī Ṭālib**, the first Shī'ī Imām, selected for their literary and rhetorical excellence. Although various **Sunnī** authors and orientalists have questioned the genuineness of this work, there is now no good reason either to doubt that he was the compiler, or to impute any kind of forgery on his part. The work has been the subject of numerous commentaries. Apart from works in ***kalām*** and ***fiqh***, al-Raḍī wrote several works on Koranic **exegesis**, among which is the *Talkhīṣ al-bayān 'an majāzāt al-Qur'ān*, one of the first works to give a literary exposition of the figurative aspects of scripture. He wrote a similar work on figures of speech in Prophetic ***ḥadīth***, the *Majāzāt al-āthār al-nabawiyya*. The high quality of his poetry, which was collected together in his *dīwān*, moved **al-Tha'ālibī** to regard him as the greatest poet of the Family of the Prophet, possibly of the entire Quraysh.

Text editions

Dīwān, Beirut, (1961).

Majāzāt al-nabawiyya, Ṭāhā Muḥammad al-Zaynī (ed.), Cairo (1967).

Nahj al-balāgha, Muḥammad 'Abdūh (ed.), Cairo (1933); Ṣubḥi al-Ṣāliḥ (ed.), (1387/1967); English trans. by Sayyid Muḥammad 'Askarī Ja'farī, Karachi, etc., numerous printings, and by Sayyid 'Alī Riḍā (rev. edn), Tehran (1979) (the more useful of the two, with indices).

Talkhīṣ al-bayān, Muḥammad 'Abd al-Ghanī Ḥasan (ed.), Cairo (1955).

J. COOPER

al-Sharīf al-Rundī *see* Ibn Sharīf al-Rundī

al-Sharīf al-Ṭalīq (*c*.347–95/958 or 9–1004 or 5)

Marwān ibn 'Abd al-Raḥmān al-Sharīf al-Ṭalīq was a poet in Córdoba. A great-grandson of the caliph 'Abd al-Raḥmān III, he was imprisoned in Madīnat al-Zahrā' at age 16 for killing his father over a girl. Among his fellow prisoners was the poet Abū 'Abd Allāh ibn Mas'ūd al-Bajjānī, who wrote love poetry to him and, later, ***hijā'***. Most of al-Ṭalīq's poetry was written in prison. Al-Manṣūr ordered his release around 379/989–90, because of a dream vision of Prophet or, in another account, thanks to the intervention of al-Manṣūr's pet ostrich, who repeatedly picked out al-Sharīf's petition from among many others and deposited it in the *ḥājib*'s lap until he was forced to read it.

Although al-Sharīf al-Ṭalīq is reported to have written much poetry, little is extant, and that only in fragmentary quotations. His friend, **Ibn Ḥazm**, called him the greatest Andalusian poet of his time, comparing his rank in al-Andalus with that of **Ibn al-**

Muʿtazz in Iraq. The extant fragments deal mostly with wine and flowers.

Text editions

Ibn Bassām, *al-Dhakhīra fī maḥasin ahl al-jazīra*, Iḥsān ʿAbbās (ed.), Beirut (1399/1979), vol. 1, 563.
Ibn Ḥazm, *Ṭawq al-ḥamāma*, L. Bercher (ed.), Algiers (1949), 72–3.
al-Maqqarī, *Nafḥ al-ṭīb*, Iḥsān ʿAbbās (ed.), Beirut (1988), vol. 3, 586–8.
Monroe, James T., *Hispano-Arabic Poetry: A Student Anthology*, Berkeley (1974), 11–12, 154–9.

Further reading

ʿAbbās, Iḥsān, *Ta'rīkh al-adab al-Andalusī: ʿaṣr siyādat Qurṭuba*, 2nd edn, Beirut (1981), 223–5.
García Gómez, Emilio, *Cinco poetas musulmanes: biografías y estudios*, 2nd edn, Madrid (1959), 67–93.

R.P. SCHEINDLIN

al-Sharqāwī, ʿAbd Allāh (d. 1812)

Egyptian historian. A renowned *shaykh* of **al-Azhar** but a relatively minor historian, al-Sharqāwī was president of the first governing council (***dīwān***) set up by Napoleon during the French occupation of 1798–1801. His two historical works are a 56-page history of **Egypt** (*Tuḥfat al-nāẓirīn fī-man waliya Miṣr min al-wulāh wa-al-salāṭīn*) and a collection of biographies of Shāfiʿī religious leaders (*imāms*) from the fifteenth century AD to his own time (*al-Tuḥfa al-bahiyya fī ṭabaqāt al-Shāfiʿiyya*). Both works are deeply flawed, the former being too brief and too annalistic to be of any value, and the latter being mostly cribbed from earlier authors.

Further reading

Crabbs, J.A., *The Writing of History in Nineteenth-century Egypt*, Detroit (1984), 57–8.

J. CRABBS

al-Sharqāwī, ʿAbd al-Raḥmān (1920–87)

Egyptian novelist, poet and dramatist. Born in the province of Munūfiyya, al-Sharqāwī studied law at Cairo University. He first became known in literary circles for his poetry, written in **free verse**, but subsequently turned to fiction and drama. His first novel, *al-Arḍ* (1953), epitomized the new mood of **commitment** following the Egyptian Free Officers' Revolt of 1952 and represents a landmark in the development of the Arabic novel; recently described as 'arguably the most widely known work of modern Arabic fiction both inside and beyond the Near and Middle East', the work was filmed by Yūsuf Shāhīn and has been translated into several languages. Two main struggles are acted out in the course of the novel, which is set in the early 1930s during the dictatorship of Ismāʿīl Ṣidqī: in the first, an attempt is made to deprive the villagers of the water needed for irrigation; the second revolves around a local landowner's scheme to build a new road across the peasants' land. In the course of the narrative al-Sharqāwī gives us a vivid picture of a number of village 'types' – the realism of the description being considerably enhanced by the use of vigorous dialogue in Egyptian colloquial. The novel is also of interest from a formal point of view, for while the first and third sections are narrated by a schoolboy returning from Cairo for his summer holidays, the central section reverts to a more conventional third-person narrative.

Though writing of the 1930s, al-Sharqāwī was almost certainly expressing in *al-Arḍ* an unspoken fear about the future course of developments under the new regime. His three subsequent novels (*Qulūb khāliya*, 1957; *al-Shawāriʿ al-khalfiyya*, 1958; *al-Fallāḥ*, 1967) continue the theme of commitment of *al-Arḍ*, but lack its artistic sophistication, degenerating at times into mere propaganda.

In addition to his poetry and fiction, al-Sharqāwī also wrote a biography of the Prophet Muḥammad (*Muḥammad, rasūl al-ḥurriyya*, 1962), in which he attempted to present his life from a Marxist viewpoint, and produced a number of verse dramas, including *Ma'sāt Jamīla* (1962) (on the life of the Algerian resistance fighter Jamīla Buhrid), *al-Ḥusayn thā'iran* and *al-Ḥusayn shahīdan* (1969).

Text edition

Egyptian Earth, Desmond Stewart (trans.), London (1962).

Further reading

Badawi, M.M., 'Islam in modern Egyptian literature', *JAL* 2 (1971), 172–4.
Kilpatrick, Hilary, *The Modern Egyptian Novel*, London (1974), 126–40.

P. STARKEY

al-Sharqī, ʿAlī (1892–1964)

Iraqi poet and prose writer. Born in al-Najaf, al-Sharqī studied Arabic philology and Islamic law there. In 1909 he began to publish neo-classical, patriotic poems on political events in Iraq and other Arab countries in newspapers and journals. In his works, he criticized the cultural and social backwardness of Iraq, urging his fellow countrymen to rise from their sleep of ignorance, to learn from European technical and cultural superiority, and to respect and educate women as future mothers. Al-Sharqī also wrote strophic poetry from the 1920s on, in which he called for the abolition of antiquated social and religious customs and ideas, and for more political freedom. His ***dīwān*** *ʿAwāṭif wa-ʿawāṣif*, originally published in Baghdad in 1953, was republished in 1979 with the addition of newly discovered poetry.

Further reading

ʿAwwād, ʿAbd al-Ḥusayn Mahdī, *al-Shaykh ʿAlī al-Sharqī: ḥayātuhu wa-adabuhu*, Baghdad (1981).

W. WALTHER

al-Sharqī al-Quṭāmī *see* al-Quṭāmī

Shārūbīm, Mīkhā'īl (1861–1920)

Egyptian historian. Largely overlooked but nevertheless important, Shārūbīm was a Copt, fluent in Arabic, English and French. He worked for a time in the Ministry of Finance but retired in 1903 to devote the rest of his life to writing.

Shārūbīm's most important work is *al-Kāfī fī tārīkh Miṣr al-qadīm wa-al-ḥadīth*, four thick volumes covering the history of **Egypt** from the time of Noah to the end of the reign of Tawfīq (1892). The sections on the nineteenth century are the most interesting and original; Shārūbīm's style is also fascinating as a transition between medieval and modern forms of historical writing.

Further reading

Crabbs, J.A., *The Writing of History in Nineteenth-century Egypt*, Detroit (1984), 133–6.

J. CRABBS

al-Shārūnī, Yūsuf (1924–)

Egyptian literary critic and short-story writer. Born in the delta governorate of Munūfiyya, al-Shārūnī studied philosophy in Cairo and worked as a teacher in the Sudan, before moving to the Supreme Council for the Arts, Literature and Science in Cairo. He has written numerous critical essays and several volumes of short stories, combining the assurance of the established generation with the experimentation of younger writers. His stories chronicle change and transformation in Egyptian society. His critical works include the seminal volume *Dirāsāt fī al-qiṣṣa al-qaṣīra* (1967), which contains studies on Najīb **Maḥfūẓ**, Yaḥyā **Ḥaqqī**, **al-Kharrāṭ** and others, in addition to al-Shārūnī's own fiction. Among his recent collections are *al-Umm wa-al-waḥsh* (1982) and *al-Karāsī al-mūsīqiyya* (1990).

Further reading

Shalabī, M., *Maʿa ruwwād al-fikr wa-al-fann*, Cairo (1982).

M. MIKHAIL

Shaʿshūʿ, Salīm (1926–)

Iraqi Jewish poet, journalist and jurist. Born in Baghdad, Shaʿshūʿ graduated from the Alliance school and the Law College in Baghdad, where he worked as a lawyer while publishing his poetry in the Iraqi newspapers. In 1951 he emigrated to Israel. He published poems and articles in *al-Yawm* and the Israel Broadcasting Service, and edited various periodicals. In 1955 he was elected chairman of the Arabic Language Association of Poets, and later chairman of the Arab Writers' Association. After his studies in the United States, he returned to Israel to work as a lawyer.

Shaʿshūʿ's love poetry, patriotic school songs and verses in praise of Israel's achievements and leaders were published in his collections *Fī ʿālam al-nūr* (Nazareth, 1960), *al-Anāshīd wa-al-maḥfūẓāt al-madrasiyya* (Nazareth, 1962) and *Ughniyāt li-bilādī* (Jerusalem, 1976). He also published a book on the co-operation between Jews and Arabs in Andalusia entitled *al-ʿAṣr al-dhahabī* (Shfaram, 1979), and a book in Hebrew on Islamic religious courts in Israel, which he subsequently translated into Arabic.

Further reading

Dictionary of International Biography, Cambridge (1976), vol. 2, 806.

Moreh, S. and Abbasi, M., *Biographies and Bibliographies in Arabic Literature in Israel 1948–86*, Jerusalem (1987), 117–19.
Snir, R., '"We were like those who dream": Iraqi–Jewish writers in Israel in the 1950s', *Prooftexts* 11 (1991), 153–73.

S. MOREH

Shawqī, Aḥmad (1868–1932)

Egyptian neo-classical poet. Probably the last of the great court poets who have graced the history of Arabic literature, Shawqī – like **al-Bārūdī** – was educated in the modern secular system, studying law and translation at the Cairo Law School. In 1887, he went to Europe to complete his higher education in law at the University of Montpellier. His remarkable poetic talent was soon recognized after he entered the Egyptian court in 1891, and he became effectively the poet laureate of the Khedive ʿAbbās. From then on Shawqī came to dominate neo-classical poetry in **Egypt** and beyond, until his death in 1932. He more than deserved the title 'Prince of Poets', and his enormous talent has ultimately always been the most effective answer to his detractors who sought to dismiss him as the 'Poet of Princes'.

The first volume of his ***dīwān*** (*al-Shawqiyyāt*) was first published in 1898, but it was only much later that his collected works appeared: volumes 1 and 2 came out in 1926 and 1930, while volumes 3 and 4 were published posthumously in 1936 and 1943. Shawqī was at the height of his powers between 1890 and 1920, and is undoubtedly the neo-classical poet of the greatest range and talent. While he was the author of many panegyrical poems as was demanded by his official position, he is not always at his most comfortable when praising the often inconsistent policies of the Khedive ʿAbbās towards the Ottoman Caliphate or the British powers in Egypt. However, he is seen at his best when he directs all the traditional power of the satire (***hijā'***) against the autocratic Lord Cromer, or when he evokes the glories of Egypt's Pharaonic past in poems such as 'The Sphinx', or 'Tutankhamon'. Equally impressive are the passages of *waṣf* in which he recreates the brilliant and colourful scenes of social life in and around the court circles of Egyptian high society. During World War 1, Shawqī was exiled to Spain because of his known attachment to the Ottoman cause, and because of his eloquent antipathy to the British. He was unable to return to Egypt until the end of 1919.

Shawqī is typical of the neo-classical school in that he imitates in a highly creative manner many of the major figures of classical Arabic poetry, not least **Ibn Zaydūn**, the great poet from Muslim Spain. **Abū Tammām**, **al-Buḥturī**, **al-Mutanabbī** and **Abū al-ʿAlā' al-Maʿarrī** were other important sources of inspiration to him from the classical tradition. His time spent in France brought him into contact with French literature: he is said to have translated Lamartine's *Le Lac* into Arabic, and he produced his own Arabic versions of La Fontaine's *Fables*, but this acquaintance with European literature never displaced classical Arabic poetry as the dominant formative influence on his work. After World War 1, Shawqī enthusiastically embraced in his verse themes celebrating the rise of Egypt as a new and independent nation-state, but he and his work were attacked by the new generations of Egyptian nationalists such as **al-ʿAqqād**, **Shukrī** and **al-Māzinī**, who saw in him a symbol of the old order which they wished to replace. However, their criticisms were motivated more by personal and political motives than by genuine literary criteria.

In addition to his poetry, Shawqī published a number of short prose romances of unimpressive quality. Much more interesting are the poetic dramas that he wrote as a result of his contact with the French theatre. The original version of *ʿAlī Bayk al-Kabīr* appeared in 1893 (revised and republished in 1932), while the period 1929–32 saw the publication of *Maṣraʿ Kilūbātrā* (1929), *Qambīz* (1931), *Majnūn Laylā* (1931), *ʿAntar* (1931), and a prose play *Amīrat al-Andalūs* (1932). A sign of the great esteem in which he was held even by those who did not share his aesthetic priorities was illustrated by the fact that he became the first president of the **Apollo Group** in 1932. Still today Shawqī's reputation remains undimmed as the greatest neo-classical poet in modern Arabic.

Further reading

Badawi, M.M., *A Critical Introduction to Modern Arabic Literature*, Cambridge (1975), 29–42.
CHALMAL, 38ff.
Khouri, M., *Poetry and the Making of Modern Egypt*, Leiden (1971), 55–77.

R.C. OSTLE

Shaybūb, Khalīl (1891–1951)

Syrian Christian Romantic poet. Born in Latakia, Shaybūb graduated from the Frère High School in commerce, then emigrated to Alexandria, where he graduated in law (1926) and in 1934 published *al-Muʿjam al-qaḍāʾī* (2nd edn, 1949). He published his revolutionary poetry in literary magazines, influenced by **Muṭrān** and the French romantic poets. He enjoyed close relations with his Egyptian contemporaries; he was elected president of the literary association Jamāʿat Nashr al-Thaqāfa in 1931, and was an active member of the **Apollo Group** headed by **Abū Shādī**. His Romantic poems composed between 1912 and 1920 were published in *al-Fajr al-awwal* (Alexandria, 1921), with an introduction by Muṭrān.

Encouraged by the Apollo Group's experiments, Shaybūb tried his hand at *shiʿr ḥurr* (see **free verse**) (using the French technique of *vers libre*), terming it *shiʿr muṭlaq*. In his two symbolic poems 'al-Shirāʿ' (1932) and 'al-Ḥadīqa al-mayyita wa-al-qaṣr al-bālī' (1934), he used various Arabic metres with an irregular rhyme scheme and enjambment, avoiding the use of the caesura in most of his verses. Although his examples were not successful, they encouraged other talented poets to follow suit and provided a model for the second, successful stage of Arabic free verse.

His book *ʿAbd al-Raḥmān al-Jabartī* (Iqraʾ series, 70: Cairo, 1948) is based on his imagination rather than on historical facts. Shaybūb also translated two books, one on the Bourse, the other (with ʿUthmān Ḥilmī) a collection of oriental poems (1936).

Further reading

Brugman, J., *An Introduction to the History of Modern Arabic Literature in Egypt*, Leiden (1984), 193–5.

Dāghir, Yūsuf Asʿad, *Maṣādir al-dirāsāt al-adabiyya*, Beirut (1956), III/1, 668–70.

Jayyusi, S.K., *Trends and Movements in Modern Arabic Poetry*, Leiden (1977), vol. 2, 543–5.

Qabbish, A., *Tārikh al-shiʿr al-ʿArabi al-ḥadith*, n.p. (1971), 264–5.

S. MOREH

al-Shāyib, Fuʾād (1910–70)

Syrian writer born in the village of Maʿlūlā. He studied law in **Damascus** and Paris, and first worked as a journalist. Later he became a director of broadcasting in Damascus, and then an offical in the Palace of the Republic.

He produced one book of short stories, *Taʾrīkh jurḥ* (Beirut, 1944), which is the earliest such collection from Syria, and he also published one play. His pioneering collection contains ten stories, which are not connected by any common theme; his style is straightforward, avoiding lengthy digressions and descriptions. He may be described as a representative of social realism.

Text edition

Azrak, M.G. and Young, M.J.L. (trans), *Modern Syrian Short Stories*, Washington, DC (1988).

Further reading

al-Aṭrash, M.I., *Ittijāhāt al-qiṣṣa fī Sūriyya*, Damascus (1982).

M.J.L. YOUNG

al-Shaykh, Ḥanān (1945–)

Lebanese novelist and short-story writer, whose writings focus on questions of sexuality and women's autonomy. Born in **Beirut**, she went to **Cairo** to study and to work with the Egyptian writer Iḥsān **ʿAbd al-Quddūs** while still a teenager. During her four years in Egypt she wrote and published her first novel, *Intiḥār rajul mayyit* (1967). Subsequently she has lived in Beirut, the Arabian Peninsula and London. Her first novel to attract critical attention was *Ḥikāyat Zahra* (1980), which tells of a young woman's struggle to come to terms with the label of madness that others have attached to her. Zahra's erotic encounters with a sniper at the height of the Lebanese Civil War earned the novel a notoriety that time and translation into English and French seem to have mitigated. In 1988, she published *Misk al-ghazāl*, a novel set in a westernized desert environment. The novel, which was almost simultaneously translated into English as *Women of Sand and Myrrh*, betrays the author's awareness of her new market. Her latest novel is *Barīd Bayrūt*. That evokes the emotions of an emigrant returning to post-bellum Lebanon.

Text editions

Beirut Blues, Catherine Cobham (trans.), London (1995).

The Story of Zahra, Peter Ford (trans.), London (1986).

Women of Sand and Myrrh, Catherine Cobham (trans.), London (1989).

Further reading

Accad, E., *Sexuality and War. Literary Masks of the Middle East*, New York (1990).

M. COOKE

Shaykhū, Le Père Luwīs (Louis Cheikho) (1859–1927)

Jesuit priest, theologian, linguist, historian and scholar. Born in Mardin (in present-day Turkey) he died in **Beirut**. After studying in **Damascus** and Lebanon, Shaykhū was sent to join the Jesuits in France, where he studied Greek, Latin and French. He travelled to England and Austria and to the East, visiting Mosul, Baghdad and Aleppo. In 1878 he taught Arabic language and literature at the secondary college of the University of Saint-Joseph in Beirut, where he became a professor of Arab philology. He collected many manuscripts and books for the Jesuit Bibliothèque orientale in Beirut, which he created. In 1898 he founded *al-Mashriq* magazine in Beirut, for twenty-five years writing most of its articles; the magazine became an encyclopaedia of Islamic and Arab Christian history and culture. Using scientific methods of criticism and analysis, he also edited books by **Badīʿ al-Zamān al-Hamadhānī**, the ***dīwān*s** of **Abū al-ʿAtāhiya**, **al-Khansāʾ**, **al-Samawʾal**, **al-Thaʿālibī**, **al-Buḥturī**'s anthology, the *Ḥamāsa*, and the animal fables of ***Kalīla wa-Dimna***. Shaykhū made an outstanding contribution to the history of Islam and the Middle East, and to the history of classical and modern Arabic literature, publishing (in addition to his editing work) on theology, philosophy, history, language, literature and bibliography.

Further reading

Dāghir, Yūsuf As'ad, *Maṣādir al-dirāsāt al-adabiyya*, Beirut (1956), ii, 515–24.
Hechaïmé, C., *Bibliographie analytique du Père Louis Cheikho*, Beirut (1986).

P.C. SADGROVE

al-Shayzarī (*fl.* fourth quarter of the sixth/twelfth century)

Little is known of Jalāl al-Dīn ʿAbd al-Raḥmān ibn Naṣr (Allāh) al-Shayzarī's personal life. He has been called 'al-Shīrāzī' rather than 'al-Shayzarī' by some copyists and biographers, but the latter name seems more likely. There is evidence in two treatises attributed to him, *Kitāb Manhaj al-sulūk fī siyāsat al-mulūk* and *Rawḍat al-qulūb*, linked by internal evidence to each other, that he was a judge in **Syria**. The latter book deals with some topics of **love theory** and offers personal anecdotes but is not long nor coherently organized. Regarding *al-Īḍāḥ fī asrār al-nikāḥ*, a work on sexual intercourse attributed to him, the Ottoman biobibliographer **Ḥājjī Khalīfa**, calling the author 'al-Shīrāzī', says that he was a physician of Aleppo who died 774/1372–3, raising questions about its attribution to this al-Shayzarī.

Text editions

Kitāb Nihāyat al-rutba fī ṭalab al-ḥisba, al-Sayyid al-Bāz al-ʿArīnī and Muḥammad Muṣṭafā Ziyāda (eds), Cairo (1946); *Islam devletinde hisbe teşkilati* (Turkish trans. of *Nihāyat al-rutba*), Istanbul (1993).
al-Manhaj al-maslūk fī siyāsat al-mulūk, ʿAlī ʿAbd Allāh Mūsā (ed.), al-Zarqa, Jordan (1987); the same, under the variant title *al-Nahj al-maslūk fī siyāsat al-mulūk*, M.A. Damāj (ed.), Beirut (1994).
L'oneïrocrite musulmane ou Doctrine de l'interprétation des songes par Gabdorrachaman fils de Nasar, P. Vattier (trans.), Paris (1664).
Der musulmannische Traumdeuter, Bey Benjamin Schillern (pub. and trans.?), Hamburg (1702) (trans of al-Shayzarī's *Khulāṣat al-kalām fī ta'wīl al-aḥlām*).

Further reading

Giffen, L.A., *Theory of Profane Love among the Arabs*, New York (1971) (on the genre to which *Rawḍat al-qulūb* belongs, although it was missed in that study).
Semah, D., 'Rawḍat al-Qulūb by al-Šayzarī, a twelfth-century book on love', *Arabica* 24 (1977), 187–206 (inc. intro. and ch. 1 of Arabic text of *Rawḍat al-qulūb wa-nuzhat al-muḥibb wa-al-maḥbūb*, ed. from Oxford and Tehran MSS).

L.A. GIFFEN

al-Shiblī (247–334/861–945)

Abū Bakr ibn Jaḥdar al-Shiblī was a Ṣūfī master. After serving as governor of Nahavand, he came under the influnce of al-Khayr Najjāj and joined the Ṣūfī circle of **al-Junayd** in **Baghdad**. Given to extreme emotions and bizarre behaviour, he engaged in painful mortifications and experienced states of ecstasy. His teachings are often expressed in paradoxical maxims and short verses or in mystical comments on verses of love poetry, especially those of Majnūn Laylā (see **Qays ibn al-Mulawwaḥ**). Though closely associated with **al-Ḥallāj**, he proved disloyal when interrogated during the latter's trial for heresy. Al-Shiblī's erratic behaviour led to his being committed to an asylum, where he continued to discourse on mysticism until his death.

Text edition

Diwan, Kāmil al-Shaybī (ed.), Baghdad (1967).

Further reading

Dermenghem, Emile, 'Abou Bakr Chibli, poète mystique bagdadien', *AIEO* 8 (1949–50), 235–64.

R.P. SCHEINDLIN

al-Shidyāq, (Aḥmad) Fāris (1804–87)

Lebanese linguist, lexicographer, critic, poet and journalist. Born in 'Ashqūt (Lebanon), he died in Istanbul. A Maronite convert to Protestantism, al-Shidyāq worked as a translator, editor and supervisor of the Arabic press for the British Church Missionary Society in Malta. *Circa* 1828/9 he went to **Cairo**, and worked on the official ***al-Waqā'i' al-Miṣriyya*** newspaper, returning to Malta in 1834, where he wrote *al-Riḥla al-mawsūma bi al-wāsiṭa fī ma'rifat aḥwāl Mālṭa*. In Britain he completed a translation of The Book of Common Prayer (1848), The New Testament, the first significant modern translation of the Old Testament, and *A Practical Grammar of the Arabic Language*. In Paris, he co-operated with Gustave Dugat on a French grammar for Arabs (1854). His most famous work, part autobiography, part criticism of the Maronite hierarchy, *al-Sāq 'alā al-sāq fī mā huwa al-Fāryāq* (Paris, 1855), has been compared to the masterpieces of Rabelais, displaying the infinite capacities of the Arabic language. In Tunis, at the invitation of the Bey, he embraced Islam, and published *Kashf al-mukhabbā 'an funūn Ūrubbā* on his travels in Europe. He was then invited by Sultan 'Abd al-Majīd to Istanbul, where he published the first great Arab newspaper ***al-Jawā'ib*** (1861–84). One of the creators of modern newspaper language, his writing demonstrated a surprising freedom from the artifices of nineteenth-century prose. He also published a thesaurus of Arabic etymology (1867), and critiques of the lexicons entitled *al-Muḥīṭ* by both **al-Fīrūzābādī** and **al-Bustānī**, and of Nāṣīf **al-Yāzijī**'s *Majma' al-Baḥrayn* (1871–2).

Text edition

La Jambe sur la jambe, R. Khawam (trans.), Paris (1991).

Further reading

CHALMAL, 406–8.
Hafez, S. *The Genesis of Arabic Narrative Discourse*, London (1993), 46–8, 129–30.
Karam, A.G., 'Fāris al-Shidyāḳ', *EI*[2], ii, 800–2.

P.C. SADGROVE

Shihāb al-Dīn Maḥmūd ibn Sulaymān *see* Ibn Fahd

Shihāb al-Dīn Yaḥyā al-Suhrawardī *see* al-Suhrawardī, Shihāb al-Dīn Yaḥyā

Shī'īs, Shī'ī literature

As a whole, the Shī'a are distinguished among the major Muslim divisions by their adherence to the doctrine that the Imāmate, or leadership, of the Islamic community resides in the *Ahl al-Bayt*, this being (with various doctrinal qualifications) the family of the Prophet through his daughter Fāṭima and her husband **'Alī ibn Abī Ṭālib**, the Prophet's cousin, the first Imām, and the fourth Caliph. Of the three major groupings within the Shī'a, the **Zaydīs**, the **Ismā'īlīs** and the Ithnā 'Asharīs (the Twelvers, or Imāmīs), it is the latter that has been the most numerous and which has consequently produced the largest body of literature.

As their name implies, the Ithnā 'Asharīs believe in a hereditary line of twelve Imāms beginning with 'Alī and ending with Muḥammad al-Mahdī, who began a continuing period of major occultation in 329/940, and who, it is believed, will return before the end of time to restore justice to the world. Meanwhile, he remains the guarantor of the *Sharī'a*, God's Proof (*ḥujja*) to humankind, among whom he lives, albeit hidden from all. The Twelver theory of the Imāmate also holds the Imām to be immune (*ma'ṣūm*) from sin and error, and divinely appointed (through *naṣṣ*).

The main doctrines of the Twelvers as well as their law (*fiqh*) were initially elaborated and systematized in the period following the Occultation, first in **Rayy** and Qum, and then in **Būyid Baghdad**. The shrine cities of Najaf and Karbalā' in Iraq subsequently became the main centres of Twelver learning, although they have sometimes been eclipsed, as at present, by the *madrasa* cities of Iran such as Qum. Iran, where all but a small minority of the population is Twelver, is the only present-day state in which Twelver Shī'ism is the constitutional religion (it was declared a Shī'ī state by the Ṣafavids at the beginning of the sixteenth century (tenth AH)), but important numbers of Ithnā 'Asharīs are also to be found in the Lebanon, Iraq and Bahrain (in each of which they are possibly the largest Muslim group), as well as in **India**, Pakistan and Afghanistan. Twelvers also form a significant proportion of emigré Muslim populations in the West, particularly among those with sub-continent origins.

Twelver law demonstrates no greater divergence from the major **Sunnī** *madhhab*s than do these latter among themselves. In ritual practice, the *ziyāra* (visitation) of the shrines of the Imāms and their descendants (Persian: *imāmzāda*) is emphatically recommended (*mustaḥabb*) and an integral part of every Shī'ī Muslim's life. A considerable body of recitational literature (also called *ziyāra*) has accumulated to accompany these devotions.

As sources of knowledge, the Imāms are considered to be equal to the Prophet, the only real difference being that, unlike the Prophet, they have not been given any revelation (*risāla*). ***Ḥadīth*** (traditions) narrated from them are therefore on a par with Prophetic *ḥadīth*, and Shī'ī *ḥadīth* literature is consequently extensive. Among the Imāms, the fifth and sixth, Muḥammad al-Bāqir (d. 114/732 or 117/735) and Ja'far al-Ṣādiq (d. 148/765), stand out as major sources both in doctrine and in law. The primary collections date from the fifth/eleventh centuries, in particular the 'Four Books' in law: the *Furū'* of *al-Kāfī* by al-Kulaynī (d. 329/941) (the *Uṣūl* of *al-Kāfī* contains non-legal traditions); *Man lā yaḥḍurūhu al-faqīh* by **Ibn Bābawayh** (d. 381/991); and *Tahdhīb al-aḥkām* and *al-Istibṣār* by the Shaykh al-Ṭūsī (d. 460/1067). Mention should also be made of the voluminous twelfth/seventeenth-century *ḥadīth* encyclopedia of Muḥammad Bāqir **al-Majlisī**, *Biḥār al-anwār*. Two extremely popular works attributed to the Imāms are ***Nahj al-balāgha*** (the first Imām, 'Alī; see also **al-Sharīf al-Raḍī**), and the collection of devotional literature *al-Ṣaḥīfa al-Sajjādiyya* or *al-Ṣaḥīfa al-kāmila* (the fourth Imām, Zayn al-'Ābidīn), both of which are considered exemplary specimens of early literary Arabic.

Early Imāmī commentaries on the **Koran** also provide a rich source for *ḥadīth* material, notably in the *Tafsīr*s of al-Qummī (d. 307/919) and al-'Ayyāshī (d. 320/932). Later *tafsīr*s, in which *ḥadīth* are still a major component, such as the Shaykh al-Ṭūsī's *al-Tibyān* and al-Ṭabarsī's (d. 548/1153) *Majma' al-bayān*, are similar in form to other *tafsīr*s of their time (see **exegesis**, **Koranic medieval**). A major modern Imāmī *tafsīr* is the 'Allāma al-Ṭabāṭabā'ī's (d. 1982) *al-Mīzān*.

Twelver law has typically stressed the necessity for the layperson to follow a living *mujtahid* (legal authority). In consequence, and also as a result of the rationalist approach of Imāmī ***kalām*** theology, the contribution of Twelver scholars to the literature in *uṣūl al-fiqh* (jurisprudence) has been particularly significant, continuing down to the present day. Notable scholars in this field have been the Shaykh al-Ṭūsī, the 'Allāma **Ibn al-Muṭahhar al-Ḥillī** (648–726/1250–1325), the Shaykh Murtaḍā al-Anṣārī (d. 1281/1864) and the Ākhūnd Muḥammad Kāẓim al-Khurāsānī (d. 1329/1911). The *fiqh* (derived law) literature is similarly extensive and has been added to in all periods.

Shī'ī *kalām* theology traces its origins back to the times of the fifth and sixth Imāms, but it witnessed its most notable flowering in the fifth/eleventh century with the writings of the Shaykh al-Mufīd (d. 413/1022), and his pupils the **Sharīf al-Murtaḍā** (d. 436/1044) and the Shaykh al-Ṭūsī. Modern Shī'ī theology, with its markedly philosophical vocabulary and style, took shape with the writings of **Naṣīr al-Dīn al-Ṭūsī** (d. 672/1274), a major Shī'ī philosopher and scientist as well as a theologian, and his pupil Ibn al-Muṭahhar al-Ḥillī.

Many of the early *falāsifa* (philosophers) either had Shī'ī leanings or Shī'ī backgrounds, but since their interests were universal rather than sectarian such attributions can be problematic. What is uncontroversial, however, is that, beginning with Naṣīr al-Dīn al-Ṭūsī, logic, metaphysics and theology together with speculative mysticism and ethics became fused together in Shī'ī learning in what came to be known as the science of *ḥikma* (wisdom, theosophy). **Mullā Ṣadrā**, Ṣadr al-Dīn al-Shīrāzī (d. 1050/1640) was the outstanding philosopher in this tradition, which continues down to the present day. Indeed, the noticeable interest in philosophy, which is such a marked characteristic of writing among many contemporary Shīʿī scholars such as Muḥammad Bāqir al-Ṣadr (exec. 1980), can be largely understood as a result of the continuation of this tradition.

In the field of ***adab*** literature, the question of the attribution of Imāmī, or even Shīʿī, beliefs to an author becomes even more problematic, for while it is virtually necessary that a scholar in the religious sciences should declare his sectarian allegiance (many religious scholars, such as the Sharīf al-Raḍī, have also been distinguished poets), such is not the case with writers in other, more popular areas of literature. Second, as adherents of a minority and frequently persecuted sect, many Shīʿīs have been, to say the least, discreet about their affiliations, supported in this by the Imāmī legal doctrine of *taqiyya* (dissimulation for the protection of the faith). Moreover, many non-Shīʿī authors have written eloquently on Shīʿī themes. It is therefore perhaps more fruitful to examine Shīʿism within *adab* and popular literature from the point of view of the development of genres. Eulogy of the *Ahl al-Bayt* has been a constant feature of Islamic religious poetry, and need not be taken as an indication of sectarian affiliation; for instance, **al-Farazdaq** (d. *c*.110/728 or 112/730) wrote panegyrics for **Umayyads** as well as ʿAlids such as Zayn al-ʿĀbidīn, the fourth Imām, and the Sunnī Imām **al-Shāfiʿī**'s poetry is often cited for its demonstration of strong love of the Prophet's family. The ***manāqib*** literature extolling the virtues of the *Ahl al-Bayt* comprises *ḥadīth* works as well as ones of a more hagiographical nature, again by both Shīʿīs (see, for example, under **Ibn Shahrāshūb**) and non-Shīʿīs (e.g. Aḥmad **Ibn Ḥanbal**'s *Manāqib* of ʿAlī ibn Abī Ṭālib). Another genre particularly developed in Shīʿī literature has been the *marthiya*, the elegy (see ***rithāʾ***), in this case, for a member of the *Ahl al-Bayt* (all the Imāms except the Twelfth are generally believed by the Imāmīs to have been murdered), and in particular al-Ḥusayn ibn ʿAlī, who was martyred at the hands of the troops of the Umayyad caliph al-Yazīd ibn Muʿāwiya at the massacre of Karbalāʾ in 61/680. An early example of this kind of *marthiya* is provided by **al-Sayyid al-Ḥimyarī** (d. 173/789), and the literary merits of the *rithāʾ* of al-Sharīf al-Raḍī have been much praised. The *marthiya* genre was successfully taken over into Persian and Urdu. Also inspired by the Karbalāʾ tragedy are the *taʿziya*s ('passion plays'), the *rawḍa*s (ritual commemorative recitations) and the *nawḥa* dirges, all of which are associated with the mourning ceremonies of Muḥarram, especially the tenth day, ʿĀshūrāʾ, the anniversary of al-Ḥusayn's death, one of the most significant days in the Shīʿī calendar. Although these forms are more often thought of in connection with Persian and Urdu, they are also developed in Arabic, particularly among the Shīʿa of southern Iraq.

Further reading

al-Amīnī, ʿAbd al-Ḥusayn, *al-Ghadīr fī al-kitāb wa-al-sunna wa-al-adab*, 4th printing, Tehran (1396/1976) (while being an extensive and authoritative contemporary work justifying Imāmī claims for the *Ahl al-Bayt*, this contains a wealth of material from *adab* sources).

Kohlberg, Etan, *A Medieval Muslim Scholar at Work: Ibn Ṭāwūs and His Library*, Leiden (1992) (an annotated bibliography of the contents of a celebrated seventh/thirteenth-century Imāmī scholar's library, important, among other reasons, for the detail it gives about many works now irretrievably lost).

Modarressi, Hossein, *An Introduction to Shīʿī Law: A Bibliographical Study*, London (1984).

al-Ṣaḥīfa al-kāmila, attributed to the fourth Imām Zayn al-ʿĀbidīn, as *The Psalms of Islam*, William C. Chittick (trans.), London (1988).

al-Ṭabāṭabāʾī ʿAllāma Muḥammad Ḥusayn, *al-Mīzān*, Sayyid Akhtar Rizvi (trans.), Tehran (1983–).

al-Tihrānī, Āghā Buzurg, *al-Dharīʿa ilā taṣānīf al-Shīʿa*, 25 vols, Tehran and Najaf (1353–98) (major modern bibliographical encyclopedia covering all Shīʿī literature, compiled alphabetically under title).

Uṣūl of al-Kāfī, Tehran (1978–) English translation.

General works on Shīʿism in English include:

Halm, Heinz, *Shiism*, Edinburgh (1991).

Momen, Moojan, *An Introduction to Shiʿi Islam: The History and Doctrines of Twelver Shiʿism*, New Haven and London (1985).

Richard, Yann, *Shiʿite Islam*, Oxford (1995).

J. COOPER

shiʿr *see* poetry

al-shiʿr al-ḥurr *see* free verse

al-shiʿr al-mursal see blank verse

al-Shirbīnī (late eleventh/seventeenth century)

Yūsuf ibn Muḥammad al-Shirbīnī was a comic writer of late eleventh/seventeenth century Egypt, famed for his satirical treatise entitled *The Shaking of Peasant Caps in Explanation of the Ode of Abū Shādūf*. Cast in the form of an elaborate parody of pedantic philological commentary, this work gives a detailed line-by-line explanation of a colloquial poem ostensibly composed by a crude peasant ('Abū Shādūf') who laments his sorry state, the whole being prefaced by a general discussion of the Egyptian peasantry. Its broad, often obscene, humour stands in the tradition of **Ibn Sūdūn**, whom the author cites a number of times, but is unique in its concentration on rural life.

Text edition

Hazz al-quḥūf fī sharḥ qaṣīd Abī Shādūf, Būlāq (1274/1857), and later editions.

Further reading

Baer, G., 'Shirbīnī's *Hazz al-Quḥūf* and its significance', in *Fellah and Townsman in Ottoman Egypt*, London (1982), 3–47.

Davies, H.T., *Seventeenth-Century Egyptian Arabic: A Profile of the Colloquial Material in Yūsuf al-Širbīnī's 'Hazz al-Quḥūf fī Šarḥ Qaṣīd Abī Šādūf'*, Ph.D. diss. Berkeley (1981).

Peled, M., 'Nodding the necks: a literary study of Shirbīnī's *Hazz al-Quḥūf*', *WI* 26 (1986), 57–75.

E.K. ROWSON

Shukrī, ʿAbd al-Raḥmān (1886–1958)

Egyptian poet. Like **al-Māzinī**, Shukrī was a graduate of the Teachers' Training College in **Cairo**, a product of the secular school system which had been established in **Egypt** in the second half of the nineteenth century. He published his first ***dīwān*** in 1909 before spending three years in England at Sheffield University College. After his return to Egypt in 1912, five further volumes of poetry were published in rapid succession between 1913 and 1918; both in the poetry itself and particularly in the prefaces that he wrote to these collections, he reveals a deep and wide-ranging knowledge of poetry and criticism in eighteenth- and nineteenth-century England.

Shukrī is the member of the **Dīwān Group** who is remembered primarily for his poetry rather than for the novels, literary criticism or polymathic writing on cultural topics that were characteristic of the work of al-Māzinī or **al-ʿAqqād**. With **Abū Shādī**, he ranks as one of the most important enthusiasts for English romanticism in modern Arabic literature and was able to adapt many of its principles to the new poetry which was beginning to supersede the neo-classical school.

Shukrī's first two collections of poetry (1909 and 1913) are the most traditional in style and theme and contain a number of elegies in honour of famous personalities and poems written for social and political occasions. Between 1915 and 1918 the full extent of his romanticism begins to emerge as he pleads for the overriding importance of the imagination and the passions, the need for simple, everyday language in poetry, and the insistence on the primacy of beauty in all things. He also claims that the poet is marked out by special gifts of vision not shared by the rest of humankind. Many of these ideas are traceable directly to Hazlitt, Keats, Coleridge or Wordsworth. Much of his amatory poetry is obsessed with the ambiguity of the spiritual and the physical nature of love, and it becomes increasingly obvious that he was unable to resolve this tension with any degree of fulfilment. This, combined with his intense concentration on the emotional ebbs and flows of his own psyche, lends his poetry a manic-depressive quality.

Although originally a close colleague of al-Māzinī and al-ʿAqqād, by the time that *al-Dīwān* was published in 1921, a bitter quarrel had broken out between Shukrī and the other two, illustrated by the vitriolic attack by al-Māzinī on Shukrī in the pages of *al-Dīwān* itself. Later al-Māzinī was to express regret for this and acknowledge the debt that he owed to him.

Unlike his two erstwhile colleagues, Shukrī shunned the rough and tumble of politics, journalism and public life. He became a teacher in Alexandria in 1912, and remained in education until retirement in 1944. Much of his later life was spent in alienated seclusion. His collected works, *Dīwān ʿAbd al-Raḥmān Shukrī*, were published in Alexandria in 1960.

Further reading

Badawi, M.M., *A Critical Introduction to Modern Arabic Poetry*, Cambridge (1975), 84–105.
CHALMAL, 92–5.

R.C. OSTLE

Shukrī, Muḥammad (1935–)

Moroccan novelist and short-story writer. Illiterate until the age of 19, and largely self-taught, Shukrī is one of the most interesting and outspoken new voices in Arabic fiction today. His initial attempts at short-story writing attracted immediate attention through their vivid depictions of the seamier side of life in which the author seems to have spent much of his youth. It is this quality that has also made it difficult for him to find publishers, at least until recently when his work has come to be more widely recognized for its originality. Besides a collection of short stories, *Majnūn al-ward* (1979), he has also published autobiographical novels, one called *al-Khubz al-ḥāfī* (published originally in an English adaptation in 1973), and a second, known under two titles *Zaman al-akhṭā'* (*Time of Errors*) for the Moroccan edition and *al-Shuttar* (*Streetwise*) for the British one (1994).

Text editions

For Bread Alone, P. Bowles (trans.), London (1973).
Streetwise, E. Emery (trans.), London (1996).

R. ALLEN

Shumayyil, Shiblī (1853–1917)

Controversial Greek Catholic doctor, scientist, journalist, philosopher, poet and social reformer, born in Kafr Shīmā (**Syria**). Shumayyil studied and taught medicine at the Syrian Protestant College, then travelled to Paris and Istanbul to complete his studies. He practised medicine in **Egypt** for ten years, and in 1886 founded *al-Shifā'* magazine in Cairo to publicize medical advances. He also wrote the programme of the Socialist Party in Egypt. Despite fierce opposition from Muslim conservatives, from the 1880s he was the foremost popularizer of Darwinism in the Arab world, considering science the key to the secrets of the universe. Apart from his works on Darwin's theory of evolution, he published articles on science, history, literature, criticism and politics; a work of Hippocrates; a treatise on the plague; a book on the urgent need for science, justice and liberty in the Ottoman Empire (1895); and a novel *al-Ḥubb 'alā al-fatra*. He also translated Racine's *Iphigénie*, and wrote a play on World War 1.

Further reading

Haroun, G., *Šibli Šumayyil, Une penseé évolutionniste arabe à l'epoque d'An-Nahda*, Beirut (1985).
Hourani, A., *Arabic Thought in the Liberal Age, 1798–1939*, London (1962), 248–53.
Lecerf, J., 'Šibli Šumayyil ... ', *BEO* 1 (1931), 153–86.
Sadgrove, P.C., 'Shumayyil, Shiblī', *EI*², IX, 501–2.

P.C. SADGROVE

Shuqayr, Shākir (1850–96)

Lebanese Melchite journalist, teacher, story writer and poet, born and died in al-Shuwayfāt. He wrote for the first magazine specializing in fictional writing in **Beirut** *Dīwān al-fukāha* (1891–3), and in **Egypt** founded *al-Kināna* (1895) magazine. Shuqayr wrote and translated about thirty stories; published a work on the Arab art of composition; and wrote several plays, including *al-'Ayla al-Muhtadiya*, promoting the education of girls. He also published an edition of **Abū al-'Alā' al-Ma'arrī**'s *Diwān Saqṭ al-Zand*.

Further reading

Dāghir, Yūsuf As'ad, *Maṣādir al-dirāsāt al-adabiyya*, Beirut (1956), ii, 488–90.

P.C. SADGROVE

al-Shushtarī (600 or 610–68/1203 or 1212–69)

Abū al-Ḥasan 'Alī ibn 'Abd Allāh al-Shushtarī was a Ṣūfī leader and poet. Born in Shushtar (near Guadix), al-Shushtarī was turned to Sufism by disciples of **Abū Madyan al-Tilimsānī** in Bougie; he became an adherent of Ibn Sab'īn, following him to **Egypt** and meeting him in Mecca. On Ibn Sab'īn's death, al-Shushtarī became head of the Mutajarridīn in **Syria** and Egypt. He is buried in his *ribāṭ* in Damietta.

As a religious poet, al-Shushtarī imitated **Ibn al-'Arabī**. He composed pieces in classical metres and ***muwashshaḥāt***; he was the first to compose ***zajal***s on religious themes. Five prose works are ascribed to him. Al-Shushtarī is venerated by the Shādhilīs and is one of the principal figures of Ṣūfism.

Text editions

Corriente, F. *Poesía estrófica atribuida al místico granadino aš-šUštari*, Madrid (1988).
Dīwān, Ḥ. al-Nashshār (ed.), Alexandria (1960).

Further reading

Massignon, L., 'Investigaciones sobre Shushtarī, poeta andaluz en Damieta', *al-Andalus* 14 (1949), 29–54.
Stern, M., *Hispano-Arabic Strophic Poetry*, Oxford (1974), index.

R.P. SCHEINDLIN

Shuʿūbiyya

The name of a cultural and literary trend discernible in the early **ʿAbbāsid** period, especially in the third/ninth century. The term derives from Koranic usage, in which the divine creation of *shuʿūb* ('peoples') and *qabā'il* ('tribes') is mentioned, all being equal in the sight of God. The original partisans of the *shuʿūb* seem to have been the **Khārijīs**, with their emphasis on piety, rather than race or membership of a particular family, as the test of true belief. But by ʿAbbāsid times, certain non-Arab elements, and especially ***mawālī*** or clients of Persian and 'Nabataean' (i.e. Iraqi Aramaic) origin, began to protest against the social and cultural discrimination against them by the Arabs. They demanded, first of all, equal treatment, but many passed on to claim superiority, because of the past glories of ancient Persian or Babylonian civilization, over the Arabs, with their miserable **bedouin** background in pre-Islamic times.

The movement was not really anti-Islamic, but it did encourage a certain scepticism towards Arab culture and to the religion of Islam which was inextricably bound up with it. Hence a fierce anti-*Shuʿūbī* reaction was engendered among the defenders of the Arab tradition, not all of whom were necessarily of unalloyed Arab blood; **al-Jāḥiẓ** had Negro blood in his veins, and **Ibn Qutayba** was of arabized Persian stock. Leading *Shuʿūbī*s included **Sahl ibn Hārūn**, the director of the caliph al-Ma'mūn's **Bayt al-Ḥikma** ('House of Wisdom'), although the great philologist and historian **Abū ʿUbayda**, who did so much to recover the literary heritage of the ancient Arabs and to record their religious traditions under Islam, often considered a *Shuʿūbī*, was probably one in the earlier Khārijī sense, concerned to ridicule Arab social pretensions but with no particular concern to vaunt the Persians. By the fourth/tenth century the controversy had died down, when the mainstream of Islamic culture and literature had absorbed enough of the Persian tradition in ethics and statecraft to disarm the partisans of the *Shuʿūbiyya* but not to damage the essentially Arab–Islamic basis of the faith.

A certain so-called *Shuʿūbī* literature appeared in Muslim **Spain** at a later date, when al-Andalus had dissolved into petty principalities or *ṭā'ifa*s representing to some extent ethnic groupings like the Berbers and Ṣaqāliba or 'Slavs'; a notable example of it is the epistle of the fifth/eleventh-century poet and secretary **Ibn Gharsiya** (Garcia). But this was of minor importance, and its few exponents tended to repeat clichés adopted from the earlier Islamic East.

Further reading

Gibb, H.A.R., 'The social significance of the Shuubiya', *Studies on the Civilization of Islam*, Boston (1962), 62–73.
Goldziher, I., *Muslim Studies*, C.R. Barber and S.M. Stern (trans), London (1967–71), vol. 1, 137–98.
Monroe, J.T., *The Shuʿūbiyya in al-Andalus*, Berkeley and Los Angeles (1970).
Norris, H.T., 'Shuʿūbiyyah in Arabic literature', in *CHALABL*, 31–47.

C.E. BOSWORTH

al-Sibāʿī, Yūsuf (1917–78)

Egyptian novelist and short-story writer. Born in **Cairo**, al-Sibāʿī was educated at the Egyptian Military Academy and at first pursued a military career. Following the 1952 overthrow of the monarchy, he held a number of prestigious cultural positions, including those of general secretary of the Higher Council for Literature and Fine Arts, minister of culture (1973–5), minister of culture and information (1975–6) and chairman of the board of ***al-Ahrām*** (1976–8). Closely identified with the policies of President Nasser and his successor, he was assassinated by a gunman at a conference in Nicosia in protest against President Sadat's Middle East policies.

Al-Sibā'ī's first published collection of short stories, *Aṭyāf*, appeared in 1947. His novel *Arḍ al-nifāq* (1949), in which he criticized the corruption of contemporary society, met with considerable success, and he consolidated his reputation as a leading Romantic novelist with *Innī rāḥila* (1950). He subsequently went on to produce a further twenty collections of short stories and some sixteen novels, as well as essays and several plays. Many of his works were adapted for the **cinema**. A frequent theme in al-Sibā'ī's work is the struggle of women to break free from traditional constraints on their freedom. Despite their popularity with the ordinary reader, al-Sibā'ī's works have tended to be despised by the literary establishment and have seldom received much serious critical attention.

Text edition

The Cobbler, and Other Stories, by Youssef el-Sebai, Cairo (1973).

Further reading

Ramsay, G., *The Novels of an Egyptian Romanticist: Yūsuf al-Sibā'ī*, Edsbruk (1996).

P. STARKEY

Sībawayhi (second/eighth century)

Abū Bishr 'Amr ibn 'Uthmān ibn Qanbar Sībawayhi, of Persian origin, was born in the mid-second/eighth century; he came to **Basra** to study religion and law, but is said to have turned to **grammar** after committing a solecism himself. He died in 177/793 or perhaps later, aged about 40.

Sībawayhi is the creator of systematic Arabic grammar. Although there is no doubt that his ideas evolved from a background of vigorous and informed discussion of the Arabic language there is no clear antecedent, either within the Muslim tradition or without it (e.g. Greek or Syriac), for the exhaustive and coherent description of classical Arabic set out in his one work known simply as *Sībawayhi's Book*, (*Kitāb Sībawayhi*). However, the *Kitāb* is considerably easier to read and understand when viewed as Sībawayhi's application of legal theory to the linguistic data provided by his great teachers and informants **al-Khalīl ibn Aḥmad**, Yūnus ibn Ḥabīb and others. Thus although most of the lexical, phonological and morphological information can safely be attributed to his masters (especially al-Khalīl, who also probably supplied him with certain basic syntactical notions, for example that compound elements can have the status of single words, and that the listener plays a role in determining the form of speech), there can be little doubt that Sībawayhi fully deserves his reputation as the author of what has been called 'the Koran of grammar'.

It is noteworthy that Sībawayhi founded no school, perhaps for reasons of personality or because he did not live long enough, and indeed the *Kitāb* was somewhat eclipsed in the decades following his death. By the fourth/tenth century, however, Sībawayhi was firmly established as the acknowledged founder of a grammatical system that has remained essentially unchanged until today.

Text editions

Kitāb Sībawayhi, Būlāq (1898–1900), rpt Baghdad (1965); A.S. Hārūn (ed.), Cairo (1968–77).
Le livre de Sībawaihi, H. Derenbourg (ed.), Paris (1881–9), rpt Hildesheim (1970).
Sībawaihi's Buch über die Grammatik, G. Jahn (trans.), Berlin (1895–1900), rpt Hildesheim (1969).

Further reading

Bernards, M., *Establishing a Reputation: The Reception of Sībawayh's Book*, Nijmegen (1992).
——, *Changing Traditions: Al-Mubarrad's Refutation of Sibawayh and the Subsequent Reception of the* Kitāb, Leiden (1997).
Bohas, G., Guillaume, J.-P. and Kouloughli, D.E., *The Arabic Linguistic Tradition*, London and New York (1990).
Diem, W., 'Bibliographie/Bibliography, Sekundärliteratur zur einheimischen arabischen Grammatikschreibung', in *The History of Linguistics in the Middle East*, C.H.M. Versteegh, K. Koerner, H.-J. Niederehe (eds), Amsterdam (1983), 195–250, items 155–214.
Owens, J., *Early Arabic Grammatical Theory: Heterogeneity and Standardization*, Amsterdam (1990).
Troupeau, G., *Lexique-index du Kitāb de Sībawayhi*, Paris (1976).
Versteegh, Kees [C.H.M.], *Landmarks in Linguistic Thought III, The Arabic Linguistic Tradition*, London and New York 1997, ch 3 and passim.

M.G. CARTER

See also: grammar and grammarians

Sibt Ibn al-Jawzī (581 or 582–654/ 1185 or 1186–1256)

Shams al-Din Abū al-Muẓaffar Yūsuf ibn Qizoghlū Sibt Ibn al-Jawzī was a historian of the **Ayyūbid** period, known as 'the grandson' (*sibṭ*) of the famous Ḥanbalī scholar **Ibn al-Jawzī**. Much of his contemporary fame stemmed from his eloquence, perhaps inherited from his grandfather, as a popular preacher, but his lasting fame comes from his great universal history, the *Mir'āt al-zamān*, in which he followed the system of Ibn al-Jawzī in his *Muntaẓam* of an annalistic listing of historical information plus obituaries of prominent people who had died during that year. For the first three Islamic centuries (based on **al-Ṭabarī**) and for the sixth/twelfth century (using **Ibn al-Qalānisī**, Ibn al-Jawzī and **ʿImād al-Dîn al-Iṣfahānī**), he appears to bring little new, but is valuable for the fourth–fifth/tenth–eleventh centuries (where he utilizes the largely lost histories of Hilāl **al-Ṣābi'** and his son Ghars al-Niʿma) and for the history of **Syria** and **Damascus** in his own time (being much used by Abū Shāma and subsequent historians).

Text editions

Les dynasties de l'Islam a travers le Mir'āt al-zamān ... partie relative aux années 447 h. à 452 h., K. Yazbeck (trans.), Beirut (1983).

al-Juz' al-thāmin min kitāb Mir'āt al-zamān fī ta'rīkh al-aʿyān (parts 1 and 2), Chicago (1907).

Kanz al-mulūk fī kaifiyyat as-sulūk, The Treasure of Princes or the Fashion of Behaviour, E.G. Vitestam (ed.), Lund (1970).

Mir'āt al-zamān fī ta'rīkh al-aʿyān (extracts for the years 1056–86), A. Sevim (ed.), Ankara (1968).

Mir'āt al-zamān fī ta'rīkh al-aʿyān (the years 335–447 AH), J.J.M. al-Hamāwundī (ed.), Baghdad (1990).

al-Sifr al-awwal min Kitāb Mir'āt al-zamān, I. ʿAbbās (ed.), Beirut (1985).

Further reading

Ahmad, M., Hilmy, M., 'Some notes on Arabic historiography during the Zengid and Ayyubid periods (521/1127–648/1250)', in *Historians of the Middle East*, Bernard Lewis and P.M. Holt (eds), London (1962), 91–2.

Cahen, C., 'Historiography of the Seljuqid period', in *Historians of the Middle East*, Bernard Lewis and P.M. Holt (eds), London (1962), 60–1.

C.E. BOSWORTH

Sicily, Siculo-Arabic poets

Among the Arabs who led the conquest of Sicily (211/827) were famous men of culture, like Asad ibn al-Furāt, a judge from Qayrawan, and Mujbār ibn Sufyān, the conqueror of Messina (228/843), who left the oldest Arabic verses of Sicily. The spread of Islamic culture and faith in Sicily did not meet with strong opposition, due to the weakness of local resistance and to the economic benefits introduced, such as a new irrigation system and new cultivation which brought a great development of commerce. Both the patronage of the Aghlabid rulers, who supported the arts, and the immigration of many Mālikīs fleeing from the spread of Shīʿism in North Africa, helped the introduction of Islamic culture. Among the immigrants were famous jurists, poets, lexicographers, grammarians and men of religion, who soon created schools of thought known all over the Mediterranean. Sicily became a halting-place for the pilgrims to Mecca and a meeting-place for men of letters.

From the tenth century Sicily was ruled by the Kalbite *amīrs* (336–445/947–1053), the **Shīʿī** emissaries of the Egyptian **Fāṭimids**, who were virtually autonomous in their rule and therefore able to suppport the arts and tolerate religious controversies with the Sicilian Mālikīs. The patronage of these princes aided the development of an autonomous cultural production that produced Sicilian representatives in every field of science. Poetry, earlier strictly linked to traditional models, developed innovative modes; much of this poetry has been preserved in anthologies, like those of **Ibn al-Qaṭṭāʿ** and al-Ṣayrafī. We know of the existence of more than 170 poets, but little is known about more than a dozen of them and a few thousand verses (a part from several complete ***dīwān*s**) that represent their production.

Along with the great poets we find the names of **secretaries**, judges, princes, grammarians and viziers. Among the panegyrists of the Aghlabids we find Ibn al-Qaṭṭāʿ, one of the earliest Siculo-Arabic poets, an exponent of the classical tradition. ʿAlī ibn Muḥammad **al-Khayyāṭ**, the official panegyrist of the Kalbid court, wrote encomia to Yūsuf Thiqat al-Dawla (381–8/990–8) and to his heir, the prince-poet Jaʿfar (388–405/998–1014/15); al-Khayyāṭ was a modern poet who excelled in describing reality. ʿAbū ʿAbd Allāh

Muḥammad ibn Qāsim ibn Zayd al-Kātib was the panegyrist of Ibn Ḥawwās, lord of Agrigento and enemy of the Kalbids. While most poets were panegyrists, there were also spiritual poets, like **al-Ṭūbī**, who lived in the first half of the eleventh century and was a grammarian, an author of ***maqāmāt***, and a poet of mystical love. **Al-Tamīmī** was the bard of the fratricidal wars that paved the way for the Norman conquest of the island; in his poems the traditional theme of parting became the bitter account of Muslim emigration to foreign lands and of torment for a beloved place ravaged by enemies.

The fame of the Sicilian poets endured after their emigration, as in the case of **al-Ballanūbī**, who was born in Villanova and travelled to **Egypt**, where he wrote poems for the viziers ʿAbū al-Ḥasan al-Anbarī (d. 438/1046) and al-Mudhabbir (453/1061). Praised both as poet and grammarian, he belongs to the modern school, but has an original skill in describing reality.

The greatest Arab poet of Sicily, **Ibn Ḥamdīs**, took part in the first attacks against the Normans and then emigrated to Seville, to the court of the prince-poet **al-Muʿtamid ibn ʿAbbād** (1048–95), whose frendship inspired sincere panegyric which won the poet the title of the best heir of **al-Mutanabbī**. Once the prince was exiled (484/1091), Ibn Ḥamdīs emigrated to the courts of Algeria and Tunisia. Later in his life he became nostalgic for Sicily, and recalled the happy banquets of his youth, reviving the conventional motifs of bacchic poetry.

In Christian Sicily there still remained an important Arab community, as was witnessed by the traveller **Ibn Jubayr**, and in **Ibn Ẓafar al-Ṣiqillī**'s *Sulwān al-mutāʿ*. The Norman kings adopted the Arab chancery, created a school of translation and opened their court to poets like ʿAbd al-Raḥmān al-Itrabanīshī, and to geographers like **al-Idrīsī**, the author of *The Book of Roger*. This tradition was kept up by Frederick II, who gathered in his court the first poets of the Italian language, Ciullo d'Alcamo and Giacomo da Lentini, as well as the Alexandrian poet Ibn al-Qalāqīs and the Provençal poets. Frederick also promoted the translation of Arabic masterpieces, and the Arab philosopher Ibn Sabʿīn (d. 670/1271) wrote for him a work on the immortality of the soul. The very fact that Arab, Sicilian and Provençal poets were attending the same assemblies makes us consider the possibility of Arab influence on early Italian poetry, even if there is no written evidence except for Petrarch's negative comment on Arabic poetry. The two share many common motifs, e.g. lovers' separation and reconciliation, the sickness of love that only the beloved can cure, the comparison of beloved and moon, the lover's obedience to both earthly and divine authority, and this contact has produced tangible results in, for example, the Arabic alliterations of Giacomo da Lentini 'Lo viso, e son diviso dallo viso,/ e per avviso credo ben visare,/ però diviso viso dallo viso/ ch'altr'è lo viso che lo divisare'.

Further reading

Ahmad, A., *History of Islamic Sicily*, Edinburgh (1975).

Amari, M., *Storia dei Musulmani in Sicilia*, Catania (1935).

Andaloro, M. (ed.), *Federico e la Sicilia dalla Terra alla Corona. Arti Figurative e Suntuarie*, Palermo (1994).

Atti del Convegno di studi Federiciani, Palermo (1952).

Atti del Convegno di Studi Ruggeriani, Palermo (1955).

Centenario della Nascita di Michele Amari, Palermo (1910).

Di Matteo, I., 'Antologia di poeti arabi siciliani', in *Archivio Storico Siciliano*, Palermo (1935), 1–28.

Gabrieli, F. and Scerrato, U., *Gli Arabi in Italia*, Milan (1979).

Mehren, M.F.A., 'Correspondance du philosophe soufi Ibn Sabʿīn 'Abd oul-Haqq avec l'empereur Frédéric II de Hohenstaufen', *JA* 14 (1879), 341–454.

Rizzitano, U., 'Un compendio dell'antologia dei poeti arabo-siciliani, *Accademia Nazionale del Lincei, Memorie* 8 (1958), 334–78.

——, 'Nuove fonti arabe per la storia dei Musulmani in Sicilia', *RSO* 32 (1957), 531–55.

——, 'Il contributo del mondo arabo agli studi arabo-siculi', *RSO* 36 (1961), 71–93.

Roncaglia, A., 'La lirica arabo-ispanica e il sorgere della lirica romanza fuori dalla penisola iberica', *Convegno di Scienze Morali. Storiche e filologiche – Oriente ed Occidente nel Medio Evo*, Rome (1957), 321–43.

Scarcia Amoretti, B.M. (ed.), *Del Nuovo sulla Sicilia musulmana – Giornata di studio 3–5–1993*, Rome (1996).

F.M. CORRAO

Sīdī ben Ammār *see* Ibn ʿAmmār

al-Sijistānī, Abū Ḥātim (d. 255/869)

Abū Ḥātim Sahl ibn Muḥammad al-Jushamī al-Sijistānī was the pupil of **Abū ʿUbayda**, **al-Aṣmaʿī** and **Abū Zayd al-Anṣārī**. A Baṣran philologist best known for his expertise in lexicography, **prosody** and the elucidation of obscure words, he was not regarded as a particularly outstanding grammarian even though he himself claimed to have read the *Kitāb* of **Sībawayhi** twice with no less an authority than al-Akhfash al-Awsaṭ. His students include **al-Mubarrad**, **Ibn Durayd** and **Ibn Qutayba**. He is credited with a large number of works, on vocabulary and morphology, **Koran** recitation, Koranic philology, popular solecisms, gender, long-lived people, etc., although only a handful survive. His contribution probably lay more in his personal influence rather than his compositions: **al-Riyāshī**'s tribute at his burial was that the knowledge lost to the world was not so much in Abū Ḥātim's books but in his heart.

Text editions

Kitāb al-aḍdād, A. Haffner (ed.), *Drei arabische Quellenwerke über die Aḍdād*, Beirut (1913).

Kitāb al-muʿammarīn, I. Goldziher (ed.), *Abhandlung zur arabischen Philologie*, Leiden (1899), vol. 2.

M.G. CARTER

al-Sijistānī, Abū Sulaymān *see* Abū Sulaymān al-Sijistānī

al-Sijistānī, Abū Yaʿqūb *see* Abū Yaʿqūb al-Sizjī

ṣināʿa

(Also *ṣanʿa*), 'craft' or 'art'. Applied by literary critics to both poetry and prose, it designates writing as a type of knowledge, a craft whose rules and principles must be mastered, and a profession practised by those who have acquired the necessary skills. The concept of poetry (or writing in general) as *ṣināʿa* generated a host of 'metaphors of craft' in which poetry, in particular, is compared to building, weaving, goldsmithing and other skilled crafts (see, for example, **Ibn Ṭabāṭabā**, *ʿIyār al-shiʿr*; **ʿAbd al-Qāhir al-Jurjānī**, *Dalāʾil al-iʿjāz*). A detailed treatment of writing as *ṣināʿa* is found in **Abū Hilāl al-ʿAskarī**'s *Kitāb al-ṣināʿatayn al-kitāba wa-al-shiʿr* (*The Book of the Two Arts, Prose and Poetry*) – by *kitāba*, 'prose', Abā Hilāl means the chancery or secretarial style; see **artistic prose**; **secretaries**). The term *ṣanʿa* is occasionally used in the sense of '(excessive) artifice, laboured art'; hence *maṣnūʿ* poetry takes on the meaning of 'artificial' or 'mannered' poetry, in opposition to *maṭbūʿ*, 'natural' or 'classical' poetry (see ***maṭbūʿ* and *maṣnūʿ***).

Further reading

Cantarino, Vicente, *Arabic Poetics in the Golden Age*, Leiden (1975), 55–62.

Kanazi, G., *Studies in the Kitāb aṣ-ṣināʿatayn of Abū Hilāl al-ʿAskarī*, Leiden (1989) 25–32.

Kilito, Abd El-Fattah, 'Sur le métalangage métaphorique des poéticiens arabes', *Poétique* 38 (1979), 162–74.

J.S. MEISAMI

See also: literary criticism, medieval; poetry, medieval; rhetoric and poetics

Sindbād

The tale of *Sindbād the Sailor* is a relatively late addition to the ***Alf layla wa-layla*** (*The Thousand and One* or *Arabian Nights*). It is absent from the earliest extant *Alf layla* text, Paris 3609–3611 (Bibliothèque Nationale), a fourteenth-century Syrian recension. Versions of *Sindbād* dating from the seventeenth and eighteenth centuries are recorded in Arabic story-collections independent of the *Alf layla*; some of these manuscripts also contain narratives such as *The Ebony Horse*, which, like *Sindbād*, was absorbed into the *Alf layla* at a relatively late date in the history of the *Nights*. It is difficult to determine the precise point in time at which *Sindbād* entered the *Alf layla*: the tale appears in both an early eighteenth-century Egyptian text of the *Nights*, Paris 3615, and in an even earlier Turkish version of the collection, Paris 356, dated 1046/1637.

Earlier scholarship sought to retrace Sindbād's voyages by matching the islands cited in the tale with known geographic sites in the East; researchers likewise conjectured the possible literary sources that might have influenced the narrative. As early as 1797, in lectures delivered to 'a literary society in Exeter', Richard Hole termed Sindbād's voyages 'the Arabian Odyssey,' citing the Cyclops and Lotus-Eaters of Homer's epic as sources for the Arabic narrative. To support such claims of Greek influence, Gustave von Grunebaum has noted that the Homeric epics were translated into Syriac by a Christian Arab astrologer at the caliphal court of al-Mahdī in the eighth century CE. Von Grunebaum also traces Sindbād's adventures to Pseudo-Callisthenes' *Life of Alexander the Great* (late third–early fourth century CE) and cites the ninth-century *Kitāb al-ḥayawān* (*Book of Animals*) of **al-Jāḥiẓ** as a possible intermediate source. But analogues to Sindbād's adventures can be found in even earlier texts, as in the ancient Egyptian *Tale of the Shipwrecked Sailor*, with its account of a solitary mariner washed up on an island who encounters a bearded serpent of lapis lazuli and gold.

In seeking more nearly proximate sources for the *Alf layla*'s Sindbād, Edward William Lane cited the thirteenth-century *'Ajā'ib al-makhlūqāt* (*Wonders of the Created World*) of **al-Qazwīnī**, with its descriptions of elephant-hunting *rukh*s and sea-creatures so huge as to be mistaken by mariners for islands. As Mia Gerhardt points out, works such as al-Qazwini's cosmography reflect the travellers' tales circulated by merchants who braved the Indian Ocean in the **'Abbāsid** age.

Recently scholars such as Gerhardt and Ferial Ghazoul have looked for some thematic unity underlying the disparate incidents of the seven Voyages. Peter Molan relates *Sindbād* to the frame-tale of Scheherazade and King Shahrayār. There is an ethical discrepancy, Molan argues, between Sindbād's professed piety and the ruthless violence he inflicts on fellow prisoners in the fourth Voyage; the fact that he conceals his actions once rescued demonstrates the hero's repressed sense of guilt. In Molan's view these tales 'become a parable for the instruction of King Shahrayār in self-deception and injustice', admonishing the monarch for his own unwarranted violence towards the young women he marries and kills.

Such a theme, if intended by the redactor, is implicit rather than overt: nowhere in the text is a comparison openly made between Sindbād and Shahrayār. Yet it is more typical of the *Alf layla* in general that moralizing themes when they occur (and they do so frequently) are asserted explicitly and repeated so as to draw the audience's attention. In *The City of Brass* and *The Fisherman and the Genie* (to take two examples), the moral is summarized in a single sentence ('This is a warning for whoever would be warned'; 'Spare me and God will spare you') which ties together each story's sub-plots by recurring in various frames of the narrative. And in the fourteenth-century Syrian version of *The Enchanted Prince* the listening Shahrayār is shown brooding over the hero's sufferings and comparing his own state with that of the prince. Unifying thematic devices such as the above seem absent from *Sindbād*.

But what the Voyages lack in sustained moral argument they make up in terms of structure. Each journey follows a cyclical pattern: **Baghdad** (prosperity) – voyage – storm – loss/isolation – perilous adventures – wealth regained – description of wonders and natural curiosities (a kind of narrative decrescendo on the voyage home) – return to the safety of Baghdad, where the hero forgets the hardships he endured. Structurally *Sindbād* calls to mind other lengthy *Alf layla* story ensembles such as *The Hunchback* and *The Barber's Six Brothers*: the tales contained in each collection constitute an example of a narrative cycle where the unity lacking at the thematic level is compensated for by a consistent formal patterning. Listeners thus know what sort of narrative entertainment to expect from each collection.

'Wondrous is this', exclaim the stranded survivors after Sindbād's men are attacked by yet another monster, 'each death is more horrible than the one before!' In the Voyages' parade of cannibals, ogres and snakes, the audience's chief pleasure is the frisson of hair-raising adventure.

Text editions

Alf layla wa-layla, 'Abd al-Raḥmān al-Sharqāwī (ed.), 2 vols, Bulaq (1835).

The Alif Laila or Book of the Thousand Nights and One Night, W.H. MacNaghten (ed.), 4 vols, Calcutta (1839–42).

The Arabian Nights' Entertainments, 3 vols, E.W. Lane (trans.), London (1839–41) (Lane's notes on the voyages of Sindbād appear in vol. 3, 80–117).

The Thousand and One Nights (Alf layla wa-layla) from the Earliest Known Sources, M. Mahdi (ed.), 2 vols. Leiden (1984).

Further reading

Gerhardt, M., *The Art of Story Telling: A Literary Study of the Thousand and One Nights*, Leiden (1963).

Ghazoul, F.J., *The Arabian Nights: A Structural Analysis*, Cairo (1980).
Hole, R., *Remarks on the Arabian Nights' Entertainments*, London (1797).
Molan, P., 'Sinbad the Sailor: a commentary on the ethics of violence', *JAOS* 98 (1978), 237–47.
Pinault, D., *Story-Telling Techniques in the Arabian Nights*, Leiden (1992).
Simpson, W.K., *The Literature of Ancient Egypt: An Anthology of Stories, Instructions, and Poetry*, New Haven (1973).
von Grunebaum, Gustave, 'Creative borrowing: Greece in the "Arabian Nights"', *Medieval Islam*, 2nd edn, Chicago (1953), 294–319.

D. PINAULT

Sindbād, Book of

The *Book of Sindbād*, or *Story of the Seven Viziers*, is an early and influential work of Arabic narrative prose (nothing to do with '**Sindbād**, the sailor'). The gist of the story is as follows: A king entrusts the education of his son to the sage Sindbād, who, in order to avert a catastrophe presaged by the prince's horoscope, orders his pupil not to speak for seven days. But no sooner has the prince begun his period of silence than one of his father's wives attempts to seduce him and, failing in this, accuses him of dishonouring her. The silent prince is unable to defend himself, and his father sentences him to death. The king's seven ministers then try to delay the execution; each day a different minister appears before the king and tells him two stories, one illustrating the dangers of precipitous action, and another warning of the wiles of women. The queen, for her part, also tries to influence the king by means of stories. At the end of the seven days the prince speaks again and reveals the truth; the treacherous queen is banished (or in some versions killed).

The *Fihrist* of **Ibn al-Nadīm** (see *Fihrist* (Dodge), vol. 2, 716–17), in its list of 'Indian books' known to Muslims, mentions a 'great' and a 'small' *Book of Sindbād*, and elsewhere in the *Fihrist* the author includes the '*Book of Sindbād*' among the titles that **Abān al-Lāḥiqī** (d. *c.*200/815) 'transmitted' (*naqala*, here evidently meaning 'translated in verse') 'from the books of the Persians and others'. However, the oldest surviving versions of the story are the Syriac, preserved in a single incomplete manuscript published, together with a German rendering, by F. Baethgen (Leipzig, 1879), and the Greek translation of the aforementioned Syriac version, made towards the end of the eleventh century by Michael Andreopoulos (critical edition by V. Jernstedt, Sankt-Peterburg, 1912). Some linguistic features of the Syriac text indicate that it is based on an Arabic original. The Greek, for its part, has an introduction mentioning 'Mousos the Persian' as the 'author' of the book, apparently meaning that a certain Mūsā was responsible for the Arabic translation (presumably from the Middle Persian) on which the extant Syriac version is based. These are followed by the neo-Persian *Sindbādh-nāma* of Muḥammad ibn 'Alī al-Ẓahīrī al-Samarqandī from around the year 556/1161 (ed. A. Ateş, Istanbul 1948). This has a rather puzzling passage in its introduction which speaks of an earlier Persian translation made in 339/950–1 and says that before that time the book had existed 'in Pahlawī' (i.e. Middle Persian) and that 'no-one had translated it' (i.e. into neo-Persian). But does this really mean that Ẓahīrī's version derives from the Middle Persian without an Arabic intermediary? There is also a fairly close translation from Arabic into Old Spanish from the mid-thirteenth century (ed. J.E. Keller, Chapel Hill, 1953) and a much freer Hebrew version from about the same time (ed. M. Epstein, Philadelphia, 1967). There are numerous medieval and Renaissance retellings of the *Book of the Seven Sages* in European languages, but their precise relationship with the Oriental versions has not been established satisfactorily. The extant Arabic manuscripts are all late and much altered; the best hitherto available text in that language is the version in non-literary Arabic published by Ateş (as part of his mentioned edition of the Persian *Sindbādh-nāma*) from an Istanbul manuscript dated 940/1533–4. A corrupt version of the story of the seven viziers is included in the older printed editions of the *Thousand and One Nights* (***Alf layla wa-layla***).

The question of whether or not the *Book of Sindbād* is really of Indian origin has been hotly debated (notably, but much too narrow-mindedly, by the classicist Perry, who denies such an origin). There is no clear Indian parallel for the frame-story although this does have some striking similarities with the frame-story of the *Pañcatantra* (in a version not retained by the Near Eastern book of ***Kalīla wa-Dimna***). As for the sub-stories, some of these do occur in Indian collections (two are clearly taken from *Kalīla wa-Dimna* and thus probably do not come *directly* from an Indian source), but most have not been traced to demonstrably early Indian books. The work also contains at least one quotation from an Indian book on state-craft, the *Cāṇakya-nīti-śāstra*. It would seem on the whole most likely that the *Book of Sindbād*, as such, was originally compiled in Sasanian Persia, in the Middle Persian language, and is not a translation of a pre-existing Sanskrit work, but that its author was familiar with Indian narrative and gnomic works, presumably in Middle Persian translations. Moreover, the strongly misogynist character of the book suggests that it originated in a Christian (rather than a Zoroastrian) environment.

Further reading

There is no up-to-date study of the interrelationship of the various versions by a competent orientalist; the best of the older studies is:

Nöldeke, T., *ZDMG* 33 (1879), 513–36 (detailed review of Baethgen's edition of the Syriac version).

See also:

de Blois, F., 'Two sources of the *Handarz* of Ōšnar', *Iran* 31 (1993), 95–7.

Perry, B.E. *The Origin of the Book of Sindbad*, offprint from *Fabula* III/1–2 (1959).

F. DE BLOIS

singers and musicians

As far as can be determined, there has always been a close connection between singing and poetry in Arabic culture. In the **Umayyad** and **'Abbāsid** periods, the best-documented before modern times, composers of songs for entertainment habitually set to music lines by recognized poets, not necessarily their contemporaries. Songs seldom had more than four lines of text, which might not be consecutive in the original poem; indeed on rare occasions composers combined lines from poems, sometimes even by different authors, modifying the rhyme-word and text where necessary.

All that can be reliably concluded from the sources for the pre-Islamic period is that entertainment music, performed by singing girls (*qayna*, pl. *qiyān*) often in taverns, existed alongside work songs and ceremonial music in Arabia. With the early Islamic conquests, which brought great wealth to the **Hijaz**, a leisure culture developed among members of the Arab aristocracy. Musicians came into contact with the Byzantine and Persian traditions, the latter in particular already highly evolved.

In the Umayyad period a Hijazi school of singing emerged and male performers are mentioned for the first time. Some of them had an ambiguous sexual status and almost all were freedmen (***mawālī***). The famous musicians of the period include Ibn Surayj, Ma'bad, Mālik, al-Gharīḍ, the *diva* Jamīla and Yazīd ibn 'Abd al-Malik's favourites Sallāma and Ḥabāba. Advances in technical proficiency and vocal artistry occurred, with songs often being accompanied either on the lute or the tambourine. Towards the end of the period the first attempt to collect and codify them was made.

It has been suggested that the Umayyad ***ghazal*** emerged as a product of this flourishing musical culture. But although poets and musicians appreciated each other's work, the arguments for singers having influenced the form, diction or choice of metre in the new poetry are not convincing. Composers re-formed poems to suit the music (see above). No correlation can be established between musical rhythms and metres (see **prosody**) and the *ghazal*'s style is dictated in the first place by the subject matter. Poets and singers certainly co-operated, but without the one necessarily influencing the other.

The 'Abbāsid era saw the centre of musical life transferred from the Hijaz to Iraq; al-Mahdī was the first caliph to issue a general invitation to singers to attend the court. Persian influence, and perhaps also that of an indigenous Iraqi tradition of **Ḥīra** and **Kufa**, became stronger. The status of the musician improved somewhat, as court singers were expected to possess a level of culture enabling them to take part in salon conversation. The *qayna*, still very often a slave, had to be witty and well educated as well as beautiful and a good singer. A luxury object, she was a symbol of sophisticated, *ẓarīf* society (see ***ẓarf***) and, if mercenary, could cause ravages among her admirers, as **al-Jāḥiẓ** has recorded. Besides professional musicians amateurs appeared; the most socially eminent were the caliph al-Wāthiq and the prince **Ibrāhīm ibn al-Mahdī**, but very many statesmen and administrators had a good knowledge of music.

Musical performance attained a high degree of professionalism, with the two schools of Isḥāq **al-Mawṣilī** and Ibrāhīm ibn al-Mahdī advocating a more conservative and technically demanding, and a more innovative and indulgent approach to the repertoire respectively. Certain changes in fashion are documented, such as the popularity of the fast *mākhūrī* rhythmic mode and the vogue for the *ṭunbūr* (long-necked lute). Instrumental music was limited to preludes and accompanying the singer, but the best instrumentalists, such as Manṣūr Zalzal, the lutenist, and Barṣawmā, the flautist, were much respected. Among the great singers of the period were Ibn Jāmiʿ, Ibrāhīm **al-Mawṣilī**, Mukhāriq, ʿAmr ibn Bāna (who was the son of a *kātib*), ʿAlluwayh and the prima donnas ʿArīb and Shāriya.

As in the Umayyad period, there is little evidence to support theories of musical fashion having influenced the development of poetry, and for the same reasons. The rare instances of a mediocre poet owing his standing to his regular co-operation with a famous singer-composer, like Ibrāhīm ibn Sayāba with Ibrāhīm and Isḥāq **al-Mawṣilī**, are the exception, not the rule. If musicians turned to contemporary poetry for their songs – and some composers, such as Isḥāq al-Mawṣilī, had a preference for older verse – this must be ascribed to a preference for texts produced in the same milieu in which they themselves were working, a milieu in which wine and love were perennial occasions for artistic inspiration.

As well as the collections of songs made by Isḥāq al-Mawṣilī and others, the third/ninth century saw the appearance of the first theoretical work on music by the philosopher **al-Kindī**; he and later writers, of whom the most important is Abū Naṣr **al-Fārābī** (d. 339/950), treated tonality and the rhythmic cycles fundamental in Arabic music, incorporating aspects of Greek theory as well as indigenous Arabic concepts. An important book on the art of singing, by **al-Ḥasan ibn Aḥmad ibn ʿAlī al-Kātib** (?fourth/tenth century), has survived.

Another genre of writings on music which appears in the third/ninth century is that of the tracts condemning it on religious grounds; the first to do so was **Ibn Abī al-Dunyā** (d. 281/894). He and his successors regarded entertainment music, associated with wine-drinking, *qiyān*, homosexuals and love poetry, as reprehensible, although the orthodox Muslim attitude to other forms of music, for instance connected with ceremonies, was more permissive.

That condemnation of music does not seem to have been very effective can be gathered from references to musicians and singers in later sources. Although there is nothing in the period after the fourth/tenth century to rival **Abū al-Faraj al-Iṣbahānī**'s *Kitāb al-Aghānī* for coverage of the world of song, entertainment music continued to be part of court life, as is shown, for instance, by the fact that a major theorist of the ninth/fifteenth century, ʿAbd al-Qādir ibn Ghaybī, was a singer at court in **Baghdād** and Samarkand. Nor is there any reason to believe that musical life declined after the fourth/tenth century, though hardly anything is known about the relationship between music and poetry. Even today famous singers in the Arab world sometimes turn to famous poets for their texts; the Egyptian Muḥammad ʿAbd al-Wahhāb's performances of Aḥmad **Shawqī**'s poems, and the Lebanese Fayrūz's of Jubrān Khalīl **Jubrān**'s are only the most obvious examples.

Text editions

Abu Naṣr al-Fārābī, *Kitāb al-mūsīqī al-kabīr*, Ghaṭṭās ʿA.M. Khashaba (ed.), Cairo (1967).

al-Ḥasan ibn Aḥmad ibn ʿAlī al-Kātib, *La Perfection des connaissances musicales*, Amnon Shiloah (trans, with comm.), Paris (1972).

Ibn Abī al-Dunyā, *Dhamm al-malāhī*, in *Tracts on Listening to Music*, J. Robson (ed. and trans.), London (1938), 1–64.

Grande traité de la musique. La musique arabe, vols. 1 and 2, Rodolphe Erlanger (trans.), Paris (1930, 1935).

Kamāl adab al-ghināʾ, Ghaṭṭās ʿA.M. Khashaba (ed.), Cairo (1975).

Further reading

Bencheikh, J.E., 'Les musiciens et la poésie: Les écoles d'Isḥâq al-Mawṣilî (m. 225 H.) et d'Ibrâhîm Ibn al-Mahdî (m. 224 H.)', *Arabica* 22 (1975), 114–52.

Farmer, Henry George, *A History of Arabian Music to the XIII Century*, London (1929, rpt 1973).

al-Kholy, S.A., *The Function of Music in Islamic Culture in the Period up to 1100 A.D.*, Cairo (1984).

Neubauer, Eckhard, *Musiker am Hof der frühen ʿAbbâsiden*, Frankfurt (1965).

Sawa, George Dimitri, *Music Performance Practice in the Early ʿAbbâsid Era 132–320 AH/750–932 AD*, Toronto (1989).

Stigelbauer, Michael, *Die Sängerinnen am ʿAbbâsidenhof um die Zeit des Kalifen al-Mutawakkil*, Vienna (1975).

Wright, O., 'Music and verse', in *CHALUP*, 433–59.

See also: music and poetry

H. KILPATRICK

sīra literature

Sīra (pl. *siyar*) means 'biography'. *Sīrat al-awwalīn* (see ***Legends of the Elders***) were the histories of the ancients. The lives of the Persian kings were known to the Arabs as the *siyar al-mulūk*, and they probably influenced the Arab *sīra* genre. Al-Naḍr ibn al-Ḥārith, who had lived for a long time at **Ḥīra**, recounted the deeds of Rustam and Isfandyār to the Meccans of the Prophet's time. **Ibn al-Nadīm** listed in his *Fihrist* about thirty Arabic *siyar* known at his time (fourth/tenth century). *Al-sīra* became the biography *par excellence* of the Prophet **Muḥammad** with *Kitāb al-sīra wa-al-mubtada' wa-al-maghāzī* (*The Book of the Biography and the Beginning of the Campaigns*, one of the titles by which the work is known), by Muḥammad **Ibn Isḥāq**, which has come down to us in the version (*riwāya*) of 'Abd al-Malik **Ibn Hishām**. The term does not appear with this meaning in the **Koran**, while in ***ḥadīth*** literature its plural form means 'military campaigns'. *Sīra*, according to Muḥibb al-Dīn al-Khaṭīb, is 'the written version (*tadwīn*) of the Prophet's vicissitudes in his *ghazawāt* and the recording in historical texts of Islamic *jihād*'s early struggles'. In his intervention on the *Sīrat Rasūl Allāh* Ibn Hishām selects passages and annotates the text. In a literary perspective the work represents a noteworthy example of Arabic historical prose; its prestige, however, is determined by the content. It incorporates many poems; much of the verse was composed by the Prophet's panegyrist, **Ḥassān ibn Thābit**, and the *Sīra* ends with a long poem of lament by him. It is this poetical component, with its interpolations and errors of metre and **grammar**, that has been a cause of puzzlement from early times; recent studies suggest evaluating these poems in the perspective of oral poetry and its formulaic character. The *Sīra*'s content has been adopted in the works of historians and biographers like **al-Ṭabarī** and **Ibn Sa'd**, who also drew on other versions. There have been important commentaries on the work, e.g. *al-Rawḍ al-unuf* by al-Suhaylī (d. 581/1185). Conspicuous among later compilations is the biography of the Prophet known as *al-Sīra al-Shāmiyya* by Muḥammad Ibn Yūsuf al-Ṣāliḥī (d. 942/1535). A ramification of the *sīra* genre is constituted by biographies of the Prophet's Companions, transmitters of traditions, scholars and Imāms, ending up in the *ṭabaqāt* ('classes') genre. There have also been biographies of single sultans, for example *al-Rawḍ al-zāhir* by **Ibn Shaddād** (d. 684/1285), a life of the **Mamlūk** Baybars.

Siyar sha'biyya is the definition of Arab folk romances, which were very popular in the **Ayyūbid** and Mamlūk periods (see also **epic poetry**, ***malāḥim***). The first *siyar* were formed round an early nucleus of poems, around the eighth or ninth century. They are part of a narrative tradition comprising *ayyām al-'Arab* (**Battle Days**) *maghāzī* and ***futūḥ***. The most important epic cycles recount the deeds of **'Antar**, **Banū Hilāl**, **Zīr Sālim**, **Sayf ibn Dhī Yazan**, **Dhāt al-Himma**, al-Ẓāhir **Baybars**, Fīrūzshāh, **Ḥamza al-Bahlawān**. ***Qiṣṣa*** is sometimes used as a synonym of *sīra* but, like ***dīwān***, it more usually refers to an episode or single story within the cycle. These *siyar* have assimilated local legends and motifs typical of fairy-tales. Their setting is that of the *samar*, or narration by poets and story-tellers during the evening vigil. The dialogues between characters are in verse, while the descriptions and the narrator's comments are generally in prose, prefaced by *qāla al-rāwī* ('the narrator said'). Contributions to this literature have come from anonymous poets, professional story-tellers, collectors (and inventors) of legends and heroic deeds. The different *siyar* have characteristics of their own. In some, e.g. the *Sīrat Banī Hilāl*, the dynamic character of the narrative tradition is more marked; some, like the *Sīrat al-Zīr Sālim*, preserve more archaic connotations; in some the figure of an 'author' and a period may be glimpsed, as in the *Sīrat al-Malik al-Ẓāhir* or the *Sīrat Sayf*; the *Sīrat 'Antar* shows more signs of intervention by obscure compilers with some claims to literary merit (the work is attributed to **al-Aṣma'ī**). The story-tellers active in coffeehouses, sometimes supported by a written text, and the *shu'arā'* ('poets' specializing in the Hilali deeds) are almost always professionals. This literature has been condemned by jurists, who discouraged scribes from copying it, and snubbed by men of letters because of the vernacular language that characterizes it.

The *siyar sha'biyya* are sited in a 'critical netherland of Middle Arabic and dialect non-literature' (B. Connelly). They are currently the object of new interest on the part of some Arab scholars, and also of reappraisal – coloured by a tinge of nationalism – in the perspectives of literature and folklore. It is Fārūq Khūrshīd's view that the *sīra* represents the *riwāya umm* (literally, 'the mother romance'), so constituting one of the original sources of Arab contemporary romances.

Further reading

Abdel-Meguid, A., 'A survey of the terms used in Arabic for "narrative" and "story"', *IQ* 1 (1954), 195–204.
Canova, G. 'Gli studi sull'epica popolare araba', *OM* 57 (1977), 211–26.
Connelly, B., *Arab Folk Epic and Identity*, Berkeley (1986).
Ghazoul, F.J., *The Arabian Nights: A Structural Analysis*, Cairo (1980), 69–89.
Grignaschi, M., 'La *Nihāyatu-l-'Arab fī aḫbāri-l-Furs wa-l-'Arab*', *BEO* 22 (1969), 15–67, 26 (1973), 83–184.
Heath, P., 'A critical review of modern scholarship on *Sīrat 'Antar ibn Shaddād* and the popular *Sīra*', *JAL* 15 (1984), 19–44.
Khūrshīd, F., *Aḍwa' 'alā al-sīra al-sha'biyya*, Cairo (1964).
Khūrshīd, Fārūq and Dhihnī, Maḥmūd, *Fann kitābat al-sīra al-sha'biyya*, Cairo (1961).
Lyons, M.C., *The Arabian Epic*, 3 vols, Cambridge (1995).
Madeyska, D., 'The language and structure of the *Sīra*', *QSA* 9 (1991), 193–218.
——, *Poetyka siratu, Studiom o arabskim romansie rycerskim*, Warsaw (1993).
Marcos Marín, F., *Poesía narrativa árabe y épica hispánica*, Madrid (1971).
Pantůček, S., *Das Epos über den Westzug del Banu Hilal*, Prague (1970).
Petráček, K., 'Volkstümliche Literatur', in *GAP*, vol. 2, 228–41.
Sulaymān, Mūsā, *al-Adab al-qaṣaṣī 'inda al-'Arab*, Beirut (1950).

G. CANOVA

See also: biography, medieval; epic poetry; *futūh*; Muḥammad the Prophet

al-Sīrāfī (*c.*290–368/*c.*903–79)

Abū Sa'īd al-Ḥasan ibn 'Abd Allāh al-Sīrāfī was a jurist and grammarian. After studies of philology and all the religious disciplines (including the legal applications of mathematics and astronomy), he settled in **Baghdad**, where he was appointed *qāḍī* and taught Ḥanafī law and **grammar**. All of his works are on grammar, following the 'Basrian' school of **Sībawayhi**; he also wrote a history of the teaching tradition of the school. An extensive commentary (*sharḥ*) of the *Kitāb Sībawayh* is his main work, and the most prestigious commentary of the *Kitāb* ever written. Although well versed in some of the mathematical sciences, he resented the intrusion of Aristotelian hermeneutic and methodology into contemporary grammar, and in a debate in the year 326/937–8, recounted by Abū Ḥayyān **al-Tawḥīdī**, he refuted the claims of the Christian translator and commentator of Aristotelian logic, Abū Bishr **Mattā ibn Yūnus**: there is no universal logic (*manṭiq*) revealing absolute truth, but the only way to 'logical speech' (*nuṭq*) is through the grammar of a particular language.

Text editions

Abū Ḥayyān al-Tawḥīdī, *Kitāb al-Imtā' wa-al-mu'ānasa*, A. Amīn and A. al-Zayn (eds), Cairo (1939–44), vol. 1, 107–29. (On the debate with Abū Bishr Mattā, see art. 'Mattā ibn Yūnus', with references.)
Akhbār al-naḥwiyyīn al-Baṣriyyīn, F. Krenkow (ed.), Beirut and Paris (1936).
Sharḥ Kitāb Sībawayh, Ramaḍān 'Abd-al-Tawwāb *et al.* (eds), Cairo (1986ff.). See also *Kitāb Sībawayh*, 'Abd-al-Salām M. Hārūn (ed.), Cairo (1966–77), in the notes.

G. ENDRESS

Sīrat Abī Zayd see Banū Hilal, romance of

Sīrat 'Antar see 'Antar, romance of

Sīrat Banī Hilāl see Banū Hilāl, romance of

Sīrat Dhāt al-Himma see Dhāt al-Himma, romance of

Sīrat al-Ẓāhir Baybars see Baybars, Romance of

Sirr al-asrār

Many works falsely ascribed to **Aristotle** were translated into Arabic, but none enjoyed the popularity of the *Sirr al-asrār* (*Secret of Secrets*). This was supposedly translated by Yaḥyā ibn al-Biṭrīq (**Eutychius**) into Syriac and thence into Arabic in the tenth century CE. The work consists of a letter from Aristotle to

Alexander the Great, giving the latter advice on the principles of kingship and in that respect it falls into the pattern of the **Mirror for Princes** literary form so popular in both the Islamic and Christian medieval period. The reported correspondence deals with advice as to how the king should select his advisers, what he should eat, how he should comport himself, and so on, and this probably reflects the original Greek text. It seems that much additional material was added later, within the context of Islamic culture, since the full text resembles an encyclopaedia rather than an exchange of letters. In addition to moral and political advice there is a compilation of diverse ideas and speculations concerning astrology, physiognomy, alchemy, magic and medicine. This proved to be a potent mixture, and the work had an extensive reception not only in the Islamic world but in Europe as well: there are more than five hundred copies of Latin manuscripts of the text, as well as many translations into more than thirteen different languages. The work even had a significant influence upon Russian culture.

The work's varied content meant that it proved useful to readers with very diverse interests. So, for example, **Fakhr al-Dīn al-Rāzī** could study with interest the medical parts, while Roger Bacon could reflect upon the Hermetic content. The provenance of the work is as mysterious as its name, and the story has it that it was only discovered by Eutychius by chance while searching for the *Politics* of Aristotle. Its popularity only went into decline with the general abeyance of medieval Aristotelianism in the early sixteenth century CE. In the Islamic world it was very widely studied, and many of the attributions to Greek thinkers come from this source. There is no doubt that much of the writing in Arabic on the wide range of subjects covered by the *Sirr al-asrār* was informed by that text. It served less as a source of definite doctrines that were to be accepted uncritically than of ideas with an eminent provenance which could be taken up, discussed, elaborated and developed. As such, it proved to be a useful aid to creative thought, as one might expect of a combination of the occult, political and natural sciences. It illustrates how, during the medieval period, the distinction between magic and science was far less rigid than later came to be the case. Although the *Sirr al-asrār* incorporates familiar literary forms, its status as a compilation of quite disparate elements made it a rather unique document, whatever version one looks at, and it was treated with great respect for a long period of Islamic and European cultural history.

Text edition

'Risalat Arisṭāṭālīs lil-Iskandar fī al-siyāsa', *Al-Machriq* 10 (1907), 311–19.

Further reading

Grignaschi, M., 'Les 'Rasā'il 'Arisṭāṭālīsa 'ilā-l-Iskandar' de Sālim Abū-l-'Alā' et l'activité culturelle à l'époque omayyade', *BEO* 19 (1965–6), 7–83.

Manzalaoui, M., 'The pseudo-Aristotelian *Kitāb Sirr al-asrār*: facts and problems', *Oriens* 23–24 (1974), 146–257.

Ryan, W. and Schmitt, C. (eds), *Pseudo-Aristotle, the Secret of Secrets: Sources and Influences*, London (1982).

O. LEAMAN

See also: Alexander the Great; Aristotle

al-Sizjī, Abū Ya'qūb *see* Abū Ya'qūb al-Sizjī

Spain

Much like Christopher Columbus's accounts of the marvels and riches he encountered in the New World, the early Arab accounts of the Iberian Peninsula speak of a green and fertile land and of jewels and treasures dating back to the time of Solomon. The almost eight centuries of Arab–Islamic civilization in that land, called *Spania* or *Hispania* by the Romans, named al-Andalus by the Arabs, are still marked by the breathtaking Great Mosque of Córdoba, the Giralda in Seville, and the Alhambra in Granada, as well as countless other buildings. Al-Andalus is remembered for its great philosophers, such as **Ibn Rushd** (Averroës) and **Maimonides**, its mystics, its poets. If for many centuries al-Andalus was mainly the province of study for a handful of specialists, a curiosity for tourists to southern Spain, a figure of loss in the Arab world, in the past fifty years it has excited ever-increasing attention. In an idealization not unworthy of those early Arab geographers, al-Andalus has become – at least in the popular imagination represented by historical novels and coffee-table books – a symbol of multicultural harmony, an oasis of culture and refinement in a medieval Europe still mired in superstition and ignorance.

Yet the question of cross-fertilization of cultures, of a *convivencia* of Muslims, Christians and Jews, is not merely a modern-day fashion. It is indeed the central issue in the history of al-Andalus, for its political fortunes rose and fell in relationship to its ability to minimize ethnic factionalism and forge a spirit of common enterprise. Even so, modern scholarship all too often projects current national and linguistic boundaries into the past, separating cultures and literatures that were deeply interwoven. Still, as in so many other times and places, the link between political stability and artistic creation is ambiguous and often paradoxical and, as we shall see, literary production in al-Andalus seems to flourish precisely at the moments of greatest chaos.

Historical overview

In the late seventh and early eighth centuries CE the Visigothic rulers of the Iberian Peninsula were consumed with problems of succession, the tax burden on the population was high, and civil unrest and revolts were commonplace. Thus in 92/711, when the governor of North Africa, Mūsā ibn Nuṣayr, sent his lieutenant Ṭāriq ibn Ziyād and a modest number of troops to the Peninsula, the Muslim forces encountered little resistance. In some places they were received as liberators and there was a good deal of popular collaboration in the overthrow of the Visigoths. Many Arabic historical accounts tell how Jewish communities – which had chafed under oppressive legal measures under the Visigoths, including a decree of forced conversion and severe restrictions on their economic activities – were especially helpful to the new rulers. By 97/716 Mūsā's forces had occupied most of the Peninsula, with the notable exception of the northwest. The period of expansion and consolidation finally came to a close in 114/732 when Charles Martel defeated the Arab forces in the Battle of Poitiers.

For the first few decades of Islamic rule, the government was under the control of the caliph in **Damascus**. The conflicts that attended the **ʿAbbāsid** overthrow of the **Umayyad** regime led to a decentralization of power, with the curious result that in 139/756, ʿAbd al-Raḥmān ibn Muʿāwiya, a young Umayyad prince who had fled the newly installed ʿAbbāsids, gathered enough local support to declare himself amīr of al-Andalus. The Umayyad emirate, roughly one and a half centuries long, was marked by the growing Arabization and Islamization of the indigenous population as well as by outbreaks of ethnic conflict.

During his long reign (912–61), ʿAbd al-Raḥmān III quelled dissent and unified al-Andalus under his control, and won several decisive victories over the Christian kingdoms of León and Navarra. In 929, in a largely symbolic challenge to his rivals in **Baghdad** and Qayrawan, he declared himself caliph and Commander of the Faithful. The new caliph and his successor, al-Ḥakam II, were especially masterful in balancing power among the different ethnic and religious groups and fostered a period of unity and economic prosperity which came to an end less than a century later with the death of ʿAbd al-Malik al-Muẓaffar in 1008. The caliphate crumbled in the quarter-century of chaos and civil war that followed. In 1031 it was abolished and al-Andalus fragmented into the Taifa (Ar. *ṭāʾifa*) kingdoms. These tiny states were in constant flux, boundaries shifting, principalities merging and breaking apart. Their rivalries allowed the Christian forces to the North to make military advances; the fall of Toledo in 1085 was an especially significant and symbolic loss. The weak and mortally threatened Taifa kings were forced to appeal several times to the Almoravids of North Africa for military support. Finally, their leader, Yūsuf ibn Tāshfīn, enraged at the antagonism between the Andalusian leaders and at evidence that they were co-operating with the Christians, deposed them one by one and took control of al-Andalus in 1091.

Although there were several decades of prosperity under the Almoravids, the military pressure exerted by the Christian kingdoms continued to grow, and increasing numbers of *mozárabes* – Christians living under Islamic rule – moved to the North. The Almoravids faced increasing attack in North Africa as well, and their persecution of Ṣūfī leaders heightened dissatisfaction among the populace. The Almoravid regime finally fell to the Almohads in 1145, although it was not until 1173 that they established near-complete control over what remained of al-Andalus. Discord among the Christian kingdoms of Castile, León, Navarra and Portugal in the second half of the twelfth century stalled the advances of the first half and reached the point that on occasion the Christian kingdoms would ally themselves with the Almohads against their rivals. Under Papal pressure Christian unity was established early in the thirteenth century and in 1212 the Almohads were dealt a decisive defeat by Alfonso VIII of Castile in the Battle of Las Navas de Tolosa. The Christian surge continued. Córdoba fell in 1236; after a two-year siege, Seville fell in 1248.

Only the tiny principality of Granada was left. The weakness of the Almohads had allowed Muḥammad ibn Yūsuf ibn Aḥmad ibn Naṣr to establish the independent kingdom centred around Granada. The Naṣrid state slowly diminished, surviving mainly through strategic alliances and with costly tribute paid alternately to its North African neighbours and the Christian kingdoms to the North. The marriage of Ferdinand and Isabel in 1479 brought about the union of Castile and Aragon that fuelled the final drive against the isolated Granadan kingdom. The capitulations signed by Muḥammad XII (Boabdil) in 1492 marked the end of al-Andalus.

Literature

Literary historians struggle to provide a clear narrative of the establishment of a peculiarly Andalusian literary sensibility and identity. There can be little doubt that literary values in the early period of Muslim rule, lasting until the early tenth century, came from the East. During the emirate and well into the caliphate, almost all of the eminent jurists travelled to the East to complete their education. The arrival at court in Córdoba in 822 of the musician **Ziryāb** (d. 857) – whose innovations included adding a fifth string to the lute, and who was considered the arbiter of style in matters ranging from clothing to cuisine – is alternately interpreted as a sign of al-Andalus's continuing dependence on the East or as symbolic of a westward shift in trend-setting.

Some of the reluctance to break with eastern models is clearly related to the problem of regional identity in a culture of *ʿArabiyya*, that is to say, a culture that places a high value on the proper use of Arabic and the models of Arabic usage: the **Koran** and the pre-Islamic poets. Both Arabs and new converts (*muwalladūn*) shared what might be called an 'anxiety of influence' living in a place far west of the defining cultural centre. The Arabs were actually a small minority of the population – most of the Berber soldiers who settled in al-Andalus were themselves recently, and imperfectly, Arabized – and the prevalence of intermarriage made it all the more important to be vigilant against corruption of the language. The new converts – many of whom faked an Arabic lineage – also sought to master a 'pure' Arabic. Jews and even Christians vied in their mastery of the language, as Alvarus, the ninth-century bishop of Córdoba, complains in his oft-quoted lament that the Christian youth were 'intoxicated with Arab elegance' (Watt and Cachia, 56). The Iraqi philologist **al-Qālī**, who arrived at court in Córdoba in 941, firmly established the study of **grammar** and lexicography there and presumably endeavoured to stamp out some of the Andalusian ill usage of the language. In the same century, the philologist al-Zubaydī al-Ishbīlī wrote a treatise on the grammatical errors and mispronunciation of Andalusian Arabic.

Perhaps tellingly, the works that most clearly celebrate Andalusian writers begin to appear as al-Andalus is receding as a military and political power, and are marked by the nostalgia of men who have personally borne some of that loss. **Ibn Bassām** (d. 542/1147) composed his *al-Dhakhīra* (*The Treasury*), now an indispensable source of Hispano-Arabic writings, after fleeing his hometown of Santarem when it fell to Alfonso V. So too, **Ibn al-Khaṭīb**'s (d. 776/1374) important collection of *muwashshaḥāt*, *Jaysh al-tawshīḥ*, appeared after he was exiled to North Africa.

Although Arabic poetry had occupied a place of great importance since pre-Islamic times, literary prose was much slower to develop. It sprang from oratory and from the letters and documents written at court, and became more ornate and more concerned with stylistics. Writers competed in elegance of expression, often employing rhymed prose (*sajʿ*) and recondite vocabulary. **Artistic prose** eventually was cultivated for its own sake and writings were collected in books of ***adab***, an equivocal term generally defined as spanning the breadth of knowledge of a cultured person, including religion, poetry, grammar, history, philosophy and the natural sciences.

As would be the case in the development of the Romance vernaculars, one of the crucial steps in the development of Arabic prose came in the form of a translation. ʿAbd Allāh **Ibn al-Muqaffaʿ**'s (d. 139/756) ***Kalīla wa-Dimna***, translated into Arabic from the Persian, was a

Mirror for Princes expressed through animal tales. Considered a model of elegance and widely circulated, it was translated into a number of languages in thirteenth-century al-Andalus: into Hebrew several times, into Castilian by King Alfonso *el sabio* and into Latin by John of Capua as the *Directorium Vitae Humanae*.

Another important development in Arabic prose composition was the establishment of the ***maqāma*** genre. **Badīʿ al-Zamān al-Hamadhānī** (d. 398/1007) and **al-Ḥarīrī** (d. 516/1122) both drew upon popular tales of tricksters and swindlers and fashioned them into a series of brief scenes linked by the same quick-witted rogue and gullible narrator.

Al-Ḥarīrī's *Maqāmāt* were much admired and imitated in al-Andalus and attracted the attention of critics and scholars, including Aḥmad al-Sharīshī (d. 619/1222), whose *Sharḥ al-Maqāmāt* is still considered the most important of the commentaries. The *maqāma* form was also adopted by Jewish writers in Spain, most notably Judah ben Solomon al-Ḥarīzī (d. 622/1225) who translated al-Ḥarīrī's work into Hebrew. He later expressed regret that in having done so he had served to exalt the Arabic language, and then proceeded to compose his own Hebrew *maqāmāt*, which he called the *Tahkemoni*. By translating and imitating al-Ḥarīrī's model, al-Ḥarīzī circumvented the Andalusian Arabic *maqāma* tradition which had focused on the idea of elegant expression and largely abandoned the trickster motif. Several critics have suggested that the Hebrew *maqāma* may have played an important role in the emergence of the Spanish picaresque novel in the sixteenth-century.

The little Andalusī poetry that has survived from the eighth and ninth centuries is conventional in themes, images and verse patterns. While in the East great poets such as **Abū Nuwās**, **Abū Tammām**, **al-Buḥturī** and **al-Mutanabbī** had already been canonized, poetry in al-Andalus had yet to enter its golden age. Among the early notables were Yayḥā **al-Ghazāl** (d. 251/865), a dashing figure who served as ʿAbd al-Raḥmān II's ambassador to Constantinople. His verse displays an unlaboured diction and a direct and intimate mode of address that seems to typify much Andalusian verse. **Ibn ʿAbd Rabbih** (d. 328/940) is remembered for his *al-ʿIqd al-farīd* (*The Unique Necklace*), a book of *adab* basically drawn from eastern sources. He wrote on diverse subjects, including many poems of ***muʿāraḍa*** on eastern models; his lengthy historical *urjūza* which relates the caliph's military exploits is noteworthy due to the rarity of narrative poetry in Arabic. Yusūf ibn Hārūn al-Ramādī (d. 403/1013) also exhibits an almost conversational style, although at times he writes with grandiose phraseology. In an unsuccessful attempt to secure his release from prison, he wrote a book of poems describing every type of bird known to him. Unfortunately the work is now lost, so scholars can only speculate as to whether it is an early expression of the type of descriptive nature poetry that would become so important in al-Andalus, or simply an invocation of the well-established trope of bird as a symbol of freedom or perhaps both of these things. (See further **nature, in classical poetry**.)

One of the most celebrated Arabic poets of this time was **Ibn Hāni'** (d. 362/973), who was known as the Mutanabbī of the West. Primarily a panegyrist, his baroque and grandiloquent style was in keeping with the literary fashion of the East. He cultivated a reputation as a libertine and was forced to flee al-Andalus after being accused of heresy. **Ibn Darrāj al-Qasṭallī** (d. 421/1030) also employed a high rhetoric and difficult style, and it might be said that these two poets represent a counter to the current of direct and unlaboured expression seen among other Andalusian writers.

It was during the caliphal period that Jews began to occupy high posts in the government and play an active role in cultural life. In the preceding centuries Jews had undergone a sociolinguistic transformation, becoming urbanized and Arabized. Ḥasday ben Shaprut (*c.*915–970), a doctor and diplomat in the court of ʿAbd al-Raḥmān III and al-Ḥakam II, is not only testament to the growing influence of the Jewish community but was also instrumental in promoting a secular Hebrew literary culture modelled on that of the Arabs. He was patron to several poets, including Dunash ben Labraṭ, who began to experiment with writing poetry in Hebrew according to the Arabic system of quantitative metre. Although this innovation was initially quite controversial – critics claimed it distorted Hebrew syntax – it was quickly accepted and was ultimately adopted not only for secular poetry but for religious verse as well. Dunash is also said to be the first Hebrew poet to adopt both the structure and themes of the Arabic ***qaṣīda***. He was followed by countless other poets who joined Arabic poetic norms with Biblical Hebrew diction and imagery. It was precisely that fusion that fuelled what is known as the 'golden age' of Hebrew letters (950–1150) illuminated by figures such as Ibn Daud, Judah Halevi and **Moses Ibn Ezra**.

The political instability and constant intrigue during the *fitna* and the Taifa kingdoms often led to drastic changes of fortune for poets and scholars. However, the different courts competed with each other in attracting the finest poets and scholars in a manner not unlike that of the city-states of Renaissance Italy, the end result being a period of enormous literary quality and productivity.

As Seville grew more powerful, incorporating some of the neighbouring states, it became a scholarly and literary centre. The generosity of the ʿAbbādī court attracted philosophers, astrologers, poets and other intellectuals. **Ibn ʿAmmār** (d. 479/1086) rose from humble origins and by virtue of his charm and eloquence won the patronage and friendship of **al-Muʿtamid ibn ʿAbbād** (1040–91), the poet–king of Seville. Yet he ultimately conspired against his benefactor, and was killed violently by the king's own hand. He writes mainly of his own experience, eschewing elaborate description and aestheticism. For his part al-Muʿtamid is cast as one of the great tragic figures of al-Andalus. Raised in an atmosphere of wealth, splendour and literary refinement, it was his lot to be deposed and banished to North Africa by Yūsuf ibn Tāshfīn, the Berber leader of the Almoravids in North Africa. Another element of romance in his life is the story of his love for Iʿtimād, a humble girl who captured his attention by finishing a verse with which he had challenged his friend Ibn ʿAmmār. His early poems celebrating a life of comfort, love and the pleasures of wine stand in opposition to the many later expressions of exile and bitter lament.

In addition to numerous writings on the Islamic sciences, **Ibn Ḥazm** (d. 456/1064) is remembered for his *Ṭawq al-ḥamāma* (*The Neck-ring of the Dove*), a systematic examination of love relationships, drawing on his own life experiences and those of his friends. Starting from the Neoplatonic idea that love is the union of souls divided by their corporality, he goes on to integrate the medical tradition of melancholia with certain Ṣūfī ideas. Ibn Ḥazm's book – written in prose punctuated by many poems – covers topics such as love at first sight, the vicissitudes of love, proscribed practices and the benefits of sexual abstinence.

The verse of Ibn Ḥazm's close friend and fellow poet **Ibn Shuhayd** (d. 426/1035) reflects the political turbulence that swirled around him. It was probably during a period of exile in Málaga that he wrote his famous *Risālat al-tawābiʿ wa-al-zawābiʿ* (*The Treatise of Familiar Spirits and Demons*), in which the poet is visited by his inspiring *jinn* who takes him on a journey to meet the *jinn* of poets past and present. Ibn Shuhayd thus engages in a sort of poetic competition with many of them, and records his ideas on poetry, comments on great poets of the past, and snipes at many of his contemporaries. Many of his most moving poems were written as he reconsidered love and death, paralysed by a stroke and slowly dying at the age of 43.

The most famous of the Andalusī poets is the Córdoban **Ibn Zaydūn** (d. 463/1090) who, like Ibn Shuhayd, was born to a prominent family and suffered the upheavals of his times. The verses that he wrote about his brief and tragic affair with the princess **Wallāda bint al-Mustakfī** (d. 484/1091?) define his literary persona. Of these, the most acclaimed is his *nūniyya*, in which he retraces their story, merging many archetypes of Arabic poetry – the tenderness of their love now vanished, the rival, the poet's constancy in the face of the beloved's betrayal – with an almost fairy-tale fascination with the trappings of royalty. Ibn Zaydūn was called 'the Buḥturī of the West' and his poetry is marked by its musicality and craftsmanship. Wallāda was a poet in her own right who entertained poets and intellectuals and paid no heed to those who criticized her lack of modesty. Although few of her poems are extant, we have several poems of sharp-tongued satire directed at Ibn Zaydūn (which, needless to say, only adds to the pathos surrounding the spurned lover).

The caliphal and Taifa periods also witnessed important developments in popular poetry. Al-Andalus was the birthplace of the ***muwashshaḥ***, a strophic poetic form which achieved great popularity and went on to be embraced by Hebrew poets in al-Andalus, and Arab poets throughout the Islamic world. The *muwashshaḥ* is characterized by its strophic form, which stands in contrast to the traditional monorhyme of the *qaṣīda*, and by its final strophe, the *kharja*, which employs non-classical Arabic diction, usually Andalusī colloquial. The discovery of some Hebrew and

Arabic *muwashshaḥāt* with varying amounts of Romance elements in their *kharja*s has excited a great deal of speculation about the origins of this form. The metre of these poems has also been the subject of much debate, with some critics arguing that it constitutes an extension of traditional Arabic **prosody**, while others promote the theory that it conforms to a Romance metrical system.

The Almoravids (1091–1145) introduced a fundamentalist regime that suppressed the secular arts. A few poets flourished, notably the great nature poet **Ibn Khafāja** (d . 533/1138). Turning away from the poems of love and pleasure of his youth, as he matured he sang of flowers, gardens, rivers and mountains. He is known for his linguistic dexterity and Jayyusi cites his originality of phraseology and syntax, his ability to transfer words from different semantic areas, and his use of verbal paradox among his many poetic gifts (see Jayyusi 1992, 367 ff.). His nephew, **Ibn al-Zaqqāq** (d. 529/1135), is also known as a nature poet. **Ibn ʿAbdūn** (late fifth–sixth/eleventh–twelfth century) wrote a useful account of life in Seville. Several of the great writers of *muwashshaḥāt* and ***zajal***s flourished during this time, including the master *washshāḥ* **al-Aʿmā** of Tudela (d. 520/1126), **Ibn Baqī** (d. 545/1150–1), and the pre-eminent *zajalist* **Ibn Quzmān** (d. 555/1160). (See further ***zajal***.)

Under the Almohads (1145–1223) there was a great revival of poetry. Notable figures include **al-Ruṣāfi** (Muḥammad ibn Ghālib), the converted Jew **Ibn Sahl** (d. 649/1251), who memorialized his conversion, first writing love-poems to an ephebe named Moses and later to another called Muḥammad, and **Ḥāzim al-Qarṭājannī** (d. 684/1285), whose work on the theory of poetry was also influential. A number of women poets arise at this time, most notably **Ḥafṣa bint al-Ḥājj al-Rukūniyya** (d. 586/1191) of Granada. Most of her poems are dedicated to her lover, the poet Abū Jaʿfar ibn Saʿīd, who was executed for his opposition to the Almohad regime. Rubiera Mata (1992, 110) has noted that in describing herself, using stock tropes of female beauty commonly used by male poets, she creates a startling effect. **Ibn Ṭufayl** (d. 581/1185) earned great fame with his **Ḥayy ibn Yaqẓān** (*Alive, Son of Awake*), a philosophical allegory about the search for truth and knowledge. Through careful observation and logic, the hero, who grows up on an uninhabited island, discovers the existence of God and his need for union with Him. In the second part of the book, Ḥayy is confronted with Asal, who teaches him human speech, then tells him of his religion, and they discover that they have reached the same conclusions through different paths. An important element in Ibn Ṭufayl's thought is the linking of philosophy with a mystical approach.

In a similar vein, the two Córdoban philosophers **Ibn Rushd** (Averroës) (d. 595/1198) and Mūsā ibn Maymūn (**Maimonides**) (d. 601/1204) endeavour to prove the compatibility between philosophy and revealed religion. Ibn Rushd, a student of Ibn Ṭufayl, fought to restore pure Aristotelianism in the face of earlier thinkers who had blended it with Neoplatonism, and he ardently defended speculative thought against its attackers. In his refutation of **al-Ghazzālī**'s *Tahāfut al-falāsifa* (*The Incoherence of the Philosophers*), the *Tahāfut al-Tahāfut* (*The Incoherence of 'The Incoherence'*), he argued that both faith and reason are valid paths to truth. Although Averroës did not gain many followers among Muslims, and his work marks the end of Arabic Aristotelianism, his writings were influential among the Christian scholastics and Jewish thinkers.

In his famous *Dalālat al-ḥā'irīn* (*Guide of the Perplexed*), Maimonides, the great Jewish doctor and theologian, attempts to point Jewish speculative thought more firmly towards Aristotelianism. Writing in **Judaeo-Arabic** (Arabic using Hebrew characters), and thoroughly influenced by **al-Fārābī** and other Islamic philosophers, he elaborates a system of elucidation to deal with the apparent anthropomorphism of the Hebrew Bible. The interpretation of the *Guide* is complicated by the author's declaration that he has designed his book to hide its true meaning from all but those who possess the wisdom not to be harmed by it.

Another towering figure of this era is the Ṣūfī mystic **Ibn al-ʿArabī** (d. 638/1240) of Murcia, who not only composed an abundance of lengthy and difficult religious treatises – at least 400 can be attributed with certainty – but also both classical and popular poetry. Among his major works are *al-Futūḥāt al-Makkiyya* (*Illuminations of Mecca*), an exhaustive exposition of Ṣūfī doctrine, and *Fuṣūṣ al-ḥikam* (*Bezels of Wisdom*), a treatise on the prophets from Adam to Muḥammad. His book of poems celebrating the love of Niẓām bint Makīn al-Dīn, the *Tarjumān al-ashwāq*, aroused a furor and he was forced to write a commentary on it explicating its religious meaning. He is also known as the first mystical poet to write *muwashshaḥāt*, and was followed in the religious use of popular poetic forms by another Andalusian, ʿAbd al-Ḥasan **al-Shushtarī**, whose *zajal*s and *muwashshaḥāt* are still sung by Ṣūfīs throughout the Arab world.

The polymath Lisān al-Dīn **Ibn al-Khaṭīb** (d. 776/1374) not only held high government posts but distinguished himself as a historian, philosopher, writer and poet. Although many of these texts have disappeared, we have titles for over sixty works including writings on medicine, Sufism and politics, as well as a history of the kingdom of Granada, an anthology of *muwashshaḥāt* including some of his own composition, a biographical dictionary of the literati of his time and his autobiography. The victim of political intrigues, accused of heresy by his former protégé turned rival, the poet **Ibn Zamrak** (d. 796/1393), he died strangled in prison. Although Ibn Zamrak's *dīwān* is lost, some of his poems have been preserved, and a number of them adorn the walls of the Alhambra. As court poet, most of his compositions were elegies, panegyrics and occasional poems.

As the Christian *Reconquista* continued its advances, culminating in the capitulation of the kingdom of Granada in 1492, many prominent and educated Muslims left the Peninsula. Even though the agreement signed between the Catholic Monarchs and Muḥammad XII (Boabdil) guaranteed Muslims the freedom to practise their religion and speak their language, the arrival in Granada of Cardinal Jiménez de Cisneros in 1499 marked the beginning of the end of those rights. The Inquisition burned Islamic books; insurrections followed. The punishment for the revolt was a 1503 decree ordering the Muslims of Granada to choose between conversion to Christianity or exile. With mosques and other centres of Arabic learning closed, the percentage of these *nuevos convertidos*, later known as Moriscos, literate in Arabic dwindled rapidly. The Moriscos attempted to preserve and pass on religious practice and doctrine, ***ḥadīth***, Morisco legends and folklore, writing them in ***aljamía*** or *aljamiado* – that is, in Castilian or other Romance vernaculars using Arabic characters. Words, phrases and passages in Arabic are often intercalated, and at times the *aljamiado* glosses the Arabic.

Most of the *aljamiado* texts that have survived are anonymous, and although the bulk of them deal with religious and legal matters, they also include prophecies (often of calamities to befall the Christians), poems, stories and short novels. Upon their expulsion from Spain in 1609, many Moriscos settled in North Africa. Yet, if they were rejected as not Spanish in Spain, they did not find ready acceptance among their fellow Muslims either. Perhaps once again as symbol of their separate Andalusī identity, the expelled Moriscos continued to write in Romance for a time, but using the Latin alphabet.

Further reading

General works

Two brief (if polemic) overviews are:

Fletcher, R., *Moorish Spain*, Berkeley (1992).

Watt, W.M., and Cachia, P., *A History of Islamic Spain*, Edinburgh (1965).

For more detailed treatment see:

Arié, R., *España musulmana (siglios XII–XV)*, Barcelona (1984).

Caro Baroja, J., *Los Moriscos del reino de Granada. Ensayo de historia social*, Madrid (1957).

Chejne, A., *Muslim Spain: Its History and Culture*, Minneapolis (1974).

——, *Islam and the West: the Moriscos, A Cultural and Social History*, Albany (1983).

Collins, R., *The Arab Conquest of Spain*, Cambridge MA (1989).

Convivencia: Jews, Muslims and Christians in Medieval Spain, Vivian B. Mann et al. (eds), New York (1992).

Domínguiz Ortiz, A., *Historia de los moriscos: vida y tragedia de una minoria*, Madrid (1985).

Glick, T.F., *Islamic and Christian Spain in the Early Middle Ages*, Princeton (1979).

Harvey, L.P., *Islamic Spain 1250–1500*, Chicago (1990).

Ibn Khaldūn, *The Muqaddimah: An Introduction to History*, F. Rosenthal (trans.), 3 vols, New York (1958).

Imamuddin, S.M., *Muslim Spain 711–1492A.D: A Sociological Study*, Leiden (1981).

Jayyusi, S.K., (ed.), *The Legacy of Muslim Spain*, Leiden (1992).

Lévi-Provençal, E., *Histoire de l'Espagne musulmane*, 3 vols, Paris (1950–3).

al-Maqqarī, *The History of the Mohammedan Dynasties in Spain*, P, de Gayangos (trans.), London (1840) (an abridged translation of his *Nafḥ al-ṭīb*).

Vernet Ginis, J. *La ciencia en el-Andalus*, Seville (1986).

Wasserstein, D., *The Rise and Fall of the Party-Kings: Politics and Society in Islamic Spain, 1002–1086*, Princeton (1985).

On Andalusian Arabic

Corriente, F., *Arabe andalusí y lenguas romances*, Madrid (1992)

——, *A Grammatical Sketch of the Spanish Arabic Dialect Bundle*, Madrid (1974).

On art and architecture

Dodds, J.D., *Architecture and Ideology in Early Medieval Spain*, University Park (1990).

——, (ed.), *Al-Andalus: The Art of Islamic Spain*, New York (1992).

Vernet Ginis, J., *Al-Andalus: el Islam en España*, Madrid and Barcelona (1984).

Literature

Benabu, Isaac (ed.), *Circa 1492: Proceedings of the Jerusalem Colloquium: Litterae Judaeorum in Terra Hispanica*, Jerusalem (1992).

de la Granja, F., *Maqāmas y risālas andaluzas*, Madrid (1976).

Garulo, T., *Diwan de las poetisas de al-Andalus*, Madrid (1986).

González Palencia, A., *Historia de la literatura arábigo-española*, 2nd edn, Barcelona (1945).

Menocal, M.R., *The Arabic Role in Medieval Literary History*, Philadelphia (1987).

——, *Shards of Love: Exile and the Origins of Lyric*, Durham, NC (1994).

Monroe, James T., *Hispano-Arabic Poetry: A Student Anthology*, Berkeley (1974).

Mujica Pinilla, *El collar de la paloma del alma: Amor sagrado y amor profano en la ensenanza de Ibn Hazm y de Ibn Arabi*, Madrid (1990).

Nykl, A.R., *Hispano-Arabic Poetry and its Relations with the Old Provençal Troubadours*, Baltimore (1946).

Pérès, H., *La poésie andalouse en arabe classique au XI siècle*, Paris (1953).

Rubiera Mata, M.J., *Bibliografia de la literatura árabe*, Alicante (1988).

Hispano-Hebraic literature

See the entry on Hebrew literature, relations with Arabic.

See also the entries for the individual authors cited.

L. ALVAREZ

story-telling

The antiquity of Arab story-telling is attested by the **Koran**, both in its condemnation of pagan entertainers and in its own reworking of ***Jāhiliyya*** legends and Biblical tales to construct moralizing narratives. The numerous genres of story-telling in the medieval era are catalogued in **Ibn al-Nadīm**'s tenth-century *Fihrist*, which also notes the ways in which tales from Babylonian, Persian and Indian sources were absorbed by Arabic narrative collections. A glimpse is offered us in the *Fihrist* of how one such collection was compiled: according to Ibn al-Nadīm, the **ʿAbbāsid** minister Muḥammad **al-Jahshiyārī** not only culled tales from manuscripts but also 'summoned to his presence the storytellers, from whom he obtained the best things about which they knew and which they did well'.

Throughout the medieval era the *ʿulamā'* viewed with suspicion the *quṣṣāṣ* or professional story-tellers who performed before large audiences especially in urban mosques. The subject matter of the reciters' speeches was unobjectionable: Koranic verses – often those concerning final judgement, hellfire, and the need to prepare for the afterlife – would be quoted and then illustrated with vivid anecdotes about well-known figures from scripture. Religious authorities acknowledged the popularity of these performances but warned against their doctrinal weakness: many *quṣṣāṣ* fabricated ***ḥadīth***, falsely ascribing utterances to the Prophet; others, influenced by Ṣūfī mysticism, mingled wine poetry and love stories with their sermons on the quest for divine union. The educated feared the sway over mosque crowds held by the *quṣṣāṣ*. To take one comic example: the thirteenth-century author **Ibn al-Jawzī** in his *Kitāb al-quṣṣāṣ* tells what happened to the celebrated Koran scholar ʿĀmir al-Shaʿbī when he interrupted a *qāṣṣ* during a Friday sermon to correct the speaker's faulty *ḥadīth* citation concerning the trumpet of Judgement Day. Encouraged by the reciter, the angry crowd pelted al-Shaʿbī with shoes and slippers till he acknowledged the *qāṣṣ* as correct. Ibn al-Jawzī understood the political implications of such power over the masses. Himself a scholar and preacher in the employ of the ʿAbbāsid government in **Baghdad**, he refrained from condemning the *quṣṣāṣ* as a class, drawing attention rather to the reciters' potential for educating the common people in their faith. But he insisted that each *qāṣṣ* meet certain standards of behaviour and education: sufficient training in orthodox Islamic law and scripture; moral integrity and the ability to resist the temptation to extract money from the audience; and the willingness to hold gatherings and preach only after being given permission by the government.

The public utterances recorded by Ibn al-Jawzī show the transition from *waʿẓ* (religious exhortation) to *qaṣaṣ* (narrative recitation/tale-telling) at the hands of popular reciters. His text illuminates the role played by the sermon genre in the history of Arab story-telling. This transition can be further illustrated by **al-Tha'labī**'s eleventh-century collection *Qiṣaṣ al-anbiyā'* (*Tales of the Prophets*). Drawing on the oral legendary traditions surrounding Koranic figures, the author quotes actual verses from the Koran but then weaves around each an entire vividly executed narrative. Note for instance Koran 37:100–107, comprising the very terse scriptural reference to Abraham's near-sacrifice of his son. Al-Tha'labī cites these verses but also dramatizes the scene with a wealth of visual detail missing from the Koran: we are treated to a description of the boy weeping, 'tears flowing down his cheeks', yet bravely urging his father to strike and obey Allah's command; Abraham approaches, binds his son, and presses the knife against his neck, only to have the weapon struck from his hand by divine agency at the last possible moment. In this redaction al-Tha'labī has retained the Koranic theme of *islām* (faithful obedience) enunciated in the Abraham tale but has elaborated it in such a way as to construct a narrative that maximizes the audience's experience of pleasurable suspense.

The *qāṣṣ*'s technique – quoting Koranic verses and then building a prose narrative around these sentences, while dramatizing the narrative with as much visual detail as possible so as to hold the audience's attention – can be discerned in a number of pietistic tales that comprise part of the ***Alf layla wa-layla***, the *Thousand and One* or *Arabian Nights*. One example is *The City of Brass*. The *Alf layla* redactor articulates his theme – God's deathless majesty contrasted with human evanescence, and our consequent need to prepare for the afterlife – through a series of exhortations (heavily influenced by Koranic phrasing) that proclaim the vanity of our attempts at constructing works of earthly splendour. The redactor merges these homilies with the story by presenting them as inscriptions carved on the walls of deserted palaces and encountered by the tale's protagonist, Mūsā ibn Nuṣayr. Mūsā leads a party of treasure-hunters who cross the Sahara, encounter demons and magical statues, and face various trials that determine whether the travellers have taken to heart the admonitory inscriptions found in the lost cities. In such stories the sermon has been made an integral part of the tale of wonder. Thus works such as *The City of Brass* can be considered the descendant of the narrative sermons preached by the early mosque story-tellers.

Story-telling as an oral performance medium has survived in the Arab Near East from the medieval era on into the late twentieth century, notwithstanding competition from the widespread publication of novels and increased literacy, as well as the advent of radio and television (recall Najīb **Maḥfūẓ**'s *Midaq Alley*, set in Cairo during World War 2, where the cafe-owner Kirsha installs a radio and dismisses the aged story-teller who once entertained patrons with narrative recitations). In the period 1978–80 Ibrahim Muḥawi and Sharif Kanaana collected some two hundred tales from Palestinian story-tellers currently active in the Galilee, Gaza and the West Bank. Bridget Connelly has shown that adventures from the ***sīra*** of the ***Banī Hilāl*** are still recited today in Upper Egypt by wandering poets who travel from village to village, performing at *mūlid*s (Muslim saints' festivals), weddings and circumcisions.

The importance of formulaic phrasing as an aid in public performance, attested by Parry and Lord with regard to Yugoslav folk singers, has also been demonstrated in Arab oral recitation. **Bedouin** poets of the Sinai and Negev recorded by Clinton Bailey employ verbal formulae and recurrent imagery in composing verses; and Muhawi and Kanaana argue that reciters of Palestinian folktales rely on 'verbal mannerisms and language flourishes not used in ordinary conversation', as well as introductory prose formulae which alert the audience that it is entering an imaginative realm distinct from that of the everyday. According to Connelly, Egyptian listeners are keenly sensitive to the proper use of conventional phrasing in recitals of *Sīrat Banī Hilāl*; any performer careless enough to hobble the story through the unfocused repetition of formulae which do not advance the narrative soon finds he has lost his audience.

Orality has left its mark on written forms of Arabic narrative literature, as can be seen in some *Alf layla* manuscripts, with their accumulation of repeated incidents, formulaic language phrased in ***saj'*** (rhymed prose), and colloquial spelling and diction. But as Ruth Finnegan has demonstrated, written literature in turn has often influenced modes of oral performance. Edward Lane described the ''Anātireh' of nineteenth-century **Cairo**, coffeehouse reciters who read aloud the 'romance of **'Antar**' from texts of the epic on the evenings of religious festivals. Muhawi and Kanaana tell of a contemporary Palestinian story-teller among the reciters they interviewed who has read various printed editions of oral narrative collections such as the *Sīrat Banī Hilāl* and the *Arabian Nights*, with the result that these texts 'have left an indelible mark on his work'. The boundary between oral and written literature is permeable; influence is mutual.

Text editions

Fihrist (Dodge), vol. 2, 712–24.
Ibn al-Jawzī, *Kitāb al-quṣṣāṣ wa'l-mudhakkirīn*, Merlin Swartz (ed. and trans.), Beirut (1971).

Further reading

Bailey, C., *Bedouin Poetry from Sinai and the Negev: Mirror of a Culture*, Oxford (1991).
Connelly, B., *Arab Folk Epic and Identity*, Berkeley (1986).
*EI*², arts 'Ḥikāya', 'Ḳāṣṣ', 'Ḳiṣṣa' (Ch. Pellat).
Finnegan, R., *Oral Poetry: Its Nature, Significance and Social Context*, Cambridge (1977).
Goldziher, I., 'The hadith as a means of edification and entertainment', *Muslim Studies*, C.R. Barber and S.M. Stern (trans.), London (1971), vol. 2, 145–63.
Lane, E.W., *The Manners and Customs of the Modern Egyptians*, London (1954).
Lord, A., *The Singer of Tales*, New York (1978).
Muhawi, I. and Kanaana, S., *Speak, Bird, Speak Again: Palestinian Arab Folktales*, Berkeley, CA (1989).
Pinault, D., *Story-telling Techniques in the Arabian Nights*, Leiden (1992).

D. PINAULT

See also: folklore; legends; oratory and sermons; popular literature

strophic poetry

Most classical Arabic poems have a single rhyme throughout, whereas the number of lines varies from one poem to another. Besides this monorhyme poetry, strophic forms such as *muzdawij* (see ***muzdawija***), *musammaṭ*, ***muwashshaḥ*** and ***zajal*** are also found.

The *musammaṭ*, with a common rhyme in the last line (*simṭ*) of each stanza (e.g. *aaaa bbba ccca* or *aaaaa bbbba cccca*), dates from the end of the second/eighth century and is considered to be the precursor of the *muwashshaḥ*. The latter form, which probably originated in **Spain** by the end of the third/ninth century, shows more intricate patterns, often with internal rhymes (rhyming schemes, e.g. *bbbaa cccaa dddaa* etc.; *cccab dddab eeeab*; *aa bbbaa cccaa dddaa*; or *abc dddabc eeeabc fffabc*). Over 90 per cent of *muwashshaḥ*s have five stanzas. The stanza, called *dawr* or *bayt*, consists of three or four *aghṣān* (sg. *ghuṣn*) and one line or more with common rhyme (*simṭ*, pl. *asmāṭ*; also *qufl*, pl. *aqfāl*). A *simṭ* line preceding the first stanza is called *maṭla'*. If such an opening line fails, the *muwashshaḥ* is called *aqra'* ('bald'); otherwise it is *tāmm* ('complete'). The poem is in classical Arabic, but ends with a *kharja* (or *markaz*) which may contain non-classical material, or in some cases be in Romance. The metre of the *muwashshaḥāt* is probably based on an extended *'arūḍ* system (see **prosody**), although other theories on its nature (stress-based, Romance scansion) have been advanced. The relationship between the *muwashshaḥ* and Romance poetry is in debate. The *muwashshaḥ* is used especially in singing. Among its subjects, comparable to those of classical poetry, the more lighter themes are especially favoured. *Zajal* also originated in Spain – probably by the end of the fifth/eleventh century – and employs non-classical Arabic. There are two types: (1) identical in everything with the *muwashshaḥ* except for its vernacular language; (2) the *zajal* proper, which has as its basic form *aa bbba ccca ddda*, etc., that is to say, the *asmāṭ* do not reproduce the scheme of the whole *maṭla'*, but half of it only, and it has no *kharja*. The number of stanzas can be much higher than in the *muwashshaḥ*. It has a greater variety of subjects including bohemian scenes in bawdy language. Its chief representative is **Ibn Quzmān** (d. 555/1160).

Further reading

Corriente, F. and Sáenz-Badillos, A. (eds), *Poesía estrófica*, Actas del Primer Congreso Internacional sobre Poesía Estrófica (...), Madrid (1991).
Stern, S.M., *Hispano-Arabic Strophic Poetry*, L.P. Harvey (ed.), Oxford (1974).
Zwartjes, O., *The Andalusian Xarjas: Poetry at the Crossroads of Two Systems?* Nijmegen (1995).

W. STOETZER

See also: *muwashshaḥ*; *zajal*

al-Subkī, Tāj al-Dīn (728–71/1327–69–70)

Tāj al-Dīn al-Subkī came from one of the great scholarly clans of the **Mamlūk** period and was the son of a well-known father, Tāqi al-Dīn al-Subkī, noted for his expertise in ***ḥadīth*** and in the religious sciences generally. Tāj al-Dīn held various teaching posts and was for a while the chief *qāḍī* in **Damascus**. He was a keen Shāfiʿī and among his thirty or more books is the *Ṭabaqāt al-kubrā*, a collection of biographies of Shāfiʿī jurists. He was an eyewitness of the Black Death and his *Risāla fī al-ṭāʿūn* places the epidemic in a religio-legal context and considers whether it is legitimate to flee a pestilence which God has ordained. Al-Subkī's treatise *Kitāb Muʿīd al-niʿam* (*Book of the Restorer of Favours*) is a work on the necessity for good intentions and good working practices on the part of all ranks of society, from caliphs and sultans down to house painters, dressers and washers of the dead. In this treatise, among other things he warns manuscript copyists against reproducing works of entertainment. (No one would ever accuse al-Subkī of being entertaining.) Al-Subkī was a much-quoted defender of Ṣūfī in a period when their doctrines and practices were opposed by many. Like **Ibn Taymiyya** before him and **al-Suyūṭī** after him, al-Subkī had many clashes with the Mamlūk miltary authorities.

Text editions

Kitab Muʿīd al-niʿam wa-muʿbīd al-niqʿam, D.W. Myhrman (ed.), London (1908).

Ṭabaqāt al-Shāfiʿiyya, 6 vols, Cairo (1906).

R. IRWIN

Ṣūfī literature, poetry

Islamic mysticism in the sense of an endeavour to establish an intimate, emotional rapport with God, indeed a rapport predicated on love, is characterized quite naturally by a tendency to poetry. Already in the second/eighth century, during Ṣūfī gatherings devoted to the enjoyment of music and dance (***samāʿ***), conventional love poetry was recited by way of expressing the lover–mystic's relationship to the divine Beloved. But to begin with, such poetry was taken from the work of 'wordly' poets, e.g. **Abū Nuwās**. Actual mystical–ascetic poetry was composed during this period by **Abū al-ʿAṭāhiya** (d. 748/825). Verses on mystical passionate love have been transmitted as the work of the female mystic **Rābiʿa al-ʿAdawiyya** (d. 183/801), although the authenticity of their attribution is doubtful.

Alongside love poetry of a mystical dimension, there also appear the genres of didactic mystical verse, as well as poetry of mystical meditation. However, the genre of mystical epic poetry as attested in Persian literature does not exist in Arabic.

Several famous personalities of the period of classical Sufism (third to fifth/ninth to eleventh centuries) were also poets. Examples that may be mentioned are Dhū al-Nūn al-Miṣrī (d. 245/860), the celebrated al-Ḥusayn ibn Manṣūr **al-Ḥallāj** (d. 910/922) and Abū Bakr **al-Shiblī** (d. 334/946). Their poetry is quoted in such Ṣūfī handbooks and biographical dictionaries as the *Ṭabaqāt al-ṣūfiyya* by Abū ʿAbd al-Raḥmān **al-Sulamī** (d. 412/1021) and the *Ḥilyat al-awliyāʾ* by **Abū Nuʿaym al-Iṣbahānī** (d. 430/1038). Handbooks of this kind which especially cite poetry are the *Kitāb al-taʿarruf* by Abū Bakr **al-Kalabādhī** (probably d. 380/990), the *Kitāb al-lumaʿ* by Abū Naṣr **al-Sarrāj**, chapter 92 of which treats exclusively of poetry, and the *Risāla* by **al-Qushayrī**.

The most important mystical poets of the post-classical period of Sufism are **Ibn al-Fāriḍ** (d. 632/1235) and **Ibn al-ʿArabī** (d. 638/ 1240). The former ranks as the greatest mystical poet in the Arabic language. As well as a *dīwān*, Ibn al-ʿArabī has left a collection of mystical love poems, the *Tarjumān al-ashwāq*.

In the later period of Sufism as in other fields of learning – e.g. medicine, philosophy and **grammar** – there arose a range of didactic poetry which presented the contents of Ṣūfī handbooks and the rule of Ṣūfī brotherhoods in versified form. An early example of this development is the *Rāʾiyya* of Aḥmad b. Muḥammad al-Sharīshī (581–641/1185–1243), a didactic poem in the *ṭawīl* metre that presents in versified form the section of ʿUmar **al-Suhrawardī**'s *ʿAwārif al-maʿārif* dealing with the relationship between the shaykh and the novice. As a representative of more recent Sufism, the *Alfiyyat al-taṣawwuf* by Muṣṭafā al-Bakrī (1099–1162/1688–1749) may be mentioned, a poem in the ***rajaz*** metre dealing with the whole of Sufism in 1,200 verses.

The poetry in later Sufism that glorifies the life and the cosmic role of the Prophet **Muḥammad** constitutes a special genre. The best-known example of the genre is the *Burda* of **al-Būṣīrī** (608–94/1213–96). Similarly, in the later centuries, along with versified eulogies of the Prophet, there has been an increase in verse praising the saints, Ṣūfī shaykhs and founders of Ṣūfī brotherhoods.

Text edition

al-Fāsī, Aḥmad ibn Yūsuf, *Sharḥ Rā'iyyat al-Sharīshī*, Cairo (1316/1898); see also the entries for the individual authors mentioned.

Further reading

Hunwick, John O., 'The Arabic qasida in West Africa: forms, themes and contexts' in *Qasida Poetry in Islamic Asia and Africa*, S. Sperl and C. Shackle (eds.), Leiden (1996), vol. 1, 83–97.

Meier, Fritz, *Abū Sa'īd-i Abū l-Ḫayr*, Leiden (1976), 210–18.

——, 'Kehrreim und Maḥyā', in *Wagner Festschrift*, vol. 2, 462–89.

Nicholson, R.A., *Studies in Islamic Mysticism*, Cambridge (1921).

O'Fahey, R.S. and Hunwick, J.O. (eds.), *Arabic Literature of Africa*, Leiden (1994–), vol. 1, chs 4 and 8 (examples of praise of the prophets and the saints).

Schimmel, A., *As Through a Veil: Mystical Poetry in Islam*, New York (1982).

——, *Mystical Dimensions of Islam*, Chapel Hill (1975).

B. RADTKE

Ṣūfī literature, prose

Like mystics everywhere, the Ṣūfīs produced an extensive literature, of poetry and prose. Although in some instances the very categories 'poetry' and 'prose' prove to be ideal types, as the literature itself is so mixed, there is a basis for the distinction in the writings.

Ṣūfī prose literature in Arabic and other Islamic languages took many forms and may be classified and viewed in various ways. A useful classificatory scheme distinguishes between the following.

1. Ṣūfī literature that is formally parallel to standard genres of Islamic religious literatures, but which has a specifically Ṣūfī content and point of view. Some main literary types here are *tafsīr* (see **exegesis, Koranic**), collections of ***ḥadīth***, theological treatises and *ṭabaqāt*-type literature (see **biography, medieval**). In each case, the literature more or less takes the form of its counterpart in the 'mainstream canon', while its contents and orientation in various ways represent Sufism. This does not mean that the entire contents of the work were necessarily Ṣūfī, for some overlap with the contents of the mainstream canon is clearly evident in many of these works. Such overlap was an indication of (a) the genuine, generally deep integration of Sufism into the broader Islamic tradition; and (b) the conscious attempt by Ṣūfī writers to base their works not only on Ṣūfī sources but on general Islamic sources as well. This was in order to show specifically that the Ṣūfī enterprise was indeed rooted in Islam and, like the other Islamic spiritual and intellectual disciplines, was derived from the **Koran** and comprised many other mainstream literatures as well. Prominent examples of this genre are the Ṣūfī *tafsīr Laṭā'if al-ishārāt* by Abū al-Qāsim **al-Qushayrī** (d. 465/1072) and the well-known *Ṭabaqāt al-Ṣūfīyya* by **al-Sulamī** (d. 412/1021).
2. Ṣūfī literature that has a specific Ṣūfī form, content and style. The range of prose works here is wide. However, two types would seem to subsume much of the field: general treatises about Sufism for both Ṣūfīs and a wider audience; specialized treatises expressing the particular orientation, ideas or sectarian purpose of an individual Ṣūfī figure or a group. Works such as **Ibn al-ʿArabī**'s *Fuṣūṣ al-ḥikam* and *al-Futuḥāt al-Makkiyya* would be examples of the specialized treatise. Less numerous and having more of a Ṣūfī 'consensual focus' in certain highly regarded books are the general treatises on Sufism. Five of these in particular attained canonical status within most Ṣūfī circles and in the general community: the *Kitāb al-Ta'arruf li-madhāhib ahl al-taṣawwuf* of **al-Kalabādhī** (d. 385/995); the *Kitāb al-Luma'* of Abū Naṣr **al-Sarrāj** (d. 378/988), the oldest Ṣūfī compendium; *Qūt al-qulūb* of Abū Ṭālib **al-Makkī** (d. 386/996), the second oldest; *al-Risāla al-Qushayriyya* of al-Qushayrī; *Kashf al-maḥjūb* of al-Hujwīrī (d. 469/1076). These treatises served to educate and inform both the Ṣūfīs themselves and the larger community and its scholars about Sufism. The most important of them, the *Ta'arruf*, was highly influential and instrumental in achieving an accommodation between Sufism and orthodox Islam. Al-Kalabādhī's time was one of great tension between the two parties, and this great achievement was never subsequently to be broken. The *Ta'arruf* has five parts whose contents are typical of the general Ṣūfī treatise: discussion and description of Sufism, its name and provenance, and the great Muslims who were Ṣūfīs; the Ṣūfī

understanding of basic orthodox doctrines; a description of the Ṣūfī 'spiritual stations' (*maqāmāt*); an explanation of the standard Ṣūfī technical terms; miscellaneous aspects of Sufism, e.g. miracles.

Further reading

Schimmel, A, *Mystical Dimensions of Islam*, Chapel Hill (1975).

R.L. NETTLER

Sufism

The etymology of the Arabic word *taṣawwuf* has been extensively debated; it is most likely that it originally referred to the ascetic practice of wearing garments of wool (*ṣūf*; hence *Ṣūfī*). Many early 'wearers of wool' were not mystics; and Sufism was only one of many manifestations of Islamic mysticism over the centuries. Its use to designate 'official' or 'mainstream' Sunnī mysticism seems to date from the late fifth/eleventh century, when the Sunnī **Saljūqs**, in particular, protected and encouraged this particular tendency.

The pre-history of Islamic mysticism is shrouded in obscurity. It is more than likely that, as Massignon suggested, it incorporated local non-Islamic (Gnostic, Manichaean, shamanistic) as well as Shī'ī elements in the course of its development (cf. Chabbi, 1977, 22). Later accounts both of the history of Sufism and of its doctrines – often uncritically accepted by scholars – represent a retrospective reconstruction of its development as continuous, linear and systematic, and trace its antecedents to the teachings and example of early ascetics like **al-Ḥasan al-Baṣrī** (d. 110/728) and of semi-legendary figures like Dhū al-Nūn al-Miṣrī (d. 246/861). The reality is far more complex. The teachings of the Iraqi schools of Sufism, which developed in the late third/ninth century in the circles of **al-Junayd** (d. 298/910) in Baghdad and **Sahl al-Tustarī** (d. 283/896) in Basra, were exported to Khurasan in the fourth/tenth century by emigrants from Iraq and by such eastern writers as **al-Kalabādhī** (d. 381/990) and Abū Naṣr **al-Sarrāj** (d. 378/988). Sufism (like other Sunnī groups) was bitterly hostile to the local pietistic movement of the Karrāmiyya, founded by Ibn Karrām (d. 255/859), who propagated an activist and ostentatious asceticism and whose travelling preachers attracted many converts. In the rewriting of Ṣūfī history, such local traditions and figures as could not be recuperated were expunged from the historical record. From the late fifth/eleventh century onwards, especially under Saljūq patronage but also under the later **Ghaznavids**, Sufism spread both westwards, to Egypt and, eventually, to North Africa and Spain, and eastwards to the Indian sub-continent.

It would be erroneous, even given the triumph of mainstream Sūfism, to speak of a unified body of Ṣūfī doctrine; the Ṣūfīs themselves, maintaining that there are many roads to the one single Truth (*ḥaqīqa*), did not hesitate to travel down a multiplicity of such roads. For the Ṣūfī, the relationship – the ancient covenant – between God and man is based not merely on obedience but also on friendship: if obedience means following God's law (*shar'īa*), the follower of the Ṣūfī path (*ṭarīqa*) seeks to fill his heart with God through perpetual remembrance (*dhikr*) of His name, and to raise himself spiritually to a state of closeness to the Divine. The Ṣūfī is the 'Friend of God'.

Some scholars have distinguished between two main 'schools' or tendencies, those of 'sober' and of 'ecstatic' mysticism – reflected, for example, in the conflict between the 'sober' school of al-Junayd and the 'ecstatic' **al-Ḥallāj**, which led to the latter's execution in 309/922 – but this too is an oversimplification. At the heart of mainstream Sufism is an emphasis on individual piety and on upward spiritual progress, from repentence through self-purification to perfection and closeness to God; but these common features have been interpreted variously. Many Ṣūfī teachers exhort abandoning the material pleasures of this world in favor of pious poverty; others find no inherent conflict between an exalted spiritual state and the possession of material wealth. While chastity may be recommended, unlike Christian pietism Sufism does not value celibacy. To follow the Ṣūfī *ṭarīqa* meant, usually, to choose a recognized teacher (though even this was not always a condition) and to follow his guidance. Endless tomes have been written on the 'stations' (*maqāmāt*) and 'states' (*aḥwāl*) of the path, and on Ṣūfī terminology in general, in an attempt to codify Ṣūfī doctrine; but Ṣūfī writings on such matters appear to be part of a didactic project aimed at the cultivation of an élite, to whom their circulation was largely confined. More public sessions of teaching, preaching, and *dhikr* (not always looked on with approval by the mainstream) attracted a broader social spectrum, particularly urban merchants and artisans and rural peasantry. Neither élite nor popular Sufism should however be seen as an other-worldly movement focused on individual piety alone; Sufism was always closely linked to its particular political, religious and social milieu. Moreover, it was never a universalist spiritualizing movement, as is assumed by some modern scholars.

With the passage of time the relatively informal structures of Ṣūfī teaching and preaching were centred in more formal institutions. Most important of these was the Ṣūfī lodge, the *khānaqāh* or *ribāṭ*. Originally instituted by the Karrāmiyya as a meeting place and a hostel for travelling preachers, the first Ṣūfī programme for the building of a large number of such lodges was initiated by Abū Isḥāq al-Kāzarūnī (d. 426/1035), who built 65 lodges in the villages of southern Iran. Such lodges spread under the Saljūqs as part of their programme of pious building activities. The second important institution was the formalizing of Ṣūfī 'brotherhoods', with specific programmes of instruction and rules of conduct, linked to specific (though often only putative) founders. The first such international brotherhood was established by the Ṣūfī *shaykh* and adviser to the caliph al-Nāṣir (r. 575–622/1180–1225) ʿUmar **al-Suhrawardī**, from whom the Suhrawardiyya brotherhood takes its name. To such brotherhoods – organized along lines similar to those of the closely related ***futuwwa*** groups – the term *ṭarīqa* (formerly used only in the sense of 'path', or more generally of 'Ṣūfī way of life') came to be applied. Increasingly, Ṣūfīs were grouped into brotherhoods whose masters traced their pedigree through a chain of masters or teachers (*silsila*) back to the Prophet. Membership in such groups did not imply exclusivity, as individuals might belong to more than one; and sub-brotherhoods constantly appeared as splits between the membership of a larger group occurred.

Some Ṣūfī groups – like that headed by Ibn Qasī, who established a small kingdom in southern Portugal which he ruled until assassinated in 525/1151 – were militant; others were pietistic and quietist. The involvement of Ṣūfīs at court, where they acquired increasing influence, became marked following the Mongol invasions of the seventh/thirteenth century; ʿUmar al-Suhrawardī is said to have advised the Ṣūfī Najm al-Dīn Dāya (d. 654/1256) to dedicate a book on Sufism to a ruler, an unusual action necessitated by the present danger to Islam. Involvement with temporal rulers increased in subsequent centuries, under the Tīmūrids, the Ottomans and the Mughal rulers of India.

The literary legacy of Sufism is both vast and varied, as Ṣūfī thought found expression not only in Arabic but in the vernaculars – especially Persian, Turkish, and the languages of South Asia – and in a wide variety of genres. Particularly noteworthy is the mystical poetry of such poets as **Ibn al-Fāriḍ** (d. 632/1235) and **Ibn al-ʿArabī** (d. 638/1240), whose vibrant lyricism has been obscured by the heavy-handed approach of later commentators, who sought to reduce their use of a vocabulary rich in allegory and symbol to the level of a 'lexical code' expressive of points of Ṣūfī doctrine (a procedure followed by many more recent scholars).

Sufism is often described as a 'humanist' movement defending the value of the individual against non- (or even anti-) humanist 'orthodox' Islam. But while both specific individuals and specific movements often incurred criticism – or worse – from conservative religious scholars or from the governing powers, this was because their sometimes radical doctrines, or those of their practices which were suspected of being morally dubious (the Ṣūfī ***samāʿ*** or musical gathering; the practice of gazing on beautiful beardless youths (*al-naẓar bil-murd*); or some of the wilder rites of specific brotherhoods) were seen – especially in times of crisis – as threats to the stability of Islam or to that of the state as conducting to immoral conduct. Sufism, by and large, co-existed with external orthopraxy based on the *sharʿīa*, as the inward-turning search for greater consciousness of God.

Further reading

Books and articles on Sufism are numerous, and I will cite only a few of interest here, in which references may be found to many others:

Baldick, Julian, *Mystical Islam: An Introduction to Sufism*, London (1989).

Chabbi, Jacqueline, 'Remarques sur le développement historique des mouvements ascétiques au Khurasan, IIIe/IXe siècle – IVe/Xe siècle', *Studia Islamica* 46 (1977) 5–72.

Dreher, J., *Das Imamat des islamischen Mystikers Abūlqāsim Aḥmad b. al-Ḥusain b. Qasī*, thesis, Bonn (1985).

Hodgson, M.G.S., *The Venture of Islam*, Chicago (1974), vol. 2, 201–54, 455–57.

Molé, M., *Les mystiques musulmans*, Paris (1965).

Schimmel, A., *Mystical Dimensions of Islam*, Chapel Hill (1975).

J.S. MEISAMI

al-Sufūr (1915–24)

Egyptian literary weekly, founded by a group of young writers from the school of Aḥmad **Luṭfī al-Sayyid** and ***al-Jarīda***, mouthpiece of the Umma Party. Among the leading editors were Muḥammad Ḥusayn **Haykal**, **Ṭāhā Ḥusayn** and the brothers Muṣṭafā and 'Alī **'Abd al-Rāziq** – all figures with a European (mostly French) education, including a university degree. *Al-Sufūr* advocated complete unveiling (*sufūr shāmil*), the emancipation of women, and social and cultural reforms in the spirit of Qāsim **Amīn**; although lacking a clear-cut programme, it also played an important role in the field of literature, providing a forum for a great number of Egyptian writers, including Muḥammad and Maḥmūd **Taymūr**, Ibrāhīm **al-Miṣrī** and others. In the 1920s the magazine began to lose influence and its role was assumed by ***al-Fajr***, the mouthpiece of the so-called 'Modern School', with its more outspoken attack on traditional literary values.

Further reading

Brugman, J., *An Introduction to the History of Modern Arabic Literature in Egypt*, Leiden (1984), 232–4.
de Moor, E., 'Quelques discussions dans la revue réformiste *al-Sufūr*', *QSA* (1993).
Ḥaqqī, Y., *Fajr al-qiṣṣa al-miṣriyya*, Cairo (1975), 75ff.

E.C.M. DE MOOR

al-Suhrawardī, 'Umar (539–632/1145–1234)

Shihāb al-Dīn Abū Ḥafṣ 'Umar al-Suhrawardī was the nephew of Abū al-Najīb al-Suhrawardī (d. 563/1168) and the real founder of the Suhrawardiyya order (*ṭarīqa*). In the **Baghdad** of his time he was considered to be the Ṣūfī *Shaykh al-Shuyūkh*; as adviser to the **'Abbāsid** caliph al-Nāṣir li-Dīn Allāh (r. 575–622/1180–1225), he conceived a policy for unifying the caliphate, the ***futuwwa***, and Sufism under the aegis of the caliph. His primary importance for Arabic mystical literature lies in his authorship of the *'Awārif al-ma'ārif*, which Trimingham characterizes as 'the medieval vade-mecum for spiritual direction', asserting that this 'deservedly has been the most popular [Ṣūfī] guide' (1971, 29). This book increased the prestige and authority of the Suhrawardiyya *ṭarīqa*, and may well have been instrumental in encouraging the spread of the order. Baldick stresses that 'one difference between [this] manual and earlier ones is that it is not just a collection of different people's opinions, but an integrated programme orientated towards real practice' (1989, 75).

Text editions

'Awārif al-ma'ārif, Cairo (1939), Beirut 1966.
The 'Awarif ul-Ma'arif..., H. Wilberforce Clarke (trans.), (1891), rpt New York (1970).
Die Gaben des Erkenntnisse, R. Gramlich (trans.), Wiesbaden (1978).

Further reading

Baldick, Julian, *Mystical Islam: An Introduction to Sufism*, London (1989).
Trimingham, J.S., *The Sufi Orders in Islam*, Oxford (1971).

I.R. NETTON

al-Suhrawardī, Yaḥyā ibn Ḥabash (549–87/1153–91)

Shihāb al-Dīn Yaḥyā ibn Ḥabash al-Suhrawardī was a mystical philosopher and proponent of the 'Illuminationist' (*ishrāqī*) school of thought, and thus often characterized by the epithet *Shaykh al-Ishrāq*; also called *al-Maqtūl*, 'the Murdered', and *al-Shahīd*, 'the Martyr'. A native of Suhraward (northern Iran), he travelled west to study religious law and philosophy at Marāgha (northern Azarbaijan) and Isfahan. Following his studies he spent some time travelling around Iran, visiting Ṣūfīs and devoting himself to meditation and prayer; finally, after travelling through Anatolia and **Syria**, he settled at the court of al-Malik al-Ẓāhir, son of the **Ayyūbid** ruler Saladin (Ṣalāḥ al-Dīn) in Aleppo. Here he met with criticism and hostility on the part of more conservative religious scholars, and on the order of Saladin was arrested on charges of heresy; he died in prison, either murdered or deliberately starved to death.

In his writings al-Suhrawardī develops a motif already apparent in **Ibn Sīnā**'s later works: that of God as light. He viewed God as *Nūr al-Anwār*, 'Light of Lights', and developed an extremely complex hierarchy of lights, with the *Nūr al-Anwār* at its peak, which owed as much to the angelology of

Zoroastrianism as to Neoplatonic emanation theory (see **Platonism**). This doctrine was expounded in what is probably his most famous work, the *Ḥikmat al-Ishrāq* (*Wisdom of Illumination*). His philosophy has had a lasting influence on Islamic mysticism, especially in Iran (where it was built upon and systematized by the great **Shī'ī** philosopher **Mullā Ṣadrā** of Shiraz, d. 1640), and his *Ḥikmat al-Ishrāq* was the subject of many commentaries.

As far as the general development of Arabic literature is concerned, al-Suhrawardī, together with **Ibn al-'Arabī**, represents a trend in Arabic mystical writing towards greater complexity. The *Ḥikmat al-Ishrāq* manifests an élitist style of writing which found admirers particularly among later Ṣūfīs and philosophers, but which, with its involved imagery of light and complex emanationist structure, can have appealed to few others. There is, however, another style of writing in the Suhrawardian corpus which is best exhibited in some of his short treatises, written both in Arabic and in Persian, which are more anecdotal in nature and allegorical in style (he is said to have been the first to introduce the allegorical tale into Persian).

Text editions

L'archange empourpré: quinze traités et récits mystiques, H. Corbin (trans.), Paris (1976).

Kitāb al-Lamaḥāt, E. Maalouf, (ed.), Beirut (1969).

Le Livre de la sagesse orientale, H. Corbin (trans.) (with commentary), C. Jambert (ed.), Lagrasse (1976).

The Mystical and Visionary Treatises of Shihabuddin Yahya Suhrawardi, W.M. Thackston (trans.), London (1982).

Oeuvres philosophies et mystiques, vols 1–2, H. Corbin (ed.), vol. 3: *Oeuvres en persan*, S.H. Nasr (ed.), 2nd edn, Tehran and Paris (1976–7) (includes the *Ḥikmat al-Ishrāq*).

Further reading

Aminrazavi, M., *Suhrawardi and the School of Illumination*, Richmond (1996).

Corbin, H., *Suhrawardi d'Alep, fondateur de la doctrine illuminative*, Paris (1939).

Hodgson, M.G.S., *The Venture of Islam*, Chicago (1974), vol. 2, 230–8, vol. 3, 44–6.

Horten, M., *Die Philosophie der Erleuchtung nach Suhrawardī*, Halle (1912), rpt Hildesheim (1981).

Nasr, S.H., 'Shihāb al-Dīn Suhrawardī Maqtūl' in *A History of Muslim Philosophy*, M.M. Sharif (ed.), Wiesbaden (1963), vol. 1, 372–98.

——, *Three Muslim Sages: Avicenna, Suhrawardī, Ibn 'Arabī*, Cambridge, MA (1964).

Netton, I.R., *Allāh Transcendent*, London (1989), 256–320.

Ziai, H., *Knowledge and Illumination: A Study of Suhrawardī's Ḥikmat al-Ishrāq*, Atlanta (1990).

I. NETTON/J.S. MEISAMI

sukhf

Obscenity and scatology, particularly as used in poetry for its shock value and humorous effect. As defined by the lexicographers, the term literally means 'light-mindedness, foolishness', but gradually developed in the direction of 'insensitivity, crudeness', and finally 'foul language'. As a literary term, it is particularly associated with the fourth/tenth-century Baghdadi poet **Ibn al-Ḥajjāj**, who went beyond the established conventions of licentious poetry (see ***mujūn***) in his day to compose verses filled with explicit sexual and excremental references. Although often paired with *mujūn* in later literature, *sukhf* is distinguished from it in referring less to hedonistic behaviour offensive to the prudish than to gross language and comportment upsetting to the squeamish. In its aggressive scurrility, it has clear links back to the traditional use of obscenity in abuse poetry (see ***hijā'***). Although never a major genre, *sukhf* does figure prominently in such works as **Abū al-Muṭahhar al-Azdī's** *Tale of Abū al-Qāsim al-Baghdādī*, the poetry of **Ibn al-Habbāriyya**, and the **shadow plays** of **Ibn Dāniyāl**.

Further reading

See *mujūn*.

E.K. ROWSON

al-Sukkarī (212–75 or 290/827–88 or 903)

Abu Sa'īd al-Ḥasan ibn al-Ḥusayn al-Sukkarī was a philologist from **Basra**; Abū Ḥātim **al-Sijistānī** was one of his teachers. He is responsible for the redaction of an extraordinarily large quantity of Arabic poetry; lists of his works are given in **Ibn al-Nadīm**'s *Fihrist* (ed. Flügel, 78, 157–9). He edited the ***dīwān***s of numerous tribes, the most important to us (because the only one that is preserved and published) being that of the tribe of **Hudhayl**, as well as the *dīwān*s of more than fifty individual poets. They include many famous ones, such as **Imru' al-Qays**, **Zuhayr**, **al-Nābigha al-Dhubyānī**, **al-Aʿshā**, **Labīd**, **Dhū al-Rumma**, **al-Farazdaq** and **Jarīr**, and even some ***muḥdathūn*** like **Abū Nuwās** and **Abū Tammām**. Other works and compilations by him include works on *luṣūs* ('robber-poets'), poetry by Jews, on wild animals (*al-Wuḥūsh*) and plants (*al-Nabāt*).

Further reading

Fihrist (Dodge), vol. 1, 345–50, and see index.

G.J.H. VAN GELDER

al-Sulamī, Abū ʿAbd al-Raḥmān (325 or 333–412/937 or 942–1021)

Abū ʿAbd al-Raḥmān Muḥammad ibn al-Ḥusayn al-Sulamī was a Ṣūfī writer. Born in Nishapur, he received an education in ***hadith*** studies, Shāfiʿī jurisprudence and **Sufism**. After years of extensive travel, he settled in Nishapur in 368/977–8 and died there. He is the most important compiler and collector of information pertinent to classical Sufism. Of his more than 100 works, 30 or so have come down to us. His chief work on the history of Sufism is the *Ta'rīkh al-ṣūfiyya*, which has only survived in the form of quotations in other authors. The extant *Ṭabaqāt al-ṣūfiyya* is an extract from this work. Al-Sulamī's most important work is his **Koran** commentary, the *Ḥaqā'iq al-tafsīr*, which attempts to gather together the whole of the earlier Ṣūfī tradition of commenting on the Koran. His numerous other smaller writings deal with individual aspects of Sufism, such as customs and practices.

Text editions

Majmūʿa-i āthār-i Abū ʿAbd al-Raḥmān-i Sulamī, 2 vols, Teheran (1369–72/1980–93).

The Minor Qur'ān Commentary of Abū ʿAbd ar-Raḥmān Muḥammad b. al-Ḥusayn as-Sulamī, G. Böwering (ed.), Beirut (1995) (an edition of the *Ḥaqā'iq al-tafsīr* by G. Böwering is forthcoming).

Ṭabaqāt al-ṣūfiyya, Nūr al-Dīn Sharība (ed.), Cairo (1953); J. Pedersen (ed.), Leiden (1960).

Further reading

Böwering, G., 'The major sources of Sulamī's minor Qur'ān commentary', *Oriens* 35 (1996), 35–56.

B. RADTKE

al-Ṣūlī, Abū Bakr Muḥammad ibn Yaḥyā (d. *c.*335/946)

Courtier and man of letters from **Baghdad**. The poet Ibrāhīm ibn al-ʿAbbās **al-Ṣūlī** was his great-uncle. He was the ***nadīm*** of the caliphs al-Muktafī, al-Muqtadir and al-Rāḍī, having also been the tutor of the last-mentioned. He wrote many works on poetry and poets, among them a commentary (lost) on **Abū Tammām**'s *Ḥamāsa*. He was chiefly interested, however, in 'modern' (***muḥdath***) poets, producing several monographs on them (on Abū Tammām and others) as well as recensions of the poems of **Abū Nuwās**, **Muslim ibn al-Walīd**, **al-ʿAbbās ibn al-Aḥnaf**, **Ibn al-Muʿtazz**, **Ibn al-Rūmī**, **al-Ṣanawbarī** and others; sometimes with a commentary, as for the poetry of Abū Tammām. His *al-Awrāq* is basically an anthology of **ʿAbbāsid** poets (including members of the ruling dynasty). A book on viziers, *al-Wuzarā'*, is known only from quotations. Informative is his *Adab al-kuttāb*, on the art of writing (on its material aspects as well as the form and content of letters). He was one of the great chess masters of all time; a book on chess written by him has been preserved. He died in **Basra**.

Text editions

Adab al-kuttāb, Muḥammad Bahjat al-Atharī (ed.), Baghdad (1922).

Akhbār Abī Tammām, wa-bi-awwalihi Risālat al-Ṣūlī ilā Muzāḥim ibn Fātik..., Khalīl Maḥmūd ʿAsākir *et al.* (eds), Cairo (1937).

Akhbār al-Buḥturī, Ṣāliḥ al-Ashtar (ed.), Damascus (1958).

al-Awrāq: ashʿār awlād al-khulafā' wa-akhbāruhum, J. Heyworth Dunne (ed.), Cairo (1936).

al-Awrāq: qism akhbār al-shuʿarā', J. Heyworth Dunne (ed.), London (1934).

G.J.H. VAN GELDER

al-Ṣūlī, Abū Isḥāq Ibrāhīm ibn al-ʿAbbās (*c.*176–243/*c.*792–857)

Secretary and poet of the early **ʿAbbāsid** period, who lived primarily in Mesopotamia. Al-Ṣūlī, stemming from a family of Turkish origin, held different administrative posts under the caliphs between al-Ma'mūn (198–218/813–33) and al-Mutawakkil (232–47/847–61). He was a friend of several prominent persons, among them the **Muʿtazilī** *qāḍī* Ibn Abī Du'ād (d. 240/854), the poet

Di'bil (d. *c*.244/859) and at some time also the secretary-poet **Muḥammad ibn 'Abd al-Malik Ibn al-Zayyāt** (d. 233/847), with whom his relationship however severely worsened (documented in several lampoons). As a ***muḥdath*** poet, he was held in high esteem. A ***dīwān*** of his poetry as it was worked out by his famous grand-nephew Abū Bakr **al-Ṣūlī** (d. 335/946) was edited; it contains (without the appendix) 182 poems of an average length of only three lines. Major genres are encomia (on several caliphs and the vizier al-Faḍl ibn Sahl), love and wine poetry and blame poems (*mu'ātabāt*).

Text edition

Dīwān, 'A. al-Maymanī (ed.), in *al-Ṭarā'if al-adabiyya*, Cairo (1937), 126–94; supplement by N.Ḥ. al-Qaysī, *al-Mawrid* 18 (1989), vol. 3, 163–4.

T. SEIDENSTICKER

Sulṭān, Nūr al-Hudā *see* Shā'rāwī, Hudā

ṣu'lūk see ṣa'ālīk

Sunnīs

Sunnīs are Muslims who hold that infallible guidance of the community ended with the death of the Prophet and that rulership over the community was rightfully exercised by those whom the community, represented by its most eminent leaders, elected. Sunnīs thus reject the **Shī'ī** belief that the Prophet had appointed his son-in-law and cousin, **'Alī ibn Abī Ṭālib**, to be ruler after him and that infallible guidance continued to be available through 'Alī and his descendants, the rightful heads of the community. Unlike Shī'īs, Sunnīs permit a diversity of schools of law (four of which – the Mālikī, Ḥanafī, Shāfi'ī and Ḥanbalī – have become predominant) and give greater importance to fallible human opinion in the shaping of the law. Their ***ḥadīth*** collections preserve only sayings and deeds of the Prophet Muḥammad, whereas those of the Shī'īs include also sayings of the 'Alid Imāms. The Sunnīs are the more widespread geographically of the two sectarian communities.

B. WEISS

Surūr, Najīb Muḥammad (1932–78)

Experimental Egyptian dramatist, director, actor and poet. He studied law at the College of Law and drama in **Cairo** and Moscow, working for several years in the Arabic section of Radio Moscow. Back in Cairo from 1964 onwards, he adopted Brechtian techniques, drawing on the Egyptian folk heritage and music, and using classical and modern poetry as source material for his colloquial plays, which describe the struggle of the ordinary Egyptian people for social justice against foreign and local forces of oppression. Four ***dīwān***s of his poetry have also been published, and his short caustic articles about cultural life in Egypt have appeared as *Hākadhā qāl Juḥā*.

Further reading

Sadgrove, P.C., 'Nadjīb Muḥammad Surūr' *EI*², vii, 869–70.

P.C. SADGROVE

Suwayd ibn Abī Kāhil (first/seventh century)

A ***mukhaḍram*** poet who traced his ancestry to the Yashkur and also, on occasion, to the Dhubyān. The tradition of his mother's marriages, first to a tribesman of the Dhubyān, who sired Suwayd, and then to Abū Kāhil of the Yashkur who acknowledged him as his son, is probably fictitious, being produced to account for conflicting ancestries within the poet's verse. He was imprisoned, possibly twice, by 'Āmir ibn Mas'ūd al-Jumaḥī, during his governorship of **Kufa** (64–5/683–5), for his attacks on the Banū Shaybān. Little of his ***dīwān*** has survived save a few scattered fragments. His long ***qaṣīda*** in the ***Mufaḍḍaliyyāt*** (no. 40) is composite, being two distinct odes joined together (40b begins with verse 45), although the medieval critics do not consider it as such. According to **al-Aṣma'ī**, it was known in the ***jāhiliyya*** as *al-Yatīma*, the unique pearl. The two poems are distinctly *mukhaḍram* in style: 40a is a tribal vaunt cast in the structural mode of the traditional, pre-Islamic tripartite panegyric; 40b, a celebration of the poet's vituperative skills, is noteworthy for its literary borrowings from earlier poets.

Text editions

Dīwān, S. al-'Ashūr (ed.), Basra (1972).

Lüling, G., *Die einzigartige Perle des Suwaid b. Abī Kāhil al-Yaškurī*, Erlangen (1973).
Lyall, C.J. (ed.), *The Mufaḍḍaliyyāt*, Oxford (1918).

J.E. MONTGOMERY

al-Suyūṭī (849–911/1445–1505)

Jalāl al-Dīn Abū al-Faḍl ʿAbd al-Raḥmān ibn Abī Bakr al-Suyūṭī was born in **Cairo** and spent most of his life there. He was a Shāfiʿi and taught the religious sciences. For a while he was *shaykh* of the Ṣūfī Baybarsiyya *Khānqāh* in Cairo and, despite quarrels with the Ṣūfīs there, he remained throughout his life an enthusiast for Sufism. He wrote copiously on an enormous number of subjects. He was the author of several history books (the *Badāʾiʿ al-ẓuhūr*, the *Tāʾrīkh al-khulafāʾ* and the *Ḥusn al-muḥāḍara*), but as a historian he is of little interest save for the occasional expressions of personal prejudice. Al-Suyūṭī was a champion of the prerogatives of the caliph and of the *ʿulamāʾ*, and (despite his Circassian mother) suspicious of irreligious innovations and encroachments of the Circassian **Mamlūk** regime.

More generally, al-Suyūṭī was the author of unoriginal works of vulgarization. He appears to have written over 500 works, although some of these were no more than pamphlets. He wrote on pyramids, women's fate in the after-life, congregations at the Friday prayers, the status of the Ethiopians, Koranic **exegesis**, the Temple of Jerusalem, philology, the reign of Qaytbay, *kunya*s (surnames), the mystical poetry of **Ibn al-Fāriḍ**, plagues, the legality of wearing garments trimmed with the fur of strangled squirrels, magical medicine, saints' birthday festivals, anatomy, his own quarrels with the Ṣūfīs of the Baybarsiyya, with other scholars, with the *mamlūk*s and much, much more. His most solid work was probably in the field of ***ḥadīth*** studies. Al-Suyūṭī was not so much an original author as a compliator. At times this sort of activity verged on outright plagiarism and this was indeed what his contemporary **al-Sakhāwī** accused him of. Predictably, a ***maqāma*** on the difference between authorship and plagiarism features in the plenum of al-Suyūṭī's writings.

This vain and opinionated scholar was convinced that he was the man of his age, a *mujtahid*, one capable of delivering legal opinions based on his individual interpretation of the **Koran** and the sayings of the Prophet. He also had ambitions to purify and revive Islam. His autobiography should be seen in this context. This book, *al-Taḥadduth bi-niʿmat Allāh*, lacks the charm of some other early Muslim autobiographies and mostly consists of a list of the teachers he had studied under as well as of the books he had published and *fatwā*s (legal opinions) he had issued. Al-Suyūṭī, who was good at making enemies, spent part of his life in hiding and part of it in seclusion.

Quite a number of works of erotica have been ascribed to him but the attributions seem doubtful and none of the pornographic books are listed in his autobiography. Similarly, because of his prestige, al-Suyūṭī had various prophecies foisted on him concerning the downfall of the Mamlūk sultanate and the rise of the Ottomans. He may or may not also have compiled an anthology of comic stories about the sixth/twelfth-century soldier Qarāqush.

Text editions

History of the Caliphs, H.S. Jarret (trans.), Calcutta (1881), rpt Amsterdam (1971).
Islamic Cosmology: A Study of as-Suyūṭī's al-Hay'a as-sanīya fī l-hay'a as-sunnīya, A.M. Heinen (ed. and trans.), Beirut (1982).
Die Maqâman des Sojûṭî, O. Rescher, (trans.) Kirchhain (1918).
The Mutawakkilī of As-Suyūtī, W.Y. Bell (ed. and trans.), Cairo (1924).
Suyūṭī's Itqān on the Exegetic Sciences of the Qor'ān, A Sprenger *et al.* (eds), Calcutta (1857).
Al-Suyuti's Who's Who in the Fifteenth Century [*Naẓm al-iqyān*], P.K. Hitti (ed.), New York (1927).

Further reading

Brustad, K., 'Imposing order: reading the conventions of representation in al-Suyūṭī's autobiography', *Edebiyât* n.s. 7 (1996) 327–44.
Garcin, J.-C., 'Histoire, opposition politique et piétisme traditionaliste dans le *Husn al Muhadarat* de Suyuti', *AI* 7 (1969), 33–89.
Sartain, E.M., *Jalāl al-Dīn al-Suyūṭī*, vol. 1: *Biography and Background*, vol. 2: *Al-Taḥadduth bini ʿmat allāh*, Cambridge (1975).

R. IRWIN

Syria, medieval

Syria included, within the confines of medieval *Bilād al-Shām*, Palestine, East Jordan, Lebanon and the northwestern parts of the Fertile Crescent. Its main towns, however, were situated along a north–south axis: Aleppo, Ma'arra, Hama, Hims, **Damascus**. In addition, Ḥarrān (situated south of Urfa, Turkey) may be mentioned as the home of **Thābit ibn Qurra** and his school of translators. Qinnasrīn was the early Arab garrison (*miṣr*) and centre of North Syria, and the newly founded Ramla became capital of Palestine under the caliph Sulaymān. The relatively scanty Arab settlement in urban environments and the rule of the **Umayyads** (661–750) who held many residences all over Syria, were unfavourable to the emergence of a predominant cultural capital. Thus for example the poet laureate **'Adī ibn al-Riqā'** and the state secretary and prose author **'Abd al-Ḥamīd al-Kātib** followed their masters to various different places. Even more so, the **bedouin** poet 'Umayr **al-Quṭāmī** (d. *c*.101/719–20) was engaged in tribal strife and kept aloof from residential life. After the heartland of Islam had moved east with the establishment of the **'Abbāsids**, the poets **Abū Tammām** (d. 231/846) and **al-Buḥturī** (d. 289/897), both of Syrian origin, spent only the beginning of their careers with local patrons. The situation changed with the splendid court of Sayf al-Dawla (d. 356/966–7; see **Ḥamdānids**) at Aleppo, who patronized characters as different as the poet **al-Mutanabbī**, the philosopher **al-Farābī** and the preacher **Ibn Nubāta al-Khaṭīb**. **Al-Tha'ālibī** opens the chapter on Syrian poets of his geographically arranged collection with the circle of this patron (*Yatīmat al-Dahr*, vol. 1); his work was continued by **'Imād al-Dīn**'s *Kharīdat al-Qaṣr* which contains many data on Syrian poets and their verses.

Fragmentation and the conflicts between North Syria, dominated by Aleppo, and South Syria, which was mostly subject to the authority of **Cairo**, continued to mark Syrian history from the fourth/tenth century, and during the Crusades, until the seventh/thirteenth-century. Even after formal unification, the **Ayyūbid** al-Malik al-Ẓāhir (d. 613/1216) governed Aleppo independently, giving this city its medieval apogee. **Ibn al-Qifṭī**, **Ibn Shaddād** and **Ibn al-'Adīm** flourished here at that time. At Hama (Ḥamāt) the Ayyūbid al-Malik al-Muẓaffar (d. 587/1191; *EI*², 7: 816–18) succeeded in establishing his lineage; **Abū al-Fidā'** was a descendant of his. Hama thus became a place of patronage to which al-Malik al-Manṣūr (d. 617/1221; *GAL* 1: 396), Ibn Abī al-Dam and the historian **Ibn Wāṣil** bear witness. Besides these cities and that of Damascus, the federal system of Ayyūbid rule generated a number of small centres. The physician **Ibn Abī Uṣaybi'a**, for example, served at Ṣarkhad, south of Damascus in the Ḥawrān.

Among medieval scholars and men of letters, travelling was quite usual, but the period of the **Crusades** was particularly unquiet, as may be examplified by **Usāma ibn Munqidh**. Poets often had to lead an itinerant life, and **Ibn al-Qaysarānī** (d. 548/1154), as well as his rival Ibn Munīr al-Ṭarābulusī (d. 548/1153) and, later, Shihāb al-Dīn al-Talla'farī (d. 675/1277) spent their lives at different courts and cities of Syria. In contrast, Ma'arrat al-Nu'mān owes its fame to **Abū al-'Alā' al-Ma'arrī** (d. 449/1053), the immortal poet and most famous member of a family of littérateurs. In the same town Ibn Abī Ḥaṣīna (d. 457/1065; *EI*², 3: 686), the poet of the Mirdāsids, won his skills.

Like Damascus, Aleppo during the fourteenth century remained a fertile ground for scholarship and literature, as testified by **Ibn al-Wardī** (749/1349). Contributions to the encyclopaedic spirit of the time were also produced later by Aleppans like Ibn al-Shiḥna (d. 890/1485; *GAL* 2: 483). At this time, however, the most flourishing period of Arabic literature in Syria had already passed.

Further reading

Badawī, A.A., *al-Ḥayāt al-adabiyya fī 'aṣr al-ḥurūb al-ṣalībiyya bi-Miṣr wa-al-Shām*, 2nd edn, Cairo (1979).

——, *al-Ḥayāt al-'aqliyya fī 'aṣr al-ḥurūb al-ṣalībiyya bi-Miṣr wa-al-Shām*, Cairo (1972).

Bāshā, Umar Mūsā, *al-Adab fī bilād al-Shām, 'uṣūr al-Zankiyyīn wa-al-Ayyūbiyyīn wa-al-Mamālīk*, Beirut (1989).

——, *Ta'rīkh al-adab al-'Arabī, al-'aṣr al-Mamlūkī*, Beirut (1989).

Bianquis, Thiery, *Damas et la Syrie sous la domination Fatimide (359–461/969–1076), Essai d'interpretation de chroniques arabes médiévales*, Damas (1989).

Canard, Marius, *Histoire de la Dynastie des Ḥamdanides de Jazīra et de la Syrie*, Algiers (1951).

Sallām, M. Zaghlūl, *al-Adab fī al-'aṣr al-Mamlūki*, 2 vols, Cairo (1971).

——, *al-Adab fī al-'aṣr al-Fāṭimī: al-kitāba wa-al-kitāb*, Alexandria (1988).

Sauvaget, J., *Alep, Essai sur le développement d'une grande ville syrienne des origines au milieu du XIX*ᵉ *siècle*, Paris (1941).

al-Ṭabbākh, M. Rāghib, *I'lām al-nubalā' bi-ta'rīkh*

Ḥalab al-shahbā, 2nd edn, Aleppo (1408/1988).

S. LEDER

Syria, modern

Syria's contribution to the ***nahḍa*** in the nineteenth and early twentieth centuries was hindered by the oppressive conditions prevailing in the Ottoman Empire, of which Syria was then a part. This led to the emigration of many Syrian writers to **Egypt**, America and elsewhere. The French occupation of Syria between the two world wars was in its turn not conducive to the encouragement of Arabic literature. Nevertheless, considering the small size of its population (15 million in 1996), Syria has made a notable contribution to modern Arabic letters – a contribution that has increased significantly since World War 2.

Syrian poets are represented among Arabic writers of the neo-classical and Romantic tendencies, while the modernist school has been dominated by ʿAlī Aḥmad Saʿīd (**Adūnīs**), whose work led to a revolution in the language of modern poetry, giving free play to an obscurity of expression and a sense of anguish and disorientation. Other prominent examples of modernism in poetry are the works of Salīm Barakāt and Muḥammad **al-Māghūṭ**.

The pioneer of Syrian drama was Aḥmad Abū Khalīl **al-Qabbānī**, who began to produce plays of his own in **Damascus** in the late 1870s. Among Syrian contributors to the genre of poetic drama was the poet ʿUmar **Abū Rīsha** (with his *Rāyāt Dhī Qār*, 1936). It was not until 1959, however, when the government set up the National Theatre Company, that serious drama began to flourish in Syria, the outstanding contemporary Syrian dramatist being Saʿd Allāh **Wannūs**.

The beginnings of modern Syrian prose fiction can be traced to the pioneering works of Fransīs **al-Marrāsh**. In the period between the first and second world wars, names that stand out are those of Maʿrūf Aḥmad **al-Arnaʾūṭ**, who was the first Syrian writer of historical novels, and Shakīb **al-Jābirī**, whose *Naham* (1937) is one of the landmarks in the development of modern fiction. Among prominent themes treated in the Syrian novel have been political reform (e.g. Ṣidqī Ismāʿīl, *al-ʿUṣāh*, 1964), the clash of generations (e.g. Hānī **al-Rāhib**, *Sharkh fī taʾrīkh ṭawīl*, 1969) the status of women (e.g. Kūlīt Khūrī, *Ayyām maʿah*, 1959), the suppression of dissent (e.g. Nabīl Sulaymān, *al-Sijn*, n.d.) and present-day alienation from society (e.g. Jūrj Sālim, *Fī al-Manfā*, 1962) Walīd **Ikhlāṣī**, *Aḥzān al-ramād*, 1975).

In the last forty years the short story has been the most significant genre in the literature of Syria – as ʿAbd al-Salām **al-ʿUjaylī** has put it, the short story has replaced the ***qaṣīda***. The early stages of its maturity are represented by the Romantic tendency of such writers as Ulfat ʿUmar **al-Idilbī** and Muẓaffar Sulṭān (b. 1913), and above all by ʿAbd al-Salām al-ʿUjaylī, who, apart from his short stories, has written novels, essays, travel books and even ***maqāmāt***.

In the 1950s and 1960s the movement of socialist realism was at its height, and in Syria was prominently represented by the members of the Rābiṭat al-Kuttāb al-Sūriyyīn. The secretary of this association was Saʿīd al-Ḥurāniyya (b. 1929), one of the leading Syrian short-story writers of the realistic school.

The 1960s and 1970s saw a flowering of creativity in the short story, with writers such as the surrealist Zakariyyā **Tāmir**, whose poetic imagination appears in his flights of fancy and excursions into the absurd, Kūlīt Khūrī, a surrealist feminist writer, and Walīd Ikhlāṣī, whose stories extend from animal fables to works of a modernist type which start from a basic refusal to accept existing values. Among the outstanding names is that of Jūrj Sālim, who uses fantasy and the bizarre to probe the basic questions of existence, and the best of whose stories rise above a Syrian or Arab horizon, and have a universal appeal.

Further reading

al-Aṭrash, Maḥmūd Ibrāhīm, *Ittijāhāt al-qiṣṣa fī Sūriyya baʿd al-ḥarb al-ʿālamiyya al-thāniya*, Damascus (1982).
al-Daqqāq, ʿUmar, *Funūn al-adab al-muʿāṣir fī Sūriyya*, Damascus (1971).
Ibn Dhurayl, ʿAdnān, *al-Riwāya al-adabiyya al-Sūriyya*, Damascus (1973).
Kayyālī, Sāmī, *al-Adab al-ʿArabī al-muʿāṣir fī Sūriyya 1850–1950*, Cairo (1959).
al-Saʿāfīn, Ibrāhīm, *Taṭawwur al-riwāya al-ʿArabiyya fī Bilād al-Shām*, Baghdad (1980).

M.J.L. YOUNG

Syriac literature

The literary tradition expressed in Syriac, a

dialect of Aramaic which emerged as a distinct language during the third century CE and became the liturgical tongue of the Jacobite and Nestorian churches. By the sixth century CE, Syriac literature, heavily influenced by Greek models and vocabulary, was fully developed in many genres, including not only such specifically religious fields as Biblical exegesis and homiletics, but also poetry, **grammar**, history, philosophy, medicine and the sciences. The great literary centres were the patriarchal libraries, and also those of leading monasteries throughout **Syria**, Iraq, southern Asia Minor and Persia. Books were readily available for visiting monks to study, and were often loaned to other monasteries for recopying.

There is some evidence of a direct Syriac influence on Arabic literature. Muslim authors occasionally refer to use of a Syriac book, but always via translation. Syriac-speaking Christian scholars, however, needed to know Arabic in order to deal with the new imperial order, and by the ninth century CE the general spread of Arabic was encouraging the growth of a Christian Arabic literature – based in part on Syriac foundations – which revealed to Muslims the extent and breadth of Syriac learning. The works of such historians as **Agapius** (*fl.* mid-fourth/tenth century) and **Eutychius** (d. 328/940), for example, were appreciated and used by Muslim historians who thereby gained access to Syriac sources underlying these works.

Far more important, however, was the role of Syriac literature as an intermediary between other literary traditions and that of Islam. Christian missions (especially Nestorian) were well established in the Far East, and a broad range of Indian and Persian texts were available in early Islamic Iraq in Syriac translation; numerous Indian literary and medical works that were to be influential on their later Arabic counterparts, for example, came from Sanskrit and Pahlavi to Arabic via Syriac.

Even greater was the impact of Syriac as a mediator of the Greek heritage to Islamic culture. During the translation movement of the third/ninth century, associated with the name of **Ḥunayn ibn Isḥāq** (d. 260/873), almost all of what had survived of Greek medical and philosophical literature was translated into Arabic either through Syriac, or by eastern Christian translators, or using codices from the network of Christian monasteries. Similar influences can also be traced in grammar, and in such literary types as the dispute essay or poem (often encountered in ***adab***) and the question-and-answer essay (frequently deployed in early Islamic theology).

Further reading

Barsaum, Ignatius Aphram I. *al-Lu'lu' al-manthūr fī ta'rīkh al-'ulūm wa-al-ādāb al-Suryāniyya*, 3rd edn, Baghdad (1976).

Baumstark, Anton, *Geschichte der syrischen Literatur*, Bonn (1922).

Conrad, Lawrence I., 'Arab-Islamic medicine', in *The Western Medical Tradition, 800 BC to AD 1800*, Lawrence I. Conrad *et al.*, (eds) Cambridge (1995), 104–10.

Fiey, Jean Maurice, 'Mārūthā de Martyropolis d'après Ibn al-Azraq (m. 1181)', *Analecta Bollandiana* 94 (1976), 35–45.

L.I. CONRAD

See also: Christian Arabic literature; Greek literature; translation, medieval

T

Ta'abbaṭa Sharran (first half of sixth century?)

Pre-Islamic poet. Thābit ibn Jābir, whose nickname ('He took evil under his arm') is explained in several anecdotes, is one of the 'outcast poets' (*ṣa'ālīk*). The stories or legends about him may be found in **Abū al-Faraj al-Iṣbahānī**'s *al-Aghānī*. Like his friend **al-Shanfarā**, on whom he wrote an elegy, he is particularly famous for one poem that is sometimes said to be a later forgery by **Khalaf al-Aḥmar**. This poem, a short *lāmiyya* (twenty-six lines) in the rare *madīd* metre, sometimes called his 'Song of Revenge', is found in **Abū Tammām**'s *Ḥamāsa*. In Europe its fame was secured by renderings by Goethe and Rückert.

Text edition

Dīwan T. Sh. wa-akhbāruh, 'Alī Dhū al-Faqār Shākir (ed.), Beirut (1984).

Shi'r, Najaf (1973).

Further reading

Abu-Khadra, Fahid, 'A new reading of an ancient poem', *Arabica* 35 (1988), 311–27.

Baur, G., 'Der arabische Held und Dichter Ṯābit Ben Ǧābir von Fahm, genannt Ta'abbata Šarran, nach seinem Leben und seinen Gedichten', *ZDMG* 10 (1856), 7–109.

Jones, Alan, *Early Arabic Poetry*, vol. 1, 205–47, 266–70.

Lyall, C.J., 'Four poems by Ta'abbata Sharra, the brigand-poet', *JRAS* (1918), 211–27.

Stetkevych, Suzanne P., *The Mute Immortals Speak: Pre-Islamic Poetry and the Poetics of Ritual*, Ithaca and London (1993), 55–118; cf. also *JSS* 31 (1986), 27–45 and *JAOS* 104 (1984), 661–78.

G.J.H. VAN GELDER

ṭabaqāt see biography, medieval

al-Ṭabarī, Muḥammad ibn Jarīr (*c.*224–314/839–923)

Al-Ṭabarī was a pre-eminent historian, jurist and commentator on the **Koran** during the early **'Abbāsid** period. Al-Ṭabarī was born in Āmul, a major city of the Caspian province of Ṭabaristān, to an affluent landowning family of uncertain ethnic origin. After completing his primary education, he travelled for further studies to **Rayy** and other cities in Iraq, **Syria**, Palestine and **Egypt** before finally settling in Baghdad where he remained until his death.

In the words of al-Nahrawānī as related by **Ibn al-Nadīm**, al-Ṭabarī became 'the sage of his time, the leader of his period, and the jurist of his age'. Among the many scholarly books on which this reputation was built, one of the most important was certainly the *Jāmi' al-bayān*, more commonly known simply as the *Tafsīr*, a voluminous commentary on the Koran. Utilizing a methodology perfected by al-Ṭabarī, it analyses the Koran phrase by phrase, generally beginning with a philological explanation of the verse followed by a seriatim listing of all the traditions by various authorities commenting on the text which al-Ṭabarī had been able to collect and compile. The traditions are often contradictory, but al-Ṭabarī typically refrains from discriminating among them; insofar as he injects his own view, it is usually to suggest ways to reconcile the differences. Although somewhat uncritical, the inclusion of such a variety of material helped to establish the opinion of al-Ṭabarī as one of the most judicious and reliable transmitters of religious traditions.

Al-Ṭabarī's fame as a historian derived from his *Ta'rīkh al-rusul wa-al-mulūk* (*The History of the Prophets and Kings*), a voluminous chronicle of history from creation to 302/915. Approximately a third of the text, arranged topically, deals with the pre-Islamic history of the Middle East, focusing on Judaeo–Christian figures, the historical and legendary rulers of Iran, and the life of **Muḥammad**. The remainder is a strictly annalistic account of the history of the Islamic world. The entries for each Hijrī year typically include descriptions of significant political events, appointments to government offices, obituary notices and various miscellanea such as reports of natural disasters, etc. Each discrete narrative is usually prefaced by a list of the authorities on whose report it is based. The text often seems disjointed and difficult to follow because of Tabari's preference for giving multiple reports about the same event and, in some cases, dividing the narrative into sections for events that spanned more than one year. Nonetheless, al-Ṭabarī's prestige as a jurist and religious scholar, his meticulousness in naming his sources, his lack of any obvious biases in the treatment of sensitive issues and the massive comprehensiveness of his work helped to establish the *History* as the most important and the most trustworthy product of early Muslim historiography.

The very fact that al-Ṭabarī's *History* bears such a stamp of orthodoxy and authority requires that it be evaluated with the degree of scepticism normally reserved for such works. Certainly, the extent to which it was a product of its times, reflecting al-Ṭabarī's own social background and political affinities, is a subject that needs investigation. Al-Ṭabarī's reliability in the use of his sources and the accuracy of extant versions of the text are also open questions. There are, for example, indications that the text of the *History* itself has been abridged or modified, as noted by Ibn al-Nadīm and evidenced by allusions to events as if they should be familiar when they are not found described elsewhere in the *History*. Many of the authorities that al-Ṭabarī names cannot be identified; some passages really seem to be taken from unnamed intermediary sources rather than the original cited by al-Ṭabarī. Not infrequently, as H. Keller first pointed out (in his edition of Ibn Abī Ṭāhir Ṭayfūr; Leipzig, 1908), there are significant differences between passages that al-Ṭabarī ascribes to a particular source and the parallel versions found in other works. These difficulties notwithstanding, Ṭabarī's *History* remains the single most important source of information about the classical Islamic world.

Text editions

Al-Ṭabarī's *Jāmiʿ al-bayān* is most readily available in the frequently reprinted Bulaq edition of 1903 and a still incomplete scholarly edition by Maḥmūd and Aḥmad Shākir (Cairo, 1955–69).

An abridged English translation of the work is under way with the appearance of J. Cooper, *The Commentary on the Qur'ān by Abū Jaʿfar Muḥammad b. Jarīr al-Ṭabarī*, vol. 1, Oxford (1987), which also provides a useful introduction to the text.

The *Ta'rīkh* is available in two published versions, one prepared by a committee of Orientalists under the direction of M.J. de Goeje (Leiden, 1879–1901) and a slightly revised edition by Muḥammad Abu al-Faḍl Ibrāhīm (Cairo, 1960–9). Neither should be regarded as definitive, and a re-edition is much to be desired.

The whole of the text is now appearing in an English translation of thirty-eight volumes under the general editorship of Ehsan Yar-Shater.

Virtually everything to be known about al-Ṭabarī's life and work may be found summarized in the introduction to the English translation by Franz Rosenthal, *The History of al-Ṭabarī*, vol. 1: *General Introduction and From the Creation to the Flood*, Albany (1989).

E.L. DANIEL

See also: exegesis, Koranic; historical literature

taḍmīn see prosody; rhetorical figures

tafʿīla see free verse; prosody.

tafsīr see exegesis, Koranic

al-Taftazānī (d. between 791/1389 and 797/1395)

Saʿd al-Dīn Masʿūd ibn ʿUmar al-Taftazānī was an eminent scholar who flourished in Samarkand during the reign of Tīmūr and is especially noted for his **commentaries** on earlier works in the fields of logic, **rhetoric**, theology and jurisprudence. Al-Taftazānī lived at a time when scholarly writing largely took the form of such commentaries, and his commentaries in particular were to be studied in subsequent centuries in *madrasa*s throughout the Islamic world. Special mention should be made of his two commentaries on **al-Khāṭīb al-Qazwīnī**'s *Talkhīṣ al-Miftāḥ*, a work on rhetoric, a longer commentary entitled *al-Muṭawwal* and a shorter commentary on the same work, *al-Mukhtaṣar*. These were widely accepted as the primary authoritative texts for the advanced study of rhetoric.

Text editions

A Commentary on the Creed of Islam, E.E. Elder (trans.), New York (1950).
al-Muṭawwal, the basic text commented upon in ʿAbd al-Raḥmān al-Shirbīnī, *Fayḍ al-fattāḥ ʿalā ḥawāshī sharḥ Talkhīṣ al-Miftāḥ*, Cairo (1905–8).

B. WEISS

Taghlib *see* tribes

Ṭāhā, ʿAlī Maḥmūd (1902–49)

Egyptian Romantic poet. Born in Mansura, Ṭāhā's professional formation (like that of **Abū Shādī** and Ibrāhīm **Nājī**) was non-literary, graduating as he did as an engineer in 1924. A member of the **Apollo Group**, his reputation was probably more widespread than any other in the inter-war period. He provided the most complete model of the bohemian avant-garde Romantic poet of the 1930s and 1940s, and it was this image that contributed to his great reputation. He had a lively enthusiasm for European culture and society, and his travels to Venice, Lake Como, Zurich and the Rhine are evoked fully both in his poems and prose accounts. He was attracted to innovation and experimentation: *Arwāḥ wa-ashbāḥ* (1942) is a poetic drama based on episodes from Greek legend and the Old Testament, while *Ughniyat al-riyāḥ al-arbaʿ* (1943) is a similar work, sections of which are designed to be sung, rather like the librettos written by Abū Shādī.

Ṭāhā's best-known collection of verse, *al-Mallāḥ al-tā'ih* (1934), contains some of the finest examples of his work. His hallmarks are introspective, Romantic malaise, atmospheres of pained bewilderment and perplexity and a strong sense of alienation from the majority of society. These qualities alone could well have been an unappealing combination, but Ṭāhā adds to them constant undertones of rebellion against prevailing norms and a vibrant sensuality. His language, although it cultivates the vague and the evocative rather than the concrete and the explicit, has remarkable musical qualities. Taken all together, these features of his work along with his personal example gained him a cult status. His popularity was enhanced by the fact that a number of his poems were set to music and reached audiences well beyond Egypt. His first collection was followed by *Layālī al-mallāḥ al-tā'ih* (1940), *Zahr wa-khamr* (1943) and *al-Shawq al-ʿā'id* (1945). His death at the relatively early age of 47 helped to underline his image as the most rebellious of the Egyptian Romantics.

Further reading

Badawi, M.M., *A Critical Introduction to Modern Arabic Poetry*, Cambridge (1975), 137–45.
CHALMAL, 118–22

R.C. OSTLE

al-Tahānawī (d. after 1158/1745)

Muḥammad Aʿlā ibn ʿAlī al-Tahānawī was an Indo-Muslim Ḥanafī scholar of whose life little is known except that he composed in **India** in 1158/1745 a useful dictionary of technical terms of all the branches of the Arabic religious and literary sciences, the *Kashshāf iṣṭilāḥāt al-funūn*. It has been frequently quoted in Western Orientalist scholarship on the basis of the 1854–62 Bibliotheca Indica edition, *A Dictionary of the Technical Terms Used in the Sciences of the Musalmans*.

C.E. BOSWORTH

Ṭāhir, Bahā' (1935–)

Egyptian novelist and short-story writer, also known for his work as a drama and television producer and critic. His first collection of short stories, *al-Khuṭūba*, appeared in 1972. Many of the stories are placed in realistic settings and depict the state or development of human relationships in careful but terse detail; events occur, conversations are recorded, yet there is little concern with explorations of causality. During the 1980s his output increased considerably, including two novels, *Sharq al-nakhl* (1985) and *Qālat ḍuḥan* (1986), and two short-story collections, *Bi-al-amsi ḥalamtu bik* (1980) and *Anā al-malik ji'tu* (1987). Since 1981 Ṭāhir has resided in Geneva where he works for the United Nations.

Further reading

Hafez, Sabry, 'Innovation in the Egyptian short story', in R.C. Ostle (ed.), *Studies in Modern Arabic Literature*, Warminster (1973), 86–98.

R. ALLEN

Ṭāhirids

A powerful family of provincial governors and other office holders, prominent in both political and cultural life in Iraq and Iran throughout the third/ninth century. They were of Iranian stock, but became early clients of the Arab tribe of Khuzā'a. Their rise to power began with Ṭāhir ibn al-Ḥusayn, a general of the caliph al-Ma'mūn, who directed the latter's successful rebellion against his brother al-Amīn, taking **Baghdad** in 198/813. Rewarded first with the governship of **Syria** and the upper Tigris–Euphrates region of al-Jazīra, he was subsequently made head of the police in Baghdad and given control of the rich revenues of southern Iraq, and then in 205/821 was appointed governor of all the eastern provinces of the empire. He died a year later, but his descendants continued to hold both the governorship of **Khurasan** and that of Baghdad virtually uninterruptedly for a century. The most prominent members of the family after Ṭāhir were his son **'Abd Allāh** (d. 230/844), governor of al-Jazīra, of Egypt, and then of Khurasan for fifteen years, and 'Abd Allāh's son 'Ubayd Allāh (d. 300/913), who pursued his career entirely in Iraq, serving as governor there several times.

Despite their Iranian origins, and a putative genealogy linking them to the hero Rustam, the Ṭāhirids exhibited little sympathy for the **Shu'ūbiyya** movement, and were major proponents of Arabic letters. Both Ṭāhir and 'Abd Allāh's epistles were collected as exemplars of fine style. Particularly celebrated were Ṭāhir's letter to al-Ma'mūn after his conquest of Baghdad and the murder of al-Amīn, and his letter of advice to his son 'Abd Allāh upon the latter's appointment to the governorship of al-Jazīra, an early example of the genre of **Mirrors for Princes**; both are extant in later sources. **Ibn 'Abd Rabbih** also preserves samples of both men's oratory. 'Abd Allāh was, moreover, an accomplished poet and musician, as was his son 'Ubayd Allāh; the latter's lost works include not only a poetic ***dīwān*** and works on prose style and on music, but also his correspondence with his good friend **Ibn al-Mu'tazz**. Another member of the family, Manṣūr ibn Ṭalḥa ibn Ṭāhir, who served as governor of Marw and Khwārazm, wrote on philosophy and music and was known as 'the Sage of the Ṭāhirids'.

The Ṭāhirids were also important as patrons of other writers and poets. Ṭāhir appointed the grammarian **al-Farrā'** as tutor to his sons, and the scholar **Ibn Sallām al-Jumaḥī** was patronized in Nishapur by 'Abd Allāh, to whom he dedicated two of his works. 'Abd Allāh also encouraged al-Farrā''s pupil **Tha'lab**, and 'Ubayd Allāh organized debates between Tha'lab and his rival **al-Mubarrad** in Baghdad. Some famous poets had more complex relations with the Ṭāhirids. **Di'bil** was notorious for his hostility to the family; **Abū Tammām**, after enjoying support in Baghdad from Ṭāhir's nephew Isḥāq al-Muṣ'abī, accepted an invitation to Nishapur from 'Abd Allāh, but was unhappy and did not linger there; **Ibn al-Rūmī** enjoyed on the whole better relations with 'Ubayd Allāh, for whom he composed numerous panegyrics.

Further reading

Bosworth, C.E., 'An early Arabic Mirror for Princes: Ṭāhir Dhū l-Yamīnain's epistle to his son 'Abdallāh (206/821)', *JNES* 29 (1970), 25–41.

——, 'The Ṭāhirids and Arabic culture', *JSS* 14 (1969), 45–79.

——, 'The Ṭāhirids and Persian literature', *Iran* 7 (1969), 103–6.

——, 'The Ṭāhirids and Ṣaffārids', in *CHIr*, vol. 4, *From the Arab Invasion to the Saljuqs*, 90–106.

E.K. ROWSON

al-Ṭahṭāwī, Rifā'a Rāfi' (1801–71)

Egyptian educator, official, journalist, translator and prose writer. Together with Muḥammad **'Abduh**, al-Ṭahṭāwī was one of **Egypt**'s two most prominent nineteenth-century *'ulamā'*. Sent by Muḥammad 'Alī to Paris in 1826 as leader of Egypt's first educational mission to France, he drank deeply and appreciatively of French and European culture, returning to Egypt in 1831 to begin a distinguished career in public service. Under Muḥammad 'Alī he headed the School of Languages and the Translation Department, whose functions were both to teach European languages to successive cadres of Egyptian students, and to help translate major European literary works into Arabic. He was also for a time editor of Egypt's first Arabic-language newspaper, ***al-Waqā'i' al-Miṣriyya***. Al-Ṭahṭāwī's career suffered some setbacks during the reigns of 'Abbās I and Sa'īd, but the more Europe-oriented Ismā'īl made him director of no less than five major government agencies: the War School, the Translation

Department, the School of Accounting, the School of Civil Engineering, and the Buildings Department.

Historians of Egypt are generally agreed that al-Ṭahṭāwī's main service to his country was as an educator. He shaped the ideas of several generations of Egyptian students, and he and his student disciples spent most of their lives editing and translating into Arabic European classics of history, biography, geography, science and engineering. In addition, al-Ṭahṭāwī himself produced four major literary works: *Anwār Tawfīq al-jalīl fī akhbār Miṣr wa-tawthīq Banī Ismā'īl* (1868–9), on Pharaonic Egypt; *Nihāyat al-Ījāz fī sīrat sākin al-Ḥijāz* (published posthumously in 1874), on the Prophet Muḥammad and early Islam; *Takhlīṣ al-ibrīz fī talkhīṣ Bārīz* (first edition, 1869), on his trip to France; and *Kitāb manāhij al-albāb al-Miṣriyya fī mabāhij al-ādāb al-'aṣriyya* (first edition, 1869), on nineteenth-century Egypt and especially the reign of Muḥammad 'Alī. The most sophisticated and fascinating of the four works, in both substance and style, is probably *Takhlīṣ al-ibrīz*, in which al-Ṭahṭāwī offers a penetrating, perceptive, and often surprisingly sympathetic account of his encounter with Western (mainly French) culture. The other three works (especially *Manāhij al-albāb*, on events in which the author had himself participated) provide an insight into how nineteenth-century Egyptian culture was becoming a blend of traditional (Egyptian) and modern (Western) elements.

Text edition

L'Or de Paris, A. Louca (trans.), Paris (1988).

Further reading

Crabbs, J.A., *The Writing of History in Nineteenth-century Egypt*, Detroit (1984), 67–86.
Hourani, A., *Arabic Thought in the Liberal Age 1798–1939*, London (1962), 67–83.

J. CRABBS

Tāj al-Dīn al-Subkī *see* al-Subkī, Tāj al-Dīn

ta'jīb

'Amazement' (transitive: 'amazing s.o.'); a technical term in philosophical poetics, i.e., in the works devoted to the *Poetics* of **Aristotle**. It plays a major role in **Ibn Sīnā** (Avicenna; d. 428/1037) and in authors dependent on him. 'Amazement' is one of the two goals of poetry, the other being 'public interests'. Both go together in Greek poetry, says Ibn Sīnā, but in Arabic poetry one finds poems exclusively geared to 'amazement'. The poetic elements that create 'wonder' (*ta'ajjub*) in the listener are twofold. First, 'amazement' is a concomitant of 'image-making' (*muḥākāt*, lit. 'imitation', a descendent of the Aristotelian μίμησις, but with a different interpretation), the latter being the most important constituent of the 'creation of mental images in the mind of the listener' (*takhyīl*, which in turn is the essential constituent of poetry. (See **imagination**.) The result of this *takhyīl*, on the part of the listener, is *takhayyul*, 'having, or receiving, mental images' and acting upon them immediately and unthinkingly; this is opposed to rational 'assent' (*taṣdīq*) to the truth of a statement and acting in accordance with it. Ibn Sīnā says that both are a submissiveness of the soul, the first to the wonder and pleasure aroused by the poetic text itself, the second to the recognition of the truth of what is being said. The other way in which 'amazement' is achieved is by the use of a rhetorical 'artifice' (*ḥīla*), either of the wording or of the meaning; this meaning is, however, only subsidiary to the first.

The theory of amazement can be traced back to certain passages in the *Poetics*, but in its generality it is Ibn Sīnā's creation. Although amazement seems to be equated with aesthetic pleasure in the passage alluded to above, in other places he keeps them apart.

In non-philosophic literature, especially of an anecdotal nature, the reaction of the listener to a poem is often described with 'wonder' (*'ajab*), 'amazement' (*ta'ajjub*), 'pleasure' (*ladhdha*, *iltidhādh*), 'being moved/rocked' (*hazza*, *ihtizāz*), and other words of similar meaning. However, a strict theory of aesthetic pleasure has not been developed from them.

Text editions

Fann al-shi'r min kitāb 'al-Shifā', in *Arisṭūṭālīs: Fann al-shi'r, ma' al-tarjama al-'Arabiyya al-qadīma wa-shurūḥ al-Fārābī wa-Ibn Sīnā wa-Ibn Rushd*, 'Abd al-Raḥmān Badawī (ed.), Cairo (1953), 159–98.
Avicenna's Commentary on the Poetics *of Aristotle*, Ismail M. Dahiyat (trans.), Leiden (1974).

Further reading

Black, D., *Logic and Aristotle's Rhetoric and Poetics in Medieval Arabic Philosophy*, Leiden (1990), 256–8.

Kemal, S., *The Poetics of Alfarabi and Avicenna*, Leiden (1991) (index, s.v. wonder).

Schoeler, G., *Einige Grundprobleme der autochthonen und der aristotelischen arabischen Literaturtheorie*, Wiesbaden (1975), esp. 57–73.

W.P. HEINRICHS

tajnīs see rhetorical figures

al-Takarlī, Fu'ād (1927–)

Iraqi author of short stories and novels. Born in Baghdad, al-Takarlī studied law in Baghdad, and served as a judge in Ba'qūba and Baghdad until his emigration to Paris in 1979. In his first short story *al-'Uyūn al-khuḍr* (1952) he handled a topic that attracted a number of Iraqi writers (e.g. the poet **al-Sayyāb**), as it had some French and Russian authors: the theme of the virtuous prostitute. Al-Takarlī's short stories published in the collection *al-Wajh al-ākhar* (1960, enlarged 2nd edn, 1982) deal with the psycho-social problems of male/female relations in a society dominated by crude patriarchal traditions. *Al-Raj' al-ba'īd* (Beirut, 1980–1993), the result of eleven years of literary work, is one of the best of all Iraqi novels; it provides a panorama of Baghdadi bourgeois society in the last months of 'Abd al-Karīm Qāsim's regime in 1962–3, as shown through three generations of a family living together in a house in the old quarter of Bāb al-Sharqī. The book relates, from a number of different viewpoints, the events and emotions of the protagonists; the love of three men for their cousin Munīra; and the fate of the men and Munīra in an atmosphere of political pressure combined with outdated traditions. His last novel *Khatam ar-Raml* (Beirut, 1996) depicts the problems of a mother-bound young egotist in the Baghdad of the 1970s.

Text edition

Les Voix de l'Aube, Paris (1985).

Further reading

al-Ṭāhir, 'Alī Jawād, *Fī al-qaṣaṣ al-'Irāqī al-mu'āṣir*, Beirut (1967), 12–35.

Walther, W., 'Distant echoes of love in the narrative work of F. al-Tikirlī', in R. Allen, H. Kilpatrick and E. de Moor (eds), *Love and Sexuality in Modern Arabic Literature*, London (1995), 131–9.

——, 'Studies in human psyche and human behaviour under political and social pressure. The recent literary work of Fu'ād al-Takarli', in *Arabic Quarterly* (forthcoming).

W. WALTHER

takhalluṣ see qaṣīda

takhyīl see imagination; metaphor

Takieddine, Khalīl *see* Taqī al-Dīn, Khalīl

Takieddine, Said *see* Taqī al-Dīn, Sa'īd

talkhīṣ see abridgements

al-Tall, Muṣṭafā Wahbī (1899–1949)

Jordanian poet. Born in Irbid, al-Tall was educated in Jordan and **Syria**. His career as teacher, lawyer and official was marked not only by exile, dismissal, resignations and imprisonment, but also by fearless outspokenness and a relentless pursuit of freedom from social restrictions.

Al-Tall's *Dīwān*, published posthumously in 1982, is an unabashed record of his tumultuous life and temperament. Flying in the face of social taboos, al-Tall sang of wine, excess and freedom, which he sought among the gypsies of Transjordan, whom he eulogized as a foil to the dominant religious and political authority whose hypocrisy he ridiculed. The verse sparkles with wit, and is enriched by apt colloquialisms and a strong local flavour.

Al-Tall is considered Jordan's foremost poet. Though a champion of the oppressed and outcast, he was personally close to King 'Abdallah. Despite the vibrancy and reach of his work (reminiscent of the *ṣu'lūk* poets, Burns and Lorca – see ***ṣa'ālīk***), it failed to make any significant impact on the contemporary literary scene.

M.R. NOURALLAH

Tambal, Hamza al-Malik (1898–1960)

Sudanese poet and literary critic. Tambal first appeared on the Sudanese literary scene in 1927, with the publication in *Ḥaḍārat al-Sūdān* (the country's sole newspaper) of a stinging attack on traditional poetry. His aim was to point out the need for a poetry of true personal feelings and originality born in moments of spiritual inspiration. The style of his criticism, however, which echoed the irreverent tone of the **Dīwān Group**, was alien to Sudanese society, and *Ḥaḍārat al-Sūdān* soon ceased publication of his articles. Tambal's anthology *Dīwān al-ṭabī'a* (1931) represents a complete departure from traditional poetry, both in form and style; its language is conversational and interwoven with Sudanese local expressions, the imagery is drawn from the local environment, and topics and feelings are drawn from personal experience of everyday life. Despite this, Tambal played no part in the Sudanese literary movement of the 1930s, and his contribution to Sudanese literature was not recognized until after his death.

Further reading

Shoush, M.I., *al-Shi'r al-ḥadīth fī al-Sūdān*, 2 edn, Khartoum (1971).

M.I. SHOUSH

Tamīm *see* tribes

Tamīm ibn al-Mu'izz li-Dīn Allāh al-Fāṭimī (337–74/948–84)

Fāṭimid poet and *amīr*. Born in al-Mahdiyya (in present **Tunisia**), he arrived as a member of his father al-Mu'izz's family in **Cairo** in 362/973, when **Egypt** had already been conquered and occupied by the Fāṭimid army under general Jawhar al-Ṣaqlabī.

Tamīm's poems belong to many different genres. In his wine poems, **Abū Nuwās**'s influence may be observed. Although Tamīm was passed over in the succession to the Imāmate, he dedicated his poems of praise exclusively to the two Imāms of his time, his father and his own brother Nizār al-'Aziz billāh. Next to his boasting (***fakhr***) on account of his Fāṭimid descent, his poetry contains many descriptions of gardens and palaces where he enjoyed staying. Characteristic of some is the transition (*takhalluṣ*) from a rather profane, introductory section on wine to the next more serious one dealing with praise (***madīḥ***) for the Enlightened Imām. Acquainted with many expressions of the Fāṭimid creed, he was able to convey these in elegant poems. In his special poems of lament (*marāthī*; see ***rithā'***), he is seen shedding profuse tears when commemorating the untimely deaths of his hallowed **Shī'ī** forefathers.

Text edition

Dīwān, Muḥammad Ḥasan al-A'ẓamī (ed.), Cairo (1957), rpt Beirut (1970).

Further reading

Smoor, P., 'Fāṭimid poets and the "Takhalluṣ" that bridges the nights of time to the Imām of time', *Der Islam* 68/2 (1991), 232–62.
——, '"The Master of the Century": Fāṭimid poets in Cairo', *Orientalia Lovaniensia Analecta, Egypt and Syria in the Fatimid, Ayyubid and Mamluk Eras*, V. Vermeulen and D. De Smet (eds), Leuven (1995), 139–62.
——, 'Wine, love and praise for the Fāṭimid Imāms, the Enlightened of God', *ZDMG* 142/1 (1992), 90–104.

P. SMOOR

Tamīm ibn 'Ubayy *see* Ibn Muqbil

al-Tamīmī (third/ninth century)

Abū Muḥammad Qāsim al-Tamīmī was an apologist of the fratricidal war (*fitra*) that paved the way for the Norman conquest of **Sicily**. Soon after, he became witness to the Muslim wars against the Christian occupation of the island. In al-Tamīmī's work the traditional theme of separation and regret for those departed becomes a bitter description of the tragic events of his days: the emigration of friends towards the distant Islamic lands, and distress for the beloved place that has now become the land of the unbelievers. His elegies are considered to be the best of the Sicilian school.

Text edition

Di Matteo, I., 'Antologia di poeti arabi siciliani', in *Archivio Storico Siciliano*, Palermo (1935), 1–28.

F.M. CORRAO

Tāmir, Zakariyyā (1931–)

Syrian short-story writer. Born in **Damascus**, Tāmir is regarded as one of the most accomplished writers of short stories in the Arab world in recent decades. Beginning in the late 1960s, he has produced a number of collections of stories that use a terse yet clear style to create nightmarish visions of a society characterized by personal alienation, sexual frustration and political oppression. His works introduce the reader to worlds in which the normal logic of life and reality is not to be found. He has also written a number of stories for children. Currently resident in Oxford, he has also served as editor of the prominent Syrian literary journal, *al-Ma'rifa*. His collections include: *Ṣahīl al-Jawād al-Abyaḍ* (1960), *Rabī' fī al-ramād* (1963), *al-Ra'd* (1970), *Li-mādhā saqaṭ al-nahr* (1973) and *Dimashq al-ḥarā'iq* (1973).

Text edition

Tigers on the Tenth Day & Other Stories, D. Johnson-Davies (trans.), London (1985).

Further reading

Allen, R., *Modern Arabic Literature*, New York (1987), 313–17.
CHALMAL, 322–4.
al-Khateeb, H., 'A modern Syrian short story: *Wajh al-qamar*', *JAL* 3 (1972), 96–105.

R. ALLEN

tamthīl see rhetorical figures

al-Tankīt wa-al-Tabkīt (June to October 1881)

Influential nationalist literary, educational and satirical weekly founded in Alexandria by 'Abd Allāh **Nadīm**. Nadīm wrote in a style as close to the vernacular as classical syntax would permit, creating a new press language accessible to a broader readership; his sketches arguably represent the beginnings of the modern Egyptian short story. In *al-Tankīt wa-al-Tabkīt* Nadīm exposed Khedive Ismā'īl's injustice and his debt problems, attacking foreign interference in Egypt, the moral decline of the young and the threats posed by modernization, and supporting the 'Urābist army officers in their call for liberty.

Further reading

al-Ḥadīdī, 'Alī, *'Abd Allāh al-Nadīm, khaṭīb al-waṭaniyya*, Cairo (n.d.).
Hafez, S., *The Genesis of Arabic Narrative Discourse*, London (1993), 120–3.

P.C. SADGROVE

al-Tanūkhī (329–84/940–994)

Abū 'Alī al-Muḥassin ibn 'Alī al-Tanūkhī, compiler of three anthologies, middle **'Abbāsid** period. Al-Tanūkhī was born in **Basra** as the son of a judge, held the office of *qāḍī* from 349/960 onwards in Mesopotamian and western Iranian towns. In the realms of ***adab***, he received instruction by such famous men as **Abū al-Faraj al-Iṣbahānī** (d. 356/967) and Abū Bakr **al-Ṣūlī** (d. 335/946). A ***dīwān*** of his poetry is now lost. His *'Unwān al-ḥikma* is a collection of gnomic wisdom, arranged according to classes or social groups of persons uttering them; in the first two-thirds of the book, the names of the persons uttering the maxims are given, whereas in the rest anonymously quoted sayings prevail. *Al-Mustajād min fa'alāt al-ajwād* mainly contains texts about generous people; it is often ascribed to al-Tanūkhī, but rather seems to be written by an anonymous author of the fifth/eleventh or sixth/twelfth century (Sellheim 1976, 348–53). *Nishwār al-muḥāḍara* is a collection of anecdotes mainly on upper-class officials, their intrigues and struggle for influence. These anecdotes were, as the author states in his introduction, put down in writing for the first time; from the original eleven sections, only four are preserved. The most famous of his books is *al-Faraj ba'd al-shidda*, which contains anecdotes on the topic 'joy follows sorrow'. Al-Tanūkhī used earlier works in this genre (namely, the books devoted to this topic by **al-Madā'inī**, **Ibn Abī al-Dunyā** and Abū al-Ḥusayn Ibn Yūsuf [d. 328/939]), but added a considerable amount of new material collected by himself from literary and oral sources. The design of the book is to convey faith in God even in hopeless circumstances. The texts are grouped in fourteen thematically arranged chapters, e.g. according to the sorts of distress or to the ways that rescue is achieved. The manuscript tradition shows substantial divergences, and until now al-Tanūkhī's role in the composition of the work is far from being clarified (Ashtiany, 115). *Al-Faraj* was translated into Persian (seventh/thirteenth century) and Turkish.

Text editions

al-Faraj ba'd al-shidda, Cairo (1955); 'A. al-Shāljī (ed.), 5 vols, Beirut (1978).

Ende gut, alles gut. Das Buch der Erleichterung nach der Bedrängnis, (partial) A. Hottinger (trans.), Zürich (1979).

Nishwār al-muḥāḍara wa-akhbār al-mudhākara, D.S. Margoliouth (ed.), London (1921); parts published in *RAAD* 10 (1930), 12 (1932), 13 (1933), 17 (1942); 'A. al-Shāljī (ed.), 8 vols, Beirut (1971–3).

The Table-Talk of a Mesopotamian Judge, D.S. Margoliouth (trans.), London (1922) and in *IC* 3 (1929) to 6 (1932), rpt Hyderabad (n.d.).

Sellheim, R., *Materialien zur Arabischen Literaturgeschichte*, vol. 1, Wiesbaden (1976).

Further reading

Ashtiany, J., 'Al-Tanūkhī's *al-Faraj Ba'd al-Shidda* as a literary source', in *Arabicus Felix*, 108–28.

Fähndrich, H., 'À propos d'une compilation de la sagesse arabe: 'Unwān al-ḥikma d'al-Muḥassin al-Tanūḫī', *QSA* 5–6 (1987–8), 241–50.

——, 'Die Tischgespräche des mesopotamischen Richters. Untersuchungen zu al-Muḥassin at-Tanūḫīs Niśwār al-Muḥāḍara', *Der Islam* 65 (1988), 81–115.

Fakkar, R., *At-Tanûḫî et son livre: La délivrance après l'angoisse*, Cairo (1955).

Kindlers Neues Literatur Lexikon, W. Jens (ed.), Munich (1991), vol. 16, 339–42 (S. Grotzfeld).

Wiener, A., 'Die Farağ ba'd aš-Šidda-Literatur', *Der Islam* 4 (1913), 290–8, 387–420.

T. SEIDENSTICKER

Taqī al-Dīn al-Fāsī *see* al-Fāsī, Taqī al Dīn

Taqī al-Dīn, Khalīl (1906–87)

Lebanese novelist, short-story writer and essayist. Born in the Shouf area of Lebanon, Khalīl Taqī al-Dīn studied law in Beirut, before embarking on a long career as a civil servant and diplomat. He began his career as a writer by publishing essays in the leading literary journals of the day under the nicknames Bashshār and al-Sādhij, and was one of the founders of al-'Uṣba al-'ashara ('The Group of Ten'), who revolutionized the Beirut literary scene in the 1930s under the influence of the **Mahjar** poets and the French naturalist school. He later published two collections of short stories, *'Ashar qiṣaṣ* (1940) and *al-I'dām* (1941), and a collection of essays, *Khawāṭir sādhij*, in which he brought to life the traditions of his native Shouf as well as tackling topical world issues. A short political, romantic story *Tamāra* (1955) dramatized his experience in Stalin's Russia. Khalīl Taqī al-Dīn's short novel *al-'Ā'id* (1968) vividly involves the reader in the Druze belief in reincarnation; his major work, however, is *Karen wa-Ḥasan* (1971), a socio-political novel set in World War 2 which brings together East and West through the love story of the two heroes. Khalīl Taqī al-Dīn is noted for his simple yet sensuous style, his unique gift for conveying local colour, and his deep love for his country and fellow human beings.

M.T. AMYUNI

Taqī al-Dīn, Sa'īd (1904–60)

Lebanese dramatist, short-story writer and essayist. Born in Baakline, in the Shouf area of Lebanon, Sa'īd Taqī al-Dīn lived half his life in the Philippines. A rebel and adventurer at heart, his writing defies categorization; his dominant mode is satirical in style, blending humour, irony, caricature and self-mockery in a manner reminiscent of Swift but rarely found in Arabic literature. Living abroad, Sa'īd took to heart the socio-political problems of Lebanon, and his native village assumed mythical status in his imagination. He broke new ground in the Lebanese theatre through his use of an everyday form of Arabic easily understood by his large audiences, well before this style was adopted by contemporary journalists and playwrights. His best-known play is *Lawlā al-muḥāmī* (1924). Sa'īd also broke new ground in his essays and aphorisms, which captured economically and incisively the deterioration in the character and lifestyle of his epoch. His complete works were published in Beirut in 1969.

Further reading

Daye, J., *Sa'īd Taqī al-Dīn*, 3 vols, Beirut (1978–91).

Shaybūb, E., *Sa'īd Taqī al-Dīn: sīratuhu wa-intājuhu*, Beirut (1980).

M.T. AMYUNI

Ṭarafa ibn al-ʿAbd (middle of the sixth century)

Important early pre-Islamic poet from the clan Qays ibn Thaʿlaba (cf. **al-Aʿshā Maymūn**), who was probably in contact with the **Lakhmids** of **Ḥīra**. Further reports about his life can hardly claim reliability. This also holds true for the famous story of 'al-Mutalammis' letter', in which he figures as the companion of his maternal uncle **al-Mutalammis**. The story tells how Ṭarafa met a premature death when he unwittingly delivered a letter containing his own death-warrant from the king of Ḥīra to the governor of the province al-Baḥrayn. But unlike al-Mutalammis, who is rather the hero of a saga interspersed with poetry ascribed to its protagonist, Ṭarafa was a skilled poet who composed long polythematic ***qaṣīda***s on a high artistic level. This is especially conspicuous in the descriptive passages in his poems which burst forth with original comparisons. The finest example of this kind is a long and famous section of 28 lines in Ṭarafa's *Muʿallaqa* in which he describes a riding camel using 24 comparisons and metaphors. Ṭarafa's fame rests nearly exclusively on this poem. Since he was one of the *muqillūn*, i.e. those who had composed only few poems; his ***dīwān*** contains less than a dozen other longer poems which can claim authenticity.

Text editions

Arberry, A.J., *The Seven Odes*, Cambridge (1957), 67–89.

Dīwān, in Ahlwardt, *Divans*; Durriyya al-Khaṭīb and Luṭfī al-Ṣaqqāl (eds), Damascus (1975).

Geiger, B., 'Die Muʿallaqa des Ṭarafa', *WZKM* 19 (1905), 323–70, 20 (1906), 37–80.

Sells, M., 'The *Muʿallaqa* of Ṭarafa', *JAL* 17 (1986), 21–33.

Further reading

Jacobi, Renate, *Studien zur Poetik der altarabischen Qaṣīde*, Wiesbaden (1971), *passim*.

T. BAUER

See also: *Muʿallaqāt*

ṭardiyya (hunting poem)

A monthematic piece (***qiṭʿa***) usually composed in ***rajaz*** and dealing with some aspect of the hunt as practised by the Arabs. The earliest examples date from the middle **Umayyad** period; the effloresence of the genre occurred in the **ʿAbbāsid** era. In the pre-Islamic era, extant treatments of hunting scenes (a probable residuum of the practice, common in many hunting societies, of bewitching the game by capturing its essence in verse) are included within the polythematic ***qaṣīda*** and are of two types; the professional, or 'primitive' hunt, and the aristocratic, or royal, hunt (Bāshā's *ṣayd* and *ṭarad* respectively). The professional hunt occurs as part of the camel description (*waṣf al-nāqa*), the prey being the oryx and the wild ass (an exception is **Muzarrid**, *Mufaḍḍaliyyāt* 17, where the depiction [vv. 63–74], intended as a virtuoso display of poetic genius, concludes the ode). The aristocratic hunt is linked with the personal vaunt (***fakhr***) and often concludes the ode: it is sometimes linked with an equine description. Both types are attested in the poetic remains of the Umayyad **Abū al-Najm al-ʿIjlī**, where the *qaṣīda* format persists but wedded to the *rajaz*, which metre was to dominate the genre. To Abū al-Najm is also attributed the first extant monothematic *ṭardiyya*, a description of coursing with cheetahs, extemporized at the request of ʿAbd al-Malik ibn Bishr. It is unlikely that this is the first instance of the practice of composing such pieces at the conclusion of a hunt.

The influence of the *qaṣīda* format is discernible in the saker falcon description composed by **Ḥumayd al-Arqaṭ** (*Ḥamāsat Abī Tammām* [ed. Freytag, 1848, rpt 1969], 393) – the saker is a simile for the poet's horse – but is dispensed with in a piece composed by **al-Shamardal** ibn Sharīk (ed. Seidensticker, Wiesbaden, 1983, 20), also a saker description, which displays the characteristics of the genre as it was to be developed by **Abū Nuwās**, the supreme cynegetic poet. His *ṭardiyyāt*, composed in both *rajaz* and other metres (commonly *mutaqārib*, *ṭawīl* and *sarīʿ*), are crisp and vivid metonymical descriptions of the chase and can be categorized as (a) the early morning expedition (the prototype of which is **Imru' al-Qays**, Ahlwardt 40.17–37, and which employs a variant of the formula *wa-qad aghtadī*, present in the poems of Abū al-Najm, al-Shamardal and Ḥumayd); and (b) the purely descriptive, introduced by the verb *anʿatu*, (cf. Smith, 172), and related to the *rajaz* imprecations of snakes and rats which **al-Jāḥiẓ** quotes in the *Kitāb al-Ḥayawān* (ed. Hārūn, Cairo 1938–45, vol. 4, 285, vol. 5, 258–9; cf.

Wagner, *Grundzüge*, vol. 2, 56). The milieu is aristocratic and the full panoply of hunting animals and techniques is celebrated. **Ibn al-Muʿtazz** shows himself to be an adherent of Abū Nuwās in his hunting poems. Other poets of the genre include **Ibn al-Muʿadhdhal** (d. 240/854), **al-Nāshi' al-Akbar** (d. 293/906), **al-Ṣanawbarī** (d. 334/944) and **Kushājim** (d. 360/971). The most prolonged and exhaustive treatment of the chase is that composed by **Abū Firās al-Ḥamdānī**, an *urjūza* of 137 lines in which various animals are featured in different narrative styles.

A *ṭardiyya* composed by **al-Mutanabbī**, description, rhyming in *lām*, of a saluki, is interesting as much for the circumstances attendant upon its composition as for its poetic merit. The poet is approached by the *kātib* Abū ʿAlī Hārūn al-Awrājī, a patron of his, who has come back from the hunt full of admiration for a saluki which, unaided by a saker, has run down a gazelle. He wishes that al-Mutanabbī could have been present to capture the occasion in verse, but the great panegyrist is reluctant: he has no truck with such things. At the insistence of Abū ʿAlī, the poet dictates an improvised *urjūza* to the secretary. The *ṭardiyya* poets will have been commissioned by enthusiastic nobles to produce descriptions of their favourites (in many instances these would have been improvised; hence the fondness for the *rajaz* metre), just as George Stubbs produced equine portraits for his eighteenth-century patrons. The *ṭardiyya* was a poetic vogue which subsequently fell into neglect.

Further reading

Bāshā, ʿA.R., *Shiʿr al-ṭarad*, Beirut (1974).

Montgomery, J.E., 'A reconsideration of some Jāhilī poetic paradigms', unpublished PhD thesis, University of Glasgow (1990).

——, 'The cat and the camel: a literary motif', in *Literary Heritage of Classical Islam: Arabic and Islamic Studies in Honor of James Bellamy*, M. Mir and J. Fossum (eds), Princeton (1993), 137–48.

Smith, G.R., 'Hunting poetry (*ṭardiyyāt*)', in *CHALABL*, 167–84.

Stetkevych, J., 'The Hunt in the Arabic *Qaṣīdah*' the Antecedents of the Ṭardiyyah', in *Tradition and Modernity in Arabic Language and Literature*, J. Smart (ed.), Richmond (1996), 102–118.

Wagner, E., *Grundzüge der klassischen arabischen Dichtung*, Darmstadt (1988), vol. 2, 46–58.

J.E. MONTGOMERY

ta'rīkh see chronogram; historical literature

tarjama see biography; translation

taṣrīʿ see prosody

al-Tawḥīdī, Abū Hayyān (*c*.315–411/*c*.927–1023)

Abū Ḥayyān ʿAlī ibn Muḥammad al-Tawḥīdī was a prose essayist and one of the greatest masters of Arabic style. He grew up in **Baghdad**, where he received an excellent religious and literary education and initially worked as a copyist. His first major work, *Insight and Treasures*, was a relatively conventional anthology of anecdotes and philological lore which, nonetheless, already displayed some of the wit and stylistic brilliance for which he was to become famous. A prickly and cantankerous person, he found it difficult throughout his life to establish good relations with patrons in positions of power; an overture to the **Būyid** vizier in **Rayy**, **Ibn al-ʿAmīd**, and a later stay at the court of the latter's successor, **al-Ṣāḥib Ibn ʿAbbād**, both ended in failure and acrimony, but provided material for his masterpiece of venomous gossip, *The Faults of the Two Viziers*. Back in Baghdad, al-Tawḥīdī somewhat more successfully served for a time as copyist and then boon companion to the vizier Ibn Saʿdān; his somewhat reworked account of evenings spent in conversation with the latter, *Delight and Entertainment*, offers a rich picture of Baghdadi intellectual life at the time, and particularly of the philosophical circles that he was beginning to frequent. He became a devoted follower of the philosopher **Abū Sulaymān al-Sijistānī**, whose views dominate his *Conversations*, which treat a variety of philosophical topics. Philosophy also has its place among the very wide-ranging series of 180 questions he addressed to his friend **Miskawayh** which, together with the latter's replies, form their joint work *The Scattered and the Gathered*. Some time around 375/985 al-Tawḥīdī left Baghdad for Shiraz, where he published a number of other works, including a *Treatise on Friendship*, originally drafted in Baghdad, and a mystical treatise, *Divine Intimations*. In 400/1010 he burnt his books, as we know from a rather bitter letter he composed to justify his act. He died at an advanced age in Shiraz. A campaign by later religious scholars accusing him of heresy and irreligion cast a shadow over his reputation, but his unique style, modelled on that of **al-Jāḥiẓ** (of whom he wrote a lost encomium) and somewhat conservative in his own day in its relative lack of artifice, has kept his memory alive.

Text editions

'Abū Ḥaiyān al-Tawḥīdī on penmanship', in *Four Essays on Art and Literature in Islam*, F. Rosenthal (trans.), Leiden (1971), 20–50.
Akhlāq al-wazīrayn, M. al-Ṭanjī (ed.), Damascus (1965).
al-Baṣā'ir wa-al-dhakhā'ir, W. al-Qāḍī (ed.), 10 vols in 6, Beirut (1988).
'Épître sur les sciences d'Abū Ḥayyān al-Tawḥīdī', M. Bergé (ed.), *BEO* 18 (1964), 241–98.
al-Hawāmil wa-al-shawāmil (with Miskawayh), A. Amīn and A. Ṣaqr (eds), Cairo (1951).
al-Imtā' wa-al-mu'ānasa, A. Amīn and A. al-Zayn (eds), 3 vols, 2nd edn, Cairo (1953).
al-Ishārāt al-ilāhiya, W. al-Qāḍī (ed.), Beirut (1973).
al-Muqābasāt, M.T. Ḥasayn (ed.), Baghdad (1970).
'La Risālat al-Ḥayāt d'Abū Ḥayyān al- Tawḥīdī', C. Audebert (trans.), *BEO* 18 (1964), 147–95.
Thalāth rasā'il li-Abī Ḥayyān al-Tawḥīdī, I. Kaylānī (ed.), Damascus (1952).

Further reading

Bergé, M., *Pour un humanisme vécu: Abū Ḥayyān al-Tawḥīdī*, Damascus (1979).
——, 'Abū Ḥayyān al-Tawḥīdī', in *CHALABL*, 112–24.
Kraemer, J., *Humanism in the Renaissance of Islam*, Leiden (1986), 212–22.

E.K. ROWSON

ta'wīl *see* exegesis, Koranic

ṭawīl *see* prosody

tawriya *see* rhetorical figures

Ṭayfūr, Aḥmad ibn Abī Ṭāhir *see* Ibn Abī Ṭāhir Ṭayfūr

Taymūr, Aḥmad (1871–1930)

Egyptian man of letters. Born in **Cairo** into a Turco-Circassian family which emigrated to **Egypt** at the beginning of the nineteenth century, Aḥmad Taymūr was educated by his elder sister, the poetess 'Ā'isha 'Iṣmat **al-Taymūriyya**. Widowed at an early age, he occupied himself with the education of his sons Muḥammad and Maḥmūd **Taymūr**, influencing their literary career through his profound knowledge of Arabic language and literature.

Aḥmad Taymūr spent his large inheritance on books and manuscripts which were consulted by scholars from the Arab world and Europe. His collection of about 20,000 volumes was donated after his death to the Egyptian **Dār al-Kutub**. His lexicographical studies of **Ibn Manẓūr**'s *Lisān al-'Arab* and Cairene proverbs still provide interesting material; and his folkloric studies on **shadow-plays**, painting, **music** and games in the Arab world demonstrate an intense interest in Arab life and culture.

Further reading

Dāghir, Yūsuf As'ad, *Maṣādir al-dirāsāt al-adabiyya*, Beirut (1956), vol. 2, 231–5.
de Moor, E., *Un oiseau en cage*, Amsterdam (1991), 40–5.
Ziriklī, Khayr al-Dīn, *al-A'lām*, 7th edn, Cairo (1986), vol. 1, 95–6.

E.C. DE MOOR

Taymūr, Maḥmūd (1894–1973)

Egyptian novelist, short-story writer, playwright and essayist. Born in **Cairo**, Maḥmūd Taymūr was the third son of Aḥmad **Taymūr** and the youngest brother of Muḥammad **Taymūr**. After secondary school he entered the Agricultural College, but had to abandon his higher studies after contracting typhoid. Choosing to follow the example of his brother Muḥammad, whom he greatly admired and who inspired him to read and imitate the works of De Maupassant, he published his first writings – partly in prose poetry – in the reformist review ***al-Sufūr***. After Muḥammad's death in 1921 he collected and edited his works, then started to write his own short stories in the realistic style of the 'Modern School', founded by his brother and some other friends. In 1925 he published his first collections of short stories, *al-Shaykh Jum'a wa-qiṣaṣ ukhrā* and *'Amm Mitwalli wa-qiṣaṣ ukhrā*. Twenty-four other volumes of short stories, seven novels, eighteen plays and sixteen volumes of essays followed, making

Maḥmūd Taymūr one of the most prolific writers in modern Arabic literature.

As he himself stressed, Maḥmūd Taymūr's work was deeply influenced by the ideas of his brother Muḥammad, by the Romantic writer **al-Manfalūṭī**, by the symbolism of **Jubrān** and the **Mahjar** school, by Russian novelists such as Chekhov and Turgenev and by the French realists. His stay in Europe between 1925 and 1927 also greatly influenced his sense of literature.

In 1939 Maḥmūd published his first novel, *Nidā' al-majhūl*, a fantastic adventure set in the Lebanese mountains and characterized as both a 'Gothic romance' and a 'novel of spiritual quest'; his best-known novel, *Salmā fī mahabb al-rīḥ*, the love story of a 'modern' Egyptian woman living in difficult social circumstances, was published in 1947.

Maḥmūd's first plays, one-acters written in 1941 in the Egyptian colloquial, deal with contemporary life in Egypt. This is also the case with some longer plays such as *Makhba' raqm 13* (1941), *Ḥaflat shāy* (1943) and *Qanābil* (1943). In other plays Taymūr uses a historical setting, Arab or pharaonic, to create his characters: examples are *Suhād* (1942), *Ḥawwā al-khālida* (1945) and *al-Yawm Khamr* (1945).

Maḥmūd Taymūr's fictional work shows a development from naturalistic description to psychological analysis, from local colour to human nature in general. As in other writers of the period, one notices a shift to socially committed literature after 1945. At first, he used colloquial Arabic in the dialogue of his short stories as an expression of his intention to create an *adab qawmī* 'national literature', but after his stay in Europe he developed into a purist who even tried to replace European loan-words by equivalents in standard Arabic. Maḥmūd Taymūr, who is sometimes known as the 'Egyptian Maupassant', was awarded the State Prize for Literature several times, and was a member of the Egyptian Arabic Language Academy.

Further reading

Badawi, M.M, *Modern Arabic Drama in Egypt*, Cambridge (1987), 88–111.

al-Ḥakīm, Nazīh, *Maḥmūd Taymūr ...*, Cairo (1946).

al-Ibyārī, Fatḥī, *'Ālam Taymūr al-qaṣaṣī*, Cairo (1976).

Peters, I., *Mahmûd Taymûr and the Modern Egyptian Short Story*; unpublished Ph.D thesis, Columbia University (1974).

Wielandt, R., *Das erzählerische Frühwerk Mahmûd Taymûrs*, Beirut (1983).

E.C.M. DE MOOR

Taymūr, Muḥammad (1892–1921)

Egyptian dramatist and prose writer. Born in **Cairo**, the second son of Aḥmad **Taymūr** and elder brother of Maḥmud Taymūr, Muḥammad Taymūr studied at the 'Abbās Khedivial School before travelling to Europe in the summer of 1911. Until the summer of 1914 he studied law in Paris and Lyon, devoting most of his time to drama and French literature. His reading of realistic writers like De Maupassant and Zola prepared him to become a pioneer of the modern Arabic short story, while his visits to the Odéon Theatre prompted the idea of becoming an actor and playwright.

After returning to Egypt, Muḥammad Taymūr performed in the clubs of Gezira, an activity frowned on both by his family and by the palace. From 1916 he began to publish poems in the reformist review ***al-Sufūr***, and theatre criticism in *al-Minbar*. He also wrote short stories in the style of De Maupassant under the name *Mā tarāhu al-'uyūn* (1917). In 1918 he married his cousin Rashīda Rashīd. In the same year he published his first play, *al-'Uṣfūr fī al-qafaṣ*, in which he avenged himself on the restrictions of his education by introducing a young hero, son of a well-to-do family, who marries his nurse, preferring freedom and poverty to family control and wealth. His second play, also performed in 1918, was a comedy based around a middle-class employee, *'Abd al-Sattār Effendi*, who is dominated by his loud-voiced wife and their spoiled son. Muḥammad Taymūr's intention was to prove that it was possible to write a comedy in Egyptian dialect without the shameless devices employed in the boulevard comedies of Najīb al-Rīḥānī and 'Alī al-Kassār.

At about the same time, Muḥammad – together with Aḥmad Khayrī al-Sa'īd – founded the literary circle Madrasat al-ādāb al-jadīda, later known as al-Madrasa al-ḥadītha (the 'Modern School'), to which belonged also Maḥmūd Ṭāhir **Lāshīn**, Yaḥyā **Ḥaqqī** and Ḥusayn Fawzī.

In 1920 Muḥammad offended the Turkish establishment with his comedy *al-'Ashara al-ṭayyiba*, an adaptation of the French comedy *Barbe-Bleu*, with music by Sayyid Darwīsh. The manuscript of his most important play, *al-Hāwiya* – in which a young aristocrat loses his fortune, his wife and his life as the inevitable consequence of drug addiction – was finished just before his death. With this play Taymūr proved that serious problems could be treated in the vernacular, which until then had been reserved for lighthearted comedies. His complete works were published after his death in three volumes by his brother Maḥmūd (Cairo, 1922, rpt 1990).

Further reading

Badawi, M.M, *Early Arabic Drama*, Cambridge (1988), 101–20.

de Moor, E., *Un Oiseau en cage ...*, Amsterdam (1991).

Khiḍr, A., *Muḥammad Taymūr, ḥayātuhu wa-adabuh*, Cairo (1965).

Waḥīd, 'Alā al-Dīn, *Masraḥ Muḥammad Taymūr*, Cairo (1975).

E.C.M. DE MOOR

al-Taymūriyya, 'Ā'isha 'Iṣmat (1840–1902)

Turco-Egyptian poet and prose writer. A member of the Taymūr family of scholars and writers, 'Ā'isha al-Taymūriyya was the daughter of Ismā'īl Pasha Taymūr, a learned high government official, and a Circassian concubine. An autobiographical preface to her allegorical tale *Natā'ij al-aḥwāl fī al-aqwāl wa-al-af'āl* (1305/1887–8) recalls her anger as a child at being barred from 'unfeminine' intellectual pursuits and forced into embroidery by her mother, whereupon her father took her education in hand, engaging tutors in Arabic and Persian and hearing her lessons himself. Her marriage to Maḥmūd Bey al-Islāmbulī in 1854 interrupted her studies and writing, which she resumed after his death in 1875, engaging the services of two women tutors. She composed poetry in Arabic, Turkish and Persian, and apparently planned to publish ***dīwān***s in all three languages, but the death of her daughter and eye disease deterred her. Her Arabic *dīwān Ḥilyat al-ṭirāz* was first published in Cairo in 1884; her Turkish *dīwān Shākūfa* was being published as Zaynab **Fawwāz** wrote her biographical dictionary in the early 1890s. Al-Taymūriyya also published a prose treatise on gender relations, *Mir'āt al-ta'ammul fī al-umūr* (1892), and articles on girls' education and literary subjects.

Text editions

'Family reform comes only through the education of girls' and 'Introduction to *The Results of Circumstances in Words and Deeds*', M. Booth (trans.), in Margot Badran and Miriam Cooke (eds), *Opening the Gates: A Century of Arab Feminist Writing*, Bloomington and Indianapolis (1990).

Fawwāz, Zaynab, *al-Durr al-manthūr fī ṭabaqāt rabbāt al-khudūr*, Cairo/Bulaq (1312/1894).

Further reading

Booth, Marilyn, 'Biography and feminist rhetoric in early twentieth-century Egypt: Mayy Ziyada's studies of three women's lives', *Journal of Women's History* 3 (1) (Spring 1991).

Kaḥḥāla, 'Umar Riḍā, *A'lām al-nisā' fī 'ālamay al-'Arab wa-al-Islām*, Beirut, 4th pr. (1982).

Ziyāda, Mayy, *'Ā'isha Taymūr: shā'irat al-ṭalī'a*, Cairo (1926); rpt Beirut (1975).

M. BOOTH

Al-Ṭayyib Bā (Abū) Makhrama (d. 947/1540)

Famous Yemeni jurist and historian of South Arabia and Aden. Born into a renowned clan of scholars and Shāfi'ī jurists who had come to Aden from Ḥaḍramawt, he studied under the best *'ulamā'* of his time and soon acquired a reputation as the most knowledgeable expert on legal affairs. He also excelled in ***ḥadīth*** studies, Koranic **commentary** and Arabic **grammar**, and was a popular teacher whose lectures attracted numerous students. Towards the end of his life the Ṭāhirid sultan of Aden appointed him chief *qāḍī* of this city. He held this post for a short time, then was afflicted by a fatal illness.

Al-Ṭayyib Bā Makhrama owes his fame to his two historical works, one of which, *Ta'rīkh thaghr 'Adan*, deals with Aden and its inhabitants, historical sites and monuments; the other, *Qilādat al-nahr*, is a collection of the biographies of South Arabian rulers, notables, scholars and mystics who lived between the sixth/twelfth and tenth/sixteenth centuries. *Qilādat al-naḥr* also includes sections that describe political developments in **Arabia** during this period. The former work is available to specialists in a splendid edition by O. Löfgren; of the latter only the historical section has been edited. Although both works are compilations based on the chronicles of earlier Arabian historians (e.g. Ibn Samura, al-Yāfi'ī, al-Janadī, al-Khazrajī, Ibn al-Dayba' and some less well-known authors from Ḥaḍramawt), they provide valuable – and sometimes unique – information on medieval **Yemen** and South Arabia.

Further reading

Ahmed, M. ʿAbd El Aal, *The First Portuguese Efforts to Control the Red Sea*, Cairo (1980) (in Arabic).
al-ʿAydarūsī, ʿAbd al-Qādir, *al-Nūr al-sāfir*, Baghdad (1353/1934), 226–8.
Löfgren, O., 'Über Abū Maḥrama's *Ḳilādat al-naḥr*', *MO* 25 (1931), 120-37.
——, *Arabische Texte zur Kenntnis der Stadt Aden im Mittelalter*, Uppsala (1936–50).
Schuman, L.O., *Political History of the Yemen at the beginning of the 16th Century*, Amsterdam (1960).
Zetterstéen, K.V., 'Über Abū Maḥrama's *Ta'rīkh thaghr ʿAdan*', in *Festschrift C. Meinhof*, Hamburg (1927), 364-70.

A. KNYSH

Tengour, Habib (1947–)

Algerian poet and novelist writing in French. Born in Mostaganem in western **Algeria**, Tengour studied the Muslim religious brotherhoods of his own region at university. As a poet, he is attracted by political and satirical fable, embellishing various types of epic poem with tinges of corrosive humour. *Tapapakitaques* (1977) ('The island of poetry') – a story-poem in which poets are seen to bow to the needs of artistic production – is a clear criticism of poetry written on demand for the Party. *Sultan Galiev* (1985), *Le Vieux de la montagne* (1983) and *L'Epreuve de l'arc* (1990) are works that mix literary genres. In these works, Algeria is put to the test: what is the point of passing the test if one then 'hides in the shadows'? The narrator draws inspiration from the fragmented style of Yacine **Kateb**, built on juxtapositions and relying on memory.

J. DÉJEUX

al-Thaʿālibī (350–429/961–1038)

Abū Manṣūr ʿAbd al-Malik ibn Muḥammad al-Thaʿālibī was a prolific anthologist and literary critic. He spent his entire life in the Eastern Islamic lands, mostly at his native Nishapur, where he was patronized by the local notables and, later, the **Ghaznavid** governor, but he also stayed for some time with a family of scholars in Jurjān and at the court of the Khwārazmshāh in al-Jurjāniyya. Living at a time when the New Persian renaissance was in full bloom (he was an exact contemporary of the Persian epic poet Firdawsī), he dedicated his life to the promotion and promulgation of Arabic literature and the Arabic language, on which he composed a number of eloquent paeans. A steady stream of anthologies, critical studies and philological works flowed from his pen; close to a hundred titles by him are known, of which at least half are extant and at least a quarter published. Of all of these, the most important is unquestionably the *Yatīmat al-dahr* (*Unique Pearl of the Age*), a large-scale anthology of poetry (and some prose) from the second half of the fourth/tenth century, arranged geographically and ranging from Andalusia (scantily covered) to eastern Iran and Transoxania (extremely rich); amidst a total of 470 poets included, such major figures as **al-Mutanabbī** and **Badīʿ al-Zamān al-Hamadhānī** are given extensive coverage. Late in his life he updated this work with a much shorter sequel, the *Tatimmat al-Yatīma*, which inspired numerous later anthologists, notably **al-Bākharzī** and **ʿImād al-Dīn al-Iṣfahānī**, to continue the series through later centuries. Typical of al-Thaʿālibī's broader ***adab*** works is his *Laṭā'if al-maʿārif* (*Book of Curious and Entertaining Information*), a grab-bag of historical and geographical lore. Among his philological works, perhaps the most significant are the *Fiqh al-lugha* (*Principles of Language*), a thematically arranged analytical lexicon, and the *Thimār al-qulūb* (*Fruit of Hearts*), a dictionary of common two-word expressions which is full of fascinating information. Somewhat exceptional within his *oeuvre* is the *Ghurar al-siyar* (*Illustrious Biographies*), a universal history with a particular accent on the pre-Islamic Persian kings (of which only the first half is extant), dedicated to the Ghaznavid governor of Nishapur.

Text editions

Fiqh al-lugha wa-sirr al-ʿArabiyya, Beirut (1984).
Ghurar akhbār mulūk al-Furs wa-siyarihim, Histoire des Rois des Perses, H. Zotenberg (ed. and trans.), Paris (1900).
Laṭā'if al-maʿārif, I. al-Ibyārī and Ḥ.K. al-Ṣayrafī (eds), Cairo (1960).
The Book of Curious and Entertaining Information, C.E. Bosworth (trans.), Edinburgh (1968).
Tatimmat al-Yatīma, ʿA. Iqbāl (ed.), Tehran (1934).

Thimār al-qulūb fī al-muḍāf wa-al-mansūb, M.A. Ibrāhīm (ed.), Cairo (1985).
Yatīmat al-dahr wa-maḥāsin ahl al-'asr, M.M. 'Abd al-Ḥamīd (ed.), 4 vols in 2, Cairo (1956–8).

Further reading

al-Jadir, Maḥmūd 'Abd Allāh, *al-Tha'ālibī*, Baghdad (1976).
——, *al-Tha'ālibi nāqidan wa-adīban*, Beirut (1991).
al-Samarrai, Q., 'Some biographical notes on al-Tha'ālibī', *Bibliotheca Orientalia* 32 (1975), 175–86 (the fullest biobibliographical treatment of al-Tha'ālibī).

E.K. ROWSON

See also: *adab*; anthologies

Thābit ibn Qurra (d. 288/901)

Abū al-Ḥasan Thābit ibn Qurra al-Ṣābī was a renowned scientist of the early Islamic period. A native of Ḥarrān in northern **Syria**, he belonged to an expanding group of Syriac-speaking Christian scholars who, well versed in both Greek and Arabic, gravitated to **Baghdad** in quest of the support and patronage available to scientists and translators who could make the ancient sciences available for study in Arabic and pursue this work in new directions. Thābit joined the Banū Mūsā in the 'Abbāsid capital, and both prepared new translations and revised those of others.

The era of Thābit was a stage in the history of Arabic science when scholars were engaging not only in translation, but also, and increasingly, in original work of their own. Thābit produced such treatises in Arabic and Syriac in most of the classical sciences. He developed the thinking of Archimedes and Euclid in the area of number theory, statics, geometry and trigonometry, and produced a unique work on sun-dial theory, although this last work seems to have escaped the notice of later writers. In medicine he wrote the earliest extant treatise on smallpox, a perennial scourge in his day.

His most important and influential work was in the application of mathematics to astronomy. His eight surviving essays in this field clearly set astronomy on new solid foundations by subjecting Ptolemaic models to rigorous mathematical proof. This set a standard followed in subsequent research, and increasingly made astronomy a scientific discipline in which empirical data, while still crucial, were judged against strict mathematical criteria. In Latin translation some of his work was also influential in medieval Europe.

Text editions

Sezgin, Fuat (ed.), *Thabit ibn Qurra (d. 288/901): Texts and Studies*, Frankfurt am Main (1996).
Thābit ibn Qurra, oeuvres d'astronomie, Régis Morelon (ed. and trans.), Paris (1987) (provides editions and French translations of the astronomical works, and a good introduction to Thābit more generally).

L.I. CONRAD

See also: translation, medieval

Tha'lab (200–91/815–904)

Abū al-'Abbās Aḥmad ibn Yaḥyā, called Tha'lab (born in **Baghdad**, and died accidentally in 291/904), was the leading representative of the 'Kūfan' school of **grammar** and an aggressive antagonist for his 'Baṣran' counterpart **al-Mubarrad**. Clearly a commanding personality rather than a systematic scholar, he was noted for his uprightness of character, his debating skills, his powerful memory and purity of accent. From early youth he showed an unusual eagerness for learning and soon acquired a mastery of ancient poetry and its obscure vocabulary. He prided himself on his grounding in the works of **al-Farrā'** and evidently saw himself as having inherited the role of champion of the 'Kūfan' position.

His listed works give the impression of a scholar more interested in the meanings of words than in the grammatical system of the language, and this is confirmed by those that survive, notably his popular and influential *Kitāb al-faṣīḥ*, an anthology of words grouped semantically, and the *Majālis* or reports of his teaching sessions, where grammatical ideas are informally present in what are primarily discussions of meaning and usage. He is also the author of a commentary on the poems of **Zuhayr**. It would be interesting to examine the contents of such works as the *Ḥadd al-naḥw*, *al-Maṣūn fī al-naḥw* and *al-Muwaffaqī*, all presumably grammatical works ascribed to him but no longer extant. A collection of grammatical disputes, also vanished, is attributed to him, as is a work on poetical 'rules', *Qawā'id al-shi'r*, which has been published.

Text editions

al-Faṣīḥ, J. Barth (ed.), Leipzig (1876), and see *GAS* vol. 8, 141–5 for other editions and commentaries.

Majālis Tha'lab, A.S.M. Hārūn (ed.), Cairo (1948–9).

Qawā'id al-shi'r, C. Schiaparelli (ed.), *Proc. 8th Int. Cong. Or.* 2:1, fasc. I, Leiden (1891), 173–214; M.'A. Khafājī (ed.), Cairo (1348/1948); R. 'Abd al-Tawwāb (ed.), Cairo (1386/1966) (for other works concerned with poetry see *GAS*, vol. 2, index).

Sharḥ Dīwān Zuhayr ibn Abī Sulmā, Cairo (1944); F.D. Qabāwa (ed.), Beirut (1982).

Further reading

Abū Deeb, K., 'Literary criticism', in *CHALABL*, 403–4.

Trabulsi, Amjad, *La Critique poétique des Arabes jusqu'au Ve siècle de l'hégire/XIe siècle de J.C.*, Damascus (1955), 81–3 and *passim*.

van Gelder, G.J.H., *Beyond the Line: Classical Arabic Literary Critics on the Coherence and Unity of the Poem*, Leiden (1982), 44–8 and *passim*.

M.G. CARTER

al-Tha'labī (d. 427/1035)

Abū Isḥāq Aḥmad ibn Muḥammad al-Nīsabūrī al-Shāfi'ī al-Tha'labī is best known for his collection of ***Legends of the Prophets***, *Kitāb 'Arā'is al-majālis fī qiṣaṣ al-anbiyā'*. In medieval Muslim biographical works he is called 'commentator and historian', the former for his Koran commentary *Kashf al-bayān*, and his *Qatlā al-Qur'ān* (*Those Killed by the Koran*), while the title 'historian' refers to his collection of prophetic legends, which form an important pre-Islamic section of universal histories.

Unlike **al-Kisā'ī**, whose work in the same genre has been seen as belonging to 'the popular narrative tradition of medieval Islam' (T. Nagel, *EI*[2] vol. 5, 176), al-Tha'labī utilizes the techniques of traditional Muslim scholarship, citing Koran and ***ḥadīth*** in most, though not all, of his tales. These are, therefore, usually not only fuller in detail, drawing on many sources, but also somewhat less fanciful than those of al-Kisā'ī.

After a lengthy opening section on the Creation, the prophets treated most fully are Adam, Abraham, Joseph, Moses, David, Solomon and Jesus, with shorter sections devoted to many other figures mentioned in the Koran, such as Job, Hūd and Ṣāliḥ. Among these, too, are the stories surrounding the strange figure of al-Khiḍr, the **Alexander** cycle, and the lengthy story of Buluqiyyā (possibly of Jewish origin) which also occurs in the conversion legends about **Ka'b al-Aḥbār** and in ***Alf layla wa-layla***. There is as yet no scholarly edition of the text or a full translation of this important work (although a translation by the author of this entry is in progress – Ed.).

Text edition

'Arā'is al-majālis fī qiṣaṣ al-anbiyā', Cairo (1347/1928).

Further reading

Nagel, T., *Die Qiṣaṣ al-anbiyā'. Ein Beitrag zur arabischen Literaturwissenschaft*, Bonn (1967).

Rosenthal, F., *A History of Muslim Historiography*, Leiden (1968), 288–90, 432.

W. BRINNER

See also *Legends of the Prophets*

Thaqīf *see* tribes

theatre and drama, medieval

In Arabic literature, and in Greek and Syriac works translated into Arabic, theatre is rendered as *mal'ab* (pl. *malā'ib*) or *dār mal'ab*, and rarely transcribed as *ṭayāṭir*. In R. Payne Smith's *Thesaurus Syriacus* (Oxford, 1897–1901, vol. 2, col. 4370) the Greek *theatron* is given in Syriac as *ṭe'aṭron* and in Arabic as *shuhra* (lit. notoriety), *manẓar* (spectacle) and *mal'ab*. On the other hand, in both Hebrew and Syriac the Greek term was adopted as the sole term: in Hebrew the term is *teaṭron* up to the present time, while in Syriac it is *ṭe'aṭron*. In Muslim **Spain** the term *mal'ab*, together with its synonym *masraḥ*, continued to be used in the sense of 'theatre' until the fall of Muslim Granada and the expulsion of the Jews from Spain in 1492. In the Muslim East, only the term *mal'ab* was current until the mid-nineteenth century, when it was replaced by *masraḥ*.

The ruins of Hellenistic and Roman theatres in Turkey, Mesopotamia, **Syria**, Lebanon, Jordan, Israel, **Egypt** and North Africa are concrete evidence of the important role that theatre played in the religious, political and cultural life of Hellenistic culture in these areas. Although Judaism, Christianity and

Islam rejected the theatrical traditions of the Greeks, Romans, Byzantines and Persians, nevertheless it is possible to observe evidence of the survival of ancient seasonal fertility rites and myths. In their dramatic performances, long after the rise of Islam, these nations portrayed death and resurrection in the rituals of agricultural festivals pertaining to the seasonal cycle of life.

A century before the rise of Islam, live theatre in the Middle East and North Africa ceased to be a high religious artistic cult. Only games, buffoonery, mimes, farces and other low-brow performances existed. Arab historians give scanty evidence of Arab awareness of theatrical performances in the Byzantine empire on the eve of Islam. The most important evidence is given by the Prophet **Muḥammad**'s poet, **Ḥassan ibn Thābit** (d. 54/674?), who mentions in one of his poems the *mayāmisu Ghazzatin* (the mimes of Gaza) as an example of something feeble. The second evidence is provided by an episode of ʿAmr ibn al-ʿĀṣ (d. 42/663); it is said that, during one of his visits to Egypt as a merchant in the ***jāhiliyya***, he attended a celebration in Alexandria where various plays were performed in a *malʿab* (theatre or amphitheatre). The third evidence lies in references to the live performances of the Jewish conjurer and actor Bustānī (or Baṭrūnī), from a village near **Kufa**, who performed 'various kinds of magic, illusion tricks and acts of buffoonery' before al-Walīd ibn ʿUqba, the governor of Iraq in 35/655. These evidences reveal that, on the eve of Islam, impersonators, clowns and buffoons had replaced the classical theatre in the Near Eastern provinces of the Roman empire. Indeed, Islam was no less hostile to theatre and drama than Judaism and Christianity. However, the original meanings of the pagan religious dramas among the Greeks, Romans and Persians had long been forgotten. Instead, these dramatic ceremonies came to be understood as commemorating some legendary or historical event and became seasonal folk theatre.

These dramas, which became secular entertainment, tended towards parody and mockery of earlier customs and rituals. This change is obvious in the Persian and Central Asian dramatic elements which entered the Muslim world, mainly the play with the hobby-horse (*kurraj* or *karj*), the *samāja* (see **masks and masquerades**) performances during the ***Nayrūz*** festivals with fire, splashing water and knocking on doors, and the performance of *Amīr al-Nayrūz* (Prince of Nayrūz). In ancient Persia and Central Asia, the hobby-horse was used in various dramatic rituals, in Shamanic rites as well as in seasonal fertility rites, to help establish contact with spirits. In Islam, hobby-horse performances, accompanied by music and dancing, were either for the sake of inducing a delirious and ecstatic state, or for celebrating feasts, combats and military exercise.

In ancient times, masks and fire were used to keep evil spirits away, because evil spirits are not attracted to ugly things and are afraid of fire, while water is a symbol of purity and prosperity. The performance of *Amīr al-Nayrūz* in carnival processions of the 'Feast of Fools' in medieval Islam resembles what Arab historicans called *rukūb al-kawsaj* (the procession of the thin-bearded), which in ancient Persia was a festival called *Kôsa nishin* which celebrated the New Year. In this festival a play of 'temporary king' or 'false amīr', which symbolizes the expulsion of winter or the driving out of the old year, was acted in market-places in Persia, Iraq and Egypt. In Egypt, it became a festival celebrated by both Copts and Muslims and was condemned by many Muslim scholars and rulers.

In medieval Islam, unlike in ancient Greece and in the Roman Empire, dramas were not acted in theatres, but in market-places, in squares near the citadels, or in the courtyards of grandees and palaces of rulers. The troupes would play their drums and music to attract the attention of the audience, who would form a circle around them to attend their plays and exchange with them sharp retorts and jokes. The North African scholar **Ibn al-Ḥājj** al-ʿAbdarī (d. 737/1336) described this dramatic play, claiming that it was performed yearly since Pharaonic Egypt up to his days. The performer would paint his face with lime or flour and stick on a beard of fur, dress himself in a red or yellow dress (*thawb shuhra*), put on his head a long conical cap (*ṭurṭūr*), and ride on an ugly donkey. Surrounded by green palm branches and bunches of dates, he sets out with his procession with a ledger in his hand, as if he is a ruler accounting with his people for the payment of taxes. The clamouring celebrators rove with him through the alleys and streets of the city, and past most of the shops and houses in the markets, knocking on doors to collect money to spend on their New Year festival.

Live theatrical performance (***khayāl***) can be a short scene (*faṣl* or ***bāba***) of pantomime or a dramatic play performed by one or more actors, with dialogue and props. The shadow-play is performed by one actor hidden behind the screen, performing his repertoire with songs and changing his voice according to the different characters appearing on the screen. These dramas, sometimes performed according to written texts, were more often improvised, resembling the *Commedia dell' Arte*.

Very few summaries of dramas are given in Arabic literary works. The oldest describes what can be called a 'morality play', an imaginary trial of the Muslim caliphs. The actor is a 'Ṣūfī' (ascetic) whose intention is to fulfil a religious duty, 'to enjoin what is right and prohibit what is disapproved'. The trial seems to have been enacted almost entirely through monologue. This Ṣūfī actor would twice a week climb a hill with a reed staff (*qaṣaba*), followed by men, women and boys, and call for one caliph after another, enumerating their good or bad deeds and sending them to Paradise or to Hell. Apart from the Ṣūfī who acts the role of the judge the actors were young boys who portrayed caliphs from Abū Bakr to the **'Abbāsid** al-Mahdī (158–69/775–85). According to other summaries, the favourite subjects were farces ridiculing Muslim judges or depicting everyday quarrels such as arguments between two wives, or improvisations ridiculing the actors' opponents or their masters' enemies in indecent colloquial or semi-colloquial verse or prose.

The text of some dramas may comprise **poetry**, **artistic prose** and ***maqāmāt*** written by famous poets and writers. The best examples are **Abū al-Muṭahhar al-Azdī**'s *Ḥikāyat Abī al-Qāsim al-Baghdādī* (*c*.400/1009–10) and the three **shadow plays** composed by **Ibn Dāniyāl** (d. 710/1310–11). The only drama descibed as *khayāl* extant in colloquial poetry and extant in full is *Misṭarat khayāl, Munādamat Umm Mujbir*, preserved by 'Abd al-Bāqī al-Isḥāqī (d. 1660) in his anthology *Dīwān sulāf al-anshā' fī al-shi'r wa-al-inshā'* (*The Anthology of those Intoxicated by the Choicest Wine in Poetry and Compositions*). The play, defined by the author as comedy (***hazl***) and scurrilous mockery (*huz' sakhīf*), has four characters: al-Rayyis (Captain), al-Qilā'ī (Sailing Master), al-Malīḥa (the Beautiful Girl) and Umm Mujbir (the Old Wife) (see Moreh, 1992, 170–8).

The Captain is informed by the Sailing Master, who has married a beautiful girl, that his old, sick and lusty wife has returned from the dead. The Captain cannot believe what he hears, as he had buried her long ago. The old woman scolds him for his new marriage and claims that she is more beautiful and sexy than his young wife. The Captain calls his frightened young wife to expose her beauty to the old wife; the latter invites her husband to make love with her, claiming that she can make him forget his young wife. The play presents the eternal struggle between beauty and ugliness, new and old, present and past. The new has its own freshness and appeal, while the old becomes obsolete and loses its role in life; yet old people cling to the present and try to prove they are more experienced and useful than the young.

The latest Arabic drama written in this conventional mode is *Nazāhat al-mushtāq wa-ghuṣṣat al-'ushshāq fī madīnat ṭiryāq fī al-'Irāq* (lithograph, Algeria, 1847; ed. by S. Moreh and P.C. Sadgrove, Oxford (1996). Most of the verses and some prose sections of this drama are taken from the Arabian Nights (***Alf layla wa-layla***) and from Ibn Ghānim al-Muqaddisī's *Kitāb Kashf al-asrār 'an ḥikam al-ṭuyūr wa-al-azhār* (Paris, 1820) ed. and trans. M Carcin de Tassy, *Les oiseaux et les fleurs, allégories morales d'Azz-Eddin Elmocaddessi*, Paris (1821). Ya'qūb Sanua (1839–1912) was accused by 'Alī **Mubārak** of being an actor and playwright of the popular types called Awlād Rābiya.

There are no summaries in classical Arabic literature of shadow-play dramas, but fortunately some shadow-plays from the nineteenth century onwards have been recorded and published. Beside Ibn Dāniyāl's medieval plays (published by Ibrāhīm Ḥamāda, 1963), Paul Kahle edited *Das Krokodilspiel (Li'b et-Timsah), ein egyptishes Schattenspiel* (Göttingen, 1915); J.G. Wetzstein edited a shadow-play which he attended in 1857 in Damascus entitled *al-'Āshiq wa-al-ma'shūq (Die Liebenden von Amasia, ein damascener Schattenspiel* (Leipzig, 1906); the Syrian scholar Salmān Qaṭāya published twelve shadow-plays (*Nuṣūṣ min khayāl al-ẓill fī Ḥalab*). Fortunately, these colloquial Syrian plays, concerning adventures which befell 'Īwāẓ and Qaraqūz, were recorded by Muḥammad al-Shaykh in Aleppo between 1935 and 1937 on discophile, were found and collected by Dr Salmān Qaṭāya and published in Damascus in 1977. Prof. J.M. Landau has discovered five plays written by Aḥmad Farīm al-Fār in a collection entitled *Kashf al-Astār ʿan Baladiyyāt Ahmad al-Fār al-Maʿrūf bi-ʾbn Rābiya* (see *JAL* 7, 1986, 120–5).

Further reading

al-Aʿrajī, Muḥammad Ḥusayn, *Fann al-tamthīl ʿinda al-ʿArab*, Baghdad (1978).

Jacob, G., *Geschichte des Schattentheaters im Morgen- und Abendland*, Osnabrück (1972).

Landau, J.M., *Shadow-plays in the Near East*, Jerusalem (1948).

——, *Studies in the Arab Theatre and Cinema*, Philadelphia (1958), 9–47.

Moreh, S., 'The background of the medieval Arabic theatre: Hellenistic-Roman and Persian influences', *JSAI* 13 (1990), 294–329.

——, *Live Theatre and Dramatic Literature in the Medieval Arab World*, Edinburgh, NY (1992).

——, 'The shadow play (*khayāl al-ẓill*) in the light of Arabic literature', *JAL* 18 (1987), 46–61.

——, and Sadan, J., *Two Medieval Plays* (in preparation).

——, and Sadgrove, P.C., *Jewish Contributors to Nineteenth-Century Arabic Theatre*, Oxford (1996).

Prüfer, C., 'Drama (Arabic)', in *ERE*, vol. 4, 872–8.

Reich, H., *Der Mimus, ein Literarentwickelungs geschichtlicher Versuch*, Berlin (1903).

Saʿd, Fārūq, *Khayāl al-ẓill ʿinda aʾl-ʿArab*, Beirut, 1991.

Woidich, M. and Landau, J.M., *Arabisches Volkstheater in Kairo im Jahre 1909: Aḥmad il Fār und seine Schwänke*, Beirut (1993).

S. MOREH

See also: actors and acting, medieval; shadow-play

Thousand and One Nights see *Alf layla wa-layla*

theatre and drama, modern

The extent of the existence of an indigenous dramatic tradition in the Arab world, and the implications that this may have for an account of the development of Arabic drama during the nineteenth and twentieth centuries, has been the subject of considerable controversy in recent years. Although proponents of various viewpoints have been vociferous in proclaiming their own interpretations, however, the essential facts are hardly in doubt: for while, on the one hand, it would be ridiculous to deny the existence of dramatic elements in Arab culture, and indeed, in popular Arabic literature, it is equally clear that until the mid-nineteenth century the Arab world had not been home to a theatrical tradition of the sort found, for example, in the classical civilizations of Greece or Rome, or in Elizabethan England.

The origins of the modern Arabic theatre are to be found, like many other literary innovations of the ***nahḍa***, in a subtle interplay of indigenous traditions and European inspiration; its coming to maturity may be ascribed to a combination of Levantine initiative and Egyptian resources. Although recent research has unearthed an Arabic play apparently published in Algiers in 1847, the first significant step towards the establishment of a modern Arabic drama was probably taken by the Lebanese Mārūn **al-Naqqāsh**, who staged an adaptation of Molière's *L'Avare* in his Beirut home in 1847; this was followed in 1849 by an original Arabic play, *Abū al-Ḥasan al-mughaffal aw Hārūn al-Rashīd*, based on a story in the *Thousand and One Nights* (***Alf layla wa-layla***). Mārūn's early death was a blow to the early Syrian theatre, but his enthusiasm (originally acquired on business trips to Europe) was passed on to other members of his family: his plays were published by his brother Niqūlā **al-Naqqāsh**, and his nephew Salīm Khalīl **al-Naqqāsh** later formed his own troupe. In Damascus, Aḥmad **al-Qabbānī** staged a number of similar productions, some of which again derived their plots from the *Thousand and One Nights*.

The next significant steps in the development of the modern theatre were taken not in the Levant but in **Egypt**. Although the Egyptians had been briefly introduced to the idea of a European theatre during the French occupation of 1798–1801, the first-known Arabic productions in Egypt were undertaken by an Egyptian Jew Yaʿqūb **Ṣanūʿ**, who staged a number of plays in Egyptian colloquial between 1870 and 1872, when his theatre was closed by order of the Khedive. The next theatrical performances in Egypt were staged by Syrian émigrés. In 1876 Salīm Khalīl al-Naqqāsh established himself in Alexandria, and the exodus of Syrian theatrical talent continued during the 1880s and 1890s with the arrival in Egypt of al-Qabbānī, Iskandar Faraḥ, Jūrj **Abyaḍ** and others.

Although use was also made of the Arab heritage, many playwrights of this period relied heavily on the technique of adapting Western drama in devising plots for their productions in Arabic. Moreover, despite some attempts by Abyaḍ and others to establish an Egyptian 'classical' theatre, most productions relied heavily on music and elements of melodrama for their popular appeal. The financial basis for serious theatrical productions remained extremely fragile and troupes had to make concessions to popular taste in order to survive; with few exceptions, the theatre was not regarded as worthy of serious literary attention. Various types of popular theatre, however, began to emerge, combining elements from the indigenous popular farce with Western comic techniques: among these were the so-called 'Franco-Arab revue' created by the Syrian 'Azīz 'Īd, and Najīb al-Rīḥānī's Kish-Kish Bey, a distinctively Egyptian character reacting slightly naïvely, but with fundamental good sense, to world affairs and social developments. Indirect descendants of this branch of theatrical activity may be found today among the Egyptian cinema and television productions which continue to dominate the Arab world.

The process of 'coming of age' of the modern Arabic theatre may by dated to the period of World War 1, when a number of Egyptian playwrights began to produce works of a new level of dramatic maturity, many of them directly related to the problems of contemporary Egypt. Among this generation, the names of Ibrāhīm **Ramzī**, Anṭūn **Yazbak** and Muḥammad **Taymūr** are of most significance. Unashamedly using Egyptian colloquial in much of their work, they brought to fruition the concept of an 'Egyptian theatre', the groundwork for which had been laid by 'Uthmān **Jalāl** and subsequently developed by Faraḥ **Anṭūn**. At the same time, the theatre was slowly beginning to acquire a new status as a respectable branch of literary activity – a process aided by the interest in it shown by Ṭāhā **Ḥusayn**, and by the neo-clasical poet Aḥmad **Shawqī**, who composed six historical dramas and a comedy in verse towards the end of his career.

Arabic theatre between 1933 and about 1956 was dominated by the towering figure of Tawfīq **al-Ḥakīm**, whose dramatic career had begun with the writing of some half-dozen colloquial plays for the popular theatre of the 'Ukāsha brothers in Cairo in the early 1920s. These early efforts were continued and developed in works (some in classical, some in colloquial Arabic) produced in the early 1930s. His most distinctive contribution to the Egyptian theatre, however – the establishment of an Arabic 'theatre of ideas' – received its main impetus from the period that he spent as a student in Paris during 1925–8, when he spent much time frequenting performances of works by avant-garde writers such as Shaw and Pirandello. The resultant series of 'intellectual' plays in classical Arabic began with *Ahl al-Kahf* (published in 1933, but written during al-Ḥakīm's stay in Paris), which broke new ground by using a Koranic story as the basis for a drama; it was followed by *Shahrazād* (1934), *Pygmalion* (1942), *Sulaymān al-Ḥakīm* (1943), *al-Malik Ūdīb* (1949) and other plays in which the author utilizes a variety of sources from both Western and Eastern traditions as a basis for a variety of intellectual debates in dramatic form; despite their eclectic nature, a number of common themes are discernible in these works, including the oppositions between fantasy and reality, art and life, and heart and mind.

Not all of al-Ḥakīm's drama falls into the category of intellectual drama, however. In 1950 he published a collection of plays on social themes in which he attacked contemporary Egyptian politicians of all persuasions for their corruption and inefficiency. His later plays, from 1954 on, also show a renewed enthusiasm for technical experimentation, with a view both to bridging the gap between theatre and public, and enriching the Egyptian stage by the importation of new ideas and techniques from contemporary Western theatre. These plays present us with a bewildering variety both of theme and of technique: whereas *Yā ṭāli' al-Shajara*, for example – perhaps the most successful – shows obvious influence of the Theatre of the Absurd, *Majlis al-'adl* is a thinly veiled Brechtian allegory on the Palestine problem. In two plays, *al-Ṣafqa* (1956) and *al-Warṭa* (1966), he attempted to resolve the old dilemma of 'classical or colloquial Arabic?' by using what he termed a 'third language' combining elements of both, but the experiment failed to find much favour.

By this stage in his career, al-Ḥakīm had been joined by a group of younger playwrights who continued to uphold Egypt's leading position in the field of drama but whose outlook reflected that of an angrier, more outspoken generation. At the same time, a number of other Arab countries were beginning to witness an increase in serious dramatic production – sometimes actively aided, as in Egypt, by new regimes who were quick to appreciate the propaganda potential of theatrical activity. In Egypt itself, the new mood was heralded by Nuʿmān **ʿĀshūr**'s *al-Nās illi taḥt* (1956), which combined social criticism with a strong element of popular comedy: this was followed by *al-Nās illi fōq* (1957), representing a wholesale condemnation of the Egyptian aristocracy, and by *ʿĀ'ilat al-Dughrī* (1962), in which the author uses the break-up of a middle-class Egyptian family to symbolize the disintegration of contemporary society. This group of dramatists, sometimes referred to as the 'new wave', also includes Luṭfī **al-Khūlī**, Saʿd al-Dīn **Wahba** and Yūsuf **Idrīs** among others: almost all politically 'committed' (often to the extent of having been imprisoned for their views), they almost all used colloquial Arabic for their plays in the interests of authenticity; at the same time, their works show an acute awareness of contemporary theatrical developments in the West, including not only the 'committed' theatre of Sartre, Brecht and others, but also the dramatists of the 'Theatre of the Absurd'. Outstanding among the productions of the 1960s was Yūsuf Idrīs's *al-Farāfīr* (1964), which the author claimed represented an example of a truly Egyptian drama and which raises fundamental questions about the nature of power and the structure of society; despite the author's theorizing, however, the play itself almost certainly owes more to contemporary Western dramatic techniques than to traditional Arab forms of entertainment. Other dramatists who made a significant contribution to Egyptian drama during the 1960s and later include Mikhā'īl **Rūmān**, Alfrīd **Faraj**, Maḥmūd **Diyāb**, ʿAlī **Sālim** and Shawqī **ʿAbd al-Ḥakīm**. A significant feature of the drama of this generation has been the creative use of folklore and other aspects of the indigenous tradition in order to try to bring the theatre 'closer to the people'.

The new blossoming of drama in Egypt following the 1952 revolution had a powerful impact elsewhere in the Middle East, and the 1950s and 1960s saw most major Arab states establishing those institutions required to underpin theatrical activity in the modern world – government troupes, drama schools and the like. Although interesting drama has been produced in countries from Iraq to Morocco, it is perhaps Syria that, after Egypt, has seen the boldest and most innovative theatrical productions in recent years – paradoxically perhaps, since the authoritarian nature of the Syrian regime has tended to stifle creativity in many other fields. The plays of Saʿd Allāh **Wannūs** in particular enjoy a wide reputation throughout the Arab world: in *Ḥaflat samar min ajli 5 Ḥuzayrān* (1968) he launched a blistering attack on the official policies and propaganda that accompanied the 1967 Arab–Israeli war; and his outspokenness has been continued in a series of daring productions, the latest of which – *Yawm min zamāninā* (produced in Damascus in 1996) – includes attacks on both religious and secular authorities. Other Syrian playwrights of note include Mamdūḥ **ʿUdwān**, Walīd **Ikhlāṣī** and Muḥammad **Māghūṭ**, most of whose plays, in varying degrees, are 'political' in character; among their counterparts in other Arab countries may be mentioned Yūsuf **al-ʿĀnī** (Iraq), ʿIzz al-Dīn **al-Madanī** (Tunisia), ʿIṣām Maḥfūz (Lebanon) and al-Ṭayyib al-Ṣiddīqī (Morocco). A small number of writers, among them Ṣalāḥ **ʿAbd al-Ṣabūr** (Egypt) and Samīḥ **al-Qāṣim** (Palestine) have continued the tradition of writing verse drama in the period following World War 2. Among other notable developments has been the rise of Palestinian theatre groups, including the Balalin Company of Jerusalem and the Hakawati Group, founded in 1977.

There is a marked contrast between the work of most of the dramatists mentioned above and the 'intellectual' drama of Tawfīq al-Ḥakīm – often designed to be read rather than acted and in many cases unwieldy when transferred to the stage. Indeed, this contrast provides a useful indicator of the main trends in the development of Arabic drama since World War 2. Although al-Ḥakīm's importation of contemporary techniques from Western theatre has been continued by succeeding generations, it has been accompanied by a new emphasis on the potential of 'theatre as theatre' rather than 'theatre as literature' – an emphasis that has often implied the use of colloquial, rather than classical, Arabic and which has involved a renewed search for specifically Arab dramatic forms, sometimes based on traditional popular modes of entertainment such as the *ḥakawātī*. At the same time (particularly following the 1967 Arab–Israeli War), Arabic theatre has become progressively more politicized – a trend that has involved considerable risks, in view of the constraints of **censorship** in most Arab states; in this connection, the use of episodes from Arab or Islamic history as a metaphor for contemporary developments may be observed in the work of several playwrights. Increasing links with television production are also a feature of contemporary drama in many Arab countries.

Text editions

Abdel Wahab, Farouk (ed.), *Modern Egyptian Drama: An Anthology*, Minneapolis (1974).

Jayyusi, S.K. and Allen, R. (eds), *Modern Arabic Drama: An Anthology*, Bloomington and Indianapolis (1995).

Manzalaoui, M. (ed.), *Arabic Writing Today: The Drama*, Cairo (1977).

Further reading

Bawadi, M.M., *Early Arabic Drama*, Cambridge (1988).

——, *Modern Arabic Drama in Egypt*, Cambridge (1987).

Ben Halima, H., *Les Principaux thèmes du théâtre arabe contemporain 1914–1960*, Tunis (1969)

Al-Khozai, M.A., *The Development of Early Arabic Drama (1847–1900)*, London (1984).

Landau, J.M., *Studies in the Arab Theater and Cinema*, Philadelphia (1958).

Tomiche, N., *Le Théâtre arabe*, Paris (1960).

P. STARKEY

al-Tīfāshī (580–651/1184–1253)

Shihāb al-Dīn Abū al-ʿAbbās Aḥmad ibn Yūsuf al-Tīfāshī was a writer on scientific and literary topics. Born in Qafṣa, in Tunisia, he studied in Tunis and then **Cairo**, where he became a student of **ʿAbd al-Laṭīf al-Baghdādī**. After some time in **Damascus**, and back in Tunis, he made his home permanently in Cairo, where he befriended **Ibn Saʿīd al-Maghribī**, but also travelled extensively in **Syria** and northern Mesopotamia. The best known of his seven surviving works is his study of precious stones, which evinces both great erudition and an empirical spirit. Of his *Eloquent Disquisition on the Perception of the Five Senses*, a vast literary encyclopaedia, only two sections of a later abridgement by **Ibn Manẓūr** survive, treating astronomical and meteorological phenomena and mixing extensive poetic citations with quotations from earlier philosophical and astrological works. Possibly also originally part of this encyclopaedia is an important treatise on music and dance (only partially published) containing much comparative material which illustrates the contrasts between the musical styles of the Middle East and of North Africa. Other extant works are an abridgement of a ***ḥadīth*** collection by **Abū Nuʿaym** on prophetic medicine, and a series of treatises on erotic topics, which enjoyed considerable popularity.

Text editions

Azhār al-afkār fī jawāhir al-aḥjār, M.Y. Ḥasan and M.B. Khafājī (eds), Cairo (1977).

Faṣl al-khiṭāb fī madārik al-ḥawāss al-khams li-ulī al-albāb, abridged by Ibn Manẓūr as *Surūr al-nafs bi-madārik al-ḥawāss al-khams*, surviving parts I. ʿAbbās (ed.), Beirut (1980).

Mutʿat al-asmāʿ fī ʿilm al-samāʿ, partial edn by M.B. al-Ṭanjī, ʻal-Ṭarā'iq wa-al-alḥān al-mūsīqīya fī Ifrīqīya wa-al-Andalus', *al-Abḥāth* 21 (1968), 93–116.

Nuzhat al-albāb fīmā lā yūjad fī kitāb, London (1991).

Les Délices des coeurs, R.R. Khawam (trans.), Paris (1981).

The Delight of Hearts, or What You Will Not Find in Any Book, E.A. Lacey (trans.), San Francisco (1988) (partial translation from the French).

Risāla fīmā yaḥtāj ilayh al-rijāl wa-al-nisā' fī istiʿmāl al-bāh mimmā yaḍurr wa-yanfaʿ, H.M. El-Haw (ed. and trans.), Erlangen (1970).

Rujūʿ al-shaykh ilā ṣibāh fī al-qūwa ʿalā al-bāh, numerous popular editions.

The Old Man Young Again. literally transl. from the Arabic by an English Bohemian, Paris (1898) (the relationship between this work and that of Ibn Kamāl Pasha of the same title remains to be investigated).

al-Shifā' fī al-ṭibb al-musnad ʿan al-sayyid al-muṣṭafā, ʻA.A. Qalʻajī (ed.), Beirut (1988).

Biography and references: treated fully by ʿAbbās in his intoduction to the *Surūr al-nafs*; see also Khawam's introduction to *Les Délices des coeurs*.

E.K. ROWSON

al-Tihāmī, ʿAlī ibn Muḥammad (d. 416/1025)

Abū al-Ḥasan ʿAlī ibn Muḥammad al-Tihāmī was a poet of mostly panegyric poetry. Of low birth, coming from the Tihāma (Red Sea coast of the Arabian Peninsula), he was active in various places in Syria and Iraq; he was a preacher in al-Ramla in Palestine. He made a career in Egypt but ended his life in prison in **Cairo**, having been apprehended by the **Fāṭimid** authorities while in the possession of secret, anti-Fāṭimid letters from the head of the tribe Ṭayyi', Ḥassān ibn Mufarrij, addressed to another tribe. Apart from panegyric poetry he made elegiac poems, among which a poem of eighty-six lines on his own son was especially admired.

Text editions

Dīwān, Muḥammad Zuhayr al-Shāwīsh (ed.), 2nd edn, Damascus (1964); ʿUthmān Ṣāliḥ al-Furayḥ (ed.), Riadh (1985); ʿAlī N. ʿAṭwī (ed.), Beirut (1986).

G.J.H. VAN GELDER

al-Tijānī Yūsuf Bashīr (1912–37)

Sudanese poet. Al-Tijānī, who came from a religious family with intimate Ṣūfī affiliations, was named by his father after the leader of the Tijāniyya Ṣūfīs. He studied at a *khalwa* and at the al-Maʿhad al-ʿIlmī in Omdurman. One of the few Sudanese poets whose name was known in the wider Arab world before the 1950s (and often compared with the Tunisian **al-Shābbī**), al-Tijānī belonged to the Romantic school which dominated the Sudanese literary scene during the 1930s and 1940s, and which was commonly known as the 'Fajr School' after the name of its magazine first published in 1934. Al-Tijānī – whose poetry fluctuates between religious doubt, a believing heart and Sudanese mystical traditions – was also a prolific writer of love poetry extolling the goddess of beauty. He had a basic love of life and an unending wonder about it. He died of consumption at the age of 25.

Text edition

Abū Saʿd, A., *al-Shiʿr wa-al-shuʿarā'*, Beirut (1959).

Further reading

Jayyusi, S.K., *Trends and Movements in Modern Arabic Poetry*, Leiden (1977), vol. 2, 452–74.
Shoush, M.I. 'Some background notes on modern Sudanese poetry', *Sudan Notes and Records*, 44 (1963), 21–42.

C.E. BERKLEY

al-Tikirlī, Fu'ād *see* al-Takarlī, Fu'ād

al-Tilimsānī, Abū Madyan *see* Abū Madyan al-Tilimsānī

al-Ṭirimmāḥ (*c.*50–110/*c.*670–728)

Al-Ḥakam ibn Ḥakīm al-Ṭirimmāḥ was a poet of the middle **Umayyad** period, who resided mainly in **Kufa**. Al-Ṭirimmāḥ ('the Elevated'), stemming from the distinguished Thuʿal clan of Ṭayyi', came to Kufa as a soldier. After a longer sojourn in Iran where he seems to have earned his living as a teacher, he returned to Kufa and died there. He composed panegyrics on the Umayyad governors Yazīd ibn al-Muhallab (d. 102/720) and Khālid al-Qasrī (d. 126/743–4). In only three of his poems, traces of his alleged **Khārijī** inclinations can be found, and they have been contested altogether by al-Ṣāliḥī (1971, 121–52) and other scholars. He is said to have been an intimate friend of the poet **al-Kumayt ibn Zayd** who had strong **Zaydī** convictions. In a series of poems he quarrelled with the Tamīmī poet **al-Farazdaq**, he on his part being a glowing advocate of the Yemenī tribes. Ḥasan's edition of his ***dīwān*** includes 37 poems with 1,450 verses containing numerous descriptions of desert travels and animals. In these descriptive parts of his poetry especially, he tends to use rare words. Al-Ṭirimmāḥ favoured short metres.

Text editions

Dīwān, ʿIzzat Ḥasan (ed.), Damascus (1968).
The Poems of Ṭufail ibn ʿAuf al-Ghanawī and aṭ-Ṭirimmāḥ, F. Krenkow (ed. and trans.), London (1927), (incomplete edn with an English translation).

Further reading

Blachère, Régis, *Histoire de la littérature arabe*, 3 vols, Paris (1952–66), 530–4.
al-Ṣāliḥī, ʿA., *al-Ṭirimmāḥ Ibn Ḥakīm al-Ṭā'ī*, Baghdad (1971).

T. SEIDENSTICKER

al-Tirmidhī, Muḥammad ibn ʿĪsā (d. between 270/883 and 279/893)

A renowned ***ḥadīth*** specialist who authored one of the collections of *ḥadīth*s in use among **Sunnī** Muslims. In contrast to the collections of **al-Bukhārī** and **Muslim ibn al-Ḥajjāj**, which bear the title *al-Saḥīḥ*, the collections of al-Tirmidhī and others are generally known under the title *al-Sunan* and occupy a somewhat lower rank. Al-Tirmidhī's collection is shorter than those of al-Bukhārī and Muslim but includes the same *ḥadīth* in two or more chapters less frequently. It furthermore is distinguished by its critical notes on the chains of transmitters and by its references, in connection with particular *ḥadīth*s, to differences between the schools of law.

Text edition

Sunan al-Tirmidhī, Medina (1965–6).

B. WEISS

Toledo *see* Spain

Ṭrād, Michel (1912–)

Lebanese colloquial poet. Born in Zahleh into a poor family, Ṭrād's childhood and adolescence were spent in village schools, where he learned French and studied Arabic language and literature, ultimately graduating from the 'school of life' as he put it. The mountain setting of his early years was essential to his poetic development. His first poems immediately attracted the attention of Mārūn **ʿAbbud**, his former teacher, who hailed him as the most genuine poet in the Lebanese dialect and credited him with transforming ***zajal*** from a poetry of occasion and verbal virtuosity to one of high literary value.

Ṭrād's poetry is a poetry of gesture apprehended by intuition, in which objects elicit moods peculiar to village life. The publication of *Jilnār* (1951) and *Dūlāb* (1957) established his reputation as a Romantic–symbolist poet of great originality, and in 1957 one of his poems appeared in *Shiʿr*, alongside those of some of the pioneers of modern Arabic *fuṣḥā* poetry. With the publication of *Laysh* (1964) Lebanese colloquial poetry took a further step towards becoming a legitimate poetic idiom, and critics who had shunned it in the 1950s and 1960s welcomed it as a source of inspiration.

Further reading

ʿAbbūd, M., *al-Shiʿr al-ʿāmmī*, Beirut (1968), 131–44.
Booth, M., 'Poetry in the vernacular', in *CHALMAL*, 472–4.
'Zajal: Michel Ṭrād fī ʿīdih al-thamānīn', *al-Nahār* (17 June 1993), 16–17.

M.T. AMYUNI

translation, medieval

Between the eighth and tenth centuries, Muslim and Christian scholars rendered into Arabic what they and their patrons deemed most valuable in the Persian, Greek and other traditions. This new knowledge, particularly Greek philosophy, became an integral part of Islamic intellectual life. 'Indian books have been transmitted, Greek wisdom translated, Persian literature passed on; some have grown in splendor, and the rest have lost nothing ... These books have been transmitted from nation to nation, from generation to generation, and from language to language, finally reaching us; we are the last to inherit them and to study them' (al-Jāḥiẓ, 1938, 2, 75). The translated texts, as well as the Arabic responses to them, aroused in turn the interest of European Christians who from the eleventh to the thirteenth century rendered into Latin numerous Arabic works both translated and original.

Chronological outline

The pre-Islamic Arab kingdom of Lakhm (see **Lakhmids**) provided bilingual **secretaries** such as **ʿAdī ibn Zayd** to the Persian court. After the Islamic conquests, however, it was the non-Arabs who had to learn Arabic. Ṣāliḥ ibn ʿAbd al-Raḥmān, a Persian convert, is credited with translating the Sasanian tax records for the new rulers. Persian secretaries, particularly **Ibn al-Muqaffaʿ** (d. 759/142), brought into Arabic from Pahlavi (Middle Persian) works on kingship, statecraft and history, as well as texts originally translated from the Sanskrit, including the fable collection ***Kalila wa-Dimna***. Since the original Pahlavi texts are lost, it is difficult to determine what Ibn al-Muqaffaʿ's ideas of transmission and translation may have been, but his style decisively influenced the development of prose composition in Arabic, and the translations that he and his colleagues produced are among the few extant literary sources for Sasanian history.

Also present in the conquered lands were Christian and pagan communities who were bearers of a tradition of Greek scholarship and, in the case of the Nestorians, of translation into Syriac. The Nestorians had renewed their contact with Greek learning when the Byzantine emperor Justinian closed the pagan academies in 529 and teachers of the Alexandrian curriculum took refuge in **Persia**.

Muslim interest in Greek science is said to have begun with the **Umayyad** prince Khālid ibn Yazīd (d, 704/84), who had scholars brought from Alexandria to translate Greek and Coptic alchemical books for him. Nevertheless, systematic translation from Greek began with the **ʿAbbāsid** caliph al-Maʾmūn (d. 833/218) who, inspired according to legend by a dream vision of **Aristotle**, established a library and translation centre in **Baghdad** under the direction of the celebrated Nestorian **Ḥunayn ibn Isḥāq al-ʿIbādī** (d. 873/260). Ḥunayn and his disciples rendered into Syriac or Arabic practically the entire available canon of Greek and Hellenistic philosophy and science, developing in the process the terminology needed to express complex new ideas in Arabic. (See further **Bayt al-Ḥikma**.)

Although the Iraqi translation movement appears to have ended by the mid-tenth century, the texts it made available were studied wherever Arabic was known. This made possible the next broad phase of translation activity, namely the transfer from Arabic to other languages, particularly Hebrew and Latin. Jewish scholars such as **Maimonides** shared with their Muslim counterparts an interest in Greek philosophy and medicine, and Hebrew translations of Arabic works played a role both in medieval Jewish intellectual life and in the transmission of learning to the West. The large-scale translations from Arabic which were to have such an influence on Christian European thought took place in **Spain** and **Sicily**, where from the eleventh to the thirteenth centuries Arabic translations and original works on philosophy, medicine, astronomy and mathematics were rendered into Latin. Less easily documentable is the diffusion of fabulous and quasi-historical narratives, such as *Kalila wa-Dimna*, *Tales of* ***Sindbād***, and the **Alexander** romance, in a profusion of versions and languages from the Middle East to Spain and Europe. Spain itself provided northern Europe not only with Arabic manuscripts and with native bilinguals who assisted in translation work, but with a variety of poetic, musical and narrative forms and elements. An Arabic account of **Muḥammad**'s journey to the other world (***Miʿrāj***), translated into Castilian at the behest of Alfonso X (d. 1284) and then into Latin, French and Italian, was known in fourteenth-century Italy, and has been credited with influence upon Dante's *Divine Comedy*.

General issues

Accounts scattered throughout the Arabic sources give a sense of the uses and occasionally the precise circumstances of medieval translation. The tenth-century chronicler **Ḥamza al-Iṣfahānī** cites as his source for Byzantine history a book read aloud for him by a Greek captive of war and translated orally into Arabic by the captive's son (*Sinī mulūk al-arḍ*, Beirut, 1961, 63). Discussing the Roman emperors, the historian **al-Masʿūdī** (d. 956/345) mentions Greek or Latin sources belonging to the Melkite Christians, but he does not describe if or how he was able to use them (al-Masʿūdī, *Murūj*, vol. 1, 310). Similarly, **Ibn Qutayba** (d. 889/276) quotes an elegant and accurate Arabic rendering of the first chapters of Genesis without naming a translator (*Maʿārif*, Cairo, 1960, 9–14). The translator Ḥunayn ibn Isḥāq, on the other hand, is more forthcoming, as attested by his list of the available works of **Galen** with an account of previous translations (ed, and trans. G. Bergsträsser, *Ḥunain b. Isḥāq uber die syrischen und arabischen Galen-Übersetzung*). A fourteenth-century author states that Ḥunayn's method of translation is superior because 'he considers a whole sentence, ascertains its full meaning and then expresses it in Arabic with a sentence identical in meaning, without concern for the correspondence of individual words' (al-Ṣafadī, trans. Rosenthal, 1975, 21).

Some medieval Muslim scholars were critical of the idea of translation, or of the content of the works being translated, but such scholars protest too much. The littérateur **al-Jāḥiẓ** comments that no one person can command two languages as well as a difficult subject matter; therefore, all translations are necessarily defective (1938, vol 1, 75–9). But al-Jāḥiẓ's own work bespeaks a familiarity with Greek thought, available to the author only through the translators whose labour he belittles. He cites Aristotle on such matters as the cross-breeding of dogs and wolves (*ibid.*, vol. 1, 183–4), and in another work puts a new twist on the old Arab practice of ridiculing misers, describing them in Galenic terms of 'contrary compositions' and 'conflicting humours' (*Bukhalāʾ*, ed, al-Ḥājirī, Cairo, 1990, 2). Similarly, in a debate in *c.*938/326 with the logician **Mattā ibn Yūnus**, the grammarian **al-Sīrāfī** argues that the distance between peoples, ages and languages makes translation impossible, and dismisses Mattā's logic as Greek grammar misapplied to Arabic sentences (al-Tawḥīdī, *Imtā'*, vol. 1, 104–28; Mahdi in von Grunebaum, 1970). However, al-Sīrāfī's knowledge of the expressions used by the philosophers suggests that he was at least acquainted with the tradition that he is criticizing. Al-Sīrāfī's position becomes even more ironic if the codification of Arabic **grammar** had indeed taken place in the eighth century along lines suggested by contact with the Greek school tradition (as proposed by C. Versteegh, 1977). Finally, an example from the beginning of the modern period illustrates how much at home the classical traditions were in Arabic literature long after the end of the translation movement. In an episode from *Ḥadith 'Isā ibn Hishām* of Muḥammad **al-Muwayliḥī** (d. 1906), the protagonist imagines what various historical figures would think of contemporary Paris, citing among others Chosroes, Julius Caesar and Plato (Cairo, 1964, 291–2).

Some misconceptions arising from tendentious views of the translation movements may be briefly discussed. First, Arabic scholarship was by no means solely responsible for Western awareness of the classical heritage. Those Greek works that have had the greatest hold on the Western imagination – the epics and tragedies – reached Europe through a later and separate process of transmission. Second, the point of translation into Arabic – in the minds of its patrons and practitioners, at any rate – was not to preserve the Greek heritage. From an Arabocentric view, the Persian element was arguably as important as the Greek, albeit in different ways; and the latter tradition was, furthermore, the object of commentaries, responses and refutations – the object not simply of preservation but of 'appropriation and naturalization' (A.I. Sabra). Finally, the re-transmission of classical scholarship to Europe should not be viewed as rendering unto the West what was the West's to begin with. Greek scholarship had been a Mediterranean phenomenon; and from the sixth to the eleventh centuries, Hellenism – as a body of texts and an intellectual style – was a rather a distinctive feature of Eastern Christian and later Islamic thought than of Western Christian. Only a tendentious mythification could maintain that Hellenism is more 'natural' to northern Europeans than to the medieval Middle Easterners who saw themselves as heirs to all the best that had been thought and said in the world.

Further reading

On translation into Arabic

Fihrist (Dodge), vol. 2, 571–711.

Morony, M.G., *Iraq after the Muslim Conquest*, Princeton (1984), 64–88.

Muḥammadī, M. *al-Tarjama wa-al-naql 'an al-Fārisiyya fī al-qurūn al-Islāmiyya al-ūlā*, Beirut, (1964).

O'Leary, D.L., *How Greek Science Passed to the Arabs*, London (1949).

Salama-Carr, M., *La Traduction à l'époque abbaside*, Paris (1990).

Walzer, R., *Greek into Arabic*, Oxford (1962).

On Islamic Hellenism

Peters, F.E., *Aristotle and the Arabs*, New York (1968).

Rosenthal, F., *The Classical Heritage in Islam*, London (1975).

Sabra, A.I., 'The appropriation and subsequent naturalization of Greek science in medieval Islam: a preliminary statement', *History of Science*, 25 (1987), 223–43.

Versteegh, C., *Greek Elements in Arabic Linguistic Thinking*, Leiden (1977).

von Grunebaum, G.E. (ed.), *Logic in Classical Islamic Culture*, Weisbaden (1970) (see esp. M. Mahdi, 'Logic and language in classical Islam').

On transmission from Arabic

Burnett, Charles, 'A group of Arabic–Latin translators working in northern Spain in the mid-12th century', *JRAS* 97 (1977), 62–108.

——, 'The translating activity in Muslim Spain', in *The Legacy of Muslim Spain*, S.K. Jayyusi (ed.), Leiden (1992), 555–79.

Gabrieli, F., 'The transmission of learning and literary influences to Western Europe', in *Cambridge History of Islam*, 2B, Cambridge (1970), 851–89.

Halkin, A.S., 'Translation and translators (medieval)', in *EJ*, vol. 15, 1318–29.

Haskins, C., *The Renaissance of the Twelfth Century*, Cambridge, MA (1927).

Lacarra, M.J., *Cuentística medieval en España: los orígenes*, Saragossa (1979).

Lindberg, D.C. (ed.), *Science in the Middle Ages*, Chicago (1978), 52–90.

Mattock, J.N., 'The early translations from Greek into Arabic: an experiment in comparative assessment', in *Akten des zweiten Symposium Graeco–Arabicum*, G. Endress (ed.), Amsterdam (1989), 73–102.

Menocal, M.R., *The Arabic Role in Medieval Literary History*, Philadelphia (1987).

van Koningsveld, P. Sj., 'La literatura christiano–arab de la España medieval y el significado de la transmision textual en arabe de la Colectio Conciliorum', in *Concilio III de Toledo: XIV Centenario 589–1989*, Toledo (1991), 695–710.

On theory and technique

Bergsträsser, G., *Ḥunain b. Isḥāq über die syrischen und arabischen Galen-Übersetzungen*, Leipzig (1925).
al-Jāḥiẓ, *Kitāb al-Ḥayawān*,, 'A.S. Hārūn (ed.), Cairo (1938), vol. 2, 75–9.
Rosenthal, F., *Technique and Approach of Muslim Scholarship*, Rome (1947).
Salama-Carr, M., *La Traduction à l'époque abbaside*, Paris (1990).
al-Tawḥīdī, Abū Ḥayyān, *al-Imtā' wa-al-mu'ānasa*, Cairo (n.d.), vol. 2, 104–28, (D.S. Margoliouth (trans.), *JRAS* (1950), 79–129).

M. COOPERSON

translation, modern

Translation from European languages into Arabic has played a major role in the shaping of modern Arabic writing since the mid-nineteenth century. During the early stages of the ***nahḍa***, translation activities were most in evidence in its two centres, **Cairo** and **Beirut**. Muḥammad 'Alī, the ruler of **Egypt**, sent several groups of young officers to Europe – mainly to France – to be trained in modern science and technology. Some of the earliest translators of European texts were members of these missions. Rifā'a Rāfi' **al-Ṭahṭāwī**, a member of one of the first delegations, established in Cairo a department of translation in the service of the government as well as a school for translators. Rifā'a also translated several French books, including Fénelon's didactic novel, *Les Aventures de Télémaque* (1696); the Arabic translation of this work was published in Beirut in 1867. In the other centre of translation activity, Beirut, European missionaries were active in producing literary and religious works for the Arabic reader. The most important product of their activity in the nineteenth century was, without doubt, the Protestant and Catholic translations of the entire Bible into Arabic from the original languages. The former was completed in 1865 by two American missionaries, Eli Smith and Cornelius Van Dyck and their Lebanese assistants, Buṭrus **al-Bustānī**, Nāṣīf **al-Yāzijī** and Yūsuf **al-Asīr**. The latter, prepared by Augustin Rodet and Ibrāhīm **al-Yāzijī**, appeared in 1886.

Towards the end of the nineteenth century, when scores of young Lebanese graduates of the missionary schools settled in Egypt, a new stage in the history of translation was inaugurated. The Lebanese emigrants launched a variety of newspapers, journals and other publications in which translations of European thought and literature occupied substantial space. In the course of the twentieth century, translation became widespread in several Arab literary centres.

The main languages from which literature has been translated into Arabic are French and English. The former was predominant until the early decades of the twentieth century, but in the inter-war period French was gradually overtaken by English as the main source language, and in recent decades English has been the central foreign language in the entire Mashriq. A 1985 survey of books translated into Arabic in Egypt indicated that 75 per cent of translated books came from English, while 10 per cent were from French (*'Ālam al-Kutub*, April–June 1985, 3). In the **Maghrib**, however, French has been the main European language, although there was also some use of Italian sources in Libya and Spanish sources in Morocco. Recently, English has been making inroads into North Africa, mainly through the influx of American culture. Other European languages, such as German and Russian, only rarely serve as source languages, although works in these and other languages are often translated through an intermediary language. Until the 1920s, Turkish and Persian sometimes served as source languages and intermediary languages through which some European literature reached Arab readers.

The literary genre in which translation is most conspicuous is the novel. Many novels were at first serialized in journals and newspapers to attract readers. The novels selected for translation were accordingly often trivial, and only rarely were the great masters of European fiction presented to Arab readers. Most of the early translators felt free to tamper with the text or at least to delete 'boring' or 'daring' episodes and descriptions. In the inter-war period, a noteworthy improvement occurred in the quality and selection of European works. It was not until the 1940s, however, that translation of the classics of European fiction was seen as a serious literary undertaking. In Egypt, Ṭāhā **Ḥusayn** initiated a series of translations when he edited the literary journal *al-Kātib al-Miṣrī* (1945–8). In the 1950s and 1960s, a similar activity was undertaken by Lebanese publishers, who translated several modernist novelists (e.g. Camus and Sartre). These works encouraged younger Arab writers to pursue modern styles of writing. Translations of such authors as Virginia Woolf and James Joyce were instrumental in promoting an Arabic equivalent to the stream-of-consciousness technique. Joyce's *Ulysses*, for example, was translated in full and published in Cairo in 1982.

European poetry has also been translated since the beginning of the twentieth century. Prominent among European poets whose works have often been translated into Arabic are Victor Hugo and Shelley. Palgrave's anthology of English poetry, *The Golden Treasury*, served in the inter-war period as a source for many translations of English lyrical poetry in Egypt. The main poetic works that interested Arab translators were, however, Shakespeare's plays (e.g. *Romeo and Juliet*, *The Merchant of Venice*) as well as plays by French classical dramatists. In the post-World War 2 period, several other European poets were translated, including Baudelaire, T.S. Eliot and St John Perse.

Translators of European poetry into Arabic were faced with difficulties exceeding those of translators of prose, mainly because of the special structure of classical Arabic **prosody** and its rhyming system. Several poets tried to produce translations in the classical Arab form (e.g. the Egyptian poet ʿAlī Maḥmūd **Ṭāhā** in his 1934 translation of Shelley's 'To a Skylark'). Most of these attempts, however, turned out to be paraphrases rather than an accurate rendering of the original. In view of these difficulties, most translators of poetry resorted to prose or to free verse. As of the 1950s, some translators were able to make use of the newly developed poetic style entitled *al-shiʿr al-ḥurr* (**'free verse'**) to reflect the original form of European poetry. However, prose is still the main vehicle for translating foreign poetry.

The earliest dramatic texts to be translated into Arabic were the comedies of Molière and the tragedies of Corneille and Racine. Muḥammad ʿUthmān Jalāl, a disciple of al-Ṭahṭāwī, translated plays by Molière and Corneille in the last two decades of the nineteenth century. His versified translations were written in colloquial Egyptian Arabic rather than in the formal literary language (*fuṣḥā*). At times he Egyptianized the characters and situation, although the translation of the text itself remained fairly loyal to the original. Shakespeare was also, as indicated above, a dramatist much sought after by translators. The early Arabic versions of his plays were often adaptations rather than faithful translations of the original text, e.g. Najīb **al-Ḥaddād**'s verse translation of *Romeo and Juliet*, entitled *Shuhadāʾ al-gharām* (i.e. *Martyrs of Love*). Of special note is a translation of this play produced by ʿAlī Aḥmad **Bākathīr** in Cairo in 1947 in which he used a kind of classical Arab prosody but in a fashion reminiscent of the later *al-shiʿr al-ḥurr* style. Jalāl's example in translating European plays into the vernacular, however, was not followed by later translators. With very few exceptions, European drama is translated and staged in *fuṣḥā*, whereas original drama is increasingly being written and staged in the vernacular.

Translation of non-fictional texts also abounds. These translations have given Arabic prose a measure of flexibility and acted as a vehicle of transmission for a variety of modern modes of discourse.

Further reading

Moosa, M., *The Origins of Modern Arabic Fiction*, Washington D.C. (1983).

Peled, M., 'Creative translation: towards the study of Arabic translations of Western literature since the 19th century', *JAL* 10 (1979), 128–50.

al-Shayyāl, Jamāl al-Dīn, *Tārīkh al-tarjama wa-al-Ḥaraka al-Thaqāfiyya fī ʿAṣr Muḥammad ʿAlī*, Cairo (1951).

Somekh, S., *Genre and Language in Modern Arabic Literature*, Wiesbaden (1991).

Tājir, Jak, *Ḥarakat al-tarjama bi-Miṣr khilāl al-qarn al-tāsiʿ ʿashar*, Cairo (n.d.).

S. SOMEKH

See also: *al-nahḍa*

transmission *see* poetry, classical

travel literature

A tradition of the Prophet enjoined his followers to seek knowledge even as far as China; but Arabic travel literature as it has come down to us is concerned, at least in the pre-modern period, primarily with travelling inside the religious and cultural unity of the land mass and the Mediterranean basin of the *Dār al-Islām* or Abode of Islam, plus a limited number of accounts of voyages along the Indian Ocean fringes of East Africa and of peninsular India to south-east Asia and the coast of China. Until the expansion of activities by the Barbary Corsairs in the sixteenth century CE, no Muslim ships seem to have braved the Atlantic Ocean waters.

Thus we have the paradox of considerable traffic within the Arab lands combined with an almost total lack of interest in, for example, the lands of northern Europe and northern Asia and of sub-Saharan Africa, regarded as *Dār al-Ḥarb* or *Dār al-Kufr*, the Abodes of War and Unbelief; since the medieval Muslim had everything necessary for salvation within his own closed world, curiosity about the outside lands was superfluous, if not indeed dangerous. Hence what the Arabs knew of such lands tended to come at second hand through trade contacts, as was brought by the Scandinavian–Slav Rūs who sailed down the river systems of Russia from Scandinavia to Byzantium and the Islamic lands, bringing some vague knowledge to the latter of the intervening peoples and lands; or else through the travels of persons marginal to the Muslim community, such as those of the Spanish Jew Ibrāhīm ibn Ya'qūb al-Ṭurṭūshī across the Frankish empire and the Slav lands of eastern Europe in the mid-fourth/tenth century, whose account is unfortunately lost but is quoted by later writers. It is a regrettable fact that the accounts of many medieval travellers both within and outside the Islamic lands are known only from citations in historical and geographical works. Of the very few early accounts of travels by Muslim Arabs into the *terrae incognitae* of northern Eurasia which have survived, we possess that of the diplomatic envoy from the caliph to the king of the Bulghars on the middle Volga, **Ibn Faḍlān** (309–10/921–2) extremely valuable for its ethnographical information, and that of the globe-trotter and poet **Abū Dulaf** who accompanied an embassy from Bukhara across Central Asia to the Emperor of China's court (*c.*328/940), useful but confused in its arrangement.

Within the Islamic world, however, there was much travel by pilgrims heading for Mecca and Medina or the **Shī'ī** shrines; by scholars seeking out famous teachers or institutions of learning; by Ṣūfī mystics attracted by a charismatic *shaykh*; by religious propagandists, such as the **Ismā'īlī** ones; by officials and diplomatic envoys; but above all, by traders. The earliest form of travel literature known to us is that of the practical manuals, the road books, from the third/ninth century onwards, developing into the classic Arabic works on geography (see **geographical literature**); most of these were based on actual travels (e.g. those of **Ibn Ḥawqal** and **al-Muqaddasī**), and might combine sober information with a more credulous interest in local marvels and other phenomena. Full-length, independent travel books (Arabic *riḥla*, 'journey') appear slightly later. That of the sixth/twelfth-century Spanish Muslim voyager **Ibn Jubayr** enshrines the experiences of a pilgrim to the Holy Places who sailed through the Mediterranean to Egypt and who was an acute observer of local conditions. Also from the far Muslim West, the lengthy *riḥla* of the Moroccan **Ibn Baṭṭūṭa** covers the experiences of thirty years of his life, spent in journeys across the whole expanse of the eighth/fourteenth-century Islamic world, from Ghana to South Russia, India, the Maldive Islands and China, at a time when the Turco–Mongol conquests had facilitated movement across the Euro–Asiatic land mass; as well as revealing the author's personal beliefs and ways of thought, insights only rarely vouchsafed from medieval Muslims, the *riḥla* contains much important historical and social information on fringe regions of the Islamic world otherwise poorly documented.

Much of Ibn Baṭṭūṭa's travelling was done by sea along the Indian Ocean and China Sea shores, while the importance of commercial voyages through the Mediterranean and Red Seas is revealed to us by the extensive **Judaeo–Arabic literature** from the Cairo **Geniza**. Certain of the Perso–Arab sea captains who operated in the eastern waters have left us accounts of their voyages which form the earliest texts for Arab maritime history, such as the *Akhbār al-Ṣīn wa-a'l-Hind* (*Information on China and India*) put together in 237/851 and dubiously attributed to a certain Sulaymān the Merchant, and the *Kitāb 'Ajā'ib al-Hind* (*Book of the Wonders of India*) (*c.*342/953), a collection of sailors' tales by the captain **Buzurg ibn Shahriyār**, who probably came from Sīrāf in the Persian Gulf. There must have been a long tradition of seafaring and travel lore in these waters, as in the Mediterranean likewise; the Indian Ocean one certainly continued up to the time of the great navigator **Aḥmad ibn Mājid** *c.*1500 CE.

It was only in the nineteenth century, when the Arab and Turkish worlds were drawn willy-nilly into the international states-system and became parts of a worldwide economy, that Arabs began to travel in significant numbers to Europe and to write accounts of their journeys, what they saw on arrival and how they reacted to an alien culture and way of life. Rifā'a Rāfi' **al-Ṭahṭāwī** wrote in 1834 his *Takhlīṣ al-ibrīz fī talkhīṣ Bārīz* on his experiences in France; and the several works of Aḥmad Fāris **al-Shidyāq** of a generation or so later contain much acute if deprecatory comment on his stays in London and Paris.

Further reading

Hourani, G.F., *Arab Seafaring*, Princeton (1951); new enlarged edn by John Carwell, Princeton (1995).

Miquel, A., *La Géographie humaine du monde musulman jusqu'au millieu du 11ᵉ siècle*, 4 vols, Paris and The Hague (1967–88).

C.E. BOSWORTH

See also: geographical literature

tribes

The importance of genealogy for the Arabs was both retrospective and prospective. To know one's ancestors and to recall their glorious deeds in verse was a source of tribal cohesion, but equally there was a solemn duty to hand on by meritorious conduct the tribe's good name to future generations. As a Prophetic ***ḥadīth*** puts it, *al-nās ma'mūnūn 'alā ansābihim* ('People are the guardians of their lineage'). The purity of the blood-line (*aṣāla*) was nowhere more highly esteemed than in pre-modern **Arabia**, where pre-eminent **bedouin** tribes were termed *sharīf* and claimed descent from one of the two original ancestors of the Arabs. Among the best known of these tribes are 'Anaza, Shammar, Ḥarb, Muṭayr, 'Ajmān, Ẓafīr, al-Murra, Qaḥṭān, 'Utayba, Dawāsir, Sba'i, Qawāsim, Ḥuwaiṭāt and Banū Tamīm. The ruling families of Saudi Arabia, Kuwait and Bahrain are descended from 'Anaza who are considered the aristocrats of the desert (Dickson, 1983).

Arab genealogists view the origin of the Arabs as descendants of Shem son of Noah in tripartite fashion: (i) *al-'Arab al-bā'ida* (the lost Arabs), the original inhabitants of Arabia such as the tribes of 'Ād and Thamūd, most of whom had vanished before the advent of Islam; (ii) *al-'Arab' al-āriba* (the true Arabs) who descend from Qaḥṭān and occupied the southwestern corner of Arabia (southern Arabs); (iii) *al-'Arab al-musta'riba* (the Arabized Arabs) whose patriarchal ancestor was 'Adnān and who occupied the central and northern areas of the peninsula (northern Arabs). The picture is complicated by the drift northwards in the centuries before Islam of the Qaḥṭān tribes, the two main branches of which were Ḥimyar and Kahlān. It was the descendants of the latter especially who migrated from southern Arabia: Lakhm and Ghassān established important states in the north of Arabia, bordering on the Persian and Byzantine empires in the pre-Islamic era (see **Ghassānids**; **Lakhmids**), while Kinda held sway for a time in central Arabia. Other descendants of Kahlān, through Azd, were the tribes of Aws and Khazraj who were settled in Medina at the time of the Hijra. Another Qaḥṭānī tribe well represented in the Syrian desert to this day is that of Kalb. Although the southern Arabs were traditionally afforded historical precedence, after the advent of Islam the northern tribes more than redressed the balance, since they counted among their number the all-important tribe of Quraysh, whose ancestor Qusayy took possession of the Ka'ba by defeating the Khuzā'a, its previous (southern) owners. The two main branches of the northern Arabs descend through Muḍar and Rabī'a. From the former, through Qays 'Aylān, spring Bāhila, Ḥawāzin and Ghaṭafān. Thaqīf are descended from Ḥawāzin, and 'Abs and Dhubyān from Ghaṭafān. Also from Muḍar through Khindīf spring **Hudhayl**, Tamīm, Ḥarb and Kināna, the ancestors of Quraysh. From Rabī'a through Asad are descended 'Anaza, 'Abd al-Qays, Taghlib and Bakr ibn Wā'il.

The tribal wars in pre-Islamic Arabia provided ample scope for poets to eulogize the virtues of their tribes, and it seems that the renowned literary fair held at **'Ukāẓ**, during which all hostilities ceased, was above all an occasion for boasting and panegyric (al-Quṭb, 1968). The first ***qaṣīda*** is said to have been an elegy composed by **al-Muhalhil ibn Rabī'a** of Taghlib on the death of his brother Kulayb in the war of Basūs between the tribes of Bakr and Taghlib. Another celebrated war of the period, between two tribes with a common ancestry, was that between 'Abs and Dhubyān which lasted for forty years and occasioned the fine *ḥamāsa* poetry of **'Antara ibn Shaddād**, who fought valiantly on the side of 'Abs. **Imru' al-Qays**'s *qaṣīda* bears witness to the hatred that existed between Kinda and Lakhm, both tribes of Qaḥṭānī origin. The bitter rivals of Aws and Khazraj also shared a common forebear (Azd) and the great satirists **al-Farazdaq** and **Jarīr** both belonged to branches of Tamīm.

One writer has posited a basic duality in bedouin society which throughout history has set tribes against each other at all levels of social structure (*EI*², vol. 4, 334–5). Operating outside the confines of the tribe provided an equally strong motivation for celebration by the ***ṣaʿālīk*** poets **al-Shanfarā** and **Ta'abbaṭa Sharran** of bedouin ideals – 'bravery in battle, patience in misfortune, persistence in revenge, protection of the weak, and defiance of the strong' (Nicholson, 1988, 79). Rivalry between northern and southern tribes has also been an abiding phenomenon in Arab history, contributing to the flow of ***fakhr*** and ***hijā'*** verse. The tribes of Kalb and Qays supported rival claimants to the caliphate after the death of Yazīd in 64/683, satire being the principal weapon used on both sides. These feuds were later transported to **Spain** where ʿAbd al-Raḥmān enlisted the support of Kalb tribesmen, anxious for revenge on their northern kinsmen, to found an **Umayyad** dynasty in 139/756. The long-running rivalry between Shammar and ʿAniza, which was not resolved until early in the twentieth century, was a modern manifestation of a tribe of southern descent pitted against one of northern ancestry with poets performing their time-honoured roles (see Sowayan, 1985).

Further reading

Dickson, H.R.P., *The Arab of the Desert*, London (1983).

Kay, S., *The Bedouin*, New York (1978).

Kazzarah, S., *Die Dichtung der Tamīm in vorislamischer Zeit: ein Beitrag zur Kenntnis der altarabischen Poesie*, inaug. diss., Erlangen and Nürnberg (1982).

Nicholson, R.A., *A Literary History of the Arabs*, Cambridge (1988).

al-Quṭb, S.A., *Ansāb al-ʿArab*, Beirut (1968).

Sowayan, S.A., *Nabati Poetry*, Berkeley (1985).

P.G. EMERY

See also: Arabia; bedouin

truth and poetry

The issue of poetic truth was widely discussed by medieval Arab critics. The saying *Aḥsan al-shiʿr akdhabuhu* ('The best poetry is the most false'); attributed to **Aristotle**, was often invoked to prove both poetry's excellence and its falsehood, which was taken as a given: only the **Koran**, the divine revelation, was absolutely true. Although the Prophet employed poets as his spokesmen, the Koran condemned (pagan) poets who 'say what they do not do' (26:25–7); the inimitability of Koranic style (see ***iʿjāz al-Qur'ān***) was opposed to that of poetry on both religious and aesthetic grounds by Koran scholars and men of letters alike. Thus the debate on poetic truth turned upon moral, linguistic or aesthetic issues; and 'truth' was designated by terms whose sense varied from one discipline to another, and shifted in the course of time.

In debates on the comparative virtues of ancient versus modern poets, the poetry of the former was often praised for its 'truth' (*ṣidq*), while that of the latter, characterized by exaggeration and by the use of figurative language, was accused of being 'false' (*kādhib*). (See further **ancients and moderns**.) *Ṣidq* connotes objectivity, sincerity and accuracy of description, qualities for which **Ibn Ṭabāṭabā** (d. 322/934) praised the ancients. By contrast, **Qudāma ibn Jaʿfar** (d. 337/948) declared that the poet need not be 'sincere' (*ṣādiq*), but must say what the topic (*maʿnā*) requires; if he contradicts himself on different occasions this does not matter so long as his treatment is skilful. Qudāma also approved the use of hyperbole (*ghuluww*) for purposes of emphasis (*mubālagha*), but warned that the poet should avoid impossibility (*istiḥāla*), shifting the ground of the discussion from moral to aesthetic–linguistic considerations.

The issue of poetic truth is clearly related to the principle of decorum: it was improper, for example, to praise someone for qualities that he clearly lacked (e.g. to praise someone who had never ridden a horse for his horsemanship) or in terms inappropriate to his position (praise of a religious figure should not include references to wine). On the other hand, panegyric poetry (see ***madīḥ***) was expected to present its subject in ideal, rather than veridical, terms, enhanced by hyperbole; while in invective and in the 'lighter' genres (e.g. ***mujūn***) the poet was allowed almost unlimited licence to exaggerate.

Another term that figured in the debate on poetic truth was *ḥaqīqa*, which for philologist–critics meant the 'literal' or 'proper' use of language, as opposed to ***majāz***, 'improper', idiomatic, or figurative usage. In this context an 'untrue' statement was an instance of 'anomalous signification' attributable to rhetorical excess (as in the many criticisms of **Abū Tammām**'s poetry), deliberate contravention of established usage, or linguistic incompetence (cf. Al-Azmeh, 1986, 109–10.) 'False' statements, in this sense, lead to impossibility or absurdity; but in some contexts (e.g. invective) a 'false' (that is, inaccurate or even patently untrue) statement might he perfectly acceptable.

The recognition that figurative language was the standard form of linguistic usage, and especially of poetic diction, meant, however, that the poet had no obligation to be 'truthful', but might employ his creativity freely. This notion was developed extensively by **ʿAbd al-Qāhir al-Jurjānī** (d. 471/1078), whose discussion of the poetic imagination elevated the mendacious poet to the level of consummate artist.

For the philosophers 'truth', in the context of discourse, had primarily a logical–semantic sense. Statements were classified on a scale ranging from demonstrative (*burhāniyya*), which were absolutely true (*ṣādiqa*), to poetic, which were both imaginative (*mukhayyila*, *takhyīliyya*; see **imagination**) and false (*kādhiba*). Abū Naṣr **al-Fārābī** (d. 339/950) defined poetic discourse as that which is 'neither demonstrative nor argumentative nor rhetorical nor sophistic' (Cantarino, 1975, 93), but maintained that while poetic statements were false they were also analogical, and differed from sophistic statements, which were deliberately misleading. **Ibn Sīnā** (d. 428/1037) emphasized the imaginative nature of poetic statements, asserting that they were more effective than rational statements, and capable of inducing 'poetic assent' (*taṣdīq shiʿrī*). **Ibn Rushd** (d. 595/1198) also stressed the relation between poetry and the imagination as well as poetry's ethical role: it was the purpose of poetry to move the hearer towards the good by its imaginative presentation of good and bad qualities. The views of Ibn Sīnā in particular were to influence later critics such as **Ḥāzim al-Qarṭājannī**, who developed the notion that poetry is characterized neither by truth not by falsehood, but by its status as imaginative and creative discourse.

Further reading

Ajami, Mansur, *The Alchemy of Glory: The Dialectic of Truthfulness and Untruthfulness in Medieval Arabic Literary Criticism*, Washington, DC (1989) (see also the review by J.S. Meisami, *JAL* 22 (1993), 166–70).

Al-Azmeh, A., *Arabic Thought and Islamic Societies*, London (1986), 108–37.

Black, Deborah L., *Logic and Aristotle's Rhetoric and Poetics in Medieval Arabic Philosophy*, Leiden (1990).

Bürgel, J.-C., 'Die beste Bedeutung: eines literarischen Streites des arabischen Mittelalters im Lichte komparatistischer Betrachtung', *Oriens* 22–4 (1974), 7–102.

Cantarino, Vicente, *Arabic Poetics in the Golden Age*, Leiden (1975), 26–40, 82–99.

Jacobi, R., 'Dichtung und Lüge in der arabischen Literaturtheorie', *Der Islam* 49 (1972), 85–99.

Shahid, Irfan, 'Another contribution to Koranic exegesis: the sura of the prophets', *JAL* 14 (1983), 1–21.

J.S. MEISAMI

See also: literary criticism, medieval

al-Ṭūbī (fourth/tenth century)

Abū ʿAbd Allāh Muḥammad ibn al-Ḥasan al-Kātib al-Ṭūbī was a Siculo-Arabic writer. His father was the chief chancellor of the emiral court and a famous grammarian, and his brother ʿAlī was also a well-known poet. Al-Ṭūbī was an excellent poet, a writer, a grammarian and also a physician. According to his critics he composed better ***maqāmāt*** than those of **al-Ḥarīrī**. Al-Ṭūbī is also a poet of spiritual love; in his poems the bacchic and erotic themes veil the classical topics of mystical love. He often uses the motif of lovesickness, a recurrent theme also of the newly born Italian poetry of the thirteenth century.

Text edition

Di Matteo, I., 'Antologia di poeti arabi siciliani', in *Archivio Storico Siciliano*, Palermo (1935), 1–28.

F.M. CORRAO

Ṭūbiyā, Majīd (1938–)

Egyptian novelist and short-story writer. Born in Upper Egypt, Ṭūbiyā worked initially as a schoolteacher before studying at the Film Institute in **Cairo**. Most recently he has held a position at the Ministry of Culture. He is one of the more prolific of contemporary Egyptian writers of fiction. His first collection, *Vostok yaṣil ilā al-qamar* (1967), was a great critical success, particularly for its ability to portray different levels of consciousness; it was soon followed by *Khams jarā'id lam tuqra'* (1970) and *al-Ayyām al-Tāliya* (1972). Since then he has produced a number of novels, including *Abnā' al-ṣamt* (1974), *Ḥanān* (1981) and *Taghribat Banī Hathut* (1988), along with further short-story collections. Ṭūbiyā has also written works for children and scenarios for films.

Further reading

Hafez, Sabry, 'Innovation in the Egyptian short story', in R.C. Ostle (ed.), *Studies in Modern Arabic Literature*, Warminster (1975), 86–98.

R. ALLEN

Ṭufayl ibn ʿAwf al-Ghanawī (sixth century CE)

Ṭufayl ibn ʿAwf (or ibn Kaʿb) of the Ghanī (Qays ʿAylān) was a pre-Islamic poet-warrior also known as Ṭufayl al-Khayl (Ṭufayl of the Horses) and al-Muḥabbir (the Embellisher) on account of his superlative equine descriptions. He is referred to by some authorities as the 'master' of the inter-tribal chain of poet–transmitters which included **Aws ibn Ḥajar** and **Zuhayr**, although, given his hostile dealings with **Zayd al-Khayl** of the tribe of Ṭayyi', he was probably a contemporary of Aws ibn Ḥajar: Zuhayr would then have served an apprenticeship to both poets; poem 8 in Krenkow's edition of the ***dīwān*** of Ṭufayl is, despite its fragmentariness, stylistically similar to several of Zuhayr's works. Ṭufayl's ***qaṣīda*s** are predominantly tribal vaunts (***fakhr***) of either a political or an annalistic nature. Poem 2 is a political, exhortative threnody, in which the poet laments the murder of Huraym ibn Sinān, and urges his fellow tribesmen to a punitive raid to avenge his death. His verse is measured and traditional; the equine pieces, which occur within depictions of his tribe on a raid, were much valued in Arab antiquity by critics and aficcionados alike. Krenkow has established that there is a connection between poem 1 and a piece by Zayd al-Khayl, and they may belong to a flyting.

Text editions

Dīwān, M. ʿAbd al-Qādir Aḥmad (ed.), Beirut (1968).

Krenkow, F., 'Ṭufail al-Ganawī', *JRAS* (1907), 815–77.

The Poems of Ṭufail ibn ʿAuf al-Ghanawī and aṭ-Ṭirrimāḥ, F. Krenkow (ed and trans.), London (1927) (incomplete edn with an English translation).

J.E. MONTGOMERY

al-Ṭughrā'ī (453–514/1061–1120 or 21)

Mu'ayyid al-Dīn Abū Ismāʿīl al-Ḥusayn ibn ʿAlī al-Ṭughrā'ī was an Arab poet. He held important administrative posts (among them that of court astrologer) under the **Saljūq** sultans Malikshāh and Muḥammad – he acquired his nickname, al-Ṭughrā'ī, from his association with the *dīwān al-ṭughrā'* (the royal signature) – but first achieved political prominence at Mosul as vizier to the Saljūq prince Masʿūd. He was executed on allegedly trumped-up charges of 'corrupt religious belief'.

Al-Ṭughrā'ī's masterpiece, his ***qaṣīda*** entitled the *Lāmiyyat al-ʿajam* (*The Verses Rhyming in* lām *of the Non-Arabs*), written in **Baghdad** in 505/1111–12 and bemoaning the corrupt times in which he lived, has excited admiration for its recherché vocabulary (*gharā'ib*); al-Ṣafadī's commentary on it explains every word and rhetorical device. Translations of it have existed in Europe since the seventeenth century. Its name is a conscious echo of the *Lāmiyyat al-ʿArab* of **al-Shanfarā**; both works rhyme in *lām*. Al-Ṭughrā'ī also composed panegyrics on Saljūq notables. He was a master of prose style too – **Ibn al-Qalānisī** quotes in full a diploma drafted by al-Ṭughrā'ī for Sultan Muḥammad. He wrote at least six works on alchemy.

Text editions

Dīwān, ʿAlī Jawād al-Ṭāhir and Yaḥyā al-Jubūrī (eds), Baghdad (1976).

al-Ṭāhir, ʿAlī Jawād, *Lāmiyyat al-Ṭughrā'ī* (text and study), Baghdad (1962).

Further reading

al-Bundārī, *Histoire des seldjoucides de l'Irâq*, Mīh. Houtsma (ed.), Leiden (1889), 110, 116, 132–3.

Ibn al-Athīr, *al-Kāmil fī al-ta'rīkh*, Beirut (1965), vol. 10, 395–6.

al-Ṣafadī, *al-Ghayth al-musajjam fi sharḥ Lāmiyyat al-ʿAjam*, Cairo (1305/1888), Beirut (1975).

Yāqūt, *Irshād al-Arīb ilā Maʿrifat al-Adīb*, D.S. Margoliouth (ed.), Leiden (1907–27), vol. 4, 51–60.

C. HILLENBRAND

Ṭūlūnids *see* Egypt; Maghrib

al-Tūnisī, Khayr al-Dīn (1822/3?–89)

Tunisian statesman and reformer, born in the Caucasus and brought up in Istanbul. Khayr al-Dīn came to **Tunisia** in 1830, entered the service of the Bey and began a military career. He lived in Paris from 1853 to 1856. In 1857, he was appointed Minister of the Navy. Between 1862 and 1869 he lived in various foreign capitals. He was prime minister from 1873 to 1877, when he was forced into exile and went to Istanbul, where he was grand vizier from 1878 to 1879. In his various capacities, Khayr al-Dīn showed himself to be a daring supporter of reform and of efficient administration, and a defender of Tunisian independence. In 1868 he wrote *Aqwam al-masālik fī ma'rifat aḥwāl al-mamālik* (ed. al-Munṣif al-Shannūfī, Carthage, 2 vols, 1990–1), the greater part of which comprises a discussion of the political and economic situation of Europe; and in a long introduction he puts forward his own ideas, in the style of **Ibn Khaldūn**. Khayr al-Dīn was a modernist who believed that it was necessary to emulate the successful system of government and technical progress of the West, which could be justified with reference to Islam, and that by doing this Muslim countries would be able to overcome their backwardness. His theories in this area influenced the Egyptian **al-Ṭahṭāwī**.

Text editions

Brown, L.C., *The Surest Path*, Cambridge (1967).
Essai sur les réformes nécessaires aux Etats musulmans, M. Morsy (ed.), La Calade (1987).

Further reading

Smida, M., *Khéiredine, ministre réformateur*, Tunis (1970).
Van Krieken, G.S., *Khayr al-dîn et la Tunisie*, Leiden (1976) and *EI*[2], vol. 4, 1185–7.

J. FONTAINE

al-Tūnisī, Maḥmūd Bayram (1893–1961)

Best known for his poetry composed in Egyptian and Tunisian vernacular modes, which is fondly recited across the Arab world, 'Bayram' is also remembered as a writer of satiric and parodic prose. Born in Alexandria into a family of *petit-bourgeois* merchants of Tunisian background and 'French protected' status, he began in 1916 to publish *fuṣḥā* poems of social–political criticism in the Alexandria newspapers *al-Najāh* and *al-Ahālī*. It was in the latter that his famous poem 'al-Majlis al-baladī' appeared (25 March 1917). In the tumultuous political circumstances of 1919, Bayram founded two satirical newspapers, *al-Misalla* and *al-Khāzūq*, in which he began to publish colloquial poems, but apparently his attacks on the royal family hit home, for the newspapers were closed and Bayram was deported as a troublesome French protegé on 21 October 1919. He spent the next nineteen years in Tunisia (1919–20; 1933–7), France (1920–33, with a brief clandestine return to Egypt in 1922), and Syria (1937–8). The vulnerability of immigrant day-labourer life in France that Bayram experienced in the 1920s is described in short stories and essays from this period; his colloquial narrative poems of the same era, published in the **Cairo** newspaper *al-Shabāb* and then the magazine ***al-Funūn***, etch the miseries of poverty sympathetically while sketching merciless and hilarious caricatured portraits of social types in **Egypt**. Other poems form a running commentary on Egyptian and Arab politics of the period, while his satiric ***maqāmāt*** explore the roles of Muslim clerics in everyday dramas of Egyptian life. Bayram's breadth of knowledge and his skill at exploiting both the folk and classical expressive traditions is evident in all of these compositions. In Tunis in the 1930s, Bayram collaborated in a series of periodicals and founded his own, *al-Shabāb*, turning his pen to dissecting the local scene until he was banished, once again a troublemaker, to **Syria**. Managing to slip into Alexandria, he lived clandestinely while seeking a royal pardon. Finally an order that the police should overlook his presence was achieved; it was not until after the Free Officers' revolution, however, that Bayram received Egyptian citizenship (1954) and then, a few months before his death, a State Prize. During these last two decades of his life he regularly contributed fine short poems of social criticism to major Egyptian newspapers; wrote songs for **Umm Kalthūm** and others; composed lyrics for comic operettas and films, and wrote radio serials. In 1975 the General Egyptian Book Organization began to issue his complete works, edited by Rushdī Ṣāliḥ. Bayram brought Egyptian ***zajal*** to a new level of artistry, influencing the next, revolutionary, generation of colloquial poets, notably Ṣalāḥ **Jāhīn** and Fu'ād **Ḥaddād**.

Further reading

al-Bannā, Muḥammad Kāmil, *Maḥmūd Bayram al-Tūnisī: qīthārat al-adab al-sha'bī*, Tunis (1980).

Booth, Marilyn, *Bayram al-Tunisi's Egypt: Social Criticism and Narrative Strategies*, Exeter (1990).

al-Jābirī, Muḥammad Ṣāliḥ, *Maḥmūd Bayram al-Tūnisī fī al-manfā: ḥayātuh wa-āthāruh*, 2 vols, Beirut (1987).

Majed, Jaafer, *La Presse littéraire en Tunisie de 1904 à 1955*, Tunis (1979).

al-Qabbānī, 'Abd al-'Alīm, *Maḥmūd Bayram al-Tūnisī: 1893–1961*, Cairo (1969).

M. BOOTH

Tunisia, modern

Modern Tunisian literature is a product of the ***nahḍa***. In its prose form, this literature is, generally speaking, journalistic – the direct link with traditional culture being provided by poetry. In about 1860, the date of the First Constitution and the founding of the Official Press, reformist chroniclers began to take up the cause of modernity. During the French occupation (1881–1956) a quest for identity developed alongside the struggle against colonialism. Thus, the beginning of the twentieth century saw both the appearance of new literary genres (the short story, novel and play) and the affirmation of a specifically Tunisian literature, within the wider context of Arabic literature in general. Names such as Abū al-Qāsim **al-Shābbī** and al-Ṭāhir **al-Ḥaddād** became bywords for innovation. In the 1930s, a rich period of literature was ushered in by the periodical *al-'Ālam al-adabī*, edited by Zīn al-'Ābidīn al-Sanūsī, and later Muḥammad al-Bashrūsh's *al-Mabāḥith*, in which Maḥmūd **al-Mas'adī** and 'Alī **al-Du'ājī** distinguished themselves. Having recovered their independence, Tunisian writers began to organize themselves, and the 1960s were characterized by attempts at collectivization. The realist novel developed under the influence of al-Bashīr **Khurayyif**, and neo-realist poetry came into vogue under Ja'far Mājid. However, this was above all the decade of avant-garde literature, first attempted by Ṣāliḥ al-Garmādī. 'Izz al-Dīn **al-Madanī** began writing historical theatre and al-Ṭāhir al-Hammāmī produced poetry '*ghayr al-'amūdī wa-al-ḥurr*'. The 1970s saw the return of economic liberalization. The 'novel of conscience' emerged with Muṣṭafā **al-Fārisī**, who challenged the idea of individual power. Ṣāliḥ **al-Jābirī** tackled the issue of the rising middle class through a use of realism very similar to the poetic realism of al-Mīdānī ibn Ṣāliḥ, while Muḥyī al-Dīn **Khurayyif** expressed his ideas through contemplative poetry. However, this was above all the decade of *nouveau théâtre*, introduced by Fāḍil al-Ja'ībī and Fāḍil al-Jazīrī, who broke the traditional rules of the drama by expressing their ideas solely in dialectal Arabic. The start of the 1980s was rather bloody. Social inequality gave rise to Islamic fundamentalism. The realist novel continued to develop under M. al-Hādī ibn Ṣāliḥ, while in her poetry Faḍīla al-Shābbī put forward an original cosmogony. Riḍā al-Kāfī wrote on the horror of death. This decade also saw the rise of the Kairouan school, which began to develop literature on the theme of expatriation, following the defeats and suffering of the people; hence the tendency to take refuge in history or mysticism (Muḥammad al-Ghuzzī) or the simplicity of the natural world (Munṣif al-Wahāybī).

Further reading

Baccar, T. and Garmadi, S., *Ecrivains de Tunisie*, Paris (1981).

Fontaine, J., *Histoire de la littérature tunisienne par les textes*, Bardo, 2 vols (1988, 1994).

——, *La Littérature tunisienne contemporaine*, Paris (1991).

Literatura tunecina contemporanea, ed. P. Martínez Montavez, Madrid (1978).

Pantuček, S., *Tunesische Literaturgeschichte*, Wiesbaden (1974).

J. FONTAINE

Ṭūqān, Fadwā (1917–)

Palestinian poet. Born into a wealthy and conservative family in Nablus, Fadwā Ṭūqān was prevented at the age of 13 from continuing her education when her elder brother learnt that a boy was following her daily to and from school and had dared to give her a jasmine flower. Confined to the traditional extended-family house, she found more kindly treatment at the hands of another elder brother, Ibrāhīm **Ṭūqān** (1905–41), a well-known nationalist poet, who undertook to teach her at home and acquaint her with the art of writing verse.

She began to publish her own poetry under the pseudonym of Danānīr a few years later. Then, under her real name, she published her first collection of poetry, *Waḥdī ma' al-ayyām* (1955), expressing her deep feelings of loneliness and of yearning for a fuller life free from social repression. Mostly in traditional verse, the collection showed some influences of the innovative Arab–American **Mahjar** poets. She wrote a few poems in **free verse** in the 1950s and others in traditional metrical verse with some variations and departures, and collected them in *Wajadtuhā* (1957) and *A'ṭinā Ḥubban* (1960). These collections established her reputation as one of the leading women poets in the Arab world, coyly expressing her tender emotions of Romantic love for an unnamed man and her pent-up feelings of social protest.

In 1963 she travelled abroad alone for the first time and spent some time in Oxford studying English literature. Her later collections written in free verse show her widening horizons but remain highly personal and confessional. In *Amām al-bāb al-mughlaq* (1967) she mourns the death of her younger brother Nimr, but in her later collections written under Israeli occupation she finally emerges to celebrate the struggle of her nation for dignity and freedom (*al-Layl wa-al-fursān*, 1969; *'Alā qimmat al-dunyā waḥīdan*, 1973; *Kābūs al-layl wa-al-nahār*, 1974; and *Tammūz wa-al-shay' al-ākhar*, 1987). Today she lives in Nablus and continues to sing the heroes of the Palestinian *intifāḍa*, putting her poetry at the service of the Palestinian resistance to the Israeli occupation of her homeland.

Text editions

Arberry, A.J., *Modern Arabic Poetry: An Anthology, with English Verse Translations*, Cambridge (1950), 17–19.
Asfour, J.M., *When the Words Burn: An Anthology of Modern Arabic Poetry, 1945–1987*, Dunvegan, ON (1988), 208–10.
Boullata, I.J., *Modern Arab Poets 1950–1975*, Washington, DC (1976) 119–23.
Boullata, K., *Women of the Fertile Crescent*, Washington, DC (1978), 145–56.

Further reading

Jayyusi, S.K., *Trends and Movements in Modern Arabic Poetry*, 2 vols, Leiden (1977), 655–7.
Malti-Douglas, F., *Woman's Body, Woman's World*, Princeton (1991), 161–78.

I.J. BOULLATA

Ṭūqān, Ibrāhīm (1905–41)

Palestinian poet. Born in Nablus, Ibrāhīm Ṭūqān studied there and at the American University of Beirut. The brother of Fadwā Ṭūqān, he is known as the foremost spokesman for the Palestinian cause in the 1920s and 1930s. Much of his poetry, which ranges between the personal and the national, was published originally in Arabic newspapers; it was collected after his death in a single-volume *Dīwān* (1988). He died prematurely from a recurrent stomach illness.

Further reading

Jayyusi, S.K., *Trends and Movements in Modern Arabic Poetry*, Leiden (1977), 284–95.

P. STARKEY

al-Turk, Niqūlā (1763–1828)

Lebanese Melchite historian and poet, born and died in Dayr al-Qamar. Al-Turk was in **Egypt** from 1798 to 1804 to report to the Druze Prince Bashīr of the Lebanon on the French occupation and various editions of his history of this period, *Histoire de l'expédition des Français en Égypte* (1839), have appeared. Several anonymous manuscripts on the history of the Shihābīs, on the battles between the French and the Austrians in 1805, and a history of the notorious Governor of Acre, Aḥmad Bāshā al-Jazzār, are also ascribed to him. His ***dīwān*** (1949), which includes some ***maqāmāt***, shows that while not a master of the poetic language, he was sometimes capable of spontaneity.

Text edition

Turc, Nicolas, *Chronique d'Egypte, 1798–1804*, G. Wiet (ed.), Cairo (1950).

P.C. SADGROVE

Turkish literature, relations with Arabic

The relationship between Turkish literature and Arabic is a rather complex one. First of all, there is not one Turkish literature but several, including literatures in Eastern (e.g.

Karakhanidic and Chaghatay) as well as Western Turkish (e.g. Azeri, Ottoman and Modern Turkish of Turkey). The earliest stage in the development of a relationship between the Turkish languages and Arabic began with the Islamization of Turkish peoples of Central Asia from the eighth century (western data) onwards. With the rise of New Persian language and literature, the Turkish languages and literatures came under the influence of Persian and their relations with Arabic were mediated by Persian. Through Persian, Arabic words, Arabo-Islamic concepts and the metrical system of *ʿarūḍ* (see **prosody**) were transferred to Turkish.

In the fifth/eleventh century, Maḥmūd of Kashgar compiled the first Turkish–Arabic dictionary, the *Dīwān Lughāt at-Turk*, and Yūsuf Ulugh (Khāṣṣ) Ḥājib composed the *Kutadgu Bilig* (*Auspicious Wisdom*) in the metre *mutaqārib*. Although the metre of this poem is Arabic, its form, the *mathnawī* (poem with rhyming couplets), is Persian. Later Turkish literatures, especially Kipchaq (**Mamlūk**), Ottoman and Chaghatay literatures, make use of all existing Arabic metres but they show the same preferences as classical Persian literature, i.e. the metres most commonly used are *ramal*, *hazaj*, *mutaqārib*, *muḍāriʿ* and *mujtathth* while the metres *ṭawīl*, *kāmil*, *wāfir*, etc., are only rarely used.

During the ninth/fifteenth century, a new phase in the relationship between Turkish literatures and Arabic set in: in the east, under Tīmūrid rule, Chaghatay emerged as a major literary language, and in the west, Ottoman literature rivalled Persian. The rise of the new literary languages was accompanied by the **translation** of numerous Arabic and Persian works (including the **Koran**, *Qābūsnāma* and Saʿdī's *Gulistān*) into Turkish languages as well as the composition of parallel poems (called *naẓīre*) to existing ones. About one century later, important philological commentaries were written in Ottoman Turkish. In the field of religious poetry, the genre of eulogy on the Prophet (*naʿt ar-rasūl*) evolved partly under the influence of Arab authors such as **al-Buṣīrī**, whose famous *Qaṣīdat al-Burda* was used as a model for *naẓīre*s and *takhmīse*s (poems in which every hemistich of an original is followed by four hemistichs of a new poem).

Ottoman intellectuals of the tenth/sixteenth and subsequent centuries most often were proficient in the 'Three Languages' (*üç lisân*), namely Arabic, Persian and Turkish, and in some cases they also spoke Albanian, Greek, Hungarian or one of the Slavonic languages. Their style of Ottoman prose-writing closely followed that of classical Persian prose with its extremely complicated syntax and heavy emphasis on **rhetoric**; in many respects it differed markedly from the style of Arabic ***adab*** prose but it did use internal rhymes (***sajʿ***).

Ottoman literature, which outranks all other pre-modern Turkish literatures in volume and intellectual weight, makes free use of Arabic words, phrases, proverbs, poetic forms and genres, and follows the aesthetic guidelines layed down by poeticians like **ʿAbd al-Qāhir al-Jurjānī**, the most important textbook used by Ottoman writers being, however, the *Talkhīṣ al-Miftāḥ* of **al-Khaṭīb al-Qazwīnī** (d. 739/1338), an epitome of the *Miftāḥ al-ʿulūm* by **al-Sakkākī** (d. 626/1229); an Ottoman commentary on the Arabic lines of the *Talkhīṣ* was published as late as 1887.

In the nineteenth century, Ottoman writers and intellectuals sought to adapt their styles of writing to European (predominantly French) standards and tastes. In 1881–2, Raja'izada Mahmud Akram (Recaizade Mahmud Ekrem) published his *Taʿlīm-i edebiyyāt* which is at least partly based on the French tradition of literary theory, while in the same year Ahmad Jawdat Pasha (Ahmed Cevdet) published his *Belāghat-i ʿothmāniyye*, a work solidly grounded in the medieval tradition of Persian and Arabic poetics.

The language reform of Atatürk, with its abolition of the Arabic script and secularist bias lent force to a movement that reduced the number of Arabic and Persian words in the Turkish language and replaced them with older Turkish ones or neologisms. Cut off from large parts of their literary heritage, modern Turkish writers, especially secularist and Marxist writers, developed a new literary language and emulated the styles of Western or socialist literatures. Only recently a trend back to forms, topics and styles of pre-modern Turkish literature has been felt; it is, however, unclear whether this movement will lead to a renewal of the ancient ties between Turkish literature and Arabic.

M. GLÜNZ

al-Ṭurṭūshī (451–520/1059 or 60–1126)

Abū Bakr al-Ṭurṭūshī, often known as Ibn Abī Randaqa, was an Arab scholar. After studying

Mālikī *fiqh*, as well as ***ḥadīth***, mathematics and ***adab*** (which he learned from **Ibn Ḥazm**) in his youth, he went east to complete his education in Iraq and **Syria**. He eventually settled in Alexandria, where he taught the religious sciences – **Ibn Tūmart** was his pupil. Several of his treatises on *fiqh* are extant. His most famous book, the *Sirāj al-mulūk*, modelled on similar works of his great rival **al-Ghazzālī**, is a long *Fürstenspiegel*, a treatise on the ruler's spiritual perfection, with edifying anecdotes from Islamic and non-Islamic sources.

Text editions

al-Du'ā' al-ma'thūr wa-ādābuh, Beirut (1988).
Kitāb al-ḥawādith wa-al bida', Tunis (1959).
Lámpara de los prĭncipes, M. Alarcón (trans.), 2 vols, Madrid (1930).
Sirāj al-mulūk, Cairo (1354/1935).

Further reading

Viguera, J.M., 'Las cartas de al-Gazālī y al-Ṭurṭusī...', *Al-Andalus* 42 (1977), 341–74.

C. HILLENBRAND

al-Tustarī, Sahl ibn 'Abd Allāh *see* Sahl al-Tustarī

U

'Ubayd, 'Īsā (18??–1922)

Syrian short-story writer living in **Egypt**. Brother of Shiḥāta **'Ubayd**, he was associated with the literary movement known as the 'Modern School', and with the Sufūr group. Influenced by French literature, he published two collections of short stories in a psychological and realistic vein. In the introduction to the first collection, *Iḥsān Hānim* (1921), he advocated an Egyptian literature that would depict the social, psychological and national life of the Egyptians in a realistic manner, in contrast with the idealistic and Romantic style of **al-Manfalūṭī**. He also advocated the use of a so-called 'middle language', subsequently adopted by realist writers such as **Maḥfūẓ** for dialogue. The title story of his second collection *Thurayyā* (1922) is a novella. The work of 'Ubayd, with its special attention to feminist questions, deserves more scholarly analysis.

Further reading

Brugman, J. *An Introduction to the History of Modern Arabic Literature in Egypt*, Leiden (1984), 246–7.

Khidr, A., *al-Qiṣṣa al-qaṣīra fī Miṣr*, Cairo (1966), 129–55.

E.C.M. DE MOOR

'Ubayd, Shiḥāta (18??–1961)

Short-story writer of Syro-Lebanese origin living in **Egypt**. Like his brother 'Īsā **'Ubayd**, Shiḥāta advocated a new realistic prose literature, and attacked the Romantic style. His stories, which have a Syro-Lebanese emigrant background, are novel-like in structure. His first collection, *Dars mu'lim*, was published in 1922, but he stopped writing after the death of 'Īsā in 1923. Shiḥāta 'Ubayd is regarded as one of the pioneers of the so-called *adab qawmī* ('national literature').

Further reading

Brugman, J., *An Introduction to the History of Modern Arabic Literature in Egypt*, Leiden (1984), 246–7.

Khidr, A., *al-Qiṣṣa al-qaṣīra fī Miṣr*, Cairo (1966), 129–39, 152–69.

E.C.M. DE MOOR

'Ubayd ibn Ayyūb (probably first half of the second/eighth century)

Outlaw poet. A ***dīwān*** of 'Ubayd is not known; the collection of fragments by N.Ḥ. al-Qaysī contains 29 pieces with 160 verses. 'Ubayd describes himself as a man persecuted by the authorities because of a crime (which is not specified) and therefore forced to lead the life of an outcast. Isolated from human company, he tries to find a surrogate in relationships with wild animals and desert demons and asks pardon from God. One of his poems (no. 18, ed. al-Qaysī) is the longest outlaw poem known so far except for **al-Shanfarā**'s *Lāmiyya*.

Text editions

Mallūḥī, 'A., *Ash'ār al-luṣūṣ wa-akhbāruhum*, Damascus (1988), 113–66.

Fragments in al-Qaysī, N.Ḥ., *al-Mawrid* 3 (1974), vol. 2, 121–36; *idem*, *Shu'arā' Umawiyyūn*, Baghdad and Beirut (1976–85), vol. 1, 193–238.

Further reading

Seidensticker, T., 'Die Lāmīya des 'Ubaid Ibn Aiyūb', *ZDMG* 138(1988), 99–127.

T. SEIDENSTICKER

'*Udhrī* poetry

Love poetry of an elegiac kind, flourishing during the **Umayyad** period among **bedouins** in the Hijaz. The term is coined after two poets of the Banū 'Udhra, a tribe of Yemeni origin (see **tribes**), **'Urwa ibn Ḥizām** and **Jamīl ibn Ma'mar**, who expressed a faithful devotion to their beloved, and allegedly died of love. Several poets of other tribes are reckoned among the 'Udhrīs, e.g. **Qays ibn Dharīḥ**, **Qays Ibn al-Mulawwaḥ**, called Majnūn, and **Kuthayyir**, Jamīl's ***rāwī***. In the course of the second/eighth century, 'Udhrī poets and their beloveds – 'Urwa and 'Afrā', Jamīl and Buthayna, Qays and Lubnā, Majnūn and Laylā, Kuthayyir and 'Azza – were transformed into heroes of romantic stories about chaste lovers, who were separated, but remained faithful and died of sorrow (cf. Blachère, *Histoire*, 760–3). About the same time, the concept of **courtly love** developed in the intellectual climate of **'Abbāsid** urban society was labelled *al-ḥubb al-'udhrī* and projected back into an idealized bedouin environment. *'Udhrī* verses, sometimes of dubious authenticity, were quoted in treatises on **love theory**, and influenced the vocabulary of **Ṣūfī** poetry. The legend of the 'Benou-Azra', who 'when loving, die', has been introduced into European literature by Stendhal's treatise *De l'amour* (1822), and inspired Heine's poem 'Der Asra'.

'Udhrī love poetry, viewed from a diachronistic aspect, constitutes an intermediate stage between the pre-Islamic *nasīb* (see ***qaṣīda***) and the 'Abbāsid ***ghazal***, where *'Udhrī* attitudes are blended with courtly elements, i.e. the beloved's despotism and superiority, and the ethical value of love. On the synchronistic level, it forms the elegiac counterpart to the frivolous eroticism of the Ḥijāzī *ghazal*, represented by **'Umar ibn Abī Rabī'a**. Although both variants of Umayyad love poetry reveal certain similarities and must have developed in contact with each other, the bedouin origin of *'Udhrī* verses is evidenced by conventional techniques of composition and style, and by a preference for traditional metres. The elegiac and emotional appeal of the *nasīb* are enhanced, for whereas pre-Islamic poets refer to a former love-affair they wish to forget, *'Udhrī* poets speak of a present love and project their hopes and wishes into the future. They are introspective, absorbed by their longing and desire, imbuing the world and its phenomena with their melancholy feelings. The beloved's beauty is praised, but not described in detail, as in the *nasīb*. The main elements of *'Udhrī* love are passionate devotion to one woman, chastity and faithfulness until death. Reflections upon death and the possibility of meeting beyond the grave are leitmotifs of *'Udhrī* poetry.

There have been several attempts to analyse and explain *'Udhrī* love within the context of early Islamic society, both from a religious and from a socio-economic aspect, beginning with Ṭāhā **Ḥusayn**'s *Ḥadīth al-arbi'ā'*. A.K. Kinany brings it into relation with Islamic monotheism, eschatology and ethics (1951, 251–86), whereas T.L. Djedidi, who also proposes a 'homologie' between monotheism and 'dame unique', thoroughly investigates its social and economic basis. He maintains that the Banū 'Udhra are a marginal group of impoverished semi-nomads, deprived of access to the wealth pouring into the Hijaz, and that economic privation is symbolically correlated with loss of the beloved and sexual renunciation (1974, 132). There are doubtless several factors to be considered when interpreting the predominantly masochistic, anti-social attitude of the 'Udhrīs. From medieval sources, e.g. the *Kitāb al-Aghānī*, it appears that 'Udhrī poets enjoyed high esteem already in the first/seventh century, and replaced the 'bedouin hero', the paragon of tribal values, as a model for identification (cf. *GAP*, vol. 2, 36–8). Their perseverance in an individual relationship, frustrated by demands of the group, and their ensuing death, were approved of by society, for according to an apocryphal ***ḥadīth***, lovers who remain chaste and die of sorrow, die as a 'martyr' (*shahīd*). The ambivalence inherent in the *'Udhrī* phenomenon is evident and seems to be related to social tensions in the Umayyad period. While advocating a new system of values in agreement with Islam, *'Udhrī* poets turn against society in renouncing life, thereby protesting, albeit in a passive way, against the loss of stability in a rapidly changing world.

Further reading

al-Aẓm, S.J., *Fī al-ḥubb wa-al-ḥubb al-'udhri*, 2nd edn, Beirut (1974).

Blachère, Régis, *Histoire de la littérature arabe*, Paris (1952–66), vol. 3, 649–60.

Djedidi, T.L., *La Poésie amoureuse des Arabes: le cas des 'Uḏrites*, Algiers (1974).

Ḥusayn, Ṭāhā, *Ḥadīth al-arbi'ā'*, 12th printing, Cairo (1972), vol. 1, 187ff., vol. 2, 18ff.

Khairallah, A.E., *Love, Madness and Poetry: An Interpretation of the Maǧnūn Legend*, Beirut (1980).

Kinany, A.K., *The Development of gazal in Arabic Literature*, Damascus (1951).
Vadet, J.-C., *L'Esprit courtois en Orient dans les cinq premiers siècles de l'Hégire*, Paris (1968), 363–78.

R. JACOBI

al-'Ujaylī, 'Abd al-Salām (1918–)

Syrian short-story writer. One of **Syria**'s best-known writers of short stories since the 1950s, al-'Ujaylī was born in al-Raqqa on the Euphrates in eastern Syria into a family that was still semi-nomadic. Throughout his life he has extended the range of his travels but retained a strong attachment to al-Raqqa where he lives most of the time. Illness interrupted his school studies but provided the opportunity to read extensively in religion, history and modern and classical literature. He attended secondary school in Aleppo and studied medicine at the University of Damascus, qualifying in 1945. For most of his professional life he practised medicine in al-Raqqa but he was also a member of the People's Assembly in the late 1940s. In 1947 he volunteered and fought in the Syrian army in Palestine. In 1962 he was briefly Minister of Culture.

Al-'Ujaylī's first short story was published in 1936 but his first book was a collection of Romantic poetry, *al-Layālī wa-al-nujūm* (1951). He has been a prolific writer of short stories that have been collected into nearly twenty volumes. He has also published two novels, *Bāsima bayn al-dumū'* (1959) and *al-Maghmūrūn* (1979), and nine volumes of essays, lectures, travels and accounts of rural life and desert life in the Euphrates valley. In his late seventies, he is still active as a writer of fiction and a critic of ancient and modern literature.

Al-'Ujaylī's realistic tales usually illustrate psychological dilemmas of modern life. Many are derived from his clinical experiences and are located among the people of eastern Syria. His earlier stories often read as if they were intended to be read aloud. Later stories have touched on how modern bureaucracy and the police state have affected the lives of ordinary people. All have a profound humanism and are written in simple, crafted Arabic.

Collections of his stories have been published in French and Spanish.

P. CLARK

'Ukāẓ

One of the 'markets of the Arabs' (*aswāq al-'Arab*) that were held periodically in pre-Islamic times on various sites on the Peninsula. These markets were associated with fairs and cultic centres. 'Ukāẓ, the market of the tribes of Qays 'Aylān and Thaqīf, was situated not far southeast from Mecca; it was held for two or three weeks in the month of Dhū al-Qa'da. It is the scene of many stories of the early poets, including **poetic contests**.

Further reading

Müller, Gottfried, *Ich bin Labīd und das ist mein Ziel*, Wiesbaden (1981), 141–53 ('Exkurs' on the markets in general).
al-Rashīd, Nāṣir ibn Sa'īd, *Sūq 'Ukāẓ fī al-Jāhiliyya wa-al-Islām*, Cairo (1980).

G.J.H. VAN GELDER

'Ulayya bint al-Mahdī (160–210/777–825)

'Abbāsid princess, musician and poet, half-sister of **Hārūn al-Rashīd** and **Ibrāhīm ibn al-Mahdī**. A cultivated, elegant and pious woman, she was married to an 'Abbāsid prince, but love-poems of hers addressed to two slaves have been preserved. Much of her poetry consists of short pieces designed to be sung; in the ***muḥdath*** style, it treats of love, friendship and longing for home, but also includes praise of Hārūn, the caliph, celebration of wine and sharp attacks on enemies. 'Ulayya is not the only princess known to have composed poetry and songs, but she was the most gifted, surpassing her brother Ibrāhīm in musicianship.

Text edition

al-Ṣūlī, Abū Bakr, *Ash'ār awlād al-khulafā' wa-akhbāruhum*, J. Heyworth Dunne (ed.), London (1936), Beirut (1982), 55–83 (many samples of poetry).

H. KILPATRICK

'Umar ibn Abī Rabī'a (23–93/644–712 or 103/721)

Famous love poet, foremost representative of the Ḥijāzī school. He belonged to a rich Meccan family of the clan Makhzūm. Later he settled in Medina, but often returned to Mecca, especially during the pilgrimage, in pursuit of amorous adventures. 'Umar played a leading part in the pleasure-oriented urban society of the **Hijaz**. He associated with singers and musicians, enjoyed the conversation of women and wrote verses to numerous ladies of the Qurayshī nobility, including the caliphal family. Charm, gaiety and a considerable vanity were his personal attributes. His poetry was highly esteemed already in his lifetime. His contemporary **Jarīr** calls him 'the best poet of love'.

'Umar's ***dīwān*** (ed. P. Schwarz) consists of 440 poems and fragments, exclusively devoted to the erotic genre. Two variants of his ***ghazal*** can be distinguished:

1 A lengthy form (50–70 vv.) in the manner of the ***qaṣīda***, i.e. a sequence of thematic units, beginning with a conventional motif of the *nasīb*, followed, as a rule, by a praise of the beloved. The *ghazal* ends with one or more individual episodes, referring to amorous conflicts or adventures and their happy end (cf. Audebert, 1975, 1977).
2 A short, monothematic *ghazal* (4–20 vv.), which was probably destined to be sung. It is closely structured by stylistic means and usually contains a lively narrative, e.g. a lovers' quarrel and reconciliation.

Excepting a few texts of doubtful authenticity, displaying a courtly attitude (cf. Blachère, 1952–66, 638), 'Umar's *ghazal* is light-hearted, even frivolous, but never obscene, and reveals a remarkable pyschological insight. He tends to elaborate the human aspect of conventional motifs, assigning to the lover's friends and the beloved's maids an active part in the relationship. Urban traits, an extensive use of dialogue, and the introduction of individual elements are his main contributions to the development of *ghazal* poetry.

Text edition

Dīwān, P. Schwarz (ed.), Leipzig (1901–9); M.M. 'Abd al-Ḥamīd (ed.), Cairo (1952), rpt Beirut (1961).

Further reading

Audebert, Claude, 'Réflexions sur la composition des poèmes de 'Umar ibn Abī Rabī'a', *Cahiers de linguistique d'Orientalisme et de Slavistique* 5–6 (1975), 17–29, 9 (1977), 5–18.

——, 'Rime et parallélisme dans un poème de 'Umar B. Abī Rabī'a: ou le jeu de l'attente déjouée', *Institut Français d'Archéologie orientale du Caire: Livre du Centenaire 1880–1980*, Cairo (1980), 355–67.

Blachère, Régis, *Histoire de la littérature arabe*, Paris (1952–66), 629–42.

Jacobi, R., 'Theme and variations in Umayyad ghazal poetry', *JAL* 23 (1992), 109–19.

Kinany, A.H., *The Development of gazal in Arabic Literature, Pre-Islamic and Early Islamic Periods*, Damascus (1950), 193–249.

Seidensticker, T., 'Anmerkungen zum Gedicht 'Umar ibn Abī Rabī'a Nr. 299 Ed. Schwarz', *Wagner Festschrift*, 131–44.

R. JACOBI

'Umar ibn Laja' (late first or early second/eighth century)

'Umar (or 'Amr) ibn al-Ash'ath ibn Laja' of Taym, ***rajaz*** and *qaṣīd* poet, was a friend of **al-Farazdaq** and was involved in a series of ***naqā'iḍ*** with **Jarīr**. He appears to have died in Ahwaz. The *naqā'iḍ* of 'Umar ibn Laja' and Jarīr were collated by **al-Aṣma'ī**, Abū 'Amr al-Shaybānī and Ibn Ḥabīb; the ten poems preserved in Muḥammad ibn al-Mubārak ibn Maymūn's *Muntahā al-ṭalab min ash'ār al-'Arab*, totalling 730 verses, form the basis of the Kuwait edition of his poetry.

Text edition

Shi'r, Y. al-Jubūrī, (ed.), Kuwait (1981).

P.F. KENNEDY

'Umar al-Nu'mān *see Alf layla wa-layla*

'Umāra al-Yamanī (515–69/1121–74)

Yemenī author of prose and poetry, born in Marṭān in al-Zarā'ib in the coastlands of **Yemen**, who studied Shāf'ī ***fiqh*** in Zabīd. As a trader he visited Aden in south Yemen, where he met *dā'īs* (propagandists) of the **Fāṭimids** in **Egypt**. In 550/1155 he was commissioned by the Sharīf of Mecca, Qāsim ibn Hāshim ibn Fulayta, to participate in an embassy to the Fāṭimid Imām al-Fā'iz in **Cairo**, just after the vizier Ṭalā'i' ibn Ruzzīk, who also had literary pretensions, had seized power and had been granted the honorific title 'al-Malik al-Ṣāliḥ'. In his poems 'Umāra praised not only the Imāms al-Fā'iz and al-'Āḍid, but this vizier and his successors. But when the poet gave evidence of his sympathy with and regret for the fall of the Fāṭimid dynasty, the Sunnī Ayyūbid sultan Ṣalāḥ al-Dīn (Saladin) had him executed in Cairo.

'Umāra's *Tārīkh al-Yaman* is an important source for Yemenī tribal history. His autobiographical *al-Nukat al-'aṣriyya fī akhbār al-wuzarā' al-Miṣriyya* deals with his youth in Yemen, but, more importantly, also describes the lives and intrigues of many Egyptian viziers and notables whom he met in Cairo. As a poet 'Umāra not only composed a lament on the downfall and the empty palaces of the Fāṭimids, but also a complaint addressed to Saladin, as well as many laudatory poems dedicated to his erstwhile Fāṭimid benefactors.

Text editions

al-Mufīd fī akhbār Ṣan'ā' wa-Zabīd, Muḥammad ibn 'Alī al-Akwa' (ed.), Cairo (1976).

'Oumāra du Yémen sa vie et son oeuvre, Hartwig Derenbourg (ed.), in *Publications de l'école des langues orientales vivantes*, IVe série – X and XI (partie française), Paris (1897, 1904) (contains a very small selection of his poetry with translation, and the text of *al-Nukat al-'aṣriyya*).

Ta'rīkh al-Yaman, Ḥasan Sulaymān Maḥmūd (ed.), Cairo (1957).

Yaman: Its Early Mediaeval History by Najm ad-Dīn 'Omārah Al-Ḥakami, H.C. Kay (ed.), London (1892).

Further reading

al-Miṣrī, Dhū al-Nūn, *'Umāra al-Yamanī*, Cairo (1966).

Smoor, P., '"The Master of the Century": Fāṭimid poets in Cairo', *Orientalia Lovaniensia Analecta, Egypt and Syria in the Fatimid, Ayyubid and Mamluk Eras*, U. Vermeulen and D. De Smet (eds), Leuven (1995), 139–62.

P. SMOOR

al-'Umarī, 'Abd al-Bāqī *see* al-Fārūqī

'Umayr ibn Ṣhuyaym al-Quṭāmī *see* al-Quṭāmī

Umayya ibn Abī al-Ṣalt (d. *c.* 9/631)

Poet from the town al-Ṭā'if. In his poems, he gives accounts of Biblical legends, the Creation, the Flood, the Day of Judgment, etc. These and other religious topics, which often display striking similarities to Koranic passages, shed light on monotheistic belief in ancient Arabia. Many of the poems, however, are of questionable authenticity.

Text editions

Dīwān, 'Abd al-Ḥafīẓ al-Saṭlī (ed.), 2nd edn, Damascus (1977).

Umayya ibn Abi ṣ Ṣalt, F. Schulthess (ed. and trans.), Leipzig (1911).

Further reading

Schulthess, F., 'Umajja b. Abi-ṣ Ṣalt', in *Nöldeke Festschrift*, vol. 1, 71–89.

Seidensticker, T., 'The authenticity of the poems ascribed to Umayya Ibn Abī al-Ṣalt', in *Tradition and Modernity in Arabic Language and Literature*, J.R. Smart (ed.), Richmond (1996), 87–101.

T. BAUER

Umayyads

(Banū Umayya), Meccan clan of Quraysh, first dynasty of caliphs (40–132/661–750). Their rise to power was the immediate result of the first civil war (see **Orthodox caliphate**), but the foundation was laid under the third caliph 'Uthmān (23–35/644–56), who had appointed members of his clan to key positions in the Islamic state. After the murder of the fourth caliph **'Alī ibn Abī Ṭālib**, Mu'āwiya ibn Abī Sufyān, governor of Syria since 18/639, seized the caliphate without serious opposition. Damascus became his residence, political power shifting from the Arabian Peninsula to **Syria**.

Since J. Wellhausen's classic *Das arabische Reich und sein Sturz* (*The Arab Kingdom and its Fall*, 1927), Umayyad rule has been viewed as an attempt to found an Arab empire with its centre in Syria (cf. also Hawting, 1986). In **'Abbāsid** sources, mainly hostile, the Umayyads are accused, moreover, of having changed the caliphate into kingship (*mulk*). In fact, Mu'āwiya (40–60/661–80), by securing the office for his son Yazīd (60–4/680–3), introduced hereditary succession, which was to be threatened continuously, in particular by the two factions emerging from the first civil war, **Shī'īs** and **Khārijīs**, both operating in Iraq. A first Shī'ī rising was easily suppressed, but it resulted in the death of Muḥammad's grandson al-Ḥusayn at Karbalā' (61/680), thus providing the Shī'ī cause with a martyr. A more serious challenge proved the anti-caliphate of ʿAbd Allāh ibn al-Zubayr at Mecca (64–73/683–92), which started the second civil war. It was widely recognized for a time, but eventually defeated under the caliph ʿAbd al-Malik ibn Mawān (65–86/685–705).

The reign of ʿAbd al-Malik and his son al-Walīd (86–96/705–15) was a period of internal stability and military expansion, both largely due to **al-Ḥajjāj ibn Yūsuf**, governor of Iraq (75–95/694–714), who mercilessly enforced Umayyad authority. ʿAbd al-Malik is credited with several reforms tending to further centralized government, e.g. the change to Arabic as official language in administration, and the introduction of a Muslim coinage, which soon superseded the former Byzantine and Sasanian currencies. During al-Walīd's caliphate Muslim troops entered **Spain** (92/711), while in the east campaigns directed by al-Ḥajjāj resulted in the conquest of Transoxania and Sind. A new Islamic and imperial consciousness is apparent in the architecture of the time, e.g. the Dome of the Rock, the Great Mosque at **Damascus**, and the Umayyad palaces in the Syrian desert.

The last period of comparative stability was the caliphate of Hishām ibn ʿAbd al-Malik (105–25/724–43), but the forces destined to overthrow the dynasty had begun to operate before his reign. Besides Shīʿī and Khārijī opposition, only temporarily checked by al-Ḥajjāj, tribal factionalism and the discontent of the 'clients' (see ***mawālī***), the underprivileged non-Arab Muslims demanding equality, had continuously threatened internal peace. The enmity between the northern (Qays) and southern (Kalb) tribal confederations (see **tribes**), politically exploited by the caliphs, proved fatal in the end, for tribal conflicts within the army contributed to the downfall of the dynasty. The problem of the mawālī remained unsolved. An attempt was made by ʿUmar II ibn ʿAbd al-Azīz (99–101/717–20), but his fiscal reform was not continued, and when a revolt broke out in **Khurasan** (129/747), carefully prepared by secret propaganda in the name of 'Muḥammad's family' (*āl Muḥammad*), all discontented groups united. Success was imminent; after three years of combat, the third civil war, the caliphate was seized by the ʿAbbāsids, their lineage going back to the Prophet's uncle al-ʿAbbās (cf. Shaban, 1970).

The internal conflicts outlined above, the uprooting of tribes dissatisfied with life in military camps, gradual urbanization and contact with non-Arab civilization, all had their impact on Arabic literature, which during the first/seventh century passed from an oral to a literate stage. Poets were forced to experiment. They adapted conventional genres and motifs to their own requirements and developed new concepts and techniques (cf. *CHALUP*, 387–432), thereby creating the basis on which ʿAbbāsid ***muḥdathūn*** were to build their brilliant edifice of the 'new style' (see ***badīʿ***). Poetry flourished in different local centres and consequently lost its former homogeneity, in spite of contact and fluctuation. In Damascus tribal poets, engaged in caliphal politics, continued to use the ***qaṣīda***, changing its structure, however, in accordance with their panegyrical purposes. Their invectives (see ***hijāʾ***; ***naqāʾiḍ***) against political or personal enemies achieved a degree of scathing and poignancy unknown before. In the **Hijaz**, cut off from the mainstream of politics, love poetry was the favourite genre. There is a gay, frivolous ***ghazal***, cultivated in the rich society of the pilgrim towns (see **ʿUmar ibn Abī Rabīʿa**), whereas **bedouin** poets composed *ghazal* verses of an elegiac kind, expressing a chaste, unfulfilled love and faithfulness until death (see ***ʿUdhrī* poetry**). Both variants are later assimilated, with added sophistication, in Syria and in Iraq.

In **Kufa** and **Basra**, the newly founded garrison towns, Shīʿī and Khārijī poets resumed the conventional genres of ***fakhr***, *hijāʾ* and ***madīḥ***, imbuing their verses with a distinctive Islamic flavour and a heightened emotional appeal (cf. *CHALABL*, 185–201). **Al-Kumayt**'s *Hāshimiyyāt*, his verses in praise of the Banū Hāshim, Muḥammad's clan, are the first important testimony of Shīʿī poetry. The passionate hatred and fanaticism of Khārijī poets, who expressed their desire to fight and die as a 'martyr' (*shahīd*), constitute an active counterpart to *ʿUdhrī* resignation, a violent reaction to the changes of bedouin life and the dissolution of tribal society.

Poetry remains the principal genre of Umayyad *belles-lettres*, but there is evidence of a gradual formation of literary prose, greatly furthered by the art of **oratory** in its religious and political function (cf. Blachère, 1952–66, 732–6). The beginning of narrative prose dates back to the late Umayyad period, e.g. romances about famous lovers and miraculous stories, as also the origin of Islamic historiography, first concerned with the Prophet's biography (see ***sīra***; Muḥammad) and with early Muslim campaigns. The first brilliant specimens of **artistic prose** were written in Umayyad chanceries. There is general consent that its founder was **ʿAbd al-Ḥamīd ibn Yaḥyā**, **secretary** (*kātib*) to the caliph Hishām, who also served the last Umayyad, Marwān II. ibn Muḥammad (127–32/744–9/50), and perished with the dynasty (cf. *CHALUP*, 154–79).

Further reading

Blachère, Régis, *Histoire de la littérature arabe*, Paris (1952–66), vol. 2.
CHALUP.
Hawting, G.R., *The First Dynasty of Islam*, London (1986).
Hodgson, M.G.S., *The Venture of Islam*, Chicago (1974), vol. 1: 217–79.
Rubinacci, R., 'Political poetry', in *CHALABL*, 185–201.
Shaban, M.A., *The Abbasid Revolution*, Cambridge (1970).
Wellhausen, J., *The Arab Kingdom and Its Fall*, M.G. Weir (trans.), Calcutta (1927).

R. JACOBI

Umayyads of Spain *see* Spain

Umm Kalthūm (1904?–75)

Egyptian singer. Accompanied by the *takht* (oriental orchestra), Umm Kalthūm followed the style of the traditional Arab musical performance in which music is used to express the meaning of the words and to highlight the various meanings of the text. The poet Aḥmad Rāmī introduced her to the best Arabic poetry and she in turn persuaded him to write songs in colloquial Egyptian Arabic. Her voice spanned two octaves. Probably the greatest Arab singer of this century, her ability to perform difficult music lasted until an advanced age.

Further reading

Saïah, Y., *Oum Kalsoum, l'étoile de l'Orient*, Denoë, Paris (1985).
Ubaydli, A., 'Umm Kalthūm: the possibility of European appreciation of an Arab singer', *Proceedings of the 1989 International Conference on Middle Eastern Studies*, Durham (1989), 213–22.

A. UBAYDLI

underworld *see* Banū Sāsān

al-Uqayshir al-Asadī (first/seventh century)

Al-Mughīra ibn ʿAbd Allāh al-Uqayshir al-Asadī was born in the ***jāhiliyya*** and died in the reign of the Umayyad caliph ʿAbd al-Malik, and was one of the first bacchic personalities of the first century. He was, in Bencheikh's well-judged résumé, a 'picturesque bohemian' who frequented the taverns and monasteries of **Ḥīra**, and formed with several companions a group called the Mujjān al-Kūfa. Judging by the small amount of his poetry that survives, he was an excellent poet, somewhat mercurial in his moods, who describes wine in a fine language, still strongly marked by the **bedouin** lexical tradition. His awareness of the traditional canon is exemplified in a poem which, in the manner of the later poet **Abū Dulāma**, parodies martial sentiments: the poet rides to battle on a donkey; but he is sidetracked, sells his mount and spends his gains in a tavern.

P.F. KENNEDY

Further reading

EI[2], art. 'Khamriyya' (J.E. Bencheikh).

al-ʿUrayyiḍ, Ibrāhīm (1908–)

Bahraini poet and literary critic. Born in **India** as the son of a Bahraini father and Iraqi mother al-ʿUrayyiḍ grew up in an environment hardly exposed to Arabic language and culture. After returning to Bahrain at the age of 20 he studied classical and modern Arabic literature, distinguishing himself by his writing on both. His first poetic attempts were in Urdu and English, in which he published poems under the title *Sonnets* (1932). His first Arabic collection was *al-Dhikrā* (1931) but his poetry drew the attention of Arab critics only after the collection *al-ʿArāʾis* (1946) was published. Al-ʿUrayyiḍ also wrote an epic about Palestine entitled *Arḍ al-shuhadāʾ* (Beirut, 1951). As a literary critic he attempted in *al-Asālīb al-shiʿriyya* (Beirut, 1950) to study the role of tone in Arabic poetry, following an earlier attempt by Muḥammad **Mandūr**.

Text edition

Jayyusi, Salma Khadra (ed.), *The Literature of Modern Arabia*, London (1988), 233–5, 549.

R. SNIR

urjūza see rajaz

al-ʿUrwa al-Wuthqā

Al-ʿUrwa al-Wuthqā ('the firm bond' – **Koran** 2:256) was a weekly periodical published by **al-Afghānī** and **ʿAbduh** in Paris between March and October 1884. Reportedly the ideas were al-Afghānī's and the words ʿAbduh's. Although only eighteen numbers were issued, it was extremely influential and was circulated widely in the Muslim world despite being banned by the British in **Egypt** and **India**. Its early lapse was probably due to financial problems. Its main themes were pan-Islamism, the necessity for *jihād* against colonialist powers (particularly the British), and the restoration of true Islamic belief and practice. It was one of the earliest publications systematically to apply Koranic verses and ***ḥadīth***s to contemporary problems.

Further reading

Keddie, N., *Sayyid Jamāl al-Dīn 'al-Afghānī': A Political Biography*, Berkeley and Los Angeles (1972), 214–28.

Riḍā, Muḥammad Rashīd, *Tarīkh al-Ustādh al-Imām al-Shaykh Muḥammad ʿAbduh*, Cairo (1931), esp. vol. 1, 290ff.

K. ZEBIRI

ʿUrwa ibn Ḥizām (d. 30/650 or later)

One of the poets of the Banū ʿUdhra who is said to have died for the love of one woman, his cousin 'Afrā'. His life, which has probably been embellished into legend in the manner of much of the ʿUdhrī romances, has been received in two principal versions: one from **Ibn Qutayba**, the other from **Abū Faraj al-Iṣbahānī**. His extant poetry consists of one long *nūniyya* and a *bā'iyya*. The *nūniyya*'s exceptional length (238 verses) and the repetition of imagery within it suggests strongly that it is an amalgam of separate compositions.

Text edition

Shiʿr, I. al-Sāmarrā'ī and A. Maṭlūb (eds), Baghdad (1961).

Further reading

Krackovskij, I.J. and Ritter, H., 'Die Frühgeschichte der Erzählung von Macnūn and Lailā in der arabischen Literatur', *Oriens* 8 (1955), 33–9.

P.F. KENNEDY

See also: *ʿUdhrī* poetry

ʿUrwa ibn al-Ward (second half of sixth century)

Pre-Islamic poet. He is sometimes called 'the ʿUrwa of the vagabonds/outlaws (*ʿUrwat al-ṣaʿālīk*)', although unlike other ***ṣaʿālīk*** he did not sever the bonds with his tribe, ʿAbs. The nickname may therefore reflect merely his affinity to and sympathy with the true outcasts, visible in the stories about him and in some of his poems. In his most famous poem (27 lines) he contrasts, after a *nasīb*, the 'good' and the 'bad' *ṣuʿlūk*.

Text editions

Dīwān, ʿAbd al-Muʿīn al-Mallūḥī (ed.), Damascus (1966).

Die Gedichte des ʿUrwa ibn Alward, T. Nöldeke (ed. and trans.), Göttingen (1863).

Further reading

Jones, Alan, (ed. and trans.) *Early Arabic Poetry*, vol. 1, Marāthī *and* Ṣuʿlūk *Poems*, Reading (1992), 127–38, 258–60.

al-Khawāja, Ibrāhīm, *ʿUrwa Ibn al-Ward: ḥayātuhu wa-shiʿruh*, Tripoli (1981).

G.J.H. VAN GELDER

Usāma ibn Munqidh (488–584/1095–1188)

Amīr of Shayzar. Usāma was fond of hunting, fighting and politics; he was also a prolific and sophisticated author. In 552/1157 an earthquake levelled the north Syrian castle of Shayzar and many of the surrounding villages; almost all his family were killed in the disaster. As he puts it in his anthology of poetry *al-Manāzil wa-al-diyār* (*Camps and Dwellings*), 'I was moved to compose this volume by the destruction which has overcome my country and my birthplace. For time has spread the hem of its robe over it'. A similar desire on the part of this long-lived survivor to make a record of a world that was in the process of vanishing may be behind his autobiographical *Kitāb al-Iʿtibār* (*Book of Instruction*), whose anecdotes, many of which are intended to give a moral message, are not in any chronological order. The work can also be seen as belonging to the genre of ***fakhr***, for it celebrates Usāma's courage and martial skill and many of the stories deal with hunting and warfare. The book is particularly valuable for its accounts of Usāma's (occasionally friendly) encounters with the Franks of the Kingdom of Jerusalem.

Usāma's *Kitāb al-ʿAṣā* (*Book of the Stick*), written at an age when he himself must have been using a walking-stick, is a rhabdophilist's anthology, dealing with the role of the stick in religion, history, folklore and poetry. Again, snippets of autobiography are embedded in this compilation. His *Kitāb al-Badīʿ*, a treatise on the poetic art, is one of about a dozen of his works which have survived. Usāma, who was steeped in *Jāhilī* poetry, wrote poetry himself, and his *dīwān* was much admired by contemporaries. Nostalgia, the problems of old age and the inscrutable nature of destiny are recurrent preoccupations in Usāma's writings. Some of his works, such as his oneirocritical treatise, the *Kitāb al-Nawm wa-al-aḥlām*, and his book about women, the *Akhbār al-nisāʾ*, do not seem to have survived.

Text editions

Dīwān, A.A. Badawī and Ḥ. ʿAbd al-Majīd (eds), Cairo (1953), rpt Beirut (1980).

Kitāb al-Badīʿ, A.A. Badawī and Ḥ. ʿAbd al-Majīd (eds), Cairo (1960).

Kitāb al-Iʿtibār, ed. Ḥasan Zayd, Beirut (1988).

Ousâma Ibn Mounkidh, un émir syrien au premier siècle des Croisades, H. Derenbourg (ed. and trans.), Paris (1889).

Usamah's Memoirs, Entitled Kitab al-Iʿtibar, P.K. Hitti (ed.), Princeton (1930).

An Arab-Syrian Gentleman and Warrior in the Period of the Crusades, P.K. Hitti, (trans.), New York (1929).

The Autobiography of Ousâma, C.R. Potter (trans.), London (1929).

Des enseignements de la vie ... souvenirs d'un gentilhomme syrien des temps des Croisades, André Miquel (trans.), Paris (1983).

Die Erlebnisse des syrischen Ritters Usāma ibn Munqid, H. Preisser (trans.), Munich (1985).

Kitāb al-Manāzil wa-al-diyar, Anis Khalidov (ed.), Moscow (1961).

Further reading

Derenbourg, H., *Anthologie de textes arabes inédits par Ousâma et sur Ousâma*, Paris (1893).

Morray, D.W., *The Genius of Usāmah ibn Munqidh: Aspects of the Kitāb al-Iʿtibār*, Durham (1987).

R. IRWIN

ʿUsayrān, Laylā (1936–)

Lebanese journalist and novelist. Born in **Beirut**, ʿUsayrān was active with the Palestinians in the south of Lebanon in the late 1960s and early 1970s. She wrote for the Palestinian newspaper *Fatḥ* and – during the Lebanese civil war – for *Filasṭīn al-Muḥtalla*; all of her writings are engaged in the Palestinian cause. She has published four novels: *ʿAṣāfīr al-fajr* (1968) and *Khaṭṭ al-afʿā* (1970) pre-date the outbreak of the Lebanese civil war; her two war novels are *Qalʿat al-usṭā* (1979) and *Jisr al-ḥajar* (1982). *Qalʿat al-usṭā* tells the story of a strong woman who learns from the war that she must first take care of herself if she is to be of any use to those many who need her. ʿUsayrān has refused to collect her journalistic writings into a book, insisting that a book must be written as a book.

M. COOKE

al-Ushnāndānī (d. 288/900–1)

Abū ʿUthmān Saʿīd ibn Hārūn al-Ushnāndānī was a Basran philologist and the teacher of the philologist and lexicographer **Ibn Durayd**, who quotes him frequently in his great dictionary *al-Jamhara*. His work *Kitāb maʿānī al-shiʿr* (*The Meanings of Poetry*) consists of difficult and mostly anonymous poetical examples with their explanations, which he used as teaching materials. It was transmitted by his pupil Ibn Durayd, who is sometimes regarded as the author of the work.

Text edition

Kitāb maʿānī al-shiʿr, Damascus (1922).

Further reading

Yāqūt, *Muʿjam al-udabāʾ*, I. ʿAbbās (ed.), Beirut (1993), vol. 4, 244–5.

R.A. KIMBER

uslūb (pl. *asālīb*)

Lit. 'way, behaviour'. Occurs in classical texts on poetics; it is rarely used as a technical term in the strict sense, but mostly in a vague manner to denote something like 'a mould for the treatment of a theme'. **Ibn Qutayba** uses it in his famous description of the structure of the ***qaṣīda*** to refer to the various thematic parts of the ode. **ʿAbd al-Qāhir al-Jurjānī** defines it *en* *passant* as 'a certain kind of, and method in, word composition'; the examples show that it is a characteristic syntactic mould created by one poet and imitated by others. Much later, **Ibn Khaldūn** incorporates it in his definition of (Arabic) poetry: 'Poetry is eloquent speech built upon metaphor and descriptions, segmented into parts that agree in metre and rhyme-consonant, each part being independent in its purport and aim from what precedes and follows, and following the methods (*asālīb*) of the Arabs peculiar to it' (G.J.H. van Gelder, 1982). He explains the meaning of *uslūb* as 'a mental form for metrical world combinations which is universal in the sense of conforming with any particular word combination. This form is abstracted by the mind from the most prominent individual word combinations and given a place in the imagination comparable to a mold or loom' (F. Rosenthal, 1967). This seems to be similar to al-Jurjānī's understanding of the term. The process by which these moulds are acquired is probably the one that **Abū Nuwās** was advised to follow by his teacher **Wāliba ibn Ḥubāb**, to wit, that to become a poet he should learn 10,000 lines of poetry and then unlearn them. Ibn Khaldūn reports from his teachers that they did not consider the poetry of **al-Mutanabbī** and **Abū al-ʿAlāʾ al-Maʿarrī** to be true poetry, as they did not follow the *asālīb* of the (ancient) Arabs.

Ḥāzim al-Qarṭājannī uses the term technically. The fourth part of his *Minhāj* is devoted to it. He establishes a neat proportion between 'words' (*alfāẓ*) and 'combination of words' (*naẓm*), on the one hand, and 'meanings, themes' (*maʿānī*) and 'combination of themes' (*uslūb*), on the other. However, the larger context of the chapter requires that the term be understood in a slightly more general way, since various attitudes of discourse are subsumed under this heading: seriouness vs. jest, coarseness vs. delicacy, and others.

In modern Arabic the term has become the equivalent of 'style'.

Further reading

'Abd al-Qāhir al-Jurjānī, *Dalāʾil al-iʿjāz*, Maḥmūd Muḥammad Shākir (ed.), Cairo (1404/1984), 468–9.

Bencheikh, Jamel Eddine, *Poétique arabe: Essai sur les voies d'une création*, Paris (1989), 56–8 (on Ibn Khaldūn's *uslūb*).

Ḥazim al-Qarṭājannī, *Minhāj al-bulaghāʾ wa-sirāj al-udabāʾ*, Muḥammad al-Ḥabīb Ibn al-Khūja (ed.), Tunis (1966), 327–80, in particular 363–4.

Ibn Khaldūn, *al-Muqaddima*, Beirut (n.d.), 569–73; Franz Rosenthal (trans.), 2nd edn, London (1967), vol. 3, 373–82.

Ibn Qutayba, *Introduction au Livre de la poésie et des poètes*, Maurice Gaudefroy-Demombynes (ed. and trans.), Paris (1947), 14.

van Gelder, G.J.H., *Beyond the Line*, Leiden (1982), index, sub radice *slb*.

W.P. HEINRICHS

al-ʿUtbī (d. 413/1022)

Abū al-Naṣr Muḥammad ibn ʿAbd al-Jabbār al-ʿUtbī was a prose stylist, historian and poet. Born in **Rayy**, he spent his life as a chancery official in the **Ghaznavid** and other courts in the East. His fame rests on his *Kitāb al-Yamīnī*, a laudatory biography of the Ghaznavid Amīr Maḥmūd (Yamīn al-Dawla), written in an ornate rhymed prose that was intended to outdo the *Kitāb al-Tājī* in praise of the rival **Būyid** dynasty by Ibrāhīm ibn Hilāl **al-Ṣābiʾ**. Celebrated for its style, the *Yamīnī* (which ends in 409/1018, twelve years before Maḥmūd's death) was the object of numerous philological commentaries, as well as a paraphrastic Persian translation by Jarbādhqānī (early seventh/thirteenth century).

Text edition

The most accessible text of the *Yamīnī* (not yet critically edited) is that printed with the twelfth/seventeenth-century commentary by al-Manīnī, *al-Fatḥ al-wahbī*, Cairo (1286/1869); passages relevant to India are translated in Sir H. M. Elliot and J. Dowson, *The History of India as told by its own Historians*, London (1869), rpt New York (1966), vol. 2, 14–52. Jarbādhqānī's *Tarjama-yi tārīkh-i Yamīnī* was critically edited by J. Shiʿār, Tehran (1966); the translation by J. Reynolds, London (1858), rpt Lahore (1975) is unsatisfactory.

Further reading

Rubinacci, R., 'Le citazione poetiche nell' *Al-Taʾrūḥ al-Yamīnī di Abū Naṣr al-Utbī*', in *A Francesco Gabrieli: Studi Orientalistici offerti nel sessantesimo compleanno ...*, Rome (1964), 263–78.

——, 'Upon the "al-Taʾrīkh al-Yamīnī" of Abū Naṣr al-ʿUtbī', *Studia Turcologico Memoriae Alexii Bombaci Dicta*, Naples (1982), 463–7.

E.K. ROWSON

al-ʿUthmān, Laylā (19??–)

Kuwaiti novelist and short-story writer. A

promising writer who joins the growing list of Arab women novelists including Collette Khūrī, Ghāda **al-Sammān** and many others, Laylā ʻUthmān has also written poetry in prose, a field usually reserved for men. Her collection *Imra'a fī inā'*, which appeared in 1976, includes a preface by the Iraqi novelist and critic ʻAbd al-Raḥmān Majīd al-Rubayʻī, in which he praised her work for its sincerity and poignancy. Her other works include the collections of short stories *al-Raḥīl, Fī al-layl ta'tī al-ʻuyūn, al-Ḥubb lahu ṣuwar* and *Lā yaṣluḥ lil-ḥubb* (1987); and the novels *al-Mar'a wa-al-qiṭṭa* and *Wasmiyya takhruj min al-baḥr*.

Further reading

Fawzī, M., *Adab al-aẓāfir al-ṭawīla*, Cairo (1987).

M. MIKHAIL

V

vices and virtues *see* ***manāqib* literature**

W

Waḍḍāḥ al-Yaman (d. *c.*93/712)

Love poet of the middle **Umayyad** period. ʿAbd al-Raḥmān (or ʿAbd Allāh) ibn Ismāʿīl, 'the Bright from the Yemen', is said to have been of Southern Arabian origin or, according to others, to be descended from the Persians who had invaded South Arabia towards the end of the sixth century CE. The *akhbār* tell us about his love for a certain Rawḍa whose family did not consent to a marriage, and about an encounter with and love poem on Umm al-Banīn, wife of the caliph al-Walīd I (86–96/705–15), who is reported to have killed him because of this. The question raised in the 1920s by Ṭāhā **Ḥusayn** of whether Waḍḍāḥ existed at all is still discussed. In recent scholarship there is a certain agreement that behind all legendary adornment a historical personage can be discerned. An ancient ***dīwān*** has not survived; the collections of fragments compiled by al-Suwaysī and by Ḥaddād contain 27/34 pieces with 237/267 lines respectively (partly of doubtful attribution). A dialogue poem of ten lines with seven sequences of speech and reply (no. 4, ed. al-Suwaysī/no. 7, ed. Ḥaddād) is of some importance for literary history.

Text editions

'Waḍḍāḥ al-Yaman, ḥayātuhū wa-mā tabaqqā min shiʿrih', Ḥ.J. Ḥaddād (ed.), *al-Mawrid*, 13 (1984) vol. 2, 103–36.

Waḍḍāḥ al-Yaman, al-shāʿir wa-qiṣṣatuhū, R. al-Ḥ. al-Suwaysī (ed.), Beirut (1974) (cf. the review by al-Ṭ. al-ʿAshshāsh, *Ḥawliyyāt al-Jāmiʿa al-Tūnisiyya* 15 (1977), 199–206).

Further reading

Fotijeva, V.S., 'K voprosy ob istorichnosti Vaḍḍākha al-Iamana' ['On the question of the historicity of Waḍḍāḥ al-Yaman'], *Pis'mennye Pamjatniki Vostoka* 1975 (1982), 136–62.

Souissi, R., 'Waḍḍāḥ al-Yaman, le personnage et sa légende', *Arabica* 17 (1970), 252–308.

T. SEIDENSTICKER

Wādī al-Nīl (1867–78)

The first independent newspaper in **Cairo**, founded by ʿAbd Allāh Abū al-Suʿūd. It disappeared on his death. *Wādī al-Nīl* contained political, scientific, commercial and literary material, including feuilletons on history, the voyages of **Ibn Baṭṭūṭa**, etc., and occasional poetry by ʿAlī **al-Laythī**, Muḥammad Ṣafwat **al-Sāʿātī** and others. Its patron was the Khedive Ismāʿīl, whom it defended in his diplomatic struggle against the Porte for greater independence for **Egypt**. Although *Wādī al-Nīl* made some contribution to the development of journalistic style, its language remained strongly influenced by ***sajʿ*** (rhymed prose).

Further reading

Ayalon, A., *The Press in the Arab Middle East: A History*, New York (1995), 41–2.

Ḥamza, ʿAbd al-Laṭīf, *Qiṣṣat al-ṣiḥāfa al-ʿArabiyya (fī Miṣr)*, Baghdad (1967), 62–3.

P.C. SADGROVE

wāfir see prosody

Wahb ibn Munabbih (34–110? or 114?/654–728? or 732?)

Along with two early Jewish converts to Islam, ʿAbd Allāh ibn Salām and **Kaʿb al-Aḥbār**, Abū ʿAlī Waht ibn Munabbih al-Yamānī al-Ṣanʿānī is considered a most important source for the pre-Islamic history of **Arabia** and for Jewish and Christian tradition. Although we have somewhat more information about him than the others mentioned above, some questions about his background and biography still remain.

Probably born a Muslim in Yemen, there is considerable debate about the background of Wahb's family. While some sources (e.g.

al-Dhahabī, **Ibn Ḥajar**) speak of his family's Persian origin in Herat and of his father's conversion to Islam in Yemen during the time of the Prophet, others (e.g. **Ibn al-Nadīm**, **al-Ghazzālī**, **Ibn Khaldūn**) assume his Jewish origin, from *ahl al-kitāb* in Persia. He became a judge in Ṣan'ā', and there are enigmatic references to his having been beaten and imprisoned. This may be connected to other references to his having held Qadarī views and having written about them, an act he is said to have regretted.

Several works are attributed to him, only fragments of which are extant. Among those listed by R.G. Khoury are *Kitāb al-Isrā'īliyyāt*, *Kitāb al-mubtada' wa-qiṣaṣ al-anbiyā'*, *Zabūr* or *Mazāmīr Dāwūd*, *Maghāzī Rasūl Allāh*, *Kitāb al-qadar*, *Tafsīr Wahb*. Most are mentioned by **Ḥājjī Khalīfa** and are often cited by **Ibn Hishām**, **al-Ṭabarī**, **al-Mas'ūdī** and **al-Kisā'ī**, among others, in dealing with early Yemenite and Arabian history and with Jewish and Christian tradition. His misquotation of Biblical verses and misreading of inscriptions are quite evident, but among Muslim scholars he was considered a trustworthy transmitter of traditional lore. Some contemporary Muslim critics of the ***Legends of the Prophets*** genre, however, include Wahb among the sources considered unreliable.

Further reading

Hirschberg, H.Z., 'Wahb ibn Munabbih', *EJ*, vol. 16, 241–2.
Horovitz, J., 'Wahb ibn Munabbih', *EI*[1], vol. 4, 1173–5.
Huart, C., 'Wahb ben Monabbih et la tradition Judéo-Chrétienne au Yemen', *JA* 10 (4) (1904), 331–50.
Ibn Ḥajar al-'Asqalānī, *Tahdhīb al-tahdhīb*, Hyderabad (1907), vol. 11, 166–8.
Khoury, R.G., *Wahb ibn Munabbih*, 2 vols, Wiesbaden (1972).

W. BRINNER

See also: *Isrā'īliyyāt; Legends of the Prophets*

al-Wahrānī (d. 565/1179)

Muḥammad ibn Muḥriz al-Wahrānī was a humorous writer. Trained in the composition of elaborate prose (*inshā'*), he arrived in **Egypt** from his native Wahrān (Oran) early in the reign of Saladin, but quickly despaired of competing with such luminaries as **al-Qāḍī al-Fāḍil** and turned instead to the satiric and parodic pieces that became his forte. Some eighteen of these have been collected from various manuscripts and published. Written in a fairly elaborate Arabic with a significant admixture of vernacular vocabulary, they are mostly highly topical, mocking al-Wahrānī's contemporaries and commenting on local events. The best known of them is the 'Grand Dream', a fantasy visit to the Afterlife clearly modelled on the *Epistle of Forgiveness* of **Abū al-'Alā' al-Ma'arrī**. Others include a formal complaint of neglect by the assembled mosques of **Damascus** and a letter of appointment for the 'judge of the dissolute' in Alexandria. Al-Wahrānī spent his later years in Damascus, winning an appointment as preacher in the mosque of the suburb of Dārayyā, where he died.

Text edition

Manāmāt al-Wahrānī wa-maqāmātuhu wa-rasā'iluh, I. Sha'lān and M. Naghash (eds), Cairo (1968),

Further reading

Fähndrich, H., 'Parodie im "Mittelalter": aus einem Werk des M. b. Muḥriz al-Wahrānī', *Wagner Festschrift*, vol. 2, 439–46.
Ibn Khallikān, *Wafayāt al-a'yān*, I. 'Abbās (ed.), Beirut (1977), vol. 4, 385–6.
al-Ṣafadī, *Biographische Lexicon*, Istanbul and Wiesbaden (1931–), vol. 4, 386–9.

E.K. ROWSON

waḥy see inspiration

Wāliba ibn Hubāb (d. *c.*170/786)

Abū Usāma Wāliba ibn al-Ḥubāb al-Asadī poet of Damascene origin, born and brought up in **Kufa**. Only fragments of his poetry survive, although **Ibn al-Nadīm** mentions a ***dīwān*** of 100 'leaves'. It was in wine poetry and ***mujūn*** (two themes that overlap) that he influenced **Abū Nuwās** (among other Kufan reprobates, such as **Muṭī' ibn Iyās**). This influence can be detected in the momentum of debauchery which culminates in the final line of a poem and in imagery that alludes to both Arab and Persion culture (giving his poetry an intertextual dimension within the canon of Arabic literature); he is anti-Arab and includes elements of ***badī'*** which is played out in the antithesis between a happy spirit and an oppressed state; he also treated the Satanic pact to be found later in Abū Nuwās.

Further reading

Ḥāwī, I., *Fann al-shi'r al-khamrī*, Beirut (1981).
Ḥusayn, Ṭāhā, *Ḥadīth al-arba'ā'*, Cairo (1960–2), vol. 2, 212–25.
Vajda, G., 'Les zindīqs en pays d'Islam', *RSO* 17 (1938), 206.
Wagner, Ewald, *Abū Nuwās*, Wiesbaden (1965).

P.F. KENNEDY

al-Walīd ibn 'Ubayd Allāh, al-Buḥturī *see* al-Buḥturī

al-Walīd ibn Yazīd (second/eighth century)

Umayyad caliph and poet, assassinated after a short reign (125–6/743–4), aged about 36. He was designated to succeed his uncle Hishām ibn 'Abd al-Malik (105–25/724–44), but had to wait twenty years for the caliphate. The enmity between him and Hishām is amply documented in the sources and in his ***dīwān***. Al-Walīd spent a life of dissipation in the Syrian desert, where he built several palaces, e.g. Khirbat Mafjar and Mshattā, and assembled poets and musicians at his court (cf. Hamilton, 1988). He used to shock his contemporaries by scandalous behaviour, excessive drinking and blasphemous verses, but he was also a sensitive poet and an accomplished musician and composer, who set his own poems to music. His thwarted passion for Salmā, his wife's sister, inspired him to some of the most original ***ghazal*** verses in Arabic literature.

Al-Walīd's ***dīwān***, 102 poems and fragments, has been collected from various sources and edited by F. Gabrieli. Love (43 texts) and wine (14 texts) are his favourite themes, apart from exaggerated boasting (see ***fakhr***) and invectives (see ***hijā'***). His poems are usually short (4–8 v.v.) and carefully structured, especially on the phonological and morphological level. By his technique of repetition, which suggests the art of the composer, his verses achieve a musical quality unknown in Arabic poetry before. A distinctive feature of his *dīwān* is the predominance of rare metres, such as *wāfir*, *ramal majdhū'* and *khafīf* (see **prosody**). Al-Walīd's *ghazal* is of the elegiac kind in the 'Udhrī mode (see ***'Udhrī* poetry**), but there is a charming playfulness about it all his own, e.g. a lover's dialogue with a bird (no. 64). His bacchic poems, by their simple language and by various motifs and images, paved the way for the **'Abbāsid** *khamriyya* and influenced, above all, **Abū Nuwās**.

Text edition

Gabrieli, F., 'Al-Walīd ibn Yazīd. Il califfo e il poeta', *RSO* 15 (1934), 1–64.

Further reading

Blachére, Régis, *Histoire de la littérature arabe*, Paris (1952–66), 646–8.
——, 'Le prince omayyad al-Walîd [II] ibn Yazîd', in *Mélanges Gaudefroy-Demombynes*, Cairo (1935–45), 115–23.
Derenk, D., *Leben und Dichtung des Omaijaden-kalifen al-Walīd ibn Yazīd*, diss., Frankfurt and Freiburg (1974).
Hamilton, R., *Walid and His Friends*, Oxford (1988).
Jacobi, R., 'Zur Ġazalpoesie des Walīd ibn Yazīd', in *Wagner Festschrift*, 145–61.
——, 'Theme and variations in Umayyad ghazal poetry', *JAL* 23 (1992), 109–19.

R. JACOBI

See also: *khamriyya*; Umayyads

Wallāda bint al-Mustakfī (d. 484/1091?)

Andalusian princess and poet; best known as **Ibn Zaydūn**'s lover. Her father, Muḥammad III al-Mustakfī, briefly held the caliphate (1024–5), ultimately fleeing the capital in disguise, only to be poisoned shortly thereafter. Little is known of Wallāda's life, save for her exploits among the literati of Córdoba, who flocked to her house. She was renowned for her beauty, charm and nobility, yet her disdain for convention, including her refusal to wear the veil or marry, and rumours of lesbianism led to accusations of immorality. Few of her poems are extant. The poems collected by her biographers include two amorous pieces directed towards Ibn Zaydūn and several satirical poems against him, apparently written after their relationship had taken a turn for the worse.

Text edition

Garulo, T., *Dīwān de las poetisas de al-Andalus*, Madrid (1986) contains biographical notes and a Spanish translation of her poetry.

Further reading

Hoenerbach, W., 'Notas para una caracterización de Wallāda', *al-Andalus* 36 (1971), 467–73.
Jayyusi, S.K., *The Legacy of Muslim Spain*, Leiden (1992), 709–12 (see also index).
Nichols, J.M., 'Wallāda, the Andalusian lyric and the questions of influence', *East and West* 21 (1977), 286–91.
Nykl, A.R., *Hispano-Arabic Poetry and its Relations with the Old Provençal Troubadours*, Baltimore (1946), 107–8.

L. ALVAREZ

Wannūs, Sa'd Allāh (1941–1997)

Syrian dramatist. Trained in **Syria**, **Egypt** and France, Wannūs was regarded as the most significant figure in recent Syrian drama, as playwright, producer and drama critic. His best-known play is *Ḥaflat samar min ajl al-khāmis min Ḥuzayrān* (1968), a work that became an event in its own right in that it forced its audiences to confront the issues surrounding the June defeat of 1967 through a wholesale condemnation of societal values. In later plays (and also in a series of articles on dramatic theory) Wannūs made further valuable contributions to modern Arabic drama, albeit to mixed critical reviews. Among his most notable plays are: *Mughāmarat ra's al-mamlūk Jābir* (1972), *Sahra ma'a Abī Khalīl al-Qabbānī* (1972) and *al-Malik huwa al-malik* (1977). Although these plays revolve around themes culled from narratives from the past, they are characterized by an experimental approach to the language of dialogue and audience reception, and represent a vigorous attempt to create an innovative Arabic drama.

Further reading

Allen, Roger, 'Arabic drama in theory and practice: the writings of Sa'dallāh Wannūs', *JAL* 15 (1984), 94–113.
Gouryh, Admer, 'Recent trends in Syrian drama', *World Literature Today* 60 (2) (Spring 1986), 216–21.

R. ALLEN

al-Waqā'i' al-Miṣriyya (1828–)

Official gazette of the Egyptian government, founded by Muḥammad 'Alī Pasha in **Cairo**. It appeared in Turkish and Arabic until *c.*1847. It became a daily in the 1880s. When Muḥammad **'Abduh** was chief editor (1880–2), it became a paper of opinion, playing a reformist and educational role, but was reduced again to a government gazette under the British occupation. From the 1860s it increasingly published occasional poetry by leading poets, including Aḥmad **Shawqī**, Maḥmūd Sāmī **al-Bārūdī** and others.

Further reading

'Abduh, Ibrāhīm, *Ta'rīkh al-Waqā'i' al-Miṣriyya, 1828–1942*, Cairo (1942).

P.C. SADGROVE

al-Wāqidī (d. 207/823)

Abū 'Abd Allāh Muḥammad ibn 'Umar al-Wāqidī was a renowned Medinan historical compiler of materials on many subjects. Though an enthusiastic and gifted student, he seems not to have attracted much notice until 170/786, when he had an opportunity to guide the caliph **Hārūn al-Rashīd** around the pilgrimage sites of Medina. After this he enjoyed lavish patronage and support until his death.

Al-Wāqidī was a prolific writer and compiled numerous monographs. Although some of his works were devoted to the **Koran**, ***ḥadīth*** and jurisprudence (see ***fiqh***), most covered historical subjects: pre-Islamic history, **Muḥammad**, the caliphate of Abū Bakr, the conquests of **Syria** and Iraq, the battles of al-Jamal and Ṣiffīn, the assassination of 'Uthmān and the minting of Islamic coinage. Some of these texts were undoubtedly short essays incorporated into his larger works. These latter included an annalistic history of Islam to 179/796 entitled *al-Ta'rīkh al-kabīr* (*The Large History*), and a biographical dictionary called *Kitāb al-Ṭabaqāt* (*Book of Classes*), extending to about 186/802. Both of these works are lost, but the latter formed the core for a work of the same title by his secretary **Ibn Sa'd**. Of all his books, the only one surviving today is his *Kitāb al-Maghāzī* (*Book of Campaigns*), a compilation on the military expeditions led or sent from Medina by the Prophet Muḥammad.

A well-organized and critical writer and an avid bibliophile (his library was enormous for his time), al-Wāqidī used the rich resources available in Medina to present a work noteworthy for its historiographical sophistication (see the entry for **Muḥammad**) and wealth of detail. But much of this material seems to have been unknown to his predecessors, and in many cases the details and chronology are undoubtedly based on arbitrary speculation; the sorting of the genuine survivals of old material from more recent accretions has thus been an important subject in a scholarly discussion with implications for the understanding of other early historical texts.

Text edition

Numerous *futūḥ* texts have been published under al-Wāqidī's name, but all such attributions are false.

Kitāb al-Maghāzī, Marsden Jones (ed.), Oxford (1966).

Muhammed in Medina. Das ist Vakidi's Kitab alMaghazi in verkürzter deutscher Wiedergabe, Julius Wellhausen (trans.), Berlin (1882) (the best translation, though outdated).

Further reading

More traditional approaches to al-Wāqidī are J. Horovitz, 'The earliest biographies of the prophet and their authors', *IC* 2 (1928), 498–521; A.A. Duri, *The Rise of Historical Writing Among the Arabs*, L.I. Conrad (trans.), Princeton (1983), 37–9 (with further bibliography); Tarif Khalidi, *Arabic Historical Thought in the Classical Period*, Cambridge (1994), 44–8; Michael Lecker, 'The death of the Prophet Muḥammad's father: did Wāqidī invent some of the evidence?', *ZDMG* 145 (1995), 9–27. For the more sceptical perspective, see J.M.B. Jones, 'The chronology of the *Maghāzī*: a textual survey', *BSOAS* 19 (1957), 245–80; Lawrence I. Conrad, 'The conquest of Arwād: a source-critical study in the historiography of the early medieval Near East', in *The Byzantine and Early Islamic Near East, I: Problems in the Literary Source Material*, Averil Cameron and Lawrence I. Conrad (eds), Princeton (1992), 364–84.

L.I. CONRAD

See also: *futūḥ*; historical literature

Waraqa ibn Nawfal (late sixth–early seventh century CE?)

A pre-Islamic ascetic and sage, member of the Asad ibn ʿAbd al-ʿUzzā (Quraysh), and a paternal cousin of Khadīja, **Muḥammad**'s first wife. He is said to have converted to Christianity, to have been a *ḥanīf*, and to have been able to read and write Hebrew. In the sources he is wrapped in the cloth of legend. He did not convert to Islam or transmit any traditions. He seems to have composed poetry, although little of his work is extant and has not been collected. His verses, generally of a monotheistic, 'religious' stamp, are often attributed to Zayd ibn ʿAmr ibn Nufayl, with whom he is closely associated, and to **Umayya ibn Abī al-Ṣalt**, a 'religious' poet from al-Ṭā'if. His two 'religious' poems are suspiciously Koranic, and there is one pleasant, unexciting piece of ***ghazal***, very much in the manner of **ʿUmar ibn Abī Rabīʿa**'s less inspired productions.

Further reading

Cheikho, L., *Kitāb Shuʿarā' al-Naṣrāniyya*, Beirut (1922–6), vol. 1, 616–18.

J.E. MONTGOMERY

al-Warrāq (d. *c*.230/845)

Maḥmūd ibn (al-) Ḥasan al-Warrāq was a poet of the middle **ʿAbbāsid** period, who lived in **Baghdad**. Al-Warrāq (trader in papers/books, copyist of books), who is said to have earned a living as a slave trader at times, mainly composed ascetic and gnomic poetry. The collection by al-ʿUbaydī, which could be enlarged from sources published since 1969, contains 215 pieces the length of which varies from single lines up to 14 lines. Topics of his ascetic poems (***zuhdiyyāt***) include obedience to God, renunciation of the wordly life and of worldly possessions, praise of generosity, modesty, truthfulness and forgiveness and blame of hypocrisy, calumny and envy. As many of the gnomic poems bear on moral topics as well, they are closely related to the *zuhdiyyāt*.

Text edition

Dīwān, ʿA.R. al-ʿUbaydī (ed.), Baghdad (1969); for a futher edition see R. Weipert, *ZGAIW* (1985), 271.

Further reading

Ḥusayn, M.ʿĀ.M., *Jawānib al-ʿiẓa wa-al-ḥikma fī shiʿr Maḥmūd al-Warrāq*, Cairo (1987).

T. SEIDENSTICKER

al-Wāsānī (d. 394/1004)

Abū al-Qāsim al-Ḥusayn ibn al-Ḥasan (or al-Ḥusayn) al-Wāsānī was a poet from **Damascus**. Almost nothing is known of his life. He had some kind of official position, from which he was removed after a scurrilous attack in verse. **Al-Tha'ālibī** calls him 'the **Ibn al-Rūmī** of his time', on account of his ***hijā'***. Most of the poems that have been preserved (*c.*450 lines in al-Tha'ālibī's *Yatīma* and **Yāqūt**'s *Mu'jam al-udabā'*) are invective of the obscene kind. In one poem, a humoristic masterpiece of nearly two hundred lines, he gives a lively description of disastrous banquet given by him in Khamrāyā, a village near Damascus.

Further reading

Walīmat Ibn Wāsān, 'Abd al-Qādir al-Maghribī (ed. and annot.), *RAAD* 10 (1930), 641–51, 705–19.

G.J.H. VAN GELDER

waṣf

Description, descriptive poetry. In pre-Islamic Arabic poetry, particular parts of the traditionally built ode (***qaṣīda***) might contain various descriptions. The poet, upon visiting the places where he used to see or meet his beloved before she travelled away with her own clan, describes the deserted camp including the remains of narrow ditches which once encircled tents, soot-covered stones used by the nomads as a fireplace, and tufts of wool still blowing about, at least for a short while after the camp had been abandoned. Descriptions of the poet's camel are also very common, whereas rain is seldom illustrated. The scenery did not vary profoundly in the first Islamic generations, although one may notice, albeit rarely, throughout **Umayyad** poetry landscapes typical of **Damascus** or other Arab sedentary places. Nevertheless, somewhat later in **'Abbāsid** poetry we find fresh descriptive themes included in the new models of poetry (especially those initiated by **Abū Nuwās**, d. *c.*197/813): ***khamriyyāt*** (wine poems) and ***ṭardiyyāt*** (hunting poems). The hunted animals, the hunting dogs and falcons which assist the hunter, are all attentively described.

If one imagines the birth of all new poetical models dedicated to specific themes as if emancipated from the traditional framework of the multi-theme *qaṣīda*, the complete freeing of *waṣf* should be ascribed apparently to the fourth/tenth century, when certain poets begin to specialize in descriptive poems. However, what seems to constitute a new offspring of well-worn elements in old poetry, which occasionally contains faunal elements and depictions of drinking parties, is sometimes misleading. The emergence of such new themes as independent poems is due to the needs of the consumers of 'Abbāsid culture and their lifestyle (hunting and wine parties were a characteristic activity of the higher class); the further development of descriptive poetical themes is one of the requirements of this society's taste. Accordingly, it is no wonder that in the third/ninth century an important phase of evolution in descriptive poetry takes place. Poets such as **Abū Tammām** (d. 228–3/842–51) and **al-Buḥturī** (d. 284/897) describe a palace, a landscape, even a snowy scene. Descriptive poetry is one of the prominent features of **Ibn al-Rūmī** (d. 283/896). In the fourth/tenth century, some poets acquire a reputation for being almost exclusively devoted to *waṣf*. **Al-Ṣanawbarī** (d. 334/945) specializes in *rawḍiyyāt*, poems describing flora-filled prairies (he is particularly fond of pine trees), whereas **Kushājim** (d. 350–60/961–71) and **al-Sarī al-Raffā'** (d. 360–2/970–3) devote short descriptive poems to a rich variety of objects: stove, wax candle, horse-drawn wagon, clouds, jug full of ale, bird trap, compass, garden flowers, etc. *Waṣf* poetry becomes progressively more elaborate (similes and metaphors), complicated and somewhat enigmatic. How can one discern what symbolizes the dancing maiden who twirls on one leg? Actually her description portrays a compass; that is what the title says: 'And he [i.e. the poet] said while describing a compass'. But if one covers up the title, the poem becomes a riddle. This is how one can explain the transition phase from descriptive poetry to genuine riddles, built upon rhyme and rhythm. For instance, the riddle poet al-Ḥaẓīrī al-Warrāq (d. 568/1172), whose collection of descriptive riddles is unpublished (a good MS is to be found in Istanbul), describes a huge animal which swallows people alive without the latter even uttering a complaint; at the end of the poem, it becomes evident that the poet has just described a tent. Other examples are to be found in a chapter containing descriptive riddles, in al-Abshīhī's (sometimes spelled al-Ibshīhī) literary anthology of the ninth/fifteenth century. (See further ***lughz***.)

All this proves that *waṣf* becomes a climax of artfulness and that the readers or listeners do not appreciate, in it, the realistic aspect, i.e. whether the descriptive verses conform to the material side, but are more concerned with the stylistic and artificial features, i.e. how the poet has developed the metaphorical side. This artfulness even engenders indirect and overt competitions in describing objects, plants, etc., by various poets. One of the themes that can be encountered within the descriptive category is represented in long groupings of poems depicting pretty maidens and handsome lads (or slave girls and male servants, as it can be understood) in a variety of situations and professions. If one is interested in examining an illustration of relatively late descriptive poetry, **Ibn al-Wardī** (d. 749/1349) provides some typical examples. **Al-Suyūṭī** (d. 911/1505) has conserved an entire series of poems describing oriental sweets (MSS are to be found in Princeton and Dublin; published recently by Dār al-Faḍīla, Cairo). During this particular time, an endless repertoire of such topics was devised, since this rather later, over-developed, descriptive poetry fit the taste of the upper social order.

In prose literature, *waṣf* is not defined as an independent genre. However, exemplary elements of ornate writing, collected for the use of any *kātib* (**secretary**, letter writer) who needs to improve his epistolary style can be found in many of **al-Tha'ālibī**'s (d. 429/1038) compositions, such as *al-Tamthīl wa-al-muḥāḍara*, *Lubāb al-ādāb* and *Siḥr al-balāgha*. **Al-Ḥuṣrī** (Abū Isḥāq; d. 413/1022, or 453/1061, according to the monograph by al-Shuway'ir), in his *Zahr al-ādāb*, copies from the latter source, entire chapters containing descriptions of food dishes, drinks, flowers and the like, calling them: 'Descriptions [*awṣāf*], by Contemporary Writers, Concerning ...'. (See further **artistic prose**.) Such prose *awṣāf* are often quoted by compilers in various ***adab*** anthologies and are skilfully elaborated in ***maqāmāt***.

Further reading

Arazi, A., *La Réalité et la fiction dans la poésie arabe ancienne*, Paris (1989).
al-Ḥāwī, I., *Fann al-waṣf*, 3rd edn, Beirut (1980).
al-Qaysī, N.Ḥ., *al-Ṭabī'a fī al-shi'r al-Jāhilī*, 2nd edn, Beirut (1984).
Schoeler, G., *Arabische Naturdichtung*, Beirut and Wiesbaden (1974).
von Grunebaum, G.E., *Die Wirklichkeitweite des früharabischen Dichtung*, Vienna (1937).
——, 'The response to nature in Arabic poetry', reprinted in his *Themes in Medieval Arabic Literature*, London (1981), item VII.

J. SADEN

See also: nature, in classical poetry

al-Washshā' (d. 325/937)

Abū al-Ṭayyib Muḥammad ibn Aḥmad al-Washshā' was a grammarian and lexicographer from **Baghdad**, best known as a compiler of books on 'good manners'. Al-Washshā', who at times earned a living as a teacher, wrote about thirty books, of which only four seem to have been preserved. Among these, only one is concerned with philology; the remaining three deal with elegance of behaviour and expression, often with a certain bias towards formalism. The *Kitāb al-Fāḍil fī ṣifat al-adab al-kāmil* presents well-turned linguistic utterances (*balāghāt*), arranged in forty-five chapters according to situations or social groups. In his *Tafrīj al-muhaj wa-sabab al-wuṣūl ilā al-faraj*, not yet edited, al-Washshā' presents in a sort of pattern-book texts suited for quotation in love-letters. The best known among his books is the *Kitāb al-Muwashshā*, which in fifty-six chapters treats morality, decent behaviour and elegant manners (***ẓarf***): 'a large collection of short verses, which were inscribed on books, portions of the dress, and on various other articles concludes the work (ch. 37–56). The passages in which the author himself speaks are written in rhymed prose; but by far the greater portion of the book consists of anecdotes, sayings, and verses, taken from other writers. It is unnecessary to point out the value of the work as showing the sentiments and manners of the educated Arabs during the most brilliant period of the Caliphate' (Brünnow, preface to his edn of *al-Muwashshā*, p. v). Within the field of Arabic love literature, chapters 15–22 are of importance; within these, chapter 20 on the phenomenon of singer–slaves deserves special mention.

Text editions

Kitāb al-Fāḍil fī ṣifat al-adab al-kāmil, Y.W. al-Jubūrī (ed.), Beirut (1991).
Kitāb al-Muwashshā, R.E. Brünnow (ed.), Leiden (1886); Fahmī Sa'd (ed.), Beirut (1985).

Das Buch des buntbestickten Kleides, D. Bellmann (trans.), 3 vols, Leipzig and Weimar (1984).

Further reading

Giffen, L.A., *Theory of Profane Love Among the Arabs*, New York (1971).
Vadet, J.C., *L'esprit courtois en Orient*, Paris (1968), 317–51.

T. SEIDENSTICKER

See also: love theory; *ẓarf*

Wāsīnī, al-Aʿraj (1954–)

Algerian novelist writing in Arabic. Born in Achach (Tlemcen), Wāsīnī received his higher education in **Damascus** from 1977 to 1985. After writing a thesis on the Arabic novel in **Algeria**, he taught at the Institut des Lettres Arabes at the University of Algiers. He published seven novels between 1981 and 1993, as well as two essays on the novel, and has also edited the journal *al-Musā'ala* for the Union of Algerian Writers. Wāsīnī believes literature to be the artistic expression of a dimension of life. He has tried to render Arabic more 'human' and less restricted to the religious sphere, making it a vivid means of expression in the modern world as it had been at the time of the ***Alf layla wa-layla***. The main characteristic of his work is tenderness. Wāsīnī's background and the posts that he has held have placed him in an ideal position to encourage young talented writers.

M. BOIS

Waṭṭār, al-Ṭahir (1936–)

Algerian novelist, short-story writer and journalist, writing in Arabic. Born in Sedrata, Waṭṭār studied at the Ben Badis Institute (Constantine), then at the Zitouna in Tunis. He began publishing short stories in Tunis in 1955. To date, he has published four collections of short stories and six novels. His first novel, *al-Lāz* (1974), owes its success to the human dimension that the author gives to the war of liberation, avoiding clichés used by other writers dealing with this theme: the story is disconcerting and brutally realistic, but also has lyrical interludes. *Al-Zilzāl* (1974) portrays a society that is both in the process of collapsing and of being reborn. *'Urs al-baghl* (1978) has been rightly called both a 'roman épique et symbolique à la fois' and a 'roman cathartique et prométhéen'. Waṭṭār's later novels – *al-Ḥawwāt wa-al-qaṣr* (1980) and *Tajriba fī al-ʿishq* (1989) – show a greater use of symbolism, which at times become disconcerting. *Al-Ḥawwāt wa-al-qaṣr* portrays a quest for solidarity and a protest against tyranny. In the preface to his final novel he notes that 'novelty ... is that which springs from myself ... as an Arab writer living in Africa on the shores of the Mediterranean, somehow bonded with the people living in Hyderabad or Alma-Ata'.

Waṭṭār tells of how, in his youth, he learned by heart the works of Jubrān Khalīl **Jubrān**, Mīkhā'īl **Nuʿayma** and Īlīyā **Abū Māḍī**, vowing then not to become tied to any particular school. As a journalist, he started two periodicals in 1962–3, founded the Al-Gahizia association (named after **al-Jāḥiẓ**) in 1989, and began a literary review, *al-Tabyīn*, in 1990.

M. BOIS

al-Wa'wā' al-Dimashqī (d. between 370/980 and 390/1000)

Abū al-Faraj Muḥammad ibn Aḥmad (or Muḥammad) al-Wa'wā' was a poet from **Damascus**. Originally a fruit-seller in the market-place, he acquired a certain fame as a poet. He made panegyrics for Sayf al-Dawla, al-Sharīf al-ʿAqīqī and others, but his strength lay rather in descriptive poems on lyrical subjects: nature, wine and love.

Text edition

Dīwān, I. Kratschkowsky, I. (ed.), Leiden and Petrograd (1913–14) (with a Russian translation and study; for a summary, by W. Ebermann, see *Islamica* 3 (1927), 238–41); Sāmī al-Dahhān (ed.), Damascus (1950).

G.J.H. VAN GELDER

waʿẓ see oratory and sermons

al-Wazīr al-Maghribī *see* al-Maghribī, al-Ḥusayn ibn ʿAlī

wine poetry *see khamriyya*

wisdom literature *see ḥikma*

wonder *see* ***ta'jīb***

wonders of the world *see* ***'ajā'ib* literature**

Y

Yacine, Kateb *see* Kateb, Yacine

Yaḥyā ibn ʿAdī (280 or 281–363 or 364/893 or 894–974)

Monophysite Christian philosopher and theologian born in Tikrit who spent most of his life in **Baghdad** where he studied with **Mattā ibn Yūnus**, and achieved considerable eminence as the philosopher of his age. His most important works were his *Tahdhīb al-akhlāq* (*Refinement of Virtues*), *Maqāla fī al-tawḥīd* (*Discourse on Unity*), and *Tabyīn ghalaṭ Abī Yūsuf Yaʿqūb ibn Isḥāq al-Kindī* (*Explication of the Error of … al-Kindī*). Yaḥyā was an intellectual disciple of the great **al-Fārābī** and his writings exhibit several of the concerns of his master, especially in their veneration for logic. But it is perhaps in the field of ethics that Yaḥyā made his most striking contribution to Arabic literature. In what is historically a very early Arabic treatise on ethics, Yaḥyā in his *Tahdhīb al-akhlāq* drew on Plato and **Aristotle** to produce one of the seminal works on ethics in Arabic. His *Maqāla fī al-Tawḥīd* is also of interest because of the unexpected influence of Procline theology. A copyist by profession and a bibliophile by inclination, Yaḥyā collected many manuscripts, and continued the tradition of editing, translating and commenting on Greek texts begun by **Ḥunayn ibn Isḥāq**.

Text editions

Maqāla fī al-tawḥīd, Khalīl Samīr (ed.), Jounieh and Rome (1980).

Petits traités apologétiques de Yaḥyā ben ʿAdī, A. Perier (ed.), Paris (1920).

Takriti, N., *Yahya Ibn ʿAdi: A Critical Edition and Study of his Tahdhīb al-Akhlāq*, Beirut and Paris (1978).

Further reading

Endress, Gerhard, *The Works of Yaḥyā ibn ʿAdī: An Analytical Inventory*, Wiesbaden (1977).

Kraemer, Joel, *Humanism in the Renaissance of Islam: The Cultural Revival during the Buyid Age*, Leiden (1986), 6–7, 104–16 and *passim*.

Netton, I.R., *Al-Fārābī and His School*, London (1992).

Perier, A., *Yahya ben ʿAdī: un philosophe arabe chrétien du Xᵉ siécle*, Paris (1920).

I. NETTON

Yaḥyā ibn ʿAlī al-Khaṭīb al-Tibrīzī *see* al-Khaṭīb al-Tibrīzī

Yakan, Walī al-Dīn (1873–1921)

Turco-Egyptian poet and prose writer. Born in Istanbul, he was educated in **Cairo**, and worked for most of his life in government service there. In 1897 he founded the periodical *al-Iʿtimād*, in which he criticized the Turkish sultan. He spent the years 1902–8 in exile in Anatolia for his liberal views. As a poet, Yakan belongs to the neo-classical school: he regularly produced poems for official occasions, although his poetry also contains works that show strong personal feeling.

Further reading

Brugman, J., *An Introduction to the History of Modern Arabic Literature in Egypt*, Leiden (1984), 53–5.

P. STARKEY

Yaʿqūb ibn Killis *see* Fāṭimids

al-Yaʿqūbī (d. 284/897)

Aḥmad ibn Abī Yaʿqūb ibn Jaʿfar al-Yaʿqūbī is one of the early historians of Islam whose writings survive. He was the descendant of a freedman of the **'Abbāsid** family and thus sometimes al-'Abbāsī was added to his name. His family, and he too, were moderate **Shī'īs**. After the fall of the **Ṭāhirid** dynasty in the eastern Islamic world, he moved to **Egypt**, where he died.

Al-Ya'qūbī's world history, known simply as *al-Ta'rīkh* (*The History*), continues its coverage until the year 259/872. It deals with the empires and rulers of world history before Islam, and its treatment of Islamic history, which is organized by caliphal reign and also gives prominence to the Shī'ī Imāms, betrays its author's Shī'ī sympathies and in that sense is a valuable corrective to the extant, predominantly **Sunnī**, historiography. Certain items of information are regularly given for each reign, such as a brief character sketch of the ruler, and lists of his campaigns and his officials. Towards the end of his life in Egypt al-Ya'qūbī also composed a geographical work, the *Kitāb al-buldān*, which claims to be based on wide travels in the author's youth and first-hand questioning of informants. **Baghdad** and Samarra are given quite detailed treatment as the centres of the Islamic world.

Text editions

Kitāb al-Buldān, M.J. de Goeje (ed.), Leiden (1892) (*BGA* vol. 7).

Ta'rīkh al-Ya'qūbī or *Ibn Wādhih qui dicitur al-Ja'qūbī Historiae*, M.T. Houtsma (ed.), 2 vols, Leiden (1883).

Further reading

Millward, W.G., 'Al-Ya'qūbī's sources and the question of Shī'a partiality', *Abr-Nahrain* 12 (1971–2), 47–74.

D.S. RICHARDS

See also: geographical literature; historical literature

Yāqūt (575–626/1179–1229)

The renowned author Shibāb al-Dīn Yāqūt ibn 'Abd Allāh al-Rūmī al-Ḥamawī had an unusual background. When young and living, presumably as a Christian, in part of Anatolia held by the Byzantines (hence his by-name al-Rūmī, 'the Greek'), he was taken captive and sold as a slave at **Baghdad** (hence the conventional patronymic 'Ibn 'Abd Allāh'). His merchant master educated him and employed him on trading visits to the Gulf, Oman and **Syria**. Manumitted in 596/1199, he became a professional copyist and then a book-seller in Baghdad, continuing to travel widely. At the first Mongol incursions in 616/1219 he fled the Islamic east to Mosul and Aleppo, where he was to die in Ramaḍān 626/August 1229.

Among his surviving writings there is an unpublished work on genealogies, but his fame rests on two large-scale compilations, both arranged alphabetically. One, the *Kitāb al-Irshād*, is a biographical dictionary of literary figures, past and present. This is a painstaking and scholarly work of synthesis, which carefully identifies its sources and argues points of detail, and is eminently useful. Of comparable utility is the other work, *Mu'jam al-buldān*, a compilation of toponyms. Apart from the basic identifying and locating of each item, the author expands into the literary and historical associations of each place, listing appropriate notable individuals and quoting apposite verses. The net result is a work that is redolent of the scholar's lamp and literary leanings more than the author's own wide travels and experience. He also wrote a monograph on duplicate place-names (*al-Mushtarik*).

Text editions

Irshād al-Arīb ilā Ma'rifat al-Adīb or *Dictionary of Learned men*, D.S. Margolioth (ed.), 6 vols, Leiden (1907–31).

Kitāb al-Mushtarik, F. Wüstenfeld, (ed.), Göttingen (1846).

Mu'jām al-buldān, Jacut's geographisches Wörterbuch, F. Wüstenfeld (ed.), 6 vols, Leipzig (1866–73); later Cairo editions.

Introductory Chapters of Mu'jam al-Buldān, W. Jwaideh (trans.), Leiden (1959).

Mu'jam al-udabā (=*Irshād al-Arīb*), Cairo (1936–8); Iḥsān 'Abbās (ed.), Beirut (1993).

Further reading

Abdur Rahman, K.M., 'Sources of Yaqut's geographical dictionary', *Dacca University Studies*, 2ii (1938), 81–3.

——, 'The Arab geographer Yāqūt al-Rūmī', *JAS Pakistan* 3 (1958), 23–8.

D.S. RICHARDS

See also: biography, medieval; geographical literature

Yāsīn, Kātib *see* Kateb, Yacine

Yazbak, Anṭūn (late 19th – early 20th century)

Syro-Egyptian dramatist. A lawyer by profession, Yazbak was one of the pioneers of the Egyptian melodrama. He worked for a time with Jūrj **Abyaḍ**, with whom he had studied in Beirut and whose troupe performed his *'Āṣifa fī bayt* at the Cairo Opera House in 1924. His best-known work is *al-Dhabā'iḥ* (1925), which revolves around a retired general's relationship with Amīna and a European woman, Noreska, whom he marries after divorcing his first wife. Written in colloquial Arabic, the play represented a significant advance in the depiction of human relationships on the Egyptian stage of the time. Despite the play's popularity, however, the author quickly fell into obscurity and his work has seldom been accorded the recognition that it deserves.

Further reading

Badawi, M.M., *Early Arabic Drama*, Cambridge (1988), 120–33.

P. STARKEY

al-Yazīdī, Abū Muḥammad Yaḥyā ibn al-Mubārak (d. 202/817 or 818)

Grammarian and man of letters. He was a *mawlā* (see ***mawālī***) from **Basra**, called al-Yazīdī because he was the tutor of the children of Yazīd, son of the caliph al-Manṣūr. He moved from Basra to **Baghdad** and was for a while the tutor of al-Ma'mūn. He was considered an expert in the reading of the **Koran**, **grammar** and lexicography. His several grammatical and lexicographical works, among them *al-Nawādir*, composed for the **Barmakid** vizier Ja'far ibn Yaḥyā, are not preserved. He appears in many anecdotes in anthologies such as **Abū al-Faraj al-Iṣbahānī**'s *al-Aghānī*. He died at an advanced age, leaving five sons who were scholars and poets like their father.

Text edition

Shi'r al-Yazīdiyyīn, Muḥsin Ghayyāḍ (ed.), Najaf (1973).

G.J.H. VAN GELDER

al-Yāzijī family

Lebanese Maronite family from Kafr Shīmā. In addition to Ibrāhīm, Khalīl, Nāṣīf and Warda (see separate entries), the family also included: **Rājī** (1803–57), younger brother of Nāṣīf, a poet with a ***dīwān*** in ms; and **Ḥabīb** (1833–70), businessman, poet and prose writer, the oldest child of Nāṣīf. Ḥabīb translated a novel from French and wrote a commentary on his father's *urjūza* on poetics (1869).

Further reading

Kratschkowsky, I., 'Yāzidjī', *EI*[1], viii, 1171–2.

P.C. SADGROVE

al-Yāzijī, Ibrāhīm (1847–1906)

Lebanese scholar, philologist, critic, poet and journalist, son of Nāṣīf **al-Yāzijī**. Born in **Beirut**, he died in **Cairo**. He taught at the Greek Catholic Patriarchal School and made a much-admired revision of the translation of the Bible for the Jesuits. In Beirut, he edited the scientific magazine *al-Ṭabīb* (1884–8), then emigrated to **Egypt**, where he published the literary magazine *al-Bayān* (1897–8), and one of the most important literary periodicals *al-Ḍiyā'* (1898–1906). He also published his ***dīwān***, *al-'Iqd*; a translation of *L'imitation de Jésus-Christ*; a critique of the language of the press (1901); an Arabic dictionary; 'The Arabs and Turks' (1910); an immensely successful dictionary of synonyms; and a criticism of the faults in Buṭrus **al-Bustānī**'s dictionary. Among his verse, he wrote a famous poem ('Awaken, O ye Arabs!') hostile to the Turkish oppressors, and glorifying the Arabs. He also edited many of his father Nāṣīf's works on grammar and morphology, and completed his commentary on **al-Mutanabbī**'s *dīwān*. He is renowned for his endeavours to purify and modernize Arabic.

Further reading

Kratschkowsky, I., 'Yāzidjī', *EI*[1], viii, 1171.
Soueid, P., *Ibrahim al-Yaziji: L'homme et son oeuvre*, Beirut (1969).

P.C. SADGROVE

al-Yāzijī, Khalīl (1856–89)

Lebanese teacher, writer and poet, the youngest son of Nāṣīf **al-Yāzijī**. Born in **Beirut**, he died in al-Ḥadath of tuberculosis. In 1882 he published a few issues of the magazine *Mir'āt al-Sharq* in **Cairo** and on his return to Beirut, taught Arabic literature at the American College and the Catholic Patriarchal College. An excellent poet, he wrote a ***dīwān***, *Nasamāt al-awrāq* (1882), and several dramas in verse, as well as a highly praised tragedy *al-Murū'a wa-al-wafā' aw al-faraj ba'd al-ḍīq* (*Chivalry and Loyalty*) (1884) on the pre-Islamic story of Hanẓala and al-Nu'mān, an opera on the pre-Islamic poetess, **al-Khansā'**; and other works. He published a school edition of ibn al-Muqaffa''s animal fables, ***Kalīla wa-Dimna***, but left in manuscript a work on natural philosophy and a unique dictionary on the synonyms of the vernacular, intended to encourage the colloquial to develop in the direction of the classical.

Further reading

Kratschkowsky, I., 'Yāzidjī', *EI*[1], viii, 1171.

P.C. SADGROVE

al-Yāzijī, Nāṣīf (1800–71)

Lebanese Maronite teacher, philologist and poet. Born in Kafr Shīmā, he died in **Beirut**. He was secretary to the Greek Catholic Patriarch, and to Prince Bashīr al-Shihābī until the latter's abdication. In 1849 he, Buṭrus **al-Bustānī** and Yūsuf **al-Asīr** helped the American missionaries in a new translation of the Bible; he also versified the translations of several hymns. He taught at the National School of al-Bustānī, at the Greek Catholic Patriarchal School, and at the Syrian Protestant College, writing some fifteen school textbooks on various aspects of language, logic and medicine. Among his published works is a letter to Baron Silvestre de Sacy correcting his edition of *al-Maqāma al-Ḥarīriyya*. His three poetic ***dīwān***s remained wedded to the fashions of the day, but his most important work, *Majma' al-baḥrayn* (1856), a collection of sixty ***maqāmāt***, was a pioneering work, important for its attempt to link the traditional style of **al-Ḥarīrī** with contemporary concerns. Considered the greatest Arabic scholar of his age, Nāṣīf al-Yāzijī helped to re-establish Arabic in Lebanon as an effective medium of self-expression, and is a key figure in the nineteenth-century Arabic literary revival.

Further reading

Jayyusi, S.K., *Trends and Movements in Modern Arabic Poetry*, 2 vols, Leiden (1977), 18–20.
Kratschkowsky, I., 'Yāzidjī', *EI*[1], viii, 1170.

P.C. SADGROVE

al-Yāzijī, Warda (1838–1924)

Lebanese poet, daughter of Nāṣīf **al-Yāzijī** and sister of Ibrāhīm **al-Yāzijī** and Khalīl **al-Yāzijī**. Warda al-Yāzijī received an early education at home in Arabic **grammar** and **prosody** and attended a French school in **Beirut**, where her family had moved in 1840 from Kafr Shīmā. Upon graduation, she taught in a school, and is thought to have started writing poetry at the age of 13. After her marriage in 1866 to Francis Sham'ūn she continued writing poetry and teaching, in addition to raising five children. She moved to Alexandria after her husband's death in 1899 and lived there until her death. Her collected poetry was published in Beirut as *Ḥadīqat al-ward: naẓm Warda bint al-shaykh Nāṣīf al-Yāzijī* (1867). Expanded editions were published in 1886/7 (Beirut) and 1914 (Cairo). Much of al-Yāzijī's poetry was ***rithā'***, in the classical traditon of poetry by women. She also wrote poems addressed to other women poets, notably Warda al-Turk and 'Ā'isha **al-Taymūriyya**. Al-Yāzijī also wrote prose essays for publication in periodicals; in particular, her brother Ibrāhīm's periodical *al-Ḍiyā'* published her four-part article 'al-Mar'a al-sharqiyya' in 1906.

Text edition

'Epistolary poem to Warda al-Turk', M. Booth (trans.), in Margot Badran and Miriam Cooke, *Opening the Gates: A Century of Arab Feminist Writing*, Bloomington and Indianapolis (1990), 21–2.

Further reading

Booth, Marilyn, 'Biography and feminist rhetoric in early twentieth-century Egypt: Mayy Ziyada's studies of three women's lives', *Journal of Women's History* 3 (1) (Spring 1991).
Ma'lūf, 'Īsā Iskandar, 'Mashāhīr al-Yāzijiyyīn al-Lubnāniyyīn', *al-Āthār* 2 (6) (December 1912).
Ziyāda, Mayy, *Warda al-Yazijī*, Cairo (n.d.) [1924].

M. BOOTH

Yemen

Arab country occupying the southern part of the Arabian Peninsula. Long before the rise of Islam Yemen possessed a developed civilization, a fact in which present-day Yemenis still take pride.

When Muḥammad preached Islam in Mecca, this civilization had long lain in ruins, devastated by wars and intrusions of militant Arabian **tribes**. Throughout the Middle Ages and until recently, Yemeni society was decentralized and dominated by tribal ideology. This factor strongly coloured its literary output, which includes an enormous body of tribal poetry, extolling the merits of one tribe and demeaning its rivals. Already in pre-Islamic times Yemen boasted a number of great tribal poets, including **Imru' al-Qays**, 'the king of Arab poets', and **'Amr ibn Ma'dīkarib**. Under Islam, tribal partisanship persisted. It found an expression in the keen rivalry between the Yemeni tribes (Qaḥṭān) and those of North Arabia ('Adnān). Among those who took an active part in this rivalry was **al-Hamdānī** (d. 334/945), undoubtedly the greatest Yemeni scholar, whose encyclopaedic works scrupulously record genealogies of South Arabian tribes (in order to prove their antiquity) and contain lengthy samples of old Yemeni poetry. Later on, Yemen's glorious past was praised in the patriotic poems of **Nashwān al-Ḥimyarī** (d. 573/1178). Since throughout the medieval period Yemeni society was highly stratified and the status of its members depended on their lineage, genealogical works and praises of one's family became part and parcel of Yemeni literature.

Yemen's stormy political history during the first centuries of Islam hindered the development of non-poetic genres. When Yemen became home to several heterodox religious communities, these started to propagate their sectarian positions among Yemeni Muslims via theological writings (see **Zaydīs**). Under the dynasties of **Sunnī** rulers (the **Ayyūbids**, Rasūlids and **Ṭāhirids**), Yemen witnessed a cultural florescence. The four centuries of their rule (sixth/twelfth–tenth/sixteenth) produced a galaxy of eminent historians and biographers (Ibn Ḥātim, al-Janadī, al-Khazrajī, Ibn al-Ahdal, Ibn al-Dayba', etc.) They established a solid tradition of annalistic historiography that was perpetuated by later authors, most notably **al-Ṭayyib Bā Makhrama** (d. 974/1540). Apart from theological and legalistic literature, Yemenis produced a voluminous corpus of Ṣūfī works which included biographies of Ṣūfī saints, moralistic admonitions, mystical poetry, apologies for mysticism, essays on occult sciences, etc. The wide spread of the cult of the Ṣūfī saints created a demand for hagiographies. It was met by 'Abd Allāh al-Yāfi'ī, al-Sharjī and al-Shillī, whose works abound in accounts of the exemplary piety of holy personages and spectacular miracles ascribed to them.

Poetry continued to occupy a place of prominence. Its most eloquent representative at that time was **Ibn al-Muqrī** (d. 837/1433), a scholar of encyclopaedic interests and knowledge. Ibn al-Muqrī's elaborate poetry as well as that of court poets were largely directed at the educated élite. Parallel to the classical poetry, some lettered Yemenis took to composing verses in colloquial Arabic that drew on the metrical and lexical riches of local folklore. This substantially increased their appeal with less sophisticated audiences.

The eleventh/seventeenth–thirteenth/nineteenth centuries did not bring about any substantial changes in the trends and genres of Yemeni literature. Innovations introduced by the later Zaydī authors were mostly theological in nature. In the **Sunnī** parts of the country, the character of literary output remained essentially the same as in the previous centuries.

Poetry in Yemen has always fulfilled an important social function, since poets were often viewed as mouthpieces of popular sentiment. Some of them defended tribal honour, others severely criticized oppressive rulers and called for social justice. This tradition has continued until our day. In the 1940s–early 1960s, a number of popular Yemeni poets (al-Mawshikī, al-Zubayrī, al-Baradūnī, etc.) were among the principal instigators of armed struggle against the regime of the Zaydī Imām which perpetuated the outdated social structure and isolationism. When the Imām was overthrown in 1962, poets served as educators of the masses, instilling in them new societal values and nationalist ideology. Yemeni poets of the post-revolutionary period have combined imagery and metre borrowed from the classical poetry with modern literary trends, e.g. romanticism, symbolism, and realism. Younger poets tended to depart from the established poetrical dogma and metrics, looking for new forms of self-expression.

Yemeni prose is still beginning to take shape. It models itself chiefly on the more sophisticated Arabic literatures of **Egypt**, Iraq and **Syria**. Therefore, in Yemen poetry remains the major form of artistic expression.

Further reading

Al-Hamdānī: A great Yemeni scholar, Yūsuf M. 'Abdallāh (ed.), Sana'ā' (1407/1986).
al-Ḥibshī, 'Abd Allāh, *Ḥayāt al-adab al-Yamanī fī 'aṣr Banū Rasūl*, 2nd edn, Ṣana'ā' (1980).
——, *Maṣādir al-fikr al-Islāmī fī al-Yaman*, Ṣana'ā' (1976).
Löfgren, O., *Arabische Texte zur Kenntnis der Stadt Aden*, 2 vols, Leiden (1936–50).
Serjeant, R.B., 'Materials for South Arabian history', *BSOAS* 13 (1950), 281–307, 581–601.
Sharaf al-Dīn, Aḥmad, *Ta'rīkh al-fikr al-Islāmī fī al-Yaman*, Cairo (1968).
Smith, G.R., *The Ayyūbids and Early Rasūlids in the Yemen*, London (1974 and 1978).
Wüstenfeld, F., *Die Çufiten in Süd-Arabien*, Göttingen (1883).
See also relevant articles in *Yemen: 3000 Years of Art and Civilisation in Arabia Felix*, W. Daum (ed.), Innsbruck and Frankfurt am Main (1988).
For contemporary literary life in Yemen one may also consult the Yemeni literary journals *al-Yaman al-jadīd*, *al-Afāq*, *Dirāsāt Yamaniyya*, etc.; for a fine study of tribal poetry see S. Caton, *Peaks of Yemen I Summon*, Berkeley (1990).

A. KNYSH

Yūsuf III ibn al-Aḥmar (d. 819/1417)

Ruler of Granada from 810/1408 to 819/1417, and poet. Yūsuf spent many years, during the reign of his brother, as a prisoner in the castle of Salobreña; it is related that as his brother was dying he ordered that Yūsuf be put to death, but he asked to finish a chess game he was playing with the governor of the gaol, and thus gained time during which his partisans released him. He pursued an active, though unsuccessful, defence of Granadan interests in the face of Christian reconquest. His poetry is marked by its adherence to a classicizing style, but he is also known as the author of ***muwashshaḥāt***. Despite the traditional **Sunnī** and Mālikī orthodoxy of Naṣrid Granada, this prince's verse contains traces of **Shī'ī** influence.

Text editions

Dīwān, 'Abd Allāh Kannūn (ed.), Cairo (1965).
Monroe, J.T., *Hispano-Arabic Poetry: A Student Anthology*, Berkeley (1974), 366–75.

Further reading

Arié, R., *L'Espagne musulmane au temps des naṣrides (1232–1492)*, Paris (1973), index (for his epitaph see the sources at 198, n.3).

D.J. WASSERSTEIN

See also: Spain

al-Yūsuf, Fāṭima (189?–19??)

Egyptian actress and journalist. Born Rūz al-Yūsuf, she adopted the name Fāṭima after marrying Muḥammad 'Abd al-Quddūs. She worked first as an actress under the director 'Azīz al-'Īd, then acted with Jūrj **Abyaḍ** and Najīb al-Rīḥānī. Her best roles were played with the Ramses troupe in the early 1920s. In 1925 she gave up acting and founded ***Rūz al-Yūsuf***, one of the most respected weekly political magazines in the Arab world. As a staunch supporter of Sa'd Zaghlūl and the Wafd Party, she gradually became more involved in politics and later published a daily newspaper bearing the same name. Her satirical caricatures angered many politicians, however, and she herself faced bankruptcy and imprisonment. She remained head of her publishing business until it was handed over to her son Iḥsān **'Abd al-Quddūs** in 1945.

M. MIKHAIL

Yūsuf, Sa'dī (1934–)

Iraqi poet. Born in **Basra**, Yūsuf started his poetic career as a poet practising **free verse**, under the influence of **al-Sayyāb**. In his free verse and poetry in prose, Yūsuf reflects the spiritual, intellectual and political situation of Iraqi intellectuals, workers and communists, persecuted by their governments. His poetry, which uses colloquial dialogue, is loaded with images derived from prisons: bars, barbed wire, police enquiries, dark nights, fugitives, murders, tombs, etc.

Yūsuf has published several anthologies, including *51 Qaṣīda* (Baghdad, 1959), *Ughniyāt laysat lil-ākharīn* (1954), *al-Najm wa-al-ramād* (1961), *Qaṣā'id mar'iyya* (Beirut, 1965) and *Taḥta jidāriyyat Fā'iq Ḥasan* (Beirut, 1974). He has also written a narrative, *al-Qurṣān* (Baghdad, 1952), and collected an anthology of writers from Basra, *Mukhtārāt min al-adab al-Baṣrī al-ḥadīth* (Basra, 1961).

Further reading

Abū Sa'd, Aḥmad, *al-Shi'r wa-al-shu'arā' fī al-'Irāq*, Beirut (1959), 326–9.

'Awwād, G.H., *Mu'jam al-mu'allifīn al-'Irāqiyyīn, fī al-qarnayn al-tāsi' 'ashar wa-al-'ishrīn (1800–1969)*, Baghdad (1969), 2, 40.

Qabbish, A., *Tārīkh al-shi'r al-'Arabī al-ḥadīth*, n.p. (1971), 733.

S. MOREH

Z

al-Zabīdī, al-Murtaḍā (1145–1205/1732–91)

al-Sayyid Abū al-Fayḍ Muḥammad ibn Muḥammad ibn ʿAbd al-Razzāq al-Murtaḍā al-Zabīdī, Arabic lexicographer. Born in the Northwest Province of **India**, al-Zabīdī was the author of the largest surviving Arabic dictionary, the *Tāj al-ʿarūs min jawāhir al-Qāmūs*, which he began in 1174/1760 and finished in 1188/1774 (published editions, Cairo, 1889–90, reprinted several times; Kuwait, 1965–). He died in **Cairo**. The author names 113 sources consulted in the compilation of his dictionary and estimates it to contain about 120,000 words. One of his sources was the equally famous *Lisān al-ʿArab* of **Ibn Manẓūr**, whose entire contents were subsumed into the *Tāj*. The *Tāj* was used by E.W. Lane as the basis of his Arabic–English lexicon *Madd al-Qāmūs*.

Further reading

Haywood, J.A., *Arabic Lexicography: Its History, and its Place in the General History of Lexicography*, 2nd edn, Leiden (1965), 89–90.

Kraemer, J., 'Studien zur altarabischen Lexikographie', *Oriens* 6 (1953), 236–8.

M.G. CARTER

See also: lexicography, medieval; lexicography, modern

al-Zafayān (*fl.* 75/695)

ʿAṭāʾ ibn Usayd (or Asīd) al-Zafayān al-Saʿdī was a ***rajaz*** poet. Very little is known of his life; he belonged to the tribe Tamīm, was a contemporary of **al-ʿAjjāj** and seems to have died at an advanced age. He is hardly ever mentioned by critics or anthologists. A small ***dīwān*** is preserved, with ten poems (265 lines) in the style of al-ʿAjjāj.

Text edition

Ahlwardt, W. (ed.), *Sammlungen alter arabischer Dichter, II. Die Dīwāne der Reğezdichter El'aǧǧāǧ und Ezzafajān*, Berlin (1903).

Further reading

Ullmann, Manfred, *Untersuchungen zur Rağazpoesie: ein Beitrag zur arabischen Sprach- und Literaturwissenschaft*, Wiesbaden (1966), index s.v. Zafayān.

G.J.H. VAN GELDER

Ẓāfir al-Ḥaddād (d. 529/1135)

A blacksmith who made his career as a poet of some talent, first in Alexandria and later in **Cairo**. He composed poems in praise of the **Fāṭimids**, in particular the Imāms al-Āmir and al-Ḥāfiẓ, and their respective viziers, especially the all-powerful al-Afḍal ibn Badr al-Jamālī. The travelling Andalusian poet and prose author Abū al-Ṣalt Umayya ibn ʿAbd al-ʿAzīz, who visited him in **Egypt** and later on sailed to al-Mahdiyya (present-day **Tunisia**), remained in correspondence with Ẓāfir in his *Risāla Miṣriyya*. Characteristic of Ẓāfir's religious attitude is the nearly total lack of wine poetry in his *dīwān*. His laudatory poems dedicated to the Imāms not only glorify their Godly Light, but also describe their victorious war effort against the Crusaders (see **Crusades**) and **Byzantines**. Remarkable are his satirical poems (***hijāʾ***) describing the forgetfulness of a certain Abū ʿĀmir and his poems of complaint (*shakwā*) which describe his real or fictitious claustrophobic fear induced by housing accommodation that was much too small.

Text edition

Dīwān, Ḥusayn Naṣṣār (ed.), Cairo (1969).

Further reading

Smoor, P., 'The poet's house: fiction and reality in

the works of the "Fāṭimid" poets', *QSA* (Venice/Rome) 10 (1992), 45–62.
——, 'Wine, love and praise for the Fāṭimid imāms, the Enlightened of God', *ZDMG* 142/1 (1992) 90–104.
Umayya ibn ʿAbd al-ʿAzīz Abū al-Ṣalt, 'Risāla Miṣriyya', in *Nawādir al-makhṭūṭāt*, ʿA.S.M. Hārūn (ed.), 2nd printing, Cairo (1972) vol. 1, 11–56..

P. SMOOR

Zafzāf, Muḥammad (1945–)

Moroccan novelist, short-story writer and journalist. Born in Kenitra, Zafzāf first wrote short stories which were published in periodicials in various Arab countires. A number of his stories paint evocative pictures of Moroccan rural life. Well known outside Morocco, Zafzāf has been instrumental in forging links between Maghribī and Middle Eastern intellectuals. He introduced Western readers to modern Arabic poetry in Morocco by co-translating into French works by thirteen Moroccan poets (*Treize poètes marocains*, 1977). The author of a number of novels, including *Arṣifa wa-judrān* (1974), *al-Shajara al-muqaddasa* (1980) and *al-Thaʿlab alladhī yaẓhar wa-yakhtafī* (1989), Zafzāf's central character is frequently portrayed as a passionate individual, desperate to express himself freely in a taboo-laden society.

Further reading

Faraḥāt, A., *Aṣwāt thaqāfiyya min al-Maghrib al-ʿArabī*, Beirut (1984).

F. ABU-HAIDAR

al-Zahāwī, Jamīl Ṣidqī (1863–1936)

Neo-classical Iraqi poet. Al-Zahāwī was born in Baghdad to Kurdish parents descended from the Baban royal family of Sulaymāniyya. After completing his traditional Koranic school education, he was given a foundation in Arabic and the classical poets by his father, a scholar and *muftī* of Baghdad. He later developed an interest in Western literature, science and thought through Turkish and Persian translations.

Al-Zahāwī occupied posts in education, publishing, journalism and law. In 1890 he became Arabic editor for the official newspaper *al-Zawrā'*. Following the proclamation of the Ottoman Constitution of 1908, he went to Istanbul as a lecturer in Islamic philosophy and teacher of Arabic literature. On his return to Baghdad he was appointed lecturer in the Law School. In 1917, during the British occupation, he convened a committee to translate the Ottoman Laws, and after Iraq gained independence in 1920 he was appointed as a member of the Senate for four years.

Al-Zahāwī first became known to the Arab literary world through his daring and stormy articles on social and scientific theories published in Syro-Egyptian journals and newspapers such as ***al-Muqtaṭaf*** and *al-Mu'ayyad*. His name has often been linked with that of Maʿruf ʿAbd al-Ghanī Maḥmud **al-Ruṣāfī**, as both represented the social and political aspirations of the Iraqi people during the turbulent first three decades of the twentieth century.

Al-Zahāwī was a prolific poet and writer. In addition to a translation of Omar Khayyām's *Quatrains* into Arabic, he produced several volumes of poetry, the main themes of which are concerned with politics, philosophy, scientific theory, nationalism, and social and moral issues including religion and the emancipation of women. His *Dīwān* was published in 1924.

Al-Zahāwī also wrote about the role and aims of poetry. He criticized many aspects of the classical tradition, calling for new metres and a content that more accurately reflected the realities of everyday life. But although he experimented with **blank verse** and was regarded as a pioneer in this form, much of his poetry remained close to the classical style and technique.

Further reading

Badawi, M.M., *A Critical Introduction to Modern Arabic Poetry*, Cambridge (1975), 47–75.
Jayyusi, S.K., *Trends and Movements in Modern Arabic Poetry*, 2 vols, Leiden (1977), 184–193.
Masliyah, S.H., 'The life and writings of the Iraqi poet: Jamīl Ṣidqī al-Zahāwī', unpublished PhD thesis, UCLA (1973).

R. HUSNI

zajal, medieval

A strophic poetic form which originated in Islamic **Spain**. Often compared with the ***muwashshaḥ***, it differs in being written entirely in the local vernacular Arabic dialect and punctuated with non-Arabic words or phrases, and in having a slightly different rhyme scheme and running longer – often much longer – than the typical five-strophe length of the *muwashshaḥ*.

There is little evidence concerning the origins of the *zajal*. The earliest known *zajal* poets are **Ibn Quzmān** (d. 555/1160) and Ibn Rāshid, yet many sources indicate that the form had existed for some time before the sixth/twelfth century, passed on orally but unrecorded by critics and anthologists because of its vernacular diction. The characteristic organization of the *zajal* is: AA bbbA cccA etc.; a more involved variant is ABAB cccAB dddAB. The rhyme of the initial refrain, the *maṭla*ʿ (which is sometimes missing in the *muwashshaḥ*) is reproduced at the end of each of the following strophes (*ghuṣn*s), but there are half as many lines as in the *maṭla*ʿ (the *muwashshaḥ* reproduces it in full).

The distinctions between the two so-called 'sister genres', the *zajal* and the *muwashshaḥ*, are blurred by the existence of poems that are structured as *muwashshaḥ*, yet are written entirely in the vernacular. While the themes of *muwashshaḥāt* tend to be those of classical poetry, the *zajal*s take on a wider variety of topics. The structural similarities between the two forms have spawned a lively debate about which preceded the other, whether the *zajal* had its origin in some now-lost oral Romance tradition or whether it was a popularization of the *muwashshaḥ*. Another theory is that the *muwashshaḥ* is a cultured version of the popular *zajal*. These controversies are but a part of the larger debate about cultural borrowing or transmission between Islamic Spain and Christian Spain and the rest of Europe. Nykl has argued that Ibn Quzmān's *zajal*s provide clear evidence for Arabic influence in the form and content of Provençal poets such as William of Acquitaine and Marcabru. In Spain, *zajal*-esque forms are widespread in thirteenth-century Galician–Portuguese poetry, including the *Cantigas* of Alphonse the Wise. By the latter half of the seventh/thirteenth century the *zajal* form is echoed in the Provençal *dansa*, the Italian *ballata* and the Old French *virelai*. Still, the question remains whether the *zajal* really moved from Arabic to Romance, as the dates of the manuscripts imply, or whether the colloquial Arabic *zajal* was based on a pre-existing unwritten Romance form (as Monroe argues), in which case the *zajal* becomes the record of a Romance influence on an Arabic poetic form rather than the opposite.

The most celebrated composer of *zajal*s was Ibn Quzmān, whose poems spanned from panegyrics to the wealthy to bawdy and obscene ditties. Another noted *zajal*ist was the seventh/thirteenth-century Ṣūfī poet Abū al-Ḥasan ʿAlī **al-Shushtarī**, whose poems, judging from the number of extant manuscripts, circulated widely in mystic circles.

Further reading

Beltrán, V., 'De zejeles y de "dansas"', *RFE* 64 (1984), 239–66.

Corriente, F., *El cancionero hispanoárabe*, Madrid (1984).

Frenk, M., *Estudios sobre la lírica antigua*, Madrid (1978).

Monroe, J.T., 'Which came first, the *zajal* or the *Muwaššaḥa*?', *Oral Tradition* 4 (1989), 38–64.

——, '*Zajal* and *muwashshaḥa*', in *The Legacy of Muslim Spain*, S.K. Jayyusi (ed.), Leiden (1992), 398–419.

Nykl, A.R., *Hispano-Arabic Poetry and its Relations with the Old Provençal Troubadours*, Baltimore (1946).

Stern, S., *Hispano-Arabic Strophic Poetry*, Oxford (1974).

L. ALVAREZ

See also: prosody, medieval; strophic poetry

zajal, modern

As used in modern Arabic, *zajal* denotes various types of poems composed in colloquial idioms. Dialectal poetry made its first appearance in medieval **Spain** and is nowadays widespread all over the Arab world. In addition to traditional kinds commonly sung or recited in public gatherings, such as ***mawāliya***, *ʿatāba*, *mējanā*, *mʿannā*, *shrūqī*, *qarrādī*, etc., it also includes more 'elevated' types published in magazines and individual collections. Whereas in **Egypt**, **Lebanon**, **Syria** and Palestine, however, *zajal* signifies all kinds of colloquial poetry, oral or written, this term is seldom used in **Arabia** and Iraq, where ***nabaṭī*** and *shiʿr ʿāmmī* respectively are preferred.

Modern *zajal* is as diverse in form and structure as in subject-matter. Scholars are not unanimous as to the nature of its **prosody**. Some argue in favour of syllabic metrics; others demonstrate that, with known adjustments (final $C\overline{V} > CV$; $C\overline{V}C > CVC$ or $C\overline{V}-CV$; $CVCC > CVC-CV$ or $CV-CVC$; initial $CC\overline{V}$ and $CCVC > C\overline{V}$ and CVC), the quantitative patterns of classical Arabic metrics are at work. While monorhymed *zajal* is not rare, strophic forms with varieties of rhyme schemes are more common. In recent decades, 'free' colloquial poems, with lines of unequal length in which rhymes are only occasionally found, have gained prominence and acquired literary status. *Zajal* handles all subjects treated also in poetry using classical Arabic. It is often put in service of politics and ideologies. Among its representatives in Egypt are Maḥmūd Bayram **al-Tūnisī**, Aḥmad Rāmī, Ṣalāḥ **Jāhīn** and Aḥmad Fu'ād **Nigm**; in Lebanon, Rashīd **Nakhla**, Sa'īd **'Aql**, Michel **Ṭrād** and the brothers Raḥbānī.

Further reading

Booth, M., *Bayram al-Tunisi's Egypt ...* , Exeter (1990).
Cachia, P., 'The Egyptian *Mawwāl*', *JAL* 8 (1977), 77–103.
Jargy, S., *La poésie populaire traditionnelle chantée au Proche-Orient Arabe*, Paris (1870).
Semah, D., 'On the metre of bedouin poetry', *Asian and African Studies* 25 (2) (July 1991), 187–200.

D. SEMAH

al-Zajjāj *see* grammar and grammarians

al-Zajjājī (d. 337/949 or later)

Abū al-Qāsim 'Abd al-Raḥmān ibn Isḥāq al-Zajjājī was a native of Nihavand but mainly active in **Baghdad**, then for a while in **Damascus** and Aleppo, dying in Tiberias. His name derives from his being a student of al-Zajjāj, and he also studied under Ibn Kaysān, Ibn al-Sarrāj and al-Akhfash al-Aṣghar. He is credited with several works of lexicography and morphology, a treatise on the etymology of the names of God, a possible supplement to **Ibn al-Sikkīt**'s *Iṣlāḥ al-manṭiq* and a number of short grammatical treatises including a commentary on the opening sections of **Sībawayhi**'s *Kitāb*. But he is best known for two texts, an extremely popular grammar *al-Jumal*, said to have inspired 120 commentaries, and the *Īḍāḥ*, a penetrating analysis of the theoretical presuppositions of **grammar** which reveals the lively intellectual environment in which the work was conceived.

Text editions

Ḥurūf al-ma'ānī, A.T. al-Ḥamad (ed.), Beirut and Irbid (1984).
Ḥurūf al-ma'ānī wa-al-ṣifāt, H.S. Farhūd (ed.), Riyādh (1982).
Īḍāḥ 'ilal al-naḥw M. al-Mubārak (ed.), Cairo (1959), rpt Beirut (1979), trans. Kees (C.H.M.) Versteegh, *The Explanation of Linguistic Causes, Az-Zağğāğī's Theory of Grammar*, Amsterdam and Philadelphia (1995).
al-Jumal fī al-naḥw, M. ben Cheneb (ed.), Paris (1957): A.T. al-Ḥamad (ed.), Beirut and Irbid (1984).
Kitāb ishtiqāq asmā' Allāh, A.H. al-Mubārak (ed.), Najaf (1974); A.Y. al-Daqqāq (ed.), Damascus (1975).
Kitāb al-lamāt, M. al-Mubārak (ed.), Damascus (1985).
Majālis al-'ulamā', A.S.M. Hārūn (ed.), Kuwait (1962).

M.G. CARTER

See also: grammar and grammarians

Zakariyyā' ibn Muḥammad al-Qazwīnī *see* al-Qazwīnī, Zakariyya' ibn Muḥammad

Zakhūr, Père Rufā'īl (Don Raphaël de Monachis) (1759–1831)

Poet and translator. Born in **Cairo**, he joined the order of the Basiliens and attended the Greek Seminary in Rome. In 1781 he entered the Monastery of the Saviour near Sidon. He returned to Egypt in 1794, later becoming the only Arab member of the French Institut d'Egypte. In 1803 he was appointed teacher of Arabic at the École des Langues Orientales in Paris; among his students was Champollion. He returned to Egypt again in 1816, working for the rest of his life as a teacher and translator in the service of Muḥammad 'Alī. He translated a number of works from Italian and French, including the fables of La Fontaine and Machiavelli's *Il Principe*, and compiled a *Dizionario italiano e arabo* (1822), the first book from the Būlāq press.

Further reading

Bachatly, Charles, 'Un membre oriental du premier Institut d'Égypte. Don Raphael', *Bulletin de l'Institut Égyptien* 17 (1934–5), 237–60.

P.C. SADGROVE

al-Zamakhsharī (467–538/1075–1144)

Abū al-Qāsim Maḥmūd ibn 'Umar al-Zamakhsharī was a philologist, theologian and **Koran** commentator. For most of his life al-

Zamakhsharī lived in the region of his birth, **Khwarazm** in Central Asia, although he did spend some time studying in Bukhara and **Baghdad**, and twice he visited Mecca. Motivated by a great appreciation of Arabic (although his native language was Persian), and influenced by rationalist **Mu'tazilī** theology, al-Zamakhsharī wrote one of the most widely appreciated commentaries on the Koran, *al-Kashshāf 'an ḥaqā'iq ghawāmiḍ al-tanzīl* (*The Unveiler of the Realities of the Sciences of the Revelation*). Despite what came to be regarded as a heretical theological slant, the work has been an essential part of the curriculum of religious education throughout the Muslim world for centuries. It attracted many super-commentaries which attempted to explain its terse style and intricacies, as well as refutations (e.g. by **Fakhr al-Dīn al-Rāzī**) and bowdlerized versions (e.g. by **al-Bayḍāwī**). Al-Zamakhsharī commented on each phrase of the Koran in sequence, providing philosophical, lexicographical and philological glosses while displaying a concern for the rhetorical qualities of the text (see ***i'jāz al-Qur'ān***). His text is also imbued with his theological vision which is characterized by a thorough-going de-anthropomorphization and support for the doctrines of human free will and the 'created Koran'. Al-Zamakhsharī also wrote a number of other works, including works on Arabic **grammar**, **rhetoric** and lexicography, and a collection of **proverbs**.

Text editions

al-Kashshāf 'an haqā'iq ghawāmid al-tanzīl, W. Nassau Lees, Khadīm Ḥusayn and 'Abd al-Ḥayy (eds), 2 vols, Calcutta (1856); Beirut (1947), rpt (1966) (many other editions).

Kitāb al-Mufaṣṣal (extracts), H. Perès, H. (trans.), Algiers (1947).

Maqāmāt, Y. Biqā'ī (ed.), Beirut (1981); O. Rescher (trans.), *Maqâmen-Literatur*, pt 6.

al-Mustaqṣā fī amthāl al-'Arab, 2nd edn, Beirut (1977).

Further reading

Goldziher, I., *Die Richtungen der islamischen Koranauslegung*, Leiden (1920), 117–77.

Ibrahim, Lutpi, 'Al-Zamakhsharī: his life and works', *IS* 19 (1980) 95–110 (L. Ibrahim has written an extensive series of articles on al-Zamakhsharī and his theological position – one useful example is 'The relation of reason and revelation in the theology of az-Zamakhsharī and al-Bayḍāwī', *IC* 54 (1980), 63–74).

A. RIPPIN

Zand ibn al-Jawn, Abū Dulāma *see* Abū Dulāma

ẓarf

Ẓarf, in its currently used, general meaning translates as 'elegance, charm, gracefulness, wittiness, resourcefulness, or esprit'. In **'Abbāsid** times it came to denote a comprehensive ideal of personal elegance and refinement, and implied such qualities as culture, urbanity, ethics, aesthetic sensibility, courtesy and amiability. Modern scholars have sometimes referred to the '*ẓarf*/***adab*** ideal', for the semantic fields of the two words overlap in some contexts (cf. Bonebakker, below). *Ẓarf* was described (and prescribed, one might say) in specific terms by Abū al-Ṭayyib **al-Washshā'** (d. 325/936 or 7) in his *Kitāb al-Muwashshā*, also entitled *al-Ẓarf wa-al-ẓurafā'* (*Elegance and Elegant People*). Al-Washshā' and those whom he quotes express the intimate interdependence of *adab*, *muruwwa*, ***futuwwa*** and *ẓarf* – 'culture, manly virtue, chivalry and refinement'. For the *ẓarīf* (m. pl. *ẓurafā'*, noun or adjective), a person pursuing this courtly ideal, an understanding of how one should conduct oneself in love and friendship was fundamental. Thus *al-Ẓarf wa-al-ẓurafā'* becomes a unique treatise on love theory (especially chs 15–22). In love and affection one should not transgress the bounds of the Holy Law nor be indiscreet or unfaithful. Chaste behaviour (*'iffa*) is essential, as well as avoidance of extremes of passion.

Similarly, al-Washshā's contemporary **Ibn Dā'ūd** (d. 297/910), head of the Ẓāhirī school of law, entitled a chapter in his *Kitāb al-Zahra* (*The Book of the Flower*) 'One Who is Refined [*ẓarīf*] Will Be Chaste'. He also insisted on the necessity of keeping one's love a secret. However, Ibn Dā'ūd's concept of the *ẓarf* ideal differed in an important respect from that of al-Washshā', who found Ibn Dā'ūd guilty of excess in love, for the latter reportedly suffered a fatal illness caused by spurned love and devotion for another young man.

In these pages, the conventions of idealized love colour the most mundane relationships and social formalities. Without a hint of incongruity, al-Washshā' also includes in his catalogue of inscriptions on the theme of love a chapter on phrases of mystical longing for Allāh. Fraternal love between Muslims 'in

Allāh', love for beautiful slave girls, the burning Ṣūfī love for God – all are expressed in notes written to a beloved, engraved on jewellery, or painted on dishes, inscribed on trays, embroidered on drapery, garments, caps, shoes, or even painted in gold upon an apple or a serving maid's forehead. Other aspects of fashion also figured in this picture: taking care, for example, to offer guests only those foods listed as suitable for the refined, and to avoid serving certain others.

In the words of J.-C. Vadet, the shared *ẓarf* ideal seems to have functioned as a 'unifying social principle' in urban circles of the cultured and lettered. Its conventions helped to bind together individuals of many ethnic, tribal and geographic origins. It seems to have been allied to a developing 'Islamic humanism' (J.L. Kraemer's phrase) that soon flourished among these élites.

Text edition

al-Washshā', *Kitāb al-Muwashshā* (or *al-Ẓarf wa-al-ẓurafā'*), Beirut (1965) (with explanatory notes and partly vocalized; based on R.E. Brünnow's Leiden 1886 edition).

Further reading

Bonebakker, S.A., '*Adab* and the concept of *belles-lettres*', in *CHALABL*, 16–30 (on the changing sense of *adab*).
Ghazi, M.F., 'Un group sociale: "Les Raffinés" (*ẓurafā'*)', *SI* 11 (1959), 39–71.
Giffen, L.A., *Theory of Profane Love among the Arabs*, New York (1971) 8–15, 70–1, n. 8, Table 1, and index.
Hamori, A., 'Love poetry (*ghazal*)', in *CHALABL*, 202–82 (esp. 208–11 on refined love and *ẓarf*).
Kraemer, J.L., *Humanism in the Renaissance of Islam*, 2nd rev. edn, Leiden (1993), esp. xi–30, 162–5.
Vadet, J.-C., *L'esprit courtois en Orient dans les cinq premiers siècles de l'hégire*, Paris (1968), 317–51.
von Grunebaum, G.E., *Medieval Islam*, Chicago (1962), 250–7.

L.A. GIFFEN

See also: *adab*; courtly love; *ghazal*; love theory

ẓarīf see *ẓarf*

al-Ẓarīfī, Ḥusayn (1909–)

Iraqi poet, dramatist and literary critic. Born in Baghdad, al-Ẓarīfī graduated in law in 1933, and in 1935 was appointed as a judge. At the same time he was embarking on his intensive literary activities; he was close to the Iraqi poet Jamīl Ṣidqī **al-Zahāwī** whom he regarded as the first to write *shi'r mursal* (**blank verse**) in modern Arabic literature, and as one of the contributors to *Apollo* himself experimented with Arabic metre. In his drama *Rasūl al-salām* he adopted, under the influence of Aḥmad **Shawqī**, the technique of using varied metres and rhymes based upon thoughts, emotions, situation and character. Defending this method, al-Ẓarīfī argued that a drama was performed by several actors speaking in different tones and that the monotonous use of metre and rhyme would distract attention from the characters and plot.

Further reading

Moreh, S., *Modern Arabic Poetry 1800–1970*, Leiden (1976), 171–2.

R. SNIR

al-Zawzanī (d. 486/1093)

Abū 'Abd Allāh al-Ḥusayn ibn Aḥmad al-Zawzanī was a philologian. He came from Zawzan (between Herat and Nishapur), wrote some works on Arabic–Persian **lexicography** (*al-Maṣādir*, *Tarjumān al-Qur'ān*) and is known especially for his commentary on the ***Mu'allaqāt***, which has often been printed both in the East and in (nineteenth-century) Europe. Its popularity is due to its relatively compact size, free from long digressions, and its clear presentation: after the explanation of the difficult words of each line, a simple prose paraphrase of the line is offered, with some attention for different interpretations, and often explicitly connecting the line with the preceding one.

Text edition

Sharḥ al-Mu'allaqāt al-sab', Cairo (1352/1953).

G.J.H. VAN GELDER

Zayd al-Khayl (*fl.* early first/seventh century)

Zayd ibn Muhalhil Abū Muknif, chief of the Nabhān, a branch of the Ṭayyi', was a ***mukhaḍram*** warrior-poet, generally known as Zayd al-Khayl (Zayd of the Horses) because he owned an unusually large number of thoroughbreds, mention of which he makes in his poems. **Abū al-Faraj al-Iṣbahānī** labels him a 'sparse' poet. He was involved in many conflicts and raids inflicted on neighbouring **tribes** and these, together with celebrations of benefactions and hospitality, the standard concerns of early Arabic aristocratic poetry, constitute the body of verse. There is also evidence of several flytings (see ***hijā'***) with **Ṭufayl al-Ghanawī**, **'Āmir ibn Ṭufayl** of the 'Āmir ibn Ṣa'ṣa'a and **Ka'b ibn Zuhayr**; he also took **al-Ḥuṭay'a** captive on a raid. In the year 9/630, he was a part of his tribe's delegation to the Prophet who changed his name to Zayd al-Khayr (Zayd the Good). He may have died during or after his return from Medina or he may have survived until the caliphate of 'Umar I (13–23/634–44).

Text edition

Dīwān, Najaf (1968).

Further reading

Aghānī (Cairo 1329/1905), vol. 14, 48–60.

J.E. MONTGOMERY

Zaydān, Jurjī (Jirjī) (1861–1914)

Syrian-Egyptian novelist, journalist and historian. A leading Syrian contributor to the Egyptian ***nahḍa*** of the late nineteenth and early twentieth centuries, Zaydān was born in **Beirut**. At least initially, he intended to go into the field of medicine, but he did not complete his studies. Like many other educated Syrian Christians, he emigrated from Ottoman **Syria** to the intellectually freer atmosphere of British-run **Egypt**, where he began a long and distinguished career as one of Egypt's most prolific authors. The journal ***al-Hilāl***, which he founded in 1892, went on to become one of Egypt's longest-lived and most successful publications.

Zaydān was fluent in several European languages and had at one point studied both Hebrew and Syriac. By 1897 his fame had extended beyond Egypt proper, and he was made a member of the Royal Asiatic Society. He has been called by some scholars 'Dean of the Syrian Egyptian historians'.

As Christians, Zaydān and most of his fellow 'Syrian Egyptians' were more committed to the Westernization process than their Muslim Egyptian counterparts. In their various journals they trumpeted the virtues of rationalism, secularism, Darwinism, socialism and even communism – ideas that made them as a group seem suspect and even dangerous to more devout Muslims and even to Egyptian nationalists like Muṣṭafā **Kāmil** and Muḥammad **Farīd**.

Zaydān's literary output was astonishing. He remained as editor of *al-Hilāl* until his death in 1914 and contributed countless articles to it and other journals. He also wrote nine major historical studies, including works on the pre-Islamic Arabs, freemasonry, the history of England and nineteenth-century biography, and major compilations on the history of Islamic civilization (*Tārīkh al-tamaddun al-Islāmī*, 5 vols, Cairo, 1902–6), the history of Arabic literature (*Tārīkh ādāb al-lugha al-'arabiyya*, 4 vols, Cairo, 1911) and Egyptian history (*Tārīkh Miṣr al-ḥadīth min al-fatḥ al-Islāmī ilā al-ān*, 2 vols, Cairo, 1911). He may also have written a history of the Arabic language (*Tārīkh al-lugha al-'Arabiyya*) and a book about national groups (*Ṭabaqāt al-umam*), but publication information on these two works is incomplete.

In addition to all this, Zaydān also wrote an astonishing total of twenty-two historical novels and romances, seeking in this way to popularize the study of history. In all his works he was a stylistic innovator, abandoning florid and stilted medieval forms for the more recently developed 'direct' (i.e. semi-journalistic) style of writing. His great service was to open up new literary and historical vistas to the Arab reader. Despite this, many scholars now feel that the originality of some of his work is suspect, and that he in fact 'borrowed' much of his material from contemporary European authors.

Further reading

Crabbs, J.A., *The Writing of History in Nineteenth-century Egypt*, Detroit (1984), 191–8.
Philipp, T., *Gurgi Zaidan: His Life and Thought*, Beirut (1979).

J. CRABBS

Zaydīs

A moderate wing of the **Shī'īs** that recognizes the imamate of Zayd ibn 'Alī, younger brother of the fifth Shī'ī Imām, Muḥammad al-Bāqir (d. 115/733). After the death of his brother, Zayd revolted against the **Umayyads** in **Kufa** and proclaimed himself leader of the Islamic community. He was supported by those Shī'īs who opposed the quietist policy of al-Bāqir and his successor, the sixth Imām Ja'far al-Ṣādiq. The revolt was suppressed, and Zayd perished in battle (122/740). Five decades later his followers founded a Zaydī state in northeast Iran. It lasted until 316/928, although some Zaydī pockets survived until the advent of the **Ṣafavids** (the first half of the tenth/sixteenth century). In the late third/ninth century Zaydism spread among the tribal populations of north **Yemen**. From then on and until 1382/1962, the Northern Highlands, and occasionally the **Sunnī** parts of Yemen also, were ruled by the Zaydī Imāms, residing in Ṣana'ā'.

Zaydī doctrine combines the features of Sunnism and Shī'ism. Like Sunnīs, the majority of Zaydīs hold the caliphs Abū Bakr and 'Umar to have been legitimate rulers and reject the notion of the hidden Imām as well as that of the Imām's infallibility. Like the **Khārijīs**, they advocate armed uprising against the impious (i.e. Sunnī) rulers with the aim of replacing them with one of their own. This should be elected from among the pious descendants of 'Alī and Fāṭima and must assert his right to the imamate on the battlefield. Theologically, the Zaydīs adhere to the **Mu'tazilī** doctrine, while their legal theory is patterned on that of the **Sunnī** schools of law.

The Zaydī communities of Iran and Yemen produced many distinguished religious scholars, who left many works on theology, history and biography. Among the most prolific writers were Zaydī rulers, for in the view of the Zaydīs, being the Imām presupposed an extensive knowledge of the religious sciences as well military prowess. Owing to Zaydism's eclecticism, later Zaydī scholars such as Ibn Ibrāhīm al-Wazīr (d. 840/1436), Ṣāliḥ al-Maqbalī (d. 1108/1696) and al-Shawkānī (d. 1250/1832) espoused a remarkably broad-minded approach to Islamic theology, abandoning the narrow factionalism and blind adherence to the tradition prevalent among mainstream Muslim doctors. The features of Zaydī learning are vividly reflected in the work of the refined courtier Aḥmad **ibn Abī Rijāl** (d. 1092/1618) of Ṣana'ā', which includes collections of Zaydī biographies, religious and secular poetry, juridical and theological tracts. Contemporary Yemeni intellectuals try to revive the progressive aspects of the Zaydī legacy with the view to reforming the traditional society of Yemen.

Further reading

al-'Amrī, Ḥusayn, *al-Imām al-Shawkānī*, Beirut and Damascus (1990).
Madelung, W., *Der Imām al-Qāsim Ibn Ibrāhīm und die Glaubenslehre der Zaiditen*, Berlin (1965).
——, *Religious Trends in Early Islamic Iran*, New York (1988), 86–92.
al-Maqāliḥ, 'Abd al-'Azīz, *Qirā'a fī fikr al-Zaydiyya wa-al-Mu'tazila*, Beirut (1982).
Strothmann, R., *Das Staatsrecht der Zaiditen*, Strasburg (1912).
van Arendonck, C., *Les Débuts de l'imamat Zaïdite au Yemen*, Leiden (1960).

A. KNYSH

See also: Yemen

Zayyād, Tawfīq (1932–1994)

Palestinian poet. Born in Nazareth, he was educated there and in Moscow, where he studied Russian literature. Like Maḥmūd **Darwīsh** and Samīḥ **al-Qāsim**, Zayyād – who also served as mayor of Nazareth – came to the attention of Arab literary circles in the wake of the 1967 war. A proponent of Marxism in both his political convictions and literary outlook, he was a committed poet (see **commitment**) who believed in social realism as a supreme literary principle. His attitude to poetry placed emphasis on its role as a force for change in society through the accessibility of its content and the humanism of its universal message. Although some of his poetry is in **free verse**, it is reminiscent of pre-1948 Palestinian poetry in its upbeat, oratorical style of delivery, as well as in its being largely '*munāsabāt*' poetry ('poetry of occasions').

Zayyād's poetry is characterized by its direct imagery, immediate symbolism, strident message, explosive discharge of raw emotions and unshakeable belief in the right of the Palestinian people to assert their identity and reclaim their land. He often used elements of Palestinian culture – including proverbs, traditional songs, folk beliefs, popular games and traditional practices – to enhance the immediacy of the thematic content of his poetry and increase its appeal to the masses. In addition to his poetry, he has translated works from Russian and published a translation of the works of Turkish poet Nazim Hikmet.

Text edition

Jayyusi, S.K. (ed.), *Anthology of Palestinian Literature*, New York (1992).

Y. SULEIMAN

al-Zayyāt, Laṭīfa (1925–)

Egyptian novelist, critic and short-story writer. From the Delta town of Damietta, al-Zayyāt earned her BA and MA degrees in English from Cairo University and her PhD from ʿAyn Shams University, then joined the English department of ʿAyn Shams. She drew on her experiences as a student activist in the oppositional politics of **Cairo** in the 1940s in her novel *al-Bāb al-maftūḥ* (1960), which tellingly interweaves the story of a middle-class girl's coming to political and sexual consciousness with that of the struggle for national identity and independence, with an intricate emphasis on the 'dailiness' that shapes the women characters' lives. Her short-story collection *al-Shaykhūkha wa-qiṣaṣ ukhrā* (1986) meditates on the identities of women growing older and incorporates formal experimentation with, for example, the diary form. Her novella *al-Rajul alladhī ʿarafa tuhmatahu* appeared in the critical journal *Adab wa-naqd* in 1991. In 1992 she published *Ḥamlat taftīsh: Awrāq shakhṣiyya*, an innovative and courageous self-examination which draws on the process and material of autobiographical writing. She ventured into playwriting with *Bayʿ wa-shirā'* (1994) and continued her career as a novelist with *Ṣāḥib al-bayt* (1994). Al-Zayyāt has published many literary studies in English and Arabic, including her *Min ṣuwar al-mar'a fī al-qiṣaṣ wa-al-riwāyāt al-ʿArabiyya* (1989) and *Najīb Maḥfūẓ: al-ṣūra wa-al-mithāl* (1989).

Text edition

The Search, S. Bennett (trans.), London (1996).

Further reading

'Laṭīfa al-Zayyāt fī mir'āt Laṭīfa al-Zayyāt', *Ibdāʿ* 11 (1) (January 1993).
Sharīf, Habba, 'Hal lil-naṣṣ al-nisā'ī khuṣūṣiyya? Dirāsa li-riwāyat Laṭīfa al-Zayyāt *al-Bāb al-maftūḥ*', in Salwā Bakr and Hudā al-Sadda (eds), *Hāgar* [Kitāb al-mar'a 1], Cairo (1993).
al-Shārūnī, Yūsuf (ed.), *Al-Layla al-thāniya baʿda al-alf: mukhtārāt min al-qiṣṣa al-nisā'iyya fī Miṣr*, Cairo (1975).

M. BOOTH

al-Zibriqān (d. second half of first/seventh century)

Pre- and early Islamic poet. Al-Ḥuṣayn ibn Badr, nicknamed al-Zibriqān, of the tribe Tamīm, was among the deputation of his tribe to the Prophet in 630. Having converted to Islam, he was appointed collector of taxes (*ṣadaqāt*) of his tribe. When **al-Ḥuṭay'a** made some forceful ***hijā'*** on al-Zibriqān, he complained to the caliph ʿUmar, who imprisoned al-Ḥuṭay'a. Only fragments of his poetry have been preserved. Rabīʿa ibn Ḥudhār, a contemporary of his, called his verse 'like warmed-up meat, neither well done so that it may be eaten, nor left raw so that it may still be useful'.

Text edition

Shiʿr al-Zibriqān Ibn Badr wa-ʿAmr Ibn al-Ahtam, Suʿūd Maḥmūd ʿAbd al-Jābir (ed.), Beirut (1984).

G.J.H. VAN GELDER

Zifzāf, Muḥammad *see* Zafzāf, Muḥammad

Zīrids *see* Spain

Zīr Sālim, romance of

The *Qiṣṣat al-Zīr Sālim* is a folk elaboration of the episode of the *ayyām al-ʿArab* (**Battle Days**) known as the war of Basūs. Traditions going back to **Abū ʿUbayda** and **Ibn al-Kalbī**, among others, tell of the long war between the **tribes** of Bakr and Taghlib, started by the tyrant Kulayb's killing of Basūs's camel. Kulayb is portrayed in the romance as a noble knight whose victory over the Yemeni *Tubbaʿ* (king) freed the Taghlib from paying tribute. His brother Zīr Sālim undertakes a terrible struggle against his murderer, Jassās, and the Banū Murra. Predominant in the *Qiṣṣa* are the theme of intertribal strife and a fierce **bedouin** character, expressed by an irrepressible desire for vengeance. The romance of Zīr is considered by storytellers the introduction to the epic cycle of the **Banū Hilāl**. Arab gypsies have seen the origin of their wanderings in Zīr's orders to Jassās's defeated people to scatter with no fixed abode.

Text edition

Qiṣṣat al-Zīr Sālam Abū Layla al-Muhalhil, Cairo (1278/1861–2), and Beirut (1866) (first edns).

Further reading

ʿAbd al-Ḥakīm, Shawqī, *al-Zīr Sālim Abū Laylā al-Muhalhil*, Beirut (1982).

Canova, G., 'Osservazioni a margine della storia di Zīr Sālim', *QSA* 3 (1985), 115–36.
Caskel, W., 'Aijām al-'arab', *Islamica* 3, suppl. (1930), 97–8.
Caussin de Perceval, Jean-Jacques Antoine, *Essai sur l'histoire des Arabes*, Paris (1847–8), vol. 2, 275–85.
Ibn Isḥāq, *Kitāb Bakr wa-Taghlib*, Bombay (1305/1887–8).
Oliverius, J., 'Aufzeichnungen über den Basūs-Krieg . . .', *ArO* 33 (1965), 44–64.
Lyons, M.C., *The Arabian Epic*, Cambridge (1995), 3: 650–60.
——, 'Themen und Motive im arabischen Volksbuch von Zīr Sālim, *ArO* 29 (1971), 129–45.
——, 'The epic and genealogical cyclization in the Arabic folk book about Zīr Sālim', *Acta Universitatis Carolinae*, Philologica, 5 (1975), 27–44.
——, 'Der Reflex der sozialen Verhältnisse und historischen Begebenheiten im arabischen Volksbuch von Zīr Sālim', *Acta Universitatis Carolinae*, Philologica, 7 (1977), 49–61.
von Kremer, A., *Aegypten*, Leipzig (1863), vol. 2, 307–22.

G. CANOVA

See also: *sīra* literature

Ziryāb (*c.*160–230/*c.*789–845)

Nickname of 'Alī ibn Nāfi' Abū al-Ḥasan, musician and courtier. The nickname refers probably to his 'golden' voice. A freedman of the caliph al-Mahdī, Ziryāb early displayed musical gifts. He studied with Isḥāq **al-Mawṣilī**, but the story that Isḥāq's jealousy of his success and popularity with the caliph drove him from Baghdad, is a later invention. After spending some time in North Africa he was invited to Córdoba, where the amīr 'Abd al-Raḥmān ibn al-Ḥakam welcomed him. He established the very important Andalusian school of music, laying down certain rules of performance; he also added a fifth string to the lute. A man of wide culture, he was a respected companion of the ruler and an arbiter on matters of taste; in the realm of cookery he introduced the refined, cosmopolitan traditions of Baghdad. Ziryāb's central role in the development of Andalusian civilization is partly due to the fact that his arrival coincided with a change in the self-image of the emirate, which was seeking a new sophistication.

Further reading

Poché, Christian, *La musique arabo-andalouse*, Arles (1995), 34–37.
Wright, Owen, 'Music in Muslim Spain', in *The Legacy of Muslim Spain*, S.K. Jayyusi (ed.), Leiden (1992), 555–79.

H. KILPATRICK

See also: singers and musicians; Spain

Ziyād al-A'jam (d. 100/718?)

Abū Umāma Ziyād ibn Sulmā (or Jābir or Sulaymān or Sulaym) was one of the *fuḥūl* of **Khurasan** who lived through most of the first century of the Hijra. He belonged to 'Abd Qays or was a *mawlā* of that tribe; while his nickname (al-A'jam) indicates he was Persian, it may be that the sobriquet simply refers to a foreign accent, for which he was mocked by al-Mughīra ibn Ḥabnā'. He was an adaptable opportunist in character who drank wine and may have been a transmitter of ***ḥadīth***. Most of his poetry survives in fragments (except an elegy rhyming in *ḥā'*); he composed ***hijā'***, ***madīḥ*** and ***rithā'*** and was known as the **Ḥuṭay'a** of the **Umayyad** age – even **al-Farazdaq** was too cautious to satirize him. His *madīḥ* was traditional and there are echoes of pre-Islamic poetry in his verse.

Text edition

Shi'r Ziyād al-A'jam, Y.H. Bakkār (ed.), Beirut (1983).

P.F. KENNEDY

Ziyāda, Mayy (born Mārī Ilyās Ziyāda) (1886–1941)

Syro-Lebanese poet, prose writer, translator and intellectual. One of many Syro-Lebanese intellectuals to emigrate to **Egypt** early this century, 'Mayy' (as she signed her essays) received her early education in Nazareth, 'Ayn Ṭūra and **Beirut** before moving to **Cairo** with her parents in 1908. Her earliest publications were essays and fiction translations in the journal that her father edited, *al-Maḥrūsa*, and a volume of French-language poems published pseudonymously (*Fleurs de rêve*, 1911, by 'Isis Copia'). New friends, notably Aḥmad **Luṭfī al-Sayyid** and Ya'qūb **Ṣarrūf**, encouraged her to supplement her French- and English-language education with an immersion in the Arabic heritage, while acquaintance with the feminist leader Hudā **Sha'rāwī** and the writer Malak Ḥifnī Nāṣif ('Bāḥithat al-Bādiya') deepened her concern with women's status and roles, a commitment that she explored in many speeches and essays (some collected in *Sawāniḥ fatāh* and *Kalimāt wa-ishārāt*, both 1922) and in her biographical–literary studies of women writers (*Bāḥithat al-Bādiya: baḥth intiqādī*, 1920; *Warda al-Yāzijī*, 1924; *'Ā'isha Taymūr: shā'irat al-ṭalī'a*, 1926). She also wrote on Arabic literature and on social thought and organization (*al-Musāwāh*, 1922), and composed prose poems (*Ẓulumāt wa-ashi''a*, 1923). In 1913 or 1914 Ziyāda had begun hosting weekly salons; continuing until the late 1920s, these drew eminent figures from the Cairo literati and beyond. The successive deaths of friends and loved ones at the end of the decade impelled a deep melancholy, however, and in 1936 relatives in Beirut placed her in an asylum against her will. Released more than a year later with the help of friends, Ziyāda lived quietly in Beirut and then Egypt until her death.

Further reading

Booth, Marilyn, 'Biography and feminist rhetoric in early twentieth-century Egypt: Mayy Ziyada's studies of three women's lives', *Journal of Women's History* 3 (1) (Spring 1991).

Ghurayyib, Rūz, *Mayy Ziyāda: al-tawahhuj wa-al-ufūl*, Beirut (1978).

al-Kuzbarī, Salmā, *Mayy Ziyāda: ma'sāt al-nubūgh*, 2 vols, Beirut (1982).

Sakākīnī, Widād, *Mayy Ziyāda fī ḥayātihā wa-āthārihā*, Cairo (1969).

M. BOOTH

Zoroaster, Zoroastrians *see* Persia

Zuhayr ibn Abī Sulmā (d. 609 CE)

A most celebrated pre-Islamic poet and the ***rāwī*** of Aws ibn Ḥajar and **Ṭufayl al-Ghanawī**. Zuhayr, whose father was an estranged member of the Muzayna and who was born into the 'Abd al-'Uzza ibn Dhubyān (of the Ghaṭafān confederacy), is renowned for the meticulous care he lavished upon his poetry, particularly his seven *Ḥawliyyāt* (*Annual Odes*), whence he was designated a 'slave of poetry' (*'abd al-shi'r*). His ***Mu'allaqa*** celebrates the peaceful conclusion of the internecine war of Dāḥis, waged between the 'Abs and Dhubyān, by two chieftains of the clan of Murra, Harim ibn Sinān and al-Ḥārith ibn 'Awf. It is an original and dramatic panegyric, combining a measured structure with gnomic sententiousness, a prominent feature which, among the medieval critics, came to epitomize the poetry of Zuhayr. Numerous other panegyrics (Ahlwardt 3, 4, 9, 14 and 18) are devoted to these chieftains and there is a threnody (Ahlwardt 2) bemoaning the death of Harim's father, Sinān ibn Abī Ḥāritha. The style and content of his panegyrics are largely **bedouin**, being adaptations of the ***qaṣīda*** of tribal ***fakhr***: there is a marked absence of the camel description, although reference should be made to Ahlwardt 15, in which a hunting scene replaces the ***waṣf***, and Qabāwa 32. A number of his poems are variations upon a theme concerning the theft of a slave and some camels (Ahlwardt 7, 8, 10, 13 and Qabāwa 23). There are political comminations addressed to other **tribes** contemplating an attack upon the Ghaṭafān (Ahlwardt 6 and 19), an ode in the style of his master Aws (Qabāwa 24) and an address to the **Lakhmid** king, al-Nu'mān ibn al-Mundhir (Ahlwardt 20), ascribed by **al-Aṣma'ī**, on stylistic grounds, to the obscure Ṣirma al-Anṣārī.

Zuhayr's ***dīwān*** has been preserved in two recensions; by the Andalusian al-A'lam **al-Shantamarī**, an edition purporting to reflect that of al-Aṣma'ī, and a more comprehensive collection by **Tha'lab**. The recension of al-Shantamarī/al-Aṣma'ī is exclusive and its concentration upon the poems dedicated to the affairs of the Ghaṭafān may suggest its provenance from a tribal collection: the native critics mention the lack of poems in praise of Zuhayr's natural tribe, the Muzayna. A comparison between the two recensions serves to emphasize the exclusive and unrepresentative nature of al-Shantamarī's collection *al-'Iqd al-thamīn fī dawāwīn al-shu'arā' al-sitta al-Jāhiliyyīn*.

Text editions

Dīwān: Ahlwardt, *Divans*; Aḥmad Zakī al-'Adawī (ed.), Cairo (1964); Ḥasan Fawr (ed.), Beirut (1988).

Shi'r Zuhayr ibn Abī Sulmā, F. Qabāwa (ed.), Aleppo (1970), rpt Beirut (1992).

Further reading

Jacobi, R., *Studien zur Poetik der altarabsichen Qaṣide*, Wiesbaden (1971).

Montgomery, J.E., *The Vagaries of the Qaṣīdah*, Warminster (1997).

J.E. MONTGOMERY

zuhdiyya

The term *zuhdiyya* (ascetic poem) is formed from the verb *zahada*, 'to renounce'/'to turn away from'/'to abstain from gratification'. The *zuhdiyya* developed as a genre in the early Islamic period and, in its maturity, is associated principally with the **ʿAbbāsid** poet **Abū al-ʿAtāhiya** (d. 211/826).

The earliest poetry to which the *zuhdiyya* owes a debt is that of the Christian **ʿAdī ibn Zayd** of **Ḥīra** (d. *c.*600), whose ***dīwān*** stands apart from the dominant strain of pre-Islamic poetry by virtue of its consistently pious, monotheistic sentiment. He preached the impotence of man in his world and reminded him, prince or pauper, of his inexorable demise. It was the pious dimension in his cognizance of death that set ʿAdī apart from the most representative of the pre-Islamic poets, who were also, to some extent, precursors of Abū al-ʿAtāhiya in their consistently voiced awareness of fleeting time; the *zuhdiyya*, in some measure, is a development of the ***ḥikma*** ('wisdom') and *naṣāʾiḥ* ('didactic poetry') to be found in some pre-Islamic and ***mukhaḍram*** poetry.

Islam, more specifically the language and tenets of the **Koran**, is an important source for the *zuhdiyya*, which took a monochrome view of the revelation's relatively more nuanced view on life: the Koran repeatedly warns against absorption in the pleasures of this life to the exclusion of the Hereafter, but nevertheless consistently celebrates the gifts of God's Creation. The *zuhdiyya*, however, adopts an almost exclusively negative view of the pleasures of this world. This asceticism is first associated with **al-Ḥasan al-Baṣrī** (d. 110/728). In the same period, a figure of lesser stature in Islamic literary history, Sābiq ibn ʿAbd Allah al-Barbarī (late first/early eighth century), composed what constitutes the earliest substantive collection of *zuhdiyyāt*. Much in this collection, with respect to both form and content, is entirely consonant with the later poetry of Abū al-ʿAtāhiya.

Also associated with the genre is **Ṣāliḥ ibn ʿAbd al-Quddūs** (d. 167/783–40), a poet who was accused of *zandaqa* (heresy). The nature of his religiosity, departing from the mainstream orthodoxy, may be responsible for this accusation yet nothing in his poetry clarifies the issue. What survives is akin to the expression of Abū al-ʿAtāhiya, against whom the same accusation was levelled (similarly, his poetry too offers no clarification of the charge, although the source of pique for the political and religious powers of the period is not hard to discern in the constant, if sometimes only implicit, reminder of their inevitable demise). The influence on the *zuhdiyya* which may have stemmed from **Khārijī** poetry is negligible.

Ranging from poems of less than ten lines to poems of over forty verses, the *zuhdiyyāt* are an admixture of general piety, practical wisdom, social etiquette (in small measure) and the *naṣīḥa* of earlier poetry. The most striking formal feature that these poems display is the use of anaphora and parallel phrases; this probably constitutes a borrowing from religious sermon material. Their language is in the main simple and accessible, hence the popularity Abū al-ʿAtāhiya is said to have enjoyed among the people of the market-place.

Although the *zuhdiyyāt* of Abū al-ʿAtāhiya may stem from a genuine piety, they exhibit a significant dimension of literary posturing: the poet manipulated some features and motifs of the classical Arabic tradition of poetry; commonly he transmuted the significance of *dār* (pl. *diyār*) from its conventional meaning, 'abode' (i.e. 'erstwhile campsite of the beloved'), to that of '(this) life (as distinct from the Hereafter)'. His use of *dār* essentially carries the same significance as *dunyā* (world); the manipulation of a number of the essential lexical items of earlier poetry is, in a few striking poems, coupled with a borrowing of the conventional ***qaṣīda*** structure, *nasīb* to ***madīḥ*** (although *raḥīl* is missing from this schema, the model is nevertheless manifestly clear; furthermore, the meaning of *raḥīl* is transformed elsewhere by the poet to signify 'passing away'). Further, the *zuhdiyya*'s dominant message of an eschewal of pleasures effectively formed a line of counterpoint against the libertine poetry of this period (the ***khamriyya*** and ***mujūn*** poetry); Abū al-ʿAtāhiya effectively set up his domain of pious poetry as a counter-genre of the wine poem. To this extent the audience of the *zuhdiyya* was a literary one, and not only the *hoi polloi* of the *sūq*. One clue to this feature is the treatment of fate (*al-dahr*) which commonly, within individual poems, constitutes a stepping stone to what emerges as a straightforwardly pious message; in this way the *zuhdiyya* is in contraflow with the poetry of *mujūn*, where an irreligious attitude may be buttressed by treatment of *al-dahr*. In some *zuhdiyyāt* the transition from the treatment of *al-dahr* to the treatment of Islam effectively provides a structure. A significant number of *zuhdiyyāt* are addressed to an anonymous, reprobate interlocutor who is urged, with echoes of a bacchic lexicon, to abandon his guileless view of fate and, in some cases, to repent.

After the latter half of the third/ninth century the *zuhdiyya* as a genre was in decline; this may be due to developments in mystical poetry and the growing popularity the latter enjoyed. (See **Ṣūfī literature, poetry**.) With mystical poetry the *zuhdiyya* shared some important themes, notably the treatment of *tawakkul* ('trust in God').

Further reading

Abdesselem, M., *Le Thème de la mort dans la poésie arabe des origines à la fin du IIIème/IXème siècle*, Tunis (1977).

——, 'Zuhdiyya', in *Dictionnaire Universel des littératures* (vol. 3), Paris (1994).

Bellamy, J.A., 'The impact of Islam on early Arabic poetry', in *Islam: Past Influence and Present Challenge*, Edinburgh (1979), 141–67.

Hamori, Andras, 'Ascetic poetry (*zuhdiyyāt*)', in *CHALABL*, 265–74.

Kannūn, A.A., *Sābiq al-Barbarī*, Damascus (1969).

Kennedy, P.F., *The Wine Song in Classical Arabic Poetry: Abū Nuwās and the Literary Tradition*, Oxford (1997) (chapters 2–4).

Kinsberg, Leah, 'What is meant by *Zuhd*?', *SI* 61 (1985), 27–44.

Martin, J.D., 'The religious beliefs of Abu al-'Atāhiya according to the *zuhdiyāt*', *Glasgow Oriental Society Transactions* 23 (1969–70).

Ritter, H., 'Studien zur Geschichte der islamischen Frommigkeit, I: Ḥasan al-Basrī', *Der Islam* 21 (1933), 1–83.

Sperl, Stefan, *Mannerism in Arabic Literature*, Cambridge (1989), 71–96.

Vajda, G., 'Les zindīqs en pays d'Islam', *RSO* 17 (1938), 215–20, 225–8.

Wagner, Ewald, *Grundzüge der klassischen arabischen Dichtung*, Darmstadt (1988), vol. 2, 120–30.

P.F. KENNEDY

See also: religious poetry

al-Zuhrī, Muḥammad ibn Muslim (d. 124/742)

A celebrated **ḥadīth** scholar of the **Umayyad** period. He flourished in the pre-literary phrase in the development of *ḥadīth* literature, and his fame thus rests upon his command of orally transmitted material rather than upon written works. His involvements in Umayyad court life – for example, he was tutor to the sons of the caliph Hishām – have earned him a unique place in Muslim historical works. He transmitted not only material relating to the prophet **Muḥammad**, but also material relating to the Companions of the Prophet. His name accordingly appears frequently in the chains of transmitters of material used by Muslim historians and biographers, not to mention authors of later *ḥadīth* collections. The great extent to which his contemporaries consulted him in regard to prophetic precedent bears witness to the importance of *ḥadīth* material in the religious life of Muslims of his time.

Text edition

al-Maghāzī al-nabawiyya, S. Dahhan (ed.), Damascus (1981).

B. WEISS

Zurayq, Qusṭanṭīn (1909–)

University teacher and Arab nationalist writer. Zurayq was born in Damascus and educated at the American University of Beirut and at the Universities of Princeton and Chicago, from which he received a doctorate in history in 1930. He spent most of his professional life as a university teacher and administrator, mostly at the American University of Beirut, where he was vice-president (1947–9, 1952–4), acting president (1954–7) and distinguished professor of history until his retirement in 1977. He also served as chairman of the Institute of Palestine Studies between 1963 and 1984. Zurayq is probably best known for three works: *al-Wa'y al-qawmī* (1940); *Ma'nā al-nakba* (1949); and *Naḥnu wa-al-mustaqbal* (1977). Zurayq was always a robust spokesman for the Palestinian cause, but also stressed the direct responsibility of the individual Arab states and of Arab society in general for many of the ills afflicting the region.

Further reading

Atiyeh, G.N. and Oweiss, J.M., *Arab Civilisation...Studies in Honor of Constantine K. Zurayk*, Albany NY (1988).

P. SLUGLETT

Glossary

Items in bold denote that a main entry can be found under that heading.

Ahl al-Kitāb
'People of the Book', i.e., non-Muslim confessions (Judaism, Zoroastrianism, Christianity) possessing a written scripture, who enjoy a special status under Islamic rule.

akhbār
See *khabar.*

ʿAlids
Descendants of **ʿAlī ibn Abī Ṭālib**.

ʿālim
See *ʿulamāʾ*.

Amālī
Literally, 'dictations'; specifically, a book dictated from memory and copied down by a scribe; usually consisting of philological observations (cf. the *Amālī* of **al-Qālī**).

amīr
Commander, governor, prince.

amīr al-umarāʾ
Commander-in-chief (of, e.g., the caliphal army or guard).

Anṣār
Literally, 'helpers'; specifically, the supporters of the Prophet **Muḥammad** in Medina, especially after his migration there in 622. An individual is termed an Anṣārī.

Atabeg (*Atābak*)
A Turkish title dating from the time of the **Saljūqs**. Originally it was bestowed on notables (usually military chiefs) placed in charge of the tutelage and protection of young princes. As such officials gained increasing power (often by marriage to the mother of their charge), they became virtually independent territorial rulers and established hereditary dynasties. The title was also used by the Saljūqs of Anatolia, by the rulers of **Khwārazm**, the **Ayyūbids** and the **Mamlūks**.

Dahrī; Dahriyya
The term Dahriyya (sg. Dahrī) was applied to the holders of various materialistic beliefs, especially in the eternity of the world (thus denying Resurrection and the Afterlife); it is sometimes used generally for 'heretic'.

dāʿī
Literally, 'he who summons', that is, who invites people to believe in the true religion; used more specifically to refer to propagandists of dissenting groups claiming leadership of the Muslim community (e.g., the **ʿAbbāsids**; various **Shīʿī** groups). Under the **Fāṭimids** the *dāʿī al-duʿāt* ('chief summoner') was head of religious matters and of the teaching and propagation of the *daʿwa* (see below).

daʿwa
Call, summons, invitation, e.g., to the true religion; to support the cause of dissenting groups claiming the right to the Imāmate (see below, 'Imām', such as the **ʿAbbāsid** *daʿwa*, the **Ismāʿīlī** *daʿwa*; also, the content and teachings of this summons, e.g., religious law (***fiqh***).

dhikr
Literally, 'reminding', and the oral mention of this memory. In **Sufism** it refers to the repetition of an ejaculatory litany (*ḥizb, wird*), composed by the founder of a Ṣūfī brotherhood (*ṭarīqa*), and often containing the name of God or some other formula, as well as to the

technique of performing this litany (aloud or softly; with accompanying gestures, etc.), to the context (collectively or privately), and to the gathering in which this litany is performed. *Dhikr* is the most common form of prayer in Sūfism.

faqīh
A specialist in Islamic religious law; see ***fiqh***.

fatwā
A legal opinion issued by a jurist (*muftī*) authorized to deliver such opinions on the basis of Islamic law (see ***fiqh***).

gharaḍ
Literally, 'purpose'; see **genres, poetic**; ***qaṣīda***.

ghayba
Absence; in **Shīʿism**, it refers to the absence or occulation of the last in the relevant line of imāms (see below), who has no successor and will remain hidden until his return at a pre-ordained time as the Mahdī ('rightly-guided'), the eschatological saviour whose appearance will precede the End of Days.

ghazw
Raid, expedition. In pre-Islamic **Arabia** it referred to inter-tribal raids; in Islamic times, to expeditions in the course of *jihād* (see below). A holy warrior is termed a *ghāzī*.

ḥadātha
Modernity, modernism; a term associated with **Adūnīs** and other members of the so-called *Shiʿr* group of poets.

ḥajj
The annual pilgrimage to Mecca, incumbent upon every Muslim who is able (physically and financially) to perform it at least once in his/her lifetime.

Ḥanafī
Follower of the legal school of **Abū Ḥanīfa**.

Ḥanbalī
Follower of the legal school of Aḥmad **Ibn Ḥanbal**.

Hijra (Hegira)
The emigration of the Prophet **Muḥammad** from Mecca to Medina in September 622. Subsequently (perhaps under 'Umar I; see **Orthodox caliphate**) the beginning of the Islamic era was fixed as 16 July 622 (1 Muḥarram 1), the beginning of the lunar year.

Imām
Generally, the individual who leads the prayer and behind whom other Muslims pray. Specifically, one who claims leadership of the Islamic community (Imāmate, *imāma*), in both **Sunnī** but more especially **Shīʿī** contexts.

Imāmī, Imāmiyya
Twelver Shīʿīs (*Ithnāʿ ashariyya*); see **Shīʿīs**.

ism
Name; specifically, that part of the name which is 'given' or 'personal' (also called [*ism*] *ʿalam*), consisting of an adjective (Aḥmad, 'most praised'), a noun (Asad, 'lion'), or a verb (Yazīd, 'he increases'). The use of 'civil' surnames in the Islamic world dates only from recent times. The traditional Arabic name typically consists of the following elements: (1) the *kunya* or agnomen (Abū, 'father of'; Umm, 'mother of'), the second part of which may be refer to an actual offspring of the person in question (Abū Muḥammad, 'father of Muḥammad') or may be a form of honorific (Abū al-Barakāt, 'father of blessings'), etc. Sometimes *kunya*s are associated with certain *ism*s (Abū Ḥafṣ 'Umar; 'Umar I's daughter Ḥafṣa was married to the Prophet). An individual may have more than one *kunya*; (2) The *ism*; (3) The *nasab*, 'patronymic', expressing the relation of a son (ibn) or daughter (bint) to his/her father (or sometimes mother) and forefathers. The name of a particularly distinguished ancestor at the end of the chain may serve as a surname by which subsequent family members are known (**Ibn Rushd**, after the philosopher's paternal grandfather). The *nasab* may express tribal or ethnic origin (**Ibn Khaldūn**, a descendant of the Spanish Arab tribe of the Banū Khaldūn; **Ibn al-Rūmī**, 'son of the Greek'), or (ancestral) occupation or profession (**Ibn al-Munajjim**, 'son/descendant of the astrologer'; **Ibn al-Nadīm**, 'son/descendant of the boon-companion'; **Ibn al-Qalānisī**, 'son/descendant of the hat-maker'). (4) The *nisba*, 'relation', which indicates place of origin (tribal or geographical: al-Qurashī, 'of Quraysh'; al-Iṣbahānī, 'from Isfahan'), birth or residence (al-Khwārazmī, 'born in Khwārazm'; al-Baghdādī, 'residing in Baghdad'), etc. *Nisba*s may also denote affiliation with a religious

school (al-Ḥanbalī, a follower of **Ibn Ḥanbal**) or a Ṣūfī brotherhood (al-Qādirī, a member of the Qādiriyya *ṭarīqa*), or be derived from one's own or an ancestor's profession (**al-Zajjājī**, 'the glass-maker'). An individual may have several different *nisba*s. (5) The *laqab*, 'honorific' or 'nickname, sobriquet'. This can be of many types: descriptive of a physical characteristic (**al-Jāḥiẓ**, 'the goggle-eyed') or a profession (**al-Sarrāj**, 'the saddle-maker'); honorifics including regnal titles (al-Hādī, 'the rightly-guided'), official titles of honour (Nāṣir al-Dawla, 'Supporter of the Realm'), or prominence in religious learning (Shams al-Dīn, 'sun of the faith'); compounds formed with Dhū/ Dhāt ('possessor': Dhū al-Wizāratayn, 'holder of both vizierates', i.e. head of the administration and the military); and many more. The *laqab* often precedes other parts of the name; and an individual may have a number of such titles. Historical personages were generally known by one (or more) of these elements, called the *shuhra* ('repute': e.g. **Abū Nuwās** al-Ḥasan ibn Hāni' al-Ḥakamī).

isnād
Chain of authorities, i.e., of those who transmit a historical account (see below, *khabar*), a ***ḥadīth***, an anecdote, etc.

jihād
Literally, 'struggle, effort'; in legal terminology, military action for the expansion and defence of Islam, holy war against infidels, unbelievers, pagans.

kātib (pl. *kuttāb*)
Copyist, scribe, secretary; see **books and book-making**; **secretaries**.

khabar (pl. *akhbār*)
Piece of information, account, whether historical, biographical, or a Prophetic tradition; see ***ḥadīth***; **historical literature**.

khānaqāh (also *khānqāh*)
Ṣūfī lodge, meeting place and home of specific brotherhoods (*ṭarīqa*; see **Sufism**). Other terms for the Ṣūfī lodge include *ribāṭ*; *zāwiya*; Turkish *tekke*.

laqab
See *ism*.

madrasa
In medieval times, a college for the study of law and other (ancillary) religious sciences, often attached to a mosque; in modern times, a college for higher religious studies; see **education**.

maghāzī
Raids, expeditions; in Islamic times, the term refers specifically to the Prophet's military expeditions during the Medinan period, and to the literary genre devoted to accounts of them; see ***futūḥ***; **Muḥammad**.

maḥmal (also *maḥmil*)
The ceremonial litter sent by Islamic rulers to Mecca at the time of the Pilgrimage; its wooden frame was richly decorated with silks, brocades and embroidery (often of gold), and it was carried by a camel. It was in later medieval times a sign of the independence of the rulers who sent it, and was considered a source of blessing (*baraka*).

majlis (pl. *majālis*)
Literally, a seat, a seated gathering; a meeting, assembly; also the hall in which such gatherings were held. The term is applied to royal ceremonial audiences; to the 'salons' of rulers and notables in which a variety of philosophical, religious, grammatical and literary topics might be discussed; to musical and drinking gatherings, tribunals, teaching sessions etc. The **Ismāʿīlī**s in particular were noted for their 'sessions of wisdom', *majālis al-ḥikma* (see **Fāṭimids**).

Mālikī
Follower of the legal school of **Mālik ibn Anas**.

mamlūk (pl. *mamālīk*)
Slave; in particular, a military slave; see **Mamlūks**.

masā'il (sg. *mas'ala*)
'Questions' – religious, philosophical, grammatical, etc. – on which two scholars dispute, often by correspondence. Such discussions were often collected in works titled *Masā'il* (or *As'ila*) *wa-ajwiba*, 'Questions and Answers'.

marthiya (pl. *marāthī*)
Elegy, threnody; see ***rithā'***.

Mashriq
'East, Orient' (literally, the direction from which the sun rises); used to refer to the

eastern part of the Islamic world, as opposed to the **Maghrib**, the western part (where the sun sets).

mawlā
Non-Arab client of an Arab tribe; see ***Mawālī***.

mawlid (pl. *mawālīd*)
Birthday; in particular, the birthday of the Prophet **Muḥammad**, and the festival which celebrates it (*mawlid al-nabī*). This festival was established as a royal ceremonial by the **Fāṭimids**, who also celebrated the anniversaries of **ʿAlī ibn Abī Ṭālib**, of his wife the Prophet's daughter Fāṭima, of the reigning imām, and several others. **Sunnī** *mawlids* are attested from the early seventh/thirteenth century. With the growth of importance of **Sufism** in Egypt the *mawlid* became a popular festival, and from there spread through the Islamic world. The panegyrics in praise of the Prophet performed at these festivals, composed in verse or mixed verse and prose, are also called *mawlid*.

muftī
See *fatwā*.

Muhājir (pl. *Muhājirūn*)
Emigrant; applied specifically to those Meccans who accompanied **Muḥammad** to Medina (see *Hijra*).

muḥtasib
An official charged with the office of *ḥisba*, whose duties are to 'command good and prohibit evil'. His specific tasks are the inspection of markets, weights and measures, and the maintenance of public morality.

muruwwa
Literally, manliness; the sum of a man's physical and related moral qualities. In pre-Islamic times *muruwwa* comprised both material and moral qualities (e.g., the possession of wealth and the related virtues of liberality, hospitality, etc.); in Islamic times the focus shifted more to abstract moral virtues (piety, abstemiousness, etc.).

nasīb
See ***qaṣīda***.

nisba
See *ism*.

qāḍī (pl. *quḍāt*)
A judge who administers Islamic law (*sharīʿa*; see below), appointed by the caliph or a provincial governor (see above, amīr) and representing his authority. Each capital or major town has its *qāḍī*; the chief judge of a city or a region is called *Qāḍī al-quḍāt*.

qaṣīd
See ***qaṣīda***.

quṭb
In **Sufism**, the most perfect human being, or one so spiritually perfect as to be a manifestation of the 'Muḥammadan Truth' (*ḥaqīqa Muḥammadiyya*). Mediating between the Divine and the human, his presence is deemed necessary to the maintenance and survival of the universe.

ribāṭ
A fortified military-religious edifice. In early Islamic times, it denoted forts built for defence as the Muslim conquests advance, later, border forts on the edge of non-Muslim territories; it also came to mean, in the Western Islamic lands in particular, a Ṣūfī lodge (see *khānaqāh*).

risāla (pl. *rasā'il*)
Treatise, letter, epistle; a written message (sometimes in the form of a poem), as opposed to an oral one. The term later came to mean either official or private correspondence; a brief prose work in the form of a letter or a short treatise; a monograph or essay on a particular topic. See **artistic prose**; **prose, non-fiction, medieval**.

Sayyid
Literally, 'chief', 'leader'; specifically, a descendant of the Prophet or, for ʿAlids (see above), of **ʿAlī ibn Abī Ṭālib** through his son al-Ḥusayn.

Shāfiʿī
Follower of the legal school of **al-Shāfiʿī**.

sharīʿa (also *sharʿ*)
Religious law; see ***fiqh***.

Sharīf
Literally, 'noble'; specifically, a descendant of the Prophet's clan of the Banū Hāshim (from his great-grandfather Hāshim ibn ʿAbd Manāf). For ʿAlids (see above), a descendent

of **'Alī ibn Abī Ṭālib** through his sons al-Ḥasan or al-Ḥusayn or other of his offspring.

shuhra
See *ism*.

sunna
Customary procedure, traditional usage; specifically, the *sunna* of the Prophet **Muḥammad**, his sayings and doings and the usages sanctioned by him, considered the guide for the individual Muslim's daily life, and later established as legally binding precedents and as a source of law. See ***fiqh***; **Sunnīs**.

Sūra
Koranic verse; see **Koran**.

ṭabaqa (pl. *ṭabaqāt*)
Class, grouping; see **biography, medieval**.

Ṭā'ifa
Refers to the 'party' kings of Spain (*mulūk al-ṭawā'if*); see **Spain**.

Ṭālibids
Descendants of **'Alī ibn Abī Ṭālib**.

ṭarīqa
The Ṣūfī 'path' or way of life (see **Sufism**); more specifically, a Ṣūfī brotherhood. See also above, *khānaqāh*.

'ulamā' (sg. *'ālim*)
Scholars, learned men; specialists in the religious sciences.

washshāḥ
A composer of *muwashshaḥāt*; see ***muwashshaḥ***.

wird
See *dhikr*.

Ẓāhirī
Member of the legal school of **Ibn Dā'ūd al-Iṣbahānī**.

zandaqa
Specifically, Manichean Dualism; also used more generally for 'heresy'.

zāwiya
See *khānaqāh*.

zindīq (pl. *Zanādiqa*)
One who holds Dualist or heretical beliefs.

zuhd
Asceticism; see ***zuhdiyya***.

Chronological tables

The Orthodox or Rightly Guided Caliphs (al-Khulafā' al-Rāshidān), 11–40/632–61

11/632	Abū Bakr
13/634	'Umar ibn al-Khaṭṭāb
23/644	'Uthmān ibn 'Affān
35–40/656–61	'Alī bin Abī Ṭālib
	Umayyad caliphs

The House of 'Alī, 40–322/661–934

- 'Alī, d. 40/661
  - Ḥasan, d. 50/670?
    - Ḥasan
      - 'Abd Allah
        - Ibrāhīm
        - Muḥammad al-Nafs al-Zakyya, d. 145/762
  - Ḥusayn, d. 61/680
    - 'Alī Zayn al-'Ābidīn, d. 94/712–13?
      - Muḥammad al-Bāqir, d. 113/731–2
        - Ja'far al-Ṣādiq, d. 148/765
          - Ismā'īl
            - Muḥammad
              - Aḥmad
                - Ḥusayn (al-Mu'ill)
                  - Muḥammad al-Qā'im, d. 322/934
                    - The Fāṭimid Caliphs
          - Mūsā al-Kāẓim, d. 183/799
            - 'Alī al-Riḍā, d. 202/817–18
              - Muḥmmad al-Jawād, d. 220/835
                - 'Alī al-Hādi, d. 254/868
                  - Ḥasan al-'Askarī, d. 260/873–4
                    - Muḥammad al-Mahdī, disappeared about 260/873–4
      - Zayd, d. 125 or 6/743–4
        - Yaḥyā
        - 'Īsā
  - Muḥammad ibn al-Ḥanafiyya, d. 81/700–1

The Hidden Imāms of the Ismā'īlīs: Muḥammad, Aḥmad, Ḥusayn (al-Mu'ill)

The Imāms of the Twelver Shī'a: Mūsā al-Kāẓim to Muḥammad al-Mahdī

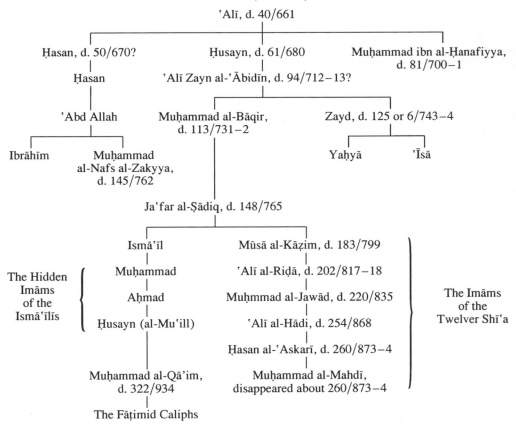

The Umayyad Caliphs, 41–132/661–750

41/661	Mu'āwiya I ibn Abī Sufyān
60/680	Yazīd I
64/683	Mu'āwiya II
64/684	Marwān I ibn al-Ḥakam
65/685	'Abd-al-Malik
86/705	al-Walīd I
96/715	Sulaymān
99/717	'Umar ibn 'Abd-al-'Azīz
101/720	Yazīd II
105/724	Hishām
125/743	al-Walīd II
126/744	Yazīd III
126/744	Ibrāhim
127–32/744–50	Marwān II al-Ḥimār
	'Abbāsid caliphs

The Spanish Umayyads, 138–422/756–1031

138/756	'Abd al-Raḥmān I al-Dākhil
172/788	Hishām I
180/796	al-Ḥakam I
206/822	'Abd al-Raḥmān II al-Mutawassiṭ
238/852	Muḥammad I
273/886	al-Mundhir
275/888	'Abd Allāh
300/912	'Abd al-Raḥmān III al-Nāṣir
350/961	al-Ḥakam II al-Mustanṣir
366/976	Hishām II al-Mu'ayyad, *first reign*
399/1009	Muḥammad II al-Mahdī, *first reign*
400/1009	Sulaymān al-Musta'īn, *first reign*
400/1010	Muḥammad II, *second reign*
400/1010	Hishām II, *second reign*
403/1013	Sulaymān, *second reign*
407/1016	Hammūdid 'Alī al-Nāsir
408/1018	'Abd al-Raḥmān IV al-Murtaḍā
408/1018	Ḥammūdid al-Qāsim al-Ma'mūn, *first time*
412/1021	Ḥammūdid Yaḥyā al-Mu'talī, *first time*
413/1022	Ḥammūdid al-Qāsim, *second time*
414/1023	'Abd al-Raḥmān V al-Mustaẓhir
414/1024	Muḥammad III al-Mustakfī
416/1025	Ḥammūdid Yaḥyā, *second time*
418–22/1027–31	Hishām III al-Mu'tadd
	Mulūk al-Ṭawā'if

The 'Abbāsid Caliphs, 132–656/749–1258

132/749	al-Saffāḥ
136/754	al-Manṣūr
158/775	al-Mahdī
169/785	al-Hādī
170/786	Hārūn al-Rashīd
193/809	al-Amīn
198/813	al-Ma'mūn
201–3/817–19	Ibrāhīm ibn al-Mahdī, *in Baghdad*
218/833	al-Mu'taṣim
227/842	al-Wāthiq
232/847	al-Mutawakkil
247/861	al-Muntaṣir
248/862	al-Musta'īn
252/866	al-Mu'tazz
255/869	al-Muhtadī
256/870	al-Mu'tamid
279/892	al-Mu'taḍid
289/902	al-Muktafī
295/908	al-Muqtadir
320/932	al-Qāhir
322/934	al-Rāḍī
329/940	al-Muttaqī
333/944	al-Mustakfī
334/946	al-Muṭī'
363/974	al-Ṭā'i'
381/991	al-Qādir
422/1031	al-Qā'im
467/1075	al-Muqtadī
487/1094	al-Mustaẓhir
512/1118	al-Mustarshid
529/1135	al-Rāshid
530/1136	al-Muqtafī
555/1160	al-Mustanjid
566/1170	al-Mustaḍī'
575/1180	al-Nāṣir
622/1225	al-Ẓāhir
623/1226	al-Mustanṣir
640–56/1242–58	al-Musta'ṣim
	Mongol sack of Baghdad

The Ḥamdānids, 293–394/905–1004

al-Jazīra and Syria

1. Mosul branch

293/905	Abū al-Hayjā' 'Abd Allāh (governor of Mosul for the Caliph)

317/929	Nāṣir al-Dawla al-Ḥasan
358/969	ʿUddat al-Dawla Abū Taghlib
369/979	*Būyid conquest*
379–89/981–91	Ibrāhīm / al-Ḥusayn — restored by the Būyids as joint rulers
	Conquest of Mosul by the ʿUqaylids, and of Diyārbakr by the Marwānids

2. Aleppo branch

333/945	Sayf al-Dawla ʿAlī I
356/967	Saʿd al-Dawla Sharīf I
381/991	Saʿīd al-Dawla Saʿīd
392/1002	ʿAlī II
394/1004	Sharīf II
	Power seized by the slave general Luʾluʾ, and then conquest by the Fāṭimids

The Fāṭimids, 297–567/909–1171

North Africa, and then Egypt and Syria

The Dāʿī *Abū ʿAbd Allāh all-Shīʿī, completed his preparatory work in 298/910*

297/909	ʿUbayd Allāh al-Mahdī
322/934	al-Qāʾim
334/946	al-Manṣūr
341/953	al-Muʿizz
365/975	al-ʿAzīz
386/996	al-Ḥākim
411/1021	al-Ẓāhir
427/1036	al-Mustanṣir
487/1094	al-Mustaʿlī
495/1101	al-Āmir
524/1130	*interregnum; rule by al-Ḥāfiẓ as regent but not yet as Caliph*
525/1131	al-Ḥāfiẓ
544/1149	al-Ẓāfir
549/1154	al-Fāʾiz
555–67/1160–71	al-ʿĀdid
	Ayyūbid conquest

The Ṭāhirids, 205–59/821–73

Khurasan

205/821	Ṭāhir I ibn al-Ḥusayn, called Dhū al-Yamīnayn
207/822	Ṭalḥa
213/828	ʿAbd Allāh
230/845	Ṭāhir II
248–59/862–73	Muḥammad
	Ṣaffārids and Sāmānids

The Ṣaffārids, 253–*c.*900/867–*c.*1495

Sīstān

253/867	Yaʿqūb ibn Layth al-Ṣaffār
265/879	ʿAmr ibn Layth
288/901	Ṭāhir ibn Muḥammad ibn ʿAmr
296/908	Layth ibn ʿAlī
298/910	Muḥammad ibn ʿAlī
298/911	*first Sāmānid occupation, and usurpations of Kuthayyir ibn Aḥmad and Aḥmad ibn Qudām*
299/912	ʿAmr ibn Yaʿqūb ibn Muḥammad ibn ʿAmr
300/913	*second Sāmānid occupation*
310/922	Aḥmad ibn Muḥammad ibn Khalaf ibn Layth ibn ʿAlī (originally appointed governor for the Sāmānids)
352/963	Walī al-Dawla Khalaf ibn Aḥmad
393/1003	*Ghaznavid occupation*
	Ṭāhir ibn Khalaf, governor under Ghaznavid suzerainty in the early part of Maḥmūd of Ghazna's reign
420/1029	Naṣr ibn Aḥmad, under Ghaznavid suzerainty in the reigns of Masʿūd and Mawdūd, then after 440/1048 under Saljūq suzerainty

The Sāmānids, 204–395/819–1005

Khurasan and Transoxania

204/819	Ahmad I ibn Asad ibn Sāmān, governor of Farghāna
250/864	Naṣr I ibn Aḥmad, originally governor of Samarqand
279/892	Ismāʿīl I ibn Aḥmad
295/907	Aḥmad II ibn Ismāʿīl
301/914	al-Amīr al-Saʿīd Naṣr II
331/943	al-Amīr al-Ḥamīd Nūḥ I
343/954	al-Amīr al-Muʾayyad ʿAbd-al-Malik I

350/961	al-Amīr al-Sadīd Manṣūr I
365/976	al-Amīr al-Riḍā Nūḥ I
387/997	Manṣūr II
389/999	'Abd-al-Malik II
390–5/1000–5	Ismā'īl II al-Muntaṣir *Division of territories among Qarakhanids (Transoxania) and Ghaznavids (Khurasan)*

The Būyids or Buwayhids, 320–454/932–1062

Persia and Iraq

1. Line in Fārs and Khūzistān

322/934	'Imād al-Dawla 'Alī
338/949	'Aḍud al-Dawla Fanā-Khusraw
372/983	Sharaf al-Dawla Shīrzīl
380/990	Ṣamṣām al-Dawla Marzubān
388/998	Bahā' al-Dawla Fīrūz
403/1012	Sulṭān al-Dawla
412/1021	Musharrif al-Dawla Ḥasan
415/1024	'Imād al-Dīn Marzubān
440/1048	al-Malik al-Raḥīm Khusraw-Fīrūz
447–54/1055–62	Fūlād-Sutūn (in Fārs only) *Power in Fārs seized by the Shabānkāra'ī Kurdish chief Faḍlūya*

2. Line in Kirmān

324/936	Mu'izz al-Dawla Aḥmad
338/949	'Aḍud al-Dawla Fanā-Khusraw
372/983	Ṣamṣām al-Dawla Marzubān
388/998	Bahā' al-Dawla Fīrūz
403/1012	Qiwām al-Dawla
419–40/1028–48	'Imād al-Dīn Marzubān *Saljūq line of Qāwurd*

3. Line in Jibāl

320/932	'Imād al-Dawla 'Alī
335–66/947–77	Rukn al-Dawla Ḥasan

(a) Branch in Hamadān and Iṣfahān

366/977	Mu'ayyid al-Dawla Būya
373/983	Fakhr al-Dawla 'Alī
387/997	Shams al-Dawla
412–*c*.419/1021–*c*.1028	Samā' al-Dawla (under Kākūyid suzerainty)

(b) Branch in Rayy

366/977	Fakhr al-Dawla 'Alī
387–420/997–1029	Majd al-Dawla Rustam *Ghaznavid conquest*

4. Line in Iraq

334/945	Mu'izz al-Dawla Aḥmad
356/967	'Izz al-Dawla Bakhtiyār
367/978	'Aḍud al-Dawla Fanā-Khusraw
372/983	Ṣamṣām al-Dawla Marzubān
376/987	Sharaf al-Dawla Shīrzil
379/989	Bahā' al-Dawla Fīrūz
403/1012	Sulṭān al-Dawla
412/1021	Musharrif al-Dawla Ḥasan
416/1025	Jalāl al-Dawla Shīrzīl
435/1044	'Imād al-Dīn al-Marzubān
440–7/1048–55	al-Malik al-Raḥīm Khusraw-Fīrūz *Saljūq occupation of Baghdad*

The Ghaznavids, 366–582/977–1186

366–87/977–97	Sebüktigin
387–8/997–8	Ismā'īl
388–421/998–1030	Maḥmūd
421/1030 and 432/1041	Muḥammad
421–32/1030/41	Mas'ūd I
432–?440/1041–?1048	Mawdūd
?440/?1048–9	Mas'ūd II
?440/?1048–9	'Alī
?440–?443/?1049–?1052	'Abd al-Rashīd
443–51/1052–9	Farrukh-Zād
451–92/1059–99	Ibrāhīm
492–508/1099–1115	Mas'ūd III
508–9/1115–16	Shīr-Zād
509–11/1116–17	Malik Arslan
511–?552/1117–?1157	Bahrām Shāh
?552–5/?1157–60	Khusraw Shāh
555–82/1160–86	Khusraw Malik

The Saljūqs, 429–590/1038–1194

1. Great Saljūqs (Iraq and Persia) 429–590/1038–1194

429/1038	Rukn al-Dunyā wa-al-Dīn Toghrïl I (Ṭughril)
455/063	ʻAḍud al-Dawla Alp-Arslan
465/1072	Jalāl al-Dawla Malik-Shāh I
485/1092	Nāṣir al-Dīn Maḥmūd I
487/1094	Rukn al-Dīn Berk-yaruq (Barkiyāruq)
498/1105	Muʻizz al-Dīn Malik-Shāh II
498/1105	Ghiyāth al-Dīn Muḥammad I
511–52/1118–57	Muʻizz al-Dīn Sanjar (ruler in eastern Persia 490–552/1097–1157; after 511/1118 supreme Sultan of the Saljūq family)

In Iraq and western Persia only:

511/1118	Mughīth al-Dīn Maḥmud II
525/1131	Ghiyāth al-Dīn Dā'ūd
526/1132	Rukn al-Dīn Toghrïl II
529/1134	Ghiyāth al-Dīn Masʻūd
547/1152	Muʻīn al-Dīn Malik-Shāh III
548/1153	Rukn al-Dīn Muḥammad II
555/1160	Ghiyāth al-Dīn Sulaymān Shāh
556/1161	Muʻizz al-Dīn Arslan
571–90/1176–94	Rukn al-Dīn Toghrïl III *Khwārazmshāhs*

The Khwārazmshāhs

1. Afrīghids of Kāth AD 305–385/995

?–385/?–995	Abū ʻAbd Allāh Muḥammad *Ma'mūnid conquest*

2. Ma'mūnids of Gurgānj 385–408/995–1017

c.382/*c*.992	Abū ʻAlī Ma'mūn I
387/997	Abū al-Ḥasan ʻAlī
399/1009	Abū al-ʻAbbās Ma'mūn II
407–8/1017	Abū al-Ḥārith Muḥammad *Ghaznavid conquest*

3. Ghaznavid governors 408–25/1017–34

408/1017	Altuntash
423/1032	Hārūn ibn Altuntash (lieutenant of the nominal Khwārazmshāh, Saʻīd ibn Masʻūd of Ghazna, later independent of Ghazna)
425/1034	Ismāʻīl Khāndān ibn Altuntash (independent of Ghazna)
432/1041	*conquest of Khwārazm by the Oghuz Yabghu, Shāh Malik of Jand*

4. Line of Anūshtigin *c*.470–628/*c*.1077–1231, originally as governors for the Saljūqs, latterly as independent rulers in Central Asia and Persia

c.470/*c*.1077	Anūshtigin Gharcha'ī
490/1097	*Turkish governor Ekinchi b. Qochqar*
490/1097	Quṭb al-Dīn Muḥammad
521/1127	ʻAlā' al-Dīn Atsïz
551/1156	Il-Arslan
567/1172	ʻAlā' al-Dīn Tekish
567–89/1172–93	*Sultān Shāh ibn Il-Arslan, rival ruler in northern Khurasan*
596/1200	ʻAlā' al-Dīn Muḥammad
617–28/1220–31	Jalāl al-Dīn Mingburnu (? The exact form of this Turkish name is uncertain) *Mongol conquest*

The Ayyūbids, 564–end of the 9th century/1169–end of the 15th century

Egypt, Syria, Diyārbakr, the Yemen

1. In Egypt

564/1169	al-Malik al-Nāṣir I Ṣalāḥ al-Dīn (Saladin)
589/1193	al-Malik al-ʻAzīz ʻImād al-Dīn
595/1198	al-Malik al-Manṣūr Nāṣir al-Dīn
596/1200	al-Malik al-ʻĀdil I Sayf al-Dīn
615/1218	al-Malik al-Kāmil I Nāṣir al-Dīn
635/1238	al-Malik al-ʻĀdil II Sayf al-Dīn
637/1240	al-Malik al-Ṣāliḥ Najm al-Dīn Ayyūb
647/1249	al-Malik al-Muʻaẓẓam Tūrān-Shāh

648–50/1250–2	al-Malik al-Ashraf II Muẓaffar al-Dīn *Baḥrī Mamlūks*

2. In Damascus

582/1186	al-Malik al-Afḍal Nūr al-Dīn ʿAlī
592/1196	al-Malik al-ʿĀdil I Sayf al-Dīn
615/1218	al-Malik al-Muʿaẓẓam Sharaf al-Dīn
624/1227	al-Malik al-Nāṣir Ṣalāḥ al-Dīn Dā'ūd
626/1229	al-Malik al-Ashraf I Muẓaffar al-Dīn
634/1237	al-Malik al-Ṣāliḥ ʿImād al-Dīn, *first reign*
635/1238	al-Malik al-Kāmil I Nāṣir al-Dīn
635/1238	al-Malik al-ʿĀdil II Sayf al-Dīn
636/1239	al-Malik al-Ṣāliḥ Najm al-Din Ayyūb, *first reign*
637/1239	al-Malik al-Ṣāliḥ ʿImād al-Dīn, *second reign*
643/1245	al-Malik al-Ṣāliḥ Najm al-Din Ayyūb, *second reign*
647/1249	al-Malik al-Muʿaẓẓam Tūrān-Shāh (with Egypt)
648–58/1250–60	al-Malik al-Nāṣir II Ṣalāḥ al-Dīn *Mongol conquest*

The Mamlūks, 648–922/1250–1517

Egypt and Syria

1. Bahrī line 648–792/1250–1390

648/1250	Shajar al-Durr
648/1250	al-Muʿizz ʿIzz al-Dīn Aybak
655/1257	al-Manṣūr Nūr al-Dīn ʿAlī
657/1259	al-Muẓaffar Sayf al-Dīn Qutuz
658/1260	al-Ẓāhir Rukn al-Dīn Baybars I al-Bunduqdārī
676/1277	al-Saʿīd Nāṣir al-Dīn Baraka [or Berke] Khan
678/1280	al-ʿĀdil Badr al-Dīn Salāmish
678/1280	al-Manṣūr Sayf al-Dīn Qalā'ūn al-Alfī
689/1290	al-Ashraf Ṣalāḥ al-Dīn Khalīl
693/1294	al-Nāṣir Nāṣir al-Dīn Muḥammad, *first reign*
694/1295	al-ʿĀdil Zayn al-Dīn Kitbughā
696/1297	al-Manṣūr Ḥusām al-Dīn Lājīn
698/1299	al-Nāṣir Nāṣir al-Dīn Muḥammad, *second reign*
708/1309	al-Muẓaffar Rukn-al-Dīn Baybars II al-Jāshankīr
709/1309	al-Nāṣir Nāṣir al-Dīn Muḥammad, *third reign*
741/1340	al-Manṣūr Sayf al-Dīn Abū-Bakr
742/1341	al-Ashraf ʿAlā' al-Dīn Kūjūk
743/1342	al-Nāṣir Shihāb al-Dīn Aḥmad
743/1342	al-Ṣāliḥ ʿImād al-Dīn Ismāʿīl
746/1345	al-Kāmil Sayf al-Dīn Shaʿbān I
747/1346	al-Muẓaffar Sayf al-Dīn Ḥājjī I
748/1347	al-Nāṣir Nāṣir-al-Dīn al-Ḥasan, *first reign*
752/1351	aṣ-Ṣāliḥ Ṣalāh al-Dīn Ṣāliḥ
755/1354	al-Nāṣir Nāṣir al-Dīn al-Ḥasan, *second reign*
762/1361	al-Manṣūr Ṣalāḥ al-Dīn Muḥammad
764/1363	al-Ashraf Nāṣir al-Dīn Shaʿbān II
778/1376	al-Manṣūr ʿAlā' al-Dīn ʿAlī
783/1382	al-Ṣālih, Ṣalāh al-Dīn Ḥājjī, *first reign*
784/1382	al-Ẓāhir Sayf al-Dīn Barqūq [Burjī]
791/1389	Ḥājjī II (*second reign, with honorific title* al-Muẓaffar)

2. Burjī line 784–922/1382–1517

784/1382	al-Ẓāhir Sayf al-Dīn Barqūq, *first reign*
791/1389	Ḥājjī II (*second reign,* Baḥrī)
792/1390	al-Ẓāhir Sayf al-Dīn Barqūq, *second reign*
801/1399	al-Nāṣir Nāṣir al-Dīn Faraj, *first reign*
808/1405	al-Manṣūr ʿIzz al-Dīn ʿAbd al-ʿAzīz
808/1405	al-Nāṣir Nāṣir al-Dīn Faraj, *second reign*

815/1412	al-ʿĀdil al-Mustaʿīn (ʿAbbāsid caliph, proclaimed sultan)
815/1412	al-Mu'ayyad Sayf al-Dīn Shaykh
824/1421	al-Muẓaffar Aḥmad
824/1421	al-Ẓāhir Sayf al-Dīn Ṭaṭār
824/1421	al-Ṣāliḥ Nāṣir al-Dīn Muḥammad
825/1422	al-Ashraf Sayf al-Dīn Barsbay
841/1437	al-ʿAzīz Jamāl al-Dīn Yūsuf
842/1438	al-Ẓāhir Sayf al-Dīn Jaqmaq
857/1453	al-Manṣūr Fakhr al-Dīn ʿUthmān
857/1453	al-Ashraf Sayf al-Dīn Ināl
865/1461	al-Mu'ayyad Shihāb al-Dīn Aḥmad
865/1461	al-Ẓāhir Sayf al-Dīn Khūshqadam
872/1467	al-Ẓāhir Sayf al-Dīn Bilbay
872/1468	al-Ẓāhir Timurbughā
872/1468	al-Ashraf Sayf al-Dīn Qā'it Bay
901/1496	al-Nāṣir Muḥammad
903/1498	al-Ẓāhir Qānṣūḥ
905/1500	al-Ashraf Jānbalāt
906/1501	al-ʿĀdil Sayf al-Dīn Tūmān Bay
906/1501	al-Ashraf Qānṣūḥ al-Ghawrī
922/1517	al-Ashraf Tūmān Bay
	Ottoman conquest

Muḥammad ʿAlī's Line 1220–1372/1805–1953

Egypt

1220/1805	Muḥammad ʿAlī Pasha
1264/1848	Ibrāhīm Pasha
1264/1848	ʿAbbās I Pasha
1270/1854	Saʿīd Pasha
1280/1863	Ismāʿīl (assumed title of Khedive in 1284/1867)
1296/1879	Tawfīq
1309/1892	ʿAbbās II Ḥilmī
1333/1914	Ḥusayn Kāmil (assumed title of Sultan)
1335/1917	Aḥmad Fu'ād I (assumed title of King in 1340/1922)
1355/1936	Fārūq
1371–2/1952–3	Fu'ād II
	Republican régime established

Index

The index is designed to draw together themes and subjects. People, places and individual works are covered within main entries and by extensive cross-referencing. Numbers in **bold** refer to main entries.

abjad, **22–3**, 157
abridgements, **23–4**, 175, 473
abuse, *see hijā'*
abyaḍ, *see mawāliyā*
actors and acting, medieval, **52–4**, 134, 208
  buffoonery, 53, 514
  ḥākī/ḥākiya, 53
  ḥikāya, 52, 53, 54, 441, 596
  khayāliyyūn, 53
  khulbus, 53
  kurraj, *karj*, 53, 54, 548, 596, 701, 767
  la''ābūn, 53
  la'b, 53, 441
  la'ib, 53, 441
  li'b, 53
  mayāmis, 53
  muḍḥik, 53, 572
  muḥabbaẓ, 53, 441
  muḥākī, 441
  mukhāyil, 441
  mukhāyilūn, 53, 54, 596
  nuqūṭ, 54
  raqqāṣūn, 53
  raqṣ, 53, 54
  ṣafā'ina, 53, 514
  yaḥkī, 54
  see also khayāl; masks and masquerades; *mukhannathūn*; shadow-play; theatre and drama, medieval
adab, **54–6**, 57, 258, 611
  abridgements, 23
  anecdotes, 55, 284
  anthologies, 94, 95, 609, 807
  artistic prose, 106, 617, 618
  boon companions, 571
  commentaries, 174
  dialect, 189
  didactic, 193
  encyclopedias, 90, 208
  epigrams, 210
  fables, 214
  fiction, 228, 229, 230
  folklore, 235
  geography and cosmography, 65, 245, 246
  hazl, 281
  Hebrew translation, 283
  ḥikma, 286
  illustration, 496
  khurāfa, 444
  legends, 465
  love, 478
  maqāma, 55, 507, 508
  mawālī, 518
  proverbs, 55, 622
  secretaries, 698
  truth, 228
  ẓarf, 821
al-adab al-hazlī, 294
al-adab al-sha'bī, *see* popular literature
adīb, **57**, 622
admonition, *see under* oratory and sermons: *maw'iẓa*
aghrāḍ, 243, 607
aghṣān, *see under* prosody; *ghuṣn*
'ajab, 754
'ajā'ib literature (*mirabilia*), **65–6**, 241, 244, 247, 611, 754
'Ajam, **66**
ajrās al-ḥurūf, 462
al-ajwiba al-muskita, 616
akhbār, *see under* anecdotes
akhbār al-shu'arā', *see under* anecdotes: poets
akhdh, *see under sariqa*
akhlāq, *see mathālib*
'aks, *see* rhetorical figures
alfāẓ, 90, 798
alif, 620
Aljamia, **80–1**
allegory, **81**, 229
allusion and intertextuality, **81–3**, 90, 396, 398, 616, 690
  ishāra, 81, **398**

talmīḥ, 82, 690
alphabet, *see abjad*
amazement, *see ta'jīb*
'āmmiyya, see under colloquial Arabic
'amūd al-shi'r, **89**, 472
analogy, *see under* rhetorical figures: *tamthīl*
ancients and moderns, **90–1**, 472, 523, 653, 655, 691–2, 781
anecdotes, 214
adab, 55
anthologies, 95
bārid, 294
biographical, 152
encyclopedias, 208
fiction, 228, 229
fukāha, 294
hazl and *jidd*, 281
hijā', 284
historical, 291
humorous, 294–5
laṭīfa, 294
love, 478
mawāliyā, 518
muḍḥika, 294
mulḥa, 294
nādira, 294
poets, 134, 167
animal poetry, 592, 606, 631, 671
animal tales, 214, 229, 235, 406–7, 476
anthologies, medieval, **94–6**, 154, 174, 190, 208, 210, 235, 285, 290, 472, 476, 478, 489, 564, 609, 638, 807
antithesis, *see under* rhetorical figures: *muṭābaqa*
anwā', see genres, poetic
aphorism, *see ḥikma*
apostrophe, *see under* rhetorical figures: *iltifāt*
'aqd, 609
aqra', see under prosody: *ṭamm/aqra'*
a'rāb, see bedouin
arḍah, see under dancers and dancing: war dance
arkān, see genres, poetic
art, *see ṣinā'a*
artifice, *see maṭbū'* and *maṣnū'*
artistic prose, 95, **105–6**, 208, 615–16, 618, 655, 677, 721, 768, 807
'arūḍ, see prosody
asālīb, see genres, poetic
asceticism, *see* mysticism; *zuhdiyya*
asmāṭ, see prosody
aṣnāf, see genres, poetic
assent, *see under taṣdīq*
astrology, 194, 257, 290, 603
astronomy, 244, 245, 246, 476, 598, 775
'atāba, see zajal, modern
aṭlāl, 249, 582, 631, 633, 806
audio cassettes, 190
autobiographical novel, 112
autobiography, medieval, **111–12**
autobiography, modern, **112–13**
awā'il, 241
Aws, *see* tribes
Ayyām al-'Arab, see Battle Days

bāba, see shadow-play; theatre and drama, medieval
badī', see rhetorical figures
badīha, see improvisation
badīhan, 592
badī'iyyāt, **124**, 543
badw, see bedouin
baḥr, see prosody
bā'iyya, see prosody
balāgha, see rhetoric and poetics
ballads, 519, 610
banquet poetry, *see khamriyya*
barāmīj, see under education, medieval: teachers
bārid, see under anecdotes
basīṭ, see prosody
bāṭil, see under truth and falsehood
Battle Days, 55, **141**, 150, 234, 237–8, 406, 609, 611, 623, 726
bayān, see rhetoric and poetics; *'ilm al-bayān*
bayt, see prosody
bedouin, 90, **146–8**, 249, 394, 406, 467, 479, 482, 547, 570, 592, 605, 623, 630, 647, 650, 652, 657, 670, 694, 717, 736, 780, 781
beggars, **134–5**, 189, 236, 610
bid'a, 602
biographical dictionaries, *see* biography, medieval
biography, medieval, **150–2**
autobiography, 111, 113
dictionaries, 151, 289, 290, 291, 505
manāqib, 504–5
mudhakkirāt, 113
mystical, 739
poets, 406, 651
prophets, 211, 401
ṭabaqāt, 151, 726, 739
birdhawniyyāt, see under horse poetry
blame, 609, 655, 693
blank verse, **154**
blood-money, *see under dīya*
boasting, *see fakhr*
book painting, *see* literature and the visual arts
books and book-making, **154–60**, 235, 470–1
boon companion, *see nadīm*

borrowing, *see under* rhetorical figures: *iqtibās*; *sariqa*
brevity, *see* *ījāz*
brigand poets, *see* *ṣaʿalīk*
buffoonery, *see* actors and acting, medieval
buṭūlī, *see* epic poetry

caesura, *see* prosody
CAL, *see under* canonical Arabic literature
calligraphy, 157, 194, 614
camel poetry, 406, 582, 606, 631, 632, 645, 646, 759, 806
campsites, deserted, *see under* *aṭlāl*
canonical Arabic literature, 228–30
cantillation, *see under* music and poetry: *tarannum*
catalogue, 694, 821
censorship, **171–2**, 615, 701, 771
centos, 83
charm, *see* *ẓarf*
chastity, 249, 821
chivalry, *see under* *futuwwa*; *muruwwa*
chronicles, *see* historical literature
chronogram, **173**
chronology, *see* historical literature
cinema and literature, **173–4**, 770
civil strife, *see under* *fitna*
classes, *see under* biography, medieval: *ṭabaqāt*
clients, *see* *mawālī*
clown, *see under* actors and acting, medieval: *khulbus*
codex, 154, 155, 157
collections, *see* *dīwān*
colloquial Arabic, 113, 189, 191, 192; *see also* dialect in literature; popular literature; *zajal*, modern
comedians, *see under* actors and acting: *mayāmis*
commentaries, 23, 124, 156, **174–5**, 194, 200, 213, 473, 508, 523, 601, 603, 618, 652, 776
commitment, **175–6**, 475, 613, 770
compilations, *see* anthologies, medieval; encyclopedias, medieval
conceits, *see under* *maʿānī*
conciseness, *see under* *ījāz*; *tawqīʿ*
condolence, *see under* *taʿziya*
congratulation, 173, 655
congruence, *see under* rhetorical figures: *mumāthala*
connection, *see under* *ribāṭ*
conquest, *see* *futūḥ*
consequence, *see under* rhetorical figures: *istitbāʿ*
contempt, *see* *hijāʾ*; satire, medieval
contradicting poems, *see* *naqāʾiḍ*
convents, *see under* education, medieval: convents
converts, 518
copyists, *see under* scribes
correspondence, *see under* rhetorical figures: *muqābala*
cosmology, 476, 556
courtly love, **176–7**, 476, 546, 565
craft, *see* *ṣināʿa*
criticism, *see* literary criticism
cryptography, 534
curtain-play, *see* shadow-play

dakhāla, 147
dancers and dancing
  ghawāzī, 134
  mukhannathūn, 548, 596
  raqṣ, 53, 513
  samāʿ, 738
  war dance, 570
  women, 134
  zaffānūn, 54
  see also masks and masquerades
dār malʿab, see theatre and drama, medieval
ḍarb, *see* prosody
ḍarūra, *see* prosody
dawʿā, 524
dawr, 737
debate literature, **186**, 583, 605
derision, *see under* *sukhriyya*; *tahakkum*
descriptive poetry, *see* *waṣf*
desert journey, *see under* *qaṣīda*: *raḥīl*
deserted campsites, *see under* *aṭlāl*
detective stories, 612
developing, *see* *sariqa*
dhamm, *see under* blame
dialect in literature
  medieval, **189–90**, 479, 623
  modern, **190–1**
  see also *zajal*
dialogue in literature
  medieval, **191**, 434, 726
  modern, **191–2**
diaries, 112
dictionaries, *see* lexicography
didactic literature, **193–4**, 593, 609, 738, 828
diffuseness, 390
digression, *see under* rhetorical figures: *istiṭrād*
dīra, 147
dirge, *see* *rithāʾ*
discipline, *see under* *fann*; *ʿilm*
disputation, 200
divination, 235
division, *see under* rhetorical figures: *taqsīm*

dīwān, **195–6**, 244, 652, 655, 690, 698, 726
dīya, 147
double entendre, *see under* rhetorical figures: *tawriya*
drama, *see under* theatre and drama
dreams and visions, 235, 236, 610, 631
du'ā', 483
dūbayt, dūbaytī, **197–8**, 210

education, medieval, **199–201**, 238, 256
  convents, 201
  law schools, 200
  learned assemblies, 199, 200
  madrasa, 193, 200, 201, 256, 470, 475, 598
  teachers, 151, 199–200, 201
  see also maqāma
education, modern, **201–3**
  literacy, 201, 202, 203, 736
  military schools, 201
  missionary schools, 202
  professional schools, 201
  universities, 202
  vocational education, 203
effeminates, *see mukhannathūn*
electronic media, 171, 615, 736, 770, 772
elegance, *see ẓarf*
elegy, *see under rithā'*; *tashbīb*
elephant poetry, 244
eloquence, *see* rhetoric and poetics
embellishments, *see* rhetorical figures
emblematic poetry, 233
emotionalism, 231
emphasis, *see under mubālagha*
emulation, *see mu'āraḍa*
encomium, *see madīḥ*
encyclopedias, medieval, 66, 90, 94, 193, **208–9**, 235, 246, 247, 281, 289, 290, 471, 534, 547, 698
endurance, *see under ṣabr*
enjambment, *see* prosody
epic poetry, 154, **209–10**, 294, 498, 570, 592, 610, 611, 726, 780
epigram, **210**, 284, 394, 479, 578, 639, 693, 694
epistles, 52, 66, 81, 105, 230; *see also* letters
equilibrium, *see under* rhetorical figures: *muwāzana*
equivalence, *see under musāwāt*
erotic poetry, *see ghazal*; *mujūn*
etymology, 468
eulogy, *see madīḥ*
exegesis, Koranic, 81, 156, **211–13**, 239, 243–4, 390, 391, 472, 473, 495, 524, 526, 739
exemplum, *see under* rhetorical figures: *tamthīl*
exhortation, *see under waṣiyya*
existentialism, 175
extemporizing, *see* improvisation

fables, 193, **214**, 229, 235, 425, 476, 507, 610, 611, 774
faḍā'il, 504–5, 516
fairy tales, 610
faithfulness, 147
fakhr, 83, 147, 210, **215–17**, 243, 249, 284, 406, 407, 433, 482, 483, 578, 582, 605, 606, 609, 630, 638, 650, 651, 759, 781
falsafa, 602
famous firsts, *see under awā'il*
fann, 244
faṣāḥa, *see* literary criticism, medieval; rhetoric and poetics
faṣl, *see* shadow-play; theatre and drama, medieval
fatalism, 146
faults, *see under* merits and faults
fertility rites, 53, 54
festivals, 53, 514, 596, 736, 767
fiction, medieval, **228–30**, 507
fiction, modern, **230–3**, 573, 610
  autobiographical novel, 112
  detective story, 612
  novel, 236, 612, 613, 736, 777
  short story, 231, 232, 233, 236, 573, 607, 612
  spy novel, 612
  thriller, 612
figural poetry, **233**
figurative language, 473, 495–6, 504, 655, 654, 661, 781, 782
figures of speech, *see* rhetorical figures
fīliyyāt, *see under* elephant poetry
fine arts and literature, *see* literature and the visual arts
fiqh, 212, **234**, 256, 470, 551, 552, 602, 616
fitna, 239
fityān, *see futuwwa*
flattery, 483
flower poetry, 244, 546, 632, 806; *see also* nature: classical poetry
flytings, *see naqā'iḍ*
folklore, **234–6**, 286, 465, 479, 514, 519, 592, 610, 612, 618, 622, 726, 771; *see also* popular literature
form, *see under ṣūra*
free prose, 677
free verse, **236–7**, 609, 619, 646, 665, 778
freedmen, *see mawālī*
fukāha, *see under* anecdotes

funūn, *see* genres, poetic
fuqahā', 599
fuṣḥā, 113, 189, 190, 191, 192, 569, 778
fuṣūl, 106, 617
futūḥ, **237–40**, 610, 611, 726
futuwwa, **240–1**, 741, 821

gambling, 684
gardens, *see under* flower poetry; nature: classical poetry
gaṣṣāds, 569
genealogy, 150, 606, 780
generosity, *see under karam*
genres, poetic, **243–4**, 609, 631, 651
  arkān, 243
  fakhr, 215
  hijā', 284
  ḥikma, 286
  madḥ, 243
  maḥāsin wa-masāwī, 489
  new, 612
  popular literature, 610, 611
  qawā'id, 243
geographical literature, **244–7**, 610–11, 617; *see also 'ajā'ib* literature; travel literature
gesture, *see ishāra*
ghajar, 134, 209
gharaḍ, 462
gharīb, 650
ghawāzī, *see under* dancers and dancing
ghazal, 244, **249–50**, 609
  anthologies, 94
  courtly love, 176
  education, 199
  epigrams, 210
  hijā', 284
  homoerotic, 250, 547
  illustration, 475
  jāhiliyya, 407, 631
  khamriyya and, 433, 434
  maqāma, 229, 507
  metaphor, 523
  muḥdathūn, 546
  mujūn and, 547
  music and, 555
  muwashshaḥ, 564, 565
  mysticism, 738
  nabaṭī, 570
  naqā'iḍ, 578
  obscene, 250
  qaṣīda, 630, 631, 632
  qiṭ'a, 638
  romanticism, 665
  see also tashbīb
ghinā', *see under* music and poetry
ghosts, 234–5
ghuluww, *see under* rhetorical figures: *mubālagha*, *ghuluww*
ghuṣn, *see* prosody
gisida, *see qaṣīda*
glosses, *see* commentaries
gnomic poetry, *see ḥikma*
good, *see under ma'rūf*
gracefulness, *see ẓarf*
grammar and grammarians, 57, 174, 175, 201, 212, 243–4, 245, **254–7**, 391, 461, 467, 472, 474, 478, 518, 523, 567, 571, 617, 652, 654, 694, 726, 738, 776
Greek literature, **257–8**, 601, 653
guilds, 240, 241, 596, 598
gypsies, *see under ghajar*

ḥabsiyya, *see under* prison poetry
ḥadātha, *see under* modernism
ḥadīth, **261**, 468, 616
  acting, 53
  adab. 55
  adīb, 57
  'ajā'ib, 65
  biography, 151, 152
  books, 155, 156
  borrowings from, 396
  commentaries, 174
  dialogue, 191
  education, 201
  encyclopedias, 208
  exegesis, 211, 212
  futūḥ, 239
  geography, 246
  khurāfa, 229, 444
  legends, 464, 465
  love, 478
  maqāma, 507
  mi'rāj, 526
  muqaddima, 551
  mysticism, 551
  nadīm, 571
  proverbs, 623
  riddles, 469
  samā', 684
  satire, 694
  sermons, 594
  sīra, 726
  style, 617, 656, 657
  transmission chain, 228, 235, 238, 261, 289
  tribes, 780
hagiography, *see manāqib* literature
ḥajj, 247
hajw, *see hijā'*; satire, medieval

ḥakawātī, *see* theatre and drama, modern
ḥākī/ḥākiya, *see* acting and actors, medieval
ḥall, 609
ḥalaq, *see under* education, medieval: learned assemblies
ḥamāsa, *see* epic poetry
ḥaqīqa, 781
Ḥarb, *see* tribes
ḥāshiya, *ḥawāshī*, *see* commentaries
hātif, *see* inspiration
hawā, *see* love theory
ḥawliyyāt, 652
hazaj, *see* prosody
hazl, 230, **281**, 294, 611, 657, 694, 768; *see also* humour
hazza, 754
Hebrew literature, relations with Arabic, **281–3**
heresy, 828
heroic tales, 610
heroism, *see under muruwwa*
hijā', 243, 244, 249, **284–5**, 473, 651, 693, 694
  anthologies, 94
  epigrams, 210
  fakhr and, 215
  jāhiliyya, 406, 407
  madīḥ, 482
  mathālib, 516
  modern poetry, 607
  moral code and, 147, 193
  naqā'iḍ, 578
  qaṣīda, 630
  qiṭ'a, 638
  sukhf, 743
  tribes, 781
ḥikāya, *see* actors and acting, medieval
ḥikma, 193, 210, 214, 243, 244, **286–7**, 476, 602, 609, 616, 623, 650, 828
ḥīla, 754
Hilālī, 569, 570
ḥilm, 215–16
Ḥimyar, *see* tribes
historical literature, 150, 193, 211, 212, 231, 244, 284, **289–82**, 609, 610, 611, 617, 779
hobby-horse, *see under* actors and acting, medieval: *kurraj*
homilectics, *see* didactic literature; oratory and sermons
homosexuality, 250, 548, 694
honour, 569; *see under 'irḍ*; *sharaf*
horse poetry, 244, 605, 606, 631
hospitality, 94, 146
ḥujja, 401
ḥumaynī, **294**
humour, 190, 214, 228, **294–5**, 483, 508, 546, 547, 578, 610, 611
  muzāḥ, 53
  nukta, 618
  see also hazl
hunting poetry, *see ṭardiyya*
ḥusn al-ta'līl, *see* rhetorical figures
huz' sakhīf, *see* theatre and drama, medieval
hyperbole, *see under* rhetorical figures: *mubālagha*

ibā', 670
Ibāḍīs, *see* Zaydīs
'ibra, 193
'iffa, *see under* chastity
iftikhār, *see fakhr*
īghāl, 658
ighāra, 690
ighrā', 243
ighrāq, *see under* rhetorical figures; *mubālagha*
īhām, *see* prosody
īhām, *see under* rhetorical figures: *tawriya*
īhām al-tadāḍd, *see under* rhetorical figures: *muṭābaqa*
ihtizāz, 754
ījāz, 210, **390**, 616, 654
i'jāz al-Qur'ān, 213, **390–1**, 585, 617, 677, 473, 781
ijāza, 605
ijtihād, 234
ikfā', *see* prosody
ikhtirā', 691
ilāhiyyāt, 422
ilhām, *see* inspiration
'illa, *see* prosody
'ilm, 235, 244, 422, 473, 616
iltidhādh, 754
iltifāt, *see* rhetorical figures
iltizām, *see* commitment; *luzūm mā lā yalzam*
imagery, 545–6, 616, 754
imagination, **393–4**, 473, 606, 754, 782
imitation, *see mu'āraḍa*
impossibility, *see under istiḥāla*
improvisation, **394**, 508, 572, 592, 593, 605, 639, 671, 760; *see also under badīhan*; oral composition; *riddiyyih*
incitement, *see under ighrā'*
inflexions, *see under i'rāb*
inḥiṭāṭ, 691
innovation, *see under bid'a*
inshā', *see* artistic prose; secretaries
inshād, *see under* music and poetry
inspiration, **396**
intention, *see under gharaḍ*
intertextuality, *see* allusion and intertextuality

intiḥāl, 690
introduction, *see muqaddima*
invective, *see hijā'*; *naqā'iḍ*; satire, medieval
iqnā', 654
iqtibās, *see* rhetorical figures
iqtiḍāb, *see* improvisation
iqwā', *see* prosody
i'rāb, 189
'irḍ, 670
irony, 694
irtijāl, *see* improvisation
irtijālan, 592
ishāb, 390
ishāra, 81, **398**
'ishq, *see* love theory
ishtiqāq, *see under* rhetorical figures: *jinās*
ishtirāk, 691
Islām, 736
Islāmiyyūn, 90, 563
isnād, 23, 208, 238, 239
isrā', 526
Isrā'īliyyāt, **400–1**
isti'āra, *see* metaphor
istiḥāla, 781
istiḥqāq, 691
istikhdām, *see* rhetorical figures
istitbā', *see* rhetorical figures
istithnā', *see under* rhetorical figures: *ta'kīd al-madḥ*
istiṭrād, see rhetorical figures
īṭā', *see* prosody
'itab, 243
i'tilāf, *see under* rhetorical figures: *murā'āt al-naẓīr*
iṭnāb, 390
izdiwāj, 677

jāhiliyya, 90, 146, 147, 154, **406–7**, 444, 475, 482, 522, 545, 548, 563, 569, 582, 598, 623, 630, 631, 632, 647, 649, 670, 767
jahl, 216
jam', *see* rhetorical figures
jam' ma'a tafrīq, *see* rhetorical figures
jam' ma'a taqsīm, *see* rhetorical figures
jam' ma'a taqsīm wa-tafrīq, *see* rhetorical figures
jazāla, 616
jester, *see under* actors and acting, medieval: *muḍḥik*
jidd, 230, 281, 294, 657
al-jidd wa-al-hazl, *see adab*; *hazl*
jihād, 239, 726
jinās, *see* rhetorical figures
jinn, 235–5, 390, 444, 671
jinnī, *see* inspiration

jokes/joking, *see hazl*; humour
journalism, *see* press
judge, *see under qāḍī*
jurist, *see under fuqahā'*
juz', *see* prosody

kādhiba, 782
kāfiyya, *see* prosody
kāhin, 609, 616, 651, 677
kalām, **422–3**, 478, 482, 495, 551, 585, 586, 602, 616, 739
kalām manthūr, 105
kāmil, *see* prosody
kān wa-kān, **425–6**
Karagöz, *see* shadow-play; theatre and drama, medieval
karam, 166, 215–16, 670
karj, *see* actors and acting, medieval
kātib, *see* secretaries
khabab, *see under* prosody: *mutadārik*
khabar, 617
khafīf, *see* prosody
khalā'a, 546
Khalīl's metrical circles, *see* prosody
khamriyya, 82, 83, 177, 191, 210, 216, 244, 250, **433–5**, 546, 547, 555, 564, 582, 583, 632, 638, 639, 684, 806, 828
khānqāh, *see under* education, medieval: converts
kharajāt, 565
kharja, *see muwashshaḥ*
khaṭīb, *see under* oratory and sermons: preachers
khayāl, 120, **441–2**, 563, 596, 631, 694, 768; *see also* acting and actors, medieval; shadow-play
khayāl al-izār, *see* shadow-play
khayāl al-sitāra, *see* shadow-play
khayāl al-ẓill, *see* shadow-play
khayāliyyun, *see* actors and acting, medieval
khiṭaṭ, *see* historical literature
khiyāl, *see khayāl*
khizāna, *see* libraries
khulāṣa, *see* abridgements
khulbus, see actors and acting, medieval
khurāfa, 229, **433–4**
khurūj, *see* prosody
khuṭba, *see* oratory and sermons
kidhb, *see under* truth and falsehood
kināya, *see* rhetorical figures
kitāb, *see* books and book-making
kitāba, 677, 721
kitābat al-inshā', *see* artistic prose
kufr, 602
kurraj/karj, *see* actors and acting, medieval
kuttāb, *see* education, medieval; secretaries

la''ābūn, *see* actors and acting, medieval
la'b, *see* actors and acting, medieval
la'ba, *see* theatre and drama, medieval
ladhdha, 754
laff wa-nashr, *see* rhetorical figures
lafẓ and ma'nā, **461–2**, 504, 585, 586, 655, 691; *see also under ma'nā*
lafẓī, 657
lāhūt, 422
lahw, 243, 244
la'ib, *see* actors and acting, medieval
lamentation, *see rithā'*
lampoon, *see hijā'*
landscape, 631, 806
laṭīfa, *see under* anecdotes
law, *see under fiqh*; *ijtihād*; *majāz*; *muṣannaf*; *qiyās*; *sharī'a*
learned class, *see under 'ulamā'*
legends, 212, 234, **464–5**, 610, 617, 726, 736
lesson, *see under 'ibra*
letters, 95, 616, 617, 678, 699, 807; *see also under* epistles
lexicography, 175, **467–9**, **469–70**, 472, 478, 518, 523, 656
li'b, *see* actors and acting, medieval
libertinage, *see mujūn*
libraries, medieval, 158–9, **470–1**
licentiousness, *see mujūn*
literacy, 201, 202, 203, 736
literalness, *see under ḥaqīqa*
literary criticism, **472–4**, **474–5**, 483, 504, 508, 587, 652, 694
literary history, 290, 291
literary journals, *see* press
literature and the visual arts, 157, 158, 233, **475–7**
logic, 472, 473, 551
love poetry, *see ghazal*
love sickness, *see under ṣibā*
love theory, 95, **477–9**
loyalty, *see under ṣidq*; *wafā'*
lughz, 479, 639, 807
luzūm mā lā yalzam, **480**, 660
lyric poetry, *see ghazal*; *qaṣīda*

ma'ānī, 82, 89, 90
ma'āthir, 504–5, 516
macaronic verse, *see mulamma'a*
madhhab, *see under* education: law schools
al-madhhab al-kalāmī, **482**, 658
madīd, *see* prosody
madīḥ, *madḥ*, 243, 244, 473, **482–4**, 583, 609, 651, 655
  allegory, 81
  courtly love, 177
  epigrams, 210
  fakhr, 216
  ghazal, 249, 250
  hijā', 284
  jāhiliyya, 406
  modern poetry, 607
  mujūn, 547
  obscenity, 397
  qaṣīda, 630, 631, 632–3
  qiṭ'a, 638, 639
  religious, 650
  rithā', 664
  ṭardiyya, 760
  truth, 781
  zajal, 819
  zuhdiyya, 828
madrasa, *see under* education
mafākhir, 504–5, 516
magazines, *see* press
maghāzī, 610, 611, 726
magic, 235, 284, 603, 654
maḥāsin, 516
maḥāsin wa-masāwī, **489**
maḥmal, 596
majāz, 473, **495–6**, 661, 781
  mursal, 496, 655, 661
majlis, *see under* education, medieval: learned assemblies
maktab, *see under* education, medieval: schools
maktaba, *see* libraries, medieval
mal'ab, *see* theatre and drama, medieval
malāḥim, 401, **498**
malḥama, *see malāḥim*; epic poetry
malḥamī, *see* epic poetry
mamdūḥ, *see* patronage
ma'nā, 95, 244, 390, 461–2, **504**, 585, 586, 781; *see also lafẓ and ma'nā*
manāqib literature, **504–5**, 516
ma'nawī, 657
manhūk, *see* prosody
m'annā, *see zajal*, modern
manẓar, *see* theatre and drama, medieval
maqāma, 52, 55, 106, 113, 134, 174, 186, 190, 193, 229, 230, 423, **507–8**, 574, 609, 622, 678, 768, 807
maqṣūra, *see qaṣīda*
maqṭū'a, *see qiṭ'a*
marāthī, *see rithā'*
mardūf, *see* prosody
markaz, *see* prosody
ma'rūf, 670
Marxism, 175, 475
masā'il, 616
mashṭūr, *see* prosody
mashyakhā, *see under* education, medieval: teachers

masks and masquerades, **513–14**, 767
maṣnū', *see maṭbū'* and *maṣnū'*
masquerades, *see* masks and masquerades
masraḥ, *masraḥiyya*, *see* theatre and drama, medieval
maṭbū' and *maṣnū'*, 89, 396, **516**, 655, 721
mathal, *see under* metaphor; parables; proverbs
mathālib, 284, **516–17**, 578, 611
mathematics, 245, 246, 257, 556, 775
maṭla', *see* prosody
mawālī, **518**, 698, 717, 724
mawalid, 611
mawāliyā, 210, **518–19**, 819
maw'iẓa, see oratory and sermons
mawlid, 54
mawsū'a, *see* encyclopedias
mawwāl, *see mawāliyā*
maxims, 55, 95, 243, 650
mayāmis, *see* actors and acting, medieval
mechanics, 257
medicine, 476, 478, 654, 738, 775
mējanā, *see zajal*, modern
merits and faults, *see maḥāsin wa-masāwī*
metaphor, 81, 82, 9 8, 90, 243, 496, **522–4**, 545, 546, 617, 622, 654, 655, 658, 661, 806
metaphysics, *see under ilāhiyyāt*; *lāhūt*
metres, poetic, *see* prosody
military schools, *see* education, modern
mirabilia, *see 'ajā'ib* literature
miracles, *see under mu'jiza*
mi'rāj literature, **525–7**
miṣrā', *see* prosody
missionaries, 201
  publications, 614
  schools, 202
mockery, *see under sukhriyya*; *tahakkum*
modernism, 606, 608–9; *see also* ancients and moderns
moral, *see* didactic literature
motifs, *see under ma'ānī*
mrādd, 570
mu'addib, *see* education: teachers
mu'allaqāt, 147, 394
mu'allim, *see under* education, medieval: teachers
mu'ammā, 479, **534**
mu'āraḍa, 390, 489, **534**, 578, 587
mu'assasa, *see* prosody
mubālagha, *see* rhetorical figures
mubālagha maqbūla, *see* rhetorical figures
mubayyat, 294
mudarris, 201
mudhakkirāt, 112–13, 593–4
muḍḥik, *see* actors and acting, medieval
muḍḥika, *see under* anecdotes
mufākhara, *see* debate literature; *fakhr*; poetic contests
mufāqara, *see under* irony
muftī, 201
mughanniyāt, *see* singers and musicians
muḥabbaẓ, *see* actors and acting, medieval
muḥaddith, 57, 152
muhājāt, *see hijā'*
muḥākāt, 754
muḥākī, *see* actors and acting, medieval
muḥakkakāt, 652
muharrij, *see* masks and masquerades
muḥdathūn, 89, 90–1, 210, 286, 472, 483, **545–6**, 563, 632, 653
muhmal, *see* prosody
mujālasa, *see under* education, medieval; learned assemblies
mujarrada, *see* prosody
mu'jiza, 654
mujtathth, see prosody
mujūn, 177, 216, 249, 250, **546–8**, 594, 639, 702, 781, 828; *see also sukhf*
mujūniyya, *see under ghazal*: obscene
mukātabāt, see under letters
mukhaḍram, 90, 406, 545, **548**, 563, 631, 828
al-mukhalla al-basīṭ, *see under* prosody: *basīṭ*
mukhammas, *see* strophic poetry
mukhannathūn, 54, **548**, 596, 694
mukhāyil, *see* actors and acting, medieval
mukhāyilūn, *see* actors and acting, medieval
mukhayyila, 782
mukhtārāt, *see* anthologies, medieval
mukhtaṣar, *see* abridgements
mulakhkhaṣ, *see* abridgements
mulamma'a, **549**
mulḥ, *see under* anecdotes
mumāthala, *see* rhetorical figures
munāqaḍāt, *see naqā'iḍ*
munāẓara, *see under* debate literature; disputation
munsariḥ, *see* prosody
munsha'āt, *see under* letters
muntakhabāt, *see* anthologies, medieval
muqābala, *see* rhetorical figures
muqaddima, **551–2**, 617
muqaṭṭa'a, *see qiṭ'a*
muqayyada, *see* prosody
murā'āt al-naẓīr, *see* rhetorical figures
murabba', *see* prosody
murdafa, *see* prosody
muruwwa, 146, 215–16, 407, 649, 670, 821
musabba', *see* prosody
musājala, *see* poetic contests
muṣālata, 690
musammaṭ, *see* strophic poetry

muṣannaf, 261
musāwāt, 390
muṣḥaf/*maṣḥaf*, 154
music and poetry
  boon companions, 572
  ghinā', 556
  inshād, 555
  medieval, 95, **555–6**
  modern poetry, 608
  renaissance, 574
  sama', **683–4**, 738, 741
  tarannum, 555
  see also singers and musicians
musnad, *see under* transmission
mustaf'ilun, *see* prosody
muṭābaqa, *see* rhetorical figures
mutadārak, *see under* prosody: *mutadārik*
mutadārik, *see* prosody
mutakallif, 516
mutakallimūn, 482
mutakāwis, *see* prosody
mutaqārib, *see* prosody
mutarākib, *see* prosody
mutawātir, *see* prosody
muṭlaq, *see* prose poem
mutūn, 194
muwalladūn, 90, **563**
muwashshaḥ, 95, 189, 236, 283, 294, 434, **563–6**, 619, 622, 737, 818, 819
  kharja, 434, 563, 564, 565, 737
muwāzana, *see* rhetorical figures
muzāḥ, *see* humour
muzāwaja, *see* rhetorical figures
muzdawij, 646
muzdawija, 194, 434, **567–8**, 619, 646, 737
mystical poetry, **738–9**
mystical prose, **739–40**
mysticism, 54, 81, 177, 240, 241, 434, 464, 505, 526, 546, 564, 594, 599, 600, 603, 639, 649–51, 683–4, 701, **740–2**, 768, 779, 822, 829

nabaṭī poetry, **569–70**, 819
nadīm, 53, 134, 191, 433, 434, **571–2**
nādira, *see under* anecdotes
al-nahḍa, 230, 231, **573–4**, 587, 614, 769, 777
naḥw, *see* grammar and grammarians
naqā'iḍ, 147, 186, 215, 284, 513, 534, **578**, 605, 693
al-naqd al-adabi, *see* literary criticism
naqīḍa, *see naqā'iḍ*
naql, *see* metaphor
narrative, *see under* fiction; poetry, narrative
naṣā'iḥ, *see* didactic literature
nasīb, *see qaṣīda*
nathr, *see under* prose
al-nathr al-fannī, *see* artistic prose
nathr mursal, 154
nathr al-naẓm, 678
nationalism, 175, 587, 726
naturalism, 231, 232, 495, 516
nature
  classical poetry, 546, **582–4**
  modern poetry, 608
  see also flower poetry
nawādir, 241, 615
nawriyyāt, 582
naẓm, **585–6**, 606, 609, 655, 798
neo-classicism, 231, 534, 574, **586–7**, 606, 607
neo-Platonism, *see* Platonism
neo-realism, 232
newspapers, *see* press
night journey, *see under isrā'*
night vision, 632
novel, *see* fiction, modern
nukta, *see* humour
nuqūṭ, *see* actors and acting, medieval
nursery rhymes, 189, 610

obscenity, 249, 397, 433, 578, 639, 737, 819
occult, *see 'ajā'ib*
office lore, 610
oneiromancy, *see under* dreams and visions
oral composition, 90, 147, 154, 191, 196, 200, 209, 234, 235, 282, 286, 394, 468, 472, 478, 565, **592–3**, 610, 611, 630–1, 726, 736, 737
oratory and sermons, 195, 286, **593–4**, 615, 618, 677, 678, 736
  khaṭīb, 593, 651
  khuṭba, 105, **449**, 593, 616
  maw'iẓa, 593, 616
  preachers, 400, 449, 593, 741
  qāḍī, 594
  qāṣṣ, 618
  wa'ẓ, 593
ornament, *see* rhetorical figures
outcast poets, *see ṣa'ālīk*
outlaws, 406

paganism, 649, 781
pageantry, **596**
pairing, *see under* rhetorical figures: *muzāwaja*
palindrome, *see under* rhetorical figures: *qalb*
panegyric, *see madīḥ*
paper-making, 470
parables, 214, 622
parody, 177, 250, 482, 508, 534, 546, 694, 767

paronomasia, *see under* rhetorical figures: *tajnīs*
patronage, 201, 477, 482, 483, 569, **598–9**, 607, 616–17, 631, 632
mamdūḥ, 631, 632
pattern poetry, 233
periodicals, *see* press
periphrasis, *see under* rhetorical figures: *kināya*
persuasion, *see under iqnāʿ*
philology, *see* grammar and grammarians
philosophical literature, 257, 393, 473, 478, 504, 606, 616, 654, 738, 775, **601–3**
plagiarism, *see sariqa*
Platonism, 176, 504, 602, **603–5**, 608
poetic contests, 394, 534, 570, 578, **605–6**, 652
poetic licence, **620**
poetics, *see* rhetoric and poetics
poetry, 57, 197, 209, 569, 570, 586, 587, 610, 652, 829
buildings, 475
commitment, 175
drama, 768
emblematic, 233
essential qualities, **89**, 472
figural, 233
goals of, 754
Jāhīli and *Islāmī*, 406
medieval, **606**
modern, **606–9**
moral effects, 473
mystical, **738–9**
narrative, 154
pattern, 233
pillars (*arkān*), 243
post-classical, 90, **563**
prose v., 229–30, 232, **609–10**, 654–5
ranking, 472
taṣdīq shiʿrī, 782
truth and, **781–2**
see also under music and poetry; singers and musicians
popular literature, 234, 394, **610–11**; *see also* folklore
post-classical poetry, *see muwalladūn*
praise, *see under madīḥ*
prayer, *see under duʿā'*
preachers, preaching, *see* oratory and sermons
prediction, *see malāḥim*
preface, *see muqaddima*
press, the, 190, 573, 610, **611–13**, 614
pride, 504–5
printing and publishing, 159, 171, 189–90, **613–15**
prison poetry, 244
professional schools, *see* education, modern
prolixity, *see under iṭnāb*
prophecy, *see malāḥim*
prose
artistic, 95, **105–6**, 208, 615–16, 617, 618, 655, 677, 721, 768, 807
assonance, 617
free, 677
kitāba, 677, 721
medieval non-fiction, **615–18**
mystical, **739–40**
nathr, 586, 609, 610
rhyming, 105, 186, 209, 230, 284, 507, 594, 609, 610, 616, 617, 618, 645, 651, 661, 663, **677–8**, 736
unadorned, 105
unrhymed, 154
versified, 609
prose poem, 609, 610, **618**, 665
prosody, **619–22**
asmāṭ, 737
baḥr, 620
bā'iyya, 620
basīṭ, 518, 519, 619, 621, 622
bayt, 425, 619, 652, 737
blank verse, **154**
caesura, 154
ḍarb, 619
ḍarūra, 620
enjambement, 154
form, **619**
free verse, **236–7**, 609, 619, 646, 665, 778
ghuṣn, 564, 737, 819
hazaj, 619, 621
īhām, 660
ikfā', 620
ʿilla, 622
iqwā', 620, 635
īṭā', 620, 635
juz', 619
kāfiyya, 620
kāmil, 194, 619, 621
khāfīf, 619, 621, 652
Khalīl's metrical circles, 467, 620–2, 646
khurūj, 620
madīd, 619, 621
manhūk, 619
mardūf, 518, 519
markaz, 564, 737
mashṭūr, 619
maṭlaʿ, 564, 619, 737, 819
metre, **619**
miṣrāʿ, 425, 619, 652, 653, 661
muʿallaqāt, 147
mu'assasa, 620
muhmal, 620

mujarrada, 620
mujtathth, 425, 619, 621
munsariḥ, 619, 621, 646
muqayyada, 620
muqtaḍab, 621
murabba', 518
murdafa, 620
musabba', 518
mustaf'ilun, 645
mutadārik, 154, 619, 621
mutakāwis, 619
mutawātir, 619
mutaqārib, 619, 621, 759
mutarākib, 619
muzdawija, 567–8
poetic licence, **620**
qāfiya, 154, 652
qawādīsi/qādūsī, **635**
qufl, 564
ramal, 475, 619, 621, 652
rawī, 620, 652
rhyme, 194, 237, 468, 480, **619–20**, 652, 660
ridf, 518, 620
rubā'ī, 518
run-on lines, 154
sabab, 622
sab'ānī, 518
sarī', 619, 621, 646, 759
ṣila, 620
simṭ, 564, 737
sinād, 620
stress, **622**
taf'īla, 619
tamm/aqra', 564
ta'sīs, 620
ṭawīl, 154, 570, 622, 738, 759
'uḍw, 425
wāfir, 619, 621
waṣl, 620
watid, 622
wazn, 154
zahr, 518
ziḥāf, 622
see also rajaz; strophic poetry
prostitutes, 514, 548
proverbs, 55, 95, 195, 208, 214, 234, 235, 243, 286, 475, 523, 594, 616, **622–4**
publishing, *see* printing and publishing
puns, *see under* rhetorical figures: *tawriya*
puzzle, *see mu'ammā*

qāḍī, 54, 201, 483, 594, 694
qādūsī, *see qawādisī*
qāfiya, *see* prosody
Qaḥān, *see* tribes
qalb, *see* rhetorical figures
qariḍ, 619, 645–6, 664
qarīn, *see* inspiration
qarrādi, *see zajal*, modern
qaṣīd, 652
qaṣīda, 210, 215, 236, 283, 294, 434, 472, 619, **630–3**, 646, 664, 797, 806
anthologies, 94
anti-*nasīb*, 632
dialect, 189
epic poetry, 209
first, 780
hijā', 284
improvisation, 394
kān wa-kān, 425
maqṣūra, 620
māwāliya, 518
naqā'iḍ, 578
nasīb, 81, 82, 83, 177, 216, 243, 249, 250, 406, 407, 433, 449, 482, 546, 582, 630, 631, 632, 633, 650, 670, 671, 828
neo-classical, 587
oral composition, 592, 593
qiṭ'a, **638–9**
raḥīl, 82, 249, 406, 482, 483, 582, 606, 631, 632, 650, 828
religion, 649
ṭardiyya, 759
tribal virtues, 147
qaṣīdat al-nathr, *see* prose poem
qaṣīr, 147
qāṣṣ, *see* oratory and sermons; story-telling
qawādisī/qādūsi, **635**
qawā'id, *see* genres, poetic
qawl, 191
Qays 'Aylān, *see* tribes
qibla, 245
qinā', *see* masks and masquerades
qiṣaṣ al-anbiyā', 611
qiṣṣa, 617
qiṭ'a, 210, 215, 283, 406, 483, 593, 619, 630, **638–9**, 759
qiyās, 551
qufl, *see muwashshaḥ*; prosody
quotations, 475; *see also under kharja*; rhetorical figures: *taḍmīn*
Quraysh, *see* tribes
quṣṣāṣ, *see under* oratory and sermons: preachers; story-telling

Rabī'a, *see* tribes
rabī'iyyāt, 582
radd al-'ajuz 'alā al-ṣadr, *see* rhetorical figures
radio, 736
rafḍ, 618

rafīq, 147
raḥīl, *see qaṣīda*
rā'iyya, 583
rajaz, 619, 621, **645–6**, 651, 652
dialect, 189
improvisation, 394
muzdawija, 567
oral composition, 593
ṭardiyya, 759
urjūza, 194, 646, 760
ramal, *see* prosody
ramz, *see* allegory
raqqāṣūn, *see* actors and acting, medieval
raqṣ, *see under* actors and acting, medieval; dancers and dancing
rare expressions, *see under nawādir*
rasā'il, *see under* letters
rationalism, 231
rawḍiyyāt, 244, 546, 582
rawī (rhyme), *see* prosody
rāwī (transmitter), 196, 209, 592, 593, **647**
realism, 231, 232, 234, 236, 393, 475, 596, 665
ḥaqīqa, 495
neo-realism, 232
socialist, 232
recitation, 639, 647
Hilālī, 569
see also under inshād; oral composition
refinement, *see ẓarf*
refuge, *see under dakhāla*
rejection, *see under rafḍ*
religious poetry, **649–51**
renaissance, *see al-nahḍa*
reproach, *see under 'itāb*
resourcefulness, *see ẓarf*
retraction, *see under* rhetorical figures: *rujū'*
revenge, *see under* vengeance
reviews, *see* press
revival, *see al-nahḍa*
revue, *see* theatre and drama, modern
rhetoric and poetics, 175, 244, 473, 504, 606, 609, 616, 639, **651–6**, 691
badī'iyyāt, **124**, 534
balāgha, 617
faṣāḥa, 652
ḥīla, 754
ījāz, 390
rhetorical figures (*badī'*), 90, 106, **122**, 173, 393, 472, 473, 474, 479, 482, 516, 523, 545, 549, 617, 632, 653, 655, **656–62**
'aks, 657, 659
hazl yurād bihi jidd, 657
ḥusn al-ta'līl, 393, 657
'ilm al-badī', 656, 661
'ilm al-bayān, 661
iltifāt, 657
iqtibās, **396–7**
istikhdām, 657
istitbā', 657–8
istiṭrād, 657, 658
jam', 658
jam' ma'a tafrīq, 658
jam' ma'a taqsīm, 658
jam' ma'a taqsīm wa-tafrīq, 658
jinās, 570, 660
kināya, 81, 398, 661
laff wa-nashr, 658
mubālagha, *ghuluww*, 483, 658, 781
mubālagha maqbūla, 658
mumāthala, 660
muqābala, 657, 659
murā'āt al-naẓīr, 658
muṭābaqa, 657, 659
muwāzana, 660, 677
muzāwaja, 659
qalb, 660
radd al-'ajuz 'alā al-ṣadr, 660
ramz, 398
rujū', 659
tabdīl, 657
taḍmīn, 82, 396, 620, 659, 690, 692
tafrīq, 659
tafwīf, 659
tajāhul al-'ārif, 569
tajnīs, 89, 518, 545, 660
tajrīd, 659
ta'kīd al-madḥ, 658, 659
tamthīl, 524, 655, 661
taqsīm, 660
tardīd, 660
tar'īḍ, 81, 398
tarṣī', 661, 678
taṣrī', 619, 639, 661
tawriya, *īhām*, 657, 660
rhyme, *see* prosody
rhythm, 618
ribāṭ (connection), 585
ribāṭ (convent), 201
riddiyyih, 578
riddles, 610; *see also under lughz*; *mu'ammā*
ridf, *see* prosody
ridicule, *see hijā'*; satire, medieval
riḥla, *see* travel literature
risāla, 52, 66, 81, 230; *see also under* artistic prose; epistles, prose, non-fiction medieval
rithā', 173, 210, 216, 243, 244, 249, 407, 482, 638, 650, 651, 655, **663–4**, 671, 678
rituals, 684, 767

riwāya, *see under* autobiography, modern; *rāwī*; fiction
romances, *see sīra* literature
romanticism, 231, 232, 474, 574, 587, 606, 607–8, 611, **665–6**
rubā'ī, *see* prosody
rubā'iyya, *see dūbayt*
rujū', *see* rhetorical figures
rukūb al-kawsaj, *see* theatre and drama, medieval
run-on lines, *see* prosody
ru'yā, *see under* dreams and visions

ṣa'ālīk, 146, 406, 598, **670–1**, 781
sabab, *see* prosody
sab'ānī, *see* prosody
ṣabr, 670
ṣadīq, 781
ṣafā'ina, *see* actors and acting, medieval
saj', 105, 186, 209, 230, 284, 507, 594, 609, 610, 616, 617, 618, 645, 651, 661, **677–8**, 736; *see also under* rhetorical figures: *tarṣī'*
samā', *see under* music and poetry
samāja, 767
samar, 726
ṣan'a, *see ṣinā'a*
sarī', *see* prosody
sariqa, 82, 90, 190, 193, 210, 461, 482, 483, 508, 546, 547, 555, 598, 606, 612, 632, 653, 655, **690–2**
satire, medieval, 631, 690, **693–5**; *see also under hijā'*; parody
science, *see under 'ilm*
scorn, *see hijā'*; satire, medieval
scribes, 154, 155, 156, 158, 159, 235, 614, 657
scrolls, 154
secretaries, 572, **698–9**
  anthologies, 95, 489
  bilingual, 774
  kātib, 193, 616
  praised, 483
  qiṭ'a, 638
  wirāqa, 156
  writings, 105, 106, 250, 609, 617, 653, 654, 655, 721, 807
self-praise, *see fakhr*
semantics, 468
separation, *see* rhetorical figures: *tafrīq*
serialization, 613, 777
sermons, *see* oratory and sermons
sex, 235–6, 478, 546, 547, 684
shadow-play, 52, 236, 441, 547, 694, **701–2**, 743, 768
  bāba, **120–1**
  faṣl, 120
  la'ba, 120
sharaf, 146
sharḥ, *see* commentaries
sharī'a, 604, 740
sharīka, 691
shatm al-dahr, 523
shaykh, *see under* education, medieval: teachers
shayṭān, *see* inspiration
shi'r, *see under* poetry
shi'r'āmmī, 819
shi'r ḥurr, *see* free verse
shi'r manthūr, *see* prose poem
shi'r mursal, *see* blank verse
shi'r qaṣaṣī, *see* epic poetry
short passages, *see under fuṣūl*
short stories, *see* fiction, modern
shrūqī, *see zajal*, modern
shuhra, *see* theatre and drama, medieval
shukr, 243
Shu'ūbiyya, 284, **717**
ṣidq, 670
siḥr, *see under* magic
ṣila, *see* prosody
silsila, *see under* education, medieval: teachers; transmission
simile, 89, 90, 243, 522, 523, 524, 546, 617, 622, 655, 661, 806
simṭ, *see* prosody
ṣinā'a, 105, 461, 472, 516, 606, **721**
sinād, *see under* poetry
ṣinf, *see* genres, poetic
singers and musicians, 250, 547, 548, 565, 622, 639, 694, **724–5**; *see also under* music and poetry
sīra literature, 112, 209, 234, 465, 498, 609, 610, 611, 612, **726–7**; *see also* biography
slaves, 250, 547, 555, 724, 807, 822
soothsayers, *see under kāhin*
sounds, *see under ajrās al-ḥurūf*
speech, *see kalām*
speeches, *see* oratory and sermons
spring, *see* nature, in classical poetry
spy novels, 612
story-telling, 106, 236, 400, 464, 572, 618, 726, **735–7**
stress, *see* prosody
strophic poetry, 82, 154, 236, 283, 294, 586, 608, 619, 622, 633, **737**, 818, 819
Sufism, *see* mysticism
sukhf, 547, 639, 702, **743**
sukhriyya, 694
ṣu'lūk, *see ṣa'ālīk*
sunna, 156

superstitions, 234, 236
ṣūra, 155, 157, 462, 586
syntax, 504, 586, 609, 620

ta'ajjub, 754
ṭabaqāt, *see* biography, medieval
tabdīl, *see under* rhetorical figures: *'aks*
tābi', *see* inspiration
tablīgh, *see under* rhetorical figures: *mubālagha*
taḍādd, *see under* rhetorical figures: *muṭābaqa*
taḍmīn, *see* rhetorical figures
tadrīs, 200
taf'īla, *see* prosody
tafrīq, *see* rhetorical figures
tafsīr, *see* exegesis, Koranic
tafwīf, *see* rhetorical figures
tahāji', *see hijā'*
tahakkum, 694
tahdhīb, *see under* abridgements
tajāhul al-'ārif, *see* rhetorical figures
taj'īb, 606, **754–5**
tajnīs, *see* rhetorical figures
tajrīd, *see* rhetorical figures
takhalluṣ, *see qaṣīda*
takhayyul, 754
takhmīs, 82–3, 651
takhyīl, *see* imagination; metaphor
takhyīliyya, 782
ta'kīd al-madḥ bi-mā yushbih al-dhamm, *see under* rhetorical figures: *ta'kīd al-madḥ*
ta'līq, 175, 618
talkhīṣ, *see under* abridgements
talmīḥ, 82, 690
talq, 618
tam'iya, *see under lughz*; *mu'ammā*
tamlit, 605
tamm, *see* prosody
tamthīl, *see* rhetorical figures
tanāsub, *see under* rhetorical figures: *murā'āt al-naẓīr*
taqfīl, 294
taqsīm, *see* rhetorical figures
tarannum, *see under* music and poetry
tardīd, *see* rhetorical figures
ṭardiyya, 83, 194, 434, 546, 567, 582, 646, **759–60**, 806
ta'rīḍ, *see* rhetorical figures
ta'rīkh, *see* chronogram; historical literature
tarjama, *see* autobiography, modern; biography; translation
ṭarsh, *see* printing and publishing
tarṣī', *see* rhetorical figures
taṣawwur, 393
taṣdīq, 754, 782; *see also* imagination
taṣdīr, *see under* rhetorical figures: *radd al-'ajuz 'alā al-ṣadr*
tashakkuk, *see under* rhetorical figures: *tajāhul al-'ārif*
tashayyu', 650
tashbīb, 243, 249, 250, 547
tashbīh, *see under* simile
ta'sīs, *see* prosody
taṣrī', *see* rhetorical figures
taṭwīl, 390
tawfīq, *see under* rhetorical figures; murā'at al-naẓīr
ṭawil, *see* prosody
ta'wil, *see* exegesis, Koranic
tawqī', 616
tawriya, *see* rhetorical figures
tawshīḥ, 294
ṭayāṭir, *see* theatre and drama, medieval
ṭayf, 631
ta'ziya, 616
television, 615, 736, 770, 772
tent-neighbour, *see under qaṣīr*
text, 200
thanks, *see under shukr*
theatre and drama
  medieval, 53, **766–9**
    bāba, 52, 53, **120–1**, 134, 768
    dialect, 190
    faṣl, 120, 514, 768
    huz' sakhīf, 768
    rukūb al-kawsaj, 53
  modern, 607, **769–72**, 573, 574, 613
    blank verse, 154
    censorship, 772
    commitment, 175, 770
    dialogue, 192
    ḥakawātī, 771
    new wave, 770
    popular, 610
    publication, 612
    renaissance, 573
    revue, 770
  see also actors and acting, medieval; masks and masquerades; shadow-play
theft, *see sariqa*
themes, *see under aghrāḍ*; *ma'ānī*; *uslūb*
theological discourse, *see kalām*
thrillers, 612
ṭibāq, *see under* rhetorical figures: *muṭābaqa*
ṭibb, *see under* medicine
traces, *see under aṭlāl*
traditionalism, 231
transference, 524
translation, 154, 190, 192, 202, 230, 231, 257–8, 283, 443, 473, 474, 567, 573,

574, 601, 612, 614, 616–17, 618, 698, 769, **774–7**, **777–8**
transmission, 228, 261, 647
travel literature, 246, **778–80**
treatise, *see under risāla*
tribes, 95, 146, 147, 195, 569, 598, 631, 632, 670, **780–1**
troubadours, 563, 565, 593
truth and falsehood, 191, 229, 443, 507, 606, 781, 782
  bāṭil, 228
  kidhb, 228
truth and poetry, 229, 473, 606, **781–2**

'Udhrī poetry, 176
'uḍw, *see* prosody
uḥjiyya, *see under lughz*
'ulamā', 400, 599, 614
unbelief, *see under kufr*
underworld, *see under* vagabonds
universities, *see under* education, modern
urjūza, *see rajaz*
uslūb **797–8**
uṣūl, 473

vagabonds, 134, 189, 236, 240
valour, 146, 237, 569, 593
vaunting, *see fakhr*
vengeance, 147
vernacular poetry, *see* nabaṭī poetry
vernacular, 155, 191, 565, 612, 818–19
verse forms, *see* prosody
vices and virtues, 215–16, 243, 284, 482, 483, 670; *see also under faḍā'il*; *manāqib*
video, 615
visions, *see under* dreams and visions
vocational education, *see* education, modern

wafā', 670
wāfir, *see* prosody
waḥy, *see* inspiration
wajh, 147
war poetry, 555, 606
warrāqūn, 155, 156–7
waṣf, 210, 243, 483, 546, 555, 639, **806–7**
waṣf al-nāqa, *see under* camel poetry
waṣiyya, 616
waṣl, *see* prosody
waswās, *see* inspiration
watid, *see* prosody
wa'ẓ, *see* oratory and sermons; story-telling
wazn, *see* prosody
wine poetry, *see khamriyya*
wisdom literature, *see ḥikma*
wit, *see ẓarf*
women, 232–3, 236, 250, 407, 663–4, 694
wonder, *see ta'jīb*
wonders of the world, *see 'ajā'ib* literature
wonders, *see khurāfa*
word-play, 587
wording, *see under lafẓī*

xerox lore, 610

yaḥkī, *see* actors and acting, medieval

zaffānūn, *see* dancers and dancing
zahriyyāt, 244, 582
zajal
  medieval, 189, 236, 434, 547, 619, 622, 737, **818–19**
  modern, **819–20**
zandaqa, *see under* heresy
ẓarf, 57, 176, 724, **821–2**
ẓarīf, *see ẓarf*
zāwiya, *see under* education, medieval: convents
ziḥāf, *see* prosody
zuhdiyya, 193, 210, 286, 639, 649–51, **828–9**